THE OXFORD HANDBOOK OF

THE QUALITY OF GOVERNMENT

THE OXFORD HANDBOOK OF

THE QUALITY OF GOVERNMENT

Edited by

ANDREAS BÅGENHOLM,
MONIKA BAUHR,
MARCIA GRIMES, AND
BO ROTHSTEIN

OXFORD

UNIVERSITY PRESS

OXFORD
UNIVERSITY PRESS

Great Clarendon Street, Oxford, OX2 6DP,
United Kingdom

Oxford University Press is a department of the University of Oxford.
It furthers the University's objective of excellence in research, scholarship,
and education by publishing worldwide. Oxford is a registered trade mark of
Oxford University Press in the UK and in certain other countries

© Oxford University Press 2021

The moral rights of the authors have been asserted

First Edition published in 2021
Impression: 3

Published in the United States of America by Oxford University Press
198 Madison Avenue, New York, NY 10016, United States of America

British Library Cataloguing in Publication Data
Data available

Library of Congress Control Number: 2020952237

ISBN 978–0–19–885821–8

DOI: 10.1093/oxfordhb/9780198858218.001.0001

Printed and bound in the UK by
TJ Books Limited

Links to third party websites are provided by Oxford in good faith and
for information only. Oxford disclaims any responsibility for the materials
contained in any third party website referenced in this work.

Contents

PART VII STATE STRUCTURE AND POLICY

PART VIII STATE-BUILDING AND BREAKDOWN

Figures

TABLES

Contributors

Pelle Ahlerup has been Associate Professor at the University of Gothenburg since May 2016. His research has addressed questions related to ethnic diversity, taxation, foreign aid, structural transformation, and the political economy of natural disasters and extreme weather events.

Amy C. Alexander is an Associate Professor in the Department of Political Science at the University of Gothenburg. Her research focuses on the sources of gender equality and its effects on politics and institutions. She has published on this in several peer-reviewed journals such as *International Organization, Comparative Politics, Politics and Gender*, and *Politics, Groups, and Identities*.

Andreas Bågenholm is a Senior Lecturer at the Department of Political Science and the Program Manager at the Quality of Government Institute at the University of Gothenburg. His research focuses primarily on various aspects of corruption and elections.

Thushyanthan Baskaran has been Professor for Applied Microeconomics at the University of Siegen since October 2015. His research mainly addresses questions of political economy, development economics, as well as public economics.

Monika Bauhr is an Associate Professor at the Department of Political Science, University of Gothenburg and a Research Fellow at the Quality of Government Institute. Her research focuses on the causes and consequences of different forms of corruption, democracy, international aid and public goods provision.

Sheri Berman is a Professor of Political Science at Barnard College, Columbia University and is the author, most recently, of *Democracy and Dictatorship in Europe: From the Ancien Régime to the Present Day*.

Arne Bigsten is Professor Emeritus of Development Economics at the University of Gothenburg. His research has concerned poverty, income distribution, trade, globalization, industrial development, foreign aid, and institutional reform.

Frida Boräng is Associate Professor at the Department of Political Science, University of Gothenburg. She is also a Research Fellow at the Quality of Government Institute at the same university.

Ruth Carlitz is an Assistant Professor of Political Science at Tulane University, where she teaches courses on international development and African Politics. Her research focuses primarily on the politics of public goods provision in low-income countries, from the perspectives of both governments and citizens.

Nicholas Charron is a Professor in the Department of Political Science and a Fellow at the Quality of Government (QoG) Institute at the University of Gothenburg. His research focuses on the causes, consequences, and measurement of QoG, multilevel governance within the EU, public opinion, and electoral behavior.

Stefan Dahlberg is the Chair Professor in Political Science at the Department of Humanities and Social Science, Mid Sweden University and Professor in Political Science at the Department of Comparative Politics, University of Bergen.

Carl Dahlström is Professor of Political Science at the University of Gothenburg, and a research fellow at the Quality of Government Institute.

Michelle D'Arcy is Assistant Professor, Department of Political Science, Trinity College Dublin, Ireland.

Stephen Dawson is a PhD candidate at the University of Gothenburg, Sweden, affiliated with the Quality of Government Institute. He studies electoral politics, political institutions, competition, corruption, and voting behavior.

Annekatrin Deglow is an Assistant Professor at the Department of Peace and Conflict Research, Uppsala University.

Donatella della Porta is Full Professor and Dean of the Faculty of Political and Social Sciences at the Scuola Normale Superiore where she directs the Center on Social Movement Studies (Cosmos). She is the author of numerous publications on social movements and political corruption.

Simone Dietrich is Associate Professor in the Department of Political Science and International Relations at the University of Geneva, Switzerland. Her research interests include foreign aid decision-making and foreign aid effectiveness as well as international organizations and global governance.

Peter Thisted Dinesen is Professor of Political Science at the University of Copenhagen. His work centers on social and political attitude formation. He has published a number of articles and chapters on the sources of generalized, especially regarding the role of institutional quality and ethnic diversity..

Eliška Drápalová is a Postdoctoral Fellow at the Department of Political Science and a Research Fellow at the QoG Institute, both at the University of Gothenburg. Her research focuses on administrative capacity, subnational quality of government, corruption in cities.

Hanne Fjelde is a Research Fellow at the Royal Swedish Academy of Letters, History and Antiquities, an Associate Professor at the Department of Peace and Conflict Research, Uppsala University and a Senior Researcher at the Peace Research Institute, Oslo (PRIO).

Francis Fukuyama is a Senior Fellow at Stanford's Freeman Spogli Institute for International Studies and Mosbacher Director of FSI's Center on Democracy, Development and the Rule of Law.

Marcia Grimes is Associate Professor at the Department of Political Science, University of Gothenburg. She is also a research fellow at the Quality of Government Institute at the same university.

Ellen Gutterman is Associate Professor of Political Science at Glendon College, York University in Toronto. Her research is focused on various aspects of the global governance of transnational crime and corruption, including a current project on transnational advocacy in the global anticorruption sphere. She has published articles in *Review of International Studies, British Journal of Politics and International Relations, Foreign Policy Analysis*, and elsewhere.

John Helliwell has been a co-editor of the World Happiness Reports since they were started in 2012. Based in the Vancouver School of Economics at the University of British Columbia, he is involved in many inter-disciplinary studies of the sources and benefits of subjective well-being.

Leslie Holmes is Professor Emeritus of Political Science at the University of Melbourne. He also teaches annually at the Graduate School of Social Research in Warsaw and the Renmin University of China in Beijing, and sometimes at the International Anti-Corruption Academy in Vienna.

Haifang Huang is an Associate Professor in the Department of Economics, University of Alberta. His areas of research include macroeconomics, urban economics and well-being. He was an associate editor for the World Happiness Report (2017–2020) as well as a contributing author.

Michael Johnston is the Charles A. Dana Professor of Political Science, Emeritus, at Colgate University in Hamilton, New York USA. He has written and edited several books on corruption and reform issues, most recently (with Scott A. Fritzen) *The Conundrum of Corruption: Reform for Social Justice* (Routledge, 2021).

Steven M. Karceski is a doctoral candidate in the Sociology Department at the University of Washington and a fellow at the UW Center for Environmental Politics. He studies political institutions, the political discourse around ideology, partisanship, and policy.

Philip Keefer is the Principal Economic Advisor of the Institutions for Development Department of the Inter-American Development Bank in Washington, DC.

Nikolas Kirby is Director of the Building Integrity Programme and Leverhulme Early Career Research Fellow in Philosophy and Public Policy at the Blavatnik School of Government, University of Oxford.

Edgar Kiser is Professor Emeritus in the Sociology Department at the University of Washington and a Visiting Professor of Sociology at NYU Abu Dhabi. Dr. Kiser has published in sociology, political science, economics, and history journals on topics including comparative-historical methods, the development of voting institutions, causes and consequences of warfare, the historical development of tax systems, and contemporary systems of taxation.

Mark Knights is Professor of History at the University of Warwick where he has directed its Early Modern and Eighteenth Century Centre. He has published many works on seventeenth- and eighteenth-century Britain, and his book *Trust and Distrust: Corruption in Office in Britain and its Empire, 1600-1850* will be published by Oxford University Press.

Staffan Kumlin is Professor of Political Science at the University of Oslo. He authored *The Personal and the Political: How Personal Welfare State Experiences Affect Political Trust and Ideology* (2004) and co-edited *How Welfare States Shape the Democratic Public* (2014).

Victor Lapuente is Professor of Political Science and Research Fellow at the Quality of Government Institute of the University of Gothenburg, and Visiting Professor at ESADE Law School.

Jonas Linde is Professor in Political Science at the Department of Comparative Politics, University of Bergen.

Mathis Lohaus is a postdoctoral research associate at the Otto Suhr Institute of Political Science at Freie Universität Berlin. His research is focused on international organizations, the diffusion of ideas, and international norms more broadly. Mathis has published *Towards a Global Consensus Against Corruption: International Agreements as Products of Diffusion and Signals of Commitment* with Routledge in 2019.

Ellen Lust is a Professor of Political Science and the Founding Director of the Programs on Governance and Local Development at Yale University (2013–16) and the University of Gothenburg (2015–present.) She has conducted research across the Middle East and Africa, and authored and edited numerous books and articles.

Simon Matti is a Professor and Chair of the Political Science Unit at Luleå University of Technology, Sweden as well as an affiliated senior researcher at the Centre for Collective Action Research (CeCAR). His main research interest concerns the politics of collective action and, in particular, the mechanisms behind public (non-)support for various policy instruments.

Alice Mattoni is Associate Professor in the Department of Political and Social Science at the University of Bologna and Principal Investigator of the ERC project *Bottom-Up Initiatives and Anti-Corruption Technologies: How Citizens Employ ICTs to Fight Corruption* (BIT-ACT).

Erin Metz McDonnell is a Kellogg Associate Professor of Sociology at the University of Notre Dame and author of *Patchwork Leviathan*. Her research fuses organizational, political, cultural, and development sociologies, with award-winning work published in the *American Sociological Review*, the *American Journal of Sociology*, and *Comparative Political Studies*.

Alina Mungiu-Pippidi chairs the European Research Centre for Anticorruption and State-building (ERCAS) at Hertie School, The University of Governance in Berlin. She is the author of *A Quest for Good Governance: How Societies Build Control of Corruption* and *Europe's Burden: Promoting Good Governance across Borders* (both with Cambridge University Press).

Marina Nistotskaya is Associate Professor at the Department of Political Science, University of Gothenburg, Sweden and a Researcher at the Quality of Government Institute.

Petrus Olander is a Post-Doc in the STANCE project at the Department of Political Science, Lund University. His main research interests include institutions, economic diversification, state capacity, and American political development.

Anna Persson is Associate Professor at the Department of Political Science, University of Gothenburg, and Research Fellow at the Quality of Government (QoG) Institute. Her research focuses on the politics of development and reform, particularly corruption, democratization, state capacity, taxation, and public goods provision.

Marina Povitkina is a Postdoctoral Researcher at the Department of Political Science at the University of Oslo, Norway, and the Centre for Collective Action Research (CeCAR) at the University of Gothenburg, Sweden. Her research interests include comparative environmental politics, in particular, the role of corruption and democracy in explaining environmental performance of states, bureaucratic politics, and the politics of collective action.

Francesca Recanatini is a Lead Economist in the Governance Global Practice at the World Bank.

Robert I. Rotberg is President Emeritus of the World Peace Foundation, Founding Director of Harvard Kennedy School's Program on Instrastate Conflict, Fellow of the American Academy of Arts and Sciences; and the author of *Anticorruption* (2020), *The Corruption Cure* (2017), and other books.

Bo Rothstein holds the August Röhss Chair in Political Science at University of Gothenburg. Together with Sören Holmberg, he founded the Quality of Government Institute in 2004 and was its Director until 2016. He served as Professor of Public Policy and Government at Oxford University 2016–17 and since 2012 he is a member of the Royal Swedish Academy of Sciences.

Carlos Scartascini is a Principal Economist in the Research Department of the Inter-American Development Bank and leader of the IDB's Behavioral Economics Group in Washington, DC.

Kim Mannemar Sønderskov is a Professor of Political Science at Aarhus University. He does research on political behavior and attitudes. Several of his publications deal with causes and consequences of generalized social trust—including the role of institutions, corruption, and ethnic diversity in shaping trust, and the role of trust in relation to pro-social behavior.

Davide Torsello is Professor of Anthropology and Organizational Behavior at Central European University. He has extensive experience of ethnographic field research in organizations and communities in Japan, Italy, and Eastern Europe. He has been studying political and business corruption, focusing in particular on the social and cultural as well as the organizational cultural aspects of the phenomenon including gift-exchange, ethics, values, informality, trust, social networks, organizational culture, change, and globalization. He has published over 60 journal articles and 10 books, in English and Italian including: *Corruption in the Public Administration: an Ethnographic Approach* (Edward Elgar, 2016); *The New Environmentalism? Civil Society and Corruption in the Enlarged EU* (Ashgate, 2012); and *Potere, legittimazione e corruzione* (A. Mondadori, 2008).

Eric M. Uslaner is Professor of Government and Politics at the University of Maryland, College Park. He is the author of 11 books, including *The Historical Roots of Corruption* and *The Moral Foundations of Trust*. He is the editor of *The Oxford Handbook of Social and Political Trust* (Oxford University Press, 2018).

Luiz Vilaça is a PhD student in Sociology at the University of Notre Dame. His research focuses on processes of administrative reform and institutional change, examining how activist bureaucrats in judicial institutions interact with political elites and social movements to promote anticorruption reform in Brazil.

Razvan Vlaicu is a Senior Economist in the Research Department of the Inter-American Development Bank in Washington, DC.

Shun Wang is a Professor in KDI School of Public Policy and Management. His research focuses primarily on development and well-being. He is a co-editor for the World Happiness Report as well as a contributing author.

Janine R. Wedel is University Professor in the Schar School of Policy and Government at George Mason University, and a Fellow at the Hertie School of Governance in Berlin. A social anthropologist, she is the author, most recently, of the award-winning *Shadow Elite (2009) and Unaccountable: How the Establishment Corrupted Our Finances, Freedom, and Politics and Created an Outsider Class* (2014/2016). She studies issues of governance, corruption, elites, accountability, and informal social networks—often focusing on Central and Eastern Europe and the United States. Her work has been reviewed or translated into more than a dozen languages.

Matthew S. Winters is Professor and Associate Head for Graduate Programs in the Department of Political Science at the University of Illinois. His research interests include the allocation and effectiveness of foreign aid, the political economy of governance, and voter attitudes toward corruption.

Jonathan Wolff is Alfred Landecker Professor of Public Policy and Values at the Blavatnik School of Government, University of Oxford.

Georgios Xezonakis is an Associate Professor of Political Science at the Department of Political Science, University of Gothenburg and Fellow at the Quality of Government Institute. His previous work appears in *Comparative Political Studies, European Journal of Political Research, Electoral Studies,* and *Party Politics.* He is also co-editor of an Oxford University Press volume *Globalization and Domestic Politics: Parties, Elections, and Public Opinion.*

Jong-sung You is Professor and Director of Inequality and Social Policy Institute at the Graduate School of Social Policy, Gachon University in South Korea. His publications include *Democracy, Inequality and Corruption: Korea, Taiwan and the Philippines Compared* (Cambridge University Press).

INTRODUCTION: QUALITY OF GOVERNMENT: WHY—WHAT—HOW

ANDREAS BÅGENHOLM, MONIKA BAUHR, MARCIA GRIMES, AND BO ROTHSTEIN

INTRODUCTION

WE want to begin this handbook by revisiting the fundamental question: why is there a need for a research enterprise on *quality of government*? Much of the research and analysis about this problem is concentrated on conceptual issues, statistics, identification of causal patterns, and the reliability and validity of various measures. Important as all this is, there is a risk that the human side of what it can mean to live in a society with dismal government institutions takes a backstage position. This is why we would like to start this introductory chapter with a few narratives about what a lack of institutional quality can imply. The first is taken from a World Bank report titled *Silent and Lethal: How Quiet Corruption Undermines Africa's Development Efforts* that was published in 2010. The report presents a number of on the ground examples to illustrate the severity of this problem. For example, in rural Tanzania "nearly four out of five children who died of malaria sought medical attention from modern health facilities. A range of manifestations of quiet corruption, including the absence of diagnostic equipment, drug pilfering, provider absenteeism, and very low levels of diagnostic effort, all contributed to this dire statistic" (World Bank 2010). These conditions most certainly result in part from a lack of quality of government. An external audit of healthcare funding in Chad found, for example, that only 1 percent of the funds allocated to non-wage expenses in fact arrived at the health facilities (Gauthier and Wane 2008).

Lack of QoG in healthcare systems has dire effects on population health in general and particularly on infant mortality. This has been shown in several studies using various measures of QoG (Factor and Kang 2015; Pinzon-Florez et al. 2015; Lin et al. 2014; Holmberg and Rothstein 2011). The problems are in no way limited to developing countries like Tanzania or Chad, however. In February 2017 when large-scale popular protests against corruption erupted in Romania, the *New York Times* asked their readers in Romania to send in personal stories about their experience of corruption. A doctor working in the public healthcare system wrote the following:

> Corruption is so embedded in the medical system that it's nearly impossible to change without the help of the judicial system. A lot of my colleagues do take bribes from their patients. Some of them won't treat someone who doesn't offer them money, although Romania's medical system guarantees free access to medical services. I don't take money from my patients, and

Monika Bauhr would like to thank RJ SAB19-0425

when I refuse their money, some get worried, thinking I refused them because they have some sort of terminal disease. Some think you're a low-quality doctor if you treat them without charge.

However, it is not only in the medical sector that corruption seems to be rampant. In the same article, a university professor wrote the following:

> I have been put under pressure to promote students who never attended class. I have been offered bribes for this and I have been sanctioned because of my integrity. I was forced to leave the country many times because of the awful corruption and because my monthly wages were insufficient for survival. My colleagues took huge amounts of money from selling graduation papers and grades... (Karasz 2017)

Low QoG in the healthcare and educational sectors does not, however, only cause severe problems for the individuals that encounter it directly. It can also have repercussions for the economic stability in countries as a whole. In an op-ed article, also in the *New York Times* (entitled "Greece's Costly Health Care Craze," July 20, 2015) Martin Makary argued that one major reason for Greece's economic problems (which in turn threatened the economic stability of the whole Eurozone) stemmed from problems in the country's healthcare sector. Lack of accountability and oversight led to a spending spree that dramatically increased costs in the public healthcare system, such as systematic overtreatment, overbilling, and the purchase of costly medical equipment by administrators who "often received kickbacks from the makers of medical devices and pharmaceutical companies." In addition, pensions for medical disabilities were easy to get "and, if denied, could still be obtained through the right connections." Hospitals in which people in positions of leadership had the "right" political contacts rarely managed to balance their budgets and instead sent the bill to the Ministry of Finance, further depleting public coffers. According to this article, these practices contributed to the debt crisis in Greece's public finances.

These "stories" are centered on various forms of corruption, which of course is a central part of what should count as the opposite of quality of government, but as will be made clear in the chapters in the first section of this handbook, there are other dimensions of this problem, such as the influence of "big money" in politics, low competence, and discriminatory and partial decision-making. However, against the backdrop of these compelling anecdotes, we zoom out and pose the question more generally: why study quality of government?

WHY QUALITY OF GOVERNMENT?

This introductory chapter sets the stage for this handbook by offering a number of answers to the question of why studying quality of government is of central importance for understanding broad based economic, social, and environmental development. Quality of government has attained even more heightened relevance in light of the recent challenges posed by both pandemics and economic recession. Representative democracy long held a privileged and almost singular status in normative definitions of what makes a government good, and many scholars have operated under this assumption for decades. One could argue that "periodic and genuine elections" based on "universal and equal suffrage" following the principles of "free voting procedures" so that its policies reflect "the will of the people," as stated in the UN Declaration of Human Rights (www.un.org/en/universal-declaration-human-rights), should be enough to claim that a government is of high quality. However, over the past two decades it has become increasingly clear that we need to expand the scope of study to include other aspects of government in order to understand government performance. This volume seeks to do just that, with in-depth explorations of quality of government, how it can be defined, measured, and identified empirically, and how it effects human well-being along with a range of other desirable outcomes. One central result is that for securing human well-being, representative democracy, which we for normative reasons certainly think is necessary in its own right, does not suffice. Without a reasonably high level of institutional quality, representative democracy is not likely to deliver increased human well-being (Holmberg and Rothstein 2012).

Research from the past decades consistently shows that quality of government is closely linked to almost all established measures of human well-being. Quality of government has important implications for public policy and socio-economic conditions in areas such as health, the environment, social policy, and poverty. As many of the chapters in this volume demonstrate, quality of government is closely linked to the root causes of poverty, population health, inequality, and public support of both domestic and international redistribution and foreign aid (You, this volume; Dietrich and Winters this volume; Kumlin this volume; Bauhr, Charron, and Nasiritousi 2013). In other words, low quality of government, for example in the form of high levels of corruption, effectively concentrates power and resources in the hands of affluent insiders, impeding redistribution and broad-based development, and entrenching or even aggravating the gap between the rich and the poor, and between the well-connected and the not so well connected. Another clear illustration of the importance of QoG is the link between corrupt healthcare systems and an increased use of antibiotics, and thereby the proliferation of bacterial resistance to existing antibiotics (Collignon 2015; Rönnerstrand and Lapuente 2017). The global over-consumption of antibiotics may lead us, in the words of the World Health Organization (WHO), to the very real possibility of "a post-antibiotic era" in the twenty-first century, where even common infections and minor injuries can become life threatening. The Covid-19 pandemic has similarly placed inordinately high demands on the functioning of government institutions, and research has already begun exploring these questions. Furthermore, QoG is also associated with a range of aspects of environmental performance (Povitkina and Matti, this volume). Thus, although only one of the United Nations' 17 sustainable development goals (SDGs) specifically call for countries to "Substantially reduce corruption and bribery in all their forms" and the development of rule of law and "effective, accountable and transparent institutions", most other goals may indeed be contingent on the achievement of these QoG-related targets. The costs of corruption are indeed breathtaking: the United Nations estimates that corruption, bribery, theft, and tax evasion cost some US$1.26 trillion per year for developing countries alone.

What, then, is QoG and why does it have such far-reaching implications? A number of chapters in the volume explore and debate QoG conceptually and historically (see the chapters by Kirby and Wolff; Mungiu-Pippidi and Rothstein in this volume), but the definition which we employ here was formulated by Rothstein and Teorell (2008). They define quality of government as the extent to which government power is exercised in a manner consistent with the norm of impartiality. In short, this means that government officials should, when exercising government power, base their decisions only on the factors and criteria stipulated in relevant law or policy directives. While a number of chapters in this volume broaden the scope of quality of government conceptually (e.g., the chapters by Ahlerup et al., Wedel, and Karceski and Kiser in this volume), we see advantages with a normative standard that applies specifically to the exercise of government power, not least because QoG does not correlate neatly with, for example, measures of democracy. Moreover, research that examines the effects of both democracy and quality of government find that they indeed have separate, though sometimes mutually reinforcing, effects on the type of valued outcomes mentioned above.

While most of the research we put forward in this volume is empirical, we want to emphasize that using the term "quality" in this enterprise stipulates that we are dealing also with a profoundly normative issue. Conceptualizing quality of government as impartiality in the exercise of government power takes its inspiration and motivation from preeminent works on social and political justice. John Rawls' landmark work *A Theory of Justice* argues that "[…] substantive and formal justice tend to go together and therefore that at least grossly unjust institutions are never, or at any rate rarely, impartial and consistently administered" (1971, 59). Rawls continues: "for if it is supposed that institutions are reasonably just, then it is of great importance that the authorities should be impartial and not influenced by personal, monetary, or other irrelevant considerations in their handling of particular cases" (1971, 59). This line of reasoning was continued by, inter alia, Brian Barry in his important book *Justice as Impartiality* published in 1995. In a comment to this book, Robert Goodin (2004) argues that the opposite to justice is *favoritism*, which is of course anathema to impartiality. QoG rests conceptually on a well-established foundation in political philosophy, and focuses on values of government that cannot be assessed within the normative standards of mainstream theories of democracy without considerable conceptual stretching.

Given the importance of the exercise of political power, or the administrative side of the state machinery, it is somewhat surprising that, until fairly recently, this was to a large extent neglected in political science and related disciplines. Until the late 1990s, interest in researching, for example, political corruption in political science and related disciplines such as economics, public administration, and policy analysis was very modest (Charron this volume; Rothstein and Varraich 2017). In political science, the main focus has been on "input" variables (e.g., elections, democratization processes, party systems) which is about the access to government power. The neglect of the equally important—if not the most important—part of the state machinery that exercises government power can, according to Fukuyama (2013), partly be understood as a symptom of the underlying ideological view inspired by neoclassical economics and the rational-choice theory, particularly strong in the United States, which emphasizes the need to limit, check, and control (and often also minimize) the state, tacitly seen as a predatory organization. In other words, how to "tame the beast" has been the central focus, not what the animal can achieve, and even less how best to design government institutions to best serve the long-term interests of the populace as a whole. What distinguishes research on the quality of government is that the ultimate dependent variable to be explained is not politics, but overall human well-being.

Theoretically, the focus on the quality of institutions owes much to what has been called the "institutional turn" in the social sciences. Around 1990, three major works were published that have had profound implications for the analysis of the importance of institutions, namely, James B. March and Johan P. Olsen's *Rediscovering Institutions*, Douglass C. North's

Institutions, Institutional Change and Economic Performance, and Elinor Ostrom's *Governing the Commons*. Although coming from different intellectual traditions, they had one thing in common, namely to challenge the then dominant societal view in studies of social and economic outcomes and development. Instead of focusing on how economic and sociological variables determined politics and outcomes of political systems, the institutional approach turned the causal logic around by arguing that the character of a society's political institutions, to a large extent, determined its economic and social development. In common language, the institutional turn in the social sciences showed why "the rules of the game" should have a more central role in social science research. The focus on institutions (instead of social structures or individual behavior) may also explain why research about QoG is both multidisciplinary and uses a wide range of research methods. As can be seen from the chapters in this volume, approaches in this area include historical and ethnographic methods, as well as statistics and comparative case methodologies (e.g., the chapters by Knights and Torsello in this volume).

QoG and Democracy

Apart from the discernible importance of QoG for a number of political, economic, and social outcomes, there are additional reasons why there is a need to focus on quality of government and not only on quality of democracy. The main reason is that it captures something that is etymologically and empirically distinct from democracy, and there are thus analytical advantages with keeping the concepts separated. Etymologically, "government" can of course refer to the "current government". However, most established dictionaries refer to the term as something that is done, namely to govern. Terms that are often used are, for example, "regulating," controlling," "administering," and "enforcing".[1] According to the *Encyclopædia Britannica 1911*, this goes back to the etymological origin in Greek of the term, which is "to steer." One definition in a leading dictionary is "the organization, machinery, or agency through which a political unit exercises authority and performs functions" (https://www.merriam-webster.com/dictionary/government). Taken together, this implies that quality of government refers to that part of the political system that David Easton (1965) labeled as the *output* side as opposed to the *input* side. The input side refers roughly to access to political power, while the output side is about the exercise of political power, usually in the form of the implementation of public policies.[2] Most conceptualizations and measures of degrees of democracy deal with the input side of the political system (Lindberg, Coppedge, Gerring and Teorell 2014), and capture elements crucial to understanding who has access to political power. These measures cannot, however, help us understand the workings of government bodies responsible for the exercise of political power in the implementation of public policies.

---

[1] See, Merriam-Webster online dictionary, Encyclopedia Britannica online, Cambridge Dictionary online.

[2] Output should not be confused with outcome, where output refers to policy decisions and outcome to the end result of policies.

Democracy, after all, relates to selecting leaders and policy directions within the normative constraint of political equality, in other words, when no actor has an inherent prerogative to exert her will over others. Disagreement, contestation, persuasion, and compromise are integral, even desirable, and some element of particularism, in which political leaders offer divisible benefits in exchange for partisan support, is inevitable (Piattoni 2001). Few find it normatively acceptable if or when these practices shape policy implementation, however, as for example if budget transfers were to be disbursed only to school districts with effective lobbying campaigns, or access to welfare programs were contingent on vote choice. Thus, not only does the word "government" clearly denote activities that go beyond the selection of leaders and policy formation, the activities of government also require normative standards that go beyond—and are entirely distinct from—those relevant to democracy.

It is sometimes argued that quality of democracy and quality of government are the same thing. However, if these two spheres of a political system are conflated, we will not be able to study how one affects the other. Simply put, we want to know if democracy serves to increase institutional quality or if the causality mainly operates in the other direction (Fukuyama 2014). The analytical advantage of conceptualizing QoG as something distinct from electoral-representative democracy is that (e)quality with respect to access to political power may be very different from the quality in how political power is exercised. In plain language, a country may in theory be of high quality with respect to the access to power (for example, impeccable free and fair elections and respect for democratic rights) but exhibit low quality in the exercise of power (for example, extensive corruption, bribe-paying, or a low level of competence in the implementation of public services).

Analytically, conceptualizing QoG as distinct from democracy thus also enables us to examine and understand how different aspects of institutional strength matter for societal outcomes, and even how, for example, corruption in public agencies shapes and is shaped by the quality of democratic institutions and processes. Empirically, most countries that score high on measures of the quality of democracy also score high on various measures of QoG. Beyond this set of best performers, however, the relationship is not always so clear (Bäck and Hadenius 2008; Bauhr and Charron 2018; Bauhr and Grimes, this volume). There are quite a number of democratic countries that suffer from high levels of corruption and, consequently, low quality in the implementation of public services.[3] Moreover, a handful of autocratic countries score quite high on indices for control of corruption.[4] Two of the most well-known cases where QoG has been much improved in recent times, Hong Kong under British rule and Singapore, managed to accomplish this rare feat without being democracies.

As mentioned above, the continued endeavor to theorize and study quality of government is also motivated by the mounting number of studies showing that QoG relates more strongly to levels of human well-being than does representative democracy. A somewhat surprising result of this research is thus that governing by the will of the people does not automatically enhance the well-being of the people. For example, comparing small countries, Rothstein (2011) shows that all standard measures of human well-being in democratic Jamaica are

---

[3] Examples are Brazil, Serbia, Greece, Jamaica, South Africa, Peru, and Bulgaria. Data from Transparency International's Corruption Perception Index 2019 and The Economist Democracy Index 2018.

[4] Examples are Singapore, United Arab Emirates, Brunei, and Qatar. Data from Transparency International's Corruption Perception Index 2019 and The Economist Democracy Index 2018.

much worse than in autocratic Singapore. However, both these former British colonies were equally poor in the early 1960s and if things like ethnic diversity, level of education, natural resources, and access to markets are considered, Jamaica had the far better prospects. Thus, democratic but highly corrupt Jamaica has been clearly outperformed by autocratic but less corrupt Singapore. The same pattern can be seen if we compare the two largest countries in terms of population. As Amartya Sen (2011) has shown, when it comes to measures of "quality of life," autocratic Communist China outperforms liberal democractic India on a large number of standard measures of human well-being. Why this is so may be connected to the particular way that Communist China organizes its public adminstration, which manages to combine a high level of competence and effectiveness with political/ideological loyalty, in organizational theory known as the "cadre type" of organization (Rothstein 2015).

A central question in much social science research is what influences citizens' attitudes about the legitimacy of their government. Broader surveys seeking to explain a range of developmental outcomes, as well as indicators measuring political legitimacy, have generated a wealth of evidence suggesting that neither democracy nor other factors such as the size of government spending or the specific policy approaches in place can explain the extensive variation in perceptions of political legitimacy that we see in the world today. Measures of quality of government have, many studies find, an independent effect on perceptions of political legitimacy. Much work in political theory would have us believe that democratic rights are the main source of political legitimacy. If people have the right to express their political opinions and vote for the political parties they prefer, and if the party or parties that get a majority of votes then formulate the policies they have promised in the election campaign, this should result in legitimacy for the political system. As shown in the chapter by Linde and Dahlberg in this volume, empirical research that has confronted this theory gives a somewhat different result. What is most important for voters when deciding if they think their governments are legitimate is not democratic rights or congruence between their values and their government's policies. Instead, it is things like control of corruption, respect for the rule of law, and the effectiveness of the public administration (Gilley 2009). Crucially, more impartiality in government institutions mitigates the gap between electoral winners and losers (Anderson and Tverdova 2003), and also neutralizes the impact of economic performance on satisfaction with democracy (Magalhães 2017). In terms of general support for the political system, QoG thus acts as a stabilizing force against the turbulence that may arise from economic ups and downs, as well as the sometimes very polarized competition inherent to democracy.

Moreover, how well representative democracy performs with respect to human well-being is, according to some studies, *contingent upon* the quality of government in the country. In most cases, representative democracy without institutional quality does not deliver increased human well-being (Halleröd, Rothstein, Daoud and Nandy 2013; Rothstein 2011). QoG is, according to empirical research, causally connected to two other variables considered important for "making democracy work." One is social trust and the other is people's satisfaction with their own lives. Social trust, a main ingredient in what has been labeled social capital, is largely generated by people's perception of the impartiality in public institutions in their societies (Dinesen and Sønderskov, this volume). Regarding life satisfaction (i.e. "happiness") results show that improved QoG has a significantly stronger effect than measures of democratic quality and measures of economic performance (Helliwell, Huang, and Wang, this volume). Dysfunctional administrative institutions and lack of QoG thus weaken democracy and its societal foundations (Bauhr and Grimes, this volume), decrease the legitimacy of the political system (Linde and Dahlberg, this volume), exacerbate difficulties in providing public goods (Persson, this volume), increase the risk of civil conflicts (Deglow and Fjelde, this volume), and may pave the way for political populism (Agerberg 2017; Keefer, Scartascini and Vlaicu, this volume).

How can we understand that democracy under conditions of low QoG may only weakly enhance human well-being? Democracy, as a system that institutionalizes competition among parties and political elites for the support of the electorate, may incentivize electoral contenders to use strategies that in and of themselves go outside the bounds of what most normative definitions of democracy prescribe. Knights (this volume) tells us that corruption in conjunction with elections was a concern from very early on, evident by the existence of a 1729 English law requiring voters to swear that they had not received a bribe or other inducement in exchange for their vote. Awareness of the potential for electoral competition to undermine democracy is thus not new.

Breaches of impartiality in institutions with core accountability functions, such as when Constitutional Courts and Supreme Audit Institutions are stacked with party loyalists, have the most severe repercussions for democracy. Basic human, political, and legal rights of government opponents become vulnerable to infringement. Incumbents may also undermine the autonomy of institutions responsible for ensuring electoral integrity, allowing for various strategies to manipulate the elections (Norris 2015). When constitutional courts, electoral commissions, and audit authorities become directly politically allied with incumbents, institutions presumed to serve as referees and rule-keepers instead become players in the political game. When incumbents capture institutions with the authority to detect and sanction corruption even at the highest level, filling them with political cronies, their effectiveness will suffer, and with it the rule of law. The rule of law principle implies that even incumbent politicians at the highest level are subject to the discipline of the law.

When the same types of breaches of QoG extend into administrative offices more generally, democracy becomes further compromised. Where QoG is low in the respect that public sector jobs are granted on the basis of personal or political loyalty rather than merit, incumbents have ampler opportunities to use strategies such as clientelism, patronage, and vote-buying. Where mid-level civil servants are loyal to incumbents, they are incentivized to allow and even organize clientelism in the form of granting access to public services in exchange for political support (Bustikova and Corduneanu-Huci 2017; Cornell and Grimes 2015) or patronage, in which lower level public sector jobs are similarly granted in exchange for party loyalty. The extent to which these strategies are available to political incumbents is to some degree a function of the extent to which elected representatives can and do fill upper and middle levels of the civil service with political allies. Granting jobs to political allies aligns civil servants' interests with those of the incumbent party, enabling incumbents to direct state resources in a targeted way to win additional votes and support, as civil servants at multiple levels of the bureaucracy are beholden to political patrons for their jobs (Dahlström and Lapuente, this volume). Taken together, these points shed light on why low QoG undermines the functioning of democracy, and helps to explain the particularly troublesome finding, namely that democratic elections in many cases do not function as a cure for corruption. Politicians that are known for being engaged in corruption quite often manage to get re-elected. Given what is known about people's overall negative attitudes towards corruption and the massive evidence that corruption is a very serious social ill, this shows that the accountability mechanism that democratic elections are supposed to produce does not always work as intended in mainstream democratic theory (Bågenholm in this volume; Xezonakis and Dawson, this volume).

These findings resonate with arguments from an intense discussion that has been labeled the "sequencing debate." The basic argument in this debate is whether successful and sustainable democratization can be achieved even absent a state machinery characterized by a well-developed administrative capacity, including a legal system where respect for the rule of law principles is established and where corruption is no longer prevalent. While this sequencing debate is far from settled, it further underscores the necessity to theorize and explore specific mechanism via which QoG might be beneficial for successful democratization (D'Arcy and Nistotskaya in this volume). Many of the possible implications of QoG for the functioning of democracy mentioned above are potentially relevant in this regard. To achieve legitimacy for elections, for example, they have to be administered in an impartial way so that voters and especially those on the losing side accept the election results. The existence of a professionalized, impartial, and uncorrupt election administration is thus necessary for electoral integrity and thereby for the legitimacy of any representative democracy (Birch 2011; Norris 2015). Similarly, when managerial civil service jobs become systematically politicized, democratic competition can politicize and weaken state structures (Cornell and Lapuente 2014). While many of these claims are often implied and seem theoretically plausible, much work remains to understand the mechanisms at work.

To sum up so far, if we want to know which political variables and institutions have an impact on human well-being, peace, social trust, life satisfaction, and the establishment of a well-working democracy, we have to conceptualize and theorize the part of the political system that *exercises* political power and that is responsible for implementing public policies. We also need this for understanding the synergies but also possible conflicts between representative democracy and the qualities of the state apparatuses that are responsible for the implementation of public policies. Given the deleterious effects of low quality of government for virtually all policy efforts to address societal problems, the question that emerges as one of the most urgent of our time is how, more precisely, we can enhance QoG. Many chapters in this volume attest to the self-reinforcing nature of corruption, not least because the development of high-quality institutions poses a collective action dilemma of the highest order. The historical accounts presented, for example, by the chapters of Berman, Knights, D'Arcy and Nistotskaya, and Uslaner in this volume, all suggest that the roots of high QoG can often seemingly be found centuries back in time. Social contract theory and the growing body of work on the political economy of state capacity tell us that once a well-functioning state is in place, democratic accountability works as intended, and corruption as well as clientelism can be kept at bay. But developing a state that effectively levies taxes, provides basic services, educates its population universally, and is no longer challenged by other sources of authority can potentially take generations. We do not in any way want to suggest that processes of democratization and democratic deepening ought to be postponed until a certain level of QoG is established. Instead, we want to emphasize that it is important for political activists and policymakers that strive to establish or secure representative democracy to also pay attention to issues related to QoG.

THE FUTURE RESEARCH OF QoG

At the time of writing, political protests are erupting across the globe. Protesters express indignation about inequality, government failures to provide services, and corruption. This groundswell of discontent clearly demonstrates a demand for redressing corruption. A number of chapters in this volume suggest that citizen engagement can prompt and sustain accountability and a broader reform agenda, but its transformative potential and positive effects cannot always be taken for granted (Boräng and Grimes; della Porta and Mattoni, this volume). We want to emphasize that despite evidence that democracy does not always weed out corruption, in many cases these protesters make use of the freedom and civil liberties promoted by democratic values, including those related to expression and association. Mobilization and coordination are certainly facilitated by a free press and social media platforms, and these institutions have been instrumental in the coordination of protests, oftentimes uniting citizens across sectarian and political party divides. This demand has driven former presidents and prime ministers from office, and in some cases has led to prosecutions of leading politicians in countries such as Argentina, Brazil, Italy, Iceland, South Korea, Romania, Peru, Ukraine, Thailand, and the Philippines (see Fukuyama and Rescanatini, this volume). Today's ongoing protests present a window of opportunity for large-scale institutional reforms. Even authoritarian China has stepped up its visible work against corruption. It is quite possible, however, that anticorruption protests may also pose a threat to democratic institutions and feed a distrust of democratically elected officials. Thus, although political power struggles are sometimes an integral part of corruption prosecutions, we have yet to see how this rising demand will translate into more effective electoral accountability mechanisms and the development of more impartial government institutions.

The cumulative evidence surveyed in the chapters of this volume does not in a convergent manner point to any single strategy to improve QoG, but taken together, they suggest a number of approaches that have contributed to improvements in the quality of government in some respects. Although the countries that in modern times have managed to make visible, large-scale, and measurable improvements in the quality of government are very few (including, e.g., Singapore and Georgia in recent years, though perhaps not sustained; South Korea and Hong Kong under British rule), the improvements should be seen in light of at least two important factors. First, improving the quality of government at the national level requires a massive effort of coalition-building, political leadership, and political clout, as well as knowledge on how anticorruption reforms fit into societies that surround them (Rotberg this volume; Johnston this volume). A partial explanation for why improvements have been modest can thus be that coordinated demand, agency, and knowledge about surrounding societal determinants do not always coincide. Second, both historically and in contemporary times, high quality of government has been an exception rather than the norm, and this state of affairs is not easily fixed by small adjustments or efforts such as anti-bribery campaigns (Persson, Rothstein, and Teorell 2013). This research agenda is one that ultimately relates to fundamental changes in how political institutions operate, as well as the direction of money flows. In well-functioning governments, resources are drawn from the population in the form of taxes, but they are also to a large extent distributed back to the population in the form of public services, infrastructure, or salaries. In corrupt systems, money to a large extent flows in the opposite direction. Bribes taken from citizens seeking services are passed upwards in the bureaucratic chain and once reaching the top level of administration, these and other forms of government revenues and resources are more likely to be placed in off-shore financial havens than brought back to serve the public good (Chayes 2015). It should be underlined that the international community has stepped up its efforts to improve QoG in fairly recent times, but global integration has also facilitated the internationalization of illicit activities as well (Holmes, this volume). While 30 years may be a long time span from the perspective of an individual's lifetime, the pace of progress in both policy and research arenas has to be related to the magnitude of the task at hand. There are certainly areas that need more research and important issues that have received less attention than they deserve. The chapters in this volume contain sections about what type of research is lacking in some of the most central subareas of QoG research.

Furthermore, the effectiveness of anticorruption measures are oftentimes evaluated using aggregate and extremely sticky perception-based measures of corruption. This provides a partial explanation for why national level improvements are seemingly difficult to achieve and why changes are not always picked up by standard measures of corruption. However, as several chapters in this volume point out, factors that contribute towards the improvements of quality of government may be better explored at alternative levels of analysis. These include variations within central state administration (see McDonnell and Vilaca, this volume); at the subnational, regional, or municipal levels (Charron this volume; Drápalová this volume); across different forms of corruption (Bauhr and Grimes, this volume); and also across different types of public service delivery sectors (Carlitz and Lust, this volume). A shift in the depth of focus may lead to a closer understanding of drivers of change. A very positive development is that the earlier concentration on the national level has been supplemented by an increasing number of studies that focus on the subnational level (regional as well as local) and on transnational networks.

This volume points to a wealth of factors and reforms that clearly warrant continued scrutiny, but also raise hopes for future improvements in QoG. One such example are studies on increased female representation, where recent studies have found a strong relationship between women in elected offices and quality of government. While more work is most certainly needed to determine if such effects will last over time and what explains the effects, work in this field may provide important keys to understanding processes of change (Alexander, this volume). Furthermore, evidence suggests that the way bureaucrats are recruited, promoted, dismissed, and incentivized (referred to by public administration scholars as "civil service systems") can have implications for opportunities to contain corruption, and in particular that an autonomous bureaucracy accountable to their professional peers rather than their political superiors may reduce corruption levels (Dahlström and Lapuente, this volume). Electoral systems can, moreover, be designed to facilitate electoral accountability by which corrupt representatives are booted out (Xezonakis and Dawson; Bågenholm, this volume). Outside the domestic arena, international cooperation and foreign aid can in some instances also produce beneficial effects (Dietrich and Winters this volume). The ratification of the United Nations Convention against Corruption (UNCAC) by over 180 countries indicates some level of commitment to the norm of QoG and universalism, and many international standards and tools are today available for those willing to use them (Lohaus and Gutterman, this volume). Going back some 30 years, we did not have UNCAC, and organizations such as the World Bank, the OECD, the African Union, the

European Union, the International Monertary Fund, and the World Economic Forum paid no attention whatsoever to this problem. No (even rudimentary) comparative measures of corruption existed, and research about this problem was almost non-existent. Political mass mobilizations for "clean government" were rare and hardly any political leaders were forced to resign because they had been implicated in corruption scandals. Writing about this problem in his study of India in the late 1960s, the Swedish Nobel Laureate Gunnar Myrdal noticed that issues about corruption were "taboo" both among academics as well as among policymakers around the world (see Rothstein and Varraich 2017, ch. 1). As can be seen from the contributions to this handbook, all these things have changed for the better during the last two decades, and this gives, we think, some room for optimism.

References

Agerberg, Mattias. 2017. "Failed expectations: Quality of government and support for populist parties in Europe." *European Journal of Political Research* 56 (3): 578–600.

Anderson, Christopher J., and Yuliya V. Tverdova. 2003. "Corruption, Political Allegiances, and Attitudes toward Government in Contemporary Democracies." *American Journal of Political Science* 47 (1): 91–109.

Bäck, Hanna, and Axel Hadenius. 2008. "Democracy and State Capacity: Exploring a J-Shaped Relationship." *Governance* 21 (1): 1–24.

Barry, Brian. 1995. *Justice as Impartiality*. Oxford: Oxford University Press.

Bauhr, Monika, and Nicholas Charron. 2018. "Insider or Outsider? Grand Corruption and Electoral Accountability." *Comparative Political Studies* 51 (4): 415–46.

Bauhr, Monika, Nicholas Charron, and Naghmeh Nasiritousi. 2013. "Does Corruption Cause Aid Fatigue? Public Opinion and The Aid-Corruption Paradox." *International Studies Quarterly* 57 (3): 568–79.

Birch, Sarah. 2011. *Electoral Malpractice*. Oxford: Oxford University Press.

Bustikova, Lenka, and Cristina Corduneanu-Huci. 2017. "Patronage, Trust, and State Capacity The Historical Trajectories of Clientelism." *World Politics* 69 (2): 277–326.

Collignon, Peter. 2015. "Antibiotic Resistance: Are We All Doomed?" *Internal Medicine Journal* 45 (11): 1109–15.

Chayes, Sarah. 2015. *Thieves of State: Why Corruption Threatens Global Security*. New York, N.Y.: WW Norton & Company.

Cornell, Agnes, and Marcia Grimes. 2015. "Institutions As Incentives for Civic Action: Bureaucratic Structures, Civil Society, and Disruptive Protests." *The Journal of Politics* 77 (3): 664–78.

Cornell, Agnes, and Victor Lapuente. 2014. "Meritocratic Administration and Democratic Stability." *Democratization* 21 (7): 1286–304.

Easton, David. 1965. *A Framework for Political Analysis*. Englewood Cliffs N.J.: Prentice-Hall.

Factor, Roni, and Minah Kang. 2015. "Corruption and Population Health Outcomes: An Analysis of Data from 133 Countries Using Structural Equation Modeling." *International Journal of Public Health* 60 (6): 633–41.

Fukuyama, Francis. 2013. "What is Governance?" *Governance: An International Journal of Policy, Administration and Institutions* 26 (3): 347–68.

Fukuyama, Francis. 2014. *Political Order and Political Decay: From the Industrial Revolution to the Globalization of Democracy*. First ed. New York: Farrar, Straus & Giroux.

Gauthier, Bernard, and Waly Wane. 2008. "Leakage of Public Resources in the Health Sector: An Empirical Investigation of Chad." *Journal of African Economies* 18 (1): 52–83.

Gilley, Bruce. 2009. *The Right to Rule: How States Win and Lose Legitimacy*. New York: Columbia University Press.

Goodin, Robert E. 2004. "Democracy, Justice and Impartiality." In *Justice and Democracy*, edited by Keith Dowding, Robert E. Goodin, and Carole Pateman, 97–111. Cambridge: Cambridge University Press.

Halleröd, Björn, Bo Rothstein, Adel Daoud, and Shailen Nandy. 2013. "Bad Governance and Poor Children: A Comparative Analysis of Government Efficiency and Severe Child Deprivation in 68 Low- and Middle-income Countries." *World Development* 48: 19–31.

Holmberg, Sören, and Bo Rothstein. 2011. "Dying of Corruption." *Health Economics, Policy and Law* 6 (4): 529–47.

Holmberg, Sören, and Bo Rothstein. 2012. *Good Government: The Relevance of Political Science*. Cheltenham: Edward Elgar.

Karasz, Palko. 2017. "In Romania, Corruption's Tentacles Grip Daily Life." *New York Times*, Feb. 9, 2017.

Lin, Ro-Ting, Lung-Chang Chien, Ya-Mei Chen, and Chan Chang-Chuan. 2014. "Governance Matters: An Ecological Association Between Governance and Child Mortality." *International Health* 6 (3): 249–57.

Lindberg, Staffan. I., Michael. Coppedge, John Gerring, and Jan Teorell. 2014. "V-DEM: A New Way to Measure Democracy." *Journal of Democracy* 25 (3): 159–69.

Magalhães, Pedro C. 2017. "Economic Outcomes, Quality of Governance, and Satisfaction with Democracy." In *Myth and Reality of the Legitimacy Crisis. Explaining Trends and Cross-National Differences in Established Democracies*, edited by Carolien Van Ham, Jacques Thomassen, Kees Aarts and Rudy Andeweg. Oxford: Oxford University Press.

Makary, Martin. 2015. "Greece's Costly Health Care Craze." *New York Times*, July 20, 2015.

March, James B., and Johan P. Olsen. 1989. *Rediscovering Institutions: The Organizational Basis of Politics*. New York: Basic Books.

Norris, Pippa. 2015. *Why Elections Fail*. Cambridge: Cambridge University Press.

North, Douglass C. 1990. *Institutions, Institutional Change and Economic Performance*. Cambridge: Cambridge University Press.

Ostrom, Elinor. 1990. *Governing the Commons: The Evolution of Institutions for Collective Action*. New York: Cambridge University Press.

Persson, Anna, Bo Rothstein, and Jan Teorell. 2013. "Why Anticorruption Reforms Fails: Systemic Corruption as a Collective Action Problem." *Governance-an International Journal of Policy Administration and Institutions* 26 (3): 449–71.

Piattoni, Simona. 2001. *Clientelism, Interests, and Democratic Representation: The European Experience in Historical and Comparative Perspective*. Cambridge: Cambridge University Press.

Pinzon-Florez, Carlos E., J. Alvaro Fernandez-Nino, Myriam Ruiz-Rodriguez, Alvaro Idrovo, and Abel Armando. A. Lopez. 2015. "Determinants of Performance of Health Systems Concerning Maternal and Child Health: A Global Approach." *PloS one* 10 (3): 27.

Rawls, John. 1971. *A Theory of Justice*. Oxford: Oxford University Press.

Rönnerstrand, Björn, and Victor Lapuente. 2017. "Corruption and Use of Antibiotics in Regions of Europe." *Health Policy* 121 (3): 250–6.

Rothstein, Bo. 2011. *The Quality of Government: Corruption, Social Trust and Inequality in a Comparative Perspective*. Chicago: The University of Chicago Press.

Rothstein, Bo. 2015. "The Chinese Paradox of High Growth and Low Quality of Government: The Cadre Organization Meets Max Weber." *Governance-an International Journal of Policy Administration and Institutions* 28 (4): 533–48.

Rothstein, Bo, and Jan Teorell. 2008. "What is Quality of Government: A Theory of Impartial Political Institutions." *Governance-an International Journal of Policy, Administration and Institutions* 21 (2): 165–90.

Rothstein, Bo, and Aiysha Varraich. 2017. *Making Sense of Corruption.* Cambridge: Cambridge University Press.

Sen, Amartya. 2011. "Quality of Life: India vs. China." *New York Review of Books* LVIII (25): 44–7.

World Bank. 2010. *Silent and Lethal: How Quiet Corruption Undermines Africa's Development Efforts.* Washington D.C.: The World Bank.

PART I

THEORY AND CONCEPTUALIZATION

....

CHAPTER 1

QUALITY OF GOVERNMENT
Theory and Conceptualization

....

BO ROTHSTEIN

INTRODUCTION: THE CONCEPTUAL MALAISE

ALMOST all important concepts used in the social sciences are contested, and what should count as quality of government (QoG) is no exception. We can just look at the endless conceptual discussions about concepts like power, democracy, violence, discrimination, governance, equality, (gender, social, economic, political) not to speak about corruption. From the outside, these discussions can easily be seen as endless (and meaningless) academic hair-splitting. Still, they are important because, as Giovanni Sartori (1970, 1038) famously pointed out, "concept formation stands prior to quantification." Without conceptual precision, operationalization in order to find empirical measures for the level and degree of QoG in different societies becomes impossible. It follows that without being able to measure the problem, we cannot compare the level of QoG between societies or study changes over time. If so, we will not be able to find out what may work as remedies for low QoG. As seen from the perspective of human well-being as put forward in the previous chapter, this is not a purely academic or insignificant problem.

One central idea for launching the QoG research enterprise has been to find a solution to the "eternal" problem of how to define corruption. In the Introduction to a *Handbook of Political Corruption*, published five years ago, the editor writes that although corruption has attracted a lot of attention, "there remains a striking lack of scholarly agreement over even the most basic questions about corruption. Amongst the core issues that continue to generate disputes are the very definition of 'corruption' as a concept" (Heywood 2014, 1). One of the main ideas behind the QoG approach has been to find a solution to this serious problem by using what in military strategy is known as the "encirclement strategy." Since corruption has been so difficult to define, the idea has been to try to find out what would be the "opposite of corruption." By this is meant an ambition to try to define what state of affairs we from a normative perspective would prefer that those who exercise public power should uphold. Or to be more precise, can we define a basic normative standard that we demand to be upheld in the exercise of public power. This implies that the QoG approach in a deliberative way combines empirical and normative theories. In earlier work, I have criticized the well-established and de facto entrenched division between normative and empirical theory in the social sciences as being highly detrimental to research efforts that aspire to say anything about real-world (policy) issues (Rothstein 1998). We may like to live in a society in which people think that the quality of their public institutions is fairly high, that the general ethical standard among their fellow citizens is reasonably high, implying that they perceive corruption to be uncommon and that they think that "most people in general" can be trusted. If this is the case, then the question of whether research in the social sciences can be relevant becomes a question of the extent to which it can contribute to increased human well-being or, to paraphrase the title of another book in this approach, whether the discipline can contribute to our understanding of why some societies are more "successful" than others (Hall and Lamont 2009). This implies that we have crossed the line between the normative (value) and empirical (fact) approaches. As argued by Gerring and Ysenowitz (2006, 105).

> We cannot conceptualize the scholarly significance of a theoretical framework or a particular empirical puzzle without also contemplating its relevance to society, its normative import-ance. This underlying feature of social science provides the missing organizing element, without which the activity of social science is, quite literally, meaningless.

FOUR CHOICES IN DEFINING QUALITY OF GOVERNMENT

Below, I will specify a number of dimensions on which this conceptual enterprise has to make choices. As stated by Hempel, "theory formation and concept formation goes hand in hand ... neither can be carried on successfully in isolation from the other" (cited in Gerring 1999, 364). In this, I rely heavily on the approach of concept formation in political science that goes back to Giovanni Sartori (1970) and that has been expanded by, for example, David Collier, John Gerring, and Andreas Schedler (for a summary, see Schedler 2010). It should be kept in mind that the goal is to establish a definition of QoG that a) resonate with important works in political philosophy and b) can be operationalized in such a way that we can actually measure the level of QoG in different countries (or regions or cities or branches of public administration within these entities). Such a process of concept formation carries a number of choices that one has to make; below I will discuss four of them.

A NORMATIVE OR AN EMPIRICAL STRATEGY?

One issue is whether QoG should be defined by a certain ethical norm that pertains to how government power is exercised or if, as argued by Fukuyama (2013), this conceptualiza-tion should be confined to more empirical "things," such as bureaucratic autonomy and capacity. One can think of four reasons for a normative definition. First, terms like "good" (as in "good governance," see below), not to mention corruption, are inherently normative.

Something is "good" in relation to a certain norm (or norms), and it is therefore necessary to specify this norm (Kubbe and Engelbert 2018; Johnston 2018). To state that a political process or a person that holds a public position is corrupt is doubtless a normative judgement. Secondly, as mentioned in the Introduction to this volume, several empirical results show that the exercise of a state's power is often the most important factor in determining whether people consider their governments to be legitimate or otherwise. Since perceptions of political legitimacy are inherently normative, we have to conceptualize this norm(s). It should be noted that the legitimacy of how the "input" side of a democratic political system should be organized is, according to Robert Dahl, based on a single basic norm, namely *political equality*, which in practice is equal voting rights and equal right to stand for office (Dahl 2006; 1989). Thus, we should be able to find the parallel basic norm for the "output" side the political system. Obviously, it cannot be "political equality" since most laws and public policies entail that citizens should be treated differently (pay different taxes, get different benefits, subsidies and services dependent on their specific situation and circumstances). Thirdly, the risk with empirical definitions is that they have a tendency to become equal to the outcome we want to explain, which makes them tantamount to tautological. One example is the definition of good institutions provided by Acemoglu and Robinson (2012). Their well-known argument is that it is institutions of a certain kind that promote economic prosperity. Such institutions, they argue, should be "inclusive." With this, they mean institutions that "allow and encourage participation by the great mass of people in economic activities that make best use of their talents and skill and enable them to make the choices they wish." Such institutions should also "secure private property, an unbiased system of law, and a provision of services that provides a level playing field in which people can exchange and contract." Moreover, such institutions "also must permit the entry of new business and allow people to choose their careers." The list goes on. The institutions that are needed for economic prosperity should also "distribute power broadly in society" and ensure that "political power rests with a broad coalition or plurality of groups" (Acemoglu and Robinson 2012, 73 and 80).

The problem with this definition is that it is very close to what the theory intends to explain. How surprised should we be that a society with such "inclusive" institutions will create the good and prosperous society and that a society with the opposite type of "extractive" institutions will be bad and poor? Their argument is close to stating that a good society will produce a good (or prosperous) society. The same can be said for definitions of QoG that includes effectiveness. The purpose of this conceptual enterprise is to explain why some states are more effective (in producing human well-being) than others, and if we include effectiveness in the very definition of QoG, we will not be able to explain variation in effectiveness.

The central issue is this: if a society decides to organize its public administration according to a certain norm (or set of norms) which states, for example, who will work in this administration and according to which principle(s) civil servants and professionals will make decisions, will this result in higher organizational capacity and competence? Furthermore, will this make it more likely that the politicians will entrust this administration with a certain degree of autonomy? The empirical answer to this question seems to be in the affirmative. For example, if civil servants are recruited based on the norm of impartiality, which means that factual competence for the job in question is what decides recruitment and promotion, this will lead to higher efficiency in the public administration and thus to higher state capacity, which in turn is likely to lead to increased levels of human well-being (Dahlström and Lapuente 2017; Rothstein 2018). Thus, the procedural principle of impartiality translates in practice into what is usually labeled *meritocracy* which, inter alia, leads to increase competence and capacity in the public sector. A final reason for a normative definition of QoG, instead of pointing at specific empirically existing institutions, is that if we look at countries that are judged to have high levels of QoG, their political and legal institutions, as well as their systems of public administration, show remarkable organizational variation (Andrews 2013). The same goes for countries that are ranked high on measures of democracy. This implies that simply exporting specific institutional configurations from high QoG to low QoG countries will not work to improve QoG. When this has been tried, the results have not been encouraging (Mungiu-Pippidi 2015). The reason seems to be that it is not the specific institutional configuration of the state and the public administration, but the basic norm (or norms) under which the institutions operate, that is the crucial factor.

A CULTURALLY SPECIFIC OR A UNIVERSAL DEFINITION?

The development of the international "anti-corruption regime" since the late 1990s has not been without its critics. One point that has been stressed in this critique is that this agenda represents a specific Western liberal ideal that is not easily applicable to countries outside that part of the world (Bracking 2007; Bukovansky 2006; Bratsis 2003; Hindess 2005; de Maria 2010). There are at least three arguments against this type of relativistic conceptual framework. The first is normative and based on a similar discussion in the areas of universal human rights and the principles of representative democracy. First, the right not to suffer discrimination by public authorities, the right not to have to pay bribes for what should be free public services, and the right to be treated with "equal concern and respect" from the courts are in fact not very distant from what counts as universal human rights (Rothstein and Varraich 2017, ch. 4). The second reason against a relativistic definition of corruption is empirical. Although the empirical research in this area is not entirely unambiguous, most of it points to the relatively surprising result that people in very different cultures seem to have a very similar notion of what should count as corruption. Survey results from regions in India and in sub-Saharan Africa show that people in these societies take a very clear stand against corruption and view the problem in much the same manner as it is understood in, for example, Denmark or by organizations such as the World Bank and Transparency International (Rothstein and Tannenberg 2015; Nichols, Siedel, and Kasdin 2004; Miller et al. 2001). For example, Widmalm (2008, 2005), studying remote and highly corrupt villages in India, finds that the Weberian civil servant model (the impartial treatment of citizens, disregarding income, status, class, caste, gender, and religion), although an absent figure in these villages, has surprisingly large support among the village population.

The existence of a universal understanding of corruption has also been questioned by postcolonial theorists (for an overview of this literature, see Gustavson 2014). However, Frantz Fanon, in his classic book, *The Wretched of the Earth*, which in many ways is ideologically the most important and founding text for the postcolonial approach to development issues, points to corruption among the new political elite as a serious malady for West Africa. In Fanon's words:

> Scandals are numerous, ministers grow rich, their wives doll themselves up, the members of parliament feather their nests and there is not a soul down to the simple policeman or the customs officer who does not join in the great procession of corruption. (Fanon 1967, 67)

The reluctance by many postcolonial scholars to regard corruption as a serious problem for the countries they study is thus difficult to understand. It is symptomatic that a recently published *Handbook of Postcolonial Politics* does not even have index entries on "clientelism," "patronage," "nepotism," or "corruption" (Rutazibwa and Shilliam 2018).

A third argument is that, ultimately, a thoroughly relativist approach in which corruption "can mean a variety of things and is context dependent" (Croeze, Vitória, and Geltner 2017, 3) will imply that we will have to operate with one theory of corruption per country, and city, and village, not to mention per century or even decade. Biologists call both hummingbirds and eagles birds, although they are utterly different in size. Corn snakes and anacondas are both snakes. One is huge and deadly while the other is often a pet. Apparently, something unique to these very different species unites them under the same category. When trying to understand what has been seen as corruption over time and space, it is this unique characteristic that we are looking for. Analyses of what counted as corruption in very distant pasts, such as Athens during the fourth century BCE (Taylor 2017), the Roman Empire (MacMullen 1988; Arena 2017), the Middle East during the tenth and eleventh centuries (van Berkel 2017), thirteenth-century France (Jordan 2009), and late medieval England (Watts 2017) give the impression of not being qualitatively different from contemporary notions of the concept. There is a common theme in these historical analysis, namely that corruption was "the promotion of one's own interest above those of the public, and the bending of rules or official powers under the influence of bribery of affection" (Watts 2017, 93). In sum, there are both normative but also strong empirical grounds for opting for a universal understanding of what should count as QoG.

THE PUBLIC GOODS APPROACH

One way to understand why there seems to exist a universal understanding of what should count as corruption despite its enormous variation both in types, frequency, and location, is what can be called the *public goods approach* to this problem. In all societies/cultures, in order to survive, all groups of people have to produce at least a minimal set of public goods such as security measures, a basic infrastructure, and organized/collective forms for the provision of food. As Fukuyama (2011, 29) has argued, the very idea proposed by rational choice–oriented contract theorists that we as humans started out as atoms in a state of nature and then decided to rationally accept a "social contract" is highly misleading. Instead, he argues, humans were from the beginning always living in some form of societal and collective arrangements.

The very nature of a good being "public" is that it is to be managed and distributed according to a principle that is very different from that of private goods. The public good principle implies that the good in question should not be distributed according to the private wishes of those who are given the responsibility for managing them. When this principle for the management and distribution of public goods is broken by those entrusted with the responsibility for handling the public goods, the ones that are victimized see this as malpractice and/or as corruption. This is why corruption is a concept that is related to the public and not the private sphere and why it is different from (or a special case of) theft and breaches of trust in the private sector. Private actors are of course very often engaged in and the source of corruption (for example by paying bribes, or getting public contracts in exchange for political support), but what they are corrupting is some public entity. Corruption is usually seen as illegal, but the reason that a special term has been used for such a long time and in so many different cultures must be that it is a special form of crime different from ordinary theft. If the public institutions are organized in a way that makes them serve private instead of public interest, this can be labeled "institutional corruption" (Thompson 2018). A well-known case is Marx's critique of Hegel's idea of the state as neutral arbiter that served to promote individual freedom and the common good. Instead, Marx argued that even a democratic state is nothing but an operation for catering to the common needs of the capitalist class (Marx and Engels 1998, 99).

Much of the confusion about cultural relativism in the discussion, about what should count as corruption, stems from the issue that what should count as "public goods" differs between different societies and cultures. For example, in an absolutist feudal country where the understanding may be that the central administration is the private property of the lord/king, the state is not seen as a public good. However, in many indigenous societies with nonstate political systems, local communities have usually produced some forms of public goods, for example, what Ostrom (1990) defined as "common-pool resources" which are natural resources that are used by members of the group, but which risk depletion if overused. Such resources are constantly faced with a "tragedy of the commons" problem and is thus in need of public goods in the form of effective regulations to prevent overuse leading to depletion.

This argument takes as a point of departure the idea that it is difficult to envision a society without some public goods. Even a small tribe has to produce some minimal public goods such as security, handling of internal conflicts, and, for example, caring for orphans. The point is: when these public goods are handled or converted into private goods, this is generally understood as corruption independent of the culture. A conclusion that follows is that we should not expect people in developing countries, whether indigenous or not, to have a moral or ethical understanding of corrupt practice that differs from, for example, what is the dominant view in Western organizations like Transparency International or the World Bank, or as that stated in the UN convention against corruption. Instead, what may differ is what is understood to fall within the public goods category.

An example could be the case in which there is no system of taxation, but there exist functions in which certain individuals have been selected to act as arbitrators or judges. These functions are to be understood as public goods because they make it possible to solve disputes between village members/families in a nonviolent way. These arbitrators may, in several cases, receive gifts from the parties involved for their services. Such gifts may, for a Westerner, look like bribes, and many anthropologists have seen them as such (Torsello and Vernand 2016). However, such gifts are usually not seen as bribes by the agents, who in general can make a functional distinction between bribes and gifts (Sneath 2006; Werner

2000; Alatas 1999). This implies that the gift is to be seen as a fee for a service, not a bribe. It would only be a bribe, and seen as such by the local populace, if it was given in a way to influence adjudication by favoring one party over another. For example, in the Muslim world, as early as the ninth and tenth centuries, a clear distinction was made between allowable gifts and illegal bribes. An "allowable gift" was something "to which no condition is attached," while a bribe was something given to a "political authority with the aim of obtaining his help or support" (van Berkel 2017, 69). In cases like this, the public good is converted into a private one and it is this that is perceived as corruption. To support this argument, Rothstein and Torsello (2014) have used data from the Human Relations Area Files (HRAF), which is the single most comprehensive and largest ethnographic database of world cultures. The HRAF database has been compiled by Yale University and includes data on 258 world cultures and over 600,000 pages of ethnographic descriptions made by professional anthropologists. The cultures covered are divided among eight world regions (Africa, Asia, Europe, Middle America and the Caribbean, Middle East, North America, Oceania, and South America). Their analysis shows that the word "bribe" is found in 113 of the 258 cultures, which is 48% of the whole HRAF sample when excluding European countries. It is also found in all four general types of societies (foragers, horticulturalists, pastoralists, and agriculturalists). The agriculturalists societies/cultures (which are also monetized and commercial) contain the largest number of bribery entries, which supports the thesis that corruption is widespread where public and private arrangements for the use of and access to resources and goods can be expected to vary. Even more interesting is their finding that pastoralist societies are apparently the least exposed to corruption among the subsistence types. This also supports the "public goods" theory, since it is in this economic type of society that one should expect to find the least ambiguity between private goods (herds and land) and public goods.

Should the Definition of QoG Be Based on Political Procedures or Policy Substance?

Is QoG something that should be defined by reference to a set of political procedures or should it be defined by reference to certain policies or outcomes? An example of the latter is the well-known definition of "good governance" provided by Daniel Kaufmann and colleagues at the World Bank, which among other things include "sound policies" (Kaufmann, Kraay, and Mastruzzi 2004). Agnafors, a political philosopher, has argued for including the "moral content" of the enacted laws or policies into the definition (Agnafors 2013). The well-known problem faced by any substantive definition of democracy and of course also QoG is why diverse people, who can be expected to have very different views about policies, should accept them. Since we are opting for a definition which can be universally accepted and applied, the inclusion of specific policies becomes problematic. To use Rawls' terminology, political legitimacy requires an "overlapping consensus" about the basic institutions for justice in a society, so that citizens will continue to support them even when they have incommensurable conceptions of "the meaning, value and purpose of human life" and even if their group would lose political power (Rawls 2005). This is of course less likely to be the case if specific (sound) policies or moral content of the laws are included in the definition of QoG.

Including as the World Bank does "sound policies" in the definition also raises the quite problematic question of how international (mostly economic) experts can be expected to be in possession of reliable answers to the question of what "sound policies" are. For example, should pensions, healthcare, or education be privately or publicly funded (or a mix of these)? To what extent and how should financial institutions be regulated? Secondly, such a definition of QoG, which is not restricted to procedures but includes the substance of policies, raises what is known as the "Platonian-Leninist" problem. If those with superior knowledge decide policies, the democratic process will be emptied of most substantial issues. The argument against the "Platonian-Leninist" alternative to democracy has been put forward by one of the leading democratic theorists, Robert Dahl, in the following way: "its extraordinary demands on the knowledge and virtue of the guardians are all but impossible to satisfy in practice" (Dahl 1989, 65).

All this implies that a strictly procedural definition of QoG is to be preferred. This also follows from the ambition to define QoG in a manner parallel with the "access side" definition for liberal representative democracy, which speaks for a strictly procedural definition. The system known as liberal representative democracy should not in itself favor any specific set of policies or moral standards (except those that are connected to the democratic procedures as such, including basic human rights).

There is a well-known drawback to all procedural definitions of political processes for decision-making, namely that they cannot offer a guarantee against morally bad decisions. There is simply no guarantee that perfectly democratically made decisions in a representative democracy will not result in severe violations of the rights of minorities and individuals. As Mann has argued, there is a "dark side" to democracy (Mann 2005). This is also the case for any procedural definition of QoG, be it ethical universalism (Mungiu-Pippidi 2015), impersonal "open access" rule (North, Wallis, and Weingast 2009), bureaucratic autonomy and capacity (Fukuyama 2013), or impartiality in the exercise of public power (Rothstein and Teorell 2008). In this approach, the strategy suggested by John Rawls may be the right one. His central idea is that if a society structures its systems for making and enforcing collective decisions in a fair way, this will increase *the likelihood* that the outcomes are normatively just. As Rawls stated: "substantive and formal justice tend to go together and therefore that at least grossly unjust institutions are never, or at any rate rarely, impartial and consistently administered" (Rawls 1971, 51).

SHOULD THE DEFINITION OF QoG BE MULTI- OR UNIDIMENSIONAL?

Several attempts to define QoG have argued for a multidimensional or "complex" strategy. QoG should entail that decisions in the public administration adhere to "efficiency," "public ethos," "good decision-making," "transparency," "accountability," and "stability" to name a few. Others have argued for a unidimensional strategy (Mungiu-Pippidi 2015; Rothstein and Teorell 2008). There are certainly advantages with the multidimensional definition since they cover more aspects of a problem. However, from an analytical standpoint, there are several drawbacks with the multidimensional strategy (also sometimes labeled "thick" conceptualizations). The first one is that we may treat what is basically an empirical question by definitional fiat. Simply put, we want to explain why high QoG makes some states' public administration more efficient than others, and this implies that we cannot include, for example, efficiency in the definition of QoG since we do not want to state that efficiency explains efficiency. The same goes for "good decision-making" (as suggested by Agnafors 2013) and "capacity" (as suggested by Fukuyama 2013). We want a definition of QoG that can be helpful in explaining why the public administration in some states has a better capacity for making good decisions than the public administration in other states (or regions, cities), and if we include what we want to explain in the definition, this explanatory purpose becomes impossible.

The problem with using *accountability* is that this term lacks a normative base (cf. Fukuyama 2014). No organization or bureaucrat can be held accountable in general since you are always held accountable according to some specified normative standard(s). The same goes for transparency—it is what you discover when a process is transparent that determines if you will think it is of low or high quality. Accountability and transparency are important for QoG, but only as tools.

A well-known problem with multidimensional definitions is how to handle a situation when a state for which we want to measure QoG shows very different values on the dimensions. The World Bank researchers on "good governance" include five different dimensions and Agnafors (2013) six. The question then becomes how to handle situations where rule of law is zero but where there is maximum efficiency (or stability, or public ethos, or good decision-making). Would that be a state with 50% QoG? As Agnafors (2013, 440) readily admits, there can be "no universal and complete weighing procedure" for solving this problem. His solution is that "one can perform an *incomplete* weighing, at least in theory, because it will be inescapably messy in practice."

Producing a definition that is so thick that it cannot be operationalized in any meaningful sense will not help us answer the question of why some states are much more successful than others in implementing policies that cater to the basic needs of their citizens. If we were to follow this conceptual strategy, the question of what politics can do to combat, for example, severe child deprivation or extremely high rates of women dying in childbirth, will never be answered. Here, Agnafors (2013), as well as many other contemporary political philosophers, stands in stark opposition to John Rawls, who argued that one aim of political philosophy "is to probe the limits of practicable political possibility" and "must describe workable political arrangements that can gain support from real people" (citation from Wenar 2017). Rawls' famous theory of justice does entail two equal basic principles, but, *nota bene*, they are lexically ordered, making it clear which of them has priority (Wenar 2017).

As argued by Van Parijs (2011, 1), "it is sound intellectual policy … not to make our concepts too fat." He continues, and we agree, "fat concepts hinder clear thinking and foster wishful thinking. By packing many good things under a single label, one is easily misled into believing that they never clash." As has been known ever since the time of William Ockham, ontological parsimony is an analytical virtue. In sum, the conceptual obesity that is suggested by Agnafors (2013) and many others for what should constitute QoG will inevitably lead to explanatory impotence and thereby become unusable for policy recommendations. This is not only a question of internal academic civilities and intellectual hair-splitting, since we now know that low QoG has severe effects on human well-being.

QoG as Impartiality in the Exercise
of Political Power

A state regulates relations between its citizens along two dimensions. One is the "input" side, which relates to *access* to public authority, institutionalized in democracies by rules concerning elections, party financing, the right to stand for office, political rights, and the formation of cabinets. The other side of the political system is the "output" side, which refers to the way in which that political authority is *exercised*. On the input side, where access to power and thereby the content of policies are determined as stated above, the most widely accepted basic regulatory principle has been formulated by Robert Dahl (1989): that of *political equality*. This is also John Rawls' (2005) basic idea of how to construct a non-utilitarian society based on his well-known principles of justice. Political equality certainly implies impartial treatment on the input side of the system, and this makes political equality and impartiality partly overlapping concepts (Rawls 2005; Goodin 2004). For example, elections have to be administered by the existing government, but if they are to be considered free and, in particular, *fair*, the ruling party must refrain from organizing them in a manner that undermines the opposition's possibilities to obtain power. However, the impartial organization of elections does not imply that the content or outcome of this process is impartial. On the contrary, the reason for why many, if not most, people are active in politics is that they are motivated by very partisan interests. A working democracy must thus be able to implement the partisan interests produced by the input side of the system in an impartial way. The question then becomes: how can this be conceptualized? Partly based on Strömberg (2000), Rothstein and Teorell (2008, 170) have suggested the following definition of QoG:

> When implementing laws and policies, government officials shall not take anything into consideration about the citizen/case that is not beforehand stipulated in the policy or the law. In this context, impartiality is not a demand on actors on the input side of the political system, but first and foremost an attribute of the actions taken by civil servants, professional corps in the public services, law enforcement personnel and the like.

To see why this definition of QoG is universal, it is useful to compare it to Dahl's idea of *political equality* as a basic norm for democracy. Every democratic state is, in its institutional configuration, different. It should suffice to point to the extreme variation in the electoral systems in, for example, the Swiss, the Danish, and the British democracies. There are in fact innumerous ways in which to organize a national democracy (presidentialism vs. parliamentarism, uni- vs. bicameralism, proportional vs. majoritarian electoral systems, variation in the power of the courts, federalism vs. unitarianism, the role of referendums, the strength of local governments, etc.). As long as the principle of equality in the access to power is not violated (for example by giving one specific political party the right to rule, or by refusing to give some specific group of citizens the right to stand for office or take part in the public debate) we can consider countries with such differing political systems as in Finland and in the USA to be democracies. The reason is that all institutional arrangements on the input side in a representative democracy should be possible to justify through the principle of "political equality." Impartiality as the parallel legitimatizing and defining principle for the "output" side can in a similar way also encompass various administrative practices or interests.

Kurer (2005, 230) has also tried to define corruption in terms of impartiality. His definition is that "corruption involves a holder of public office violating the impartiality principle in order to achieve private gain." As Kurer argues, the advantage with this definition of corruption is that what counts as a breach of impartiality is fairly universally understood and thus not related to how things like "abuse" or "misuse" of public power are viewed in different cultures. The advantage of this definition is that impartiality does not only rule out all forms of corruption, but also practices such as clientelism, patronage, nepotism, political favoritism, discrimination, and other forms of "particularisms."

John Rawls states that "it is supposed that if institutions are reasonably just, then it is of great importance that the authorities should be impartial and not influenced by personal, monetary, or other irrelevant considerations in their handling of particular cases" (Rawls 1971, 58). In the political philosophy discussion about impartiality, this distinction between which norms should guide the content versus the procedural sides of the political system is readily seen in Brian Barry's important book *Justice as Impartiality*. Barry argues that impartiality should be a normative criterion in the exercise of political power: "like cases should be treated alike" (Barry 1995, 126). His idea of "second order impartiality" implies that the input side of the political system should be arranged so that it gives no special favor to any conception of "the good." However, as Barry readily admits, his theory "accepts that a demand of neutrality cannot be imposed on the outcomes" (Barry 1995, 238). Accordingly, when it comes to decisions about the content of the policies that governments should pursue, it is not neutrality or impartiality but "reasonableness" that is his main criterion (Barry 1995, 238). In Barry's words: "What is required is as far as possible a polity in which arguments are weighed and the best arguments win, rather than one in which all that can be said is that votes are counted and the side with the most votes wins" (Barry 1995, 103).

The implication is the one argued for here, namely that impartiality cannot be a moral basis for the content of policies that individuals, interest groups, and political parties pursue on the input side of the political system since reasonableness is not the same as impartiality. For example, in a given situation, there may be good reasons for lowering public pensions and increasing support to families with children. This is, however, not the same as being impartial between these two groups, because there is no such thing as an impartial way to decide in a case like this.

What is presented here is thus not of the grand ambition that Barry, Rawls, and other political philosophers have pursued, namely to construct a universal theory of social and political justice. The ambition is more modest, namely to construct a theory of what should count as QoG. In other words, when a policy has been decided upon by the representative democratic system, be it deemed just or unjust according to whatever universal theory of justice one would apply, QoG demands that it be implemented in accordance with the principle of impartiality.

The conclusion is that there is a higher probability that a political system that institutionalizes access to power on the fairness principle of "political equality" will produce outcomes that increase social and political justice than if access to power is organized in a different manner. The equivalent for the administrative side of the state would then be that if implementation of policies is based on a norm such as impartiality, the *probability* of normatively good outcomes would increase.

An often used argument against this definition of QoG in terms of the principle of impartiality in the exercise of public power is that, in theory, a Nazi extermination camp could be administered in an impartial way (Agnafors 2013; Fukuyama 2013). The first thing to be said about comments like this is that an overwhelming part of the historical research about how the Third Reich was administrated gives a completely different picture. Instead of impartiality, the *modus operandi* of the Nazi state was systematic politically and ideologically motivated favoritism, personalistic rule, clientelism, disregard and manipulation of the rule of law principles, disregard of professional knowledge, and ad hoc decision-making (Evans 2009; Broszat 1981; Aly 2007). The idea of the impartially administrated Nazi state or concentration camp belongs to the "crazy cases" approach in political philosophy which, according to Goodin (1982), strongly increases the discipline's irrelevance. As he stated:

> First we are invited to reflect on a few hypothetical examples—the more preposterous, the better apparently. Then, with very little further argument or analysis, general moral principles are quickly inferred from our intuitive responses to these "crazy cases." ... Whatever their role in settling deeper philosophical issues, bizarre hypotheticals are of little help in resolving real dilemmas of public policy. (Goodin 1982, 8)

Secondly, the same problem exists for the procedural principles following from political equality which form the basic norm for representative democracy—there is nothing in this norm that hinders the majority in an ever so correct procedural representative democracy to decide illiberal policies that seriously violate human rights for individuals or minorities (King 1999; Zakaria 2003). This problem of the possibility of normatively unwanted outcomes is unavoidable if we want to arrive at a procedural definition of QoG (or liberal democracy). That is why most democratization activists and organizations nowadays usually speak of "democracy and human rights" as if these are inseparable. There is certainly nothing that hinders policy activists and policy organizations to start promoting "quality of government and human rights." However, from a theoretical perspective, democracy, corruption, and QoG are separate concepts and should not be conflated, since we want to know how they are empirically related. As stated by Fukuyama (2013, 351), we probably would not want to "argue that the US military is a low-quality one because it does things we disapprove of, say, invading Iraq?" If we define QoG by "good outcomes" or include "the moral status of the laws" and/or the "public ethos" (Agnafors 2013), we will be creating a conceptual tautology by saying that society with a high moral standard and a good "public ethos" will result in good outcomes. That is like saying that the good society is a prerequisite for achieving the good society. Simply put, we must have the intellectual courage to admit that a public organization can have a high quality and low corruption in doing what it does even if, from a moral perspective, we disapprove of the policies it is carrying out. It goes without saying that we as individuals can often think that a public policy is grossly unfair and unjust even if it is decided by a perfectly correct democratic procedure. As we see it, this is just one side of how majoritarian democracy is supposed to work. After all, most people become engaged in politics because they are partisan to some cause, group, or idea. However, the point we want to make implies that we should normatively prefer even policies that we disagree with to be implemented in an impartial way. If we include the substance of policies in the definition, QoG becomes simply the efficient implementation by a public authority of the policies that we happen to like. Moreover, a reasonably high level of QoG can be seen as a prerequisite for establishing democracy (Fukuyama 2014). Almost all stable "elite" democracies in

Northwestern Europe first managed to create state capacity and get corruption under control, and it was after that they became democracies.

Alternative I: The Rule of Law

Impartiality is a central ingredient in most definitions of the rule of law (Versteeg and Ginsburg 2017). However, to limit QoG to rule of law principles is problematic because this would exclude many professional and semi-professional groups that implement public policies but for which the *modus operandi* of the rule of law is not directly applicable. Teachers and school principals, doctors and nurses, social workers, urban planners, and engineers responsible for infrastructure projects are of course supposed to work within the laws that exist in their areas of expertise. However, when professionals are asked to implement projects related to public policies, they cannot refer back to a formal legal code because no such laws exist. This is because it is impossible to create laws with enough precision. There can be no law guiding exactly how doctors should act when deciding what medical treatments should be given to their patients, or when social workers should decide if a child is in such dire circumstances that it should be taken into custody, or how teachers should deal with unruly students in the classroom. In cases like these (and they are many), the rule of law principle does not work because there is no applicable law. Thus, in cases like these, it is not legal devices but *established professional knowledge and ethics* that should guide what the public servants are doing (Rothstein 1998). Moreover, in many cases, we do not want these professions to act like Weberian bureaucrats but to tailor their actions according to the very specific needs of every case. However, when doing so, we expect them not to be engaged in various forms of favoritism but to adhere strictly to their professional knowledge and ethics.

An analysis of four different comparative measures[1] of to what extent the "rule of law" principles are respected and implemented in different countries finds some very interesting results. Although the four indexes are built on quite different conceptual strategies, empirically they correlate to a surprisingly high degree. The pair-wise correlation between three of them exceeds 0.95 (the forth is about 0.80) and they also correlate at this high level with the measure of corruption constructed by Transparency International (Versteeg and Ginsburg 2017) and with the measure of "impartial administration" constructed at the Quality of Government Institute (Dahlström et al. 2015). From this, the authors conclude that the reason why the differently constructed indexes of the "rule of law" correlate so highly is that they seem to "fit into a broader umbrella concept of impartiality" which they argue might be "a higher order concept" that connects corruption and the "rule of law," thereby capturing the "essence" of both indicators (Versteeg and Ginsburg 2017, 124). The authors also argue that although impartiality is a "thin" concept, relating only to procedures and excluding the normative substance of the rules, the "thicker" conceptualization of the "rule of law" does not add anything. In other words, the "thicker" conceptualizations of the "rule of law" that includes the normative substance of the rules do not matter. One conclusion from this is that

---

[1] The indexes are constructed by the Heritage Foundation, Freedom House, the World Bank, and the World Justice Project.

we here may have found empirical support for John Rawls' presumption that "thin" procedural justice is likely to result in "thick" substantive justice.

Alternative II: Good governance

The concept of "good governance" was introduced, in part, by various development organizations as a code word for the opposite of corruption. It reflects very much the "institutional turn" in the social sciences inspired by North (1990). The term refers mainly to traditional Weberian-style organization (meritocracy, legality, hierarchy, impersonality) of the implementation process by state institutions. However, in some approaches, it also includes the "input" side of the political system, thereby blurring the important distinction between quality of democracy and QoG (Fukuyama 2016). Another problem with "good governance" is that the term *governance* is used in very different and sometimes quite opposite ways in other areas of the social sciences. In public administration and public policy, it very much refers to a critique of the Weberian model as being "rigid and bureaucratic, expensive and inefficient" (Pierre and Peters 2005, 5). Here, governance means the establishment of more or less loose networks for social coordination, including public, private, and semi-private institutions. In yet a different approach, governance means social coordination without the involvement of government institutions (Rhodes 1996). A fourth approach to "governance" is what has become known as "participatory governance" or "democratic governance." This approach emphasizes the role that ordinary citizens can play in influencing politics outside (or beside) the traditional channels in representative democracy. A strong focus in this approach is given to various forms of deliberative practices in which citizens can discuss and form opinions about how to solve various collective problems (Bevir 2010). Global governance is a fifth approach that refers to international networks of both public and transnational private institutions that cooperate to set standards and regulate both public policies and business operations, mainly through "codes of conduct" and other forms of soft law (Fukuyama 2016).

These various (and the many other[2]) approaches to governance identify important processes and changes in the contemporary political landscape, but problems arise from the fact that the term is used to denote very different processes and that the conceptualization of governance in none of these approaches is overwhelmingly precise (Fukuyama 2016). On the contrary, leading scholars of this approach make a virtue of the ambiguousness of the concept (Levi-Faur 2012; Lynn 2012). In a critical analysis, Offe (2009) has highlighted two problems: the concept lacks boundaries and is empty of agency. Moreover, there is no verb form of the word like there is for government. Members of the government can govern, but what is it that members of a network of governance are doing? In reality, the concept tends to capture all forms of collective social coordination, outside pure market relations or the family. The problem is that such a broad understanding of governance makes it difficult to distinguish it from all other forms of social coordination. To empirically operationalize a concept like this and to make it measurable seem to be out of reach.

---

[2] Wikipedia lists 20 different types of governance, see https://en.wikipedia.org/wiki/Governance

Alternative III: Impersonal or objective rule

Fukuyama (2016) and North, Wallis, and Weingast (2009) use the term "impersonal" instead of the term we suggest ("impartial"). The term "the objectivity principle" is sometimes also used (Rothstein and Sorak 2017). This is usually seen merely as a terminological and not a conceptual difference. However, in dictionaries, "impersonal" is defined as "having or showing no interest in individual people or their feelings: lacking emotional warmth," or as "without human warmth, not friendly and without features that make people feel interested or involved," or as "lacking friendly human feelings or atmosphere, making you feel unimportant." In contrast, "impartial" is typically defined as "not supporting one person or group more than another" or as "not prejudiced towards or against any particular side or party; fair; unbiased."[3]

The reasons why we should prefer "impartial" to "impersonal" or "objective" is based on the notion that states, when producing public goods/services, do not only or even for the most part rely on personnel that have legal training or orientation. Instead, both Western and developing states use a number of professions or semi-professions such a doctors, teachers, school principals, nurses, urban planners, architects, engineers, and social workers when implementing public policies. For many of these professions, the idea that they would be working according to the "rule of law" in the sense that they implement rules in an "impersonal" or "objective" manner makes little sense. They do, of course, follow the laws, but as is well-known from the literature about policy implementation, the laws that are supposed to guide what these professions do have to be quite general, and thus they cannot entail precise information about how to handle each and every case (Hill and Hupe 2002). Instead, as indicated above, what is important for these groups, when implementing public services, is the standards, knowledge, and ethics established by their professional organizations. Moreover, we do not want nurses, teachers, people who care for the elderly, or doctors to have "no interest in individual people or their feelings" or to be "lacking emotional warmth" when they do their jobs. On the contrary, we want them (and they usually also want) to be personally engaged in and committed to their jobs. Feminist scholars have rightly pointed to the existence of a "public ethics of care" that differs from mechanical rule-following as well as from an impersonal orientation (Stensöta 2010). In sum, the professional groups working in the public sector are expected to exercise some autonomy or discretion over their professional competence and judgement, but this should not be used in a way that can be deemed as giving undue favors. In other words, they should be impartial but not impersonal.

IMPARTIALITY—THE CRITICS

For some, the notion of impartiality in the execution of public policies may seem uncontroversial, since it is akin to rule of law principle. There are, however, at least four strong approaches in the social sciences which in an almost axiomatic way deny the possibility of impartiality. Inspired by neoclassical economics, the public choice approach to government

---

[3] For references to these dictionaries, see Rothstein and Varraich (2017, 100f).

starts from the assumption that civil servants are operating according to the "rent-seeking model" in which agents are self-interested utility maximizers (Mueller 1997). This is of course an axiom that is antithetical to impartiality. The same can be said of most economic analyses built on the notion that what dominates human motivation is self-interest (Weingast and Wittman 2006). In Marxism, the state usually is seen as an organization for supporting the common interest of the ruling capitalist class or international capital, which of course rules out the notion of impartiality (Therborn 2008). In addition, several identity-oriented approaches where the idea that a person with identity X could make an impartial evaluation of the merits of a person with identity Y, is seen as impossible (Burke and Stets 2009). Iris Marion Young, for example, states the following: "the ideal of impartiality serves ideological functions. It masks the ways in which the particular perspectives of dominant groups claim universality, and helps justify hierarchical decision making structures" (1990, 97). She also stated that impartiality is an "impossible ideal because the particularities of and affiliation cannot and should not be removed from moral reason" (ibid.). In addition, the approach in development studies known as "post-colonialism" understands principles such as impartiality as an expression of Western semi-imperialist ideology (de Maria 2010). In sum, the notion of impartiality as the basic norm for what should count as QoG is far from uncontroversial.

One way to respond to the critique of impartiality is to adapt a "Churchillian" approach. Like liberal representative democracy, impartiality as QoG may be far from a perfect system, but given the empirical results presented above and in many of the chapters in this volume, it may be the best we can devise, since all the alternatives are worse. Another comparison is with political equality as the basic norm for liberal representative democracy, suggested by noted democracy theorist Robert Dahl (1989). Given the very large and usually accumulative differences between citizens in economic resources, human capital, and usable networks, every known democracy today must be light years away from anything that comes even close to the realization of political equality. It is far from certain that the problem of actually implementing the principle of impartiality in the execution of public policies is greater than that exposed by the vast differences in equality of opportunity to influence politics offered by the system of representative democracy. In both cases, as the political philosophers would state it, we are in for nonideal theory (Erman and Möller 2018). If we could find a way to measure how far the two ideals are from reality, my guess is that the principle of impartiality is closer to the ideal than the principle of political equality.

Conclusions

There are several reasons that explain why representative democracy does not suffice for what should count as high-quality government. Theoretically, when analyzing a political system, it makes sense to make a distinction between the *access* to power and the *exercise* of power. Empirically, available measures show that high-quality democracy (access to power) and high QoG (exercise of power) in many cases do not correlate. Several empirical studies show that variables connected to the quality of the institutions that implement public policies are very important for establishing political legitimacy. A third reason is that historically, increased institutional quality in many cases preceded democratization. An additional argument is that QoG is highly correlated to measures of human well-being, in most studies more so than measures of democracy. We have also identified a number of potential conflicts between electoral-representative democracy and QoG.

In defining QoG, the argument presented is that we should strive for a normative, procedural, universal, and parsimonious definition that can be operationalized and measured. The definition should not include the system of access to power (e.g., representative democracy) since we want to be able to explain the relation between representative democracy and QoG. It should also not include things like efficiency or capacity, since we want to be able to explain if QoG has a positive or negative impact on these things. Following the "Rawls-Machiavelli" Programme as suggested by Van Parijs, this conceptual strategy can be seen as resting on the assumption (or hope) that if we as political scientists can suggest "just institutions" for implementing collectively binding decisions, the people that come to operate these "just institutions" are also likely to produce morally good outcomes. The alternative, that we should suggest specific ("sound") policies or prescribe the "moral status" of the laws runs in the face of the need to reach an "overlapping consensus" for how collectively binding decisions should be made and implemented. We have also cast some doubts on the ability of experts and researchers to find correct and legitimate answers to these questions.

It has been emphasized that no such procedural definition (of democracy or QoG) can work as a guarantee against morally bad outcomes—we are dealing with probabilities, not absolute certainty. Since empirical research shows that higher levels of QoG (but not representative democracy) are related to higher levels of human well-being (and political legitimacy), one can argue that we as social and political scientists have a moral obligation to increase our ambitions to define, measure, and study what takes place at the "output" side of the political system. This is not an entirely academic affair in which real-world implementation is sacrificed for an ideal (but un-implementable) definition. There are good reasons to argue that a major part of human misery in modern times is caused by the fact that a majority of the world's population is forced to live under dysfunctional (low-quality) government institutions.

As has been shown in other studies from the Quality of Government Institute, this definition of QoG can be operationalized and measured in both expert surveys and surveys with representative samples of the population (Charron, Lapuente, and Rothstein 2013; Dahlström and Lapuente 2017; Dahlström, Lapuente, and Teorell 2011). Neither experts nor ordinary people seem to have problems understanding and answering the battery of survey questions that follows from this definition of QoG. Moreover, these measures largely perform in the expected way when correlated with various outcome measures such as measures of human well-being. In closing, we argue that the opposite of corruption can be defined, measured, and operationalized. This implies that we can find explanations for the huge variation in QoG that exists between societies over time and in space. Some of these explanations may be situated in historical and structural factors that are beyond our capacity to change, while others may be within the reach of effective policies (Rothstein and Teorell 2015). While increasing QoG in a systemically corrupt society may well be an Herculean task, a number of historical cases show that this can be done (Mungiu-Pippidi and Johnston 2017; Rotberg 2017; Uslaner 2019).

References

Acemoglu, Daron, and James A. Robinson. 2012. *Why Nations Fail: The Origins of Power, Prosperity and Poverty*. London: Profile.

Agnafors, Marcus. 2013. "Quality of Government: Toward a More Complex Definition." *American Political Science Review* 107 (3): 433–45.

Alatas, S. Hussein. 1999. *Corruption and the Destiny of Asia*. Englewood Cliffs, N.J.: Prentice-Hall.

Aly, Götz. 2007. *Hitler's Beneficiaries: Plunder, Race War, and the Nazi Welfare State*. 1st U.S. ed. New York: Metropolitan.

Andrews, Matt. 2013. *The Limits of Institutional Reform in Development: Changing Rules for Realistic Solutions*. Cambridge: Cambridge University Press.

Arena, Valentina. 2017. "Fighting Corruption: Political thought and practice in the Late Roman Republic." In *Anticorruption in History*, edited by Ronald Kroeze, André Vitória, and Guy Geltner. Oxford: Oxford University Press.

Barry, Brian. 1995. *Justice as Impartiality*. Oxford: Oxford University Press.

Bevir, Mark. 2010. *Democratic Governance*. Princeton: Princeton University Press.

Bracking, Sarah, ed. 2007. *Corruption and Development. The Anti-Corruption Campaigns*. New York: Palgrave.

Bratsis, Peter. 2003. "The Construction of Corruption, or Rules of Separation and Illusions of Purity in Bourgeois Societies." *Social Text* 21 (4): 9–33.

Broszat, Martin. 1981. *The Hitler State: The Foundation and Development of the Internal Structure of the Third Reich*. London: Longman.

Bukovansky, Mlada. 2006. "The hollowness of anti-corruption discourse." *Review of International Political Economy* 13 (2): 181–209.

Burke, Peter J., and Jan E. Stets. 2009. *Identity Theory*. Oxford; New York: Oxford University Press.

Charron, Nicholas, Victor Lapuente, and Bo Rothstein. 2013. *Quality of Government and Corruption from a European Perspective: A Comparative Study of Good Government in EU regions*. Cheltenham: Edward Elgar.

Croeze, Ronald, André Vitória, and G. Geltner, eds. 2017. *Anticorruption in History: From Antiquity to the Modern Era*. Oxford: Oxford University Press.

Dahl, Robert A. 1989. *Democracy and Its Critics*. New Haven: Yale University Press.

Dahl, Robert A. 2006. *On Political Equality*. New Haven: Yale University Press.

Dahlström, Carl, and Victor Lapuente. 2017. *Organizing the Leviathan: How the Relationship between Politicians and Bureaucrats Shapes Good Government*. Cambridge: Cambridge University Press.

Dahlström, Carl, Victor Lapuente, and Jan Teorell. 2011. "The Merit of Meritocratization: Politics, Bureaucracy, and the Institutional Deterrents of Corruption." *Political Research Quarterly* 65 (3): 656–68.

Dahlström, Carl, Jan Teorell, Stefan Dahlberg, Felix Hartman, Annika Lindberg, and Marina Nistotskaya. 2015. "The QoG Expert Survey: Report II." Working Paper 2015: 9. Gothenburg: The Quality of Government Institute, University of Gothenburg.

de Maria, William. 2010. "Why is the president of Malawi angry? Towards an ethnography of corruption." *Culture and Organization* 16 (2): 145–62.

Erman, Eva, and Niklas Möller. 2018. *Practical Turn in Political Theory*. Edinburgh: Edinburgh University Press.

Evans, Richard J. 2009. *The Coming of the Third Reich*. Peterborough: Royal National Institute for the Blind.

Fanon, Frantz. 1967. *The Wretched of the Earth*. Harmondsworth: Penguin Books.

Fukuyama, Francis. 2011. *The Origins of Political Order: From Prehuman Times to the French Revolution*. New York: Farrar, Straus and Giroux.

Fukuyama, Francis. 2013. "What is Governance?" *Governance: An International Journal of Policy, Administration and Institutions* 26 (3): 347–68.

Fukuyama, Francis. 2014. *Political Order and Political Decay: From the Industrial Revolution to the Globalization of Democracy*. New York: Farrar, Straus & Giroux.

Fukuyama, Francis. 2016. "Governance: What Do We Know, and How Do We Know It?" In *Annual Review of Political Science, Vol 19*, edited by Margaret Levi and Nancy L. Rosenblum, 89–105. Palo Alto: Annual Reviews.

Gerring, John. 1999. "What makes a concept good? A criterial framework for understanding concept formation in the social sciences." *Polity* 31 (3): 357–93.

Gerring, John, and Joshua Ysenowitz. 2006. "A Normative Turn in Political Science." *Polity* 38 (1): 101–33.

Goodin, Robert E. 1982. *Political Theory and Public Policy*. Princeton: Princeton University Press.

Goodin. 2004. "Democracy, Justice and Impartiality." In *Justice and Democracy*, ed. K. Dowding, R. E. Goodin, and C. Pateman. Cambridge: Cambridge University Press.

Gustavson, Maria. 2014. *Auditing Good Government in Africa: Public Sector Reform, Professional Norms and the Development Discourse*. New York: Palgrave Macmillan.

Hall, Peter A., and Michèle Lamont, eds. 2009. *Successful Societies: How Institutions and Culture Affect Health*. New York: Cambridge University Press.

Heywood, Paul M., ed. 2014. *Routledge Handbook of Political Corruption*. London: Routledge.

Hill, Michael J., and Peter L. Hupe. 2002. *Implementing Public Policy. Governance in Theory and Practice*. London: Sage.

Hindess, Barry. 2005. "Investigating international anti-corruption." *Third World Quarterly* 26 (8): 1389–98.

Johnston, Michael. 2018. "Democratic Norms, Political Money, and Corruption." In *Corruption and Norms: Why Informal Rules Matter*, edited by Ina Kubbe and Annika Engelbert, 13–30. Basingstoke: Palgrave Macmillan.

Jordan, William Chester. 2009. "Anti-corruption campaigns in thirteenth-century Europe." *Journal of Medieval History* 35: 204–19.

Kaufmann, Daniel, Art Kraay, and Massimo Mastruzzi. 2004. "Governance Matters III: Governance Indicators for 1996–2002." The World Bank Policy Research Working Paper 3106.

King, Desmond S. 1999. *In the Name of Liberalism: Illiberal Social Policy in the USA and Britain*. Oxford: Oxford University Press.

Kubbe, Ina, and Annika Engelbert, eds. 2018. *Corruption and Norms: Why Informal Rules Matter*. Basingstoke: Palgrave Macmillan.

Kurer, Oscar. 2005. "Corruption: An Alternative Approach to Its Definition and Measurement." *Political Studies* 53 (1): 222–39.

Levi-Faur, David. 2012. "From 'Big Government' to 'Big Governance.'" In *The Oxford Handbook of Governance*, edited by David Levi-Faur. Oxford: Oxford University Press.

Lynn, Laurence E. Jr. 2012. "The Many Faces of Governance." In *The Oxford Handbook of Governance*, edited by David Levi-Faur. Oxford: Oxford University Press.

MacMullen, Ramsay. 1988. *Corruption and the Decline of Rome*. New Haven: Yale Univ. Press.

Mann, Michael. 2005. *The Dark Side of Democracy: Explaining Ethnic Cleansing*. New York: Cambridge University Press.

Marx, Karl, and Friedrich Engels. 1998. *The German Ideology*. Amherst, N.Y.: Prometheus Books.

Miller, William L., Grødeland Åse B., and Tatyana Y. Koshechkina. 2001. *A Culture of Corruption? Coping with Government in Post-Communist Europe*. Budapest: Central European University Press.

Mueller, Dennis C. 1997. *Perspectives on Public Choice: A Handbook*. New York: Cambridge University Press.

Mungiu-Pippidi, Alina. 2015. *The Quest for Good Governance: How Societies Develop Control of Corruption*. New York: Cambridge University Press.

Mungiu-Pippidi, Alina, and Michael Johnston, eds. 2017. *Transition to Good Governance*. Cheltenham: Edward Elgar.

Nichols, Philip M., George J. Siedel, and Matthew Kasdin. 2004. "Corruption as a Pan-Cultural Phenomenon: An Empirical Study in Countries at Opposite Ends of the Former Soviet Empire." *Texas Journal of International Law* 39 (2): 215–36.

North, Douglass C. 1990. *Institutions, Institutional Change and Economic Performance*. Cambridge: Cambridge University Press.

North, Douglass C., John J. Wallis, and Barry R. Weingast. 2009. *Violence and Social Orders: A Conceptual Framework for Interpreting Recorded Human History*. Cambridge: Cambridge University Press.

Offe, Claus. 2009. "Governance: An 'Empty Signifier'?" *Constellations* 16 (4): 550–61.

Ostrom, Elinor. 1990. *Governing the Commons: The Evolution of Institutions for Collective Action*. New York: Cambridge University Press.

Pierre, Jon, and B. Guy Peters. 2005. *Governing Complex Societies: Trajectories and Scenarios*. Basingstoke: Palgrave MacMillan.

Rawls, John. 1971. *A Theory of Justice*. Oxford: Oxford University Press.

Rawls, John. 2005. *Political Liberalism (expanded edition)*. New York: Columbia University Press.

Rhodes, R. A. W. 1996. "The New Governance. Governing without Government." *Political Studies* 44 (4): 652–67.

Rotberg, Robert I. 2017. *The Corruption Cure: How Leaders and Citizens Can Combat Graft*. Princeton: Princeton University Press.

Rothstein, Bo. 1998. *Just Institutions Matter: The Moral and Political Logic of the Universal Welfare State*. Cambridge: Cambridge University Press.

Rothstein, Bo. 2018. "Epistemic Democracy and the Quality of Government." *European Politics and Society*. Online version Sept 7, 2017.

Rothstein, Bo, and Nicholas Sorak. 2017. "Ethical Codes for the Public Administration." QoG Working Paper 2017:12. Gothenburg: The Quality of Government Institute, University of Gothenburg.

Rothstein, Bo, and Marcus Tannenberg. 2015. "Making Development Work: The Quality of Government Approach." Report 2015:17. Stockholm: Swedish Government Expert Group for Aid Studies.

Rothstein, Bo, and Jan Teorell. 2008. "What is Quality of Government: A Theory of Impartial Political Institutions." *Governance: An International Journal of Policy, Administration and Institutions* 21 (2): 165–90.

Rothstein, Bo, and Jan Teorell. 2015. "Causes of Corruption." In *Routledge Handbook of Political Corruption*, edited by Paul M. Heywood, 79–94. London: Routledge.

Rothstein, Bo, and Davide Torsello. 2014. "Bribery in pre-industrial societies: Understanding the universalism-particularism puzzle." *Journal of Anthropological Research* 70 (2): 263–82.

Rothstein, Bo, and Aiysha Varraich. 2017. *Making Sense of Corruption*. Cambridge: Cambridge University Press.

Rutazibwa, Olivia, and Robbie Shilliam. 2018. *Routledge Handbook of Postcolonial Politics*. New York: Routledge.

Sartori, Giovanni. 1970. "Concept misformation in comparative politics." *American Political Science Review* 64 (4): 1033–53.

Schedler, Andreas. 2010. Concept Formation in Political Science. Mexico City: CIDE.

Sneath, David. 2006. "Transacting and enacting corruption, obligation and the use of money in Mongolia." *Ethnos* 71 (1): 89–122.

Stensöta, Helena O. 2010. "The Conditions of Care: Reframing the Debate about Public Sector Ethics." *Public Administration Review* 70 (2): 295–303.

Strömberg, Håkan. 2000. *Allmän förvaltningsrätt*. Mamlö: Liber.

Taylor, Clare. 2017. "Corruption and Anticorruption in Democratic Athens." In *Anticorruption in History*, edited by Ronald Kroeze, André Vitória, and Guy Geltner, 21–34. Oxford: Oxford University Press.

Therborn, Göran. 2008. *What Does the Ruling Class Do When It Rules: State Apparatuses and State Power under Feudalism, Capitalism and Socialism*. New ed. London: Verso.

Thompson, Dennis F. 2018. "Theories of Institutional Corruption." *Annual Review of Political Science* 21: 495–513.

Torsello, Davide, and Bertrand Vernand. 2016. "The Anthropology of Corruption." *Journal of Management Inquiry* 25 (1): 34–54.

Uslaner, Eric M. 2019. *The Historical Roots of Corruption: Mass Education, Economic Inequality, and State Capacity*. New York: Cambridge University Press.

van Berkel, Maaike. 2017. "Fighting Corruption between Theory and Practice." In *Anticorruption in History*, edited by Ronald Kroeze, André Vitória, and Guy Geltner, 65–76. Oxford: Oxford University Press.

van Parijs, Philippe. 2011. *Just Democracy: The Rawls-Machiavelli Programme*. Colchester: ECPR press.

Versteeg, Mila, and Tom Ginsburg. 2017. "Measuring the Rule of Law: A Comparison of Indicators." *Law & Social Inquiry* 42 (1): 100–37.

Watts, John. 2017. "The Problem of the Personal. Tackling Corruption in Later Medieval England, 1250–1550." In *Anticorruption in History*, edited by Ronald Kroeze, André Vitória, and Guy Geltner, 91–102. Oxford: Oxford University Press.

Weingast, Barry R., and Donald A. Wittman. 2006. *The Oxford Handbook of Political Economy*. New York: Oxford University Press.

Wenar, Leif. 2017. "John Rawls." In *Stanford Encyclopedia of Philosophy*, edited by Edvard N. Zalta. Center for the Study of Language and Information: Stanford University. https://plato.stanford.edu/archives/spr2017/entries/rawls/

Werner, Cynthia. 2000. "Gifts, Bribes and Development in Post-soviet Kazakhstan." *Human Organization* 59 (1): 11–22. Widmalm, Sten. 2005. "Explaining Corruption at the Village Level and Individual Level in India." *Asian Survey* XLV (5): 756–76.

Widmalm, Sten. 2008. *Decentralisation, Corruption and Social Capital: From India to the West.* Thousand Oaks: SAGE Publications.

Young, Iris M. 1990. *Justice and the Politics of Difference.* Princeton: Princeton University Press.

Zakaria, Fareed. 2003. *The Future of Freedom: Illiberal Democracy at Home and Abroad.* 1st ed. New York: W. W. Norton & Co.

CHAPTER 2

....

THE UNIVERSALIZATION
OF ETHICAL UNIVERSALISM

....

ALINA MUNGIU-PIPPIDI

INTRODUCTION

In spring of 2019, French President Emmanuel Macron announced his intention to abolish the École nationale d'administration (ENA), the elite postgraduate institution that counts presidents, prime ministers, and chief executives among its ranks (indeed Macron himself graduated from ENA). The decision stunned both French and international public opinion, as ENA stood as a symbol of the selection by merit of modern European bureaucracy, something that many developing countries would pay dearly to have. ENA worked like many elite schools, drawing on its networks of alumni, political connections, and "revolving doors" to connect top decision-makers. "If we want to build a society of equal opportunity and national excellence, we must reset the rules for recruitment, careers and access to the upper echelons of the civil service," Macron said, according to a leaked text of his speech on the reform (*Agence France-Presse* 2019). "That's why we will change the system of training, selection and career development by suppressing ENA and several other institutions," the president went on to say. For many, it appeared as if President Macron chose to defend himself from the Yellow Vests by giving the populists exactly what they wanted: the symbolic destruction of the quintessential political elite establishment.

And yet President Macron, aside from the national debates on what was wrong with France before taking this decision, can resort to the highest authority. Already in 1835, Alexis de Tocqueville (1954: 6) wrote that the advancement of "the equality of conditions" is "a providential fact, and it possesses all the characteristics of a divine decree: it is universal, it is durable, it constantly eludes all human interference, and all events as well as all men contribute to its progress" (6). Since then, ethical universalism—defined as the moral principle that all persons ought to be treated with equal and impartial positive consideration for their respective goods or interests—has seemingly conquered the world: many constitutions and in particular the United Nations Declaration of Human Rights and the United Nations Convention against Corruption have truly universalized the principle, if not the practice.

This chapter is a succinct introduction to the intellectual and policy course of ethical universalism from the specific (if not really narrow) angle of "quality of government" as defined by Rothstein and Teorell (2008), that is, impartiality in the exercise of public authority in a democratically elected government. Its glorious road to universal recognition, if not universal implementation, could fill several dissertations and books on political development (and some very good ones have already been written). However, unlike the human rights angle of ethical universalism, which has received ample coverage, the relation of ethical universalism to quality of government has been understudied. This chapter attempts to fill this gap. It is organized as follows: in the following section, I define and trace the history of ethical universalism as a governance norm and benchmark; then, I look at the progress in government practice over time and across the world; and finally, I briefly review current trends and challenges to adopting and implementing this new international norm.

WHAT IS ETHICAL UNIVERSALISM?

Ethical universalism can be defined as the moral principle that all persons ought to be treated with equal and impartial positive consideration for their respective goods or interests (Gewirth 1988). Three interrelated concepts in political theory meet here: first, that of *equity*, making people who are equal in respect to contribution also equal in respect to outcomes; second, that of *reciprocity*, the assumption that fairness should be responded to in kind; and third, that of *impartiality*, in other words, of judgment free of favoritism and observant of rules only (Wilson 1993, 70). At the interpersonal level, psychologists discuss *reciprocity*, while game theorists label it *reciprocal altruism* (Trivers 1971), the inner attribute which makes an individual treat another fairly and cooperatively due to the expectation of reciprocation of such treatment. In the sphere of governance, ethical universalism has been from time immemorial the most basic moral principle, resulting in equality before the law and therefore of an impartial and nonselective justice: the basics of what we today call "rule of law." Control of corruption, or the capacity of a state to operate autonomously from private interest for the greatest social welfare possible, is the implementation of the same ethical universalism principle in the distribution of public goods and allocation of public resources. Both utilitarianism, the main philosophy underpinning modern public policy, and the doctrine of human rights draw on ethical universalism, as both provide for the equal and impartial consideration of interests (Gewirth 1988). While utilitarianism requires individuals to be weighted equally when adding up their utilities to the greatest possible overall sum of individual welfares, the principle of human rights, on the other hand, requires that all persons be treated equally and impartially with the aim to secure their individual entitlement. Of course, the two doctrines can only clash in situations when individual and collective entitlements do not coincide. But for our purpose here, it is enough to notice how their nineteenth-century progress has contributed to infusing modern governance with the principle of ethical universalism, each in its own separate way.

Ethical universalism rose to salience with the Enlightenment, but it has always been enshrined in the ancient debate on justice and public virtue. Cicero provided the best outline of the argument and thus became the influential source for later thinkers, from theologians to lawyers (Mungiu-Pippidi 2015, ch. 3). He argued for this moral principle to be upheld basically due to its practicality in a republic defined as "an association of rights": "by what rule can the association of citizens be held together, if the condition of the citizens be not equal?" (Cicero 1877, 383). We thus endorse ethical universalism because it is the only principle allowing a rational human organization, and as such it has become part of what James Q. Wilson called "the moral sense." During the Enlightenment the same reason underpinned the social contract concept, which can only conceivably be based on ethical universalism.

Cicero synthesized previous Greek and Roman thought on the matter when explaining in his *De Officiis* (*On Duties*) that:

> Those who propose to take charge of the affairs of government should not fail to remember two of Plato's rules: first, to keep the good of the people so clearly in view that regardless of their own interests they will make their every action conform to that; second, to care for the welfare of the whole body politic and not in serving the interests of some one party to betray the rest. For the administration of the government, like the office of a trustee, must be conducted for the benefit of those entrusted to one's care, not of those to whom it is entrusted. Now, those who care for the interests of a part of the citizens and neglect another part, introduce into the civil service a dangerous element—dissension and party strife (Cicero 2006, 66).

Thus, corruption has always been central to political philosophy and inseparable from every conceptualization of just government, due to the early intuition that unchecked power leads to partiality in the act of governing. If Enlightenment thinkers did not use the term "corruption" often—or used it more to indicate the decay of morals—this is largely on account of the fact that corruption was institutionalized as *privilege* (hereditary or status bound), and equality was their concern far more than *venality* related to the public function (hereditary or for-sale offices). John Locke (2003) does not mention corruption, for instance, but defines "tyranny" in fairly Aristotelian terms as "making use of the power any one has in his hands, not for the good of those who are under it, but for his own private, separate advantage" (188). This view of good government as *nonpartisan government* and of the good state as *autonomous from private interest* has been gradually built up, becoming nearly dominant in Europe after the Enlightenment in different forms of social contracts and political legitimacy ideas.

Between Cicero and the French Revolution, many legal privileges co-existed with the ethical universalistic principle as stated in both canon and secular European law (Mungiu-Pippidi 2015, ch. 3). By the end of the eighteenth century, despite the rise of a new ideology and the erosion of privileges of the top status groups—nobles and clergymen—European society was largely a society of estates, where privilege was prevalent (Hufton 1980, 46). In the New World, Cicero and Montesquieu strongly influenced the American Federalists' understanding of good governance. Despite scarce mentions of the word "corruption," the Constitution of the United States embeds a structural "anti-corruption principle, much like the separation-of-powers principle, or federalism," and "its framers saw the document as a structure to fight corruption" (Teachout 2009, 342).[1]

In the nineteenth century, important headway towards democracy was made with the gradual elimination of official privileges, the extension of education, and secularization. Among other effects, these developments facilitated the *equalization of political resources*, defined by Robert Dahl (1996) as "whatever can be used by a specific collection of people to influence the decision of a government" (639). Among the resources that Dahl lists are

---

[1] Chapter 3 of Mungiu-Pippidi (2015) connects Cicero to Thomas Jefferson.

wealth, coercion, status, and connections (even offering the Chinese term *guanxi*, familiar to students of corruption). He also remarks that "the extent to which democracy and political equality are attainable depends, among other things, on the distribution of access to political resources." Political equality, also called equality of opportunity, is thus merely an ideal, as dissimilar access to political resources results in uneven influence over the government, itself conducive to policies meant to conserve the advantages of some group over another. In other words, Dahl (1996) opposes particularism (as in status, connections, wealth) with the principle of ethical universalism, which can only be implemented against particular privileges. Corruption is therefore the companion of political inequality, and the two are locked in a vicious circle.

The debate over economic equality has generally treated inequality as arising from luck (birth factors) and personal choice (merit), the two main variables dictating the distribution of resources, with emphasis put on individual responsibility versus collective responsibility. Somehow the endorsement by the state of ethical universalism has been taken for granted in this grand ideological debate (with the state's autonomy from private interest), as all modern constitutions (at least on paper) bow to the first article of the French Declaration of the Rights of Man and of the Citizen: "Men are born and remain free and equal in rights." But implementation of this principle is problematic when political resources are so unequal. John Rawls (1999, sections 12–13) introduced further challenge with his "fair equality of opportunity" and "impartiality." Fair equality of opportunity is satisfied if those with the same level of talent and ability, and the same willingness to use them, have the same prospects of success regardless of their initial place in the social system (Rawls 1999, 63). This creates a spectrum between a minimal implementation of the ethical universalism principle (as in equality before the law, public contracts granted impartially, or every pensioner being entitled to a pension in virtue of her contribution) and a maximum of implementation, where the state would in fact invest significant resources to ensure that full equality of opportunity is ensured for people with initially unequal endowments. Full satisfaction of the ethical universalism principle in governance would thus far exceed the full elimination of any procedural favoritism, as the original unequal endowment with political resources remains a subversive factor of universal fair treatment.

The pursuit of absolute equality, however, can also generate risks. As Baron de Montesquieu (1777) noticed three centuries ago, the principle of democracy may be corrupted "not only when the spirit of equality is extinct" but also in the opposite situation, when a spirit "of extreme equality" takes hold, so that "each citizen would fain be upon a level with those whom he has chosen to command him" (book VIII, ch. II). The people would then want to judge instead of magistrates, teach instead of teachers, legislate instead of legislators, and contest all professional elites—even if not corrupted—in the name of equality.

This story of the autonomy of the state from private interest and therefore its enabling to treat citizens equally and impersonally seems marginal in the grand story of political equality as chronicled in classic political development theory (Lipset 1960) or in light of more recent theories of human rights promotion and diffusion (Risse, Ropp, and Sikkink 1999). But that should perhaps be reconsidered. Before grand ambitions of equality of opportunity can be satisfied, experience shows that even the minimal implementation of the ethical universalism principle—the elimination of any favoritism—requires a remarkable capacity of the state to enforce public versus private interest. This is a fundamental feature of governance defining and determining institutional quality, and consensus is increasingly emerging

Table 2.1 Ideal types of governance by state autonomy from private interest

Author	Continuum "bad" extreme	Continuum "good" extreme
Weber (1968)	Patrimonialism; patriarchalism	Universalism; impersonality of bureaucracy
Krueger (1974) on rent-seeking societies	Government restrictions on economic freedom	No government restrictions
Mungiu (2006) and Mungiu-Pippidi (2015) on control of corruption	Particularism (favoritism and venality)	Ethical universalism
North, Wallis, and Weingast (2009) on social order and violence	Limited access order	Open access order
Rothstein and Teorell (2008) on quality of government	Favoritism/discrimination	Impartiality
Acemoglu and Robinson (2012) on prosperity	Extractive institutions	Inclusive institutions
Fukuyama (2015)	Personalism	Impersonalism

across disciplines that governance can be ranged on a continuum between an extreme where the state is used in the private interest of ruling elites, and one where it functions for broader public interest. Table 2.1 renders a simplified overview of the various conceptualizations of this continuum in the last 100 years, which seems to indicate some convergence across disciplines, if not language. The quality of governance of any given country falls somewhere in between the two extremes: the good governance end (the "open access order" of North, Wallis, and Weingast [2009], "inclusive institutions" of Acemoglu and Robinson [2012], and ethical universalism/impersonalism/impartiality of Mungiu-Pippidi [2015; Mungiu 2006], Fukuyama [2015], and [Rothstein and Teorell 2008] following Weber [1968]) and the bad governance/low quality of government end (patrimonialism, limited access orders, extractive institutions, particularism, and so on).

THE LONG ROAD FROM THEORY TO PRACTICE

While the development of political thought from the ancients to the moderns has always given virtue and equality a central place, political development itself is more of a constant struggle to build up a practice of governance respectful of ethical universalism. This does not happen in a vacuum, but against the particular interests of privileged groups who own the most lucrative rents and are endowed with superior political resources translated both into superior rights and status; as Rousseau (2012) put it in his *Social Contract*, "The strongest is never strong enough to be master all the time, unless he transforms force into right and obedience into duty" (159). The historical advance of ethical universalism is a story of conflict, with the norm (in a Durkheimian sense) evolving faster than the practice. Political challengers used it to advance their power bids. Such individual attempts seem to have led to the formulation and further advocacy of the principle, and not the other way around. Cicero, for instance, built his fame as a lawyer and politician fighting corruption in the famous case of Verres, governor of Sicily. He had no choice, if he wanted to win as a challenger against a patrician system controlling de facto, if not *de jure*, the courts. A jury formed of senators only was more likely to look favorably on one of their own than on any challenger: status and justice were thus intertwined, and the problem of equal treatment was the central problem from the onset. To win the case was not a matter of evidence, but a matter of establishing equal grounds: the evidence contributed rather to what we would today call "naming and shaming," in other words, of increasing the reputation costs of patricians to defend a notoriously corrupt man when irrefutable evidence could be presented. Establishing equality before the law is thus the first landmark of applied ethical universalism.

The elimination of legal privileges came next. Privileges in Europe did not concern only the aristocracy and the clergy: towns, regions, and various groups of people had their particular privileges as well, some to the detriment of others (mostly peasants). Pushed from the top due to the need to increase the tax base and from the bottom due to political emancipation, the battle for privilege elimination was a long and protracted one. That perfect Enlightenment disciple, Emperor Joseph II, came to power in 1780 with a program to transform society by promoting social equality, uniform treatment by the law, and the autonomy of the state from private interest. Enlightened despotism made some steps to build a modern state, in particular by secularization and building a merit-based bureaucracy autonomous from any private interest other than the ruler's. However, the constituency for ethical universalism in the Habsburg Empire was feeble, and the kind of *tabula rasa* needed to build an empire based on reason and equality on the ruins of old particularisms was beyond the means even of an absolute monarch. Although Joseph II eliminated some privileges and discriminations, for instance, regarding the serfs, his reforms mobilized too many of those who stood to lose and not enough of those who stood to win (Hufton 1980, 187–95). From Northern Italy to the Low Countries, resistance was fierce. At his death in 1790, he left a self-composed epitaph, "Here lies Joseph II, who was unfortunate in all his enterprises" (Hufton 1980, 185).

The French Revolution was more efficient in promoting a similar agenda not only due to its brutality, but because, as Daniel Mornet (1967) showed in his extensive study on the intellectual origins of the French Revolution, extensive propaganda for ethical universalism preceded the action by many years and created strong public support. By the 1780s, the view that the Third Estate was being overtaxed and had been paying to cover legal exemptions of the First and Second Estates had become widespread. Pre-revolutionary propaganda had managed in particular to discredit the clergy by presenting it as the chief profiteer of such legal inequities. Although such a statement needs serious qualifying to fit the evidence, the lack of universal criteria in the historical taxation system of France (also varying across regions) made the absence of equality and the lack of accountability of tax farmers easy targets of radical propaganda. The system was less corrupt by present-day standards than it seemed to contemporaries: in fact, there is the evidence of remarkable public works in various regions in the eighteenth century (Tocqueville [1998] cites Languedoc) as proof that there was value for money, despite tax collection inefficiencies. The inequality of an organically grown and highly complicated system bothered people more than the burden of taxation itself or the corruption of tax farmers in a narrow sense (for instance, by embezzlement). As Tocqueville (1998) stated, hate towards inequality was the deeper and older of the two entrenched motivations of the revolution—freedom being the weaker and more recent aspiration. The "violent and inextinguishable hatred of inequality … born and nourished by [its] sight … had long pushed the French, with constant and irresistible strength, to want to destroy all that remained of medieval institutions and … to build a society where men were as alike, and conditions as equal, as humanity would admit" (Tocqueville 1998, 244).

By the early twentieth century, Max Weber (1968, pt. 2, ch. 11) argued in his *Economy and Society* that a new type of authority, the rational–legal one, had already emerged in several European states from the patrimonial and feudal struggle for power. By that time, various status groups in Western Europe had found the promotion of ethical universalism as well as of government rationalization to be both in their own best interest and inherently just causes. Rationalization meant an evolution from the brutal material interests as espoused, for instance, by the Spanish conquistadors who had spoiled the gold and silver of the New World to the more rationalistic, capitalistic channeling of the economic surplus, with an adjacent ideology highlighting personal austerity and achievement (Weber 1968). The market and capitalism, despite their obvious limitations, gradually emerged in these cases as the main means of allocating resources, replacing the previous discretionary allocation by means of more or less organized violence. The process needed the state to become impersonal, and hence the evolution.

While nearly modern bureaucracies preceded the French revolutions and could already be found surrounding Joseph II or the Prussian King Frederick Wilhelm I (the father of Friedrich the Great), it was the new, postrevolutionary "rational" French state—promoted by Napoleon Bonaparte with Enlightenment missionary zeal from Egypt to the German states—that made a decisive step towards creating and enabling modern bureaucracies (Breuilly 2003). The blueprint interventions to promote ethical universalism in the wake of the French Revolution can be studied in several Italian republics created during the French Directorate (in Milan, Genoa, Naples, and so on), each with its own name and a constitution written in Paris which proclaimed ethical universalism as the new governance norm (Gaffarel 1895). Perhaps Switzerland, wrongly credited to have had an independent path to the successful governance it enjoys today, is the most successful example of good governance promotion (Fischer 1946; Mungiu-Pippidi 2019, ch. 1). By the mid-eighteenth century, Switzerland was a country dominated by privileges and restrictions on economic freedom (Tilly 2009). Furthermore, it was plagued by religious, ethnic, and political conflicts which would continue for more than 100 years to come. The public ethic was nonexistent: offices of governor were sold in return for presumed benefit (in the form of bribes or appropriation received) during tenure; crimes were punishable mostly by fines because that seemed more convenient for an ever deficient budget. If top officials were caught embezzling funds, they were simply replaced by way of punishment and suffered no other inconvenience (Fischer 1946). To cap it all off, there were no roads, schools, or hospitals. The absence of any centralized power and the lack of solidarity across territories and social groups meant that most Swiss cantons faced the same collective action problems as do developing countries nowadays, namely that nobody wanted to pay for public benefits (Mungiu-Pippidi 2019, ch. 1). Still, at the beginning of the nineteenth century, the various contentious and self-centered interest groups somehow managed to form a nation, and a highly successful one which took off economically from the beginning of the nineteenth century until nearly surpassing

England, Europe's first industrial nation, as the most competitive European economy (Biucchi 1973).

The rational government as the solution to social dilemmas was not a Swiss national innovation. The first French occupation, initiated in 1798, introduced the basics of a revolution in government—equal rights, separation of powers, centralization, bureaucracy—according to the new rational and enlightened philosophy (Mungiu-Pippidi 2019). The French replaced the political system of the thirteen-canton Confederation with the centralized unitary state of the Helvetic Republic, which soon collapsed due to underfunding and permanent conflict between federalist and centralist factions. A succession of coups and a civil war followed, plus a temporary retreat by the French state, although the French later intervened again as "mediator of the Swiss Confederation." In his words to the Swiss representatives in 1802, First Consul Napoleon Bonaparte himself introduced ethical universalism as part of the inevitable advance of history:

> A new environment and mood, changed from that of the past and closer to reason have established the equality of rights between all parts of your territory. The wish and interest of both you and the states surrounding you, therefore, favor:
>
> 1. The equality of rights between your eighteen cantons;
> 2. A voluntary and earnest renunciation to the privileges from the part of patrician families;
> 3. A federal organization, so that each Canton organizes itself according to its religion, customs, interests and opinions. (quoted in Monnier, Dufour, and Hanisch 2003)

The embodiment of his thought was the French-designed Act of Mediation, or Malmaison Constitution, a largely federalist constitution which also introduced the abovementioned political modernization elements which shaped the future of Switzerland. Present-day Switzerland resembles fairly closely the blueprint established by the Act of Mediation, certainly more so than all its other constitutional documents (Biucchi 1973; Tilly 2009). In a society dominated by inequality between town and country, between patricians and the people, and between various linguistic, ethnic, and religious groups, ethical universalism could hardly have come easily. In fact, it took far longer for it to become the dominant norm than the brief French Revolution and Empire. But the foreign intervention, based on political principles derived from the Enlightenment, managed to solve local collective action problems and set a course that Swiss liberals fought to defend for decades afterwards (Tilly 2009, 328).

The important instrument in the promotion of ethical universalism which outlasted the French occupations was the Napoleonic Code, which replaced the organically grown complex body of French laws implementing Enlightenment ideas. Before the revolution, French law had consisted of a mix of Roman, canon, and local customs, with many exemptions, privileges, and special charters granted by kings or other feudal lords. Privileged groups opposed any uniformization attempted in the Ancien Régime. The magistrates, as Tocqueville (1998) showed in his *The Old Regime and the Revolution*, were also a status group in their own right, opposing the king in virtue of their class interests aside from any principled opposition. The drafting process of a single civil law code had started in 1793, then continued under the chairmanship of Napoleon Bonaparte after 1800. The resulting code underwent several simplifications and was adopted piecemeal, with final promulgation in 1804. It introduced—beyond the main gain of a simplified universal law that any ordinary person could understand—principles such as transparency (laws became valid only after being published) and equality, making all male citizens equal and abolishing primogeniture, hereditary nobility, and class privileges. Also, civilian institutions were emancipated from ecclesiastical control and freedom of person, freedom of contract, and inviolability of private property were enacted (Tunc 1954). French influence in much of continental Europe, on the one side, and the qualities of the legal text, on the other, allowed the Napoleonic Code to spread rapidly throughout Europe and the world, precipitating the end of feudalism and the liberation of serfs. It was not only adopted in many countries occupied by the French during the Napoleonic War (like Poland), but had a lasting impact on civil law codes in other regions of the world which sought top-down modernization by constitutional means: Eastern Europe, the Middle East (where it was combined with Islamic law), and Latin America (where its influence has survived) (Mirow 2004).

The British, despite Edmund Burke's praise of liberties when compared to the French, had in fact numerous privileges and a highly unequal, status-based society by the time of the French Revolution; change took over a century and has progressed only gradually. From the elimination of slavery to that of royal privileges, this is a glorious story, but the true extent of meritocracy and equality in British society should not be overrated. Public positions, including in the colonies and the church, continued to be distributed by patronage, while a wild press and a self-assertive class of barristers pushed for equality. It is highly tempting to present a coherent retrospective story of incessant progress with certain "thresholds," except that after every step forward problems still persisted for decades (as in venality of military positions and electoral corruption). It was due to a succession of blunders in the Crimean War that William Gladstone commissioned a review of the Civil Service in 1853; the resulting Northcote–Trevelyan Report of February 1854 recommended a system of examination ahead of entry and promotion on merit through open competition which was eventually adopted as part of a civil service act (Neild 2002, 69). Again, it took quite a long time for some basic ethical universalism-based practices to catch up: late in the twentieth century, Foreign Office officials still came from privileged backgrounds as a rule, and the colonial administration had always been filled with recruits on the basis of family ties and patronage, with varying degrees of competence. The British did try to leave behind in Africa some foundation for an autonomous civil service on the basis of the indigenous population (Public Service Commissions), but their effort arrived too late, and the need to nationalize the former colonial administration by the new African governments subverted it altogether (Adu 1965, 29). Their legacy was more positive where courts were concerned.

The United States waited until 1883 to pass its own equivalent, the Pendleton Act. This provided for the open selection of government employees, administered by a Civil Service Commission and thus guaranteeing the right of citizens to compete for federal appointment on an ethical universalism basis, without regard to politics, religion, race, or national origin (Hoogenboom 1959). Even if their full implementation took decades, such British and American reforms enjoyed great reputation, and considerable emulation followed, since the rest of the world tried to copy whatever in the European organization explained its superior prosperity and international influence. Most notably, in 1905 China abolished its traditional Confucian examination system for civil servants, which had endured over 1,300 years, and reorganized it closer to these Western models (Simon 2013).

How universal is ethical universalism, actually? Some ancient Chinese teachings on political governance also teach impartiality. For instance, two chapters of the eclectic text *Lü Shi Chun Qiu* (*The Annals of Lü Buwei*) are entitled "*Gui gong*" ("Honoring impartiality") and "*Qu si*" ("Dispensing with partiality") (Lü, Knoblock, and Riegel 2000). Despite some scholars arguing that ethical universalism exists also in Confucianism or Islamism (which is true for virtue, integrity, trust, social cohesion, and other concepts relevant for good governance [Kamali 2008]), ethical universalism as such advanced in the rest of the world thanks to modern Western promotion and is fairly tied with Western individualism. While a number of remarkable personalities have spoken eloquently against the incompatibility of liberal democracy with religions such as Buddhism, Hinduism, Confucianism, and Islamism,[2] there is no evidence that a governance regime based on equal and fair treatment of every individual, with the complete suspension of any privilege, originated anywhere else than the source shown here: the French Revolution and the administrative revolution that followed it. To be clear, that still did not mean the success of the full norm, or the practice of equality even in the French Empire. Women were excluded from the onset, French dominions overseas had different rules, and the courts hardly treated everybody impartially: it needed the Dreyfus affair and many years of campaigning to create full rule of law (Neild 2002, ch. 4). But the Napoleonic Code and the administrative codes derived from it laid down the norm of ethical universalism in public life for the most part. Norm and practice then advanced on specific paths country by country: some more revolutionarily, others more gradually; some more formally (Latin American and East European countries adopted highly advanced constitutions based on France or Belgium but were unable to implement them), others more substantially (a self-governing British colony, New Zealand, became an ethical universalism champion for being among the first in the world to adopt women's suffrage and for addressing more equitably than others the rights of its indigenous population). As for the alleged incompatibility of ethical universalism with religion, the successful examples of Japan, Uruguay, South Korea, and Taiwan clearly show that this is not the case.

The Swiss account is thus just the first in a long series of Western "interventions" or attempts to change governance in another country with the self-avowed objective of promoting or restoring ethical universalism (Mungiu-Pippidi 2019, ch. 1). According to the degree of development of the society where the intervention takes place, goals might range from the abolition of slavery or feudal institutions, as in certain nineteenth-century interventions (some accompanying colonialism), to the restoration of constitutional order or the rule of law. As Emperor Napoleon III, the nephew of the first Napoleon, put it to the Duke of Malakoff, the general governor of Algeria, "We need to persuade the Arabs that we have not come to Algeria to press and spoil them, but to bring them the benefits of civilization. And the first condition of civilization is the reciprocal respect of everybody's rights" (quoted in Séguin 2014). As side effects of colonialism, legal codes based on more advanced versions of the Napoleonic Code and individual rights based on British common law also spread the doctrine and practice of ethical universalism around the world, though in different proportions.

---

[2] A discussion on the question of democracy as a universal value can be found in Diamond and Plattner (2009, 289–392), with answers in the positive from many distinguished scholars, politicians, and even the Dalai Lama.

Reforms accompanying external interventions promoting ethical universalism may vary considerably, from land reforms by the United States in Taiwan and South Korea to the European Union's attempt to build rule of law and control of corruption in the Balkans. By and large, such reforms have similar aims, namely the elimination of privileges, favoritism, and discrimination by authorities and the final aim of producing "modern," Western-modeled government everywhere. Tools might include development aid, conditionality and sanctions policies, membership or offers of privileged trade status, and even direct government by external powers, as in Kosovo or Iraq (Mungiu-Pippidi 2019, ch. 2).

The record of such interventions also varies greatly, though. Modern constitutions generally strike off all traditional privileges (like rank or church tax exemptions) immediately. Of all the elements of "modernization," impersonality and impartiality of the bureaucracy or, to put it better, the state's autonomy from private interest have proved the most difficult to achieve, despite continuous growth in literacy and urbanization in the last decades. The early models of successful bureaucracies are associated with "enlightened despots," for instance, in Denmark, Prussia, the Habsburg Monarchy, and Napoleonic France, where strong monarchs seeking greater social control, a better performing military, and an extension of their tax base developed the merit system as a by-product (Mungiu-Pippidi 2015, ch. 3). Conversely, where free universal elections preceded the development of bureaucracy, as in the United States, modernization of the state took far longer—many decades in the American case—even when rule of law was present. The reasons for such cases were the politicization of bureaucracy and the slow progress of a merit-based system. The path of democratization and the path of ethical universalism are therefore not entirely congruent, and Tocqueville was the first to note the paradox involved:

> In aristocratic governments the individuals who are placed at the head of affairs are rich men, who are solely desirous of power. In democracies statesmen are poor, and they have their fortunes to make. The consequence is that in aristocratic States the rulers are rarely accessible to corruption, and have very little craving for money; whilst the reverse is the case in democratic nations. But in aristocracies, as those who are desirous of arriving at the head of affairs are possessed of considerable wealth, and as the number of persons by whose assistance they may rise is comparatively small, the government is, if I may use the expression, put up to a sort of auction. In democracies, on the contrary … the number of citizens who confer that power is extremely great … [so] buyers are rarely to be met with; and, besides, it would be necessary to buy so many persons at once that the attempt is rendered nugatory (Tocqueville 1954, ch. XIII).

THE PRESENT AND FUTURE OF ETHICAL UNIVERSALISM

Closer to our times, institutional quality—an economics paradigm translated into political science as "governance" or "quality of government" and into plain language as corruption—emerged as an international problem in the aftermath of the controversial Washington Consensus reforms in the last decade of the twentieth century, and it has grown exponentially ever since. Following increased awareness and individual agency of various kinds, an international normative framework against corruption began to develop. On October

31, 2003, the United Nations (UN) General Assembly (resolution 58/4) adopted the United Nations Convention against Corruption (UNCAC). Fifteen years on, 181 UN member states have already ratified the convention alongside parties like the Cook Islands, Niue, the Holy See, the State of Palestine, and the European Union, reaching near global unanimity. Unlike its older and more famous antecessor the Universal Declaration of Human Rights (1948) and the subsequent UN human rights covenants, UNCAC did not meet with official expressions of dissent or claims that it imposed some form of Western institutional hegemony on the rest of the world. No equivalent exists for UNCAC of the historical reservations made by Saudi Arabia or Iran towards the universality of human rights, which resulted in a separate Islamic document known as the Cairo Declaration on Human Rights in Islam (entered as A/CONF.157/PC/62/Add.l8 at the 1993 World Conference on Human Rights in Vienna). In fact, the Cairo Declaration lays the ground for UNCAC by stating that "All individuals are equal before the law, without distinction between the ruler and the ruled" (Article 19) and "Authority is a trust; and abuse or malicious exploitation thereof is absolutely prohibited" (Article 23). The 1948 Universal Declaration of Human Rights, although apparently not dealing with corruption, already included two fundamental provisions for good governance by stating in Article 7 that "All are equal before the law and are entitled without any discrimination to equal protection of the law. All are entitled to equal protection against any discrimination" and in Article 21(2) that "Everyone has the right to equal access to public service in his country." UNCAC itself brings it all together, spelling out in the preamble the principles of "proper management of public affairs and public property, fairness, responsibility and equality before the law and the need to safeguard integrity and to foster a culture of rejection of corruption" to then give them operational substance.

UNCAC does not define corruption but rather its opposite, the standards of good governance: transparency, accountability, equal access and treatment, and participation in decisions that impact one's life. The more than 180 ratifying parties of the convention (some of which are not democracies) thus agreed on the norms of good governance, putting an end to the moral relativist arguments where governance is concerned. Relativism will always remain insofar as individual "agent" choices are under discussion—is it moral to bribe a prison guard to help an innocent detainee escape?—but not nation-state or government choices. After the end of apartheid, no UN member state in the world has made discrimination a constitutional option. The constitutional choice has been made, once and for all, in favor of equality and nondiscrimination. And corruption (or anticorruption) is just a particular case of that. As Mark Warren (2004) showed, "corruption is always a form of duplicitous and harmful exclusion of those who have a claim to inclusion in collective decisions and actions" (328). Regardless of whether a government is elected or not, the promise of fair and nondiscriminative treatment exists in every present constitutional contract. The only remaining reservations are with the 12 countries who had not ratified UNCAC by the end of 2019 (Syria, Tonga, Eritrea, North Korea, Somalia, Monaco, San Marino, Barbados, Saint Kitts and Nevis, Saint Vincent, Surinam, and Andorra), but some ratifications might still follow.

Ratification does not necessarily mean implementation where corruption is concerned, and UNCAC as all UN conventions is based on peer reviews and carries no sanctions. It should come as no surprise then that global evaluations of how the new international anticorruption norms impact practices are rather pessimistic (Mungiu-Pippidi 2015, ch. 7; Cole 2015). But seeing how long it took for ethical universalism to become a global norm, it is still very early to assess impact. After all, it is rather extraordinary that in the roughly 200 years since the French revolutionaries tried to enshrine such principles into basic law, most of the world has come to an agreement on this, both in public opinion support and international legislation.

So what is the future of ethical universalism, or at least of the minimalist interpretation of it from the angle in this chapter? Two broad categories of approaches exist, which vary both in their respective theories of change as well as in the international intervention required.

The developmental approach presumes that ethical universalism can only advance by the maturation of society, which will itself generate sufficient constraints on elites' corrupt behavior and therefore will gradually—or, taking advantage of unexpected windows of opportunity—adjust the suboptimal control of corruption to more optimal levels. Roughly, this is what Michael Johnston (2014) argues in his "deep democratization" approach: that internal demand and capacity to enforce accountability of office holders by their own societies is the only sustainable way to advance ethical universalism as a governance principle. That being said, views on how to do this vary widely, from the minimalist Rothstein and Tannenberg (2015) approach (universal education should be seen as core good governance policy) to the maximalist "seven steps" proposed by Mungiu-Pippidi (2018) for countries where anticorruption is driven mostly by external donors. These steps are based on a comprehensive equilibrium model of corruption as a result of controlling opportunities for corruption by constraints, which presume wide intervention both on the state side (transparency, administrative simplification) and in society (autonomy for the judiciary and the press, a critical mass of civic-minded citizens empowered by digital tools) in order to modify the framework enabling public integrity (Mungiu-Pippidi and Dadašov 2016). This approach sees international donors as either sponsors (more or less benevolent, as they are neither disinterested nor aware of the unintended consequences of their anticorruption actions) or coalition builders or even leaders (as external agency may be the only exogenous factor able to break social dilemmas), but presumes that *domestic political agency is the only essential element which can step up implementation of ethical universalism* and that the essential work is within the nation-state.

The legal enforcement approach, on the contrary, relies heavily on international legislation—of which UNCAC is only a small part—and asks for ever increasing regulations to be transposed at the country level, but somehow enforced internationally. Its theory of change (often understated) is therefore some sort of conditionality, as it presumes that *increased international oversight (which could only happen if some leverage exists) can determine domestic enforcement of good governance*. A successful example is the United States Foreign Corrupt Practices Act of 1977, which is enforced more and more often against companies from other countries —Sweden, Brazil, the United Kingdom, France, Israel, Netherlands, Switzerland—which bribe internationally, as it is rather difficult for any multinational to not have some American connection and to escape American jurisdiction thus broadly conceived. Most proposals on this line are hosted by the Brookings Institution in the United States. Three are worth mentioning:

- The Extractive Industries Transparency Initiative (EITI), which has existed since 2003 and reaches a wide membership, asks countries to publish timely and accurate information on key aspects of their natural resources management. By holding countries to an international standard, EITI seeks to curb corruption and improve accountability, thus preventing the resource curse. So far, more progress has been made in extending member-ship than in generating actual impact, according to evaluations (Sovacool et al. 2016).

- The International Anti-Corruption Court (IACC) is a proposal for the establishment of a court similar to the International Criminal Court, or as a part of it, for the criminal en-forcement of laws prohibiting grand corruption. Judge Mark L. Wolf (2014) outlined the proposal in a paper for the Brookings Institution in July 2014 and at a governance forum in Prague. Under the proposed court, states could voluntarily accede to the IACC, granting it jurisdiction over investigating and prosecuting domestic acts of grand corruption, which would operate under the principle of "complementarity" (conducting prosecutions only when domestic courts are unwilling or unable). Judges and prosecutors would be selected internationally, thus ensuring independence.

- Last but not least, the international community is asked to adopt a new human right: freedom from official corruption (Murray and Spalding 2015). Some argue that the progression of ethical universalism as a legal norm, as seen in both human rights and anticorruption law, justifies the establishment of a stand-alone right defined as "freedom from corruption." That would have an essential role in upholding and enforcing other human rights. The pan European courts' jurisprudence is also cited as having advanced its jurisdiction on anticorruption and rule of law, therefore setting a precedent for trans-national work.

Domestic and international agency intersect differently in the two approaches. Internationalists admit that the political will of domestic governments would be needed for the IACC to function, but if such political will were to exist, such a court might not be needed at all. Developmentalists see a role for external donors as sponsors or catalysts, forgetting the Samaritan dilemma: that the simple intervention of outsiders in the governance equilib-rium of another country may create unintended consequences and, instead of helping local agency, may disincentivize it (Gibson et al. 2005). It is easier to find arguments against both schools rather than in their favor: the evidence clearly shows that emulation, and not pro-motion, is what works for countries to adopt ethical universalism (Mungiu-Pippidi 2015, ch. 7). But the two approaches may also prove complementary in the end. Ethical universalism progressed far more as a norm than as a practice in contemporary times due to activism by lawyers, but there may be still some role for development actors (entrepreneurs, investors, technocrats, charities) to take it further.[3]

References

Acemoglu, Daron, and James A. Robinson. 2012. *Why Nations Fail: The Origins of Power, Prosperity and Poverty*. 1st ed. New York: Crown Publishers.
Adu, A. L. 1965. *The Civil Service in New African States*. London: Allen & Unwin.
Agence France-Presse. 2019. "End of the Road for ENA, France's Elite Training School?" April 24, 2019. https://www.france24.com/en/20190425-end-road-ena-frances-elite-training-school

---

[3] Part of the material used in this chapter was presented as the 2019 Seymour Martin Lipset Lecture "The Trials and Tribulations of Western Good Governance Promotion." The description of Switzerland and the French intervention is a compressed version of the one found in Mungiu-Pippidi (2019).

Biucchi, Basilio M. (1973). "The Industrial Revolution in Switzerland." In *The Fontana Economic History of Europe, Volume 4 Part 2: The Emergence of Industrial Societies*, edited by Carlo M. Cipolla, 639–47. Glasglow: Collins.

Breuilly, John. 2003. Napoleonic Germany and State-Formation. In *Collaboration and Resistance in Napoleonic Europe: State Formation in an Age of Upheaval, c. 1800–1815*, edited by Michael Rowe, 121–52. New York: Palgrave Macmillan.

Cicero, Marcus Tullius. 1877. *Cicero's Tusculan Disputations*. Translated by C. D. Yonge. New York: Harper & Brothers.

Cicero, Marcus Tullius. 2006. *De Officiis*. Translated by Walter Miller. Sydney: Read How You Want.

Cole, Wade M. 2015. "Institutionalizing a Global Anti-Corruption Regime: Perverse Effects on Country Outcomes, 1984–2012." *International Journal of Comparative Sociology* 56 (1): 53–80.

Dahl, Robert A. 1996. "Equality Versus Inequality." *PS: Political Science and Politics* 29 (4): 639–48.

Diamond, Larry, and Marc F. Plattner. 2009. *Democracy: A Reader*. Baltimore: Johns Hopkins University Press.

Fischer, Ernest. 1946. *Histoire de la Suisse: des origines à nos jours*. Paris: Payot.

Fukuyama, Francis. 2015. *Political Order and Political Decay: From the Industrial Revolution to the Globalization of Democracy*. New York: Macmillan.

Gaffarel, Paul. 1895. *Bonaparte et les républiques italiennes (1796–1799)*. Edited by Felix Alcan. Paris: Ancienne Librairie Germer Baillère.

Gewirth, Alan. 1988. "Ethical Universalism and Particularism." *The Journal of Philosophy* 85 (6): 283–302.

Gibson, Clark C., Krister Andersson, Elinor Ostrom, and Sujai Shivakumar. 2005. *The Samaritan's Dilemma: The Political Economy of Development Aid*. Oxford: Oxford University Press.

Hoogenboom, Ari. 1959. "The Pendleton Act and the Civil Service." *The American Historical Review* 64 (2): 301–18.

Hufton, Olwen. 1980. *Europe: Privilege and Protest 1730–1789*. London: Fontana.

Johnston, M. 2014. *Corruption, Contention, and Reform: The Power of Deep Democratization*, Cambridge: Cambridge University Press.

Kamali, Mohammad H. 2008. *Shari'ah Law: An Introduction*. Oxford: Oneworld Publications.

Krueger, A. O. 1974. "The Political Economy of the Rent-Seeking Society." *The American Economic Review* 64 (3): 291–303.

Lipset, Seymour M. 1960. *Political Man*. New York: Doubleday.

Locke, John. 2003. *Two Treatises in Government and a Letter Concerning Toleration*. Edited by Ian Shapiro. New Haven: Yale University Press.

Lü, Pu-wei, John Knoblock, and Jeffrey Riegel. 2000. *The Annals of Lü Buwei*. Stanford: Stanford University Press.

Mirow, M. C. 2004. "The Code Napoléon: Buried but Ruling in Latin America." *Denver Journal of International Law & Policy* 33 (2): 179–92.

Monnier, Victor, Alfred Dufour, and Till Hanisch, eds. 2003. *Bonaparte, la Suisse et l'Europe: Actes du Colloque européen d'histoire constitutionnelle pour le bicentenaire de l'Acte de médiation (1803–2003)*. Brussels: Bruylant.

Montesquieu, Charles de Secondat, Baron de. 1777. *The Complete Works of M. de Montesquieu*, Vol. 1. London: T. Evans. https://oll.libertyfund.org/titles/montesquieu-complete-works-vol-1-the-spirit-of-laws

Mornet, Daniel. 1967. *Les origines intellectuelles de la Révolution française*. Paris: Colin.

Mungiu, Alina. 2006. "Corruption: Diagnosis and Treatment." *Journal of Democracy* 17 (3): 86–99.

Mungiu-Pippidi, Alina. 2015. *A Quest for Good Governance. How Societies Build Control of Corruption*. Cambridge, UK: Cambridge University Press.

Mungiu-Pippidi, Alina, and Ramin Dadašov. 2016. "Measuring Control of Corruption by a New Index of Public Integrity." *European Journal on Criminal Policy and Research* 22 (3): 415–38.

Mungiu-Pippidi, Alina. 2018. "Seven Steps to Control of Corruption: The Road Map." *Dædalus* 147 (3): 20–34.

Mungiu-Pippidi, Alina. 2019. *Europe's Burden: Promoting Good Governance Across Borders*. Cambridge, UK: Cambridge University Press.

Murray, Matthew, and Andrew Spalding. 2015. *Freedom from Official Corruption as a Human Right*. Governance Studies, January 2015. Washington, DC: Brookings. https://www.brookings.edu/research/freedom-from-official-corruption-as-a-human-right/

Neild, Robert. 2002. *Public Corruption: The Dark Side of Social Evolution*. London: Anthem Press.

North, Douglass C., John Joseph Wallis, and Barry R. Weingast. (2009). *Violence And Social Orders: A Conceptual Framework For Interpreting Recorded Human History*. Cambridge, UK: Cambridge University Press.

Rawls, John. 1999. *A Theory of Justice: Revised Edition*. Cambridge, MA: Harvard University Press.

Risse, Thomas, Stephen C. Ropp, and Kathryn Sikkink, eds. 1999. *The Power of Human Rights: International Norms and Domestic Change*. Cambridge, UK: Cambridge University Press.

Rothstein, Bo, and Jan Teorell. 2008. "What Is Quality of Government? A Theory of Impartial Government Institutions." *Governance* 21 (2): 165–90.

Rothstein, Bo, and Marcus Tannenberg. 2015. *Making Development Work: The Quality of Government Approach*. Rapport 2015:07 till Expertgruppen för biståndsanalys (EBA). Stockholm: The Expert Group for Aid Studies.

Rousseau, Jean-Jacques. 2012. *The Basic Political Writings*. 2nd ed. Translated and edited by Donald A. Cress. Indianapolis: Hackett Publishing.

Séguin, Philippe. 2014. *Louis Napoléon le Grand*. Paris: Grasset.

Simon, Karla W. 2013. *Civil Society in China: The Legal Framework from Ancient Times to the "New Reform Era*. Oxford: Oxford University Press.

Sovacool, Benjamin K., Götz Walter, Thijs Van de Graaf, and Nathan Andrews. 2016. "Energy Governance, Transnational Rules, and the Resource Curse: Exploring the Effectiveness of the Extractive Industries Transparency Initiative (EITI)." *World Development* 83: 179–92.

Teachout, Zephyr. 2009. "The Anti-Corruption Principle." *Cornell Law Review* 94 (341): 341–413.

Tilly, Charles. 2009. "Astonishing Switzerland." *Swiss Political Science Review* 15 (2): 321–31.

Tocqueville, Alexis de. 1998. *The Old Regime and The Revolution, Volume I: The Complete Text*. Translated by Alan S. Kahan. Edited by François Furet and Françoise Mélonio. Chicago: University of Chicago Press.

Tocqueville, Alexis de. 1954. *Democracy in America, Volume 1*. Translated by Henry Reeve. New York: Vintage Books. https://en.wikisource.org/wiki/Page:Democracy_in_America_(Reeve,_v._1).djvu/

Trivers, Robert L. 1971. "The Evolution of Reciprocal Altruism." *The Quarterly Review of Biology* 46 (1): 35–57.

Tunc, André. 1954. "The Grand Outlines of the Code Napoleon." *Tulane Law Review* 29: 431–52.

United Nations. 1948. Universal Declaration of Human Rights. Accessible at eng.pdf (ohchr. org)

Warren, Mark E. 2004. "What Does Corruption Mean in a Democracy?" *American Journal of Political Science* 48 (2): 328–43.

Weber, Max. 1968. *Economy and Society: An Outline of Interpretive Sociology.* New York: Bedminster Press.

Wilson, James Q. 1993. *The Moral Sense.* New York: The Free Press.

Wolf, Mark L. 2014. *The Case for an International Anti-Corruption Court.* Governance Studies, July 2014. Washington, DC: Brookings. https://www.brookings.edu/research/the-case-for-an-international-anti-corruption-court/

CHAPTER 3

"QUALITY OF GOVERNMENT"
A Philosophical Assessment

NIKOLAS KIRBY AND JONATHAN WOLFF

CONTEXT: THE NEED FOR A PHILOSOPHY
OF GOVERNANCE

UNTIL recently, with some notable exceptions,[1] contemporary political philosophy has had little to say about topics of "governance." Over the last decades, the discipline has investigated the *"why"* of government: debating its aims largely in terms of social justice. The discipline has also investigated thoroughly the *"who"* of government: debating who, if anyone, should have state authority, and the right to coerce citizens. However, it has largely neglected, the *"how"*; how government should implement the policies determined by its leadership when using its discretion. Unlike earlier thinkers,[2] contemporary theorists have largely ignored topics such as bureaucracy, institutions, corruption, public integrity and public service. Accordingly Rothstein and Jan Teorell's idea of "Quality of Government" ("QoG"),[3] combined with the work of other political scientists and public administration theorists,[4] invites a welcome and long overdue return to topics of governance for political philosophy.

The initial challenge, however, is to get a grip on the topic. One approach would be to look at existing accounts of good governance and to consider whether they stand up to the usual forms of philosophical scrutiny. In this respect, the work of Rothstein and colleagues stands as an impressive focal point. Yet without a firmer account of what problem the concept of "good governance" is intended to address, or what phenomenon it is intended to describe, we risk doing little more than trading philosophical intuitions. In this

---

[1] See for example, on "dirty hands" (Walzer 1973); on institutions, (Waldron 2016); on institutional ethics, (Thompson 1995); and institutional corruption, (Lessig 2013).

[2] (Plato 1871; Aristotle 1996; Confucius 1971; Machiavelli 1984; Weber 2019; Machiavelli 2008; Hamilton et al. 2003; Weber 1994).

[3] (Rothstein and Teorell 2008; Strömberg 2000).

[4] (Heywood 2015; Mungiu-Pippidi 2015; Huberts 2014; Fukuyama 2013).

case, it can be useful to start the analysis from the opposite direction. If good governance is what we seek, what, then, is it that we wish to avoid? Many theorists of the quality of governance, for good reason, are greatly concerned with the levels of corruption, favoritism, or cronyism that are increasingly apparent. Rothstein (2011) is entitled *The Quality of Government: Corruption, Social Trust and Inequality in International Perspective*. These concerns lead Rothstein to highlight impartiality as the key aspect of quality of government. Yet it is an open question whether good governance should be measured in terms of resistance to this set of defects alone, and, therefore, whether impartiality has the importance it is afforded.

Our strategy in this chapter is to start from both ends. First, we clarify the question by explaining why good governance cannot be reduced to either of justice and legitimacy. Second, we present one, fictionalized, account of bad government, as a checkpoint against which to test theories. Third, we review the limited philosophical landscape. Fourth, we engage in a critique of the Quality of Government theory. Finally, we tentatively outline an alternative account, and consider directions for future research.

"QUALITY OF GOVERNMENT" IS THE ANSWER TO *WHAT* QUESTION?

"Quality of Government," (QoG) is a putative answer to a question. But what is that question? As Rothstein and other political scientists put it, QoG (capitalized) is the answer to the question: "what is *quality* of government?" (not capitalized).[5] But what does this question actually mean? Is it simply another way of asking "what should we most want from government in general?"

Not exactly. There is an implicit scope restriction. They are only asking what we should want from the executive bureaucracy.[6] It directs our attention away from the legislature and the judiciary—the typical concerns of contemporary political philosophy—to an arm of government largely ignored by the discipline: the sphere of ministries and state departments, civil service employees and state officials, with responsibility for putting you in gaol and doling out state benefits. Though relatively neglected by political philosophers, questions of how the executive bureaucracy should act remain strongly normative and are not merely matters of efficiency.

To understand this particular concern with norm(s) of *bureaucracy*, we begin by showing why the norms of "justice" and "legitimacy" fail to meet the expectations required in answers

---

[5] Rothstein and Teorell, perhaps confusingly, put forward "quality of government" as this abstract virtue, and also name their particular concrete conception, "Quality of Government": (Rothstein and Teorell 2008).

[6] Sometimes Rothstein and Teorell seem to argue as if Quality of Government stretches as a norm across all three branches of government (Rothstein and Teorell 2008, 170). This would be a much bolder claim, running into a much greater wealth of philosophical literature on legislative and judicial arms of government. In this chapter, we shall presume the more limited focus on executive bureaucracy, which in truth is undoubtedly their primary concern.

to the question: "what should we most want from the executive, bureaucratic branch of government?"

"Justice" is central to general political thinking yet although it is important that no bureaucrat acts "unjustly" in *some* sense, we also do not expect most bureaucrats, most of the time to act on the basis of their own substantive conception of justice, even if correct. For example, take tax policy. In most cases, we think it would be an abuse of office for a bureaucrat to rely on his or her personal sense of ideals of justice rather than what is required by law. There are exceptional circumstances, of course,[7] but in the general case it is natural to think that the bureaucrat's role is instead defined and constrained by law, policy and the responsibilities of office. Their primary purpose is to implement the directions of higher authorities, ultimately determined by political leadership. When more exceptionally, within normal procedures bureaucrats should pursue what they think most just, they should do so *only because* this task has been permitted and delegated to them. But judgment will be heavily hemmed in. Thus, for example, in normal times no street level bureaucrat can legitimately decline to collect income tax because of the belief that tax rates are unjustly too high.

If "justice" is not what we should most want from bureaucratic decision-making, does this mean, therefore, that "legitimacy" *instead* is the central norm of bureaucracy?

"Legitimacy" has numerous meanings. When applied to a government, or an officer of government, it generally implies that the agent has authority qua the "right to rule," in the sense that they are able to give orders that others are morally obliged to obey, and/or they have the right to coerce others to comply with such legitimate orders.[8] Once again, this definition explains well a key feature of legislative and judicial actors, as well as some aspects of executive action, but it misses what "legitimacy" might mean for great swaths of bureaucracy that neither order nor push anyone around. Much of government is *administration* in the purest sense, administering public resources, using public assets, offering services, spending public money, and so on. The defining feature of hospitals, schools, libraries and nursing homes are not their rule-making and coercive powers, if any, but their discretionary power over entrusted public resources.

For administrative institutions legitimacy means that the scope of their discretionary powers, are sourced in the prior exercise of some "right to rule," either held by itself or another, higher agent. As such, a hospital or any other such institution, can be said to be legitimate insofar as it continues to retain its powers at the will of the higher power.

Legitimacy is of limited relevance to understanding what we want from bureaucracy. While legitimacy is the minimum standard of government action, it is a permissive concept. It does not constrain or determine what one should *do with the power it grants*. Yet *that* is the

---

[7] Consider the Chinese diplomat Feng Shan Ho who, against orders, issued perhaps thousands of visas to Jews in Austria during the Second World War (Holocaust Memorial Day Trust 2019).

[8] Raz exemplifies the view that prioritizes "authority" in its account of (political) legitimacy: (Raz 1986). By contrast, other authors like (Ladenson 1980; Rawls 2005; Ripstein 2004) exemplify the prioritization of the rightful coercive power. However, the distinction does not matter much for our purposes, as both put forward normative accounts of legitimacy, that is the relevant "right" to rule is understood as a *moral* right held irrespective of whether other people respect or recognize its existence. This is opposed to the descriptive accounts of legitimacy more common in political science (Weber 1994).

central question of executive, bureaucratic action: what to do with the discretion that the law, and other authoritative directions, permit? Intuitively, that discretion can be exercised "well" or "poorly," in ways that neither raise questions of legitimacy nor justice. To illustrate, let us turn to one of the most famous, although fictional, depictions of executive malfunction: *The Trial* (Kafka [1925] 2015).

THE TRIAL

When someone has had an encounter with a government agency that seems to exemplify the lowest grade of poor governance they may well describe it as "Kafkaesque," drawing comparison with Kafka's *The Trial*, in which legal proceedings are instigated against the central character Joseph K, in a way that exemplifies a multitude of failures. Given the title of Kafka's book, one might think of Joseph K as caught up in his country's judicial system, rather than its executive. However, it is not clear Joseph K ever even reaches his own trial, remaining stuck within the bureaucracy surrounding it. In a way, the judicial idea of *a trial*, sits within the novel as a normative ideal of how a government should treat its citizens, which is infiltrated and corrupted by bureaucratic behaviour associated with a malfunctioning executive.

Among the indignities Joseph K suffers within this bureaucratic nightmare, the most memorable is that an accusation is made against him which is sufficient to place him under arrest, and subject to legal proceedings, but the nature of the charge is never explained. In this system cases drag on, the nature of the proceedings is very unclear, and it is not known who has any formal role in the process. Anything Joseph K says or does is in danger of being interpreted in a way that is detrimental to his case. The proceedings are exceedingly slap-dash, and take place within premises that seem inappropriate. Communication inside and outside of court is highly problematic, and sometimes deliberately deceptive. Steps are made to put Joesph K at a disadvantage at every point, and his own advocate is not permitted to tell him how the case is progressing, although it is also unclear whether his advocate has any legal standing. There are also some more familiar examples of partiality or corruption. On initial arrest, the wardens try to trick him out of his high-quality clothes and at several places it is indicated that his case will go better if he employs someone who has a personal connection with the court or the officials. These, we say, are "Kafkaesque circumstances," and provide one example of low-quality governance, in that it is a very bad example of state inter-action with an individual.

In more abstract term, we see the following defects in the handling of Joseph K's case, and, by extension, the sort of defects that could afflict any interaction between the state and its citizens. These include:

1. Poor communication.
2. Deliberate cultivation of uncertainty.
3. Lack of known procedure.
4. Lack of assurance of fairness of procedure.
5. Attempt at bribery/theft.
6. Lack of conditions that are conducive to trust.

7. Unknown probability or nature of adverse outcome.
8. Highly stressful procedure.
9. Importance of personal connection.

We do not suggest that this comprises an exhaustive list of executive failings, but it is interesting how few are failings of "legitimacy," or "justice," at least as we have characterized them above. We might presume that bribery and theft breach the limits of power of any state actor. However, the rest do not necessarily reflect the actions of illegitimate agents, or actions that go beyond their power, or fail some norm of distributive justice. The action reflects a bad use of the discretionary power of government, regardless of its substantive policy aims; a failure of the *quality* of bureaucratic government. But what would make bureaucracy not just legitimate, but *good*? Let us call this the question of "good governance."[9]

NORMS OF GOOD GOVERNANCE IN POLITICAL THOUGHT

To our knowledge, very little in contemporary political philosophy addresses the question of good governance. Others have also noted this absence.[10] Yet, as we will show in this section, there are writings that shed some light on the issues at hand.

Canonical authors

The question of the quality of government has not always been neglected by philosophers. For example, it is possible to read much of the work of Jeremy Bentham as a lengthy exploration of precisely these questions (e.g. Bentham 1996). Yet it is not, perhaps, surprising that during a period of rapid political change and development, with the creation of new types of governing institutions around the world, theorists should pay attention to how they should function. Over the following centuries, as the novelty of bureaucratic government wore off, philosophical interest faded alongside.

John Rawls' canonical *A Theory of Justice* (Rawls 1971) contains several discussions that are of relevance to our topic, such as those on institutions, the basic structure and the rule of law, and the role of the virtue of integrity. Nevertheless, the context of the discussion is always that of how a substantive theory of justice can be advanced and implemented, rather than quality of government in its own right. Robert Nozick's defense of libertarianism (Nozick 1974), understandably, has even less to say. Ronald Dworkin's work, though often relevant, also functions more at the level of abstract principle to inform government action rather than the concrete principles by which such governments should act

---

[9] Some version of this "distinctiveness thesis," that is, that there are distinct moral norms that govern the exercise of executive power aside from legitimacy and justice is also found in more or less explicit form in (Rohr 1986; Heath 2014, 20–1; Zacka 2017, 17, 20–1; Rosanvallon 2018).
[10] (Green 2007, 165; Heath 2014; Zacka 2017, 247).

(Dworkin 1978). Brian Barry has been helpful to Rothstein in developing some of his own thinking, but Barry does not advance any direct thesis concerning the quality of government (Barry 1989).

In the wake of Rothstein's work a number of recent works of political philosophy have more systematically explored the mechanisms of government, engaging both with the history of political thought (Rosanvallon 2018) and contemporary empirical studies and social theory (Herzog 2018; Zacka 2017). Interest in this topic is likely to increase given great concerns about the behaviour of many holders of high office. In addition, other authors are providing the initial threads of a political theory. There are three major categories: political ethics, institutional ethics, and theories of power.

Political Ethics

At least since Machiavelli, there has been an argument that the moral norms (if any) that apply to those with political power are distinct from those that apply to the rest of us in normal life. This "distinctiveness thesis" is putatively grounded upon the fact that political leaders are in a special position to create and/or sustain certain preconditions for the rest of moral life—stability, order, and security (Philp 2007; MacIntyre 1967, 125; Schmitt 2007)—and can use a unique tool to do so—legitimate violence (Weber 1994). There is then a question of what precisely these distinct norms of political ethics might be: whether they constitute a certain kind of amoral realism often credited to Machiavelli himself (Machiavelli 1984); or alternatively a morality of *virtu* valorizing flexibility, shrewdness, decisiveness, resolution, cunning and other traits that dispose a leader to gain power and glory (Machiavelli 2008, ch. 2; Philp 2007, ch. 2); or in the further alternative a consequentialist "ethic of responsibility" that permits political leaders to act contrary to normal deontological rights and obligations for the greater good (Weber 1994). Further, the existence of such distinct political norms then creates what others have referred to as the "problem of dirty hands," when these norms run contrary to our duties in normal moral life (Walzer 1973). For example, can we lie for the good of the nation? Kill the few in order to save the many? Cheat, in order to push forward worthy ends?

Such theories of political ethics, however, do not offer normative theories of executive power per se. This is really no surprise, since it is a line of thought that arises before the state, bureaucracy and separation of powers, as we know it, existed. As such, these theories offer less to societies where power and responsibility to maintain stability, order, and security, and the right to use violence lies with *institutions* placed in an articulated structure regulated by the rule of law, rather than *individuals* (qua "princes") holding unconditional sovereignty.[11]

---

[11] Waldron discusses the separation of power in particular as an articulated structure necessary to preserve to rule of law:(Waldron 2016, ch. 3). Although, following Schmitt, we might hold that even within such structures sovereignty does lie in those in the position to decide the exception to the rules (Schmitt 2005).

Institutional ethics

A second thread of thought models government institutions primarily as hierarchies, with superiors and subordinates in relations of authority, starting with the legislative branch, or the political and electorally accountable leadership of the executive, and reaching down to the lowest street-level bureaucrat. Within this model, for some theorists, the only real moral question facing bureaucrats below is whether or not to follow their orders (Quinlan 1993; Applbaum 1993).

Other theorists argue that, in practice, bureaucracies are akin to a string of *principal–agent relationships*, where the principal (ultimately the people, or at least the political leadership), has much less information than its agents (bureaucrats). Thus, the fundamental problem of governance is to align agent behaviour with their principal's interests. This latter line of thought has driven a series of analyses of corruption as a form of misalignment (Philp 1997; Ceva and Ferretti 2017; Warren 2004), as well as the particular responsibilities that bureaucrats might have to prevent corruption, and other principal–agent failures (Buchanan 1996).

Finally, still other theorists take seriously the idea that such hierarchies and principal–agent relationships fall within institutions (qua organizations) which at least *prima facie* we treat as collective agents with their own rights, permission and/or responsibilities (Thompson 1995; Lessig 2013; Kirby 2020). Whilst this field is nascent, the primary concern has been on how the responsibilities, and accountability of individual bureaucrats relate to that of their collective (Thompson 2005).

Any comprehensive theory of good governance will have to embrace these three themes addressed by institutional ethics. However, such institutional ethics misses the primary concern of any theory of good governance: the discretion of bureaucrats. The hierarchical models presuppose that the directions of the superior to the subordinate are clear, and that the only question is whether or not to follow them. It does not address what to do when a direction is missing, vague, incomplete, or ambiguous. Similarly, the principal–agent theories presuppose a clear idea of the principal's interest, rather than one which is inchoate, controversial, and/or politically unresolved. Finally, institutional models tend to presuppose clear institutional purposes and responsibilities, rather than necessarily offering such clarity.

Theories of Power

A third thread of thought concerns the proper distribution of power within society in general, and thus has implications for how bureaucracy may affect such distributions of power in particular.

First, a theme that runs back at least as far as the neo-Roman republicans of the Renaissance (Pettit 1997; Skinner 1998; Skinner 1998), and the Enlightenment constitutionalists (Waldron 2016, ch. 2) is the need of the "people" to *restrain, limit,* and *control* the government. The primary value at stake is the avoidance of domination by government, as it might use its powers arbitrarily, or for illegitimate ends. Secondly, another theme that runs back to classical Athens, but finds its foundational modern proponent in Rousseau, is for the need to share equally in the power of government, rather than the need to restrain it (Rousseau 1968). Today's "deliberative democrats" are the inheritors of this line of thought. Finally, we might see a complex interaction of both of these lines of thought in more radical thinkers who are more inclined to see freedom and respect for equality in insurgent actions against the state, and a return of much of its powers to localized groups and communities (Young 1990).

Without being theories of "good governance," these theories imply certain conditions on any form of governance in order for it to be consistent with justice and/or legitimacy. Many themes of contemporary governance emerge from this line of thought: the imperative to reduce and minimize discretion, or at least to make its exercise transparent and accountable; the deference to community collaboration, deliberation and representation in making bureaucratic decisions; the drive for inclusive organizations, and the principle of subsidiarity. The limits of such theories, of course, is that they do not take much heed of the ineliminability and the value of bureaucratic discretion, let alone how it might be exercised when such "power-sharing" with the community is impossible or inappropriate. Any comprehensive theory of good governance, by contrast, will presumably make the case for genuine bureaucratic discretion, informing its institutional structure and norms. Let us approach QoG as an attempt to do just that.

Defining "Quality of Government"

According to Rothstein, QoG is (at least part) of what we most want for bureaucratic government. It is the norm that should guide bureaucratic discretion beyond simply complying with the minimum standards of legitimacy. However, what does QoG mean?

The canonical formulation

Rothstein and Teorell (2008) offer a very explicit definition of "QoG as Impartiality":

> Our definition of impartiality in the exercise of public power is the following: When implementing laws and policies, government officials shall not take into consideration anything about the citizen/case that is not beforehand stipulated in the policy or the law (Strömberg 2000).[12]

In order to understand this principle, we need to clarify its relationship with the discretion of government officials. We need to distinguish between three senses of the term "discretion": "*de facto*," "*legal*," and "*pure*."

"Discretion" can refer to the ability to choose between doing X or Y, conjoined with a lack of anyone else to control that choice (or punish it *ex post*). We might call this "*de facto*" *discretion*, as one may have it regardless of one's *de jure* (that is, legal) situation. A law, therefore, does not necessarily constrain an officer's *de facto discretion*, if it is not likely to be enforced against her. This is the meaning of "discretion" that Rothstein (and his co-authors) often deploy. For example, he writes with Varraich that professionals like "nurses, postal workers

---

[12] (Rothstein and Teorell (2008), 170). Reference original. They also go onto to seemingly equate this with excluding bias, but we address this below.

and even police officers" have "discretion" insofar as they have the "power to withhold their specialisations from citizens," perhaps seeking some form of bribe, even though in doing so they would be contravening the law to "deny people their rights."[13]

De facto discretion must be distinguished from "legal discretion" as defined in administrative law. Legal discretion is contrasted with "legal duties." Acting contrary to legal duties is beyond the legal power of the public officer. It would be *ultra vires* and is liable to judicial accountability. By contrast, legal discretion is the domain of legally permissible choice left for public officials by such legal duties. Within this domain, there is no legal requirement to act one way or another. However, such discretion may still be regulated by other nonlegal (or more accurately nonjusticiable) standards of accountability: policy, values, principles, norms and so forth. However, such accountability must be administrative or political, as opposed to legal. Thus, for example, a public official's boss may hold her accountable for her compliance with government policy, but a judge cannot necessarily do the same in court.

With these two senses of "discretion" in hand, we can clarify the manner in which the canonical QoG principle seeks to inform the exercise of discretion by public officials.

First, the principle presumably entails that when any public official has *de facto discretion*, she should exercise it only within the limits of her legal discretion. This follows if we interpret "implementing" laws to also mean "complying" with laws in general. Obviously, we might otherwise distinguish between a particular law or policy being implemented (e.g. a new law lowering the national speed limit), its implementation (e.g. public officials travelling around the country changing road signs), complying with that particular law during its implementation (e.g. those public officials obey the new speed limit when so travelling around the country) and complying with—but not implementing—others laws in general during implementation of this particular law (e.g. following general procurement regulations whilst implementing the particular new speed limit law).

However, QoG also requires that one exercises one's legal discretion in accordance with considerations that are not tantamount to legal duties. Let us call these "policy considerations," although some policy considerations might be set out or implied by a law, but they may not be enforceable as legal duties.[14] So, we might say, as a first pass as a principle informing bureaucratic decision-making, QoG holds that public officials should always comply with their legal duties, and only exercise their remaining legal discretion on the basis of considerations stipulated beforehand in the relevant *government* policy being implemented.

This preliminary interpretation, however, needs to be amended. At a number of points in his work, Rothstein (along with co-authors), explicitly includes professional standards as further considerations that may be taken into account when implementing government laws and policy. Public doctors may draw upon the professional standards of the medical profession, and so on.[15] However, *why* should this be case? Why should a private professional group or its representative organizations in their name literally determine the exercise of government discretion? Presumably, the implicit reason is that the government has delegated some of its standard-making powers to these professions, and thus can override such standards if it so wishes. For example, if a profession becomes so progressive that it now considers

---

[13] (Rothstein and Varraich 2017, 57, see also, 119, 121ff.)

[14] This is the distinction between "law" and "policy" in administrative law: (Cane 1996, 116).

[15] (Rothstein and Varraich 2017, 101f).

structural injustice to be a reason to prioritize certain clients over others, but a conservative government policy is explicitly opposed to such a consideration, then the conservative government's policy overrides the professional standard. Thus, to this end, we should distinguish valid and invalid professional standards. Valid professional standards are only those that for some reason (most likely delegation of standard-making powers or incorporation of those standards once made, by government), should direct public officers. Invalid standards would be those without such "public" standing.

So to complete our interpretation of the canonical QoG principle, it requires that public officials comply with their legal duties, and with any remaining legal discretion only take into account considerations stipulated in the relevant government policy, and valid professional standards.

On this interpretation, however, QoG both assumes the existence of but does not itself inform one further kind of discretion. We shall call this "pure discretion." Such pure discretion exists within the domain of legal discretion, but it is not governed by any particular policy or standards. Thus, QoG cannot apply. There are no relevant policies or standards to stipulate considerations "beforehand." QoG must assume the existence of just such discretion because it must exist at some level within bureaucracies and professional bodies in order for those decision-makers to set the policies and standards that stipulate the considerations to be taken into account in other decisions. After all, someone, somewhere has to have the ultimate discretion to set the (nonlegislative) considerations, and not just follow the considerations set by others. So, QoG must assume the existence of such pure discretion, but cannot act as a standard to determine its good exercise. If it is to be assessed as being exercised well or poorly, against any standard, QoG cannot be that standard. Thus, the more prevalent such "pure discretion" is within government, the less explanatory QoG can be as an account of good government.

This leads to a final question: when do bureaucrats have pure discretion? When can decision-makers take into account considerations not yet stipulated in law, relevant policy, or professional standard beforehand? If it were *all the time*, then of course QoG would vanish as an informative principle. But it must be *some of the time* or else there would never be any policies or standards for QoG to refer to. So when? No clear answer lies within Rothstein et al.'s work, but it seems consistent with the logic of QoG that pure discretion should only exist where it is explicitly contemplated by a relevant superior law, policy, or standard. For example, where the law gives the minister discretion to determine some matter, "as she sees fit," or where stated considerations are said not to be "exhaustive," then the law clearly contemplates pure discretion. We should assume that QoG otherwise operates to create a strong presumption against a public officer having any pure discretion. Thus, for example, where a policy is strictly, but not explicitly open-ended, like most policies, it should be interpreted to be "closed." By this we mean, that when a law (or policy or standard) is of the form "in deciding the case, the decision-maker should take X, Y, and Z into consideration," strictly speaking it does not exclude being interpreted to mean "in deciding the case, the decision-maker should take X, Y, and Z into consideration *and can take into account any other considerations she so determines, so long as they are consistent with her legal duties, and professional standards*." But, the force of QoG operates to interpret such a law to mean "in deciding the case, the decision-maker should take X, Y and Z into consideration, *and only those considerations, her legal duties and her professional standards*."

However, as we shall argue later, this presumption against pure discretion might just be the Achilles' heel of the QoG principle (at least under its canonical formulation).

The bias principle

Before commencing our substantive assessment of the canonical formulation of QoG, as analysed above, it is worth noting what Rothstein and Teorell assert immediately afterwards:

> As Cupit writes: "To act impartially is to be unmoved by certain sorts of considerations—such as special relationships and personal preferences. It is to treat people alike irrespective of personal relationships and personal likes and dislikes" (Cupit 2000).[16]

Let us call this the "bias principle." Now, Rothstein and Teorell put forward this principle as if it were a mere elaboration of the QoG principle. But it is not. They are neither identical nor necessarily consistent. Let us demonstrate.

First, we could take into consideration something about a citizen/case not beforehand stipulated in the law, the government policy or valid professional standards (breaching QoG), without it being a special relationship or a personal preference (failing to breach the bias principle). For example, when implementing a policy to build school halls, a bureaucrat might prioritize funding for one school hall in one community over another because the former is poorer and has had less public investment over recent years. Poverty, and lack of recent public investment may not be considerations "stipulated beforehand" in the immediate government policy or any relevant government policy, but the bureaucrat need not have any special relationship with, or personal preference or liking for either community.

Secondly, a consideration about a citizen/case could be stipulated in the law, government policy or professional standard beforehand (consistent with QoG) but turn upon the existence of a personal relationship (breaching the bias principle). We could imagine a law, government or professional standard that explicitly *requires* an officer to act on the basis of personal relationships, likes, or dislikes. For example, if a policy of recusal were to require a decision-maker to recuse herself from making any decision about a person with whom they have a personal relationship, then it would mean making a decision on the basis of a personal relationship. Now this example might be dismissed on the grounds that recusal is not the sort of decision considered in the scope of the policy, as its point is precisely to protect decisions from the intrusion of personal relationships. But consider something that Rothstein et al. themselves introduce that could arise within advocacy services. Imagine a professional standard for a community services caseworker that encourages the worker to empathize for their client, predictably coming to care for them, and thus fight harder for their rights within a general system. This means acting on the basis of a special relationship, involving a particular, purposefully created, preferential concern for the client.[17]

The bias principle, therefore, is distinct from the canonical formulation of QoG. They should not be confused. Instead, as we shall do below, it should be assessed on its own merits. However, first let us assess the canonical formulation.

---

[16] (Rothstein and Teorell 2008, 170). Reference original.
[17] See (Zacka 2017).

"QUALITY OF GOVERNMENT" AS A SUFFICIENT CONDITION FOR GOOD GOVERNMENT

Sometimes, Rothstein et al. appear to claim that QoG, under its canonical formulation, offers a *full conception* of good government, in the sense that it alone is a sufficient condition. It is "good governance." it defines the "opposite of corruption." it provides a (the?) "basic normative standard for how people entrusted to provide public services ought to behave" (Rothstein and Varraich 2017). Impartiality, so defined, has the same conceptual primacy and fertility for interpreting good governance as basic moral equality has for interpreting the first virtue of social institutions (Rothstein and Teorell 2008).

At other times, however, Rothstein et al. back away from this claim: "Impartiality could hardly be considered the sole normative yardstick for assessing all aspects of a political system. Self-evidently, normatively despicable policies, such as an apartheid system, can in theory be implemented impartially" (Rothstein 2011). As others have noted, this latter position must be correct (Agnafors 2013; Fukuyama 2013). Impartiality is consistent not merely with illegitimate bureaucratic behaviour but also a range of more quotidian, intuitive government failings. Decision-making can be impartial, but inefficient, ineffective, capricious, without an evidence base, lack robustness, lack clarity, create uncertainty, be inconsistent with another officeholder's decision, and so on. At best, QoG is a necessary but not a sufficient condition for "good governance."

However, Rothstein *et al.* do have a reply. They argue that QoG is sufficient—at least in practice—because, *empirically*, impartiality leads to whatever else we might want from good governance (rule of law, human rights compliance, efficiency, well-being, and so on). However, we believe that in the light of the considerations emerging from the Kafka example, this claim stretches plausibility. Many of the problems encountered by Joseph K seem entirely detached from impartiality. And indeed, we would argue that whether or not that is the case, it remains important to articulate the full set of conditions that define good governance, regardless of their empirical relationship. In particular, this is important in *nonideal* situations, where one intuitive governance goal (e.g. efficiency) can only come at the expense of another (e.g. impartiality). Only a full theory of good governance can explain how to resolve such conflicts. Once again, we will return to this below.

Finally, Rothstein *et al.* have a further argument, in the alternative, that QoG is sufficient because it exhausts the *procedural* requirements of good governance, and no theory of good governance should include "controversial" substantive requirements (Rothstein 2011; Rothstein and Varraich 2017). Yet it is unclear to us at least that even their theory does, or at least should, actually avoid substantive commitments. For example, shortly after the introduction of the theory, the authors remark:

> One example ... is support to poor families with children. The enactment of such policies would not break the principle of impartiality, while denying such allowances for families from a certain ethnic group or parents with a certain sexual orientation when implementing the policy would.[18]

---

[18]   (Rothstein and Teorell 2008, 170).

But what would the authors say about a policy that withdrew support from poor families in order to fund tax breaks for the superrich? Could we say that a government that deliberately diverts resources from the poor to the rich, without even having the grace to claim that the policy is better for the poor in the long term, meets the criteria of good governance? If not, how can we justify the asymmetry between rich and poor without appealing to a substantive element?

"Quality of Government" as a Necessary Condition for Good Governance

Intuitively, Rothstein *et al.* appear to be on stronger ground in positing that QoG is a necessary condition of good governance. Rothstein and Teorell never explicitly put forward a case for *why* QoG might be plausible. We can think of three possible reasons. However, on closer inspection, we argue each has difficulties, revealing that QoG might be a less plausible necessary condition of good government that it might first appear.

First, there is what we might call the "republican argument": QoG is effectively a presumption against "pure" discretionary power being delegated to the executive bureaucracy. Such discretionary power is dangerous within the hands of the executive, as they can effectively implement their own will rather than that of the legislature, or decision-makers, including professional bodies, to whom they have explicitly delegated that will. This is a form of tyranny or "unfreedom."

The trouble with this argument is that the primary reason that the executive bureaucracy needs discretion is to implement the perceived legislative "will" to the best of its abilities. Often, considerations not stipulated in the law in general, the relevant policy, or professional standards beforehand must be taken into account. Often, in fact, this is to ensure that this particular policy can be made consistent with other policies. For example, a procurement process might make no reference to environmental considerations, but another policy highlights the need for government to decrease environmental impacts. Or, alternatively, limiting costs as much as possible may not be an explicit consideration in one legislated project, but such savings will help support another. Rothstein *et al.* might argue that so long as there is *some* policy, *somewhere* in government that supports a consideration, then consistent with QoG it can be relied upon in implementing any *particular* policy. However, this leads to a form of hidden pure discretion. Within government there will always be a veritable multitude of often conflicting policies, with even more conflicting considerations. If QoG is consistent with reference to any consideration from any other government policy, then in effect the decision-maker has the ability to find most considerations that they might possibly hope to rely upon, and the discretion to exclude any others they do not.

But even assuming this form of "backdoor" pure discretion exists, no set of laws and policies can cover every case, even collectively. It is very common for "street-level bureaucrats" to have to fill in grey areas of policies themselves (Lipsky 2010; Zacka 2017), a point well understood in respect to the law by legal theorists (Dworkin 1978).

It is the task of the executive to implement, make concrete and collectively coherent, each individual, abstract, and minimal directions of the legislature. It seems to be a more plausible principle of governance to presume pure executive bureaucratic discretion to achieve this aim, and place the onus upon the legislature to explicitly rule it out. Furthermore, this should be combined with legislative oversight and accountability such that if the bureaucracy misinterprets the legislative will when exercising its discretion, or otherwise misuses its powers, then it can be corrected by the legislature. In other words, a pure bureaucratic discretion broader than QoG seems much more plausible when laws are seen within a dynamic, agile, ongoing relationship between legislative and executive branches, rather than a static, one-shot interaction in which a rule is determined and then implemented.

Second, a "fairness argument": suggests that citizens live under laws and policies that are as clear (easily understood), certain (individuals can be sure that they will be applied), and consistent (various rulings will not conflict with one another) as possible. However, so the argument goes, presuming an indeterminate scope of bureaucratic discretion when implementing such laws and policies disrupts clarity, certainty and consistency. Thus, it is best to restrict such decision-making to those considerations clearly and certainly set out within the law or policy beforehand, and consistently only apply them.

This argument underestimates the clarity, certainty and consistency that *good* bureaucratic governance can achieve whilst using discretion. A bureaucracy can act in respect to a new consideration not contemplated by current law, policy or standards, but then seek to generalize that *ad hoc* action as new policy, publicize it, and ensure that each of its decision-makers are coordinated to apply the same considerations in each case. Today's acts of pure discretion can become tomorrow's policy or standard. Just as uncertainty is an acceptable cost for a sufficiently responsive, agile, and adaptive common law in certain countries, it can apply equally well although less formally for bureaucracy.

Finally, the "abuse of power" argument suggests legal discretion is often an opportunity for abuse of power. For example, if a bureaucrat is permitted to consider factors not "stipulated beforehand," then they may have the opportunity to consider their own personal interests, or those of others they know. Or, they might start to factor in other dubious factors such as personal likes and dislikes or political partisanship.

Empirically, this is true.[19] Discretion—*de facto*, legal, and pure—can create opportunities for abuse of power. However, this in itself is not decisive against discretion. Instead, it recommends weighing the risks and potential benefits of such discretion, and mitigating its risks with accountability and positive incentive.

However, if the ultimate argument for QoG is that it is needed in order to exclude certain types of factors being taken into consideration, such as corrupt, partial, and partisan reasons, then why not reformulate the principle to merely explicitly exclude those considerations? Why not have a principle that explicitly defines what *cannot* be considered (corrupt, partial and partisan reasons), rather than implausibly limiting the scope of what *can* be considered (only those considerations "stipulated beforehand")? Indeed, Rothstein and Teorell themselves mention a similar principle just after their canonical formulation: the bias principle, described above.

Before turning to an assessment of the bias principle, let us make one final note on the canonical formulation. One way in which all three critiques above, might be blunted, is if the set of considerations "beforehand stipulated in the policy or the law" includes additional

---

[19] (Klitgaard 1988).

implicit as well as explicit considerations.[20] On this interpretation, some of the inflexibility we have attributed to QoG is alleviated, as decision-makers may claim that considerations of resource allocation, efficiency, ongoing relationships with stakeholders, other government priorities, whole of government coordination and consistency, and so on are all additional *implicit* considerations. They can then be relied upon when making decisions, consistent with QoG.

In response, first, the line between considerations implied by a policy or law, and additional considerations simply thought to be important is fuzzy at best. Rarely will such considerations be logically entailed by the explicit considerations. Instead background normative assumptions—about how government should and should not operate—themselves not in the policy or law, will have to be deployed. For example, to claim that it is implicit that government should act consistently across policies might seem obvious but is based on a normative assumption that consistency is valuable. Many ministers might well disagree.

Secondly, even if implicit considerations exist and can be relied upon by decision-makers, consistent with the canonical formulation of QoG, the problem for Rothstein and Teorell, however, is that this merely suggests that the real work, the real theory of governance, lies in articulating these very background, substantive normative claims rather than simply acknowledging the formal point that, once they are justified then obviously they should be deployed by decision-makers. Good governance would be defined by some theory that brought together something like the norms of efficiency, consistency and coordination, stable relationships with stakeholders, and so on that should *always* be considerations in public decision-making. QoG would simply be a formal implication of this substantive theory.[21]

"Quality of Government" as an Opposition to Bias

To recall our point, above, the bias principle is *not* the same as the QoG principle. And, we have argued in the previous section that the QoG principle has difficulties when posed as a necessary condition of good government. So we might now ask, whether the bias principle as an alternative interpretation of "impartiality" is more plausible instead?

First, let us clarify the scope of the principle. It is a principle that aims to define explicitly what should *not* be considered in bureaucratic decision-making. Cupit restricts this to consideration of "special relationships," "personal preferences," and "likes and dislikes." To this we should add corrupt abuse of public office for private gain or using discretion and power to further party-political purposes. These considerations may not be exhaustive, there may be more. Our general point is that it is more plausible to work out and clarify gradually explicit considerations to *exclude* from government decision-making, than isolate an exhaustive and exclusive account of what can be included (like the canonical QoG principle).

---

[20] This was helpfully suggested during review.
[21] And this seems to be the approach begun by authors such as (Zacka 2017; Heath 2014; Kirby 2020; Agnafors 2013) as discussed in the conclusion below.

Secondly, with this clarification in hand, we must account for intuitively acceptable practices such as recusal on the basis of a special relationship, or a caseworker giving preferential concern to the client with whom she empathizes. Arguably, these cases can be held consistent with the bias principle *if* they are explicitly permitted by a prior rule, and that prior rule itself was decided upon in a way that did not breach the bias principle. For example, suppose the head of the department of community services is simply given the direction to create a series of policies for caseworkers and how they relate to clients. The head of department *knows* that caseworkers will tend to identify with their clients as an instinctive human reaction, and that any attempt to stop such identification will be counterproductive. So she permits her caseworkers to so identify. However, she creates a robust, adversarial system in which other actors hold the caseworker's recommendations to account. She, therefore, institutes a policy that, as a whole, shows no bias or preference for the clients, against, say, other actors whose interests are at stake, consistent with the bias principle. Some philosophers have distinguished different levels of impartiality and have argued that impartiality at a systems level is consistent with partiality at a personal level. For example, utilitarians have argued that we maximize utility overall by encouraging people to develop close relationships within their family and friendship groups (for discussion see Parfit (1984)). Here we see a similar logic: that partiality between individuals could be the best way of running a service which is impartial overall.

Further, consider a case of government cuts that fall on a disadvantaged group that, as it happens, is socially stigmatized, including by the government bureaucrats who share common prejudices. If the disadvantaged group complains about how it is affected, is it sufficient for the bureaucrats to reply that the decision was based not on personal preferences but on grounds clearly stipulated in the policy beforehand? In some cases, the policy will be the result of honestly applied policy, but equally there will be cases where allowing the cut to fall on the relatively powerless is the easy way out for officials, knowing that the protests would be greater if the cuts fell elsewhere. Here, we would judge that the bias principle is violated.

Finally, consider a tax official having to decide whether a prize counts as income for the purposes of income tax. If the official is influenced by personal considerations—for example if someone they admired won the prize, which led them not to question a colleague's decision—then there is a strong case again that the bias principle has been violated.

Is "Quality of Government" Anything More than Just a Constraint of Legitimacy?

The canonical formulation of QoG, we have argued, has difficulties if posed as either a sufficient or necessary condition of "good government." But we have suggested that reformulating QoG as a bias principle is highly plausible as a necessary condition. Perhaps, it might even be what Rothstein and Teorell actually intended. However, there is one final critique that questions whether QoG, so understood, actually advances the "good government" question much at all, beyond the traditional demand for legitimacy in decision-making. The real, new, and interesting task, for philosophy at least, is to explore what else *if anything* constitutes good government.

However, one might now suspect that the bias principle is *nothing more* than an implication of legitimacy, by which governments are already bound. Furthermore, it accords with some of the key principles of administrative law.[22] To put it another way: well of course government actors do not legitimately have power to act in a biased manner, and thus they cannot exercise a power they do not have.

We think, however, that this critique—whilst plausible—grants too much to the ordinary concept of "legitimacy." An actor has legitimacy if they have the right to rule, and their decision has legitimacy if it falls within their scope of power. However, it is too fast to assume that only unbiased decisions are ever legitimate. In truth, many countries around the world have laws and policies that allow for partial decision-making by systemic *design*. For example, in many countries incoming administrations have the right to appoint political advisers within ministerial officers (e.g. UK special advisers). Further, in other jurisdictions ministers can also nominate whomever they please to senior posts in the administration (the US appointment system). In part, the theory behind such systems is that public administration will be aligned and responsive to the political imperatives of the government. Further, in most systems, it is widely accepted that senior positions, such as ambassadorial appointments, are appointed as rewards for political support. In all these cases, the bias principle is contravened. *Politics*, and partisan considerations and preferences, have infiltrated the decision-making. However, if impartiality was only a derivative concern of legitimacy, then we would be committed to dismissing all such real world practice as *illegitimate*, as if laws and policies made by such officials should simply be dismissed as failed attempts to exercise a power they do not have.

This seems implausible. It demands too much of the concept of "legitimacy," which instead should remain a very permissive concept, only curtailing the very moral limits of possible power. While there remains a problem with such "politicization" of government, the problem is independent of legitimacy. Rather, it fails the test of impartiality understood as the bias principle. It is legitimate, but *bad* government. In this way, the bias principle does advance (even if only partially) our central question: what should we most want from bureaucratic government *beyond* mere legitimacy?

CONCLUSION: DIRECTIONS
FOR FURTHER RESEARCH

Rothstein *et al.* have exposed an important gap both in the thinking and priorities of contemporary political philosophy. Traditional debates about justice, especially distribution, rights, and inequality, remain important, as do debates about legitimacy and the value of democracy. But it is also a pressing time to consider what makes good bureaucratic government. As trust in government falls, and concern about corruption rises, as public institutions have been privatized and public functions contracted out, and traditional Weberian public values have been eroded, a philosophy of governance is needed to explore the normative principles of the bureaucratic arm of government.

---

[22] At the rule against bias is *nemo iudex in sua causa* (a person must not be judge in his own case or own cause). See (Cane 1996, 160).

QoG attempts to do that, and whilst we have spoken against its canonical formulation, interpreted instead as a "bias principle" it is plausibly an important part of an answer. However, as others have argued a philosophy of good government will involve a number of different values. In response to Rothstein et al., Agnafors recommends a six-part, "complex" definition of quality of government combining a "minimal morality and public ethos," a compliance with formal norms of decision-making (like noncontradiction) and the need to give reasons, a "principle of beneficence," efficiency, rule of law and impartiality, and institutional "stability."[23] Similarly, Zacka, whilst not an explicit critic of Rothstein et al., puts forward a four-part account of the disposition guiding the discretion of street-level bureaucrats: "efficiency," "fairness," "respect," and "responsiveness" (Zacka, 2017, 11–12, 20–2). Heath puts forward the rule of law, Pareto efficiency, and citizen equality (Heath, 2014).

Nevertheless, such lists as they stand, are theoretically weak in three ways. First, currently such lists are largely asserted in an intuitive fashion, without any deeper justification or structural unity. Bare "intuition" does a lot of epistemic work, without leading to any form of reflective equilibrium. Secondly, much work is needed to find a principled way to balance or prioritize the factors unless intuition, once again, is to be our only recourse. And finally, recall the suggestion that while pro-poor policies were said to be consistent with impartiality, pro-superrich policies presumably were not. This appears to assume that good governance presupposes a theory of justice, despite efforts to keep the topics apart. Whether this is correct, how it is to be done, what theory is appropriate, and what it implies in practice are unexplored topics.

Future research into the philosophy of good government should aim to find greater theoretical coherence and justification for the factors of good government. For example, it might explore precisely *why* QoG as the bias principle is a necessary condition of good government. Oddly enough, that is a question Rothstein et al. have not yet sought to answer. Perhaps, it is time for the philosophers to take up the burden.

REFERENCES

Agnafors, Marcus. 2013. "Quality of Government: Toward a More Complex Definition." *American Political Science Review* 107 (3): 433–45. https://doi.org/10.1017/s0003055413000191.

Applbaum, Arthur Isak. 1993. "The Remains of the Role." *Governance* 6 (4): 545–57. https://doi.org/10.1111/j.1468-0491.1993.tb00164.x.

Aristotle,. 1996. *The Politics; and, The Constitution of Athens*. 2nd ed. *Cambridge Texts in the History of Political Thought*. tr. Stephen Everson. Cambridge: Cambridge University Press.

Barry, Brian. 1989. *A Treatise on Social Justice. Theories of Justice*. London: Harvester Wheatsheaf.

Bentham, Jeremy, 1996. *An Introduction to the Principles of Morals and Legislation. Principles of Legislation*. Oxford: Clarendon Press.

---

[23] (Agnafors 2013). The "principle of beneficence" holds that "Under conditions of uncertainty, public agents ought, when exercising public authority, to treat the subjects under their authority in accordance with the most beneficial alternative that is materially and ethically available" (439).

Buchanan, Allen. 1996. "Toward a Theory of the Ethics of Bureaucratic Organizations." *Business Ethics Quarterly* 6 (4): 419–40. https://doi.org/10.5840/10.2307/3857497.

Cane, Peter. 1996. *An Introduction to Administrative Law*. 3rd ed. *Administrative Law*. Oxford: Clarendon Press.

Ceva, Emanuela, and Maria Paola Ferretti. 2017. "Political Corruption." *Philosophy Compass* 12 (12). https://doi.org/10.1111/phc3.12461.

Confucius. 1971. *The Analects of Confucius*. tr. Arthur Waley. London: George Allen & Unwin Ltd.

Cupit, Geoffrey. 2000. When Does Justice Require Impartiality. Presented at the Political Studies Association-UK 50th Annual Conference, London.

Dworkin, Ronald. 1978. *Taking Rights Seriously*. New impression, with a reply to critics. ed. London: Duckworth.

Fukuyama, Francis. 2013. "What Is Governance?" *Governance* 26 (3): 347–68. https://doi.org/10.1111/gove.12035.

Green, Leslie. 2007. "The Duty to Govern." *Legal Theory* 13 (3–4): 165–85. https://doi.org/10.1017/s1352325208070079.

Hamilton, Alexander, James Madison, and John Jay. 2003. *The Federalist. Cambridge Texts in the History of Political Thought*. Cambridge, U.K.; New York: Cambridge University Press.

Heath, Christopher. 2014. *A General Framework for the Ethics of Public Administration*. Unpublished Manuscript. University of Toronto.

Herzog, Lisa. 2018. *Reclaiming the System: Moral Responsibility, Divided Labour, and the Role of Organizations in Society*. Oxford: Oxford University Press.

Heywood, Paul. 2015. *Routledge handbook of political corruption*. Milton Park, Abingdon, Oxon; New York, NY: Routledge.

Holocaust Memorial Day Trust. 2019. "Feng Shan Ho." Accessed March 3rd 2021. https://www.hmd.org.uk/resource/feng-shan-ho/.

Huberts, L. W. 2014. *The Integrity of Governance: What It Is, What We Know, What Is Done, and Where to Go. Governance and Public Management Series*. Basingstoke: Palgrave Macmillan.

Kafka, Franz. [1925] 2015. *The Trial. Penguin Modern Classics*, edited by Idris Parry. London: Penguin Books.

Kirby, Nikolas. 2020. "An "Institution-First" Conception of Public Integrity." *British Journal of Political Science*, 1–16. doi: 10.1017/S000712342000006X.

Klitgaard, Robert E. 1988. *Controlling Corruption*. Berkeley: University of California Press.

Ladenson, Robert. 1980. "In Defense of a Hobbesian Conception of Law." *Philosophy and Public Affairs* 9 (2): 134.

Lessig, L. 2013. "Foreword: "Institutional corruption" defined." *Journal of Law, Medicine & Ethics* 41 (3): 553–5. https://doi.org/10.1111/jlme.12063. https://www.ncbi.nlm.nih.gov/pubmed/24088144.

Lipsky, Michael. 2010. *Street- Level Bureaucracy: Dilemmas of the Individual in Public Services*. Updated ed. New York: Russell Sage Foundation.

Machiavelli, Niccolò. 1984. *The Prince. World's Classics*, edited by Peter Bondanella. Oxford: Oxford University Press.

Machiavelli, Niccolò. 2008. *Discourses on Livy. Oxford World's Classics*, edited by Julia Conaway Bondanella and Peter Bondanella. Oxford: Oxford University Press.

MacIntyre, Alasdair C. 1967. *A Short History of Ethics*. London: Routledge & Kegan Paul.

Mungiu-Pippidi, Alina. 2015. *The Quest for Good Governance: How Societies Develop Control of Corruption*. Cambridge, United Kingdom: Cambridge University Press.

Nozick, Robert. 1974. *Anarchy, State and Utopia*. Oxford: Basil Blackwell.

Parfit, Derek. 1984. *Reasons and Persons*. Oxford: Oxford University Press.

Pettit, Philip. 1997. *Republicanism: a theory of freedom and government. Oxford political theory*. Oxford: Clarendon Press.

Philp, Mark. 1997. "Defining Political Corruption." *Political Studies* 45 (3): 436–62. https://doi.org/10.1111/1467-9248.00090.

Philp, Mark. 2007. *Political Conduct*. Cambridge, Mass.; London: Harvard University Press.

Plato, 1871. *The Dialogues of Plato*. Tr. Benjamin Jowett. Oxford: Clarendon Press.

Quinlan, Michael. 1993. "Ethics in the Public Service." *Governance* 6 (4): 538–44. https://doi.org/10.1111/j.1468-0491.1993.tb00163.x.

Rawls, John. 1971. *A Theory of Justice*. Original ed. Cambridge, Mass: Belknap Press of Harvard University Press.

Rawls, John. 2005. *Political Liberalism*. Expanded ed. *Columbia Classics in Philosophy*. New York: New York: Columbia University Press.

Raz, Joseph. 1986. *The Morality of Freedom. Ebook Central*. Oxford [Oxfordshire]: New York: Clarendon Press: Oxford University Press.

Ripstein, Arthur. 2004. "Authority and Coercion." *Philosophy & Public Affairs* 32 (1): 2–35. https://doi.org/10.1111/j.1467-6486.2004.00003.x.

Rohr, John A. 1986. *To Run a Constitution: The Legitimacy of the Administrative State. Studies in Government and Public Policy*. Lawrence: University Press of Kansas.

Rosanvallon, Pierre, 2018. *Good Government: Democracy Beyond Elections*. Tr. M. B. DeBevoise. Cambridge, Massachusetts: Harvard University Press.

Rothstein, Bo. 2011. *The Quality of Government: Corruption, Social Trust, and Inequality in International Perspective*. Chicago; London: University of Chicago Press.

Rothstein, Bo, and Jan Teorell. 2008. "What Is Quality of Government? A Theory of Impartial Government Institutions." *Governance* 21 (2): 165–90. https://doi.org/10.1111/j.1468-0491.2008.00391.x.

Rothstein, Bo, and Aiysha Varraich. 2017. *Making Sense of Corruption*. Cambridge, United Kingdom: Cambridge University Press.

Rousseau, Jean Jacques. 1968. *The Social Contract*. Translated by M. Cranston. London: Penguin Books.

Schmitt, Carl. 2005. *Political Theology: Four Chapters on the Concept of Sovereignty*. Chicago; London: University of Chicago Press.

Schmitt, Carl, 2007. *The Concept of the Political*. Expanded ed. Chicago; London: University of Chicago Press.

Skinner, Quentin. 1998. *Liberty Before Liberalism*. Cambridge: Cambridge University Press.

Strömberg, H. 2000. *Allmän Förvaltningsrätt*. Malmö: Liber.

Thompson, Dennis F. 1995. *Ethics in Congress: From Individual to Institutional Corruption*. Washington, DC: Brookings Institution.

Thompson, Dennis F. 2005. *Restoring Responsibility: Ethics in Government, Business and Healthcare*. Cambridge: Cambridge University Press.

Waldron, Jeremy. 2016. *Political Political Theory: Essays on Institutions*. Cambridge: Harvard University Press.

Walzer, Michael. 1973. "Political Action: The Problem of Dirty Hands." *Philosophy and Public Affairs* 2 (2): 160.

Warren, Mark. 2004. "What Does Corruption Mean in a Democracy?" *American Journal of Political Science* 48 (2): 328–43.

Weber, Max. 1994. *Political Writings. Cambridge Texts in the History of Political Thought*, edited by Peter Lassman and Ronald Speirs. Cambridge: Cambridge University Press.

Weber, Max,. 2019. *Economy and Society: A New Translation*. Tr. Keith Tribe. Cambridge, Massachusetts: Harvard University Press.

Young, Iris Marion. 1990. *Justice and the Politics of Difference*. Princeton: Princeton University Press.

Zacka, Bernardo. 2017. *When the State Meets the Street: Public Service and Moral Agency*. Cambridge, Massachusetts: The Belknap Press of Harvard University Press.

CHAPTER 4

....

SHADOW ELITES
Beyond Institutional Corruption Theory
and Ill-Conceived Anticorruption Regimes
And Toward a New Research Agenda

....

JANINE R. WEDEL

A new breed of influencers, with "shadow elites" at the helm, has arisen amid transformational developments over the past several decades. "Institutional corruption," systemic and fully legal corruption, appears to have taken root in the United States and may also be making a debut in some other liberal democracies. Impartial government, a cornerstone of quality of government, may be compromised. It is tempting to think that this state of affairs emerged overnight, spurred by the success of anti-system movements in liberal democracies and beyond. In fact, it has been decades in the making.

How did we get to where we are now? What are the reforms, developments, and trends, both inside and outside government, that in recent decades have fostered this evolution? How do the influencers who have emerged to capitalize on the changes operate and organize themselves vis-à-vis government, and how do these ways and means relate to the concept of institutional corruption? Further, how is it that shadow elites and institutional corruption have established themselves over roughly the same time frame as international anticorruption regimes?

This chapter, grounded in a social anthropological perspective, seeks to address these questions by outlining common patterns of organization and operation, illustrated with specific examples. It deals with crucial indicators of quality of government, including rule of law and corruption, that are not typically captured in the literature because most indices and tools employed to assess government quality cannot detect such patterns. That is a serious omission because these patterns contribute to long-term erosion of governance that cannot easily be reversed.

Analyzing the emergence of a potentially new phenomenon such as shadow elites requires a methodological approach that allows for detailed consideration of the contextual developments that have spawned it. Examples here presented rely on multiple data collection methods and varying sources, which may include public documents, public interest and investigative reports, journalists' findings, published accounts from insiders, and scholarly works, enabling triangulation of evidence (Yin 2014, 239, 241). A core task of this work is to "thickly" describe the *modus operandi* and organization of shadow elites and offer interpretation and implications thereof (Denzin 2001; Geertz 1973; Ryle 1971). Thick description of multiple examples enables a within and cross-case analysis of shadow elites who operate in diverse institutional environments (Eisenhardt 1989; Yin 2014). Grounded theory (Glaser and Strauss 2009), which conceptualizes what is happening through empirical research, can then be developed to rectify lack of fit between empirical research and theory. Examples are useful both for theory building (Glaser and Strauss 2009) and for examining their implications for corruption, quality of government, and democracy. Most examples here provided are from the United States, where some of the developments and practices associated with shadow elites are perhaps most visible. Yet evidence suggests that these developments and practices, which are systemic and institutional and employed by actors from across the political and ideological spectrum, enjoy wide reach across liberal democracies, if not well beyond.

That is because gathering transformational developments over the past roughly 40 years have spawned new spaces of policy and what has become known as "governance" and created the conditions for the attenuation of impartial government and accountability. Impartiality and accountability are fundaments of the classic (ideal) hierarchic, legal, meritocratic, and impersonal bureaucracy elucidated by Max Weber (1947, 1994), providing a bulwark against favoritism, politicization, and corruption, along with theoretical foundations for modern democracy. The "procedural norm" of impartiality is the very essence of quality of government, contend political scientists Bo Rothstein and Jan Teorell (2008, 165, 171).

Yet transformational reforms within the U.S. and many other governments, the first part of this chapter explains, have crippled the capacity to act impartially and accountably, thus setting the stage for corruption. Additional transformational developments that arose over roughly the same period and with momentous consequences that touch nearly everywhere are then introduced. They have rendered governance vulnerable to a new breed of influencers and encouraged shadow elites, the most insidious of them, and ushered in systemic, structural corruption, in which activities are mostly legal but nevertheless violate an official institution's public, impartial mission and, often, its perceived integrity.

The sections that follow explore the organization and *modus operandi* of shadow elites as compared with their "power elite" forebears and clarify their relationship to structural and personal corruption. Shadow elites not only personalize bureaucracy, flout transparency, circumvent accountability structures, threaten the impartiality needed to ensure quality government, and betray public trust, they fuse state and private power to achieve their own agendas.

Subsequent sections lay out the organization and *modus operandi* of shadow elites and evaluate theories of institutional corruption in view of shadow elite practices. While definitions vary, institutional corruption "broadly refers to legal, systemic corruption rather than illegal, quid-pro-quo corruption" (Amit et al. 2017, 448). Although institutional corruption threatens both impartiality and accountability (Thompson 2018, 17), as do shadow elites, and the two theories converge on some key points, there also are points of divergence. We ask whether theories of institutional corruption, as thus far elaborated, adequately account for the operations of shadow elites and the merging of state and private power that they achieve.

A following section discusses the co-emergence of shadow elites and international *anti*corruption regimes over the past quarter century. We inquire why these regimes have largely failed to recognize the impact and interactions of the transformational developments and the modes of corruption that arose with them, let alone address them.

Finally, we note the pressing need for further research and a wide-ranging and multi-disciplinary approach to identify and study shadow elite practices, ecosystems, and implications.

Governance Ecosystem, Transformed

The first transformational development—the redesign of government by way of privatization and deregulation—originated in the Anglo-Saxon world,[1] gaining great momentum in the 1980's era of U.S. President Ronald Reagan and U.K. Prime Minister Margaret Thatcher.[2] A cornerstone of the reforms—and enduring drive in many contexts—has been to model government after business, expressed both in efforts to make government itself more like business and to enlist private actors in its work (Osborne and Gaebler 1992; Osborne and Plastrik 1997). Yet making government more like business endangers the distinctive qualities and purposes of both and implicitly contradicts impartial government.

The contracting of government services to private entities is a major case in point (Guttman and Willner 1976; Guttman 2006). The "Reagan revolution" sanctified the practice of outsourcing government services, and with public-private partnerships and nongovernmental entities substantially engaged in the work of government, "government" began to give way to "governance."[3]

U.S. "shadow government" has since mushroomed, under both Republican and Democratic administrations. In 2015, there were 2.6 contract workers (bound by fewer rules than their government counterparts) for each government employee (Light 2017). Companies, consulting firms, and NGOs daily stand in for government. Contractor companies have long helped drive public priorities, sometimes with government officials only signing on the dotted line.

So-called "inherently governmental functions," discretionary decision making and actions "so intimately related to the public interest as to mandate performance by Government employees" (Office of Management and Budget 1992), are often, in fact, done by contractors.

---

[1] While the reforms have tended to be most fully implemented and taken root most completely in the Anglo-Saxon world, they have been exported around the globe, spun off in various forms (with international financial institutions frequent sponsors), and adapted in varying assemblages.

[2] "Reinventing government," which incorporated the New Public Management and similar reforms, was eagerly embraced by the 1990's presidential administration of Bill Clinton.

[3] While the definition of "governance" has been inconsistent, the term took off during the decades of the reforms and transformational developments here detailed. In 2006, ECOSOC observed that "governance" "has gained great usage in contemporary public administration." See Rothstein (this volume, 16) for a rundown of meanings.

Since at least the mid-2000s, private contractors have been routinely carrying out such functions—running intelligence operations, most government information technology work, and databases tracking foreigners as they enter and exit the United States (Verkuil 2007; Wedel 2009, 73–110; Wedel 2010). Even regulation is sometimes outsourced to private companies. For example, certain consulting firms, in sectors like finance, have been tasked by the government to financially oversee private banks *at the same time* that these same banks have been their clients (Douglas 2013), a state of affairs that has resulted in regulatory lapses (Freifeld 2015). The contracting trend presents serious challenges to governmental control and accountability and to impartial government.[4]

Another trend poses a more direct challenge: the enervating and politicizing of civil service. Impartial government mandates that civil servants must be chosen on the basis of "merits and qualifications," write Rothstein and Teorell (2018, 170), not by elections or political appointment. Steps taken threatening that standard have included reducing the number of civil service positions and weakening rules. In the United States, rules that had governed civil servants for the better part of a century came under threat during the George W. Bush administration. Following the 2001 terrorist attacks, the work of civil servants may have become more open to network- and politics-influenced decisions.[5]

Fast forward to President Donald Trump, who took a wrecking ball to the system, now no longer even under the guise of reforming government—but often of dismantling it (e.g., Osnos 2018). The civil service has been a particular target.[6]

Clearly, when parts of the government apparatus and civil service are being eroded, the capacity for both impartial government and accountability are threatened. Moreover, new forms of less-than-accountable governance ever farther from the Weberian vision are created through both de jure and de facto reorganizing.

---

[4] Four reasons for this have been noted with regard to the United States. First, for decades, contracted-out services have gone far beyond ancillary tasks like food or printing services to government functions, as described above (Verkuil 2007; Wedel 2009, 73–110; Wedel 2011). Second, contractors and the entities they work for are not subject to the same rules as government employees and function with less visibility. Third, the complexity injected into government via the increase in actors involved in its work creates often-complicated chains of command and reporting among government agencies, contractors, and subcontractors, who, as stated above, are subject to fewer constraints than government employees. Four, while officially government officials monitor contracting and quality of work, that becomes problematic when expertise and information are outsourced; oversight by actual government employees routinely falls short (United States House of Representatives 2007; Wedel 2009, 73–110; Wedel 2011).

[5] While the reforms met with fierce opposition, Bush attempted to relax civil service rules in the Department of Defense and the new Department of Homeland Security on a limited basis and slated other departments to follow suit (e.g., Barr and Lee 2005). However, a "thickening" did occur, in which political appointees filled more management layers and there was "very tight coordination from the White House on down to the political appointees," according to Light (quoted in Barr 2004).

[6] The Trump administration has reorganized governance, sometimes by design (Clark 2018), as in slashing agency budgets (Reuters 2018a; Reuters 2018b) and furloughs (Ogrysko 2019), and often de facto, as in appointing "acting" officials then made permanently provisional (Seipel 2019). Targeting the civil service, the administration has made firing civil servants easier (Scheiber 2018), limited the regulatory guidance they can provide (Katz 2019), created an atmosphere that encourages their departure (Rein 2017), and starved agencies by not filling numerous jobs (Schoen 2018). In October 2020, at the tail end of his administration, President Trump issued a sweeping executive order that would eliminate job

In addition to this government redesign, several transformational developments have emerged. These include the Cold War's end; the Internet's rise soon after, occasioned by the earlier advent of digital technology; and financialization (Carroll 2008; Davis and Walsh 2017; Davis and Williams 2017; Wedel 2009, 23–45; 2014/2016, 23–7; 2017, 154–7). The close of the Cold War dispersed global authority and opened up sparsely governed arenas, generating opportunities for players from transnational networks laundering money or promoting human rights to currency traders conducting instant global transactions (additionally enabled by the Internet). The emergence of digital and then social media has squeezed out old political and media gatekeepers and, at the same time, provided those in or seeking power with inexpensive and easily exploitable new platforms. Thanks to digital media, all manner of influencers and countries can advance self-interested narratives, "information," and modes of deception such as trolls and bots directly to readers (Rainie, Anderson, and Albright 2017). Also crucial is financialization. While capital used to move from financial centers to corporations, now bankers and traders trade their own portfolios, reaping large profits (Carroll 2008); capital markets exert considerable influence on economic and political institutions (Savage and Williams 2008). States have ceded the upper hand in important decisions to business (e.g., Bowman et al. 2015, 4; Crouch 2004, 4) and seen their autonomy and "public" character dwindle (e.g., Kapferer 2005; Vogl 2015). Financialization has also multiplied the number of lucrative intermediary financial positions (Savage and Williams 2008) while, at the same time, weakening managerial elites (Davis and Williams 2017). With policymaking bodies more diversified and dispersed, the space for elite intermediaries and experts has greatly expanded (e.g. Davis and Williams 2017; Dezalay and Garth 2002; Zald and Lounsbury 2010).

The transformational developments, both on their own and through their interactions, have reconfigured the institutional ecosystem in which states, corporations, and other institutions shape themselves and interact. They have, for better and for worse, forged new spaces of governance and policy and created fresh capacity for a plethora of individuals and entities, including think tank, philanthropic, grassroots, and consulting organizations, to perform novel roles in governance and policy. They have fashioned an ecosystem riddled with what's been called "structured unaccountability" (Honegger, Neckel, and Magnin 2010), in which unaccountability is baked into the DNA of many of today's governmental and corporate workings (Wedel 2014/2016, 3–47). Amid this new ecosystem, a novel breed of influencers, including shadow elites, has emerged to capitalize on the developments and, through their actions, nudge unaccountability forward.

These influencers and the entities they empower connect to formal government, governance, and policy both through interactions with government and those independent of it. To examine how this works, let's look at how the influencers are organized and operate vis-à-vis formal government, and how that organization and *modus operandi* compares to their counterparts prior to the transformational developments.

---

protections for many civil servants and ease politicization of policy decisions (e.g., Mueller 2020). The policy met with legal and time constraints and was not implemented (Rein 2021). As of this writing, it is unclear what action the subsequent Joe Biden administration will take with regard to the issue.

From Power Elites to Shadow Elites

Describing the American power structure 65 years ago, sociologist C. Wright Mills famously theorized the existence of a "power elite" organized into three distinct pillars of power—government, corporations, and the military. The strength of these pillars rests on command and control, following Weber's bureaucratic model, in which hierarchical structures are distinct and bureaucrats wield executive power. This interlocking constellation of government officials, military leaders, and corporate executives effectively control major political and social decision-making, Mills (1956) maintained.

Today, however, the transformational developments have reorganized how government interacts with social networks. Of course, institution-based forms of power that rest on formal position and hierarchy still thrive. But Mills's model does not account for either (1) the plethora of entities such as consulting organizations, corporations, and think tanks that today are contracted to do government work or (2) the labyrinth of networks involved in governance that perform the invaluable role of connecting—be they networks linking these entities to formal government or networks linking individuals and entities among themselves.

Indeed, the potency of today's influencers resides substantially in their roles as connectors; an influencer's position in informal networks and links to organizations and venues is pivotal to his power. Influencers wield and coordinate sway from multiple, often moving perches in official and private organizations. They are more flexible, mobile, and global in reach than their forebears (Davis and Williams 2017; Wedel 2009; 2017).

The result is that *Mills's hierarchies are nowadays subject to competition from, and compelled to interact much more with, forms of power grounded in networks, often blurring boundaries among state and private spheres of activity and authority in the process* (Wedel 2017). In this remade ecosystem, with policy and governance more indirect and difficult to detect, accountability becomes much more challenging.

In sum, in generating new spaces of policy and governance, the transformational developments—the redesign of government, the Cold War's end, the rise of the Internet, and financialization—could not help but facilitate the blurring of state and private relationships and authority and with it, unaccountability. The developments could not help but enable greater influence by agenda-bearing individuals whose actions are less visible and less accountable than their power elite predecessors.

At the top of the food chain of these novel influencers are shadow elites (Wedel 2009), the most insidious and elusive of them. Shadow elites, defined by their *modus operandi* and organization rather than family or class background, wealth, or institutional position (Wedel 2009; 2014/2016; 2017), are able to deploy this *modus operandi* and means of organizing, of course, because they are operating in the reshaped governance ecosystem formed by the transformational developments. A unique term for shadow elites is warranted because they debuted to take advantage of a new ecosystem and because their *modus operandi* and organization are distinctive. Individual shadow elite players are labeled "flexians," after one of their characteristic features—flexibility (Barth 1969, Ong 1999). When these operators work together in longstanding groups, thus multiplying their influence, they are called "flex nets" (Wedel 2009, 15–19).

Shadow elites fuse state and private interests as they assume a tangle of roles across state and private spheres to achieve their goals, exhibiting scant loyalty to official organizations on behalf of whom they work, such as those of government. These influencers know no *particular* ideology or political affiliation or leaning. Entrée to insider information and access is their most vital resource.

Shadow elites are defined by their positionality in the structure, as reflected in their combination of practices, which include: (1) their *informality* and supplanting of formal structures and processes (while still using them when beneficial); (2) their *flexibility*, shifting and overlapping roles in pursuit of strategic goals; (3) the *vehicles of influence they mobilize*, including consultancies, think tanks, and nongovernmental organizations; (4) *their roles as connectors*, among government, corporate, and nongovernmental organizations and venues, and their networks vis-à-vis each other; (5) *their lack of fixed attachment* to any specific sector or organization; and (6) the *flexible, mobile, malleable, and multipurposed character of the vehicles of influence they employ*. Taken together, these practices and features characterize shadow elites (Wedel 2017, 166–9).

Shadow elites' organization and *modus operandi* design them to defy democratic standards of accountability. Unaccountability is an essential but incomplete condition for today's systemic, structural, and legal corruption; shadow elites typically also violate public trust (Wedel 2009, 205), harking back to ancient understandings of corruption.[7]

Years before the rise to power of Trump and other such anti-system leaders, many of the ways and means of shadow elites became established practice for many influencers across political lines. Many players would surely view their own activities as simply the "way things are done." Their activities, while not as in your face as was much corruption under Trump, are also not completely hidden. In the next section we show how shadow elite ways and means interact with government and governance and how these players further shape the evolution of the governance ecosystem.

SHADOW ELITE PRACTICES, ADVANCING

Only a subset of today's influencers engage in activities in which they employ all characteristic shadow elite ways of operating and organizing—"practices" for short. And hence *only some qualify as shadow elites*. This section focuses on four (of six) shadow elite practices. These practices can—and often do—appear separately; informality, for instance, is frequently employed alone. Moreover, the six practices can—and often do—appear in different combinations. As we shall see, the first two practices, (1) *informality* and (2) *flexibility*, sometimes work together with the second two practices, (3) *mobilizing vehicles of influence* and (4) *serving as connectors*. The last two practices—(5) *lack of fixed attachment* to any specific sector or organization and (6) the *flexible and mobile character of the vehicles of influence the players employ*—also often are carried out in conjunction with the other practices.

---

[7] Betrayal of the public trust is at the core of age-old notions of corruption found in the Bible and the Qur'an (Wedel 2014/2016, 8, 276–7).

In reflecting on shadow elites and the recent evolution of the American system, we clarify that Donald Trump is *not* a shadow elite exemplar. As a wealthy celebrity and real estate developer before becoming commander-in-chief, he appears to have had little need to employ shadow elite practices in tandem to manipulate public policy or the federal bureaucracy to achieve his goals. However, many of those who helped him rise to office or served as part of his inner circle while in office are shadow elite exemplars.[8] Moreover, as president, Trump employed certain shadow elite practices. The most obvious is informality.

Informality has been studied most robustly and extensively outside the United States, in non-Western societies. Still, informality has been charted in U.S. governance—and began years before the rise of Trump.

Let's look at two kinds of informality—informal social networks and what are known as "informal practices." They have been observed in the United States in recent decades in the service of circumventing time-honored bureaucratic and governance procedure.

With regard to informal social networks, many of the most agile players work together in tight-knit, trust-based, enduring personal-professional networks that defy characterization as interest groups or lobbies. The longstanding network around U.S. Treasury Secretary Robert Rubin, former CEO of Goldman Sachs and treasury secretary from 1995 to 1999 under President Bill Clinton, provides an example. The personal and professional histories of the Rubin network have long intersected in venues ranging from Goldman Sachs and the U.S. Treasury (under multiple presidential administrations) to Harvard University and the Brookings Institution.

While the concept of informal social networks illustrates players' linkages and interactions over time, informal practices are what players do. A concept elaborated by sociologist Alena Ledeneva (2006, 22), informal practices are strategies that involve navigating formal rules and informal norms to achieve personal goals. They are regular, recurring activities that exhibit clear patterns, structure, logic, and predictability (Wedel 2017).

The following three examples from U.S. administrations over recent decades demonstrate the use of informal practices via informal social networks that bypass standard bureaucratic and governance procedure, thereby undermining impartiality.

In the Iran-Contra affair of the 1980s, rogue officials employed shadow elite practices in creating alternative, informal governing structures and processes to circumvent bureaucracy, as well as the checks and balances of Congress, which had outlawed the officials' activity. Simultaneously they were also enjoying the tacit approval of President Reagan, who had secretly blessed the operations. These informal structures and processes, although substantially embedded within government bodies and often carried out by officials, were off the books. They skirted formal bureaucratic and chain-of-command arrangements and enabled the players to carry out illegal operations in secret, thereby derailing official U.S. foreign policy (Wedel 2009, 161–5).

---

[8] Those include former New York City mayor Rudy Giuliani, the president's personal lawyer, who has for years run an eponymous consulting firm in which he parlays his connections to corporations and foreign governments. He is, of course, well-known for accusations that he helped engineer a shadow diplomacy channel in Ukraine to serve Trump's political ends, while at the same time allegedly conducting his own business (e.g., Dawsey, Hamburger, and Parker 2018; Protess, Rashbaum, and Rothfeld 2019).

A decade later major decisions that would greatly and adversely affect the global economy were taken eschewing formal procedure in favor of informality. During the late 1990s of the Clinton administration, as unregulated financial derivatives were proliferating, members of the network around Treasury Secretary Rubin excluded officials from key decisions— officials who would have been included if official position, rather than membership in the network, were guiding their decision-making processes. At the same time, they brought in others from outside government who were part of their network: members who were top bankers, the very people whose activities government was supposedly regulating. With members in key finance posts and others on Wall Street, the Rubin network excluded the chair of the Commodity Futures Trading Commission, who should have been included and able to exercise formal power, but stood well outside the Rubin network (Morgenson 2010). The network prevailed in its decisions (Stein and Dickinson 2006). Its advocacy of unregulated derivatives, the 1999 repeal of the Glass-Steagall Act, and other policies championed by the Rubin network bear significant responsibility for the 2008 financial crisis (e.g., Morgenson 2010). Here standard procedure is undermined as the network incorporates its fellows (private bankers) who, in terms of impartial government, should be kept at arm's length, while dismissing a government regulator who, by definition, should be included in the deliberations.

In the George W. Bush administration of the early 2000s, another episode of bureaucratic and procedural circumvention unfolded at the behest of the dozen or so members of the "Neocon Core" and their allies who helped take the United States to war in Iraq. They did so substantially by thwarting bureaucratic and professional authority, creating within government personalized practices and network-based entities while circumventing standard ones and marginalizing officials who were not part of their network. Neocon Core members in government duplicated job descriptions of existing government units, setting up their own units manned largely with loyalist allies (e.g., Stein and Dickinson 2006) and creating supposed "intelligence" and propaganda positing, for example, a (nonexistent) connection between al-Qaeda and Saddam Hussein and the 9/11 attacks (Kessler 2016). The Core operated informally and through a cross-agency clique; in fact, the decision to go to war was made outside the usual interagency procedures, according to a host of insiders in key agencies, including those within the Pentagon and the Department of State (Wedel 2009, 177).[9]

These examples demonstrate, well before Trump, the various informalizing, personalizing, politicizing, and sidelining of standard procedure, a red flag in terms of the requirements of impartial government (Rothstein and Teorell 2008). Impartial government is spurned when bureaucratic procedure is subverted or bypassed. In these examples impartiality is threatened both on the "*input*" side (pertaining to access to political power) and the "*output*" side (pertaining to "the exercise of political power, usually in the form of the implementation of public policies") (Rothstein, this volume, 12–13). Moreover, alternative governing structures are being forged, an affront to the checks and balances of democratic governance.

Under Trump bureaucracy-busting exploded, reaching unprecedented levels (e.g., Devaney 2017; McFaul 2018), from the shelving of expertise (e.g., LaFraniere, Confessore, and Drucker 2017), installing of family members as official and unofficial advisors (e.g.,

---

[9] While the foreign policy of intervention in Vietnam failed, key insiders argue, the system of decision-making worked (Gelb and Betts 1979; Haass 2009).

Abramson 2018), and placing of senior aides in agencies to monitor loyalty (e.g., Dawsey and Cook 2017) to the denigration and dismissal of diplomats (e.g., Gramer, Luce, and Lynch 2017; Harris 2017).

An eroding government apparatus and bureaucracy leaves governance vulnerable to still more informalization, personalization of policy, and loss of expertise, as well as enforcement of loyalty to the leader.

A second practice of shadow elites is *flexibility*. A flexible player juggles multiple roles and uses the information and other resources gathered in one professional role to his advantage in other roles. Flexibility enables both opportunity and deniability.

Consider, for instance, the recent history of U.S. retired generals and admirals. A quarter century ago, most retired generals stopped working in the defense field upon retirement. Today, most continue working in the defense business, many forming dense, complex networks of associates and companies.[10] Many embark on sprawling, postretirement careers that mix government advisory roles with private sector work, consulting for defense companies or setting up their own firms (e.g., Bender 2010; Smith 2012). They may additionally assume university and think tank roles that afford them an impartial imprimatur, as well as media roles to build their brand and influence (Wedel 2014/2016, 19; Barstow cited in Wedel 2014/2016, 160).

Built into the structure of some of these overlapping roles is the ability of players to deny responsibility and unaccountability. Consider the overlapping roles of Retired General X, who serves on a government advisory board shaping defense policy or procurement directions and gaining access and proprietary information while at the same time owning a firm or consulting for a defense company that can benefit from this invaluable information and entrée as it seeks military contracts.[11] X can plausibly deny that his own firm's or company's decisions are influenced by information from his government role. And here we add an important characteristic of shadow elites to their six structural practices outlined earlier: When in the public eye and seeking to influence public policy, shadow elites present themselves using their most impartial, neutral roles and hide, obscure, or minimize the most partial sounding roles. Appearing on CNN, X might be identified as a retired general years after leaving public service and perhaps more currently as a think tank or university fellow. Almost never is X identified as an owner of or consultant for a defense enterprise. Herein lies the accountability problem. The difficulty of establishing whether he is acting in the interest of a private entity or national defense challenges accountability. When such influencers help shape the priorities of government and are thus in a position to profit financially from these decisions, state and private power merge. Walls separating state and private interests and authority dissolve, along with accountability.

Let us now consider flexibility from the vantage point of players whose base of power is a substantially merged, state–private interest. With well over half of U.S. government work now outsourced, including substantial parts of key government functions like intelligence and regulation, government contractors can blur government and business in

---

[10] A comprehensive dataset based on publicly available data (started by the *Boston Globe* [e.g., Bender 2010] and further developed by the Mapping Shadow Influence Project directed by Janine R. Wedel at George Mason University), covers the postretirement activities of all two, three, and four-star officers retiring between 1992 and 2018.

[11] A number of retired generals fit this pattern.

ways that are new over the past several decades and that undermine public accountability and even state functions, potentially compromising some of the most sensitive work of any government.

The flexible maneuverings of two players who have moved between state and private roles over the past two decades, under both Democratic and Republican administrations, provide an example. They have helped to fuse core functions of key parts of the government responsible for intelligence operations with major government contractor Booz Allen Hamilton Inc., one of the Washington, DC, region's biggest employers. Nearly all (97%) of the company's revenue comes from government contracting (Rosenberg 2016).

The maneuverings of retired Vice Admiral John Michael "Mike" McConnell and that of his colleague retired Air Force Lieutenant General James Clapper show how the walls between state and private have become porous at best. McConnell has woven back and forth between Booz Allen and top intelligence jobs within government, including the Director of National Intelligence, a Cabinet-level position formed following 9/11 to better coordinate a fragmented intelligence community. Clapper exemplifies this same pattern, but with a greater variety of private sector posts. He has worked for or advised not only Booz Allen but at least a half dozen other contractors (Dilanian 2010).

The work of Booz Allen has become thoroughly integrated with government work; McConnell and Clapper have had their feet firmly planted in both sectors. McConnell's public comments make clear that he sees little difference between his government role and his lucrative Booz Allen role (Mazzetti and Sanger 2007).

Such arrangements have helped reshape the intelligence world into a hybrid and accountability-challenged behemoth. The media and even government investigators have little way to know whether work is conducted with the public's best interest in mind and whether expansions to the surveillance state are warranted by national security considerations or driven by a powerful contractor's desire to expand profits.

The third practice of shadow elites is that they set up or use *vehicles of influence* such as think tanks, nonprofits or "grassroots" organizations, and consulting firms. Vehicles of influence can endow powerbrokers with flexibility that enables them to achieve their own agendas while escaping public notice. While basing their operations in such a vehicle, players flexibly move between official and private roles to achieve private goals.

These operators work not only from *outside* government, but also from *inside* government or the seat of power. When considering think tanks or nonprofits or consulting firms, we tend to think of them swaying legislators or media from the *outside* (as do interest groups or lobbies), rather than exerting influence by positioning their players to also operate from *inside*, swaying those with direct power from the inside. Yet the positionality of players who empower these vehicles of influence is often multiple and moving within the same time frame; the players' multiple positionality sometimes appears designed to undercut official institutions.

We see such outside/inside, back-and-forth positionality in the consulting entity Promontory Financial Group set up in 2001. Founded and staffed largely by former regulators, banks hire Promontory for a large array of tasks. The U.S. government has dispersed and diluted its own authority by enlisting Promontory and firms like it to do financial oversight that in the past was the government's sole province. Thus, while also being paid by banks to manage a crisis or to suss out government regulations in the making, Promontory serves as an ersatz government regulator through several means.

One means is the *formal* outsourcing of authority, in which the government itself mandates that banks use Promontory or a similar firm to do financial oversight (Douglas 2013). In performing potentially overlapping roles as both regulator and vendor, Promontory's influence goes well beyond the classic "revolving door," predicated on C. Wright Mills's pillars of power, where government and business are separate, even as players have close contacts across these spheres. However, when such entities are entrusted by government to carry out functions of government, they are able to shape outcomes from *inside* the regulatory process, even as they stand *outside* formal government. This structure has led to big accountability breaches, including accusations of whitewashing the records and reputations of troubled banks who were often the very clients paying Promontory's bills (e.g., Horwitz and Aspan 2013; Freifeld 2015; Hallman and Melendez 2013; Sherred 2013).

The ultimate unaccountable vehicles of influence are known as "flex organizations." Flex organizations themselves have changing positionality; they can legitimately and variously claim both official and private status. Neither clearly official nor clearly private, they exhibit features of each.[12] With little power or influence independent of the players who empower them, flex organizations enable those players and the organizations themselves to shift their status (from official to private standing or the reverse) to serve their own agendas as called for in a given situation. Their players thus avail themselves of the best of both worlds—the authority and ability to act on behalf of the state (or an international institution) and to allocate its resources, and the profits of the private sector—while skirting accountability to the state.

A fourth practice of shadow elites is that they *serve as connectors (among entities and players) and additionally often operate in close-knit, exclusive networks, or "flex nets," the most insidious of networks.* United by shared activities and close interpersonal histories, members of a flex net work together as part of an exclusive long-term, self-propelling network to pursue their mutual agendas—ideological and sometimes financial (Wedel 2009, 15–19). They fuse official and private power most completely as they reorganize governance processes, authorities, and bureaucracies to suit the group's purposes (Wedel 2009, 19). Inside information and access is their currency. Members of flex nets, like all shadow elites, exercise mobile positionality, assuming shifting and overlapping roles in government, business, and think tank organizations (the latter sometimes being vehicles of influence they themselves set up) and coordinating their power and influence from multiple vantage points to achieve their goals (Wedel 2009, 17–18).

A quintessential flex net is the Neocon Core (that helped take the United States to war in Iraq in the 2000s) (Wedel 2009, 147–91), discussed earlier with a focus on informality. Its dozen or so members have worked with each other in various incarnations—some for as

[12] Flex organizations were first charted in 1990's postcommunist Russia in conjunction with the foreign-aid funded privatization and economic reform agenda. Bankrolled by international financial institutions and Western governments, flex organizations were frequently the sites of the most important economic reform activity, including the most important policy decisions and policy implementation. Often, these organizations assumed more authority *on behalf of the Russian state* than the relevant government agencies. Empowered by their players, flex organizations have no mechanism for true succession. When the players depart, no real institution is left, only an empty shell. This is but one reason why flex organizations must not be confused with static hybrids like "quangos" that conduct government work, "parastatals," or "government-sponsored enterprises" such as the American Fannie Mae and Freddie Mac (Wedel 2001, 145–53).

long as 40 years—to realize their goals through the assertion of military power. The 9/11 terrorist attacks lent them the requisite political *casus belli* to both flout standard bureaucratic
procedure and to set up duplicative units in government to achieve their ends, as described
under *informality*. They had long been laying the groundwork for that opportunity: In
the 1990s, members of the group were prime movers in the *vehicles of influence* they had
created—"letterhead" organizations variously pegged as think tanks and educational associations to sway public opinion and policymakers toward their goals in the Middle East
(Wedel 2009, 170–4). A cornerstone of the Core's success has been its skill in challenging official U.S. intelligence, creating alternative versions, and branding its versions as official and
definitive for politicians, government, and the media.

Flex nets are a paradox in terms of political influence: As uninstitutionalized, unregis-
tered, and unannounced sets of people, they are more amorphous and less transparent than
conventional lobbies and interest groups, yet also more coherent and less accountable. While
administrations come and go, flex nets (like all shadow elites) persist; they are not instruments of any particular administration even when their members occupy official positions
in it. The implications of flex nets for democracy are enormous, perhaps best expressed by
a player close to the Core: "There is no conflict of interest, because we define the interest"
(Wedel 2009, 19).

And herein lies the fusion of state and private power, the antithesis of a democratic system.
Operating at the nexus of official and private power, shadow elites not only co-opt public policy
agendas, crafting policy with their own purposes in mind. They test the time-honored principles of *both* the canons of accountability of the modern democratic state and the codes of competition of the "free market." In so doing, they reorganize relations between government and
business to their advantage, creating new iterations of governance, eroding the distinct walls
envisioned by Weber. Then, building on the new ecosystem that has been established, shadow
elites continue their ways and means, precipitating further changes in the same direction.

President Trump exploited this state of affairs to the hilt, but it obviously predates him.[13]
Shadow elites and these four practices here detailed—*informality* and supplanting of formal
structures and processes (while still using them when beneficial); *flexibility* in maneuvering shifting and overlapping roles; *mobilizing vehicles of influence*, including consultancies, think tanks, and NGOs; and *roles as connectors*, among government, corporate,
and nongovernmental organizations and venues, as well as networks vis-à-vis each other
(along with the two additional shadow elite practices)—were securely entrenched well before Trump.

***

Examining these examples, we observe the players exhibiting more than just the one or two
practices showcased in a specific example. Retired General X, who uses inside information

---

[13] Trump encouraged loyalists to enmesh state and private agendas across the executive branch,
staffing it with officials with deep ties to the industry they were supposed to police or expressly
antagonistic positions towards their own agencies (Przybyla 2017; Schuck 2017). This led to a Wild West
of "capture," in which an industry co-opts its appointed watchdogs (Whitehouse 2018), in education, the
environment, finance, and perhaps especially the energy sector (e.g., Banerjee 2018, Michaels 2017, Miller
and Jimenez 2017, Shuster and Marritz 2020).

gleaned from his government advisory role (*flexibility*) in his consulting firm (*vehicle of influence*) is also obviously connecting to the government (performing *the role of connector*).

In the examples of both the Rubin network and the Neocon Core, we see government officials, part of tight-knit, enduring networks, pursuing (and often achieving) their group's longstanding agendas through means that are not quite consistent with their official roles and responsibilities. In both cases, as we have shown, there is plenty of *informality*, enabling the officials to skirt bureaucratic practice and to exclude government officials outside their network who should have been included. *Flexibility* of roles and the setting up of *vehicles of influence* are also well documented with regard to the Neocon Core, and both groups achieved their goals at least in part by serving as *connectors* across state and private spheres. Additionally, Neocon Core members' *lack of fixed attachment* to any specific sector or organization and the *flexible and mobile character of the vehicles of influence* they set up-practices five and six-are on display.

In the Booz Allen example, we highlighted the practice of *flexibility* and, with that of Promontory, the practices of *flexibility* and setting up *vehicles of influence*. But the players who empower these firms are additionally acting as *connectors* between state and private sectors.

Thus, in all these cases—Retired General X; the Rubin network; the Neocon Core; Booz Allen; and Promontory—multiple, if not most, shadow elite practices are certainly or likely employed, including the final two. In all cases, state and private power appear to merge. In all cases, the result is that impartial government, both with regard to input and output (Rothstein, this volume, 12–13), and the Weberian vision of bureaucracy as one separate and protected from political influence are flouted, along with democratic accountability. In fact, with unaccountability structured into the governance ecosystem, systemic legal and structural corruption is not only likely to occur, but in some cases even becomes enshrined and legitimized as established practice.

IMPLICATIONS OF SHADOW ELITES FOR THEORIES OF INSTITUTIONAL CORRUPTION

How do the practices of shadow elites jibe with theories of institutional corruption? To explore this issue, we provide further background on the concept of institutional corruption.

Political scientist Dennis Thompson coined the term in the mid-1990s using the case of the "Keating five," five U.S. senators who assisted a campaign contributor during the savings-and-loan banking crisis of the 1980s. He believed a broader definition of corruption was warranted, noting the need for legislators to raise funds, as well as some of the senators' apparent lack-of-corrupt motivation (Thompson 1993). This form of corruption, Thompson (2018, 4) writes, "can cause as much damage to the democratic process as conventional corruption, if not more." Legal scholar Lawrence Lessig (2013, 553) later elaborated that institutional corruption

> is manifest when there is a systemic and strategic influence which is legal, or even currently ethical, that undermines the institution's effectiveness by diverting it from its purpose or weakening its ability to achieve its purpose, including, to the extent relevant to its

purpose, weakening either the public's trust in that institution or the institution's inherent trustworthiness.

Lessig further developed the theory to help make sense of a system of campaign finance in which lobbyists both directly and indirectly "get a better chance at changing government policy" (Lessig 2015, 101–8). He then helped generate a groundswell of interest in the subject. Under his leadership and the auspices of Harvard University's Safra Center, a broader range of scholarship applying institutional corruption theory to government as well as nongovernmental organizations such as investment banks, ratings agencies, pharmaceutical companies, and think tanks was produced (for an overview, see, e.g., Newhouse 2014, 569–78).

While shadow elite and institutional corruption theory share some important premises, there are points of departure. We begin with areas of agreement.

Contexts of applicability

In a review article of institutional corruption literature, Thompson (2018, 16) reports that institutionalists agree that their approach "can be installed into a wide variety of theories of democracy (and other institutional forms of governance)." Both institutional corruption and shadow elite theories have been primarily applied in the United States (although shadow elite theory is substantially informed by knowledge of post-communist eastern European corruption). Both theories purport to be applicable elsewhere and are being employed by (often) non-American analysts to examine corruption outside the United States.

Accountability and impartial government

Both shadow elites and institutional corruption challenge impartial government and democratic accountability. Shadow elites, however, are *structurally* unaccountable and not only can hardly be held to account by existing legal and regulatory mechanisms; they enjoy the resource of deniability. Retired General X, for instance, can plausibly deny using information and access from his government advisory board in his consulting firm that does business with the government. There is little way, aside from self-disclosure, for the public to know if he is using his information and access gleaned from his government role in his business role(s) (and in any additional media and think tank or academic roles). Nor is there an established regime to hold him to account.

Institutions, organizations, and informality

Shadow elite theory employs a sociological definition of "institutions" as broad, stable social arrangements, either formal or informal, and distinguishes between institutions and organizations. Institutional corruption theory does not generally make this distinction: Often, "institution" appears to mean large-scale social arrangements or rule regimes, while other times the term refers to formal organizations (sometimes with both meanings used alternately in the same article by the same author). Institutional corruption theory, while well developed in legal and philosophical terms, especially in the U.S. context, appears less developed in terms of charting the actual operations of individuals, networks, and organizations; informality is scarcely considered. The theory thus is poised to miss the mechanisms and drivers of some of today's most egregious legal corruption.

Individual vs. institutional corruption

Thompson (2018, 11–12) specifies three conditions that distinguish institutional corruption from individual corruption:

> (*a*) the gain an official receives is more institutional than personal, (*b*) the advantage the official provides takes the form of access more than action, and (*c*) the connection between the gain and the advantage manifests a tendency to subvert legitimate procedures of the institution, regardless of whether an improper motive is present.

Examining these conditions, institutional corruption theory does not fully apply to the operations of shadow elites. Consider Retired General X, who enjoys inside access and information from the government advisory board he sits on. With regard to (*a*)—"the gain an official receives is more institutional than personal," the gain X receives in his official capacity when using information or access from his government role to gain the upper hand in his consulting firm cannot be said to be "more institutional than personal."

Condition (*b*)—"the advantage the official provides takes the form of access more than action"—appears predicated on one official giving an advantage to another (presumably non-official) individual; however, X provides *himself* with the advantage. Institutional corruption theory here falls short in envisioning influencers whose roles overlap as they straddle organizations and whose sway and success derives from this overlap. It also does not account for the morphing positionality of an actor like Promontory that operates outside/ inside, back-and-forth in the liminal spaces between government and private regulatory fixing. Further, while X's advantage is certainly *access* (to information and people), it is also *action* when he uses that information in his own firm. On the other hand, X definitely fits Thompson's (2018, 13–14) formulation that "the advantage sought or received is … a greater opportunity to exercise influence than most other citizens enjoy."

The violation of institutional procedures and purpose

With respect to Thompson's (*c*) above—"the connection between the gain and the advantage manifests a tendency to subvert legitimate procedures of the institution, regardless of whether an improper motive is present"—shadow elite theory and institutional corruption theory seem to agree. The *structural* positioning of X serves to undermine the purpose of his official affiliation, that of the government—be it national security or cost efficiency— regardless of any "improper motive" on the part of X. However, this undermining extends beyond Thompson's "procedures"; the institutional purpose is at stake. Indeed, some institutionalists maintain that the institution's purpose is additionally violated (Lessig 2013,

553; Miller 2017, 82–88; Thompson 2018, 15). Shadow elite theory concurs; X clearly violates the government's institutional purpose.

Public trust

Theorists are divided as to whether this violation of institutional purpose (resulting from institutional corruption) damages public trust in institutions (Amit et al. 2017, 455–9; Thompson 2018, 15). Philosophers Emanuela Ceva and Maria Paola Ferretti, writing from an institutionalist perspective, hold that institutional corruption hurts not only the proper functioning of the institution in question, but also public faith in it, "even in the absence of corrupt individuals" (Thompson 2018, 15). Shadow elite theory suggests that the activities of shadow elites typically violate public trust. While this betrayal does appear sometimes to lead to loss of public trust in an institution, that result is not necessarily the case.

Institutional defects and institutional change

Lessig concentrates on what he calls "dependence corruption," defined as "when officials have to depend on support from persons other than those to whom they owe exclusive allegiance" (Thompson 2018, 10; Lessig 2015, 245–1). For instance, congresspeople, in securing financing through super PACs, compensate for an institutional defect (the necessity of raising millions of dollars), yet their agenda (running for office) is publicly justifiable.

However, most institutionalists do not agree with the idea that the corruption lies primarily in the defects of institutions (Thompson 2018, 16). Neither does shadow elite theory. Engines of change, shadow elites are not typically merely responding to defects in the official institutions with which they affiliate, and the way they operate cannot accurately be understood in terms of dependence corruption. Consider flex nets, self-propelling groups with their own agendas that persist through and can outlast numerous governmental administrations. The Neocon Core, pioneers in governance innovation—from the "Team B" exercise of the mid-1970s to challenge official intelligence assessments; to "letterhead" organizations set up in the 1990s to influence government, media, and public opinion; to duplicative intelligence units created within government in the early 2000s to manufacture a case for war (Wedel 2009, 158–87)—helped lay the groundwork for more of the same from actors of all stripes and agendas; these organizational modes have since proliferated. Shadow elites not only bend governance and policy to achieve their agendas, their collective choices often serve to further reshape the governance and policy ecosystem, creating conditions for still more partiality and unaccountability.

Motivation

Shadow elites typically appear to be motivated by some combination of ideology, brand-, or empire-building, prestige, or money. Institutional corruption theorists have tended to concentrate on the role of money, although some have questioned that emphasis (suggesting, for instance, that factors such as "a desire for prestige" should be included) (Lessig 2019; Thompson 2018, 19).

Personal corruption

A debate in the institutional corruption literature concerns whether the protagonists in such corruption are personally corrupt, with much literature arguing that they are not (Thompson 2018, 8). Shadow elite writing is somewhat equivocal on this issue. While shadow elites' systemic, legal, and structural corruption generally violates public trust, can shadow elites definitively be said necessarily to be personally corrupt? Further clues can be found in the fact that while much of shadow elites' activity is in the open, they seek to conceal some of their activity, prioritizing the covert over the civic. Here shadow elite theory concurs with Ceva and Ferretti's (2018, 4) assessment that "An agenda is surreptitious . . . when its rationale may not be publicly vindicated" as part of an official's mandate. Indeed, when in the public eye, shadow elites present themselves with their most impartial, neutral roles, hiding those that might reveal a self-interested agenda. (In fact, to the extent that the public is aware of shadow elite activity at all, it is usually due to the reports of investigative journalists or official investigators.) This element of deception is crucial to shadow elites' effectiveness and would indicate that, when undermining their official institution's public mission, they do so knowingly.

Fusion of official and private power

While theories of institutional corruption do not appear to preclude the fusion of official and private power brought about by shadow elites, they also do not fully account for it. In the institutional corruption view, "institutions" do not appear to include those that involve merged conglomerations of state and private, as seen, for instance, in the case of Booz Allen. In this regard, shadow elite theory can be said to capture the mechanisms of some of today's most nefarious corruption, as well as its consequences in the form of the fusing of state and private power.

***

Institutional corruption theory has made crucial contributions to the study of systemic, legal corruption. In drawing attention to institutional arrangements and away from focus on the behavior of isolated individuals, institutional corruption theories are having groundbreaking impact in the way corruption is conceptualized. Still, as thus far elaborated, these theories may fall short in conceptualizing the full range of today's systemic, legal, and structural corruption.

INTERNATIONAL ANTICORRUPTION REGIMES, ILL-CONCEIVED

What is the relationship between these theories of systemic, legal corruption and anticorruption regimes? The transformational developments discussed earlier have evolved together with shadow elite practices since the early to mid-1990s—a time frame that also coincides with the establishment of the international anticorruption regimes. These regimes got their start with the founding of the NGO Transparency International in 1993 and the World Bank's launch of its anticorruption work in 1996, when its president warned of the "cancer of corruption." With these organizations taking the lead, and under the tutelage largely of economists, international anticorruption efforts begun in the mid-1990s were in full swing by the end of the century, with international institutions and Western governments devoting big budgets. The money was mainly spent on studying and diagnosing corruption and instituting programs to alleviate corruption in "developing" or "underdeveloped" countries.

The idea that corruption was a problem for the less developed, far-off countries flourished just as Western experts and aid monies were helping reform the economies of the former Soviet Union and Eastern Bloc. The collapse of the Soviet Union provided not only a huge new swath for the implementation of anticorruption programs and studies; many 1990s efforts were first tried in formerly communist nations.

Just which corruption—and causes thereof—the economists at the helm of these efforts chose as their focus helps explain their difficulty in seeing new forms of corruption in the making or observing shadow elite practices. Several interrelated reasons account for this.

First, while these new forms of corruption, along with shadow elites and their practices, cross borders, the indices for measuring and ranking corruption measure and rank specific countries. This focus implies that corruption is country-specific and emanates from the inside, yet shadow elites and the vehicles of influence they create often span borders.

Second, while shadow elites meld official and private activities for maximum influence, the anticorruption industry homed in on governments, not on the larger lattice work of power. In the economists' and World Bank perspective, [p]ublic sector corruption is arguably a more serious problem in developing countries [than private sector corruption]" (e.g., World Bank 1997, 11). With the public sector a fount of corruption in this approach, minimizing it supposedly contains corruption. This, as well as the idea that markets are best left to self-regulate, were prevailing tenets during this period. In this view, the state is evaluated according to its friendliness toward business, with corruption treated "as both effect and cause of incomplete, uneven, or ineffective economic liberalization," as political scientist Michael Johnston (2005, 6) has written.

This perspective has been expressed in two distinct anticorruption and aid approaches, often undertaken in tandem. The first was to streamline government by reforming the bureaucracy or shrinking opportunities for corruption by decreasing the number of bureaucracies with which an entrepreneur needs to engage to start a business (e.g., World Bank, 1999: 2). The second form of this containing-government approach was the push to privatize state-owned companies (e.g., World Bank, 1997: 8).

The argument fit perfectly with the no-holds-barred rush to privatization of the early to mid-1990s, underwritten by abundant Western resources, that I saw firsthand in Russia. This was little surprise, since the drive to privatize and deregulate had been gathering steam since the Reagan era and found currency in the Clinton White House. But when deployed unregulated, in lands where virtually everything had been owned by the state, such divestiture was a virtual guarantor of corruption, not to mention kleptocracy, sometimes on a colossal scale, as scholars and analysts documented in real time in the 1990s. Throughout the post-Soviet region, powerful oligarchs, "clans," and political-business networks with inside information and access routinely "grabitized"—that is, privatized—for themselves heretofore state enterprises at fire-sale prices (e.g., Appel 1997; Glinkina 1994; Grabher and Stark 1997; Levitas and Strzałkowski 1990; Millar 1996; Nelson and Kuzes 1994; Nelson and Kuzes1995; Kosals 2007; Shelley 1995; Stark 1990; Stark 1996; Stark and Bruszt 1998; Wedel 2009: 124–5). Many privatization schemes fostered corruption, the fusion of state and private power, and shadow elite practices that have now found their way to the West. Clearly, any anticorruption program concentrating on just one sector or the other, and neglecting the essential organizational impact of state–private networks will, by definition, miss key drivers of corruption. Moreover, it may actually foster corruption.

Third, the prevailing conceptualization of corruption essentially boiled down to bribery and illegal activity, not systemic, legal corruption, which only more recently has gained attention in anticorruption circles. In effect, economists treated corruption as a synonym for bribery (Johnston 2005). The World Bank's definition of corruption as "the abuse of public office for private gain" could be interpreted more broadly. But the working definition within international anticorruption regimes had it that most acts of corruption are committed by public-sector bureaucrats, with the typical act a bribe—an illegal, one-off transaction in a single venue. The task of the analyst, a leading economist of corruption, Susan Rose-Ackerman, has written, is "to isolate the incentives for paying and receiving bribes and to recommend policy responses based on that theory" (Rose-Ackerman 2006, xv). The concentration on bribery and single transactions also meant that anticorruption prescriptions tended to target the rank and file, not elite players. Yet shadow elites aren't rank and file and have little need to engage in bribery; their *modus operandi* and means of organizing themselves is legal and far more sophisticated.

Fourth, the economic models employed also focused on the individual, not the network, as the crux of the problem (which is also a limitation of institutional corruption theory). The individual bureaucrat taking bribes was the guilty party. Overlooked were the informal networks and groups that underwrote corruption across state and private venues. New forms of corruption whose protagonists specialize in crossing boundaries—state and private, national—were scarcely a blip on the economists' radar screen.

In short, the international anticorruption regimes that debuted in the 1990s, focusing substantially on context-free metrics and simple models, cannot begin to track the complex processes of shadow elite corruption. The regimes' longtime foci left little room for attention to systemic, legal corruption or other insights from institutional corruption and shadow elite research. The regimes' models have been ill-equipped to grapple with new forms of corruption and shadow elite practices. As political scientist Johnston (2014, 10) assessed it, a "generation of reform effort has produced mixed results at best."[14]

However, there are welcome signs. While the original approaches carry with them much path dependency, attention to systemic, legal corruption has increased in anticorruption organizations. For example, more consideration is being given to transnational networks (for instance as represented by Cooley and Heathershaw 2017), even incorporating such approaches into anticorruption efforts.

[14] See also Krastev 2004; Ivanov 2007; Bauhr and Nasiritousi 2011; Sampson 2010; Hansen 2011; Hansen 2012; Wedel 2012; and Wedel 2014/2016, 74–100.

REFLECTIONS TOWARD A RESEARCH AGENDA

It is difficult to overestimate the impact of the past several decades' transformational developments. They created myriad new spaces of governance and policy and myriad openings for private players to perform policy and governance roles—along with opportunities to blur state and private relationships and authority. Shadow elites—flexians and flex nets—have taken advantage of these opportunities most fully, ushering in the possibility or even likelihood of systemic, structural, and legal corruption. This directly affronts the tenets of impartial government.

The new normal represented by shadow elites is a far cry from the bureaucrat who took a bribe or who served his personal interests at the expense of the client and the public good; *that* corruption was the pathology of the system (as Weberian bureaucracy might have it). That corruption clearly broke the rules, was against the law, and could be held to account. But because the ecosystem has undergone a sea change and unaccountability is structured into it, today's (shadow elite) corruption must be understood differently. Now, too, it must be understood differently because unaccountability allows the corruption of shadow elites to be far more indirect and difficult to detect than their power elite forebears. Now, too, corruption must be understood differently because unaccountability has also emasculated the old ways of detecting, deterring, and punishing corruption.

What do we need to consider to better understand and investigate shadow elite corruption?

First, many more empirical studies of shadow elite practices are needed, especially outside the United States. Studies of flexians, flex nets, and flex organizations in various governance ecosystems, along with the specific factors that most encourage their flourishing, are called for. What new forms of governance are being created? And how is quality of government in the form of impartial government affected?

This kind of research is captivating and achievable, even if very labor intensive. It requires the skills of investigative reporting, as well as those of critical analysis, including the ability to scrutinize phenomena in context, move beyond specific cases, and spot patterns of activity, relationships, and change. As an example, I became involved in this kind of research not by being embedded with elite networks but by honing skills as an observer and social analyst, following leads and instincts, and developing relationships widely. My effectiveness has been greatly bolstered through informal collaboration with investigative journalists, government auditors, and NGO watchdogs.

Second, we suggest that institutional corruption theory and corruption theory more generally could benefit considerably from cross-fertilization and engagement with anthropology, sociology, geography, and other disciplines to broaden its scope. Areas that warrant further empirical and theoretical elaboration include the mechanisms of systemic change and analyses of how players and networks maneuver formal and informal institutions and transform governance ecosystems. No one discipline can adequately capture phenomena that cut across so many boundaries. More robust collaboration would be an extremely welcome addition to the quality of government research agenda.[15]

[15] I thank Andreas Bågenholm, Monika Bauhr, Hülya Demirdirek, Marcia Grimes, Linda Keenan, Bo Rothstein, and June Sekera for their helpful feedback and suggestions on drafts of this chapter.

References

Abramson, Jill. 2018. "Nepotism and Corruption: The Handmaidens of Trump's Presidency." *The Guardian*, March 6, 2018. https://www.theguardian.com/commentisfree/2018/mar/06/nepotism-corruption-handmaiden-trump-presidency

Amit, Elinor, Jonathan Koralnik, Ann-Christin Posten, Miriam Muethel, and Lawrence Lessig. 2017. "Institutional Corruption Revisited: Exploring Open Questions within the Institutional Corruption Literature." *Southern California Interdisciplinary Law Journal* 26 (3): 447–68.

Appel, Hilary. 1997. "Voucher Privatisation in Russia: Structural Consequences and Mass Response in the Second Period of Reform." *Europe-Asia Studies* 49 (8): 1433–49.

Banerjee, Neela. 2018. "Trump's EPA Is on the Verge of 'Regulatory Capture', Study Says." insideclimatenews.org. May 1, 2018. https://insideclimatenews.org/news/01052018/trump-epa-regulatory-capture-industry-influence-climate-pruitt-compared-reagan-gorsuch-journal-public-health.

Barr, Stephen. 2004. "Appointees Everywhere, But Try to Count Them." *Washington Post*, October 17, 2004, p. C2, http://www.washingtonpost.com/wp-dyn/articles/A38874-2004Oct16.html.

Barr, Stephen, and Christopher Lee. 2005. "Director of Civil Service Resigns: James Oversaw Key Rule Changes." *Washington Post*, January 11. A13, http://www.washingtonpost.com/wp-dyn/articles/A63283-2005Jan10.html.

Barth, Fredrik. 1969. *Ethnic Groups and Boundaries: The Social Organization of Culture Difference.* Boston, MA: Little, Brown & Co.

Bauhr, Monika, and Naghmeh Nasiritousi. 2011. "Why Pay Bribes? Collective Action and Anticorruption Efforts." *QoG Working Paper*, December Gothenburg: The Quality of Government Institute, University of Gothenburg.

Bender, Bryan. 2010. "From the Pentagon to the Private Sector." *Boston Globe*, December 26, 2010. www.boston.com/news/nation/washington/articles/2010/12/26/defense_firms_lure_retired_generals/

Bowman, Andrew, Ismail Ertürk, Peter Folkman, Julie Froud, Colin Haslam, Sukhdey Johal, and Adam Leaver. 2015. *What a Waste: Outsourcing and How It Goes Wrong.* Oxford: Oxford University Press.

Carroll, William K. 2008. "The Corporate Elite and the Transformation of Finance Capital: A View from Canada." In *Remembering Elites*, edited by Mike Savage and Karel Williams, 44–63. Malden, MA: Blackwell Publishing.

Ceva, Emanuela, and Maria Paola Ferretti. 2018, "Political Corruption, Individual Behavior and the Quality of Institutions." *Politics, Philosophy & Economics* 17 (2): 216–31. doi:10.1177/1470594X17732067

Clark, Charles S. 2018. "White House Proposes a Massive Reorganization of Federal Agencies." *Government Executive.* June 21, 2018. n.d. Retrieved December 5, 2019, from Government Executive website: https://www.govexec.com/management/2018/06/trump-reorganization-plan-would-merge-education-and-labor-recast-hhs/149183/

Cooley, Alexander, and John Heathershaw. 2017. *Dictators Without Borders: Power and Money in Central Asia.* New Haven, CT: Yale University Press.

Crouch, Colin. 2004. *Post-Democracy.* Cambridge: Polity Press.

Davis, Aeron and Catherine Walsh. 2017. "Distinguishing Financialization from Neoliberalism." *Theory, Culture & Society* 34 (5–6): 27–51.

Davis, Aeron and Karol Williams. 2017. "Elites and Power after Financialization." *Theory, Culture & Society* 34 (s): 3–26.

Dawsey, Josh, and Nancy Cook. 2017. "Trump Assembles a Shadow Cabinet." politico.com, January 24, 2017. https://www.politico.com/story/2017/01/trumps-shadow-cabinet-234088.

Dawsey, Josh, Tom Hamburger, and Ashley Parker. 2018. "Giuliani Works for Foreign Clients While Serving as Trump's Attorney." *The Washington Post*, July 10, 2018. Retrieved December 5, 2019, from: https://www.washingtonpost.com/politics/giuliani-works-for-foreign-clients-while-serving-as-trumps-attorney/2018/07/09/e21554ae-7988-11e8-80be-6d32e182a3bc_story.html

Denzin, Norman K. 2001. *Interpretive Interactionism*. Berkeley, CA: Sage.

Devaney, Tim. 2017. "Dems: Trump 'Ignoring' Rulemaking Procedures." *The Hill*, March 27, 2017. https://thehill.com/regulation/energy-environment/324990-dems-trump-ignoring-rulemaking-procedures

Dezalay, Yves, and Bryant G. Garth. 2002. *The Internationalization of Palace Wars: Lawyers, Economists, and the Contest to Transform Latin American States*. Chicago: University of Chicago Press.

Dilanian, Ken. 2010. "Intelligence Nominee's Contractor Ties Draw Scrutiny." *Los Angeles Times*, July 25, 2010. https://www.latimes.com/archives/la-xpm-2010-jul-25-la-na-clapper-contractors-20100725-story.html.

Douglas, Danielle. 2013. "The Rise of Promontory." *The Washington Post*, August 2, 2013. www.washingtonpost.com/business/economy/the-rise-ofpromontory/2013/08/02/c187a112-f32b-11e2-bdae-0d1f78989e8a_story.html.

Eisenhardt, Kathleen M. 1989. "Building Theories from Case Study Research." *Academy of Management Review* 14 (4): 532–50.

Freifeld, Karen. 2015. "Promontory to pay $15 million to N.Y. over work for Standard Charter." Reuters, August 18, 2015. https://www.reuters.com/article/us-promontory-stanchart-settlement/promontory-to-pay-15-million-to-n-y-over-work-for-standard-chartered-idUSKCN0QN1ZO20150818

Geertz, Clifford. 1973. *The Interpretation of Cultures: Selected Essays*. New York: Basic Books.

Gelb, Leslie H., and Richard K. Betts. 1979. *The Irony of Vietnam: The System Worked*. Washington, DC: Brookings Institution Press. www.jstor.org/stable/10.7864/j.ctt15hvr3r.

Glaser, Barney G., and Anselm L. Strauss. 2009. *The Discovery of Grounded Theory: Strategies for Qualitative Research*. London: Transaction.

Glinkina, Svetlana P. 1994. "Privatizatsiya and Kriminalizatsiya: How Organized Crime Is Hijacking Privatization." *Demokratizatsiya* 2: 385–91.

Grabher, Gernot, and David Stark. 1997. eds. *Restructuring Networks in Post-Socialism: Legacies, Linkages, and Localities*. Oxford: Oxford University Press.

Gramer, Robbie, Dan de Luce, and Colum Lynch. 2017. "How the Trump Administration Broke the State Department." *Foreign Policy*, July 31, 2017. https://foreignpolicy.com/2017/07/31/how-the-trump-administration-broke-the-state-department/

Guttman, Dan. 2006. "Contracting, an American Way of Governance: Post 9/11 Constitutional Choices." In *Meeting the Challenge of 9/11: Blueprints for More Effective Government*, edited by Thomas H. Stanton, 230–73. Armonk, NY: M. E. Sharpe Publishers.

Guttman, Daniel, and Barry Willner. 1976. *The Shadow Government: The Government's Multi-Billion-Dollar Giveaway of Its Decision-Making Powers to Private Management Consultants, "Experts," and Think Tanks*. New York, NY: Pantheon.

Haass, Richard N. 2009. *War of Necessity, War of Choice: A Memoir of Two Iraq Wars*. New York: Simon and Schuster.

Hallman, Ben, and Eleazar David Melendez. 2013. "Foreclosure Review Insiders Portray Massive Failure, Doomed from the Start." *Huffington Post*, January 14, 2013. www. huffingtonpost.com/2013/01/14/foreclosure-review-failurestart_n_2468988.html

Hansen, Hans Krause. 2011. "Managing Corruption Risks." *Review of International Political Economy* 18 (2): 251–75.

Hansen, Hans Krause. 2012. "The Power of Performance Indices in the Global Politics of Anti-Corruption." *Journal of International Relations and Development* 15 (4): 506–31.

Harris, Gardiner. 2017. "Diplomats Sound the Alarm as They are Pushed Out in Droves." *The New York Times*, November 24, 2017. https://www.nytimes.com/2017/11/24/us/politics/state-department-tillerson.html.

Honegger, Claudia, Sighard Neckel, and Chantal Magnin. 2010. *Strukturierte Verantwortungslosigkeit: Berichte aus der Bankenwelt*. Berlin: Suhrkamp Verlag GmbH und Co. KG.

Horwitz, Jeff, and Maria Aspan. 2013. "OCC Pressures Banks to Clean Up Card Debt Sales." *American Banker*, July 2, 2013. https://www.americanbanker.com/news/occ-pressures-banks-to-clean-up-card-debt-sales

Ivanov, Kalin S. 2007. "The Limits of a Global Campaign Against Corruption." In *Corruption and Development: The Anti-Corruption Campaigns*, edited by Sarah Bracking, 28–45. New York: Palgrave Macmillan.

Johnston, Michael. 2005. *Syndromes of Corruption: Wealth, Power, and Democracy*. New York: Cambridge University Press.

Johnston, Michael. 2014. *Corruption, Contention and Reform: The Power of Deep Democratization*. Cambridge, UK: Cambridge University Press.

Katz, Eric. 2019. "Trump Signs Orders to Restrict 'Unaccountable Bureaucrats' from Creating 'Backdoor Regulations.'" Government Executive. October 9, 2019. n.d. Retrieved December 5, 2019. https://www.govexec.com/management/2019/10/trump-signs-orders-restrict-unaccountable-bureaucrats-creating-backdoor-regulations/160493/

Kapferer, Bruce. 2005. "New Formations of Power, the Oligarchic-Corporate State, and Anthropological Ideological Discourse." *Anthropological Theory* 5 (3): 285–99.

Kessler, Glenn. 2016. "The Pre-war Intelligence on Iraq: Wrong or Hyped by the Bush White House?" *The Washington Post*, December 13, 2016. https://www.washingtonpost.com/news/fact-checker/wp/2016/12/13/the-pre-war-intelligence-on-iraq-wrong-or-hyped-by-the-bush-white-house/

Kosals, Leonid. 2007. "Essay on clan capitalism in Russia." *Acta Oeconomica* 57 (1): 67–85.

Krastev, Ivan. 2004. *Shifting Obsessions: Three Essays on the Politics of Anticorruption*. Budapest: Central European University Press.

LaFraniere, Sharon, Nicholas Confessore, and Jessie Drucker. 2017. "Prerequisite for Key White House Posts: Loyalty, Not Experience." *The New York Times*. March 14, 2017. https://www.nytimes.com/2017/03/14/us/politics/trump-advisers-experience.html

Ledeneva, Alena V. 2006. *How Russia Really Works: The Informal Practices That Shaped Post-Soviet Politics and Business*. Ithaca; London: Cornell University Press. www.jstor.org/stable/10.7591/j.ctt7zdpw.

Lessig, Lawrence. 2013. FOREWORD: "Institutional Corruption 'Defined.'" *The Journal of Law, Medicine & Ethics: A Journal of the American Society of Law, Medicine & Ethics* 41 (3): 553–5.

Lessig, Lawrence. 2015. *Republic Lost: The Corruption of Equality and the Steps to End It*. New York, NY: Hachette Book Group.

Lessig, Lawrence. 2019. *Institutional Corruption*. Harvard University: Edmond J. Safra Center for Ethics website, n.d. Retrieved December 5, 2019. https://ethics.harvard.edu/lawrence-lessig-institutional-corruption-0

Levitas, Anthony, and Piotr Strzałkowski. 1990. "What Does 'Uwłaszczenie Nomenklatury' (Propertisation of the Nomenklatura) Really Mean?" *Communist Economies* 2 (3): 413–16.

Light, Paul. C. 2017. "The True Size of Government," *Issue Papers*, The Volcker Alliance, Oct. 5, 2017, https://www.volckeralliance.org/publications/true-size-government.

Mazzetti, Mark, and David. E. Sanger. 2007. "Bush Aides See Failure in Fight With Al Qaeda in Pakistan." *The New York Times*, July 18, 2007. https://www.nytimes.com/2007/07/18/washington/18intel.html

McFaul, Michael. 2018. "Why Trump's Personalized Approach to Diplomacy Is Bad for America." *The Washington Post*, June 28, 2018. https://www.washingtonpost.com/news/global-opinions/wp/2018/06/28/why-trumps-personalized-approach-to-diplomacy-is-bad-for-america/

Michaels, Dave. 2017. "SEC Chair Nominee Clayton's Ethics Report Reveals Range of Possible Conflicts, *The Wall Street Journal*, March 8, https://www.wsj.com/articles/sec-chair-nominee-claytons-ethics-report-reveals-range-of-possible-conflicts-1488988744.

Millar, James R. 1996. "From Utopian Socialism to Utopian Capitalism: The Failure of Revolution and Reform in Post-soviet Russia." *George Washington University 175th Anniversary Papers* (2). Washington, D.C.: George Washington University.

Miller, Ben and Laura Jimenez. 2017. "Inside the Financial Holdings of Billionaire Betsy DeVos, Washington, DC: Center for American Progress, January 27, https://www.americanprogress.org/issues/education-postsecondary/news/2017/01/27/297572/inside-the-financial-holdings-of-billionaire-betsy-devos/.

Miller, Seumus. 2017. *Institutional Corruption: A Study in Applied Philosophy*. Cambridge, UK: Cambridge University Press.

Mills, C. Wright. 1956. The Power Elite. New York: Oxford University Press.

Morgenson, Gretchen. 2010. "3,000 Pages of Financial Reform, but Still Not Enough." *The New York Times*, May 29, 2010. http://www.nytimes.com.mutex.gmu.edu/2010/05/30/business/30gret.html.

Mueller, Eleanor. 2020. "Trump executive order strips protections for key federal workers, drawing backlash." *Politico*, October 22, 2020. https://www.politico.com/news/2020/10/22/trump-order-strips-worker-protections-431359.

Nelson, Lynn D., and Irina Y. Kuzes. 1995. *Radical Reform in Yeltsin's Russia: Political Economic and Social Dimensions*. Armonk, NY: M. E. Sharpe.

Nelson, Lynn D., and Irina Y. Kuzes. 1994. *Property to the People: The Struggle for Radical Economic Reform in Russia*. Armonk, NY: M. E. Sharpe.

Newhouse, M.E. 2014. "Institutional Corruption: A Fiduciary Theory." *Cornell Journal of Law and Public Policy* 23 (3): 553–94.

Office of Management and Budget. 1992. "Policy Letter 92-1 To The Heads Of Executive Agencies And Departments. Subject: Inherently Governmental Functions," September 23, 1992. https://georgewbush-whitehouse.archives.gov/omb/procurement/policy_letters/92-01_092392.html.

Ogrysko, Nicole. 2019. "Waiting for Additional Leave Guidance, New Shutdown Furlough Notices Go Out and More." *Federal News Network*, January 22, 2019. https://federalnewsnetwork.com/government-shutdown/2019/01/waiting-for-additional-leave-guidance-new-shutdown-furlough-notices-go-out-and-more/

Ong, Aihwa. 1999. *Flexible Citizenship: The Cultural Logics of Transnationality*. Durham and London: Duke University Press.

Osborne, David, and Peter Plastrik. 1997. *Banishing Bureaucracy: The Five Strategies for Reinventing Government*. Reading, MA: Addison-Wesley Publishing Company, Inc.

Osborne, David, and Ted Gaebler. 1992. *Reinventing Government: How the Entrepreneurial Spirit is Transforming the Public Sector*. Reading, MA: Addison Wesley.

Osnos, E. 2018. *Trump vs. The "Deep State."* https://www.newyorker.com/magazine/2018/05/21/trump-vs-the-deep-state

Protess, Ben, Rashbaum, William K., and Michael Rothfeld. 2019. "Giuliani Pursued Business in Ukraine While Pushing for Inquiries for Trump." *The New York Times*. November 27, 2019. https://www.nytimes.com/2019/11/27/nyregion/giuliani-ukraine-business-trump.html.

Przybyla, Heidi M. 2017. "Trump's Cabinet Is His Team of Disrupters at Agencies They've Battled." *USA Today*. January 12, 2017. https://www.usatoday.com/story/news/politics/2017/01/12/some-trump-cabinet-picks-skeptical-their-agencies-missions/96417756/.

Rainie, Lee, Janna Anderson, and Jonathan Albright. 2017. "The Future of Free Speech, Trolls, Anonymity and Fake News Online." Pew Research Center: Internet & Technology. March 29, 2017. Retrieved December 5, 2019. https://www.pewresearch.org/internet/2017/03/29/the-future-of-free-speech-trolls-anonymity-and-fake-news-online/

Rein, Lisa. 2017. "How Trump's First Year Has Decimated Federal Bureaucracy." *The Independent*, December 31, 2017. https://www.independent.co.uk/news/world/americas/president-donald-trump-white-house-first-year-inauguration-federal-bureaucracy-barack-obama-a8135921.html

Rein, Lisa. 2021. "Trump's 11th-hour assault on the civil service by stripping job protections runs out of time." *The Washington Post*, January 18, 2021. https://www.washingtonpost.com/politics/trump-civil-service-biden/2021/01/18/5daf34c4-59b3-11eb-b8bd-ee36b1cd18bf_story.html.

Reuters. 2018a. "Trump Turns Attention to Budget Cutting after Slashing Taxes." *Reuters*, October 17, 2018. https://www.reuters.com/article/us-usa-trump-budget-idUSKCN1MR2G9.

Reuters. 2018b. "Trump Seeks to Shrink Cabinet Agencies' Budgets." *Reuters*, October 17, 2018. https://www.reuters.com/article/usa-trump-budget/trump-seeks-to-shrink-cabinet-agencies-budgets-idUSL2N1WX105

Rose-Ackerman, Susan, ed. 2006. *International Handbook on the Economics of Corruption*. Cheltenham, U.K./Northampton, MA: Edward Elgar.

Rosenberg, Matthew. 2016. "At Booz Allen, A Vast U.S. Spy Operation, Run for Private Profit." *The New York Times*, October 7, 2016. https://www.nytimes.com/2016/10/07/us/booz-allen-hamilton-nsa.html.

Rothstein, Bo, and Jan Teorell. 2008. "What Is Quality of Government? A Theory of Impartial Government Institutions." *Governance* 21 (2) (April): 165–90. https://papers.ssrn.com/sol3/papers.cfm?abstract_id=1328817

Rothstein, Bo. 2021. "Quality of Government: Theory and Conceptualization." In *The Oxford Handbook of the Quality of Government*. Oxford: Oxford University Press.

Ryle, Gilbert. 1971. *Collected Essays, 1929–1968: Collected Papers*, vol. II. London: Hutchinson.

Sampson, Steven. 2010. "The Anti-corruption Industry: From Movement to Institution." *Global Crime* 11 (2): 261–78.

Savage, Mike, and Karel Williams. 2008. "Elites: Remembered in Capitalism and Forgotten by Social Sciences." *The Sociological Review* 56 (1 suppl) (May): 1–24. doi:10.1111/j.1467-954X.2008.00759.x.

Scheiber, Noam. 2018. "Trump Moves to Ease the Firing of Federal Workers." *The New York Times,* May 25, 2018. https://www.nytimes.com/2018/05/25/business/economy/trump-federal-workers.html.

Schoen, John W. 2018. "After 500 days, Hundreds of White House Jobs Remain Unfilled by Trump Administration." CNBC.com, June 4, 2018. https://www.cnbc.com/2018/06/04/after-500-days-dozens-of-white-house-jobs-remain-unfilled.html.

Schuck, Peter H. 2017. "Trump's Bureaucratic Showdown." *The New York Times,* November 27, 2017. https://www.nytimes.com/2017/11/27/opinion/trump-cfpb-appointment-independence.html.

Seipel, Arnie. 2019. "Trump's 'Acting' Cabinet Grows with Acosta Departure." NPR.org, July 12, 2019. n.d. Retrieved December 5, 2019. https://www.npr.org/2019/07/12/741094931/trumps-acting-cabinet-grows-with-acosta-departure

Shelley, Louise I., 1995. "Privatization and Crime: The Post-soviet Experience." *Journal of Contemporary Criminal Justice* 11 (4): 244–56. https://doi.org/10.1177/104398629501100405

Sherred, Brown. 2013. "Brown Chairs Banking Hearing on Role of Independent Consultants in Financial Services Industry." Washington D.C., April 11, 2013. https://www.brown.senate.gov/newsroom/press/release/brown-chairs-banking-hearing-on-role-of-independent-consultants-in-financial-services-industry

Shuster, Simon, and Ilya Marritz. 2020. "As Energy Secretary, Rick Perry Mixed Money and Politics in Ukraine. The Deals Could be Worth Billions." *Time.* September 10, https://time.com/5887230/rick-perry-deals-energy-ukraine/.

Smith, R. Jeffrey. 2012. "Generals No Longer Retire to Vermont—They Lobby for Contractors in Washington." *Center for Public Integrity,* November 21, 2012. www.publicintegrity.org/2012/11/21/11839/generals-no-longer-retire-vermont-they-lobby-contractors-washington.

Stark, David, and Lazlo Bruszt. 1998. *Postsocialist Pathways: Transforming Politics and Property in East Central Europe.* Cambridge: Cambridge University Press.

Stark, David. 1990. "Privatization in Hungary: From Plan to Market or from Plan to Clan?" *East European Politics & Societies* 4 (3): 351–92.

Stark, David. 1996. "Recombinant Property in East European Capitalism." *American Journal of Sociology* 101 (4): 993–1027.

Stein, Jonathan, and Tim Dickinson. 2006. "Lie by Lie: A Timeline of How We Got into Iraq." *Mother Jones.* https://www.motherjones.com/politics/2011/12/leadup-iraq-war-timeline/

Thompson, Dennis F.1993. "Mediated Corruption: The Case of the Keating Five." *American Political Science Review* 87 (2): 269–381.

Thompson, Dennis F. 2018. "Theories of Institutional Corruption." *Annual Review of Political Science* 21 (1) (May): 495–512. doi:10.1146/annurev-polisci-120117-110316.

United States House of Representatives, 2007. "More Dollars, Less Sense: Worsening Contractor Trends under the Bush Administration," United States House of Representatives, Committee on Oversight and Government Reform, Majority Staff, June 2007, https://www.hsdl.org/?view&did=475628

Verkuil, Paul R. 2007. *Outsourcing Sovereignty: Why Privatization of Government Functions Threatens Democracy and What We Can Do about It.* Cambridge: Cambridge University Press. doi: https://doi.org/10.1017/CBO9780511509926.

Vogl, Joseph. 2015. *Der Souveränitätseffekt [The Sovereignty Effect].* Zurich: Diaphanes.

Weber, Max. 1994. *Political Writings.* Edited by Peter Lassman, translated by Ronald Speirs. Cambridge: Cambridge University Press. https://doi.org/10.1017/CBO9780511841095.

Weber, Max. 1947. *The Theory of Social and Economic Organization.* Translated by A. M. Henderson and Talcott Parsons. New York: Free Press of Glencoe.

Wedel, Janine R. 2001. *Collision and Collusion: The Strange Case of Western Aid to Eastern Europe.* New York, NY: Palgrave.

Wedel, Janine, R. 2009. *Shadow Elite: How the World's New Power Brokers Undermine Democracy, Government, and the Free Market.* New York, NY: Basic Books.

Wedel, Janine R. 2010. "Selling Out Uncle Sam: How the Myth of Small Government Undermines National Security." Washington, DC: New American Foundation, August, http://janinewedel.info/SellingOutUncleSamAug10.pdf.

Wedel, Janine. 2011. "Federalist No. 70: Where Does the Public Service Begin and End?" *Public Administration Review* 71 (1) (December): 118–27.

Wedel, Janine R. 2012. "Rethinking Corruption in an Age of Ambiguity." *Annual Review of Law and Social Science* 8: 453–98. https://doi.org/10.1146/annurev.lawsocsci.093008.131558.

Wedel, Janine R. 2014/2016. *Unaccountable: How the Establishment Corrupted Our Finances, Freedom, and Politics and Created an Outsider Class.* New York, NY: Pegasus (updated paperback & kindle editions 2016).

Wedel, Janine R. 2017. "From Power Elites to Influence Elites: Resetting Elite Studies for the 21st Century." *Theory, Culture & Society* 34 (5–6): 153–78. http://journals.sagepub.com/eprint/CVTt62SuM5jNaUIekDdN/full.

Whitehouse, Sheldon. 2018. "Legal Responses to Regulatory Capture." American Constitution Society Expert Forum, November 9, 2018. https://www.acslaw.org/expertforum/blog-post-for-the-american-constitution-society-legal-responses-to-regulatory-capture/

World Bank. 1997. *Helping Countries Combat Corruption: The Role of the World Bank.* Washington, D.C.: World Bank. Poverty Reduction and Economic Management.

World Bank. 1999. *Anti-Corruption Program in the ECA Region.* Washington, D.C.: World Bank. Poverty Reduction and Economic Management.

Yin, Robert K. 2014. *Case Study Research: Design and* Methods. 5th ed. Beverly Hills, CA: Sage.

Zald, Mayer N., and Michael Lounsbury. 2010. "The Wizards of Oz: Towards an Institutional Approach to Elites, Expertise and Command Posts." *Organization Studies* 31(7): 963–96.

PART II

DATA AND METHODOLOGICAL APPROACHES

CHAPTER 5

....

MEASURING THE UNMEASURABLE? TAKING STOCK OF QOG MEASURES

....

NICHOLAS CHARRON

INTRODUCTION

....

CITIZENS and policymakers in countries worldwide are becoming increasingly aware of problems associated with corruption and poor-quality institutions. In addition, aid donor organizations are keen on having their resources allocated efficiently; while researchers have grown increasingly interested in the causes and consequences of high-quality institutions. These trends have increased demand for a wide scope of indictors that diagnose governance problems to find solutions for improvement. This chapter seeks to highlight recent trends in the measurement of "good governance," to elucidate differences, strengths, and weakness among current tools, and to discuss fertile areas of development for future research.

Various stakeholders within the good governance regime have provided a wealth of tools in recent years. Most readers are now familiar with the initial efforts of the Corruption Perceptions Index (CPI) and Worldwide Governance Indicators (WGI) from Transparency and the World Bank respectively. Set up as international 'benchmarks', such governance indicators served as a valuable 'nudging' alternative to strict aid conditionality (Zürn 2018), while simultaneously providing policymakers, researchers, and civil society actors a set of freely available tools to compare countries and begin to do empirical analyses of the causes and consequences of corruption and other governance dimensions. Based on the initial, "first generation" measures, the empirical evidence is clear—poor governance has a negative effect on economic and societal development (Mauro 1995; La Porta et al. 1999; Holmberg et al. 2009).

Yet, definitional concerns regarding corruption, let alone a concept as broad as "good governance" or "quality of government" (QoG), are many (see, for example, Fukuyama 2013) and proper measurement of any concept relies on a valid conceptualization of what exactly ought to be measured (Adcock and Collier 2001). The concept's complexity has led scholars interested in measuring QoG down multiple pathways, which will be elaborated further in this chapter, with a specific emphasis on measures of corruption. What are the key components of "QoG," and which are the main ways in which scholars have attempted to operationalize them? How have these measures changed and adapted over time to critiques? What are some potential fruitful ways forward? This chapter will address these questions.

It is worth pointing out early on that no one indicator offers a definitive measurement. As Kaufmann et al. (2007, 2) note, "no measure of corruption "objective" or subjective, specific or aggregate, can be 100 percent reliable—in the sense of giving precise measures of corruption." In addition, Heller (2009, 30) argues that the multitude of indicators are "complementary rather than inimical to each other." Moreover, as this chapter will cover in subsequent sections, there is no unified definition of the concept, nor is the field unified whether the concept is unidimensional or multidimensional. Thus, given a lack of consensus on the scope of the concept of QoG, and the abstract, often unobservable nature of the concept it is not likely that the unifying "holy grail" of measures exists somewhere on the horizon. All data—whether subjective, experience-based, or objective—are in essence assessments, and thus subject to "noise." Measures that indicate a lack of impartiality or corruption in one region, sector, or institution in a country might not be indicative of corruption in another, thus aggregated country-level measures will inevitably contain a substantial degree of variation among their constituent parts. Most current mainstream measures focus mainly on public sector, rather than private sector behavior. With these caveats in mind, available QoG indicators can nonetheless provide rich information to interested users, yet there is still much room for development in this field.

This chapter takes stock of the proliferation of QoG data available to researchers and policymakers. I begin with an overview of common indicators and the various dimensions on which data is and can be constructed, and the implications for users. Next, correlations among several commonly used indicators of corruption are presented. The following section summarizes a literature on several main critiques of existing QoG data. Next, I offer some suggestions that users of the data should consider when assessing a quality of a QoG measure. In the final section, I present some thoughts about measurement of QoG going forward.

Broad Trends and History

While there are many critiques of contemporary governance indicators, a lack of abundance is certainly not one of them. Even in the mid-2000s, over 140 indicators were available (Arndt and Oman 2010), and the available measures have only risen since then, many of the newer indicators with a country or regional specific focus. Yet it is not enough to simply build a measure, but it must also be used and legitimized by relevant stakeholders, in this case high-quality peer-reviewed research. The first major studies to compare corruption across countries ("or institutional quality") were published by Knack and Keefer, and Mauro in 1995, in which expert assessment data on corruption risks were employed from for-profit firms from the International Country Risk Guide (ICRG), and BI (The Economist Unit) were used for a subset of countries. In 1999, the first major scientific study to use the CPI measure from Transparency International (a freely available measure) as a proxy for a country's corruption was by Ades and di Tella, while the "Worldwide Governance

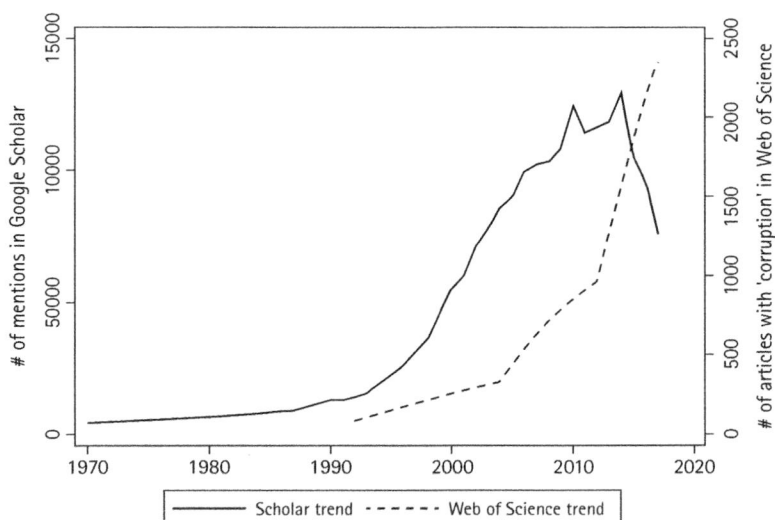

FIGURE 5.1 Studies with the word "corruption": 1970–2018

Source: Google Scholar and Thompson Web of Science.

Indicators" (WGI) was unveiled by Kaufmann et al. in the same year. Persson et al. (2003) then soon legitimized the WGI's control of corruption as an alternative proxy of cross-country corruption levels to the ICRG and CPI. These three measures led to a subsequent boom in research, and Figure 5.1 highlights the trends over time of the studies mentioning the word "corruption," which researched its peak of 129,000 in 2015. To put this in context, the nearly ubiquitous word "democracy" within political science yields 145,000 mentions in the same year of 2015. A similar trend line is observed for the Web of Science mention of the term "corruption" as a keyword.

The use of such measures led to a surge in empirical, cross-country corruption research in the first decade of the 2000s, as is indicated in Figure 5.1. Studies incorporating QoG and corruption have thus become mainstream within political science and economics and are some of the most commonly written about topics today due to the expansion of data.

Mapping Methodological Approaches

As the industry of measuring various aspects of good governance has blossomed, so have the diverse ways in which indicators are constructed (Heinrich and Hodess 2011). Prior to selecting a measure for academic or practical usage, one should be aware of the measure's variations, dimensions, and features and select any measure based on the goals of one's study or project, and underlying concepts for which the indicator serves as proxy. Here we can identify several lenses through which contemporary governance indicators vary using the example of corruption indicators, a taxonomy for which is shown in Figure 5.2. The inner circle represents the core concept "corruption," and the indicators of this concept are shaped by six

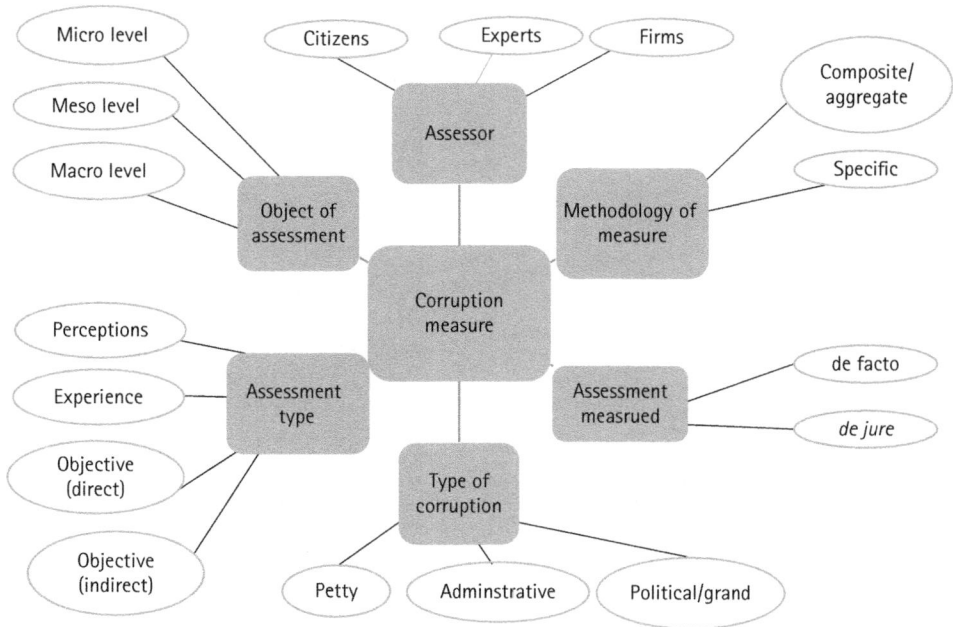

FIGURE 5.2 Taxonomy of governance indicator dimensions—example of corruption

factors, shown in the inner orbit of the core concept. The outer bubbles represent some of the ways (yet not exhaustively) in which these six dimensions can vary across various indicators.

First, is the *object* being assessed? So-called "first generation" indicators focused almost exclusively on the country level, while later measures offer more decentralized indicators, such as the subnational (Alt and Lassen 2008; Charron et al. 2014), or municipal level (Olken 2007; da Cruz et al. 2016). Others work on the meso level and compare variation institutions within countries, such as the executive, legislature, courts, parties, media, or elections; while others capture corruption in specific public services: healthcare, education, and policing, for example.

Second, measures of corruption are essentially assessments of some object in question, yet *who the assessor is* varies from indicator to indicator and has critical implications for usage. Initial measures such as the CPI, ICRG, and WGI relied almost exclusively on experts, which can range from experienced researchers, to experienced professionals in the public or private sector, oftentimes with specific country expertise, such as in Freedom House's Nations in Transit measure. Others, for example, from the "barometers" surveys, such as Eurobarometer, Afrobarometer, and Latinobarometer, Global Corruption Barometer, and the European Quality of Government Index (EQI) rely on citizen assessment. The Business Environment and Enterprise Performance Survey (BEEPS) and the Bribe Payers Index (BPI) employ assessments from firms, and are thus better equipped to assess corruption experiences and perceptions of private actors. More recently, several studies have relied on public bureaucrats (Charron et al. 2016; Meyer-Sahling et al. 2018) which constitutes something between average citizens and experts, or what could be known as "experience-based perceptions".

Such surveys that track individual- or firm-level assessments can be employed, aggregated to various levels, or used at the micro level for various research questions. For example, researchers might be interested in explaining variation in causes perceptions of corruption among certain populations (Sharafutdinova, 2010). Or explore the consequences of perceptions or experiences of corruption on support for various EU policies (Bauhr and Charron 2020), the satisfaction with public service or one's democratic participation (Dahlberg and Solevid 2016), or general life satisfaction (Ciziceno and Travaglino 2019) to name a few. Micro-level data also offers the added advantage of disaggregation of perceptions of wealthy versus poor citizens or males versus females, a strategy used, for example, by the African Peer Review Mechanism.

The third dimension is the *type* of assessment. As corruption is most often not directly observable, many earlier (and later) indicators rely on aggregate perceptions, which can come from any of the assessors. As critiques and skepticism of the perception indicators grew, in particular, regarding the composite perceptions approach to measuring corruption, other measures were developed. Following trends in public administration studies, which had begun to proxy quality institutions with citizen satisfaction measures (Bouckaert and Van de Walle 2003), some corruption studies moved to more "experience-based" measures. Here indicators such as personal experience with petty corruption or experience of vote-buying or some closely related concept, such as nepotism or favoritism, were seen as remedying the weakness of perception measures (for example, Fan et al. 2009). In addition, firms are also asked their experience of bribery in their own as well as host countries, for example, the World Bank's Productivity and Investment Climate Private Enterprise Surveys (PICS). However, experience-based measures were argued to be inequivalent and invalid across countries with diverse political systems, due to issues of underreporting and false responses in more repressive countries (Jensen et al. 2010). And while in and of themselves, these studies led to new and important research insights, they also led to a debate about whether such perceptions reflect "actual" corruption experienced by residents of the particular country in question (Donchev and Ujhelyi 2014; Rose and Mishler 2010; Razafindrakoto and Roubaud 2010; Charron 2016; Gutmann et al 2020).

The debates and questions over the validity of perception measures and the limitations of experience-based measures due to issues such as social desirability bias in surveys and validity issues of using experienced-based measures or corruption increased the demand for more "objective" measures. Such concerns have led to an ever growing and diverse set of indicators that vary on several key dimensions. While experience-based measures are not typically expert-based, objective assessments generally are. Here we observe a recent boom in ways in which corruption is measured objectively, with tools such as audits, procurement, and public spending patterns to elucidate either corruption "red flags" (indirect) or via direct measures. With respect to direct objective measures, Golden and Picci (2005) use deviations in infrastructure spending as a way of capturing corruption in Italian regions; and Olken (2007) uses discrepancies in actual infrastructure spending with independent estimates in Indonesian villages. Ferraz and Finan (2008) use data from random municipal audits in Brazilian municipalities. Other such objective measures also include corruption convictions (Alt and Lassen 2008; Glaeser and Saks 2006; Bågenholm and Charron 2020). Expenditures, audits, and convictions as objective measures of corruption are, however, much more useful at the subnational level within single countries, as differences in judicial and media effectiveness in discovering and prosecuting corruption, as well as differences in the laws, can lead to very misleading comparisons across countries. Regarding the more indirect side, Fazekas and Kocsis (2020) collected data on public procurement contracts in European countries to generate "red flags," such as single bidding on contracts and other items that indicate lack of competition in procurement. In addition, indicators from the Open Budget Index or the Comparative Constitutions Project (CCP) can be used as objective measures of corruption and transparency. Perceptions and objective indicators are not mutually exclusive, however; the Ibrahim Index of African Governance is an example of combining measures of expert perceptions with objective data on education and health outcomes.

Fourth, specifically regarding corruption, more and more attention is given to understanding and distinguishing different *types* of the phenomenon (Bauhr 2017). Many of the citizen assessments, for example, track petty corruption, while grand corruption is often captured by expert perceptions or objective measures. Administrative corruption can be proxied with experiences or perceptions or citizens, bureaucrats, experts, or firms.

Fifth, measures differ on whether they are *de jure* or *de facto*. *De jure* measures are mainly on the input side: those that focus on rules, laws, institutions, and procedures concerning a certain aspect of governance. Conversely, *de facto* measures proxy outputs: results or outcomes concerning some aspect of governance, or how governance happens in practice. Measures of governance that rely on *de jure* inputs, such as Bertelsmann, Global Integrity Index, or the International Budget Project, provide data on strength and weakness of existing laws and regulations, or the presence or absence of various oversight agencies intended to affect corruption and improve governance, such as ombudsmen, anticorruption agencies, or auditing agencies. These measures are of course clear and (mostly) actionable—countries, regions, or sectors can improve their score by adjusting their laws or practices, or by adding various commissions, oversight functions, or agencies intended to improve governance and fight corruption. While these measures themselves tend to be objective, subjective decisions by the user are sometimes required to assess their validity in a given context.

De facto measures are the result of the performance of government institutions and can be direct or indirect. For example, within the anticorruption field, most have concluded that direct measures, such as convictions or indictments, might not provide a valid picture of actual corruption to compare across countries, but might be a valid measure within (certain) countries or clusters of countries with similar political and legal systems. Thus, such indicators as results from audits, infrastructure expenditures, corruption risks in procurement, corruption convictions, experiences or perceptions with corruption, and satisfaction with public services, tend to be proxies rather than direct output measures.

The distinction between input and output measures is essential, and the two are complementary rather than rivals. For example, let's say we want to know if the rate of petty corruption goes down in a given area that has adopted stronger ombudsmen laws, or invested more in transparency. In this case, we would want to use an input measure to explain an output one. Moreover, consumers of the data should also be aware that certain aggregate governance indicators combine inputs and outputs, such as the WGI, which takes input data from sources like Global Integrity and combines them with outputs, such as citizen perceptions from Gallop or Barometer sources. This can be both positive, in that these measures provide a very comprehensive picture, and negative, in that they contain underlying data that might inadvertently capture both the cause and the outcome of one's theoretical model.

Finally, there is the methodological question of *type* of measure—either composite (e.g., "poll of polls") types of measure or single item indicators, which are more specifically targeted. Composite indicators offer a big picture, aggregate snapshot of governance or corruption of the object in question, oftentimes allowing for cross-country/regional comparisons among many units. These might be best at capturing what Fisman and Golden (2017, 4) describe as "corruption-as-equilibrium," or a large-scale system of incentives toward or against corrupt activities. The CPI and WGI measures are the clearest examples of these, aggregating multiple underlying indicators of corruption to provide near global coverage to be used to compare and contrast countries en masse. In contrast to composite indicators, which also generally rely on secondary data, single item or indicators offer a more fine-tuned assessment of one specific object in question, often providing primary data collected by the providing source. For example, the International Country Risk Guide (ICRG), Bertelsmann Stiftung, and Nations in Transit (NIT) from Freedom House are examples of indicators in which experts classify countries based on preselected specific criteria of inputs and outputs. Within-country measures of specific sectors, such as the Indian Corruption Study of corruption in various public sector services, conducted by Transparency International, could also be used as single item measures at the meso or subnational levels. Some offer a combination of the two; for example, the corruption measure provided by the Varieties of Democracy project (McMann et al. 2016), which provides single item measures of specific institutions, such as the legislature and executive, while also providing a composite by country-year of all institutions collected. The WGI (Kaufman et al. 2009) also provides the main composite index, along with the underlying indicators.

How Well Do Some of the Current Measures Correlate?

As noted in the previous section, the taxonomy highlighted shows that there are at least six dimensions by which a given governance (or in this case corruption) measure can be distinguished, which allows hundreds of possible combinations. While the space allowed in this chapter does not permit a complete analysis, for the sake of parsimony, 18 various indicators of corruption/'control of' corruption are taken from the QoG's standard dataset (Teorell et al. 2016) to investigate country-level variation and correlations. Table 5.1 highlights the pairwise correlations between the various commonly used measures ($p<0.05$ in bold), along with a comparison of two additional measures that proxy for economic development—infant mortality rate and GDP per capital (logged)—with which we expect corruption measures to be negatively and positively correlated, respectively. All measures are rescaled so that higher values equate to less (or "control of") corruption.

On the whole, we find that most all measures correlate in the direction expected with the two measures of development, as well as with each other. Not surprisingly, we see that there is remarkably high correlation between and among the two main composite indicators (CPI and WGI) with the other single-source expert assessments—the Heritage, Vdem, ICRG, Bertelsmann, and QoG's measure of civil service impartiality (e.g., "opposite of corruption" (Rothstein 2014)); many of which are in fact included in the composite measures themselves. Note that while all measures pertain to the public sector, there are differences in emphasis and scope—some combining all institutions (Vdem), while others focusing on the civil service for example (QoG). Moreover, all of these composite and expert perception-based measures correlate strongly with the two measures of development, with the ICRG showing the strongest correlation, and the Bertelsmann the weakest.

Table 5.1 Pairwise correlations of corruption and integrity measures

Variables	1	2	3	4	5	6	7	8	9	10	11	12	13	14	15	16	17	18
(1) log_gdppc	1																	
(2) inthnt mort.	−0.79	1.00																
(3) CPI	0.69	−0.61	1.00															
(4) WGI	0.66	−0.61	0.99	1.00														
(5) Heritage	0.67	−0.57	0.98	0.96	1.00													
(6) Vdem	0.64	−0.58	0.88	0.90	0.87	1.00												
(7) ICRG	0.75	−0.68	0.93	0.93	0.93	0.86	1.00											
(8) Bertelsmann	0.47	−0.45	0.87	0.85	0.85	0.74	0.69	1.00										
(9) QoG	0.71	−0.59	0.91	0.90	0.90	0.84	0.84	0.76	1.00									
(10) GCB bribe rate	0.20	−0.35	0.06	0.10	0.08	0.16	0.02	0.01	−0.09	1.00								
(11) WDI bribe firm	0.56	−0.46	0.57	0.58	0.57	0.55	0.51	0.47	0.56	0.01	1.00							
(12) CCP ac com	0.10	−0.02	0.03	0.01	0.05	−0.03	0.01	0.14	0.01	−0.12	0.07	1.00						
(13) CCP merit	0.03	−0.01	0.02	0.03	0.02	0.01	0.03	−0.02	0.08	0.05	0.06	0.17	1.00					
(14) GII	0.93	−0.89	0.73	0.71	0.69	0.66	0.78	0.49	0.71	0.32	0.50	−0.09	−0.02	1.00				
(15) All civil service	0.08	−0.03	0.31	0.26	0.36	0.16	0.09	0.36	0.47	0.10	0.55	0.20	0.11	0.03	1.00			
(16) WVD	0.12	−0.24	0.13	0.12	0.13	0.14	0.03	0.11	0.37	0.25	0.15	0.06	0.11	0.26	0.69	1.00		
(17) GCB officials	0.23	−0.19	0.43	0.46	0.44	0.40	0.51	0.10	0.48	0.14	0.03	0.16	0.18	0.22	0.30	0.23	1.00	
(18) GCB police	0.55	−0.45	0.62	0.65	0.62	0.57	0.70	0.27	0.68	0.11	0.28	0.02	0.12	0.54	0.18	0.30	0.78	1.00

Note: Pairwise correlation with p<.05 in bold. See appendix for further description of source data.

Next, we observe two measures of aggregated corruption experiences—citizen bribe rates (GCB) and those of firms (WGI). Although weaker than the expert assessments, these two measures still show statistically significant correlations in the expected direction with the development indicators, yet only the WGI shows significant correlations with the expert/composite indicators.

In our next set of indictors—the *de jure* objective ones, mainly assessing the input side of the equation—we find much less consistency. The two measures from the Comparative Constitutions Project (CCP)—whether a country has an anticorruption commission and whether meritocratic recruitment is mentioned in the constitution for civil service hiring—show little to no relationship with any of the output measures based on perceptions or experiences. Nor do they relate empirically with the measure of development. The African Integrity Index's (AII) measure of Civil Service Integrity (available for African states only), does correlate with some expert perceptions and experience measures, but not measures of development. Yet the Global Integrity Index (GII), which also assess the input side, has a much stronger set of pairwise correlations. This also might be due to the fact that the GII is also a composite index of many underlying input indicators, giving it a more comprehensive makeup than single objective indicators.

Our last set of indicators are perceptions of citizens, from the World Value Survey, and two measures from the Global Corruption Barometer (GCB) on the degree of perceived corruption of public officials and the police. Here we find somewhat mixed results, with the correlations from the GCB showing stronger pairwise correlations with the other corruption indicators as well as GDP per capita, in particular the perceptions of corruption in the police. The WVS item, which asks the extent to which people feel corruption is "never justified" shows weaker correlations across the board. In sum, while the measures all proxy some aspect of "control of corruption," some show greater correlations with the other indicators as well as related concepts, e.g., "construct validity" (Adcock and Collier 2001), than others. However, this should not dissuade researchers and policymakers from using the objective, de facto indicators if these in fact more closely match the concepts one seeks in their work.

MAIN CRITIQUES OF THE DATA

As with many abstract concepts that we are interested in measuring in social sciences, such as *democracy*, *legitimacy*, or *inequality*, measures of QoG have been met with a number of critiques. The critiques, which are mainly aimed at the more established measures, such as the WGI or CPI (yet apply to others as well), fall into several camps. Although space does not allow for an exhaustive list, I highlight some key issues raised in the literature below.

Conceptual/definitional issues

Many divergent definitions of concepts

Klitgaard et al. (2005, 414) argue that there has been "an explosion of measures, with little progress toward theoretical clarity or practical utility." A key reason for this is highlighted by Fukuyama (2013) in his discussion of "what is governance?" Those interested in this concept span multiple disciplines and thus have overlapping, yet quite distinct understandings of what this is. On the definition of QoG itself, Rothstein and Teorell (2008) are clear—QoG is defined as *impartiality*. Rothstein (2014) argues further that impartiality is the "opposite of corruption." Moreover, the norm of impartiality of interest is on the input—not output—side of governing, that is to say, they seek to measure how power is exercised, not what governments produce. However, the field is far from unified on this (see for example Fukuyama 2013), as noted in the chapter by Rothstein in this handbook. Moreover, while there are many near-neighbor proxies of impartiality, such as rule of law and corruption, yet there are few that attempt to measure this concept directly; an exception being the QoG Institute's expert cross-national survey (Dahlström et al. 2015).

While many measures are labelled "governance," "rule of law," or "corruption" indicators, their underlying definitions can differ depending on the source of the data (Versteeg and Ginsburg 2017). For example, even among leading international organizations which helped to pioneer large-scale measurement, there are clear disagreements about what one means with concepts of "governance" or corruption, for example. Most definitions of QoG imply a set of processes and rules by which citizen express their interests, which encompass a panoply of underlying concepts, such as rule of law, lack of corruption, impartiality, human rights, and civil society; all of which themselves are broad and contested concepts. For example, corruption alone has multiple contemporary definitions. The United Nations posits a broad definition of "the abuse of power for private gain," while WGI defines it as "the abuse of public office for private gain" (Kaufmann et al. 2011). Transparency International refers to it as "the misuse of public power for private benefit" (Lambsdorff 2006). Thus even among these three well-cited definitions, there is disagreement over whether what is being abused is "public sector/office" power, or simply "power" more broadly, which would include actors outside the public sector, rendering measures based on these various definitions different.

Vagueness of concepts

Several critics argue that there is a vagueness and lack of clarity of underlying concepts of contemporary QoG data. Thomas (2010) questions the "construct validity" of the WGI data, arguing that the scope of the definition of the QoG indicators themselves is too vague to be meaningful. For example, in terms of corruption, the main indicators, such as CPI or WGI, often conflate petty corruption with grand corruption, for example, or even include nepotism and "favoritism." These can be very different forms of corruption that imply different solutions (Rohwer 2009; Bauhr 2017); the broad, mainstream indicators render it difficult to test more specific research questions.

A multidimensional or unidimensional concept?

The field is divided over whether the broad idea of QoG is a unidimensional or multidimensional concept. While this does not imply that the measure per se cannot contain multiple dimensions—corruption in health services versus police, for example—it does have implications for how many underlying concepts we should include in our measures. On the multidimensional side, Kaufman et al. (1999) set the standard that the concept should be wide, and the WGI include six dimensions,[1] while Agnafors (2013) argues for six, if not

---

[1] These are: "government effectiveness," "regulatory quality," "voice and accountability," "rule of law," "control of corruption," and "Political Stability and Absence of Violence."

more, dimensions. Fukuyama (2013) elucidates two dimensions—bureaucratic autonomy and capacity. On the unidimensional side, Rothstein (2014) asserts that QoG is impartiality, and argues that we should measure this via a procedural lens—whether bureaucrats, civil servants, and lawmakers apply laws equally to all citizens irrespective of their background—not by policies or outputs, which he argues are a consequence of QoG, rather than QoG itself.

This debate is highly relevant in terms of the range of outcomes we can validly ask our QoG measures to explain. If one wants to explain the democratic performance or level of violent conflict in a country, for example, then these concepts obviously must be separate from our conceptions and measures of QoG, otherwise we introduce a tautology.

Lack of equivalence and Western centrism

A valid measure of QoG and its components rests on the assumption of "equivalence" (Stegmueller 2011)—that the concepts we are measuring are valid and comparable across our units of interest (countries, regions, etc.). That the vast majority of experts and organizations that assess country-level QoG are Western has led to a conceptual critique of the data is that QoG, and in particular corruption as a concept, is conceived in, and driven by, Western institutions, and imposed on countries with different histories, cultures, and traditions, which are not comparable outside of the West. De Maria (2010) argues that this Western-led effort to define and measure corruption in developing areas like Africa is essentially a Trojan Horse to help international corporations exploit resources more efficiently by forcing local leaders to adopt neoliberal reform. He argues that many of the instances defined in the West that constitute corrupt are seen as reciprocity or gift-giving in other contexts, which render cross-country measures like the CPI invalid in some contexts. Others argue that modern Western distinctions between public and private sector (e.g., "abuse of public resources for private gain") do not translate into many non-Western societies, and even in Western societies this distinction is often less relevant practice than in theory (Bratsis 2003). Heidenheimer (2002) argues that non-Western countries have different legal standards, different citizen understandings of what "corruption" is, even to the extent that corruption and low QoG can be seen as beneficial at times (Heidenheimer 2002, 38). Such critiques in essence argue for a relativistic conceptual understanding of impartiality and corruption, and thus the implication for current measures is that they lack valid equivalence across countries. However, without some minimal universal understanding—Western or not—of QoG, measurement and comparison is not possible (Rothstein 2014, 740).

Methodological issues

Data type—subjective, indirect, invalid measures

The earlier indicators relying on subjective, expert perceptions were subject to several criticisms. Firstly, that a subjective assessment does not necessarily present a fully accurate picture about "actual corruption" (Søreide 2006; Arndt and Oman 2010). Two, some assert that the expert assessors were biased toward business/market interests, not necessarily the public interest. As several earlier indicators of QoG, such as the ICRG, are in fact generated by private companies that explicitly intended to be "relevant to our clients' proprietary interests."[2] Other indicators, such as the WGI, have come under fire for similar criticism, as some of their underlying data is based on sources including the ICRG (Kurtz and Shrank 2007). A third argument in this vein concerns the use of heuristics by experts. Since corruption is clandestine, and impartiality is a subjective judgment, these concepts are difficult to observe, and experts might therefore be relying on the observable causes or consequences that researchers assert are related to corruption in the first place (Treisman 2007). For example, if experts believe that political gender equality relates to lower levels of corruption, and they observe that country x elects more women into parliament, this might lead to them rating country x as less corrupt. This clearly creates problems of causal inference when investigating the effect of gender equality on corruption (or vice versa). Finally, there is the issue of "bandwagoning," or "group-think," in which experts are influenced by one another and generally reticent to offer an assessment that differs from that of their peers for fear of criticism (Iqbal and Shaw 2008).

Whole-country bias

While some researchers and practitioners might be interested in a measure that provides the general "context" of a given country's level of corruption or QoG, we now have a much better sense of the degree to which QoG can vary within countries across subnational regions or various agencies. On the former, Charron et al. (2013) have shown via the EQI that QoG varies considerably within many European countries. For example, in Italy, northern regions such as Bolzano, Trento, or Fruili Venezia-Giulia perform much closer to a typical Austrian or German region, while in southern regions, such as Calabria or Campania, the QoG is similar to a typical region in Romania or Bulgaria. Nistotskaya (2009) finds striking regional variation in Russian Oblasts in terms of meritocratic recruitment of civil servants, while Seligson (2006) finds sizable disparity of corruption experience rates across provinces within Latina America, with Bolivia offering a prime example.

Not only do single-country QoG scores overrepresent some regions and underrepresent others, but studies of civil servants have found significant variation across agencies within countries with regard to measures of integrity, willingness to engage in corruption, and professionalism in developing countries (Roll 2014; Meyer-Sahling et al. 2018). Others have found noteworthy differences across agencies in terms of corruption risks in US agencies (Dahlström et al. 2019). Based on this within-country evidence across regions and agencies, researchers and practitioners should be aware that the country-level measures overgeneralize and that they are not indicative of all areas or institutions within a single country.

Data rescaling

One of the key features of some of the most prominent indicators of QoG, such as the WGI or CPI, is the method of data normalization or standardization; in other words the rescaling of multiple data items to match a common scale. Each of these composite indicators are composed of a number of underlying variables which may or may not be on the same scale (0–4, 0–10, etc.), and in order to aggregate them, a rescaling process is necessary (Nardo et al. 2005).

---

[2] https://www.prsgroup.com/about-us/the-prs-story/

For example, the CPI (since 2012) uses a simple z-score standardization[3] to combine 13 independent data sources, and then a simple average is taken and adjusted to aggregate the data for each country. The WGI also normalizes all underlying source data and produces z-scores for each country on all governance indicators from −2.5 to 2.5, with a mean of "0" and standard deviation of "1." This process has the obvious advantage of allowing researchers to combine multiple data sources (thus reducing the misleading effect of outlying data) and increasing the number of countries that can be compared in a single metric. However, normalization of data arbitrarily constrains the variation of QoG within a certain range, and thus while the rankings are reliable; we are unable to discern the "real distance" between units (Lambsdorff 2006).

Comparability over time

A central weakness in much of the current QoG data is its lack of valid comparison over time (Knack 2006; Arndt and Oman 2010; Heywood and Rose 2014). First, related to the issue of data normalization or standardization, while any observed changes in a country's position *can* occur for reasons that have to do with improvements or declines of QoG, they also can have *nothing* to do with such reasons. Since normalization and standardization implies that a country's score is in relation to all other countries (e.g., the mean) of a given year, one country's decline necessarily means a set of other countries' increases and vice versa. For example, since the Fidesz government assumed power in Hungary in 2010, the country's score in "Voice and Accountability" on the WGI has declined from 0.91 to 0.32 in 2018, or roughly 60% of a full standard deviation in the data. Each country around Hungary's score during this decline (given they also do not decline) will necessarily increase, if only by a small margin, but increase nonetheless. Moreover, the addition of any new country into the normalized data affects other countries' rankings. For instance, when low-ranked South Sudan was included in the dataset in 2011, this increased scores of all other countries above it, whether they "actually" improved or not. Finally, this process implies a constant global mean—thus, any changes we observe are not "absolute," but changes that are relative to other countries. In other words, if all countries simultaneously improved or declined in QoG from one year to the next, the data would not be able to tell us this. The CPI have taken measures to address this critique by anchoring all years post-2012 to the 2012 mean and standard deviation, but many of these issues still remain.

Irrespective of normalization rescaling, the issue of over-time comparisons persists, even when data is a single-source measure assessed by experts. Measures such as those of Freedom House, Nations in Transit, or ICRG rely on experts assessing countries on a number of criteria, but expert assessors change over time and as QoG is often unobservable, we are seldom privy to any heuristics they use to make assessments. If experts are relying (consciously or unconsciously) on cues such as economic growth (Kurtz and Shrank 2007) or gender equality, for example, which they now know to be related with QoG, this further complicates what the data signify in terms of over-time trends. The problem becomes even murkier when experts are asked to assess past periods for which research and information can be lacking and no current living person has first-hand experience, such as in the Vdem measure (McMann et al. 2016).

---

[3] In other words, $x_i - \bar{x} / \sigma$ where each country's observation is subtracted from the sample mean $\bar{x}$ and divided by the standard deviation (σ) They then set the mean of each of these to 45 and standard deviation of 20 (e.g., the 2012 baseline year) and fit them to a scale between 0 and 100.

How do we assess a "good" measure?

While it is certainly important to understand the weaknesses and common critiques of existing QoG data prior to its usage, one should certainly not be dissuaded entirely from using such data. The high correlation across a number of various indicators provides a degree of validity—despite differences in conceptualization—suggesting that they are tapping into a similar, coherent latent concept. In terms of the type indicator, level of analysis, temporal validity, etc. (as per Figure 5.2), there is no "one size fits all," perfect measure—the best available measure will depend primarily on the research question and the purpose of the project. For example, it makes little sense to use a county-level measure when testing ideas about corruption in certain sectors (defense, health, etc.) given indicators are available at the appropriate levels of analysis and focus on the desired unit. Conversely, if one is interested in a "bird's-eye view" of how well institutions work across countries, it is probably best to use a comprehensive measure that best captures QoG at the systems levels. One should stay away from perception-based measures when testing for short-term effects of policy changes, although such measures are at times more appropriate when testing causes and consequences of public/firm political/economic behavior. Below are a few points to consider when selecting an indicator:

- Clear conceptual definition which is clearly linked to the empirical measurement.
- Transparent process by which units are assessed and ranked. Replicability is a plus if possible.
- Sufficient equivalence across space and time for units in the sample. A "best practice" for the authors of corruption data is to report some type of test of equivalence via confirmatory factor analysis or some type of item response theory (IRT) approach where appropriate.
- Validity for over-time comparisons can increase by using a more specific, single-item indicator, rather than a composite indicator that relies on data standardization. However, if using a standardized composite indicator, make certain that the sample is consistent throughout the time period in question.
- If there is a trade-off between the number of observations and precision, it is oftentimes better in these cases to "sacrifice" observations for a more precise measure that best matches the goals of the research question.
- Finally, measures of QoG should also be able to "get past the gatekeepers" of peer review. If measures appear in high-quality peer-reviewed journals, this is a sign that they have received some/much scrutiny. If one wants to introduce and market a new measure, testing its fitness via peer review is highly encouraged.

GOING FORWARD

Although we have seen the recent boom in governance indicators in recent years, there remains many gaps left to fill. In this final section, while certainly not an exhaustive list, I highlight several thoughts regarding governance indicators moving forward. First, a key weakness of most measures is their lack of availability and/or ability to assess trends over time. In particular, in the absence of experimental data, we need data that can track trends in governance over time in order to investigate which factors cause change. At the risk of sounding mundane, we should simply continue with collecting valid measures that have been more or less accepted by the research and policy communities in coming years, in particular, those based on annual/semi-annual survey data, keeping in mind the limitations of data rescaling. In due time, even those that are limited to a handful of years will develop into a useful time series. *The Oxford Handbook of the Quality of Government* published in 2050 should not have to highlight this issue as prominently as this one.

Two, the emphasis on the meso-level within countries, in which the unit of analysis is focused at the sectoral or institutional level, has been a positive advancement. NGOs, policymakers, and scholars should continue to invest in this path in the future. These data allow for much more precision and specificity to test research questions and to offer specific policy recommendations. However, many of these instruments have been within single countries. A new exception is Transparency International's cross-country measures on corruption risks in defense sectors,[4] which offers a promising way forward. Future measures would thus make a significant contribution if such work were harmonized across a set of countries. For example, we should work to develop standardized civil servant surveys of perceptions and experiences with corruption and related concepts (meritocracy, favoritism, nepotism, etc.) in order to compare patterns of corruption and impartiality within various sectors and institutions across countries. This would open up vast new avenues of research, offer much more fine-grained analyses, and help to better elucidate "best practices." The recent OECD report from 2017 offers several useful pathways forward on this front (van Dooren 2018), shown in Table 5.2.

The table shows that the majority of OECD countries conduct regular or semi-regular employee surveys of those working in the central bureaucracy, while others such as the Netherlands or Slovakia offer sector-level surveys. Others conduct both, such as the U.S. or Chile. The surveys ask questions ranging from job qualifications, to work–life balance, to workplace integrity, discrimination, and effectiveness of the workplace, any of which could be feasibly used to construct fruitful output or input measures of governance. However, comparison across countries is difficult, as each survey (and thus question wording and content) is country-specific, allowing for valid comparison across sectors *within* countries, yet not sectors *across* countries. Moreover, even some OECD countries still do not conduct regular or even semi-regular public administration surveys. Thus, international organizations such as the OECD, and in particular the EU, should push states to adopt standardized portions of the employee surveys in order to compare best practices. For example, we might want to know if antidiscrimination laws in various sectors systematically lead to perceptions and experiences of less discrimination among public sector workers, among other questions. Such surveys offer a highly fruitful way forward.

Three, the recent move to use open data to build objective measures is a promising avenue for future measures of corruption, or corruption risk. Although costly and time

---

[4] http://government.defenceindex.org/#close

Table 5.2 Employee surveys and frequencies in OECD countries

Country	Central public administration survey?	Frequency	Minster/sector–level surveys?
Australia	x	Yearly	
Austria	x	Biannual	
Belgium			
Canada	x	Biannual	
Chile	x	Yearly	x
Czech Rep.	x	Yearly	
Denmark			
Estonia	x	Yearly	
Finland	x	Yearly	
France	x	Biannual	
Germany			
Greece			
Hungary			
Iceland	x	Yearly	
Ireland	x	Irregular	
Israel	x	Yearly	
Italy			
Japan			
Korea	x	Biannual	
Latvia	x	Irregular	
Lux.			
Mexico	x	Yearly	x
Netherlands			x
New Zealand			
Norway	x	> 2 years	
Poland			
Portugal	x	Irregular	
Slovakia			x
Slovenia			
Spain			
Sweden			
Switzerland	x	Yearly	
Turkey			x
UK	x	Yearly	
USA	x	Yearly	x

consuming forms of data collection, these sources have proven highly valuable, given the re-sources of data organization that are available (Fazekas and Kocsis 2020).

Fourth, another possible avenue for future measures of governance and corruption is better understanding the role in which the private sector plays, and if governance practices are similar in the public and private sectors within countries. It would be interesting, for example, to understand how bribery or kickbacks in a country's private sector to achieve a deal or contract relate to such occurrences in the public sector. For example, firm-level surveys that inquire about connections, kickbacks, nepotism, etc. in doing business in the private sector would be of interest. Another relatively uncharted territory is the role of trans-national, superrich individuals and corporations. For example, the wealthiest eight people in the world have as much wealth as the poorest 50% (Elliot 2017), and their outsized footprint allows them many offshore channels for tax avoidance and to exercise immense pressures on governments (Rogers 2018). Due to their monumental wealth and access to world markets, this renders such individuals and corporations highly relevant when assessing governance (Giridharadas 2018). The breathtakingly large (€200 billion) 2017–18 money-laundering corruption scandal involving Danske Bank illustrates this point. The Danish-based bank's local branch in Tallinn, Estonia, through a whistleblower, detected a high-level money-laundering scheme involving the family of Vladimir Putin and the Russian security service (FSB), among others. The scandal involved laundered money from primarily Estonia, Latvia, Russia, Cyprus, and the U.K., yet over 150 countries were listed as the source of the money, in 32 currencies via shell companies that had been established in the U.K., New Zealand, Cyprus, and Moldova. Ultimately, the Danish bank, and its Danish CEO, who resigned, were held responsible. The Organized Crime and Corruption Reporting Project (OCCRP) named Danske Bank the 2018 "actor of the year" which has done the most to advance corruption and organized crime in the world, and which had overlooked this massive corruption for years.[5] Yet how do current measures take such high-level corruption into account? While Russia's reputation among international experts is poor at best, Denmark continues to sit atop the world rankings on most leading indicators, while Estonia has been climbing steadily up the rankings for the past 20 years. Corruption at this level involving super-wealthy individuals across so many countries and entities makes identifying the "source" of the problem as diffi-cult as identifying the origin country of a type of goods with a complex, international supply chain. In this example, while actors from neither Denmark nor Estonia "robbed the bank" so to speak, they did provide a police escort for the getaway car. This begs the question—what would the proper unit of analysis be to help us better understand these phenomena? Here, typical data collection methods such as surveys or open public data sources are unlikely to yield useful information sufficient to build some type of measure, so researchers will have to be creative, yet there are recent precedents in measuring the wealth and influence of the world's wealthy elite (see for example Alvaredo et al. 2013).

Finally, researchers and practitioners should not forget that, within the corruption "in-dustry" (Sampson 2010), there are many actors with numerous motivations for measuring corruption and/or QoG. A caveat for researchers and other good faith actors—we should not believe that our current measures are not useful simply because some political actors claim they are not "actionable." An actionable measure implies that governments or bureaucracies

---

[5] https://www.occrp.org/en/poy/2018/

can improve their score via direct action on one or more of the measurement's items—for example, by instituting an anticorruption agency or making transparent its annual budget. On the one hand, if they are "good faith" actors seeking to improve governance and fight corruption, political actors might genuinely want an overview of the degree to which corruption exists, in which institutions it is most prominent, and specifically what reforms can be made to improve the situation. On the other hand, some political leaders and policymakers, in particular those that seek to maintain the status quo of a corrupt system that benefits them, hail QoG measurements that expose poor governance with as much fanfare as the fossil fuel industry acknowledges measures of CO_2 omissions used to track climate change. For political reasons, they will do what they can to discredit them. Thus, we should not be under the illusion that all actors, in particular those that obtain power in, and benefit from, corrupt systems, are interested in reforms to curb corruption or in measurements that expose poor governance. Such actors will likely exploit such "actionable" measures by making necessary cosmetic changes without altering anything fundamental that puts their status and power in question. Thus, corruption measures that are not directly, but *indirectly* actionable are in fact preferable in many cases. And while perceptions and even experience-based measures might lag behind government action, people will eventually experience and perceive less corruption when there is less corruption.

REFERENCES

Adcock, Robert, and David Collier. 2001. "Measurement Validity: A Shared Standard for Qualitative and Quantitative Research." *American Political Science Review* 95 (3): 529–46.

Ades, Alberto, and Rafael Di Tella. 1999. "Rents, Competition, and Corruption." *American Economic Review* 89 (4): 982–93.

Agnafors, Marcus. 2013. "Quality of government: Toward a more complex definition." *American Political Science Review* 107 (3): 433–45.

Alt, James, and David Lassen. 2008. "Political and Judicial Checks on Corruption: Evidence from American State Governments." *Economics and Politics* 20 (1): 33–61.

Alvaredo, Facundo, Anthony B. Atkinson, Thomas Piketty, and Emmanuel Saez. 2013. "The Top 1 Percent in International and Historical Perspective." *Journal of Economic Perspectives* 27 (3): 3–20.

Arndt, C., & Oman, C. (2010). "Measuring governance. *OECD Development Centre Policy Briefs"* 39: 1.

Bauhr, Monika, and Charron, Nicholas. (2020). The EU as a savior and a saint? Corruption and public support for redistribution. *Journal of European Public Policy* 27 (4): 509–27.

Bauhr, Monika. 2017. "Need or Greed? Conditions for Collective Action against Corruption." *Governance* 30 (4): 561–81.

Bouckaert, Geert, and Steven van de Walle. 2003. "Comparing Measures of Citizen Trust and User Satisfaction as Indicators of "Good Governance": Difficulties in Linking Trust and Satisfaction Indicators." *International Review of Administrative Sciences* 69 (3): 329–43.

Bratsis, Peter. 2003. "The Construction of Corruption, or Rules of Separation and Illusions of Purity in Bourgeois Societies." *Social Text* 21 (4): 9–33.

Bågenholm, Andreas, & Charron, Nicholas. 2020. "Accountable or Untouchable? Electoral accountability in Romanian local elections." *Electoral Studies* 66: 102183.

Charron, Nicholas. 2016. "Do Corruption Measures have a Perception Problem? Assessing the Relationship between Experiences and Perceptions of Corruption among Citizens and Experts." *European Political Science Review* 8 (1): 147–71.

Charron, Nicholas, Carl Dahlström, and Victor Lapuente. 2016. "Measuring Meritocracy in The Public Sector in Europe: A New National and Sub-National Indicator." *European Journal on Criminal Policy and Research* 22 (3): 499–523.

Charron, Nicholas, Lewis Dijkstra, and Victor Lapuente. 2014. "Regional Governance Matters: Quality of Government within European Union Member States." *Regional Studies* 48 (1): 68–90.

Charron, Nicholas, Victor Lapuente, and Bo Rothstein. 2013. *Quality of Government and Corruption from a European Perspective: A Comparative Study on the Quality of Government in EU Regions.* Cheltenham, UK: Edward Elgar Publishing.

Ciziceno, Marco, and Giovanni A. Travaglino. (2019). "Perceived corruption and individuals' life satisfaction: The mediating role of institutional trust." *Social Indicators Research* 141 (2): 685–701.

da Cruz, Nuno Ferreira, António Tavares, Rui Cunha Marques, Susana Jorge, and Luís de Sousa. 2016. "Measuring Local Government Transparency." *Public Management Review* 18 (6): 866–93.

Dahlberg, Stefan, and Maria Solevid. 2016. "Does corruption suppress voter turnout?" *Journal of Elections, Public Opinion and Parties* 26 (4): 489–510.

Dahlström, Carl, Mihály Fazekas, and David E. Lewis. 2019. "Agency Design, Favoritism and Procurement in the United States." QoG Working Paper 2019: 4.

Dahlström, Carl, Jan Teorell, Stefan Dahlberg, Felix Hartmann, Annika Lindberg, and Marina Nistotskaya. 2015. "The QoG Expert Survey Dataset II." University of Gothenburg: The Quality of Government Institute.

De Maria, William. 2010. "Why is the President of Malawi Angry? Towards an Ethnography of Corruption." *Culture and Organization* 16 (2): 145–62.

Donchev, Dilyan, and Gergely Ujhelyi. 2014. "What do Corruption Indices measure?" *Economics and Politics* 26 (2): 309–31.

Elliot, Larry. 2017. "World's Eight Richest People Have Same Wealth as Poorest 50%." *The Guardian*, January 16, 2107. https://www.theguardian.com/global-development/2017/jan/16/worlds-eight-richest-people-have-same-wealth-as-poorest-50

Fan, Simon, Chen Lin, and Daniel Treisman. 2009. "Political Decentralization and Corruption: Evidence from around the World." *Journal of Public Economics* 93 (1–2): 14–34.

Fazekas, Mihály, and Gábor Kocsis. 2020. "Uncovering High-Level Corruption: Cross-National Objective Corruption Risk Indicators Using Public Procurement Data." *British Journal of Political Science*: 50 (1): 155–64.

Ferraz, Claudio, and Fredrico Finan. 2008. "Exposing Corrupt Politicians: The Effects of Brazil's Publicly Released Audits on Electoral Outcomes." *The Quarterly Journal of Economics* 123 (2): 703–45.

Fisman, Raymond, and Miriam Golden. 2017. *Corruption: What Everyone Needs to Know.* New York: Oxford University Press.

Fukuyama, Francis. 2013. "What is Governance?" *Governance* 26 (3): 347–68.

Giridharadas, Anand. 2018. *Winners Take All: The Elite Charade of Changing the World.* New York: Alfred A. Knopf.

Glaeser, E. L., & Saks, R. E. (2006). Corruption in America. *Journal of public Economics* 90 (6–7): 1053–72.

Golden, Miriam, and Lucio Picci. 2005. "Proposal for a New Measure of Corruption, Illustrated with Italian Data." *Economics and Politics* 17 (1): 37–75.

Gutmann, Jerg, Fabio Padovano, and Stefan Voigt (2020). Perception vs. experience: explaining differences in corruption measures using microdata. *European Journal of Political Economy* 65: 101925.

Heidenheimer, Arnold. 2002. "Perspectives on the Perception of Corruption." In *Political Corruption—Concepts and Contexts*, edited by Arnold J. Heidenheimer and Michael Johnston, 3–36. New Brunswick, NJ: Transaction Books.

Heinrich, Finn, and Robin Hodess. 2011. "Measuring Corruption." In *Handbook of Global Research and Practice in Corruption*, edited by Adam Graycar and Russell G. Smith, 18–33. Cheltenham, UK: Edward Elgar Publishing.

Heller, Nathaniel. 2009. "Defining and Measuring Corruption: from Where Have We Come, Where Are We Now, and What Matters for the Future?" In Corruption, Global Security, World Order, edited by Robert I. Rotberg, 47–66. Baltimore, US: Brookings Institution Press.

Heywood, Paul, and Jonathan Rose. 2014. "Close but No Cigar: The Measurement of Corruption." *Journal of Public Policy* 34 (3): 507–29.

Holmberg, Sören, Bo Rothstein, and Naghmeh Nasiritousi. 2009. "Quality of Government: What you Get." *Annual Review of Political Science* 12 (1): 135–61.

Iqbal, Kazi, and Anwar Shah. 2008. "How do the Worldwide Governance Indicators Measure Up?" http://siteresources.worldbank.org/PSGLP/Resources/Howdoworldwidegovernancei ndicatorsmeasureup.pdf

Jensen, Nathan, Qaun Li, and Aminur Rahman. 2010. "Understanding Corruption and Firm Responses in Cross-National Firm-Level Surveys." *Journal of International Business Studies* 41 (9): 1481–504.

Kaufmann, Daniel, Art Kraay, and Massimo Mastruzzi, 2011. "The Worldwide Governance Indicators: Methodology and Analytical Issues." *Hague Journal on the Rule of Law* 3 (2): 220–46.

Kaufmann, Daniel, Art Kraay, and Massimo Mastruzzi. 2009. *Governance Matters VIII: Aggregate and Individual Governance Indicators 1996–-2008*. Washington, DC: The World Bank.

Kaufmann, Daniel, Aart Kraay, and Massimo Mastruzzi. 2007. "Measuring Corruption: Myths and Realities." Africa Region Findings & Good Practice Infobriefs; no. 273. Washington, DC: World Bank. https://openknowledge.worldbank.org/handle/10986/9576

Kaufmann, Daniel, Aart Kraay, and Pablo Zoido-Lobaton. 1999. "Governance Matters (English)." Policy, Research working paper; no. WPS 2196. Washington, DC: World Bank. http://documents.worldbank.org/curated/en/665731468739470954/Governance-matters.

Klitgaard, Robert, Johannes Fedderke, and Kamil Akramov. 2005. "Choosing and Using Performance Criteria." In *High Performance Government: Structure, Leadership, Incentives*, edited by Robert Klitgaard and Paul Light, 407–46. Santa Monica, CA: RAND Corporation.

Knack, Stephen. 2006. *Measuring Corruption in Eastern Europe and Central Asia: A Critique of the Cross-Country Indicators*. Washington, DC: The World Bank.

Knack, Stephen, and Phillip Keefer. 1995. "Institutions and Economic Performance: Cross-Country Tests Using Alternative Institutional Measures." *Economics and Politics* 7 (3): 207–27.

Kurtz, Marcus, and Andrew Shrank. 2007. "Growth and Governance: Models, Measures, and Mechanisms." *Journal of Politics* 69 (2): 538–54.

La Porta, Rafael, Florencio Lopez-de-Silanes, Andrei Shleifer, and Robert Vishny. 1999. "The Quality of Government." *The Journal of Law, Economics, and Organization* 15 (1): 222–79.

Lambsdorff, Johann Graf. 2006. "Measuring Corruption – The Validity and Precision of Subjective Indicators (CPI)". In *Measuring Corruption*, edited by Charles Sampford, Arthur Shacklock, Carmel Connors, and Fredrik Galtung, 81–100. Aldershot: Ashgate.

Mauro, Paolo. 1995. "Corruption and Growth." *The Quarterly Journal of Economics* 110 (3): 681–712.

McMann, Kelly, Daniel Pemstein, Birgette Seim, Jan Teorell, and Staffan I. Lindberg. 2016. "Strategies of Validation: Assessing the Varieties of Democracy Corruption Data." V-Dem Working Paper 23.

Meyer-Sahling, J.-H., Schuster, C., & Mikkelsen, K. S. 2018. *Civil service management in developing countries: What works? Evidence from a survey with 23,000 civil servants in Africa, Asia, Eastern Europe and Latin America.* Report for the UK Department for International Development (DFID), London.

Nardo, Michela, Michaele Saisana, Andrea Saltelli, Stefano Tarantola, Anders Hoffman, and Enric Giovannini. 2005. "Handbook on Constructing Composite Indicators: Methodology and User Guide." OECD Statistics Working Paper STD/DOC 3.

Nistotskaya, Marina. 2009. "Organizational Design of Welfare-Enhancing Public Bureaucracy: A Comparative Analysis of Russia's Regions." PhD diss. Budapest, Hungary: Central European University.

OECD. 2017. "OECD at a Glance 2017." https://www.oecd.org/gov/government-at-a-glance-2017-highlights-en.pdf

Olken, Benjamin. 2007. "Monitoring Corruption: Evidence from a Field Experiment in Indonesia." *Journal of Political Economy* 115 (2): 200–49.

Persson, Torsten, Guido Tabellini, and Francesco Trebbi. 2003. "Electoral Rules and Corruption." *Journal of the European Economic Association* 1 (4): 958–89.

Razafindrakoto, Mireille, and François Roubaud. 2010. "Are International Databases in Corruption Reliable? A Comparison of Expert Opinion Surveys and Household Surveys in Sub-Saharan Africa." *World Development* 38 (8): 1057–69.

Rogers, Stephen. 2018. "Super-rich Pose 'Significant' Tax Risks." *The Irish Examiner*, September 29, 2018. https://www.irishexaminer.com/news/arid-30872286.html

Rohwer, Anja. 2009. "Measuring Corruption: A Comparison between the Transparency International's Corruption Perceptions Index and the World Bank's Worldwide Governance Indicators." *CESifo DICE Report* 7 (3): 42–52.

Roll, Michael. ed. 2014. *The Politics of Public Sector Performance: Pockets of Effectiveness in Developing Countries.* Abingdon, UK: Routledge.

Rose, Richard, and William Mishler. 2010. "Experience versus Perception of Corruption: Russia as a Test Case." *Global Crime* 11 (2): 145–63.

Rothstein, Bo. 2014. "What is the Opposite of Corruption?" *Third World Quarterly* 35 (5): 737–52.

Rothstein, Bo, and Jan Teorell. 2008. "What is Quality of Government? A Theory of Impartial Government Institutions." *Governance* 21 (2): 165–90.

Sampson, Steven. 2010. "The Anti-Corruption Industry: From Movement to Institution." *Global Crime* 11 (2): 261–78.

Seligson, Mitchell. 2006. "The Measurement and Impact of Corruption Victimization: Survey Evidence from Latin America." *World Development* 34 (2): 381–404.

Sharafutdinova, G. (2010). What explains corruption perceptions? The dark side of political competition in Russia's regions. *Comparative Politics*, 42(2), 147–166.

Søreide, Tina. 2006. *Is It Wrong to Rank? a Critical Assessment of Corruption Indices*. Bergen, Norway: Chr. Michelsen Institute.

Stegmueller, Daniel. 2011. "Apples and Oranges? The Problem of Equivalence in Comparative Research." *Political Analysis* 19 (4): 471–87.

Teorell, Jan, Stefan Dahlberg, Sören Holmberg, Bo Rothstein, Anna Khomenko, and Richard Svensson. 2016. *The Quality of Government Standard Dataset*, version Jan 16. University of Gothenburg: The Quality of Government Institute.

Thomas, Melissa. 2010. "What Do the Worldwide Governance Indicators Measure?" *The European Journal of Development Research* 22 (1): 31–54.

Treisman, Daniel. 2007. "What Have We Learned about the Causes of Corruption from Ten Years of Cross-National Empirical Research?" *Annual Review of Political Science* 10 (10): 211–44.

Van Dooren, Wouter. 2018. "Measuring Public Administration: A Feasible Study for Better Comparative Indicators in the E.U. European Commission."

Versteeg, Mila, and Ginsburg, Tom. 2017. "Measuring the Rule of Law: A Comparison of Indicators." *Law and Social Inquiry* 42 (1): 100–37.

Zürn, Michael. 2018. A Theory of Global Governance: Authority, Legitimacy, and Contestation. Oxford: Oxford University Press.

CHAPTER 6

....

DOWN-TO-EARTH. WHAT CAN WE LEARN FROM LOCAL CASE STUDIES?

....

ELIŠKA DRÁPALOVÁ

Introduction
....

IN recent years, the term "quality of government" has emerged as one of the most popular and keenly touted concepts (Rothstein and Teorell 2008). In the economic-political debate, the impartiality and capacity of government institutions are often sustained as prerequisites for governments' legitimacy, sustained economic growth, as well as a universal remedy against financial crises. High quality of government is associated with stronger trust in the political system and government (Rothstein and Uslaner 2005), better delivery of public services (Morris and Klesner 2010), a lower poverty rate, inclusiveness, and equal opportunities for minorities and females (Sundström and Wängnerud 2016). An increasing body of research and chapters in this book emphasize its importance for the equal distribution of resources, economic growth, environmental protection, human and civil rights, the performance of democracy, and even democratic survival.

Despite the increasing relevance of the topic, the local government is seldom mentioned. In 2008, Erlingsson and his colleagues complained that research on corruption is "biased towards cross-section studies" and called for more multilevel approach that "investigate why levels of corruption may vary over time, within a political system" (Erlingsson, Bergh, and Sjölin 2008, 598). Since then, we have seen a radical proliferation of regional-level comparative studies that aim to address corruption and quality of government across different levels of government (see Rönnerstrand and Lapuente 2017; Agerberg 2017; Alexander and Parhizkari 2018; Charron, Dahlström, and Lapuente 2016; Melo, Pereira, and Souza 2014). Although these studies contributed with much-needed knowledge to the field, they generally do not go "below" the regional level and only exceptionally include local government in the multilevel perspective. This lack of consideration of the local level is a significant limitation of the quality of government research agenda and a missed opportunity for reforms.

Local governments are crucial for the implementation of reforms and policies, whereby their performance has a direct impact on the life opportunities of citizens and the vitality of companies. Indeed, one could argue that the consequences of corruption materialize and are overwhelmingly felt at the local level. Corruption in local governments influences the quality of regulation, urban planning, and housing safety (Jiménez, Villoria, and Romero 2012; Jiménez 2009). It influences business entrepreneurship and local economic development (Lapuente and Nistotskaya 2009; Malesky and Taussig 2009). Public money that is pocketed by politicians is lost to local budgets, as evidenced by unpaved streets, missing and obsolete infrastructure, and poor public utilities (Golden and Picci 2005; Abrate et al. 2014). Cities struggling with corrupt governments run larger deficits, deliver fewer public goods, and invest less in more socially productive areas (Bandiera, Prat, and Valletti 2009; Diaz-Cayeros, Estévez, and Magaloni 2016). Citizens migrate from cities with low quality of government to better-governed cities, thus deepening the regional disparities (World Bank 2013). Low quality of government is associated with a vote for populist and anti-establishment parties in subsequent local and regional elections (Agerberg 2017; Vampa 2015). Low quality of local government is associated with low levels of participation, a lack of transparency, and favoritism in the decision-making process (Broms, Dahlström, and Fazekas 2019), as well as high levels of informality and violence (Hilgers and Macdonald 2017; Moncada 2016). Municipalities with a low quality of government present fewer opportunities for women and discriminate more against minorities (Sundström and Wängnerud 2016).

This QoG "farsightedness" also disregards that the performance of governments and corruption largely vary within countries, as well as among them. Recent research reports indeed highlight a considerable subnational variation in quality of and access to public services (Herrera 2017a; 2017b), level of transparency (da Cruz et al. 2016),[1] diffusion of clientelist practices (Weitz-Shapiro 2014; Mares, Muntean, and Petrova 2017) and corruption (Klašnja 2015; 2016; Drapalova 2016; Frye, Reuter, and Szakonyi 2014) across cities in the US, Europe, Asia and Latin America. Moreover, current theories face difficulties in explaining this wide subnational variation captured by the growing number of studies. This yet unexplained variation shows the limitation of cross-country studies and points to the potential for a fruitful combination between the quality of government research agenda and the bottom-up focus on cities and local governments.

This chapter adds the local government to this growing subnational and multilevel research agenda on the QoG. This chapter focuses on cities, municipalities, towns, and villages and explores how local government case studies contribute to understanding the factors that determine the quality of government and corruption. In particular, it shows where the local-level case studies have improved existing theories, and provided alternative mechanisms and new venues for research. Considering that local government provides a large share of public goods, spending and hiring, as well as the methodological benefits of studying institutions at the subnational level, the time seems ripe to include the local level in the QoG agenda and systematically compare findings from cities within and across countries.

The remainder of this chapter is organized as follows. The first section describes the local government and its rising importance. The second section makes a case for studying the

---

[1] Several Transparency International's national chapters provide indicators of transparency at the level of municipalities, see for example Transparency International's national chapters of Slovakia, Portugal, Spain, and Ukraine.

quality of government in a subnational setting, emphasizing in particular the potential of a subnational focus in uncovering new theoretical explanations and mechanisms. It also shows some methodological advantages of studying corruption in a local context and highlights possible problems such as a lack of reliable and comparable indicators disaggregated below the national level. The third and fourth sections respectively deal with assessing the variation in the quality of government locally, and provide some explanations for the causes of this variation, drawing on insights from both quantitative and qualitative empirical analysis, mainly—but not exclusively—from Southern and Eastern European cities. The final part outlines an agenda of empirical and theoretical questions that deserve attention in future research. As such, the chapter not only offers new evidence on the given topic but also provides a glance into how future works can further improve existing knowledge.

WHAT IS THE LOCAL-LEVEL FOCUS ON THE QUALITY OF GOVERNMENT?

In 2008, the share of urban population reached 50% and according to the UN by 2050 more than 70% of the world's population will be urban. This rapid global urbanization trend runs in parallel with the rise of the decentralized provision of essential public services in many jurisdictions (Vampa 2016; Keating 1998). This political decentralization and the associated problems have increasingly directed the comparative politics focus at the local level (Giraudy, Moncada, and Snyder 2019). The subnational focus is gaining prominence in electoral studies (Dandoy and Schakel 2013; Hooghe, Marks, and Schakel 2010), in economic development theories (Storper 2013; Florida 2014; Moretti 2012), as well as in social movements literature (Jacobsson 2015). However, only a few studies with an urban focus primarily deal with the quality of government (da Cruz and Marques 2019).

Most importantly, the lack of attention paid to cities has resulted in limited conceptual work on how to define the quality of government at the municipal level. So far, only a handful of researchers have attempted to define the local quality of government and how to assess it (da Cruz and Marques 2019; Huberts and Six 2012; Transparency International 2014 among others). Identifying the most fitting definition of the quality of local government is beyond the scope of this chapter. This chapter adopts the definition of quality of government offered by Rothstein and Teorell (2008) as the impartial exercise of public power. Rothstein and Teorell define impartiality as "when implementing laws and policies, government officials shall not take anything into consideration about the citizen/case that is not beforehand stipulated in the policy or the law" (Rothstein and Teorell 2008, 170). Additionally, the lion's share of subnational measurement efforts stops at the regional level (Golden and Picci 2005; Charron, Dijkstra, and Lapuente 2015), even though cities are the oldest political configurations that predate nation-states.

Despite national specificities, subnational governments comprise legislative, executive, or administrative units, which are generally organized into regional, provincial, or municipal levels. Cities, towns, and districts are usually the lowest level of political organization, closest to the ground. Local governments mostly provide basic public services, maintain infrastructure, and oversee the implementation of laws and reforms enacted at higher levels.

The process of political decentralization, along with subnational political dynamics, has marked an increase in power of regional and local governments in Europe and across the world (Keating 1998). Local governments have gained significant powers in federal countries as well as previously centralized states like those in Eastern Europe. Political decentralization is associated with greater power, responsibilities, and spending. For example, in Spain, subnational spending accounts for 23% of national GDP (Khalil and Navarro 2012). However, the greater resources (own taxes) and competencies (procurement) that this brings endows greater responsibilities—as well as opportunities for mismanagement and corruption.

Why We Should Study the Quality
of Government at the Local Level

Theoretically, local government is seen as a domain in which politicians are in direct contact with citizens, offering citizens greater control over politicians and thus corruption in politics (Kriesi and Erlach 2007). Local communities are places where bottom-up collective action—which is vital for anticorruption endeavors—takes place. However, empirical findings seem to contradict or at least fall short of confirming these propositions. An increasing number of studies demonstrate the greater cohesiveness of interest groups, the low effectiveness of civil society, and the relative weakness of the government. Local governments appear to be at a higher risk of corruption, even in countries with low corruption levels (Bergh et al. 2016). For example, many of the recent corruption scandals in Spain involved regional and local politicians and entrepreneurs (Jiménez, Villoria, and Romero 2012; Jiménez, García-Quesada, and Villoria 2014).

This higher vulnerability is accounted for by a combination of local political and institutional factors such as the strong availability of resources (real estate, public procurement), proximity between actors, and the greater discretion of local bureaucrats who deal with implementation and regulation (Chubb 1982). Local governments often play a prominent role in managing the delivery of services to citizens, including for registration and licensing, road maintenance, city planning, and public utilities. In many countries, local bodies also deliver core services, such as public security, healthcare, and education, and they can hold cross-cutting responsibilities for economic development or poverty alleviation. Moreover, politicians usually relate to particular places for their electoral support, where they make contact with their followers (Weitz-Shapiro 2014; Eisenstadt and Roniger 1984). Local governments have a lower probability of audit, closer ties between actors, and lower capacity of local administration to effectively scrutinize their operations (especially the smaller towns). Except for capital and large cities, the media scrutiny is weaker, as well as the activity of watchdog organizations and NGOs. Research by Filipe Campante and Quoc-Anh Do (2014) shows that US cities situated further from the capital have less media scrutiny and higher corruption.

Leaving aside the theoretical reasons, there are several methodological, and policy motivations for studying corruption across municipalities. Perhaps the main reason for the rediscovery of local government in comparative politics is the availability of a large number and diversity of cases (John 2009). This large number of cases makes cities a quantitative scholar's cornucopia. The availability of data at the local level, which was previously a limiting factor, has considerably improved with the increasing decentralization of service provision and strengthening of local democracy.[2] Especially with open data government initiatives, administrations release substantial data on expenditure, procurement, and budgets that can be used to trace corruption and can be matched with other public and privately collected datasets (for example Broms, Dahlström, and Fazekas 2019; Riera et al. 2013). This combination of different government data allows linking corruption with other social, political, and economic phenomena. Public opinion surveys are increasingly sampling and providing information at the city level and allow for comparisons between many cities (see Urban Audit 2015).

Additionally, the large number of cities allows for larger samples, greater variation, and more precise specification, which is of utmost importance for quantitative analysis. This large number is a considerable advantage compared with national-level studies, where there is only a limited number of cases. A large-N makes it easier to find control variables or match cases. Experimental research, discontinuity studies, and difference-in-difference analysis have recently been extensively used at the municipal level. Large research projects conduct surveys in villages and settlements and run field experiments (some examples include Mares, Muntean, and Petrova 2016; Olken 2005). Historical borders of empires or arbitrarily set thresholds (population or municipal size) for municipal funding and salary schemes are an excellent opportunity for external treatment in discontinuity studies (see Klašnja 2015). Perhaps the most known is the random distribution of audits in Brazilian municipalities that have been used in many quasi-experimental research design studies (see Mondo 2016; Ferraz and Finan 2011).

A large number of cities is an even greater boon to the qualitative researcher, whereby the embeddedness of cities in national institutional contexts offers good possibilities of intranational comparison among cities, an analysis that allows for full control of national policies or factors related to political culture (Sellers 2002). More cases allow for a more precise and thoughtful case selection based on the variety of independent and dependent variables, increasing the control and rigor of the case study (Gerring and Cojocaru 2016; Nielsen 2014). Comparative analysis of cities within the same national context is a strategy that conveniently allows the researcher to control for a number of political and institutional variables.

At city level, policy and its implementation are close to the institutional political process and frequently extend far beyond formal institutions into the realm of civil society. Qualitative comparison of cities and villages is sensitive to cultural backgrounds and informal institutions (Chubb 1982; Graham, Desai, and McFarlane 2013), a sensitivity that makes cities an excellent site for ethnography and other qualitative and interpretative techniques. Numerous excellent ethnographic studies deal with the quality of government, informality, crime, and corruption in European and US cities and towns (see Chubb 1982; Verdery 2003; Pardo 1996; Menes 2003; Muir and Gupta 2018; Glaeser and Goldin 2007; Riordan 1995; Schneider and Schneider 2013).

For example, the ethnographic work by Judith Chubb (1981, 1982) traces the relationship between local economic structure, social relations, and political patronage in Naples and

---

[2] For example, Transparency International, OECD, or Doing Business Survey by World Bank all have local government chapters and indicators.

Palermo. Chubb showed with great precision how local political machines have used different strategies to target different electoral constituencies and social groups. She found that, whereas the citizens' support was bought off by the discretionary offer of scarce public jobs and subsidies, local businesses were disciplined by much less resource-intensive means, mainly by discretionary applied regulation. Schneider and Schneider (2005, 2013) focus on the relationship between what they called "industrialization without development" and clientelism in Sicily. Although they do not deal directly with the quality of government but with state capture and mafia, their research provides important mechanisms that link the formation of mass political parties with intense industrial development, internal migration, and clientelism in Sicilian towns and countryside. Katherine Verdery (2003) mapped the relationship between economic and political transformation in postsocialist Romania and the persistence of clientelism. These books have demonstrated the importance of a deep understanding of the local social, economic, and political interaction; they have also provided mechanisms that lead not only into vicious circles but also out of them.

The local level has strong potential for a combination of both methods within the mix-method framework, namely combining quantitative and qualitative data collection and analysis to reinforce the final findings (Lieberman 2005). This combination extends beyond simple triangulation of findings and uses a range of methods as complementary parts of research design (Seawright and Gerring 2008; Seawright 2016). Despite this double advantage, studies combining a within- and cross-country focus are rather scarce.

Finally, the local approach also offers more practical outcomes that can be used in the public policy design, implementation, and evaluation process of anticorruption reforms. Cities provide the opportunity to observe the implementation and performance of laws within the same institutional setting. Accordingly, the subnational focus can contribute to a body of knowledge that could potentially be useful to policymakers and those who seek to improve the implementation of reforms.

WHAT WE CAN LEARN FROM STUDYING THE QUALITY OF GOVERNMENT IN CITIES

While many have highlighted the advantages of subnational comparisons holding "things" constant, the subnational focus also enables scholars to generate new research questions and theories, as well as learning more about processes and mechanisms. The local level provides "a suitable balance between reducing the complexity to uncover causal mechanisms and providing the contextual richness of the case" (Pierre 2005, 456). The strength of cities lies not only in numbers, but also the fact that cities are, above all, a complex set of interactions. At the local level, different actors (politicians, businesspeople, bureaucrats, and civil society) must interact directly with each other on a regular basis, and in ways that are readily observable (Stone 2005).

Adopting a subnational perspective on the quality of government can uncover new research gaps. Researchers focusing on the subnational dimension have found a surprising intercity variation for a wide range of governmental outcomes, which established theories struggle to account for. Whereas the institutional framework, cultural, and administrative theories would expect an even distribution of outcomes, cities show remarkable variation in the quality of public services (Herrera 2017a; Lu 2015; Drapalova 2017), transparency (Dragos and Neamtu 2013; Spáč, Voda, and Zagrapan 2018), administrative performance (Parrado, Dahlström, and Lapuente 2018; Urban Audit 2015), clientelism (Weitz-Shapiro 2014; Mares, Muntean, and Petrova 2017), and corruption (Klašnja 2015; Frye, Reuter, and Szakonyi 2014). This puzzling variation points to existing gaps in the literature and demonstrates the opportunity for scholars to generate new explanations.

An important contribution of this subnational focus to the QoG research agenda has been theories of collective action (Ostrom 1990; Ostrom, Walker, and Gardner 1992; Persson, Rothstein, and Teorell 2013). Collective action theories have been critical within the QoG research agenda in terms of highlighting the social nature of corruption while pointing to the limitations of principal–agent theory (PA). Collective action theories that focus on the local level have returned academic attention to important factors, such as informal arrangements and local coalitions, as well as the role played by nonstate actors such as local political factions (Auerbach 2017), social movements (instead Verdenicci and Hough 2015), and businesses in providing public goods and leading the anticorruption efforts in areas where the state is weak or inexistent (Börzel and Risse 2016). Additionally, city-level case studies have brought greater awareness and understanding of how the quality of government and corruption operates in a multilevel setting (Piattoni 2010). Do the mechanisms of corruption differ across levels? The local level approach is better equipped to incorporate a multilevel perspective that takes into account the interactions between national and subnational factors. The context-sensitivity of subnational approaches "prompts building theories that are aware of scope conditions on which they operate" (Giraudy, Moncada, and Snyder 2019, 13).

However, "cities are most rewarding for comparative research that can take the analysis towards causal explanations" (Pierre 2005, 449). At the city level, one can observe close linkages between norms, institutions and politics, and policy outcomes. Focusing on corrupt local government in the otherwise well-functioning system serves to highlight the weak points of anticorruption policies, whereas "pockets of good government" in areas with high corruption can elucidate new mechanisms or a specific set of conditions that enable reforms. The following subsections will focus on three main explanatory factors and show how the subnational level has contributed to clarifying or uncovering the causal mechanisms. The common understanding is that the quality of (local) government is affected, on the one hand, by the resources available (natural and financial resources, inequality, political power), and on the other, by political (party) competition, and other more contextual or historical factors such as social capital (civil society strength, organized economic actors) that constrain the discretionary use of these resources (Mungiu-Pippidi 2015).

Resources for (anti-)corruption

The subnational level is an excellent focal point to examine the link between the quality of government and financial resources. It is relatively well established that corruption negatively affects public finances (Caamaño-Alegre et al. 2011; Craw 2008). However, does the quality of government depend on the size of the budget and financial support, or is

it dependent upon the management of resources? In Europe and elsewhere, municipal finances still rely on the central transfers that are intended to compensate for possible inequalities among cities. This budgetary reliance helps to insulate the effect of finance on
a range of indicators of government performance and administration. Existing research
shows that the level of corruption is not affected only by the level of funding, as much as
what the budget is spent on—whether improving public services or expensive and un-
necessary public works like empty airports, disproportionate sports stadiums, or fast-speed
trains to nowhere (García-Quesada and Jiménez 2019). In Italy, although corruption is
higher mostly in more impoverished communities concentrated in the southern part of
the country, many wealthy cities also suffer from corruption, for example, Milan—Italy's
economic center, was the epicenter of *Tangentopoli* (della Porta and Vannucci 2012)—or
Rome, known for the *Mafia Capitale* scandal (Pezzi 2019). During the building boom on
the Spanish coast and in large cities, before the economic crisis, many wealthy cities in
Spain faced corruption scandals related to real-estate speculation (Jiménez, Villoria, and
Romero 2012). By contrast, many relatively poor cities perform well in terms of controlling
corruption, such as Ragusa in Sicily (Drapalova 2016).

Moreover, natural-resource endowment is another important factor determining the
level of corruption in cities. While most of the subnational research supports the "resource
course" hypothesis, it also shows why the association between resources and quality of government has not always translated well at the subnational level. On the one hand, the research shows that when natural resources are unequally distributed across the territory,
these extra assets influence political competitiveness at the municipal level by providing incumbents with additional resources. Incumbents can spend these extra funds on patronage
in the form of public employment, social subsidies, and vote-buying (Bertholini, Pereira,
and Renno 2018). On the other hand, Monteiro and Ferraz (2014) found in the Brazilian
case that regional laws mitigated this effect, setting limits on the use of this type of revenue
for public contracts. Interestingly, the lack of resources and isolation can also have the opposite effect and produce a more controlled distribution of resources and local cooperation
(Drapalova 2016; Petrovici 2017). The lack of external interference and the need to share
scarce resources can help to build dense cooperative networks that organize themselves as
alternative public service suppliers and additional accountability mechanisms (Petrovici
and Simionca 2011).

Scholars have also highlighted the demand side of the quality of government and included factors like the socioeconomic level of citizens, unemployment, and education. Low
socioeconomic status and high employment are associated with lesser citizen engagement
and reduced transparency (Tavares and da Cruz 2018). At the national level, the size of
the middle class is considered as an essential factor driving the quality of government. Yet
Rebeca Weitz-Shapiro (2012) has shown that socioeconomic well-being in cities is only relevant if parties are vulnerable to middle-class claims. Moreover, while more corrupt countries also have higher levels of inequality, at the local level there are numerous examples of
highly unequal cities that perform well or have substantively improved in controlling corruption (Moncada 2016; Conger 2014; Herrera 2017b; Drapalova 2016). Comparing the income levels of Spanish municipalities, both corrupt (Majadahonda and Pozuelo de Alarcón)
and clean cities (Alcobendas, San Cugat) feature among the cities with the highest income
inequality (Drapalova 2016).

Political competition and electoral accountability

In democratic systems, electoral accountability and interparty competition figure as widely accepted explanations driving governmental performance and efficiency (Bardhan and Mookherjee 2007; Melo, Pereira, and Souza 2014; Schnell 2018). These theories broadly argue that when electoral pressure is high and incumbents face possible defeat, they are more receptive to citizens' demands, more cooperative with the opposition, and more careful not to deplete public resources. The subnational studies confirm the electoral competition theory. Using data on 234 South African municipalities, Daniel Berliner (2017) found that political competition can generate endogenous incentives for higher transparency and compliance even under conditions of weak capacity and enforcement. Likewise, municipalities with more competition also provide more public goods (Besley and Burgess 2002; Kroth, Larcinese, and Wehner 2016).

However, municipal studies show the limits of political competition and point to other factors that are at least as important as holding competitive elections (Costas-Pérez, Solé-Ollé, and Sorribas-Navarro 2012; Esaiasson and Muñoz 2014; Jiménez, Quesada and Villoria 2014). In political systems with high levels of corruption, party competition and the electoral accountability mechanisms might also not perform as expected. Instead of policy preferences, votes might signal support for a local chief or be traded for private goods (Manzetti and Wilson 2007). Paradoxically, in cities with high corruption, elections can transform into an auction for votes, whereby citizens trade their votes for goods or local investment (Anduiza, Gallego, and Muñoz 2013; Muñoz, Anduiza, and Gallego 2016; Fernandez-Vazquez, Barberá, and Rivero 2016). Rebeca Weitz-Shapiro (2012) shows in her sample of Argentinian cities that the socioeconomic composition of the local electorate interacts with the electoral competition. Competitive elections push mayors to opt out from the clientelistic distribution of public resources only when a sizable middle-class constituency is also present and able to switch to an alternative party. However, electoral competition increases clientelism when the size of the poor population is large. In some local constituencies, citizens are willing to condone corrupt mayors if they deliver or provide public services and infrastructure (Esaiasson and Muñoz 2014; Anduiza, Gallego, and Muñoz 2013). Figueiredo, Hidalgo, and Kasahara (2012) conducted a randomized field experiment in Brazil and found that corruption is filtered by the ideology, whereby the left-wing candidates charged with corruption suffer higher losses on average. Ferraz and Finan's (2011) well-known study of randomized audits in Brazilian municipalities show that the electoral punishment of mayors was stronger when information was publicly disclosed.

Although interparty competition remains important, attention has slowly shifted to other related factors like the intensity of elite rotation, political alternatives, and the structure of cleavages within local elites, ethnic cleavages, or multilevel party dynamics (Klašnja 2015; Broms, Dahlström, and Fazekas 2019; Nye and Vasilyeva 2015). Nye and Vasilyeva (2015) show that the intensity of political competition influences the type of accountability mechanisms and their limits. The authors find that when the competition is fierce, informal mechanisms of accountability (local political pressure) are less efficient than formal institutions. The vertical accountability from the central and regional government is an important factor, as well as how embedded political elites are. National parties frequently collect votes in cities by strategically distributing subsidies, aid, and strategic investment. Adam Auerbach's (2017) study of the effect of party networks on the public goods delivery in Indian slums discovers that slums more embedded within local party networks have better infrastructure and access to services. Lili Tsai observed a similar mechanism in her groundbreaking book on Chinese villages (Tsai 2007). These results also translate to the European context, whereby politicians with links to a particular local community tend to redistribute more benefits to such communities or target specific communities (Mares, Muntean, and Petrova 2017).

The personal characteristics of leaders, education, and professional trajectory can also influence the local quality of government (Besley, Pande, and Rao 2012). Where other than at the local level would personal characteristics and leadership skills make a difference? The research finds a difference in performance and corruption depending on the gender and education of mayors. Municipalities run by female mayors have better economic performance, higher public spending, and more transparency (Tavares and da Cruz 2018; Suzuki and Avellaneda 2018). However, many questions remain unanswered: Is personal integrity a sufficient condition in fragile institutional settings? How does leadership interact with the political competition? For example, in municipalities in Madrid and Catalonia, it was the strong local leader with majoritarian political support who initiated administrative reforms to increase the local government capacity of control corruption (Drapalova and Di Mascio 2020).

Other sources of accountability: Informal institutions, social capital, and business associations

Besides electoral competition and formal checks and balances, there are many other possible accountability mechanisms. Especially at the city level, informal institutions, social norms, and collective action can potentially play an even greater role. Indeed, a subnational focus has significantly contributed to consolidating the research on the link between social capital and quality of government (Rothstein and Uslaner 2005). For many—including Robert Putnam and his groundbreaking book investigating the effects of social capital on regional government performance in Italy—social capital has roots in local communities. According to Putnam, Leonardi, and Nanetti (1994) and subsequent research, higher social capital activates citizens to engage politically, control public servants, and consequently to increase the likelihood that corruption is detected and punished. Studies including social capital in their analysis in different cities and localities mostly confirm Putnam's results (Bigoni et al. 2013; Guiso, Sapienza, and Zingales 2004; Solt 2004, Bandiera 2003).

A local focus also enables us to delve deeper and further in history to uncover the origin of social capital and solve the conundrum of the direction of causality between social capital and quality of government. Bigoni et al. (2013) ran experiments in southern and northern Italian cities and argue that conflicts and wars play a role in creating social ties. Cities that were attacked and besieged by an external army in the past created strong bonds within communities because they were forced to collaborate. Other studies point to the socioeconomic organization of communities and private ownership as the origins of social capital. Solt's (2004) historical analysis of Italian land ownership structure shows that social capital is higher in communities with small landowners. Guiso, Sapienza, and Zingales (2004) provide a mechanism through which social capital generated a long time ago can be transmitted across generations and influence current public policy outcomes. Nevertheless, there is also research contradicting the deep historical roots of social capital, showing that even in cities with high criminality, corruption, and low social capital, effective civil society action and better government performance are possible (Conger 2014; Gunnarson 2014; Chubb 1982). Also, Dinesen and Sönderskov argue that government corruption is a key factor undermining social capital (see Dinesen and Mannemar Sønderskov, in this volume).

Moreover, studies on local community power structures provide a much-needed mechanism to social capital theory. Building on collective action theories, these studies investigate the community power structure and embeddedness of local elites in the community (Auerbach 2017; Herrera 2017a; Lu 2015; Petrovici and Simionca 2011). In this sense, these studies connect horizontal mobilization with vertical administrative structures. According to Lily Tsai, Chinese local leaders embedded in socioeconomic structures of local communities are more effectively pressured to deliver better governance for everyone, regardless of the type of accountability regime (Tsai 2007). Lu (2015) shows the negative impact of migration on Chinese local community structures. Locally focused studies have also described the dark side of social capital, warning that unhealthily close connections between politicians and economic actors lead to collusive networks, capture, or inefficient and partial use of resources (Frye, Reuter, and Szakonyi 2014, 2018). This situation is more likely in cities and villages, where contacts between local political and economic elites are particularly close.

In the debate about the impact of organized societal actors on the quality of public institutions, economic actors and business associations rarely appear as possible drivers of good governance (Dávid-Barrett 2019; Börzel and Risse 2016). While the quality of government is regarded as a fundamental condition for the vitality of the business sector and the local economic conditions (measured as the number of companies per capita) (Nistotskaya and Cingolani 2016; Nistotskaya, Charron, and Lapuente 2015), only a few studies set out to unpack the mechanisms between local firms and quality of government (see Malesky and Taussig 2009; Zhu and Zhang 2016). Most current theoretical treatments view business associations as rent-seekers: special interest groups that promote their own interests (Kartner and Warner 2015). Business–political collusion is frequently reported in media and scholarly research as a source of corruption and low quality of government (Fazekas 2017). Mares et al. (2017, 2016) show that companies act as brokers for the local patronage system. Frye Reuter and Szakonyi (2018, 2014) investigate the role of employers as the brokers of party machines, mobilizing and intimidating voters. Their research finds that Russian cities with a prominent employer—so-called single-company towns—have a lower quality of government and a higher incidence of voter intimidation and clientelism.

However, not all economic actors benefit from corrupt networks (loyalty) or quit the market (exit). Economic actors such as international investors or small firms are also victims of corrupt politicians and administration. Under certain circumstances, these companies decide to act on their economic and political environment (voice). Firms excluded from clientelistic networks, newcomers, and especially SMEs suffer under corrupt governments due to excessive or uncertain regulation, a waste of organizational resources in dealing with administration, and deficient public infrastructure, which increases their costs (Hedberg 2015). Accordingly, in many cities one can witness locally organized businesses that demand enforcement, better regulation, and even voluntary cooperation to reduce corruption (Drapalova 2016; Conger 2014). Research in a number of developing countries reveals a broad range of benign functions and activities undertaken by business associations, many of which focus on government performance and public services (Börzel and Deitelhoff 2018;

Doner and Schneider 2000; Dávid-Barrett 2019; Conger 2014). These positive functions address crucial development such as strengthening the regulatory framework, facilitating vertical and horizontal coordination, reducing information costs, enforcing rules, policing, and shielding businesses from corrupt civil servants (Markus 2014; Duvanova 2014). The associations that engage in these activities tend to have high member density, valuable se-lective benefits, and effective internal control mechanisms and mediation of member inter-ests. When local businesses are organized within the association, their coordination can significantly increase information circulation and constrain the opportunities for corrup-tion within the business community (Drapalova 2016).

FRAMEWORK: MULTILEVEL PARTY DYNAMICS AND LOCAL ECONOMIC ORGANIZATION

This section presents examples of how the focus on local government can contribute to the QoG research agenda. Concretely, this section focuses on cities with better-than-expected quality of government in regions and countries with high corruption and inefficient govern-ment, and attempts to provide clues and elucidate mechanisms of change and resilience. This approach is illustrated with examples from Southern and Eastern Europe.

Perhaps the most intriguing aspect of the subnational variation presented earlier is the existence of cities that are exemplars of transparency, quality of government, and public in-novation in countries and regions with a high incidence of corruption. In other words, in regions plagued by corruption we find "islands of good government" with a high quality of government, which offer sites for policy learning. We find these surprising pockets of good government in Sicily in the city of Ragusa and Lecce in the Southern Italian region of Apulia, as well as, in Spain (in Alcobendas), and in Romania (Cluj and Sibiu) (Drapalova 2016, 2018). These "pockets of good government" (Roll 2014), "deviant cases" (Gerring and Cojocaru 2016) or "good apples on bad trees" (Drapalova 2016) might prove fruitful sites for under-standing how to potentially break the vicious circles of corruption and create resilient bur-eaucracies. Uncovering the mechanisms and conditions under which these cities manage to control corruption despite being placed in countries with a low quality of government can add valuable contributions to the current scholarship on quality of government.

From the cross- and within-country comparative case study of similar pairs of cities in Italy, Spain, and Romania, two factors emerge that seem especially relevant for controlling corruption and the quality of government, namely multilevel party dynamics and local eco-nomic organizations that influence access to resources (Drapalova 2018). In political systems with corruption and clientelism (like Romania and parts of Italy), the local leaders' access to funds is highly dependent on the political connections to higher levels of government. In other words, if the incumbent party matches that of the central government, access to public funds and vertical transfers might be easier. Connected political leaders might feel little pressure to deliver services, build a meritocratic administration, organize procurement competitively, or restrain their appetite for rent-seeking, as their access to resources is pro-vided by the central government. By contrast, parties in opposition or political outsiders might have their access to state resources reduced. This resource scarcity and the political vulnerability from above push the "disconnected" local representatives to seek more sustainable and efficient solutions to the provision of public services and search for broader constituencies or outside allies to finance their policies and programs. The Italian city of Ragusa and Sibiu and Cluj-Napoca in Romania are not only islands of good government but also strongholds of political opposition. They were all found to be governed by opposition parties, ethnic minority parties, or political newcomers. This political vulnerability from above and the subsequent resource access disadvantage were necessary factors that increased the control and pushed the incumbents to seek alternative sources of finance and find efficient policy solutions (Drapalova 2018).

The second relevant factor was the role and organization of local economic actors in determining both the local administrative capacity and the type of public services that the city delivers. For cities that are coping with financial uncertainty, the business sector becomes one of the possible—if not the most likely—government allies (Savitch and Kantor 2002). Cabria, Magnier, and Pereira (2018) show that municipal political leaders with financial difficulties regard the business sector as a crucial ally. In the current phase of centrally promoted austerity policies and political decentralization, local business taxes and contributions form an increasingly important part of local budgets. Large companies might contribute large sums to municipal coffers, but they also have more power to influence government and the content of local policies. International and more mobile companies can also more effectively resist extortive pressures from the government without the need to coordinate (Frye 2002; Frye, Reuter, and Szakonyi 2014). Smaller companies, however, need to coordinate to influence the local political agenda.

Locally organized SMEs can successfully counteract extractive governments, police their members, and coordinate the provision of vital public goods. Local business organizations fulfill multiple roles that potentially limit the opportunities for corruption. Firstly, they control and discipline their members from rent-seeking, such as by seeking unilateral deals with politicians and bribing administration (Ostrom 1990). Second, business organizations act as a sort of shield against extractive public administration, providing up-to-date information and legal assistance (Drapalova 2016; Duvanova 2014). Third, they can be a sort of alternative policy platform and act as a trustee and intermediary between the public administration and individual firms. Powerful and encompassing local associations can exert a decisive influence over the government, and their diverse membership base limits their possible particularistic or narrow tendencies (Drapalova 2016).

Moreover, the local economic structure and organization can influence the governance style. Local business organizations in many cases actively push for transparency and commitment to administrative impartiality on behalf of their members (Drapalova 2016). The local IT and international hi-tech sector in Cluj are responsible for the city's implementation of open government initiative and transparent procurement. Foreign investors in Sibiu (mainly German) have brought with them a German public administration model and bargaining. An active community of export-oriented SMEs in Ragusa have self-organized a sort of private enforcement mechanism among the local businesses, imposing antimafia certificates and controls. While competing for local business with other municipalities in Madrid, Alcobendas has reformed its municipal administrative structure and simplified procurement procedures (Drapalova 2016). Business self-regulation leading to positive pressure on local administration has been established in municipalities in Mexico (Conger 2014) and Venezuela (Moncada 2016). These findings signal the existence of similar dynamics in the subnational government outside Europe. Dávid-Barrett (2019) found business-political coordination that aimed to reduce corruption in the international sphere, while Börzel and Risse (2016) observed these semi-private arrangements in parts of the world where states and governments fail to provide essential goods, security or infrastructure.

This section has shown that other organized actors such as businesses and local entrepreneurs counterbalance and check political power. Thus, the organization of business interests at the subnational level should also be part of the QoG debates. Moreover, research should pay more attention to how local government finances the provision of necessary public goods and what consequences different national and subnational finance schemes have for the quality of government and the level of corruption. Decentralization without financial autonomy makes local governments vulnerable to political pressures from the central government.

CONCLUSIONS

In most countries, local governments manage a large portion of the public procurement, planning and licensing, which are considered risk zones for corruption. Municipalities deliver core public services and thus local government quality has far-reaching consequences for economic development and citizens' well-being. The government decentralization and rise of multilevel governance in Europe and the fast urbanization in Latin America and Asia—which exacerbates existing urban social, economic, and political challenges—have contributed to the increasing interest in the impact and causes of quality of government in cities. Despite the crucial responsibilities and the role that the cities perform within the political and administrative system, remarkably little attention has been paid to the local level in the QoG research agenda. This chapter has argued for cities as a useful unit of analysis for studying the quality of government. Urban case studies provide rich empirical data that enables more detailed, controlled, and context-sensitive comparisons and analysis. Local case studies have the potential to inform and amend existing theories and provide more precision and detail to the mechanisms and arguments compared with national case studies. Within-country comparisons better isolate the effect of institutions, uncover the basis for collective action, and allow explicitly establishing scope conditions. By adopting a more multilevel approach to studying local government, we can better grasp the interaction between national and local factors.

Subnational studies have already provided some valuable contributions to existing theories on the drivers and effects of quality of government, as well as more fine-grained information about the mechanisms and processes. While such studies confirm the importance of political factors such as party competition, they also point to other factors—such as the structure of local cleavages, elite rotation, and multilevel party alliances—that influence the government quality and administrative capacity at the regional and national level. Moreover, in the wake of massive societal mobilization against corruption and the rise to power of despots and populist leaders, social movements and anticorruption protests should be better included in the current research. It is important to understand under which conditions citizens mobilize for cleaner government and what drives them. Adopting a local focus can help to solve empirical, theoretical puzzles of why and under which conditions citizens mobilize to punish corruption, when they protest, and when they re-elect corrupt despots.

While the influence of civil society is part of the QoG research agenda, local studies suggest that growing efforts to understand corruption and the quality of government should not ignore organized economic interests. By contrast, efforts aiming to strengthen intermediary institutions responsible for interest aggregation and representation can make positive contributions to local governance, and push the government to adopt reforms to limit corruption. Some of the examples presented here also weigh into the debate on the role of business associations and the influence of economic actors on the quality of government by showing that coordinated local markets can be associated with lower municipal corruption.

We still need to better understand whether local government quality qualitatively differs from the national quality of government. Is the quality of government perceived differently at the national and local level? Are the perceptions driven by different factors like efficiency, type, or form of public policies? Among the empirical and theoretical issues that deserve attention in future research are empirical assessment of whether the factors that drive the quality of government in cities are applicable across government levels: in other words, to uncover the scope conditions of bottom-up generated theories.

Although technology becomes an increasingly salient focal point to study the effect of digital capabilities and the quality of government, the relation between technology and anticorruption has not yet established reliable conclusions. The potential of information technology (IT) has been harnessed—especially in the case of cities—to reduce corruption and to promote transparency in public administration by engaging citizens in the oversight of services (Bearfield and Bowman 2017). The current trend to implement ICT technology in urban governance is an excellent opportunity to provide context-sensitive studies. Many cities across the globe are implementing ICT solutions to limit discretion and increase transparency and efficiency, like Guadalajara in Mexico, Seoul in South Korea, and Cluj in Romania. However, the effects of these policies have yet to be assessed empirically.

Finally, in order to make generalizable conclusions based on municipal cases, we need more comparative case studies to build and coherently test the remaining questions. There are still only a relatively small number of truly comparative local government studies that cover both intranational and international dimensions and rigorously combine quantitative and qualitative methods. These mix-methods studies can contribute immensely to disaggregating the effects of culture, institutional factors, and local context on the quality of government and public policies. Rigorous comparative studies would provide an evidence base for understanding and evaluating urban government reforms and interventions in the quality of government that might be relevant to all levels of government.

References

Abrate, Graziano, Fabrizio Erbetta, Giovanni Fraquelli, and Davide Vannoni. 2014. "The Costs of Disposal and Recycling: An Application to Italian Municipal Solid Waste Services." *Regional Studies* 48 (5): 896–909. https://doi.org/10.1080/00343404.2012.689425

Agerberg, Mattias. 2017. "Failed Expectations: Quality of Government and Support for Populist Parties in Europe." *European Journal of Political Research* 56 (3): 578–600. https://doi.org/10.1111/1475-6765.12203

Alexander, Amy C., and Sara Parhizkari. 2018. "A Multilevel Study of Gender Egalitarian Values across Muslim-Majority Provinces: The Role of Women and Urban Spaces." *International Review of Sociology* 28 (3): 474–91. https://doi.org/10.1080/03906701.2018.1473124

Anduiza, Eva, Aina Gallego, and Jordi Muñoz. 2013. "Turning a Blind Eye Experimental Evidence of Partisan Bias in Attitudes Toward Corruption." *Comparative Political Studies* 46 (12): 1664–92. https://doi.org/10.1177/0010414013489081

Auerbach, Adam Michael. 2017. "Neighborhood Associations and the Urban Poor: India's Slum Development Committees." *World Development* 96 (August): 119–35. https://doi.org/10.1016/j.worlddev.2017.03.002

Bandiera, Oriana. 2003. "Land Reform, the Market for Protection and the Origins of the Sicilian Mafia: Theory and Evidence." *Journal of Law, Economics and Organization* 19 (1): 218–44.

Bandiera, Oriana, Andrea Prat, and Tommaso Valletti. 2009. "Active and Passive Waste in Government Spending: Evidence from a Policy Experiment." *The American Economic Review* 99 (4): 1278–308.

Bardhan, Pranab, and Dilip Mookherjee. 2007. "Decentralization, Corruption and Government Accountability." In *International Handbook on the Economics of Corruption*, edited by Susan Rose-Ackerman, 161–83. Cheltenham: Edward Elgar Publishers.

Bearfield, Domonic A., and Ann O'M Bowman. 2017. "Can You Find It on the Web? An Assessment of Municipal E-Government Transparency." *The American Review of Public Administration* 47 (2): 172–88. https://doi.org/10.1177/0275074015627694

Bergh, Andreas, Gissur Ó Erlingsson, Mats Sjölin, and Richard Öhrvall. 2016. *A Clean House: Studies of Corruption in Sweden*. Lund: Nordic Academic Press.

Berliner, Daniel. 2017. "Sunlight or Window Dressing? Local Government Compliance with South Africa's Promotion of Access to Information Act." *Governance* 30 (4): 641–61. https://doi.org/10.1111/gove.12246

Bertholini, Frederico, Carlos Pereira, and Lucio Renno. 2018. "Pork Is Policy: Dissipative Inclusion at the Local Level." *Governance* 31 (4): 701–20. https://doi.org/10.1111/gove.12331

Besley, Timothy, and Robin Burgess. 2002. "The Political Economy of Government Responsiveness: Theory and Evidence from India." *The Quarterly Journal of Economics* 117 (4): 1415–51. https://doi.org/10.1162/003355302320935061

Besley, Timothy, Rohini Pande, and Vijayendra Rao. 2012. "Just Rewards? Local Politics and Public Resource Allocation in South India." *World Bank Economic Review* 26 (2): 191–216. https://doi.org/10.1093/wber/lhr039

Bigoni, Maria, Stefania Bortolotti, Marco Casari, Diego Gambetta, and Francesca Pancotto. 2013. "Cooperation Hidden Frontiers: The Behavioral Foundations of the Italian North-South Divide." SSRN Scholarly Paper ID 2267266. Rochester, NY: Social Science Research Network. http://papers.ssrn.com/abstract=2267266

Börzel, Tanja, and Nicole Deitelhoff. 2018. "Business." In *The Oxford Handbook of Governance and Limited Statehood*, edited by Thomas Risse, Tanja A. Börzel, and Anke Draude, 250–71. Oxford: Oxford University Press.

Börzel, Tanja, and Thomas Risse. 2016. "Dysfunctional State Institutions, Trust, and Governance in Areas of Limited Statehood." *Regulation & Governance* 10 (2): 149–60. https://doi.org/10.1111/rego.12100

Broms, Rasmus, Carl Dahlström, and Mihály Fazekas. 2019. "Political Competition and Public Procurement Outcomes." *Comparative Political Studies* 52 (9): 1259–92. https://doi.org/10.1177/0010414019830723

Caamaño-Alegre, José, Santiago Lago-Peñas, Francisco Reyes-Santias, and Aurora Santiago-Boubeta. 2011. "Budget Transparency in Local Governments: An Empirical Analysis." International Center for Public Policy Working Paper Series, at AYSPS. International Center for Public Policy, Andrew Young School of Policy Studies, Georgia State University. https://ideas.repec.org/p/ays/ispwps/paper1102.html

Cabria, Marcello, Annick Magnier, and Patricia Pereira. 2018. "Mayor's Agendas: Emerging Variations on the Theme of Entrepreneurialism." In *Political Leaders and Changing Local Democracy*, edited by H. Heinelt, A. Magnier, M. Cabria, and H. Reynaert, 243–72. Basingstoke: Palgrave Macmillan.

Campante, Filipe R., and Quoc-Anh Do. 2014. "Isolated Capital Cities, Accountability, and Corruption: Evidence from US States." *American Economic Review* 104 (8): 2456–81.

Charron, Nicholas, Carl Dahlström, and Victor Lapuente. 2016. "Measuring Meritocracy in the Public Sector in Europe: A New National and Sub-National Indicator." *European Journal on Criminal Policy and Research* 22 (April): 499–523. https://doi.org/10.1007/s10610-016-9307-0

Charron, Nicholas, Lewis Dijkstra, and Victor Lapuente. 2015. "Mapping the Regional Divide in Europe: A Measure for Assessing Quality of Government in 206 European Regions." *Social Indicators Research* 122 (2): 315–46. https://doi.org/10.1007/s11205-014-0702-y

Chubb, Judith. 1981. "The Social Bases of an Urban Political Machine: The Case of Palermo." *Political Science Quarterly* 96 (1): 107–25. https://doi.org/10.2307/2149679

Chubb, Judith. 1982. *Patronage, Power, and Poverty in Southern Italy: A Tale of Two Cities*. Cambridge Studies in Modern Political Economies. Cambridge; New York: Cambridge University Press.

Conger, Lucy. 2014. "The Private Sector and Public Security: The Cases of Ciudad Juárez and Monterrey." Working Paper Series on Civic Engagement and Public Security in Mexico. https://www.wilsoncenter.org/sites/default/files/conger_private_sector.pdf

Costas-Pérez, Elena, Albert Solé-Ollé, and Pilar Sorribas-Navarro. 2012. "Corruption Scandals, Voter Information, and Accountability." *European Journal of Political Economy* 28 (4): 469–84.

Craw, Michael. 2008. "Taming the Local Leviathan: Institutional and Economic Constraints on Municipal Budgets." *Urban Affairs Review* 43 (5): 663–90. https://doi.org/10.1177/1078087407311588

da Cruz, Nuno Ferreira da, and Rui Cunha Marques. 2019. "An Application of a Multicriteria Model to Assess the Quality of Local Governance." *Urban Affairs Review* 55 (4): 1218–39.

da Cruz, Nuno Ferreira da, António F. Tavares, Rui Cunha Marques, Susana Jorge, and Luís de Sousa. 2016. "Measuring Local Government Transparency." *Public Management Review* 18 (6): 866–93. https://doi.org/10.1080/14719037.2015.1051572

Dandoy, R., and Arjan H. Schakel. 2013. *Regional and National Elections in Western Europe. Territoriality of the Vote in Thirteen Countries*. Houndmills: Palgrave Macmillan.

Dávid-Barrett, Elizabeth. 2019. "Business Unusual: Collective Action against Bribery in International Business." *Crime, Law and Social Change* 71 (2): 151–70. https://doi.org/10.1007/s10611-017-9715-1

Della Porta, Donatella, and Vannucci, Alberto. 2012. *Hidden Order of Corruption: An Institutional Approach*. Farnham: Ashgate.

Diaz-Cayeros, A, Federico Estévez, and Beatriz Magaloni. 2016. *The Political Logic of Poverty Relief: Electoral Strategies and Social Policy in Mexico*. Cambridge: Cambridge University Press. https://doi.org/10.1017/CBO9781316492710

Doner, Richard F., and Ben Ross Schneider. 2000. "Business Associations and Economic Development: Why Some Associations Contribute More Than Others." *Business and Politics* 2 (3): 261–88.

Dragos, Dacian C., and Bogdana Neamtu. 2013. "Effectiveness of Administrative Appeals - Empirical Evidence from Romanian Local Administration." *Lex Localis - Journal of Local Self-Government* 11 (1): 71–85. https://doi.org/10.4335/11.1.71-85

Drapalova, Eliska and Fabrizio Di Mascio. 2020. "Islands of Good Government: Explaining Successful Corruption Control in Two Spanish Cities." *Politics and Governance* 8 (2): 128–39. http://dx.doi.org/10.17645/pag.v8i2.2730

Drapalova, Eliska. 2016. "Good Apples on Bad Trees: Explanation of Variation in Corruption Level in Southern European Local Government." Ph.D. diss. European University Institute.

Drapalova, Eliska. 2017. "Building Roads to Good Government? The Effect of EU Funds on Spanish Regional Governance." In *Beyond the Panama Papers. The ANTICORRP Project: Anticorruption Report 4*, edited by Alina Mungiu Pippidi. Berlin: Barbara Budrich Publishers.

Drapalova, Eliska 2018. "Explaining the Variety of Local Government Performance. The Case of Romania." Paper presented at *Democracy and Its Discontents Conference*. American Political Science Association General Conference, Boston (MA).

Duvanova, Dinissa. 2014. "Economic Regulations, Red Tape, and Bureaucratic Corruption in Post-Communist Economies." *World Development* 59 (July): 298–312. https://doi.org/10.1016/j.worlddev.2014.01.028

Eisenstadt, Shmuel. N., and Luis Roniger. 1984. *Patrons, Clients and Friends: Interpersonal Relations and the Structure of Trust in Society*. Cambridge: Cambridge University Press.

Erlingsson, Guissoro, Andreas Bergh, and Mats Sjölin. 2008. "Public Corruption in Swedish Municipalities: Trouble Looming on the Horizon?" *Local Government Studies* 34 (5): 595–608.

Esaiasson, Peter, and Jordi Muñoz. 2014. "Roba pero Hace? An Experimental Test of the Competence-Corruption Tradeoff Hypothesis in Spain and Sweden." QoG Working Paper. Gothenburg: The Quality of Government Institute, University of Gothenburg. http://qog.pol.gu.se/digitalAssets/1474/1474905_2014_02_essaiasson_jordi.pdf

Fazekas, Mihály. 2017. "Red Tape, Bribery and Government Favouritism: Evidence from Europe." *Crime, Law and Social Change* 68 (4): 403–29. https://doi.org/10.1007/s10611-017-9694-2

Fernandez-Vazquez, Pablo, Pablo Barberá, and Gonzalo Rivero. 2016. "Rooting out Corruption or Rooting for Corruption? The Heterogenous Electoral Consequences of Scandals." *Political Science Research and Methods* 4 (2): 379–97.

Ferraz, Claudio, and Frederico Finan. 2011. "Electoral Accountability and Corruption: Evidence from the Audits of Local Governments." *The American Economic Review* 101 (4): 1274–311.

Figueiredo, Miguel, Daniel Hidalgo, and Yuri Kasahara. 2012. "When Do Voters Punish Corrupt Politicians? Experimental Evidence from Brazil." http://cega.berkeley.edu/assets/cega_events/44/CEGA_ResearchRetreat2012_deFigueiredo_Paper.pdf

Florida, Richard. 2014. *The Rise of the Creative Class—Revisited: Revised and Expanded*. New York: Basic Books.

Frye, Timothy. 2002. "Capture or Exchange? Business Lobbying in Russia." *Europe-Asia Studies* 54 (7): 1017–36. https://doi.org/10.1080/0966813022000017113

Frye, Timothy, Ora John Reuter, and David Szakonyi. 2014. "Political Machines at Work: Voter Mobilization and Electoral Subversion in the Workplace." *World Politics* 66 (2): 195–228.

Frye, Timothy, Ora John Reuter, and David Szakonyi. 2019. "Hitting Them with Carrots: Voter Intimidation and Vote Buying in Russia." *British Journal of Political Science* 49 (3): 857–81. https://doi.org/10.1017/S0007123416000752

García-Quesada, Mónica, and Fernando Jiménez Sánchez. 2019. "Persuasive Corrupters: Arguments Made to Corrupt Public Officials." In *Political Corruption in a World in Transition*, edited by Jonathan Mendilow and Eric Phélippeau, 107–23. Malaga: Vernon Press.

Gerring, John, and Lee Cojocaru. 2016. "Selecting Cases for Intensive Analysis: A Diversity of Goals and Methods." *Sociological Methods & Research* 45 (3): 392–423. https://doi.org/10.1177/0049124116631692

Giraudy, Agustina, Eduardo Moncada, and Richard Snyder. 2019. *Inside Countries: Subnational Research in Comparative Politics*. Cambridge: Cambridge University Press.

Glaeser, Edward L., and Claudia Goldin. 2007. *Corruption and Reform: Lessons from America's Economic History*. Chicago: University of Chicago Press.

Golden, Miriam A., and Lucio Picci. 2005. "Proposal for a New Measure of Corruption, Illustrated with Italian Data." *Economics and Politics* 17: 37–75.

Graham, Stephen, Renu Desai, and Colin McFarlane. 2013. "Water Wars in Mumbai." *Public Culture* 25 (1 (69): 115–41. https://doi.org/10.1215/08992363-1890486

Guiso, Luigi, Paola Sapienza, and Luigi Zingales. 2004. "The Role of Social Capital in Financial Development." *American Economic Review* 94 (3): 526–56. https://doi.org/10.1257/0002828041464498

Gunnarson, Carina. 2014. "Changing the Game: Addiopizzo's Mobilization against Racketeering in Palermo." *The European Review of Organised Crime* 1 (January): 39–77.

Hedberg, Masha. 2015. "Top-Down Self-Organization: State Logics, Substitutional Delegation, and Private Governance in Russia." *Governance* 29 (1): 67–83. https://doi.org/10.1111/gove.12140

Herrera, Veronica. 2017a. *Water and Politics: Clientelism and Reform in Urban Mexico*. Ann Arbor: University of Michigan Press.

Herrera, Veronica. 2017b. "From Participatory Promises to Partisan Capture: Local Democratic Transitions and Mexican Water Politics." *Comparative Politics* 49 (4): 479–99.

Hilgers, Tina, and Laura Macdonald, eds. 2017. *Violence in Latin America and the Caribbean: Subnational Structures, Institutions, and Clientelistic Networks*. Cambridge: Cambridge University Press.

Hooghe, Liesbet, Gary Marks, and Arjan H. Schakel. 2010. *The Rise of Regional Authority: A Comparative Study of 42 Democracies*. Abington: Routledge.

Verdenicci, Serena and Dan Hough. 2015. "People Power and Anti-Corruption: Demystifying Citizen-Centred Approaches." *Crime, Law and Social Change* 64: 23-35.

Huberts, Leo, and Frédérique Six. 2012. "Local Integrity Systems: Toward a Framework for Comparative Analysis and Assessment." *Public Integrity* 14 (2): 151–72.

Jacobsson, Kerstin. 2015. *Urban Grassroots Movements in Central and Eastern Europe*. Farnham: Ashgate Publishing, Ltd.

Jiménez, Fernando. 2009. "Building Boom and Political Corruption in Spain." *South European Society and Politics* 14 (3): 255–72.

Jiménez, Fernando, Mónica García-Quesada, and Manuel Villoria. 2014. "Integrity Systems, Values, and Expectations: Explaining Differences in the Extent of Corruption in Three Spanish Local Governments." *International Journal of Public Administration* 37: 67–82.

Jiménez, Fernando, Manuel Villoria, and Juan Romero. 2012. "(Un)Sustainable Territories: Causes of the Speculative Bubble in Spain (1996–2010) and Its Territorial,

Environmental and Socio-Political Consequences." *Environment and Planning C: Government and Policy* 30: 467–86.

John, Peter. 2009. "Why Study Urban Politics?" In *Theories of Urban Politics*, edited by Jonathan S. Davies and David Imbroscio, 17–25. London: SAGE Publications.

Kartner, Jennifer, and Carolyn Marie Warner. 2015. "Multi-Nationals and Corruption Systems: The Case of Siemens." ERCAS Working Paper No. 45. https://www.againstcorruption.eu/publications/multi-nationals-corruption-systems-siemens/

Keating, Michael. 1998. *The New Regionalism in Western Europe: Territorial Restructuring and Political Change*. Cheltenham: Edward Elgar.

Khalil, Nadia, and Carmen Navarro. 2012. "Relationships Between Mayors and Economic Elites at the Local Level in Southern European Countries." In *Panel on Mayors in Comparative Perspective. Session on Comparative Studies on Local Government and Politics*. ECPR General Conference, Madrid.

Klašnja, Marko. 2015. "Corruption and the Incumbency Disadvantage: Theory and Evidence." *The Journal of Politics* 77 (4): 928–42. https://doi.org/10.1086/682913

Klašnja, Marko. 2016. "Increasing Rents and Incumbency Disadvantage." *Journal of Theoretical Politics* 28 (2): 225–65. https://doi.org/10.1177/0951629815586873

Kriesi, Hans Peter, and Emanuel Erlach. 2007. "Small-Scale Democracy: The Consequence of Action." In *Citizenship and Involvement in European Democracies: A Comparative Analysis*, 255–79. London: Routledge.

Kroth, Verena, Valentino Larcinese, and Joachim Wehner. 2016. "A Better Life for All? Democratization and Electrification in Post-Apartheid South Africa." *The Journal of Politics* 78 (3): 774–91. https://doi.org/10.1086/685451

Lapuente, Victor, and Marina Nistotskaya. 2009. "To the Short-Sighted Victor Belong the Spoils: Politics and Merit Adoption in Comparative Perspective." *Governance* 22 (3): 431–58. https://doi.org/10.1111/j.1468-0491.2009.01446.x

Lieberman, Evan S. 2005. "Nested Analysis as a Mixed-Method Strategy for Comparative Research." *American Political Science Review* 99 (3): 435–52. https://doi.org/10.1017/S0003055405051762

Lu, Jie. 2015. *Varieties of Governance in China: Migration and Institutional Change in Chinese Villages*. Oxford: Oxford University Press.

Malesky, Edmund J., and Markus David Taussig. 2009. "Out of the Gray: The Impact of Provincial Institutions on Business Formalization in Vietnam." *Journal of East Asian Studies* 9 (2): 249–90.

Manzetti, Luigi, and Carole J. Wilson. 2007. "Why Do Corrupt Governments Maintain Public Support?" *Comparative Political Studies* 40 (8): 949–70. https://doi.org/10.1177/0010414005285759

Mares, Isabela, Aurelian Muntean, and Tsveta Petrova. 2016. "Economic Intimidation in Contemporary Elections: Evidence from Romania and Bulgaria." *Government and Opposition* 53(3): 486–517.

Mares, Isabela, Aurelian Muntean, and Tsveta Petrova 2017. "Pressure, Favours, and Vote-Buying: Experimental Evidence from Romania and Bulgaria." *Europe-Asia Studies* 69 (6): 940–60. https://doi.org/10.1080/09668136.2017.1364351

Markus, Stanislav. 2014. *Property, Predation, and Protection: Piranha Capitalism in Russia and Ukraine*. New York: Cambridge University Press.

Melo, Marcus André, Carlos Pereira, and Saulo Souza. 2014. "Why Do Some Governments Resort to 'Creative Accounting' but Not Others? Fiscal Governance in the Brazilian Federation." *International Political Science Review* 35 (5): 595–612.

Menes, Rebecca. 2003. "Corruption in Cities: Graft and Politics in American Cities at the Turn of the Twentieth Century." National Bureau of Economic Research Working Paper Series No. 9990. http://www.nber.org/papers/w9990

Moncada, Eduardo. 2016. *Cities, Business, and the Politics of Urban Violence in Latin America.* Stanford: Stanford University Press.

Mondo, Bianca Vaz. 2016. "Measuring Political Corruption from Audit Results: A New Panel of Brazilian Municipalities." *European Journal on Criminal Policy and Research* 22 (3): 477–98.

Monteiro, Joana, and Claudio Ferraz. 2014. "Learning to Punish: Resource Windfalls and Political Accountability in Brazil." Working Paper.

Moretti, Enrico. 2012. *The New Geography of Jobs.* Boston: Houghton Mifflin Harcourt.

Morris, Stephen D., and Joseph L. Klesner. 2010. "Corruption and Trust: Theoretical Considerations and Evidence from Mexico." *Comparative Political Studies* 43 (10): 1258–85. https://doi.org/10.1177/0010414010369072

Muir, Sarah, and Akhil Gupta. 2018. "Rethinking the Anthropology of Corruption: An Introduction to Supplement 18." *Current Anthropology* 59 (S18): S4–15. https://doi.org/10.1086/696161

Mungiu-Pippidi, Alina. 2015. *The Quest for Good Governance.* Cambridge: Cambridge University Press.

Muñoz, Jordi, Eva Anduiza, and Aina Gallego. 2016. "Why Do Voters Forgive Corrupt Mayors? Implicit Exchange, Credibility of Information and Clean Alternatives." *Local Government Studies* 42 (4): 598–615. https://doi.org/10.1080/03003930.2016.1154847

Nielsen, Richard A. 2014. "Case Selection via Matching." *Sociological Methods & Research* 45 (3): 569–97. https://doi.org/10.1177/0049124114547054

Nistotskaya, Marina, Nicholas Charron, and Victor Lapuente. 2015. "The Wealth of Regions: Quality of Government and SMEs in 172 European Regions." *Environment and Planning C: Government and Policy* 33 (5): 1125–55.

Nistotskaya, Marina, and Luciana Cingolani. 2016. "Bureaucratic Structure, Regulatory Quality, and Entrepreneurship in a Comparative Perspective: Cross-Sectional and Panel Data Evidence." *Journal of Public Administration Research and Theory* 26 (3): 519–34. https://doi.org/10.1093/jopart/muv026

Nye, John V. C., and Olga Vasilyeva. 2015. "When Does Local Political Competition Lead to More Public Goods?: Evidence from Russian Regions." *Journal of Comparative Economics* 43 (3): 650–76. https://doi.org/10.1016/j.jce.2015.03.001

Olken, Benjamin A. 2005. "Monitoring Corruption: Evidence from a Field Experiment in Indonesia." Working Paper 11753. National Bureau of Economic Research. http://www.nber.org/papers/w11753

Ostrom, Elinor. 1990. *Governing the Commons: The Evolution of Institutions for Collective Action.* Cambridge; New York: Cambridge University Press.

Ostrom, Elinor, James Walker, and Roy Gardner. 1992. "Covenants with and Without a Sword: Self-Governance Is Possible." *The American Political Science Review* 86 (2): 404–17.

Pardo, Italo. 1996. *Managing Existence in Naples: Morality, Action and Structure.* Cambridge: Cambridge University Press.

Parrado, Salvador, Carl Dahlström, and Víctor Lapuente. 2018. "Mayors and Corruption in Spain: Same Rules, Different Outcomes." *South European Society and Politics* 23 (3): 303–22.

Persson, Anna, Bo Rothstein, and Jan Teorell. 2013. "Why Anticorruption Reforms Fail—Systemic Corruption as a Collective Action Problem." *Governance* 26 (3): 449–71.

Petrovici, Norbert. 2017. "The Politics of Mobilizing Local Resources for Growth: 'Urban Areas' in Romania." *Studia Universitatis Babes-Bolyai Sociologia* 62 (1): 37–64. https://doi.org/10.1515/subbs-2017-0004

Petrovici, Norbert, and Anca Simionca. 2011. "Productive Informality and Economic Ties in Emerging Economies: The Case of Cluj Business Networks." *School of Slavonic and East European Studies, UCL* 8: 134–44.

Pezzi, Maria Giulia. 2019. "'Mafia Capitale': Judicial and Symbolic Constructions of the New Italian Corruption." *Journal of Modern Italian Studies* 24 (3): 512–30.

Piattoni, Simona. 2010. *The Theory of Multi-Level Governance*. Oxford, UK: Oxford University Press.

Pierre, Jon. 2005. "Comparative Urban Governance: Uncovering Complex Causalities." *Urban Affairs Review* 40 (4): 446–62. https://doi.org/10.1177/1078087404273442

Putnam, Robert D., Robert Leonardi, and Raffaella Y. Nanetti. 1994. *Making Democracy Work: Civic Traditions in Modern Italy*. New Jersey: Princeton University Press.

Riera, Pedro, Pablo Barberá, Raúl Gómez, Juan Antonio Mayoral, and José Ramón Montero. 2013. "The Electoral Consequences of Corruption Scandals in Spain." *Crime, Law and Social Change* 60 (5): 515–34. https://doi.org/10.1007/s10611-013-9479-1

Riordan, William L. 1995. *Plunkitt of Tammany Hall: A Series of Very Plain Talks on Very Practical Politics*. Signet Classics.

Roll, M. 2014. *The Politics of Public Sector Performance: Pockets of Effectiveness in Developing Countries*. Abington: Routledge.

Rönnerstrand, Björn, and Victor Lapuente. 2017. "Corruption and Use of Antibiotics in Regions of Europe." *Health Policy* 121 (3): 250–56. https://doi.org/10.1016/j.healthpol.2016.12.010

Rothstein, Bo, and Jan Teorell. 2008. "What Is Quality of Government? A Theory of Impartial Government Institutions." *Governance* 21 (2): 165–90. https://doi.org/10.1111/j.1468-0491.2008.00391.x

Rothstein, Bo, and Eric M. Uslaner. 2005. "All for One: Equality, Corruption, and Social Trust." *World Politics* 58 (1): 41–72.

Savitch, H. V., and Paul Kantor. 2002. *Cities in the International Marketplace: The Political Economy of Urban Development in North America and Western Europe*. Princeton: Princeton University Press.

Schneider, Jane, and Peter Schneider. 2005. "Mafia, Antimafia, and the Plural Cultures of Sicily." *Current Anthropology* 46 (4): 501–20. https://doi.org/10.1086/431529

Schneider, Jane, and Peter Schneider. 2013. *Culture and Political Economy in Western Sicily*. Elsevier.

Schnell, Sabina. 2018. "Cheap Talk or Incredible Commitment? (Mis)Calculating Transparency and Anti-Corruption," *Governance* 31 (3): 415–30. https://doi.org/10.1111/gove.12298

Seawright, Jason. 2016. *Multi-Method Social Science: Combining Qualitative and Quantitative Tools*. Cambridge: Cambridge University Press.

Seawright, Jason, and John Gerring. 2008. "Case Selection Techniques in Case Study Research: A Menu of Qualitative and Quantitative Options." *Political Research Quarterly* 61 (2): 294–308.

Sellers, Jefferey M. 2002. *Governing from Below: Urban Regions and the Global Economy*. New York: Cambridge University Press.

Solt, Frederick. 2004. "Civics or Structure? Revisiting the Origins of Democratic Quality in the Italian Regions." *British Journal of Political Science* 34 (01): 123–35.

Spáč, Peter, Petr Voda, and Jozef Zagrapan. 2018. "Does the Freedom of Information Law Increase Transparency at the Local Level? Evidence from a Field Experiment." *Government Information Quarterly* 35 (May): 408–17. https://doi.org/10.1016/j.giq.2018.05.003

Stone, Clarence N. 2005. "Looking Back to Look Forward: Reflections on Urban Regime Analysis." *Urban Affairs Review* 40 (3): 309–41. https://doi.org/10.1177/1078087404270646

Storper, Michael. 2013. *Keys to the City: How Economics, Institutions, Social Interaction, and Politics Shape Development*. Princeton: Princeton University Press.

Sundström, Aksel, and Lena Wängnerud. 2016. "Corruption as an Obstacle to Women's Political Representation: Evidence from Local Councils in 18 European Countries." *Party Politics* 22 (3): 354–69. https://doi.org/10.1177/1354068814549339

Suzuki, Kohei, and Claudia N. Avellaneda. 2018. "Women and Risk-Taking Behaviour in Local Public Finance." *Public Management Review* 20 (12): 1741–67. https://doi.org/10.1080/14719037.2017.1412118

Tavares, António, and Nuno Cruz. 2020. "Explaining the Transparency of Local Government Websites through a Political Market Framework." *Government Information Quarterly* 37 (3): 1–13. https://doi.org/10.1016/j.giq.2017.08.005

Transparency International. 2014. "Local Integrity System Assessment Toolkit." Transparency International Secretariat Policy and Research Department.

Tsai, Lily L. 2007. *Accountability without Democracy: Solidary Groups and Public Goods Provision in Rural China*. New York: Cambridge University Press.

Urban Audit. 2015. "Urban Audit Database." Eurostat. https://ec.europa.eu/eurostat/web/gisco/geodata/reference-data/administrative-units-statistical-units/urban-audit

Vampa, Davide. 2015. "Local Representative Democracy and Protest Politics: The Case of the Five-Star Movement." *Contemporary Italian Politics* 7 (3): 232–50. https://doi.org/10.1080/23248823.2015.1087120

Vampa, Davide. 2016. *The Regional Politics of Welfare in Italy, Spain and Great Britain*. Basingstoke: Palgrave Macmillan.

Verdery, Katherine. 2003. *The Vanishing Hectare: Property and Value in Postsocialist Transylvania*. Culture and Society after Socialism. Ithaca, NY: Cornell University Press.

Weitz-Shapiro, Rebecca. 2012. "What Wins Votes: Why Some Politicians Opt Out of Clientelism." *American Journal of Political Science* 56 (3): 568–83. https://doi.org/10.1111/j.1540-5907.2011.00578.x

Weitz-Shapiro, Rebecca. 2014. *Curbing Clientelism in Argentina*. Cambridge: Cambridge University Press.

World Bank. 2013. *The Competitive Cities. Reshaping the Economic Geography of Romania*. World Bank.

Zhu, Jiangnan, and Dong Zhang. 2016. "Does Corruption Hinder Private Businesses? Leadership Stability and Predictable Corruption in China." *Governance* 30 (3): 343–63. https://doi.org/10.1111/gove.12220

CHAPTER 7

WHAT CAN WE LEARN ABOUT CORRUPTION FROM HISTORICAL CASE STUDIES?

MARK KNIGHTS

THIS chapter will argue that history can offer something important to the study of corruption and quality of government—and of course can in turn learn from other disciplines. This may seem a surprising claim when quantitative studies, based on large datasets from opinion surveys, such as the various indices that are routinely subjected to mathematically informed interrogation, are simply not available for the past. But what may seem like an obstacle to cross-disciplinary conversation may actually be an advantage, since the historian is freed from sometimes dubious datasets, correlations, and abstractions; is able to test some of the models and conclusions put forward in other disciplines; and can offer vital contextual analysis. Indeed, history offers a mass, and many different types, of data—press reports, legal cases, legislative debates, diaries, correspondence, and governmental inquiries, to name but a few—that are seldom explored by social scientists because they do not easily lend themselves to treatment by some of their methodologies and perhaps because the past is conceived of as "not relevant" to the present. But historians have studied quality of government and corruption, albeit in a somewhat patchy way, and there are always echoes and resonances of their themes across time as well as space (Aylmer 1980; Burns and Innes 2007; Dirks 2006; Geltner, Kroeze, and Vitoria 2017; Graham 2015; Harling 1996; Harling and Mandler 1993; Hellmuth 1999; Hurstfield 1967, 1973; Kramnick 1994; Kreike and Jordan 2004; Marshall 1976; Peck 1990). If we accept that concerns about good government, and corruption in particular, are not just a "modern" phenomenon, history offers a huge array of data to help us explore which reform processes worked, which didn't and why. History offers the scholar and the policymaker another important and useful tool. So this chapter is a plea for a multidisciplinary approach that includes history far more than at present, though it is not an argument for the superiority of that discipline over others.

The discussion that follows seeks to set out how a historical approach based on the collection and analysis of empirical, archival data can be useful. The focus will be on corruption as a quality of government issue, though quality of government more generally generated a vast and useful pre-modern literature, as numerous treatises and pamphlets were written

as advice and counsel to rulers, primarily to monarchs but also to assemblies, republican regimes, and the wider public. Political theory considers works by Machiavelli, Hobbes, Locke,
Montesquieu, and others but these writers were part of a much larger public discussion
about good kingship and good government that penetrated far down the social scale, not
least because the Reformation in church government, as well as rebellions and revolutions
in Britain and across Europe, and participation in both local government and imperial ventures, required many to take a position about whether government was working well, needed
reform, or had to be overturned. Analysis of this extensive public debate would merit a book
in its own right, so the subtheme here of corruption will be used to illustrate some broader
themes.

The chapter's brief is to explain the methodology of the historian—*how* we can learn about
corruption through historical case studies and *why* we should embrace them—rather than
the conclusions of *what* particular lessons history might suggest, though some of the latter
will nevertheless surface and more are available in a freely downloadable report written for
Transparency International (Knights 2016a). Both the latter and subsequent observations
in this chapter are informed by my work on corruption and office-holding in Britain between 1600 and 1850 (Knights, forthcoming, 2021b). During that time there were some very
significant changes in the way that corruption was conceptualized, how it proliferated, and
how it was reformed (for the wider evolution of the concept see Rothstein and Varraich 2017,
chapter 3). Corruption shifted from what was primarily a religious concept to one concerned
with politics, economic, and the state; opportunities for corruption expanded as the state
and empire expanded; and reforms abolished the sale of office, curbed gift-giving and embezzlement, defined what constituted public money, and introduced an actionable concept
of "abuse of trust." In other words the "early modern" period, as it is known, was a key one in
the evolution of about the evolution of corruption and anticorruption and therefore worthy
of study for what it can tell us about the development of good government.

The Importance of Case Studies and Context

History is a broad discipline with a range of different methodologies, ideologies, and concepts (for overviews of history and its methods see Tosh 2008, 2015, 2018; Jordanova 2006,
2012). Nevertheless, most historians use archival material that is often generated by institutions or individuals, enabling historians to marshal evidence and create or test theories
through compilations of case studies. Some in the social sciences may find this approach
problematic and overly concerned with a particular moment in the past at the expense of
broader conclusions. Case studies can indeed be unhelpful when the love of telling a particular story or the detail of reconstructing the past obscures the wider point that such evidence can illuminate or when the compilation of evidence becomes an end in itself, with
little analytical framework to guide the reader or draw out more general conclusions; but
the latter is simply poor history rather than a reason to avoid history altogether. A good
case study will, in fact, highlight the importance of context for understanding the challenges facing government, something that anticorruption studies are gradually accepting
as more and more important (Heywood and Johnson 2017; Heywood 2018; Johnston 2006,
2012; Nicoletti 2017). Indeed, there has been something of a "historical turn" to the study of

corruption, a recognition that the past has important things to tell us about what has or has not worked, why they did or did not succeed, and what conditions needed to prevail for reform to be successful. Different legal, economic, religious, and moral as well as political and social cultures all shape government and attitudes to corruption. It matters, for example, if a country has a tradition of fiduciary law: the legal concept and practice of a "trust" by which a principal entrusts property or powers to an agent to act as a "trustee." A trust thus carries legal duties and responsibilities for which the agent can be held accountable but also much more discretion than a contract. Without that notion or framework, the idea of "entrusted power" is unlikely to take firm root. Britain and Spain, which developed legal histories along different lines, thus had different anticorruption trajectories.

An effective case study—or even a microhistory—can also explore the role and beliefs of individuals within the macro data often studied by social scientists, adding an important layer of analysis that examines the behavior of agents within the game being played (Ginzburg 1993; Center for Microhistorical Research. http://www.microhistory.org/). By drilling down into detail, a case study's particular spatial or temporal focus can help us better understand the factors driving or preventing reform; and global and transnational case studies (for example, the study of transnational corporations, such as the European East India Companies) can explore processes of interaction and points of comparison. Cumulatively, case studies provide data from which generalizations are possible even if they are contextually colored.

If social scientists appreciate the value of the notion of path dependency, they will necessarily have to engage with the history that helped to shape it (Hellmann 2017). And that requires a recognition of the role of contingency and local circumstance. Britain's history of pre-modern anticorruption was thus fundamentally shaped by its religious reformation; parliamentary tradition; acquisition of empire; legal and print culture; and its process of socioeconomic transformation. But none of these factors was a fixed determinant. Each of them was vigorously contested and hence fluid: history suggests that there were often multiple paths that might have been taken and that the path pursued reflected a complex of contingent and contested factors. Venality of office, for example, was removed in Britain by a protracted legal and legislative process; but in France it took a relatively swift revolution. Path dependency does not mean historical inevitability, since both the direction and nature of the pathways were often bitterly fought over—the direction of the reformation, the triumph of parliamentary sovereignty, the freedom of the press, an increasingly independent judiciary, and economic liberalism were all deeply controversial and disputed. So the particular context matters. And this applies to peoples as well as institutions and structures. People are themselves conditioned by their historical context. And the choices made at one time shaped the mentalities of the next generation(s) because individuals are partly conditioned by their historical environment: "different historical circumstances make different kinds of actors" (Little 2017, 324). That means that there is no one single, universal, timeless right path but rather a variety of different strategies that have worked (or not) in different contexts. If the problems of government were the same over time and space, universal laws and practices would surely have been developed by now to prevent it.

A historical understanding of change thus challenges "one-size-fits-all" solutions. A good deal of research and international policy in the late twentieth and early twenty-first centuries assumed that corruption is universal and that universal remedies are therefore appropriate. A historical view, which involves reconstructing different ways of thinking about and tackling corruption in the past, challenges this and suggests that corruption and anticorruption evolved according to local contexts, and that these contingent factors should be taken into account by modern policymakers if they want to be successful.

The reconstruction of the past requires imagination—and imagining ourselves back into past lives and contexts helps us appreciate that although basic emotional responses of fear, love, hatred, and greed have always existed, their expression and form have always been constructs, the result of pressures from society, culture, religion, law, the economy, and the state (for the history of emotions see Plamper 2017; Reddy 2001; Rosenwein 2006). The universal, rationally calculating, self-interested actor beloved by some economists would be hard to find in history: such a view of human nature is itself a construct. Understanding the different mindsets of the past should thus be of interest to policymakers because they challenge current assumptions.

CHANGE AND CONTINUITY

One obvious area that history can help with is change and continuity over time. A "long view" can correct any assumption that corruption and anticorruption are, as has sometimes been claimed, very recent phenomena and intrinsically connected either with "modernity" (Engels 2017) or with the wave of NGO policies developed from the late 1990s onwards. Corruption and anticorruption have existed throughout history, even if the types and even concept of corruption have themselves changed over time (Geltner, Kroeze, and Vitoria 2017; Buchan and Hill 2014). One way of charting this evolution is through historical discourse analysis (Brett 2002; de Bolla 2013; Pocock 1987; Skinner 2002). Increasing quantities of historical, printed material have been digitized and are now searchable in interesting (though not always unproblematic) ways. History can thus help chart the evolution of the terms and concepts in which we are all interested and suggest that although the discourse of "corruption" does similar work across time—giving a moral and often political charge to accusations that something has decayed from its original or ideal purity—its specificity was given to it by its context. What was once described or conceptualized as corrupt in the past (charging interest on money, for example, which was known as usury) are now no longer seen as such or hold much less sway, in many countries at least (Fontaine 2014; Hawkes 2010; Nelson 1969).

Another important aspect of the historical study of change and continuity has to do with causality and processes of reform and innovation—essential features of any anticorruption strategy or policy for the improvement of government. Given that there is now a general awareness that modern corruption policies may not have been as swiftly effective as their designers hoped, understanding the speed and nature of change is clearly central to current policy formation. By looking at the past we can suggest how, and in what conditions, reform processes came about and flourished; and, more generally, how transformations of government have worked. Historians, together with social scientists and political thinkers such as Weber and Marx, have developed a large range of theories to help explain different types of change and reform processes (for overviews see Kramer and Maza 2002; Little 2000; 2007). Indeed, the word "reform" is itself one with a deep history, a contraction of the word "reformation," the term applied to the major changes brought about by the birth and development of the protestant church when it broke away in the sixteenth century (Innes 2007). It is therefore instructive to reflect briefly on how historians have explained and characterized the fundamental shift of views, practices and institutions during the Reformation—not least since "corruption" was a term most frequently applied in the pre-modern British context to religious belief to denote original sin or sins of the body and mind and because corruption has always had a moral connotation. Historians have had, of course, more than one interpretation of the Reformation: it used to be seen as a rapid process, dictated from above, but the growing consensus is now that although there were some early adopters it was generally a slow process, burning from below and taking several centuries to complete—not least because belief was embedded in social and cultural practices that shaped mind-sets and often proved stubbornly resistant to reform (Clark 2000; Haigh 1990; Ryrie 2013; Shagan 2003; Tyacke 1998, 2007). So a study of the Reformation will caution against thinking that a major set of reforms can ever be achieved simply by dictat or legislative frameworks, necessary though those may be: changing cultural values takes time. There was a "big bang" of legislative change in the 1530s, both in terms of religion and administration, but this took far longer to be implemented at the local, parish level; and historians increasingly talk of a "long reformation" that, for some, lasted from the early sixteenth until the eighteenth century.

Thinking about how big shifts in institutional and individual culture come about is thus an essential part of the historian's remit but is also the task of those seeking to escape the collective action problem of a prevalent culture of corruption. So another interesting model to "think with" is provided by historical sociologist/philosopher of science Thomas Kuhn's ideas about the "Scientific Revolution" (Kuhn 2012). He argued that a fundamental change in basic concepts and practices of scientific discipline could constitute a paradigmatic shift. This occurred when practitioners encountered anomalies that could no longer be explained by the universally accepted paradigm, which was not just a way of understanding science but a complete worldview in which that understanding operated: "science" was not a single strand of activity but one embedded in much larger worldviews. When enough anomalies had been accumulated, the study of science was thrown into a crisis in which new ideas were tried out—though this process involved a series of protracted attacks before a new paradigm prevailed. The term "revolution" may imply quick and sudden change, but in reality the process was more protracted, involved social and intellectual change, and was messy. Kuhn's ideas are now contested—the history of science has generally seen apparently-conflicting ideas as far more able to coexist than Kuhn allowed (Toulmin 1972; Iliffe 2017)—but the question of what leads to paradigmatic change is still a relevant one. In the context of quality of government, we might talk of a paradigmatic shift in the notion of office-holding, for example, during the period 1600–1850 in Britain. This involved a series of scandals and contests that cumulatively chipped away at the old paradigm of office as either a piece of personal property or as something responsible only to the monarch, making that paradigm ultimately untenable (Johnston 1991; Knights forthcoming 2021b). During this process there were rival and contested versions of what should be the right paradigm. Rather than a single factor or set of policies explaining all change, a complex of factors was at play. And even once a paradigmatic shift had been achieved, remnants of the old paradigm still prevailed: in Britain, administrative reform did not remove some of the social attributes of corruption—such as securing jobs for friends and cronies or for members of a similar class and background. Even Charles Trevelyan, the man most associated with civil service reform in mid-nineteenth century Britain and who hated patronage as a fundamentally corrupting phenomenon, argued that his plans for a more professional and efficient civil service were designed to bolster the strength of the educated social elite. In a private memorandum he asked,

> Who are so successful in carrying off the prizes at competing scholar ships, fellowships, &c. as the most expensively educated young men? Almost invariably, the sons of gentlemen, or those who by force of cultivation, good-training and good society have acquired the feelings and habits of gentlemen. The tendency of the measure will, I am confident, be decidedly aristocratic (Hughes 1949, 72).

History can thus highlight how and why some things remain stubbornly resistant to change (even whilst other elements are reformed), and governmental powers embedded in social hierarchies would be one of them. Another might be imperial exploitation: some (though not all) historians argue that anticorruption may actually have served to legitimize colonial rule (Dirks 2006; Epstein 2012).

My own view is that change has often been cyclical or wave-like—a *process*—rather than a single event or a linear progression from one state to another. Whilst some social science has suggested that societies become "modern" after tipping irrevocably over a threshold to become societies where the quality of government enables economic prosperity (North, Wallis, and Weingast 2009), historians might want to stress a series of recurring crises and reform processes, perhaps even occurring in different fields (administrative, economic, political, social, legal) at different times, that cumulatively brought about change (and which therefore also left some aspects unchanged). Such waves of reform were necessary because new forms of corruption emerged as the state, society, and economy developed in new ways. And anticorruption often coincided with repeated campaigns for moral reform—waves of anxiety that the moral fabric of society needed repair through a return to moral codes (Dabhoiwala 2012; Ingram 1996; Lemmings and Walker 2009; Roberts 2004). Such moral reform campaigns punctuated the pre-modern period, and arguably continue to shape the modern, and they provided a macro framework within which the moralizing spirit of anticorruption could prevail. Moral reform, we might say, was a macro factor—a context adding weight to micro factors such as personal agency and meso factors such as governmental or institutional initiatives. The combination of macro, meso, and micro factors helps to explain change—and hence also to underline that each context is sui generis even if there may be general principles at work (Knights 2017a). It is not that we should think of personal integrity, institutional reform, and societal reform as *alternative* or *rival* strategies—a mixture of all three were necessary. History thus urges analysts of the quality of government to avoid single-factor explanations and to think, as Michael Johnston does, of how different complexes of factors require different solutions (Johnston 2006).

Another macro factor, much studied by historians, is the role that war has played in state formation and hence also in the development of corruption and anticorruption. War has often opened up huge challenges for good government as states struggled to meet the logistical demands of conflict and to regulate the provisioning and supply of troops (Baker 1971; Brewer 1990; Brewer and Hellmuth 1999; Graham 2015; Graham and Walsh 2016). Defeat— or even mismanaged victory—has historically led to major reform processes, forcing states to confront the reasons for their inadequacies and their spiraling costs (Christie 1962). A historical approach will thus pay attention to exogenous factors as well as internal or institutional ones. Such factors are, of course, difficult for policymakers—recommending losing a war is clearly not such a great anticorruption solution—but they might help us define what elements of postwar reform can be replicated in more peaceful contexts.

History never repeats itself in the same ways; but challenges can recur in ways that are constructive to think about. The developing world, in Africa and Eastern Europe, is of course a collection of many different local and national stories and we should be very cautious about uncritically applying the lessons of the European experience to other contexts; but in some ways many of the processes at work in developing countries bear marked similarities with the pre-modern European world in terms of the importance accorded to social institutions such as friendship, patronage, kinship, and gift-giving which shaped how office-holding was/is regarded. The analysis of a historian will thus chime closely with the anthropological approaches to corruption developed by Oliver de Sardan and others (Blundo, Sardan, and Arifari 2006; de Sardan 1999). The European history of the ways in which corruption was socially embedded and constructed may help us better understand the complexities of such processes in our own day—and make us pause for thought before simplistic condemnation of practices that have been ubiquitous in the past in Western societies. Indeed, pre-modern Britain was a developing country, offering a well-documented case study of a prolonged struggle against corruption.

The history of the pre-modern is also instructive for insights into the notion of office and the interplay between the "state" and private or semi-private enterprises. Many modern definitions of corruption tend to focus on "public office," but in the pre-modern world, office was something far larger (Braddick 2000; Condren 2006; Goldie 2001; Withington 2005). It extended to the unpaid officers in the parishes and towns, the trustees of road and rail improvement schemes, the unpaid magistrates whose responsibility it was to enforce the law at the local level. Indeed, the pre-modern state was very rudimentary: it had few paid officials, no police force until the mid-nineteenth century, and was hugely reliant on the integrity of local power brokers. And these local officers owed their authority in part to royal or government appointment, but also, and as much, to their social and cultural standing in their communities. This meant that for much of the pre-modern period, Britain had a weak, dispersed "central" state and was reliant on officials whose authority stemmed as much from their social and cultural capital as it did that of the office itself. This will be a familiar scenario to those investigating development and corruption.

There are other ways in which a dialogue between past and present can be helpful. The "dispersed" and voluntary pre-modern state was also reliant on private entrepreneurs to fill what we might now see as state functions, another issue that faces many current policy concerns about procurement. The early state had to make use of a tribe of contractors, especially in order to meet the demands of war, which were frequent and unprecedentedly expansive, particularly after the late seventeenth century, when war between continental rivals tended to spill out across an imperial and hence increasingly global theater. Contractors supplied the troops with food, drink, clothing, and transport—in an era when army commissions were for sale and when commanders sought profit from the contracts they could award. The army and navy contracts or were private, profit-seeking individuals fulfilling a public role in which the national interest was paramount. The resulting tensions played out in scandal after scandal of contractors abusing their positions to make excessive profits. The pre-modern state was thus composed of hybrid private–public partnerships that should be of interest to anyone concerned about how these operate today.

Two other examples of public–private hybrid institutions may be instructive. The Bank of England was for most of its life a semi-private, semi-public institution: it raised money from private investors but made loans to the state and became the custodian of public money. It was able to float the national debt because private investors received a profit from the interest on the money they loaned and the interest payments were secured on the receipts of public taxation. There were plenty of critics of the Bank which saw it as a corrupting force, advancing the "monied men" at the expense of the "true interest" of the nation, the landed classes. Another excellent example of a hybrid public–private body is the international trading companies on which the British Empire was in part founded, such as the East India Company and the Royal Africa Company. These were given state monopolies over certain regions or types of trade and in return they often gave or loaned money to the state; but they were also private companies (Bowen 2006; Brenner 1993; Lawson 1993; Pettigrew 2013; Stern 2011). Those in authority in these companies were officers who had a duty to the public as well as to the company. The East India Company called their members "servants," and those in the non-military arm of the company "civil servants," from which the term moved in the nineteenth century to become a descriptor for public state servants.

Studying these hybrid public–private institutions should offer insights into the inherent conflicts of interest that lay in their structure and how these were tackled in the past. The history of the East India Company is of a "company state" with extensive political and civil powers as well as economic ones and its officials had to be reined in over the course of the later eighteenth and nineteenth centuries because of their widespread corruption and rapacity. Such a history is a reminder that good governance is not just about "state" officials unless we interpret that category in very broad terms; that the state has struggled in the past to regulate private–public relationships; but that some successes were possible. In 1782, for example, MPs in the House of Commons were barred from acting as contractors or having a personal interest in such concerns. As a Commons report—on such a lowly issue as hiring wagons and horses—put it, the private contractor was in effect a public officer:

> The Officer is a Trustee for the Public; as such, he is bound to husband the Public Money committed to his Charge with as much frugality as if it were his own; what he saves, or what he gains, he save and gains not for himself, but for the Public. He ought not to be permitted, by any management or contrivance, to carve out for himself an interest in the execution of a public trust (Commissioners of Public Accounts 1782).

Remarkably, the pre-modern period was actually stricter than the modern era about forcing MPs to withdraw from voting on issues in which they had a personal financial interest. Across the seventeenth and eighteenth centuries this was established convention, consolidated in a 1797 ruling by the Speaker (Platt 1961). The reasons why this is no longer in force are something of a mystery, but the revival of this older procedure in the modern Parliament could only be beneficial (Knights 2019a).

The Benefits Offered by Varieties of Historical Data

Historical sources can offer data that other material about corruption might offer far less readily or not at all. What, then, is the type of data that historical analysis yields and how might it be useful? Diaries and correspondence, in particular, but also trial transcripts and memoirs offer insights into the mindsets of perpetrators of corruption and of those observing corruption in others. If corruption is often secretive, "ego" and legal documents can help to recover something of the private world that can help explain why people acted in the way they did. And this is illuminating, since very few individuals accused of corruption saw themselves as corrupt and offered plenty of justifications and vindications of their behavior (Knights 2018a). Such comments can be supplemented by the many instances of public professions of innocence—some of them successful defenses against prosecution. These underline that corruption is always a contested concept, that can be viewed in very different ways and that can be legitimized, at least in the eyes of the accused. But it is not just ego documents that can be revealing. Corporations such as the East India Company amassed huge archives (Ogborn 2007) that enable us to examine how corruption worked in a semi-public, semi-private institution, and what measures it took to curb it. Literary and cultural works, including graphic satire, and material culture (house-building, art collection, precious objects) can also tell us much about the emotive display and ridicule of corruption and how these too change over time. This section will explore two key types of sources that both generate questions about corruption and help us to answer them. The first relates to legal and institutional history; the second to personal and cultural history.

One of the most useful and numerous types of evidence is the legal or quasi-legal: the documents generated by official or semi-official investigations or accounting bodies (undertaken by government departments, by Parliament, and by semi-private corporations such as the East India Company) together with the trials or hearings, and their verdicts or judgments. Such material almost immediately raises a number of questions: about the legal framework, both in terms of legal concepts and of institutions to enforce them; about who brought the prosecutions and why; and about the effectiveness of legal remedies. The cases themselves are also highly revealing, setting out contested notions of what constituted corruption and how behavior that was condemned by the prosecution could be redescribed as benign; about how cases and processes could be frustrated and undermined; and about institutional and personal failings. Each of these dimensions is worth expanding on further and illustrating.

Anticorruption is in part a history of the law and legal culture and here too a historical approach yields results, since legal history shows that legal cultures took time to evolve. Legislation surrounding corruption in pre-modern Britain was extremely patchy. Bribery was a concept limited in the courts to subornation of judges and magistrates, or to electoral malpractice, and it was not until the late eighteenth and early nineteenth century that prosecutions for bribery became possible under common law. Until then, extortion and exaction were far more frequent crimes, placing the blame squarely on the officer rather than those making the payment. Bribery thus has a history; it was not a universal constant (Noonan 1984). It was, for example, closely linked to electoral as well as judicial malpractice. From the late seventeenth century onwards, legislation sought to limit the amount of money spent to influence voters and from 1729 voters were required to swear that they had not accepted a bribe or other inducement. Outside of the fields of justice and elections, the statute book was virtually empty in relation to bribery. There were some medieval laws against bribes given to procure office, reinforced a little in 1555, but only applicable to the realms of justice and the king's revenue; but there was otherwise something of a legal vacuum until 1809 when "sale" of office was banned.

The paucity of anticorruption legislation had two consequences. First, public law had to borrow from private law. A trust was initially a legal instrument to protect private property by vesting land in the hands of another; but the trustee was supposed to act for the beneficiary of the trust and not himself, an altruism that made the concept attractive when applied to public office. That move was made in the mid-seventeenth century, as a result of the disputes that led to civil war: when the King claimed that he was only entrusted by God, Parliament responded that he was entrusted by the people (Knights 2018b; Maitland 2003; Maloy 2008; 2009; Mendle 1995). Very rapidly, the application of the notion of trust to public offices of all sorts became quite widespread, at home and in the empire; and in turn this led to the development of a body of law around the "abuse" or "breach" of trust. Indeed, it was this fiduciary concept that underpinned a landmark case in 1783 (still invoked today) that set out both who counted as a public official and the common law on misconduct in office (Law Commission 2016). It is interesting that a developing area of public law seeks to apply these older fiduciary concepts to the present day (Criddle et al. 2018; Finn, 1995; Fox-Decent 2011).

Second, serious cases of corruption tended to be pursued under the rather flexible charge of "high crimes and misdemeanours" prosecutable via an impeachment in Parliament, that is to say, a trial that took place when the House of Commons brought a prosecution on which the House of Lords passed judgement (Knights, forthcoming, 2021a). An alternative route was to bring a statute, called a bill of pains and penalties, against someone that the House of Commons had judged guilty of a crime and who had fled prosecution. Neither route was very satisfactory: impeachment, revived in 1621 to try a corruption case after a 150-year gap, was last used in 1806 after two failed impeachments of high-profile figures undermined confidence in the process (Fry 1992; Marshall, 1965; Tite 1974). And in 1781-3 Sir Thomas Rumbold, who had amassed an enormous fortune in India under highly dubious circumstances, escaped a "bill of pains" because it seemed unjust to prosecute him in Parliament rather than the courts, where a higher standard of proof was required. Such cases remind us that the laws surrounding corruption must be invented and that it takes a long while for legal cultures to adapt to changing circumstances. It also reminds us that the law is often a blunt instrument for tackling corruption and that prosecutions of individuals can often back-fire. Tackling corrupt individuals alone—as opposed to the system in which they flourish—is both difficult and insufficient to effect reform. And processes such as impeachments very often become politicized to such an extent that the legal process is undermined. In Britain, trials were no substitute for systematic regulation at the administrative and corporate level or for a set of internalized and explicit ethical guides for behavior. Not that those were easy either. Numerous investigations and reports were conducted by government departments and within corporations such as the trading companies to try to tackle corruption and these provide wonderfully detailed information about malpractice and reform processes. Sometimes investigations into abuses or suggestions for how to change the system were initiated by internal whistleblowers, who generally came out badly from these encounters, and there was very little attempt at a higher level to create a framework in which this type of internal exposure of misgovernment could become routine, a problem that faces many institutions and governments today (Knights 2007; Neufeld 2014).

History also underlines the gradual nature of the evolution of proper accounting procedures, which can be explored through analysis of attempts to establish national auditing bodies. As a result of the unprecedented amount of money raised by Parliament to fight the Crown in the civil wars of the 1640s, a number of committees were established to oversee and audit payments and pressure mounted for an overarching public accounts commission (Peacey 2013). Although the latter was abolished in the 1650s, there were new attempts, again in the light of expenditure on war against the Dutch in the 1660s, to institute a parliamentary oversight of accounts. Britain's entry into large-scale continental (and at times global) war after 1689 reanimated concerns for better national auditing and parliament created a commission of public accounts (Brooks 1984; Downie 1976; Seaward 2002). Yet this, too, rapidly became a partisan tool and was allowed to lapse in 1716. It was only under the pressure of the (failing) war with the North American colonists that a new commission of accounts was created in 1780. Nor would such a history merely tell us about accounting, since the numerous and highly detailed reports that the new body generated were instrumental in changing administrative and remunerative practices across a wide number of government departments, even if the recommendations took a long time to implement fully (Harling 1996). Thus, higher pay was introduced for public officers to remove the incentive for corrupt practices; best practice was shared across departments; and better auditing techniques were inculcated. The reports—and the minutes of earlier committees and commissions—are a superb resource for anyone interested in the nature of corruption in Britain and the innovations undertaken to curb it and promote good governance.

Turning to the legal cases and investigations themselves, many of which are readily available in published form or on modern databases of archival material, the courtroom or the floor of the Houses of Parliament or the minutes and papers of trading companies offer abundant evidence about attitudes to corruption and to reform. Indeed, some of the cases generated so much material that the problem is too much data rather than too little. The Governor General of India, Warren Hastings, for example, was impeached in a process that lasted from 1786 to 1795 with speeches made by Edmund Burke and Sheridan that went on for days at a time (Marshall 1965). Or, to give another example, when Charles Trevelyan, the future author of the Northcote-Trevelyan report which is generally seen as the blueprint for the modern civil service, prosecuted his boss, Sir Edward Colebrooke, Resident of Delhi, in 1828, the papers generated by the case fill five large volumes in the East India Office archive in the British Library (Prior, Brennan and Haines 2001). Indeed, as both the Hastings and Colebrooke cases illustrate, the data available relates not only to domestic corruption but increasingly to imperial corruption across a wider and wider sphere of influence and control. The Delhi materials allow us to reconstruct two very different views on what constituted corruption and hence also what constituted good government. From Trevelyan's standpoint his superior, Colebrooke—egged on by his wife——had accepted presents from Indian princes that compromised the East India Company's integrity. Trevelyan thus condemned a "system of corruption" operating in Delhi that was, in his eyes and those of the Governor General, extensive and damaging (British Library, IOR/F/4/1371/54509, 216, Trevelyan to the Governor General 1830; *Papers* 1833, 15). Yet Colebrooke had a very different take on his behavior. He came from a family with extensive Indian connections and he regarded the acceptance of gifts from Indian princes as an essential and customary lubricant for cordial relations between the Company and the Indians. Indeed, Colebrooke thought Trevelyan's attitudes were part of a growing distaste among the British for intimate relations with the native population, who were increasingly being thought of as a corrupt race. And this, Colebrooke believed, would lead to an inevitable breach between the Company and the Indians. The prosecution, and the documents it generated, thus allow us to reconstruct two contrasting views of how to govern and hence also what were the legitimate boundaries for officials. For Trevelyan, quality of government meant never taking gifts; for Colebrooke, they were an essential part of good government. "Corruption," then, involved clashing visions of how to conduct affairs—it was not a neutral term but part and parcel of the contest.

Such detailed sources allow us to reconstruct cases very fully—indeed more completely perhaps than some modern investigations and trials which are often held in secret, outside of the public domain, or only partially reported. And because many of the key actors left caches of private papers—correspondence, memoirs and vindications—it is possible to see a case in its round and through the eyes of the participants in a way that is seldom possible today. The diary of Samuel Pepys, for example, who faced a number of investigations for corruption, is a highly revealing document—not only does he record the sexual favors he sought in return for the disposal of the patronage he held for the Navy Office, but he also recorded a number of instances when he received "gifts" that were intended to influence his decisions (Knights 2014). Such a personal and revelatory document gives us insights into how Pepys could both be horrified by the corruption of others—he reacted strongly against one official who told him that that "his horse was a bribe, and his boots a bribe and told us he was made up of bribes and that he makes every sort of tradesman to bribe him; and invited me home to his house to taste of his bribe-wine"—and yet also justify his own nest-feathering. Pepys, and indeed others accused of corruption, created a personal code of morality that saw some bribes as honorable. Lord Clive, for example, explained to a committee of the House of Commons what presents he thought were honorable (those that were freely given, not extorted, and rewarded good service) and those that were dishonorable (those that were extorted by force and were simply the result of avarice) (*First Report* 1772, 148). The committee thus forced the articulation of assumptions that might otherwise have remained unsaid.

The historical evidence enables us to reconstruct not only the facts of a case but also to explore the contested and blurred boundary between public and private interests that often lies at the heart of corruption and misgovernment. Alfred Hirschman showed that the language of "interest," on which self-interest depended, was an early modern innovation that took hold over the course of the seventeenth and eighteenth centuries (Hirschman 1977; Force 2003). Historical allegations of corruption produced counterclaims that private interest was not necessarily incompatible with the public interest. To give an example, Samuel Vaughan was alleged in 1769 to have tried bribing the prime minister of the day to buy a legal office on the island of Jamaica, where he had considerable interests. Vaughan was part of a radical group in London that was a thorn in the government's side; it was very convenient to smear one of their number with corruption, especially when the radicals alleged the government of misgovernment. But Vaughan tried to put a "public good" defense: he claimed he had wanted the post because it had previously been mismanaged and he could bring order and regularity to it by employing a competent deputy. Moreover, his defense team said, if corruption was prevalent it could not be resisted by a single man—swimming against the tide was an unreasonable expectation (Vaughan 1769, 1770). At the heart of the case was therefore a judgment about where the public interest really lay and how far an individual should sacrifice their private interests to pursue it. If we are interested in the process by which the dividing line between public and private interests became firmer and clearer, we will need a historical explanation of a process by which waves of scandals gradually shifted public opinion and state action.

How and Why Key Concepts
and Discourses Change

This final section will return to how history can help us think about change in order to make two further points: that studying the history of how the concept and language of corruption changed over time can be instructive and that such a history will be one that is not focused solely on the history of institutions and governmental administration but will also include both an ethical debate and a more popular element, charting popular engagement and pressure. Reform cannot be simply a top-down, formalistic process, but must also have an ethical dimension and engage and reflect, as well as lead, popular opinion.

Political scientists have spent a good deal of time trying to define and therefore fix what we mean by corruption (summarized in Philp 1997). A historical view will show that the meaning and concept of corruption has evolved over time and that it has always been a contested and ambiguous notion. As has already been noted, for much of the pre-modern period, the word corruption was mostly used in a religious context. After the protestant reformation of the sixteenth centuries it meant original or committed sin—man was a corrupt and sinful creature—but was also associated in Britain with a Catholic Church that was doctrinally corrupt (having moved away from scriptural purity) and institutionally corrupt (selling salvation for money in the form of "indulgences"). At the same time, "government" meant regulation of the self as well as of a nation, and government was only partially conceived of along the lines of a principal-agent model: officials were empowered by the Crown, it is true, but they were ideally to be guided by an internalized sense of public duty, an ethos inculcated both by Christian sensibilities and by classical literature, in which the pre-modern world was steeped. Aristotle and Cicero, in particular, offered influential guides to understanding corruption and quality of government. In the republican tradition of civic humanism, the classics underlined the importance of virtuous governors and of a virtuous population: corruption was the decay of this virtue in both rulers and ruled. These are very different ways of thinking about corruption to today, though echoes of them still survive and they remind us that Western cultures have thought about corruption in very different ways at different times. The focus on the abuse of office emerged in fits and starts over the best part of three hundred years.

One of the reasons why it did was public interest in scandals surrounding corruption and poor government. Whilst there has been a good deal of stress on the importance of civil society in anticorruption, there has been less of a concern with involving a wider public in the process of reform. A historical approach would nevertheless emphasize the importance of this, both because public pressure acted as an important force for change—there is a considerable history on the importance of popular culture, social action and non-elite actors as well as more elite shapers of public opinion—and because public debate helped to define what was acceptable and unacceptable. One way of exploring such forces is to study print culture. Pre-modern Britain had a particularly free press—the government lost control over pre-publication censorship in 1641, on the eve of the civil war, and although it regained some control on and off over the next half-century, after 1695 the government no longer required material to be published under licence. The press not only exposed corruption but was also a participant in the production of corruption scandals, with writers and publishers having their own agendas. These factors made for robust public discussion, with numerous pamphlets, newspapers and printed images—all highly illuminating data sources for anyone interested in the quality of government or in the public management of corruption scandals, and a testament to the depth of public discussion which itself played a significant part in the anticorruption process by increasing pressure on politicians (Barker 2000; Clark 2004; Gatrell 2006; Knights 2006; O'Connell 1999; Peacey 2013; Raymond 2003; Sommerville 1996). The press articulated anxieties about corruption, either in the abstract or in relation to particular scandals. To be sure, such scandal-mongering was not always productive—a concern with the individual tended to obscure what needed to be structurally reformed—but corruption was a persistent and widespread popular concern, not least because it was used for political and electioneering purposes. Partisan rivalries were a key driver of the anticorruption campaigns as much in the past as now. But this also meant that politicians and polemicists were interested in using corruption to engage and inflame their audiences. This pressure brought about significant change—in the 1640s, for example, and again in the early 1830s, when popular pressure was instrumental in pushing through electoral reform in 1832 (Aidt 2015). Fear of revolution concentrated the minds of the elite very well.

Graphic satires are another useful resource and can illustrate the point about the changing concept of, and attitudes to, corruption as well as the importance of engaging the public and showing how anticorruption became part of the creative and imaginative life of a country. Although the protestant reformation was somewhat distrustful of images, graphic satire could be justified where it had an anti-Catholic purpose (Morton 2014); and one of the most enduring of biblical metaphors was the corrupt tree bringing forth corrupt fruit (Mathew 7:18–19; Luke 6: 43; Job 14:7). Anti-Catholicism and the biblical metaphor of corruption were combined in an image of the later sixteenth century, which showed the roots of a corrupted tree being nourished with money by "the worlde" and being watered by "ignorance" (British Museum 1916, 0212.2, Object reference number: PPA93310, analyzed by Watt, 1991, 150–4). Lying on the right-hand side is Judas, who had betrayed Jesus for money; and on the other a figure from the Acts of the Apostles, Simon Magus, who gave his name to simony, that is, the buying and selling of clerical office. In this image, the reform(ation) of corruption was being lauded (Figure 7.1).

We might contrast this with an image from over two hundred years later (Figure 7.2).

In this satire, it is reform that is being attacked: John Bull is being tempted by a populist politician Charles James Fox with an apple labeled "reform" and the corrupt tree represents an association of negative attributes of reform, since its apples are labeled "conspiracy," "revolution," "Age of Reform," "Slavery," "Blasphemy," and even "Treason." In the background a flourishing tree has a trunk of "Justice" with roots in the "Commons," "King," "Lords," branches of "Laws," and "Religion" and fruit inscribed "Freedom," "Happiness," "Security." Here, then, is a very different vision of government, in which reform could be dangerous.

The image is a useful reminder that reform was not universally welcomed or popular, and that it could be a pejorative term, particularly at times of crisis—during the French revolution and consequent revolutionary wars, reform was often seen as dangerous. Such prints may have been primarily intended for a fairly elite audience but we also know that they reflected a much more extensive public debate—one of the factors pushing reform in the early nineteenth century was a flood of cheap print that contained some biting critiques of corruption that deeply worried the governments of the day (Gilmartin 1996; Knights 2017b; Rickwood 1971; Wood 1994, 2009). Moreover, allegorical depictions of "good" and "bad"

FIGURE 7.1 A detail of an untitled, uncatalogued satire from the later sixteenth century (British Museum 1916,0212.2, Object reference number: PPA93310).

government adorned public spaces, including municipal buildings where governance actually took place. We should not underestimate the power of the visual and the metaphorical to inculcate lessons—and to create visions of both the ideal and the corrupt. Indeed, using prints or historical case studies as a basis for ethical training may have distinct advantages, since they can be tailored to particular local cultures and also defuse the confrontational risks of directly tackling an individual's moral compass (as an example, a discussion sheet about Pepys is available at Knights 2016b). The past can help a dialogue with the present.

CONCLUSION AND FUTURE AGENDA

History, then, offers a vast dataset of when and why quality of government was compromised or improved; it offers qualitative insights into the mentalities of individuals, groups, and societies that quantitative data alone cannot provide; it offers interpretations of and models for change; and it can show the ways in which corruption was and is part of a larger set of interrelated phenomena. Corruption is a topic in its own right; but it is also a lens through which larger societal problems are visible, that have to do with the process of state formation, the nature of the economy, religious and moral culture, the legal system, and the extent of

FIGURE 7.2 BM Satires 9214, James Gillray, *The Tree of Liberty* (1798)

informed public debate. History suggests that corruption cannot be seen in isolation from these other factors and that policy has to take this larger picture into account if it is to be successful.

All this helps to set an agenda for future research on national but also comparative histories. Although there are some interesting studies of corruption in different European and non-European countries in the pre-modern period, so that we know something about Denmark, Sweden, Italy, the Netherlands, France, Germany, colonial Spanish America, colonial British North America, and China (Doyle 1996; Frisk Jensen 2014; Geltner, Kroeze, and Vitoria 2017; Kerkhoff 2013; Little and Posada-Carbó 1996; Moutoukias 1988; Paquette

2008; Park 1997; Teachout 2014; Uslaner and Rothstein 2016; Waquet 1991), there has been relatively little attempt to compare such experiences in order to analyze when and why anticorruption strategies worked and failed, and how different countries navigated their way through reform (though see Brewer and Hellmuth 1999; Crook and Crook 2011; Elliott 2006, chapter 11; Innes and Philp 2013; 2018; Kroeze and Martinez 2018; Swart 1949; Wagenaar, Kerkhoff, and Kroeze 2013). Such a project would in turn throw up important conclusions about the evolution of the quality of government more generally, indicating which political, economic, religious, legal, and print cultures created the best environments (there may well have been more than one type) in which good government could emerge and flourish. Moreover, such a comparative European framework would also embrace an imperial dimension, since many continental nations, and the corporations they spawned, developed overseas colonies and empires that posed very considerable challenges in terms of government and corruption. And that history matters because imperial legacies have been important in shaping contemporary cultures. So understanding our European and imperial histories is not just an academic exercise but should tell us useful things about the processes and frameworks underpinning good government. If history has so far been slightly marginal to cross-disciplinary discussions about corruption and good government, this chapter has sought to make the case that in future it might usefully and routinely have a seat at the table.

References

Aidt, Toke. 2015. "Democratization Under the Threat of Revolution: Evidence From the Great Reform Act of 1832." *Econometrica* 83 (2): 505–47.

Aylmer, Gerald. 1980. "From Office-holding to Civil Service: The Genesis of Modern Bureaucracy." *Transactions of the Royal Historical Society* 5th series 30: 91–108.

Baker, Norman. 1971. *Government and Contractors: the British Treasury and War Supplies, 1775–1783*. London: Athlone Press.

Barker, Hannah. 2000. *Newspapers, Politics and English Society 1695–1855*. Harlow: Longman.

Blundo, Giorgio, Olivier de Sardan, and N. B. Arifari. 2006. *Everyday Corruption and the State: Citizens and Public Officials in Africa*. Chicago: Chicago University Press.

Bowen, Huw. 2006. *The Business of Empire: The East India Company and Imperial Britain, 1756–1833*. Cambridge: Cambridge University Press.

Braddick, Michael. 2000. *State Formation in Early Modern England, c.1550–1700*. Cambridge: Cambridge University Press.

Brenner, Robert. 1993. *Merchants and Revolution: Commercial Change, Political Conflict and London's Overseas Traders 1550–1653*. Cambridge: Cambridge University Press.

Brett, Annabel. 2002. "What is Intellectual History Now?" In *What is History Now?* Edited by David Cannadine, 113–31. Basingstoke: Palgrave.

Brewer, John. 1990. *The Sinews of Power: War, Money and the English State 1688–1783* Cambridge MA: Harvard University Press.

Brewer, John, and Eckhart Hellmuth, eds. 1999. *Rethinking Leviathan: The Eighteenth Century State in Britain and Germany*. Oxford: Oxford University Press.

Brooks, Colin. 1984. "The Country Persuasion and Political Responsibility in England in the 1690s." *Parliamentary Estates and Representation* 4: 135–47.

Buchan, Bruce, and Lisa Hill. 2014. *An Intellectual History of Political Corruption* Basingstoke: Palgrave.

Burns, Arthur, and Joanna Innes, eds. 2007. *Rethinking the Age of Reform: Britain 1780–1850*. Cambridge: Cambridge University Press.

Christie, Ian. 1962. *Wilkes, Wyvill and Reform: the Parliamentary Reform Movement in British Politics, 1760–1785*. Basingstoke: Macmillan.

Clark, Anna. 2004. *Scandal: The Sexual Politics of the British Constitution*. Princeton: Princeton University Press.

Clark, Jonathan. 2000. *English Society 1660–1832: Religion, Ideology and Politics during the Ancien Regime*. 2nd ed. Cambridge: Cambridge University Press.

Commissioners of Public Accounts. 1782. 7th Report, 19 June 1782, *Commons Journal* xxxviii: 1071.

Condren, Conal. 2006. *Argument and Authority in Early Modern England: The Presupposition of Oaths and Offices*. Cambridge: Cambridge University Press.

Criddle, Evan J., and Evan Fox-Decent, Andrew S. Gold, Sung Hui Kim, Paul B. Miller, eds. 2018. *Fiduciary Government*. Cambridge: Cambridge University Press.

Crook, Malcolm, and Tom Crook. 2011. "Reforming Voting Practices in a Global Age: The Making and Remaking of the Modern Secret Ballot in Britain, France and the United States, c.1600–c.1950." *Past & Present* 212: 199–237.

Dabhoiwala, Faramerz. 2012. *The Origins of Sex: A History of The First Sexual Revolution*. London: Allen Lane.

de Bolla, Peter. 2013. *The Architecture of Concepts: The Historical Formation of Human Rights*. New York: Fordham University Press.

De Sardan, J. P. Olivier. 1999. "A Moral Economy of Corruption in Africa?" *The Journal of Modern African Studies* 37 (1): 25–52.

Dirks, Nicholas. 2006. *The Scandal of Empire: India and the Creation of Imperial Britain*. Cambridge MA: Harvard University Press.

Downie, J. A. 1976. "The Commission of Public Accounts and Formation of the Country Party." *English Historical Review* 91: 33–51.

Doyle, William. 1996. *Venality. The Sale of Offices in Eighteenth Century France*. Oxford: Oxford University Press.

Elliott, Sir John. 2006. *Empires of the Atlantic World*. New Haven: Yale University Press.

Engels, Jens Ivo. 2017. "Corruption and Anticorruption in the Era of Modernity and Beyond. In *Anticorruption in History. From Antiquity to the Modern Era*, edited by Guy Geltner, Ronald Kroeze, and Andre Vitoria. Oxford: Oxford University Press.

Epstein, James. 2012. *The Scandal of Colonial Rule: Power and Subversion in the British Atlantic during the Age of Revolution*. Cambridge: Cambridge University Press.

Finn, Paul. 1995. "The Forgotten 'Trust': The People and the State." In *Equity: Issues and Trends*, edited by Malcolm Cope, 131–51. Sydney: Federation Press.

First Report from the Committee Appointed to Enquire into the Nature, State, and Condition of the East India Company. 1772. London.

Fontaine, Laurence. 2014 (first printed in France, 2008). *The Moral Economy. Poverty, Credit and Trust in Early Modern Europe*. Cambridge: Cambridge University Press.

Force, Pierre. 2003. *Self-Interest before Adam Smith: A Genealogy of Economic Science*. Cambridge: Cambridge University Press.

Fox-Decent, Evan. 2011. *Sovereignty's Promises: The State as Fiduciary*. Oxford: Oxford University Press.

Frisk Jensen, Mette. 2014. "The Question of How Denmark got to be Denmark—Establishing Rule of Law and Fighting Corruption in the State of Denmark 1660 – 1900." *Quality of Government Working Papers Series 2014:06*. Gothenburg: University of Gothenburg.

Fry, Michael. 1992. *The Dundas Despotism*. Edinburgh: John Donald.

Gatrell, Vic. 2006. *City of Laughter: Sex and Satire in Eighteenth Century London*. London: Atlantic Press.

Geltner, Guy, Ronald Kroeze, and Andre Vitoria, eds. 2017. *Anti-Corruption in History. From Antiquity to the Modern Era*. Oxford: Oxford University Press.

Gilmartin, Kevin. 1996. *Print Politics: The Press and Radical Opposition in Early Nineteenth-Century England*. Cambridge: Cambridge University Press.

Ginzburg, Carlo. 1993. "Microhistory, Two or Three Things That I Know about It." Translated by John Tedeschi and Anne C. Tedeschi. *Critical Inquiry* 20 (1): 10–35.

Goldie, Mark. 2001. "The Unacknowledged Republic; Officeholding in Early Modern England." In *The Politics of the Excluded c.1500–c.1850*, edited by Tim Harris, 153–94. Basingstoke: Palgrave.

Graham, Aaron. 2015. *Corruption, Party, and Government in Britain, 1702–1713*. Oxford: Oxford University Press.

Graham, Aaron, and Patrick Walsh, eds. 2016. *The British Fiscal-Military States 1660–1783*. London: Routledge.

Haigh, Christopher. 1990. *The English Reformation Revised*. Cambridge: Cambridge University Press.

Harling, Philip. 1996. *The Waning of "Old Corruption": The Politics of Economical Reform in Britain, 1779–1846*. Oxford: Clarendon Press.

Harling, Philip and Mandler, Peter. 1993. "From Fiscal-Military State to Laissez-faire State 1760–1850." *Journal of British Studies* 32: 44–70.

Hawkes, David. 2010. *The Culture of Usury in Renaissance England*. Basingstoke: Palgrave.

Hellmann, Olli. 2017. "The Historical Origins of Corruption in the Developing World: A Comparative Analysis of East Asia." *Crime, Law and Social Change* 68: 145–65.

Hellmuth, Eckhart. 1999. "Why Does Corruption Matter? Reforms and Reform Movements in Britain and Germany in the Second Half of the Eighteenth Century." *Proceedings of the British Academy* 100: 5–24.

Heywood, Paul. 2018. "Combating Corruption in the Twenty-First Century: New Approaches." *Daedalus* 147 (3): 83–97.

Heywood, Paul, and Elizabeth Johnson. 2017. "Cultural Specificity versus Institutional Universalism: a Critique of the National Integrity System (NIS) Methodology." *Crime, Law & Social Change* 68: 1–16.

Hirschman, Alfred. 1977. *The Passions and the Interests*. Princeton: Princeton University Press.

Hughes, Edward. 1949. "Sir Charles Trevelyan and Civil Service Reform, 1853–5." *The English Historical Review* 64 (250): 53–88.

Hurstfield, Joel. 1967. "Political Corruption in Modern England: The Historian's Problem." *History* 52 (174): 16–34.

Hurstfield, Joel. 1973. *Freedom, Corruption and Government in Elizabethan England*. London: Case.

Iliffe, Robert. 2017. *Priest of Nature: The Religious Worlds of Isaac Newton*. Oxford: Oxford University Press.

Ingram, Martin. 1996. "Reformation of Manners in Early Modern England." In *The Experience of Authority in Early Modern England*, edited by Adam Fox, Paul Griffiths, and Steve Hindle, 47–88. Basingstoke: Macmillan.

Innes, Joanna. 2007. "'Reform' in English Public Life: The Fortunes of a Word." In *Rethinking the Age of Reform: Britain 1780–1850*, edited by Arthur Burns and Joanna Innes, 71–97. Cambridge: Cambridge University Press.

Innes, Joanna, and Mark Philp. 2013. *Re-imagining Democracy in the Age of Revolutions: America, France, Britain, Ireland 1750–1850*. Oxford: Oxford University Press.

Innes, Joanna, and Mark Philp. 2018. *Re-Imagining Democracy in the Mediterranean, 1780–1860*. Oxford: Oxford University Press.

Johnston, Michael. 1991. "Historical Conflict and the Rise of Standards." *Journal of Democracy* 2 (4): 48–60.

Johnston, Michael. 2006. *Syndromes of Corruption: Wealth, Power and Democracy*. Cambridge: Cambridge University Press.

Johnston, Michael. 2012. *Corruption and Reform: One Size Does Not Fit All*. Laxenburg: International Anti-Corruption Academy.

Jordanova, Ludmilla. 2006. *History in Practice*. 2nd ed. London: Hodder Arnold.

Jordanova, Ludmilla. 2012. *The Look of the Past: Visual and Material Evidence in Historical Practice*. Cambridge: Cambridge University Press.

Kerkhoff, Toon. 2013. "Hidden Morals, Explicit Scandals: Public Values and Political Corruption in The Netherlands (1748–1813)." Ph.D. diss. University of Leiden.

Knights, Mark. 2006. *Representation and Misrepresentation in Later Stuart Britain: Partisanship and Political Culture*. Oxford: Oxford University Press.

Knights, Mark. 2007. "Parliament, Print and Corruption in Later Stuart Britain." *Parliamentary History* 26 (1): 49–61.

Knights, Mark. 2014. "Samuel Pepys and Corruption." *Parliamentary History* 33 (1): 19–35.

Knights, Mark, 2016a. "Old Corruption: What British History can tell us about Corruption Today." http://www.transparency.org.uk/publications/old-corruption-what-british-history-can-tell-us-about-corruption-today/#.W4eemPZFxoI

Knights, Mark, 2016b. "Was Samuel Pepys Corrupt?" https://www.transparency.org.uk/publications/was-samuel-pepys-corrupt/

Knights, Mark. 2017a. "Anticorruption in Seventeenth- and Eighteenth-Century Britain." In *Anti-Corruption in History. From Antiquity to the Modern Era*, edited by Guy Geltner, Ronald Kroeze, and Andre Vitoria, 181–96. Oxford: Oxford University Press.

Knights, Mark. 2017b. "Corruption, Satire, Parody and the Press in Early Modern Britain." In *The Power of Laughter and Satire in Early Modern Britain*, edited by Mark Knights and Adam Morton, 190–210. Woodbridge: Boydell and Brewer.

Knights, Mark. 2018a. "Explaining Away Corruption in Pre-modern Britain." *Social Policy and Philosophy* 35 (2): 94–117.

Knights, Mark. 2018b. "Corruption as the Abuse of Entrusted Power." In *Jus Gentium Europaeum*, edited by Nicoletta Parisi, Gianluca Potesta, and Dino Rinoldi, 149–73. Naples: Editoriale Scientifica.

Knights, Mark. 2019a. "Parliament and Conflicts of Interest." https://blogs.warwick.ac.uk/historyofcorruption/entry/parliament_and_conflicts/

Knights, Mark. 2021a, forthcoming. "Corruption and Later Stuart State Trials." In *State Trials: The Politics of Justice in Later Stuart England*, edited by Brian Cowan and Scott Sowerby. Woodbridge: Boydell and Brewer.

Knights, Mark, 2021b, forthcoming. *Trust and Distrust: Corruption in Office in Britain and its Empire c.1600–c.1850*. Oxford: Oxford University Press, 2021.

Kramer, Lloyd, and Sarah Maza. 2002. *A Companion to Western Historical Thought*. Oxford: Blackwell.

Kramnick, Isaac. 1994. "Corruption in Eighteenth-Century English and American Political Discourse." In *Virtue, Corruption and Self-Interest*, edited by Richard Matthews, 55–75. Bethlehem PA: Lehigh University Press.

Kreike, Emmanuel and Jordan, William Chester, eds. 2004. *Corrupt Histories*. Rochester N.Y.: Rochester University Press.

Kroeze, Ronald, and F. Gil Martínez. 2018. "The Transformation of Corruption in 1700–1900: A Comparison between Spain and the Netherlands." In *La Corrupción Política en la Espana Contemporánea*, edited by B. Borja de Riquer, Joan Luis Pérez Francesch, G. Gemma Rubí, and Lluís Ferran Toledano, 483–96. Madrid: Marcial Pons Historia.

Kuhn, Thomas. 2012. *The Structure of Scientific Revolutions*. 4th ed. Chicago: University of Chicago Press.

Law Commission. 2016. "The History of the Offence of Misconduct in Public Office." https://s3-eu-west-2.amazonaws.com/lawcom-prod-storage-11jsxou24uy7q/uploads/2016/01/apa_history.pdf

Lawson, Philip. 1993. *The East India Company: A History*. London: Longman.

Lemmings, David, and Claire Walker, eds. 2009. *Moral Panics, the Media and the Law in Early Modern England*. Basingstoke: Macmillan.

Little, Daniel, 2017. "Character and History." In *Questions of Character*, edited by Iskra Fileva, 323–39. Oxford: Oxford University Press.

Little, Daniel. 2000. "Explaining Large-Scale Historical Change." *Philosophy of the Social Sciences* 30 (1): 89–112.

Little, Daniel. 2007 (revised 2016). "Philosophy of History." Stanford Encyclopedia of History. https://plato.stanford.edu/entries/history/#CauHis

Little, Walter, and Eduardo Posada-Carbó. 1996. *Political Corruption in Europe and Latin America*. Basingstoke: Macmillan.

Maitland, William. 2003. *State, Trust, and Corporation*. Edited by David Runciman and Magnus Ryan. Cambridge: Cambridge University Press.

Maloy, Jason S. 2008. *The Colonial American Origins of Modern Democratic Thought*. Cambridge: Cambridge University Press.

Maloy, Jason S. 2009. "Two Concepts of Trust." *The Journal of Politics* 71 (2): 492–505.

Mendle, Michael. 1995. *Henry Parker and the English Civil War: The Political Thought of the Public's "Privado."* Cambridge: Cambridge University Press.

Marshall, Peter. 1965. *The Impeachment of Warren Hastings*. Oxford: Oxford University Press.

Marshall, Peter. 1976. *East Indian Fortunes: The British in Bengal in the Eighteenth Century*. Oxford: Clarendon Press.

Morton, Adam. 2014. "A Product of Confession or Corruption? *The Common Weales Canker Worms* (c.1625) and the Progress of Sin in Early Modern England." In *Illustrated Religious Texts in the North of Europe, 1500–1800*, edited by Adam Morton, Feike Dietz, Lien Roggen, 135–64. Farnham: Ashgate.

Moutoukias, Zacarias. 1988. "Power, Corruption and Commerce: The Making of the Local Administrative Structure in Seventeenth-century Buenos Aries." *Hispanic American Historical Review* 68 (4): 771–801.

Nelson, Benjamin. 1969. *The Idea of Usury, from Tribal Brotherhood to Universal Otherhood*. Chicago: University of Chicago Press.

Neufeld, Mathew. 2014. "Parliament and some Roots of Whistle Blowing during the Nine Years War." *The Historical Journal* 57 (2): 397–420.

Nicoletti, Michele. 2017. "Promoting Integrity in Governance to Tackle Political Corruption, Council of Europe Parliamentary Assembly Report 14344. http://assembly.coe.int/nw/xml/XRef/Xref-XML2HTML-EN.asp?fileid=23790&lang=en

Noonan, John. 1984. *Bribes*. New York: Macmillan.

North, Douglass, John Joseph Wallis, and Barry Weingast. 2009. *Violence and Social Orders: A Conceptual Framework for Interpreting Recorded Human History*. Cambridge: Cambridge University Press.

O'Connell, Sheila. 1999. *The Popular Print in England 1550–1850*. London: British Museum Press.

Ogborn, Miles. 2007. *Indian Ink: Script and Print in the Making of the English East India Company*. Chicago: University of Chicago Press.

Paquette, Gabriel. 2008. *Enlightenment, Governance and Reform in Spain and its Empire, 1759–1808*. Basingstoke: Palgrave.

Papers relative to the Case at Issue between Sir Edward Colebrooke Bt and the Bengal Government. 1833. London.

Park, Nancy. 1997. "Corruption in Eighteenth Century China." *The Journal of Asian Studies* 56 (4): 967–1005.

Peacey, Jason. 2013. *Print and Public Politics in the English Revolution*. Cambridge: Cambridge University Press.

Peck, Linda Levy. 1990. *Court Patronage and Corruption in Early Stuart England*. London: Routledge.

Pettigrew, Will. 2013. *Freedom's Debt: The Royal African Company and the Politics of the Atlantic Slave Trade 1672–1752*. Chapel Hill: University of North Carolina Press.

Philp, Mark. 1997. "Defining Political Corruption." *Political Studies* 45 (3): 436–62.

Plamper, Jan. 2017. *The History of Emotions: An Introduction*. Oxford: Oxford University Press.

Platt, D. C. M. 1961. "The Commercial and Industrial Interests of Ministers of the Crown." *Political Studies* 9 (3): 267–90.

Pocock, John G. A. 1987. "The Concept of a Language and the Métier d''Historien: Some Considerations on Practice.' In *The Languages of Political Theory in Early-Modern Europe*, edited by Anthony Pagden. Cambridge: Cambridge University Press.

Prior, Katherine, Lance Brennan, and Robin Haines. 2001. "Bad Language: The Role of English, Persian and other Esoteric Tongues in the Dismissal of Sir Edward Colebrooke as Resident of Delhi in 1829." *Modern Asian Studies* 35 (1): 75–112.

Raymond, Joad. 2003. *Pamphlets and Pamphleteering in Early Modern Britain*. Cambridge: Cambridge University Press.

Reddy, William. 2001. *The Navigation of Feeling: A Framework for the History of Emotions*. Cambridge: Cambridge University Press.

Rickwood, Edgell. 1971. *Radical Squibs and Loyal Ripostes: Satirical Pamphlets of the Regency Period 1819–1821*. Bath: Adams and Dart.

Roberts, M. J. D. 2004. *Making English Morals: Voluntary Association and Moral Reform in England, 1787–1886*. Cambridge: Cambridge University Press.

Rosenwein, Barbara. 2006. *Emotional Communities in the Early Middle Ages*. Ithaca, N.Y.: Cornell University Press.

Rothstein, Bo, and Aiysha Varraich. 2017. *Making Sense of Corruption*. Cambridge: Cambridge University Press.

Ryrie, Alec. 2013. *Being Protestant in Reformation Britain*. Oxford: Oxford University Press.

Seaward, Paul. 2002. "The Cavalier Parliament, the 1667 Accounts Commission and the Idea of Accountability." In *Parliament at Work. Parliamentary Committees, Political Power and Public Access in Early Modern England*, edited by Chris Kyle and Jason Peacey, 149–68. Woodbridge: Boydell and Brewer

Shagan, Ethan. 2003. *Popular Politics and the English Reformation*. Cambridge: Cambridge University Press.

Skinner, Quentin. 2002. *Visions of Politics*. 3 vols. Cambridge: Cambridge University Press.

Sommerville, Johann. 1996. *The News Revolution in England: Cultural Dynamics of Daily Information*. Oxford: Oxford University Press.

Stern, Philip. 2011. *The Company-State: Corporate Sovereignty and the Early Modern Foundatin of the British Empire in India*. Oxford: Oxford University Press.

Swart, Koenaraad. 1949. *Sale of Offices in the Seventeenth Century*. The Hague: Martinus Nijhoff.

Teachout, Zephyr. 2014. *Corruption in America. From Benjamin Franklin's Snuff Box to Citizens United*. Cambridge MA: Harvard University Press.

Tite, Colin. 1974. *Impeachment and Parliamentary Judicature in Early Stuart England*. London: Athlone Press.

Tosh, John. 2008. *Why History Matters*. Basingstoke: Palgrave.

Tosh, John. 2015. *The Pursuit of History: Aims, Methods and New Directions in the Study of History*. 6th ed. London: Routledge.

Tosh, John, ed. 2018. *Historians on History*. 3rd ed. London: Routledge.

Toulmin, Stephen. 1972. *Human Understanding*. Oxford: Clarendon Press.

Tyacke, Nicholas, ed. 1998. *England's Long Reformation 1500–1800*. London: Routledge.

Tyacke, Nicholas. 2007. *The English Revolution c.1590–1720*. Manchester: Manchester University Press.

Uslaner, Eric, and Bo Rothstein. 2016. "The Historical Roots of Corruption: State Building, Economic Inequality, and Mass Education." *Comparative Politics* 48 (2): 227–48.

Vaughan, Samuel. 1769. *A Refutation of a False Aspersion First thrown out upon Samuel Vaughan*. London.

Vaughan, Samuel. 1770. *An Appeal to the Public on behalf of Samuel Vaughan Esq*. London.

Waquet, Jean-Claude. 1991. *Corruption. Ethics and Power in Florence 1600–1770*. English translation by Linda McCall. London: Polity.

Wagenaar, Pieter, Toon Kerkhoff, and Ronald Kroeze. 2013. "Corruption and the Rise of Modern Politics in Europe in the Eighteenth and Nineteenth Centuries: A Comparison between France, the Netherlands, Germany and England." *Journal of Modern European History* 11 (1): 19–30.

Watt, Tessa. 1991. *Cheap Print and Popular Piety 1550–1640*. Cambridge: Cambridge University Press.

Withington, Philip. 2005. *The Politics of Commonwealth: Citizens and Freemen in Early Modern England*. Cambridge: Cambridge University Press.

Wood, Marcus. 1994. *Radical Satire and Print Culture 1790–1820*. Oxford: Oxford University Press.

Wood, Marcus. 2009. "Radical Publishing." In *The Cambridge History of the Book in Britain*, vol. 5, edited by Michael F. Suarez and Michael L. Turner, 834–48. Cambridge: Cambridge University Press.

CHAPTER 8

THE ETHNOGRAPHIC STUDY OF CORRUPTION

DAVIDE TORSELLO

THE ethnographic study of corruption is a comparatively recent scholarly field. Classical anthropological scholarship has not dealt programmatically with this phenomenon for a number of reasons that will be discussed below. Here, it may be beneficial to frame the potential contribution that ethnographic approaches may make to the study of corruption. First, this chapter will analyze the pros and cons of studying corruption via ethnographic methods; second, it will describe the main difficulty that disciplines making use of ethnography (mostly anthropology and sociology) as their main research methodology encounter; and lastly, it will present some of the main fresh and innovative insights that have been gained from the use of this methodology and its promising current and future applications.

The origin of ethnographic research methodology can be ascribed to the work of twentieth-century anthropologists who made field research the main methodology for studying different world populations and cultures. Anthropology was committed to dealing with the cultural and social aspects of life in indigenous and colonial environments, about which scarce written literature and scholarship in European languages existed. Most of the second-hand data that could be used in the sociocultural contexts in which anthropological research was conducted were mostly derived from the work of local historians (who wrote in local languages), travelers, conquerors, or missionaries. Some scholars suggest that these were the early steps of ethnography, which are situated in a particular time, distinct from the conventions of the first half of the twentieth-century, when Bronislaw Malinowski and Franz Boas conducted field research (Hodgen 2011).

The most recent features of ethnography were developed according to a range of conditions that field research was to meet. The most important of these were proximity to the studied culture, duration of the field research project, direct communication in the language of the studied population, and observance of several epistemological and deontological indications which would render the observation "tolerable" and ensure ethical conformity to the safeguards of the studied population. Each of these conditions was problematic in nature for several and sometimes conflicting reasons. Towards the beginning of the 1980s, this contributed towards the emergence of a tendency to problematize the fieldwork research method by advocating for a more reflexive turn in anthropology that would take into more serious consideration the abuses of anthropological research under colonial domin-ation or in dealing with indigenous populations undergoing acculturation (Salzman 2002). Reverberations of the abuses of ethnography have remained, particularly through post-modern influences (Spiro 1996).

The difference between disciplines that make use of qualitative data and those that do not becomes particularly heavy in an age of quantophrenia, as scholars in the social sciences seek validation of their research data through mathematical formulae and statistical evidence. Consequently, it may not be an exaggeration to state that ethnography has remained one of the "last frontiers" of qualitative research methods. Such an affirmation puts particular strains on the role of anthropology, which, unlike sociology, has remained largely immune to quantophrenia. At the same time, anthropology is often found in the position of having to resolve its internal disconnect between researchers who question the epistemological val-idity of field research methodology in the "classical sense" and those who embrace it as the real strength of qualitative methodology. While both positions have pros and cons, the true value of ethnographic methods cannot be questioned if one considers that other social sci-ence disciplines, such as geography, political science, cultural and organization studies, in the last two decades, have been ready to adopt ethnography in addition to other qualitative research methods.

The methodology applied in classical anthropological field research is based on par-ticipant observation. According to the "canonical view" developed by Malinowski, the researcher would have to spend a prolonged period of time (according to some anthro-pologists, at least a year) living in the community or social group where the research is planned. The very idea of participant observation is contradictory for the study of sen-sitive topics, such as corruption. For one thing, if the participant observation method is based on personal interaction between the observer and the observed, a degree of noise provided by this interaction should be taken into account. In my research experience, I have come across cases of interaction with persons who refused to talk about corruption-related issues in their own town or village and, conversely, I have met persons who were very outspoken about corruption. Both positions may appear to be influenced by some degree of noise due to the presence of the fieldworker. However, because of the direct interaction with the observed, the ethnographer is in the position of being able to gather extremely interesting and fine-grained data which cannot be accessed from a quantitative perspective.

Moreover, ethnographic field research is not only about participant observation and interviews. If it is true that this is the most efficient methodology in ethnographic research, in many cases, other qualitative methods can and must be deployed. In the course of com-parative field research undertaken with public administrations in eight countries (Torsello and Venard 2016), I have found it extremely helpful to use focus groups to triangulate data gathered through participant observation. This has proved very useful for dealing with cor-ruption, as the justification for the choice of focus groups has been that they involve the pres-ence of "experts" on the topic at hand (e.g. personnel working in anticorruption and integrity units in administrations, in audits, and in compliance). Focus groups became the channel for conveying information about both the procedural aspects of corruption and concrete cases that specialized personnel encountered. Moreover, they helped in reducing the noise that common talk on corruption may generate.

PROS AND CONS OF STUDYING CORRUPTION
USING THE ETHNOGRAPHIC METHOD

Corruption is a pervasive phenomenon both socially and culturally. Nonetheless, corruption has not been sufficiently studied through ethnographic methods (Torsello 2012). There are many reasons explaining this gap. First, the very feasibility of ethnographic fieldwork research on corruption must be questioned. What, from the very start, may jeopardize successful field research on this topic is the way that the observer is deemed to encounter corruption in the daily practices of the research. Participant observation of corrupt acts and transactions may indeed take place, as it has in a limited number of works by anthropologists and sociologists (see Smith 2007). However, as Blundo (2007) questions, are these occasional encounters with corruption—the "real thing"—sufficient to provide an empirical basis for the research? More importantly, what tools may the ethnographer have to ensure that such practices can be classified as corruption, particularly in cases where more complex transactions are at stake? The observer's judgment is in several cases the only looking glass science has to elicit a scientific approach to the study of corruption. However, this may not be enough, as decades of postmodernist criticism of "field authority" or researchers have proved.

Thus, the principal choice for observing corruption in social realities may be to focus on petty or small-scale corruption-related transactions. It is not by chance that, in most ethnographic accounts of corruption, this is the prevalent form of illicit action studied (de Sardan 1999). It is far more likely that the researcher will observe a customs officer receiving a small kickback than a bureaucrat accepting a substantial gift for allowing a concession. The difference is not, however, about the entity of the bribe only. Growing ethnographic evidence points to the need to draw a line between what corruption is at the level of official, public, and media debates and what it may be in reality for the citizens of states that have to deal more extensively with it. The essentialization of such a position would lead a scholar who is concerned with the feasibility of ethnographic research to maintain that petty corruption is the only type of corruption that the ethnographer may observe, or study from first-hand data, and that this does not constitute a reason for conducting qualitative research on the topic. If half of the corruption scandals which are increasingly involving multiple actors (business, public sector, professionals, and third-sector organizations) cannot be studied through participant observation, then is the corruption studied by ethnographers the "real thing"? The answer is probably not, unless the focus on methodology is shifted from observing the practice to collecting ideas and ideologies on it. In other words, the only way out of relativistic essentializations which may lead to the position that petty corruption is not corruption at all, as may indeed be the case in some geographical and societal contexts, is to shift focus from the action itself to the discourses of corruption.

In another chapter, I have stressed the importance of studying public discourses on corruption in different social contexts (Torsello 2014). One of the main achievements of ethnographic research in this field has been pointing out that corruption becomes a discourse which is contextualized and acquires significance in Foucauldian terms (During 1992, 26) when its meaning is shared by citizens. The study of the discursive aspects of corruption is a recent endeavor, which has made an innovative contribution to knowledge of the topic. When emphasizing the discursive approach, it is possible to generate a new set of premises concerning the public role of corruption, some of which are completely unknown to the more canonical approaches to the phenomenon. These aspects include, among others, the complex mix of corruption with social practices, such as networking, favors, clientelism, nepotism, cronyism, trust, some forms of social capital and weak ties, "solidarity," cohesion, sociability, reciprocity, and exchange. All of these practices are well known in anthropology and sociology, and some of them were studied by political scientists some decades ago (Landè 1983). If ethnographic field research is applied to the study of corruption with an "open mind," the encounter with descriptions and narratives of such a phenomenon will generate considerable data on different forms of social interaction that may lead to the deployment of corruption in a society.

If it is true that anthropologists and ethnographers are most likely to encounter corruption casually (de Sardan 1999), what is new in the anthropological approach informed by a focus on discourses over practices is that ethnographic data gathered over the last quarter-century underline the significance of studying the hermeneutical aspects of corruption, which contribute to rendering it a topic of public discourse, from media coverage to chats in a bar.

The focus on discursive aspects of corruption may allow researchers to reconstruct the meta-language of corruption through symbols, images, and metaphors that are commonly used to describe such a practice. This is a complex effort owing to the extremely rich range of symbols and metaphors involved. Some of them include forms of social association (the magic circle, old boys club, jelly system, magnificent trio, share the cake, eat together, invite to the table, the world in between, etc.), violent actions (to strike, pinch, stick, cut in pieces, chop), bodily expressions (belly politics, to eat, fast, cut the umbilicus, shake hands, pass from hand to hand, have an eye for, etc.) and supernatural aspects (witchcraft, magic power, blood pact, supernatural power, etc.). The absolute richness of these expressions and metaphors alone proves the social relevance that citizens attribute to widespread corruption in their countries of origin. It goes without saying that the richness of such discursive attributes is positively correlated with the incidence of the phenomenon in a society. Yet changes in the discursive aspects of corruption may well relate to changes in the way that corruption takes place in a societal context. This was the case in Italy when, in the famous peak years of the Clean Hands Movement (1990–93), corruption was symbolically described in terms of envelopes (*bustarelle*), or yellow envelopes (*buste gialle*), and making a deal was related to cutting a cake (*tagliare la torta*). These were metaphors from a time when corruption was happening at the convergence of bureaucracy, business, and political parties as the main actors. Conversely, more recent corrupt deeds in Italian politics have been described with more evocative terms, such as the magic circle (*il cerchio magico*), jelly system (*il sistema gelatinoso*), friend circle (*il circolo degli amici*), and, eventually, to use Tolkien's philosophy, "the theory of the world in-between" *(la teoria del mondo di mezzo)*. This discursive shift may be explained by the change in corrupt practices that have brought about the diminishing involvement of political parties, a more "participative" and colluding aspect of corruption, and the increasingly key role of in-between or middle men who, resorting to violence, threats, or blackmail, have significant connections with the business and bureaucratic worlds, without which these activities would be difficult to execute.

Another positive, innovative aspect of the discursive approach to corruption regards the fact that this enables the researcher to discern between commonsensical notions of the harms of corruption in society from focused dialogical perspectives. Corruption is an extremely plastic phenomenon which not only proves to be resilient and resistant to reforms and policies but also to acquire different faces and forms as some of them become obsolete. From a bird's-eye view, corruption is tied to other criminal activities and associations, which allows flexibility and opacity to its active forms; this, in turn, renders it difficult to study the changing forms of corruption. One demonstration may be the eclectic nature of the anthropology of corruption—a new field of research which, as mentioned above, has not always been able to clearly disentangle this from other practices (Torsello and Venard 2016). In other words, the positive contribution that ethnographic studies of corruption may make relates to their departure from a holistic perspective which, grounded in the social reality under investigation, can paint a broader picture, populated by metaphors, discourses, narrative, and conflicting moral standpoints. In these contexts, corruption appears not as a black box, static and resistant to policy attacks, but as a form that is continuously changing and is strongly adaptable to changing socioeconomic and political milieus. Culture, in this approach, has a privileged position, in the sense that it works to justify reasons why corruption is mistaken with other tangent phenomena, or it is nonetheless tolerated even when citizens of a country are well aware of the dangers and risks tied with its presence in society. Therefore, the analysis of discourses that veil and unveil the actual significance of corruption in a society is a powerful methodological instrument for keeping an eye on changing tropes and topics related to this changing state of things.

Some of the obstacles that a researcher may face when deciding to undertake fieldwork on corruption-related topics also merit discussion. Apart from epistemological and deontological considerations that refer to the ethical codes for ethnographic research (developed by the major professional organizations in anthropology; Torsello 2014), I would like to pay attention to the aforementioned "noise" aspects of studying corruption through ethnography. If discursive corruption or petty corruption are the most typically studied aspects in ethnography, these are also those which may be subject to continuous alteration in form and meaning. One thing would be to study a large corruption scandal in a corporation that, through its complexity, a factor of the sophistication of processes and relationships within an organization and between it and an institutional framework, nonetheless has a consolidated process through which the transaction takes place. This structure is common to most organizations; it changes its extent and delineation due to an influence from the external (institutional) environment and the culture of the corporation, but the patterns, forms, liabilities, and internal mechanisms of compliance are more or less similar. What local people define as corruption, the linguistic idiosyncrasies introduced to feed narratives of cheating, violating norms, paying kickbacks of various sorts (from cash to house rent, discounted estate purchases, trips/holidays, memberships in prestigious clubs, sexual favors, sport events, jobs and projects, and many more) and providing favors that may appear to be no more than gray areas, violations are more liable to be confused and overlooked.

The kind of corruption that ethnography may encounter, deliberately or unintentionally, is very different from the standard bribery scandal to which the public may be accustomed. This may become a limit for ethnography because it ties the gravity of the act (in case of grand-scale corruption) to mechanisms and processes that, to most, are exotic, to say the least, thus allowing for the generation of noise around the topic. The task of ethnographers, then, becomes to situate the different sociocultural, organizational, and institutional nuances emerging from the study of corruption in a wider frame that informs the holistic perspective described above.

Is this the only limitation of the ethnographic study of corruption? Some anthropologists have identified another shortcoming of ethnographic research which relates to the performative aspects of field research (Muir and Gupta 2018). A stream of literature has recently reflected not only on the power and authority of the fieldworker, as well as on the epistemological aspects that fieldwork entails, but also on the ways in which ethnography can deal with performative behavior of interviewees and participants in the research (LeCompte 1987; Thapar-Björkert and Henry 2007). As stated before, not only is corruption liable to be encountered accidentally by the researcher, but its incidence and significance may be severely affected by the modes and tones of descriptions of events related to it. As de Sardan (1999) puts it, an ethnographer may encounter three different attitudinal reactions from the ground to corruption deals: apathy and cynicism, disinterest, and deep emotional involvement. Among these, from my personal experience, the first and third are the most frequently observable. The point is that anthropologists need the instruments to discern the research implications of these attitudes—namely, they must be informed of what corruption means and entails at the level of practices, but also of socially grounded ideas related to corruption (poverty, legitimacy, exchange, moral trust, to mention a few); otherwise, the true message is not conveyed.

There are, of course, ways out of these limitations. The most obvious one is an increase in the quantity of ethnographic studies of corruption, which is already a present reality (Torsello and Venard 2016). Increased interest in what constitutes one of the hottest global topics can only welcome the availability of a larger number of ethnographic works. However, it is foreseeable that a larger availability of ethnographies will accompany a stronger interest in modeling and theoretical contributions, which can advance the dialogue between anthropology and other disciplines. Additionally, if the ethnographer has the opportunity to employ her work to confront a larger existing literature, it will be easier to avoid commonsensical and biased first-hand descriptions that have, at times, impoverished the quality of work on the topic and, in general, undermined its cross-fertilization with empirical research results in other social science disciplines.

A second aspect which can provide further solidity and replicability to ethnographic accounts concerns the cross-spatial study of social phenomena. Anthropology, as mentioned above, has always had the "privilege" of studying a plurality of geographical and cultural spaces and, thus, being able to gain insights that are often unique. Naturally, this applies to corruption as well. Corruption is a complex phenomenon that oscillates between replications of common forms and patterns of interaction and a well consolidated public discourse on the toxicity of its spread in society and political systems. Here, the anthropological study of corruption has the potential advantage of owning the empirical keys to gain comparative insights at the levels of institutional and people's experiences. Legal anthropologists, for instance, have pointed to the porosity of state institutions and the law in conditions of postcolonialism or when the notion of legal pluralism may apply (Nuijten and Anders 2007). It is also because, in some cases, the law is a construct tied to the customary, colonial, and postcolonial laws of the countries studied for these ethnographic works that in the everyday negotiation of the meaning and applicability of these different jurisprudence registers, corruption finds its space in different ways and through different public discourses. Here, the comparative perspective based on ethnographic research may provide fresh insights into a relationship that, between the law and the corrupt act, has too often been taken for granted (Misangyi, Weaver and Elms 2008).

Another shared concern is that of looking more attentively at what can be defined as a "processual view of corruption." Far from accepting the idea of conceiving of corruption as a one-shot univocal event, some anthropological works have looked at how corruption becomes entangled in contexts in which actors (political, business, and even third-sector organizations) are intertwined in long-term processes of exchange. It has been argued, for instance, that aid development projects may contribute to creating tight links between local and international actors or donors that favor the increase of gray area situations as well as the consolidation of interests, circles, and cliques or eventually fake organizations that benefit from the processes of funding in recipient countries. Ethnographic evidence has proved that this can happen at the EU level as well as in pre-EU accession Eastern European countries, South America, Southeast Asia, and Africa (Goldstein 2003; Bähre 2005; Hoag 2010; Torsello 2012).

Countries that have experienced large-scale political decentralization may experience similar forms of institutional distress, which may be tied to cultural reactions to political reforms that are ultimately poorly compatible with citizens' ideas and experiences of the state and local governments. Indonesia is an interesting case, where the transition from Suharto's totalitarian regime to a state-making process that has pressed towards large-scale delocalization of power has allowed for the formation of pockets of corruption in some areas, particularly where rich natural resources mark the geography. Here, as elsewhere in the world, the notion of witchcraft has come to the forefront of the attention of ethnographers rather often (Hutton 2004). Large ethnographic expertise on the phenomenon of witchcraft in different cultures has taught anthropologists to deal carefully with local descriptions of such a complex phenomenon. In the case of corruption, the narratives that local citizens used to inform the ethnographer of the growing oddities of delocalization and growing inequality in the country and among regions was imbued with morbid touches. Corruption was compared to witchcraft (Bubandt 2006) because of its power to alter a "regular" state of things in which power is visible (such as in the ostentation of leaders), and yet there is little space to tackle sudden and unexplainable changes in the access to, and distribution of, resources. Witchcraft has its language and metaphors, as corruption does, and sophisticated stories about rapidly enriched politicians and bureaucrats who died in unknown circumstances or as victims of witchcraft are probably telling of the power of corruption, which segregates through its invisible violence and contributes to loosening a social order that, although unreal, may still be followed by local populations who wish to give a sense to the individual–state and individual–economy connections in the everyday.

ON MORAL RELATIVISM

Anthropologists have found it problematic to deal with the implications of cultural relativism for ethnographic research (Spiro 1986). Towards the second half of the twentieth-century, when anthropology was coming out of an uncomfortable debate on its applicability to study war enemies, particularly in the United States, another task challenged it—namely, acceptance of the Universal Human Rights Declaration in 1948. Cultural relativism, which marked the initial steps of anthropology in the American school led by Franz Boas, was not yet at issue; it was indeed how anthropologists had done research. Cultural relativism has been seen as informing the reluctance of (mainly) American anthropologists to accept a Declaration that was allegedly constructed on ethnocentric premises (Brown 2008). In particular, the key criticism was directed from the standpoint of the human rights of indigenous populations, who could not be easily conceived under the same standards as other cultures, particularly when they did not possess a historiographic tradition of their own. The relativism of this criticism of the Declaration is what, across years and with the final end of the colonial regimes, put anthropology in a uneasy position—that of maintaining cultural relativism as a "method" for studying social groups and cultures in their idiosyncrasies ("anti-anti relativism," as Clifford Geertz [2000] put it) and that of avoiding discussing more about what could still be considered as a missing bridge with other social science disciplines, particularly when dealing with extremely sensitive topics, such as human rights violations and ethics. For about two decades, anthropologists have been trying to revitalize the notion of relativism not as a main research agenda but more as a tool for ensuring that they do not lose the exclusiveness of knowledge generated in the course of field research. This includes, as postmodern anthropology rightly required, reflections on the presence of ethnographers in the field—that is, the epistemological and behavioral implications of such distortion of reality. In sum, the most recent standpoints vis-à-vis cultural relativism have not been towards adopting it blindly but towards problematizing it and weighing its pros and cons. One way of doing this is by presenting some of the societal, psychological, and historical variations that this method allowed a better understanding of (Brown 2008). As Spiro (1986) puts it, one can distinguish among three types of relativism: descriptive, normative, and epistemological. Descriptive relativism refers to the theory of cultural determinism in maintaining that humans' social and psychological characteristics are defined by culture. Normative relativism, however, refers to the idea that all judgments about culture are valid; there is no such thing as a "better" or "worse" cultural form or expression. This entails that there would be no moral standard that can express a condition of judgment of a validity of merit (Spiro 1986, 260). Finally, epistemological relativism starts from the assumption that virtually all "human social and psychological characteristics are culturally determined" (Spiro 1986, 261). The corollary is that generalizations about human cultures are valid only insofar as they are group-specific and culturally relative.

The specific tension between the cultural relativistic position and the study of corruption-related ideas and practices is to be measured in terms of the proposition of what moral relativism stands for. There is abundant literature, mostly outside of anthropology—including philosophy, history, social psychology, and sociology—debating the issue of whether moral standards are relative or whether they have an inherent degree of "universal" ethic (McDonald 2010). This is not the space to debate such theoretical standpoints. However, what can be pinpointed is that the ethnographic methodology on which anthropological research typically develops often provides a space for relativizing about moral assumptions. However, what tends to be interpreted as anthropological "moral relativism" is more a hyperbole than a factual variable. The notion of moral relativism is itself of little help in understanding corruption because it departs from the assumption that morality (etymologically derived from the Latin *mores*—i.e. social customs) is the application of a sociocultural lens to define what human behavior ought to be like to meet the main recognized standards. The point is that these standards are set by social customs, making them culturally relative.

When I was conducting field research on corruption in public administration, a middle manager of a northern Italian municipal office commented on a misdoing of a colleague of hers, who had been convicted of accepting a bribe on a municipal concession of street-cleaning in public spaces. Her comment indicated a perceived gap between what she termed illicit acts that bring social stigma to the administration and those which do not, and were, thus, more tolerable. Her differentiation between these two levels of morality was not simply judged on the type of act (bribe instead of a favor) but more precisely on two aspects: the value of the bribe and its visibility. As the interviewee went on to comment, a difference may have been considered as to whether the administrator's kickback exceeded a determinate amount (€1,500, for instance) and whether the outcome of the bribery would have been buying a garden pool for the children or an expensive car. Of course, the pool was less visible and, therefore, provided lower stigmatization than an expensive car, which, when considering the salary level of Italian public officials, is quite a striking acquisition.

The ethnographic literature is rich in examples of, typically, citizens recounting stories of small bribes paid in the belief that this is the way of behaving, as others will do the same. Such deeds are usually related to the interaction between single actors (corruptors) and public officers of some kind, with this interaction being either an eliciting (extortion) of a bribe or the classic kickback to "fix things." Due to the smaller amount of money associated with these practices, ethnographic accounts have provided rich insights into the moral side of petty corruption (de Sardan 1999). Many of these insights are, however, largely ignored by mainstream literature. Paying bribes is not commonly considered moral by local populations, since the direct (and to a lesser extent indirect) consequences of corruption are often very well known (Rothstein and Torsello 2014). Thus, the degree of relativism that ethnographic research brings to the picture does not apply to general ideas about what corruption means for society. Many relativistic perceptions of corruption concern comparatively smaller amounts of money or benefits whose exchange may become part of a circle of giving and taking and, therefore, a practice sustained through cultural beliefs. If taking a bribe of up to €1,500 can still be socially "acceptable," the relativism is provided by the socially acceptable judgment regarding the value and visibility of the exchange. A similar consideration can be made for the widespread practice of the "banknote sandwich," where customs officials may solicit small donations as tips to speed up their work of checking cars or trucks. The moral relativism of these two examples is that officers, who earn poor salaries, may be "forgiven" for certain practices, as long as they do not create a stigmatization for the organization and its members. The question which arises from these beliefs is as follows: is it moral to accept that such officers get a "tip" for their poorly recognized and sometimes highly risky work?

The petty corruption practices indicated above cannot have universal acceptability; therefore, the kind of relativism that is applicable to them relates more to epistemic relativism and less to normative relativism. This relativism depends on an array of conditions: the social status of actors involved in the bribing transaction; the purpose of the bribe; the industry or institutional environment; the societal perception of corruption; and the individual-level knowledge, familiarity, and normalizing aspects of corruption. In assessing the number and complexity of these variables, it becomes easier to understand why an overarching ethical explanation of corruption is only forcedly applicable. One must understand that relativism is naturally introduced when attempting to take into account these very diverse variables.

The risk of missing the advantages of a deep ethnographic analysis of these practices lies, on one hand, in a ready-made relativism that does not provide sufficient thickness to descriptions of a socially unique pattern of behavior. On the other hand, the attempt to explain corruption-related moral views as deviance of a more or less standardized ethical order is itself self-defeating because it misses the crucial nuances of the practices and discourses of corruption, which are increasingly useful for grasping the cognitive mechanisms through which this phenomenon is accepted in society.

QUESTIONS AND FINDINGS: THE TRANSGRESSION OF CORRUPTION IN STATE INSTITUTIONS

What follows is a brief review of some of the main questions and findings that ethnographic research on corruption have provided internationally. This is not meant to be an exhaustive review, as this would require much more space. However, some examples of such discussions may be found elsewhere (Torsello and Venard 2016; Muir and Gupta 2018).

One initial question concerns the role of the state in the institutionalization of corrupt deals and the transgression of such (institutional) boundaries. How does corruption contribute to blurring the commonly perceived boundaries between state, politics, bureaucracy, public vs. private spheres, legal and illegal, and moral and immoral practices?

Concerning the relationship between corruption and the state, strong degrees of state control and intrusion in social and economic institutional relations are not deterrents to corruption. This argument has been "traditionally" used to explain the widespread presence of corruption in authoritarian regimes as well as in monopolistic states, which economists call "kleptocracies," "rent-seeking states," or "predatory states." Corruption is conceived as an outcome of widespread interpenetration of the economic and political sphere, which reduces competition and increased privileges, the creation of powerful elites and cliques operating as—to use a popular term in Italian politics—castes (Sun 2004; Johnston 2005; Varese 2005).

However, a state which appears to be porous enough to allow for the transgression and migration of practices across boundaries is also bred for corruption. Here, the case of postcolonial countries is paramount: the dissolution of colonial and postcolonial states is often considered the historical origin of the everyday presence of corruption at all levels of social interaction (Apter 1999; Bayart, Ellis, and Hibou 1999; Comaroff and Comaroff 2006; Sharma 2018). The weakness of the state structure is seen as providing porous interstices to the multiplication of power battlefields and actors. As in the strong state argument, no single solution against the phenomenon can be envisaged.

Anthropology has provided sophisticated ethnographies of the state in relation to a number of political and social phenomena and cultural practices (Sharma and Gupta 2006). Following the influence of Foucauldian interest in issues of power, knowledge, discourses, and governmentality (despite sometimes neglecting government; see Holmes 2000; Wilson 2000), ethnographic accounts of the role of the state in relation to corruption have taken different standpoints. One has been to analyze the legislative functions and spaces in which the state deals with corruption in different societal contexts. This approach is evident in Pardo

(2004) and in the book by Nuijten and Anders (2007). Nuijten and Anders, who title their edited volume *Corruption and the Secret of Law*, stress the idea that the common Western-informed notion of corruption as dichotomic between public and private also applies to the state–society dichotomy. In this perspective, they argue, it is difficult to grasp corruption through the traditional Western legalistic understanding. As the possibility of transgression is always present in law, corruption is to them the very secret of law, which defines its fields of application and intervention, but meanwhile allows for its depletion in society. In other words, in social contexts where lawmakers and political forces can introduce ad hoc regulations that allow for impunity after corruption, the rule of law may become a weak response. Thus, a normative approach to corruption, which departs from a lawmaking state at the top, is misleading because dichotomies, such as legal and illegal, in contexts where law is plural, are of little help.

Some anthropologists have sought to resolve this impasse by focusing on the transgressive aspects of corruption—that is, by identifying alternative types of social order that have been established through direct relationships between the corrupters and the corrupted (Bratsis 2003; Bubandt 2014; Lomnitz 1995; Pardo 2018). For instance, where the main focus is on means of achieving political legitimacy in times of institutional crisis, it may be useful to make use of corruption as a strong public discourse which instils a sense of urgency. Conversely, when power consolidation is at stake, the transgressive aspect of corruption needs to be as hidden as possible, giving an apparent sense of good governance.

A related aspect is that corruption as a notion seems to avoid definitions which render its conceptualization an effort marked by inherent ambiguities. This has driven ethnographic research away from other social science disciplines' concerns about good governance, the rule of law, market competition, and ethics in public and private organizations. Rather, as Haller and Shore (2005) and Muir and Gupta (2018) maintain, the type of corruption that ethnography studies in relation to the state is hardly definitional; it is much more performative and evaluative. Following the Foucauldian tradition, corruption is one of the ways in which people make sense of politics and of the state, like a conversation, a ritual or, for some, even like sorcery (Bubandt 2006). The issue is not whether the state has been able to set boundaries between what is legal and illegal, morally acceptable or not, neither whether the state makes use of corruption to obtain public (rather than private) legitimacy. It is to understand the ways in which local citizens use corruption to make sense of how state institutions work and to approach them. This standpoint is not aimed at justifying the existence of corruption in society but at explaining the reasons for its resiliency.

Muir and Gupta (2018, S60) push this argument further by stating that "in many contexts, opposition to corruption has become the very definition of 'good governance', gathering together under a single, unassailable and remarkably anodyne banner policies and social movements that pursue divergent, even irreconcilable, ends."

This is a rather strong statement which provides little space for conciliation of the diversity of disciplinary approaches vis-à-vis corruption and the state, but it is nonetheless telling of the difficulty of reaching this end after decades of corruption research.

Another approach to the state considers its relation to local governments in the case of corruption. The focus here is on the failure of the state to successfully expand to encompass local government or pursue an incomplete bureaucratization process. Thus, competition between local governments and the state becomes a potential subject of analysis in reference to different institutional contexts. In a study on the effects of EU structural transport projects in Central Eastern Europe, Torsello (2012) deals with whether corruption has been fostered by the state's attempt to enforce its decision-making processes at the local level or the opposite, by the localities' attempt to seek autonomy from state intervention. Corruption has, in these cases, also emerged often in discourses about state or local power, but in different ways compared to the ethnographies of Asian countries so far discussed. Due to the nature of the state under postsocialism, the state–society opposition is also in Central Eastern Europe a weak theoretical framework. Local practices have been directed towards using corruption as a way to express fear of the delocalization of central power. This fear is often informed more by the visible growing social inequality at the local level than by shared knowledge of a corrupt state, already present under the socialist regime. In case studies, the state is not the central focus of public discussion on corruption but local governments, which in the years preceding EU accession implemented widely decentralized administrative reforms, are believed to use corruption to remold the state. This is another argument in favor of the idea developed by anthropologists that corruption allows for transgression and blurring of bureaucratic and political boundaries in a society, rendering clear-cut definitions of the institutions affected by this phenomenon problematic.

THE DOMINANCE OF PETTY CORRUPTION

As seen above, many ethnographic works on corruption have pointed to (more or less) hidden and relativistic morality based on the importance of mutual ties of solidarity, gift exchange, and interpersonal trust. Petty corruption is the paramount field of research in this approach owing to the epistemological limitations and methodological aspects described above. The main question that this scholarship has developed is as follows: is there a socially justifiable form of corruption that intersects with norms and practices of social interaction? If so, what are the social and cultural features of this form, and what forces compete in the cultural production and reproduction of such?

Petty corruption is the field in which ethnographers can more effectively study the phenomenon, whereas larger corruption deals and scandals are not the common field of anthropological investigation owing to the obvious methodological difficulties in undertaking field research in organizations (Torsello 2016). Among those scholars who have directly or indirectly dealt with petty corruption, one can read an almost general tendency to relate this to other forms of social practices for which anthropology has an established theoretical tradition: friendship, kinship, patronage, gift exchange, solidarity, reciprocity, and resistance. This equation is understandable from a mere methodological point of view, but is problematic from a heuristic perspective.

Methodologically, the ethnographer may often observe informality in economic transactions, semi-legal or illegal practices, clientelism, and bribery and be in the troublesome position of having to judge whose good is served by those practices. The tendency is to objectivize the meaning of those practices, framing them in the sociocultural context of belonging, which leads to the distaste of many anthropologists for clear-cut categories.

Some anthropologists have debated whether the morality of corruption may itself become an alternative form of social exchange, particularly in contexts where petty forms of corruption are common everyday practices (de Sardan 1999; Smith 2007). The stigmatization of such practices is itself a double-edged sword since, on one hand, it allows for considering the frequency and salience of such practices in social interactions; thus, it produces important insights into cultural processes of meaning-building. On the other hand, the tendency to oversimplify and stigmatize cultural responses to corruption may devoid this phenomenon of the socio-institutional setting in which it is deployed. Ideas such those of "neo-patrimonial states," the "belly state," "network cultures," "gift-exchange cultures" and many others, then, become comfortable expressions of models of democracy, transparency, maximization of profit, and civil society (Torsello 2018).

The focus on petty, rather than large-scale, corruption has allowed ethnographic research to reach a different dimension as compared to other disciplines that depart from a deductive model-building process. For one thing, if it is well acknowledged that citizens of countries that experience corruption tend to denounce with vehemence its impact on social and public morality (Rothstein and Torsello 2014), this outcry is stronger and more visible in cases of large-scale scandals. These are far from individuals. They involve a reflection and reasoning about their ethical involvement, but less so about individual processes of rationalization of such involvement; therefore, it is good to judge negatively a corrupt politician or business executive. Yet the differentiation of sociocultural attitudes and perceptions of practices of petty corruption is one of the most striking findings in ethnographic research. By focusing on petty corruption, which is by far less procedural and systemic than, for example, paying a bribe to win a bid in a public procurement case, ethnographic research has been able to penetrate those sociocultural domains that allow corruption to match, at some point in the process of signification, existing patterns and models of social interaction that are by no means equal across cultures. What is similar are the ways in which a single individual may seek to conform to practices that each social context expects to become acceptable because of pressure to conform morally. Thus, petty corruption is the ideal field of study to attribute the semantic and cultural mechanisms in which this phenomenon becomes part of the daily life experiences and may be legitimized.

Concluding Remarks

The ethnographic study of corruption is a promising field that has slowly but steadily provided new insights into the social and political implications of this complex and rapidly changing practice. There are two highly promising aspects. First, the discursive aspect of corruption is an innovative topic which is deemed to gain increasing significance when attempting to detect the meaning that citizens and economic and political actors attribute to practices related to corruption. Anthropologists have developed nuanced views of what corruption means in a society and how it relates to the local culture by dealing with narratives, symbolisms, and metaphors relating to this phenomenon in different world regions. This is a field in which ethnographic research can generate a large amount of data that can be analyzed to provide new insights and missing connections that mainstream literature does not have the tools to grasp, such as the relationship between culture and what is morally reprehensible.

Second, through its focus on petty corruption, ethnographic research has the methodological instruments to follow the pathways through which corruption may become accepted (if not legitimized) via local cultural and social constructs. Again, it is because some of the topics that have been studied in different countries and regions have a long tradition in ethnographic research that fresh approaches to analyzing the resiliency of corruption and, for instance, the relativistic aspects of morality, are not totally unknown to this research method. If corruption is likely to strengthen in countries where it already constitutes a problem and, as different examples testify, also in countries where it has been less visible a phenomenon, the strength of fine-grained qualitative research that ethnography entails constitutes a promising future approach, which cannot be overlooked, to inform organizational and institutional policymaking at different levels.

The ethnographic study of corruption is dealing with a growing number of topics, some of which are more exclusively part of the anthropological tradition and some of which belong to a wider scope of research in the social science discipline. Those discussed in this chapter include the role of the state, institutional relationships, morality, and petty corruption. In particular, in the study of petty corruption, ethnographic research has been able to produce innovative results in aspects that are still rather new and insufficiently studied in the social sciences. These relate to the process of meaning creation of practices and ideas of social exchange, gift-giving, and reciprocity. Such practices may inform the diversity of sociocultural patterns of acceptance and refusal of petty corruption in governance.

References

Apter, Andrew. 1999. "Nigerian Democracy and the Politics of Illusion." In *Civil Society and the Political Imagination in Africa*, edited by Jean Comaroff and John L. Comaroff, 267–308. Chicago: University of Chicago Press.

Bähre, Erik. 2005. "How to Ignore Corruption. Reporting the Shortcomings of Development in Africa." *Current Anthropology* 46 (1): 107–13.

Bayart, J. Francois, Sthephen Ellis, and Beatrice Hibou. 1999. *The Criminalization of the State in Africa*. Translated by Stephen Ellis. Bloomington: Indiana University Press.

Blundo, Giorgio. 2007. "Hidden Acts. Open Talks. How Anthropology Can 'Observe' and Describe Corruption." In *Corruption and the Secret of Law: A Legal Anthropological Perspective*, edited by Monique Nuijtel and Gerhart Anders, 1–17. Aldershot: Ashgate.

Bratsis, Peter. 2003. "The Construction of Corruption, or Rules of Separation and Illusions of Purity in Bourgeois Societies." *Social Text* 21 (4): 9–33.

Brown, Michael F. 2008. "Cultural Relativism 2.0." *Current Anthropology* 49 (3): 363–83.

Bubandt, Nils. 2006. "Sorcery, Corruption and the Dangers of Democracy in Indonesia." *Journal of the Royal Anthropological Institute* (New Series) 12: 413–31.

Bubandt, Nils. 2014. *Democracy, Corruption, and the Politics of Spirits in Contemporary Indonesia*. New York: Routledge.

Comaroff, Jane, and John L. Comaroff. 2006. *Law and Disorder in the Postcolony*. Chicago: University of Chicago Press.

de Sardan, Oliver. 1999. "A Moral Economy of Corruption in Africa?" *The Journal of Modern African Studies* 37 (1): 25–52.

During, Simon. 1992. *Foucault and Literature: Towards a Genealogy of Writing*. London and New York: Routledge.

Geertz, Clifford. 2000. "Anti-anti Relativism." *American Anthropologist* New Series, 86 (2): 263–78.

Goldstein, Luis. 2003. "'In Our Hands': Lynching, Justice and the Law in Bolivia." *American Ethnologist* 30 (1): 22–43.

Haller, Dieter, and Chris Shore, eds. 2005. *Corruption. Anthropological Perspectives*. London: Pluto Press.

Hoag, Colin. 2010. "The Magic of the Populace: An Ethnography of Illegibility in the South Africa Immigration Bureaucracy." *Political and Legal Anthropology Review* 33 (1): 6–25.

Hodgen, Margaret T. 2011. *Early Anthropology in the Sixteen and Seventeenth Centuries*. Philadelphia: University of Pennsylvania Press.

Holmes, Douglas R. 2000. *Integral Europe: Fast-Capitalism, Multiculturalism, Neofascism*. Princeton: Princeton University Press.

Hutton, Ronald. 2004. "Anthropological and Historical Approaches to Witchcraft: Potential for a New Collaboration?" *The Historical Journal* 47 (2): 413–34.

Johnston, Michael. 2005. *Syndromes of Corruption: Wealth, Power, and Democracy*. Cambridge University Press.

Landè, Carl H. 1983. "Political Clientelism in Political Studies: Retrospect and Prospects." *International Political Science Review* 4 (4): 435–54.

LeCompte, Margaret D. 1987. "Bias in the Biography: Bias and Subjectivity in Ethnographic Research." *Anthropology & Education Quarterly* 18 (1): 43–52.

Lomnitz, Larissa A. 1995. "Ritual, Rumour and Corruption in the Constitution of Polity in Modern Mexico." *Journal of Latin American Anthropology* 1 (1): 20–47.

McDonald, Gael. 2010. "Ethical Relativism vs. Absolutism: Research Implications." *European Business Review* 22 (4): 446–64.

Misangyi, Vilmos F., Gary R. Weaver, and Heather Elms. 2008. "Ending Corruption: The Interplay among Institutional Logics, Resources and Institutional Entrepreneurs." *The Academy of Management Review* 33 (3): 750–70.

Muir, Sarah, and Akhil Gupta. 2018. "Re-thinking the Anthropology of Corruption: An Introduction to Supplement 18." *Current Anthropology* 59 (S18): S4–S15.

Nuijten, Monique, and Gerhard Anders, eds. 2007. *Corruption and the Secret of Law: A Legal Anthropological Perspective*. Aldershot: Ashgate.

Pardo, Italo, ed. 2004. *Between Morality and the Law. Corruption, Anthropology and Comparative Society*. London: Ashgate.

Pardo, Italo. 2018. "Corrupt, Abusive, and Legal: Italian Breaches of the Democratic Contract." *Current Anthropology* 59 (suppl. 18): S60–71.

Rothstein, Bo, and Davide Torsello. 2014. "Corruption among Indigenous Cultures: Understanding the Universalism-Particularism Puzzle." *Journal of Anthropological Research* 70 (2): 263–84.

Salzman, Philip C. 2002. "On Reflexivity." *American Anthropologist* 104 (3): 805–13.

Sharma, Aradhana. 2018. "New Brooms and Old: Sweeping up Corruption in India, One Law at a Time." *Current Anthropology* 59 (suppl. 18): S72–82.

Sharma, Aradhana, and Akhil Gupta, eds. 2006. *The Anthropology of the State: A Reader*. Maldern: Blackwell.

Smith, Daniel J. 2007. *A Culture of Corruption: Everyday Deception and Popular Discontent in Nigeria*. Princeton: Princeton University Press.

Spiro, Melford E. 1986. "Cultural Relativism and the Future of Anthropology." *Cultural Anthropology* 1 (3): 259–86.

Spiro, Melford E. 1996. "Postmodernist Anthropology, Subjectivity and Science: A Modernist Critique." *Comparative Studies in Society and History* 38 (4): 759–80.

Sun, Yang 2004. *Corruption and Market in Contemporary China.* Ithaca: Cornell University Press.

Thapar-Björkert, Suruchi, and Marsha Henry, M. 2007. "Re-assessing the Research Relationship: Position and Power in Fieldwork Accounts." *International Journal of Social Research Methodology* 7 (5): 363–81 https://doi.org/10.1080/1364557092000045294

Torsello, Davide. 2012. *The New Environmentalism? Civil Society and Corruption in the Enlarged EU.* Farnham: Ashgate.

Torsello, Davide. 2014. "Corruption as Social Exchange: The View from Anthropology." In *Debates on Corruption*, edited by D. Torsello, P. Hardi, and P. Heywood, 159–83. New York: Palgrave MacMillan.

Torsello, Davide, and Bertrand Venard. 2016. "The Anthropology of Corruption." *Journal of Management Inquiry* 25 (1): 34–54.

Varese, Federico. 2005. *The Russian Mafia Private Protection in a New Market Economy.* Oxford: Oxford University Press.

PART III

DEMOCRACY, ACCOUNTABILITY, AND PARTICIPATION

CHAPTER 9

··

DEMOCRACY AND THE QUALITY OF GOVERNMENT

··

MONIKA BAUHR AND MARCIA GRIMES

Introduction

··

INTERNATIONAL organizations, experts, and policymakers promote democracy as a means to secure better quality of government, here conceptualized as government free of corruption and venality.[1] Indeed, many of the least corrupt countries in the world are democracies, and democracy embodies several principles conducive to reducing corruption. Democracy ensures vertical accountability, which is the ability of citizens to monitor and sanction politicians. Competitive elections, an institutional cornerstone of democracy, provide perhaps the most important means through which citizens can remove corrupt politicians from office and replace them with representatives more inclined to serve the public good. Democracy also increases horizontal accountability, or politicians' incentives to monitor each other, as members of the opposition stand to gain from uncovering corruption and mismanagement among incumbents, and strengthens incumbents' incentives to monitor the bureaucracy to improve performance (Shleifer and Vishny 1993; Montinola and Jackman 2002). In the logic of principal–agent theory, introducing elections should thus increase the likelihood that electoral victors will work to deliver public goods efficiently, which requires mitigating corruption (Becker and Stigler 1974; Klitgaard 1988; Rose-Ackerman 1978). In short, democracy reduces both political monopoly and discretion, both seen as conditions that allow the abuse of public office for private gain (Klitgaard 1988, 75).

[1] Quality of government connotes that government officials when exercising public power base their decisions only on the considerations stipulated in the law; they should in other words act impartially (Rothstein and Teorell 2008; Rothstein this volume). At a more operational level, this means that the exercise of public power is not tainted by informal payments, party affiliation, bonds of kinship or affect, or biases based on race, ethnicity, gender, or any other factors unless they are expressly noted as relevant in the policy or law in question. Although corruption does not capture the full spectrum of ways in which the exercise of public power can deviate from the norm of impartiality, it is indeed a stark violation and this chapter focuses specifically on this aspect.

While the corruption-reducing effect of democracy may be seemingly self-evident in light of the theoretical expectations, a wealth of empirical literature suggests that democracies are not always as effective as theories would predict. Large-N studies present a more muddled picture regarding the power of key elements of democracy—elections, transparent government, free press, a strong civil society—to eradicate corruption, and suggest that democratization is not necessarily positively associated with improved quality of government. Rather, a number of country-comparative studies suggest it is curvilinear, or has a "j-shaped" pattern (Bäck and Hadenius 2008; Charron and Lapuente 2010; McMann et al. 2019; Sung 2004). Corruption appears in other words to increase in newly democratized countries, and does not always disappear in the medium to long term either. Figure 9.1 illustrates this curvilinear relationship. Thus, while more mature and full-fledged democracies consistently evince lower levels of corruption, some countries considered democratic but with comparatively lower scores on a range of components of democracy, or with shorter histories of democracy, have higher levels of corruption than autocratic regimes (Montinola and Jackman 2002). Case studies document how democratization may increase clientelism and corruption in, for example, Africa (Lemarchand 1972), Southeast Asia (Scott 1972), India (Wade 1985), and Latin America (Weyland 1998), as well as in postcommunist countries (Varese 1997).

This chapter surveys relevant country comparative studies as well as examinations of individual-level mechanisms in terms of voting and vote choice, and takes stock of both the

Electoral Democracy and Control of Corruption

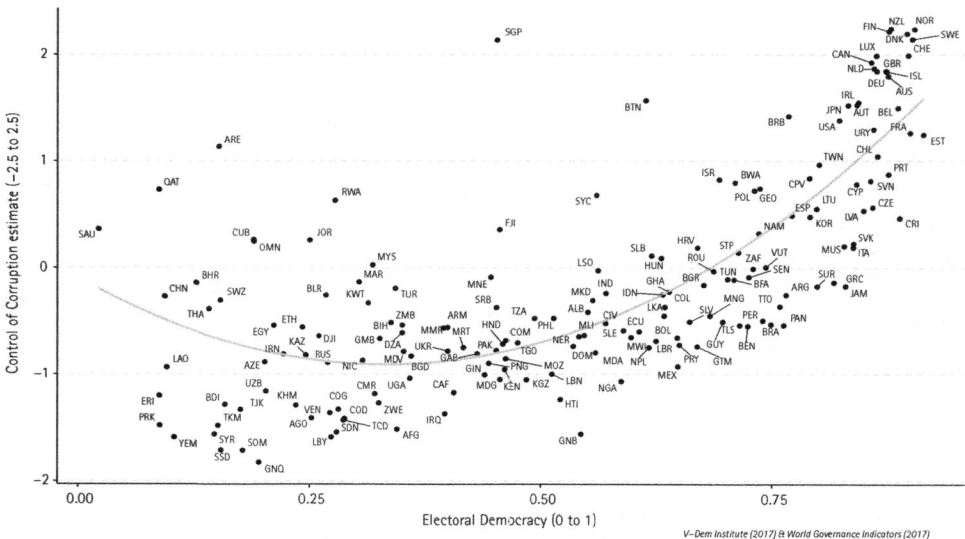

V–Dem Institute (2017) & World Governance Indicators (2017)

FIGURE 9.1 The relationship between democracy and corruption

Source: The Electoral Democracy measure is from the Varieties of Democracy Institute and combines assessments of freedom of association, clean elections, freedom of expression, constraints on elected officials, and suffrage. The corruption measured is the World Bank Control of Corruption indicator and includes perceptions of both petty and grand forms of corruption, as well as "capture" of the state by elites and private interests. For more information about these variables, see Teorell et al. (2019).

empirical evidence and theorized mechanisms for why some democracies are more suc-cessful than others in reducing corruption and improving the quality of government. We suggest that although cross-country studies on the aggregate level link between democracy and corruption have indeed raised a very important research question—i.e. if democracy reduces corruption—answers to this question are better found in adjacent fields of research. In the following, we review literature that seeks to explain the varying performance of dem-ocracies, beginning with factors closely related—if not integral to—democracy itself, such as freedoms of expression and association, moving then to voters' preferences and demands, and ending with a consideration of two major factors that affect the workings of democ-racy: state organization and economic conditions. The final section takes stock, summar-izing the main findings and pointing out directions for future research.

EVIDENCE FOR THE EFFECT OF DEMOCRACY ON CORRUPTION: THE BROAD BRUSHSTROKES

The fairly straightforward question addressed in this chapter—does democracy lead to less government corruption—defies a straightforward answer. Two early and influential studies found that a longer period of uninterrupted democratic rule between 1950 and 1995 was asso-ciated with lower contemporary levels of corruption, but that levels of democracy according to ratings such as Freedom House Political Rights, had no association at all with corruption (Treisman 2000, 434; Serra 2006, 248). Democracy does not, based on these results, display a neat, linear relationship in which any movement from autocracy to full democracy prompts an incremental reduction in corruption. And indeed, numerous studies instead observe a curvilinear relationship, in which countries considered democracies but in which basic free-doms and electoral institutions are not yet fully-fledged, perform significantly worse than more developed democracies—but also worse than autocracies—on a range of indicators of quality of government, including corruption (Montinola and Jackman 2002; Sung 2004) and administrative capacity (Bäck and Hadenius 2008). These findings prompted a number of large N studies investigating this relationship (see Table 9.1 for selective overview).

Observations of this curvilinear relationship raise the question of whether democ-racy simply requires time to mature and if so what conditions more precisely are expected to emerge? Alternatively, does the transition to democracy present new challenges? While it is most certainly debatable whether some of the autocracies that score well on the con-trol of corruption indicators actually exhibit such low levels of corruption, a number of au-thors have pointed out that authoritarian states can have a strong coercive capacity and can thereby effectively maintain control over the administrative apparatus. However, as states democratize "this capacity deteriorates, and it is replaced only slowly by the controls exer-cised by various actors in society, which can be developed in open democratic states" (Bäck and Hadenius 2008, 2). That autocratic governments lack electoral accountability does not imply that they lack accountability mechanisms or incentives to limit their own rent-seeking behavior altogether. Autocrats cannot rely on elections as a source of legitimacy and extreme misgoverning might generate a critical mass of discontent, which can ultimately lead to a revolution or ousting. In addition, some types of autocratic regimes may have longer time

Table 9.1 Large N–studies on the link between democracy and corruption selective overview

Author	Data	Measurement of democracy	Measurement of Quality of Government	Main conclusion
Sandholz and Koetzle (2000)	1996, 54 countries	Politicarights, civil liberties (Frredom House-FH), Democratic years	Transparency International Corruption Perception Index (TI CPI)	Democracy reduces corruption
Treisman (2000)	1996–1998, 64 countries	Political liberties (FH), Democratic years	TI CPI	Uninterrupted democracy reduces corruption
Paldam (2002)	1990–1998, 99 countries	Democracy index (FH)	TI CPI	Democracy decreases corruption but independent effect "dubious"
Montinola and Jackman (2002)	1980–92, 66 countries	Measure by Bollen (1993)	Business International (BI) Corruption index (also TI CPI)	Curviliinear (U-shaped) relationship
Sung (2004)	1995–2000, 103 countries	Political rights index (FH)	TI CPI	Curvilinear (S-shaped) relationship
Chowdhury (2004)	1995–2002, 155 countries	Vanhanen's democratization index, Press Freedom (FH)	TI CPI	Democracy and press freedom reduce corruption
Serra (2006)	1990–98, 62 countries	Political rights (FH), uninterrupted democracy 1950-95	Graft index and TI CPI	Uninterrupted democray reduces corruption
Billger and Goel (2009)	2001–3, 99 countrires	Political rights and civil liberties (FH)	TI CPI	Democracy reduces corruption in the most corrupt countries
Rock (2009)	1982–97, 84 countries	Democratic years (Durability of democracy Polity IV)	Corruption (ICRG/IRIS Political Risk Service)	Curvilinear (U-shaped) relationship
Bäck and Hadenius (2008)	1984–2002, 125 countries	FH and Polity	Bureaucratic Quality and Corruption (ICRG)	Curvilinear (J-shaped) relationship
Charron and Lapuente (2010)	1984–2002, 157 countries	FH and Polity	Bureaucratic Quality and Corruption (ICRG), Government Effectiveness (WB)	Positive effect, conditional on economic development
Iwasaki and Suzuki (2012)	1998–2006, 32 countries	Democratization policy index (World Bank)	Control of Corruption (WB)	Democracy reduces corruption
Kalenborn and Lessman (2013)	1996–2010, 175 countries	Vanhanen's democratization index (PRIO)	TI CPI, also ICRG and WB data	Elections control corruption given sufficient press freedom
Jetter, Agudelo and Hassan (2015)	1998–2012, 155 countries	Polity IV (Polity2)	TI CPI	Democracy reduces corruption when GDP/c >US$2000, increases corruption otherwise
Kolstad and Wiig (2016)	1998–2012, 155 countries	IV:war with a democracy in the period 1946–2008, FH, Polity	Control of Corruption (WB) and TI CPI	Democracy reduces corruption
McMann et al. (2019)	1900–2015, 173 countries	V-Dem Democracy indicators	V-Dem Political Corruption indicators	Well-functioning democracy reduces corruption

horizons than democratically elected leaders, and the competitive nature of elections may in fact incentivize rent-seeking (Charron and Lapuente 2011; Mohtadi and Roe 2003, 447). Upon transition to democracy, most observers and scholars nonetheless projected that the building blocks of democratic accountability would emerge, leading to subsequent improvements in quality of government (Rock 2009, 60). These studies all point to the plausible assumption that democratic accountability mechanisms may take time to emerge, which should account for the observed j-shaped curve. The passage of time calls these expectations into question, however, as do studies examining the micro-level mechanisms thought to link democracy to improved QoG. These mechanisms have been dealt with in adjacent fields of research, discussed in depth below.

Why Does Democracy Seemingly Fail to Improve Quality of Government?

The underlying theory of change and assumptions upon which the beneficial effect of democracy rests are not always made explicit. Recalling the skeletal conceptualization of accountability and principal–agent theory, democratic accountability requires that citizens and societal actors more broadly 1) have the information needed to assess agents' behavior and performance, 2) have effective means to issue sanctions and rewards, 3) are willing to play the role of principals, 4) value improvements in quality of government and reductions in corruption above other issues, 5) are able to overcome collective action problems (i.e that they believe that fellow citizens will become involved or base vote choice on ideology and long-term programmatic thinking). Each of these conditions, all of which need to be met in order for democracy to reduce corruption, depend on other factors, such as the media landscape, civil society strength, the existence of political elites and parties willing and able to implement reform, the prevalence of clientelism and vote-buying, citizens' trust in institutions and in each other, and several more. In this section we examine some of the mechanisms implied in this larger theory of change, and in subsequent sections turn to what institutional conditions might precede these conditions, i.e. the causes behind the causes.

Lack of democratic experience and hybrid regimes

The notion that democracy requires specific conditions to reduce corruption, and that those conditions may emerge only after a more prolonged period of democratic development, runs through a number of country-level studies. Several cross-country studies find that a longer history of democratic rule reduces corruption (Treisman 2000; Serra 2006; Rock 2009). Keefer (2007) suggests that parties are a key set of actors in understanding why young democracies underperform in reducing corruption: "policy reputation takes time to build. Political competitors in younger democracies have had less opportunity, on average, to build reputations than competitors in older democracies" (Keefer 2007, 806). Hence, in younger democracies, politicians rely more often on clientelistic networks. Norms regarding the proper use of delegated power, and in particular the condemnation of corruption, as well as citizens' understanding of their own rights and of elections as an opportunity to punish officials for corrupt behavior, take time to disseminate and take root (Mungiu-Pippidi 2006).

The varying length of experience with democracy may thus partly explain the variation in democracy's ability to weed out corruption. Democratic deepening is not, according to others, only a matter of time, however. Several authors have noted that the norms, organizations, and behaviors needed for democracy to function as intended have not developed in all countries nominally considered democracies. The emergence of regimes that combine democratic and nondemocratic/authoritarian features, sometimes called hybrid regimes, suggest that the nonlinear relationship between democracy and corruption is based on a misconception of intermediate levels of democracies as "passing sequences." This type of regime has also been described as "illiberal democracy" (Zakaria 1997, Levitsky and Way 2002 and Schedler 2009). Zakaria (1997; 22) contends that Western conceptions of democracy means liberal democracy—"a political system marked not only by free and fair elections, but also by the rule of law, a separation of powers, and the protection of basic liberties of speech, assembly, religion, and property." He notes that in fact few illiberal democracies have "matured" into liberal democracies. Some liberal democracies seem to revert to illiberal ones, continuing to hold elections while at the same time restricting basic rights and freedoms (Zakaria 1997; see also Rose and Shin 2001, 333), a tendency which many observers note seems to have accelerated in recent years in virtually all regions of the world (Bogaards 2018; Curato 2017; Hunter and Power 2019; Lührmann and Lindberg 2019). One possible driving force of democratic backsliding may well be the underperformance of democracies in enhancing human well-being, which to some extent stems from corruption, suggesting a mutually reinforcing dynamic. We return to this issue below.

It is also important to keep in mind that electoral accountability is far from given, even in issue areas other than corruption. Achen and Bartels' (2017) recent survey of research on voter behavior primarily in the United States argues the controversial case that elections do little if anything to make governments responsive to the will of the people. Vote choice, they argue, derives from group identity rather than ideology and performance evaluation. That said, a corruption scandal is an unusually strong and clear "performance" signal, and does indeed have electoral consequences, though not always and in all settings.

How can we understand that some political systems remain in states of limited democracy with levels of corruption that clearly undermine both market conditions and the provision of public goods and services? Some clues emerge in subsequent sections on the importance of government transparency, freedom of expression and association, as well as limited demand for better quality of government. Furthermore, we explore two major underlying and interrelated factors that can affect the funtioning of democracy and thus democratic accountability: institutional aspects of the state itself, and economic conditions.

Insufficent democracy: transparency, freedom of expression and association

The reason for the failure of democracy to reduce corruption is often attributed to specific deficiencies in how democracy functions in some contexts (Keefer 2007; Mohtadi and Roe

2003; Bauhr and Charron 2018). For instance, transparency in the form of easily available, accurate and salient information about both individual power holders as well as about policy output and outcomes is so central to democracy that some consider transparent government and a free press to be component parts of, rather than conditions complementary to, democracy. For analytical purposes, however, distinguishing between elections, party systems, transparent government, and the basic freedoms of expression and association allows each to be examined separately.

Transparency, defined as the timely publication of information on government revenue flows and operations, is frequently advocated as a necessary condition for improving quality of government, promoting accountability, and reducing the scope for corruption with impunity (UNODC 2004; Stiglitz 2002; Islam 2006; Kosack and Fung 2014; Bauhr and Grimes 2014; Bauhr and Nasiritousi 2012; De Renzio and Wehner 2017). There is considerable empirical support for the beneficial effects of increased transparency on public demand for accountability and government performance (e.g., Alt et al. 2002; Besley and Burgess 2002; Brunetti and Weder 2003; Reinikka and Svensson 2005; Winters and Weitz-Shapiro 2013; Chang et al. 2010; Costas-Perez et al. 2012), lending support to the contention that access to information may reduce government corruption. In particular, transparency may enable citizens to detect corruption, which even in autocracies may increase the risk that public discontent translates into coordinated uprising and disruptive protests (Hollyer, Rosendorff, and Vreeland 2015). Some studies demonstrate that information and transparency can constrain corruption in public service delivery in particular sectors (Bauhr and Carlitz 2020; Björkman and Svensson 2009; Lieberman et al. 2014; Keefer and Khemani 2014; Fox 2015; Olken 2007).

However, a recent study, using seven coordinated randomized control trials in six countries found no evidence overall that information campaigns shaped voters' propensity to punish corruption (Dunning et al. 2019). Scholars have suggested that the beneficial effect of government transparency may be contingent on the demand for accountability and the nature of the accountability systems in place. The effectiveness of transparency reforms thus builds upon assumptions about stakeholders' willingness and ability to act upon the information received (Fenster 2005; Kolstad and Wiig 2009; Bauhr et al. 2020; see also Fox 2007). For instance, Bauhr and Grimes (2014) showed that government transparency may lead to demobilization and resignation in highly corrupt countries (see also Chong et al. 2015).[2]

The demobilizing effect of exposing corruption can be understood in light of the logic of collective action and, in particular, that citizen mobilization is highly contingent upon evidence that others will do the same (Bauhr and Grimes 2014; Persson et al. 2013; Karklins 2005; Ostrom 1998). In contexts in which corruption reaches systemic levels, citizens may perceive most others to be corrupt and therefore see few potential collaborators and even perceive the risk and costs of mobilizing against corruption to outweigh any chances of success. Exposure of corruption may therefore lead to political resignation and alienation rather than protest and voting out of rascals.

Another plausible expectation is that a free media enables citizens and civil society to hold government accountable. While voters collectively have the power to renew or end an officeholder's mandate, each voter rarely follows the goings-on of government sufficiently

---

[2] Relatedly, Bac (2001) found that transparency in the rules and the identities of decision-makers also increased corruption by making it easier to identify who to bribe in order to get access to services or jobs.

closely to make an informed decision, instead relying on the media to collect, compile, verify, and make sense of relevant information. In line with expectations, the presence of a free press exhibits a strong relationship with levels of corruption in cross-sectional analyses (Brunetti and Weder 2003), but also in time-series analyses with country-fixed effects, which capture change within countries and not only patterns in differences between countries (Bhattacharyya and Hodler 2015; McMann et al. 2019). The effect of a free press on reducing corruption may be greater where media reach is greater (Dutta and Roy 2016), in countries with laws requiring that members of parliament disclose information on finances and conflicts of interest (Djankov et al. 2010), and in countries with a greater degree of social and political integration into the international community (Charron 2009). Information can, as noted above, only reduce corruption if institutional mechanisms exist that enable principals to exercise accountability (Fox 2007; Worthy and McClean 2015). Several studies note that a free press in combination with higher voter participation (Camaj 2013; Chowdhury 2004), or simply the holding of elections (Kalenborn and Lessmann 2013; Serra 2006), is greater than each of these factors independently.

The third integral component of democracy, freedom of association, also rests on strong theoretical footing. By merit of being outside the realm of the state, civil society, like the media, is accredited with a beneficial intent and ability to expose and protest corruption. A vast body of case studies substantiate these hopes, with evidence that civil society has successfully contributed to bringing about legal reforms, and also to bringing down corrupt officials (Beyerle 2014; Landell-Mills 2013; della Porta and Mattoni, this volume; Pollack and Allern 2018).

However, a few attempts to examine the link between a strong civil society and lower levels of corruption offer evidence that might temper optimism somewhat. Examinations of the relationship between a strong civil society and corruption reveal a more complex story, and also face considerable data challenges. Analyses of civil society strength have relied on estimates of the percent of the labor force employed in the nonprofit sector (Themudo 2014; 2013), a count of organizations listed in a global directory (Grimes 2013), a measure of civil liberties more generally (Ades and Di Tella 1999; Themudo 2013), and survey data (Lee 2007). While all of these measures have drawbacks, the results nonetheless yield a consistent composite picture; civil society strength, or civil liberties, only show a relationship to lower levels of corruption where conditions are favorable, as where press freedom is above the global mean (Grimes 2013; Themudo 2013), or where political competition and government transparency are sufficiently strong to enable civil society activism (Grimes 2013). Absent conditions that enable civil society to obtain information and gain traction when expressing complaints and grievances, civic engagement seems to have limited effect on reducing corruption in the aggregate.

Limited demand for Quality of Government

While international organizations, policy experts, and nongovernmental organizations promote electoral accountability as a critical component to curb corruption, citizens do not always exercise their right to protest or voice complaints, and sometimes refrain from using their electoral right to punish corrupt politicians (Bauhr and Charron 2018; de Vries and Solaz 2017). Empirical evidence for the extent to which voters' punishment of corrupt politicians leads to reduced corruption remains mixed (see e.g. Crisp et al. 2014; Basinger 2013; Bågenholm 2013). Furthermore, studies from the U.S. (Welch and Hibbing 1997; Rundquist, Strom, and Peters 1977), Greece (Konstantinidis and Xezonakis 2013), Brazil (Ferraz and Finan 2008), Italy (Chang et al. 2010), the U.K. (Eggers 2014), Mexico (Chong et al. 2015), Japan (Reed 1996), Spain (Fernández-Vázquez, et al. 2016), and Sweden and Moldovia (Klašnja and Tucker 2013), suggest that politicians are only under certain circumstances punished for being implicated in corruption scandals.

An emerging literature seeks explanations for why electoral accountability sometimes fails to contain corruption. Explanations range from understanding the deep complex loyalty ties of clientelism, to voters' preferences, i.e. simply not caring enough about corruption compared to other benefits such as local economic growth. Relatedly, citizens may indeed care about corruption and understand its negative effects but lack perceived self-efficacy and trust in other citizens' willingness to vote against corruption.

Thus, this body of research typically assumes that political corruption triggers indignation in voters minds, but that this indignation is for various reasons not channeled into electoral punishment (see, for instance, de Sousa and Moriconi 2013). One reason why corrupt politicians survive in office is that voters simply do not prioritize having a noncorrupt political representative. Other factors, such as politicians' ability to attract investment, build successful coalitions, generate short-term or local economic growth, or make otherwise popular decisions may be valued more highly by voters (see Bågenholm this volume; Zechmeister and Zizumbo-Colunga 2013; Konstantinidis and Xezonakis 2013).[3]

One key to understanding why citizens seem to express a limited demand for clean government is to recognize that political representatives manage to induce loyalty among certain groups of citizens despite or even because of their corruptness. Bauhr and Charron (2018) suggest that patronage and clientelistic ties increase loyalty to corrupt politicians, demobilize the citizenry, and craft a deep divide between insiders, or potential beneficiaries of the system, and outsiders, excluded from the spoils of the corrupt system. Citizens are oftentimes embedded in clientelist relationships driven by norms of reciprocity and a sense of obligation towards the network (Auyero 2001), and perhaps even more decisively by a fear, real or not, that access to government programs and entitlements are linked to vote choice (Stokes et al. 2013; Kitschelt 2000). The broader literature on voting behavior suggests that an electorate bound by strong loyalty ties to the incumbent will be more likely to disregard improper or even immoral behavior, including corruption. When voters and parties share clientelistic ties, we can expect such loyalty effects to be particularly strong (Golden 2003; Brusco et al. 2004; Wantchekon 2003). Relatedly, studies show how elites use patronage jobs in the public administration to help support and shore up their own party base. When informal rules (as opposed to impartiality and merit) influence hiring, it produces particularly strong loyalty ties which undermine the ability to protest and voice complaints.

---

[3] Fernández-Vázquez et al. (2016) suggest that Spanish mayors are reelected if they engage in "welfare enhancing corruption." Rundquist, Strom, and Peters (1977) suggest that economic performance and the alignment of economic preferences between voters and politicians matter more than corrupt behavior. Klašnja and Tucker (2013) find in an experimental study in Sweden and Moldovia in 2005 and 2007 that Moldovan respondents punish corrupt behavior only if the economy performs badly, but otherwise tolerate it. Konstantinidis and Xezonakis (2013) find similar evidence in an experimental study in Greece, claiming that economic benefits or tax cuts decrease the likelihood of punishment of corrupt officials.

Political change in such contexts often comes at a great risk since it threatens job prospects and even subsistence opportunities for many citizens and their extended families. Thus, pervasive practices in which government contracts and employement are granted in exchange for political support fundamentally shape loyalty structures in society as well as perceptions of "how things get done" (Ledeneva 2013; Hale 2015).[4]

New democracies may be particularly vulnerable to self-reinforcing clientelism and patronage. Democratization processes provides incentives for leaders to promise job opportunities to supporters in order to secure power after democratic transitions. The stronger the dominant network becomes, the more difficult it is for those who want to challenge it to succeed in their endeavor. Such contexts may both reduce the supply of non- or marginally corrupt candidates that run for office (see e.g. Pavão 2018), and undermine the potential of competing patronage-based networks to mobilize support, since such mobilization tends to work better for incumbents or dominant parties, than for challengers (Remmer 2010; Wantchekon 2003). A recent study on how patronage divides societies in Africa tellingly finds that patronage insiders are more tolerant to malfeasance (Chang and Kerr 2016). Several recent studies suggest that voters actively demand help and support from politicians in return for electoral support (Nichter and Peress 2017; Auerbach and Thachil 2018).

Relatedly, partisan bias can also influence the extent to which voters punish corrupt politicians, where voters that identify strongly with a particular party may be more likely to downplay or disregard malfeasance in their preferred party in order to avoid cognitive dissonance (Anduiza et al. 2013; Muñoz et al. 2016). However, other studies do not find this relationship between partisanship and corruption on voting patterns (e.g. Ecker et al. 2016; Konstantinidis and Xezonakis 2013; Rundquist et al. 1977) questioning the generalizability of the results. While somewhat a matter of speculation, it would seem likely that these effects would be more pronounced where parties to a larger extent extensively use clientelistic strategies to court voters.

Finally, as noted above, citizens may fail to mobilize against corruption if they feel their efforts would be ineffective, or they lack trust in other citizens' willingness to participate in the fight against corruption, making corruption mobilization seem futile. Some studies show that exposure to corruption leads to resignation, demobilization, and voter abstention (Bauhr and Grimes 2014; Chong et al. 2015; Sundström and Stockemer 2015). Mobilization can also depend on what forms of corruption are prevalent in the setting (Bauhr 2017). Making a distinction between "need" and "greed" corruption, Bauhr (2017) suggests that need corruption is more likely to motivate civic engagement, since it is less hidden and has more direct implications for everyday life. This explains why greed corruption can be very sticky, even in established democracies.

Furthermore, a number of institutional explanations may account for the effectiveness of electoral accountability to curtail corruption. The type of factors that the literature has directed particular attention to is the difference between presidentialism vs. parliamentarism, unitarism vs. federalism, and electoral rules, such as the difference between proportional

---

[4] Clientelism may induce citizens to vote for corrupt politicians and parties, but may also mobilize otherwise disengaged voters, i.e. "turnout buying" (Nichter 2008) or "participation buying" (Schaffer and Schedler 2007:25), or induce abstention from voting, i.e. "abstention buying" (Cox and Kousser 1981).

and majoritarian electoral systems (Persson and Tabellini 2005; Gerring and Thacker 2004). These variations are seen to influence several factors of potential importance for democracy's ability to contain corruption, such as the number of veto points in the system, the clarity of responsibility (Tavits 2007), and the extent to which citizens find viable alternatives if they decide to switch parties (Charron and Bågenholm 2016). Furthermore, studies consistently find that gender influences both citizens' and political representatives' demand for anticorruption, and that democracies with a higher share of women in elected office exhibit lower levels of corruption (Swamy et al. 2001; Dollar et al. 2001; Bauhr, Charron and Wängnerud 2019; Bauhr and Charron 2020; Esarey and Schwindt-Bayer 2018; Esarey and Chirillo 2013; Stensöta and Wängnerud 2018). These and other explanations are covered elsewhere in this volume (Bågenholm; Xezonakis and Dawson; Alexander, this volume). The extent to which citizens express demand for lower levels of corruption and better quality of government is also contingent on other institutional factors, not least state capacity, an issue to which we turn next.

The State, the Economy and the Functioning of Democratic Accountability

State capacity, which is conceptually distinct from quality of government (see D'Arcy and Nistotskaya this volume), affects the functioning of democracy and democratic accountability via a number of mechanisms, only some of which have been explored in depth to date. State capacity is a necessary precondition for tax collection as well as the overall provision of public goods and services, which have been observed to affect citizens' political interest and democratic disenchantment respectively. Moreover, state capacity contributes to the accurate collection of data and information about societal, economic and environmental conditions, a necessary prerequisite for evidence-based policymaking and thus programmatic electoral platforms. Finally, key institutional features considered central to state capacity may also tie the hands of incumbents and prevent them from using the resources of the public sector—such as access to government programs, local infrastructure projects, or jobs—in a targeted partisan way to win elections. Various facets of state capacity may in other words affect the strategies of candidates, parties, and voters and thus electoral accountability as a whole, with implications for whether elections will aid in diminishing corruption. This section unpacks these mechanisms theoretically and presents the evidence, to date fairly limited, on each point.

State capacity as an umbrella concept comprises primarily three aspects: *bureaucratic quality*, the *territorial reach* of the state, and the extent to which the state has *information* about the myriad attributes of the territory, its population, and the activities that transpire within its borders (D'Arcy and Nistotskaya, this volume). Each of these elements may have distinct implications for democratic accountability and the functioning of democracy more broadly.[5]

[5] The elements of state capacity are also interrelated. Strong local and regional elites have been argued to prevent the development of an autonomous, professional bureaucracy in contexts such as India, Sri Lanka (Kenny 2015), and Mexico (Garfias 2018).

These three facets of state capacity determine whether political decisions are implemented and translate into societal reality (Acemoglu et al. 2015; Berwick and Christia 2018, 74; Dincecco and Katz 2016; Knutsen 2013), but also together form both the rules and the playing field of all political activity in a polity.

Bureaucratic quality

Bureaucratic quality refers to the extent to which civil servants have the skills and knowledge to operationalize and implement the decisions taken by political rulers (D'Arcy and Nistotskaya, this volume). Practically, this means that staffing of bureaucracies occurs through meritocratic hiring. Bureaucratic quality defined as such implies that civil servants are *not* politically appointed, a condition which subsequently fundamentally shapes the relationship between politicians and bureaucrats. When politicians have little or no influence over the hiring and firing of civil servants, they are limited in their ability to direct how individual civil servants should perform their jobs. Limiting politicians' power in this regard restricts their ability to fire an individual bureaucrat for failing to do his or her bidding. Incumbents who have extensive powers to hire or fire civil servants thus have greater opportunities to channel government goods, services, jobs, and contracts to further their own political ends, in other words, to reward constituents or court voters (Cornell and Grimes 2015; Geddes 1994; Gingerich 2013; Kenny 2015; Shefter 1994; Keefer 2007).[6] Misallocating state resources for use in electoral campaigns entails a breech of the norm of impartiality in and of itself, but it also makes some voters beneficiaries of one form of corruption and thus, presumably, less willing to punish corruption more generally. As elaborated above, the use of clientelistic strategies may induce citizens to see elections as an opportunity to extract particularistic benefits rather than as an opportunity to reward parties for performance or policy programs. Receiving particularistic benefits may thus both undermine citizens' willingness to punish corruption, but also alter voters' views of the nature of politics itself. Politics and elections may, in voters' minds, become a *quid pro quo*, in other words a series of one-shot exchanges of votes for rewards, rather than instruments of representation and accountability.

While plausible, the implications of politicization of the bureaucracy for democratic accountability have not been explored empirically in a comprehensive and systematic manner. Cornell and Grimes (2015) show that bureaucratic politicization correlates with the prevalence of clientelism using country-level measures, and that the association is independent of other political and economic factors. More research is needed, however, to determine whether the relationship is causal by substantiating the mechanisms empirically. Research on more developed democracies, and in particular the United States,

---

[6] It is necessary here to distinguish between the concept of bureaucratic politicization and patronage. While both denote that party affiliation affects who is selected for public sector jobs, politicization of the bureaucracy refers to appointments at higher levels in government bureaucracies, while patronage jobs tend to be low-skilled but secure jobs with little discretionary power. Both types of partisan-based appointees may be called upon during electoral campaigns, but their expected contributions would differ markedly, with higher level bureaucrats generally controlling the allocation of government resources, and lower-level workers attending rallies and knocking on doors.

has gone farther in this regard, examining individual agencies and government spending at the subnational level. While some federal government agencies are stacked with political appointees, others are more meritocratic. The proportion of patronage appointments has been shown to correlate with spending decisions (Berry and Gersen 2017), and that appointees help funnel money to battleground states or to the president's core supporters (Dahlström, Fazekas, and Lewis 2019; Hudak 2014). The findings of this research do not prove that political appointments distort democratic accountability in the United States. They do, however, strongly indicate that incumbents *attempt* to sway electoral outcomes by directing government spending, and that political appointees are a crucial set of actors in these strategies. In order to better understand how political appointees affect what strategies are available to and used by incumbents, and what implications these practices have for electoral outcomes and even civic engagement more generally, studies of this kind are needed from a broader range of political settings.

State reach

The second aspect of state capacity that may affect electoral accountability is the reach of the state (Herbst 2000; Mann 1984; Migdal 1988; Soifer 2008). Even in established democracies, but especially in newer democracies and former colonies, the state is present to varying degrees, with tracts lacking government infrastructure (transportation and communication), services (schools and health clinics), and the organizational presence needed to enforce laws and regulations (including the collection of taxes). When citizens have no access to and do not benefit from state-provided public goods such as education and healthcare, they are unlikely to see the state as a source of solutions. Afrobarometer 2005/6 data indicates, for example, that having visited a clinic in the past year or having been in contact with state-provided education made individuals more likely to turn to official state channels instead of nonstate actors to express demands and grievances (MacLean 2011). A lack of institutions and linkages between citizens and the state will result in "leaders who are less than fully committed to democracy, (that) resist responding to popular needs and, as a result, citizens withdraw still further from the orbit of an already marginal state" (Bratton and Chang 2006:1063). Moreover, where state reach and informational capacity are weak, the state will be unable to collect taxes effectively, which undermines the social contract and with it, citizens' interest in politics. Also in the context of Africa, paying taxes is a strong and robust predictor of individuals' interest in politics (Broms 2015; Persson and Rothstein 2015). Thus, where state capacity is low, citizens may come to doubt democracy as an effective system of government, may increasingly expect or even demand particularistic payoffs rather than large-scale solutions, or feel indifference toward politics entirely. In sum, state reach may substantially affect the degree to which citizens are willing and interested to play the role of principals and exercise their right to vote to improve government quality.

Informational Capacity

The importance of information for electoral accountability was discussed above in relation to government transparency. It is important to remember, however, that some states not only refuse to disclose information but may even lack the capacity to collect information in the first place. States weak in informational capacity are ill-equipped to identify and track the taxable assets and activities in its own domain, or to assess the needs in the population, without which policy formation becomes guesswork. A lack of reliable statistics on societal and economic conditions also liberates political debates and campaign pledges from any burden of proof or, indeed, constraints of reality (Boräng et al. 2018). As with the other aspects of state capacity, the effect of informational capacity on electoral accountability is rather indirect in that it affects a precondition of both programmatic campaigning as well as programmatic voting. It thus conditions citizens' ability to assess both incumbents' performance as well as the credibility of parties' policy promises, i.e. both retrospective and anticipatory voting.

These facets of state capacity are mutually constitutive and while analytically distinct, can be difficult to delineate empirically. Yet all may undergird democracy and increase the likelihood that elections work as intended to reduce corruption. First, they shape the availability and quality of basic infrastructure and services, as well as levels of corruption in the various spheres of government operations. Rule of law and perceptions of corruption emerge as the two strongest predictors of citizens' satisfaction with democracy, suggesting that democratization of a weak state in the longer term may undermine support for democracy (see also Dahlberg et al. 2015; Dahlberg and Linde this volume). Levels of corruption in European regions also drives voters to opt for populist, anti-establishment, and increasingly anti-liberal parties (Agerberg 2017). When state capacity is weak, it may thus result in a low accountability trap (Fox 2015).

Democracy and State Formation: The question of sequencing

Evidence on the level of parties, agencies, and voters is lacking with respect to how the state's institutional features affect electoral accountability with respect to corruption. A more extensive literature in historical institutionalism argues convincingly, however, that introducing elections and universal suffrage in polities with weak state capacity may contribute to trapping a country in a state of low quality of democracy and low quality of government. Known as the question of sequencing, this debate centers on the issue of whether the institution-building needed to enhance government performance and better sustain democratic accountability can, in fact, be developed under democratic rule (Rose and Shin 2001). Where government offices have a weak or highly politicized presence in the territory, voters may feel that parties' programmatic promises, however appealing, lack credibility (Keefer 2007), and electoral contenders may feel compelled to offer particularistic goods to voters (Geddes 1994). These mutually reinforcing dynamics have prompted a number of authors to doubt whether democracy will, on the whole, result in better quality of government at all. Democracy may paradoxically undermine rulers' incentives to develop the state institutions needed to enhance the effectiveness of electoral accountability and reduce corruption. As Fukuyama (2015, 16) observes:

> High-performing governments have been created, either historically or under contemporary circumstances. Many states with relatively high performing governments—China, Japan, Germany, France, and Denmark, for example—created modern "Weberian" bureaucracies

under authoritarian conditions; those that subsequently went on to become democracies in-herited meritocratic state apparatuses that simply survived the transition. The motive for cre-ating modern governments was not grassroots pressure from informed and mobilized citizens but rather elite pressure, often for reasons of national security.

Most affluent, established democracies extended universal franchise on a foundation of a modern state structure, while many third wave democracies instead experienced "backwards democratizing," i.e. "introducing free elections before establishing such basic institutions as the rule of law and civil society—and they have yet to complete the process of becoming both modern and democratic" (Rose and Shin 2001, 333). When au-tonomous bureaucracies are in place before political parties develop, organizational and professional norms and interests lead bureaucracies to resist politicization; civil servants collectively become advocates and constituents of bureaucratic autonomy (Shefter 1994). Where autonomous bureaucracies are not in place prior to democratization, parties face a classic collective action dilemma with respect to developing an autonomous and profes-sional bureaucracy (Geddes 1994). While the best outcome for all electoral contenders in the longer term is to develop bureaucratic quality, incumbents in the shorter term benefit from politicizing the bureaucracy and using state resources for partisan ends. This may help to explain why political competition lowered the use of patronage in Eastern Europe (Grzymala-Busse 2007; O'Dwyer 2006), where bureaucracies were fairly professional-ized at the time of transition to democracy, but in contexts such as Ghana and Argentina, where state capacity was weaker, political competition instead increased the use of pa-tronage and undermined efforts to reform the civil service (Driscoll 2018; Weitz-Shapiro 2012).[7]

From the perspective of rulers, competitive elections may diminish rather than increase the likelihood of replacing patronage-based bureaucratic structures with more meritocratic Weberian bureaucracies. As noted above, most states considered to have higher capacity today indeed emerged under autocratic rule, substantiated by both historical and more con-temporary examples such as Spain under Franco (Charron and Lapuente 2011; Lapuente and Rothstein 2014). Reform is not, however, impossible. Mikkelsen (2018) shows that major dis-ruptions of administrative apparatuses, as in some postcommunist states, created a window of opportunity that in some cases led to the development of professionalized bureaucracies or neo-patromonial states. Such events are by definition rare, however, and difficult to in-duce with ethically acceptable policy measures.

From the perspective of the voters, if states were capable of providing public goods before democratizing, citizens will have a higher level of trust in state institutions while simultan-eously developing a "healthy" level of mistrust towards politicians, which together induce citizens to expect solutions from government and to punish and reward representatives ac-cordingly (Bustikova and Corduneanu-Huci 2017). Contrastingly, in states with low bureau-cratic capacity at the time of democratization, programmatic linkages between politicians and voters are less likely to develop, as voters are more likely to turn to politicians to secure particularistic goods.

---

[7] Interestingly, Buckley and Reuter's (2019) study of Russia also shows that increased electoral competition increases the incidence of clientelism.

Economic well-being and democratic accountability

Although notable exceptions exist, many studies observe that an overwhelming majority of countries considered democratic but which are in fact thoroughly corrupt also have comparatively low levels of economic development. One explanation for the pattern is that institutions develop as a function of economic factors, such as human capital or income, and that these factors cause institutional development (Lipset 1960; Glaeser et al. 2004; Svensson 2005). Others argue that specific policies can foster entrepreneurship and start up firms (Djankov et al. 2002) or economic openness (Ades and Di Tella 1999; see also Svensson 2005), which then promotes institutional development (Olander, this volume).

Citizens' inclinations to demand institutional improvements may be partly a function of economic well-being, which has been shown in the aggregate to change the prevalent value set in a polity (Inglehart and Welzel 2010), and to lower people's future discount rates, lengthening their time horizons. Interestingly, Charron and Lapuente (2010) show that only above a certain level of GDP per capita is democracy associated with lower levels of corruption. They show that once the effect of democracy at different levels of wealth is modeled, democracy no longer exhibits a curvilinear relationship with corruption (Charron and Lapuente 2010). Similarly, Jetter et al. (2015) show that democracy reduces corruption but "only in economies that have already crossed a GDP/capita level of approximately US$2,000 (in 2005 US$)." In poorer countries, democracy may instead increase corruption. The lack of income opportunities in the productive or private sector in poor countries may lead elites to regard attaining political offices as the only viable way to increase one's income. In the spirit of Becker (1974), criminal acts are more likely to be committed if alternative options are scarce and not promising substantial income. Higher levels of economic development means more lucrative opportunities in the private sector for those individuals that are primarily interested in higher levels of income.

CONCLUSION: RESEARCH GAPS AND IDEAS FUTURE RESEARCH

Taken together, studies consistently demonstrate that newly democratized countries exhibit, on average, higher levels of corruption than either more established democracies or even than autocracies. We now see that even decades on, democratic deepening in these newly democratized countries is not a given. This chapter takes stock of the many crucial and notable advances in attempts to understand how, whether, and when democracy contributes to the weeding out of corrupt leaders, as well as the ways in which corruption shapes and undermines democracy and democratic accountability. Despite advances, questions remain regarding when democracy actually contributes to a decrease in corruption and when it does not.

This chapter has discussed several plausible reasons why democracies vary in their ability to contain corruption and improve the quality of government. The reviewed literature suggests that factors such as transparency, freedom of association and speech, clientelism and citizens' demand for low levels of corruption in their representatives, state capacity, and economic factors may all explain the varying effectiveness of democratic rule in reducing corruption. While this literature highlights several reasons why democracy oftentimes is less effective than theories would predict, autocratization as a measure to curb corruption is, for obvious reasons, not a viable policy recommendation. Furthermore, numerous examples, both historical and contemporary, demonstrate that autocrats most certainly do not uniformly contribute to institutional development, and that the ones that succeeded in this regard are, in recent times, very few.

It is thus imperative to continue the investigation of what factors improve democracies' ability to contain corruption. In doing so, it is useful to keep in mind the underlying theory of change of democracy, and in particular the basic assumptions about actors that these theories rest upon. As discussed earlier in this chapter, the beneficial effect of democracy rests on a number of quite specific assumptions about voters, parties, and politicians. For voters, these include that voters have access to sufficient and relevant information, perceive that improvement in the quality of government and reduced corruption is compatible with the fulfillment of other immediate concerns, have means to issue sanctions and rewards, are able to overcome collective action problems, and that they at all see government institutions as a source of solutions to societal problems. A closer investigation of the determinants of these preconditions for accountability along the lines suggested in this chapter, and especially on their interdependencies, will move the research field forward. In other words, the field may benefit from more explicit acknowledgment of these assumptions and investigation of the conditions under which they are met. Will increased transparency induce or undermine citizens' collective action capacity? Will increased freedom of association enable mobilization for programatic policies or better enable citizens to make clientelistic demands? What manifestations of increased state capacity make citizens see government insitutions as a source of solutions to societal problems and intensify demands for cleaner government? And more plausibly, what combinations of conditions seem to be necessary in order to effect change? Contemporary political developments also suggest a need to pay attention to how political polarization and disinformation also affect voters' confidence in information pertaining to corruption and, consequently, their propensity to act on it.

Moreover, drilling down to understand what forms of corruption democracy incentivizes and what forms it helps contain would appear to be a particularly promising avenue for future research. We would expect democracies to be more capable of reducing certain forms of corruption as opposed to others (Bauhr 2017). An emerging literature seeks to examine how electoral systems and term limits shape competition, and how this may incentivize certain forms of corruption among politicians and parties (e.g. Nyblade and Reed 2008; Vaishnav 2018; Gingerich 2013; Klašnja and Titiunik 2017). Closer examination of the kinds of corruption incentivized by different electoral systems and term limits may prove an interesting and productive way forward. Furthermore, insights about how and when improved democratic accountability improves quality of government and reduces corruption may also be gained from distinguishing between different types of state operations and public services. Public services differ on a number of important dimensions, including their visibility, targetability and the extent to which improvements are attributable to executive action (Batley and McLoughlin 2015; Harding and Stasavage 2014; Harding 2015). Studies show, for instance that democracy is associated with spending on some public services, such as primary education (i.e Stasavage 2005), but less so with others, including access to health services (Lieberman 2015; Carlitz and Lust, this volume). A promising avenue for future empirical research would be to investigate why democracy may be better suited to redress corruption in some sectors as opposed to others, which may hold the key to a more fine-grained understanting of when and how democracy reduces corruption.

A set of factors explored in more depth in this chapter relate to the capacity of the state itself. The literature reviewed here suggests that the degree of bureaucratic politicization may enable and induce incumbents to use access to public services in a targeted way, as a means of amassing support. The research and evidence on if and how bureaucratic autonomy affects parties' linkage strategies and voters' electoral behavior—and thus electoral accountability more broadly—remains limited. Similarly, how state absence influences how citizens come to think about their role as democratic citizens can also yield new and important insights relevant to the sequencing debate as well as to our understanding of the functioning of democracy. The research on corruption voting (Bågenholm, this volume) and clientelism have both yielded a wealth of insights helping us to understand how elections do not always lead to the removal of corrupt politicians from office. Coordinated field experiments such as the Metaketa initiative (Dunning et al. 2019) could moving forward continue to explore how characteristics of the state in each context affect corruption voting. These literatures only rarely seek to understand how state capacity affects political behavior. We welcome more studies of political behavior that pay systematic attention to these institutional factors.

The review presented here also raises questions about the validity and mechanisms discussed in relation to the j-shaped curve between democracy and corruption at the country level. The curvilinear relationship suggests that democracy, given time, will lead to lower levels of corruption. As noted above, some scholars point to the fact that authoritarian regimes may also have the means to conceal corruption to a greater extent than newly democratized states (e.g. Montinola and Jackman 2002:163), in other words that the nonlinear finding may be a figment of measurement rather than an actual effect. Efforts to determine which country cases are driving the results can potentially make a valuable contribution in this regard. Given the stability over time in many measures of quality of government and democracy, it is also plausible that only a few polities show movement on these parameters in past decades, and closer examinations of those specific country cases may better reveal whether it in fact is democracy that is leading to better quality of government, and if so, how.

Despite important advances, many questions thus remain. In particular, we welcome concerted efforts to identify and explore instances in which democratic accountability has contributed to noticeable and impactful change. Research, like journalism, has a built-in bias to focus on the factors that inhibit positive change, and while it is necessary to understand the possible pitfalls, more attention to the conditions that prompt and sustain change are needed as well.

REFERENCES

Acemoglu, Daron, Camilo García-Jimeno, and James A. Robinson. 2015. "State Capacity and Economic Development: A Network Approach." *American Economic Review* 105 (8): 2364–409.

Achen, Christopher H., and Larry M. Bartels. 2017. *Democracy for Realists: Why Elections Do Not Produce Responsive Government.* Princeton, NJ: Princeton University Press.

Ades, Alberto, and Rafael Di Tella. 1999. "Rents, Competition, and Corruption." *American Economic Review* 89 (4): 982–93.

Agerberg, Mattias. 2017. "Failed Expectations: Quality of Government and Support for Populist Parties in Europe." *European Journal of Political Research* 56 (3): 578–600.

Alt, James E., David Dreyer Lassen, and David Skilling. 2002. "Fiscal Transparency, Gubernatorial Approval, and the Scale of Government: Evidence from the States." *State Politics & Policy Quarterly* 2 (3): 230–50.

Anduiza, Eva, Aina Gallego, and Jordi Muñoz. 2013. "Turning a Blind Eye: Experimental Evidence of Partisan Bias in Attitudes Toward Corruption." *Comparative Political Studies* 46 (2): 1664–92.

Auerbach, Adam M., and Tariq Thachil. 2018. "How Clients Select Brokers: Competition and Choice in India's Slums." *American Political Science Review* 112 (4): 775–91.

Auyero, Javier. 2001. *Poor People's Politics: Peronist Survival Networks and the Legacy of Evita.* Durham, NC: Duke University Press.

Bac, Mehmet. 2001. "Corruption, Connections and Transparency: Does a Better Screen Imply a Better Scene?" *Public Choice* 107 (1–2): 87–96.

Bäck, Hanna, and Axel Hadenius. 2008. "Democracy and State Capacity: Exploring a J-Shaped Relationship." *Governance* 21 (1): 1–24. https://doi.org/10.1111/j.1468-0491.2007.00383.x

Bågenholm, Andreas. 2013. "Throwing the Rascals out? The Electoral Effects of Corruption Allegations and Corruption Scandals in Europe 1981–2011." *Crime, Law and Social Change* 60 (5): 595–609.

Basinger, Scott J. 2013. "Scandals and Congressional Elections in the Post-Watergate Era." *Political Research Quarterly* 66 (2): 385–98.

Batley, Richard, and Claire Mcloughlin. 2015. "The Politics of Public Services: A Service Characteristics Approach." *World Development* 74 (Supplement C): 275–85. https://doi.org/10.1016/j.worlddev.2015.05.018

Bauhr, Monika. 2017. "Need or Greed? Conditions for Collective Action against Corruption." *Governance* 30 (4): 561–81. https://doi.org/10.1111/gove.12232

Bauhr, Monika, Nicholas Charron. 2020. Will Women Executives Reduce Corruption? Marginalization and Network Inclusion. *Comparative Political Studies*, 0010414020970218. https://doi.org/10.1177/0010414020970218

Bauhr, Monika, and Ruth Carlitz. 2020. "When does transparency improve public services? Street-level discretion, information and targeting." *Public Administration* 1–17. https://doi.org/10.1111/padm.12693

Bauhr, Monika, and Nicholas Charron. 2018. "Insider or Outsider? Grand Corruption and Electoral Accountability." *Comparative Political Studies* 51 (4): 415–46. https://doi.org/10.1177/0010414017710258

Bauhr, Monika, Czibik, Ágnes, de Fine Licht, Jenny, & Fazekas, Mihaly (2020). Lights on the shadows of public procurement: Transparency as an antidote to corruption. *Governance* 33 (3): 495–523. https://doi.org/10.1111/gove.12432

Bauhr, Monika, and Marcia Grimes. 2014. "Indignation or Resignation: The Implications of Transparency for Societal Accountability." *Governance* 27 (2): 291–320. https://doi.org/10.1111/gove.12033.

Bauhr, Monika, and Naghmeh Nasiritousi. 2012. "Resisting Transparency: Corruption, Legitimacy, and the Quality of Global Environmental Policies." *Global Environmental Politics* 12 (4): 9–29.

Bauhr, Monika, Nicholas Charron, and Lena Wängnerud. 2019. "Exclusion or Interests? Why Females in Elected Office Reduce Petty and Grand Corruption." *European Journal of Political Research* 58 (4): 1043–65. https://doi.org/10.1111/1475-6765.12300

Becker, Gary S. 1974. "A Theory of Social Interactions." *Journal of Political Economy* 82 (6): 1063–93.

Becker, Gary S., and George J. Stigler. 1974. "Law Enforcement, Malfeasance, and Compensation of Enforces." *Journal of Legal Studies* 1: 1–18.

Berry, Christopher R., and Jacob E. Gersen. 2017. "Agency Design and Political Control." *Yale Law Journal* 126 (4): 908–1241.

Berwick, Elissa, and Fotini Christia. 2018. "State Capacity Redux: Integrating Classical and Experimental Contributions to an Enduring Debate." *Annual Review of Political Science* 21: 71–91.

Besley, Timothy, and Robin Burgess. 2002. "The Political Economy of Government Responsiveness: Theory and Evidence from India." *The Quarterly Journal of Economics* 117 (4): 1415–51.

Beyerle, Shaazka M. 2014. *Curtailing Corruption: People Power for Accountability and Justice.* Boulder, CO: Lynne Rienner.

Bhattacharyya, Sambit, and Roland Hodler. 2015. "Media Freedom and Democracy in the Fight against Corruption." *European Journal of Political Economy* 39 (September): 13–24.

Billger, Sherrilyn M., and Rajeev K. Goel. 2009. "Do Existing Corruption Levels Matter in Controlling Corruption?: Cross-Country Quantile Regression Estimates." *Journal of Development Economics* 90 (2): 299–305.

Björkman, Martina, and Jakob Svensson. 2009. "Power to the People: Evidence from a Randomized Field Experiment on Community-Based Monitoring in Uganda." *The Quarterly Journal of Economics* 124 (2): 735–69.

Bogaards, Matthijs. 2018. "De-Democratization in Hungary: Diffusely Defective Democracy." *Democratization* 25 (8): 1481–99.

Bollen, Kenneth A. 1993. "Liberal Democracy: Validity and Method Factors in Cross-national Measures." *American Journal of Political Science* 37 (4): 1207–30.

Boräng, Frida, Agnes Cornell, Marcia Grimes, and Christian Schuster. 2018. "Cooking the Books: Bureaucratic Politicization and Policy Knowledge." *Governance* 31 (1): 7–26.

Bratton, Michael, and Eric C. C. Chang. 2006. "State Building and Democratization in Sub-Saharan Africa." *Comparative Political Studies* 39 (9): 1059–83.

Broms, Rasmus. 2015. "Putting Up or Shutting Up: On the Individual-Level Relationship between Taxpaying and Political Interest in a Developmental Context." *The Journal of Development Studies* 51 (1): 93–109.

Brunetti, Aymo, and Beatrice Weder. 2003. "A Free Press Is Bad News for Corruption." *Journal of Public Economics* 87 (7–8): 1801–24.

Brusco, Valeria, Marcelo Nazareno, and Susan Stokes. 2004. "Vote Buying in Argentina." *Latin American Research Review* 39 (2): 66–88.

Buckley, Noah, and Ora John Reuter. 2019. "Performance Incentives under Autocracy: Evidence from Russia's Regions." *Comparative Politics* 51 (2): 239–66.

Bustikova, Lenka, and Cristina Corduneanu-Huci. 2017. "Patronage, Trust, and State Capacity." *World Politics* 69 (2): 277–326.

Camaj, Lindita. 2013. "The Media's Role in Fighting Corruption: Media Effects on Governmental Accountability." *The International Journal of Press/Politics* 18 (1): 21–42.

Chang, Eric C. C., Miriam A. Golden, and Seth J. Hill. 2010. "Legislative Malfeasance and Political Accountability." *World Politics* 62 (2): 177–220.

Chang, Eric C. C., and Nicholas N. Kerr. 2016. "An Insider–Outsider Theory of Popular Tolerance for Corrupt Politicians." *Governance* 30 (1): 67–84. https://doi.org/10.1111/gove.12193

Charron, Nicholas. 2009. "Government Quality and Vertical Power Sharing in Fractionalized States." *Publius: The Journal of Federalism* 39 (4): 585–605.

Charron, Nicholas, and Andreas Bågenholm. 2016. "Ideology, Party Systems and Corruption Voting in European Democracies." *Electoral Studies* 41 (March): 35–49.

Charron, Nicholas, and Victor Lapuente. 2010. "Does Democracy Produce Quality of Government?" *European Journal of Political Research* 49 (4): 443–70. https://doi.org/10.1111/j.1475-6765.2009.01906.x

Charron, Nicholas, and Victor Lapuente. 2011. "Which Dictators Produce Quality of Government?" *Studies in Comparative International Development* 46 (4): 397–423.

Chong, Alberto, Ana L. De La O, Dean Karlan, and Leonard Wantchekon. 2015. "Does Corruption Information Inspire the Fight or Quash the Hope? A Field Experiment in Mexico on Voter Turnout, Choice, and Party Identification." *The Journal of Politics* 77 (1): 55–71. https://doi.org/10.1086/678766

Chowdhury, Shyamal K. 2004. "The Effect of Democracy and Press Freedom on Corruption: An Empirical Test." *Economics Letters* 85 (1): 93–101. https://doi.org/10.1016/j.econlet.2004.03.024

Cornell, Agnes, and Marcia Grimes. 2015. "Political control of bureaucracies as an incentive for party behavior." In Carl Dahlström and Lena Wängnerud (eds). *Elites, Institutions and the Quality of Government*, 205–23. London: Palgrave Macmillan.

Costas-Perez, Elena, Albert Sole-Olle, and Pilar Sorribas-Navarro. 2012. "Corruption Scandals, Voter Information, and Accountability." *European Journal of Political Economy* 28 (4): 469–84.

Cox, Gary W., and J. Morgan Kousser. 1981. "Turnout and Rural Corruption: New York as a Test Case." *American Journal of Political Science* 25(4): 646–63.

Crisp, Brian F., Santiago Olivella, Joshua D. Potter, and William Mishler. 2014. "Elections as Instruments for Punishing Bad Representatives and Selecting Good Ones." *Electoral Studies* 34 (June): 1–15. https://doi.org/10.1016/j.electstud.2013.08.017

Curato, Nicole. 2017. "Flirting with Authoritarian Fantasies? Rodrigo Duterte and the New Terms of Philippine Populism." *Journal of Contemporary Asia* 47 (1): 142–53.

Dahlberg, Stefan, Jonas Linde, and Sören Holmberg. 2015. "Democratic Discontent in Old and New Democracies: Assessing the Importance of Democratic Input and Governmental Output." *Political Studies* 63 (1): 18–37.

Dahlström, Carl, Mihály Fazekas, and David E. Lewis. 2019. "Agency Design, Favoritism and Procurement in the United States." QoG Working Paper Series 2019: 4 (May). Gothenburg: The Quality of Government Institute, University of Gothenburg.

De Vries, Catherine E., and Hector Solaz. 2017. "The Electoral Consequences of Corruption." *Annual Review of Political Science* 20 (1): 391–408. https://doi.org/10.1146/annurev-polisci-052715-111917

Dincecco, Mark, and Gabriel Katz. 2016. "State Capacity and Long-run Economic Performance." *The Economic Journal* 126 (590): 189–218.

Djankov, Simeon, Rafael La Porta, Florencio Lopez-de-Silanes, and Andrei Shleifer. 2002. "The Regulation of Entry." *The Quarterly Journal of Economics* 117 (1): 1–37. https://doi.org/10.1162/003355302753399436

Djankov, Simeon, Rafael La Porta, Florencio Lopez-de-Silanes, and Andrei Shleifer. 2010. "Disclosure by Politicians." *American Economic Journal: Applied Economics* 2 (2): 179–209.

Driscoll, Barry. 2018. "Why Political Competition Can Increase Patronage." *Studies in Comparative International Development* 53 (4): 404–27.

Dollar, David, Raymond Fisman, and Roberta Gatti. 2001. "Are Women Really the 'Fairer' Sex? Corruption and Women in Government." *Journal of Economic Behavior & Organization* 46 (4): 423–9. https://doi.org/10.1016/S0167-2681(01)00169-X

Dunning, Thad, Guy Grossman, Mccartan Humphreys, Susan D. Hyde, Craig Mcintosh, Gareth Nellis. 2019. *Information, Accountability and Cumulative Learning: Lessons for the Metaketa 1*. Cambridge: Cambridge University Press.

Dutta, Nabamita, and Sanjukta Roy. 2016. "The Interactive Impact of Press Freedom and Media Reach on Corruption." *Economic Modelling* 58 (November): 227–36.

Ecker, Alejandro, Konstantin Glinitzer, and Thomas M. Meyer. 2016. "Corruption Performance Voting and the Electoral Context." *European Political Science Review* 8 (3): 333–54.

Eggers, Andrew C. 2014. "Partisanship and Electoral Accountability: Evidence from the UK Expenses Scandal". *Quarterly Journal of Political Science* 9 (4): 441–72. doi: 10.1561/100.00013140.

Esarey, Justin, and Gina Chirillo. 2013. "'Fairer Sex' or Purity Myth? Corruption, Gender, and Institutional Context." *Politics & Gender* 9 (4): 361–89. https://doi.org/10.1017/S1743923X13000378

Esarey, Justin, and Leslie A. Schwindt-Bayer. 2018. "Women's Representation, Accountability and Corruption in Democracies." *British Journal of Political Science* (January): 1–32. https://doi.org/10.1017/S0007123416000478

Fenster, Mark. 2005. "The Opacity of Transparency." *Iowa Law Review* 91 (March): 885–949.

Fernández-Vázquez, Pablo, Pablo Barberá, and Gonzalo Rivero. 2016. "Rooting Out Corruption or Rooting for Corruption? The Heterogeneous Electoral Consequences of Scandals." *Political Science Research and Methods* 4 (2): 379–97.

Ferraz, Claudio, and Frederico Finan. 2008. "Exposing Corrupt Politicians: The Effects of Brazil's Publicly Released Audits on Electoral Outcomes." *The Quarterly Journal of Economics* 123 (2): 703–45.

Fox, Jonathan. 2007. "The Uncertain Relationship between Transparency and Accountability." *Development in Practice* 17 (4–5): 663–71.

Fox, Jonathan A. 2015. "Social Accountability: What Does the Evidence Really Say?" *World Development* 72 (August): 346–61. https://doi.org/10.1016/j.worlddev.2015.03.011

Fukuyama, Francis. 2015. "Why Is Democracy Performing So Poorly?" *Journal of Democracy* 26 (1): 11–20. https://doi.org/10.1353/jod.2015.0017

Garfias, Francisco. 2018. "Elite competition and state capacity development: Theory and evidence from post-revolutionary Mexico." *American Political Science Review* 112 (2): 339–57.

Geddes, Barbara. 1994. *Politician's Dilemma: Building State Capacity in Latin America*. Berkeley, CA: University of California Press.

Gerring, John, and Strom C. Thacker. 2004. "Political Institutions and Corruption: The Role of Unitarism and Parliamentarism." *British Journal of Political Science* 34 (02): 295–330. https://doi.org/10.1017/S0007123404000067

Gingerich, Daniel W. 2013. *Political Institutions and Party-Directed Corruption in South America: Stealing for the Team*. Cambridge: Cambridge University Press.

Glaeser, Edward L., Rafael La Porta, Florencio Lopez-de-Silane, and Andrei Shleifer. 2004. "Do Institutions Cause Growth?" *Journal of Economic Growth* 9 (3): 271–303.

Golden, Miriam A. 2003. "Electoral Connections: The Effects of the Personal Vote on Political Patronage, Bureaucracy and Legislation in Postwar Italy." *British Journal of Political Science* 33 (2): 189–212.

Grimes, Marcia. 2013. "The Contingencies of Societal Accountability: Examining the Link Between Civil Society and Good Government." *Studies in Comparative International Development* 48 (4): 380–402.

Grzymala-Busse, Anna. 2007. *Rebuilding Leviathan: Party Competition and State Exploitation in Post-Communist Democracies*. Cambridge: Cambridge University Press.

Harding, Robin. 2015. "Attribution and Accountability: Voting for Roads in Ghana." *World Politics* 67 (4): 656–89. https://doi.org/10.1017/S0043887115000209

Harding, Robin, and David Stasavage. 2014. "What Democracy Does (and Doesn't Do) for Basic Services: School Fees, School Inputs, and African Elections." *The Journal of Politics* 76 (1): 229–45. https://doi.org/10.1017/S0022381613001254

Hale, Henry E. 2015. *Patronal Politics: Eurasian Regime Dynamics in Comparative Perspective*. Cambridge: Cambridge University Press.

Herbst, Jeffrey. 2000. *States and Power in Africa: Comparative Lessons in Authority and Control*. Princeton NJ: Princeton University Press.

Hollyer, James R., Peter B. Rosendorff, and James Raymond Vreeland. 2015. "Transparency, Protest, and Autocratic Instability." *American Political Science Review* 109 (4): 764–84.

Hudak, John. 2014. *Presidential Pork: White House Influence over the Distribution of Federal Grants*. Washington, DC: Brookings Institution Press.

Hunter, Wendy, and Timothy J. Power. 2019. "Bolsonaro and Brazil's Illiberal Backlash." *Journal of Democracy* 30 (1): 68–82.

Inglehart, Ronald, and Christian Welzel. 2010. "Changing Mass Priorities: The Link between Modernization and Democracy." *Perspectives on Politics* 8 (2): 551–67.

Islam, Roumeen. 2006. "Does More Transparency Go along with Better Governance?" *Economics & Politics* 18 (6): 121–67.

Iwasaki, Ichiro, and Taku Suzuki. 2012. "The Determinants of Corruption in Transition Economies." *Economics Letters* 114 (1): 54–60. https://doi.org/10.1016/j.econlet.2011.08.016

Jetter, Michael, Alejandra Montoya Agudelo, and Andrés Ramírez Hassan. 2015. "The Effect of Democracy on Corruption: Income Is Key." *World Development* 74 (October): 286–304. https://doi.org/10.1016/j.worlddev.2015.05.016

Kalenborn, Christine, and Christian Lessmann. 2013. "The Impact of Democracy and Press Freedom on Corruption: Conditionality Matters." *Journal of Policy Modeling* 35 (6): 857–86. https://doi.org/10.1016/j.jpolmod.2013.02.009

Karklins, Rasma. 2005. *The System Made Me Do It: Corruption in Post-Communist Societies.* New York, NY: M.E. Sharpe.

Keefer, Philip. 2007. "Clientelism, Credibility, and the Policy Choices of Young Democracies." *American Journal of Political Science* 51 (4): 804–21.

Keefer, Philip, and Stuti Khemani. 2014. "Mass Media and Public Education: The Effects of Access to Community Radio in Benin." *Journal of Development Economics* 109 (July): 57–72.

Kenny, Paul D. 2015. "The Origins of Patronage Politics: State Building, Centrifugalism, and Decolonization." *British Journal of Political Science* 45 (1): 141–71.

Kitschelt, Herbert. 2000. "Linkages between Citizens and Politicians in Democratic Polities," *Comparative Political Studies,* 33 (6–7): 845–79. doi: 10.1177/001041400003300607

Klašnja, Marko, and Rocío Titiunik. 2017. "The Incumbency Curse: Weak Parties, Term Limits, and Unfulfilled Accountability." *American Political Science Review* 111 (1): 129–48. https://doi.org/10.1017/S0003055416000575

Klašnja, Marko, and Joshua A. Tucker. 2013. "The Economy, Corruption, and the Vote: Evidence from Experiments in Sweden and Moldova." *Electoral Studies* 32 (3): 536–43.

Klitgaard, Robert. 1988. *Controlling Corruption.* Berkeley, CA: University of California Press.

Knutsen, Carl Henrik. 2013. "Democracy, State Capacity, and Economic Growth." *World Development* 43 (March): 1–18.

Kolstad, Ivar, and Arne Wiig. 2009. "Is Transparency the Key to Reducing Corruption in Resource-Rich Countries?" *World Development* 37 (3): 521–32.

Kolstad, Ivar, and Arne Wiig. 2016. "Does Democracy Reduce Corruption?" *Democratization* 23 (7): 1198–215. https://doi.org/10.1080/13510347.2015.1071797

Konstantinidis, Iannis, and Georgios Xezonakis. 2013. "Sources of Tolerance Towards Corrupted Politicians in Greece: The Role of Trade Offs and Individual Benefits." *Crime, Law and Social Change* 60 (5): 549–63.

Kosack, Stephen, and Archon Fung. 2014. "Does Transparency Improve Governance?" *Annual Review of Political Science* 17 (1): 65–87.

Landell-Mills, Pierre. 2013. *Citizens against Corruption: Report from the Front Line.* Leicestershire, UK: Troubador Publishing Ltd.

Lapuente, Victor, and Bo Rothstein. 2014. "Civil War Spain Versus Swedish Harmony: The Quality of Government Factor." *Comparative Political Studies* 47 (10): 1416–41.

Ledeneva, Alena V. 2013. *Can Russia Modernise: Sistema, Power Networks and Informal Governance.* Null edition. Cambridge: Cambridge University Press.

Lee, C. S. 2007. "Labor Unions and Good Governance: A cross-national, comparative analysis." *American Sociological Review* 72 (4): 585–609.

Lemarchand, René. 1972. "Political Clientelism and Ethnicity in Tropical Africa: Competing Solidarities in Nation-Building." *The American Political Science Review* 66 (1): 68–90. https://doi.org/10.2307/1959279

Levitsky, Steven, and Lucan A. Way. 2002. "Elections Without Democracy: The Rise of Competitive Authoritarianism." *Journal of Democracy* 13 (2): 51–65. https://doi.org/10.1353/jod.2002.0026

Lieberman, Evan S., Daniel N. Posner, and Lily L. Tsai. 2014. "Does Information Lead to More Active Citizenship? Evidence from an Education Intervention in Rural Kenya." *World Development* 60 (August): 69–83.

Lieberman, Evan S. 2015. "The Comparative Politics of Service Delivery in Developing Countries." In *The Oxford Handbook of Politics of Development,* edited by Carol Lancaster and Nicholas van de Walle. Oxford: Oxford University Press.

Lipset, Seymour Martin. 1960. *Political Man: The Social Bases of Politics*. New York, NY: Doubleday & Company.

Lührmann, Anna, and Staffan I. Lindberg. 2019. "A Third Wave of Autocratization Is Here: What Is New about It?" *Democratization* 26 (7): 1095–113.

MacLean, Lauren M. 2011. "State Retrenchment and the Exercise of Citizenship in Africa." *Comparative Political Studies* 44 (9): 1238–66.

Mann, Michael. 1984. "The Autonomous Power of the State: Its Origins, Mechanisms and Results." *European Journal of Sociology* 25 (2): 185–213.

McMann, Kelly M., Brigitte Seim, Jan Teorell, and Staffan Lindberg. 2019. "Why Low Levels of Democracy Promote Corruption and High Levels Diminish It." *Political Research Quarterly* (July). 1065912919862054. https://doi.org/10.1177/1065912919862054

Migdal, Joel S. 1988. *Strong Societies and Weak States: State-Society Relations and State Capabilities in the Third World*. Princeton, NJ: Princeton University Press.

Mikkelsen, Kim Sass. 2018. "Old Habits Die Hard, Sometimes: History and Civil Service Politicization in Europe." *International Review of Administrative Sciences* 84 (4): 803–19.

Mohtadi, Hamid, and Terry L. Roe. 2003. "Democracy, Rent Seeking, Public Spending and Growth." *Journal of Public Economics* 87 (3–4): 445–66.

Montinola, Gabriella R., and Robert W. Jackman. 2002. "Sources of Corruption: A Cross-Country Study." *British Journal of Political Science* 32 (1): 147–70. https://doi.org/10.1017/S0007123402000066

Mungiu-Pippidi, Alina. 2006. "Corruption: Diagnosis and Treatment." *Journal of Democracy* 17 (3): 86–99.

Muñoz, Jordi, Eva Anduiza, and Aina Gallego. 2016. "Why Do Voters Forgive Corrupt Mayors? Implicit Exchange, Credibility of Information and Clean Alternatives." *Local Government Studies* 42 (4): 598–615.

Nichter, Simeon. 2008. "Vote Buying or Turnout Buying? Machine Politics and the Secret Ballot." *American Political Science Review* 102 (1): 19–31.

Nichter, Simeon, and Michael Peress. 2017. "Request Fulfilling: When Citizens Demand Clientelist Benefits." *Comparative Political Studies* 50 (8): 1086–117.

Nyblade, Benjamin, and Steven R. Reed. 2008. "Who Cheats? Who Loots? Political Competition and Corruption in Japan, 1947–1993." *American Journal of Political Science* 52 (4): 926–41. https://doi.org/10.1111/j.1540-5907.2008.00351.x

O'Dwyer, Conor. 2006. *Runaway State Building: Patronage Politics and Democratic Development*. Baltimore, MD: Johns Hopkins University Press.

Olken, Benjamin. 2007. "Monitoring Corruption: Evidence from a Field Experiment in Indonesia." *Journal of Political Economy* 115 (April): 200–49.

Ostrom, Elinor. 1998. "A Behavioral Approach to the Rational Choice Theory of Collective Action: Presidential Address, American Political Science Association." *American Political Science Association* 92 (1): 1–22.

Paldam, Martin. 2002. "The Cross-Country Pattern of Corruption: Economics, Culture and the Seesaw Dynamics." *European Journal of Political Economy* 18 (2): 215–40. https://doi.org/10.1016/S0176-2680(02)00078-2

Pavão, Nara. 2018. "Corruption as the Only Option: The Limits to Electoral Accountability." *The Journal of Politics* 80 (3): 996–1010.

Persson, Anna, Bo Rothstein, and Jan Teorell. 2013. "Why Anticorruption Reforms Fail—Systemic Corruption as a Collective Action Problem." *Governance* 26 (3): 449–71. https://doi.org/10.1111/j.1468-0491.2012.01604.x

Persson, Anna, and Bo Rothstein 2015. It's my Money: Why Big Government may be Good Government. *Comparative Politics* 47 (2): 231–49.

Persson, Torsten, and Guido Tabellini. 2005. *The Economic Effect of Constitutions.* Boston, MA: MIT Press.

Pollack, Ester, and Sigurd Allern. 2018. "Disclosure of Scandinavian Telecom Companies' Corruption in Uzbekistan: The Role of Investigative Journalists." *European Journal of Communication* 33 (1): 73–88.

Reed, Steven R. 1996. "Political Corruption in Japan." *International Social Science Journal* 48 (149): 395–405.

Reinikka, Ritva, and Jakob Svensson. 2005. "Fighting Corruption to Improve Schooling: Evidence from a Newspaper Campaign in Uganda." *Journal of the European Economic Association* 3 (2–3): 259–67.

Remmer, Karen L. 2010. "Political Scale and Electoral Turnout: Evidence From the Less Industrialized World." *Comparative Political Studies* 43 (3): 275–303.

Renzio, Paolo de, and Joachim Wehner. 2017. "The Impacts of Fiscal Openness." *World Bank Research Observer* 32 (2): 185–210. https://doi.org/10.1093/wbro/lkx004

Rock, Michael T. 2009. "Corruption and Democracy." *The Journal of Development Studies* 45 (1): 55–75. https://doi.org/10.1080/00220380802468579

Rose, Richard, and Don C. Shin. 2001. "Democratization Backwards: The Problem of Third-Wave Democracies." *British Journal of Political Science* 31 (2): 331–54.

Rose-Ackerman, Susan. 1978. *Corruption: A Study in Political Economy.* New York, NY: Academic Press.

Rothstein, Bo, and Jan Teorell. 2008. "What Is Quality of Government? A Theory of Impartial Government Institutions." *Governance* 21 (2): 165–90. https://doi.org/10.1111/j.1468-0491.2008.00391.x

Rundquist, Barry S., Gerald S. Strom, and John G. Peters. 1977. "Corrupt Politicians and Their Electoral Support: Some Experimental Observations." *American Political Science Review* 71 (3): 954–63.

Sandholtz, Wayne, and William Koetzle. 2000. "Accounting for Corruption: Economic Structure, Democracy, and Trade." *International Studies Quarterly* 44 (1): 31–50.

Schaffer, Fredric, and Andreas Schedler. 2007. "What is vote buying?" In *Elections for Sale. the Causes and Consequences of Vote Buying*, edited by Andreas Schedler. Boulder, CO: Lynne Rienner Publishers.

Schedler, Andreas. 2009. "The New Institutionalism in the Study of Authoritarian Regimes." *Totalitarianism and Democracy* 6 (2): 323–40.

Scott, James C. 1972. *Comparative Political Corruption.* Englewood Cliffs, NJ: Prentice-Hall.

Serra, Danila. 2006. "Empirical Determinants of Corruption: A Sensitivity Analysis." *Public Choice* 126 (1): 225–56. https://doi.org/10.1007/s11127-006-0286-4

Shefter, Martin. 1994. *Political Parties and the State.* Princeton, NJ: Princeton University Press.

Shleifer, Andrei, and Robert W. Vishny. 1993. "Corruption." *The Quarterly Journal of Economics* 108 (3): 599–617.

Soifer, Hillel. 2008. "State Infrastructural Power: Approaches to Conceptualization and Measurement." *Studies in Comparative International Development* 43 (3): 231–51.

Sousa, Luís de, and Marcelo Moriconi. 2013. "Why Voters Do Not Throw the Rascals out?—A Conceptual Framework for Analysing Electoral Punishment of Corruption." *Crime, Law and Social Change* 60 (5): 471–502. https://doi.org/10.1007/s10611-013-9483-5

Stasavage, David. 2005. "Democracy and Education Spending in Africa." *American Journal of Political Science* 49 (2): 343–58.

Stiglitz, Joseph. 2002. *Globalization and Its Discontents*. New York, NY: W. W. Norton & Company.

Stokes, Susan C., Thad Dunning, Marcelo Nazareno, and Valeria Brusco. 2013. *Brokers, Voters, and Clientelism: The Puzzle of Distributive Politics*. Cambridge: Cambridge University Press.

Stensöta, Helena and Lena Wängnerud. 2018. *Gender and Corruption: Historical Roots and New Avenues for Research*. New York, NY: Springer International Pub. https://www.palgrave.com/gp/book/9783319709284

Sundström, Aksel, and Daniel Stockemer. 2015. "Regional Variation in Voter Turnout in Europe: The Impact of Corruption Perceptions." *Electoral Studies* 40 (December): 158–69. https://doi.org/10.1016/j.electstud.2015.08.006

Sung, H. E. 2004. "Democracy and Political Corruption: A Cross-National Comparison." *Crime, Law and Social Change;* 41 (2): 179–94.

Svensson, Jakob. 2005. "Eight Questions about Corruption." *The Journal of Economic Perspectives* 19 (3): 19–42. https://doi.org/10.1257/089533005774357860

Swamy, Anand, Stephen Knack, Young Lee, and Omar Azfar. 2001. "Gender and Corruption." *Journal of Development Economics* 64 (1): 25–55. https://doi.org/10.1016/S0304-3878(00)00123-1

Tavits, Margit. 2007. "Clarity of Responsibility and Corruption." *American Journal of Political Science* 51 (1): 218–29.

Teorell, Jan, Stefan Dahlberg, Sören Holmberg, Bo Rothstein, Natalia Alvarado Pachon and Richard Svensson. 2019. The Quality of Government Standard Dataset, version Jan19. University of Gothenburg: The Quality of Government Institute, http://www.qog.pol.gu.se

Themudo, Nuno S. 2013. "Reassessing the Impact of Civil Society: Nonprofit Sector, Press Freedom, and Corruption." *Governance* 26 (1): 63–89.

Themudo, Nuno S. 2014. "Government Size, Nonprofit Sector Strength, and Corruption: A Cross-National Examination." *American Review of Public Administration* 44 (3): 309–23.

Treisman, Daniel. 2000. "The Causes of Corruption: A Cross-National Study." *Journal of Public Economics* 76 (3): 399–457. https://doi.org/10.1016/S0047-2727(99)00092-4

UNODC. 2004. "United Nations Convention Against Corruption."

Vaishnav, Milan. 2018. When Crime Pays: Money and Muscle in Indian Politics. New Haven, CT: Yale University Press.

Varese, Federico. 1997. "The Transition to the Market and Corruption in Post-Socialist Russia." *Political Studies* 45 (3): 579–96. https://doi.org/10.1111/1467-9248.00097

Wade, Robert. 1985. "The Market for Public Office: Why the Indian State Is Not Better at Development." *World Development* 13 (4): 467–97. https://doi.org/10.1016/0305-750X(85)90052-X

Wantchekon, Leonard. 2003. "Clientelism and Voting Behavior: Evidence from a Field Experiment in Benin." *World Politics* 55 (3): 399–422.

Weitz-Shapiro, Rebecca. 2012. "What Wins Votes: Why Some Politicians Opt Out of Clientelism." *American Journal of Political Science* 56 (3): 568–83. https://doi.org/10.1111/j.1540-5907.2011.00578.x

Welch, Susan, and John R. Hibbing. 1997. "The Effects of Charges of Corruption on Voting Behavior in Congressional Elections, 1982-1990." *The Journal of Politics* 59 (1): 226–39. https://doi.org/10.2307/2998224

Weyland, Kurt Gerhard. 1998. "The Politics of Corruption in Latin America." *Journal of Democracy* 9 (2): 108–21. https://doi.org/10.1353/jod.1998.0034

Winters, Matthew S., and Rebecca Weitz-Shapiro. 2013. "Lacking Information or Condoning Corruption: When Do Voters Support Corrupt Politicians?" *Comparative Politics* 45 (4): 418–36.

Worthy, Ben, and Tom McClean. 2015. "Freedom of Information and Corruption." In *Routledge Handbook of Political Corruption*, edited by Paul M. Heywood, 347–59. London and New York: Routledge.

Zakaria, Fareed. 1997. "The Rise of Illiberal Democracy." *Foreign Affairs*. 76 (6): 22–43. https://doi.org/10.2307/20048274

Zechmeister, Elizabeth J., and Daniel Zizumbo-Colunga. 2013. "The Varying Political Toll of Concerns About Corruption in Good Versus Bad Economic Times." *Comparative Political Studies* 46 (10): 1190–218. https://doi.org/10.1177/0010414012472468

....

CHAPTER 10

ELECTORAL ACCOUNTABILITY AND CORRUPTION

....

ANDREAS BÅGENHOLM

INTRODUCTION

....

THE research field on electoral accountability, i.e. to what extent voters reward or punish their elected representatives based on their performance, was for a long time dominated by economic issues (Healy and Malhotra 2013; Schwindt-Bayer and Tavits 2016, 12). Even though a few early studies focused on corruption, it was not until about 10 to 12 years ago that the "corruption voting" literature really took off. As late as 2013, De Sousa and Moriconi in a review article wrote that "[t]he literature on electoral punishment of corruption is still scarce" (2013, 496), but today there is an abundance of studies which, from numerous methodological approaches and with very different types of data, explore to what extent and why corrupt politicians are punished at elections. This has thus become a thriving subfield of corruption research in its own right.

The point of departure for what has been labeled corruption voting is the seemingly paradoxical observation that corrupt politicians continue to receive support and be reelected, despite a universally strong popular aversion against corrupt practices. One would assume that voters would be merciless with candidates and representatives who are not only ineffective in combating corruption, but who also purposely enrich themselves in an illicit fashion. As the corruption voting paradox suggests, this is far from always the case, however, which implies that the vital cornerstone of democratic politics—effective electoral accountability—is not functioning. If corrupt practices, in turn, go unpunished, and oftentimes even rewarded, the incentives for policymakers to stay clean and honest are limited at best, and the prospects of combating corruption will be severely curtailed. There are, naturally, other means through which criminal and corrupt politicians can be and have been removed from office, such as the judicial system or other monitoring bodies (horizontal accountability) or widespread popular protests (societal accountability), but such actions are less likely to be successful where corrupt incumbents enjoy substantial popular support.[1] Hence, effective electoral accountability is crucially important in order to keep corruption at bay.

As corruption has been found to have an array of detrimental consequences for any society (see for example the Introduction to this volume), the lack of effective electoral accountability mechanisms related to corruption is a serious problem and the main motivation as to why scholars have started to explore why or under which conditions corrupt politicians get punished and under which they do not. During the past decade, the empirical and theoretical knowledge on this subject has increased substantially, and today there are several competing, but most often complementary, explanations as to why corruption voting occurs.

A perhaps paradoxical observation is that most of these explanations seem highly intuitive and reasonable, which to some extent makes the original paradox less paradoxical. Some authors even seem to dismiss the paradox altogether by claiming that "[v]oters punish corrupt politicians if they have the opportunity to do so" (see De Vries and Solaz 2017, 395). Others are more pessimistic, however, suggesting that "electoral punishment of political corruption is hardly a reality in many democracies" (De Sousa and Moriconi 2013, 472).

What is considered to be the proper degree of electoral punishment for corrupt practices naturally varies among scholars in the field, which is why some are more optimistic than others. In this chapter, I review the findings in the corruption voting literature. I start out by looking at the theoretical point of departure, i.e. how the electoral accountability mechanism is supposed to work and, in the ideal world, lead to less corruption. Thereafter, I review the studies looking at the extent to which corrupt politicians and parties get punished and the different types of methodological approaches and data that have been used. In the following section, I turn to the different explanations on corruption voting and then to the limited research on the effects of electoral accountability for curbing corruption. Finally, I point out existing gaps in the literature and propose a way forward.

THE THEORY OF ELECTORAL ACCOUNTABILITY

Electoral accountability is a crucial component of democratic governance as it ideally incentivizes politicians to perform well and to be responsive to voters' wishes (see Anderson 2007, 273; Schwindt-Bayer and Tavits, 2016, 13–14). It is thus linked to retrospective voting, which implies that voters should reward good performance and punish bad performance on election day (for an overview, see Achen and Bartels 2016; Healy and Malhotra 2013, 286; Fearon 1999). Research on electoral accountability and retrospective voting has historically focused on voters' material well-being and how well the economy is (perceived) to be handled by the incumbents (Achen and Bartels 2016; Anderson 2007; Fiorina 1981), and this strand of research—the economic voting literature—has consistently found such issues to matter substantially (Stegmaier, Lewis-Beck and Brown 2019; Achen and Bartels 2016, 97–8; Lewis-Beck and Stegmaier 2000). Well-functioning electoral accountability processes

---

[1] In such contexts, the laws can be changed in favor of the incumbents, which for instance happened in Italy during the investigations into Prime Minister Silvio Berlusconi, and in Romania, where the government in 2017 sought to decriminalize large-scale political corruption. Monitoring bodies may also be stacked with political supporters, or get their mandates curtailed, thereby effectively undermining their effectiveness, which recently happened to the Romanian anticorruption agency (DNA).

do, however, put high demands on the electorate. In order to make a well-informed choice, voters must be knowledgeable, be able to correctly assess the personal consequences of the government's policies, as well as those for society at large, and, finally, be able to distinguish between outcomes that the government can reasonably be held responsible for and those that it cannot (Healy and Malhotra 2013; Anderson 2007). It is therefore not surprising that scholars disagree on the extent to which electoral accountability actually works and leads to the intended outcomes (see Gailmard 2019 for a short overview).

Even though there are older studies that look at corruption rather than the economy (for example Rundquist, Strom, and Peters 1977; Peters and Welsh 1980; Dimock and Jacobsen 1995; Welch and Hibbing 1997), it was only in the wake of the burgeoning interest in the effects of corruption in general, which found indisputable evidence of its negative effects on almost all societal spheres, not least human well-being (see the Introduction to this volume), that scholars also started to become more interested in the electoral effects of corruption, thereby expanding the research field on electoral accountability (Healy and Malhotra 2013).

Unsurprisingly, the corruption voting literature and the economic voting literature are in many respects very similar. They both start from the assumption that voters reward good performance and sanction bad, although in practice the corruption voting literature strongly emphasizes the punishing aspects, i.e. "booting out" corrupt politicians, whereas the economic voting literature looks at both consequences. They both also acknowledge that there are a number of conditions that need to be met in order for this process to be successful, such as the importance of accurate information so that voters can correctly single out who is responsible for the policies pursued, and that voters, moreover, need to find the issue salient enough to influence their vote choice. Herein lies the reason why the accountability process, which looks straightforward on paper, quite easily breaks down. These stages will be revisited in the section that reviews explanations as to why corruption voting occurs. The two strands of research also implicitly assume that well-functioning accountability processes, through which competent, honest, well-intentioned, and hard-working politicians are elected, will lead to better policy outcomes, which, in these specific cases, mean a stronger economy and less corruption. This latter part of the process, in which electoral accountability is the independent variable, has only rarely been subject to empirical research and is thus a neglected aspect in both strands of accountability research (Healy and Malhotra 2013; De Vries and Solaz 2017; see Ferraz and Finan 2011 as an early exception).

In contrast to the economic voting literature, where the problem for voters to correctly assess the impact of the economic policies pursued and to identify those responsible for them, has been widely discussed, the corruption voting literature takes its point of departure from the fact that almost all people detest corruption (Kurer 2001) and moreover think it is a widespread problem in their country (see for example Special Eurobarometers 397 and 470). Corruption is, thus, a so-called valence issue (a nonpolicy-based valence issue), i.e. something that everyone agrees on regardless of ideological position (Curini 2018, 1). Some parties and representatives emphasize this issue more strongly than others, for various reasons, but no one would argue that corruption is a good thing that should not be curbed. It has been argued that the economy is also a valence issue (a nonpositional policy-based one, Curini 2018, 1), as (almost) everyone agrees that a strong economy with high growth, low unemployment, and low inflation etc. is better than the opposite. An important difference, however, is that as soon as we move beyond simply agreeing that more growth is better than less, the issue becomes a positional one, as the measures required to reach the economic goals and how to prioritize them are highly ideologically divisive. This in turn complicates voters' ability to "objectively" assess government economic performance, whereas anticorruption policies, let alone involvement in corrupt practices, are arguably less contentious and should hence be an easier issue for voters to hold elected representatives accountable (see for instance Kurer 2001; for an opposite view, see De Vries and Solaz 2017). In addition, one may also argue that corruption makes it easier for voters to react, as a corruption scandal is a concrete event in which information will most likely reach many voters, either through the media or via political opponents, and where it is easy to identify the individuals responsible and thus punishable for it (Ferraz and Finan 2008; Chang, Golden, and Hill 2010). In contrast, it has been argued that it is very difficult for ordinary voters to assess a government's economic performance, as they oftentimes lack both willingness and capacity to evaluate such complex processes (Anderson 2007, 277; Healy and Malhotra 2013, 286–7). As discussed later in this chapter, the reality is not so clear-cut, as corruption is a shady business which all involved has an interest to hide, but the main components for holding representatives accountable are arguably easier to identify for corruption than the economy.

The majority of studies on corruption and electoral accountability focus either on the more descriptive aspects of the subject, namely to what extent corrupt elected representatives are punished at the polls, or on the explanatory aspects—the causes behind successful and unsuccessful accountability processes. The findings of these two strands of research are reviewed in the following sections. In the remaining part of this section, the theory linking electoral accountability and levels of corruption are discussed, i.e. how a well-functioning process may result in reduced levels of corruption. As mentioned above, this is hardly a literature in its own right but rather a side issue that is usually addressed only briefly in most studies (De Vries and Solaz 2017).

In a polity in which the electoral accountability procedures are known to function well, elected representatives who wish to remain in office should be incentivized to perform well, i.e. being effective in curbing corruption and, perhaps more importantly, avoiding being engaged themselves in self-enriching, corrupt behavior. Voters will select honest and well-intentioned politicians who make an effort to combat corruption and stay away from such activities themselves, and deselect, i.e. punish, the "rascals" that are unsuccessful, neglectful, or implicated in corrupt dealings (Schwindt-Bayer and Tavits 2016). This is mainly done through retrospective voting, which is when voters base their choice on the representatives' previous track record (Healy and Malhotra 2013). Ineffective and corrupt politicians will have a hard time convincing voters that they are best suited to combat corruption in the future, regardless of their electoral platform. There are, however, also aspects of prospective voting involved when it comes to corruption. When new parties, which by definition lack a previous track record, campaign on anticorruption (see Bågenholm and Charron 2014; Engler 2016), voters must first make a retrospective decision as to whether to trust any of the established parties, and in the case that they do not, vote prospectively, choosing the new party that has the most credible and effective anticorruption proposals. There can, thus, also be a small element of prospective voting when holding representatives accountable.

Thus far, we have only talked about the incentive structures that, ideally, will select honest politicians and "boot out" dishonest ones, and as we will see in the following sections, the empirical evidence for such a well-functioning process is, unfortunately, not as straightforward as popular corruption perceptions would have us believe. But if we, for a moment, accept that the accountability mechanisms work effectively, the question remains: How are they supposed to generate less corruption and thus result in the effective responsiveness that electoral accountability should ideally produce?

It does not seem too far-fetched to assume that a polity that works in the manner described above, in which honest, competent politicians who promise to fight corruption get elected, would face fewer problems with corruption in comparison to those in which politicians get away with illicit malfeasances and are reelected. It is very hard to see how the latter polity, in which corrupt and dishonest politicians frequently get reelected, would stand any chance of reducing corruption, as there would be very few incentives for anyone not to enrich themselves, let alone make any effort to hinder such practices. Recent findings accordingly suggest that politicians are more likely to be involved in corrupt dealings when the risk of being punished is considered to be low (Solaz, De Vries, and de Geus 2019) and/or when they lack reelection incentives (Ferraz and Finan 2011). Here, there is an obvious risk of a downward spiral, resulting in a stable corrupt equilibrium (De Vries and Solaz 2017, 402).

But even in a scenario in which such accountability mechanisms are working well, there are no guarantees that corruption will decrease.[2] First of all, corruption is a phenomenally difficult problem to solve even with the best intentions, as is attested to in several chapters of this volume, and it will therefore take more than just political will to fix it (Fukuyama and Recanatini this volume; Johnston this volume). Secondly, even if corrupt politicians are removed from office, there is nothing to guarantee that they will actually be replaced with more honest ones. There are multiple examples of candidates that promise change but instead quickly become accustomed to the prevalent political culture and soon find themselves involved in corruption scandals (see for instance Bågenholm 2013a). In such situations it is of little help that voters remove them, as it will still not lead to any improvements in the level of corruption. Well-functioning electoral accountability processes should thus be seen as a necessary, but far from a sufficient, condition for reducing corruption. This subject is revisited in the final section. In the next, the question as to what extent corrupt politicians get punished by the voters at the polls is discussed.

TO WHAT EXTENT ARE CORRUPT POLITICIANS PUNISHED?

Even though the corruption voting paradox is a frequent point of departure for studies in this field, there is still some disagreement on how to answer the above question. Most studies find at least some negative electoral effects for politicians or parties involved in corrupt activities, but scholars seem to have different opinions as to how to summarize the general findings. Some claim enthusiastically that electoral accountability works, insofar that voters do punish corrupt officials when they have a reasonable chance to do so (Winters and Weitz-Shapiro 2016), whereas others, rather pessimistically, point to the fact that the vote loss is so

---

[2] McMann, Seim, Teorell, and Lindberg (2019) do find a strong negative correlation between the quality of elections and levels corruption, which they attribute to effective electoral accountability. However, they do not look specifically at the extent to which voters punish corrupt incumbents. This mechanism is only assumed.

limited that it oftentimes results in successful reelection (see De Sousa and Moriconi 2013). To some extent this debate is about different expectations, but it also reflects the fact that different types of studies have come up with quite different results. Studies relying on observational data (real electoral results and real corruption scandals), including field experiments, tend to report far less of a punishment effect than studies that rely on survey experimental data, where voting intentions are hypothetical and corruption scandals are fictitious (see Incerti 2019; Boas, Hidalgo, and Melo 2019; Eggers and Fisher 2011).

Boas, Hidalgo and Melo (2019) find, for instance, that the same Brazilian respondents strongly punish hypothetically corrupt mayors but completely refrain from doing so at the polls, despite being treated with exactly the same information as in the experimental setting. Likewise, Eggers and Fisher (2011) report a mere 1.5 percentage point drop for MPs implicated in the U.K. expenses scandal, whereas in an opinion poll just before the election as many as 38% responded that they would not vote for a scandal-tainted MP. If the voters had acted according to the opinion polls, the difference would instead have been close to a 20 percentage point drop. Cobb and Taylor reach a similar result when analyzing the state legislative elections in North Carolina, concluding "that voters might in theory prefer 'clean' parties, but their political actions are uninfluenced by that preference" (2015, 923). Moreover, Incerti (2019) confirms this bias in a meta-analysis comparing field experimental studies and survey experiments, finding no corruption effect on average in the former type of studies and a 32 percentage point average drop for corrupt incumbents in the latter. Hence, the research field is dealing with two quite contradictory sets of results, one which emphasizes the lack of functioning electoral accountability mechanisms and one that suggests the opposite. It is therefore relevant to discuss the different findings in relation to the type of method and data used.

Observational data studies

Those studies that employ field experiments and/or use real world electoral data quite consistently find that politicians involved in corruption scandals lose support, but oftentimes not enough to also lose the election (see Incerti 2019; Boas, Hidalgo, and Melo 2019; Bågenholm 2013b; Eggers and Fisher 2011).

A large number of studies use observational data in order to find out the extent to which corrupt politicians are punished (see for instance Peters and Welsh 1980; Dimock and Jacobsen 1995; Welch and Hibbing 1997; Chang, Golden, and Hill 2010; Eggers and Fisher 2011; Basinger 2013; Bågenholm 2013b). As noted above, a general finding is that corrupt incumbents do suffer a vote loss, but only occasionally is this large enough to prevent them from being reelected.

The dependent variables in these types of study are usually either the shift in vote share of the incumbent politicians or parties, at the national or subnational level, between two elections, and/or whether they get reelected or not and/or whether the candidate decides to retire and not stand for reelection.

The data on corruption scandals differ somewhat between these studies. Some studies use hard evidence, such as judicial convictions and/or indictments (Ceron and Mainenti 2018; Costas-Pérez, Solé-Ollé, and Sorribas-Navarro 2012), parliamentary reports on misbehavior (Chang, Golden, and Hill 2010; Basinger 2013), and audit reports (Ferraz and Finan

2008). Others use media coverage (Chang, Golden, and Hill 2010; Ferraz and Finan 2008) or allegations made by competing parties and politicians (Bågenholm 2013b). Still others have used perception-based data in order to capture the extent to which voters' opinions on how widespread corruption is among politicians affect their party choice (Ecker, Glinitzer, and Meyer 2016).

Peters and Welch (1980) and Welch and Hibbing (1997) were among the first to explore the electoral effects of corruption. Analyzing corruption charges against members of the U.S. House of Representatives between 1968–78 and 1982–90, respectively, they found that the likelihood of an incumbent losing his/her seat increased markedly if corruption allegations had been made, although the incumbents still retained their seat in 75% of cases, compared to more than 97% when no corruption allegations were made. Moreover, regardless of winning or losing the seat, a corruption-charged incumbent lost, on average, around 10 percentage points, depending on the type of charges, and the challenger gained, on average, even more. Thus, the main conclusion reached was that corruption affects a substantial share of the still quite limited Congressional turnover. Dimock and Jacobson (1995) found similar effects when analyzing one particular scandal in the 1992 Congressional elections. Here incumbents lost, on average, 4 percentage points.

Basinger (2013) however found stronger effects studying Congressional scandals between 1972 and 2010. He concluded that 40% of the corruption-affected incumbents did not get reelected, which partly depended on a high retirement rate. Around 80% of those who chose to run were reelected, with an average vote drop of around 8%.

In one of the most cited studies in this area, Chang, Golden, and Hill (2010) found that 51% of Italian parliamentarians charged with corruption between 1948 and 1994 got reelected, compared to 58% of the clean representatives. Only during the last period included (1992–94) was the reelection rate drastically reduced, which the authors attributed to the extensive press coverage of the huge corruption scandal and investigation (the so called "Tangentopoli").

In a broader comparative study comprising 215 parliamentary elections in 32 European countries between 1981 and 2011, Bågenholm (2013b) found that governments implicated in corruption scandals and accused by the opposition of corruption in the electoral campaign lost, on average, more than ten percentage points compared to the previous election, whereas clean governments, on average, lost less than six percentage points. Even though governments implicated in corruption were "booted out" more often than clean ones, the difference did not reach statistical significance, thus confirming the rather limited effects of corruption when using real electoral results.

There are, naturally, both advantages and disadvantages with this set of approaches. The most obvious advantage is that the outcomes and assumed causes are real, i.e. the incumbent's losses or gains are based on actual electoral results and not on hypothetical vote intentions, and the corruption scandals have taken place and are not made up. The drawbacks are equally obvious. It is difficult to establish causality, i.e. that the choice of vote had to do with corruption and that it was not influenced by other factors that were unaccounted for in the study. Most studies, naturally, control for the most commonly used explanations in terms of vote choice, but as the data is aggregated one cannot connect specific voters' perceptions or predispositions to their specific vote choices. Another drawback is the possibility that voters, however large the scandal, are actually unaware of it or have insufficient information to make an informed decision, for instance by correctly identifying the main actors responsible. There are, in addition, other campaign related contingencies that may influence voters and which may be hard for researchers to control for (Boas, Hidalgo, and Melo 2019).

Experimental data studies

During the last decade, experimental studies have become increasingly popular in the corruption voting literature. Here, some of the deficiencies with real world data can be overcome and causality claims strengthened. As mentioned above, the electoral effects of corruption differ quite substantially depending on the type of experimental study. Studies employing field experiments, in which respondents receive different information about real corruption scandals, after which they indicate who they voted for in the election, generally result in limited electoral punishment, whereas survey experiments (vignettes or conjoint experiments), where the scandal and candidate information are fictitious, make people react more strongly against corrupt behavior (Incerti 2019).

Ferraz and Finan's study (2008) on Brazilian voters' reaction to audit reports is one of the most cited studies within the whole corruption voting literature. It is also one of few field survey studies that actually finds evidence of substantial electoral punishment.[3] Ferraz and Finan showed that the likelihood for incumbent local politicians to get reelected decreased substantially the more violations the audit reports contained (up to 14 percentage points). They also showed the importance of information, as voters in "corrupt" municipalities with a local radio station were even more likely to punish the incumbents. Conversely, the reelection rate among politicians in noncorrupt municipalities was higher where there was also a local radio station.

In contrast to field experiments, where manipulations have to be held within the parameters of what actually happened, a survey experiment can freely manipulate all sorts of information, for instance on the type, timing, and magnitude of the scandal, the source of information, as well as the track record and party affiliation of the competing candidates, in order to tease out the extent of electoral punishment, but, above all, to identify under which conditions voters tend to punish and under which they tend to corruption vote. The dependent variable in these studies is usually also vote intention, with the three main alternatives being i) stay loyal to the corrupt alternative; ii) switch to a clean one; or iii) abstain from voting altogether.

As mentioned above, there is a quite large discrepancy between the extent to which corrupt incumbents get punished in experimental settings and at the polls, which implies that quite a few respondents are not completely honest, perhaps due to social desirability bias, or that they do not consider the experimental setting as sufficiently realistic. Incerti (2019) includes 18 survey experiments (from 15 papers), covering five Latin American countries, six European, and one Asian country in his meta-analysis. Of these, all but two report a minimum of a 20 percentage point negative change in vote share when corruption is at hand. Only one study fails to reach statistically significant results (2019, 10). Given the much more conservative results in other types of studies, there is still a substantial uncertainty

---

[3] Incerti analyzes ten field experimental studies (from eight papers), covering Uganda, Brazil, Mexico, and India, where no significant negative effect of corruption on vote intention was found (2019, 10).

regarding the extent to which hypothetical vote intentions translate into actual voting behavior, making the external validity of the results from these latter studies hard to interpret.

Why and Under What Conditions Do Voters Support Corrupt Politicians?

The literature on corruption voting has primarily, if not exclusively, studied democratic or semi-democratic polities, as reasonably free and fair elections are seen as prerequisites for effective electoral accountability. In more authoritarian settings, elections are by definition manipulated one way or another, usually heavily biased in favor of the incumbents and in the least democratic states there are no alternatives whatsoever. It then becomes irrelevant to ask whether a corrupt officeholder was supported or not. In a democratic setting, this is still somewhat puzzling however, given people's strong aversion to corruption. But as we will see, there are a number of stages in the chain of accountability that need to be passed before voters can punish corrupt politicians, and each of these stages contains a set of hurdles that make the passage anything but simple and smooth (see for instance De Vries and Solaz 2017; Jiménez and Caínzos 2006). In contrast to the economic voting literature, it is interesting to note that voters' cognitive ability to understand and correctly evaluate government performance are not discussed to any greater extent in the corruption voting literature, again underscoring that corruption is seen as a more simple issue than the economy about which voters can make an informed choice. It also suggests that one of the main arguments as to why democratic elections fail to produce responsive governments in general, as suggested by Achen and Bartels (2016), is less applicable when focusing on corruption (an issue which they ignore). Apart from this, the lines of argumentation resemble, to a large extent, those of the economic voting literature.

The first stage in the chain of electoral accountability is that there should be awareness among voters about the occurrence of political corruption. Provision of information about corruption is therefore a prerequisite for voters to be able to act (De Vries and Solaz 2017; Jiménez and Caínzos 2006, 195–6). The main hurdle to pass at this stage is the quality and credibility of the information (De Sousa and Moriconi 2013, 488), so that voters do not just dismiss it as partisan propaganda. Hence, both the amount and type of information, as well as the source, matter. Uninformed voters will, naturally, not be able to punish a corrupt politician or party—at least not for that particular reason—but neither will voters who simply do not trust the information they receive. From a scholarly perspective, a research design that ensures that voters or respondents actually are informed about the corruption scandals that they are supposed to react to is therefore important.

For experimental studies this is not an issue, as they, by design, provide exactly the type of information—regarding the candidates, the type, timing, and magnitude of the corruption scandal etc.—that the participants should react (or not react) to. For studies relying on observational data, this is a key issue, however. As discussed above, such studies usually focus on high-profile scandals which one can assume voters would have heard about, either by assessing the extent to which the media has covered them or if they have been politicized during the election campaign, i.e. whether corruption allegation have been made against the incumbents by the opposition. Without asking voters directly, there is, however, no way to be completely sure about their level of scandal awareness, which casts some doubts on the real motives for voting behavior.

There is a quite broad consensus among scholars that information has a negative effect on corruption voting, i.e. the more aware citizens are, the stronger the vote loss for incumbents and the lower the chances of them being reelected (see Weitz-Shapiro and Winters 2017, 61; Boas, Hidalgo, and Melo 2019, 386). Chang, Golden, and Hill (2010), for instance, attribute the much stronger electoral punishment in the 1994 Italian election, compared to previous ones, to the extensive media coverage of a big corruption scandal. Ferraz and Finan (2008) find that the presence of local radio stations in Brazil impacts voters' willingness to both punish and reward politicians for their (anti-) corruption performance, measured by audit reports, implying that awareness is the key factor. McNally (2016) on the other hand finds that increased information about Silvio Berlusconi's corrupt dealings rather had a positive effect on him, as voters' tolerance for corruption supposedly increased with increasing awareness of it taking place.

As mentioned above, it is not only the amount of information that matters, however. Several studies have shown that the information also has to be credible in the eyes of the voters. The source of information is thus highly important. What constitutes a credible source varies however, depending on the context. In Colombia, voters reacted more strongly to information coming from a major national, and most importantly nonpartisan, newspaper than from the judiciary and NGOs (Botero et al. 2015), whereas Spanish voters only reacted to media stories on corruption if they also led to a court conviction (Costas-Pérez, Solé-Ollé, Sorribas-Navarro 2012). A notoriously dubious source is corruption allegations made by opposing parties. A survey experiment in Spain shows that voters discard such information and continue to vote for their preferred, but corrupt candidate (Muñoz, Anduiza, and Gallego 2016), and a Brazilian survey experiment shows that voters react more strongly to an audit report than to allegations made by the opposition party (Weitz-Shapiro and Winters 2017). A broader study covering more than 200 parliamentary elections in Europe, however, finds that corruption allegations made against political opponents significantly reduce their vote share, but this is even more strongly so if there was also an ongoing corruption scandal at the time of the election, thus lending credibility to the accusations (Bågenholm 2013b).

There are, moreover, differences in how different sources are perceived by voters, depending on their level of sophistication, i.e. knowledge and education. Weitz-Shapiro and Winters (2017) find that compared to less sophisticated respondents, the more sophisticated are better able to distinguish between sources with high and low credibility, suggesting that education may improve accountability.

But, even with adequate and credible information, there are reasons to believe that voters oftentimes tolerate and continue to support corrupt representatives, as already noted by Rundquist, Strom, and Peters (1977). There are both micro (individual) as well as macro (system-oriented) explanations for voters' reluctance to punish corruption (De Sousa and Moriconi 2013). From an individual point of view, there may be many reasons for corruption voting. For one, voters must correctly attribute the blame to the politicians implicated in corruption, which is the second stage in the accountability chain (De Vries and Solaz 2017; Jiménez and Caínzos 2006). Several studies have found that strong partisanship biases voters' assessment and makes them less likely to punish candidates from their preferred party (Anduiza, Gallego, and Muñoz 2013; Solaz, De Vries, and de Geus 2019; Breitenstein 2019; for an exception though see Xezonakis, Kosmidis, and Dahlberg 2015). There can be several reasons for this, some of which imply that voters disregard credible corruption information and some which directly connect strong party affiliation with how information is perceived.

First, voters may unconsciously filter information on corruption against their party and simply find that information less credible by default (Anduiza, Gallego, and Muñoz 2013), regardless of the source of information. Second, voters may ignore credible corruption information because they do not perceive corruption as a sufficiently salient issue in relation to other issues, which implies that ideology or specific policy positions on important issues trump transgressions, and therefore corrupt politicians will not be blamed.

There are also contexts in which voters who are not strongly partisan may turn a blind eye to corruption. First, voters may acknowledge the seriousness of the corruption information but may face a situation where all parties are considered as equally corrupt, and "[i]f the people can choose only from among rascals, they are certain to choose a rascal," as Key elegantly put it (Key 1966, 2; see also Agerberg 2019; Cordero and Blais 2017; Pavão 2018). Second, voters may be well aware of politicians' corrupt dealings, but simply think that they will benefit from them. Several studies have found that voters are more prone to corruption voting when the corrupt dealings benefit their community (Fernández-Vázquez, Barberá, and Rivero 2016; Muñoz, Anduiza, and Gallego 2016) or when state institutions are weak and clientelistic relationships are strong (Manzetti and Wilson 2007). In contrast, voters are more willing to punish when the politicians just enrich themselves personally, which three survey experiments from Brazil (Avenburg 2019), India (Weschle 2016), and Argentina (Botero et al. 2019) demonstrate. Three, there are also studies suggesting that voters are less inclined to care about corruption when the economy is perceived to be good, suggesting that voters rather reward politicians for good economic performance than punish them for being corrupt (Klašnja and Tucker 2013; Zechmeister and Zizumbo-Colunga 2013; Choi and Woo 2010; Jastramskis, Kuokstis, and Baltrukevicius 2019).

Closely related to partisanship is other in-group attributes, which, for various reasons, people may prioritize over corruption (Chang and Kerr 2017; Solaz, De Vries, and de Geus 2019). Studying 18 sub-Saharan countries, Chang and Kerr find for instance that "patronage insiders" are more likely to perceive higher levels of corruption, but also a higher tolerance of corruption than "identity insiders", i.e. co-ethnics and co-partisans of the incumbents as well as outsiders. Both insider groups were more likely to corruption voting compared to outsiders (2017). Bauhr and Charron (2018) reach the same conclusion, studying 21 European countries; the insiders, i.e. the winners in society with high corruption remain loyal to corrupt politicians, thereby sustaining the corrupt equilibrium. The mechanisms in these cases can be similar to those discussed above, such as material motives and direct personal benefits (see Bauhr and Grimes in this volume), but it could also be attributed to in-group loyalty which does not necessarily imply material gains (Solaz, De Vries and de Geus 2019).

Factors such as education, gender, and age are highly contested when it comes to electoral accountability (see De Sousa and Moriconi 2013). However, some recent studies still indicate that education, political interest, and awareness may matter. As noted above, Weitz-Shapiro and Winters (2017) conclude that education might be an effective weapon with which to punish corruption, and Klašnja (2017) reaches similar results when analyzing U.S. Congressional elections, in which voters with higher political awareness (which not necessarily corresponds to higher educational levels) are less likely to support corrupt politicians.

Gender has been more or less absent from the corruption voting literature until recently, which is surprising given that quite a few studies have found that women tend to be less tolerant towards corruption than men and also less engaged in corrupt practices (see Alexander this volume). In line with these findings, some recent studies have found evidence of some gender differences also when it comes to electoral accountability. In an experimental study of British students, Eggers et al. (2018) find that women tend to punish corrupt representatives and candidates harsher than do men, but also that female voters are harsher on female wrongdoers than on male wrongdoers. Moreover Stensöta, Wängnerud, and Agerberg (2015) as well as Alexander, Bågenholm, and Charron (2019), using survey data from 21 European countries, find that women indeed are more prone to punish corruption than men, but that the gender gaps are greater in countries where more is at stake for women's well-being, i.e. in more advanced welfare states. More studies that draw on observational data are needed before any firm conclusions on the impact of gender can be drawn, however.

On the macro or system side, there are also factors that may make it hard for voters to correctly identify those responsible for engaging in corruption. Along these lines, it has been argued that clarity of responsibility, i.e. features that help voters to evaluate the performances of their representatives and identify those responsible for them, has a positive effect on people's ability to punish corrupt politicians and, perhaps even more importantly, to reduce the level of corruption (Tavits 2007; Schwindt-Bayer and Tavits 2016). The most important indicators of clarity of responsibility are the number of parties in government and their parliamentary support. Single-party and/or majority governments facilitate clarity of responsibility, whereas coalition and/or minority governments make it harder for voters to identify whom to reward and whom to punish (Schwindt-Bayer and Tavits 2016, 13–14). Schwindt-Bayer and Tavits find that voters who perceive high levels of political corruption votes against the incumbents to a higher extent when clarity of responsibility is high, indicating that the electoral accountability mechanism works better under such institutional conditions. These findings are challenged by Rudolph and Däubler (2016) who find that German voters use their two ballots differently when encountering corrupt candidates. Analyzing the state elections in Bavaria, they find that voters to a higher extent punish corruption under the open list proportional representation election rules than in the single-member districts. More research also on the effects of different electoral system is thus warranted.

Just as in the case with information, most studies, and in particular experimental studies, do their best to solve the question of responsibility by clearly singling out who is corrupt and who is not. It is no surprise then that mayoral elections, real or fictitious, have, by far, been the most commonly studied in the corruption voting literature. The real world is often more complex for voters to handle, however, as corruption may also appear at the national level, where voters in many instances have no opportunity to punish a particular corrupt politician but instead have to punish a party, perhaps by punishing a clean representative. There are, therefore, few studies that focus on the national party level (for an exception see Bågenholm 2013b). Another instance where voters face difficulty in handling the issue of responsibility is when it is not the politicians themselves but rather unelected individuals, such as civil servants, that are involved in corrupt activities. In another survey experimental study in Brazil, Winters and Weitz-Shapiro (2016) find that mayors who are not personally involved in corruption, although they are to some extent responsible for it, get punished by the voters, but to a lesser extent than those mayors that are involved directly themselves.

There are thus both micro and macro factors that complicate voters' ability to correctly identify whether to punish and who should be punished. The final step in the accountability chain is the actual act of voting. The main accountability hurdle for voters is when voters who are informed about malfeasances, know who is responsible for them, and, without finding any attenuating circumstances, still find it hard to punish a corrupt representative or candidate. In a context where all alternatives are perceived as corrupt, the electoral accountability chain naturally breaks down, as it is simply impossible for voters to punish corrupt practices if they do decide to turn out to vote (Agerberg 2019; Cordero and Blais 2017). In an ideal setting, where people's frustration and the track records of all the established parties are well-known facts, political entrepreneurs should exploit that niche by campaigning on anticorruption, thereby providing the voters with a clean alternative. During the past 20 years, this is precisely what has happened all around the world, but this is most frequently the case in Central and Eastern Europe. The tactics here have oftentimes been to position the new alternative around the midpoint of the ideological spectrum, making it relatively easy for most people to switch to that alternative (Bågenholm and Charron 2014).

For voters further away from the center, it is naturally harder to switch to an alternative that is ideologically distanced from their own preferences. Whereas the clarity of responsibility literature emphasizes the benefits of electoral systems that produce single-party majority governments, i.e. majoritarian systems, there are other studies that argue that such systems may be detrimental when it comes to providing viable and clean alternatives. Some recent studies suggest that voters actually want to punish corrupt incumbents, even if they belong to their own party, but only as long as there is a clean alternative in place (Charron and Bågenholm 2016; Agerberg 2019). Charron and Bågenholm find that voters on the ideological fringes are less inclined to switch to a clean alternative, compared with voters who place themselves more towards the middle of the ideological spectrum. But the reason is not so much their ideological position as such, but rather the lack of viable, i.e. reasonably ideologically close, alternatives, to which these voters can switch. In countries with a large number of effective parties, the difference between fringe and middle of the road voters are diminished or even eliminated, which suggests that electoral systems that facilitate a substantive number of parties able to compete and win parliamentary representation, i.e. proportional representation systems, are conducive to effective electoral accountability. Thus, scholars disagree on the effects of electoral systems for an effective electoral accountability mechanism.

WHAT ARE THE EFFECTS OF ELECTORAL ACCOUNTABILITY ON THE LEVELS AND DIRECTION OF CORRUPTION?

Well-functioning electoral mechanisms should thus be a necessary condition for effectively combating corruption. It is hard to imagine that politicians in already corrupt societies would make any efforts to curb corruption if there are no electoral incentives that force them to do so. It is not a sufficient condition however. The old corrupt guard may just be replaced with new but equally corrupt successors, of which there have been numerous examples of over the years. But even with well-intentioned, ambitious newcomers at the helm, there is no guarantee that corruption will decrease. Corruption has been found to be extraordinarily sticky and hard to combat even with the best intentions, for reasons that are discussed elsewhere in this volume (for instance Fukuyama and Recanatini this volume; Johnston this volume).

That dysfunctional electoral accountability mechanisms have negative consequences for corruption levels in a society is clear, however, and research clearly suggests that corruption increases and countries get stuck in vicious corruption cycles when the chain of electoral accountability breaks down (Solaz, De Vries, and de Geus 2019). Few, if any, studies examine the inverse, i.e. how well-functioning mechanisms create a virtuous cycle.

There are actually very few studies that explore the direct effects of effective electoral accountability on corruption overall. Most studies that treat electoral accountability as the independent variable focus on different aspects of the electoral system (as a proxy) and correlate them with the level of corruption. In a seminal and widely cited study, Persson, Tabellini, and Trebbi (2003) show that certain aspects of the electoral system, such as open lists under proportional representation systems and majoritarian systems in general, positively relate to less corruption. The implicit assumption is that the incentive structures actually work and deter officeholders from engaging in corruption or facilitate the replacement of corrupt politicians with noncorrupt ones. In line with these findings, Kunicova and Rose-Ackermann (2005) show that proportional representation systems are more susceptible to corrupt political rent-seeking than plurality systems and are thus associated with higher levels of corruption. Chang (2005), however, finds the opposite, namely that the more personal the vote is, the more vulnerable it is to corrupt transactions.

A similar argument to that of Persson, Tabellini, and Trebbi (2003) is provided by Tavits (2007) and Schwindt-Bayer and Tavits (2016). As mentioned above, they focus on clarity of responsibility, which they relate to the government's majority status, its longevity, the extent of oppositional influence through, for instance, committees and second chambers, and finally the effective number of parties, where fewer is associated with higher clarity. In contrast to most other studies, they actually measure also the mechanism, i.e. whether electoral accountability is stronger where clarity of responsibility is higher and whether levels of corruption are impacted by these two variables. Their results confirm, not only the assumed relationship between the three variables discussed above, but also that the elites are more incentivized to take measures against corruption and to campaign on anticorruption in elections, when clarity of responsibility is high.

ELECTORAL ACCOUNTABILITY 2.0. HOW TO IMPROVE THE RESEARCH FIELD?

The research field on corruption and electoral accountability has expanded dramatically over the past ten years, gradually providing answers to important research questions. Even though some countries are strongly overrepresented in the corruption voting literature, there are by now few if any regions of the world that have been left out. Methodologically there is more plurality as well, but to an increasing extent different types of experimental approaches seem to dominate the research field for the time being. The pros and cons of those types of studies are discussed elsewhere in this chapter, but the fact that results systematically tend to differ compared to studies using observational data, and what that in turn implies in terms of real world outcomes, should be kept in mind. In order to really get a sense of whether voters actually punish corrupt politicians, there is a need for innovative studies linking real electoral outcomes with voters' actual preferences and motivations for their vote choices.

One potential way forward would be to use exit polls in countries or regions where corruption is known to be a campaign issue and/or where large-scale scandals occurred close to the election, as voters should have an easier time remembering both who they voted for and the reason why they voted, minutes after casting their ballot. In counties where corruption is never a campaign issue, such studies are, naturally, less relevant.

The research field is completely dominated by quantitative studies and for good reasons. I do think, however, that it would benefit from more qualitative approaches as well. There are very few studies where we can know for certain the extent to which an individual's vote choice is based on corruption, let alone ascertain the more elaborate reasons why this is the case. That is, we hardly know anything about how voters actually argue and motivate their real vote choice.[4] Interviewing voters in close proximity to an election would enable us to verify existing hypotheses and theories on corruption voting as well as potentially suggesting new ones.[5]

I also believe that observational studies have so far underestimated the level of voter punishment when large-scale corruption scandals occur. Remember that the general conclusion from these studies is that corrupt politicians or parties get punished but are most often still reelected. Considering that quite a few governments around the world have been removed after large-scale scandals, efforts are needed to determine if these general findings hold regardless of the magnitude and timing of the scandals.

As has been pointed out several times in this chapter, effective electoral accountability is not a sufficient condition for reducing corruption. Strangely enough, the research field to a great extent lacks studies that examine the direct connection between electoral accountability and levels of corruption. In particular, given that some scholars find a strong connection between clarity of responsibility, basically implying that majoritarian systems are conducive to reduce corruption, whereas others find a relationship between number of parties and willingness to punish, thus arguing for the benefits of a PR system, at least for facilitating electoral accountability, an urgent research task would be to look more closely at how electoral systems affect both outcomes (electoral accountability and levels of corruption). Are corrupt politicians more likely to be ejected under some electoral rules than

[4] The only exception that I have found that explicitly deals with corruption voting from a qualitative perspective is a section in Nara Pavão's dissertation (Pavão, 2015), in which she interviews Brazilian voters in focus groups.
[5] In contrast to previous studies on tax compliance, Umar, Derashid, and Ibrahim (2017), for instance, interview self-employed people in Nigeria about why they do not pay their taxes, thereby gaining much more detailed and nuanced information.

others? If so, are their successors more likely to promote anticorruption reforms and stay clean themselves? If this is indeed the case, does the level of corruption improve? And are these patterns, both negative and positive, self-sustaining, leading to virtuous and vicious cycles?

Even though results have been quite persistent when it comes to the extent of electoral punishment, I am convinced that it is worthwhile to continue studying this phenomenon, as developments around the world suggest that corruption is increasingly becoming more salient to voters. It is not too far-fetched to assume that the somewhat gloomy findings so far will be replaced with more positive ones in the near future, implying that corruption is not just considered unacceptable in theory, but also in practice.

References

Achen, Christopher H., and Bartels, Larry M. 2016. *Democracy for Realists. Why Elections Do Not Produce Responsive Government*. Princeton and Oxford: Princeton University Press.

Agerberg, Mattias. 2019. "The Lesser Evil? Corruption Voting and the Importance of Clean Alternatives." *Comparative Political Studies*. https://doi.org/10.1177/0010414019852697

Alexander, Amy C., Andreas Bågenholm, and Nicholas Charron. 2019. "Are Women More Likely to Throw the Rascals Out? the Mobilizing Effect of Social Service Spending on Female Voters." *Public Choice* 184: 235–61.

Anderson, Christopher J. 2007. "The End of Economic Voting? Contingency Dilemmas and the Limits of Democratic Accountability." *Annual Review of Political Science* 10: 271–96.

Anduiza, Eva, Aina Gallego, and Jordi Muñoz. 2013. "Turning a Blind Eye: Experimental Evidence of Partisan Bias in Attitudes toward Corruption." *Comparative Political Studies* 46 (12): 1664–92.

Avenburg, Alejandro. 2019. "Public Costs versus Private Gain: Assessing the Effect of Different Types of Information about Corruption Incidents on Electoral Accountability." *Journal of Politics in Latin America* 11 (1): 71–108.

Bågenholm, Andreas. 2013a. "The Electoral Fate and Policy Impact of 'Anti-corruption Parties' in Central and Eastern Europe." *Human Affairs* 23 (2): 174–95.

Bågenholm, Andreas. 2013b. "Throwing the Rascals Out? the Electoral Effects of Corruption Allegations and Corruption Scandals in Europe 1981–2011." *Crime, Law and Social Change* 60 (5): 595–609.

Bågenholm, Andreas, and Nicholas Charron. 2014. "Do Politics in Europe Benefit from Politicising Corruption?" *West European Politics* 37 (5): 903–31.

Basinger, Scott J. 2013. "Scandals and Congressional Elections in the Post-Watergate Era" *Political Research Quarterly* 66 (2): 385–98.

Bauhr, Monika, and Nicholas Charron. 2018. "Insider Or Outsider? Grand Corruption and Electoral Accountability." *Comparative Political Studies* 51(4): 415–46.

Boas, Taylor C., F. Daniel Hidalgo, and Marcus André Melo. 2019. "Norms versus Action: Why Voters Fail to Sanction Malfeasance in Brazil." *American Journal of Political Science* 63 (2): 385–400.

Botero, Sandra, Rodrigo Castro Cornejo, Laura Gamboa, Nara Pavao, and David W. Nickerson. 2019. "Are All Types of Wrongdoing Created Equal in the Eyes of Voters?" *Journal of Elections, Public Opinion and Parties*. doi.org/10.1080/17457289.2019.1651322.

Botero, Sandra, Rodrigo Castro Cornejo, Laura Gamboa, Nara Pavao, and David W. Nickerson. 2015. "Says Who? an Experiment on Allegations of Corruption and Credibility of Sources." *Political Research Quarterly* 68 (3): 493–504.

Breitenstein, Sofia. 2019. "Choosing the Crook: A Conjoint Experiment on Voting for Corrupt Politicians." *Research & Politics* 6 (1): 1–8.

Ceron, Andrea, and Marco Mainenti. 2018. "When Rotten Apples Spoil the Ballot: The Conditional Effect of Corruption Charges on Parties' Vote Shares." *International Political Science Review* 39 (2): 242–55.

Chang, Eric C. C. 2005. "Electoral Incentives for Political Corruption under Open-List Proportional Representation." *The Journal of Politics* 67 (3): 716–30.

Chang, Eric C. C., Miriam A. Golden, and Seth J. Hill. 2010. "Legislative Malfeasance and Political Accountability." *World Politics* 62 (2): 177–220.

Chang, Eric C. C., and Nicholas N. Kerr. 2017. "An Insider–Outsider Theory of Popular Tolerance for Corrupt Politicians." *Governance* 30 (1): 67–84.

Charron, Nicholas, and Andreas Bågenholm. 2016. "Ideology, Party Systems and Corruption Voting in European Democracies." *Electoral Studies* 41: 35–49.

Choi, Eunjung, and Jongseok Woo. 2010. "Political Corruption, Economic Performance, and Electoral Outcomes: A Cross-National Analysis." *Contemporary Politics* 16 (3): 249–62.

Cobb, Michael D., and Andrew J. Taylor. 2015. "An Absence of Malice: The Limited Utility of Campaigning against Party Corruption." *American Politics Research* 43 (6): 923–51.

Cordero, Guillermo, and André Blais. 2017. "Is a Corrupt Government Totally Unacceptable?" *West European Politics* 40 (4): 645–62.

Costas-Pérez, Elena, Albert Solé-Ollé, and Pilar Sorribas-Navarro. 2012. "Corruption Scandals, Voter Information, and Accountability." *European Journal of Political Economy* 28 (4): 469–84.

Curini, Luigi. 2018. *Corruption, Ideology, and Populism: The Rise of Valence Political Campaigning.* Palgrave Macmillan. https://doi.org/10.1007/978-3-319-56735-8

De Sousa, Luis, and Marcelo Moriconi. 2013. "Why Voters Do Not Throw the Rascals Out?— A Conceptual Framework for Analysing Electoral Punishment of Corruption." *Crime, Law and Social Change* 60 (5): 471–502.

De Vries, Catherine E., and Hector Solaz. 2017. "The Electoral Consequences of Corruption." *Annual Review of Political Science* 20: 391–408.

Dimock, Michael A., and Gary C. Jacobson. 1995. "Checks and Choices: The House Bank Scandal's Impact on Voters in 1992." *The Journal of Politics* 57 (4): 1143–59.

Ecker, Alejandro, Konstantin Glinitzer, and Thomas M. Meyer. 2016. "Corruption Performance Voting and the Electoral Context." *European Political Science Review* 8 (3): 333–54.

Eggers, Andrew C., and Alexander C. Fisher. 2011. "Electoral Accountability and the UK Parliamentary Expenses Scandal: Did Voters Punish Corrupt MPs?" Available at SSRN 1931868.

Eggers, Andrew C., Nick Vivyan, and Markus Wagner. 2018. "Corruption, Accountability, and Gender: Do Female Politicians Face Higher Standards in Public Life?" *The Journal of Politics* 80 (1): 321–26.

Engler, Sarah. 2016. "Corruption and Electoral Support for New Political Parties in Central and Eastern Europe." *West European Politics* 39 (2): 278–304.

European Commission. 2014. "Corruption." *Special Eurobarometer* 397.

European Commission. 2017. "Corruption." *Special Eurobarometer* 470.

Fearon, James D. 1999. "Electoral Accountability and the Control of Politicians: Selecting Good Types versus Sanctioning Poor Performance." In *Democracy, Accountability, and Representation*, edited by Adam Przeworski, Susan Stokes, and Bernand Manin. Cambridge: Cambridge University Press.

Fernández-Vázquez, Pablo, Pablo Barberá, and Gonzalo Rivero. 2016. "Rooting Out Corruption or Rooting for Corruption? the Heterogeneous Electoral Consequences of Scandals." *Political Science Research and Methods* 4 (2): 379–97.

Ferraz, Claudio, and Frederico Finan. 2008. "Exposing Corrupt Politicians: The Effects of Brazil's Publicly Released Audits on Electoral Outcomes." *The Quarterly Journal of Economics* 123 (2): 703–45.

Ferraz, Claudio, and Frederico Finan. 2011. "Electoral Accountability and Corruption: Evidence from the Audits of Local Governments." *American Economic Review* 101 (4): 1274–311.

Fiorina, Morris. P. 1981. *Retrospective Voting in American National Elections*. New Haven: Yale University Press.

Gailmard, Sean. 2019. "Optimism, Pessimism, and Dialogue in Electoral-Accountability Research." *PS: Political Science & Politics* 52 (4): 630–33.

Healy, Andrew, and Neil Malhotra. 2013. "Retrospective Voting Reconsidered." *Annual Review of Political Science* 16: 285–306.

Incerti, Trevor. 2019. "Corruption Information and Vote Share: A Meta-Analysis and Lessons for Survey Experimental Design." Unpublished manuscript.

Jastramskis, Mažvydas, Vytautas Kuokštis, and Matas Baltrukevičius. 2019. "Retrospective Voting in Central and Eastern Europe: Hyper-Accountability, Corruption or Socio-Economic Inequality?" *Party Politics*. https://doi.org/10.1177/1354068819880320

Jiménez, Fernando, and Miguel Caínzos. 2006. "How Far and Why Do Corruption Scandals Cost Votes." In *Scandals in Past and Contemporary Politics*, edited by John Garrand and James L. Newell, 194–212. Manchester and New York: Manchester University Press.

Key, Valdimer O. 1966. *The Responsible Electorate*. Cambridge, MA: Harvard University Press.

Klašnja, Marko. 2017. "Uninformed Voters and Corrupt Politicians." *American Politics Research* 45 (2): 256–79.

Klašnja, Marko, and Joshua A. Tucker. 2013. "The Economy, Corruption, and the Vote: Evidence from Experiments in Sweden and Moldova." *Electoral Studies* 32 (3): 536–43.

Kunicova, Jana, and Susan Rose-Ackerman. 2005. "Electoral Rules and Constitutional Structures as Constraints on Corruption." *British Journal of Political Science* 35 (4): 573–606.

Kurer, Oskar. 2001. "Why do voters support corrupt politicians?" In *The Political Economy of Corruption*, edited by Arvind K. Jain, 75–98. London & New York: Routledge.

Lewis-Beck, Michael S., and Mary Stegmaier. 2000. "Economic Determinants of Electoral Outcomes." *Annual Review of Political Science* 3 (1): 183–219.

Manzetti, Luigi, and Carole J. Wilson. 2007. "Why Do Corrupt Governments Maintain Public Support?" *Comparative Political Studies* 40 (8): 949–70.

McMann, Kelly M., Brigitte Seim, Jan Teorell, and Staffan I. Lindberg. 2019. "Why Low Levels of Democracy Promote Corruption and High Levels Diminish It." *Political Research Quarterly*. https://doi.org/10.1177/1065912919862054

McNally, Darragh. 2016. "Norms, Corruption, and Voting for Berlusconi." *Politics & Policy* 44 (5): 976–1008.

Muñoz, Jordi, Eva Anduiza, and Aina Gallego. 2016. "Why Do Voters Forgive Corrupt Mayors? Implicit Exchange, Credibility of Information and Clean Alternatives." *Local Government Studies* 42 (4): 598–615.

Pavão, Nara. 2015. *The Failures of Electoral Accountability for Corruption: Brazil and Beyond.* University of Notre Dame.

Pavão, Nara. 2018. "Corruption as the Only Option: The Limits to Electoral Accountability." *The Journal of Politics* 80 (3): 996–1010.

Persson, Torsten, Guido Tabellini, and Francesco Trebbi. 2003. "Electoral Rules and Corruption." *Journal of the European Economic Association* 1 (4): 958–89.

Peters, John G., and Susan Welch. 1980. "The Effects of Charges of Corruption on Voting Behavior in Congressional Elections." *American Political Science Review* 74 (3): 697–708.

Rudolph, Lukas, and Thomas Däubler. 2016. "Holding Individual Representatives Accountable: The Role of Electoral Systems." *The Journal of Politics* 78 (3): 746–62.

Rundquist, Barry S., Gerald S. Strom, and John G. Peters. 1977. "Corrupt Politicians and Their Electoral Support: Some Experimental Observations." *American Political Science Review* 71 (3): 954–63.

Schwindt-Bayer, Leslie A., and Margit Tavits. 2016. *Clarity of Responsibility, Accountability, and Corruption.* Cambridge: Cambridge University Press.

Solaz, Hector, Catherine E. De Vries, and Roosmarijn A. de Geus. 2019. "In-Group Loyalty and the Punishment of Corruption." *Comparative Political Studies* 52 (6): 896–926.

Stegmaier, Mary, Michael S. Lewis-Beck, and Lincoln Brown. 2019. "The Economic Voter Decides." In *Oxford Research Encyclopedia of Politics.* Oxford.

Stensöta, Helena Olofsdotter, Lena Wängnerud, and Mattias Agerberg. 2015. "Why Women in Encompassing Welfare States Punish Corrupt Political Parties." In *Elites, Institutions and the Quality of Government*, edited by Helena Olofsdotter Stensöta and Lena Wängnerud, 245–62. London: Palgrave Macmillan.

Tavits, Margit. 2007. "Clarity of Responsibility and Corruption." *American Journal of Political Science* 51 (1): 218–29.

Umar, Mohammed Abdullahi, Chek Derashid, and Idawati Ibrahim. 2017. "What Is Wrong with the Fiscal Social Contract of Taxation in Developing Countries? A Dialogue with Self-Employed Business Owners in Nigeria." *Sage Open* 7 (4): 1–11.

Weitz-Shapiro, Rebecca, and Matthew S. Winters. 2017. "Can Citizens Discern? Information Credibility, Political Sophistication, and the Punishment of Corruption in Brazil." *The Journal of Politics* 79 (1): 60–74.

Welch, Susan, and John R. Hibbing. 1997. "The Effects of Charges of Corruption on Voting Behavior in Congressional Elections, 1982–1990." *The Journal of Politics* 59 (1): 226–39.

Weschle, Simon. 2016. "Punishing Personal and Electoral Corruption: Experimental Evidence from India." *Research & Politics* 3 (2): 1–6.

Winters, Matthew S., and Rebecca Weitz-Shapiro. 2016. "Who's in Charge Here? Direct and Indirect Accusations and Voter Punishment of Corruption." *Political Research Quarterly* 69 (2): 207–19.

Xezonakis, Georgios, Spyros Kosmidis, and Stefan Dahlberg. 2015. "Can Elections Combat Corruption? Accountability and Partisanship." In *Elites, Institutions and the Quality of Government*, edited by Carl Dahlström and Lena Wängnerud, 283–304. London: Palgrave Macmillan.

Zechmeister, Elizabeth J., and Daniel Zizumbo-Colunga. 2013. "The Varying Political Toll of Concerns about Corruption in Good versus Bad Economic Times." *Comparative Political Studies* 46 (10): 1190–218.

CHAPTER 11

....

QUALITY OF GOVERNMENT AND POLITICAL SUPPORT

....

JONAS LINDE AND STEFAN DAHLBERG

INTRODUCTION

....

THE question of how political systems generate legitimacy and trust has for a long time
been a central issue within political science. Why are citizens in some countries more supportive of their political system, institutions, and incumbents than are their counterparts
in other countries? Decades of empirical research have generated a long list of potential explanatory factors, where institutional arrangements, political and economic outcomes, and
intergenerational value change have come to be the cornerstones in mainstream theories of
system support. With the benefit of hindsight, however, it may seem somewhat surprising
that mainstream research on political support and trust for quite some time tended to neglect one of the most challenging problems in the world—that of poor governance—and the
myriad of political and economic problems following from it. In this chapter, we provide an
overview and discussion of the growing stock of research on *the relationship between different aspects of quality of government (QoG) and political support*. It should be noted from
the start that this is a relatively recent subfield within the field of "political support" that has
not yet produced a wealth of studies, although the stock of research and the number of publications have been growing quite rapidly in recent years. Nevertheless, the empirical evidence
suggest that QoG is a key variable when it comes to explaining variation in political support,
between countries as well as between individuals.

We start out by briefly presenting the main analytical frameworks in empirical analyses of
political support, emphasizing the multidimensional nature of the concept, and the importance to distinguish between different objects of support, both theoretically and empirically
(Easton 1965, 1975; Norris 1999, 2011). We then turn to the concept of quality of government. We argue and show that QoG on the output side of the political system (Rothstein
and Teorell 2008) is a crucial determinant of political support and, as a consequence, key to
generating regime legitimacy (Rothstein 2009; Gilley 2009). In doing so, we emphasize the
importance to distinguish between QoG on the macro level (e.g. a country's *level* of corruption) and on the micro level, i.e. citizens' *perceptions* of QoG in their country of residence.

We also discuss the relationship between the concepts of QoG and procedural fairness, two concepts that sometimes are treated interchangeably in the literature. We conclude with a discussion of some challenges facing future research on quality of government and political support.

POLITICAL SUPPORT, TRUST, AND LEGITIMACY

During the last decade, several aspects of quality of government have spawned the research field of political support and have come to challenge many of the established explanations pertaining to the input side of democracy. It has been shown that representational devices often have a rather limited impact in explaining political support without successful policy implementations, a high quality of public service provisions, and impartial bureaucracies (Dahlberg and Holmberg 2014). However, before digging into this relatively recent subfield, we need to discuss briefly the concept of political support, and how the concept has been operationalized in empirical analyses of the relationship between QoG and political support. Within this research field, political support is closely connected to the concept of legitimacy. While there is broad consensus about the importance of political legitimacy, it is nevertheless a widely debated concept.[1] This comes as no surprise considering that "the concept of political legitimacy is central to virtually all of political science because it pertains to how power may be used in ways that citizens consciously accept" (Gilley 2006a, 499). However, along with the boom in publicly available cross-national opinion data in the last decades, what Wheatherford (1992) calls "the view from the grass roots" has become the norm in empirical studies of legitimacy. This perspective is concerned with citizens' evaluations of the legitimacy of their political system. Today, it is commonly accepted that all definitions of the concept ultimately rely on public perceptions about the political system (Booth and Seligson 2009; Gilley 2009).

Most empirical research within this field takes as its point of departure the pioneering work of David Easton (1965, 1975), which places legitimacy within the framework of what he calls "political support." Easton defines legitimacy as "the conviction 'that it is right and proper ... to accept and obey the authorities and to abide by the requirements of the regime'" (1975, 541). Easton's conceptualization of political support makes an important distinction between *specific* (oriented towards the performance of political authorities responsible for making and implementing political decisions) and *diffuse* (more abstract feelings towards the political community and the regime as such) support (Easton 1975). In more recent theorizing about political support, Easton's framework has been refined and expanded. In two influential contributions to the field, Pippa Norris (1999, 2011), outlines an analytical framework ranging from the most diffuse level of the political community to the most specific

---

[1] Some common definitions hold that "an entity has political legitimacy if and only if it is morally justified in wielding political power, where to wield political power is to attempt to exercise a monopoly, within a jurisdiction, in the making, application, and enforcement of laws" (Buchanan 2002, 695). A similar but more developed definition offered by Gilley (2009,11) states that "a state, meaning the institutions and ideologies of a political system, is more legitimate the more it holds and exercises political power with legality, justification, and consent from the standpoint of all of its citizens."

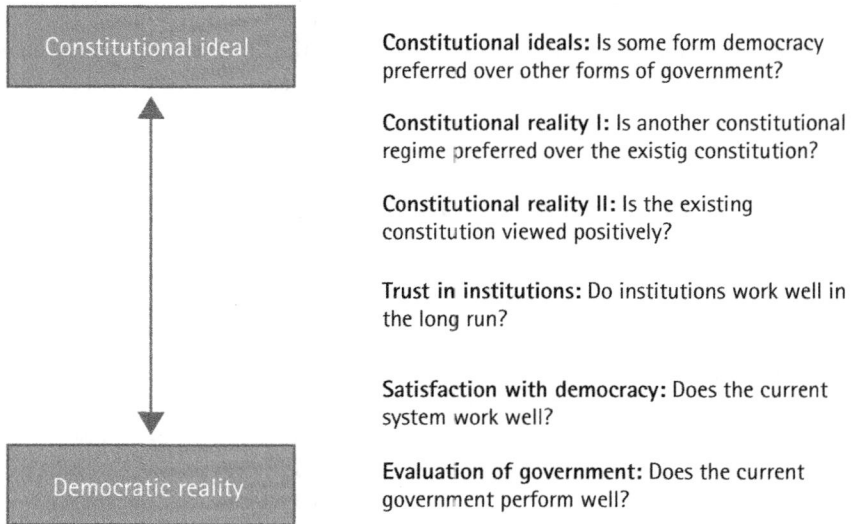

Constitutional ideals: Is some form democracy preferred over other forms of government?

Constitutional reality I: Is another constitutional regime preferred over the existig constitution?

Constitutional reality II: Is the existing constitution viewed positively?

Trust in institutions: Do institutions work well in the long run?

Satisfaction with democracy: Does the current system work well?

Evaluation of government: Does the current government perform well?

FIGURE 11.1 A conceptual framework for analyzing democratic evaluations

Source: Peffley and Rohrschneider (2014, 184–5).

level of specific political actors. According to Norris, political support has five distinct components: the political community (feelings towards the nation-state), regime principles (the underlying values of the political system), regime performance (the functioning of the system in practice), regime institutions (actual government institutions), and political actors (actual incumbent officeholders). Empirical analyses of different surveys have demonstrated the fact that the theoretical dimensions proposed by Norris are indeed reflected in the minds of citizens (Norris 2011; Booth and Seligson 2009). Another conceptualization of regime support is proposed by Peffley and Rohrschneider (2014) (Figure 11.1). They argue for distinguishing between six different types of political support, from "constitutional ideals" to "democratic reality."

Although this conceptualization comes close to Norris's framework, it sets itself apart by its explicit focus on constitutional aspects of the political system and the distinction between assessments of abstract constitutional ideals and more concrete evaluations of the democratic reality as perceived by citizens. It also nicely reflects the variation in terms of indicators used in the literature on QoG and political support, where researchers have assessed the importance of QoG for satisfaction with democracy, trust in institutions, and both constitutional ideals and reality.

Measures of political support as a dependent variable in research on quality of government

The vast majority of empirical studies of the relationship between QoG and political support has focused on what Peffley and Rohrschneider (2014) label the "democratic reality" and in particular the "satisfaction with democracy" dimension in their framework. This dimension is most frequently measured by a survey question asking about respondents' "satisfaction with the way democracy works," which is generally perceived to tap respondents' evaluation of the general performance of the political system (Linde and Ekman 2003) or "the constitutional reality" of a country (Fuchs, Guidorossi, and Svensson 1995, 332; cf. Hernández 2016; Ferrín 2016). A growing body of studies has come to investigate the importance of QoG for political *trust*, which in Figure 11.1 is located on a somewhat higher level of abstraction of political support but still clearly related to "democratic reality." In the literature, political trust is regularly viewed as one particular object of support (Norris 2017). Most often, political trust—sometimes referred to as institutional trust—is empirically measured by survey items tapping citizens' level of trust in particular political institutions, such as the parliament, the government, the judiciary, or the police (van der Meer and Zmerli 2017; Norris 2017; Marien and Werner 2018; Dahlberg and Linde 2018; Mishler and Rose 2001). Although most studies have been concerned with how the quality of government affects specific support—or the "democratic reality" dimension in Figure 11.1—a few studies have studied whether QoG also is of importance for diffuse support, or "constitutional ideals" (e.g. Magalhães 2014; Peffley and Rohrschneider 2014; Linde 2012).

The Importance of Impartiality and Fair Procedures

There is clearly a lack of conceptual consensus in the research investigating the relationship between quality of government and political support. A wide range of labels are used: "quality of government," "institutional quality," "bureaucratic quality," "good governance," and so on. Broadly speaking, we are here talking about empirical studies that highlight the importance of *how* public policy is implemented rather than *what* these policies are, or the *outcomes* of such policies. Common for most contributions to this field of research is that they to some extent can be connected to Rothstein's and Teorell's (2008) definition of quality of government, in which *impartiality in the implementation of public policy* is the fundamental principle. According to Rothstein and Teorell this means that "when implementing laws and policies, government officials shall not take anything about the citizen/case into consideration that is not beforehand stipulated in the policy or the law" (2008, 170).

The idea that impartiality and fair procedures are important for people's legitimacy beliefs stems from social psychology rather than political science. Social psychological theories of justice and fairness have for long argued that leaders and authorities are not only being evaluated by their performance, in terms of their ability to deliver favorable outcomes, but also—and to an even larger extent—on the basis of the perceived fairness of the process in which decisions are being made (Tyler, Rasinski, and McGraw 1985; Tyler, Caspar and Fisher 1989). Procedural fairness research has for a long time argued in favor of the importance of impartial, transparent, and predictable decision-making in contexts such as courts, workplaces, organizations, and other settings. However, the ideas of procedural fairness also seem to extend to the domains of politics and political science (Magalhães 2016, 524). As argued by Lind and Tyler (1988, 147–8), "because the political system, like the legal system, is a collection of institutions and rules, it is another arena within which procedural justice-based evaluations might occur."

From this perspective, it is the (perceived) fairness of the procedures through which institutions and authorities exercise authority which is the key to the willingness of individuals to defer to the decisions and rules created and implemented by those authorities and institutions (Tyler 2006; Esaiasson 2011). Since the 1970s, a large number of studies have shown that citizens attach substantial importance to the process by which outcomes are reached. If the process is perceived as fair, citizens are much more likely to accept an unfavorable outcome. Scholars like Tom R. Tyler and Allan E. Lind have repeatedly argued and demonstrated the key role that procedural fairness have for citizens' views of the legitimacy of government authorities and institutions (Lind and Tyler 1988; Tyler, Casper and Fisher 1989; MacCoun 2005). However, it should be noted that many of these studies operationalize procedural fairness as either instrumental fairness (a person feels that s/he has been able to influence the decision outcome) or relational fairness (a person feels that the authority showed respect and listened attentively), which is not directly tapping into Rothstein and Teorell's concept of QoG as the *impartial implementation* of public policies. Differences in the interpretation and implementation of the procedural fairness literature have therefore resulted in a somewhat confused usage and understanding of the concept, although its theoretical core is rooted in the impartial treatment of citizens.

It is the way in which an authority treats its citizens that signals whether it may be trusted or not (Grimes 2017). If citizens perceive the treatment they receive from institutions and public officials as fair, they will be more inclined to view the entire political system as more trustworthy, which in turn will make them more supportive of the political system and its institutions (Marien and Werner 2018, 3). Thus, experience of fair and impartial procedures on behalf of an institution generates trust in that particular institution, which spills over to a positive notion of other public institutions and the political system in general, contributing to increased regime legitimacy and system support.

But what is fair treatment, and how is it achieved? According to Galbreath and Rose (2008, 53), "fairness is achieved when everyone with the same entitlement to a public service is treated the same by public officials applying laws and regulations consistently." Thus, to be considered fair, the authorities need to treat individuals *impartially* in its exercise of public power (Rothstein and Teorell 2008). For example, "impartiality involves the application of rules in the same way to everyone with the same characteristics; for example, paying the same pension to people who, on the basis of their age and contributions, are entitled to receive the same sum" (Galbreath and Rose 2008, 55).

Thus, on the individual level it is primarily people's subjective perceptions of fairness and impartiality that lay the ground for their more general assessments of the political system and, accordingly, their legitimacy beliefs. This argument is related to the fact that the quality of public institutions is actually of greater importance for people's daily life than are elections and institutional arrangements on the input side. Rothstein (2009: 323) goes as far as arguing that:

> The idea that legitimacy has more to do with the exercise of government power than the access to this power by participation in elections makes a lot of sense. Your ability to vote is unlikely to have a clear and significant impact on your life chances: The likelihood that your vote will be decisive is, of course, miniscule. Many citizens voluntarily abstain from voting and

from participating in other forms of political activity on the input side of the political system. However, if the police do not protect you because you are an X-type citizen, if the fire-brigade does not come to your house because you are a Z-type citizen, if your children are systematically discriminated against in the schools because they are Y-type children, and if the doctors at the hospital ignore you because you are a P-type person, then you are in real trouble. To be blunt, whereas what happens on the input side usually has little consequence for individual citizens, what the state does on the output side may be life threatening (Rothstein 2009, 323)

Drivers of Political Support

Empirical research on political support has traditionally been occupied with two broad types of explanatory factors (Dahlberg and Linde 2018; Mishler and Rose 2001). For quite some time, the prevailing theoretical perspective emphasized the importance of *political culture* and *socialization* in the formation of political values and trust. Through a process of socialization early in life, political values, such as trust and support, are transferred from one generation to the next through family, peers, and school. These attitudes and value patterns will characterize a person throughout the rest of her life (Easton and Dennis 1969; Almond and Verba 1963; Inglehart 1977). Thus, political trust is exogenous, since it originates outside the political system "in long-standing and deeply seeded beliefs about people that are rooted in cultural norms and communicated through early-life socialization" (Mishler and Rose 2001, 31).

The cultural perspective has been criticized by scholars who argue that political attitudes and values are likely to change over the course of a person's life, implying that political trust and support are endogenous to the political system. Political trust and support are contingent on personal experiences and could be described as a *rational response* to the functioning and performance of the political system. People continuously form and reform their attitudes and support based on interaction with the political system, and subsequent evaluations of its performance (Mishler and Rose 2001; Kumlin 2004). Satisfaction with the performance of democratic regimes could thus be "expected to reflect an informed assessment about the cumulative record of successive government, whether judged by normative expectations about the democratic decision-making process or by the achievement of certain desired policy outputs and outcomes" (Norris 2011, 190). Since this "trust-as-evaluation"— or experiential—approach has demonstrated the strongest explanatory power and has come to dominate empirical political science research in the recent decades (van der Meer and Hakhverdian 2017), it will be at the forefront of our interest in the following section.

What kind of experiences matter the most?

This experiential approach can roughly be divided in two camps between those who emphasize that political support and trust is generated, first and foremost, on the input side of the political system, and those who argue that it is what is produced at the output side of the political system that matters the most (Rothstein 2009). A vast amount of empirical research has shown that variables relating both to the input side (e.g. democratic representation,

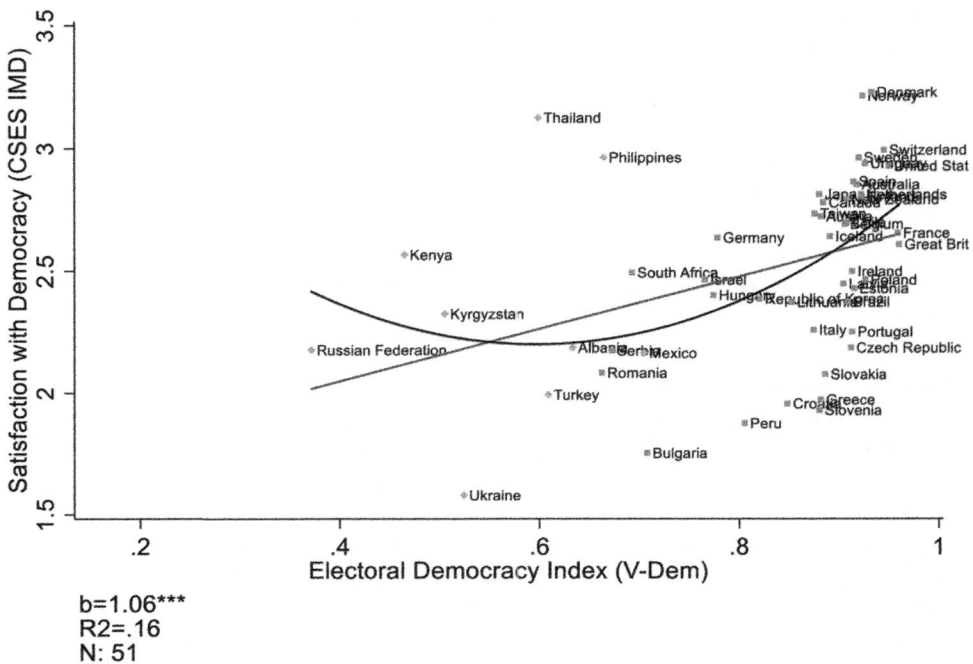

FIGURE 11.2 Electoral democracy and satisfaction with the way democracy works

Sources: Coppedge et al. (2018); *The Comparative Study of Electoral Systems* (2018); Teorell et al. (2016).

Note: The V-Dem electoral democracy index measures the existence of electoral democracy through the core values of democratic responsiveness and competitive elections, extensive suffrage, freely operating political and civil society organizations; that elections are clean without corruption and the existence of freedom of expression and media independence (see Coppedge et al. 2018). Countries classified as "free" by Freedom House are marked by squares.

accountability, and institutional arrangements) as well as policy outcomes (e.g. economic performance and welfare arrangements) influence citizens' evaluations of the way the democratic political system works in practice.

There is no doubt that both democracy on the input side and performance outcomes on the output side are likely to contribute to the legitimacy of political systems. This becomes clear when looking at correlations between those factors and average citizen satisfaction with the way democracy works around the world. Figure 11.2 illustrates the relationship between the measure "electoral democracy" from the Varieties of Democracy dataset and aggregate levels of satisfaction with the way democracy works in a wide range of countries included in the Comparative Studies of Electoral Systems (CSES) integrated database.

The relationship between electoral democracy and satisfaction with democracy is positive and statistically significant. However, the explanatory power is limited. Electoral democracy explains only 16 per cent of the variation in satisfaction with democracy. It is clear that citizens' satisfaction with democracy is determined by other factors than democracy itself.

In most country comparative research on political support, economic factors are highlighted as an important aspect to account for. When it comes to economic outcomes in terms of GDP per capita, which is probably the most frequently used indicator of macro-economic performance in comparative politics, Figure 11.3 tells a story very similar to the one in Figure

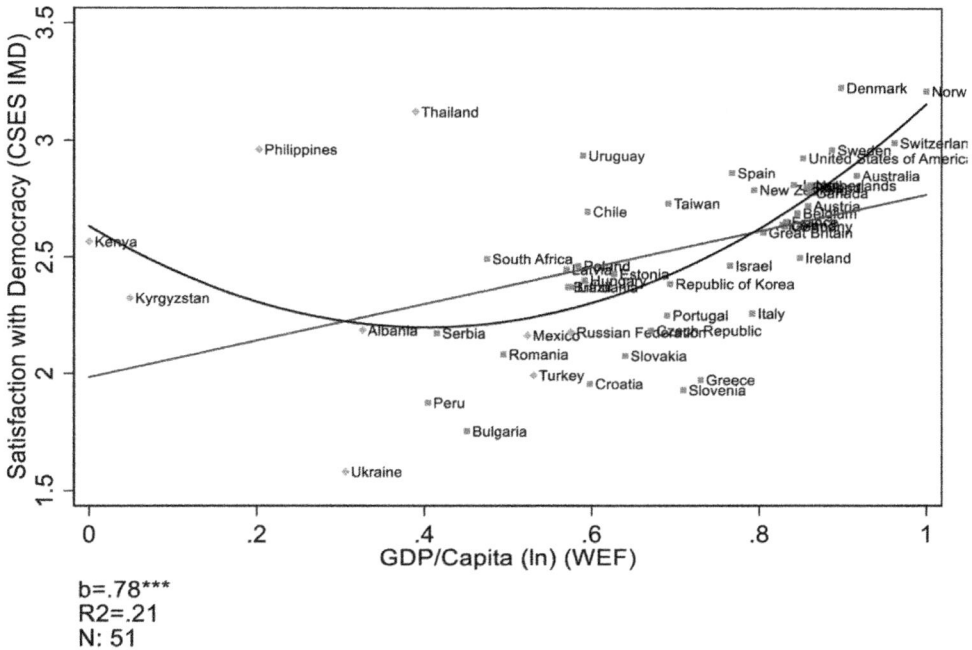

FIGURE 11.3 Economic development (GDP/capita) and satisfaction with the way democracy works

Sources: Schwab and Sala-I-Martin (2015); *The Comparative Study of Electoral Systems* (2018); Teorell et al. (2016).

Note: Countries classified as "free" by Freedom House are marked by squares.

11.2. The relationship is positive but relatively weak. However, economic performance does a slightly better job than democracy in explaining variation in satisfaction with the way democracy works ($R^2=0.21$).

The strong interest in democratic input and performance outcomes within the field of political support implied that, for quite some time, processes involving the exercise of state power and the implementation of public policy were to a certain extent mistakenly left out of the equation. So, to what extent is quality of government related to political support? How well does the argument above about QoG being more important than democracy hold up against comparative data? Figure 11.4 presents the association between satisfaction with democracy and the QoG index of impartiality, which is constructed from Rothstein and Teorell's definition of QoG.

The relationship is positive and not radically different from the ones presented in Figures 11.2 and 11.3, except for the fact that the level of impartiality in the public administrations does a much better job in explaining the variation in satisfaction with democracy across the world. The explained variance is more than twice compared to that of electoral democracy and 16 percentage points larger than for economic performance.

Considering the simple empirical evidence presented here, it seems surprising that variables relating to the quality of government, such as corruption and public administration impartiality, for so long enjoyed very limited interest among scholars working on determinants of political support. However, the last decade has seen a growing interest in QoG

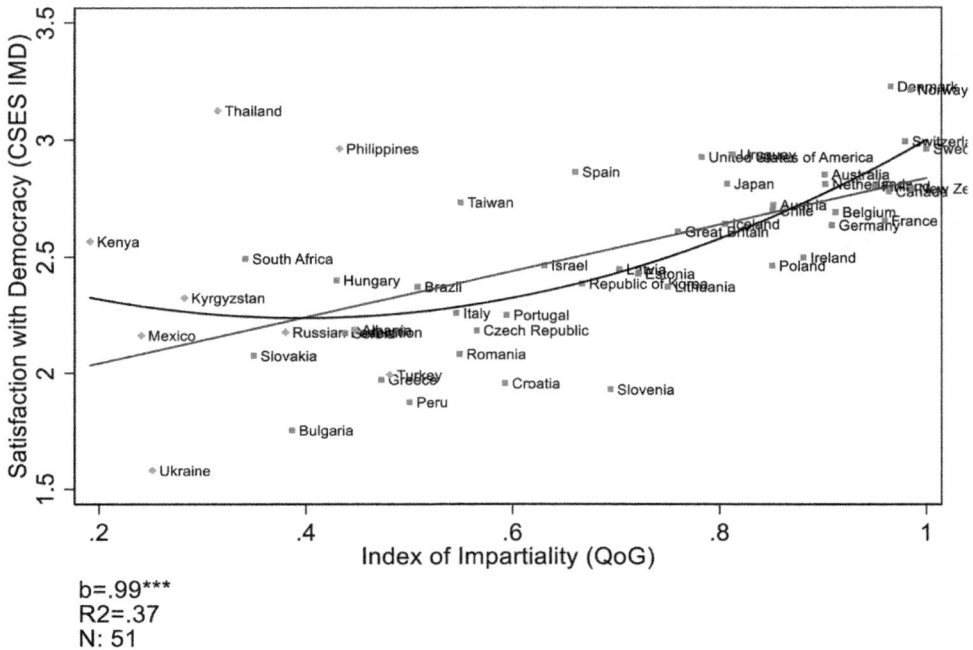

FIGURE 11.4 Quality of government and satisfaction with the way democracy works

Sources: Dahlström et al. (2015); *The Comparative Study of Electoral Systems* (2018); Teorell et al. (2016).

Note: The Index of Impartiality measures to what extent government institutions exercise their power impartially. The index is based on five items from the QoG Expert Survey 2015. It is constructed by adding each measure weighted by the factor loading obtained from a principal component factor analysis. Missing values on one or more of the questions have been imputed on the individual expert level. After that, aggregation to the country level has been made (mean value of all experts per country).

Countries classified as "free" by Freedom House are marked by squares.

related explanatory factors. In fact, in a recent volume on the state of democratic legitimacy in Europe (van Ham et al. 2017), one of the main conclusions is that QoG—together with policy controversies—appears to be the most promising factor for explaining variation and change in political support (Andeweg and Aarts 2017, 199; see also Martini and Quaranta 2020; van der Meer 2017; Magalhães 2017; Esaiasson, Gilljam, and Persson 2017). In the following sections, we will present and discuss important contributions to the relatively recent body of research focusing on the importance of quality of government for political support and trust.

QUALITY OF GOVERNMENT AND POLITICAL SUPPORT: TAKING STOCK OF THE EMPIRICAL EVIDENCE

When assessing the empirical research on the association between quality of government and political support it is important to distinguish between QoG on the macro level and

QoG on the micro level. Macro level studies are concerned with, for example, the actual extent of corruption in geographical entities such as countries, regions or municipalities and investigate covariation between levels of corruption and levels of political support. The variation sought to be explained may be either aggregated levels (e.g. country means aggregated from individuals representative survey samples) or between citizens or groups of citizens by way of multilevel statistical techniques. Studies of QoG on the micro—or individual—level are mainly concerned with citizens' *perceptions* of QoG, where people's evaluations of the quality of government in their country (or region/municipality) are thought to form the basis for their trust in political institutions and their general support for the political system.

Institutional quality on the country level

Quality of government in relation to political support has, at the macro level, mainly been operationalized by using cross-country indices measuring government effectiveness and efforts to control corruption around the world. Transparency International's *Corruption Perception Index* and the World Bank's *Worldwide Governance Indicators* have been the most frequently used data sources (see Table 11.1). Indicators of political support are gathered from large-scale cross-national surveys, such as the *World Values Survey*, the *Comparative Study of Electoral Systems*, and the *European Social Survey*, and analyzed either as country averages or at the individual level. To some extent, this field of research is still in an early stage. The first studies to explicitly focus on the connection between different aspects of institutional quality and political support did not surface until the early 2000s. Table 11.1 presents a simplified overview of empirical studies assessing the relationship between QoG on the country level and different dimensions of political support on the individual or country level.

In a pioneering study, Anderson and Tverdova (2003) demonstrated the importance of taking system-level variables into account in analyses of political support and trust. Applying a multilevel research design, they found that the level of corruption in a country has a significant negative effect on citizens' general evaluations of the political system, as well as on trust in civil servants. However, they also found that this effect is moderated by citizens' political allegiances in terms of party vote in the latest election. In countries with high levels of corruption, citizens that voted for a losing party evaluated the functioning of democracy substantially less favorable than did "winners." It was also shown that the gap in support between winners and losers is increasing with level of corruption. The study thus represents important contributions both to the research on quality of government and political support and the advancing research field investigating the importance of electoral outcomes for citizens' evaluations of the way democracy works.

However, more recent studies investigating the moderating effect of QoG on the winner–loser gap has produced mixed results, depending on research designs in terms of data coverage and the indicator used for measuring QoG (e.g. Dahlberg and Linde 2016; Palacios 2018; Martini and Quaranta 2019). For example, when using broad indicators from the World Bank in combination with more detailed survey data, one runs the risk of ending up with ceiling effects. This since the availability of survey data often are greater in less corrupt countries. Nevertheless, the strong direct effect of the extent of corruption on political support that Anderson and Tverdova uncovered has been demonstrated in many studies—covering a wide range of democracies—over the last two decades.

Table 11.1 Examples of studies assessing the importance of system level QoG for political support

Author(s)	Dependent variable(s)	System level variable(s)	Empirical scope	Main results
Anderson & Tverdova (2003)	Evaluation of democratic performance & trust in civil servants	Corruption (CPI)	*International Social Survey Programme* (16 countries)	Corruption level has an independent negative effect on support and trust. The winner–loser gap in support is moderated by level of corruption.
Wagner et al. (2009)	SWD (country)	Institutional quality (WGI)	*Eurobarometer* 1990–2000 (16 countries)	Institutional quality is more important for SWD than economic factors.
Magalhães (2014)	Legitimacy/ Diffuse support (3 dimensions/indices)	Government effectiveness (WGI)	*World Values Survey* (several waves)	In democracies, government effectiveness leads to greater diffuse support. In nondemocracies, effectiveness weakens support for democracy.
Dahlberg & Holmberg (2014)	SWD (country & individual)	Government effectiveness (WGI),	*Comparative Study of Electoral Systems* (32 countries)	Governmental output more important for SWD than democratic input.
Peffley & Rohrschneider (2014)	Diffuse and specific support (SWD)	Institutional quality (WGI)	*Comparative Study of Electoral Systems* (21 countries)	Institutional quality most important for both SWD and diffuse support.
Donovan & Karp (2017)	SWD, parties presenting clear alternatives, free and fair elections	Corruption (CPI)	*European Social Survey* 6 (28 countries)	Corruption has strong influence on all dependent variables. The effect of electoral rules disappears when taking corruption and inequality into account.
Van der Meer & Hakhverdian (2017)	SWD & institutional trust	Corruption (CPI)	*European Values Study* (42 countries)	Corruption highly important for SWD and trust, while economic performance is not.
Dahlberg & Linde (2018)	SWD & institutional trust	Corruption (CPI)	*World Values Survey* & *Comparative Study of Electoral Systems*	Institutional quality more important than socialization for SWD and institutional trust.

Note: SWD = Satisfaction with the way democracy works, WGI = Worldwide Governance Indicators (World Bank), CPI = Corruption Perceptions Index (Transparency international).

Later studies have broadened the scope by assessing the importance of a wider set of QoG related explanatory variables as well as alternative dependent variables. Rohrschneider (2005) demonstrated the importance of institutional quality for citizen's feelings of being represented in the political system. In contrast to earlier studies that had emphasized the importance of formal institutional arrangements (regime *type*), Rohrschneider found that the *procedural quality* of the bureaucracy and judiciary works to inform citizens about how seriously a regime takes their preferences. When national administrative and judicial institutions work well, citizens are also more likely to believe that parliaments and governments work in their interests. The fact that political support is to a large extent contingent of the quality of government has been documented in a continuously growing body of research. Testing the explanatory power of democratic input and governmental output variables in 32 democracies, Dahlberg and Holmberg (2014) demonstrated that aggregate levels of satisfaction with democracy correlate substantially stronger with four different QoG measures (e.g. government impartiality and government effectiveness) than with four democratic input measures (e.g. electoral rules and effective number of parties). QoG—measured by government effectiveness—also showed to be more important than absolute ideological congruence between politicians and voters when it comes to satisfaction with democracy on the individual level.

Applying a macro-level panel analysis of Eurobarometer data from 1990 to 2000, Wagner, Schneider and Halla (2009) found that high-quality institutions like the rule of law, low levels of corruption and other institutions that improve resource allocation are important determinants of satisfaction with democracy. In a comparative study covering 21 countries, Peffley and Rohrschneider (2014) found that on the country level, institutional quality is the only statistically significant predictor of satisfaction with the way democracy works. Neither the democratic input-related variables nor level of human development affect satisfaction in a significant way. Moreover, the authors find the same pattern when it comes to "democratic ideals," i.e. diffuse support for the principles of democracy. Although this dimension of political support has received less attention, some studies have indicated that the quality of output institutions does not only affect citizens' evaluations of the *functioning* of the democratic system but also seem to make people more supportive of democracy as a system of government (e.g. Magalhães 2014). Recent studies also demonstrate strong effects on political trust (Dahlberg and Linde 2018; van der Meer and Hakhverdian 2017; van der Meer 2017), and citizens' expectations about the fairness of elections and about parties presenting meaningful alternatives (Donovan and Karp 2017). In general, the findings demonstrate that the procedural quality of output institutions is significantly more important for citizens' representational judgments than the structure of input institutions.

It should be noted that most of the studies concerned with QoG and different dimensions of political support have measured the dependent variable on the individual level, i.e. using one or more survey items. However, the importance of QoG has also been demonstrated in studies employing more advanced measures, drawing on different types of data sources. In a series of studies, Gilley (2006a, 2006b, 2009) investigated the sources and effects of regime legitimacy. After constructing a measure of legitimacy based on a multitude of both attitudinal and behavioral variables, he found "general governance"—measured by the government effectiveness, control of corruption, and the rule of law indicators provided by Worldwide Governance Indicators—to be the most powerful predictor of regime legitimacy around the world.

The negative economic and societal effects of dysfunctional institutions are today well documented by economists and political scientists (see Dimant and Tosato 2019 for a recent overview). Judging by the growing number of studies of the relationship between institutional quality and political support, it also seems clear that the detrimental consequences of corruption and other violations of impartiality in the exercise of public power go beyond poor economic and political performance. Corruption and bad governance also hurt the most important source of democratic legitimacy, namely ordinary citizens' trust in political institutions and support for democracy as a form of government. Although the number of studies is still quite limited, the empirical evidence remains solid. Countries that are successful in taming corruption, upholding the rule of law and have well-functioning bureaucracies enjoy higher levels of public support and trust than countries where public institutions are corrupt and cannot be trusted to act in the interest of the public. Even though different aspects of QoG are well integrated in the literature today, it is mainly indicators relating to specific political support that has been scrutinized. In order to gain a fuller understanding of the underlying processes and mechanisms underlying these macro-level relationships, it is important to move focus to the individual level, where citizens' perceptions and experience of the functioning and performance of institutions and bureaucracies may provide important insights about the seemingly solid positive relationship between quality of government and political support.

Perceptions of quality of government on the individual level

Within social science, people have most often been viewed as rational actors that evaluate political authorities and institutions based on the outcomes they receive, and thus that support for these authorities and institutions can be explained by such outcome-based judgments (Lind and Tyler 1988). This has to a large extent also been the case in political science. Following David Easton (1975), political support has tended to be viewed as an evaluative response to regime performance in terms of actual outcomes. The authorities will thus be evaluated according to the extent to which people's demands have been met (Easton 1975, 438). However, Easton also argues that people's evaluations are determined by assessments of more general performance that goes beyond narrow self-interest. Citizens may also assess the moral character and style of behavior of those holding office (Easton 1975, 439). In other words, political authorities need to *earn* citizens' trust and support (Mishler and Rose 1997) in terms of providing both effective performance in terms of outcomes and institutional quality. If citizens suspect or experience that their political representatives and public officials are devoted to their own enrichment rather than to the public interest, this will likely have a negative influence on political support and trust.

In mainstream political support research, the empirical focus has most often been on different aspects of corruption and its effect on political support and citizens' legitimacy beliefs. Not very surprisingly, early studies concerned more recently democratized countries where corruption and bad governance were widely viewed as severe threats to democratic consolidation and economic development, such as the Latin American and post-communist countries in Central and Eastern Europe. In a large study on regime support in nine new East European democracies, Rose and collaborators found that higher levels of corruption (on the country level) make people less inclined to reject nondemocratic regime alternatives, but not more likely to explicitly support the current democratic regime (Rose, Mishler, and Haerpfer 1998).

One of the first studies to explicitly assess the effect of corruption on legitimacy on the individual level investigated how *personal experience* with corruption in the public sector affects legitimacy beliefs in Bolivia, El Salvador, Nicaragua, and Paraguay (Seligson 2002). Using survey data, Seligson constructed an index of corruption victimization based on eight questions about experiences with public corruption (e.g. being asked to pay bribes to the police, public officials and in the court system) over the year prior to the survey. The respondents' legitimacy beliefs were measured by an index consisting of five survey items tapping different aspects of respondents' trust in and support for the political system and core democratic institutions (e.g. the courts and the police). The findings show that people that has been exposed to corruption demonstrate substantially lower levels of support for the legitimacy of the regime than those without experiences of corruption, also when controlling for vote for incumbent party, which has consistently been shown to be a strong predictor of political support (Anderson et al. 2005).

Seligson's pioneering work set the stage for empirical analyses of the importance of corruption and other aspects of bad governance on political support in other parts of the world. Some of these are presented in Table 11.2. However, instead of focusing on people's actual *experiences* of corruption most of the work in this field has come to investigate the importance of citizens' *perceptions* of different aspects of quality of government, such as the extent of corruption in the public sector. Drawing on surveys from ten postcommunist democracies, Linde (2012) found public perceptions of both the extent of corruption among public officials as well as fair treatment by the authorities to be strongly associated with citizens' evaluations of regime performance (measured by satisfaction with the way democracy works) as well as with support for democratic regime principles (measured by rejection of nondemocratic regime alternatives).

The strong association between citizens' perceptions of the extent of corruption and political support has not only been found in new democracies and countries that are generally viewed as having problems with public sector corruption. Perceptions of corruption have also been shown to be an important predictor of political support in the Nordic countries, which are generally perceived as being among the least corrupt in the world (Linde and Erlingsson 2013; Erlingsson, Linde, and Öhrvall 2014, 2016).

Interestingly, contemporary studies based on broader samples of countries have shown that the importance of QoG is conditional on institutional settings. For example, it has been demonstrated that citizens' perceptions of the extent of corruption are actually a stronger determinant of discontent in established democracies than in newly democratized countries (Dahlberg, Linde, and Holmberg 2015). The authors argue that this may be explained by the fact that citizens in established democracies have greater expectations in terms of general performance. While corruption and clientelism have become part of day-to-day politics in many new democracies, people in established democracies expect politicians and public officials to behave in an impartial and noncorrupt manner. When citizens recognize or perceive public misconduct where it is not supposed to occur, such perceptions become more important for discontent. Citizens in newer democracies who in the first place are less politically trusting

Table 11.2 Examples of studies assessing the importance of perceptions of QoG for political support

Author(s)	Dependent variable(s)	Individual level variable(s)	Empirical scope	Main results
Seligson (2002)	Confidence in key government institutions	Experience of corruption	4 Latin American countries	Exposure to corruption erodes legitimacy and trust.
Linde (2012)	SWD & diffuse support	Perceptions of corruption and fairness in public administration	*New Europe Barometer* 2004 (10 East European countries)	Both SWD and diffuse support strongly affected by corruption and fairness.
Linde & Erlingsson (2013)	SWD	Perceived corruption (politicians, officials, local level), corruption development	Sweden	Perceptions of corruption strongly affects SWD.
Dahlberg et al. (2015)	Democratic discontent	Perception of corruption among politicians	*Comparative Study of Electoral Systems* (26 countries)	Corruption perceptions most important in old democracies, general performance in new democracies.
Magalhães (2016)	SWD	Procedural Fairness	*European Social Survey* 6 (29 countries)	Perceptions of procedural fairness moderates the effects of outcome favorability.
Marien & Werner (2018)	Institutional trust	Fair treatment & Corruption	*European Social Survey* 6 (27 countries)	Perceptions of fair treatment by police officers are associated with higher levels of trust in political institutions. The effect is moderated by level of corruption.

Note: SWD = Satisfaction with the way democracy works.

and more used to corruption seem to care more about the government's ability to deliver in terms of economic development and basic welfare (Dahlberg et al. 2015, 31).

A similar pattern of varying effects of perceptions of procedural fairness has been demonstrated by Marien and Werner (2018). Drawing on data from the *European Social Survey*, they show that perceptions of fair treatments by the police are associated with higher levels of trust in political institutions. However, the strength of the effect is mediated by the level of corruption, as measured by the Corruption Perceptions Index. In line with the findings by Dahlberg et al. (2015), the strongest associations between fairness perceptions (QoG) and institutional trust are found in countries with the lowest levels of corruption. Marien and

Werner argue that in such contexts, "in which fair treatment is expected, a violation of the normative expectation of fair treatment is likely to have a stronger effect on citizens' institutional trust than in contexts characterized by systematic corruption" (2018, 89).

It has also been shown that QoG (on both the system and individual level) has a moderating impact on the relationship between economic variables/outcomes and political support. The process–outcome interaction—through which procedural fairness moderates the effect of outcome favorability—has for long been an important insight of procedural fairness theories in organizational psychology. Recently, a series of studies have established that the importance of outcome favorability for political support is moderated by the quality of government. When rules and procedures are impartial and transparent—or perceived by citizens to be so—economic performance becomes less important in people's evaluations of the general performance of the political system (Magalhães 2016, 2017; Magalhães and Aguiar-Conraria 2018).

Concluding Remarks and Implications

Acknowledging the fact that research on political support in general constitutes a significant subfield with a long tradition within comparative politics, surprisingly little attention has been paid to questions about how support is related to the quality and functioning of output institutions, such as government bureaucracies and local level public administrations, which many people actually interact with in their daily lives. After having been preoccupied with institutions on the input side of the political system, such as electoral rules, and economic performance, the last decades have seen a growing interest in the way the quality of government affect public evaluations of the democratic political system. This relatively new subfield has made important contributions to the field of political support and today we know a great deal about the importance of QoG for political support and why people seems to care a lot about impartial and incorrupt government institutions and public administrations.

Over time, many novel findings have been replicated and confirmed using different datasets, country selections, operationalizations, and statistical techniques. Yet, there is a great deal of potential for improving the research field. The most obvious shortcoming is that most studies have been based on correlational research designs based on cross-section data. Although the theoretical foundations most often are solid and the empirical coverage broad, causality has not been a priority in most contributions dealing with perceptions of QoG and political support. One important reason for this is that QoG is a concept that has rendered relatively limited attention in survey settings. While institutional quality varies across countries and over time, and are continuously scored in international indices, such as the *Worldwide Governance Indicators* and *Corruption Perceptions Index*, there is a serious shortcoming of comparative individual level panel data covering relevant indicators of citizen perceptions of QoG. In relation to this, there is also ample room for more experimental work in general, and in particular when it comes to the relationship between procedural fairness, outcome favorability, and different dimensions of political support. Despite the relatively large interest in experimental studies of the importance of the process–outcome interaction when it comes to decision acceptance in general (e.g. Esaiasson et al. 2019), studies that explicitly deal with political support and trust are rare (but see Bøggild 2016).

As should be evident from this overview, there has hitherto been an overweight of studies assessing the impact of QoG on more specific levels of support, i.e. satisfaction with democracy and trust in political institutions. Although there are notable exceptions (e.g. Magalhães 2014; Peffley and Rohrschneider 2014; Linde 2012), our knowledge about the relationship between the quality of output institutions and more diffuse objects of support—or support for constitutional ideals—is rather limited. Future research should thus devote more theoretical and empirical work focusing on the link between QoG and diffuse regime support.

Another important avenue for future research is the development of more valid and reliable indicators of QoG—both on the macro as well as on the micro level. For example, most often available measures of corruption perceptions do not differentiate between different forms of corruption, such as grand or systemic corruption on the state level and petty corruption on the micro level. Personal experience of petty corruption on the micro level will most likely affect perceptions of corruption on other levels as well. Moreover, in low-corrupt countries, a broad survey question asking citizens about the extent of corruption in general are likely to also capture different forms of political dissatisfaction and distrust that are not related to actual corruption (Dahlberg and Solevid 2016). This since corruption is a term frequently used for putting blame on the ruling elite among many populist parties that have achieved electoral successes in most European countries during the last decades (Mudde and Rovira Kaltwasser 2017).

Another limitation in the field is that most indices capturing QoG or institutional quality are based on several sources (e.g. surveys of experts and citizens). Each indicator might by itself be both detailed and fine-grained, but when combined into an overall index, it becomes hard to evaluate it in more detail. Exactly what dimensions of such broad indices actually affects citizens' political support, what aspects of institutional quality are most pivotal, and in what country settings? To have several indicators of the latent concept is of course a strength but it is not only the set of indicators that often make the measures too broad. Often the index indicators are derived from different types of data, e.g. citizen surveys in combination with expert ratings. Relying on several different data sources can of course also be considered a strength but many times it is still indicators based on subjective perceptions of e.g. corruption, which is an activity occurring in the shadows and behind closed doors.

At last, we would like to emphasize this subfield's openness to incorporate theoretical perspectives and empirical findings from other disciplines. A large majority of the contributions draw quite heavily on insights from social and organizational psychology, where the theory of procedural fairness has its origins. To a certain extent it could be argued that the concept of quality of government—as defined by Rothstein and Teorell (2008) and operationalized in the empirical studies discussed in this chapter—on the individual level overlaps heavily with the concept of procedural fairness, as used and developed by Tom R. Tyler and other social psychologists and law scholars. This theoretical pluralism—which also includes inspiration from political psychology in general—should arguably constitute an important asset in future efforts to disentangle the relationship between QoG and political support.

References

Almond, Gabriel A., and Sidney Verba. 1963. *The Civic Culture: Political Attitudes and Democracy in Five Nations*. Princeton: Princeton University Press.

Anderson, Christopher J., and Yuliya V. Tverdova. 2003. "Corruption, Political Allegiances, and Attitudes Toward Government in Contemporary Democracies." *American Journal of Political Science* 47 (1): 91–109.

Anderson, Christopher J., André Blais, Shaun Bowler, Todd Donovan, and Ola Listhaug. 2005. *Losers Consent: Elections and Democratic Legitimacy*. Oxford: Oxford University Press.

Andeweg, Rudy, and Kees Aarts. 2017. "Studying Political Legitimacy: Findings, Implications, and an Uneasy Question." In *Myth and Reality of the Legitimacy Crisis*, edited by Carolien van Ham, Jacques Thomassen, Kees Aarts, and Rudy Andeweg, 193–206. Oxford: Oxford University Press.

Buchanan, Allen. 2002. "Political Legitimacy and Democracy." *Ethics* 112 (4): 689–719.

Bøggild, Troels. 2016. "How Politicians' Reelection Efforts Can Reduce Public Trust, Electoral Support, and Policy Approval." *Political Psychology* 37 (6): 901–19.

Booth, John A., and Mitchell A. Seligson. 2009. *The Legitimacy Puzzle in Latin America: Political Support and Democracy in Eight Nations*. Cambridge: Cambridge University Press.

Comparative Study of Electoral Systems. CSES INTEGRATED MODULE DATASET (IMD) [dataset and documentation]. December 4, 2018 version. doi:10.7804/cses.imd.2018-12-04. www.cses.org

Coppedge, Michael, John Gerring, Carl Henrik Knutsen et al. 2018. "V-Dem [Country-Year/Country-Date] Dataset v8." *Varieties of Democracy (V-Dem) Project*. https://doi.org/10.23696/vdemcy18

Dahlberg, Stefan, and Jonas Linde. 2018. "Socialization or Experience? Institutional Trust and Political Support among Emigrants in Different Institutional Settings." *Journal of Politics* 80(4): 1389–93.

Dahlberg, Stefan, and Jonas Linde. 2016. "Losing Happily? The Mitigating Effect of Democracy and Quality of Government on the Winner–Loser Gap in Political Support." *International Journal of Public Administration* 39 (9): 652–64.

Dahlberg, Stefan, Jonas Linde, and Sören Holmberg. 2015. "Democratic Discontent in Old and New Democracies: Assessing the Importance of Democratic Input and Governmental Output." *Political Studies* 63 (S1): 18–37.

Dahlberg, Stefan, and Sören Holmberg. 2014. "Democracy and Bureaucracy: How their Quality Matters for Popular Satisfaction." *West European Politics* 37 (3): 515–37.

Dahlberg, Stefan, and Solevid, Maria. 2016. "Does Corruption Suppress Voter Turnout?" *Journal of Elections, Public Opinion and Parties* 26 (4): 489–510.

Dahlström, Carl, Jan Teorell, Stefan Dahlberg et al. 2015. *The QoG Expert Survey Dataset II*. Gothenberg: The Quality of Government Institute, University of Gothenburg.

Dimant, Eugen, and Guglielmo Tosato. 2019. "Causes and Effects of Corruption: What Has Past Decade's Empirical Research Taught Us? A Survey." *Journal of Economic Surveys* 32 (2): 335–56.

Donovan, Todd, and Jeffrey A. Karp. 2017. "Electoral Rules, Corruption, Inequality and Evaluations of Democracy." *European Journal of Political Research* 56 (3): 469–86.

Easton, David. 1975. "A Re-Assessment of the Concept of Political Support." *British Journal of Political Science* 5 (4): 435–57.

Easton, David. 1965. *A Systems Analysis of Political Life*. New York: John Wiley.

Easton, David, and Jack Dennis. 1969. *Children in the Political System: Origins of Political Legitimacy*. New York: McGraw-Hill.

Erlingsson, Gissur Ó., Jonas Linde, and Richard Öhrvall. 2016. "Distrust in Utopia? Public Perceptions of Corruption and Political Support in Iceland before and after the Financial Crisis of 2008." *Government and Opposition* 51 (4): 553–79.

Erlingsson, Gissur Ó., Jonas Linde, and Richard Öhrvall. 2014. "Not so Fair after All? Perceptions of Procedural Fairness and Satisfaction with Democracy in the Nordic Welfare States." *International Journal of Public Administration* 37 (2): 106–19.

Esaiasson, Peter. 2011. "Electoral Losers Revisited—How Citizens React to Defeat at the Ballot Box." *Electoral Studies* 30 (1): 102–13.

Esaiasson, Peter, Mikael Persson, Mikal Gilljam, and Torun Lindholm. 2019. "Reconsidering the Role of Procedures for Decision Acceptance." *British Journal of Political Science* 49 (1): 291–314.

Esaiasson, Peter, Mikael Gilljam, and Mikael Persson. 2017. "Political Support in the Wake of Policy Controversies." In *Myth and Reality of the Legitimacy Crisis*, edited by Carolien van Ham, Jacques Thomassen, Kees Aarts, and Rudy Andeweg, 172–90. Oxford: Oxford University Press.

Ferrín, Mónica. 2016. "An Empirical Assessment of Satisfaction with Democracy." In *How Europeans View and Evaluate Democracy*, edited by Hanspeter Kriesi and Mónica Ferrín, 283–306. Oxford: Oxford University Press.

Fuchs, Dieter, Giovanna Guidorossi, and Palle Svensson. 1995. "Support for the Democratic System." In *Citizens and the State*, edited by Hans-Dieter Klingemann and Dieter Fuchs, 323–53. Oxford: Oxford University Press.

Galbreath, David J., and Richard Rose. 2008. "Fair Treatment in a Divided Society: A Bottom-up Assessment of Bureaucratic Encounters in Latvia." *Governance* 21 (1): 53–73.

Gilley, Bruce. 2009. *The Right to Rule: How States Win and Lose Legitimacy*. New York: Columbia University Press.

Gilley, Bruce. 2006a. "The Meaning and Measure of State Legitimacy: Results for 72 Countries." *European Journal of Political Research* 45 (3): 499–525.

Gilley, Bruce. 2006b. "The Determinants of State Legitimacy: Results for 72 Countries." *International Political Science Review* 27 (1): 47–71.

Grimes, Marcia. 2017. "Procedural Fairness and Political Trust." In *Handbook on Political Trust*, edited by Sonja Smerli and Tom W.G. van der Meer, 256–69. Cheltenham: Edward Elgar.

Hernández, Enrique. 2016. "Europeans' Views of Democracy: The Core Elements of Democracy." In *How Europeans View and Evaluate Democracy*, edited by Hanspeter Kriesi, and Mónica Ferrín, 43–63. Oxford: Oxford University Press.

Inglehart, Ronald. 1977. *The Silent Revolution: Changing Values and Political Styles Among Western Publics*. Princeton: Princeton University Press.

Kumlin, Staffan. 2004. "*The Personal and the Political - How Personal Welfare State Experiences Affect Political Trust and Ideology*." New York: Palgrave Macmillan.

Lind, E. Allan, and Tom R. Tyler. 1988. "*The Social Psychology of Procedural Justice*." New York: Plenum Press.

Linde, Jonas. 2012. "Why Feed the Hand That Bites You? Perceptions of Procedural Fairness and System Support in Post-communist Democracies." *European Journal of Political Research* 51 (3): 410–34.

Linde, Jonas, and Gissur Ó. Erlingsson. 2013. "The Eroding Effect of Corruption on System Support in Sweden." *Governance* 26 (4): 585–603.

Linde, Jonas, and Joakim Ekman. 2003. "Satisfaction with Democracy: A Note on a Frequently Used Indicator in Comparative Politics." *European Journal of Political Research* 42 (3): 391–408.

MacCoun, Robert J. 2005. "Voice, Control, and Belonging: The Double-Edged Sword of Procedural Fairness." *Annual Review of Law and Social Science* 2005 (1): 171–201.

Magalhães, Pedro C. 2016. "Economic Evaluations, Procedural Fairness, and Satisfaction with Democracy." *Political Research Quarterly* 69 (3): 522–34.

Magalhães, Pedro C. 2014. "Government Effectiveness and Support for Democracy." *European Journal of Political Research* 53 (1): 77–97.

Magalhães, Pedro C. 2017. "Economic Outcomes, Quality of Governance, and Satisfaction with Democracy." In *Myth and Reality of the Legitimacy Crisis: Explaining Trends and Cross-National Differences in Established Democracies*, edited by Caroline van Ham, Jacques Thomassen, Kees Aarts, and Rudy Andeweg, 156–71. Oxford: Oxford University Press.

Magalhães, Pedro C., and Luís Aguiar Conraria. 2018. "Procedural Fairness, the Economy, and Support for Political Authorities." *Political Psychology* 40 (1): 165–81.

Marien, Sofie, and Hannah Werner. 2018. "Fair Treatment, Fair Play? the Relationship between Fair Treatment Perceptions, Political Trust and Compliant and Cooperative Attitudes Cross-Nationally." *European Journal of Political Research* 58 (1): 72–95.

Martini, Sergio, and Mario Quaranta. 2019. "Political Support among Winners and Losers: Within- and between-Country Effects of Structure, Process and Performance in Europe." *European Journal of Political Research* 58 (1): 341–61.

Martini, Sergio, and Mario Quaranta. 2020. *Citizens and Democracy in Europe: Contexts, Changes and Political Support*. London: Palgrave Macmillan.

Mishler, William, and Richard Rose. 1997. "Trust, Distrust and Skepticism: Popular Evaluations of Civil and Political Institutions in Post-Communist Societies." *Journal of Politics* 59 (2): 418–51.

Mishler, William, and Richard Rose. 2001. "What Are the Origins of Political Trust? Testing Institutional and Cultural Theories in Post-communist Societies." *Comparative Political Studies* 34 (1): 30–62.

Mudde, Cas, and Cristóbal Rovira Kaltwasser. 2017. *Populism: A Very Short Introduction*. Oxford: Oxford University Press.

Norris, Pippa. 2017. "The Conceptual Framework of Political Support." In *Handbook of Political Trust*, edited by Tom W.G. van der Meer and Sonja Zmerli, 19–32. Cheltenham: Edward Elgar.

Norris, Pippa. 2011. *Democratic Deficit: Critical Citizens Revisited*. Cambridge: Cambridge University Press.

Norris, Pippa, ed. 1999. *Critical Citizens: Global Support for Democratic Governance*. Oxford: Oxford University Press.

Palacios, Irene. 2018. *Making Democratic Attitudes Work: The Effect of Institutions on Europeans' Aspirations and Evaluations of Democracy*. Ph.D. diss. Florence: European University Institute.

Peffley, Mark, and Robert Rohrschneider. 2014. "The Multiple Bases of Democratic Support: Procedural Representation and Governmental Outputs." In *Elections and Democracy: Representation and Accountability*, edited by Jacques Thomassen, 181–200. Oxford: Oxford University Press.

Rohrschneider, Robert. 2005. "Institutional Quality and Perceptions of Representation in Advanced Industrial Democracies." *Comparative Political Studies* 38 (7): 850–74.

Rose, Richard, William Mishler, and Christian Haerpfer. 1998. *Democracy and its Alternatives: Understanding Post-Communist Societies*. Baltimore: The Johns Hopkins University Press.

Rothstein, Bo. 2009. "Creating Political Legitimacy: Electoral Democracy versus Quality of Government." *American Behavioral Scientist* 53 (3): 311–30.

Rothstein, Bo, and Jan Teorell. 2008. "What is Quality of Government? A Theory of Impartial Government Institutions." *Governance* 21 (2): 165–90.

Schwab, Klaus, and Xavier Sala-I-Martin. 2015. *The Global Competitiveness Report 2014–2015*. World Economic Forum.

Seligson, Mitchel A. 2002. "The Impact of Corruption on Regime Legitimacy: A Study of Four Latin American Countries." *Journal of Politics* 64 (2): 408–33.

Teorell, Jan, Stefan Dahlberg, Sören Holmberg, Bo Rothstein, Anna Khomenko, and Richard Svensson. 2016. The Quality of Government Standard Dataset, version Jan16. University of Gothenburg: The Quality of Government Institute, http://www.qog.pol.gu.se doi:10.18157/QoGStdJan16

Tyler, Tom R. 2006. *Why People Obey the Law*. Princeton: Princeton University Press.

Tyler, Tom R., Kenneth A. Rasinski, and Kathleen M. McGraw. 1985. "The Influence of Perceived Injustice on the Endorsement of Political Leaders." *Journal of Applied Social Psychology* 15 (8): 700–25.

Tyler, Tom R., Jonathan D. Caspar, and Bonnie Fisher. 1989. "Maintaining Allegiance toward Political Authorities: The Role of Prior Attitudes and the Use of Fair Procedures." *American Journal of Political Science* 33 (3): 629–52.

Van Ham, C., Thomassen, J., Aarts, K. and Andeweg, R. (eds.) 2017. *"Myth and Reality of the Legitimacy Crisis: Explaining Trends and Cross-National Differences in Established Democracies."* Oxford: Oxford University Press.

van der Meer, Tom W. G. 2017. "Dissecting the Causal Chain from Quality of Government to Political Support." *Myth and Reality of the Legitimacy Crisis*, edited by Carolien van Ham, Jacques Thomassen, Kees Aarts, and Rudy Andeweg, 136–55. Oxford: Oxford University Press.

van der Meer, Tom W.G., and Armen Hakhverdian. 2017. "Political Trust as the Evaluation of Process and Performance: A Cross-National Study of 42 European Countries." *Political Studies* 65 (1): 81–102.

van der Meer, Tom W.G., and Sonja Zmerli. 2017. "The Deeply Rooted Concern with Political Trust." In *Handbook of Political Trust*, edited by Tom W.G. van der Meer and Sonja Zmerli, 1–15. Cheltenham: Edward Elgar.

Wagner, Alexander F., Friedrich Schneider, and Martin Halla. 2009. "The Quality of Institutions and Satisfaction with Democracy in Western Europe—A Panel Analysis." *European Journal of Political Economy* 25 (1): 30–41.

Wheatherford, M. Stephen. 1992. "Measuring Political Legitimacy." *American Political Science Review* 86 (1): 149–66.

CHAPTER 12

....

TRUST, POPULISM, AND THE QUALITY OF GOVERNMENT

....

PHILIP KEEFER, CARLOS SCARTASCINI, AND RAZVAN VLAICU

INTRODUCTION

....

WHY does electoral competition often fail to drive societies inexorably towards higher quality government?* Why do voters sometimes opt for populist politicians who advocate ultimately disastrous policies? This chapter reviews recent research on the relationship between social and political trust, on the one hand, and the quality of government and populism, on the other. It identifies a new channel through which social trust might affect both the quality of government and preferences for populism, operating through the impact of social trust on collective action by voters. Voters who cannot act collectively can less credibly threaten to punish politicians who renege on their commitments, reducing politician incentives to pursue sustainable, welfare-improving economic policies and to preserve institutions that yield impartial, credible, and sustainable policies. Low trust among voters is a basic obstacle to collective action.

A rich literature has linked politicians' inability to make credible commitments to both populism (Alesina 1987) and the quality of government (e.g. Keefer and Vlaicu 2008, Keefer and Vlaicu 2017). Other work points to the ability of voters to act collectively, for example through political parties, as key to their ability to hold politicians to account for breaking their promises (e.g. Aldrich 1995, Knack 2002). Voter mistrust in politicians implies that politicians' ability to make credible pre-electoral commitments is weak. Low voter trust in each other is an even more fundamental concern: if voters do not trust fellow voters to act with them to hold politicians accountable, politicians have less reason to fear the electoral consequences of breaking their promises, and more generally of welfare-reducing policy and institutional choices.

* The findings and interpretations in this paper are those of the authors and do not necessarily reflect the views of the Inter-American Development Bank or the governments it represents.

New survey evidence from Latin America provides support for this novel theoretical mechanism centered on voter trust and politician commitment. The Latin American data indicate a strong correlation between low trust and preferences for policies associated with low quality and populist governments. The evidence yields a significant correlation between various dimensions of voter trust and voter support for policies associated with high-quality government. An implication of this evidence is that low social and political trust reduce voter incentives to support candidates who promise high-quality government and increases their incentives to support populist candidates.

The first section reviews the central notions of trust, populism, and quality of government, and touches on issues of measurement that challenge empirical research on these issues. The second section summarizes the main theoretical arguments linking social trust to quality of government and political trust to populism. It then advances a novel theoretical mechanism that elucidates why voters may tolerate suboptimal policies and institutions. The third section reviews empirical work to date on the causal effect of social trust on government quality and of political trust on populism. It argues that micro-level evidence on mechanisms is necessary to better interpret the accumulating evidence from a mostly reduced-form literature. The fourth section examines individual-level evidence in support of the novel argument that links voter trust to voter preferences for populist policies such as targeted transfer payments and low public investment in public safety and education.

Trust: Concepts and Measurement

Individuals trust others when they believe that others will not act opportunistically to take advantage of them. Trust therefore involves the risk of loss, which can be material, psychological or relational. However, trust enables individuals to develop relationships and cooperate with other individuals to exchange goods and information and to achieve common goals. Beliefs about others' honesty, fairness, or benevolence are crucial to the emergence of trust: if individuals believe that others are not trustworthy, trust is difficult to sustain. These beliefs can be personality traits formed early in life. They can also be developed over time through repeated interactions with others: a trusting individual is more likely to act in a trustworthy manner as they are expecting others to reciprocate; experience with trustworthy behavior therefore also encourages trust.

Trust has long been studied in psychology and philosophy as a key variable shaping human behavior and interactions. Taking advantage of the increasing availability of quantitative data, economics and political science have more recently embraced the study of trust to identify its beneficial effects for the economy and society more generally. Trust is a key component of social capital, a community-level variable shown to associate strongly with good democratic governance (Putnam 1993) and sustained economic growth (Knack and Keefer 1997).

Social scientists have distinguished between generalized interpersonal trust, also described as social trust, and particularized interpersonal trust; and between out-group trust and in-group trust. Social trust reflects the societal propensity for a member of a society to trust strangers. Particularized interpersonal trust captures trust in specific and known persons. Out-group trust refers to trust in persons outside the social group, and in-group trust as trust in persons belonging to one's social or professional circle.

Trust in organizations—in political parties, legislatures, firms, the Church, the military, or the police, for example—is also key. Can individuals trust the commitments that organizations make to them? This is distinct from social trust to the extent that the internal norms of organizations lead their members to act differently inside compared to outside of the organization. Organizations can expend resources, or not, to select as members the most trustworthy members of society or to instill norms of trustworthiness; they can reward, or not, member behavior that enhances individuals' trust in the organization.

The World Values Survey (WVS) first began collecting data on social and political trust in the early 1980s. Other major survey organizations (e.g., the Pew Research Center and Latinobarómetro) have also collected time series data on social and political trust from multiple countries. The typical variable is a categorical discrete-scale measure of self-reported degree of trust in others (social trust), or in political institutions such as political parties, congress, or president (political trust).[1]

Experimental measures of interpersonal trust address the issue that survey respondents may give answers to trust questions that do not correspond to their actual beliefs and behavior. Laboratory experiments offer monetary rewards that incentivize participants to act as they would outside of the lab. Fortunately, experimental measures of trust, based on trust, investment or public good games, correlate well with survey-based measures of interpersonal trust (Naef and Schupp 2009), validating the use of survey-derived measures of social trust. Survey-based measures of political trust, however, have yet to be backed by experimental counterparts.

QUALITY OF GOVERNMENT AND POPULISM: CONCEPTS AND MEASUREMENT

In contrast to trust, there is less agreement about how to define the quality of government and populism. Some apply economic criteria and focus on the policies that governments pursue to determine the quality of government and the presence of populism. Others use institutional and political criteria more focused on the processes through which public policies are adopted. We suggest in this section that a close relationship exists between the economic and institutional definitions of each, and between low-quality government and populism. Given the conceptual proximity that we posit, it is reasonable to consider common origins for them. We turn to one such origin, mistrust, in the next section.

From an economic perspective, the quality of government is best measured by the degree to which government decision making yields policies that increase social welfare (see La Porta, et al. 1999). To the extent that government provides valuable public goods (from

---

[1] A standard survey question for measuring social trust is: "In general, do you think that most people can be trusted? (or you can never be too careful when dealing with people)." For political trust, a standard formulation is: "How much confidence do you have in the following [organizations, institutions, groups of people]?"

highways to security), uses regulation to solve serious market failures (from pollution to product safety), and efficiently redistributes income to meet society's demands for egalitarianism, the economic assessment of the quality of government is higher.

A persuasive institutional yardstick for measuring government quality is the degree to which government impartially applies the law without taking "into consideration anything about the citizen/case that is not beforehand stipulated in the policy or law" (Rothstein and Teorell 2008, 170). Corruption, for example, violates the principle of impartiality (Rothstein 2011). Governments *impartially* adopt new laws when they do not vary the procedures they use to approve those laws depending on the citizens who are affected by them or the cases that have prompted them. For example, events that trigger outrage or fear are not used to justify shortcuts in the procedures used to adopt new laws.

Economic and institutional definitions of the quality of government are related, since impartiality has all the characteristics of a public good. The benefits of impartiality, ranging from predictability to the diffusion of norms of fairness across a society, are non-rivalrous. They extend to all citizens and do not decline with the number of citizens who enjoy them. The benefits are also non-excludable: governments cease to act impartially when they deny the benefits of impartiality to some citizens. Hence, in societies in which citizens cannot easily persuade governments to provide public goods, they also find it difficult to ensure impartial government.

Most measures of governance are related to, but do not directly capture the notion of impartiality that is at the center of the quality of government literature. The World Bank Worldwide Governance Indicators (WGI) (Kaufmann, Kraay, and Mastruzzi 2003) is a country-level database that reports six indices, namely "voice and accountability," "government effectiveness," "the rule of law," "political stability," "regulatory quality," and "control of corruption." These do not directly capture the notion of "impartiality." Nevertheless, partial governments are likely to receive lower scores on measures of effectiveness and the rule of law. Partial governments are also less likely to protect property rights (e.g. as measured in an index of legal quality by Gwartney and Lawson 2007).

Weak property rights are only one possible manifestation of partial government. So also is corruption, which usually entails the purchase of favorable treatment – that is, of partiality. The World Bank control of corruption index mentioned above, or the Corruption Perceptions Index (CPI) developed by Transparency International, are based on the perceptions of experts and businesspeople.

The Quality of Government Institute in Gothenburg measures impartiality directly.[2] The QoG Expert Survey asks 1,294 experts who are knowledgeable about 159 countries to rate countries on such key dimensions as politicization, professionalization, openness and impartiality. The European Quality of Government Index is constructed from a 24-country survey of European citizens that elicits information about their experiences and perceptions regarding partiality in public sector organizations.

As with the quality of government, economic and institutional views yield two definitions of populism. In this case, however, the two definitions have given rise to two almost entirely independent bodies of research; this chapter suggests greater substantive overlaps than this bifurcation would suggest.

---

[2] https://qog.pol.gu.se/data

Economic analyses of populism emphasize the adoption of expansive fiscal and credit policies and an over-valued currency meant to accelerate economic growth and redistribute income. Populists achieve these goals in the short run but, in the end, real wages plummet as inflation surges, leaving the economic system on the verge of collapse and most of the beneficiaries of the previous expansion worse off than they were before (Dornbusch and Edwards 1991, 7). Despite evidence in their own countries' histories of the inevitability of this sad denouement, voters elect populist candidates.[3]

Countries where politicians have pursued populist economic policies necessarily score poorly according to the economic yardstick of the quality of government. The economic policies associated with each ultimately reduce the welfare of citizens. More fundamentally, both are associated with inadequate public good provision. The policy failures of populist governments include the deterioration of public good provision to finance transfers to favored constituencies; and private sector collapse, as a consequence of the distortionary tax and regulatory policies that they adopt to support those constituencies when more efficient sources of fiscal revenue are exhausted.

The research of political scientists and sociologists focuses on the institutional dimensions of populism. Populist politicians make personalistic (rather than partisan) appeals to voters, dismantle existing intermediary institutions (political parties or labor unions), and establish their own, personally controlled institutions (Kaufman and Stallings 1991; Weyland 1999; Panizza 2005). In its 1944 manifesto, the Liberal Party of Ecuador emphasized the institutional dimension of populism when it contrasted its own principles with those of José María Velasco Ibarra, a frequent, successful candidate for president who did not have a formal party organization:

> The times are not made for idolatry. They cannot be because the time for providential men has gone away. The true statesman who embodies principles, personifies collective aspirations and synthesizes ideals has replaced the demagogue and the caudillo. The organization of political parties as orienting forces of the political life of nations implies the extinction of old-fashioned personalistic forms of government (quoted in Panizza 2005, 19).

Populist leaders attempt to undermine the influence of institutions that aggregate individual demands and to identify themselves as the authentic and sole interpreters of popular will. This is, for example, how Panizza interprets the declaration by Hugo Chávez that "the people [are] the only and the true owners of their sovereignty" (Panizza 2005, 4). In defining the popular will, populist parties and politicians distinguish the people from the elite (see contributions by De Cleen and others in Kaltwasser, et al. 2017) and, by identifying the elite with the institutions of a country, they gain support for an agenda that entails dismantling or displacing those institutions.

---

[3] Other economic definitions of populism emphasize only two elements: a distributional conflict over economic resources, and a group that claims privileged access to this resource based on the assertion that it represents society (Williamson and O'Rourke 2001; Rodrik 2018a). This definition appears to center on the lack of "sustainable" redistribution, as opposed to the downward spiral towards crisis emphasized by Dornbusch and Edwards. However, research discussed below (e.g. Alesina 1987) emphasizes the dynamic consequences of group competition for state resources and the incentives that it creates for groups, once in power, to pursue unsustainable policies.

The institutional definition of populism parallels the institutional measure of the quality of government. Leaders who are not bound by institutions are free to execute government policies unconstrained by law. Populist government is necessarily partial: it can exercise authority taking account of any considerations it chooses, regardless of whether these are established by law. One manifestation of partiality emerges when populist politicians also make nationalist appeals, typically with the idea of identifying and rewarding a national identity that some in the country exhibit, at the expense of those who do not.

Given the nuances and variations in the institutional and political definitions of populism, it is not surprising that empirical measures are either somewhat opaque or partial, often emphasizing parties that are nationalist (in the sense of anti-foreigner) and anti-elite. Van Kessel (2015) presents one of the most comprehensive efforts to classify European populist parties, covering the period 2000–13. Rodrik (2018b) constructs another list of populist parties for a global sample of countries spanning the period 1960–2013. He codes as populist those parties that pursued an electoral strategy stressing cleavages between an in-group and an out-group and where this strategy was recognized in the academic literature or in the press. Both distinguish between left and right variants of populism.[4]

Whether the quality of government and populism are viewed economically or institutionally, the question therefore arises, why would a rational voter prefer a candidate who lowers the quality of government or embraces populism? Certainly, some voters benefit from partiality: they belong to the group targeted for benefits, who will receive privileged access to otherwise poor public services, and who will not be victims of government decisions that bypass institutional restraints. However, the historical and economic record yield ample evidence that the median voter, and even many voters who initially benefit from partiality, are ultimately worse off under such governments. Nevertheless, these same voters often prefer politicians who promise particularistic benefits and express disregard for institutional constraints on their authority.

THEORETICAL MECHANISMS LINKING TRUST TO GOVERNMENT QUALITY AND POPULISM

Although it would be tempting to invoke voter ignorance or irrationality to explain voter support for politicians who make them worse off, scholars who have investigated populism have largely discarded this facile explanation (e.g. Remmer 2012). Survey data indicate *positive* correlations between citizen satisfaction with democracy, the state of the economy, and support for leftist-populist presidents. Variation in voter trust across countries, on the other hand, can account for their tolerance of low-quality government and support for populism. This section briefly reviews research that has explored different dimensions of the relationship among these various phenomena. It then proposes a novel pathway from low social trust to low political trust to both low quality of government and populism.

---

[4] In all, he identifies 33 populist parties in Europe and Latin America. The underlying data on parties and elections is from the Global Elections Database (GED) and the Constituency-Level Elections Archive (CLEA).

Political Trust, the Quality of Government, and Populism

The link from low political trust to support for populism is a well-established proposition. Populist parties typically emerge to cater to popular dissatisfaction with the workings of the current political system. At the core of populist rhetoric is an anti-establishment message where the populists identify with the concerns of ordinary people and vow to take on the corrupt and elitist establishment.[5] Hence, political mistrust—voters' belief that established political actors will take advantage of them—should promote support for populism (Van Kessel 2015).

An equally well-established literature documents that experiences with low quality government reduce political trust. Rothstein (2009) argues that negative experiences with government and government services erode political trust. In contrast, perceptions that political institutions promote integrity and fairness increase political trust (Levi and Stoker 2000; Grimes 2016). These conclusions mirror the earlier arguments of Rawls (1971) that perceptions of fairness are grounded in individuals' experiences with procedural and distributive justice. Left open in this work is the question of why the quality of government is low in the first place, an issue we return to below.

Another body of research ties populism to social polarization and fractionalization. Trust, though not explicitly discussed in this work, plays a key role. For example, Kaufman and Stallings (1991, 30) argue that in polarized political settings, political competitors are caught in a prisoner's dilemma in which the pursuit of unsustainable policies is the dominant strategy no matter who is in office. Of course, the prisoner's dilemma would be solved if competitors could trust each other. Since they cannot, incumbents are more likely to pursue winner-take-all policies. In a series of articles, Alesina and co-authors formally model the logic underlying this argument. Parties cannot trust commitments that the other parties make regarding the future treatment of their social groups when the parties representing the groups are not in power. Hence, incumbents seek to ensure the welfare of their social group into the future by increasing borrowing and distributing the proceeds to their social groups. The winner not only takes all the resources currently available for redistribution, but also redistributes future resources (see, e.g. Alesina 1987; Alesina and Tabellini 1990). Hence, competition between polarized parties that do not trust each other generates large deficits that are contrary to the interests of all of them.

Alesina, Campante, and Tabellini (2008) establish an explicit link between pro-cyclical fiscal policy, a variant of populist macroeconomic policy in which governments raise spending in good times and cut it in bad times—exactly the opposite of welfare-optimizing fiscal policy, and the quality of government. Voters, confronted with corrupt politicians, demand that spending, e.g., on transfers to them, rise in good times to prevent politicians from converting the wealth of new resources into rents.[6] Hence, one type of populist macroeconomic policy is more common in corrupt countries.

---

[5] Of course, for populism to prevail, candidates need to emerge or parties need to form that supply a populist agenda that taps into voter discontent and mistrust. This mechanism may be more likely to be activated particularly in periods of increased economic and cultural anxiety, e.g., due to spreading globalization and technological change.

[6] Acemoglu, Egorov, and Sonin (2013) also link government quality and (left-wing) populism. Using a formal model, they argue that when voters fear that politicians might become beholden to the rich

Social Trust, the Quality of Government, and Populism

Social trust appears to underlie the relationships among political trust, the quality of government and populism documented in the literature. Individual-level data certainly reveal a strong link between social (interpersonal) trust and perceptions of organizational, institutional, or societal fairness (Begue 2002; Van Den Bos 2001). You (2018) summarizes evidence arguing that social trust deters corruption, but that evidence does not rule out the reverse hypothesis, that corrupt government reduces social trust.

Two basic mechanisms can explain why social trust might engender higher quality government. One has to do with the supply of trustworthy public officials in charge of implementing public policies. When social trust is high, public officials incur a larger intrinsic cost from treating citizens badly, regardless of citizen demand for quality government. In Bjørnskov (2010), a principal (politician), oversees the activities of an agent (bureaucrat) whose role is to provide a service for a client (citizen, firm). The agent can choose to provide special treatment to the client in exchange for an illegal bribe rather than provide normal treatment in exchange for the legal service fee set by the principal. A higher level of social trust increases the bribe needed to sway the agent into providing special treatment and thus reduces the incidence of these illegal transactions. This effect operates independently of any political incentives of the principal to be responsive to voters.

The supply-side channel linking social trust to good government reflects the Weberian notion of the "ideal bureaucrat" whose trustworthiness is key to improving the implementation of policies handed down from the political principals. This feature of quality government is captured in the data sources mentioned earlier (e.g., by indicators in the Quality of Government databases or by the WGI component of "government effectiveness").

The supply side argument explains why high social trust can lead to better government, but not necessarily why it makes populism less likely. Nor does it explain why voters cannot demand high-quality government when social trust is low. We identify a second, demand-side mechanism that links social trust to good government through electoral accountability. It also explains how low social trust can spur the rise of populism.

This novel demand-side mechanism begins with the basic observation that the economic and institutional failures of low-quality government and populist parties impose costs on most voters. Civic action to contain them is therefore a public good: the group is better off if every member contributes to the public good (collective action), but every member of the group has an incentive to free ride on the efforts of the others. If voters were able to act collectively, as Keefer (2015) explains, they could credibly threaten to expel from office the incumbents responsible for reducing the quality of government, deterring this behavior. In many democratic settings, however, voters lack the capacity to act collectively.

Social trust is central to this capacity: if voters cannot trust each other to incur the personal costs of contributing to the collective good of monitoring and expelling the poorly

---

right-wing elite, adopting policies lowering general welfare, honest politicians signal that they are not aligned to the right-wing elite by choosing policies to the left of the median voter.

performing incumbent, no voter has an incentive to do so.[7] Political parties can mitigate this problem, but only if they are sufficiently organized to impose sanctions on free riders (for example, social ostracism or expulsion from the party). Again, in many democracies, parties are not capable of imposing sanctions. When they are, the sanctions are often aimed at ensuring continuing party access to resources rather than improving the quality of government.

In the absence of sanctions for free-riding, collective action might still occur. Intrinsic motivation—solidarity with other citizens, outrage, patriotism—could persuade citizens to overcome the individual costs of voting and of supporting better government. In environments where low trust among voters prevails, such intrinsic incentives are weaker.

Of course, incumbents understand the collective action challenges that voters confront and pursue strategies to make free riding more attractive. Clientelism is one such strategy. By offering clientelist benefits to individuals and narrow groups of voters in exchange for their votes, free riding becomes more attractive to them. This precipitates a corresponding decline in their willingness to participate in collective action on behalf of candidates who promise to improve the quality of government.[8] High social trust gives voters greater confidence that other voters will not free ride.

Low social trust and its deleterious effects on voters' collective action mean that voters cannot credibly threaten to punish politicians who renege on their commitments.[9] This, in turn, means that politicians can less easily make credible commitments. Prior research has shown that where the credibility of politicians' commitment is low, the quality of government falls. Politicians engage in targeted transfers and rent extraction (Keefer and Vlaicu 2008). Vote-buying is high and public good provision is low (Keefer and Vlaicu 2017). The rule of law, related to the threat of partiality and the institutional dimensions of the quality of government, is weaker in younger democracies where political credibility is low (Keefer 2007). But younger democracies are precisely where organizations such as political parties are least likely to be sufficiently institutionalized to help overcome voters' collective action challenges.

In sum, low social trust and the inability of voters to act collectively lead to an electoral equilibrium in which political trust is low, politicians renege on (or do not make) electoral promises, voters therefore demand and politicians pursue suboptimal policies that yield low quality government (echoing an argument in Keefer, Scartascini, and Vlaicu 2020).

Populism is a natural corollary of this equilibrium. Low political trust provides an opportunity for political entrepreneurs to appeal to voters with anti-establishment rhetoric.

---

[7] You (2018) observes that resisting corruption requires collective action that social trust facilitates. However, the literature he summarizes is unclear about the exact nature of the collective action that citizens must undertake to reduce corruption. The argument here aims to fill this gap.

[8] For two reasons, aggregate benefits to voters from clientelist payoffs are lower than the benefits they would have received in the form of public goods from high-quality government. First, low-quality and populist governments tend to extract more private rents, reducing the resources available for spending on citizens. Second, by definition, public goods deliver greater welfare to voters, on average, than the same resources transferred in the form of particularistic payoffs.

[9] This argument does not exclude the possibility of social media-fueled demonstrations and bursts of public dismay at corruption revelations, all of which we have seen in Eastern Europe, the Middle East, and Latin America. Sustained change requires that these movements translate into more organized political movements. Low social trust impedes this transition.

Voters understand that if electoral dynamics yield only mediocre benefits from government, their best hope is to identify politicians whose sense of personal well-being is most likely to be linked with their own. The appeals of those politicians will be populist: they know the interests of voters and they are best able to serve them if institutional arrangements that constrain them are removed. But voters, seeing such politicians as their best chance of receiving benefits from government, have no reason to resist their efforts to free themselves from the constraints of law and institutions, shifting authority for public policy choices to themselves.

Of course, the best outcome would be that voters converge on the politician whose intrinsic interests lie in serving *all* of them, a search for a "principled agent" detailed in Besley (2006). But this outcome is subject to the same collective action obstacles as the effort to expel the low-performing incumbent. On the one hand, voters can more reliably identify politicians who place their own interests above those of other voters. On the other hand, the same lack of trust among voters that impedes them from acting collectively to expel nonperforming incumbents also affects their ability to collectively select politicians who are intrinsically motivated to serve the broad public interest.

The supply-side argument is rooted in the intrinsic incentives of government officials—the moral costs they incur in a high trust society when they treat citizens badly. The demand-side focuses on the extrinsic incentives of politicians: voters who can act collectively can offer politicians a tangible reward, reelection. However, intrinsic voter incentives can also play a role on the demand side. High social trust leads to a citizenry with a strong sense of civic-mindedness (Putnam 2001). These voters have intrinsic incentives to participate in the political process by acquiring information and turning out to vote, offsetting extrinsic incentives to free ride.

Empirical Evidence Linking Trust to Government Quality and Populism

Since Putnam's (1993) seminal contribution linking social trust to political corruption in Italy, empirical research has sought to find evidence of a causal effect of social trust on government quality as well as evidence for the causal mechanisms between the two. An early influential study was La Porta et al. (1997) using trust data from the World Values Survey, who found cross-national evidence of a positive effect of social trust on corruption control and bureaucratic quality, controlling for GNP per capita. Uslaner (2004) extended this analysis to a panel of countries observed over the 1980s and 1990s, and found a similar beneficial effect of social trust on reducing corruption, as measured by the Transparency International's CPI.

Methodologically, attempts at establishing causality remain a challenge in this line of inquiry. It is difficult to isolate credible exogenous variation in trust that would eliminate the influence of confounders and reverse causality. Instrumental variables for social trust have been proposed, e.g., monarchy, cold winters (Bjørnskov 2010), or obsolete historical borders (Becker et. al 2016), but concerns may still linger about the validity of what are ultimately untestable exclusion restrictions.

Other studies exploit the time variation in the data to establish causality. Graeff and Svendsen (2013) use a Granger causality model and find stronger support for the hypothesis that social trust reduces corruption than the other way around. Using the same standard data sources, Robbins (2012) estimated a structural model with instrumental variables to test for a reciprocal relationship between institutional quality and generalized trust. His results indicate that generalized trust and institutional quality exhibit a positive reciprocal relationship, but again finds that the stronger connection is from generalized trust to institutional quality. However, studies relying on time series variation in longitudinal data suffer from the short time spans in the data which make it difficult to separate real changes from measurement error that can lead to spurious correlation. Several additional decades of data may be needed to produce convincing causal evidence using panel data.

In the meantime, a promising empirical direction is to explore micro-level evidence for the possible mechanisms through which social trust leads to high-quality government. Uslaner (2008) uses individual-level data from Romania and Estonia to show that less trusting individuals are more likely to perceive high corruption in the public sector. These data cannot, however, test whether these individuals are more willing to report or resist corruption. This further causal link remains to be empirically tested.

Bjørnskov (2010) finds that the quality of governance is more strongly associated with social trust when electoral competition is intense, which can be interpreted as a demand-side mechanism where voters in high-trust environments use their vote to demand better policies. However, the negative association of corruption with social trust does not depend on the competitiveness of elections, suggesting that the supply-side mechanism is also at work: the supply of trustworthy public officials is higher in high-trust polities.

Empirical research on the link between quality of government and populism remains largely correlational. Some studies find evidence for a reduced-form relationship between low government quality and populism. Using national-level data from 31 countries, Van Kessel (2015) concludes that high levels of perceived corruption, measured by the CPI, are associated with better electoral performance of populist parties. This effect is stronger in periods of high nativism and economic hardship. The populist parties identified in Agerberg (2017) are known more for their nationalist and/or anti-elitist appeals (e.g. the National Front in France or the Five Star Movement in Italy). He finds a high correlation at the individual level with perceptions of low quality of government and support for these parties. Aggregating at the regional level, the vote share of populist parties is higher in regions where citizens report low quality of government. His data and methodology allow him to rule out other explanations for the success of populist parties, such as the electoral system or the unemployment rate.[10]

In terms of mechanisms, several studies have found evidence that low government quality is associated with a decline in political trust (e.g. Kumlin 2004; Dahlberg and Holmberg 2014) and that a decline in political trust is associated with populist support (e.g. Denmark and Bowler 2002 for New Zealand and Australia; Hooghe, Marien, and Pauwels 2011 for Belgium). These studies define political trust in terms of generalized support for the institutions of the political system, as opposed to particularized distrust in specific partisan groups. This suggests that the results are not driven by voter disaffection for specific political parties or leaders, but by a more fundamental lack of trust in established political institutions.

---

[10] This data was compiled at the Quality of Government (QoG) Institute of the University of Gothenburg.

Trust plays a role in the literature on polarization and the quality of government, but the specific type of trust is not easy to identify. Reduced-form evidence indicates that polarization (ethnic or economic) yields lower quality government. Keefer and Knack (2002) conclude that where polarization, including inequality, is high, property rights are less secure and growth is lower. Alesina, Baqir, and Easterly (1999) further show that polarization (here defined in terms of ethnic division) reduces public good provision. One interpretation of these results is that polarized environments reduce political trust, suppressing political incentives to pursue policies that raise the quality of government. Another is that in environments characterized by social mistrust, politicians can exacerbate benign social divisions to further reduce the degree to which voters are willing to hold them accountable for the low quality of their policies.

The two are difficult to disentangle. We can only say with some certainty that an association between mistrust and polarization exists. Bjørnskov (2008) identifies a relationship between inequality, political (though not ethnic) diversity, and social trust. Keefer and Knack (2002) observe, however, that polarization and fractionalization are not the same—highly fractionalized societies, characterized by many small ethnic groups, need not be polarized. Consistent with this, Uslaner (2010) shows that generalized trust is lower in societies with large minority groups living apart from majority groups.

Prior research assumes that these groups are well organized and behave monolithically (e.g. Alesina 1987). Keefer (2015) argues, however, that the incentives of politicians to engage in destructive policies, including unsustainable policymaking, are greatest precisely when their voters cannot act collectively to discipline them—as when social trust is low or when political parties *cannot* provide a mechanism for citizens to discipline party leaders or the heads of social movements. The inability of voters—even of the same ethnic group—to act collectively means that politicians cannot easily make credible commitments to them. They respond to their inability to make credible commitments even to members of their own social groups by raising the specter of winner-take-all behavior by other social groups.

Similarly, the high levels of corruption that Alesina, Campante, and Tabellini (2008) associate with populist fiscal policies, or the insecure property rights that Keefer and Knack (2002) link to polarization, are both more likely to emerge in countries where citizens find it most difficult to hold political leaders accountable for their actions. These are linked to the weakness of collective action and political parties, not to their strength. Keefer (2007) shows that corruption is significantly higher in younger compared to older democracies, and Cruz and Keefer (2015) demonstrate that public sector reforms—the reforms that are most directly intended to combat corruption—are least likely to succeed where political parties are weakest.

The apparent weakness of institutions, including political parties, in countries with low quality government and a proclivity to populism suggests that the most salient problem of trust and credible commitment may not be the one that divides social groups, but the one that separates citizens from each other and from their elected representatives. In these settings, not only is it difficult for polarized elites to make credible agreements with each other, the focus of research on populism, it is also difficult for them to commit to provide welfare-enhancing policies to voters.

This difficulty explains why the personalization of political appeals by populist politicians plays such a significant role in many analyses of populism. Absent institutional guarantees that promises will be fulfilled, politicians use personality to convince voters that their interests and those of their base are entirely aligned—that for the politician to cheat them or deprive them of promised benefits would hurt the politician as much as it would hurt them.

TRUST AND POLICY PREFERENCES: WHAT DO MICRO DATA REVEAL?

Knack (2002) was the first to link trust to voter behavior, finding that voter turnout is negatively correlated with social trust. Doyle (2011) uses data from 48 presidential elections in 18 Latin American countries to show that where public trust in political institutions is low, voters are attracted to candidates who portray themselves as radical "outsiders", crusading against the established political order (corresponding, therefore, to the "anti-elite" and "anti-institutional" definition of populism). Keefer, Scartascini and Vlaicu (2018; 2019; 2020) fill the gap that remains: the interaction of trust and populism with the quality of government.

They use data from the 2017 survey of seven Latin American countries undertaken by the Inter-American Development Bank (IDB) in collaboration with the Latin American Public Opinion Project (LAPOP).[11] They identify links between specific types of trust and specific public policies, showing an association of low voter trust with weak support for taxes to pay for public goods (Keefer, Scartascini, and Vlaicu, 2019) and between low trust and a policy bias characteristic of populist governments, to favor transfer payments at the expense of public investment.

Their research focuses on the economic definitions of populism and the quality of government. The public policy questions were designed to establish preferences for the *sustainable* provision of public goods or universalist policies, by linking them with the taxes to pay for them. Sustainability and public-ness are two crucial elements of high-quality government. Populist, low-quality governments promise broad benefits without the means to pay for them, leading to rationing and partiality; and they prefer the particularistic to the public.

However, the previous discussion makes the case that the economic and institutional or political definitions of the two concepts are tightly linked: neither anti-elitist, anti-institutionalist populists nor governments that exhibit significant partiality are likely to support the provision of institutionally demanding public goods and are more likely to prefer the selective distribution of private benefits to favored groups.

The survey also introduced innovations in the assessment of trust. In addition to standard trust questions, it elicited respondent beliefs about whether different types of people keep their promises, and whether they obey the laws and regulations of the country. Is it very common, somewhat common, not very common, or not at all common for politicians in general to keep their promises? Obey the law? Similarly, is it common for public officials, members of the respondents' families, businessmen, and union leaders to keep their promises or obey the law? Questions also focused on the credibility of specific policies. For example, respondents were asked how likely it was that, if the government implemented a

---

[11] The countries are Chile, Colombia, Honduras, México, Panamá, Perú, and Uruguay. The country samples are representative of residents of their capital cities.

policy of taxing the rich to redistribute to the poor, the revenue collected would actually reach the poor.

Table 12.1 summarizes the results of the analysis in Keefer, Scartascini, and Vlaicu (2019), omitting the many control variables in their regressions. One of the central questions in their analysis is whether social trust affects policy preferences through its influence on political trust. To examine this question, they first estimated the effects of social trust on political trust, and then asked how the estimated effect of political trust influenced preferences for sustainable policies.[12]

The first column examines the pathway from trust to support for sustainable redistribution. The natural measure of political trust in this policy setting is whether the respondent believes that tax revenues raised to finance redistribution will go to the poor: that is, whether government will fulfill its commitment to finance redistribution or divert the additional revenues to other uses. It could be that individuals who disapprove of redistribution are inclined to say that they do not trust the government to redistribute tax revenues to the poor. The specification responds to this concern by estimating a two-stage least squares model in which generalized trust is used as an instrument for confidence in the redistributive commitments of government. The component of political trust that is correlated with social trust is a highly significant predictor of support for sustainable redistribution.[13]

Public safety is the fundamental task of government and would be expected to suffer in countries with weak incentives to improve the quality of government or that encourage populist appeals to voters. If trust plays a role in shaping the electoral incentives of voters and their willingness to support or tolerate these adverse outcomes, an association should also exist between trust and support for tax-financed policing. The survey captures a dimension of trust that is most appropriate to the policy context: whether respondents believed politicians and government officials are likely to obey the law.

As in the redistribution analysis, generalized trust is used as an instrument for the proxy variable and is highly significant in the first stage regression. The substantive relationship between the two is compelling: voters who mistrust each other are less likely to believe that voters will act collectively to punish politicians who break the law; they are therefore less likely to believe that politicians will in fact obey the law. Once again, higher trust is significantly associated with support for more tax-financed resources for the police and judiciary.

Governments have significant discretion over how they use the substantial budgets allocated to education, particularly whether they use them to improve student learning rather that dissipate them in the form of rents for other actors in the system. Low quality and populist governments are more likely to permit dissipation. Hence, as with expenditures on security and redistribution, citizen trust in government should play a large role in whether citizens prefer higher taxes to fund the state provision of education or lower taxes to allow households to acquire education privately.

[12] That is, they used two-stage least squares, where the first stage regressed political trust on social trust and numerous controls, and the second stage regressed policy preferences on that component of political trust accounted for by social trust and numerous controls.
[13] The analysis in Yamamura (2014) also concludes that higher trust in government is associated with greater support for redistribution, but does not incorporate the sustainability dimension—the necessity of raising taxes to finance the policy—nor the relationship between generalized trust and trust in politicians.

Table 12.1 Trust and support for sustainable public policies

Dependent variable:	Support for tax-financed redistribution	Support for tax-financed police and judiciary	Support for tax-financed public education
TRUST: Believe that higher tax revenues will go to the poor	0.17** (0.020)		
TRUST: Believe that politicians obey the law		0.34*** (0.001)	
TRUST: Belief that politicians fulfill their promises			0.35*** (0.006)
Constant	1.67*** (0.000)	1.34*** (0.000)	0.81** (0.017)
Observations	4460	4399	4467

$^* p < 0.10,$ $^{**} p < 0.05,$ $^{***} p < 0.01$
Note: All estimates are based on two-stage least squares estimates, where social trust is an instrument for political trust. p-values in parentheses, based on standard errors clustered by area of the country in which the survey took place (28 primary strata). All estimations control for country-fixed effects. All estimations control for the following variables: gender, age of the respondent, last year of respondent education, household income and assets, whether the street in front of respondent's house is paved, the number of minor children (under 18) in the household, whether the respondent has health insurance, whether respondent has a retirement plan, whether household receives government assistance, whether interviewer regards respondent as politically informed, the patience score (discount rate) calculated from responses to discrete choice questions, and the gender of the enumerator.
Source: IDB-LAPOP 2017 survey and Keefer, Scartascini, and Vlaicu (2019).

The third column in Table 12.1 shows that another measure of trust, whether respondents believe politicians fulfill their promises (e.g., about how they will spend education budgets), is significantly associated with tax-financed increases in education spending. As before, only that component of this political trust variable that is correlated with social trust is used in the estimation: respondents who do not trust others also cannot rely on collective action by others to remove politicians who renege on their promises.

All results in Table 12.1 are robust to using alternative measures of political trust. In addition, they are significant even after controlling for the importance that respondents attach to the different problems. Controlling for whether respondents believe that aid to the poor, improving police and the courts, or better education are important for solving the country's most pressing problems does not weaken the connection between trust and preferences for sustainable public policies.

CONCLUSION

This systematic review of the literature on the quality of government and populism reveals fundamental but neglected similarities between two important phenomena, and between different, sometimes competing definitions of each of them. Each has an economic and institutional or political definition. However, the institutional and political characteristics of populism and low-quality government each give rise to government incentives to pursue unsustainable policies characterized by a heavy reliance on often unsustainable particularistic benefits at the expense of public goods. Partiality is a central characteristic of low-quality government, but it is also at the heart of populism: the institutions that populist rulers aim to supplant constitute the essential machinery for impartial government. Researchers frequently characterize populists as having a disdain for elites and institutions, but professionalism and coherent organization are necessary for impartial government and the efficient provision of public goods.

This review also presents a new argument that links social trust to these phenomena. Low social trust, by hindering citizen collective action, leads to the emergence of low-quality government and populism. When they cannot act collectively, they cannot punish politicians who break their promises and therefore cannot trust those politicians to keep their promises. New data from a 2017 survey of Latin Americans demonstrates how low social trust—citizens' low trust in each other—is a key obstacle to collective action; therefore strongly associated with low political trust; and, finally, that low political trust strongly affects support for policies that are incompatible with the quality of government and consistent with populism.

The review raises many questions for future research, especially related to the need for more evidence regarding the direct effects of social trust on voter collective action, the role of political parties in solving problems of trust, and the effects of political trust on support for democratic institutions, a central feature of definitions of the quality of government and populism. Documenting the mechanisms through which high social trust leads to greater support for institutions that ensure impartiality remains an important area for future research into the determinants of the quality of government.

REFERENCES

Acemoglu, Daron, Georgy Egorov, and Konstantin Sonin. 2013. "A Political Theory of Populism." *Quarterly Journal of Economics* 128 (2) (May): 771–805.

Aldrich, John H. 1995. *Why Parties? The Origin and Transformation of Political Parties in America*. Chicago: University of Chicago Press.

Alesina, Alberto. 1987. "Macroeconomic Policy in a Two-Party System as a Repeated Game." *Quarterly Journal of Economics* 102 (3): 651–78.

Alesina, Alberto, Reza Baqir, and William Easterly. 1999. "Public Goods and Ethnic Divisions." *Quarterly Journal of Economics* 114 (4): 1243–84.

Alesina, Alberto, Filipe R. Campante, and Guido Tabellini. 2008. "Why is Fiscal Policy often Procyclical?" *Journal of the European Economic Association* 6 (5): 1006–1036.

Alesina, Alberto, and Guido Tabellini. 1990. "A Positive Theory of Fiscal Deficits and Government Debt." *Review of Economic Studies* 57 (3): 403–14.

Agerberg, Mattias. 2017. "Failed Expectations: Quality of Government and Support for Populist Parties in Europe." *European Journal of Political Research* 56: 578–600.

Becker, Sascha O., Katrin Boeckh, Christa Hainz, and Ludger Woessmann. 2016. "The Empire is Dead, Long Live the Empire! Long-Run Persistence of Trust and Corruption in the Bureaucracy." *Economic Journal* 126 (590): 40–74.

Begue, Laurent. 2002. "Beliefs in Justice and Faith in People: Just World, Religiosity and Interpersonal Trust." *Personality and Individual Differences* 32: 375–82.

Besley, Timothy. 2006. *Principled Agents? The Political Economy of Good Government.* Oxford: Oxford University Press.

Bjørnskov, Christian. 2008. "Social Trust and Fractionalization: A Possible Reinterpretation." *European Sociological Review* 24 (3): 271–83.

Bjørnskov, Christian. 2010. "How Does Social Trust Lead to Better Governance? An Attempt to Separate Electoral and Bureaucratic Mechanisms." *Public Choice* 144: 323–46.

Cruz, Cesi, and Philip Keefer. 2015. "Political Parties, Clientelism and Bureaucratic Reform." *Comparative Political Studies* 48 (14): 1942–73.

Dahlberg, Stefan, and Soren Holmberg. 2014. "Democracy and Bureaucracy: How Their Quality Matters for Popular Satisfaction." *West European Politics* 37 (3): 515–37.

De Cleen, Benjamin. 2017. "Populism and Nationalism." In *Handbook of Populism*, edited by Cristóbal Rovira Kaltwasser, Paul Taggart, Paulina Ochoa Espejo, and Pierre Ostuguy, 342–62. Oxford: Oxford University Press.

Denemark, David, and Shaun Bowler. 2002. "Minor Parties and Protest Votes in Australia and New Zealand: Locating Populist Politics." *Electoral Studies* 21 (1): 47–67.

Dornbusch, Rudiger, and Sebastian Edwards, eds. 1991. *The Macroeconomics of Populism in Latin America.* Chicago: The University of Chicago Press.

Doyle, David. 2011. "The Legitimacy of Political Institutions: Explaining Contemporary Populism in Latin America." *Comparative Political Studies* 44 (11): 1447–73.

Graeff, Peter, and Gert T. Svendsen 2013. "Trust and Corruption: The Influence of Positive and Negative Social Capital on the Economic Development in the European Union." *Quality and Quantity* 47 (5): 2829–46.

Grimes, Marcia. 2016. "Organizing Consent: The Role of Procedural Fairness in Political Trust and Compliance." *European Journal of Political Research* 45 (2) (March): 285–315.

Gwartney, James, and Robert Lawson. 2007. *Economic Freedom of the World: 2007 Annual Report.* Vancouver: Fraser Institute.

Hooghe, Marc, Sofie Marien, and Teun Pauwels. 2011. Where Do Distrusting Voters Turn If There Is No Viable Exit or Voice Option? The Impact of Political Trust on Electoral Behaviour in the Belgian Regional Elections of June 2009." *Government and Opposition* 46 (2): 245–73.

Kaufman, Robert R., and Barbara Stallings. 1991. "The Political Economy of Latin American Populism". In *The Macroeconomics of Populism in Latin America*, edited by Rudiger Dornbusch and Sebastian Edwards. Chicago: University of Chicago Press.

Kaufmann, Daniel, Aart Kraay, and Massimo Mastruzzi. 2003. "Governance Matters III: Governance Indicators for 1996–2002." World Bank Policy Research Working Paper 3106.

Keefer, Philip. 2007. "Clientelism, Credibility and the Policy Choices of Young Democracies." *American Journal of Political Science* 51 (4) (October): 804–21.

Keefer, Philip. 2015. "Organizing for Prosperity: Collective Action, Political Parties and the Political Economy of Development." In *The Oxford Handbook of the Politics of Development*, edited by Carol Lancaster and Nicholas van de Walle, 431–57. New York: Oxford University Press.

Keefer, Philip, and Stephen Knack. 2002. "Polarization, Politics and Property Rights: Links Between Inequality and Growth." *Public Choice* 111 (1–2): 127–54.

Keefer, Philip, and Razvan Vlaicu. 2008. "Democracy, Credibility and Clientelism." *Journal of Law, Economics, & Organization* 24 (2) (October): 371–406.

Keefer, Philip and Razvan Vlaicu. 2017. "Vote Buying and Campaign Promises." *Journal of Comparative Economics* 45 (4) (December): 773–92.

Keefer, Philip, Carlos Scartascini, and Razvan Vlaicu. 2018. "Shortchanging the Future: The Short-Term Bias of Politics." In *Better Spending for Better Lives: How Latin America and the Caribbean Can Do More with Less*, edited by Alejandro Izquierdo, Carola Pessino, and Guillermo Vuletin, 325–58. Washington, DC: Inter-American Development Bank.

Keefer, Philip, Carlos Scartascini, and Razvan Vlaicu. 2019. "Social Trust and Electoral Populism: Explaining the Quality of Government." Working Paper, Inter-American Development Bank.

Keefer, Philip, Carlos Scartascini, and Razvan Vlaicu. 2020. "Voter Preferences, Electoral Promises, and the Composition of Public Spending ." Working Paper, Inter-American Development Bank.

Knack, Steven. 2002. "Social Capital and the Quality of Government: Evidence from the States." *American Journal of Political Science* 46 (4) (October): 772–85.

Knack, Steven and Philip Keefer. 1997. "Does Social Capital Have an Economic Payoff? A Cross-Country Investigation." *Quarterly Journal of Economics* 112 (4): 1251–88.

Kumlin, Staffan. 2004. *The Personal and the Political: How Personal Welfare State Experiences Affect Political Trust and Ideology*. Basingstoke: Palgrave Macmillan.

La Porta, Rafael, Florencio Lopez-de-Silanes, Andrei Shleifer, and Robert Vishny. 1997. Trust in Large Organizations." *American Economic Review: Papers and Proceedings* 87: 333–8.

La Porta, Rafael, Florencio Lopez-de-Silanes, Andrei Shleifer, and Robert Vishny. 1999. "The Quality of Government." *Journal of Law, Economics, & Organization* 15 (1) (April): 222–79.

Levi, Margaret, and Laura Stoker. 2000. "Political Trust and Trustworthiness." *Annual Review of Political Science* 3: 475–507.

Naef, Michael, and Jurgen Schupp. 2009. "Measuring Trust: Experiments and Surveys in Contrast and Combination." SOEP paper No. 167.

Panizza, Francisco, ed. 2005. *Populism and the Mirror of Democracy*. London: Verso.

Putnam, Robert. 1993. *Making Democracy Work: Civic Traditions in Modern Italy*. Princeton: Princeton University Press.

Putnam, Robert. 2001. "Social Capital: Measurement and Consequences." *Canadian Journal of Policy Research* 2 (Spring): 41–51.

Rawls, John. 1971. *A Theory of Justice*. Cambridge: Harvard University Press.

Remmer, Karen L. 2012. "The Rise of Leftist-Populist Governance in Latin America: The Roots of Electoral Change." *Comparative Political Studies* 45 (8): 947–72.

Robbins, Blaine G. 2012. "Institutional Quality and Generalized Trust: A Nonrecursive Causal Model." *Social Indicators Research* 107 (2): 235–58.

Rodrik, Dani. 2018a. "Is Populism Necessarily Bad Economics?" *American Economic Review: Papers and Proceedings* 108: 196–99.

Rodrik, Dani. 2018b. "Populism and the Economics of Globalization." *Journal of International Business Policy* 1 (1–2): 12–33.

Rothstein, Bo, and Jan Teorell. 2008. "What is Quality of Government? A Theory of Impartial Government Institutions." *Governance* 21 (2) (April): 156–90.

Rothstein, Bo. 2009. "Creating Political Legitimacy: Electoral Democracy Versus Quality of Government." *American Behavioral Scientist* 53 (3): 311–30.

Rothstein, Bo. 2011. *The Quality of Government: Corruption, Social Trust and Inequality in International Perspective*. Chicago, IL: University of Chicago Press.

Uslaner, Eric M. 2004. "Trust and Corruption." In *The New Institutional Economics of Corruption*, edited by J. G. Lambsdorff, M. Taube, and M. Schramm, 90–106. London: Routledge.

Uslaner, Eric M. 2008. *Corruption, Inequality, and the Rule of Law: The Bulging Pocket Makes the Easy Life.* New York: Cambridge University Press.

Uslaner, Eric M. 2010. "Segregation, Mistrust and Minorities." *Ethnicities* 10 (4): 415–34.

Van Den Bos, Kees. 2001. "Uncertainty Management: The Influence of Uncertainty Salience on Reactions to Perceived Procedural Fairness." *Journal of Personality and Social Psychology* 80 (6): 931–41.

Van Kessel, Stijn. 2015. *Populist parties in Europe: Agents of discontent?* Basingstoke: Palgrave Macmillan.

Weyland, Kurt. 1999. "Neoliberal Populism in Latin America and Eastern Europe." *Comparative Politics* 31 (4) (July): 379–401.

Williamson, Jeffrey and Kevin O'Rourke. 2001. *Globalization and History.* Cambridge: MIT Press.

Yamamura, Eiji. 2014. "Trust in Government and Its Effect on Preferences for Income Redistribution and Perceived Tax Burden." *Economics of Governance* 15 (1) (February): 71–100.

You, Jong-Sung. 2018. "Trust and Corruption." In *The Oxford Handbook of Social and Political Trustm*, edited by Eric M. Uslaner, 457–80. Oxford: Oxford University Press.

CHAPTER 13

....

SOCIAL ACCOUNTABILITY AND QUALITY OF GOVERNMENT
Effectiveness and Recursive Effects

....

FRIDA BORÄNG AND MARCIA GRIMES

INTRODUCTION

....

GOVERNMENT corruption is by now pinpointed to be a primary obstacle preventing basic services and infrastructure from coming to the benefit of marginalized populations throughout the world. The effectiveness of anticorruption reforms designed to strengthen horizontal accountability, often by increasing politicians' and/or top bureaucrats' ability to exercise oversight over public sector activities (Rose-Ackerman 1999), have proven underwhelming. Especially in settings plagued by corruption, such reforms have, even decades on, had little if any impact at all (Persson et al. 2013). As these reform failures have become evident, policy actors and scholars alike increasingly directed their focus towards anticorruption approaches based instead on strengthening social accountability, institutional arrangements to increase citizen involvement to reduce corruption, and improve the quality of public goods and services. Social accountability includes various initiatives that aim to increase citizen monitoring and voice (Fox 2015; Grandvoinnet et al. 2015; Malena and Forster 2004). A number of examples, with bewilderingly similar names, include citizen report cards, community scorecards, community monitoring, community oversight, social audits, citizen councils, participatory budgeting, and participatory planning, to name a few (for an overview, see Grandvoinnet et al. 2015).[1]

---

[1] A few words are in order about what we do not include in our review of social accountability. First, our focus is on local initiatives, and thus we do not discuss multi-stakeholder initiatives such as the Extractive Industries Transparency Initiative or the Construction Sector Transparency Initiative, which generally include representatives from government, civil society, and corporations, but are national or transnational

Participatory governance and civic engagement have strong normative appeal and are posited to increase the representativeness of government work and, above all, empower citizens to monitor and detect improprieties and sound fire alarms in the face of corruption, discrimination and favoritism, all stark departures from the principle of impartiality, and thus from quality of government (Johnston 2005; Paul 1992).

The idea of meeting government failures with social accountability reforms has indeed gained enormous traction in policy circles, with the World Bank as a leading actor. The World Bank Group's goals state explicitly that ending poverty and promoting shared prosperity includes "enhancing voice and participation of all segments of society in economic, social, and political spheres" (Manroth et al. 2014, 8) and the World Bank aims to make citizen engagement an integral part of its operations.

The enthusiasm for and subsequent proliferation of social accountability initiatives (SAIs) has prompted a groundswell of evaluative research to assess the extent to which they work, and the field has matured to a point that we now see a number of reviews of research on SAIs in specific sectors and areas such as health (Danhoundo et al. 2018), natural resource management (Mejía Acosta 2013), local development (Fox 2015), education (Westhorp et al. 2014); and of transparency and accountability initiatives in budget processes (Carlitz 2013; Joshi and Houtzager 2012; Kosack and Fung 2014). As this field has developed and uncovered mixed results, the evaluative question "Do they work?" has been replaced by questions about *under what conditions*, in *what respects*, and *through which mechanisms* they work (Grandvoinnet et al. 2015).

This chapter surveys the existing empirical and theoretical accounts of institutional arrangements designed to empower citizens to hold incumbents and government officials accountable. While SAIs have many goals, we focus in particular on the potential for such initiatives to improve QoG. In order to understand how SAIs may affect QoG it is necessary, we argue, to pay attention also to how QoG affects SAIs. Many before us have pointed to the Catch-22 that social accountability is less likely to succeed where corruption is more prevalent. The mechanism mostly suggested is that in high-corruption contexts, citizen complaints are not picked up and acted upon by authorities with investigative and sanctioning powers. To preview the main argument, we point out that the broader institutional environment can also affect participants themselves, and—since there can be no participation without participants—thus also participatory initiatives.

The approach we take is, first, to delineate various types of initiatives from the perspective of citizens and classify them based on the role for participants: What are the potential benefits, but also costs, of involvement? What individual level of interest, preferences, motivations but also local capacity for coordinated action do the initiatives presuppose? Based on this, what are potential weak spots of various types of initiatives? We then bring in insights from institutionalist research on how higher order institutions may affect citizens'

in scope (Brockmyer and Fox 2015). Second, while some authors include government transparency reforms under the social accountability umbrella, we see some channel for citizen voice as a necessary component for it to be called social accountability. Third, societal accountability, while terminologically similar, is different in that it refers to campaigns initiated by nonstate actors using whatever strategies (media campaigns, street protests, alliances with opposition politicians) and institutional mechanisms (ombudsman office complaints, lawsuits, elections) necessary to redress corruption (see della Porta and Mattoni this volume; Smulovitz & Peruzzotti 2000). Some authors consider these campaigns social accountability as they are citizen-led (Gaventa and McGee 2013) but they are here treated as distinct.

political attitudes and behavior—their expectations, beliefs, and demands of the participatory initiative, of the government, and even of their fellow citizens. In exploring this aspect, we identify both avenues for future research, but also possible ways to address the Catch-22.

The chapter first unpacks the theoretical foundations upon which social accountability rests in order to develop an analytical categorization of the different initiatives. We then delineate three main types of initiatives and survey the research on whether they serve to redress corruption. The chapter then takes stock of what contextual factors previous literature has pointed to as relevant to the success and failure of social accountability, and the final section then lays out the argument that government institutions can matter in ways previously overlooked.

THEORETICAL FOUNDATIONS

The 2004 World Development Report (Ahmad et al. 2003), highly influential in the social accountability discourse, makes the distinction between 'short' and 'long' routes of accountability. The long route—running through elections, elected politicians, bureaucratic oversight to service providers—was seen as ineffective in ensuring service provision to the poor. The report promotes social accountability as a means to put citizens in direct dialogue with service providers, shortening the accountability chain.

While improved service provision is the main motivation behind SAIs, reducing corruption is often a necessary component, if not the express aim of the processes. As Lodenstein et al. summarize:

> Depending on the perspective, the expected results of social accountability initiatives can vary, but include a reduction in corruption; better governance and policy design; enhanced voice, empowerment and citizenship of marginalized groups; responsiveness of service providers and policymakers to citizens' demands and, ultimately, the achievement of rights, health and developmental outcomes (2013, p 2).

Gaventa and McGee make explicit that better development outcomes will materialize because corruption and waste in government operations, seen as a root cause of poor government performance, will come to light and be redressed:

> In the development and aid context, the argument is that, through greater accountability, the leaky pipes of corruption and inefficiency will be repaired, aid and public spending will be channeled more effectively and development initiatives will produce greater and more visible results (2013, 4).

The genesis of ideas culminating in social accountability solutions far predate the 2004 World Development Report, however, and stem from two very distinct intellectual roots (Joshi 2013). Thinkers from both the left and right recognized the failure of governments to provide services for some populations, and the evident insufficiency of elections to correct the problems. While the two perspectives shared a recognition of state failure, they advanced SAIs for different reasons, with implications for how initiatives were ultimately structured and designed.

First, endorsement of SAIs can be traced to the larger agenda of structural reforms of the state and specifically New Public Management (NPM). The NPM agenda advocates the simulation of market forces as a means to improve government performance (Fukuyama and Recanatini, this volume). From the NPM perspective, social accountability allows citizens to provide customer feedback on public services, increasing so called "client power" (Grandvoinnet et al. 2015; Ahmad et al. 2003).

Individuals are from this perspective first and foremost viewed as consumers of services rather than citizens; focus is on individual action rather than collective action; and activities in the public arena serve as communicating (already existing) preferences (Baiocchi and Ganuza 2016; Carlitz 2013; Grandvoinnet et al. 2015; Joshi 2013). Information is a key component in any model of accountability, though even more so in SAIs that aim to introduce the logic of the market into public services. Such initiatives consequently primarily seek to reduce information deficits regarding service provider operations as well as client preferences and satisfaction, by channeling information and complaints about service delivery.

The empowerment perspective, attributed to the Left, emphasizes first and foremost the poor track record of many states to serve marginalized populations. From this perspective, social accountability is both a means to improve service provision but also to promote greater inclusion, ultimately deepening democracy (Avritzer 2009; Fox 2007; Fung and Wright 2003; Gaventa and McGee 2013; Pateman 2012).[2] This view acknowledges the shared interests of populations that have historically been poorly served by states, and sees acting collectively as a crucial means to secure better government services not only for participants personally but for marginalized communities at large. Proponents of SAIs from the empowerment perspective note that information and transparency about government performance and revenue flows is a necessary but far from sufficient ingredient for strengthening accountability (Fox 2007, 2015). Accessible avenues for participation are, from this view, essential. This approach thus emphasizes collective rather than individual action, and participation in accountability initiatives is seen as having intrinsic democratic value as well as being instrumental for better service provision (Grandvoinnet et al. 2015; Joshi 2013).

Common for both theoretical perspectives is that the micro-foundations of the implied theories of change are not always made explicit; it is not always clear what type of behavior is expected from participants and what these behaviors presuppose in terms of prior attitudes and beliefs. Implicitly, however, both approaches assume that citizens who lack access to high-quality public goods and services will prioritize improving those services over other ends (e.g. their own private economy), hold beliefs that positive change is possible (i.e. that they have the right to make demands and that service providers can and will respond appropriately), and are willing to invest effort into bringing about such change, even when the beneficiary of that change is the community as a collective.

As such, SAIs to a greater extent than other accountability mechanisms, such as elections, presuppose that citizens' will be willing to make significant investments of time and effort for the betterment of their community. In a general sense, citizens when engaging politically may be motivated by self-interest or alternatively by a concern for the broader public good, whether it be national or local. In research on voter behavior, these driving forces are denoted as pocketbook or sociotropic concerns, and both are considered equally valid bases for vote choice. In other words, electoral accountability is expected to function regardless of whether voting is driven by pocketbook or sociotropic concerns. When it comes to social accountability, as we will develop below, many initiatives are dependent on prosocial behavior by participants in order to function well.

---

[2] Normative arguments for social accountability build upon work on participatory and deliberative democracy (Pateman 1970; Gutmann and Thompson 1996; Fishkin 1997).

Paying explicit attention to what SAIs expect of participants brings to light that some initiatives may entail considerable costs to participants, and a full appreciation of these costs will help to assess which SAIs may be likely to realistically succeed, and which less so. A core argument of this chapter is that research on SAIs has overlooked the fact that the institutional environment may be a key determinant of participants' willingness to behave prosocially. Research on common pool resources shows that collaboration, i.e. opting for the prosocial strategy, is far from rare but is contingent on numerous factors such as the rules in place, rule enforcement systems, and the characteristics of other actors who would also need to choose prosocial behavior in order to secure the common resource (Ostrom 1990). Evidence exists that corrupt institutions depress citizens' willingness to engage politically (Bauhr and Grimes 2014; Chong et al. 2015), while government effectiveness tends to stimulate citizens' political engagement (Broms 2015; MacLean 2011), and even local collective action activity (Dell et al. 2018).

While some of these insights have been incorporated into analyses of social accountability, important lines of inquiry remain unexplored (see also Booth and Cammack 2013). The next section develops a typology of SAIs based on expectations of participants' efforts and incentives to participate, taking stock of findings and laying the foundation for the subsequent analysis.

TYPES OF SOCIAL ACCOUNTABILITY INITIATIVES AND THEIR IMPACT

Political accountability, according to Schedler (1999) includes both answerability—that is information disclosure and justification—and enforcement, i.e. "the capacity of accounting agencies to impose sanctions" (Schedler 1999, 14, cf. Bovens 2007). SAIs differ in terms of which part of the accountability chain they primarily address. We delineate three types of initiatives: 1) the first focus only on the informational aspect of accountability (as a necessary component in monitoring); 2) the second institutionalize answerability with designs that force officials or service providers to answer and justify actions; while 3) the third type go farther and devolve considerable authority to participatory bodies including tools to monitor, enforce and sanction. This also means that for each of these types, the role assigned to participants—and thus the potential costs and benefits for them—is different. This, in turn, entails that these types face different challenges. Below, we discuss these various types and their impact on QoG and service delivery.

Initiatives to address information asymmetries

Most SAIs rest on the foundations of principal–agent theory.[3] As information asymmetries between a principal and agent are often seen as the central obstacle of accountability, many

---

[3] This makes them less radically different from other anticorruption reforms than one might initially assume. Indeed, they have been subject to the same type of criticism as other anticorruption reforms based on the principal–agent framework, namely that they underestimate the challenges of collective action (Booth and Cammack 2013).

SAIs are designed specifically to facilitate the flow of information. While all models treat service providers as agents, the role of principal can be assigned to different types of actors, which has consequences for which information is seen as most important and to whom it should be provided. Some SAIs assign the role of principal to government officials, and thus are designed to gather and funnel upwards citizens' end-of-pipe experiences and observations regarding goods, services, support, infrastructure, wages, benefits, and fair (or not) treatment. These models seek to stimulate and increase the effectiveness of supply-side accountability. Other models instead treat citizens as principals, hoping to stimulate so-called demand-side accountability (Brinkerhoff and Wetterberg 2016; Dewachter et al. 2018; Gaventa and McGee 2013), and thus consist of providing citizens with performance information such as teacher absenteeism or children's learning outcomes. Such initiatives hope to prompt citizens to turn directly to service providers and demand answers or improvements.[4] Initiatives that mainly aim at reducing information asymmetries are normally dependent on the responsiveness of actors outside of the initiative.

Among those that aim to compile citizens' assessments, some mimic private sector efforts to gather customer feedback, ranging from minimalist exercises such as smiley-ratings (what Peixoto and Fox 2016 term "Yelp" mechanisms), to more involved efforts. Peixoto and Fox review the evidence on the use of 23 information and communication technology (ICT) platforms to capture citizen feedback. They find that in the majority of ICT-enabled platforms, the institutional response, and consequently the effect of the intervention, was low (2016, 21).

Some initiatives of this type have emerged from civil society actors themselves with the aim to compile information on the quality of, and prevalence of corruption in, service delivery in order to exert pressure on government. The Bangalore Citizen Report Card (CRC), pioneered in 1994, has since been replicated elsewhere. While compiling information about citizen satisfaction with services constitutes the first step in these initiatives, the aim is that this information will facilitate and stimulate pressure on service providers. Ravindra (2004) concludes that the impact of the Bangalore CRC was positive overall, but results varied not least depending on agency leadership (Ravindra 2004, 17). The results of both Peixeto and Fox (2016) and Ravindra (2004) thus highlight the dependence of an institutional response for information-based initiatives to be effective.

International policy actors or researchers have also arranged initiatives which instead aim to provide citizens with information about government operations (budget, revenue flows, commitments and performance) to prompt citizens to take action. Some of these have indeed stemmed the leakage of resources. For example, in a community-based, randomized controlled trial (RCT), Pandey et al. (2007) found that an information campaign in Uttar Pradesh—including meetings, posters, and leaflets—contributed to a reduction in excess school fees charged (as reported by parents). Studying a rice subsidy program in Indonesia, Banerjee et al. (2018) found significant improvements following an information campaign.

---

[4] There is some terminological inconsistency in the accountability literature. Some authors use the term horizontal accountability to describe all intragovernmental accountability, and vertical accountability to denote any efforts in which citizens are involved (elections, social accountability, societal accountability). We adopt this terminology. Others, however, use the term vertical accountability to describe the supply side, i.e. when higher level government offices (national or regional) exert pressure upon local governments (Brinkerhoff and Wetterberg 2016; Fox 2015)

In *Public expenditure tracking surveys* (PETS) accounting experts trace revenue flows and consult citizens to determine where public revenues and resources are, and are not, reaching the intended target activities to detect corruption and leakage (Reinikka and Smith 2004; Reinikka and Svensson 2004, 2005). This information is then made public with the hope that both citizens and oversight authorities will take corrective action. The use of Public Expenditure Tracking Surveys is most prevalent in sub-Saharan Africa, and often in contexts where QoG is particularly low. A tracking survey in Chad estimated that only 1% of nonwage health expenditures arrived at the health facility level. The potential gains of such tracking exercises are thus potentially enormous (Gauthier 2010).

Gauthier (2010) reviews all PETS carried out in sub-Saharan Africa prior to 2010, finding that they often succeed in identifying leakage as well as where in the supply chain leakage occurred. Despite success in identifying problem spots, few countries actually addressed the identified problems by implementing the needed reforms. Such inaction is often attributed to a lack of political will to put in practice reforms (Gauthier 2010; Sundet 2008; Schatz 2013).

In Uganda, a PETS effort conducted in 1996 found substantial leakage, and that schools in poorer communities suffered most from the capture of resources (Reinikka and Svensson 2004). The government subsequently carried out a newspaper campaign and published information on monthly transfers to districts. A follow-up survey in 2002 showed substantial improvement in terms of reduced resource capture and student enrollment and learning (Reinikka and Svensson 2005; 2011). While the positive change was substantial and robust, the mechanisms behind the improvement are uncertain. Reinikka and Svensson suggest that the information campaign sparked a "bottom-up route of citizen enforcement" (Reinikka and Svensson 2005, 261), but Hubbard (2007) points out that other major reforms of the educational system transpired around the same time, probably also contributing to the outcomes.[5]

In summary, then, the SAI discussed in this section have often been effective in exposing corruption and other malfeasance, but results in terms of reducing corruption are more disputed. These mixed empirical results point to a general weakness in the design of these initiatives: while the information provided upwards in the system may be useful to service providers and oversight bodies, it is not in itself a guarantee for the appropriate response in the form of investigations and corrective action (Fox 2007; Fox 2015; Gaventa and McGee 2013; Joshi 2013; Peixoto and Fox 2016; Ravindra 2004).

From the perspective of participants, the information-based initiatives require comparatively limited effort. While these initiatives presume that once information is compiled and presented to a principal, whether it be citizens or government officials, that principal will take action, collecting or consuming the information itself may require attending a single meeting, but not much more. Even if the effort of providing feedback and information on services rendered is minimal, it is important to point out that citizens' incentives to make any effort may be weak, as any potential benefit is dispersed among many, introducing a

---

[5] Devarajan et al. (2013) also point out that improvements in societal outcomes subsequent to information campaigns such as the Reinikka and Svensson intervention may not have come about via an accountability mechanism at all. Parents may simply have become more attentive to and supportive of their children's learning.

collective action dilemma. Also, even a minimal action presupposes that the prospective participant feels the action is not futile. They thus presuppose some minimal level of confidence in a government response, a belief that government should and may feasibly deliver the services in question, and an inclination to express one's opinion, which presupposes a belief that one is entitled to do so.

Institutionalized answerability

An important part of accountability is justification. As Schedler writes, "being accountable to somebody implies the obligation to respond to nasty questions and, vice versa, that holding somebody accountable implies the opportunity to ask uncomfortable questions" (1999, 14). The initiatives discussed in this section in one fashion or another institutionalize citizens' opportunity to ask, and authorities' obligation to answer, uncomfortable questions.

Community monitoring initiatives have been subject to some of the most rigorous and methodologically sophisticated examinations, yielding mixed results regarding their effect on detecting and deterring corruption.[6] Olken's (2007) landmark field experiment analyzes 608 road projects in Indonesia with different accountability mechanisms: official audits or input from the community via comment cards, the results of both of which were presented and discussed at village meetings. A commonly discussed problem in SAIs is elite capture, and in order to examine if social hierarchies interfered with public monitoring, some comment cards were distributed through schools and others distributed by neighborhood heads. Those distributed by neighborhood heads indeed yielded less critical commentary than those distributed through schools. Olken finds that comment cards helped to reduce leakage in the form of underpaid wages—an outcome of significant personal importance for many participants—but had no effect on reducing leakage due to the theft of materials (2007, 233–6), in all likelihood due to collective action problems. Thus, where reporting was shielded from elite capture *and* was incentivized by individual self-interest, it worked. But where local elites could dissuade monitoring or when it related to efficient use of public resources, it did not. The audit treatment yielded the largest reduction of corruption, and the effect was even greater where village heads were up for reelection (2007, 226). Many policy actors, including the Indonesian government itself, have taken Olken's findings to indicate that audit alone reduces corruption, but recall that the audit treatment institutionalized answerability through village meetings. It is impossible to know if the audits would have been effective absent parallel participatory initiatives (Fox 2015, 349).

Social audits also aim to institutionalize answerability by gathering assessments of services, which then are discussed in public meetings with all stakeholders present (Joshi 2013; see also Grandvoinnet et al. 2015, 295–7). A key feature is that service providers participate and partake of citizens' composite assessments and reports, and are expected to address

[6] Mixed results are common also when measuring outcomes other than corruption. While Björkman and Svensson's (2009) landmark study "Power to the people" found strong effects of community monitoring on healthcare quality and various health outcomes, these results could not be replicated in a subsequent study which was modeled closely on the original study, but much larger in sample size (Raffler et al. 2019). See also Banerjee et al. (2010).

questions about service delivery failures, and—together with citizens—to develop action plans for improvements.

Evidence from social audits, mainly from India, shows that these have been effective in terms of exposing corruption and malfeasance among local politicians, officials, and contractors (Aiyar and Samji 2009; Jenkins and Goetz 1999; Singh and Vutukuru 2010). "[M]any people discovered that they had been listed as beneficiaries of anti-poverty schemes, though they had never received payment. Others were astonished to learn of large payments to local building contractors for works that were never performed" (Jenkins and Goetz 1999, 605). The state of Andhra Pradesh institutionalized social audits in conjunction with the National Rural Employment Guarantee Act (NREGA) (Aiyar and Samji 2009). Aiyar and Samji (2009) report that these audits resulted in more than exposure of corruption: large sums of embezzled funds were recovered, and over 500 people were charged and dismissed. Most of them were field assistants, indicating that sanctions materialized mainly "where cases of petty corruption are unearthed" (Aiyar and Samji 2009, 16). Whether this actually had an effect on overall corruption in the NREGA is more uncertain. Afridi and Iversen (2013) do not find a significant reduction in overall corruption, but instead a shift in the nature of corruption: from labor-related irregularities to material-related irregularities that are harder to detect. They conclude that "while audits may be effective in *detecting* irregularities, their impact, if any, on *deterring* malpractice is modest" (2013, 300).

The success of the initiative in detecting corruption was also highly dependent on the support from the Andhra Pradesh government, which "has willingly opened itself up for scrutiny and done so by proactively mobilizing citizens to monitor its programs" (Aiyar and Samji 2009, 23). It has been difficult to replicate the success in other Indian states (Grandvoinnet et al. 2015, 66).

Few review studies focus specifically on SAIs and corruption, but Molina et al. (2017) perform a meta-analysis of five studies of effects of SAI (information campaigns, scorecards and citizen report cards, social audits and grievance redress mechanisms—some of which belong to the previously discussed category of information-based initiatives) on corruption. They find that these SAI reduced corruption to some extent, but stress that the results should be interpreted carefully due to the small number of studies included.

What effort and potential gains do initiatives that institutionalize answerability entail from the perspective of participants? Institutionalizing answerability requires more of participants than initiatives to address information asymmetries alone. Participation entails sharing information and in some cases thoughts on how operations can be improved, but in most cases do not require participants to gain detailed knowledge of revenue flows and constraints, program objectives, or other aspects of a policy operation. They do, however, presume that citizens will be willing to dedicate some amount of time and effort—and sometimes take certain risks in voicing critical views in public—with an aim to improve services for the benefit of the community as a whole.

It is therefore not surprising that a number of studies highlight problems of collective action in these initiatives. In addition to Olken's (2007) finding that community monitoring reduces fraud related to wages (private) but not related to materials (public), Björkman and Svensson (2010) show that information dissemination improves health services but only in ethnically homogeneous areas, which they see as a factor that lowers coordination costs in the community. Barr et al. (2012) test the claim more directly in a study of an initiative that involved members of the community in monitoring schools with a standardized scorecard.

In one treatment, the scorecard was simply provided while in the other, participants discussed beforehand and adapted the card to local conditions. Even this small amount of collaborative work in the early stage stimulated a collaborative spirit and increased the effectiveness of the intervention (Barr et al. 2012).

Taken together, SAIs that institutionalize answerability pose collective action dilemmas that are more difficult to overcome than in those only designed to gather or disseminate information; the individual level effort is greater, and the expected benefit is better government services collectively. Moreover, they also presuppose that participants will overcome the barriers presented by social hierarchies, i.e. that they will not be dissuaded by local elites to participate as well as contest, question and criticize officials. And similar to the more minimalist SAIs discussed above, these initiatives also presuppose confidence in government corrective response, a belief that government should and may feasibly deliver the services in question, and an inclination to express one's opinion, which, again, presupposes a belief that one is entitled to do so.

Devolved authority

The third category of participatory initiatives are those characterized by stable member sets, in which participants make commitments to participate over a series of meetings, to become knowledgeable about public sector activities, and to engage extensively in policy formation and/or the monitoring of policy implementation. For these types of initiatives, the terminology is also rich and sometimes confusing, including community oversight and community management, citizen councils, user management committees, participatory planning, and participatory budgeting (Grandvoinnet et al. 2015, 297–8). These participatory bodies often have significant authority, at times managing a portion of local government budgets.

One of the more well-known examples of devolved authority is *participatory budgeting*. These participatory bodies often monitor policy implementation and the execution of budgets, and in that sense have social accountability functions, although they also have other tasks. Participatory budgeting exists worldwide and varies in terms of mechanisms for the selection of participants and the degree of authority. The more extensive forms entail the creation of an auxiliary city council with councilors elected to represent each city district who together decide over a portion of the municipal budget. Moreover, the participatory budgeting body then can monitor how allocated funds are subsequently spent. When functioning properly, participatory budgeting thus strengthens both information regarding citizens' needs and preferences (representation) but also more effective detection when policy commitments fall short (Abers 1998; Goldfrank 2011; Gonçalves 2014; McNulty 2012; McNulty and Garcia 2019; Mayka 2019; Saguin 2018; Wampler 2008). In Peru, participatory budgeting in municipal and regional governments is required by law, a measure that expressly grew out of frustration with corruption and clientelism in the wake of scandals surrounding former president Alberto Fujimori (McNulty 2012).

In a large-N study, Gonçalves (2014) examines whether Brazilian municipalities with participatory budgeting see, on average, an increase in social spending, and whether this in turn reduces infant mortality. Though only 169 of Brazil's 5,561 municipalities have participatory budgeting bodies, those municipalities are home to 27% of Brazil's population (Gonçalves 2014, 97). The analyses reveal that participatory budgeting is linked to larger budget allocations to health and sanitation and significant decreases in infant mortality. Moreover, the analyses show that spending on health and sanitation has a stronger impact on infant mortality in municipalities with participatory budgeting. This suggests that participatory budgeting leads not only to higher spending on health and sanitation, but also that these funds are administered more effectively where participatory bodies exist to exercise oversight (Gonçalves 2014, 105).

Public policy management councils, prevalent in the Brazilian context as well, further exemplify this type of initiative. Similar to participatory budgeting, participants contribute to both policy formation and monitoring of implementation and performance (Touchton et al. 2017). Touchton et al. (2017) examine under what conditions public policy management councils affect infant mortality, and if so under what conditions, also using large-N municipal level data. They find that municipalities that have councils in all six policy areas deemed relevant—women's or hildren's rights, food security, sanitation, women's health, and urban policy" (Touchton et al. 2017, 75)—show greater reductions in infant mortality, and that the effect is stronger in municipalities with higher levels of administrative capacity (using an assessment from a federal agency). While this study focuses on infant mortality and not corruption, the results indicate the importance of the institutional context for the capacity of participatory initiatives to effect positive change.

As this form of participatory initiatives entails negotiations of budgets as well as the monitoring of their execution, the demands on participants are higher than other forms, and the collective action dilemma thus also more difficult to resolve. Moreover, while free-riding in other SAIs may take the form of staying home while others do the work to monitor operations and report suspected improprieties, SAIs with devolved authority offer more extensive opportunities for pocketbook participation. An ethnographic study of participatory budgeting in Recife, Brazil reveals that some neighborhood leaders have participatory careers that they then may convert to political careers (Montambeault and Goirand 2016) and in order to do so use the same clientelistic strategies as political candidates: seeking political support in exchange for food, transportation, or access to public goods and services (see also Wampler 2008).

Contextual Determinants of Success

Most reviews to date point to how the impact of SAIs is not uniform, but contingent on enabling factors in the social and political context (Carlitz 2013; Fox 2015; Gaventa and Barrett 2010; Grandvoinnet et al. 2015; Joshi 2013; Mansuri and Rao 2013; McGee and Gaventa 2011; Ringold et al. 2011). This discussion sometimes implies, as noted above, a Catch-22: where governance problems are persistent, the enabling factors are lacking—but these governance problems may be precisely what prompts a need for SAIs in the first place. Zinnbauer (2017) points to the paradox that the enumeration of success factors sometimes results in the message that "social accountability can help tackle accountability problems when the accountability problem is almost not there in the first place" (2017, 16).

Discussions of which contextual conditions can affect the prospects for SAIs to reduce QoG or affect societal outcomes fall in two camps. First, numerous studies note the importance of the social context: social and economic conditions which can inform both who participates but also participants' preferences and demands. A second approach focuses on what has been called the overall "accountability ecosystems" (Dewachter et al. 2018, 159), which refers to the capacity and effectiveness of government institutions to respond to and act upon information and accusations from citizens.

With regard to the social context, critics of participatory governance have pointed to how the emphasis on local level processes and actors in SAIs involves a risk that "the local" becomes romanticized, and local power relations and inequalities downplayed (Mohan and Stokke 2000). For example, Conning and Kevane (2002) point to how it is not evident that local preferences are always pro-poor.

Indeed, inequalities at the local level emerge in the literature as a major obstacle to successful social accountability. SAIs like many other policy projects are subject to elite capture and unequal engagement. Mansuri and Rao (2013) review almost 500 studies on local participation and conclude that: "Overall, the evidence suggests that participants tend to be disproportionately from wealthier, more educated, and more politically connected households. They also tend to belong to ethnic or tribal groups that enjoy higher status" (Mansuri and Rao 2013, 128; see also Arcand and Fafchamps 2012; Gugerty and Kremer 2008). Initial conditions such as inequality matter for who participates and the outcomes of that participation (Labonne and Chase 2009).[7]

Existing social inequalities also make the cost of participation a much heavier burden for some participants than others. Not only can there be monetary costs and opportunity costs in terms of lost working time for participants (McNulty 2012), there can also be significant social costs involved and in particular for those lower in the social hierarchy. In all initiatives that invite participants to "ask uncomfortable questions," participation may entail speaking out in public against more powerful persons in society (Mansuri and Rao 2013, 18). Given the uneven weight of these burdens for different individuals, the voices of the most disadvantaged may be heard less in participatory processes.

With regards to the accountability ecosystem, it is evident from the literature that social accountability processes do not unfold independent of higher level institutions. This is true not least in the context of improving QoG: in his review, Schatz (2013) points to factors such as civil liberties, government transparency, and electoral accountability as being helpful for the effectiveness of SAIs to curb corruption. Indicative of this is how initiatives tend to be more effective at exposing problems of corruption than at redressing them. When it comes to the enforcement part of accountability, the participatory initiatives often depend on the very government institutions that are failing as accountability actors in the first place. In their comprehensive review, Mansuri and Rao (2013) express skepticism about the potential for induced local participation to improve service provision where state institutions are weak. They write:

> In sum, far from being a substitute for weak and corrupt formal institutions of accountability, local oversight over the use and management of public resources is effective only when

---

[7] How inequalities in participation will impact on the results of a participatory process is, however, not always evident. Studying community driven development projects in Indonesia, Dasgupta and Beard (2007) find, counterintuitively, that it was in the community where power was most evenly distributed, where the poorest residents were excluded most in order to secure financial sustainability of the project. Dasgupta and Beard (2007, 243) describe the situation as "an example of a democratic process that was not captured by elites and yet it failed to identify helping the poorest residents as the highest priority."

institutions of accountability at the center function well and communities have the capacity to effectively monitor service providers and others in charge of public resources. This finding appears to increase, rather than diminish, the need for a functional and strong center and vigilant and able implementing agencies (Mansuri and Rao 2013, 147).

In World Bank parlance, the effectiveness of long and short routes of accountability are dependent on one another, and examining each in isolation risks missing crucial explanations for why the same type of social accountability initiative may have varying levels of success (Devarajan et al. 2013; Dewachter et al. 2018; Halloran, 2016). Instead, it is argued, we need to understand how the "accountability ecosystems" work (Dewachter et al. 2018, 159).

In such accountability systems, legal institutions that can serve as a third-party enforcer play an obvious role, as do strong audit institutions and courts. Legal institutions are also needed to protect basic rights and freedoms necessary for civil engagement (Brinkerhoff and Wetterberg 2016). Many also highlight factors that can pressure political actors to be more responsive, such as functioning electoral institutions, the presence of a viable political opposition, and free and active media (Grandvoinnet et al. 2015; McGee and Gaventa 2011; Fox 2015; Dewachter et al. 2018; Olken 2007; Schatz 2013).

While previous research has pointed to the importance of the institutional environment, in the final section we point to how some aspects of the institutional framework may impact on SAIs in more fundamental ways than is commonly discussed in the literature. We also suggest research questions that deserve more attention if we are to better understand the prospects for SAIs to improve QoG.

How Institutions Affect Social Accountability's Effect on QoG

The fact that participatory initiatives tend to yield better results in settings with comparatively less corruption or stronger administrative structures is by now virtually a matter of consensus (Beuermann and Amelina 2014; Fox 2015; Grandvoinnet et al. 2015; Mansuri and Rao 2013). As described above, the reason most commonly put forward is that SAIs mostly are dependent on some kind of institutional response to have an effect. In this section, we suggest an alternative set of mechanisms through which the characteristics of the institutional environment may affect SAIs: by affecting participants themselves.

Individual motivations for political engagement can, as noted above, come in the form of either self-interest or a concern for the broader public good. Research on issues such as taxation, corruption, and state presence show that the institutional environment can influence which motivation will be more prevalent, and thus also affect political behavior (Bauhr and Grimes, this volume; Broms 2015; Dell et al. 2018).

These findings have implications for SA policy initiatives and research efforts to understand their likelihood of success. SAIs and participatory arrangements more generally tend to rest on an underlying assumption that participants will *not* primarily be motivated by self-interest (Montambeault and Goirand 2016). Even when the aim is to propose, develop or prioritize policy, or even to decide on budget allocations, participants are implicitly expected to represent their community as a whole, or perhaps a social category (women/poor/

poor women) to which they are ascribed a representative capacity, and are not expected to seek to advance their own material or political interests.[8] As noted above, SAIs thus tend to make high demands on participants compared to other accountability mechanisms. While individuals everywhere may intrinsically have similar propensities to behave in a prosocial or collective manner, we argue that the research on comparative political behavior plausibly suggests that government institutions can alter the logic of what seems most rational and in particular with regard to engaging to affect government programs. In short, participants' willingness both to engage in SA efforts, and to do so in a way that furthers the public good, may be inversely related to corruption in government institutions. Where government officials behave in a more self-interested manner, citizens may be inclined to follow suit, or opt not to participate at all. How can we theorize this expected effect, both in terms of which aspects of state structures matter and how they may affect citizens' priors?

The conceptual discussion of state capacity developed by D'Arcy and Nistotskaya (this volume) delineates three components of state capacity, two of which are relevant here: state reach and bureaucratic quality. State reach refers to the presence of the state throughout the territory of a country. When the state has only a weak presence, in other words when basic security, infrastructure, services, as well as tax collection efforts are lacking, local residents may simply not see themselves in the role of democratic citizens, and may also not see the state as a credible provider of solutions to problems (MacLean 2011; Miller 2000). Why make the effort to formulate and express demands on an entity that has previously never delivered?

Bureaucratic quality may potentially pose the most serious challenges to SA initiatives, however, as a particularist state may have more lasting and deleterious effects on citizen behavior than an absent state (Dell et al. 2018). A principal component of bureaucratic quality is the extent to which political rulers are constrained from using the bureaucracy and state resources more generally for short-term political gains. The main purpose of the bureaucracy is to carry out the wishes of politicians expressed in policy decisions, and institutional firewalls in many states prevent political rulers from interfering in the more operative aspects of policy implementation, such as hiring of personnel and deciding which citizens qualify as beneficiaries of welfare programs. In short, these firewalls are designed to prevent the logic of politics—which is one of partisanship and competition between competing interests, grievances, values, and ideologies—from spilling into the bureaucracy, which should ideally follow a rational/legal logic (Miller 2000; Weber 1978). Such firewalls are intended to protect the processes and activities related to the *exercise* of power from the logic of politics, which is inevitable in matters related to *access* to power (Mazzuca 2010; Piattoni 2001; Rothstein and Teorell 2008).

When the logic of politics infiltrates activities related to the exercise of power, partisanship and particularism may inform the allocation of public resources, which may also have

---

[8] While beyond the scope of this paper, a number of authors have made the important critique that participatory arrangements may fail in the aim of empowerment because they grant influence on minor issues, and very little power over policy in a meaningful way. The scope of initiatives is in some cases restricted to a narrow set of issues, with no opportunity to address larger injustices and underlying problems (Botchway 2001). O'Meally (2014) examines for example an initiative that invited fishermen to discuss fishery management in Lake Victoria. He observes that overarching development priorities were never discussed. Participation may in other words fragment policy discussions in a way that hides underlying conflicts and grievances, and as such even shift the responsibility away from government to communities and individuals (Baiocchi and Ganuza 2016, 7).

implications for citizens' political behavior (e.g. Cornell and Grimes 2015). Research on clientelism attests to the fact that where clientelism is prevalent, in other words where access to government services becomes contingent on party loyalty, citizens may themselves begin making particularistic demands, in other words demands for private goods and benefits (Medina and Stokes 2002; Montambeault and Goirand 2016; Nichter and Peress 2017; O'Donnell 1996; Roniger 2004).

Citizens are known to at times behave in a self-interested manner within the framework of SAIs, but little attention is paid to why this may be more prevalent in some contexts than others. We suggest that the institutional context may influence SA success by conditioning what participants—as individuals as well as in the role of representatives for civil society organizations—bring into the participatory process. As Devarajan and co-authors note:

> In political economy environments characterized by high degrees of clientelism and rent-seeking, such as are widespread in the Africa region, an unqualified faith in civil society as a force for good is more likely to be misplaced. The evidence base on the organization of civil society suggests that historic institutions of poverty and inequality, or of ethnic identity, can inhibit collective action in the broader public interest, promote more narrow sectarian interests, and nourish clientelist political competition (Devarajan et al. 2011, 3).

Civil society can and of course has across many contexts also worked for inclusion, social justice, and better quality of government (Alvarez et al. 2017; Avritzer 2000; Beyerle 2014; Landell-Mills 2013). Though seemingly contradictory, civil society may, just as individuals, justifiably opt for self-interested over prosocial strategies, seeking club goods or privileged benefits for members. We theorize that where government bureaucracies heavily follow a logic of particularism, citizens and civil society associations are more likely to see participatory processes as a forum to advance their own interests rather than the public good, and welcome more systematic attention to this mechanism moving forward.

Somewhat relatedly, SAIs often require participants to overcome collective action problems. Participation requires effort, and when the benefits are a public good, such as better monitoring of government or improved government services, there are incentives to free ride on others. As corruption and particularism in government institutions also tends to erode social trust (Dinesen and Sønderskov this volume; Rothstein and Eek 2009), which exacerbates local efforts to engage in coordinated action, SAIs face an additional challenge in low QoG settings.

Finally, prosocial behavior with respect to SAIs more generally entails two things: showing up to participate and, once involved, contributing to the production of public goods rather than seeking to advance one's own personal interests. Inducing prosocial behavior may be more difficult in efforts relating to the monitoring of government programs due to the fact that monitoring is a public good. Recall Olken's (2007) finding that local residents were less willing to report the theft of building materials than fraud related to their own wages.

From a policy perspective, SAIs designs must consider strategies to foster prosocial behavior. This is especially true in initiatives in which the participatory body both has authority to formulate policy, which may induce a more political, partisan logic, *and* authority related to the exercise of power (implementing policy and executing budgets), which requires participants to think prosocially. Even in participatory initiatives, in other words, institutional firewalls that safeguard policy implementation from a particularistic logic may help to improve outcomes. In participatory budgeting in Peru, a special subcommittee monitors the execution of the budget (McNulty 2012), suggesting an awareness of these issues among designers of the initiative.

Taken together, this discussion points to a number of issues that are underexplored in the literature. We welcome efforts to understand the behavioral logics participants bring into participatory initiatives, the contextual factors that may induce these logics, and, perhaps most importantly, the conditions under which they are subject to change. In order to explore these dynamics, examinations of social accountability need to explore in a more systematic fashion each of three sets of variables. First, what is the nature of state–citizen relations, and specifically: To what extent does the state have a presence in terms of service provision and tax collection? And, where present, to what extent is access to government services governed by a logic of particularism?[9] Björkman and Svensson (2010) hypothesize that ethnic heterogeneity inhibits local collective efforts while others contend that how governments deal with ethnic heterogeneity has a much larger impact (Persson, this volume). These and similar questions need continued attention. Without systematic attention to the institutional environment, it will be impossible to assess and evaluate the generalizability of the findings of even highly rigorous randomized control trials and field experiments (Dunning 2016). Second, and relatedly, what priors do participants bring into the process in terms of their own sense of efficacy, beliefs about government and politics, and expectations and trust regarding other participants' behavior?

Third, and perhaps most importantly, what factors explain instances when SAIs or other forms of participatory initiative succeed despite adverse conditions? Does the institutional design of the process support and sustain collective efforts, and if so, how? Are social institutions in the locality relevant in this regard? What leadership strategies induced the necessary logics? Understanding the micro-foundations of successful initiatives and in particular how individual logic is a function of, and can be changed through, the design of the SAI can both enhance our understanding of political behavior as well as SAIs' prospects for effectiveness.

On a final methodological note, research that more systematically documents and reports the characteristics of the institutional setting noted above will also help to resolve a seeming impasse between two needs in the field. On the one hand, the best available knowledge suggests that isolated initiatives, which Fox (2015) calls "tactical" approaches, are unlikely to have a lasting impact, and that combinations of interventions (for example official audits that are also presented and discussed at village meetings) are more likely to curtail corruption than audits or meetings alone, what Fox terms "strategic" social accountability. That said, when interventions are rolled out in parallel, studies struggle to identify the exact mechanism through which effects occur (Devarajan et al. 2013; Ringold et al. 2011). Ringold et al. (2011) discuss how simultaneity of interventions—that interventions often come in packages—poses a challenge for those aiming to evaluate the specific mechanisms. More cumulativity and systematic documentation of the characteristics of the institutional setting within which SAI initiatives are launched will contribute to the generation of more generalizable lessons and knowledge.

---

[9] The Metaketa research agenda has begun doing exactly this in research on the role of information in electoral accountability (Dunning et al. 2019), allowing not only for an analysis of how information informs vote choice but how information campaigns might play out differently in different institutional contexts to affect voter behavior.

References

Abers, Rebecca. 1998. "From Clientelism to Cooperation: Local Government, Participatory Policy, and Civic Organizing in Porto Alegre, Brazil." *Politics & Society* 26 (4): 511–37.

Afridi, Farzana, and Vegard Iversen. 2013. "Social Audits and MGNREGA Delivery: Lessons from Andhra Pradesh." In *Brookings-NCAER India Policy Forum*, Shekhar, Shah, Barry, Bosworth and Arvind Panagariya (eds). New Delhi: Sage Publications.

Ahmad, Junaid, Stephen Commins, Shantayanan Devarajan, Deon Filmer, Jeffrey Hammer, Lant Pritchett, Ritva Reinikka, Shekhar Shah, and Agnès Soucat. 2003. *World development report 2004: Making services work for poor people*. No. 26895. Washington DC: The World Bank.

Aiyar, Yamini, and Salimah Samji. 2009. "Transparency and Accountability in NREGA: A Case Study of Andhra Pradesh." New Delhi: Center for Policy Research.

Alvarez, Sonia E., Gianpaolo Baiocchi, Agustín Laó-Montes, Jeffrey W. Rubin, Millie Thayer. 2017. "Interrogating the Civil Society Agenda: Reassessing Uncivic Political Activism. Alvarez, Sonia E., Jeffrey W. Rubin, Millie Thayer, Gianpaolo Baiocchi, and Agustín Laó-Montes, eds. *Beyond civil society: Activism, participation, and protest in Latin America*, 1–26. Durham NC: Duke University Press.

Arcand, Jean-Louis, and Marcel Fafchamps. 2012. "Matching in Community-based Organizations." *Journal of Development Economics* 98 (2): 203–19.

Avritzer, Leonardo. 2000. "Democratization and Changes in the Pattern of Association in Brazil." *Journal of Interamerican Studies and World Affairs* 42 (3): 59–76.

Avritzer, Leonardo. 2009. *Democracy and the Public Space in Latin America*. Princeton, NJ: Princeton University Press.

Baiocchi, Gianpaolo, and Ernesto Ganuza. 2016. *Popular Democracy: The Paradox of Participation*. Stanford, CA: Stanford University Press.

Banerjee, Abhijit, Rema Hanna, Jordan Kyle, Benjamin A. Olken, and Sudarno Sumarto. 2018. "Tangible Information and Citizen Empowerment: Identification Cards and Food Subsidy Programs in Indonesia." *Journal of Political Economy* 126 (2): 451–91.

Banerjee, Abhijit V, Rukmini Banerji, Esther Duflo, Rachel Glennerster, and Stuti Khemani. 2010. "Pitfalls of Participatory Programs: Evidence from a Randomized Evaluation in Education in India." *American Economic Journal: Economic Policy* 2 (1): 1–30.

Barr, Abigail, Frederick Mugisha, Pieter Serneels, and Andrew Zeitlin. 2012. "Information and collective action in the community monitoring of schools: Field and lab experimental evidence from Uganda." Available at: http://www.bristol.ac.uk/media-library/sites/cmpo/migrated/documents/zeitlin.pdf

Bauhr, Monika, and Marcia Grimes. 2014. "Indignation or Resignation: The Implications of Transparency for Societal Accountability." *Governance* 27 (2): 291–320.

Beuermann, Diether W., and Maria Amelina. 2014. "Does Participatory Budgeting Improve Decentralized Public Service Delivery?" IDB Working Paper Series.

Beyerle, Shaazka M. 2014. *Curtailing Corruption: People Power for Accountability and Justice*. Boulder, CO: Lynne Rienner.

Björkman, Martina, and Jakob Svensson. 2009. "Power to the People: Evidence from a Randomized Field Experiment on Community-Based Monitoring in Uganda." *The Quarterly Journal of Economics* 124 (2): 735–69.

Björkman, Martina, and Jakob Svensson. 2010. "When Is Community-Based Monitoring Effective? Evidence from a Randomized Experiment in Primary Health in Uganda." *Journal of the European Economic Association* 8 (2–3): 571–81.

Booth, David, and Diana Cammack. 2013. *Governance for Development in Africa: Solving Collective Action Problems*. New York, NY: Zed Books Ltd.

Botchway, Karl. 2001. "Paradox of Empowerment: Reflections on a Case Study from Northern Ghana." *World Development* 29 (1): 135–53.

Bovens, Mark. 2007. "Analysing and Assessing Accountability: A Conceptual Framework 1." *European Law Journal* 13 (4): 447–68.

Brinkerhoff, D. W., and A. Wetterberg. 2016. "Gauging the Effects of Social Accountability on Services, Governance, and Citizen Empowerment." *Public Administration Review* 76 (2): 274–U336. doi: 10.1111/puar.12399

Brockmyer, Brandon, and Jonathan A. Fox. 2015. "Assessing the Evidence: The Effectiveness and Impact of Governance-Oriented Multi-Stakeholder Initiatives." *Transparency & Accountability Initiative*. London UK: Open Society Foundation.

Broms, Rasmus. 2015. "Putting up or Shutting up: On the Individual-Level Relationship between Taxpaying and Political Interest in a Developmental Context." *The Journal of Development Studies* 51 (1): 93–109.

Carlitz, Ruth. 2013. "Improving Transparency and Accountability in the Budget Process: An Assessment of Recent Initiatives." *Development Policy Review* 31: s49–67.

Chong, Alberto, Ana L. De La O, Dean Karlan, and Leonard Wantchekon. 2015. "Does Corruption Information Inspire the Fight or Quash the Hope? a Field Experiment in Mexico on Voter Turnout, Choice, and Party Identification." *The Journal of Politics* 77 (1): 55–71.

Conning, Jonathan, and Michael Kevane. 2002. "Community-Based Targeting Mechanisms for Social Safety Nets: A Critical Review." *World Development* 30 (3): 375–94.

Cornell, Agnes, and Marcia Grimes. 2015. "Institutions as Incentives for Civic Action: Bureaucratic Structures, Civil Society, and Disruptive Protests." *The Journal of Politics* 77 (3): 664–78.

Danhoundo, G., K. Nasiri, and M. E. Wiktorowicz. 2018. "Improving Social Accountability Processes in the Health Sector in sub-Saharan Africa: A Systematic Review." *BMC Public Health* 18 (1): 497. doi: 10.1186/s12889-018-5407-8.

Dasgupta, Aniruddha and Victoria A. Beard. 2007. "Community Driven Development, Collective Action and Elite Capture in Indonesia." *Development and Change* 38 (2): 229–249.

Dell, Melissa, Nathan Lane, and Pablo Querubin. 2018. "The Historical State, Local Collective Action, and Economic Development in Vietnam." *Econometrica* 86 (6): 2083–121.

Devarajan, Shantayanan, Stuti Khemani, and Michael Walton. 2011. *Civil Society, Public Action and Accountability in Africa*. Washington, DC: The World Bank.

Devarajan, Shantayanan, Stuti Khemani, and Michael Walton. 2013. "Can Civil Society Overcome Government Failure in Africa?" *The World Bank Research Observer* 29 (1): 20–47.

Dewachter, Sara, Nathalie Holvoet, Miet Kuppens, and Nadia Molenaers. 2018. "Beyond the Short Versus Long Accountability Route Dichotomy: Using Multi-Track Accountability Pathways to Study Performance of Rural Water Services in Uganda." *World Development* 102: 158–69.

Dunning, Thad. 2016. "Transparency, Replication, and Cumulative Learning: What Experiments Alone Cannot Achieve." *Annual Review of Political Science* 19: S1–23.

Dunning, Thad, Guy Grossman, Macartan Humphreys, Susan D. Hyde, Craig McIntosh, and Gareth Nellis. 2019. *Information, Accountability, and Cumulative Learning: Lessons from Metaketa I*. Cambridge: Cambridge University Press.

Fishkin, James S. 1997. *The Voice of the People: Public Opinion and Democracy*. New Haven, CT: Yale University Press.

Fox, Jonathan A. 2007. *Accountability Politics: Power and Voice in Rural Mexico*. Oxford: Oxford University Press.

Fox, Jonathan A. 2015. "Social Accountability: What Does the Evidence Really Say?" *World Development* 72: 346–61.

Fung, Archon, and Erik Wright. 2003. *Deepening Democracy: Institutional Innovations in Empowered Participatory Governance*. London: Verso.

Gauthier, Bernard. 2010. *PETS-QSDS in sub-Saharan Africa: A Stocktaking Study*. Washington, DC: World Bank.

Gaventa, J., and R. McGee. 2013. "The Impact of Transparency and Accountability Initiatives." *Development Policy Review* 31 (s1): S3–28. doi: 10.1111/dpr.12017

Gaventa, John, and Gregory Barrett. 2010. "So What Difference Does It Make? Mapping the Outcomes of Citizen Engagement." *IDS Working Papers* 2010 (347): 01–72.

Goldfrank, Benjamin. 2011. *Deepening Local Democracy in Latin America: Participation, Decentralization, and the Left*. University Park, PA: Penn State Press.

Gonçalves, Sónia. 2014. "The Effects of Participatory Budgeting on Municipal Expenditures and Infant Mortality in Brazil." *World Development* 53: 94–110.

Grandvoinnet, Helene, Ghazia Aslam, and Shomikho Raha. 2015. *Opening the Black Box: The Contextual Drivers of Social Accountability*. Washington, DC: World Bank Group.

Gugerty, Mary Kay, and Michael Kremer. 2008. "Outside Funding and the Dynamics of Participation in Community Associations." *American Journal of Political Science* 52 (3): 585–602.

Gutmann, Amy. and Dennis Thompson. 1996. *Democracy and Disagreement*, Cambridge, MA: Belknap Press.

Halloran, Brendan. 2016. "Accountability Ecosystems: Directions of Accountability and Points of Engagement." Brighton: IDS © Institute of Development Studies.

Hubbard, Paul. 2007. "Putting the Power of Transparency in Context: Information's Role in Reducing Corruption in Uganda's Education Sector." Available at SSRN 1100131.

Jenkins, Rob, and Anne Marie Goetz. 1999. "Accounts and Accountability: Theoretical Implications of the Right-to-Information Movement in India." *Third World Quarterly* 20 (3): 603–22.

Johnston, Michael. 2005. *Civil Society and Corruption: Mobilizing for Reform*. Landham, MD: University Press of America.

Joshi, Anuradha. 2013. "Do They Work? Assessing the Impact of Transparency and Accountability Initiatives in Service Delivery." *Development Policy Review* 31: s29–48.

Joshi, Anuradha, and Peter P. Houtzager. 2012. "Widgets or Watchdogs? Conceptual Explorations in Social Accountability." *Public Management Review* 14 (2): 145–62.

Kosack, Stephen, and Archon Fung. 2014. "Does Transparency Improve Governance?" *Annual Review of Political Science* 17: 65–87.

Labonne, Julien, and Robert S. Chase. 2009. "Who Is at the Wheel When Communities Drive Development? Evidence from the Philippines." *World Development* 37 (1): 219–31.

Landell-Mills, Pierre. 2013. *Citizens against Corruption: Report from the Front Line*. Leicestershire UK: Troubador Publishing Ltd.

Lodenstein, Elsbet, Marjolein Dieleman, Barend Gerretsen, and Jacqueline E. W. Broerse. 2013. "A Realist Synthesis of the Effect of Social Accountability Interventions on Health Service Providers' and Policymakers' Responsiveness." *Systematic Reviews* 2 (1): 98.

MacLean, Lauren M. 2011. "State Retrenchment and the Exercise of Citizenship in Africa." *Comparative Political Studies* 44 (9): 1238–66.

Malena, Carmen, and Reiner Forster. 2004. "Social Accountability: An Introduction to the Concept and Emerging Practice." *Social Development Papers* No. 76. Washington, DC: The World Bank.

Manroth, Astrid, Zenaida Hernandez, Harika Masud, Jad Zakhour, Miguel Rebolledo, S Mahmood, Aaron Seyedian, Qays Hamad, and Tiago Peixoto. 2014. "Strategic framework for mainstreaming citizen engagement in World Bank Group operations: engaging with citizens for improved results." Washington, DC: World Bank Group.

Mansuri, Ghazala, and Vijayendra Rao. 2013. "Can Participation Be Induced? Some Evidence from Developing Countries." *Critical Review of International Social and Political Philosophy* 16 (2): 284–304.

Mayka, Lindsay. 2019. *Building Participatory Institutions in Latin America: Reform Coalitions and Institutional Change.* Cambridge: Cambridge University Press.

Mazzuca, Sebastián L. 2010. "Access to Power versus Exercise of Power Reconceptualizing the Quality of Democracy in Latin America." *Studies in Comparative International Development* 45 (3): 334–57.

McGee, Rosie, and John Gaventa. 2011. "Shifting Power? Assessing the Impact of Transparency and Accountability Initiatives." *IDS Working Papers* 2011 (383): 1–39.

McNulty, Stephanie. 2012. "An Unlikely Success: Peru's Top-down Participatory Budgeting Experience." *Journal of Public Deliberation* 8 (2): 4.

McNulty, Stephanie L., and Gustavo Guerra Garcia. 2019. "Politics and Promises: Exploring Fifteen Years of Peru's Participatory Decentralization Reform." *Public Organization Review* 19 (1): 45–64.

Medina, Luis Fernando, and Susan Stokes. 2002. "Clientelism as Political Monopoly." Paper presented at the 2002 Annual Meeting of the American Political Science Association, Boston.

Mejía Acosta, Andrés. 2013. "The Impact and Effectiveness of Accountability and Transparency Initiatives: The Governance of Natural Resources." *Development Policy Review* 31: s89–105.

Miller, Gary. 2000. "Above Politics: Credible Commitment and Efficiency in the Design of Public Agencies." *Journal of Public Administration Research and Theory* 10 (2): 289–328.

Mohan, Giles, and Kristian Stokke. 2000. "Participatory Development and Empowerment: The Dangers of Localism." *Third World Quarterly* 21 (2): 247–68.

Molina, Ezequiel, Laura Carella, Ana Pacheco, Guillermo Cruces, and Leonardo Gasparini. 2017. "Community Monitoring Interventions to Curb Corruption and Increase Access and Quality in Service Delivery: A Systematic Review." *Journal of Development Effectiveness* 9 (4): 462–99.

Montambeault, Françoise, and Camille Goirand. 2016. "Between Collective Action and Individual Appropriation: The Informal Dimensions of Participatory Budgeting in Recife, Brazil." *Politics & Society* 44 (1): 143–71.

Nichter, Simeon, and Michael Peress. 2017. "Request Fulfilling: When Citizens Demand Clientelist Benefits." *Comparative Political Studies* 50 (8): 1086–117.

O'Donnell, Guillermo. 1996. "Another Institutionalization: Latin America and Elsewhere." *Journal of Democracy* 7 (2): 34–51.

O'Meally, Simon. 2014. "The Contradictions of Pro-poor Participation and Empowerment: The World Bank in East Africa." *Development and Change* 45 (6): 1248–83.

Olken, Benjamin A. 2007. "Monitoring Corruption: Evidence from a Field Experiment in Indonesia." *Journal of Political Economy* 115 (2): 200–49.

Ostrom, Elinor. 1990. *Governing the Commons: The Evolution of Institutions for Collective Action*. Cambridge: Cambridge University Press.

Pandey, Priyanka, Ashwini R. Sehgal, Michelle Riboud, David Levine, and Madhav Goyal. 2007. "Informing Resource-Poor Populations and the Delivery of Entitled Health and Social Services in Rural India: A Cluster Randomized Controlled Trial." *Jama* 298 (16): 1867–75.

Pateman, Carole. 1970. *Participation and Democratic Theory*. Cambridge: Cambridge University Press.

Pateman, Carole. 2012. "Participatory Democracy Revisited." *Perspectives on Politics* 10 (1): 7–19.

Paul, Samuel. 1992. "Accountability in Public Services: Exit, Voice and Control." *World Development* 20 (7): 1047–1060.

Peixoto, Tiago, and Jonathan Fox. 2016. "When Does ICT-Enabled Citizen Voice Lead to Government Responsiveness?" World Development Report 2016. Washington, DC: World Bank Group.

Persson, Anna, Bo Rothstein, and Jan Teorell. 2013. "Why Anticorruption Reforms Fail— Systemic Corruption as a Collective Action Problem." *Governance* 26 (3): 449–71.

Piattoni, Simona. 2001. *Clientelism, Interests, and Democratic Representation: The European Experience in Historical and Comparative Perspective*. Cambridge: Cambridge University Press.

Raffler, Pia, Daniel N. Posner, and Doug Parkerson. 2019. "The Weakness of Bottom-up Accountability: Experimental Evidence from the Ugandan Health Sector." *Los Angeles: Innovations for Poverty Action*. Unpublished manuscript available at: https://www. poverty-action.org/sites/default/files/publications/RPP_0.pdf

Ravindra, Adikeshavalu. 2004. "An Assessment of the Impact of Bangalore Citizen Report Cards on the Performance of Public Agencies." Evaluation Capacity Development Working Paper 12.

Reinikka, Ritva, and Nathanael Smith. 2004. *Public Expenditure Tracking Surveys in Education*. UNESCO, International Institute for Educational Planning.

Reinikka, Ritva, and Jakob Svensson. 2004. "Local Capture: Evidence from a Central Government Transfer Program in Uganda." *The Quarterly Journal of Economics* 119 (2): 679–705.

Reinikka, Ritva, and Jakob Svensson. 2005. "Fighting Corruption to Improve Schooling: Evidence from a Newspaper Campaign in Uganda." *Journal of the European Economic Association* 3 (2–3): 259–67.

Reinikka, Ritva, and Jakob Svensson. 2011. "The Power of Information in Public Services: Evidence from Education in Uganda." *Journal of Public Economics* 95 (7–8): 956–66.

Ringold, Dena, Alaka Holla, Margaret Koziol, and Santhosh Srinivasan. 2011. *Citizens and Service Delivery: Assessing the Use of Social Accountability Approaches in Human Development Sectors*. Washington, DC: World Bank Group.

Roniger, Luis. 2004. "Political Clientelism, Democracy, and Market Economy." *Compartive Politics*. 36 (3): 353–75.

Rose-Ackerman, Susan. 1999. *Corruption and Government: Causes, Consequences, and Reform*. Cambridge: Cambridge: Cambridge University Press.

Rothstein, Bo, and Daniel Eek. 2009. "Political Corruption and Social Trust: An Experimental Approach." *Rationality and Society* 21 (1): 81–112.

Rothstein, Bo O., and Jan A. N. Teorell. 2008. "What Is Quality of Government? a Theory of Impartial Government Institutions." *Governance* 21 (2): 165–90.

Saguin, Kidjie. 2018. "Why the Poor Do Not Benefit from Community-Driven Development: Lessons from Participatory Budgeting." *World Development* 112: 220–32.

Schatz, Florian. 2013. "Fighting Corruption with Social Accountability: A Comparative Analysis of Social Accountability Mechanisms' potential to Reduce Corruption in Public Administration." *Public Administration and Development* 33 (3): 161–74.

Schedler, Andreas. 1999. "Conceptualizing Accountability." In *The Self-Restraining State: Power and Accountability in New Democracies*. Andreas Schedler, Larry Diamond, and Marc Plattner (eds). Boulder, CO: Lynne Rienner Publishers.

Singh, Ritesh, and Vinay Vutukuru. 2010. "Enhancing Accountability in Public Service Delivery through Social Audits: A Case Study of Andhra Pradesh, India." New Delhi: Accountability Initiative, Centre for Policy Research.

Smulovitz, Catalina, and Enrique Peruzzotti. 2000. "Societal Accountability in Latin America." *Journal of Democracy* 11 (4): 147–58.

Sundet, Geir. 2008. "Following the Money: Do Public Expenditure Tracking Surveys Matter?" *U4 Issue* 2008:8. Bergen: Christer Michelsen Institutet.

Touchton, Michael, Natasha Borges Sugiyama, and Brian Wampler. 2017. "Democracy at Work: Moving beyond Elections to Improve Well-Being." *American Political Science Review* 111 (1): 68–82.

Wampler, Brian. 2008. "When Does Participatory Democracy Deepen the Quality of Democracy? Lessons from Brazil." *Comparative politics* 41 (1): 61–81.

Weber, Max. 1978. *Economy and society: An Outline of Interpretive Sociology*, Vol. 1. Berkeley, CA: University of California Press.

Westhorp, Gill, Bill Walker, Patricia Rogers, Nathan Overbeeke, Daniel Ball, and Graham Brice. 2014. "Enhancing community accountability, empowerment and education outcomes in low and middle-income countries: A realist review." *EPPI-Centre, Social Science Research Unit, Institute of Education, University of London*.

Zinnbauer, Dieter. 2017. "Social Accountability-Taking Stock of All the Stock-Taking and Some Interesting Avenues for Future Practice and Research." Available at SSRN: https://ssrn.com/abstract=2913597

CHAPTER 14

....

CIVIL SOCIETY AGAINST CORRUPTION

....

DONATELLA DELLA PORTA AND ALICE MATTONI[1]

INTRODUCTION

....

IN the past decade, protest campaigns and broad mobilizations against corruption have developed in many countries across the world, including China, Brazil, Russia, and Turkey but also in Europe and North-America. The uprisings in the MENA region at the beginning of the 2010s—frequently grouped under the umbrella term Arab Spring—had already linked demands of democracy and freedom to the denunciation of the corruption of the elites in power. Inspired by the Arab Spring, the Indignados in Spain mobilized against the increasing inequalities that people had to face due to the corruption of their elected representatives (della Porta 2013, 2015). Similarly, in Greece's Syntagma Square, MPs were considered traitors as they had violated a basic democratic contract (Sotirakopoulos and Sotiropoulos 2013). In a similar vein, Italian anti-austerity protestors pointed out that they wanted "more democracy and less politicians," also expressing their outrage against the political elites (cf. della Porta 2015). The slogans shouted during these protests pointed, in fact, at the convergence of businesses and politicians, stigmatizing that "banks got bailed out, we got sold out." In particular, institutional democracy was seen as representative not of people, but of banks and financial power. A few months later, the Occupy Wall Street mobilizations in the US imported similar frames, expressing them in the influential slogan of the 99% against the 1%. During these protests, the occupants of Zuccotti Park declared: "No true democracy is attainable when the process is determined by economic power" (van Gelder and the staff of YES! Magazine 2011, 36).

In all these cases, civil society actors have denounced the recourse to bribes in exchange for favors—but also the development of small elites made of politicians and businessmen with common interests, and often also common assets—not only as immoral, but also as concrete causes of a systemic development considered unjust. Calls for dignity were hence linked to the stigmatization of the elites' kleptocracy. Despite their diversity, what all these mobilizations

---

[1] Alice Mattoni acknowledges that this publication has been made possible by funding from the European Research Council (ERC) under the European Union's Horizon 2020 research and innovation program, Grant agreement No. 802362 BIT-ACT).

had in common was the perceived corruption of representative democracy, which was coupled with a persistent demand for the accountability of public affairs and the prosecution of political corruption, as people stigmatized the injustice of, for example, paying the "bills of a crisis whose authors continue to enjoy record benefits" (Perugorría and Tejerina 2013, 436). Also as a result of these mobilizations, in recent decades, a growing popular awareness has emerged of the relevance of corruption as a hidden factor that negatively influences political and economic decision-making processes, in both liberal-democratic and authoritarian regimes.

This chapter aims at discussing these anticorruption efforts in order to understand their main features, challenges, and potential future developments. It is structured as follows. First, it briefly reviews how scholars in the field of corruption, and those in social movement studies, have addressed the issue of anticorruption efforts outside institutional settings. Next, it underlines the dimensions and conditions that characterize different civil society actors who struggle against corruption, with regard to the resources they employ, the forms of collective action they enact, and the discourses on corruption they elaborate. Finally, the chapter discusses the consequences of civil society's efforts against corruption. The conclusion will focus on future lines of investigation into the struggle of civil society against corruption.

A Brief Literature Review on Anticorruption Struggles from the Grassroots

Civil society and social movement actors who have mobilized against corruption seems to be particularly important. Indeed, many efforts to counter corruption across the globe rest on the initiatives of foreign donors, transnational institutions, and NGOs. These have achieved some degree of success in fighting corruption, also because:

> many [anticorruption] interventions are based on new institutions, often established by donors, which thus neither have legitimacy nor necessarily fit well in the local context. [...] More important is that donors generally do not have a good understanding of the local political incentives, that important drivers of change include groups often ignored by the donors, and that even when donors acquire good political insights they do not use these for programming their AC [anticorruption]activities in a more coherent manner and in a more appropriate longer-term perspective (Disch, Vigeland and Sundet 2009, 10).

In other words, initiatives sponsored by transnational actors, like NGOs, are often detached from the local context in which they intend to operate, a problem that might be addressed through an increased involvement of civil society and social movement actors present in a given country.

While this highlights the importance of studying the mechanisms and processes involved in grassroots anticorruption efforts, and the expectations held by the social and political actors, yet the actual research in the field is scarce. Social science research on anticorruption belongs to a well-developed and interdisciplinary field that has flourished in the last decades. For many years now, scholars who investigate anticorruption strategies have recognized the importance of civil society actors in limiting corruption (e.g., Hough 2013; Johnston 2005, Mungiu-Pippidi 2013; Mungiu-Pippidi 2015), with social change being one of the three recognized approaches to counter corruption, together with administrative change and law enforcement (Shim and Eom 2009). However, research on anticorruption has traditionally been "top-down and elite-driven with attention directed mainly toward administrative graft. Citizens and the potential of people power did not factor into the equation" (Beyerle 2014, 26). As a result, while we know a lot about corruption, how it works, and with what consequences for societies, we know much less about anticorruption, especially when considering campaigns and protests that develop outside political institutions, thanks to the grassroots participation of citizens.

In the past few years, some studies on anticorruption have emerged in the social movement literature. An investigation of protests in Spain and other countries suffering from the consequences of austerity measures casts a light on how the protesters who took the streets in 2011 addressed anticorruption through a paradigm that is different from the neoliberal one (della Porta 2017). Literature has also focused on how opposition to corruption from the grassroots might take different forms, as it happened for instance in Eastern Europe where Bulgarian activists mobilized against corruption in large demonstrations both in 1994 and in 2013–14, while in Hungary the fight against corruption remained more fragmented, involving small numbers of activists trying to influence public opinion through small-scale events (Pirro 2017). While in both Bulgaria and Hungary, activists did not succeed in obtaining changes at the institutional level (Pirro 2017), in Romania, between 2012 and 2017, a wave of four mobilizations addressed, amongst other issues, the corruption of political elites; these obtained some level of success, and managed to trigger a civic awakening in the country (Olteanu and Beyerle 2017).

Despite a growing interest in anticorruption efforts from the grassroots, a fruitful combination between social movement studies and (anti-)corruption literature is however still in the making, since the two subfield of studies have only very rarely crossed paths. The focus of attention has been very different in the two fields, as have the theories usually applied: rational choice and game theory, respectively, to address corrupt exchanges on one hand, and political processes, cultural/symbolic dimensions, and resource mobilization in research on social movements. While both have looked at very noninstitutional ways to affect public decisions, research on corruption has focused on the hidden relations between entrepreneurs, on the one hand, and politicians or public administrators, on the other, with the recourse to bribes in exchange for favors, whereas research on social movements has looked at the most visible forms of contestation: protest. Also, while the former research field has examined either the micro or the macro levels, the latter has mainly investigated the meso-level of mobilizations, mostly focusing on collective actors. With a few exceptions, social movements have been considered a positive force of politics, marked by altruistic motivation and cosmopolitan framing; corruption, by contrast, is representative of selfish behavior and the rejection of democratic values.

Nevertheless, there is some potential overlap between the two fields. In fact, both focus on the less institutionalized, but not less influential, aspects of politics; both present a sort of theoretical eclecticism, and employ interdisciplinary approaches combined with methodological pluralism (della Porta and Keating 2008); and both are committed to normative concerns with good politics. Drawing on social movement studies, the remainder of this chapter discusses in greater detail how the dimensions, processes, and mechanisms that scholars have elaborated with regard to grassroots mobilizations might help understanding what civil society actors do to fight corruption outside political institutions.

DIMENSIONS OF ANTICORRUPTION STRUGGLES
FROM THE GRASSROOTS

In the past decades, social movement studies have developed a rich conceptual toolbox to understand how collective action emerges outside institutional and political channels, how it develops in protest campaigns and mass mobilizations, and what consequences it has on the societies in which it occurs. When considering anticorruption efforts that become prominent thanks to social movement and civil society actors, there are three dimensions that seem to be particularly useful to analyze: the types of actors that engage in collective action; the types of collective action that they decide to employ; and the types of frames that they use to interpret the present situation and imagine future societies.

First, social movements have to be understood as processes in which a variety of actors might have a role—often in alliance with one another—in the fostering of protest campaigns, involving mass mobilizations but also and other forms of collective action. Understanding the type of actors that promote grassroots anticorruption efforts is therefore important not only in order to know who is behind these efforts, with what interests and objectives, but also to grasp how and why certain anticorruption efforts differ from one another. Social movement literature, indeed, shows that there is a strict link between the types of actors that mobilize, their cultural and political preferences, and the actual forms of the mobilizations that they organize (Jasper 1997).

When looking for actors outside of institutional and political channels might mobilize against corruption, we find actors who are positioned outside of the state—although they might have instrumental relationships with state actors, like controlling agencies—and outside of the market, hence do not follow a profit motive. Amongst them, there might be individuals who denounce various forms of corruption of democracy, acting as whistleblowers and calling for transparency in governmental action, as in the case of Edward Snowden. More frequently, though, behind grassroots anticorruption efforts we find collective actors, for example, civil society organizations that focus on the national level, like I Paid a Bribe in India, or transnational nongovernmental organizations such as Transparency International. Beyond their degree of collectiveness and the territorial scope of their actions, the types of actors involved in anticorruption efforts differ with regard to how they organize internally. In this regard, social movement scholars usually differentiate between horizontal and vertical organizational patterns.

On the one hand, there are constellations of civil society and social movement actors that coordinate and organize collective actions according to horizontal and decentralized patterns. For instance, corruption has been denounced forcefully at protest *acampadas* in places as distant and different as Tahrir Square, Placa de Catalunya, Sintagma Square, Zuccotti Park, or Taksim Square (della Porta 2013). In these cases, digital media were used within a logic of crowdsourcing, producing a mass aggregation of individuals that acted together independently from any formal social movement organization (Bennett and Segerberg 2013). On the other hand, there are constellations of civil society and social movement actors that organize in a more vertical and centralized fashion. An example is the Italian national campaign named "Without Corruption... The Future Starts Again," in which a national association, engaged in the fight against organized crime, launched a campaign to sensitize politicians to the issue of corruption, and to change Article 416ter of the Italian penal code, so as to expand corruption types of offenses in the country (Mattoni 2017).

Thanks to digital media, in the past decades we have seen the emergence of collective actors that had a prominent role in the struggle against corruption worldwide, and who mostly gathered and acted online: among them, the best known are Anonymous and WikiLeaks. Both these collective actors link anticorruption with information rights, through actions that aim at sensitizing the public and, at the same time, punishing corrupt elites. While WikiLeaks operates as an intermediary between those who have information and the public, Anonymous hacks listservs and other databases to acquire information (McCarthy 2015). WikiLeaks is an organization that publishes whistleblowers' information, using advanced technologies to protect the providers of information. It allows files to move across the Internet anonymously, directing the materials through countries where freedom of the press is well protected, using mirroring technologies so that content cannot be removed. Anonymous represents an evolution in digital activist tactics (Ravetto-Biagioli 2013), operating at the intersection of trolling and political reactions against institutional practices perceived as limiting free speech—"I came for the lulz but stayed for the outrage," stated an Anon (Coleman 2011a, 3). The shared interest of both organizations is "to break open structures that distort or block the flow of information" (McCarthy 2015, 440). The aim of WikiLeaks is to make those in power accountable through the leaking of sensitive information. While WikiLeaks revolves around the figure of Julian Assange, Anonymous emphasizes its rejection of leadership, as anonymity is also aimed at promoting an anti-celebrity discourse (Coleman 2011b). In both cases, transparency is of utmost importance in the fight against corruption. If, for WikiLeaks, the disclosure of information about the corruption of the elites was at the very core of its whistleblowing activities, for Anonymous, corruption became important especially when the organization campaigned in favor of Assange, defined as a symbol of "everything we hold dear."

Second, civil society and social movement actors select the forms of protest that they want to employ from a rich repertoire of collective action (Tilly 1995), which ranges from more contentious to less contentious, and from more public to less visible forms. Any "repertoire of contention" includes a wide range—although situated and finite—of "contentious performances" that activists can select to render visible their demands and proposals (Tilly and Tarrow 2007). Moreover, the diversity of strategies and tactics in the context of contentious performances also reflects the varying preferences of the diverse types of collective actors that decide to engage in the promotion of societal accountability (della Porta and Diani 2020, ch. 7). Indeed, as we have already noted above, there might be groups of citizens that are less formal and more loosely organized around common issues, without strict routines and procedures. At the other end of an ideal continuum, though, there might also be a more formal organization of citizens, structured around organizational routines and hierarchies.

All organizations face a series of strategic dilemmas (Jasper 2004), dealing with various trade-offs between the different choices they face. When considering anticorruption efforts from below, Grimes (2013) underlines the fact that social movement and civil society actors usually engage in two broad types of collective action: on the one side, there might be forms of protest that are reactive, in that activists organize them in reaction to some kind of corruption scandal and/or governmental misconduct; on the other side, collective actions exist that are more proactive and do not involve protest, which represent, rather, organized efforts to monitor, control, and contrast corruption, independently from contingent conditions.

Reactive collective actions against corruption usually involve some form of public protest, from mass demonstrations to online petitions, and also aim to achieve some kind of visibility in the short term within mainstream media. Proactive collective actions against corruption, instead, usually involve less visible but equally important social practices, oriented "to change systems of favoritism, clientelism and corruption" (Grimes 2013, 6). The anti-austerity protests that erupted in 2011 are good examples of reactive collective actions, in the sense that they aimed to hold governments across the globe accountable for their misconducts and wrongdoings, some of them with the clear intention of overthrowing those political elites that proved to be heavily corrupted and unresponsive. At the same time, these demonstrations offer a clear example of collective action that rests on noninstitutional resources, and which relies upon the massive participation of citizens in street protests (della Porta 2015). On the contrary, the campaign "Without Corruption... The Future Starts Again," outlined above, is a good example of proactive societal accountability, since the campaigners exploited the elections to foster anticorruption in the political agenda of the newly elected parliament (Mattoni 2017). Moreover, it depended on institutional resources, in that it mobilized political candidates, and subsequently the elected parliamentarians, in order to promote the institutional course of actions that eventually resulted in a change to the Italian penal code.

The Internet also provides a relevant space in which to perform collective actions against corruption. Drawing on a repertoire of contention that expanded due to the potential offered by Internet services and online platforms, both Anonymous and WikiLeaks organize collective actions that are primarily to be performed online. Distributed denial of service attacks is the main tool Anonymous uses to spread a political message (Barnard-Wills 2011). Digital sit-ins (i.e., DoS or denial of service attacks) are "the cyberspace equivalent of a protest march that blocks access to a factory. [...] Much like a sit-in at a lunch counter or government office, a DoS attack disrupts the public face of a target to draw attention to its actions and provoke a response" (Jarvis 2014, 338). Anonymous targets machines that limit access to information (Deseriis 2013, 34). Actions are often aimed against the websites and communication infrastructures of organizations that are accused of limiting access to information and information technologies (Deseriis 2013, 34). Through this type of action, Anonymous sought revenge for the repression directed towards whistleblowers such as Chelsea Manning (formerly Bradley Manning) and Edward Snowden (Coleman 2011a). After "operation Chanology" against the Scientology church, Anonymous took action against the censorship of dictators—such as Operation Tunisia or Operation Syria—by hacking governmental and private websites to show the force of civil society in challenging governments' capacity to censor access to information (Ferrada Stoehrel and Lindgren 2014). In terms of their logic of action, both groups have been defined as "e-bandits," reacting to informational asymmetry:

> By taking information, defacing websites, or otherwise using digital means to act against the powers that be, e-bandits effectively take from the rich through disabling commercial and government websites, and try at times to give back to the community, either in terms of revelation (releasing videos, previously unavailable materials), reporting, or providing previously unavailable tools (DDoS attacks) (Wong and Brown 2013, 1018).

Third, social movement actors are also engaged in the production of new meanings of contentious issues, often developing alternative norms and discourses, which then circulate in societies (Melucci 1996; Snow and Benford 1992). More specifically, social movement actors primarily engage in the construction of "collective action frames" (Benford and Snow 2000) that consist of three interrelated framing activities: first, prognostic framing, which usually defines the active subjects of mobilization, hence providing an "identity component" (Gamson 1992) through which activists define the "we" and the (social, political, economic, and cultural) problems they are fighting against, including an "injustice component" that refers to "moral indignation" (Gamson 1992); next, diagnostic framing, which elaborates the potential solution to the problems that the protests confront, as well as the demands attached to them; finally, motivational framing, which focuses on the reasons why other people should join the mobilization, hence including an "agency component" that signals the possibility to change the present situation thanks to collective action (Gamson 1992). Framing is crucial to connect the issue of corruption to other contentious issues. For instance, the leaders of the movements Y'en a Marre in Senegal, which developed in 2011 and 2012, and Balai Citoyen in Burkina Faso, which emerged in 2013, were able to unite the fight against corruption with the struggle against third-term amendments. They did so through a framing based on the concept of citizenship, "in its three dimensions of rights, duties, and empowerment [that] has proved to be a persuasive concept that allowed them to bond issues of corruption, the rule of law, and socio-economic grievances with their struggles against another presidential term" (Prause and Wienkoop 2017). In Italy, too, activists have developed collective action frames that have linked crimes against the environment to illegal activities managed by mafia organizations and facilitated by the collusion of political actors. These collective action frames occur, for instance, in the long-lasting and highly participated protests to oppose the construction of major infrastructural projects, such as the high-speed train tunnel in Val di Susa, Piedmont, or the bridge connecting Sicily and Calabria in Southern Italy (Piazza and Sorci 2017; della Porta and Piazza 2008).

As we have pointed out so far, apart from strategic choice, normative concerns are particularly relevant in social movements that have to mobilize their constituencies on the basis of symbolic rather than material incentives. In this regard, social movement and civil society actors go beyond the production of meanings through which they interpret the present times in which they are active. Indeed, they are usually also projected onto the future, elaborating ideas about the way their collective actions should change societies in the long term, hence constructing specific worldviews on what a good society means. Of course, this also applies to anticorruption struggles from the grassroots, which tend to develop a wide spectrum of views not just on what corruption means today, but what a society without corruption should look like.

However, in this regard, too, we are not dealing with fixed and rigid categories of anticorruption from the grassroots. Rather, we may witness a wide spectrum that spans from social movement and civil society actors who link anticorruption to the deep transformation of society as a whole to those that, instead, seek changes in specific sectors of societies without considering systemic change as their ultimate goal. An example of the latter is the way the mass mobilizations that took place in India, in 2011, originated. While activists mobilized against corruption as a whole, they also had a more specific objective in mind as they demanded that a stricter anticorruption law be passed by the Parliament, and that mobilized citizens might contribute to its drafting (Chowdhury and Abid 2019). Another example is the "15MParato" campaign, organized by the activist organization XNet in Spain, shortly after the peak of anti-austerity protests; their objective was to start an investigation against Rodrigo Rato, the former president of Bankia, and his collaborators, whom activists blamed for corrupt behavior in managing the bank (Mattoni 2017). By contrast, an example of those who seek a deep transformation of society as a whole are the anti-austerity movements that erupted in 2011 in many countries across Europe, claiming radical changes in societies so as to counter the corrupt political elites. Not only did they present anticorruption efforts as a matter of social justice, to be addressed through contextual knowledge, but also their very existence represented a call for anticorruption politics from the grassroots. Taking a stance against a capitalism, they targeted the neoliberal corruption of democracy caused by the growing collusion between political and financial elites. According to activists, privatization, deregulation, and liberalization are—by and large—part of the disease, bringing about unhealthy levels of collusion between politicians and business. Activist collectives like Anonymous also aimed at a systemic change of societies, publishing the text *Principles: An Anonymous Manifesto* calling for an "open, fair, transparent, accountable and just society," in which information is "unrestricted and uncensored" and citizens' "rights and liberties" (such as the right to privacy against surveillance) are upheld. Cyber-libertarianism is often linked to claims for social justice, stigmatizing the "abuse and corruption of corporations, banks, and governments," as "[t]he time has come to say: Enough! The abuse and corruption of corporations, banks, and governments can no longer be tolerated" (in Fuchs 2013, 367). It is clear, then, that anti-austerity movements and activist collectives like Anonymous embed the fight against corruption into broader mobilizations, which are intended to enact a deeper and broader change paradigm across all aspects of society.

THE CONDITIONS FOR ANTICORRUPTION MOVEMENTS FROM THE GRASSROOTS

Taken together, the dimensions of social movements discussed above can describe different aspects of social movements against corruption, as well as the campaigns and mobilizations that they organize. Using them as analytical lenses, we can also explain better the choice of specific tactics and strategies that characterizes the grassroots opposition against corruption. Focusing on the endogenous dimensions of social movement and civil society actors, though, is not enough to fully understand why anticorruption efforts develop the way they do. In this regard, contextual exogenous factors are also important. Some authors have begun to ask which kind of external conditions might influence the capacity of civil society to mobilize, and its effectiveness in fighting corruption. For instance, Grimes (2013) has investigated under what conditions the existence of a prosperous civil society may enhance societal accountability. Three conditions, in particular, proved to be decisive: The presence of political competition, a high degree of press freedom, and government transparency with regard to its own actions and decisions. According to the author, only if these three conditions are in place, a richer civil society can sustain a lower level of corruption. By contrast, in the absence of these three conditions, the author argues, the density of civil society has no bearing on the prevalence of corruption in a country (Grimes 2013, 18). Consistently, another longitudinal and cross-national study on civil society and corruption also claims that press freedom has a strong effect on "civil society efforts to generate public pressure against corrupt officials" (Themudo 2013, 65).

Government transparency, amongst other factors, is certainly linked to the widespread presence and adoption of digital media, which—in fostering a culture of transparency—seem to play a crucial role in decreasing corruption, also through the collective actions of citizens. Inspired by the work of Heald (2006) on varieties of transparency, Davies and Fumega (2014) underline the fact that the governmental uses of digital technologies for the purpose of increasing transparency can move in two opposite directions: while "upward transparency" grants the state the ability to monitor its citizens, "downward transparency" should empower citizens to control their rulers. Most of the time, transparency mechanisms are linked to the availability of data related to the phenomena that citizens and their governments scrutinize (Davies and Fumega 2014); downward transparency is often dependent on the presence of regulations that allow citizens to access data, like the Freedom of Information Act, or to create open data portals, like USAspending.gov, which shows how the tax dollars of American citizens are spent. Moreover, the success of digital media in increasing transparency and reducing corruption is also linked to citizens' acceptance of e-government initiatives (Bertot, Jaeger, and Grimes 2010), which should be citizen-centered in their development and implementation in order to be efficient and effective (Jaeger and Bertot 2010). The presence of downward transparency, however, is not clearly linked to the ability of citizens to engage in collective actions aimed at monitoring and denouncing their rulers. In this regard, Grimes (2013) shows, for instance, that government transparency might be a relevant intervening factor in curbing corruption only in those countries where a dense network of civil society actors is already in place. At the same time, Bauhr and Grimes argue that, in highly corrupted countries, the presence of transparency seems to lead to resignation rather than to civil society actors expressing their anger towards corruption and making claims to overcome it (Bauhr and Grimes 2014).

That said, the debate is ongoing in the field of grassroots anticorruption struggles. Indeed, contrary to the findings suggested above, Beyerle (2014, 15–17) argues that there are three myths about the power that citizens may exert in fighting against corruption. The first myth implies that governments—or institutions—need to have a political will to fight corruption for citizens' collective action to succeed. The second myth suggests that citizens need a specific legislative framework, which includes civil liberties and access to information, in order to organize successful initiatives against corruption. Finally, the third myth contends that citizens need institutional spaces granted by their governments in order to express their voice. In fact, many successful campaigns across the globe show that such structural factors may be less important than expected in fighting corruption, since grassroots collective action could also happen—and actually happened—in the following cases: when governments are not just ignoring corruption as a relevant issue to be addressed, but when they are corrupted themselves; when the legislative framework does not allow for civil liberties and access to information; and when there are no institutional spaces in which the citizens can express their concerns and demands related to corruption. Of course, when looking at case-based research on successful campaigns in unfavorable contexts, it is possible to argue that when they occasionally succeeded in achieving their goals this required activists to invest far more effort and taking more personal risks than in less hostile settings. Not only did they often have to rely upon the alliance of international actors, but results were frequently also more difficult to consolidate.

When referring to contextual factors, we have to acknowledge that social movement and civil society actors are embedded in a political structure that provides opportunities and constraints for collective action, influencing the struggles against corruption, their features, and their outcomes. When corruption is systemic, corrupt exchanges are themselves rooted in certain informal political rules. In these contexts, anticorruption actors need to fight a system of power that privileges illicit deals while marginalizing those who do not participate in them (della Porta and Vannucci 2012, 2014). The point is, therefore, also to consider the main structural elements that social movement and civil society actors need to address when planning and organizing mobilizations against corruption.

As social movement studies have suggested, four kinds of signals are particularly relevant in encouraging collective actors to invest their internal resources for the formation of social movements (Tarrow 1996, 32): First, the opening up of access to power due to specific and contingent factors that allow social movement actors to have a say at the level of the polity, and in the policymaking process; second, the presence of unstable political alignments between institutional political actors that operate within the realm of institutional politics, but also between institutional political actors—such as political parties—and their electorate; third, the presence of influential allies that might provide the necessary support to intervene at the policymaking level; and fourth, the presence of divided elites whose conflicts might increase the likelihood of social movement actors accessing power, especially when one part of the conflicting elites explicitly decides to support social movement actors.

More specifically, for social movement and civil society actors to succeed, pluralism and competition in the party system emerge as particularly important, as is the presence in the political system of ideological versus clientelistic structures of representation, as well as the abovementioned transparency in decision-making and the presence of channels of access to decision-making for civil society. What is more, civil society must be free in its expression and autonomous from political parties. At the same time, research on social movements also stresses the importance of the framing of political opportunities; social actors act upon their construction of the external reality and activists, indeed, interpret the elements of the political opportunity structure (Goodwin and Jasper 2004; Gamson and Meyer 1996), and might also partially change them by intervening at the level of the political process (Meyer and Staggenborg 1996; Gamson and Meyer 1996; Tarrow 1993).

Besides structural conditions, the agency of civil society organizations is, however, important in developing successful strategies to sensitize citizens to the problems related with corruption. Discursive opportunities are, in this sense, relevant in making anticorruption calls resonant (Koopmans and Statham 1999). Research on anti-austerity protests points out how social movement and civil society actors manage to create their own opportunities while they engage in collective action, through the development of a diagnostic frame based upon the stigmatization of the corruption of the elites (della Porta 2015).

Since the struggle against corruption has been linked to the claim for social justice, corruption has been defined as outrageous, given the extreme levels of enrichment of "the 1%" against the suffering of "the 99%." Thus, in Iceland—a country that, before the crisis, had been considered as having most encouraging levels of transparency in government—the citizens mobilized against the power of criminal bankers and colluding politicians. Inspired by the Arab Spring, the Indignados in Spain denounced the corruption of the political class, through the convergence of the center-right and center-left into a 'PPSOE' (a hybrid of the two main parties, PP and PSOE). The connivances of politicians from both parties with large and greedy corporations—with generous private contributions to parties and politicians being protected by the right of expression—have been stigmatized also in Greece and by Occupy Wall Street (hereafter OWS) in the US (della Porta et al. 2017). Claims in Puerta del Sol included the fight against corruption through the development of norms aimed at establishing political transparency, and also the creation of a mechanism of control by the citizens, with an effective separation of powers (Nez 2011). In OWS, demands also focus on a greater political transparency, and on getting corporate money out of politics (Blumenkranz et al. 2011). The radically decreasing trust in parties is reflected in slogans such as "No les votas" (Do not vote for them) and "No nos representan (They do not represent us) which were used widely within the Spanish protests and translated in Greek and Portuguese. Anticorruption frames—such as those against the *casta*—have been resonant with a diverse base of support, also appealing to personal experiences with perceived injustice. The corruption of the 1% reflects the breaking of a moral pact. The immorality of the system is denounced, with a sense of injustice being linked to greedy politicians and businessmen. Bribes in exchange for favors, but also the development of collusive elites of politicians and businessmen, were considered as immoral and unjust. As the narrative of the anti-austerity protests points at the convergence of businesses and politicians, institutional democracy is, in particular, seen as not representative of people, but of banks and financial power. The object of blame is mainly the corruption of representative institutions in neoliberalism, "through revolving doors, practiced deregulation and administrative collusion, [which] organized themselves into combinations in the name of competition" (Gitlin 2012, 11). So, a much used slogan is: "We are not commodities in the hands of politicians and bankers." Against the corruption of representative democracy, there is a call for the accountability of public affairs and the prosecution of political corruption (Perugorría and Tejerina 2013, 436). Similarly, daily protests have been organized in the main square of Sophia, capital of Bulgaria, to denounce the oligarchic development of economic and political power in an elitist system. Not by chance, the main demand was for the resignation of the prime minister, considered as the embodiment of a system dominated by the country's monopoly of the energy sector, with strong collusive support from political elites. The protesters grew increasingly critical of those in power, framing parties as either allies or interlocutors, and demanded clean politics, denouncing widespread patronage as well as rampant corruption (Rone 2017).

THE OUTCOMES OF ANTICORRUPTION STRUGGLES FROM THE GRASSROOTS

Civil society and social movement actors who engage in collective actions against corruption play an important role in signaling problems by naming and shaming wrongdoers, controlling and monitoring public powers, and reinforcing and consolidating representative institutions (Peruzzotti 2012, 71–2). While this might be the case for many collective actions aimed at fighting corruption, recent mass demonstrations in many countries across the globe also show that the mobilization against corruption—and, to some extent, the engagement with societal accountability politics—may also rest on a more systemic opposition to the institutions of representative democracy, which protesters considered to be corrupt almost by definition. It is not a coincidence that alternative democratic ideals, like participatory democracy, are advanced in such contexts.

Given these differences concerning social movement and civil society actors, the protest campaigns and mass mobilizations that they organize, and the contexts in which they develop, some questions are relevant to discuss: what are the consequences of anticorruption struggles from below? When should a protest campaign be considered successful, and why? What are the relevant—although sometimes unexpected—consequences of anticorruption efforts beyond the short-term goals that activists set for their mobilizations? Understanding social movement outcomes is a growing concern in social movement studies, which can so usefully complement literature on corruption, which has been mostly focused on assessing social movements' impact on anticorruption measures taken by governmental agencies and other institutional actors.

Scholars who focus on social movement outcomes usually make an analytical distinction between political, biographical, and cultural outcomes (Bosi, Giugni, and Uba 2016). Biographical outcomes are certainly important with respect to struggles against corruption; individual citizens who act as whistleblowers face considerable changes in their own lives once the corruption they expose becomes a very public—and often political—scandal. Furthermore, as happens in many other social movements, the participation in contentious collective action against corruption has a transformative potential at the level of individual activists. The attitudes of those who protest could change considerably due to participation in protest activities, both towards the protest targets against which they mobilize and towards the contentious issue at stake.

While personal and biographical outcomes are centered on the individual, at the meso level of protest we might position political and cultural outcomes of struggles against corruption. Amongst the political outcomes of anticorruption efforts, we may certainly include the passing of specific anticorruption bills, but also, on a more general level, the increase in societal accountability. Societal accountability is a mechanism of control according to which citizens monitor the actions of their representatives, with the ultimate aim of mitigating corruption through the triggering of other forms of control (Peruzzotti & Smulovits 2006; Smulovitz and Peruzzotti 2000). When citizens organize collective action in order to target their elected representatives and other state institutions, the changes they ask for are thus situated within the institutional political realm. As with any social movement's political outcomes, those referring to anticorruption, too, could be distinguished with reference to the following stages of policy change: Obtaining access to the arenas in which institutional political actors take decisions; making visible specific contentious issues within the agenda of institutional political actors; achieving the drafting and approval of specific policies; the allocation of resources to and implementation of specific policies; and finally, triggering a long-term change in the priorities of political institutions, instead of just affecting the agenda of specific political actors, like political parties obtaining an accord (Andrews and Edwards 2004). We should note, however, that while these stages might be important for proactive campaigns against corruption, not all of them play the same role in the reactive campaigns that civil society actors organize against specific political events related to corruption.

The outcomes are, however, not only of a political kind. When civil society and social movement actors mobilize, they also act at the cultural level, which has consequences for language, discourses, values, and attitudes. Although early literature on social movement outcomes tended to focus more on changes at the level of policymaking, several authors also stress the importance of social movement outcomes at the cultural level (e.g. Staggenborg 1995; Soule and Olzak 2004; Soule and King 2006). Cultural outcomes refer exactly to the meaning-making activities of social movement and civil society actors, in that they can be defined as "changes in social norms, behaviors and ways of thinking that extend beyond movement constituents or beneficiaries" (Staggenborg 1995, 341).

The cultural outcomes of anticorruption struggles may be seen at work in anti-austerity movements, which have, in fact, defined corruption as a problem of social justice, rather than as a mere obstacle towards good government. According to the citizens who mobilized in these movements, the fight against systemic corruption—considered as a factor of degeneration and injustice—cannot be a single-issue policy, nor can it be delegated to experts; rather, it must be linked to a rethinking of policy and participation (della Porta 2013). From this viewpoint, activists have operated a change at the cultural level, in that they have reframed the fight against corruption as something related to the public good, as well as to the presence of adequate regulation. Activists so denounced the spread of political corruption, arguing that it was the result of the privatization of common goods and services, like water, and that it contributed to opacity and inefficiency during the corresponding processes. Anti-austerity mobilizations attributed the increase in prices paid by citizens, and the deterioration in the quality of services provided, to the greed of large corporations, as well as to their capacity to corrupt politicians at all levels. An effective fight against corruption also requires a defense of citizens' rights, since without certainty of rights, the power of the patrons and political bosses—to whom particularistic demands are addressed—increases.

Conclusion

In this chapter, we have discussed at length how the conceptual toolbox developed in social movement studies might help understanding the different facets of anticorruption efforts from the grassroots. We have considered three main endogenous dimensions of social movements: the types of actors that mobilize; the types of collective action that they decide to employ; and the construction of meanings and interpretations about both present social problems and future societies. We then considered some relevant exogenous factors, including the political opportunity structure in which social movement and civil society actors are embedded, as well as the more general level of government transparency that might increase the emergence of anticorruption efforts from below. Finally, we also discussed the outcomes of mobilizations against corruption, pointing out that the consequences are not only at the political level. Biographical consequences at the micro level of activists' lives as well as political and cultural consequences at the macro level of public discourse on corruption, are equally crucial. In so doing, we presented examples of anticorruption efforts from the grassroots, making clear that different viewpoints—sometimes overlapping, other times contradicting each other—populate the debate on the characteristics, conditions, and consequences of such mobilizations. Other than qualitative, case-based research and quantitative, comparative research, we believe that a comparative and mixed-method approach to grassroots anticorruption struggles could make a strong contribution to the current discussion on the subject matter. To conclude, in what follows we will outline three areas that will undoubtedly offer further insight into the qualities, contexts, and impacts of the anticorruption efforts that have arisen worldwide.

First, the study of grassroots efforts against corruption would benefit from further analysis of and discussions about the emergence of different anticorruption paradigms. In fact, anticorruption has, until now, been seen as a matter of good governance, with highly technical content being spread top-down and implemented from above (e.g., by the judiciary, independent authorities, international organizations). Within a neoliberal paradigm, anticorruption efforts have often preached a reduction in state spending and regulation (della Porta 2013)—as in the inherently authoritarian anticorruption approach that authorities have implemented in Singapore and Hong Kong (Heilbrunn 2004). In short, privatization, deregulation, and liberalization have been seen as the main cures for the disease of corruption. However, in recent years in particular, social movements that denounce kleptocratic practices, as well as corrupt politicians and entrepreneurs, have developed a radically different explanatory framework. Not only do they present anticorruption as a matter of social justice, to be addressed through contextual knowledge, but their very existence represents a call for anticorruption politics from the grassroots: horizontal and participatory. Taking a stance against a neoliberal vision, they target not only the corruption of democracy produced by specific forms of capitalism, but they also see privatization, deregulation, and liberalization—by and large—as part of the problem, causing harmful levels of collusion between politicians and business. To understand how different conceptions of anticorruption efforts emerge in different settings, and with what consequences, is necessary in order to develop more effective and inclusive anticorruption strategies.

Second, anticorruption efforts from the grassroots do not only offer new paradigms to interpret corruption: they also experiment with new forms of public participation. Since the fight against corruption is a basic constituent of a wider effort by citizens to oppose the deterioration of the quality of democratic processes, the policy toolkit has broadened as a consequence of many anticorruption mobilizations. In order to fully understand the meanings and consequences of grassroots resistance against corruption, it is therefore necessary to address new accountability and transparency mechanisms that will permit a more effective control of the rulers by citizens. This would help to develop a better understanding of the experiences and the experiments that increase the citizens' opportunities to participate in the development of public policies—that is, in the formulation, decision-making, and implementation phases—as well as the information available to the public. In doing so, they encourage widespread awareness and understanding of issues that, in the "technocratic" conception of politics, are instead jealously kept hidden (Font, della Porta, and Sintomer 2014).

Third, many of the experiences and experiments mentioned above rest on the use of digital media. In the past few years, scholars interested in political mobilization and participation have noted that civil society actors are increasingly able to engage with big data, either to resist the governments and corporations' extraction of data on what people do in their daily lives, or to employ "big data" as an additional tool in the activists' repertoire of contention, in order to sustain their mobilizations (Gutierrez and Milan 2018; Milan 2018; Schrock 2016). This holds true also in frameworks of anticorruption efforts from the grassroots. Albeit with changing fortunes, in the past few years activists have attempted to exploit the potential of crowd-reporting platforms in many countries across the world, in order to monitor corruption from below, asking citizens to report the extortion of bribes on platforms like I Paid

A Bribe in India, or Not In My Country, in Kenya and Uganda (Zinnbauer 2015). Using "big data" to increase transparency and discover wrongdoings, data activists constitute an increasingly relevant part of anticorruption efforts from the grassroots. It is therefore important to understand the extent to which the increased employment of big data in the fight against corruption from the grassroots is affecting the way social movement and civil society actors organize collectively, engage citizens, and protest publicly. Furthermore, finding ways to measure the consequences of the deployment of big data in the struggle against corruption from the grassroots is relevant both at the regional and national level.

References

Andrews, Kenneth T., and Bob Edwards. 2004. "Advocacy Organizations in the U.S. Political Process." *Annual Review of Sociology* 30 (1): 479–506.

Bauhr, Monika, and Marcia Grimes. 2014. "Indignation or Resignation: The Implications of Transparency for Societal Accountability." *Governance* 27 (2): 291–320.

Barnard-Wills David. 2011. "This Is Not a Cyber War, It's a …?": Wikileaks, Anonymous and the Politics of Hegemony." *International Journal of Cyber Warfare and Terrorism* 1(1): 13–23.

Benford, Robert D., and David A. Snow. 2000. "Framing Processes and Social Movements: An Overview and Assessment." *Annual Review of Sociology* 26: 611–39.

Bennett, W. Lance, and Alexandra Segerberg. 2013. *The Logic of Connective Action: Digital Media and the Personalization of Contentious Politics*. Cambridge: Cambridge University Press.

Bertot, John C., Paul T. Jaeger, and Justin M. Grimes. 2010. "Using ICTs to Create a Culture of Transparency: E-Government and Social Media as Openness and Anti-Corruption Tools for Societies." *Government Information Quarterly* 27 (3): 264–71.

Beyerle, Shaazka. 2014. *Curtailing Corruption: People Power for Accountability and Justice*. Boulder: Lynne Rienner Pub.

Blumenkranz, Carla, Keith Gessen, Mark Greif, Sarah Leonard, and Sarah Resnick, eds. 2011. *Occupy!: Scenes from Occupied America*. 1st ed. London: Verso.

Bosi, Lorenzo, Marco Giugni, and Katrin Uba, eds. 2016. *The Consequences of Social Movements*. New York: Cambridge University Press.

Chowdhury, Arnab, and Ahmed Abid. 2019. "Emergent Protest Publics in India and Bangladesh: A Comparative Study of Anti-Corruption and Shahbag Protests." In *Protest Publics: Toward a New Concept of Mass Civic Action*, edited by Nina Belyaeva, Victor Albert, and Dmitry G. Zaytsev, 49–66. Societies and Political Orders in Transition. Cham: Springer International Publishing.

Coleman, E. Gabriella. 2011a. "Anonymous: From the Lulz to Collective Action." The New Everyday: A Mediacommons Project. April 6, 2011. http://mediacommons.futureofthebook.org/tne/pieces/anonymous-lulz-collective-action

Coleman E. Gabriella. 2011b. "Hacker Politics and Publics." *Public Culture* 23 (3): 511–16.

Davies, Tim, and Silvana Fumega. 2014. "Mixed Incentives: Adopting ICT Innovations for Transparency, Accountability, and Anti-Corruption." *U4 Issue* 2014: 4. https://www.cmi.no/publications/5172-mixed-incentives

della Porta, Donatella. 2017. "Anti-Corruption from Below. Social Movements Against Corruption in Late Neoliberalism." *Partecipazione e conflitto* 10 (3): 661–92.

della Porta, Donatella. 2015. *Social Movements in Times of Austerity: Bringing Capitalism Back into Protest Analysis*. Cambridge, UK; Malden, MA: Polity Press.

della Porta, Donatella. 2013. *Can Democracy Be Saved: Participation, Deliberation and Social Movements*. Cambridge, UK; Malden, MA: Polity Press.

Della Porta, Donatella and Mario Diani. 2020. *Social Movements: An Introduction*. London: Blackwell, 3rd edition.

della Porta, Donatella, Joseba Fernandez, Hara Kouki, and Lorenzo Mosca. 2017. *Movement Parties Against Austerity*. Oxford: Wiley.

della Porta Donatella, and Alberto Vannucci 2014. *State of the Art Report on Theories and Harmonised Concept of Corruption*. D1.1. Anticorrp http://anticorrp.eu/wp-content/uploads/2014/10/D1.1-State-of-the-art-report-on-theories-and-harmonised-concepts-of-corruption.pdf

della Porta Donatella, and Alberto Vannucci 2012. *The Governance of Corruption*. London: Ashgate.

della Porta, Donatella, and Michael Keating. 2008. *Approaches and Methodologies in the Social Sciences. A Pluralist Perspective*. Cambridge: Cambridge University Press.

della Porta, Donatella, and Gianni Piazza. 2008. *Voices of the Valley, Voices of the Straits*. New York, Oxford: Berghahn Books.

Deseriis, Marco 2013. "Is Anonymous a new form of Luddism? A comparative analysis of industrial machine breaking, computer hacking, and related rhetorical strategies." *Radical History Review* 117: 33–48.

Disch, Arne, Endre Vigeland, and Geir Sundet. 2009. "Anti-Corruption Approaches: A Literature Review." *Study* 2. http://www.sida.se/globalassets/publications/import/pdf/sv/anti-corruption-approaches-a-literature-review.pdf

Ferrada Stoehrel Rodrigo and Simon Lindgren. 2014. "For the Lulz: Anonymous, Aesthetics and Affect." *TripleC: Communication, Capitalism & Critique. Open Access Journal for a Global Sustainable Information Society* 12 (1): 238–64. https://doi.org/10.31269/triplec.v12i1.503.

Font, Joan, Donatella Della Porta, and Yves Sintomer, eds. 2014. *Participatory Democracy in Southern Europe: Causes, Characteristics and Consequences*. Lanham: Rowman & Littlefield International.

Fuchs, Christian. 2013. "The Anonymous movement in the context of liberalism and socialism." *Interface: A Journal for and About Social Movements* 5 (2): 345–376.

Gamson, William A. 1992. *Talking Politics*. Cambridge [England]; New York, NY, USA: Cambridge University Press.

Gamson, William A., and David S. Meyer. 1996. "Framing Political Opportunity." In *Comparative Perspective on Social Movements*, edited by Doug McAdam, John D. McCarthy, and Mayer N. Zald, 275–90. Cambridge: Cambridge University Press.

Gitlin, Todd. 2012. *Occupy Nation: The Roots, the Spirit, and the Promise of Occupy Wall Street*. New York: HarperCollins.

Goodwin, Jeff, and James M. Jasper. 2004. "Caught in a Winding, Snarling Vine; The Structural Bias of Political Process Theory." In *Rethinking Social Movements. Structure, Meaning, and Emotion*, edited by Jeff Goodwin and James M. Jasper, 3–30. Lanham (Maryland): Rowman & Littlefield.

Gutierrez, Miren, and Stefania Milan. 2018. "Technopolitics in the Age of Big Data: The Rise of Proactive Data Activism in Latin America." In *Networks, Movements & Technopolitics in Latin America: Critical Analysis and Current Challenges*, edited by Francisco Sierra Caballero and Tommaso Gravante, 95–109. London: Palgrave.

Grimes, Marcia. 2013. "The Contingencies of Societal Accountability: Examining the Link Between Civil Society and Good Government." *Studies in Comparative International Development* 48 (4): 380–402. https://doi.org/10.1007/s12116-012-9126-3

Heald, David. 2006. "Varieties of Transparency." In *Transparency: The Key to Better Governance?*, edited by Christopher Hood and David Heald, 25–43. Oxford: Oxford University Press.

Heilbrunn, John R. 2004. "Anti-Corruption Commissions Panacea or Real Medicine to Fight Corruption?" 37234. Washington, D.C.: The World Bank. https://www.acauthorities.org/publications/anti-corruption-commissions-panacea-or-real-medicine-fight-corruption

Hough, D. 2013. *Corruption, Anti-Corruption and Governance*. London: Palgrave Macmillan.

Jaeger, Paul T., and John Carlo Bertot. 2010. "Designing, Implementing, and Evaluating User-Centered and Citizen-Centered E-Government." *International Journal of Electronic Government Research (IJEGR)* 6 (2): 1–17. https://doi.org/10.4018/jegr.2010040101

Jarvis, Jason L. 2014. "Digital image politics: the networked rhetoric of Anonymous." *Global Discourse: An Interdisciplinary Journal of Current Affairs and Applied Contemporary Thought Publication* 4 (2–3): 1–24.

Jasper, James. 2004. "A Strategic Approach to Collective Action: Looking for Agency in Social-Movement Choices." *Mobilization: An International Quarterly* 9 (1): 1–16. https://doi.org/10.17813/maiq.9.1.m112677546p63361

Jasper, James M. 1997. *The Art of Moral Protest: Culture, Biography, and Creativity in Social Movements*. Chicago (Illinois): University of Chicago Press.

Johnston, Michael. 2005. *Civil Society and Corruption: Mobilizing for Reform*. Lanham (Maryland): Rowman & Littlefield.

Koopmans, Ruud, and Paul Statham. 1999. "Ethnic and Civic Conceptions of Nationhood and the Differential Success of the Extreme Right in Germany and Italy." In *How Social Movements Matter*, edited by Marco Giugni, Doug McAdam, and Charles Tilly, 225–52. Minneapolis: University of Minnesota Press.

Mattoni, Alice. 2017. "From Data Extraction to Data Leaking. Data-Activism in Italian and Spanish Anti-Corruption Campaigns." *Partecipazione e Conflitto* 10 (3): 723–46. https://doi.org/10.1285/i20356609v10i3p723

McCarthy, Matthew T. 2015. "Toward a Free Information Movement." *Sociological Forum* 30 (2): 439–58. https://doi.org/10.1111/socf.12170

Melucci, Alberto. 1996. *Challenging Codes: Collective Action in the Information Age*. Cambridge Cultural Social Studies. Cambridge [England]; New York: Cambridge University Press.

Meyer, David S., and Suzanne Staggenborg. 1996. "Movements, Countermovements, and the Structure of Political Opportunity." *American Journal of Sociology* 101 (6): 1628–60.

Milan, Stefania. 2018. "Data Activism as the New Frontier of Media Activism." In *Media Activism in the Digital Age*, edited by Victor W. Pickard and Guobin Yang. London: Routledge.

Mungiu-Pippidi, Alina. 2013. "Controlling Corruption Through Collective Action." *Journal of Democracy* 24 (1): 101–15. https://doi.org/10.1353/jod.2013.0020

Mungiu-Pippidi, Alina. 2015. *The Quest for Good Governance*. Cambridge: Cambridge University Press.

Nez, Héloïse. 2011. " 'No es un botellón, es la revolución !' " *Mouvements des Idées et des luttes*, June 7, 2011. http://mouvements.info/no-es-un-botellon-es-la-revolucion/

Olteanu, Tina and Shaazka Beyerle. 2017. "The Romanian People Versus Corruption. The Paradoxical Nexus of Protest and Adaptation." *Partecipazione e Conflitto* 10 (3): 797–825.

Peruzzotti, Enrique. 2012. "Accountability Struggles in Democratic Argentina: Civic Engagement from the Human Rights Movement to the Néstor Kirchner Administration." *Laboratorium: Russian Review of Social Research* 2 (2): 65–85.

Peruzzotti, Enrique, and Catalina Smulovitz. 2006. *Enforcing the Rule of Law: Social Accountability in the New Latin American Democracies*. Pittsburgh: University of Pittsburgh Press.

Perugorría, Ignacia, and Benjamín Tejerina. 2013. "Politics of the Encounter: Cognition, Emotions, and Networks in the Spanish 15M." *Current Sociology* 61 (4): 424–42. https://doi.org/10.1177/0011392113479743

Piazza, Gianni, and Giuliana Sorci. 2017. "Do Lulu Movements in Italy Fight Mafia and Corruption? Framing Processes and 'Anti-system' Struggles in the No Tav, No Bridge and No Muos Case Studies." *Partecipazione e Conflitto* 10 (3): 747–72.

Pirro, Andrea. 2017. "Screaming at a Wall. Societal Accountability from below in Bulgaria and Hungary." *Partecipazione e Conflitto* 10 (3): 773–96.

Prause, Louisa, and Nina-Kathrin Wienkoop. 2017. "Who is Responsible for Corruption? Framing strategies of social movements in West Africa mobilizing against presidential term amendments." *Partecipazione e Conflitto* 10 (3): 850–73.

Ravetto-Biagioli, Kriss. 2013. "Anonymous: Social as Political." *Leonardo Electronic Alma-nac* 19 (4): 178–95.

Rone, Julia. 2017. "Left in Translation. The Curious Absence of Austerity Frames in the 2013 Bulgarian protests." In *Global Diffusion of Protest: Riding the Protest Wave in the Neoliberal Crisis*, edited by Donatella della Porta, 137–66. Amsterdam: Amsterdam University Press.

Schrock, Andrew R. 2016. "Civic Hacking as Data Activism and Advocacy: A History from Publicity to Open Government Data." *New Media & Society* 18 (4): 581–99. https://doi.org/10.1177/1461444816629469

Shim, Dong Chul, and Tae Ho Eom. 2009. "Anticorruption Effects of Information Communication and Technology (ICT) and Social Capital." *International Review of Administrative Sciences* 75 (1): 99–116. https://doi.org/10.1177/0020852308099508

Smulovitz, Catalina, and Enrique Peruzzotti. 2000. "Societal Accountability in Latin America." *Journal of Democracy* 11 (4): 147–58. https://doi.org/10.1353/jod.2000.0087

Snow, David A., and Robert D. Benford. 1992. "Master Frames and Cycles of Protest." In *Frontiers in Social Movement Theory*, edited by Aldon D. Morris and Carol McClurg Mueller, 133–55. New Haven, Conn.: Yale University Press.

Staggenborg, Suzanne. 1995. "Can Feminist Organizations Be 'Effective?'" In *Feminist Organizations: Harvest of the New Women's Movement*, edited by Ferree Myra Marx and Patricia Yancey Martin, 339–55. Philadelphia, PA: Temple University Press.

Sotirakopoulos, Nikos, and George Sotiropoulos. 2013. "'Direct Democracy Now!': The Greek Indignados and the Present Cycle of Struggles." *Current Sociology* 61 (4): 443–56. https://doi.org/10.1177/0011392113479744

Soule, Sarah A., and Brayden G. King. 2006. "The Stages of the Policy Process and the Equal Rights Amendment, 1972–1982." *American Journal of Sociology* 111 (6): 1871–1909. https://doi.org/10.1086/499908

Soule, Sarah A., and Susan Olzak. 2004. "When Do Movements Matter? The Politics of Contingency and the Equal Rights Amendment." *American Sociological Review* 69 (4): 473–97. https://doi.org/10.1177/000312240406900401

Tarrow, Sidney. 1993. "Modular Collective Action and the Rise of the Social Movement: Why the French Revolution Was Not Enough." *Politics & Society* 21 (1): 69–90. https://doi.org/10.1177/0032329293021001004

Tarrow, Sidney. 1996. "States and Opportunities. The Political Structure of Social Movements." In *Comparative Perspectives on Social Movements: Political Opportunities, Mobilizing Structures, and Cultural Framings*, edited by Doug McAdam, John D. McCarthy, and Mayer N. Zald, 41–61. Cambridge: Cambridge University Press.

Themudo, Nuno S. 2013. "Reassessing the Impact of Civil Society: Nonprofit Sector, Press Freedom, and Corruption." *Governance* 26 (1): 63–89. https://doi.org/10.1111/j.1468-0491.2012.01602.x

Tilly, Charles. 1995. "Contentious Repertoires in Gret Britain, 1758–1834." In *Repertoires & Cycles of Collective Action*, edited by Mark Traugott, 15–42. Durham and London: Duke University Press.

Tilly, Charles, and Sidney G. Tarrow. 2007. *Contentious Politics*. Boulder, CO: Paradigm Publishers. http://www.loc.gov/catdir/toc/ecip068/2006003610.html

Van Gelder, Sarah, and The staff of YES! Magazine, eds. 2011. *This Changes Everything: Occupy Wall Street and the 99% Movement*. 1st ed. San Francisco: Berrett-Koehler Publishers.

Wong, Wendy H., and Peter A. Brown. 2013. "E-Bandits in Global Activism: WikiLeaks, Anonymous, and the Politics of No One." *Perspectives on Politics* 11 (4): 1015–33. https://doi.org/10.1017/S1537592713002806

Zinnbauer, Dieter. 2015. "Crowdsourced Corruption Reporting: What Petrified Forests, Street Music, Bath Towels, and the Taxman Can Tell Us About the Prospects for Its Future." *Policy & Internet* 7 (1) (March 1): 1–24. https://doi.org/10.1002/poi3.84

CHAPTER 15

....

ELECTORAL RULES AND CORRUPTION
A Meta-Analysis

....

GEORGIOS XEZONAKIS AND STEPHEN DAWSON

INTRODUCTION

....

CONSTITUTIONAL effects on quality of government (mostly on various aspects of graft or corruption) have been the focus of a significant part of research in political science and economics. The debate is centered across three main constitutional dimensions: The composition of the executive (presidentialism vs. parliamentarism), the territorial locus of power (unitarism vs. federalism), and the rules that govern elections (Persson and Tabellini 2005; Gerring and Thacker 2004).[1] We consider all important constitutional design aspects as they pertain to issues of quality of government. However, in this chapter we contribute to the latter part of the debate through a systematic review of the relevant literature, in search of an answer to the question: Does the choice of electoral system affect levels of corruption?

Our study is motivated by three main considerations. First, we have, by now, a corpus of research that provides the opportunity for a meta-analysis. To our knowledge, this is the first effort that applies this specific methodology in the area, and one of the few which concentrates on a review of the causes and consequences for political corruption, rent-seeking, clientelism, and other aspects of QoG (see Ugur and Dasgupta 2011 for a systematic review of the evidence on corruption and economic growth). We have collected a sample of 34 papers and a total of 476 estimates for this analysis. As such, this study has the potential to contribute to pioneering work in the area (see Treisman 2007) and provide some answers to the question on what we have learned from about three decades of research. Second, a meta-analysis provides more than a simple summary of the literature and the presentation of the findings thus far. Indeed, our literature review on the theory behind the relationship between electoral rules and corruption (this is really the main aspect of QoG that the research

---

[1] In unitary systems there is also by now a substantial debate about the effects of decentralization (see Fisman and Gatti 2002, for a review).

is focusing on) and the sketch of the relevant mechanisms are an important endeavor in their own right. However, the systematic review of the findings that is performed in this chapter gives not only a summary presentation of the results but also an opportunity to gauge the robustness of these effects and the generalizability of the findings.

Finally, and most importantly, our research is motivated by our desire to address what we view as theoretical ambiguity and empirical contradictions in the literature. For example, from a cursory review of the literature, an apparent consensus emerges regarding the superiority of majoritarianism in dealing with political corruption as opposed to proportional representation (PR) (Blume 2009; Kunicová and Rose-Ackerman 2005; Treisman 2007). This goes against established theoretical propositions on "barriers to entry" effects (Myerson 1993) and classic works on political science about the "kinder and gentler" nature of PR systems (Lijphart 1999). It also fails to pass a reality check, since the majority of countries who do best at controlling corruption use PR in their electoral systems (e.g. Sweden, Norway, Netherlands, Denmark), while countries such as Canada or the United Kingdom that have majoritarian electoral systems have a somewhat lower score in the Corruption Perceptions Index (2016–18). A consistent leader is also New Zealand—a country which replaced its first past the post (FPTP) system with a mixed-member proportional system in 1993.

The puzzle is complicated further when one considers the predictions that stem from theoretical mechanisms presented in the literature, but also from what the results suggest. For example, original theoretical treatments regarding these effects seem to suggest, simultaneously, that larger districts and plurality formulas have a positive effect on corruption (Myerson 1993; Persson 2000; Persson and Tabelini 2005; Persson, Tabellini, and Trebbi 2003). Since features of the electoral system such as the district magnitude and the electoral formula tend to be highly correlated by that logic, one would expect to find high performers both in PR and plurality systems. These ambiguities cannot be attributed to the fact that the research on these issues lacks nuance. Most studies avoid crude distinctions and incorporate different dimensions of the electoral rules in their models. However, if the statistical findings that are reported tend to point in either direction, then it begs the question whether the choice of electoral system is really related to corruption or whether we should be looking elsewhere in order to identify institutional engineering conducive to QoG.

We do find in our results that nuance is indeed important. For example, while we confirm findings about the positive effects of majoritarianism, we also find similar effects for larger districts. In trying to clarify these findings, we pursue further the "personal vote" hypothesis (Carey and Shugart 1995; Kunicová and Rose-Ackerman 2005; Chang and Golden 2005) that is applicable both in plurality and PR systems. It is among the systems that emphasize the connection between candidate performance and reelection chances—the systems that amplify accountability—where we find the most robust results. This is irrespective of the electoral formula. Therefore, PR systems can be as effective in combating corruption as majoritarian ones, as long as they offer an open-list ballot structure.

An additional finding has to do with the uncovering of potential file drawer effects. Our sample of papers is based—almost exclusively—on published research pieces. Since null results are less likely to be published, our sample of papers is likely to be biased towards statistically significant results. Following Smets and Van Ham (2013), we replicate our analysis focusing only on papers where the independent variable of interest (the electoral system) is not the theoretical focus of the paper but is rather included only as a control variable. In these cases, we find no robust electoral system effects for electoral formula and district magnitude.

Although this is based on a very limited number of papers/estimates, it is an interesting piece of information that gives cause for concern. We proceed with caution in interpreting this finding, but as published research on these issues grows, similar tests of file drawer effects are a necessity in order to establish the robustness of electoral system effects.

The chapter is organized as follows. In the next section we review the main theoretical arguments and causal stories that have been employed in the literature to support the link between electoral rules and corruption. We proceed by outlining meta-analysis as a methodology, before describing the way we arrived at the sample of papers analyzed in the section that follows. We conclude with a discussion of the main findings.

THEORY AND FINDINGS

A growing literature reviews the effects of constitutional arrangements, in the form of electoral rules, on various aspects of QoG. In this section, we review the causal mechanisms that have been offered in the literature to theoretically motivate this body of research. It is worth noting that scholarship on this subject is driven mainly by the disciplines mostly concerned with whether and how political institutions influence governance outcomes: economics and political science. The vast majority of the papers that have been collected for this meta-analysis have been published in discipline-specific journals. While research on constitutional effects is in no way nascent, its roots as it pertains to quality of government cannot be traced too much further than the early 1990s. As we will see later on, the theoretical heavy lifting is done by a handful of papers, while the rest involve either extended empirical tests or marginal refinements that attempt to add nuance and relevant conditionalities.[2]

Electoral systems, by definition, are not singular institutions. They are rather distinguished by their four main characteristics: The electoral formula, the district magnitude, the ballot structure, and the electoral threshold. In the literature, theory is motivated by all four of these characteristics (and their combinations) and as such there is no single mechanism that is offered.[3] Depending on the characteristic that the theory locks on to, different predictions follow and nuanced theoretical arguments tend to dominate crude distinctions between "plurality" and "proportional representation." However, one can distinguish between two main classes of mechanisms: one that emphasizes market-like competition, and another that is concerned with the various aspects of accountability.

Regarding the former, one of the earliest attempts applies economic arguments and is concerned with the different equilibria (virtuous or vicious) that can be a product of electoral

---

[2] The literature on electoral system effects on performance aspects of a democratic system is vast. By design, this study does not focus on research that traces effects on economic performance (e.g. Knack and Keefer 1995) or electoral misconduct (e.g. Birch 2007). There are also a number of papers which focus on conditional electoral system effects either by combining different aspects of a system (Chang and Golden 2005; Kunicova and Rose-Ackerman 2005) or in conjunction with other political variables (Charron 2011; Alfano, Baraldi, and Cantabene 2013). For the sake of space and clarity, we do not include conditional effects in the review of theory. The empirical findings from that work are, of course, part of the systematic review.

[3] We should note, however, that rarely has the effect of the electoral threshold been tested. Empirical models tend to focus predominantly on the other three aspects.

rules. The classic formulation is that of Myerson (1993), who employs arguments from in-dustrial organization (Kunicová and Rose-Ackerman 2005) under a "barriers to entry" type of idea. Central to his argument is the district magnitude, that is, the number of legislators elected in a specific district, and the electoral formula. Myerson's approach is based on the trade-off between a voter's ideology and her preferences for corruption. Rational voters will support corrupt and proximate (ideologically) candidates even in the presence of honest (but not proximate) alternatives. This is more likely to be the equilibrium under plurality electoral rules (and single member districts). This is a product of the "winner-takes-all" as-pect of the system which encourages strategic voting (along ideological lines): "some elect-oral systems can make it disadvantageous for individual voters to transfer away support from corrupt candidates, when others' expected vote is taken into account" (Myerson 1993, 119). This is the essence of the "barriers to entry" that Myerson attributes to plurality elect-oral rules. Under proportional representation and larger districts on the other hand, voters do not face similar trade-offs and strategic voting behavior is limited. As the seats that are awarded in each district increase, voters can legitimately expect to have their cake and eat it too by supporting honest and proximate candidates (Myerson 1993; Persson, Tabellini, and Trebbi 2003). The prediction here is clear: PR systems will be more effective at combating political corruption. In the case of district magnitude, similar arguments have been put for-ward by Persson and associates (see Persson and Tabellini 2000; 2005; Persson, Tabellini, and Trebbi 2003).

The accountability class of mechanisms tends to be larger, but the causal stories offered, again, vary substantially. These stories frequently (but not exclusively) use a collective action angle (e.g. among, parties, candidates, and voters) to guide their predictions (Panizza 2001; Persson and Tabellini 2000; Persson, Tabellini, and Trebbi 2003; Kunicová and Rose-Ackerman 2005).[4] Electoral systems affect QoG through the opportunities and incentives they offer to voters and opposition politicians to monitor and sanction corrupt incumbent behavior (Kunicová and Rose-Ackerman 2005; Tavits 2007; Persson and Tabellini 2005). This in a turn, is a function of clarity of responsibility for policy and the degree of individual voting as opposed to party lists (Tavits 2007; Persson, Tabellini, and Trebbi 2003), but also on the coordination problems that different actors face as they try to exert oversight in different systems (Kunicová and Rose-Ackerman 2005). For example, plurality electoral systems and proportional representation with open-list (OLPR) ballot structure provide more direct ac-countability avenues between voters and individual candidates under a retrospective voting framework (Persson, Tabellini, and Trebbi 2003; Chang and Golden, 2005; cf. Chang 2005). Both features of the electoral system are therefore expected to be more desirable from a quality of government perspective than closed list proportional representation. On the other hand, in plurality systems, opposition parties have a much higher incentive to uncover mal-feasance through oversight, since large swings are more crucial in winner-takes-all systems. In PR systems, however, it is far from clear that the benefits from uncovering incumbent corruption will flow directly to the party responsible and not be shared among parties (Rose-Ackerman 2005; Kunicová and Rose-Ackerman 2005, 584). Moreover, since coalitions are

---

[4] As is the case for various aspects of party/government performance, such as the handling of the economy, voters can hold opposition and incumbent parties accountable for corruption on election day. Further, this class of mechanisms explores both vertical and horizontal aspects of corruption accountability.

more likely in PR systems parties might be reluctant to expose future potential coalition partners (Kunicová and Rose-Ackerman 2005, 584). In this case, therefore, PR systems appear to be less equipped to deal with political corruption.

Another crucial distinction that is frequently made in this class of mechanisms is how electoral systems affect the distribution of rent-seeking opportunities between individual candidates and party leadership (Kunicová and Rose-Ackerman 2005; Gingerich 2011). This is important because it affects who should ultimately be the focus of control for rent-seeking (by voters and potentially of opposition politicians). The tighter the control of leadership over ballot structures (e.g. closed lists), the more control leadership has over rents, while in the cases of individual voting (plurality and OLPR) individual legislators are better positioned for rent extraction (see Kunicová and Rose-Ackerman 2005). Observing behavior of individual candidates is likely to be easier than monitoring party leaders, and therefore these aspects of an electoral system ultimately impede or facilitate more effective accountability.

Party leadership control over the composition of party lists has an added effect on the "career concerns" of individual legislators and therefore on their performance and effort (Holmström 1982; Persson and Tabellini 2000; Persson, Tabellini, and Trebbi 2003). Party leadership-drawn lists decrease the incentives for individual candidates to perform well when in office (or avoid pursuing rents), since intra-party procedures and politics are at least as important as constituency service (Persson 2000). In such cases, the most important component of accountability, the direct link between individual performance and reappointment, is lost (Persson, Tabellini, and Trebbi 2003). The implication is that PR systems are more likely to suffer by these effects, albeit less severely under OLPR.

The above review exposes a clear tension in the literature regarding the theoretical predictions on electoral system effects. To the degree that different features of the electoral systems tend to be correlated (e.g. PR systems have larger districts than SMD plurality systems and use some form of open or closed party list), it is difficult to see how some—but admittedly not all—predictions from the competition class of mechanisms can be squared with those from the accountability class. In the former case, large district magnitudes (found mostly in PR) should perform better while the latter class emphasizes the importance of plurality. There is, however, a clear consensus regarding the inferiority of CLPR at least as regards its effects on rent-seeking opportunities.

Even this finding, however, does not go completely unchallenged. The theoretical evaluation of the literature is complicated somewhat further when one considers additional theoretical propositions that are not emphasizing competition between but rather within parties and the cultivation of the "personal vote" (Carey and Shugart 1995; Chang 2005; Chang and Golden 2007). When electoral competition takes the form of intra-party competition (under OLPR) uncertainty and the cost of each individual "personal" vote increases the chances that politicians will seek illegal funds in order to finance their campaigns (Chang 2005). Under this approach, the "personal vote," instead of strengthening accountability, becomes a corruption-generating mechanism suggesting that, contrary to previous theoretical postulates, CLPR might be a more sustainable option.

In summary, reviewing the most often employed theoretical arguments regarding electoral system effects, one comes across plausible mechanisms that offer contradictory predictions and ambiguity. This is noted repeatedly in more recent theoretical and empirical treatments of the issue (Gagliarducci, Nannicini, and Naticchioni 2011). The tests that have been employed and the findings obtained could potentially provide some empirical regularities to counteract any theoretical contradictions.

These tests have been exhaustive and extend far beyond the initial theoretical treatments of the issue. In most cases these studies are exclusively focused on testing the relationship between electoral systems and aspects of quality of government (some examples have been cited above), while in other cases these questions form only part of a more encompassing review of QoG-related explanations (e.g. Treisman 2007; Serra 2006). Finally, in a limited number of cases, features of an electoral system are used primarily as control variables in models where these aspects of constitutional design are not the primary focus (e.g. Keefer, 2007; Dahlström, Lapuente, and Teorell 2012). It is not surprising that all predictions that have been presented above find some theoretical support. This likely reflects the validity of these predictions, but potentially also some publication bias. Empirical findings in studies that are motivated by the original or well-established theoretical models tend to support expectations for the most part. This goes for the majority of the studies. Others yield either insignificant results or results that go against the conventional wisdom regarding electoral system effects. In the meta-analysis, we will present these results in their entirety, but we would like at this stage to make some reference to those that stand out for a number of reasons.

The work of Persson and associates (Persson 2002; Persson and Tabellini 1999; Persson, Tabellini, and Trebbi 2003) is very frequently cited as confirmation of the superiority of majoritarian systems as instruments to combat corruption (Blume, Müller, and Voigt 2009; Kunicová and Rose-Ackerman 2005; Treisman 2007). This is often considered as a central and well-established finding in the literature. However, Persson and associates in their work advance a much more nuanced argument, not only theoretically, as we have seen above, but also in terms of their findings. First, in none of their work, that we are aware of, do we come across robust strictly electoral formula results (majoritarian vs. proportional systems). It is true that some of their variables are strongly correlated with electoral formula variables (e.g. the percentage of legislators elected by FPTP procedures), but they are nevertheless not a crude plurality—proportional dichotomous distinction. Incidentally, studies that focus exclusively on the electoral formula frequently return either null results (Adserà, Boix, and Payne 2003; see also Dahlström, Lapuente, and Teorell 2012 for similar results) or suggest that the direction of the effects run in the opposite direction (Keefer 2007). Second, their theoretical expectations regarding positive district magnitude effects are also supported by their results, which hints towards more proportional systems. It is actually the importance of the "personal vote" hypothesis, the vote for individual candidates, that comes out as the more robust finding, irrespective of whether this is a product of plurality rules or OLPR. This is confirmed by Kunicová and Rose-Ackerman's study (2005) and also by the work of Chang and Golden (2007), *but only under certain conditions* (i.e. the number of legislators that are elected in a district).

A cursory or even more thorough review of the literature adds to the puzzle and the ambiguity that the theoretical treatments of the issue have generated. This is a product of some counterintuitive findings but also findings that support the already contradictory theoretical propositions. However, it also seems to hint at some robust patterns, especially regarding the importance of the personal vote. In any event, the systematic review that is presented in the next section is designed to address the puzzles and provide an informed answer to the question of what we have learned from research on electoral system effects on QoG.

META-ANALYSIS METHODOLOGY

The overarching goal of meta-analyses is the pursuit of literary integration (Cooper 1988; Card 2012). Given the convoluted and, for the most part, inconclusive findings regarding electoral systems and QoG, a meta-analysis can aid this pursuit in two primary ways. First, by consolidating results of previous studies across time and space, this approach can improve the generalizability of findings produced by previous research. The aggregation and analysis of previous efforts in this field can potentially produce a more reliable estimation of the purported relationship between electoral systems and QoG. Second and relatedly, meta-analysis can systematically demonstrate the possible heterogeneity of previous results. This is of particular pertinence in this case, as demonstrated in the discussion above. Notably referred to as an analysis of analyses (Glass 1976), meta-analytic techniques can take stock of the results of previous efforts, thus enlightening us as to what the aggregate results are, and in doing so helping to synthesize the field.

A growing number of examples of meta-analysis in political science have taken considerably different approaches depending on the conceptual interest. Smets and Van Ham (2013), for example, explored a plethora of explanatory factors of a single outcome: individual level voter turnout. Doucouliagos and Ulubasoglu (2008), on the other hand, assessed empirical research on the specific relationship between democracy and growth. The design here will combine elements of each of these approaches. Although the relationship between electoral systems and QoG is broadly the subject of the analysis, we have opted to decompartmentalize electoral systems along the same lines taken by previous research. Namely, the constituent elements to be addressed here are the electoral formula, district magnitude, and ballot structure.

Study Collection

A thorough and comprehensive search process was undertaken to identify studies to be included in the analysis. Suitability criteria were established which stipulated that studies would need to (1) contain a quantitative empirical analysis, (2) assess an indicator of QoG as an output variable, and (3) assess an aspect of electoral systems as an input variable. Restrictions were not initially placed on the year range, population, or type of publication as has been the case in previous meta-analyses (e.g. Doucouliagos and Ulubasoglu 2008; Smets and Van Ham 2013), as the possible number of studies was not anticipated to be as extensive in this case. Accordingly, we consider working papers, book chapters, conference papers, and doctoral theses in addition to peer-reviewed journal articles. Removing restrictions based on source type will help alleviate publication bias, as there is a possibility that studies producing inconclusive or statistically insignificant results may fall short of publication.

In developing our selection protocol, we follow previous literature and scientific practices developed and applied in similar approaches (for example, Doucouliagos and Ulubasoglu 2008; Ugur and Dasgupta 2011; Smets and van Ham 2013). The process began with an identification of key terms related to both electoral systems and QoG. While this process is relatively straightforward in the case of the former, for the latter we relied heavily on concepts surrounding corruption practices that have been used in similar searches before (e.g. Ugur and Dasgupta 2011). In total, 15 such terms were identified for electoral systems and 16 for QoG (see Appendix 1 for an example of the search conducted in Web of Science). In order to produce a search result, the study must contain at least one key term from each of the two conceptual categories. The search process was conducted in several major relevant academic resource databases including Web of Science, JSTOR, IBSS (international Bibliography of the Social Sciences), and EBSCO (Business and Economics Databases).[5] These sources vary in their inclusion of unpublished papers. Once the searches were completed, the results were compiled and duplicates removed to produce an initial pool of studies that satisfied the relevance criteria.[6] The search process produced a total of 744 citations for further investigation.

As a second stage of the study identification process, abstracts were screened and graded according to their potential suitability for the analysis (i.e. "completely relevant," "potentially relevant," "not relevant"). This grading was based on the centrality of the key terms to the topic of the study, with a particular focus on QoG and its related concepts as an outcome variable. For example, even if electoral systems were not mentioned in the abstract, there would still remain a possibility that they could be included in model estimations as control variables and as such would be graded as "potentially relevant." Studies graded as such were subjected to an additional full-text screening, whereupon a final sample was established for coding. A total of 34 studies were identified which include quantitative estimates the impact of electoral systems on QoG.

Data Extraction

The studies included in the final sample varied significantly in terms of the number of observations (estimates) that needed to be extracted from each. A total of 476 estimates from 237 statistical models across the 34 studies were identified that used data gathered between 2002 and 2018.[7] Due to the complexity and volume of the data extraction process, a codebook was created to guide the coding procedure, detailing the aspects of each study that were to be recorded. To enhance the reliability of the coding process, a subset of the sample was coded by each coder as well as one of the authors. The extracted aspects included various study-level, model-level, and estimate-level factors such as source type, characteristics of the data, the variables and their operationalization, statistical methods employed, the results themselves, and whether the results were reported in the main text or the appendix. Information was also collected on whether the electoral system indicator was a key variable of interest to the study (whether it relates to a hypothesis) or is simply employed as a control variable, which may be a significant driver of results. Of the 476 estimates gathered, 89.5% were variables of interest and 10.5% were controls. Given that there are multiple dimensions to electoral systems that are typically operationalized distinctly (i.e. ballot structure, electoral

---

[5] The search process was conducted between September and October 2018.
[6] Search results were collated using referencing software JabRef.
[7] The mean estimate per study is 18.5. The lowest recorded estimate per study is 1 (Halim 2008), whereas the highest is 76 (Faller, Glynn, and Ichino 2005, including appendices). The standard deviation is 19.9.

Table 15.1 The distribution of independent variables across source type

Source type	Independent variable			Total
	Electoral formula	District magnitude	Ballot structure	
Journal	139	117	130	386
article	(78.5)	(80.7)	(84.4)	(81.1)
Book	2	0	0	2
chapter	(1.1)	(0)	(0)	(0.4)
Working	6	0	6	12
paper	(3.4)	(0)	(3.9)	(2.5)
Doctoral	30	28	18	76
thesis	(169)	(19.3)	(11.7)	(16)
Total	177	145	154	476
	(100)	(100)	(100)	(100)

Note: Figures in the table represent the breakdown of estimates relating to each independent variable dimension by source type. Percentages of source-type distribution are in parentheses.

formula, district magnitude), there are many instances in which more than one of these dimensions is included separately in the same model. We therefore code each estimate and operationalization separately, which often results in the extraction of multiple parameters in the same statistical model. The database was therefore constructed with a three-level nested structure of estimates-within-models-within-studies. The distribution of independent variable dimensions across source types is illustrated in Table 15.1.

Dependent Variable

A fundamental assumption of meta-analysis is that results across studies are comparable. More precisely, this analysis assumes that the various measurements of QoG are related in that they attempt to capture the same underlying phenomenon. Of the estimates included in this analysis, 92.8% use what have become conventional measures of institutional quality from either the World Bank, the International Country Risk Guide (ICRG), or Transparency International. The remainder operationalize QoG either using alternative measures of corruption (or the lack thereof) or institutional quality. There are no estimates that relate specifically to clientelism, for example, which—although closely related to corruption—may have distinct incentive structures. We are therefore confident in suggesting that any findings derived from this analysis are not driven by studies systematically capturing different phenomena in their operationalization process. Nevertheless, the specific operationalizations of QoG across the included studies vary significantly in terms of their scales and direction. For example, Persson, Tabellini, and Trebbi's (2003) dependent variable ranges from

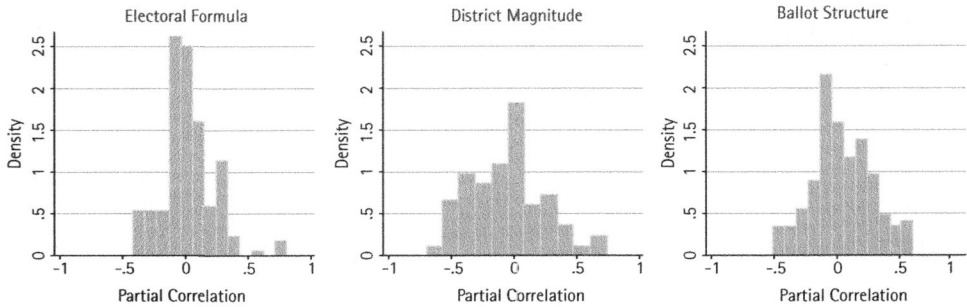

FIGURE 15.1 The distribution of effect size estimations (r) by electoral system dimension

0 (clean) to 10 (corrupt), whereas most of Panizza's (2001) institutional quality indicators range from 0 (low quality) to 100 (high quality). Indeed, this is also the case for many electoral system indicators that use contrary calculations of district magnitude, for example. This was therefore accounted for by normalizing the direction of the estimates according to the scales of both variables. To compare effects across operationalizations and studies, we estimate a proxy of the standardized effect size using the partial correlation coefficient, which is derived in the following way:

$$r_i = \frac{t_i}{\sqrt{t_i^2 + df_{ij}}}$$

where r is the partial correlation for estimate i, t_i is its derived t-statistic, and df_{ij} is the degree of freedom of model j of estimate i. Given that this transformation produces exclusively positive values, signs were reversed for observations with a negative beta value to produce an effect size estimation ranging from −1 to 1 (Greene 2000). For consistency in this analysis, positive values in this scale indicate higher QoG (i.e. better quality of government) whereas negative values indicate lower QoG. Effects are generally considered to be small if r is less than (−)0.1 and large when higher than (−)0.4 (Cohen 1988). 95% confidence intervals are calculated for each partial correlation using the sample variance.[8] Effect size estimations were gathered at both the estimate- and study-levels, with the latter taking the form of a mean effect size for a given independent variable operationalization across a study. The distribution of effect sizes by electoral system dimension is illustrated in Figure 15.1.

---

[8] 95% confidence intervals were constructed using the variance of the standardized effect size following Aloe and Thompson (2013). The confidence intervals are not illustrated in Figure 15.1, which considers only the effect size estimates.

Analysis and Results

In this analysis, we attempt to provide clarity to the purported relationship between the separate dimensions of electoral systems and QoG by calculating average effect sizes from each relevant study in the sample. Essentially, this method is able to consolidate and aggregate results produced by all previous studies included in the sample as well as quantitatively demonstrating instances of heterogeneity between studies. We assess each dimension in turn, beginning with the proportionality of the electoral formula—the institutional dimension most commonly tested in our sample. This is then followed by an independent assessment of the impact of district magnitude. By way of development and extension, we then proceed to dig deeper into the concept of proportionality by investigating the impact of ballot structure on QoG. Specifically, in this intra-proportionality test we assess the effect when ballot lists take an open or closed form. Following previous literature, we conceive this dichotomy to resemble a continuum of personalism and thus label this dimension as the personal vote.[9] By taking this approach, we aim to provide some clarity as to the genuine relationship between the various dimensions of electoral systems and the quality of government.

Proportionality

The proportionality of the electoral system here refers to the extent to which party divisions in the electorate are accurately reflected by legislative seat allocation. As some measures of this concept in the sample are continuous (e.g. proportion of officials elected under plurality rules) and others discrete (e.g. PR or majoritarian dummy variables), all variables are considered to indicate higher or lower degrees of proportionality. By combining estimates across studies, we are able to calculate the average effect of the electoral formula as represented by a forest plot in Figure 15.2.[10] The "indicator" column demonstrates the significant variation with which electoral formula has been operationalized in the field in the past two decades.[11] Each marker in the figure represents the average effect and confidence intervals for an independent operationalization of proportionality in each study. For example, some authors use alternative measurements in supplementary analyses or robustness checks, which we observe independently of one another. It is important to note that estimates should be interpreted in relative rather than absolute terms. The "scale" of proportionality as measured by each observation therefore refers to "more" or "less" proportional. This is of

---

[9] It is important to note that although we have descriptively treated these dimensions and their measurement as independent, this is not strictly the case. There are two variables in particular that we include in both the proportionality and personal vote tests: (1) PINDP (the proportion of members elected directly through plurality rules) and (2) CLPR (closed list proportional representation). In instances where the latter is a categorical variable, it is included in the proportionality test only if the reference category is a plurality system.

[10] All meta-analysis output in Figures 15.2–15.5 were produced using Stata command "metan" (Harris et al. 2008).

[11] For a full list of the variables used in the analysis along with their definitions, see Appendix 2.

Proportionality

Author	Indicator	ES (95% CI)	% Weight
Control Variable			
Adsera et al. 2003	PR	0.03 (−0.22, 0.29)	2.64
Keefer 2007	Majoritarian	0.07 (−0.13, 0.28)	7.35
Campante et al. 2009	Plurality	−0.03 (−0.25, 0.20)	2.20
Dahlström et al. 2012	Majoritarian	−0.08 (−0.46, 0.31)	3.32
Subtotal (I-squared = 0.0%, p = 0.874)		0.02 (−0.12, 0.16)	15.50
Variable of Interest			
Mudambi et al. 2002	Majoritarian	−0.74 (−0.94, −0.55)	3.54
Panizza 2002	PR	0.13 (−0.07, 0.34)	2.20
Persson 2002	Majoritarian	−0.13 (−0.36, 0.11)	12.28
Persson et al. 2003	Majoritarian	−0.14 (−0.22, −0.07)	6.68
Persson et al. 2003	PINDP	−0.20 (−0.27, −0.12)	6.68
Verardi 2004	Majoritarian	0.27 (0.18, 0.36)	1.97
Faller et al. 2005	Majoritarian	0.05 (−0.03, 0.13)	1.97
Faller et al. 2005	PINDP	−0.02 (−0.10, 0.06)	1.97
Faller et al. 2005	Mixed	0.02 (−0.03, 0.08)	1.97
Faller et al. 2005	OLPR	−0.03 (−0.09, 0.02)	1.97
Faller et al. 2005	CLPR	0.04 (−0.10, 0.18)	1.97
Kunicova & Rose-Ackerman 2005	PR-mixed	−0.18 (−0.39, 0.03)	3.76
Kunicova & Rose-Ackerman 2005	OLPR	−0.08 (−0.30, 0.13)	3.76
Kunicova & Rose-Ackerman 2005	CLPR	−0.29 (−0.49, −0.09)	3.76
Serra 2006	Majoritarian	−0.22 (−0.47, 0.02)	3.54
Treisman 2007	Majoritarian	−0.25 (−0.49, −0.01)	3.54
Halim 2008	Majoritarian	0.09 (−0.02, 0.20)	3.09
Blume et al. 2009	Majoritarian	−0.26 (−0.53, 0.01)	3.54
Teorell & Lindstedt 2010	PINDP	−0.19 (−0.44, 0.07)	3.32
Charron 2011	Multi-party PR	0.07 (−0.01, 0.14)	3.54
Charron 2011	Two-party PR	0.05 (−0.02, 0.12)	3.54
Johnson 2014	Non-PR System	−0.23 (−0.52, 0.06)	1.97
Treisman 2014	Proportional	−0.07 (−0.29, 0.15)	1.97
Treisman 2014	Mixed PR/Plurality	−0.12 (−0.34, 0.10)	1.97
Subtotal (I-squared = 91.6%, p = 0.000)		−0.13 (−0.18, −0.08)	84.50
Overall (I-squared = 88.6%, p = 0.000)		−0.11 (−0.15, −0.06)	100.00

−1   −.5   0   .5   1

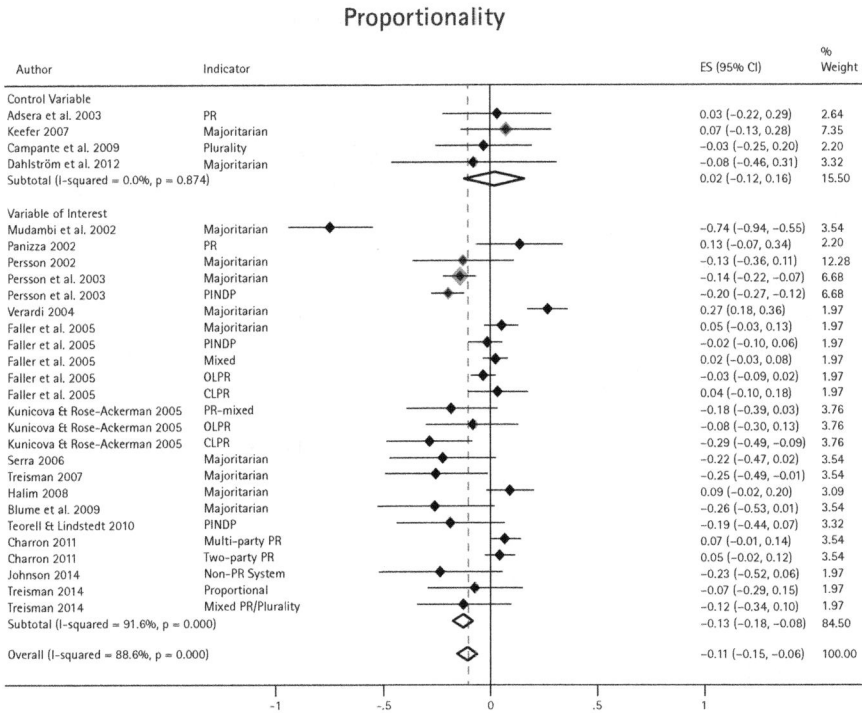

FIGURE 15.2 Forest plot illustrating the reported effect of the proportionality of the electoral formula on the quality of government

Note: Positive values on the X-axis indicate a positive correlation between proportionality and quality of government (the direction of IVs has been adjusted for consistency). Results are stratified according to the theoretical focus of the study. Each marker indicates the effect size reported and weight assigned to that estimate, with 95% confidence intervals. The dotted line reports the overall effect size.

particular importance since some observations are derived from categorical variables. The derivation of the effect size estimates therefore equates a majoritarian system dummy variable where majoritarian equals "1" to a continuous measure such as "PINDP" (the proportion of members individually elected through plurality rules) or a categorical variable such as "CLPR" where the reference category is plurality systems. In this analysis, we consider each to signify "more" or "less" proportionality relative to the variable scale and direction. We also elect to weight the observations by the Eigenfactor value of the publication source as a proxy for study quality.[12]

This strand of the analysis contains 28 observations from 19 studies. The overall average effect across studies is −0.11 (p=0.000), suggesting that a greater degree of proportionality on average decreases QoG. Although there is some heterogeneity in terms of the magnitude of

---

[12] Due to the fact that this analysis includes sources unaddressed by Eigenfactor scores (e.g. working papers and doctorial theses), we place a base value of the mean on all estimates to center the variable. Eigenfactor-scored sources are therefore in addition to this base value.

the association,[13] these results appear to support the general literary consensus that more dis-proportional electoral systems increase the quality of government. Nevertheless, these results are not unanimous, and there are indeed several studies that suggest the opposite, albeit with varying degrees of precision. To probe this further, we split the analysis according to whether the variable is a variable of interest or a control variable in the original study. This step is taken to address possible positive-result bias, whereby studies are more likely to be published when reporting conclusive, statistically significant results (Rosenthal 1979; Smets and Van Ham 2013). While we cater for this issue elsewhere by including non-published sources in the sample and centering estimate weights in the meta-analysis, this additional test pertains to the emphasis granted to variables of interest. Indeed, control variable parameters may not be subject to such biases in the same way as hypothesized variables. In a sense, we anticipate pro-portionality control variables to go "under the radar" of such biases for the most part.

The results here are substantially less secure, albeit with only four studies included. The average effect is minimal and statistically insignificant (p=0.874), thus preventing us from asserting the result with this restricted sample. When utilized as control variables, we are therefore unable to conclude a significant relationship between the degree of proportionality and QoG. There may well, therefore, be a "file drawer problem" at play.

District Magnitude

Turning to the second dimension of electoral systems we investigate here, the effect of dis-trict magnitude on QoG is presented in Figure 15.3. District magnitude refers to the (average) number of legislators elected from a district. In a seemingly contradictory finding, we find rather a positive overall effect on QoG ($r=0.17$, p=0.004). Once again, however, these find-ings are not replicated in studies only utilizing the variable as a control. Nevertheless, the overall effect of district magnitude uncovers one potential source of confusion with regard to the effect of electoral systems more generally. While proportional electoral systems seem on average to reduce the quality of government relative to plurality systems, greater district magnitude—and hence more members elected from each district—seems to improve QoG. Given the systematic correlation between electoral formula and district magnitude (i.e. plurality/majoritarian systems tend to imply that districts only elect a single member), this finding may at first glance be perplexing. Nevertheless, the direction of the effect is broadly consistent across studies, and its magnitude is even greater than that in the proportionality dimension. From the studies included in the sample, there is also much more consistency with regard to the operationalization of district magnitude, with most taking the conven-tional measure of *seats/districts* as opposed to the inverse measure *districts/ seats* .[14,15]

[13] Mudumbi et al., for example, report a consistently high t-statistic for majoritarian systems in their study. The magnitude and consistency of this effect is not replicated elsewhere. One reason for this may be their operationalization of rent-seeking, which refers to economic freedom in emerging market economies.
[14] The inverse measure is otherwise referred to as MGN or MAGN.
[15] A cautionary note, and we thank the editors of this volume for raising this point, is that this measure of district magnitude might mask the true intra-country variation in the number of legislators elected in each district. That number in a country like Sweden can vary from anything between 2 and about 30 legislators, but the national average (in the more recent data from the Database of Political Institutions) currently

District Magnitude

Author	Indicator		ES (95% CI)	% Weight
Control Variable				
Tavits 2007	District Magnitude		−0.09 (−0.46, 0.29)	11.16
Campante et al. 2009	District Magnitude		−0.00 (−0.20, 0.19)	3.33
Dahlström et al. 2012	Inverse District Size		0.05 (−0.33, 0.44)	5.03
Subtotal (I-squared = 0.0%, p = 0.820)			−0.04 (−0.28, 0.20)	19.52
Variable of Interest				
Mudambi et al. 2002	Number of Districts		0.48 (0.14, 0.81)	5.37
Panizza 2002	District Magnitude		−0.02 (−0.23, 0.18)	3.33
Persson 2002	District Magnitude		0.20 (−0.04, 0.44)	18.64
Persson et al. 2003	PDM		0.29 (0.06, 0.53)	10.14
Persson et al. 2003	MGN		0.22 (−0.03, 0.48)	10.14
Verardi 2004	District Magnitude		0.28 (0.16, 0.40)	2.99
Faller et al. 2005	MAGN		0.12 (0.01, 0.22)	2.99
Serra 2006	District Magnitude		−0.08 (−0.34, 0.17)	5.37
Chang & Golden 2007	District Magnitude		0.45 (0.18, 0.71)	5.71
Treisman 2007	District Magnitude		0.00 (−0.26, 0.26)	5.37
Blume et al. 2009	MGN		0.44 (0.20, 0.67)	5.37
Teorell & Lindstedt 2010	MAGN		0.23 (0.01, 0.46)	5.03
Subtotal (I-squared = 59.9%, p = 0.004)			0.23 (0.14, 0.31)	80.48
Overall (I-squared = 56.6%, p = 0.004)			0.17 (0.09, 0.26)	100.00

X-axis: −1   −.5   0   .5   1

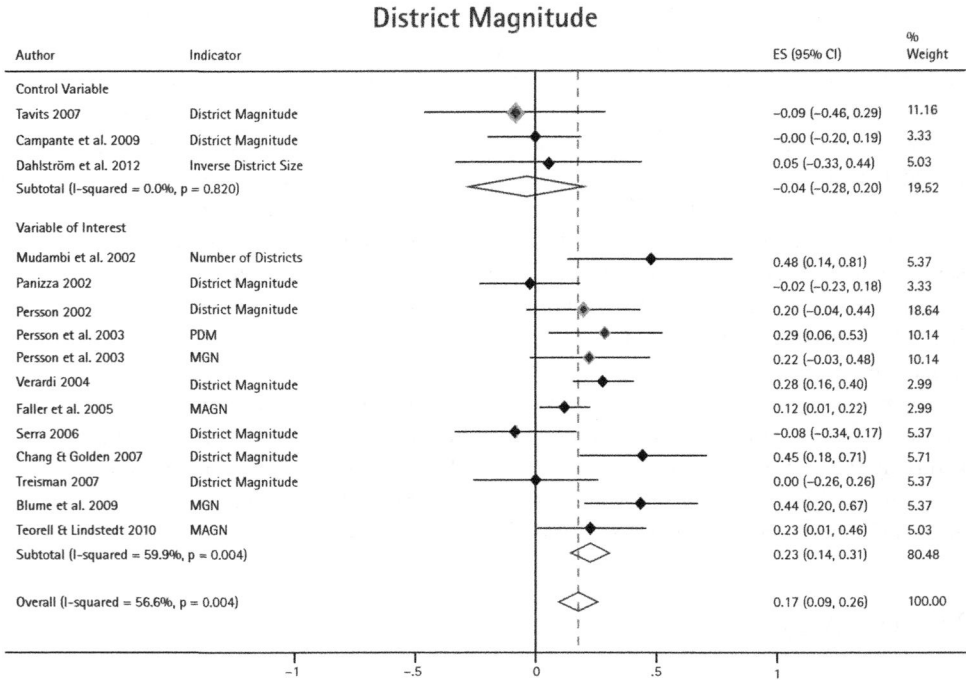

FIGURE 15.3 Forest plot illustrating the reported effect of district magnitude on the quality of government

Note: Positive values on the X-axis indicate a positive correlation between district magnitude and quality of government (the direction of IVs has been adjusted for consistency). Results are stratified according to the theoretical focus of the study. Each marker indicates the effect size reported and weight assigned to that estimate, with 95% confidence intervals. The dotted line reports the overall effect size.

Ballot Structure

Figure 15.4 illustrates the replicated test for ballot structure, which we operationalize as a scale ranging from incentivizing less to more of a personal vote.[16] The primary indicator of personalism here is whether an individual is able to vote for a specific candidate (as a

stands at around 12. Similar countries would therefore stand between a pure SMD country like the U.K. and countries like Netherlands where all MPs are elected in one country-wide district. The prediction that follows from a linear interpretation of the district magnitude effects is that in these "middle" cases, QoG would be lower (e.g. QoG in Sweden lower than QoG in the Netherlands). It is likely, though, that the effects of district magnitude are primarily driven by these middle cases, together with the SMD cases. A look at the most recent data from the DPI reveals that about 60% of cases in the district magnitude measure fall between one and 21 legislators and about 27% of the cases are SMD countries. It is the remaining 15% that has districts larger than 20 and, to be sure, very few countries in triple digits. It is true, however, that a country like the Netherlands (high QoG and 150 legislators elected in one district) would potentially be a very influential case and an outlier worth exploring in models of district magnitude.

[16] For a full review of the incentives to cultivate a personal vote in electoral systems, see Carey and Shugart (1995), who rank systems according to four dimensions (ballot control, vote pooling, control of votes, and district magnitude).

Personal Vote

Author	Indicator		ES (95% CI)	% Weight
Panizza 2002	Particularism		0.10 (−0.10, 0.30)	2.53
Persson 2002	Party List		0.28 (0.05, 0.50)	14.17
Persson et al. 2003	PPROPN		0.29 (0.05, 0.52)	7.70
Persson et al. 2003	PINDP		0.20 (0.12, 0.27)	7.70
Persson et al. 2003	PINDO		0.14 (0.07, 0.22)	7.70
Damania et al. 2004	Party List		0.04 (−0.20, 0.27)	4.08
Verardi 2004	Closed system		0.15 (0.01, 0.28)	2.28
Faller et al. 2005	PINDP		0.20 (−0.06, 0.10)	2.28
Faller et al. 2005	PINDO		0.08 (0.00, 0.16)	2.28
Faller et al. 2005	CLPR		−0.04 (−0.18, 0.10)	2.28
Kunicova & Rose-Ackerman 2005	Particularism		0.27 (0.08, 0.47)	4.34
Kunicova & Rose-Ackerman 2005	CL-Share		0.26 (0.02, 0.49)	4.34
Kunicova & Rose-Ackerman 2005	CLPR		0.29 (0.09, 0.49)	4.34
Lederman et al. 2005	CLPR		−0.01 (−0.09, 0.07)	2.53
Serra 2006	Party List		0.12 (−0.15, 0.39)	4.08
Chang & Golden 2007	Open List		0.45 (0.18, 0.71)	4.34
Tavits 2007	Personal Vote		0.30 (−0.05, 0.64)	8.48
Blume et al. 2009	PIND		0.34 (0.13, 0.55)	4.08
Teorell & Lindstedt 2010	PINDP		0.19 (−0.07, 0.44)	3.83
Johnson 2014	Open List		−0.05 (−0.45, 0.35)	2.28
Esarey & Schwindt-Bayer 2018	Personalism		−0.05 (−0.10, 0.00)	4.34
Overall (I-squared = 87.9%, p = 0.000)			0.20 (0.14, 0.25)	100.00

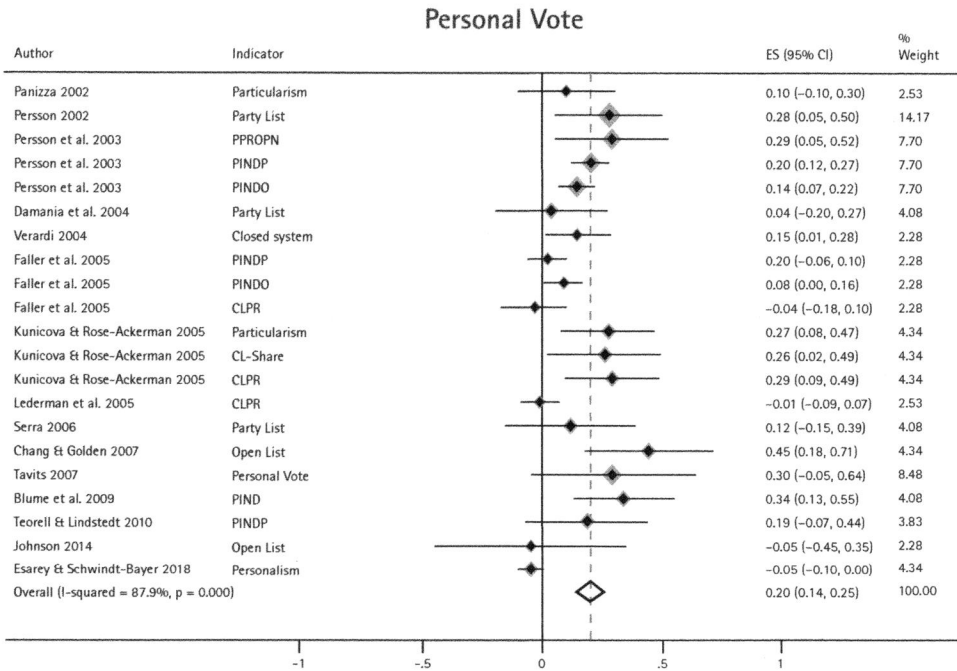

FIGURE 15.4 Forest plot illustrating the reported effect of the personal vote on the quality of government

Note: Positive values on the X-axis indicate a positive correlation between more personalism and quality of government (the direction of IVs has been adjusted for consistency). Each marker indicates the effect size reported and weight assigned to that estimate, with 95% confidence intervals. The dotted line reports the overall effect size.

member of a party or otherwise) or can only indicate a party preference. Some examples of systems that encourage a more personal vote include Westminster FPTP as employed in the U.K., or OLPR in Sweden or the Netherlands. Conversely, closed-list PR systems such as those used in South Africa and Portugal tend not to incentivize a personal vote, as it is party leadership rather than the electorate that determines the rank ordering of candidates. An average effect size of 0.2 (p=0.000) indicates that an increase in the personalism of the electoral system (i.e. more candidate- than party-centered structure) is associated with greater QoG.[17] This is also the strongest effect found in any dimension considered in this analysis. These findings seem to be largely consistent across variables and studies, with only few exceptions. Note, however, that several of the observations included in Figure 15.4 contain elements of the proportionality–plurality dimension. That is, there is a risk of cross-dimension contamination with variables such as PINDO (the proportion of legislators elected under OLPR *or* plurality rules). These measures are therefore not entirely isolated from the already-established effects of plurality systems.

---

[17] As ballot structure is very rarely (if ever) used as a contextual control variable, splitting the sample as in previous tests was not required here.

Personal Vote (de-contaminated)

Author	Indicator	ES (95% CI)	% Weight
Panizza 2002	Particularism	0.10 (−0.10, 0.30)	3.18
Persson 2002	Party List	0.28 (0.05, 0.50)	17.80
Persson et al. 2003	PPROPN	0.29 (0.05, 0.52)	9.68
Persson et al. 2003	PINDO	0.14 (0.07, 0.22)	9.68
Damania et al. 2004	Party List	0.04 (−0.20, 0.27)	5.13
Verardi 2004	Closed system	0.15 (0.01, 0.28)	2.86
Faller et al. 2005	PINDO	0.08 (0.00, 0.16)	2.86
Kunicova & Rose-Ackerman 2005	Particularism	0.27 (0.08, 0.47)	5.46
Kunicova & Rose-Ackerman 2005	CL-Share	0.26 (0.02, 0.49)	5.46
Lederman et al. 2005	CLPR	−0.01 (−0.09, 0.07)	3.18
Serra 2006	Party List	0.12 (−0.15, 0.39)	5.13
Chang & Golden 2007	Open List	0.45 (0.18, 0.71)	5.46
Tavits 2007	Personal Vote	0.30 (−0.05, 0.64)	10.66
Blume et al. 2009	PIND	0.34 (0.13, 0.55)	5.13
Johnson 2014	Open List	−0.05 (−0.45, 0.35)	2.86
Esarey & Schwindt-Bayer 2018	Personalism	−0.05 (−0.10, 0.00)	5.46
Overall (I-squared = 89.5%, p = 0.000)		0.21 (0.14, 0.27)	100.00

−1   −.5   0   .5   1

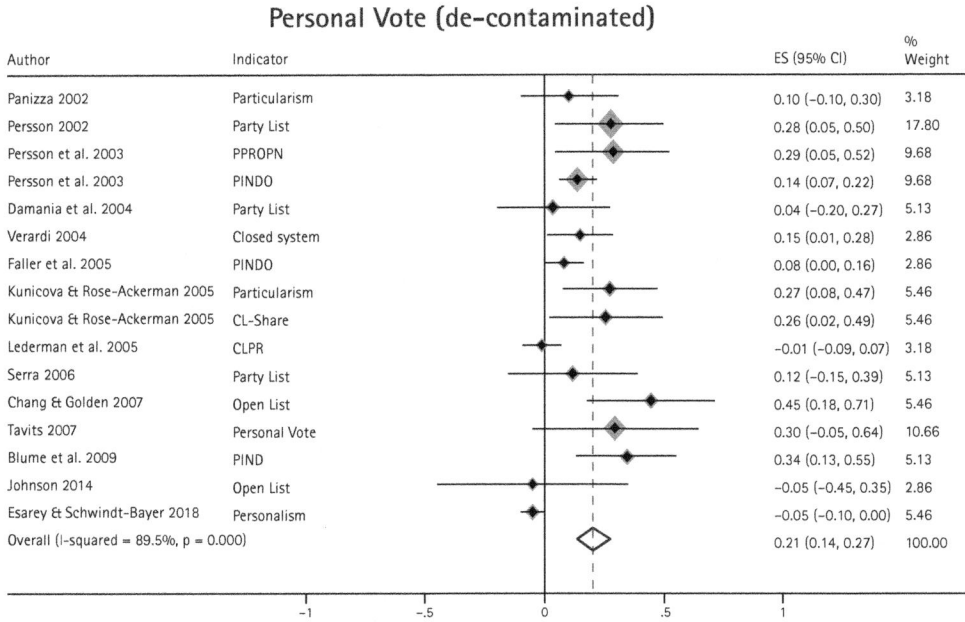

FIGURE 15.5 Forest plot illustrating the reported effect of the personal vote on the quality of government

Note: Positive values on the X-axis indicate a positive correlation between more personalism and quality of government (the direction of IVs has been adjusted for consistency). Each marker indicates the effect size reported and weight assigned to that estimate, with 95% confidence intervals. The dotted line reports the overall effect size.

As one of the key aspects of the field we wish to assess is the purported disparities between closed-list and open-list proportional representation systems, we re-run a "clean" test in Figure 15.5 which excludes all variables containing plurality contamination. The results in this restricted sample remain robust (r=0.21), suggesting that the positive effect of the personal vote on QoG applies in the intra-proportional dimension in addition to, and independent of, the plurality–proportional dimension. With regard to the personal vote, previous research efforts seem to point in a very clear direction: when citizens cast their vote for an individual rather than a party, the quality of government tends to be significantly higher. And, whilst the selection of more personalistic systems has been demonstrated to often be endogenous to QoG indicators in new democracies (e.g. Shin 2017), the consistency of this finding suggests that this relationship is not sensitive to alterations in the samples of the constituent studies.

DISCUSSION

In the analysis we highlighted one possible cause of confusion in the literature surrounding the relationship between electoral rules and the quality of government. Contrary effects were found regarding the proportionality of the electoral formula and district magnitude; while proportionality was found overall to be detrimental to QoG, greater district magnitude—which is typically associated with proportional systems—tends also to be associated with better quality of government. While is it difficult to definitively identify the cause of this disparity beyond conceptual differences, one explanation could be a potential nonlinear effect of district magnitude. Although the crude differentiation between proportional and plurality electoral systems is able to speak to the difference between single-member districts and average district magnitude levels "greater than 1," it is otherwise restricted. Estimates utilizing a continuous measure of district magnitude, on the other hand, can more precisely estimate the difference between observations with large and mid-range districts, for example. Thus, there may in fact be two junctures along the spectrum of proportionality/district magnitude where each respective indicator is a more valid measure. For discrete differences between single-member districts (plurality systems) and multi-member districts per se (proportional systems), the plurality–proportional distinction appears to demonstrate that SMDs improve QoG. When the scale of district magnitude is taken in its full extent, however, the analysis above demonstrates that larger districts increase government quality. It is therefore plausible that both single-member districts under plurality rules *and* large, multi-member districts under proportional rules have a positive impact on the quality of government relative to small-to-mid-range multi-member districts using proportional rules.

This finding produces two further implications. First, measures of proportionality and district magnitude should not be used interchangeably. The contrary findings illustrated in the analysis here suggest that these concepts, although highly correlated, do not capture the same structural phenomena. Or, perhaps more accurately, they may capture the opposite ends of the same continuum. Several studies—especially those employing institutional control variables—tend to select either one of district magnitude or electoral formula as a model parameter. When considered alongside one another, Figures 15.2 and 15.3 rather demonstrate that these variables are anything but equitable and in fact have opposing effects on the quality of government.

Secondly, taken together, the results of the meta-analysis suggest support for an individual accountability mechanism that transcends the crude majoritarian–proportional distinction (Persson and Tabellini 2005). In this systematic review, we show that the quality of government can be positively correlated with systems in which district magnitude is at its lowest (plurality systems) and its highest (proportional systems), and importantly that these findings do not necessarily contradict one another. The most important aspect of the electoral rule is therefore not the electoral formula per se, but rather the individual accountability mechanism that operates within both. The strongest and most robust of our findings is that of ballot structure and the personal vote. In addition to, and independent of SMDs, the studies included in this analysis have consistently found that more personalistic electoral systems increase the quality of government.

That being said, one limitation of this study—and, indeed, the field as a whole—is the inability to directly and meticulously test the mechanisms alluded to throughout the chapter, and especially the supported personal vote hypothesis. The theory refers specifically to the incentive structure of the official who may or may not engage in corrupt activities. However, the studies in this analysis rely overwhelmingly on aggregated country-level estimates of QoG (such as measures from the World Bank or Transparency International) rather than individual-level or even political official-specific measures. Indeed, the vast majority of common corruption measures are broader in scope than the official-specific implications of the individual accountability hypothesis. As such, while this analysis finds considerable support for such a mechanism, it is bound by the limits of its constituent studies in falling short of unreservedly affirming the personal accountability hypothesis.

Testing the actual mechanisms that are implied in electoral system models, as in the above example, are a clear avenue for further research on these issues. There also exist, by now, cross-country datasets that provide ample opportunities to extend research done at the national level (e.g. Chang, 2005). This would help to adjudicate between findings that support the theory of the detrimental effects of OLPR (as in Chang 2005) and research, such as ours, which underlines the importance of clear lines of accountability between voters and legislators. Measures of clientelistic efforts and effectiveness at the party level (see, Kitchelt 2013) combined with system-level data can provide answers to the above questions (see Kitchelt 2011 for a recent attempt).

Additionally, we believe that the potential file drawer effects that have been presented earlier are a matter that we need to draw attention to. In our study we have a very limited number of cases that we can build on to test for these effects, but further research should take this finding under consideration. We have not been able with this design to effectively test the robustness of findings that address the conditional system effect (Charron 2011; Kunicová and Rose-Ackerman 2005; Alfano, Baraldi, and Cantabene 2013; Chang and Golden 2007). Inevitably, even with the extensive efforts made for the research presented in this chapter, the compilation of relevant studies is likely to fall some way short of a comprehensive collection. Indeed, it is also likely that those studies that evaded the collection process here may well share some commonalities such as statistically insignificant results. This chapter has attempted to alleviate these concerns by including variables from studies that were not of key concern to the others. This can only go some way, however, toward compensating for null studies.

As with the research on which this analysis is based, we have sought to answer the question of whether the choice of electoral system affects corruption levels. Our findings suggest that electoral system configurations that strengthen accountability between voters and individual legislators are effective allies in the fight against corruption. This is neither a counterintuitive nor surprising finding. Our research does pinpoint, however, which levers we should be paying more attention to, and provides support to claims that have been offered in the literature about the importance of combining plurality and proportional elements (Persson and Tabellini 2005). It also suggests, though, that on the whole, our options in order to improve government quality through changes in the mechanics of elections are very limited. From a policy perspective, we might be better off focusing our efforts elsewhere.[18]

REFERENCES

Sources marked with an * are included in the meta-analysis.

*Adserà, Alícia, Carles Boix, and Mark Payne. 2003. "Are You Being Served? Political Accountability and Quality of Government." *The Journal of Law, Economics, and Organization* 19 (2): 445–90.

---

[18] The authors would like to thank Djordje Milosav and Jana Schwenk for valuable assistance during this project.

*Alfano, Maria R., Anna L. Baraldi, and Claudia Cantabene. 2013. "The Role of Political Competition in the Link between Electoral Systems and Corruption: The Italian Case." *Journal of Socio-Economics* 47: 1–10.

*Alfano, Maria R., Anna L. Baraldi, and Erasmo Papagni. 2016. "Effect of the Proportionality Degree of Electoral Systems on Corruption." *Environment and Planning C: Government and Policy* 34 (8): 1895–916.

Aloe, Ariel M., and Christopher G. Thompson. 2013. "The Synthesis of Partial Effect Sizes." *Journal of the Society for Social Work and Research* 4 (4): 390–405.

Birch, Sarah. 2007. "Electoral Systems and Electoral Misconduct." *Comparative Political Studies* 40 (12): 1533–56.

*Blume, Lorenz, Jens Müller, and Carsten Wolf. 2009. "The Economic Effects of Constitutions: Replicating—and Extending—Persson and Tabellini." *Public Choice* 139 (1–2): 197–225.

*Campante, Filipe R., Davin Chor, and Quoc-Anh Do. 2009. "Instability and the Incentives for Corruption." *Economics and Politics* 21 (1): 42–92.

Carey, John M., and Matthew S. Shugart. 1995. "Incentives to Cultivate a Personal Vote: A Rank Ordering of Electoral Formulas." *Electoral Studies* 14 (4): 417–39.

Cohen, Jacob. 1988. *Statistical Power Analysis for the Behavioral Sciences*. New Jersey: Erlbaum.

Chang, Eric C. 2005. "Electoral Incentives for Political Corruption under Open-List Proportional Representation." *The Journal of Politics* 67 (3): 716–30.

*Chang, Eric C., and Miriam A. Golden. 2007. "Electoral Systems, District Magnitude and Corruption." *British Journal of Political Science* 37 (1): 115–37.

*Charron, Nicholas. 2011. "Party Systems, Electoral Systems and Constraints on Corruption." *Electoral Studies* 30 (4): 595–606.

Cooper, Harris M. 1998. *Synthesizing Research: A Guide for Literature Reviews*. Oaks, California: Sage.

*Dahlström, Carl, Victor Lapuente, and Jan Teorell. 2012. "The Merit of Meritocratization: Politics, Bureaucracy, and the Institutional Deterrents of Corruption." *Political Research Quarterly* 65 (3): 656–68.

*Damania, Richard, Per G. Fredriksson, and Muthukumura Mani. 2004. "The Persistence of Corruption and Regulatory Compliance Failures: Theory and Evidence." *Public Choice* 121 (3–4): 363–90.

Doucouliagos, Hrlstos, and Mehmet All Ulubasoglu. 2008. "Democracy and Economic Growth: A Meta-Analysis." *American Journal of Political Science* 52 (1): 61–83.

*Esaray, Justin, and Leslie A. Schwindt-Bayer. 2018. "Women's Representation, Accountability and Corruption in Democracies." *British Journal of Political Science* 48 (3): 659–90.

*Faller, Julie K., Adam N. Glynn, and Nahomi Ichino. 2005. "Electoral Systems and Corruption." *Essays on Political Corruption*. Ph.D. diss. Harvard University, Graduate School of Arts and Sciences.

Fisman, Raymond, and Roberta Gatti. 2002. "Decentralization and Corruption: Evidence across Countries." *Journal of Public Economics* 83: 325–45.

Gagliarducci, Stefano, Tommaso Nannicini, and Paolo Naticchioni. 2011. "Electoral Rules and Politician's Behavior: A Micro Test." *American Economic Journal: Economic Policy* 3 (3): 144–74.

Gerring, John, and Strom C. Thacker. 2004. "Political Institutions and Corruption: The Role of Unitarism and Parliamentarism." *British Journal of Political Science* 34 (2): 295–330.

Gingerich, Daniel W. 2011. "Ballot Structure, Political Corruption, and the Performance of Proportional Representation." *Journal of Theoretical Politics* 21 (4): 509–41.

Glass, Gene V. 1976. "Primary, Secondary, and Meta-Analysis Research." *Educational Researcher* 5 (10): 3–8.

Greene, William H. 2000. *Econometric Analysis 4th Edition*. New Jersey: Prentice Hall.

*Halim, Nafisa. 2008. "Testing Alternative Theories of Bureaucratic Corruption in Less Developed Countries." *Social Science Quarterly* 89 (1): 236–57.

Harris, Ross J., Michael J. Bradburn, Jonathan J. Deeks, Roger M. Harbord, Douglas G. Altman, and Jonathan A.C. Sterne. 2008. "Metan: Fixed- and Random-Effects Meta-Analysis." *The Stata Journal* 8 (1): 3–28.

Holmström, Bengt. 1982. "Managerial incentive problems—A dynamic perspective." In *Essays in Economics and Management in Honor of Lars Wahlbeck*. Helsinki: Swedish School of Economics.

*Johnson, Joel J. 2014. "Electoral Systems and Political Corruption." *SSRN Electronic Journal*. https://ssrn.com/abstract=2488834

*Keefer, Philip. 2007. "Clientelism, Credibility, and the Policy Choices of Young Democracies." *American Journal of Political Science* 51 (4): 804–21.

Knack, Stephen, and Philip Keefer. 1995. "Institutions and Economic Performance: Cross-Country Tests Using Alternative Institutional Measures." *Economics and Politics* 7 (3): 207–27.

*Kunicová, Jana, and Susan Rose-Ackerman. 2005. "Electoral Rules and Constitutional Structures as Constraints on Corruption." *British Journal of Political Science* 35 (4): 573–606.

*Lederman, Daniel, Norman V. Loayza, and Rodrigo R. Soares. 2005. "Accountability and Corruption: Political Institutions Matter." *Economics and Politics* 17 (1): 1–35.

Lijphart, Arend. 1999. *Patterns of Democracy: Government Forms and Performance in Thirty-Six Countries*. Yale: Yale University Press.

*Mudambi, Ram, Pietro Navarra, and Chris Paul. 2002. "Institutions and Market Reform in Emerging Economies: A Rent Seeking Perspective." *Public Choice* 112 (1–2): 185–202.

Myerson, Roger. 1993. "Effectiveness of Electoral Systems for Reducing Government Corruption: A Game-Theoretic Analysis." *Games and Economic Behavior* 5 (1): 118–32.

*Panizza, Ugo. 2001. "Electoral Rules, Political Systems, and Institutional Quality." *Economics and Politics* 13 (3): 311–42.

*Persson, Torsten. 2002. "Do Political Institutions Shape Economic Policy?" *Econometrica* 70 (3): 883–905.

Persson, Torsten, and Guido Tabellini. 1999. "The Size and Scope of Government: Comparative Politics with Rational Politicians." *European Economic Review* 43 (4-6: 699–735.

Persson, Torsten, and Guido Tabellini. 2005. *The Economic Effects of Institutions*. Cambridge: MIT Press.

*Persson, Torsten, Guido Tabellini, and Francesco Trebbi. 2003. "Electoral Rules and Corruption." *Journal of the European Economic Association* 1 (4): 958–89.

Rosenthal, Robert. 1979. "The File Drawer Problem and Tolerance for Null Results." *Psychological Bulletin* 86 (3): 638–41.

*Serra, Danila. 2006. "Empirical Determinants of Corruption: A Sensitivity Analysis." *Public Choice* 126 (1–2): 225–56.

Shin, Jae Hyeok. 2017. "The Choice of Candidate-Centered Electoral Systems in New Democracies." *Party Politics* 23 (2): 160–71.

Smets, Kaat, and Carolien Van Ham. 2013. "The Embarrassment of Riches? a Meta-Analysis of Individual-Level Research on Voter Turnout." *Electoral Studies* 32: 344–59.

*Tavits, Margit. 2007. "Clarity of Responsibility and Corruption." *American Journal of Political Science* 51 (1): 218–29.

*Teorell, Jan, and Catharina Lindstedt. 2010. "Measuring Electoral Systems." *Political Research Quarterly* 63 (2): 434–48.

*Treisman, Daniel. 2007. "What Have We Learned about the Causes of Corruption from Ten Years of Cross-National Empirical Research?" *Annual Review of Political Science* 10: 211–44.

*Treisman, Daniel. 2015. "What Does Cross-National Empirical Research Reveal about the Causes of Corruption?" In *Routledge Handbook of Political Corruption*, edited by Paul M. Heywood, 95–109. New York: Routledge.

Ugur, Mehmet, and Nandini Dasgupta. 2011. "Corruption and Economic Growth: A Meta-Analysis of the Evidence on Low-Income Countries and beyond." MPRA Paper 31226, University Library of Munich, Germany, revised 31 May 2011.

*Verardi, Vincenzo. 2004. "Electoral Systems and Corruption." *Latin American Journal of Economic Development* 3: 117–50.

APPENDIX 1.

DOCUMENTATION OF THE SEARCH PROCESS

Database	Date	Set	Search Team	Hits (Studies)
Web of Science	20/07/2018	#1	TS=("electoral system" OR "proportional representation" OR "first-past-the-post" OR "electoral formula" OR "electoral rule") OR TS=("voting system" OR majoritarian OR proportional OR "ballot structure" OR "mixed system") OR TS=("open-list" OR "closed-list" OR "district magnitude" OR "multi-member" OR "single member") *Timespan*=1990-2018> 244,442	2,710
		#2	TS=(corruption OR misgovernance OR "rent-seeking" OR :speed money" OR birbery) OR TS=("side-payment" OR "institutional quality" OR graft OR fraud) OR TS=(sleaze OR misconduct OR malpractice OR clientelism OR "quality of government") *timespan*=1990-2018>44,461	
		#3	#1 AND #2	

APPENDIX 2.

VARIABLE OPERATIONALIZATIONS INCLUDED IN THE ANALYSIS

Dimension	Variable	Definition
Electoral formula	PR	Proportional Representation: most legislative seats are distributed proportionately (dummy)
	Majoritarian	Majoritarian electoral formula: most legislative seats are distributed through SMDs (dummy)
	Plurality	Majoritarian electoral formula: most legislative seats are distributed through SMDs (dummy)
	PINDP	The proportion of individually elected members from plurality rules
	Mixed	Mixed electoral system (dummy)
	OLPR	Open-list Proportional Representation (categorical)
	CLPR	Closed-list Proportional Representation (categorical)
	PR-Mixed	Proportional electoral system with mixed features
	Multi-Party PR	Multi-party Proportional Representation system
	Two-Party PR	Two-party Proportional Representation system
	Non-PR System	Majoritarian electoral formula: most legislative seats are distributed through SMDs (dummy)
	Mixed PR/Plurality	Mixed electoral system (dummy)

Dimension	Variable	Definition
District Magnitude	District Magnitude	Total legislative seats divided by the number of districts
	Inverse District Magnitude	Total electoral districts divided by the number of seats
	Number of Districts	The number of districts. The implication is fewer districts equals larger magnitude
	MGN	Total electoral districts divided by the number of seats
	MAGN	Total legislative seats divided by the number of districts
	PDM	Total legislative seats divided by the number of districts
Ballot Structure	Particularism	Index of electoral system particularism: Incentives for the cultivation of personal reputation
	Party List	The percentage of members elected from a party list.
	PPROPN	The proportion of members elected through proportional rules
	PINDP	The proportion of individually elected members from plurality rules
	PINDO	The proportion of individually elected members from plurality rules and open-lists.
	Closed System	Closed-list Proportional Representation (dummy)
	CLPR	Closed-list Proportional Representation (categorical)
	CL-Share	The percentage share of members elected through closed lists
	OLPR	Open-list Proportional Representation (categorical)
	Open List	Open-list Proportional Representation (dummy)

Dimension	Variable	Definition
	Personal Vote	Index of electoral system personalism: Incentives for the cultivation of personal reputation
	PIND	The proportion of individually elected members from plurality rules and open lists
	Personalism	Index of electoral system personalism: Incentives for the cultivation of personal reputation

PART IV

SUSTAINABILITY AND DEVELOPMENT

CHAPTER 16

....

INEQUALITY AND CORRUPTION

....

JONG-SUNG YOU

INTRODUCTION

CORRUPTION is a primary problem for the quality of government. Corruption is a serious threat to democracy and human well-being, and there is mounting evidence of its detrimental effects on economy and society (Fisman and Golden 2017; Rose-Ackerman and Palifka 2016; Rothstein and Varraich 2017). It violates equal treatment before the law and impartial administration of institutions (Rothstein 2011). Since most corrupt exchanges, especially those that involve substantial financial gains, favor the wealthy and the powerful rather than the poor and the powerless, corruption tends to reinforce and widen existing inequalities of wealth, power, and influence (Johnston 2005). Cross-national studies show evidence that corruption indeed increases economic inequality (Chong and Calderon 2000; Dincer and Gunlap 2012; Gyimah-Brempong 2002; Gyimah-Brempong and de Camacho 2006; Gupta, Davoodi, and Alonso-Terme 2002; Li, Xu, and Zou 2000; Ullah and Ahmad 2016; You 2016).

Higher inequalities in income and wealth may lead to higher levels of corruption by undermining democratic accountability mechanisms (You 2015). Wealthy elite may capture policymaking and implementation processes and corrupt electoral process through sponsoring clientelistic politics. The incentives for the wealthy to rely on state capture and clientelism are higher at higher levels of inequality, and the poor are more vulnerable to clientelism and corrupt demands at higher levels of absolute and relative poverty. Hence, economic inequality is likely to fuel clientelism and capture, thereby increase corruption, especially in democracies. There is cross-national evidence that supports these causal effects and mechanisms (Policardo and Carrera 2018; You 2015; You and Khagram 2005). Also, high inequality is likely to affect norms and perceptions about corruption, eroding social trust and encouraging corruption (Ariely and Uslaner 2017; Loveless 2017; You 2012; You and Khagram 2005).

Thus, corruption is likely to increase inequality, which in turn will increase corruption. The reciprocal causality may create a vicious cycle of high corruption and high inequality as well as a virtuous cycle of low corruption and low inequality (Apergis et al. 2010; Chong and Gradstein 2007; Rothstein 2011; Uslaner 2008; You 2015).

The purpose of this chapter is to explore the relationship between inequality and corruption theoretically and empirically. The chapter examines causal effects from inequality to corruption, from corruption to inequality, and bidirectional causality. Then, it explores interaction effects between inequality and democracy on corruption and the joint effect of inequality and corruption on social trust and development. It also discusses data and methodological issues in the study of inequality and corruption. The concluding section discusses policy implications and future research agenda.

THE EFFECT OF INEQUALITY ON CORRUPTION

Whereas earlier cross-national studies failed to find a significant effect of economic inequality on corruption (Husted 1999; Paldam 2002), a number of empirical studies have confirmed significant impact of inequality on corruption since the publication of You and Khagram's (2005) cross-national study (Easterly 2007; Policardo and Carrera 2018; Uslaner 2008; 2017; Uslaner and Rothstein 2016; You 2014; 2015; Zhang, Cao, and Vaughn 2009). Glaeser, Scheinkman, and Shleifer (2003) proposed a theory in which inequality encourages institutional subversion, including corruption, by the wealthy. Dutta and Mishra (2013) presented a formal model in which inequality increases corruption in the presence of an imperfect credit market.

Why will economic inequality increase corruption? Various explanations for causal mechanisms have been proposed by the literature, focusing on the role of state capture, electoral clientelism, bureaucratic patronage, education, social support, and perceptions of corruption and social trust.

First, high inequality increases the risks of state capture or institutional subversion by the wealthy elite, especially in countries with formal institutions of democracy (Glaeser, Scheinkman, and Shleifer 2003; You and Khagram 2005; You 2015, 33–4). Inequality encourages the rich to subvert the political, regulatory, and legal institutions of society for their own advantages. The wealthy can subvert the institutions through political contributions, bribes, or deployments of legal and political resources. This "King John redistribution" from the have-nots to the haves (as opposed to the "Robin Hood redistribution" from the haves to the have-nots) renders the property rights of those less well positioned—including small entrepreneurs and small shareholders—insecure (Glaeser, Scheinkman, and Shleifer 2003). The incentives for institutional subversion are particularly high in democracies. Since democracy is supposed to allow equal voice to every citizen, redistributive pressures of the masses will be high in democratic countries with high inequality. At higher levels of inequality, the gap between the median income and mean income will be larger. Hence, as inequality increases, the median voter with presumably the median income will support larger redistribution (Meltzer and Richard 1981). Then, the rich will have higher stakes and greater expected returns in influencing policymaking and policy-implementing processes. Hence, the wealthy elite will try to defend and further advance their interests, often subverting the political, regulatory, and legal institutions through lobbying, corruption, intimidation, and other forms of influence. Acemoglu and

Robinson's (2008) model of "captured democracy," in which *de jure* political power of citizens is offset by de facto political power of the elite, is more likely to occur at higher levels of inequality.

Although state capture by the wealthy elite could occur without corruption (i.e. through legal lobbying and campaign contributions), it often involves corruption. Moreover, capture by the elite tends to spread corruption to the entire private sector (You 2015, 176–7). As large firms and business groups exert great capacities for state capture, smaller firms are compelled to engage in corruption. Since the latter typically have weaker influence and connections to state power, they tend to rely more on extralegal means, such as bribery and illegal political contributions. Kathy Fogel (2006) finds that countries with higher inequality experience greater oligarchic family control of the economy, worse corporate governance, lower shareholder rights, and less strict accounting disclosure rules. Xun Wu (2005) also finds a significant effect of corporate governance on the level of corruption. It can be inferred that higher inequality is associated with worse corporate governance and higher corruption (You 2015, 34).

There is some empirical evidence that supports the effect of inequality on state capture. Hellman, Jones, and Kaufmann (2000) created a dataset on "capture economy index" for 22 transition economies, which incorporates firms' responses to questions such as how much their business is influenced by the sale of parliamentary votes on laws and presidential decrees to private interests, the sale of court decisions, and illicit political contributions by private interests. The capture economy index was found to be a significant predictor of Corruption Perceptions Index (CPI) and a measure of corporate corruption across these countries. When the capture economy index was regressed on per capita income and inequality of income, the effect of per capita income was not significant, but that of income inequality was significantly positive (You 2015, 242).

Second, economic inequality is likely to increase prevalence and persistence of clientelism in electoral mobilization (You 2015, 11–12, 32–3). Electoral clientelism involves exchanges of particularistic benefits for political support between politicians and voters. Clientelism is not necessarily illegal or corrupt, but it often involves petty electoral corruption such as vote-buying in cash, gifts, entertainment, etc. Moreover, electoral clientelism encourages high-level political corruption, because politicians are often compelled to collect clientelistic resources through corrupt means (Hicken 2011; Stokes 2007). Clientelistic politicians typically lack the genuine will to combat corruption, and their call for anticorruption reform is merely rhetorical. Furthermore, clientelistic voters lose the ability to punish corrupt politicians at the poll.

The literature on clientelism agrees that the poor are more prone to clientelism than middle-class voters (Hicken 2011; Jensen and Justesen 2014; Stokes 2007). Since countries with higher levels of inequality have higher shares of the poor population at a given level of economic development, inequality will be associated with clientelism controlling for economic development. Higher inequality will also encourage the wealthy elite to promote clientelism rather than programmatic politics. Since programmatic competition under high levels of inequality is likely to strengthen leftist parties that pursue redistributive policies, the rich will be motivated to support clientelistic politicians. In return, clientelistic politicians are likely to be captured by wealthy donors. Both the demand side (the poor) and the supply side (the rich) of clientelism suggest that high economic inequality is likely to intensify clientelistic competition.

Robinson and Verdier (2013) show through formal modeling that clientelism becomes an attractive political strategy for the elite under high levels of inequality. Acemoglu, Ticchi, and Vindigni (2011) propose a theory that emergence and persistence of inefficient states based on patronage politics are more likely when there is higher income inequality. Debs and Helmket (2010) find that the probability of a leftist candidate being elected was lower at higher levels of inequality, from the data on 110 elections in 18 Latin American countries from 1978 to 2008. They interpret that this is because the rich bribed the poor voters to avoid redistribution. Thomas Markussen (2011) also finds strong association between economic inequality and political clientelism across local governments in South India.

Herbert Kitschelt's (2013) dataset on democratic accountability and linkages provides cross-national data on clientelism. Employing both ordinary least squares (OLS) and instrumental variable (IV) regressions, You (2015, 236–9) finds that income inequality is strongly associated with clientelism across countries, when both the duration of electoral democracy and the level of economic development are taken into account. Also, clientelism is significantly associated with political corruption.

Third, high inequality is likely to increase bureaucratic patronage and corruption (You 2015, 33). Clientelism typically involves provision of public sector jobs in exchange for political support (Calvo and Murillo 2004). Meritocratic recruitment of civil servants is hindered by political interference for patronage jobs. Also, the rich may penetrate the bureaucracy through political appointments. For example, land inequality led to the penetration of local institutions by landed elites in late nineteenth-century Germany (Ziblatt 2009).

Bureaucratic patronage will increase bureaucratic corruption. Public officials who have obtained their jobs through patronage are likely to seek promotion via patronage, engaging in corruption to reward their patrons (Hodder 2009). Weberian bureaucracy, and in particular meritocratic recruitment, is found to be closely associated with lower corruption (Rauch and Evans 2000; Dahlström, Lapuente, and Teorell 2012). Rauch and Evans (2000) constructed a dataset on bureaucratic structure for 35 developing countries, based on expert survey. They found that their measure of meritocratic recruitment is a statistically significant determinant of ICRG index of corruption. Using the QoG survey data on "professional bureaucracy" (absence of patronage appointments in bureaucracy) and the World Bank Institute's Control of Corruption Indicator, Dahlström, Lapuente, and Teorell (2012) reach the same conclusion.

You (2015, 240–1) finds that income inequality is significantly and negatively associated with "professional bureaucracy" using the QoG survey data. Also, professional bureaucracy is strongly associated with lower levels of perceived corruption (higher CPI) and experience of bureaucratic corruption (percentage of respondents whose family members have bribed public officials during the last year, from TI's Global Corruption Barometer Survey data).

Fourth, high inequality is likely to increase corruption via its negative effect on educational attainment of the poor population. High inequality of income and land tends to lower educational level by constraining the poor population's investment in education (Cingano 2014; Cinnirella and Hornung 2016; Easterly 2007; Galor, Moav, and Vollrath 2009). Also, studies show that education has been linked to lower levels of corruption (Botero, Ponce, and Shleifer 2012; Goldin and Katz 1999; Uslaner 2017; Uslaner and Rothstein 2016). Uslaner and Rothstein (2016) find that countries with a more egalitarian distribution of land were more likely to introduce universal education in the late nineteenth century, which in turn is strongly linked to corruption levels in 2010 across 78 countries.

Fifth, inequality is likely to increase perceptions of corruption and erode social trust (generalized interpersonal trust), which in turn may foster a norm of corruption as acceptable behavior. Under high levels of inequality, relatively poor people are likely to perceive that the rules of the game are unfair or that the rich have made their fortunes through corrupt means (You 2012). Hence, the overall perceptions of corruption will rise and the level of social trust will decline as economic inequality increases (You 2018). High perceptions of corruption as well as low social trust are likely to justify their own corruption (Uslaner 2004; 2008). People are more likely to honestly follow the rules of the game when they trust that others will do the same. When they do not trust others to act honestly, their own incentives for cheating and corruption will increase as well. In this sense, corruption can be understood as a problem of collective action (Persson, Rothstein, and Teorell 2013; Rothstein 2011, 99–110). It will be harder to overcome collective action problems at lower levels of generalized trust and with higher perceptions of corruption.

Eric Uslaner (2008) presents cross-national evidence to support this causal chain from inequality through social trust to corruption. His earlier study (Uslaner 2002) presents empirical evidence that high inequality leads to low generalized (out-group) trust and high particularized (in-group) trust. Other cross-national studies have also found significantly negative effect of income inequality on social trust (Leigh 2006; You 2012; Zak and Knack 2001). In addition, income inequality was found to be negatively associated with social trust across U.S. cities and states (Alesina and La Ferrara 2002; Kawachi et al. 1997). Public perceptions of corruption were higher in countries with higher levels of income inequality (Ariely and Uslaner 2017; You and Khagram 2005), and individual perceptions of corruption were higher for those with high perceptions of inequality (Loveless 2017).

Lastly, social support theory in criminology suggests that economic inequality inhibits the development of social support networks, and thereby increase crime, including white-collar crime such as corruption (Cullen 1994, 537; Zhang, Cao, and Vaughn 2009). Social support is broadly defined as the willingness of governments to commit scarce resources to the aid and comfort of their citizens. Cullen (1994, 534) proposes that crime rates vary inversely with the level of social support across nations and across communities. While traditional criminological theories focused on *something bad or negative* as causes of crime, he argues that social support, or *something positive*, can prevent or insulate the occurrence of crime. Zhang, Cao, and Vaughn (2009) propose that democracy reduces corruption by promoting human development and social support for citizens' well-being, and that inequality fosters corruption through reduced human development and reduced social support. Using public expenditure on healthcare as a measure of social support and employing structural equation model, they find indirect effect of inequality on corruption through reduced social support and human development as well as indirect effect of democracy on corruption through enhanced social support and human development.

So far, we have reviewed various explanations on the causal mechanisms from inequality to corruption and empirical evidence supporting these explanations. Although multiple empirical studies have confirmed the significant effect of inequality on corruption, not all studies have reached the same conclusion. Sulemana and Kpienbaareh (2018) find that higher levels of inequality are associated with lower levels of corruption in sub-Saharan Africa, using unbalanced panel data for 48 countries from 1996 to 2016. In fact, they find the reverse causality, i.e., that corruption causes inequality. However, Policardo and Carrera (2018) robustly find that income inequality increases corruption, while corruption does not appear to be significant in the determination of income inequality, using a dynamic GMM model with panel data of 50 countries from 1995 to 2015. On the other hand, Stevens (2016) provides evidence that income inequality affects corruption in configuration with democracy, human development, and culture (two value orientations: traditional/rational-secular and survival/self-expression), using a fuzzy set qualitative comparative analysis (fsQCA) on a sample of 77 countries. He shows that the effect of each of these conditions such as income inequality, democracy, human development, and two cultural orientations are configurational and dependent upon the presence or absence of other conditions.

THE EFFECT OF CORRUPTION ON INEQUALITY

Corruption creates unequal influence, typically benefiting the "haves" at the expense of "have-nots" (Johnston 2005). Corruption undermines the principles of impartial administration and equal treatment before the law (Mungiu-Pippidi 2006; Rothstein and Teorell 2008). Thus, corruption is likely to reinforce and widen existing inequalities of power and wealth. Grand corruption is likely to favor the wealthy and the powerful while petty corruption is likely to impose higher costs to the poor. There is plenty of empirical evidence to support these claims.

Empirical studies of state capture by the large corporations and conglomerates show that state policies are often bought by the special business interests (Hellman, Jones and Kaufmann 2000; Hutchcroft 1998; Kang 2002). In transition economies, fear of a leviathan state has given way to an increased focus on oligarchs who capture the state. In the capture economy, the policy and legal environment are shaped to the captor firm's huge advantage, at the expense of the rest of the enterprise sector (Hellman, Jones, and Kaufmann 2000). State capture by the industrial-financial conglomerates, or crony capitalism, was an important cause of the Asian financial crisis of 1997 (Haggard 2000). State capture is pervasive in the extraction of natural resources, according to the UNDP (2008, 92). In the Pacific Islands, international logging companies were accused of bribing government officials to influence policy decisions. In Mongolia, political elites entered into numerous deals and joint ventures with mining companies. These examples demonstrate that the wealthy elite gain from corrupt deals at the expense of the general public.

Transparency International's Global Corruption Barometer Survey (2010) shows that the poor suffer from petty corruption much more than the rich do. The survey asked the people around the world if they had paid bribes in the previous year when they contacted public service agencies. The survey shows that the poorer around the globe are more frequently forced to pay bribes. In eight out of nine public services, users who belong to the lowest income quintile pay bribes more frequently than those with higher income levels. In order to receive basic social services, poorer people are effectively paying higher prices (You 2016).

The UNDP's (2008) Asia-Pacific human development report on corruption documents in detail how petty corruption imposes costs on the poor, particularly in developing countries. The poor are "vulnerable to police corruption because they lack the influence needed to defend themselves when they get into difficulties." Street vendors are particularly vulnerable to police extortion. The sums extorted by the police constitute a significant proportion of the income for the poor. On the other hand, poor people get less attention when they register a complaint to the police (UNDP 2008, 44).

The poor also suffer from judicial corruption, especially at the lower tiers of the court. A household survey conducted by TI Bangladesh in 2005 shows that two-thirds of the respondents who went through the lower tiers of courts in the previous year paid bribes of $108 per case on average. This amounted to about a quarter of the average annual income for them. The poor cannot rely on the legal system to defend their rights and properties, being subject to arbitrary judgments that cause them to lose their land, homes, or livelihoods (UNDP 2008, 50).

An experimental study by Fried, Lagunes, and Venkataramani (2010) demonstrates that the poor are more likely to be targeted by corrupt police officers than affluent people are. In their field experiment in a major Latin American city, four automobile drivers committed identical traffic violations across a randomized sequence of crossroads, which were monitored by transit police. They identified the effect of citizens' perceived wealth on officers' propensity to solicit bribes and on the size of the bribes that they solicit. Their core finding is that officers are more likely to target lower-class individuals and let more affluent drivers off with warnings. Their subsequent interviews with police officers suggest that officers associate wealth with the capacity to exact retribution and therefore are more likely to demand bribes from poorer individuals. This study demonstrates that the poor bear the brunt of police corruption.

Corruption is likely to hinder the development of welfare state programs. While a capitalist market economy tends to increase inequality of income and wealth, welfare state policies intended for redistribution and social insurance tend to reduce inequality. However, the enactment of social policies requires large taxation. When the citizens do not believe that taxes are collected in a fair and uncorrupt manner, they will not support large taxation and redistribution. High quality of government such as low levels of corruption is essential to develop encompassing welfare states, as Bo Rothstein (2011, 127–30) argues. He presents empirical evidence that high quality of government is significantly associated with social spending and welfare state generosity across 18 OECD countries (Rothstein 2011, 135–9).

A number of cross-national studies have examined the effect of corruption on inequality. Li, Xu, and Zou (2000) find that corruption affects income distribution in a slightly inverted U-shaped way (the least corrupt countries are the most equal and the countries with medium-high levels of corruption are the most unequal) and that corruption alone explains a large proportion of the Gini differential across developing and developed countries. Chong and Calderon (2000) also find that institutional quality (as measured by a composite index based on measures of corruption of government, quality of bureaucracy, law and order tradition, risk of expropriation, and risk of contract repudiation) displays a quadratic relationship with income inequality that is significant and robust. For poor countries, institutional quality is positively linked with income inequality, but for rich countries, institutional quality is negatively linked with the distribution of income. This finding appears to be consistent with a recent theory of augmented Kuznets curve where institutional reform first increases inequality, but subsequent improvements lower it (Acemoglu and Robinson 2000; Bourguignon and Verdier 2000).

Gupta, Davoodi, and Alonso-Terme (2002) suggest that corruption increases inequality and poverty by perpetuating an unequal distribution of asset ownership and unequal access to education, minimizing the progressiveness of the tax system, lowering the level and effectiveness of social spending, and lowering economic growth. Their cross-country analysis largely confirms their arguments. Ullah and Ahmad (2016) confirm the significant contribution of corruption to unequal income distribution based on Generalized Method of Moments (GMM) estimation, using panel data of 71 developed and developing countries.

Dincer and Gunlap (2012) analyze the effects of corruption on income inequality across American states. They use an objective measure of corruption, i.e., the number of public officials convicted in a state for crimes related to corruption. Exploiting both time series and cross-sectional variation in the data, they find robust evidence that an increase in corruption increases income inequality across the United States.

Gyimah-Brempong (2002) uses panel data from African countries and a dynamic panel estimator and finds that increased corruption is positively correlated with income inequality. The study also finds that corruption decreases economic growth directly and indirectly through decreased investment in physical capital. The combined effects of decreased income growth and increased inequality suggest that corruption hurts the poor more than the rich in African countries.

Gyimah-Brempong and de Camacho (2006) use panel data from 61 countries over a 20-year period to investigate regional differences in the effect of corruption on economic growth and income distribution. They find that there are statistically significant regional differences in the growth and distributional impacts of corruption. The largest growth impact of corruption is found in African countries, and the largest distributional impact of corruption is found in Latin America. A one standard deviation reduction in corruption decreases Gini coefficient of income distribution (0–1 scale) by 0.05 points, 0.14 points, 0.25 points, and 0.33 points in OECD, Asian, African, and Latin American countries, respectively.

However, Andres and Ramlogan-Dobson (2011) find the opposite for Latin America. They find that lower corruption is associated with higher income inequality in Latin America. Dobson and Ramlogan-Dobson (2012a; 2012b) suggest that this is due to the large informal sector in the region. Using data on a large sample of countries, they find that the informal sector impacts the link between corruption and inequality. The marginal impact of corruption on income inequality becomes negative once the informal sector becomes large. Once the informal sector accounts for a little over one-fifth of GDP, lowering corruption does not reduce inequality.

THE MUTUALLY REINFORCING EFFECTS OF CORRUPTION AND INEQUALITY

A number of empirical studies have found the causal effect of inequality on corruption and/or causal effect of corruption on inequality, although there are some exceptions. There may be a reciprocal causality, or mutually reinforcing effects between inequality and corruption. Also, this suggests the existence of a vicious cycle of high inequality and high corruption as well as a virtuous cycle of low inequality and low corruption.

Some studies have empirically tested the bidirectional causality. Chong and Gradstein (2007) find supporting evidence in a cross-country panel framework. They exhibit a model in which inequality and corruption may dynamically reinforce each other and test this relationship with a broad array of institutional measures including corruption. The double causality between institutional strength and more equal distribution of income is empirically established using dynamic panel and linear feedback analysis.

Apergis, Dincer and Payne (2010) find evidence for the two-way causal relationship between inequality and corruption using a panel data set of all 50 U.S. states over the period 1980 to 2004. The Granger-causality results associated with a panel vector error correction model indicate both short-run and long-run bidirectional causality between corruption and income inequality.

Rothstein (2005; 2011) and Uslaner (2008) add social trust to the circular relationship between inequality and corruption. Rothstein proposes a theory of "social trap," or the existence of a vicious cycle of "high corruption ⇒low social trust ⇒ low redistribution ⇒ high inequality ⇒ high corruption." Uslaner proposes a theory of "inequality trap," or a vicious cycle of "high inequality⇒low social trust ⇒ high corruption ⇒ high inequality." They both reach the same conclusion, irrespective of precise causal directions and mechanisms. It will be difficult for countries trapped in a vicious cycle of "high corruption, high inequality, and low trust" to break out of this trap. You (2012) finds cross-national evidence that high inequality, in particular skewed distribution of income, and corruption increase the sense of unfairness among the people and hence erode social trust, which in turn makes it difficult to organize collective actions to reduce inequality and corruption.

THE EFFECT OF INEQUALITY AND CORRUPTION ON DEVELOPMENT

Since the pioneering study of Paolo Mauro (1995), a number of empirical studies have shown the harmful effect of corruption on economic and social development (Johnson, LaFountain and Yamarik 2011; Kaufmann and Kraay 2002; Keefer and Knack 1997; Mo 2001). Also, there has been growing consensus about the negative effect of income inequality on economic growth (Alesina and Rodrik 1994; Benabou 1996; Berg et al. 2018; Cingano 2014; Deininger and Olinto 2000; Easterly 2007; Perotti 1996; Persson and Tabellini 1994). In particular, some studies have examined the joint effect of inequality and corruption (or institutional quality) on development or the sequential effect from inequality to corruption (or institutional quality) to development.

Glaeser, Scheinkman, and Shleifer (2003) test the joint effect of income inequality and institutional quality (rule of law) on economic growth. Their growth regression suggests that inequality is detrimental for growth, but only in countries with poor rule of law. For the countries with good rule of law, inequality has no effect on economic growth. Note that rule of law is closely correlated with the absence of corruption.

Easterly (2007) proposes that income inequality negatively affects economic growth via human capital accumulation and institutional quality, including the level of corruption. He finds cross-national evidence for the effect of inequality on corruption and institutional quality as well as the latter's effect on growth. You and Lee (2018) conduct causal mediation analysis, using structural equation modeling. They find that the indirect effect of inequality on growth through corruption is highly significant, while the direct effect from inequality to growth is insignificant.

You (2014; 2015) conducts a comparative historical analysis of three East Asian countries of South Korea, Taiwan, and the Philippines to examine the effect of inequality on corruption and development. The study shows a compelling story of how different levels of inequality have led to different levels of corruption and thereby different paths of economic development. The three countries were all similarly poor, very corrupt, and highly unequal at the time of independence after the Second World War. In fact, the Philippines had somewhat higher per capita income and substantially higher educational attainment than South Korea and Taiwan. Also, inequality of land was the greatest in South Korea. However, South Korea and Taiwan implemented far-reaching land reforms in the early years of post-independence, while the Philippines failed to do so.

Successful land reform in South Korea and Taiwan and failed reform in the Philippines produced starkly different levels of inequality of land and income, which in turn led to different levels of corruption and development. In the Philippines, failed land reform has maintained domination of the landed elite and led to the persistent electoral clientelism, bureaucratic patronage, and capture of the policymaking and implementation processes by the elite. The Philippine state, captured by the powerful landed-industrial-financial family conglomerates, has never been able to formulate and implement coherent industrial policy. The persistent clientelism and capture have not only constrained the anticorruption efforts but hindered economic development.

In contrast, sweeping land reform in Korea and Taiwan dissolved the landed elite and created relatively egalitarian societies. Land reform contributed to the rapid expansion of education by enabling the tenant-turned-owner cultivators to educate their children. Educational expansion led to increased pressures for meritocracy. Clientelism was somewhat limited due to the separation of the political and economic elites and by relatively low levels of absolute poverty and the growing size of educated middle class. The gradual development of meritocratic bureaucracy was accompanied by declining bureaucratic corruption. Both Korea and Taiwan enjoyed high state autonomy in the absence of an influential economic elite and were able to formulate and implement coherent industrial policies.

Although both South Korea and Taiwan had achieved rapid economic growth, Korea's *chaebol*-centered industrialization led to increasing economic concentration and policy capture by powerful business interests compared to the small-and-medium-sized-enterprises-centered industrialization in Taiwan. This explains Korea's historically higher level of corruption than that of Taiwan.

The divergent developmental trajectories of these countries that initially shared similar conditions provide compelling evidence for the vicious and virtuous cycles hypothesis. The Philippines represents a case trapped in a vicious cycle of high inequality, high corruption, and underdevelopment, while South Korea and Taiwan represent a virtuous cycle of low inequality, low corruption, and high economic development. It is notable, however, that South Korea and Taiwan started at no better conditions than the Philippines did. These countries demonstrated that the vicious cycle should not be a destiny. They were able to break the vicious cycle by implementing sweeping land reforms and a series of anticorruption reforms, including the establishment of meritocratic bureaucracies.

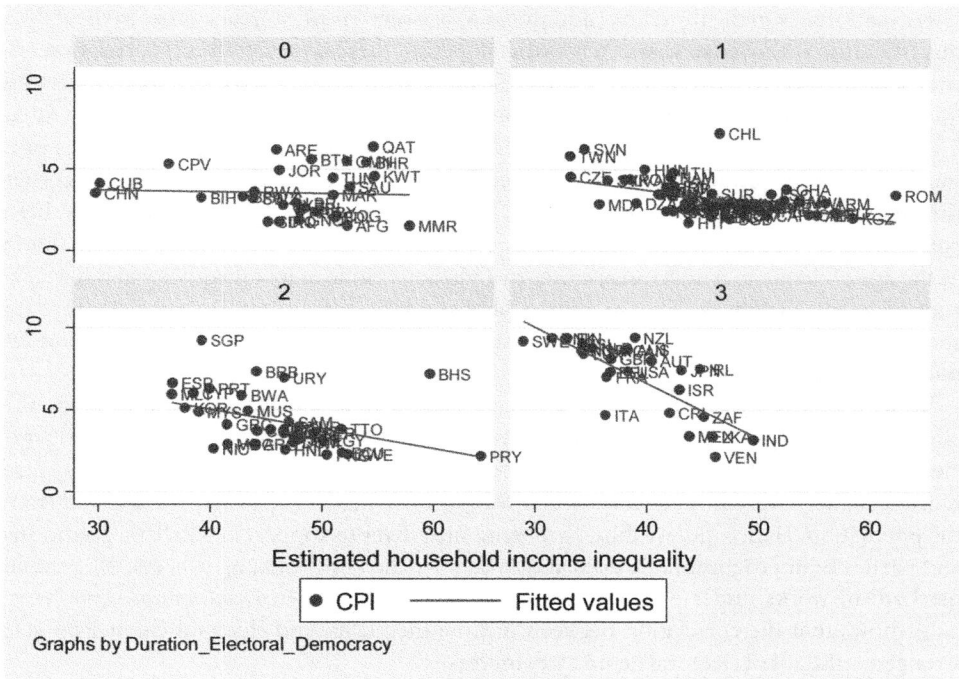

FIGURE 16.1 The association between inequality and corruption, by duration of democracy

Source: You (2015, 243).

Note: Duration of electoral democracy variable takes the value of 0 for dictatorships, 1 for countries with up to ten consecutive years of electoral democracy, 2 for countries with between 11 and 30 consecutive years of electoral democracy, and 3 for countries with more than 30 consecutive years of electoral democracy. Each box displays the scatter plots of estimated household income inequality for 2002 from UTIP data on the X-axis and average CPI for 2002–6 on the Y-axis.

DIFFERENT PATTERNS OF INEQUALITY AND CORRUPTION UNDER DEMOCRACIES AND DICTATORSHIPS

So far, we have discussed the relationship between inequality and corruption without distinguishing its different patterns between under democracies and under dictatorships. In fact, the correlation between inequality and corruption is quite strong across democracies but it is quite weak across dictatorships, as You and Khagram (2005) show. In particular, You (2015, 243) finds that the correlation tends to become stronger among democracies of longer duration.

Figure 16.1 displays four separate scatter plots of income inequality (Gini on X axis) and corruption (CPI on Y axis; a higher score denotes a lower level of perceived corruption) by the age of electoral democracy. The countries in the first box (duration = 0) are dictatorships; those in the second box (duration = 1) have been electoral democracies for ten or fewer years; those in the third box (duration = 2) between 11 and 30 years; those in the fourth box (duration = 3) over 30 years. Across dictatorships, there is no significant correlation between inequality and corruption. Across electoral democracies, the correlation between inequality and corruption becomes stronger as the age of democracy increases. The fitted lines are steeper in the scatter plots for older democracies. In particular, those countries with more than 30 years of electoral democracy tend to be concentrated toward the top left corner (low inequality and low corruption) or the bottom right corner (high inequality and high corruption) of the box. This suggests that countries converge into either of the two equilibria as the age of democracy increases, either in a virtuous circle of low inequality and low corruption or in a vicious circle of high inequality and high corruption. Democracies that are successful/unsuccessful in controlling corruption tend to be successful/unsuccessful in reducing inequality, and vice versa.

What explains these differences between dictatorships and democracies? First, the effect of inequality on clientelism and capture is likely to be more pronounced in democracies than in dictatorships. When there are competitive elections, the wealthy elite may lose more at higher levels of inequality, which will produce higher redistributive demand from the population. Hence, the wealthy have more incentives to support clientelistic politicians and parties than programmatic ones and to capture the policymaking process. This causal mechanism works under electoral democracies, but not under dictatorships. You (2015, 244) shows that the correlation between income inequality and electoral clientelism gets stronger as the age of electoral democracy increases.

Second, both controlling corruption and reducing inequality through redistributive programs require substantial degrees of collective action by the citizens in democracies (Mungiu-Pippidi 2015). Since both inequality and corruption undermine generalized interpersonal trust, which is important in enhancing collective action capacity, there will be mutually reinforcing relationships among high inequality, high corruption, and low interpersonal trust (or among low inequality, low corruption, and high interpersonal trust) in democracies. You (2018) finds that control of corruption and generalized interpersonal trust are strongly correlated across democracies but not across dictatorships.

DATA AND METHODOLOGICAL ISSUES IN THE STUDY OF INEQUALITY AND CORRUPTION

The often contradicting findings of different empirical studies on the relationship between inequality and corruption indicate the difficult problems faced by quantitative study of corruption and inequality: data quality and endogeneity (Treisman 2007; You and Khagram 2005).

First, both inequality and corruption are difficult to measure. The problem of data quality for inequality arises from many sources. While most data are based on household surveys, they are often not representative of the whole population. Moreover, survey data are based on different measures and units of analysis such as income vs. expenditure, market income vs. disposable income, and individual-level vs. household-level. Also, there are various metrics of inequality such as Gini index, Theil index, coefficient of variation, ratio of percentiles, share of income, etc. High-quality data on income inequality is available for only a small number of rich countries, notably the data from the Luxembourg Income Study (LIS). Greater coverage across countries and over time is available only at the cost of significantly reduced comparability across observations (Solt 2019). Researchers should be very careful about different definitions and metrics of inequality, particularly for cross-national studies (Deininger and Squire 1996; Solt 2019; You and Khagram 2005).

Frederick Solt's (2019) Standardized World Income Inequality Database (SWIID) is an attempt to meet the needs of those engaged in broadly cross-national research by maximizing the comparability of income inequality data while maintaining the widest possible coverage across countries and over time. The SWIID (version 8.1.) currently provides comparable Gini indices of disposable and market income inequality for 196 countries for as many years as possible from 1960 to the present; it also includes information on absolute and relative redistribution.

Corruption is even more difficult to measure because most corrupt acts are conducted secretly. Because of the inherent difficulty in objectively measuring corruption, measures of "perceived corruption" such as Transparency International's Corruption Perceptions Index (CPI) and Control of Corruption in the Worldwide Governance Indicators have been widely used by cross-national studies. Another frequently used data is the International Country Risk Guide (ICRG) index of corruption, published by Political Risk Services Group (PRS). However, these perceived measures are likely to contain large measurement error as well as systemic bias. Country analysts and survey respondents may assume that richer countries are less corrupt, producing bias in favor of richer countries (Donchev and Ujhelyi 2014). This kind of bias should be a concern although such bias may not be very large (Charron 2016).

An alternative measure of corruption is data on "experienced corruption" such as data from the TI's Global Corruption Barometer (GCB) surveys. However, surveys of experienced corruption are likely to reflect only the petty bribery, and the definition of bribery or corruption may differ for peoples of different cultures. The GCB data on "experience of bribery" displays large yearly fluctuations within countries, which may be due to substantial measurement errors rather than actual changes in the frequency of bribery.

Secondly, in addition to the problem of data quality, there is a problem of endogeneity in the study of inequality and corruption. Since inequality and corruption are likely to affect each other, it is difficult to sort out causal effects. There are two ways of dealing with the endogeneity problem in quantitative studies: longitudinal data analysis and the use of instrumental variables. Some studies have employed longitudinal data analysis, but the lack of reliable quantitative cross-national data on corruption for a sufficiently long time is still a problem. The ICRG data is available from 1984, but Johanne Lambsdorff (2006), the architect of the CPI, notes that ICRG index measures "political risks" rather than "degrees" of corruption. Stephen Knack (2006) finds evidence that the ICRG was readjusted to conform more closely to the CPI in 2001, which makes it problematic to conduct longitudinal analysis because the data before and after the readjustment are not comparable. The CPI and Control of Corruption data may be slightly more reliable, but they are available only from 1995 and 1996, respectively. There are large variations in these measures across countries for any given year, but there are only small variations across time within countries. A large part of yearly fluctuation is likely to come from measurement error rather than actual changes in the level of corruption. Hence, reliability of cross-national longitudinal analysis is still problematic.

Some longitudinal studies have used corruption prosecution statistics that are available for American states for a considerable time (Apergis, Payne, and Dincer 2010; Dincer and Gunlap 2012; Johnson, LaFountain, and Yamarik 2011). However, prosecution statistics may reflect the rigor and effectiveness of prosecution as well as the frequency of corruption. This problem may be less serious across American states but more serious across countries.

A number of studies have used instrumental variable methods to address the endogeneity issue. None of the instruments that have been used for corruption by various studies, however, look valid. Mauro (1995) and some researchers have used ethnolinguistic fractionalization (Mocan 2008; Neeman, Paserman, and Simhon 2008; Dreher and Schneider 2006) or legal origin (Fredriksson and Svensson 2003; Pellegrini and Gerlagh 2004; Dreher and Schneider 2006) as an instrument for corruption in growth regressions, but neither is a good instrument for corruption. Both ethnolinguistic fractionalization and legal origin are only weakly correlated with corruption, suffering from the problem of weak instruments as Shaw, Katsaiti, and Jurgilas (2011) have argued. Predicted trade share that Shaw et al. (2011) have used as an instrument for corruption is likely to be directly correlated with economic development other than through corruption. Trade openness with which predicted trade share is highly correlated is likely to be correlated with economic development. Gupta, Davoodi, and Alonso-Terme (2002) used "democracy" as an instrument for corruption in their study of the causal effect of corruption on inequality. However, democracy is likely to be directly correlated with inequality other than through its correlation with corruption. All of the above instruments seem to violate the exclusion restrictions.

As for instruments for inequality, existing studies have used "*mature cohort size*" and "*wheat to sugar ratio.*" You and Khagram (2005) used "mature cohort size" (ratio of population aged 40–59 to the whole adult population) as an instrumental variable for inequality. Higgins and Williamson (1999) found that mature cohort size is a powerful predictor of inequality. Easterly (2007) used "wheat to sugar ratio," or the log of [(1 + share of arable land suitable for wheat)/(1 + share of arable land suitable for sugar)], as an instrument for inequality. It is based on Engerman et al.'s (2002) finding that factor endowments such as the exogenous suitability of land for wheat vs. sugarcane were a central determinant of inequality across the Americas. Both instruments seem to reasonably satisfy the exclusion restriction. When both instruments are used together, they pass the overidentification test (You 2015, 233–5).

Although most studies of causes and consequences of corruption have relied on quantitative methods such as multivariate regressions, qualitative study can be also used for such studies. Comparative historical analysis can be used to explore the causes and consequences of corruption (Mahoney and Rueschemeyer, 2003). Systematic and contextualized comparisons of similar and contrasting cases paired with careful analysis of historical sequences can be a powerful tool for causal analysis. Comparative historical investigation can help reveal not only the causal direction between the variables of interest, but also the causal mechanisms. You's (2015) comparative historical analysis of inequality and corruption in South Korea, Taiwan, and the Philippines demonstrates the usefulness of this approach.

Fuzzy set qualitative comparative analysis (fsQCA) is another useful research method in identifying configurations of causal conditions (Ragin 2008). While regression analysis attempts to isolate the independent, additive effect of each predictor variable on the response variable, causal effects may be configurational rather than independent and combinatorial rather than additive. Thus, there may be multiple causal pathways to the same outcome. In the fsQCA process, raw data on the conditions (outcomes and potential causes) of cases can be calibrated into fuzzy set scores, and fuzzy set scores can then be calculated for cases' membership of configurations of conditions. This process can identify more than one condition/configuration that is necessary or sufficient to cause an outcome. Using a fuzzy set qualitative comparative analysis (fsQCA) on a sample of 77 countries, Stevens (2016) shows that inequality affects corruption in configuration with democracy, human development, and culture.

POLICY AND RESEARCH IMPLICATIONS

The significant effect of inequality on corruption and mutually reinforcing effects between inequality and corruption have important policy implications, in particular for democracies. We observe that democracies that are successful/unsuccessful in controlling corruption tend to be successful/unsuccessful in reducing inequality, and vice versa. Successful anticorruption reform requires not only combating corruption per se, but reduction of economic inequality. Also, effective anticorruption reform will likely help to alleviate inequality.

The importance of tackling inequality as an anticorruption strategy has implications for libertarian approaches to corruption control. The literature on corruption tended to focus on bureaucratic and political corruption, ignoring the problems of state capture by the wealthy elite. The narrow focus on corrupt incentives for public officials led to a neoliberal policy prescription for anticorruption reform: "if you want to cut corruption, cut government" (Becker 1995). Deregulation, privatization, and minimization of bureaucratic discretion were proposed as remedies. However, many developing and transition economies saw privatization processes riddled with rampant corruption (Bello et al. 2004; Hellman, Jones, and Kaufmann 2000). Also, empirical studies show that larger government size is not associated with a higher level of corruption (Gerring and Thacker 2005). Indeed, the large governments of Scandinavian countries have both the lowest levels of inequality and corruption in the world.

While both reducing inequality and curbing corruption benefit the majority of the population, both require collective action. While few people benefit from increasing inequality and corruption, it is not easy for those who lose from high inequality and corruption to overcome collective action problems to successfully fight against both inequality and corruption. Since high inequality and corruption tend to erode social trust that helps to overcome collective action problems, societies can be trapped in a vicious circle of high inequality, high corruption, and low trust. However, the relationship among inequality, corruption, trust, and collective action capacity is not deterministic but probabilistic. We should not underestimate the role of human agency. The experiences of successful land reform in South Korea and Taiwan that reduced inequality in wealth and income should serve as an example that a vicious circle can be cut. The experiences of successful anticorruption reform in Singapore and Hong Kong are another example (Rothstein 2011).

Both inequality and corruption seem to erode both interpersonal and institutional trust, and there seems to be a feedback mechanism from trust to inequality and corruption (Rothstein 2011; Uslaner 2008). The role of trust and collective action in reducing inequality and corruption seems to be particularly important in democracies. The presence of high correlations between inequality and corruption as well as between corruption and trust across democracies, but not across dictatorships, suggests this (You 2015; 2018). However, the different patterns in the correlations and their feedback mechanisms among inequality, corruption, and trust between democracies and dictatorships have not been studied. This will be an important topic for future research.

The relationship between inequality and corruption has broader implications on some important topics in comparative politics and political economy. For example, capture and clientelism may explain the puzzle of persistence of inequality in democracies. The median voter theorem predicts that higher market income inequality should lead to higher redistribution in democracies (Meltzer and Richard 1981). In fact, higher levels of market income inequality do not produce higher levels of redistribution across industrialized democracies (Iversen and Soskice 2006). This puzzle may be explained by the effect of inequality on capture and clientelism. In a captured democracy, the redistributive demand of the median voter will not translate into government policies because the wealthy elite can influence the policy outcomes in their favor (Acemoglu and Robinson 2008). Under clientelistic politics, programmatic parties that can represent the interests of the poor do not develop, and the poor voters tend to support a perverse system dominated by clientelistic politicians "that keeps them poor" (Diaz-Cayeros, Estévez, and Magaloni 2011). Thus, higher market income inequality does not lead to higher redistribution. This may explain the persistence of inequality observed in many democracies, contrary to the Meltzer-Richard (1981) model (You and Khagram 2005).

The effect of inequality on clientelism and capture also helps to explain the difficulty of transition from a "limited access order" to an "open access order" in many societies with high levels of economic inequality. North, Wallis, and Weingast (2009) posit that in limited access order societies, access to valuable rights and activities are limited to the privileged few who have violence potential. These privileges enjoyed by the dominant coalition of powerful groups and individuals generate rents. In open access order societies, access to political and economic rights and organizational activities are open to everyone. Open competition in political and economic arenas is the driving force for development. Their "theory of double balance" implies that societies tend to have both open access polity and open access economy or both limited access polity and limited access economy. If open access polity (formal institutions of democracy) is introduced in a limited access economy, the formally open access polity may retreat to a limited access polity (authoritarian reversal) or function like a limited access polity. Clientelism and capture can make the formally open access polity function like a limited access polity, in which privileges and associated rents are preserved. Clientelism distributes part of the rents to the poor voters, but it helps the powerful and wealthy elites to largely maintain the privileges of limited access to rents. Capture enables the wealthy elite to preserve rents based on privileges.

The effect of clientelism on inequality is another topic that needs further research. While capture-type of corruption clearly favors the wealthy over the poor, it is not clear whether clientelism helps or hurts the poor. It is hard to compare the total amount of the particularistic benefits the poor get from politicians and the overall loss to the poor due to clientelistic politics, because it is difficult to estimate how much benefit the poor might have received collectively from programmatic politics in the absence of clientelism.

The study of corruption needs to transcend its narrow focus on corrupt incentives for public officials. More studies are needed on corrupt incentives for firms, politicians, and voters, focusing on the problems of clientelism and capture. There should be more studies on whether, why, and how inequality increases clientelism and capture as well as how clientelism and capture affect inequality. In particular, more studies are needed on how different kinds and degrees of economic inequality affect perceptions of inequality and fairness, and thereby perceptions of corruption and interpersonal trust. Finally, further study is needed on the role of social trust and collective action capacity in tackling inequality and corruption.

References

Acemoglu, Daron, and James A. Robinson. 2000. "Why Did the West Extend the Franchise? Democracy, Inequality, and Growth in Historical Perspective." *The Quarterly Journal of Economics* 115 (4): 1167–99.

Acemoglu, Daron, and James A. Robinson. 2008. "Persistence of Power, Elites, and Institutions." *American Economic Review* 98 (1): 267–93.

Acemoglu, Daron, Davide Ticchi, and Andrea Vindigni. 2011. "Emergence and Persistence of Inefficient States." *Journal of the European Economic Association* 9 (2): 177–208.

Alesina, Alberto, and Eliana La Ferrara. 2002. "Who Trusts Others?" *Journal of Public Economics* 85: 207–34.

Alesina, Alberto, and Rodrik, Dani. 1994. "Distributive Politics and Economic Growth." *Quarterly Journal of Economics* CIX (2): 465–90.

Andres, Antonio R., and Carlyn Ramlogan-Dobson. 2011. "Is Corruption Really Bad for Inequality? Evidence from Latin America." *Journal of Development Studies* 47 (7): 959–76.

Apergis, Nicholas, James E. Payne, and Oguzhan C. Dincer. 2010. "The Relationship between Corruption and Income Inequality in U.S. States: Evidence from a Panel Cointegration and Error Correction Model." *Public Choice* 145: 125–35.

Ariely, Gal, and Eric M. Uslaner. 2017. "Corruption, Fairness, and Inequality." *International Political Science Review* 38 (3): 349–62.

Becker, Gary S. 1995. "If You Want to Cut Corruption, Cut Government." *Business Week* 3454: 26.

Benabou, Ronald. 1996. "Inequality and Growth." *NBER Macroeconomics Annual* 11: 11–92.

Bello, Walden, Herbert Docena, Marissa de Guzman, and Marylou Malig. 2004. *The Anti-Development State: The Political Economy of Permanent Crisis in the Philippines*. Quezon City: University of the Philippines.

Berg, Andrew, Jonathan D. Ostry, Charalambos G. Tsangarides, and Yorbol Yakhshilikov. 2018. "Redistribution, Inequality, and Growth: New Evidence" *Journal of Economic Growth* 23 (3): 259–305.

Botero, Juan, Alejandro Ponce, and Andrei Shleifer. 2012. "Education and the Quality of Government." *NBER Working Paper*, available at www/nber.org/papers/w18119.

Bourguignon, Francois, and Thierry Verdier. 2000. "Oligarchy, Democracy, Inequality and Growth." *Journal of Development Economics* 62 (2): 285–313.

Calvo, Ernesto, and Maria Victoria Murillo. 2004. "Who Delivers? Partisan Clients in the Argentine Electoral Market." *American Journal of Political Science* 48 (4): 742–57.

Charron, Nicholas 2016. "Do Corruption Measures Have a Perception Problem? Assessing the Relationship between Experiences and Perceptions of Corruption among Citizens and Experts." *European Political Science Review* 8 (1): 147–71.

Chong, Alberto, and Cesar Calderon. 2000. "Institutional Quality and Income Distribution." *Economic Development and Cultural Change* 48: 761–86.

Chong, Alberto, and Mark Gradstein. 2007. "Inequality and Institutions." *Review of Economics and Statistics* 89 (3): 454–65.

Cingano, Federico. 2014. "Trends in Income Inequality and its Impact on Economic Growth." OECD Social, Employment and Migration Working Papers, No. 163, OECD Publishing. http://dx.doi.org/10.1787/5jxrjncwxv6j-en

Cinnirella, Franceso, and Erik Hornung. 2016. "Landownership Concentration and the Expansion of Education." *Journal of Development Economics* 121: 135–52.

Cullen, Francis T. 1994. "Social Support as an Organizing Concept for Criminology: Presidential Address to the Academy of Criminal Justice Sciences." *Justice Quarterly* 11 (4): 527–59.

Dahlström, Carl, Victor Lapuente, and Jan Teorell. 2012. "The Merit of Meritocratization: Politics, Bureaucracy, and the Institutional Deterrents of Corruption." *Political Research Quarterly* 65 (3): 658–70.

Debs, Alexandre, and Gretchen Helmket. 2010. "Inequality under Democracy: Explaining the Left Decade in Latin America." *Quarterly Journal of Political Science* 5 (3): 209–41.

Deininger, Klaus, and Pedro Olinto. 2000. "Asset Distribution, Inequality and Growth." World Bank Research Working Paper No. 2375.

Diaz-Cayeros, Alberto, Federico Estévez, and Beatriz Magaloni. 2011. *The Political Logic of Poverty Relief: Electoral Strategies and Social Policy in Mexico.* Cambridge University Press.

Deininger, Klaus, and Lyn Squire. 1996. "A New Data Set Measuring Income Inequality." *World Bank Economic Review* 10: 565–91.

Dincer, Oguzhan C., and Burak Gunalp. 2012. "Corruption and Income Inequality in the United States." *Contemporary Economic Policy* 30 (2): 283–92.

Dobson, Stephen, and Carlyn Ramlogan-Dobson. 2012a. "Why Is Corruption Less Harmful to Income Inequality in Latin America?" *World Development* 40 (8): 1534–45.

Dobson, Stephen, and Carlyn Ramlogan-Dobson. 2012b. "Inequality, Corruption and the Informal Sector." *Economics Letters* 115: 104–107.

Donchev, Dilyan, and Gergely Ujhelyi 2014. "What Do Corruption Indices Measure?" *Economics and Politics* 26 (2): 309–31.

Dreher, A., and Schneider, F. 2006. "Corruption and the Shadow Economy: An Empirical Analysis." IZA discussion papers 1936, Institute for the Study of Labor (IZA).

Dutta, Indranil and Ajit Mishra. 2013. "Does Inequality Foster Corruption?" *Journal of Public Economic Theory* 15 (4): 602–19.

Easterly, William. 2007. "Inequality Does Cause Underdevelopment: Insights from a New Instrument." *Journal of Development Economics* 84 (2): 755–76.

Engerman, Stanley L., Kenneth L. Sokoloff, Miguel Urquiola, and Daron Acemoglu. 2002. "Factor Endowments, Inequality, and Paths of Development among New World Economies." *Economía* 3 (1): 41–109.

Fisman, Ray, and Miriam A. Golden. 2017. *Corruption: What Everyone Needs to Know.* New York, NY: Oxford University Press.

Fogel, Kathy. 2006. "Oligarchic Family Control, Social Economic Outcomes, and the Quality of Government." *Journal of International Business Studies* 37 (5): 603–22.

Fredriksson, Per G., and Jakob Svensson. 2003. "Political Instability, Corruption and Policy Formation: The Case of Environmental Policy." *Journal of Public Economics* 87 (7–8): 1383–405.

Fried Brian J., Paul Lagunes, and Atheendar Venkataramani. 2010. "Corruption and inequality at the crossroad: A multimethod study of bribery and discrimination in Latin America." *Latin American Research Review* 45 (1): 76–97.

Galor, Oded, Omer Moav, and Dietrich Vollrath. 2009. "Inequality in Landownership, the Emergence of Human-Capital Promoting Institutions, and the Great Divergence." *Review of Economic Studies* 76: 143–79.

Gerring, John, and Strom C. Thacker. 2005. "Do Neoliberal Policies Deter Political Corruption?" *International Organization* 59 (1): 233–54.

Glaeser, Edward, Jose Scheinkman, and Andrei Shleifer. 2003. "The Injustice of Inequality." *Journal of Monetary Economics* 50 (1): 199–222.

Goldin, Claudia, and Lawrence F. Katz. 1999. "Human Capital and Social Capital: The Rise of Secondary Schooling in America, 1910–1940." *Journal of Interdisciplinary History* 29: 683–723.

Gupta, Sanjeev, Hamid R. Davoodi, and Rosa Alonso-Terme. 2002. "Does Corruption Affect Income Inequality and Poverty?" *Economics of Governance* 3: 23–45.

Gyimah-Brempong, Kwabena. 2002. "Corruption, Economic Growth and Income Inequality in Africa." *Economics of Governance* 3: 183–209.

Gyimah-Brempong, Kwabena, and Samaria Muñoz de Camacho. 2006. "Corruption, Growth, and Income Distribution: Are There Regional Differences?" *Economics of Governance* 7: 245–69.

Haggard, Stephan 2000. *The Political Economy of the Asian Financial Crisis.* Washington, DC: Institute for International Economics.

Hellman, Joel S., Geraint Jones, and Daniel Kaufmann. 2000. "Seize the State, Seize the Day: State Capture, Corruption, and Influence in Transition." World Bank Policy Research Working Paper No. 2444. Washington DC: World Bank.

Hicken, Allen. 2011. "Clientelism." *Annual Review of Political Science* 14: 289–310.

Higgins, Matthew, and Jeffrey G. Williamson. 1999. "Explaining Inequality the World Round: Cohort Size, Kuznets Curves, and Openness." NBER Working Paper 7224. Cambridge, MA: National Bureau of Economic Research.

Hodder, Rupert. 2009. "Political Interference in the Philippine Civil Service." *Environment and Planning C: Government & Policy* 27 (5): 766–82.

Husted, Bryan W. 1999. "Wealth, Culture, and Corruption." *Journal of International Business Studies* 30: 339–60.

Hutchcroft, Paul. 1998. *Booty Capitalism: The Politics of Banking in the Philippines.* Ithaca, NY: Cornell University Press.

Iversen, Torben, and David Soskice. 2006. "Electoral Systems and the Politics of Coalitions: Why Some Democracies Redistribute More than Others." *American Political Science Review* 100 (2): 165–81.

Jensen, Peter Sandholt, and Mogens K. Justesen. 2014. "Poverty and Vote Buying: Survey-Based Evidence from Africa." *Electoral Studies* 33: 220–32.

Johnston, Michael. 2005. *Syndromes of Corruption: Wealth, Power, and Democracy.* Cambridge, UK: Cambridge University Press.

Johnson, Noel D., Courtney L. LaFountain, and Steven Yamarik. 2011. "Corruption is Bad for Growth (Even in the United States)." *Public Choice* 147: 377–93.

Kang, David. 2002. *Crony Capitalism: Corruption and Development in South Korea and the Philippines.* Cambridge University Press.

Kaufmann, Daniel, and Aart Kraay. 2002. "Growth Without Governance." *World Bank Policy Research Working Paper* No. 2928.

Kawachi, Ichiro, Bruce P. Kennedy, Kimberly Lochner, and Deborah Prothrow-Stith. 1997. "Social Capital, Income Inequality, and Mortality." *American Journal of Public Health* 87 (9): 1491–98.

Keefer, Philip, and Stephen Knack. 1997. "Why Don't Poor Countries Catch up? A Cross-National Test of an Institutional Explanation." *Economic Inquiry* 35 (3): 590–602.

Kitschelt, Herbert 2013. Dataset of the Democratic Accountability and Linkages Project (DALP). Duke University. https://web.duke.edu/democracy/index.html

Knack, Stephen. 2006. "Measuring Corruption in Eastern Europe and Central Asia: A Critique of the Cross-Country Indicators." *World Bank Policy Research Working Paper* No. 3968.

Lambsdorff, Johann Graf. 2006. "Measuring Corruption: The Validity and Precision of Subjective Indicators (CPI)," in *Measuring Corruption*, edited by C. Sampford, A. Shacklock, C. Connors, and F. Galtung, 101–30. Aldershot, UK; Burlington, VT: Ashgate.

Leigh, Andrew. 2006. "Trust, Inequality and Ethnic Heterogeneity." *Economic Record* 82 (258): 268–80.

Li, Hongyi, Lixin C. Xu, and Heng-fu Zou. 2000. "Corruption, Income Distribution, and Growth." *Economics and Politics* 12: 155–82.

Loveless, Matthew. 2017. "How Individuals' Perceptions of Inequality May Affect Their Perceptions of Corruption: A Challenge to New Democracies." *Research on Economic Inequality* 24: 247–70.

Mahoney, James, and Dietrich Rueschemeyer, eds. 2003. *Comparative Historical Analysis in the Social Sciences*. Cambridge University Press.

Markussen, Thomas. 2011. "Inequality and Political Clientelism: Evidence from South India." *Journal of Development Studies* 47 (11): 1721–38.

Mauro, Paolo. 1995. "Corruption and Growth." *Quarterly Journal of Economics* 110: 681–712.

Meltzer, Allan H. and Scott F. Richard. 1981. "A Rational Theory of the Size of Government." *Journal of Political Economy* 89: 914–27.

Mo, Pak Hung. 2001. "Corruption and Economic Growth." *Journal of Comparative Economics* 29 (1): 66–79.

Mocan, Naci. 2008. "What Determines Corruption? International Evidence from Micro Data." *Economic Inquiry* 46 (4): 493–510.

Mungiu-Pippidi, Alina. 2006. "Corruption: Diagnosis and Treatment." *Journal of Democracy* 17 (3), 86–99.

Mungiu-Pippidi, Alina. 2015. *The Quest for Good Governance: How Societies Develop Control of Corruption*. Cambridge University Press.

Neeman, Zvika, M. Daniele Paserman, and Avi Simhon. 2008. "Corruption and Openness." *B.E. Journal of Economic Analysis & Policy* 8 (1): 1–38.

North, Douglass C., John J. Wallis, and Barry R. Weingast. 2009. *Violence and Social Orders: A Conceptual Framework for Interpreting Recorded Human History*. New York: Cambridge University Press.

Paldam, Martin. 2002. "The Cross-Country Pattern of Corruption: Economics, Culture, and the Seesaw Dynamics." *European Journal of Political Economy* 18 (2): 215–40.

Pellegrini, Lorenzo, and Reyer Gerlagh. 2004. "Corruption's Effect on Growth and Its Transmission Channels." *Kyklos* 57 (3): 429–56.

Perotti, Roberto. 1996. "Growth, Income Distribution, and Democracy: What the Data Say." *Journal of Economic Growth* 1: 149–88.

Persson, Anna, Bo Rothstein, and Jan Teorell. 2013. "Why Anticorruption Reforms Fail—Systemic Corruption as a Collective Action Problem." *Governance* 26 (3): 449–71.

Persson, Torsten, and Guido Tabellini. 1994. "Is Inequality Harmful for Growth?" *American Economic Review* 84: 600–21.

Policardo, Laura, and Edgar J. Sanchez Carrera. 2018. "Corruption Causes Inequality, or Is it the Other Way Around? An Empirical Investigation for a Panel of Countries." *Economic Analysis and Policy* 59: 92–102.

Rauch, James E., and Peter B. Evans. 2000. "Bureaucratic Structure and Bureaucratic Performance in Less Developed Countries." *Journal of Public Economics* 75 (1): 49–71.

Ragin, Charles C. 2008. *Redesigning Social Inquiry: Fuzzy Sets and Beyond.* Chicago, IL: University of Chicago Press.

Robinson, James, and Thierry Verdier. 2013. "The Political Economy of Clientelism." *Scandinavian Journal of Economics* 115 (2): 260–91.

Rose-Ackerman, Susan, and Bonnie J. Palifka. 2016. *Corruption and Government: Causes, Consequences, and Reform.* Cambridge University Press.

Rothstein, Bo. 2005. *Social Traps and the Problem of Trust.* Cambridge: Cambridge University Press.

Rothstein, Bo. 2011. *The Quality of Government: Corruption, Social Trust, and Inequality in International Perspective.* Chicago: University of Chicago Press.

Rothstein, Bo, and Jan Teorell. 2008. "What Is Quality of Government: A Theory of Impartial Political Institutions." *Governance* 21 (2): 165–190.

Rothstein, Bo, and Aiysha Varraich. 2017. *Making Sense of Corruption.* Cambridge University Press.

Shaw, Philip, Marina-Selini Katsaiti, and Marius Jurgilas. 2011. "Corruption and Growth under Weak Identification." *Economic Inquiry* 49 (1): 264–75.

Solt, Frederick. 2019. "Measuring Income Inequality Across Countries and Over Time: The Standardized World Income Inequality Database." Draft. http://myweb.uiowa.edu/fsolt/swiid/swiid.html

Stevens, Alex. 2016. "Configurations of Corruption: A Cross-National Qualitative Comparative Analysis of Levels of Perceived Corruption." *International Journal of Comparative Sociology* 57 (4): 183–206

Stokes, Susan C. 2007. "Political Clientelism." In *The Oxford Handbook of Comparative Politics,* edited by Carles Boix and Susan C. Stokes, 604–27. New York: Oxford University Press.

Sulemana, Iddisah, and Daniel Kpienbaareh. 2018. "An Empirical Examination of the Relationship between Income Inequality and Corruption in Africa." *Economic Analysis and Policy* 60: 27–42.

Treisman, Daniel. 2007. "What Have We Learned about the Causes of Corruption from Ten Years of Cross-national Empirical Research?" *Annual Review of Political Science* 10: 211–44.

UNDP. 2008. *Tackling Corruption, Transforming Lives: Accelerating Human Development in Asia and the Pacific.* Macmillan India Ltd.

Ullah, Muhammad Aman and Eatzaz Ahmad. 2016. "Inequality and Corruption: Evidence from Panel Data." *Forman Journal of Economic Studies* 12: 1–20.

Uslaner, Eric M. 2002. *The Moral Foundations of Trust.* Cambridge: Cambridge University Press.

Uslaner, Eric M. 2004. "Trust and Corruption." In *The New Institutional Economics of Corruption,* edited by J. G. Lambsdorff, M. Taube, and M. Schramm, 76–92. London: Routledge.

Uslaner, Eric M. 2008. *Corruption, Inequality, and the Rule of Law: The Bulging Pocket Makes the Easy Life*. Cambridge and New York: Cambridge University Press.

Uslaner, Eric M. 2017. *The Historical Roots of Corruption: Mass Education, Economic Inequality, and State Capacity*. Cambridge University Press.

Uslaner, Eric M., and Bo Rothstein 2016. "The Historical Roots of Corruption: State Building, Economic Inequality, and Mass Education." *Comparative Politics* 48 (2): 227–48.

Wu, Xun 2005. "Corporate Governance and Corruption: A Cross-Country Analysis." *Governance* 18 (2): 151–70.

You, Jong-sung 2012. "Social Trust: Fairness Matters More Than Homogeneity." *Political Psychology* 33 (5): 701–21.

You, Jong-Sung. 2014. "Land Reform, Inequality, and Corruption: A Comparative Historical Study of Korea, Taiwan, and the Philippines." *The Korean Journal of International Studies* 12: 191–224.

You, Jong-Sung. 2015. *Democracy, Inequality, and Corruption: Korea, Taiwan, and the Philippines Compared*. Cambridge: Cambridge University Press.

You, Jong-Sung. 2016. "Corruption and Inequality in Asia." In *Routledge Handbook of Corruption in Asia*, edited by T. Gong and I. Scott, 97–112. Abingdon, UK: Routledge.

You, Jong-Sung. 2018. "Trust and Corruption." In *The Oxford Handbook of Social and Political Trust*, edited by Eric Uslaner, 473–96. New York, NY: Oxford University Press.

You, Jong-sung, and Eunro Lee. 2018. "Inequality, Corruption, and Growth." Unpublished paper.

You, Jong-sung, and Sanjeev Khagram. 2005. "A Comparative Study of Inequality and Corruption." *American Sociological Review* 70 (1): 136–57.

Zak, Paul J., and Stephen Knack. 2001. "Trust and Growth." *The Economic Journal* 111 (470): 295–321.

Zhang, Yan, Liqun Cao, and Michael S. Vaughn. 2009. "Social Support and Corruption: Structural Determinants of Corruption in the World." *Australian and New Zealand Journal of Criminology* 42 (2): 204–17.

Ziblatt, Daniel. 2009. "Shaping Democratic Practice and the Causes of Electoral Fraud: The Case of Nineteenth-century Germany." *American Political Science Review* 103 (1): 1–21.

CHAPTER 17

THE QUALITY OF GOVERNMENT AND ECONOMIC GROWTH

PELLE AHLERUP, THUSHYANTHAN BASKARAN, AND ARNE BIGSTEN

INTRODUCTION

AT the end of last century, the development policy discussion focused on what came to be called the "Washington Consensus" (Williamson 1990). This consensus emphasized the role of markets in development and led to a package of reforms launched by the Washington institutions in poor or stagnant countries via structural adjustment. The structural adjustment programs (SAPs) typically included policies for macro-economic stabilization and regulatory reform. However, at least in the case of Africa, the SAP period did not bring sustained growth. This gradually led to a shift in the emphasis towards the role of institutions and the quality of government with a growing realization that successful development requires both functioning markets and a functioning state.

An important trait of well-functioning states are good institutions. The importance of institutions was brought into the center of academic discourse on development by Douglass North (1990).[1] His argument was that institutions could reduce inefficiencies due to transaction costs and asymmetric information. Institutions were believed to be particularly important for the protection of property rights and the enforcement of contracts. This idea was later picked up and elaborated further by Acemoglu and Robinson (2012), who emphasized the central role of inclusive institutions to bring about economic development. The new mainstream approach thus added institutional reform to market reform and may be referred to as the post–Washington Consensus. While the focus was now on good institutions, there was only a limited understanding of how good institutions could be achieved or,

---

[1] North (1990, 3) writes that "institutions are the rules of the game in a society or, more formally, are the humanly devised constraints that shape human interaction. In consequence they structure incentives in human exchange, whether political, social, or economic."

more precisely, how one could administer institutional change. For example, although there was often agreement on the policies needed e.g. to fight corruption, the implementation of these policies might be infeasible if opposed by local elites. The implementation of reform and the quality of government would thus depend on the distribution of political and economic power. More generally, reformers had to not only identify institutional shortcomings, but at the same time also deal with the political economy of how to implement institutional changes: To create good governance one needs to identify which institutions matter, how they should be reformed, and how such reforms can be implemented (Bourguignon and Wangwe 2018).

Against this background, this chapter reviews the literature on the relationship between the quality of government and economic growth. Since there is limited evidence on the link between quality of government as such and growth, we chose to devote more space to discuss the role of related aspects, such as democracy, formal institutions, and cultural norms, in the context of the literature on economic growth. We discuss institutional challenges in generating high growth rates and, once they emerge, of sustaining them. The focus is on developing countries, but we will also cover studies that explore this question for more developed ones.

We start by discussing the concept of quality of government in the context of the literature on economic growth. Then we review the evidence of the impact of the quality of government and related aspects of political and economic life, on growth and pay attention to the mechanism or channels through which the quality of government is seen to affect growth. Next, we discuss determinants of institutional quality in particular, and by doing so illustrate the empirical difficulty in establishing the direction of causality between the quality of institutions and economic development. Thereafter we discuss whether it is harder to sustain growth if it increases inequality. Finally, we summarize the key conclusions and point to ways forward in future research.

DEFINING QUALITY OF GOVERNMENT

This study focuses on the role of quality of government for growth. However, this is a broad concept that covers numerous aspects. In this section, we discuss how it could be defined in the context of the literature on what causes the great global disparities in economic growth.

There is a large literature in Economics on the role of *institutions* for good *governance*. The most cited definition of *governance* in this literature is due to Kaufmann, Kraay, and Mastruzzi (2008), who define governance as the traditions and institutions that determine how authority is exercised in a particular country. Their definition includes three dimensions, namely (i) the process by which governments are selected, held accountable, monitored, and replaced; (ii) the capacity of governments to manage resources efficiently and formulate, implement, and enforce sound policies and regulations; and (iii) the respect of citizens and the state for the institutions that govern economic and social interactions among them. The extensive debate on institutions and development clearly shows that institutions as defined above tend to be persistent and difficult to change in the short run. This means that it is hard to sustain growth when such institutions are poor to begin with (Acemoglu, Johnson, and Robinson 2001; Acemoglu and Johnson 2005).

The definition by Kaufmann, Kraay, and Mastruzzi (2008) is a good starting point for structuring our thinking about QoG. However, Rothstein and Teorell (2008) argue that the definition is too broad. According to them, good governance only requires *political equality* on the "input" side of the relationship between a state and its citizens and *impartiality* on the "output" side. On the one hand, political equality is needed in order to ensure equal access to political power. Impartiality, on the other hand, is the marker of good governance on the output side. It is defined as follows: "when implementing laws and policies, government officials shall not take anything about the citizen/case into consideration that is not beforehand stipulated in the policy or the law" (Rothstein and Teorell 2008, 168). Impartiality, by their definition, is thus a procedural norm for how to exercise authority and does not concern the *content* of policies (or for that matter, how policymakers are elected). More specifically, Rothstein and Teorell (2008, 182) are not concerned about the *quality* of policies or the *efficiency* of the government and argue that "impartiality is always preferable to efficiency," since rights are more important and fundamental than utility. Yet, they contend that impartiality, since it implies meritocratic recruitment rather than recruitment based on political or clientelistic connections, may enhance efficiency.

Following Rothstein and Teorell, we acknowledge that government impartiality and various forms of inequalities are important for the sustainability of economic growth. Empirically, we think that more impartiality could be positively correlated with sustained economic growth for two main reasons. It may either be at the core of what constitutes QoG in the context of economic growth, as is suggested by the discussion in Rothstein and Teorell (2008), or it may proxy for the broad aspects of governance suggested by Kaufmann, Kraay, and Mastruzzi (2008). It is plausible that an impartial government is also rational and efficient in terms of policy choice. An impartial approach to government may also be associated with secure property rights and equality of opportunity, i.e. no ethnic favoritism, which may reflect the inclusive institutions emphasized by Acemoglu and Robinson (2012).

It may be more challenging to achieve and sustain growth in a situation of high inequality. In the case of Africa, there has been an extensive discussion about the role of ethnic divisions. The effect of ethnic divisions on sustainable growth could be either direct or indirect. One could envisage that there is a direct effect of ethnic diversity or lack of social cohesion on economic growth and the sustainability thereof. This could take the form of a lack of trust among economic agents, making it harder to do business or to organize different forms of collective action. Additionally, in a divided society, it is harder to not only form an agreement on the content of policies but also to ensure that they are implemented without favoring specific groups. This affects the government's willingness or ability to decide on and implement policies that improve the prospects for sustained economic growth. Easterly and Levine (1997) hold that "Africa's growth tragedy" can be explained by reference to how ethnic divisions have fed into rent-seeking behavior and difficulties in agreeing on the provision of public goods that, in turn, are needed for economic growth. This is in consonance with more recent findings that the quality of government and the provision of public goods are lower in societies with more social and economic inequalities between ethnic groups (Baldwin and Huber 2010; Kyriacou 2013) and where ethnic groups are spatially more segregated (Alesina and Zhuravskaya 2011).

Further, it is commonly asserted that African policymakers often favor their co-ethnics and their home region. For instance, Kramon and Posner (2016) find evidence of ethnic favoritism when it comes to educational outcomes in Kenya. Similarly, Hodler and Raschky

(2014) find that foreign aid is disproportionately located to the leaders' home regions. There is indirect evidence that higher levels of perceived government impartiality do reflect less actual ethno-regional favoritism. Ahlerup and Isaksson (2015) show that respondents in the Afrobarometer surveys are less likely to say that the government treats their group unfairly if they are co-ethnics with the president, live in the president's home region, or live in a region where a large share of the population belongs to the president's ethnic group. It seems likely that lower levels of impartiality in Africa are in large part due to higher ethnic or regional favoritism.

Ethnic or regional favoritism implies that governments do not allocate resources according to objective economic criteria. Hence, in countries where the government is more impartial, common resources are probably more often allocated to individuals, regions, or sectors where they fulfill commonly agreed on goals, such as to ensure sustained economic growth. A plausible assumption is that the pressure for between-group distribution will be lower when people know that the government acts impartially.

Governments may invest less if there is more uncertainty about future domestic revenues or foreign aid. If revenues plummet, government investments may too, as the resource constraint become binding. If resources suddenly rise, the government capacity constraint may bind instead. It has been shown that economic growth in sub-Saharan Africa suffers from the volatility of government revenues, public investments, and aid (Museru, Toerien, and Gossel 2014). A reason for this could be that divided societies that lack social cohesion may find it harder to respond effectively against economic shocks, in the wake of which the government may be forced to allocate adjustment burdens across groups. Transitions between governments after elections can become more disruptive, since the new government may feel that it is now their group's turn to get their "fair share." Impartiality could thus be linked to more stable public policies, as an impartial government could be a sign that the government does not benefit primarily those groups that happen to be in power at the time. Consider, for example, the disastrous consequences in the form of ethnic clashes killing thousands of people that followed the Kenyan elections in 2007, where the opposition felt that the incumbent government had "stolen" the election (Wrong 2009).

Let us sum up our discussion about the concept of quality of government. From the discussion so far, one could argue that there are three dimensions of it that may matter for growth. The first dimension is about the input side of politics, i.e. the quality of democracy or political equality. The second dimension relates to the competence, efficiency, and capacity of the government to formulate and implement policies and plans, and to formulate and enforce rules and regulations (rule of law, property rights, etc.). More efficiency within the government is likely to lead to more efficiency outside the government in terms of, e.g., an efficient allocation of resources in the private sector. The third dimension is the impartiality by which the government implements the policies that have been formulated. Since we believe that political equality mainly captures the extent to which citizens can and will elect governments with good characteristics, we hold that the concept of quality of government as such should refer primarily to the second and third dimensions, that is, the efficiency within the government and the impartiality in implementation.

With regard to the effects of impartiality of policy implementation, we contend that there are three broad categories of mechanisms whereby impartiality may be linked to sustained growth. First, impartiality implies less ethno-regional favoritism. Second, impartiality implies less room for rent-seeking. Third, as the stake in elections will be lower, there will be more stability in economic and political conditions. Together, these mechanisms suggest that impartiality could lead to a more efficient use of available resources and higher social acceptance of potential relative changes in the income distribution resulting from economic growth.

QUALITY OF GOVERNMENT AND GROWTH

A lack of direct evidence

If QoG is defined as efficiency within the government and impartiality in implementation of government policies, there are no empirical studies that assess how important this complete package is for economic growth, Yet, there are many studies on the role of related aspects of the political and economic life of countries, such as the level of democracy, quality of formal institutions, cultural norms, and policies. In this chapter, we present a brief overview of this literature. There are both backward and forward linkages between QoG and these related aspects. QoG is likely to be higher in more democratic countries, as governments in these countries tend to cater more to the welfare of a broad section of the population than do governments in more autocratic countries. At the same time, more people will have capacity and possibility to influence politics in countries with higher levels of QoG, since they are less likely to face discrimination that would prevent such participation. QoG will be higher in countries with better formal institutions, such as stronger protection of property rights and a stronger legal system, since these institutions level the playing field when it comes both to political and economic interactions, and discipline the bureaucracy. It seems fair to assume that QoG may be higher in societies where cultural norms are egalitarian or individualistic, rather than hierarchical or collectivistic, since these norms influence all interactions, both between citizens and between citizens and the state. Over time, if QoG is improved and people are treated equally, fairly, and impartially, this is likely to affect deep cultural norms.

Positive or normative?

Quality of government in the sense of impartiality is a normative concept—but whether it is also good for growth is an empirical question.

Ahlerup, Baskaran, and Bigsten (2016) argue that the way in which governments approach the ethnic question within their country will significantly affect the likelihood that any sparks of growth can be sustained over a long period. Their argument is that economic growth initially tends to exacerbate inequality. This rise in inequality may particularly affect the income distribution across different ethnic groups. If, in such a context of newly emerging growth and rising inequality, the government is (perceived to be) partial toward certain ethnic groups, then this may lead to political divisions and internal conflicts that may preclude the possibility that any growth episode turns into prolonged spells. That is, episodes of growth may be short-lived and dissipate quickly when political tensions increase simultaneously.

They explore this issue for 20 sub-Saharan African countries using survey data from the Afrobarometer. They construct an *Impartiality index* that captures the share of the respondents holding that the government never treats the ethnic group to which they belong unfairly. This index conveys a powerful signal of the extent of partiality in Africa, and that more than half of the respondents in this set of countries see their government as acting partial along ethnic lines is an indication of the magnitude of the potential problem, both in this and in other contexts. The authors find that this measure has a statistically significant positive relationship with the probability of sustaining growth at the national level also when income inequality, fractionalization in terms language, ethnicity, and religion, formal institutions, conflict, and country-fixed effects are included in the regressions. There are also indications that impartiality may matter even more in countries that are initially poorer. Worthy of note is that they do not find any effect on the growth rate as such, which indicates that what impartiality does here is more to help countries stay on a path of moderate economic growth than to be a sufficient condition for high economic growth. Hence, they indeed find that countries whose governments are perceived to be relatively impartial tend to be more likely to experience periods of sustained growth. Their conclusion is that to foster growth, governments should not only implement the "right" policies but should also implement those policies in an impartial manner. In fact, impartiality in itself may have a positive effect on growth irrespective of the specific content of policies.

Is this a generalizable result, to growth more broadly defined, and for other regions or time periods? Currently, only a small literature is concerned with these specific questions. A more fruitful way to inform us about the effect of the quality of government on growth could then be to look at it from another perspective, and ask what differentiates governments in countries with high economic growth from those with lower growth. Accordingly, in this section, we present the findings from studies that explore the role of democracy, institutions, policies, and culture in the growth process.

Democracy

In a recent paper, Acemoglu et al. (2019) argue that *democracy* does lead to higher economic growth. Using a binary democracy indicator, they find that transitioning from autocracy to democracy is associated with an increase in income by 20 percent. The proposed mechanisms are that democracy is associated with more investments, more economic reforms, more public goods, and less social unrest. While democracies tax more, which in itself is often thought to be bad for growth, they also tend to provide more public goods and political stability.

In a meta-analysis, Doucouliagos and Ulubaşoğlu (2008) argue that there is no solid case to be made for a direct effect of democracy on economic growth, but that democracy does have a positive indirect effect, going through higher human capital, more economic freedom, lower inflation, and lower political instability. The theoretical arguments for an effect of democracy on growth proposed by these authors include that democracies are more likely to be free and provide secure property rights, which improves resource allocation. On the other hand, responsiveness to popular demands may imply that democracies are more sensitive to rent-seeking, to allocation of common resources for immediate consumption rather than long-term investments, or to allow ethnic, social, or economic cleavages to transform into various forms of disruptive conflict. Overall, if quality of government is measured by indicators sensitive to public goods provision, economic freedom, economic reforms, or political stability, then the findings in this strand of the literature suggest both that quality of government is likely to have positive effects on the growth rate and that democratizing reforms are one way to improve the quality of government.[2]

Studying the link between democracy and inequality, Acemoglu et al. (2015) note that elites often dominate in nondemocratic countries but that democracies cannot be assumed to always promote more equality either, since they can be captured by elites or richer segments of the population, cater only to the middle class interests, or open up new possibilities only for some groups which could result in more inequality ("inequality-increasing market opportunities"). Empirically, the authors find that democracy has a positive effect on the tax rate and on secondary education but no robust effect on inequality. That democracies provide public goods that are of interest to broad segments of the population, e.g., secondary education, and collect more taxes to be able to do so, suggests that democracies may have higher quality of government and may act more impartially vis-à-vis the general interests of the whole population.

Institutions

The argument by Acemoglu, Johnson, and Robinson (2001) that *institutions* are a fundamental determinant on long-term economic growth has been met with some criticism. Albouy (2012) raises concerns whether their instrumental variable, "settler mortality," really captures the perceived mortality of potential European settlers in different locations, but this criticism is forcefully discarded by Acemoglu, Johnson, and Robinson (2012). Another line of criticism is due to Glaeser et al. (2004), who posit that the true reason why institutions are correlated with development may be that Europeans brought with them human capital rather than institutions, and that the resulting difference in human capital then is as likely a candidate for causing long-term economic development as are formal institutions. Drawing on an exercise where they simultaneously instrument for institutions and human capital, Acemoglu, Gallego, and Robinson (2014) find that both factors matter for long-term economic growth and that the critique launched by Glaeser et al. (2004) is unfounded.

Supposing that we accept that institutions are a fundamental force in the growth process, the question naturally becomes "then which institutions matter more?" Acemoglu and Johnson (2005) argue that it is property rights institutions that matter for long-term economic growth, investment, and financial development, while contracting institutions matter only for the form of financial intermediation. Hence, not all forms of institutions are equally important for growth. It appears to be especially important to have institutions that shape vertical exchanges by limiting the power that governments have over their citizens. The existence of secure property rights means a more predictable economic environment and a more level playing field, and this is why we see positive effects on investments, private

---

[2] The modernization hypothesis posits that with economic development countries will also become more democratic. Acemoglu et al. (2009) find that this is not generally the case. Instead, they suggest that certain historical factors, such as colonial experience which is captured by country-fixed effects in their analyses, are determinants of both democratization and long-term economic growth.

credit, and stock markets development. In the context of this review, it is worth noting that Acemoglu and Johnson (2005) use three different indicators of property rights that all capture the level of certainty about ownership of assets. Similar to the idea of impartiality, they all capture the degree of predictability in the ownership of returns to investments. However, they could also mask preferential treatment of certain groups since they just capture the average for the society as a whole.

Leaving the quantitative world of cross-country regressions, Acemoglu and Robinson (2010) present a more in-depth qualitative analysis of the issue of African underdevelopment that they have touched upon in a number of papers (some of which are cited in this text). The analysis consists of illuminating anecdotes about African precolonial development, European colonial policies, and postcolonial events, all placed in a coherent theoretical framework. The authors argue that state institutions in Africa have often been absolutist and patrimonial, and that this is the key reason for the lack of development. Specifically, they argue that the institutional transition that has led to economic growth in many parts of the world never took place in Africa. State formation was delayed, and state institutions were more patrimonial (rule by a strategy of exchanging rights for support from certain people or groups) and absolutist (unconstrained). In addition, Africa was negatively affected by slave trade and colonial rule. The combination of absolutist and patrimonial institutions implies, e.g., less secure property rights, that the quality of government is lower, and that the government by definition is not impartial.

At the individual level, with experience comes capacity. Arguing that this could be the case also at the level of the state, Borcan, Olsson, and Putterman (2018) show that more or longer experience with state structures is not linearly related to more economic development. Instead, the relationship is hump-shaped, where countries with medium state experience have higher income levels. There is a learning process that benefits old states, leading to higher quality institutions, but younger states have the possibility to pick best practice institutions, which gives them an advantage over some states that are locked into their specific institutional setups. The empirical analysis does not inform us whether the impact of state history is to give us better rules or that states have acquired more capacity to ensure that those rules are enforced. That younger states may have an advantage over "middle-aged" states actually suggests that the content of policies or the quality of government/institutions is a more fundamental growth determinant than the experience with the state apparatus as such.

Another strand of the literature puts more emphasis on the role of actual *policies*. Fatás and Mihov (2013) find that policy volatility, a measure of discretionary changes in government consumption, has a negative effect on economic growth. Importantly, they show that the role of formal institutions, in their case constraint on the executive, have only an indirect effect on economic growth in that they affect degree of policy volatility. The authors do not investigate the content of the policy volatility in the sense of who gets more spending or benefit from tax reductions, but suggest that the theoretical mechanism could be either tax rate volatility, which is known to have negative effects on growth, or an increase in uncertainty about future tax rates leading to less investment and hence growth. While stability in, or lack of uncertainty about, government spending and tax rates is not impartiality as such, there are similarities. Both stability and impartiality point to the role of a level playing field, in either time or space. Other papers make similar arguments, albeit more informally. Henry and Miller (2009) argue that while institutions surely matter, one must not forget that policies do too. They exemplify this notion with Barbados and Jamaica, which they argue were very similar in terms of geography, population, colonial history, and institutions, but where different macroeconomic policies still led to large differences in economic growth over a sustained period of time.

Culture

The empirical distinction between institutions and policies, institutions and culture, or formal institutions and informal institutions is not always clearly spelled out. In their review of the literature on the links between *culture* and institutions, Alesina and Giuliano (2015) distinguish between "culture," using a definition similar to the one North (1990) uses for informal institutions, and "institutions," which is what North would call formal institutions. Empirically, it is still difficult to disentangle culture from institutions. The cultural traits discussed by the authors include generalized trust (which has been found to be good for growth[3]), individualism versus collectivism (where individualism is good for growth), strength of family ties (where societies with stronger ties have less generalized trust, more often accept selfish behavior outside the family network while demanding good behavior within the network, and have more family firms with more nepotism in hiring), generalized versus limited morality (see discussion below), and attitudes towards work and perception of reason for individual poverty.

Tabellini (2008) finds that while people with "limited morality" are more likely to follow codes of good conduct and behave honestly when interacting with individuals belonging to the same family or clan, they may find it morally acceptable to behave differently when interacting with people outside their group, people with "generalized morality" are more likely to follow the same codes of good conduct and behave honestly regardless of with whom they interact. He finds that generalized morality, as captured by higher levels of generalized trust and tolerance and respect for other people as measured in the World Values Surveys, is associated with more well-functioning formal institutions, measured by country-level assessments of "government anti-diversion policies" and "bureaucratic quality." He shows both that generalized morality affects formal institutions, and, following the strategy in Nunn (2007), that countries with a higher level of generalized morality export more from industries that rely relatively more on good institutions. While a possible mechanism could be that people behave better in private organizations (or in horizontal exchanges), it is also possible that officials and public administrators act more in the interest of the common good (or behave better in vertical exchanges). The latter comes very close to capturing the impartiality of government highlighted by Rothstein and Teorell (2008) and Ahlerup, Baskaran, and Bigsten (2016). In a related paper, Tabellini (2010) shows that cultural values cause different economic development at the level of European regions. The measure of culture used is wider than just generalized versus limited morality, as it includes also the extent to which people think that individual efforts are likely to pay off and the value parents put on their children being obedient, intended to capture (a lack of) individualism, but it is still

---

[3] The empirical cross-country macroeconomic literature often finds a positive effect of trust on growth, starting with seminal work by Knack and Keefer (1997) and Zak and Knack (2001), where the latter also include a measure of formal institutions.

sufficiently similar that we can hypothesize that some of the positive effects could be due to generalized morality. In fact, in his ordinary least squares estimations with country-fixed effects, Tabellini (2010) finds that both trust and respect at the regional level are individually correlated with regional output growth.

Institutions, culture, or policies

On the one hand, studies such as Fatás and Mihov (2013) find that policies do matter, even when institutions are held constant. Anecdotes, such as in Henry and Miller (2009), also suggest that policies matter. On the other hand, Acemoglu et al. (2003) argue that it is institutions rather than policies that explain development. Similarly, Rodrik, Subramanian, and Trebbi (2004) argue that once institutions are held constant, neither geography nor openness matter for growth.

We do not aim to act as judges in this still ongoing debate on the relative importance of institutions, geography, policy, or culture. Instead, we note that, to some extent, studies may be either measuring other factors than what they claim to be measuring, or to actually end up measuring the same factors while using different terms for what they have measured. For instance, Acemoglu et al. (2003) use as indicators for institutional quality the outcome of (formal and informal) institutions. The indicator they use, the risk that private foreign investments are expropriated, is determined both by formal constraints for what the government can do, and more informal norms about what agents of the governments should do. Similarly, several of their policy variables are also outcomes, such as inflation etc. Accordingly, we would here side with the critique in Glaeser et al. (2004), who argue that measures such as protection against expropriation are outcomes, not institutions, and that many institutional indicators in fact measure policy choices, are unstable, and do not measure actual constraints.

Quite problematically, the confusion of institutions and governance is ubiquitous in the empirical literature. For instance, one can note how the World Bank Governance Indicators are by their creators called "governance indicators," but still regularly used as indicators of *institutions*. These indicators are also by construction measures of how people perceive matters such as "the rule of law," not whether this perception is due to formal institutions, informal institutions, or just due to temporary policy that may be quickly malleable.

Before discussing the relative importance of institutions, culture, and policies, let us present recent contributions on the historical growth performance of China and the role of Islam (notably in the Middle East).

China is indeed an interesting case in this context. As convincingly argued by Brandt, Ma, and Rawski (2014), economic and political institutions are fundamental both for China's historical success, its demise during colonization, and its recent rapid growth. To highlight two characteristics, China has a long history of meritocratic recruitment, which has contributed to the high value its people put on education. However, the powerful bureaucracy also implied an absence of checks and balances, which has led to pervasive patronage structures that today contribute to rising economic inequality. Due to this lack of constraint on the executive and lack of formal property rights, one could view China as a counterargument to the necessity for high quality of government. At the same time, we are not (yet) at the end of history, and many observers see the system as inherently unstable in that it continues to build up fundamental inequalities, which eventually may block further growth.[4]

In a comprehensive survey of the connections between Islam and economic performance, Kuran (2018) discusses possible reasons for the weak economic performance of Muslim-majority countries. The author discusses how the historically relatively more egalitarian inheritance system in the Middle East, as compared to institutions in Western Europe, prevented the rise of larger commercial enterprises and the accumulation of private capital. This became especially problematic during the Industrial Revolution with its increased returns to large-scale production and corporations. Additionally, that the concept of corporation is lacking from Islamic law may be part of the explanation for why historical experience with impersonal exchange has been low, which may have caused lower levels of generalized trust. Here we have a case of a societal characteristic, egalitarianism, that, on the one hand, should be associated with more impartial governments, but which, on the other hand, may hamper economic growth.

Now, do institutions ("formal institutions") or culture ("informal institutions") matter more for growth? Drawing from history, the answer seems to be that both matter. For instance, the weak performance of East Germany compared to West Germany, or North Korea compared to South Korea, cannot be attributed to differences in population structure, history, or culture. Hence, good formal institutions and good policies are key in some situations. On the other hand, economic performance in southern vs northern Italy cannot be explained by differences in formal institutions since they are the same. Instead, the story of the importance of long-term disparities in cultural values and beliefs has often been told in economics and political science (Putnam 1993; Guiso, Sapienza, and Zingales 2016; Tabellini 2008, 2010). Kuran (2018) explains how the egalitarian Islamic law delayed the introduction of impersonal exchange and corporations in the Middle East, and how this became a hindrance to growth, especially from the start of the Industrial Revolution. Brandt, Ma, and Rawski (2014) discuss how different features of Chinese culture have been positive or negative for growth in different times during history. The Chinese growth miracle has apparently not been hindered by fundamental inequalities or a patrimonial system where political connections have been essential for successful businesses. Evidently, quality of government in the sense of impartiality is not a necessary condition for growth.

Rothstein (2015) argues that the institutional theory of development has failed to note a special kind of institutional feature in the Chinese system of governing. He characterizes this as a cadre organization, which is different from the Weberian bureaucracy model of civil service neutrality. In this system, higher levels of government set targets for lower levels, but leave a lot of discretion for the latter as to how they achieve the targets (delegated discretion). The basis for the model is strong, ideologically based commitment by the civil servants to the specific political doctrine. The notion is that the agents will choose measures that the principal would have chosen had s/he been in the same situation with the same information. Rothstein argues that this type of flexible operative ideology may be successful in a rapidly

---

[4] In a discussion on the overall robustness of 67 common correlates of growth, Sala-I-Martin, Doppelhofer, and Miller (2004) find 18 variables to be robustly correlated with growth. Among these 18 are the share of the population that are Confucian. Political rights or civil liberties are not among the factors robustly correlated with growth. However, their method cannot solve the issue of causality.

changing society such as China, but it might not work in a multiparty system where the ideological orientation of the rulers may change.

Economic growth is determined by the interplay between both formal and informal institutions as well as politics. What constitutes high quality of government, in the sense of what is good for growth, is a combination of these factors, and the importance of individual elements in this mix is different under different circumstances. The literature on the economic impact of culture shows that factors outside the *government* codetermine the quality of institutions more broadly defined. Using the normative and narrow definition of quality of government as impartiality, history tells us that it is good for growth in general, but also that high and sustained growth can be possible even with low quality of government.

Determinants of Institutional Quality

While there is broad agreement that good quality of government correlates positively with economic growth, the direction of causality is still debated. Acemoglu, Johnson, and Robinson (2001) argue that there are four fundamental potential causes of growth, namely geography, institutions, culture, and luck. They identify institutions as the key factor and argue that they cause growth through good governance. This view has dominated the development literature since the turn of the century.

However, there is also a literature arguing that it is economic development *per se* that leads to better institutions and more democracy (rather than the other way around). Glaeser et al. (2004), in particular, are skeptical of over-emphasis of historical determinants of institutions. They argue that education and human capital go a long way in explaining recent institutional improvements and are hence a more fundamental cause of growth. They criticize the institutional camp for ignoring human capital, despite massive evidence that it predicts growth (Barro 2001; Mankiw, Romer, and Weil 1992). For example, when comparing initial executive constraints with initial human capital in longitudinal data, Glaeser et al. (2004) find that the latter predicts growth much better and that institutions have little predictive power for growth.

Acemoglu, Johnson, and Robinson (2001) sought to explain the quality of institutions with colonial history arguing that settlement patterns shape institutions. Glaeser et al. (2004) argue that the data certainly shows that history matters, but not specifically that institutions matter. They point to an identification problem and ask the question: Did colonizers, when they settled, bring with them institutions or themselves and their human capital? They agree that institutions (capitalism is a set of institutions) matter for growth, but find that it is harder to establish that certain rules and constraints matter. They conclude that the best candidate as a fundamental cause of growth is human capital.

Both the institution and human capital camps think it is important to understand institutional change and its determinants. While the former camp focuses on internal political mechanisms, the latter notes that there are other important factors that should not be ignored. Firstly, there are shocks, such as wars, revolutions, and changes in commodity prices. Secondly, modernization drives institutional change. Institutions are much better in richer and more educated countries. The question then is what drives modernization. There are both political forces (Lipset 1959; Hirschman 1970; Barro 1999) and economic ones. The human capital camp argues that institutional quality is driven by human capital, especially management. There have obviously been enormous institutional improvements in recent decades alongside rapid improvements in education.

We think that there are good arguments for both standpoints, i.e., that both institutions and human capital are fundamental for long-term growth. The two stories focus on two components of our initial definition of quality of government, namely rules and regulations on the one hand and competence and capacity on the other. It is not self-evident which of the two mechanisms that is more important for sustainable growth.

Inequality and Growth

A question that is poised to become increasingly central to the economic policy debate, especially for countries such as China, is whether economic growth accompanied by growing economic inequality is harder to achieve and sustain. Problems with sustaining growth are found both when it benefits primarily ethnic minorities and when it benefits a politically powerful majority. When minorities believe that the government actively discriminates against them, the consequence may be ethnic strife, political conflicts, or attempts toward secession. These effects may lead to lower growth.

The fact that some countries, especially in Africa, has had such dismal economic and political performance for a sustained period of time has often been explained by reference to their high levels of ethnic diversity. Easterly and Levine (1997) famously attributed a large part of Africa's poor growth performance to the link between ethnic fragmentation and a distorted public goods provision, an effect studied more directly by, e.g., Miguel and Gugerty (2005); Miguel (2004); Alesina et al. (2003); Alesina, Baqir, and Easterly (1999); and La Porta et al. (1999). That ethnic diversity leads to distorted provision of public goods is in line with recent findings suggesting that the quality of government and the provision of public goods is lower in societies with more social and economic inequality between ethnic groups (or where ethnic groups are spatially more segregated).

The classical Economics literature posits that there is a growth–equity trade-off. The arguments for why inequality could be good for growth are, for example, that it provides incentives for investments, increases savings since the wealthy generally save a higher share of their income than the poor, and makes it possible for at least some individuals to accumulate the minimum capital needed to start a business (Barro 2000). In his classical book on the trade-off, Okun (1975) argues that redistribution tends to hurt growth by dampening incentives to save and invest. However, the impact of redistribution policies on growth would also depend on how they are implemented. The overall impact of tax and expenditure reform may be positive if the tax revenues are used for growth-enhancing public expenditures such as investment in education, health, and infrastructure.

In contrast to the classical hypothesis, much of recent empirical literature has found that inequality can be harmful for both the rate of growth and the sustainability of growth (Persson and Tabellini 1994; Easterly 2007; Halter; Oechslin, and Zweimüller 2014; Berg, Ostry, and Zettelmeyer 2012). The literature has also identified the channels whereby inequality can be harmful for growth. Firstly, the political economy channel implies that inequality leads to pressure for redistributive policies that may harm growth (Alesina and

Rodrik 1994; Persson and Tabellini 1994; Perotti 1996). Secondly, there are explanations focusing on credit market imperfections. For example, Galor and Zeira (1993) focus on the interaction between credit market imperfections and fixed costs of investment in education, and show that inequality may lead to underinvestment in education, which can reduce growth. Thirdly, it can be argued that inequality leads to social and political tensions, which in turn may hinder growth in various ways, e.g., by diverting resources from production to security, by distorting resource allocation, or by reducing trust leading to less efficient cooperation. Inequality may also be related to ethnic conflicts. Such social polarization may reduce the security of property rights, thus eventually causing lower growth (Keefer and Knack 2002). Generally, uncertainty tends to decrease investments and thus reduce growth (Alesina and Perotti 1996). Rodrik (1999) argues that it is easier to adjust to shocks and to sustain growth when there is social consensus. Although the literature is somewhat divided on the effects of redistribution on growth, there has been a shift in the balance in recent decades away from the classical perception.

Berg et al. (2018) examine how inequality and redistribution affect growth in a joint framework. They use a new comprehensive panel data set covering both developed and developing countries and focus on the growth rate over a five-year period as well as the duration of growth spells. They also investigate whether the effects vary by the extent of inequality and seek to identify the channels through which inequality and redistribution affect growth. The authors demonstrate that there is a strong negative relationship between inequality and growth in income per capita in the subsequent period, and a weak positive relationship between redistribution and subsequent growth. They also note that higher inequality is associated with shorter growth spells. When analyzing the effects of redistribution, they combine the direct growth effect of redistribution with the growth effect of the resulting decline in inequality. In their basic model, growth depends on initial income, inequality, and redistribution. Inequality is always negatively and significantly associated with growth. Among the control variables, one is of particular interest: The one for political institutions, that is, the Polity IV measure of democracy. This variable is positive but insignificant and its inclusion does not change the relationship between inequality and growth. Next, they find that inequality has a significant negative relationship with the duration of growth spells. When redistribution is large (top quartile), it is harmful to growth. This, however, is not the case when redistribution is more limited (bottom three quartiles). They find that the quality of political institutions has a significantly positive effect on the duration of growth spells. One reason for why inequality has a negative effect on growth spells is that inequality seems to have a negative effect on the accumulation of both human and physical capital.

The main result of their study is thus that lower net inequality (after redistribution) is linked to faster growth. Redistribution is generally positive for growth unless it is very pronounced. If it is very pronounced, it can negatively affect the durability of growth. It thus seems harder to initiate and sustain growth when inequality is high, and the main reasons appear to be intermediate effects on human capital and physical capital investments. These factors, in turn, depend on the quality of government in a broad sense. Noting that high quality of government requires the formulation of sound policies as well as competent and impartial implementation, high-income inequality reduces the likelihood of achieving all this by contributing to conflicts, instability, and a lack of trust.

CONCLUSIONS AND WAYS FORWARD

In this chapter, we have discussed the importance of the quality of government for economic growth. We first noted that there is a variety of ideas about what is meant by quality of government. One of our aims was thus to decide what to include in this concept in the context of a discussion on the determinants of economic growth. We used a popular definition of good governance as a starting point, and then argued that only some of the components of good governance should be included in a narrower concept of quality of government. In our review of the literature on the determinants of growth, we discussed both quality of government narrowly defined as well as wider concepts and definitions, since they are closely related, and since the narrow definition has only rarely been used in the empirical literature. As far as the concept of quality of government goes, we conclude that it is unreasonable to restrict the definition to impartiality only, as is suggested by Rothstein and Teorell (2008). It needs to have at least two dimensions—impartiality and efficiency. We have noted repeatedly in our review that both these dimensions matter. A government needs to be both efficient and impartial to achieve good results. These two dimensions need to be there in the formulation and implementation of government policy. In the concept of governance from which we started, there was also the component of democracy, but the latter should not as such be part of quality of government. Democracy can be perceived as only the procedure by which voters select good-quality governments. Governance also included a range of (informal) institutions (culture), but they can be perceived as part of only the environment within which the government operates and thus not part of quality of government.

We have reviewed some limited evidence that impartiality is good for growth and shown that there is an abundance of studies showing that a level playing field is good for growth. The discussion pointing to the importance of secure property rights is a case in point, but there are many other examples of why biased government decision-making (corruption, rent-seeking) distorts resource allocation and reduces growth or its sustainability.

Our review found that both formal and informal institutions as well as politics can be important for economic growth, and that the relative importance of each of these factors differ by time and place. There is no one-size-fits-all type of institution to be found to always trump all others in the empirical literature. Notably, the economic impact of cultural beliefs and values demonstrate how factors beside the state and its bureaucracy and beyond formal laws and regulations can in some cases be fundamental determinants of long-term economic development.

Impartiality is not sufficient for good quality of government and certainly not for economic growth. In fact, while the historical evidence supports the notion that quality of government thus narrowly defined is good for growth, cases such as the recent growth miracle in China demonstrate that high growth is possible without it. We maintain that the government must also be competent and effective in policy formulation and implementation, including the building up of stable formal governance institutions. The literature on institutions and state capacity has made this point emphatically. It is also clear that efficient provision of public goods such as education and infrastructure are crucial for growth. It is not enough that these are impartially distributed. We conclude that a government that is both efficient and impartial has the best chance of achieving and sustaining economic growth.

Again, while there are persuasive theoretical reasons to expect that quality of government should be good for economic growth, there is still scant empirical evidence that this is the case also in practice. The literature covered in this chapter, showing how there is suggestive empirical evidence that democracy, formal institutions, cultural norms, and policies, matter for economic growth, supports the notion that also QoG should matter, but more empirical research is needed to establish that this is indeed the case, and also, if so, give us estimates of the strength of the relationship. Ahlerup, Baskaran, and Bigsten (2016) show that QoG matters for sustained growth in Africa, but until we see the results from other studies using data from other parts of the world, we do not know if this result is specific to this particular context, or if it can be generalized to context with other historical (colonial) experiences, and other demographic (ethnic) challenges. Researchers could embrace the multidimensionality of QoG, by measuring QoG along several dimensions and empirically link each of these dimensions to plausible mechanisms and possible outcomes. Aggregate-level data on these dimensions could, as in Ahlerup, Baskaran, and Bigsten (2016), be constructed using responses in individual-level surveys. Researchers could also benchmark indicators of QoG against indicators of democracy, formal institutions, and cultural norms in order to inform us about the importance of QoG relative to the importance of related aspects. We also need to know more about where QoG comes from, what builds it up, maintains, or destroys it. How malleable is QoG? We need to connect potentially deep historical roots and more recent influences. We could here be informed by detailed analyses of the relationship between long-term historical factors and trends, and geography on the one hand, and QoG on the other. How have shocks, such as colonization, wars, natural disasters, and climate change affected QoG? We also need more qualitative evidence of deliberate attempts to improve QoG and why these were successful or not, and analyses of the role of different agents and structures for determining the eventual outcomes.

REFERENCES

Acemoglu, Daron, Francisco A. Gallego, and James A. Robinson. 2014. "Institutions, Human Capital, and Development." *Annual Review of Economics* 6: 875–912.

Acemoglu, Daron, and Simon Johnson. 2005. "Unbundling Institutions." *Journal of Political Economy* 113 (5): 949–95.

Acemoglu, Daron, Simon Johnson, and James A. Robinson. 2001. "The Colonial Origins of Comparative Development: An Empirical Investigation." *American Economic Review* 91 (5): 1369–401.

Acemoglu, Daron, Simon Johnson, James A. Robinson, and Yunyong Thaicharoen. 2003. "Institutional Causes, Macroeconomic Symptoms: Volatility, Crises and Growth." *Journal of Monetary Economics* 50: 49–123.

Acemoglu, Daron, Simon Johnson, James A. Robinson, and Pierre Yared. 2009. "Reevaluating the Modernization Hypothesis." *Journal of Monetary Economics* 56: 1043–58.

Acemoglu, Daron, Simon Johnson, and James A. Robinson. 2012. "The Colonial Origins of Comparative Development: An Empirical Investigation: Reply." *American Economic Review* 102 (6): 3077–110.

Acemoglu, Daron, and James A. Robinson. 2010. "Why is Africa Poor?" *Economic History of Developing Regions* 25 (1): 21–50.

Acemoglu, Daron, and James A. Robinson. 2012. *Why Nations Fail: The origin of power, prosperity, and poverty*. New York: Crown Business.

Acemoglu, Daron, Suresh Naidu, Pascual Restrepo, and James A. Robinson. 2015. "Democracy, redistribution, and inequality." In the *Handbook of Income Distribution, Volume 2B*, edited by Anthony B. Atkinson and François Bourguignon, Chapter 21, 1885–966. Amsterdam: Elsevier.

Acemoglu, Daron, Suresh Naidu, Pascual Restrepo, and James A. Robinson. 2019. "Democracy Does Cause Growth." *Journal of Political Economy* 127 (1): 47–100.

Ahlerup, Pelle, Thushyanthan Baskaran, and Arne Bigsten. 2016. "Government Impartiality and Sustained Growth in sub-Saharan Africa." *World Development* 83: 54–69.

Ahlerup, Pelle, and Ann-Sofie Isaksson. 2015. "Ethno-Regional Favouritism in Sub-Saharan Africa." *Kyklos* 68 (2): 143–52.

Albouy, David Y. 2012. "The Colonial Origins of Comparative Development: An Empirical Investigation: Comment." *American Economic Review* 102 (6): 3059–76.

Alesina, Alberto, Reza Baqir, and William Easterly. 1999. "Public Goods and Ethnic Divisions." *Quarterly Journal of Economics* 114 (4): 1243–84.

Alesina, Alberto, Arnaud Devleeschauwer, William Easterly, Sergio Kurlat, and Romain Wacziarg. 2003. "Fractionalization." *Journal of Economic Growth* 8 (2: 155–94.

Alesina, Alberto, and Paola Giuliano. 2015. "Culture and Institutions." *Journal of Economic Literature* 53 (4): 898–944.

Alesina, Alberto, and Roberto Perotti. 1996. "Income Distribution, Political Instability and Investment." *European Economic Review* 40 (6): 1203–28.

Alesina, Alberto, and Dani Rodrik. 1994. "Distributive Politics and Economic Growth." *Quarterly Journal of Economics* 109 (2): 465–90.

Alesina, Alberto, and Ekaterina Zhuravskaya. 2011. "Segregation and the Quality of Government in a Cross Section of Countries." *American Economic Review* 101 (5): 1872–911.

Baldwin, Kate, and John D. Huber. 2010. "Economic versus Cultural Differences: Forms of Ethnic Diversity and Public Goods Provision." *American Political Science Review* 104 (4): 644–62.

Barro, Robert J. 1999. "Determinants of Democracy." *Journal of Political Economy* 107 (S6): 158–83.

Barro, Robert J. 2000. "Inequality and Growth in a Panel of Countries." *Journal of Economic Growth* 5 (1): 5–32.

Barro, Robert J. 2001. "Human Capital and Growth." *American Economic Review* 91 (2): 12–17.

Berg, Andrew, Jonathan D. Ostry, and Jeromin Zettelmeyer. 2012. "What Makes Growth Sustained?" *Journal of Development Economics* 98 (2): 149–66.

Berg, Andrew, Jonathan D. Ostry, Charalambos G. Tsangarides, and Yorbol Yakhsilikov. 2018. "Redistribution, Inequality, and Growth: New Evidence." *Journal of Economic Growth* 23 (3): 259–305.

Borcan, Oana, Ola Olsson, and Louis Putterman. 2018. "State History and Economic Development: Evidence from Six Millenia." *Journal of Economic Growth* 23 (1): 1–40.

Bourguignon, F and Wangwe, S. 2018. "Introduction," in Tanzania Institutional Diagnostic, Economic Development and Institutions. https://edi.opml.co.uk/wpcms/wp-content/uploads/2018/09/00-TID_Introduction-1.pdf

Brandt, Loren, Debin Ma, and Thomas G. Rawski. 2014. "From Divergence to Convergence: Reevaluating the History Behind China's Economic Boom." *Journal of Economic Literature* 52 (1): 45–123.

Doucouliagos, Hristos, and Mehmet Ali Ulubaşoğlu. 2008. "Democracy and Economic Growth: A Meta-Analysis." *American Journal of Political Science* 52 (1): 61–83.

Easterly, William. 2007. "Inequality Does Cause Underdevelopment: Insights from a New Instrument." *Journal of Development Economics* 84 (2): 755–76.

Easterly, William, and Ross Levine. 1997. "Africa's Growth Tragedy: Policies and Ethnic Divisions." *Quarterly Journal of Economics* 112 (4): 1203–50.

Fatás, Antonio, and Ilian Mihov. 2013. "Policy Volatility, Institutions, and Economic Growth." *Review of Economics and Statistics* 95 (2): 362–76.

Galor, Oded, and Joseph Zeira. 1993. "Income Distribution and Macroeconomics." *Review of Economic Studies* 60: 35–52.

Glaeser, Edward L., Rafael La Porta, Florencio Lopez-de-Silanes, and Andrei Shleifer. 2004. "Do Institutions Cause Growth?" *Journal of Economic Growth* 9: 271–303.

Guiso, Luigi, Paola Sapienza, and Luigi Zingales. 2016. "Long-term Persistence." *Journal of the European Economic Association* 14 (6): 1401–36.

Halter, Daniel, Manuel Oechslin, and Josef Zweimüller. 2014. "Inequality and Growth: The Neglected Time Dimension." *Journal of Economic Growth* 19 (1): 81–104.

Henry, Peter Blair, and Conrad Miller. 2009. "Institutions versus Policies: A Tale of Two Islands." *American Economic Review* 99 (2): 261–67.

Hirschman, Albert O. 1970. *Exit, Voice, and Loyalty: Responses to Decline in Firms, Organizations, and States.* Cambridge, Massachusetts: Harvard University Press.

Hodler, Roland, and Paul A. Raschky. (2014). "Regional Favoritism." *Quarterly Journal of Economics* 129 (2): 995–1033.

Kaufmann, Daniel, Aart Kraay, and Massimo Mastruzzi. 2008. "Governance Matters VII: Aggregate and Individual Governance Indicators for 1996–2007." Policy Research working paper (WPS 4654). Washington, DC: World Bank

Keefer, Philip, and Stephen Knack. 2002. "Polarization, Politics and Property Rights: Links Between Inequality and Growth." *Public Choice* 111 (1–2): 127–54.

Knack, Stephen, and Philip Keefer. 1997. "Does Social Capital Have an Economic Payoff? A Cross-Country Investigation." *Quarterly Journal of Economics* 112 (4): 1251–88.

Kramon Eric, and Daniel N. Posner. 2016. "Ethnic Favoritism in Education in Kenya." *Quarterly Journal of Political Science* 11 (1): 1–58.

Kuran, Timur. 2018. "Islam and Economic Performance: Historical and Contemporary Links." *Journal of Economic Literature* 56 (4): 1292–359.

Kyriacou, Andreas P. 2013. "Ethnic Group Inequalities and Governance: Evidence from Developing Countries." *Kyklos* 66 (1): 78–101.

La Porta, Rafael, Florencio Lopez-de-Silanes, Andrei Shleifer, and Robert Vishny. 1999. "The Quality of Government." *The Journal of Law, Economics, & Organization* 15 (1): 222–79.

Lipset, Seymour Martin. 1959. "Some Social Requisites of Democracy: Economic Development and Political Legitimacy." *American Political Science Review* 53 (1): 69–105.

Mankiw, N. Gregory, David Romer, and David N. Weil. 1992. "A Contribution to the Empirics of Economic Growth." *Quarterly Journal of Economics* 107 (2): 407–37.

Miguel, Edward. 2004. "Tribe or Nation? Nation Building and Public Goods in Kenya versus Tanzania." *World Politics* 56 (3): 327–62.

Miguel, Edward, and Mary Kay Gugerty. 2005. "Ethnic Diversity, Social Sanctions, and Public Goods in Kenya." *Journal of Public Economics* 89 (11–12): 2325–68.

Museru, Malimu, Francois Toerien, and Sean Gossel. 2014. "The Impact of Aid and Public Investment Volatility on Economic Growth in Sub-Saharan Africa." *World Development* 57: 138–47.

North, Douglass C. 1990. *Institutions, Institutional Change, and Economic Performance*. Cambridge: Cambridge University Press.

Nunn, Nathan. 2007. "Relationship-Specificity, Incomplete Contracts and the Pattern of Trade." *Quarterly Journal of Economics* 122 (2): 569–600.

Okun, Arthur M. 1975. *Equality and Efficiency: The Big Trade-Off*. Washington: Brookings Institution Press.

Perotti, Roberto. 1996. "Growth, Income Distribution, and Democracy: What the Data Say." *Journal of Economic Growth* 1 (2): 149–87

Persson, Torsten, and Guido Tabellini. 1994. "Is Inequality Harmful for Growth?" *American Economic Review* 84 (3): 600–21.

Putnam, Robert D. 1993. *Making Democracy Work: Civic Traditions in Modern Italy*. Princeton: Princeton University Press.

Rodrik, Dani. 1999. "Where Did All the Growth Go? External Shocks, Social Conflict, and Growth Collapses." *Journal of Economic Growth* 4 (4): 385–412.

Rodrik, Dani, Arvind Subramanian, and Francesco Trebbi. 2004. "Institutions Rule: The Primacy of Institutions Over Geography and Integration in Economic Development." *Journal of Economic Growth* 9 (2): 131–65.

Rothstein, Bo. 2015. "The Chinese Paradox of High Growth and Low Quality of Government: The Cadre Organization Meets Max Weber." *Governance* 28 (4): 533–48.

Rothstein, Bo, and Jan Teorell. 2008. "What is Quality of Government? A Theory of Impartial Government Institutions." *Governance* 21 (2): 165–90.

Sala-I-Martin, Xavier, Gernot Doppelhofer, and Ronald I Miller. 2004. "Determinants of Long-Term Growth: A Bayesian Averaging of Classical Estimates (BACE) Approach." *American Economic Review* 94 (4): 813–35.

Tabellini, Guido. 2008. "Presidential Address—Institutions and Culture." *Journal of the European Economic Association* 6 (2–3): 255–94.

Tabellini, Guido. 2010. "Culture and Institutions: Economic Development in the Regions of Europe." *Journal of the European Economic Association* 8 (4): 677–716.

Williamson, John. 1990. *Latin American Adjustment: How Much Has Happened?* Washington DC: Institute for International Economics.

Wrong, Michela. 2009. *It's Our Time to Eat: The Story of a Kenyan Whistleblower*. London: Fourth Estate.

Zak, Paul J., and Stephen Knack. 2001. "Trust and Growth." *The Economic Journal* 111 (470): 295–321.

CHAPTER 18

....

ECONOMIC DIVERSIFICATION, HOMOGENEITY OF INTERESTS, AND THE IMPARTIALITY OF GOVERNMENT

....

PETRUS OLANDER

Ambition must be made to counter ambition.

James Madison, Federalist 51

INTRODUCTION

....

INSTITUTIONS have been linked to a range of economic factors, most prominently researchers have found economic growth to be an outcome affected by the prevailing institutions (North 1990; see Ahlerup, Baskaran and Bigsten this volume). Others have focused on how economic factors condition what institutions are created, for example, see Jong-sung You this volume, details the research connecting economic inequality to quality of government by way of corruption, and there is an extensive body of literature on how resource extraction could lead to worse institutional quality (e.g. Ross 2001). In this chapter, I focus on another economic factor: how the mix of economic activities in a polity, the economic diversity, affects institutions and the exercise of public power.

The quality of government is the result of the design of institutions, and to the extent that they can do so, elites shape the institutions of government to their own advantage. The reason for poor quality of government and failed reform efforts is not that we do not know what high quality of government looks like; we do (e.g. Evans and Rauch 1999; Dahlström, Lapuente, and Teorell 2011; Mauro 1995). The problem is instead that having a high quality of government is frequently not in the interests of those who have the power to shape it (e.g. Acemoglu and Robinson 2000; Glaeser, Scheinkman, and Shleifer 2003; Sonin 2003;

Carothers 2007; Chaudhry and Garner 2007; Engerman and Sokoloff 2008; North, Wallis, and Weingast 2009; Menaldo and Yoo 2015). Improved quality of government is therefore largely a matter of understanding what might constrain those with the power to shape institutions from shaping these institutions in their own favor. The question is not if elites shape institutions, but rather how they design the institutions under different constraints. This is where diversity of interests comes in.

There is no canon of literature devoted to the relationship between economic diversity and institutions or the quality of government, yet economic interests are central to our understanding of why institutions take the shape they do, and diversity is crucial to many accounts of the causes of institutional designs and the ways in which governments operate. In this chapter, I highlight that, while not always explicit, the concept of economic diversity and competing interests has influenced our thinking about institutions and governments. To do this, I draw on a wide range of research, research that is not always cohesive in terms of the institutions they focus on but that is nonetheless united in its focus on institutions that result from the degree of diversity of economic interests among those who devise the institutions. After reviewing the previous research, I discuss how considering diversification in future research can help us better understand ongoing institutional developments.

As the quote above from Madison suggests, the idea that diversity of interest can help restrain the powerful from dominating the less powerful is old. The specter, or the promise, of homogeneity of interest is an omnipresent workhorse, but, at the same time, often anonymous in social science theory and empirics. Adam Smith, Montesquieu, and James Madison all grappled with the risk that one segment of society united in common interest would unjustly impose themselves on the rest (Montesquieu 1777; Smith 1776; Madison 1778). What concerned the three was that a coalition united by a narrow common interest would devise institutions perpetuating their power and position at the expense of the rest. Without counterweights, the system could be made to work for the benefit of the coalition and to the disadvantage of outsiders. This notion has echoes in social and political commentary throughout history, from the muckraker journalists of the late nineteenth-century United States who detailed the corruption of politics and business of the era, to contemporary worries about giant global corporations, and the influence of monopolies of industries.

Ranked by revenue, 69 out of 100 of the world's largest government and corporate entities are now corporations (Zingales 2017). This suggests that many individual companies can have a great deal of leverage in interactions with governments, and if they join forces with other actors who have similar interests, their influence can be enhanced even further. The consequences of such coalitions can be dire, even when they only seek to tailor institutions in their own sector. Several accounts, for example, attribute the consequences of the global financial crisis in 2007–8 to the comingling of investment and commercial banking made possible by the repeal of the Glass-Stegall legislation, which, going back to the United States 1933 Banking Act, had previously hindered the joint operation of both types of banking within one bank (Zingales 2012).

The concept of diversity is also present in recent social science, both in empirical findings and theoretical models, but the role played by uniformity of interest is rarely placed at the center. Nonetheless, heterogeneity is one of the factors argued to have facilitated the glorious outcome of the 1688 English revolution in the influential work of both North, Wallis, and

Weingast (2009), and later Acemoglu and Robinson (2012). Much of the literature on the so-called resource curse focuses on the dominance or reliance on resource extraction industries to explain adverse outcomes (Ross 2015). Cohesiveness of interests is used to explain lobbying (Olson 1965), changes in democratic institutions (e.g. O'Donnell and Schmitter 1986; Ansell and Samuels 2010), and the emergence of religiously neutral schooling (Ravitch 1974). Some recent additions to the scholarly literature have placed economic diversification generally as a factor contributing to democracy and institutional quality (Kolstad Wiig 2017; Olander 2019).

In this chapter, I highlight how various versions of this theme permeate the literature related to institutions. I discuss how diversity, especially economic diversity, or cohesiveness of interest, facilitates or hinders the reform and endurance of institutional arrangements. In the next section, I start by discussing how institutions are designed and suggest that economic elites will often seek to take an active role in the setup of institutional frameworks. I then outline the theoretical perspective, starting from Montesquieu, Smith, and Madison. The purpose of this section is not to give an exhaustive history of the concept of diversified and competing interests, only to show how it is not alien to political theory. This is followed by a review of contemporary research and is then linked to ongoing economic, social, and political processes. Finally, I summarize and offer some concluding remarks.

Who Designs Institutions?

Institutions are often defined as "humanly devised constraints that shape human interaction" (North 1990, 3). This definition has at least two implications. *First*, there is agency, or at least indirectly, there is agency affecting the shape institutions take; the institutions are devised. This does not imply that all institutions are effective in creating the outcomes those who devised the institutions had in mind, institutions may have unintended outcomes, and can end up benefitting outsiders. *Second*, institutions are a form of exercise of power and, by extension, this means that the designer of institutions exerts power over the behavior of others. This follows from the definition of power as the ability to make someone do what they otherwise would not (e.g. Dahl 1968; Morgenthau 1948; Olson 2000). The people who are able to influence the design of institutions might be referred to as elites. I follow Robert D. Putnam, who suggests elites should be defined on the outcomes of their action (1976, 73), and I define the actors who are able to influence the institutional setup as actors to be part of the elite. This influence can be active or passive; others may consider groups powerful without that group taking an active part in the design of the institutions. Therefore, actors can be part of the elite without always having to actively influence institutional designs.

By conscious choice or not, this definition is regularly used but is often not explicit in works on institutions. Acemoglu and Robinson simply define elites as "politically powerful groups" (2006, 115) and North, Wallis and Weingast define elites as "members of the dominant coalition" (2009, 18). While not all would agree it is sufficient, having some type of power is necessary for membership in the elite even in more elaborate definitions. In his classic work on elites, C. Wright Mills lists a litany of attributes characterizing the elites, but, pivotally, the elite "are in positions to make decisions having major consequences" (1956, 4). Similarly, Vilfredo Pareto's enumeration of requirements for what makes someone part of the elite acknowledges that at least for membership in his first class of elites they must "directly or indirectly play a significant part in government and political life" (Pareto 1966, 248).

Defining the actor on the outcome of their actions is not perfect since we cannot predefine the relevant actors. There is, however, no real alternative, as the resource elites deal in is power and the only way of knowing if an actor has power or not is to see if they have the ability to make people do what they otherwise would not. If they cannot, they were powerless anyway, and it would have been a mistake to define them as elites to begin with. Being able to influence the behavior of others is a necessary condition, and it is sufficient since we could not avoid categorizing a person or group of persons who influence human interaction as part of the elite. Conversely, we cannot define someone occupying an ostensibly powerful office, but who is powerless to influence the behavior of others, as being part of the elite.

Defined as such, these elites may be categorized as political, something they are, but it does not limit the concept to groups based in any specific resource, as it is the outcome of their action that defines them. This implies that the elites can have their base in wealth, land, religion, violence, fame, or whatever other resource that they can transform into power and use to influence outcomes. It gives elites a dynamic character to the composition of the elite, what groups we can consider elites, and the sectors they have their base in can change.

In practice, no individual is powerful enough to impose their own will on a polity; imposing institutions on others will always require a coalition and the institutions the coalitions design will have to be a compromise between the preferences of the members. How closely the institutional design reflects the preferences of each member will depend on the importance of that member - the power of the member, and the cohesiveness of the preferences of the members of the coalition. When the preferences of elites are more cohesive it makes it easier for them to form a coalition that can change institutions in their common interest.

In this chapter, I primarily focus on elites based in economic activities, which have been the predominant focus of previous research. Economic elites are part of the political elite, but, generally, they do not make up the whole political elite. They are part of the political elite as far as they influence institutions and political decisions; being exceedingly rich does not, in itself, suffice for membership in the elite. People who are wealthy but do not influence institutions are just rich people. Theoretically, there could be an economic elite who are not engaged in politics, only passively influencing politics by their economic activity. Empirically, however, no markets are that free; as research in new institutional economics has shown, markets do not operate in a vacuum (cf. North 1990), and success in the economic realm requires extensive interaction with the state.

The interaction between state and economic actors has taken various forms in different polities and times, and the different forms of interaction have frequently become the study of different fields of research. These include, among other things, lobbying (e.g. Olson 1965), corporatism (Schmitter 1974), development states (Johnson 1982), and institutional economics (North 1990). From the viewpoint of economic actors, each of these offer a way for the actor to complement their performance in the market with their performance in what we may call the economy of influence. Through the economy of influence, economic actors seek to create advantageous rules, practices, and in some cases direct transfers to increase the benefits from their business activities. Alternatively, they seek to prevent the creation of rules and practices that would be to their disadvantage.

Because asking outright for money for their own enrichment might stand little chance of success, the actors will frequently articulate their demands in terms of public interest and common good. Using terms from Anthony Downs (1957), we can think of this in terms of a private motive, and a social function. Economic actors seek political power to benefit their private motive, but in order to effect this they need to phrase their pursuit in terms of social function. Thus, the actors argue that the tariffs they lobby for, the bargains and rules they create through corporatism, and the institutions they support that structure markets, are not only for the benefit of themselves but also for the benefit of the polity as a whole. In different polities and at different times, the extent to which public power lends itself to economic actors, and the extent to which the deals made actually do fill a social function and do not just serve a private motive will vary. As long as there is a state, however, economic actors will always monitor what it does, might do, or what other actors might make it do. Economic actors must take into account the possibility of government action, and prudent economic actors will seek political power to enhance the performance of their economic ventures, or preempt the creation of adverse institutions.

Herein lies what I consider quality of government. I am largely in agreement with the definition provided by Rothstein and Teorell, quality of government as impartiality, or: "when implementing laws and policies, government officials shall not take into consideration anything about the citizen/case that is not beforehand stipulated in the policy or the law" (2008, 170). I would, however, suggest this is not enough, since it fails to capture favoritism taking place before the policies and laws are created. Regulatory capture and favoritism that brings about new laws is excluded, Rothstein and Teorell's conceptualization does not capture if the policy or law is the result of a corrupt process unless the process violates some preexisting law. Since, for example, regulatory capture often takes place while the laws are being written, this is a problem.

It is true, however, as Rothstein and Teorell would interject, that all laws favor someone, but this does not mean that all laws are cases of favoritism to the same extent. Some laws, while designed with the private motive of elites in mind, will have a better social function than other laws.

Offering a glimpse of a case discussed further on in this chapter, any tax exemption will favor the people who qualify, but a general tax exemption available to broad segments of society is something very different from when the Nevada state legislature was called into special session in 2013 to pass a series of bills giving an incentive package worth in excess of $1.25 billion to Tesla Motors. I argue we can and should take this difference in favoritism into account, and conceptualize quality of government as adherence to a norm of impartiality in the exercise of public power. Doing so opens the concept to a consideration of the extent of favoritism going into the design of the laws and not just how the laws and regulations are implemented.

To avoid confusion, however, I will only use the term quality of government in this chapter when it is in reference to the impartiality of implementation of laws and policies. When referring to the adherence to the norm of impartiality, I will use impartiality or institutional quality.

BACKGROUND TO THE CONCEPT OF
COMPETING INTERESTS AND DIVERSITY

In one of the great feats of investigative journalism, Ida Tarbell, exposed the business prac-tices of the Standard Oil Company in the late nineteenth-century United States in a series of articles for McClure's Magazine. Tarbell showed how the company and its leader, J.D. Rockefeller, had structured the market for oil and its transportation in a way that ensured the company's market dominance and made Rockefeller himself enormously rich. Rockefeller is still today consistently considered to have been the richest American of all time. Prefacing the compilation of Tarbell's articles published in 1904 is a quote from Ralph Waldo Emerson's essay Self-Reliance: "*An institution is the lengthened shadow of one man!*" (Tarbell 1904). Yet, no one, not even J.D. Rockefeller, is powerful enough to unilaterally design the institutions of a polity to their own liking; all who venture to do so must rely on a coalition to devise the institutions that are later to shape human interaction.

A successful coalition must control a majority of the relevant power resource, in democ-racies this should be enough of the votes that are cast in the election. In contrast, in autoc-racies, or soon to be autocracies, it is often other resources and not just popular support. Geddes, Wright, and Frantz, studying how dictatorships work, describe the motivation of non-incumbents seeking to become incumbents as the will "to change public policy and re-distribute the fruits of control of the state" (2018, 37). We might think of the people trying to extract government favoritism in much the same way. The members of a coalition must formulate their program—how they want to alter or maintain the current distribution of spoils produced by the institutional system. Some communality of interest must therefore exist between members of a coalition. The minimum amount of communality of interest would be non-incumbents who consider the current state of affairs so unfavorable that liter-ally any other possible arrangement would be better. At the other end of the spectrum are in-cumbents who can conceive of no practically possible alternative distribution better than the current one. This latter position will, however, only ever be arrived at after having taken into account that others have other preferences, no *possible* alternative distribution is key, and compromise is therefore necessary. All polities must have some coalition to escape anarchy, but equipped with that power the coalition must be constrained from using the public power they have from enriching themselves and cementing their position at the expense of others. This is not only one of the central issues in thinking about institutions but also of politics and exchange in general.[1]

The separation of powers advocated by Montesquieu is one of the more well-known at-tempts to deal with this issue using institutional designs to balance interests (1748). In *The Spirit of the Laws*, Montesquieu lays out the argument for how government might be ar-ranged so that different branches of the government counteract the power of each other, preventing the power instilled in any one of them from being misused (1748). Montesquieu's focus is on formal institutions; it is through rules that good institutions are to be secured. Adam Smith instead came at the problem from the perspective of a fear that people of the

---

[1] For a perspective on the problem of making sure that there is actual power to go with the authority of government, see D'Arcy and Nistotskaya's this volume.

same trade would come together and form a conspiracy against the public. Smith had a bleaker view of the chances of having formal institutions constrain the behavior of business, as any tool to do so might also provide them with a vehicle for their conspiracy (1776). This thinking has informed contemporary research on regulatory capture, which has repeatedly uncovered how rules and government intervention meant to prevent certain practices have become a means for those very practices (Huntington 1952, Stigler 1971, Dal Bo 2006).

James Madison, famous for his role in shaping the Constitution of the United States, combined both views, arguing that both formal and informal institutions would help prevent the misuse of power. In Federalist 51, Madison, under the pen name Publius, not only argues that the formal power instilled in government should be broken up with the aim of balancing the power held by any one branch, but also that:

> "... society itself will be broken into so many parts, interests, and classes of citizens, that the right of individuals, or of the minority, will be in little danger from interested combinations of the majority." (Madison, Federalist Papers 51).

Since Madison's thinking permeates the United States Constitution with its separation of the government into judicial, executive, and legislative branches, with the legislative branch being further divided into the House and Senate, it has been carried forward to the present day in very concrete ways. Outcome, however, should not be inferred from intent. A neat theoretical concept, the virtue of the idea of balancing interests is, as these very brief examples suggest, an empirical question.

DIVERSITY AND COHESIVENESS OF INTERESTS IN CONTEMPORARY SOCIAL SCIENCE

Researchers working on regulatory capture have considered the impact of diversification of interests. Mancur Olson, in *The Logic of Collective Action*, suggested diversification might be a factor in lobbying (1965). His idea is that when firms or industries lobby legislators on questions of trade, they will try to make the legislators tailor the deals to their particular interest, but when more industries are engaged, their interests may be adversarial and their lobbying efforts can offset one another's. The mechanism has been tested empirically and the findings indicate that competing interests can lead to trade liberalization instead of protection for industries (Gawande, Krishna, and Olarreaga 2012). The mechanism has been used to explain the effects of industry homogenization and the corrosive effect of one-sided lobbying on the regulation of banking (Nourse and Schacter 2002; Whitford 2007; Zingales 2012). Conversely, In Song Kim has found that more fine-grained trade deals tend to contain more trade barriers, as each category often only concerns one party, which means companies can dictate the terms of trade without having to overcome a collective action problem (2017). Here we see diversification working as envisioned; when ambition counters ambition, neither side is able to gear institutions in their own favor. When, in contrast, barriers keeping ambitions adversarial are lifted, institutions are reshaped to the advantage of the industry at the expense of consumers. In Song Kim's research further shows that, facing the problem of adversarial interests, actors adapt to avoid having to coordinate with adversaries, seeking instead to make the rules apply to a more limited set of products.

This idea of diversification and competition between interests is present in the broader literature on institutions such as North, Wallis, and Weingast's (2009) and Acemoglu and Robinson's prominent accounts (2012). Acemoglu and Robinson generally stress their model of institutions as being the central cause of economic development and thus the cause of economic diversification, but credit the decline in the use of public power for favoritism following the Glorious Revolution[2] to: "[p]erhaps most critically, the emergence and empowerment of diverse interests ... [which] ... meant that the coalition against Stuart absolutism was not only strong but also broad." Had it instead been the case that "all those fighting against the Stuarts had the same interests and the same background, the overthrow of the Stuart monarchy would have been much more likely to ... [re-create] ... the same or a different form of extractive institutions" (2012, 210).

In other words, the challenge that faces a coalition is what institutions it should strive to create. How narrowly self-serving those institutions can be is, in part, a function of how cohesive the interests of the coalition are. Had the coalition against the Stuarts been more cohesive, they could have recreated a system of extractive institutions, but because they were a broad coalition, such narrowly extractive institutions would hurt other members of the coalition. They were forced to settle for institutions that were more neutral which, while not benefitting any one of them to the extent they might most prefer, at least did not hurt them. While Acemoglu and Robinson in the quote stress the importance of the broad-based coalition representing a diverse set of interests, the notion is largely mute in their empirical work on institutional determinants. In a recent article, Olander tests an elaborated version of the argument using cross-national data; the empirical results support the theory that economic diversification leads to improvements in institutional quality, at least during the period 1984–2010 (Olander 2019).

The development of the institutions of democracy is arguably a separate field of inquiry, but it is relevant since it relates to the extent to which there is favoritism in the access to public power. Further, there are results important for the discussion here since economic diversification has figured among the factors facilitating democratization (e.g. Ahlquist and Wibbels 2012; Boix 2011). Barrington Moore's account of historical regime development goes beyond the ruler–ruled model and distinguishes between urban and rural elites, and their interaction with the peasantry and the middle class, showing how ways of allying the actors leads to different outcomes (1966). Rueschemeyer, Stephens, and Stephens focus their theory on the power relations and the structure of class-coalitions, with regime outcomes being determined by the interplay between classes as well as the organization of the state, civil society, and international relations. In this account, it is the landed upper class that most strongly oppose democratization, and breaking their historical hold on power is therefore necessary for democracy to emerge (1992). Differentiating between income and land inequality, Ben Ansell and David Samuels make the argument that disenfranchised rising economic actors seek credible commitment from the state. When landholdings are more equally distributed, pressure for democracy mounts, as more people fear the extractive state. In terms of income

---

[2] There are those who argue that financial innovation was the cause of the economic outcomes following the revolution, not less extractive government (see Coffman, Leonard, and Neal 2013). This debate, however, lies outside the scope of this chapter.

inequality, the prediction goes in the other direction, when disenfranchised yet economically successful actors emerge, they fear having their assets stripped from them and mount pressure for democracy in response. They conclude that, "political transitions are primarily a function of intraelite conflict rather than a function of a small but monolithic elite's fear of the impoverished multitudes" (Ansell and Samuels 2010, 1544). This in some sense echoes the prominence O'Donnell and Schmitter place on the cohesiveness of military regimes if they are to be able to resist calls for reform. When the military splits between hardliner and softliners, they elect to go back to the barracks, facilitating moves towards democracy, rather than force the risk of intra-military fighting (1986). In a more explicit theory and test of diversification, Kolstad and Wiig find support for the hypothesis that economic diversification leads to improvements in democracy. They argue that diversification can enhance the bargaining power of the downtrodden as diversification increases outside opportunities but can also be detrimental to elite cohesiveness and the ability of incumbents to oppose the clamor for reform (Kolstad and Wiig 2017).

Diversification, or rather its inverse, concentration, is also a factor in theories on the so-called resource curse literature. This literature focuses on how different economic activities such as the extraction of oil (Karl 1997; Ross 2015), diamonds (Olsson 2007), mining (Knutsen et al. 2017), forestry (Harwell, Farah, and Blundell 2011), but also foreign remittances and foreign aid (Ahmed 2012), have detrimental effects on a range of outcomes such as economic growth (e.g. Sachs and Warner 1995), conflict (Fearon and Laitin 2003), institutions broadly (e.g. Isham et al. 2005), and democracy (Ross 2012).[3] This is an extensive body of literature. While some of these accounts focus on features of the particular resources, others indirectly focus on the dependence on single economic sectors, in other words the effect of having a highly concentrated economy. Rephrasing this approach in the language used in this chapter, resource curse research looking at the impact of dependence of natural resources is interested in the impact of having an economy that is not diverse. The growth of any single economic activity can cause either economic diversification or concentration, and the effect depends on the composition of the rest of the economy. Economic diversification/concentration is therefore not analogous to resource dependence, but resource dependence is a case of lack of economic diversity.

There are several mechanisms proposed in the resource curse literature that can aggravate such concentration. If commodity prices increase, the relative cost of extracting resources in politically unstable environments decreases, and thus there will be more oil extraction where there is little economic development but a considerable level of strife. Michael Ross hypothesizes that this rather than any detrimental effect specific to oil might be driving the correlation between oil and various adverse outcomes (2015). Diversification further links to resource extraction through the so-called Dutch Disease. This could materialize in two ways. For instance, high growth in an exporting sector, say natural gas, can cause an influx of foreign currency, raising the exchange rate and making other goods in the economy more expensive to buy for foreign customers. As these other sectors might not benefit from the productivity increase in the oil/gas sector, they lose competitiveness and cannot export their products. It could also be the case that, directly or indirectly, a boom in one sector pushes up

---

[3] While most commonly, scholars report having found a negative correlation between a natural resource and an outcome, Haber and Menaldo (2011), as well as Dunning (2008) find oil sometimes has a positive correlation with democracy.

labor costs, which will make non-booming sectors less competitive as their labor costs increase (Corden and Neary 1982; Corden 1984). Thus, while not all proposed effects of natural resource extraction hinge on lack of diversification, there are several mechanisms that tie resource extraction to economic concentration and lack of diversification.

Going beyond economic diversification, there are other types of diversification thought to influence institutions, most prominently among these in relation to the broader institutional literature is ethnic and linguistic fractionalization. Those finding a negative relationship between this type of fractionalization, institutional quality, and desirable outcomes generally argue that ethnic fractionalization drives polarization, leading to problems in agreeing on policy and to competitive rent-seeking (e.g. Easterly and Levine 1997; Alesina et al. 2003). While the outcome of diversification must here be considered normatively undesirable, the mechanisms relied upon are similar to those related to economic diversification. To the extent that ethnic fractionalization really does have negative effects, it focuses our attention on the importance of the arena and the type of diversification. The coordination problems diversification can cause may facilitate negative outcomes, if, for example, actors perceive there to be no acceptable compromises. Importantly however, later research has offered qualifiers to the idea that ethnic fractionalization has negative effects, such as the idea that the relevance of ethnic fractionalization depends on how and to what extent it is politicized (Posner 2004; Miguel 2005; Eifert, Miguel, and Posner 2010). Others have found the effect of ethnic diversity might be positive (Gerring, Hoffman, and Zarecki 2016). Some caution is therefore advised before stating that ethnic fractionalization has either a negative or a positive relationship with institutional quality.

Related to both our discussion of diversification and non-economic diversification is the research on religious fractionalization and institutional outcomes. Looking at religious freedom, here the argument is rather that religious fractionalization has led to more neutrality in the institutions governing religious practices. James Madison attributed the disestablishment of state funding for churches to the mutual hatred of the religious sects in his native Virginia (1785). Similarly, it was the inability in the early nineteenth century of Catholics and Protestant denominations to reconcile their differences that led the legislature of New York to cut the previous subsidies to Protestant schools rather than establish funding for Catholic schools as well (Ravitch 1974). Diversity of interest can thus be an integral part of studies of institutions beyond economic diversity.

Going Forward

Having highlighted how diversity features in previous research, I now shift focus to look forward; why should the impact of economic diversity be a focus of future research and what developments make it a worthwhile effort? I will here focus on four areas: reconcentration of economic output in advanced economies; the local impact of economic concentration and its impact on transient populations; state intervention and diversification; and, finally, how diversification can link institutions and stable economic growth.

There are theoretical reasons to think that as countries become wealthier their economies become either more or less diversified. Countries might at first exploit natural endowments before diversifying, and diversified countries might be better at avoiding the negative effects of sectoral volatility, leading to higher aggregated wealth in the longer term (Wagner and Deller 1998; Koren and Tenreyro 2007, 2013; Haddad et al. 2013). However, it could be that since economic activities tend to cluster in certain areas such as countries, they become hubs for a particular trade, leading to more concentration as the specific sector develops. Since diversification is an aggregate concept, it is the diversity of the economy as a whole, different mechanisms could work in different directions, and which mechanism dominates is an empirical question.

In their empirical inquiry into the relationship between diversification and income, Imbs and Wacziarg find a positive relationship: countries that are more prosperous have more diverse economies, but at fairly high levels of GDP, economies tend to reconcentrate (2003), which has been corroborated in findings on export diversification (Cadot, Carrere, and Strauss-Kahn 2011). Should this pattern persist, it might spell trouble in polities that we regularly consider as having consolidated a high quality of government. In lobbying, legal, illegal, or just questionable, as was discussed above, when interests are more cohesive, lobbying efforts will increasingly speak with one voice, and politicians and bureaucrats might allow institutions to become increasingly tailored to fit those requests. With regional concentration, this effect might become more pronounced. Having an industry or company settling or emerging in an area could be a big hit, but there is the risk that individual economic interests capture local politics and wield immense power over both working and private life through terms of employment and the institutional system.

In a globalized world, polities compete to attract employers and investors. There are numerous examples of how politicians bend or change the rules or offer tailored packages in terms of taxes and subsidies to get a company to open a factory in their country or districts. The car company Tesla was given $1.25 billion in subsidies and tax breaks to set up a gigantic battery factory in Nevada (Hidalgo 2015), and tech giant Amazon calculated they would receive $573 million in performance-based incentives following the establishment of their second headquarters in Virginia (Amazon Company News 2018). These kinds of subsidies can be criticized based on the notion that the risks of investment should be borne by the owners of the corporations rather than the public. When governments try to create an institutional environment that is conducive to investment and economic development it does not necessarily represent a grave violation of the norm of impartiality, but when governments tailor the institutional environment for specific investors it does.

An additional question, less debated, but no less interesting seen through the lens of this chapter, is what influence might be exercised by an industry that not only provides most of the jobs in a limited area but in which local politicians have invested heavily. Steve Hill, director of the Nevada Governor's Office of Economic Development, and central to creating the incentive package for the Tesla battery factory, explained to one reporter: "We have to make sure we do everything we can to help them get to the finish line as quickly as possible because it's in all of our best interests" (Hidalgo 2015). When we consider the Nevada legislature had already been called into special session to pass a series of new acts, rewrite existing acts, and transfer favorable tax exceptions from other industries to provide Tesla with the first incentive package, [4] it appears Hill was not overstating the willingness of the

---

[4] Tesla was not named in any of the acts and all were passed in general terms, *technically* applying to all who could meet the standard set. S.B. 1-3, 2013 Spec. Sess. (Nev. 2013). A.B. 1-2, 2013 Spec. Sess. (Nev. 2013). Be that as it may, calling a special session and rewriting laws nonetheless sends a clear signal that the government is open for business on a bilateral basis.

government to accommodate Tesla's requests. Moving beyond the study of the interaction between business, labor, and politics, taking into account the cohesiveness of the relevant economic interests will help us better understand the impact such public–private partnerships and competition between polities have on local economic and institutional changes. Since, as noted in the introduction, 69 out of 100 of the world's largest government and corporate entities are now corporations if ranked by revenue (Zingales 2017), we cannot assume the public, as represented by the government, will be the stronger party in such partnerships and interactions.

Another set of issues related to the regional clustering of economic activity within a polity linking to favoritism and impartiality in the exercise of public power is what happens to the areas which are not in a cluster. What is good for the cluster or even the many is sometimes bad for the few, and vice versa.

Allowing free market entry in the form of free trade is good for the many, but, as the work of David Autor and co-authors shows, is likely bad for some; many workers who have had their jobs creatively destroyed fail to adjust, with lasting effects on their life quality (e.g. Autor et al. 2014; Autor, Dorn, and Hanson 2016). Understanding the degree of impartiality of government related to economic development is therefore complex. While, for example, we regularly associate stronger property rights with better institutions, it and the adoption of stricter land-use institutions that push up housing prices have prevented low-skilled workers from moving to where they can make a better living, while benefitting high-skilled workers who own property in those areas (Glaeser 2014; Hsieh and Moretti 2015; Herkenhoff, Ohanian, and Prescott 2017). Local institutions can have consequences far beyond the area immediately affected. It is therefore not only relevant to study the local impact of concentrated economic interests but also what impact such concentration might have on other areas since that is where the adverse outcomes may hit. The impact of local institutions in one place can be positive but have local negative consequences elsewhere.

Similarly, the influence of cohesive economic interests at the national level may boost aggregate economic development, as in the case of freer trade, and create sprawling clusters of new and exciting industries. However, to more fully comprehend the outcomes generated, the distribution across the population must be considered. Studying how future political entrepreneurs exploit these conditions and how economic actors choose to deal with these rifts will be important.

Furthermore, as things are and have been, the dominant research approach to quality of government has been cross-national, sometimes coupled with time series data. This approach might hide the issues of spatial within-country variation discussed above, but it might obscure the transient population. Transient populations and workers are not a new phenomenon; substantial segments of migrants to the United States during the nineteenth century were so-called Birds of Passage who came for a period before returning home, some staying for only a season at a time (e.g. Piore 1979; Wyman 1993). Without getting entangled in the relative virtues of labor migration, it is plain to see that this poses a problem for the cross-country approach to quality of government, for it begs the question: Quality of government for whom?

Just as, when studying democracy, we need to know who the people are, so we also need to know in relation to whom there is impartiality in the exercise of public power. For example, the often used ICRG indicator of quality of government (e.g. Menaldo 2016; Charron and Lapuente 2010; Besley and Persson 2011) gave a score of 0.64 (0–1 range) to

Qatar in 2018. At the same time, 9 out of 10 people in Qatar were migrant workers who have a hard time achieving even the most basic of property rights or freedom of movement, and their rights are still connected to the arbitrary will of their employers (HRW 2016). Similarly, the Chinese economic model currently relies on large swaths of internal temporary labor migration, migrants that frequently are treated as second-class citizens (Solinger 1999; Chan and O'Brien 2019). Because these migrants, domestic or international, tend to work in particular sectors, actors in those particular sectors are likely to have an outsized influence on the institutions that govern their lives, even when those institutions are ostensibly government ones. Integrating transient populations into the future study of diversity and quality of government will allow us to understand more of the institutional system and bring groups likely to experience the worst quality of government to the fore—those who lack citizenship or who are often not considered part of the geographical constituency where they reside. These are not only normative or conceptual questions, but important empirical ones. For example, will the economic growth we might expect following institutional improvements depend on the extension of those improvements to the whole population or is it enough that a certain class has those rights? North, Wallis, and Weingast, in their comprehensive account of institutional change, distinguished between rights for the elite and the extension of such rights to everyone (2009), a distinction that would seem to apply here. Haber, Maurer, and Razo show how, in Mexico, property rights were used to prevent economic collapse in times of instability but still excluded large segments of society from those rights (2003). To improve our understanding of the effects of institutions, future research might consider if a sector is dominated by a limited set of actors and the role it plays in the institutions that are designed pertaining to the people whose lives are tied to that sector.

Economic diversification and concentration are not the only factors affecting the institutional makeup of a polity, and the effect diversification has on the institutions is conditioned on other factors as well as preexisting institutions. The case of Norway, which, following the exploitation of the country's vast oil and gas reserves, has experienced a sharp decrease in the diversity of its overall economy from the 1970s onwards but has nonetheless been able to maintain impartial institutions, suggests the impact of concentration is conditioned on already established institutions. This assertion is also made in the resource curse literature (cf. Ross 2012). Deepening our understanding of what the institutions are that can act as a counterweight to increased cohesion of economic interests is, and remains, an important task for researchers.

The knowledge about what allows countries to diversify is limited. Michael L. Ross has provided a descriptive base for future research related to oil exporters and diversification (2019). The picture that emerges is, however, bleak: Resource-rich countries have increasingly diverged from non-oil states, and in relative terms they have moved towards even more concentrated economies since the 1980s. This development is especially distinct for African oil producers. Since diversification has been an explicit goal in many countries, these results are disappointing, but they echo previous findings by economists (Cadot, Carrère, and Strauss-Kahn 2013). A factor contributing to the difficulty of diversifying a polity's economy is that diversification can threaten the power base of incumbent elite groups (Wiig and Kolstad 2012). The threat that diversification can pose to the power of incumbents is also a theme in research on the impact of slavery on the economic diversification and institutions of the South of the United States (e.g. Bateman and Weiss 1981;

Olander 2015).[5] Expanding our knowledge about how incumbent concentrated interests resist and hinder efforts to diversify the economy, and what interventions might ease this resistance, could be instrumental for successful diversification and facilitate improved quality of government.

Efforts to diversify the economy connect institutions, governments, and what has been called developmental states, as well as government intervention in the economy more broadly. Frequently, governments seemingly engage in attempts to facilitate economic growth and economic diversification (cf. Johnson 1982; Leftwich 1995). This type of government intervention in the economy touches on the very core of institutional quality and impartiality. Preferably, the institutions created to facilitate growth should do so without impeding the growth of economic sectors even more productive than the ones envisaged and promoted by incumbent elites and bureaucrats. The extent to which government intervention in the economy promotes or hinders economic development is not the focus here as there are other strands of research engaged in providing answers to those questions. However, related to the discussion in this chapter is the interplay between the state and various economic actors and how those interactions produce different institutions. When do interventions result in functioning markets and when does it result in an economy captured by incumbents and made to serve their interests? When does state support for economic activity result in economic actors focused on making profits through the economy of influence, and when does it result in economic actors focused on making profits in the marketplace? In more concrete terms, this is the question of what will happen to the Chinese institutional system or the institutions of the Gulf States should their efforts to diversify prove successful. Will the agents tasked by the Gulf State governments break free from their government masters and seek to change the institutions or will they seek to conserve the institutional system that elevated them in the first place, capturing both the economy and the state? Here, combining the study of the role of diversification to the ongoing discussion of transformations of developmental states (cf. Evans and Heller 2015) seems a promising avenue.

Relatedly, does it matter if the economic change that creates diversification takes place at the frontier or if it is catch-up growth? It may be easier for incumbents to foresee how to design institutions that maintain their control while there is catch-up growth than to design a system allowing them to maintain control while there is growth at the frontier, since more of the factors related to catch-up growth are known from other contexts. For example, the growth of textile manufacturing is likely to produce economic elites with a certain set of institutional preferences, something the incumbents can prepare for, but what the preference set of an economic elite who make their fortune at the frontier of economic development looks like is more uncertain. It could also be that catch-up growth is more transformative in scope than growth at the frontier, and since there will always be an interaction with the local context the magnitude of the transformation as it interacts with the unique features of the local context it still could make catch-up growth unwieldy to manage. There is still much that we do not know about the institutional response of incumbents to economic change.

Bringing economic diversification into our analysis can improve our understanding of institutions and economic growth. Lant Pritchett has described how countries experience different patterns of growth (2000). Countries that have better institutional systems frequently

---

[5] While related, it is not the same as the question of the relative profitability of slavery.

experience a more stable economic growth that is enduring but it might not be spectacular in any single year. Countries with poor institutional quality instead often experience violent boom and busts with a lower mean growth rate as a result (Acemoglu et al. 2003). As mentioned above, more diversified economies tend to be more stable, experiencing less fluctuation in overall growth rates (Wagner and Deller 1998; Koren and Tenreyro 2007, 2013; Haddad et al. 2013). Economic diversification therefore offers a link between economic stability and higher institutional quality, but research is still lacking if we are to understand more precisely how this plays out.[6]

Conclusions

In this chapter, I have highlighted how diversity of interests relates to institutions and the quality of government. First, I pointed to how institutions per the common definition as "humanly devised constraints shaping human interaction" are designed, and I argued we should therefore pay attention to the makeup of the actors engaged in designing institutions. I then argued those engaged in designing institutions can be labeled elites, and that elites can, in turn, be defined as those able to influence institutional outcomes. While this is tautological, I argued and showed that this is not only reasonable but how elites are defined in some of the central works on institutions. Additionally, I offered a brief account of why economic actors will engage in activities to affect the design of institutions and why they are central to our understanding of institutional outcomes.

Following this, I discussed how diversity of elite interests is argued to be central for preventing governments and institutions from being captured by narrow interests. Montesquieu, Smith, and Madison all considered and sought remedies to the risk that elites unified in interest would form collusive coalitions bent on gearing institutions in their own favor. I concluded that while an attractive concept, the soundness of pitting ambition against ambition is an empirical question.

Reviewing contemporary social science for findings related to the diversity of interests, I started in the literature on regulatory capture where it has been found that more cohesive lobbying efforts led to institutions tailored to the interests of incumbents. Similar mechanisms have been argued in the broader literature on institutions but are largely absent in empirical applications. Further, I outlined how diversity of interests and intra-elite competition are linked to the emergence of democratic institutions. Focusing on its inverse concentration of interests, I linked the literature on the so-called resource curse and institutions to diversification, arguing that dependence on any one economic activity will facilitate more narrow coalitions. I considered two non-economic cases of diversification, ethnic fractionalization and religious fractionalization, outlining how the former has sometimes been linked to adverse economic outcomes, but the latter has been linked to the establishment of more impartial government institutions relating to religious life.

---

[6] Acemoglu, Johnson, Robinson, and Thaicharoen suggest linking institutional quality to volatility, but while they are aware of the role that diversification might play (see Acemoglu and Zilibotti 1997; Acemoglu et al. 2003, n19) they do not link diversification and institutions.

In the last section before the conclusions, I looked forward and outlined a few areas where the idea of diversification might be applied in future research. Specifically, I did this in relation to ongoing economic transformations: The reconcentration of economic activities likely taking place in high-income countries and its regional clustering. The impact of narrow interests in relation to transient populations, the employment of whom is concentrated to certain sectors but whose conditions might escape the country-year unit of analysis. Finally, the effects of efforts by governments to facilitate economic growth and what effects that might have on the behavior of economic and political actors.

While this chapter shows that there is enough research to suggest diversity of interests matters for how institutions are designed and change over time, it is clear that it is a factor often absent in accounts of institutional outcomes. Ongoing economic transformations and government reforms means diversity is likely to continue to be important, but how it will impact institutions cannot be taken for granted as incumbents might hope to benefit from diversification without losing control. To better understand its impact, it is imperative that future research is attentive to where institutional reforms might produce adverse outcomes, be it among transient populations or in certain regions.[7]

REFERENCES

Acemoglu, Daron, and Fabrizio Zilibotti. 1997. "Was Prometheus Unbound by Chance? Risk, Diversification, and Growth." *Journal of Political Economy* 125 (4): 709–51.

Acemoglu, Daron, and James A. Robinson. 2000. "Political Losers as a Barrier to Economic Development." Political Economy. *Governance and Development* 90 (2): 126–30.

Acemoglu, Daron, and James A. Robinson. 2006. *Economic Origins of Dictatorship and Democracy*. Cambridge: Cambridge University Press.

Acemoglu, Daron, and James A. Robinson. 2012. *Why Nations Fail: The Origins of Power, Prosperity, and Poverty*. London: Profile Books.

Acemoglu, Daron, Simon Johnson, James A. Robinson, and Yunyong Thaicharoen. 2003. "Institutional causes, macroeconomic symptoms: volatility, crises and growth." *Journal of Monetary Economics* 50 (1): 49–123.

Ahlquist, John S., and Erik Wibbels. 2012. "Riding the Wave: World Trade and Factor-Based Models of Democratization." *American Journal of Political Science* 56 (2): 447–64.

Ahmed, Faisal Z. 2012. "Perils of Unearned Foreign Income: Aid, Remittances and Government Survival." *American Political Science Review* 106 (1): 146–65.

Alesina, Alberto, Arnaud Devleeschauwer, William Easterly, Sergio Kurlat, and Romain Wacziarg. 2003. "Fractionalization." *Journal of Economic Growth* 8: 155–94.

Amazon Company News. 2018. "Amazon Selects New York City and Northern Virginia for New Headquarters." Accessed October 29, 2019. https://blog.aboutamazon.com/company-news/amazon-selects-new-york-city-and-northern-virginia-for-new-headquarters

Ansell, Ben and David Samuels. 2010. "Inequality and Democratization: A Contractarian Approach." *Comparative Political Studies* 43 (12): 1543–74.

---

[7] Research for this chapter was made possible by funding from Riksbankens Jubileumsfond, Grant M14-0087:1, "State-Making and the Origins of Global Order in the Long Nineteenth Century and Beyond" (STANCE).

Autor, David H., David Dorn, and Gordon H. Hanson. 2016. "The China Shock: Learning from Labor-Market Adjustment to Large Changes in Trade." *Annual Review of Economics* 8: 205–40.

Autor, David H, David Dorn, Gordon H. Hanson, and Jae Song. 2014. "Trade Adjustment: Worker-Level Evidence." *The Quarterly Journal of Economics* 129 (4): 1799–860.

Bateman, Fred, and Thomas Weiss. 1981. *A Deplorable Scarcity: The Failure of Industrialization in the Slave Economy*. Chapel Hill, North Carolina: UNC Press Books.

Besley, Tim, and Torsten Persson. 2011. *Pillars of Prosperity*. Princeton: Princeton University Press.

Boix, Carles. 2011. "Democracy, Development, and the International System." *American Political Science Review* 105 (4): 809–28.

Cadot, Olivier, Celine Carrere, and Vanessa Strauss-Kahn. 2013. "Trade diversification, income, and growth: what do we know?" *Journal of Economic Surveys* 27 (4): 790–812.

Cadot, Olivier, Celine Carrere, and Vanessa Strauss-Kahn. 2011. "What's Behind the Hump?" *The Review of Economics and Statistics* 93 (2): 590–605.

Carothers, Thomas. 2007. "How Democracies Emerge: The 'Sequencing' Fallacy." *Journal of Democracy* 18 (1): 12–27.

Chan, Alexsia T., and Kevin J. O'Brien. 2019. "Phantom Services: Deflecting Migrant Workers in China." *The China Journal* 81 (1): 103–22.

Charron, Nicholas, and Victor Lapuente. 2010. "Does democracy produce quality of government?" *European Journal of Political Research* 49: 443–70.

Chaudhry, Azam, and Phillip Garner. 2007. "Do Governments Suppress Growth? Institutions, Rent-Seeking and Innovation Blocking in a Model of Schumpeterian Growth." *Economics and Politics* 19 (1): 35–52.

Coffman, D'Maris, Adrian Leonard, and Larry Neal. 2013. *Questioning Credible Commitment: Perspectives on the Rise of Financial Capitalism*. Cambridge: Cambridge University Press.

Corden, Max W. 1984. "Booming Sector and Dutch Disease Economics: Survey and Consolidation." *Oxford Economic Papers* 36: 359–80.

Corden, Max W., and Peter Neary. 1982. "Booming Sector and De-Industrialisation in a Small Open Economy." *The Economic Journal* 92: 825–48.

Dahl, Robert A. 1968/1986. "Power as Control of Behavior." In *Power*, edited by Steven Lukes. Oxford: Basil Blackwell.

Dahlström, Carl, Victor Lapuente, and Jan Teorell. 2011. "The Merit of Meritocratization: Politics, Bureaucracy, and the Institutional Deterrents of Corruption." *Political Research Quarterly* 65 (3): 656–68.

Dal Bó, Ernesto. 2006. "Regulatory Capture: A Review." *Oxford Review of Economic Policy* 22 (2): 203–25.

Downs, Anthony. 1957. "An Economic Theory of Political Action in a Democracy". Journal of Political Economy 65 (2): 135–50.

Dunning, Thad. 2008. *Crude Democracy Natural Resource Wealth and Political Regimes*. Cambridge: Cambridge University Press.

Easterly, William, and Ross Levine. 1997. "Africa's Growth Tragedy: Policies and Ethnic Divisions." *The Quarterly Journal of Economics* 112 (4): 1203–50.

Eifert, Benn, Edward Miguel, and Daniel N. Posner. 2010. "Political Competition and Ethnic Identification in Africa." *American Journal of Political Science* 54 (2): 494–510.

Engerman, Stanley L., and Kenneth L. Sokoloff. 2008. "Debating the Role of Institutions in Political and Economic Development." *Annual Review of Political Science* 11: 119–35.

Evans, Peter, and James E. Rauch. 1999. "Bureaucracy and Growth: A Cross-national Analysis of the Effects of 'Weberian' State Structures on Economic Growth." *American Sociological Review* 64 (5): 748–65.

Evans, Peter, and Patrick Heller. 2015. "Human development, state transformation and the politics of the developmental state." In *The Oxford Handbook of Transformations of the State*, 691–713. Oxford: Oxford University Press.

Fearon, James D., and David D. Laitin. 2003. "Ethnicity, Insurgency, and Civil War." *American Political Science Review* 97 (1): 75–90.

Gawande, Kishore, Pravin Krishna, and Marcelo Olarreaga. 2012. "Lobbying Competition Over Trade Policy." *International Economic Review* 53 (1): 115–32.

Geddes, Barbara, Joseph Wright, and Erica Frantz. 2018. *How Dictatorships Work: Power, Personalization, and Collapse*. Cambridge: Cambridge University Press.

Gerring, John, Michael Hoffman, and Dominic Zarecki. 2016. "The Diverse Effects of Diversity on Democracy." *British Journal of Political Science*: 1–32. doi: 10.1017/S000712341600003X

Glaeser, Edward L. 2014. "Land Use Restrictions and Other Barriers to Growth." Technical report. Cato Institute.

Glaeser, Edward, Jose Scheinkman, and Andrei Shleifer. 2003. "The Injustice of Inequality." *Journal of Monetary Economics: Carnegie-Rochester Series on Public Policy*, L: 199–222.

Haber, Stephan, Noel Maurer, and Armando Razo. 2003. *The Politics of Property Rights: Political Instability, Credible Commitments, and Economic Growth in Mexico, 1876–1929*. Cambridge: Cambridge University Press.

Haber, Stephen, and Victor Menaldo. 2011. "Do Natural Resources Fuel Authoritarianism? A Reappraisal of the Resource Curse." *American Political Science Review* 105 (1): 1–24.

Haddad, Mona, Jamus Jerome Lim, Cosimo Pancaro, and Christian Saborowski. 2013. "Trade Openness Reduces Growth Volatility When Countries Are Well Diversified." *Canadian Journal of Economics* 46 (2): 765–90.

Harwell, Emily, Douglas Farah and Arthur Blundell. 2011. *Forests, Fragility, and Conflict: Overview and Case Studies*. Washington DC: Prog. Forests, World Bank.

Herkenhoff, Kyle F, Lee H. Ohanian, and Edward C. Prescott. 2017. "Tarnishing the Golden and Empire States: Land-Use Restrictions and the U.S. Economic Slowdown." NBER Working Paper No. 2379. Issued in September 2017.

HRW. 2016. Human Rights Watch—Qatar Events of 2016. https://www.hrw.org/world-report/2017/country-chapters/qatar

Hsieh, Chang-Tai, and Enrico Moretti. 2015. "Why Do Cities Matter? Local Growth and Aggregate Growth." Technical report, National Bureau of Economic Research.

Huntington, Samuel P. 1952. "The Marasmus of the ICC: The Commision, the Railroads, and the Public Interest." *The Yale Law Journal* 61 (4): 467–508.

Imbs, Jean, and Romain Wacziarg. 2003. "Stages of Diversification." *The American Economic Review* 93 (1): 63–86.

Isham J. M. Woolcock, Lant Pritchett, and G. Busby. 2005. "The Varieties of the Rentier Experience: How Natural Resource Export Structures Affect the Political Economy of Growth." *World Bank Economic Review* 19 (2): 141–74.

Johnson, Chalmers A. 1982. *MITI and the Japanese Miracle: The Growth of Industrial Policy, 1925–1975*. Stanford, CA: Stanford University Press.

Karl, Terry Lynn. 1997. *The Paradox of Plenty: Oil Booms and Petro-States*. Berkeley: University of California Press.

Knutsen, Carl Henrik, Andreas Kotsadam, Eivind Hammersmark Olsen, and Tore Wig. 2017. "Mining and Local Corruption in Africa." *American Journal of Political Science* 61 (2): 320–34.

Kolstad, Ivar, and Arne Wiig. 2017. "Diversification and Democracy." *International Political Science Review*: 1–19.

Koren, Miklos, and Silvana Tenreyro. 2007. "Volatility and Development." *The Quarterly Journal of Economics* 122 (1): 243–87.

Koren, Miklos, and Silvana Tenreyro. 2013. "Technological Diversification." *The American Economic Review* 103 (1): 378–414.

Leftwich, Adrian. 1995. "Bringing Politics Back in: Towards a Model of the Developmental State." *The Journal of Development Studies* 31 (3): 400–27.

Madison, James. 1778. *Federalist 51*. In *The Federalist: A Collection of Essays, Written in Favour of the New Constitution, as Agreed Upon by the Federal Convention September 17, 1787*. New York: J. and A. McLean.

Madison, James. 1785. Letter from James Madison to Thomas Jefferson August 20, 1785. http://www.beliefnet.com/resourcelib/docs/2/Letter_from_James_Madison_to_Thomas_Jefferson_2p.html. Retrieved 01/09/17

Mauro, Paolo. 1995. "Corruption and Growth." *Quarterly Journal of Economics* 110 (3): 681–712.

Menaldo, Victor. 2016. "The Fiscal Roots of Financial Underdevelopment." *American Journal of Political Science* 60: 456–71.

Menaldo, Victor, and Daniel Yoo. 2015. "Democracy, Elite Bias, and Financial Development in Latin America." *World Politics* 67 (4): 726–59.

Miguel, Edward. 2005. "Tribe or Nation? Nation Building and Public Goods in Kenya versus Tanzania." *World Politics* 56 (3): 328–62.

Mills, C. Wright. 1956. *The Power Elite*. Oxford: Oxford University Press.

Montesquieu, Charles de Secondat. 1777 [1748]. Charles Louis de Secondat. Baron de Montesquieu. 1777. *The Complete Works of M. de Montesquieu*. London: T. Evans, 1777, 4 vols. Vol. 1. http://oll.libertyfund.org/titles/837

Moore, Barrington Jr. 1966. *Social Origins of Dictatorship and Democracy: Lord and Peasant in the Making of the Modern World*. Boston: Beacon Press.

Morgenthau, Hans. 1948/2006. *Politics Among Nations: The Struggle for Power and Peace*. New York: McGraw Hill.

North, Douglass C. 1990. *Institutions, Institutional Change and Economic Performance*. Cambridge: Cambridge University Press.

North, Douglass C., John J. Wallis, and Barry R. Wiengast. 2009. *Violence and Social Orders— A Conceptual Framework for Interpreting Recorded Human History*. Cambridge: Cambridge University Press.

Nourse, Victoria F., and Jane S. Schacter. 2002. "The Politics of Legislative Drafting: A Congressional Case Study." *New York University Law Review* 77 (3): 575–624.

O'Donnell, Guillermo, and Philippe C. Schmitter. 1986. *Transitions from Authoritarian Rule: Tentative Conclusions about Uncertain Democracies*. Baltimore, MD: Johns Hopkins University Press.

Olander, Petrus. 2015. "Dynamic Economic Growth as a Constraint on Elite Behavior." In *Elites, Institutions and the Quality of Government*, edited by Carl Dahlström and Lena Wängnerud, 187–203. UK: Palgrave Macmillan.

Olander, Petrus. 2019. "Economic Diversification and Institutional Quality—Issues of Concentrated Interests." *Studies in Comparative Political Development* 54 (3): 346–64.

Olson, Mancur. 1965. *The Logic of Collective Action*. Cambridge, MA: Harvard University Press.

Olson. Mancur. 2000. *Power and Prosperity: Outgrowing Communist and Capitalist Dictatorships*. Oxford: Oxford University Press.

Olsson, Ola. 2007. "Conflict Diamonds." *Journal of Development Economics* 82: 267–86.

Pareto, Vilfredo. 1966. *Vilfredo Pareto: Sociological Writings, Selected and Introduced by S.E. Finer*. New York: Praeger.

Piore, Michael J. 1979. *Birds of Passage: Migrant Labor and Industrial Societies*. Cambridge: Cambridge University Press.

Posner, Daniel N. 2004. "Measuring Ethnic Fractionalization in Africa." *American Journal of Political Science* 48 (4): 849–63.

Pritchett, Lant. 2000. "Understanding Patterns of Economic Growth: Searching for Hills among Plateaus, Mountains, and Plains." *The World Bank Economic Review* 14 (2): 221–50.

Putnam, Robert D. 1976. *The Comparative Study of Political elites*. New Jersey: Prentice-Hall Englewood Cliff.

Ravitch, Diane. 1974. *The Great School Wars: New York City, 1805–1973: A History of the Public Schools as Battlefield of Social Change*. New York: Basic Books.

Hidalgo, Jason. 2015. "Art of the Tesla deal: How Nevada won a Gigafactory." *Reno Gazette Journal*, June 4, 2015. https://eu.rgj.com/story/news/2014/09/13/art-tesla-deal-nv-won-gigafactory/15593371/

Ross, Michael L. 2001. *Timber Booms and Institutional Breakdown in Southeast Asia*. New York: Cambridge University Press.

Ross, Michael L. 2012. *The Oil Curse: How Petroleum Wealth Shapes the Development of Nations*. Princeton, NJ: Princeton University Press.

Ross, Michael. L. 2015. "What Have We Learned about the Resource Curse?" *Annual Review of Political Science* 18: 239–59.

Ross, Michael. L. 2019. "What Do We Know about Export Diversification in Oil-Producing Countries?" *The Extractive Industries and Society* 6 (3): 792–806.

Rothstein, Bo, and Jan Teorell. 2008. "What is Quality of Government? A Theory of Impartial Government Institutions." *Governance* 21 (2): 165–90.

Rueschemeyer, Dietrich, Evelyne Stephens, and John D. Stephens. 1992. *Capitalist development and democracy* 22. Polity: Cambridge.

Sachs, Jeffrey D., and Andrew M. Warner. 1995. "Natural Resource Abundance and Economic Growth." No. w5398. National Bureau of Economic Research.

Schmitter, Philippe. C. 1974. "Still the Century of Corporatism?" *The Review of Politics* 36 (1): 85–131.

Smith, Adam. 1776. *An Inquiry into the Nature and Causes of the Wealth of Nations by Adam Smith, edited with an Introduction, Notes, Marginal Summary and an Enlarged Index by Edwin Cannan*. London: Methuen, 1904.

Solinger, Dorothy J. 1999. *Contesting citizenship in urban China: Peasant migrants, the state, and the logic of the market*. Berkeley: University of California Press.

Song Kim, In. 2017. "Political Cleavages within Industry: Firm-level Lobbying for Trade Liberalization." *American Political Science Review* 111 (1): 1–20.

Sonin, Konstantin. 2003. "Why the Rich May Favor Poor Protection of Property Rights." *Journal of Comparative Economics* 31: 715–31.

Stigler, George J. 1971. "The Theory of Economic Regulation." *The Bell Journal of Economics and Management Science* 2 (1): 3–21.

Tarbell, Ida, M. 1904. *The History of the Standard Oil Company*. New York: McClure and Phillips Company.

Wagner, John E., and Steven C. Deller. 1998. "Measuring the Effects of Economic Diversity on Growth and Stability." *Land Economics* 74 (4): 541–56.

Whitford, William C. 2007. "A History of the Automobile Lender Provisions of BAPCPA." *University of Illinois Law Review*: 143.

Wiig, Arne, and Ivar Kolstad. 2012. "If Diversification Is Good, Why Don't Countries Diversify More? the Political Economy of Diversification in Resource-Rich Countries." *Energy Policy* 40: 196–203.

Wyman, Mark. 1993. Round-Trip to America: The Immigrants Return to Europe, *1880–1930*. Ithaca, New York: Cornell University Press.

Zingales, Luigi. 2017. "Towards a Political Theory of the Firm." *Journal of Economic Perspectives* 31 (3): 113–30.

Zingales, Luigi. 2012. *A Capitalism for the People: Recapturing the Lost Genius of American Prosperity*. New York, New York: Basic Books.

CHAPTER 19

....

QUALITY OF GOVERNMENT AND ENVIRONMENTAL SUSTAINABILITY

....

MARINA POVITKINA AND SIMON MATTI

INTRODUCTION

ALTHOUGH the various facets of Quality of Government (QoG) time and time again have been identified as significant factors contributing to governmental effectiveness and the possibility both to avoid and solve pressing problems (see Chapters 3, 4, 5, and 7 in this volume), the study of QoG in relation to environmental (un)sustainability is rather scant. Instead, scholars attempting to identify and explain variations in environmental performance either on the macro (between countries) or the micro (between individuals) level tend to focus on other explanatory factors, ranging from regime type to individual motivation. Although such studies have proved highly valuable for understanding the complexity of addressing contemporary environmental problems, this chapter argues that QoG both conditions and interacts with the effects of other institutional and behavioral variables.

From previous research we can conclude that achieving environmental sustainability goals has two main dimensions. First, it requires national commitments and, therefore, political systems that could secure adoption and implementation of environmental sustainability policies. Second, it requires cooperative and coordinated action among resource users or emitters in order to prevent overuse and depletion of common resources, as well as their compliance with policies and rules to this effect. Considering the significance of QoG for the actions of both governments and other societal actors, we believe it is an essential part of further understanding whether and how governments respond to environmental sustainability challenges.

Our chapter is motivated by three main limitations in the current state of art. First, there is a clear lack of research on the relationship between quality of government and an environmental dimension of sustainable development, which calls for developing a theory for understanding such relationship. Second, the existing literature is scattered between different disciplines and subfields, from economics to public administration and political science, which calls for a study that connects the various arguments and findings through a comprehensive survey of the field. Third, the studies on the effects of QoG on the various elements of environmental sustainability on a macro level are distinct and somewhat disconnected from the studies on the effects of QoG on the behavior of actors on the micro level, which calls for bridging these strands of literature and explaining the relationship between the two.

This chapter addresses all three of these gaps. It begins by conceptualizing environmental sustainability as a political problem and proceeds by theorizing the necessity of a capable and largely uncorrupt state for delivering environmental public goods and services, both in terms of decision-making and implementation. Furthermore, it discusses the role of quality of government in encouraging cooperative behavior among individuals and other actors in collective action dilemmas characterizing natural resource use. In this endeavor, we review previous research on how quality of government both directly and indirectly can affect decision-making over such long-term projects as environmental sustainability, implementation of environmental sustainability policies, as well as public support of and compliance with these policies. Certainly, there are numerous factors that explain why countries differ in the way they address problems of environmental sustainability, including history, economy (Grossman and Krueger 1995), geography, demographics, and other factors external to the political process, as well as political factors such as the level of democracy (e.g. Eckersley 2004), party composition (e.g. Kamieniecki 1995), and the relationship between state and society (Scruggs 1999). Therefore, it is here relevant to talk about the *relative* effect of governmental quality on environmental outcomes, and about the *interplay* between QoG and other relevant factors. The chapter concludes by pointing towards avenues for future research on the relationship between QoG and environmental sustainability.

Environmental Sustainability as a Problem

In 2015, member states of the United Nations set the agenda to reach 17 global goals for sustainable development (the SDGs) to solve pressing problems that the world faces today. These goals include eradicating poverty and hunger, improving health and education quality, securing people's access to water, sanitation, and clean energy, achieving gender equality and social justice, addressing climate change, and taking care of the environment, among others. All goals aim towards sustainable development—a development that, following the Brundtland Commission's definition, "meets the needs of the present without compromising the ability of future generations to meet their own needs" (World Commission on Environment and Development 1987) and implies improving people's economic and social well-being while protecting the environment and ensuring longevity of natural resources. Among the social, economic, and environmental pillars of sustainable development, this chapter will focus specifically on the latter: *environmental* sustainability. However, although our focus here is centered on environmental issues in particular, the importance of quality of government for reaching other global goals could nonetheless be assumed equally significant. On the one hand, several of the SDGs target environmental quality indirectly, as a requirement for achieving them, e.g. poverty reduction or promoting public health. On the other hand, the overarching problems behind environment-related and other SDGs, e.g.

education, hunger, or health and well-being, are of a similar type, requiring similar amendment strategies.

Conceptualizing a healthy environment as a global free-access good, the presence of environmental degradation can be attributed to two kinds of institutional failures: market failures and governance failures. *Market failures* denote situations in which the allocation of goods and services by a free market is not efficient. Such situations can arise for various reasons, for example, time-inconsistent preferences (Hoch and Loewenstein 1991), information asymmetries (Stiglitz 1998), noncompetitive markets (Tirole 1988), principal–agent problems (Hart and Holmström 1987), or externalities (Laffont 2008), and are rooted in a classic collective action problem where rational actors' failure to cooperate around a common benefit leads to outcomes that are societally suboptimal (e.g. Olson 1965; Hardin 1982).

In his seminal work *The Logic of Collective Action* (1965, 2), Mancur Olson argues that without "coercion or some other special device," rational and self-interested individuals will not voluntarily cooperate in collective action situations "unless the group is very small." Although this claim has been partly refuted (e.g. Ostrom 2005; Lubell, Zahran, and Vedlitz 2007), examples of actors voluntarily cooperating on a larger scale are still strikingly rare. For environmental goods in particular, the non-excludability problem (i.e. the difficulty to control access to a resource leading to overuse or noncontribution) shared by all free-access goods is also coupled with additional issues, making voluntary collective action unlikely. For example, both the temporal dimension of the problem, which implies that many environmental consequences become visible long after their causes, and spatial dimension, which implies that causes and consequences are geographically separated and problems are therefore not visible to those bringing them about, make it increasingly difficult to assign personal responsibilities and prompt a voluntary behavior change as a response (cf. Jagers et al. 2020).

Addressing environmental problems in a comprehensive manner thus requires a range of governmental responses both to correct such market failures and handle their consequences. In short, it requires the involvement of the state or some other third party that can facilitate or regulate cooperation when it does not voluntarily arise. On the national level, such governmental interventions take the form of policy measures, or what Jane Mansbridge (2014, 10) characterizes as "legitimate coercion" by governments. These either target unsustainable behavioral patterns to mitigate the causes of the problem itself, or treat the symptoms by adapting natural or human systems such that damage from environmental degradation is reduced (Adger et al. 2007).

At the same time, due to a high risk of externalities, private markets are unlikely to provide public goods related to environmental sustainability if left to their own devices (Min 2015). This leaves also the task of securing the delivery of environmental public goods in the hands of government administrations. Thus, to reach environmental goals and secure environmental sustainability, the state requires both institutions or "rules of the game" (North 1990, 3) that stimulate or regulate cooperative behavior in collective action dilemmas in their territories, as well as institutions that favor commitment to and delivery of sustainability-related public goods and services to their populations. As will be further discussed in this chapter, quality of government—a set of institutions that shape how political power is exercised—is beneficial for both.

Governance failures, however, denote situations in which governments are unsuccessful in correcting market failures and thus in both securing cooperation as well as providing public goods. Although governance failures commonly are explained by poor or misdirected implementation processes (Howlett 2019; Smith and Larimer 2018; Pressman and Wildavsky 1973), their sources might be a direct result of low levels of QoG, as they suggest a situation where decision-makers and the public administration either lack capacity or are unwilling to properly decide on, implement, monitor, and enforce environmental policies. Furthermore, a range of literature also points towards a possible indirect effect of QoG on the state's capacity for environmental protection, as the quality of decision-making and administrative processes, or "good governance," in various ways affect the formation of public support and preferences for governmental interventions.

Certainly, not all situations can be conceptualized as pure social dilemmas where governmental intervention is necessary to steer actors towards the one single Pareto optimal solution. In reality, environmental problems come in many different shapes and forms, with a range of different causes, and therefore also potential solutions. For example, in difference to classic prisoner's dilemma-type situations that assume equal preferences among actors, real life problems often arise as both individual factors (e.g. values, experiences, and resources) and contextual factors (e.g. culture, history, and social environment) affect how we evaluate different outcomes. In fact, asymmetric preferences are far more common than perfect symmetry, making the possible solutions to a collaborative game much more difficult to predict. Moreover, many problematic situations do not only contain one, but several, equilibria, where collectively beneficial outcomes rather require that actors coordinate around one out of several possible alternatives. Again, this makes the opportunities for governmental intervention slightly different than in pure social dilemmas, as asymmetric preferences, unequal power relations, and a multitude of potential routes ahead need to be accounted for.

Lastly, using the well-known typology of goods into private, club, common, and public goods, developed by Ostrom, Gardner and Walker (1994), as an example, the very nature of the resource in question affects what kind of governmental intervention is called for. Whereas the free rider problem characterizing public goods requires institutional measures to ensure their continuous production, common-pool resources rather need governments to target over-consumption. Given this variety, we can also assume that the specific ways in which QoG affects attempts to reach sustainability differs across types of environmental goods and empirical cases. For example, in environmental sustainability problems connected to the overuse of natural resources, such as deforestation or overexploitation of marine fish stocks, QoG influences the behavior of actors using these resources. In problems connected to the provision of public goods, such as universal supply of clean water or air, apart from influencing the behavior of polluters of water and air resources, QoG affects the success of implementation of the respective public policy programs. Nonetheless, in all instances where government is in any way involved, the need for good quality institutions is believed to be imminent.

In the following, we consider two broad aspects of the QoG-environment relationship. First, it is the macro level, where we suggest ways in which QoG might determine the extent to which governments succeed in upholding the production of environmental public goods. Second, it is the micro level, where we suggest that QoG should also be seen as a factor facilitating collective action over resource use, limiting overexploitation of natural resources.

QUALITY OF GOVERNMENT AND THE PROVISION OF ENVIRONMENTAL PUBLIC GOODS

In our definition of the quality of government, we refer to the seminal work by Rothstein (2011), who broadly defines it as impartiality in the exercise of power. Impartiality implies that "When implementing laws and policies, government officials shall not take into consideration anything about the citizen/case that is not beforehand stipulated in the policy or the law" (Rothstein and Teorell 2008, 170, refering to Strömberg and Lundell 2000). The existing empirical literature on the relationship between QoG and environmental sustainability does not, however, directly mention concepts of impartiality or quality of government. Rather, most of the studies focus on various elements of quality of government instead, commonly without further discussing the conceptual links between these elements and the overarching concept itself. In their conceptual paper on the definition of QoG, Rothstein and Teorell (2008) discuss how quality of government relates to different competing conceptions of QoG and emphasize that quality of government or the principle of impartiality implies the absence of corruption, encompasses rule of law, and is likely to affect the effectiveness of public administration (see also Versteeg and Ginsburg 2017). Therefore, in our review, we specifically focus on these elements of or close concepts to QoG discussed in the previous research and connect them under the umbrella of the overarching QoG concept.

Overall, research on the connection between QoG (or its related concepts) and environmental sustainability is scant, calling for future research to further explore and explain how, and to what extent, QoG affects environmental sustainability efforts both directly and indirectly. Several large-N studies report positive and significant association between QoG and various national environmental sustainability outcomes, such as protection of population from natural disasters (Persson and Povitkina 2017) and water quality (Povitkina and Bolkvadze 2019). However, of all QoG elements, most of the large-N studies focus specifically on corruption. For example, Damania, Fredriksson, and List (2003), Fredriksson and Svensson (2003), and Pellegrini (2011) report that more corrupt countries have weaker stringency of environmental policies. Welsch (2004), using data on various indicators of air quality, including urban sulphur dioxide (SO_2), nitrogen dioxide, and total suspended particulate concentrations, as well as water quality such as dissolved oxygen demand, phosphorus concentration, and suspended soils in river basins, finds that all these types of pollution increase with corruption, either through the direct effect of corruption on law enforcement or through its effect on countries' income. Cole (2007), using data both across countries and over time, shows that more corruption is associated with higher carbon dioxide (CO_2) and SO_2 emissions. Povitkina (2018) further suggests that corruption has a moderating effect on the relationship between democracy and CO_2 emissions, and that democracies only emit less if their corruption levels are low. If corruption is high, no statistically significant difference between CO_2 emissions in democracies and authoritarian regimes is found.

Figure 19.1 shows that countries with higher QoG score higher on Environmental Performance Index, which is an aggregated measure of countries' efforts towards environmental sustainability. It consists of various indicators of environmental quality, ranging

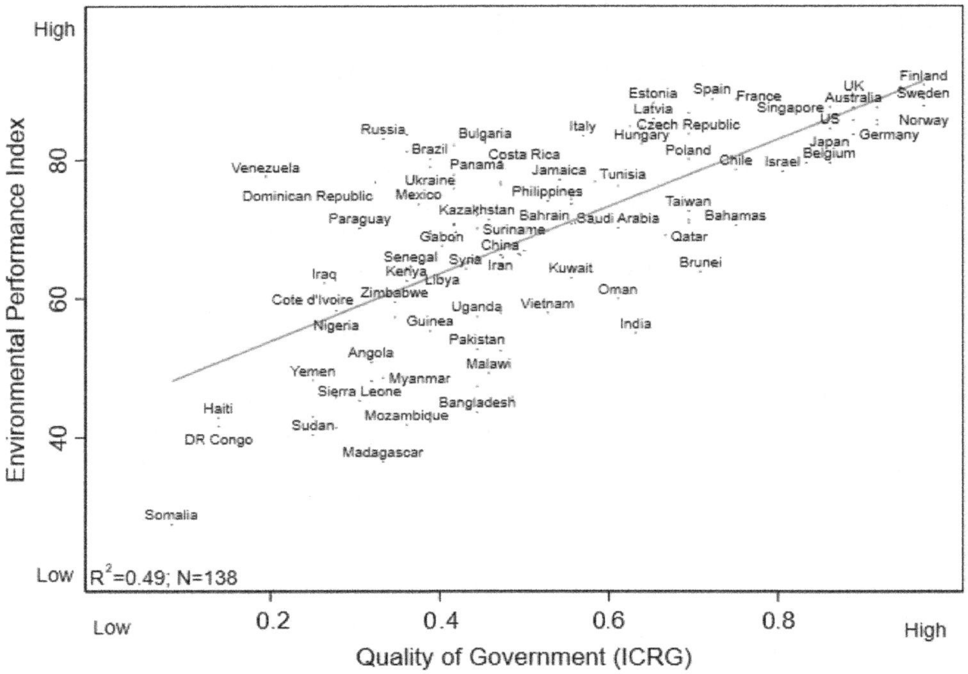

FIGURE 19.1 World countries plotted according to their quality of government and environmental performance

Note: ICRG = International Country Risk Guide, N = number of countries. Data on the Environmental Performance Index comes from Wendling et al. (2018). Data on the Quality of Government Index comes from the Political Risk Services (PRS) group (2018). Both indicators are taken from the Quality of Government Dataset, version Jan19, for the year 2015 (Teorell et al. 2019).

from air and water emissions to the condition of fisheries and forests, and to environmental policy actions, such as the size of protected areas (Wendling et al. 2018). Such correlations, however, have to be interpreted with caution. Many of the countries that have a high QoG have also reached a high level of economic development (Mauro 1995; Ahlerup, Baskaran, and Bigsten, Chapter 4 in this book). This leads to a strong positive correlation between the two in cross-country statistical samples[1] and a difficulty in disentangling the effect of QoG from that of economic development.

The effect of economic development itself on the environmental quality is ambiguous. A number of studies suggest that the relationship between the two follows an inverse U-shaped pattern. At low levels of economic development, more development is associated with more environmental degradation but after a country reaches a certain income level, further affluence is associated with a lower environmental impact (e.g. Grossman and

---

[1] The correlation between gross domestic product (GDP) per capita and QoG is estimated to be around 75% in 2015, which implies that 75% of countries with higher QoG also have higher GDP per capita. The correlation is calculated by the authors with GDP data from Gleditch (2011) and QoG data from the International Country Risk Guide by the PRS Group (2018), both taken from Teorell et al. (2019).

Krueger 1995). Among the hypothesized mechanisms behind the turn of the curve towards environmental improvement in economically developed states is believed to be the adoption of environmental policies as well as introduction of green technologies and standards into industrial production (Leal 1994; Stern 2002)—processes that are often influenced by the level of QoG (Lægreid and Povitkina 2018).

What complicates the picture even more is that many economically developed countries with high QoG that are now at the forefront of addressing environmental problems, have in the past also contributed greatly to the current level of environmental degradation and climate change. As shown in Figure 19.2, countries with higher QoG have higher ecological footprint for consumption per capita, implying that they exert a higher pressure on the ecological systems. However, given that QoG and gross domestic product (GDP) per capita, which is a commonly used measure of countries' wealth, usually go hand-in-hand, the observed patterns on the figures might as well be due to the level of economic development of states rather than QoG, or some other confounding factors. Therefore, despite the findings in the large-N studies, it is difficult to disentangle the positive effect of QoG from the ambiguous effect of economic development on the environment. In addition, current literature still does not inform us on how high the effect of QoG is on achieving environmental sustainability, independent of its statistical connection to or through economic development.

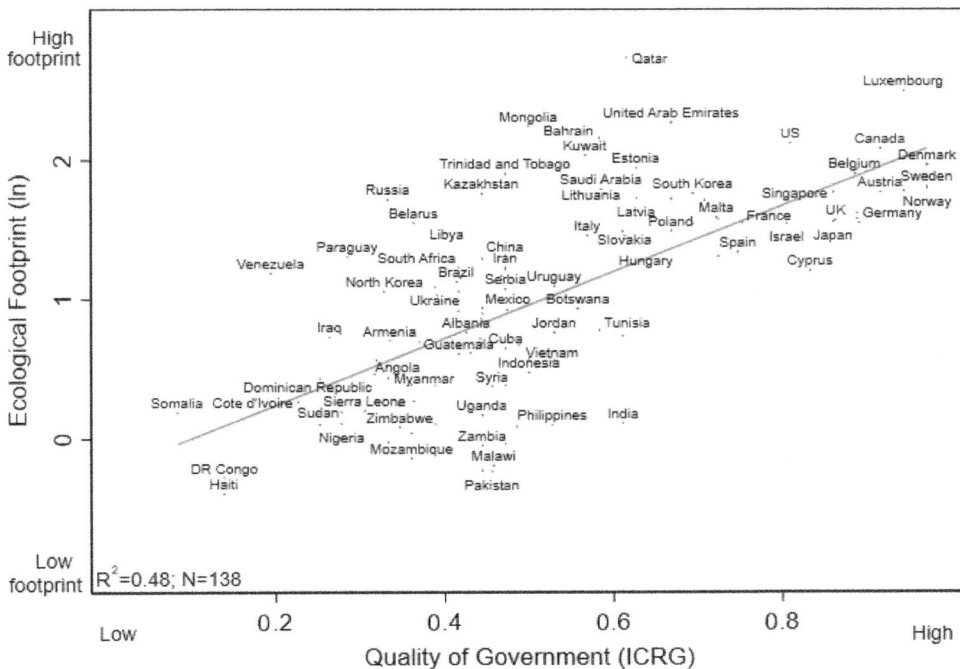

FIGURE 19.2 World countries plotted according to their quality of government and ecological footprint per capita for consumption

Note: ICRG = International Country Risk Guide, N = number of countries, ln = natural logarithm. Data on Ecological Footprint comes from Global Footprint Network (2018). Data on the Quality of Government Index comes from the PRS group (2018), both indicators are taken from the Quality of Government Dataset, version Jan19, for the year 2015 (Teorell et al. 2019).

406 MARINA POVITKINA AND SIMON MATTI

The evidence from existing case studies instead provides a more in-depth insight into how different aspects of QoG impact environmental sustainability. The majority of studies focus on the role of corruption as an impediment to successful enforcement (e.g. Sundström 2016), and a few—on the role of bureaucratic capacity (e.g. Ringquist 1993) in implementing environmental sustainability goals. We discuss these studies in the next sections and, given the scant literature, we additionally turn to the previous research on QoG and its role in the provision of other public goods such as social welfare. By analyzing this literature and characterizing environmental sustainability as a free-access good, we construct a theoretical foundation for better understanding the relationship between QoG and environmental public good provision, which covers both the adoption and implementation of environmental policies. Nonetheless, as with all theoretical models, it requires rigorous empirical testing throughout future research.

QoG, law enforcement and environmental sustainability

The most discussed concept (inversely) related to QoG in the existing literature is corruption, which hampers effective enforcement of environmental laws. In the presence of corruption in public administration, which is responsible for monitoring compliance and sanctioning defection in the implementation of policies, regulations are rarely followed and ultimately environmental laws do not get implemented (López and Mitra 2000; Damania, Fredriksson, and List 2003). Users of natural resources, such as emitters, illegal loggers, or poachers, be it individuals or firms, can offer bribes to government officials and pay their way out of the prescribed codes of behavior instead of complying with regulations (Desai 1998; O'Connor 1994), while inspectors may take bribes in return for allowing overuse of natural resources, for example, underreporting emissions, allowing illegal logging, overfishing, and poaching, instead of enforcing compliance with the standards (Damania 2002; Robbins 2000; Sundström 2015, 2016).

On the example of South African fisheries, Sundström (2015) shows how such poor enforcement can look in practice. Corrupt norms incentivize inspectors to remain blind to violations, either by inadequate monitoring, by sharing information on their patrolling times thus helping fishermen avoid being detected, or by being directly involved in overfishing practices and facilitating them. By summarizing the existing case studies in a comprehensive review, Sundström (2016) also describes how corruption disrupts law enforcement in the forest management sector. Numerous case studies demonstrate that corrupt rules allow illegal resource extraction through four main mechanisms: Companies can pay bribes for permits or obtaining falsified licenses to harvest on areas larger than initially authorized (Robbins 2000; Smith et al. 2011), reuse already utilized permits (Miller 2011) or increase their quotas (Gore, Ratsimbazafy, and Lute 2013); they can pay bribes for expanding harvesting in the protecting areas (Bettinger 2015); for illegal transporting of the resources (Pellegrini 2011); and for smuggling the resources on the international markets for trade (Milledge, Gelvas, and Ahrends 2007). Sundström and Wyatt (2017), on the examples of illegal trade in falcons and abalones, provide additional detailed evidence of how corruption facilitates conservation crime—the violation of existing conservation regulations—showing that bribes help wrongdoers obtain false permits or escape inspections by the customs.

The capacity of states to enforce their formal institutions is also influenced by the degree of rule of law, that is the absence of arbitrary power. Yet another concept under the QoG umbrella, although strongly related to corruption (cf. Versteeg and Ginsburg 2017), rule of law is crucial for securing (quasi-) voluntary compliance and the cooperation of actors in collective action dilemmas over natural resource protection, as further elaborated in the next section. At the same time, the equality of public officials before the courts prevents derailing from long-term policy implementation to short-term goals and thus secures commitments to the long-term policy objectives (Raz 1979; Skaaning 2010; Møller and Skaaning 2012; Fukuyama 2014). Rulers often have an incentive to prioritize projects that produce visible results quickly and can generate legitimacy among the public for their performance in the short term. If the rule of law is weak, rational and utility-maximizing rulers could more easily divert resources from already adopted long-term policies to short-term projects, which provide them with more personal gain.

Bureaucratic capacity and environmental sustainability

Previous research uniformly agrees that any public policy benefits from a strong public administration capable of achieving the set goals (Miller 2000; Rauch and Evans 2000; D'Arcy and Nistotskaya 2017; Nistotskaya and Cingolani 2016) and environmental sustainability policies are not an exception. A strong bureaucracy is necessary for the efficient design and effective implementation of public policies, for securing and maintaining a system for tax collection to finance political programs, and for establishing a countrywide infrastructure for the land oversight (Geddes 1994).

However, environmental sustainability as a public policy program possesses a few characteristics that make strong bureaucracy even more crucial. Reaching environmental sustainability is a complex task, requiring in-depth knowledge on ecosystems and the interconnectedness of ecosystems. Therefore, it calls for public administration employees to be competent in their duties. Employment by meritocratic recruitment, through formal examination or selection by education, rather than political reasons, makes it more likely that civil servants will be competent (Dahlström and Lapuente 2017). Competent employees are more likely to seek out and incorporate the relevant knowledge and expertise faster and design effective policies and action plans that account for the breadth and interconnected nature of environmental sustainability issues.

Political appointments to the top positions in the public administration, on the contrary, could bring less competent leaders to public agencies than employment by merit. Such agency heads might not be capable of developing effective action plans or account for all the necessary elements for achieving such complex goal as sustainability. Huber and McCarty (2004) show in their game-theoretic model that incompetence also decreases the incentives of civil servants to comply with policy goals, as they recognize that their ability to implement necessary policies is limited.

Employment by merit additionally helps civil servants develop an *esprit de corps* (from French: "group spirit"), an impression of the shared knowledge and abilities with colleagues. Such group spirit favors joint commitment to the goals and, as a consequence, coherence within public administration structures (Evans and Rauch 1999). Given that environmental sustainability goals can sometimes have low short-term compatibility either with other political goals, for example, economic development or expansion of transport infrastructure, or with other environmental policy goals (cf. Söderberg and Eckerberg 2013; Söderberg 2016), such coherence can favor the resolution of policy conflicts. Political appointments, on the other hand, often result in frequent changes of agency heads, creating "leadership vacuums," and thereby obscuring agency goals (Lewis 2007, 1075). This leads both to incoherence within the implementation bodies as well as the inability of civil servants to actually commit to implementation under the unstable leadership (Cornell 2014). Incoherence and inability to commit are detrimental to such long-term and complex projects as environmental sustainability programs commonly constitute.

To develop commitment to projects that require long-term implementation such as achieving environmental sustainability, it is beneficial that civil servants retain motivation to pursue these projects. Attractive employment conditions incentivize civil servants to stay within the government structures longer. This lengthens time horizons of civil servants, increases their competence over time, reduces staff turnover, and prevents the loss of institutional memory. Loss of institutional memory can hamper the implementation of such long-term commitments as environmental policies, as implementation of initiatives may be disrupted before any results are reached. Furthermore, when career prospects and salaries are tied to job performance rather than to the good will of political leaders, this also reduces civil servants' incentives for corrupt behavior for personal short-term gain (Evans and Rauch 1999; Dahlström and Lapuente 2017), which might otherwise obstruct the attainment of professional (e.g. environmental sustainability) goals. Commitment to professional goals is also one of the conditions for generating effectiveness in public policy implementation (Dahlström and Lapuente 2017; Ujhelyi 2014), including implementation of policies aimed at environmental sustainability.

Few studies explore the role of bureaucratic quality in executing public policies related to environmental sustainability in particular. Among them, Ringquist (1993) shows the necessity of competent professionals for the environmental laws to be implemented. Teodoro (2010a) demonstrates that local governmental structures affect the politics of water conservation and the adoption of water conservation policies in the U.S. Switzer (2019) unpacks the role of citizens' preferences in law compliance by the local government agencies. Teodoro (2010b) additionally finds that professional bureaucrats are indeed loyal to their professional norms in the agencies dealing with water issues, but also specifies that mobility is needed to spur innovation and achieve higher conservation rates. Although there is a broad scholarship on the role of public administration in dealing with environmental problems, for example, on administrative and organization behavior in the forestry sector (Kaufman 1960), the success of municipal solid waste recycling programs (Feiock and West 1993), capacity of local governments and cities to address the challenges of climate change (Bulkeley and Kern 2006; Bulkeley 2013; Betsill and Bulkeley 2007), this literature does not incorporate QoG aspects in explaining environmental outcomes and mostly looks at structural conditions or specifics of governance.

To sum up, previous studies point towards the necessity of a well-functioning bureaucracy for attaining public policy goals of various kinds. We here suggest that environmental sustainability goals are no different. In fact, given the nature of environmental problems discussed above, they are perhaps even more likely to benefit from the "ideal" Weberian (Weber 1978) model of a capable bureaucracy, prescribing meritocratic recruitment, autonomy of the public administration from politics, and a predictable career ladder, which provides long-term rewards for civil servants.

Quality of government and decision-making for environmental sustainability

Environmental sustainability goals do not only present a complicated challenge for bureaucracies but also for decision-makers. As many aspects of environmental health have a low visibility in general, and the effect of most policy interventions on the environment becomes visible only after a fairly long time, it can be difficult for citizens to correctly assess both the state of the environment as well as the environmental policy actions taken by the governments. Harding and Stasavage (2014) argue that due to repeated elections, democratic leaders tend to have short time horizons and therefore have an incentive to prioritize public services that have visible outcomes and can be quickly delivered instead of committing to goals that take a long time to reach. In addition, environmental sustainability policies are usually not the first priority for the majority of citizens, as there are often other pressing issues to address. Special interests that represent such pressing issues can furthermore acquire considerable political influence, prompting governments to deprioritize environment on the political agenda. The combination of these factors makes environmental decision-making especially difficult in both high- and low-QoG settings.

However, the current literature also gives us reasons to believe that a combination of institutions under high quality of government is more favorable for developing political commitments to environmental sustainability policies. Quite the reverse, a combination of institutions under low quality of government makes up for a system where politicians are more likely to attend to short-term interests rather than prioritize sustainability. This is due to the following reasons:

First, if public administration is incapable of designing and implementing effective policies, there are few incentives for politicians to pursue such policies, as it will be difficult to justify policy choices and their financing to the public (Dahlström, Lindvall, and Rothstein 2013). Weir and Skocpol (1985, 149), in their analysis of policy choices during the Great Depression, also show that political parties tend to define their goals taking into consideration the "capacities of the state." Capabilities of public administration, Dahlström, Lindvall and Rothstein (2013) argue, depend on the level of corruption and the overall competence of civil servants to carry out long-term complicated policies efficiently and in a legitimate manner. Lack of competence and the presence of corruption are clearly different types of problems, but they both create a perception of the incapability of civil service, which will make politicians deter the adoption of such policies.

Second, when careers of bureaucrats are separated from those of politicians, strong well-functioning bureaucracy can impose "checks and balances" and constrain democratic leaders, preventing their interference with the policy revisions, securing policy implementation despite the change of leadership (Cornell 2014; Dahlström and Lapuente 2017). Numerous public administration scholars argue that in meritocratic bureaucracies the hands of politicians are tied when dealing with public administration (e.g. Horn 1995). Cornell and Lapuente (2014), on the examples of Spain and Venezuela, empirically show that meritocratic employment to public administrations, which depends on peer review and is independent from political influence, constrains political leaders in managing the staffing policy, and thus prevents them from pursuing partial policies through manipulating bureaucracy. Povitkina and Bolkvadze (2019) additionally posit that an independent public administration and strong rule of law can reduce the short-termism inherent to democracies, making commitments to long-term policies such as environmental sustainability more likely. Their analysis shows that even when dealing with one policy issue, such as provision of safe drinking water, political leaders in Moldova—a democratic country with low QoG—only tend to address a visible part of the problem and build water pipes that can bring votes in the short term. In the absence of the constraints on democratic leadership that QoG provides, a long-term aspect of safe drinking water provision, that is maintaining high water quality, gets neglected.

Third, it is easier for special interests opposing environmental sustainability goals to gain political influence in a system where aspects of QoG are failing. For example, a corrupt system provides an opportunity for representatives of polluting industries to bribe policymakers and push their interests through to decisions that deviate from environmental protection (Wilson and Damania 2005). Nonetheless, following Campos and Giovanni (2007; see also Harstad and Svensson 2011; Damania, Fredriksson, and Mani 2004), the increasing influence of special interests over decision-making might present a problem also in high QoG contexts. As both business lobbying within the framework of the law and political corruption are means for exerting political influence, they can be thought of as both substitutes and complements, although it is not conventionally conceptualized this way. Nonetheless, if judges are not independent but subject to political influence or open for bribery, it is also easier for powerful interest groups to impose their preferences on the legal system and override environmental laws. In their investigation of the reasons behind poor water management in Moldova, Povitkina and Bolkvadze (2019, 1206) show that due to close connections between law enforcement and politicians, public officials in the law enforcement bodies "turned a blind eye" to wrongdoings from polluting businesses that had close ties with politicians.

QUALITY OF GOVERNMENT AND COLLECTIVE ACTION

There are also good reasons to suspect the link between QoG and environmental sustainability that not only applies to the macro (state) level, but is also valid on the micro (individual) level, albeit in a less direct fashion. In short, the distortion of governmental functionality caused by low levels of QoG could be expected to spill over to citizen–state relationships. As argued above, due to the low visibility and diluted sources of responsibility of environmental problems, voluntary collective action over resource use is unlikely (Hardin 1982; Olson 1965). Although high-profile examples of voluntary environmental collective action on a large scale do exist, for example the Greta Thunberg-initiated youth movement *Fridays for Future*, cooperation among actors in social dilemmas requires for the most part some form of "legitimate coercion" by a third party, typically the state (Mansbridge 2014,

10). In social dilemmas, the task for the third party is to regulate collective action behaviors, monitor and sanction defectors, and ensure compliance with regulations. For this, however, public support is crucial especially where the state targets the cooperative behavior of individuals by introducing policies and institutions to this effect (cf. Matti 2010). For example, support reduces the government's cost of monitoring and enforcing compliance as those affected by the policies will refrain from attempts to cheat or free ride to a greater extent (March and Olsen 2004). If, on the other hand, the measures introduced to govern cooperation are perceived as inappropriate, unjust, or disproportional, the cost of monitoring will rise rapidly, making it increasingly difficult for the state to maintain collective ventures (Ostrom 2005).

Furthermore, for representative democracies in particular, there is ample evidence that public opinion both constrains (Sobel 2001; Foyle 2004) and directs the actions of decision-makers (Stimson 2007; Soroka and Wlezien 2009), as vote-maximizing politicians are unlikely to risk unpopularity by introducing or sustaining policies that might be received poorly by the electorate (Page and Shapiro 1983; Stimson, Mackuen, and Erikson 1995; Burstein 2003; Connelly et al. 2012; Wallner 2008). Public policy attitudes seem to also matter for the specific issue of environmental policy, with several studies arguing that the introduction of effective policies to curb climate change is constrained by a lack of public support. Several studies point towards a lack of public support as a key obstacle slowing down governmental attempts to implement sustainability transitions (cf. Drews and Van den Bergh 2016; Löfgren and Nordblom 2009), with examples from Britain (e.g. Jagers, Löfgren, and Stripple 2010), Canada (Harrison 2010, 2012), Australia (Crowley 2017), and the U.S. (Shwom et al. 2010; Feldman and Hart 2018). The French *gilets jaunes* protests during the winter of 2018–19, sparked by the proposal to introduce a domestic carbon tax, is a further case in point (cf. Carattini, Kallbekken, and Orlov 2019).

Given this, increased scholarly attention has been directed towards better understanding the conditions for public policy support and the variation in national policy use it prompts. A range of potential explanations analyzed in the previous research includes the degree of political polarization (Linde 2018), economic conditions and dependencies (Jagers and Matti 2018.; Ščasný et al. 2017; Kenny 2018), and political culture (Cherry et al. 2014).

However, recent studies also suggest that differences in institutional quality explain why policy attitudes differ across countries. In particular, some evidence suggests that higher levels of corruption and related problems of institutional quality correlate negatively with attitudes towards the use of economic policy tools, such as taxes and subsidies, but positively with a preference for command-and-control regulation. Focusing on welfare policies, Svallfors (2013; see also Holmberg, Rothstein, and Nasiritousi 2009; Rothstein, Samanni, and Teorell 2012) concludes that an overall perception of institutions as efficient and fair drive positive attitudes towards higher taxes and governmental spending. Di Tella and MacCulloch (2007) suggest that perceived corruption is connected to support for more governmental market regulation, and several authors demonstrate how the anticipated efficacy of noncorrupt governments' market interventions is higher and thus more readily supported (Acemoglu and Verdier 2000; Shleifer and Vishny 1993). In a country-comparative study of attitudes towards environmental policy measures, Harring (2014, 2016) concludes that the general public in countries with higher levels of corruption has weaker preferences for economic policy measures, as they are perceived as being less efficient (see also Damania 2002; Aghion et al. 2010). Although not entirely conclusive and worthy of further in-depth scrutiny, these effects of the level of QoG on public policy attitudes should be highly relevant in the environmental domain, as most policy specialists agree that market-based interventions, such as carbon taxes, are among the most effective tools for addressing collective environmental problems.

There are several possible mechanisms through which the macro-level QoG factor could affect micro-level attitudes towards policy instruments among individuals. From an overarching perspective, the state leads by example in a sense that well-functioning political institutions and noncorrupt officials spill over to boost more cooperative social norms among the general public. Such norms, in turn, lead people to more readily accept limitations in personal utility in favor of the collective good (e.g. Levi 1997; Letki 2006; Rothstein and Stolle 2008). Thus, higher levels of institutional quality are suggested to increase the overall levels of support for state intervention aiming towards collective action. Moreover, the general reluctance of people in low-QoG systems both to grant an untrustworthy government more control of financial means, e.g. through an increased use of economic policy measures, and to let potentially corrupt private actors escape governmental control on unregulated markets, seems entirely rational given the importance of perceived effectiveness for policy support, which a range of studies document (Schuitema, Steg, and Forward 2010; Jaensirisak, Wardman, and May 2005; Kallbekken and Sælen 2011; Jagers and Hammar 2009). It is simply not effective to, for example, pay higher taxes in support of a common good, if the revenues are not put to proper use but rather disappear in the pockets of corrupt public officials, or to restrain individual consumption if market actors can continue to overuse natural resources without being sanctioned by the state.

Quality of government, trust, and policy attitudes

More specifically, QoG, as numerous studies suggest, is highly significant for developing and sustaining trust, both in fellow citizens and in government itself (Delhey and Newton 2005; Rothstein and Stolle 2008; Dinesen 2013, 2012). This link between QoG and trust, and the subsequent indirect link between QoG and environmental sustainability, is crucial, in particular as high levels of trust are believed to benefit the stability and effectiveness of a number of societal processes, including the support of and compliance with political decisions (Rudolph and Evans 2005; Hetherington 1998; Braithwaite and Levi 1998). As the solution to collective action problems depends on the joint efforts by both community and elite actors, there are good reasons to anticipate that perceptions of cooperative success depend on the level of trust in the intentions and capacity of other actors to perform the necessary tasks. There are also reasons to believe that individuals will refrain from cooperative behavior unless they perceive a reasonable chance of collective efficacy; that is, whether the relevant collective will be able to perform a given task (Finkel, Muller, and Opp 1989; Lubell, Zahran, and Vedlitz 2007; Bonniface and Henley 2008; Finkel and Muller 1998; Koletsou and Mancy 2011). For example, ample evidence suggests that people in high-trust countries are more willing to pay higher environmental taxes than those living in low-trust countries (e.g. Harring and Jagers 2013; Fairbrother 2016), as they trust the measures to both be complied with (efficacy) and effectively attain their goal (outcome expectancy).

As successful cooperation in any collective action situation depends on a sufficiently large number of actors choosing cooperative strategies, beliefs about others' intentions to comply also affect personal attitudes toward political decisions and policy instruments to this effect (Biel and Thøgersen 2007; Ostrom and Walker 2003; Ostrom 1998). Of particular interest is the conclusion by Ostrom (2005, 54) and Torgler (2003, 124) that many individuals are "conditional cooperators," ready to engage in collective action only to the extent they perceive others as willing to do the same. In small-scale settings, characterized by regular interactions and face-to-face communication, previous experiences and reputation guide these expectations of reciprocity. In contrast, in large-scale situations the extent to which other people are believed to cooperate is rather based on estimated trustworthiness, or generalized trust, where high levels of trust increase personal willingness to cooperate (cf. Sønderskov 2011). Thus, if you trust that other actors will reciprocate your actions, either through the assurance of third party-sanctions or as a normative rule of thumb (cf. Yamagishi 2003), you are more likely to cooperate yourself. This is also the conclusion from several studies addressing the relationship between generalized trust and different forms of environmental behaviors. In a large-N cross-national study Taniguchi and Marshall (2018) find trust to be positively related to three forms of environmental behaviors—intended action, informal action, and formal action; Duit (2011) concludes that generalized trust is related to public (although not private) sphere behaviors; and Sønderskov (2009, 2011) highlights a significant relationship between trust and large-scale collective action in public goods provision.

In guiding public support for policy instruments more specifically, generalized trust works in several ways. On the one hand, distrust in others' predisposition to voluntary behavioral change can be expected to drive general support for the introduction of policy measures mandating change or compensating for defective behavior, in particular if the policy problem is perceived as highly pressing (Johansson Sevä and Kulin 2018). On the other hand, low levels of interpersonal trust also affect evaluations of a policy measure's effectiveness negatively, and can therefore reduce support for a particular measure if perceived as too easy for free riders to evade (Hammar, Jagers, and Nordblom 2009; Harring and Jagers 2013). In fact, using cross-national data, Harring (2014) finds that low levels of interpersonal trust increase the support for stricter regulation and policy instruments that punish noncooperation, whereas high interpersonal trust rather drives preferences for policy measures that instead focus on rewarding cooperation.

Trust in government refers broadly to the confidence the public have in the representative and administrative bodies responsible for deciding on (political trust) and implementing (institutional trust) public policies (Rothstein and Stolle 2008; Citrin and Muste 1999). High levels of trust thus indicate that citizens not only approve of their government or various governmental bodies, but also that they believe that the government acts according to standing political and institutional principles (Levi and Stoker 2000). Trust in government is, as such, based in more than simply affective motives. Rather, trusting a governmental body "entails having confidence that the institution is reliable, observes rules and regulations, works well, and serves the general interest" (Devos, Spini, and Schwartz 2002, 484). Citizens who trust their government will, therefore, to a greater extent comply with government regulations, even at the risk of personal costs. Conversely, with a lack of trust in government, public policies aimed at motivating or enforcing collective action will risk being seen as both unfair and ineffective and will most likely be harder to effectively implement (Citrin and Muste 1999; Tyler 1990; Sandmo 2005; Dresner et al. 2006; Kallbekken and Sælen 2011; Kallbekken, Garcia, and Korneliussen 2013). As proposed by Dietz and colleagues (2007) as well as Kellstedt and colleagues (2008), there are also good reasons to expect the effect of trust in government to be particularly tangible in shaping attitudes in complex and contested issues such as the environment, as the public has to rely more heavily on political elites to accurately evaluate the need for different policies. Furthermore, the effect of trust on policy attitudes is most pronounced for redistributive policies and those implying tangible personal sacrifices (Hetherington 1998; Rudolph and Evans 2005).

On the global level, where coordination and cooperation between individuals or other actors operating within the territory of a sovereign state is replaced by the need for collective action among states themselves, international environmental regimes may instead serve as a third-party enforcer (Lövbrand 2014; Breitmeier, Underdal, and Young 2011; Young 2004). International regimes, broadly defined as a set of implicit or explicit principles, norms, rules, and decision-making procedures (cf. Krasner 1983) address collective action problems by reducing transactions costs, creating a forum for consensus-making and negotiation, and increasing transparency by providing a platform for reporting and assessment. Although lacking the authoritative enforcement capacities of the state, the rapid growth of the number of multilateral environmental agreements such as treaties, protocols, and amendments (e.g. Mitchell 2017) suggests that international regimes serve an important role. By binding states and other global actors to a set of behavioral principles, such as setting emission levels or fishing quotas, they can counteract the negative effects of low trust (brought on by low levels of QoG) within a national system, constituting a supranational framework to which national authorities have to relate and in which other actors' trust might be placed.

Conclusions and Agenda for Future Research

In this chapter we have reviewed the previous work on the relationship between the elements of the quality of government and environmental sustainability. The relationship is believed to operate both on the macro level, where varying levels of QoG benefit or hamper the environmental performance of states, and on the micro level, where QoG guides the behavior of key actors in natural resource use and management. Given that the existing studies with an empirical focus on the QoG–environmental sustainability relationship are scant and scattered across different academic fields, the main goals of the chapter have been to define the overlaps between research on the topics of QoG and the environment, bridge previous work addressing the effect of QoG on environmental sustainability on the macro and micro levels, as well as further theorize the relationship between QoG and environmental sustainability.

Bringing previous research from the different fields and traditions together, we conclude that a low governmental quality, whether it comes in the form of high corruption, weak rule of law, or low bureaucratic capacity, can be expected to negatively impact the adoption and implementation of environmental policies, and thus state capacity to reach the sustainability goals. In our theoretical exercise we determined that independence of civil service and strong rule of law constrain the short-termism of political leaders and favor a continuation of policy implementation despite changes in leadership, political goals, or temporary shifts in public opinion. Competent and relatively uncorrupt public administration is, furthermore, more likely to design efficient action plans for policy implementation, while strong control over corruption increases the quality of monitoring, inspections, and enforcement of legal rules. As these consequences of QoG are evident in a range of empirical cases related to the provision and maintenance of free-access goods, we should expect, and have indeed also some evidence to this effect, that they are equally valid also for the achievement of environmental sustainability.

In addition, although most empirical models of environmental policy support fail to address the connection between a well-functioning government and individual policy attitudes, some recent studies suggest that quality of government affects the attainment of environmental sustainability goals also indirectly, through affecting individual behavioral choices. High levels of QoG increase public trust both in the policy compliance of fellow citizens as well as in the ambitions and abilities of governmental authorities to decide upon and monitor such policies. Therefore, it positively affects public support for government interventions in achieving environmental sustainability goals, including support for environmental taxes and other policy instruments, as well as public preferences for the type of policy measure used. Public support, in turn, increases the compliance with governmental policies and therefore also contributes to collective action for achieving environmental sustainability.

While many of the theoretical claims put out in this chapter are based on the previous arguments and findings, they need rigorous empirical testing in the future research. In addition, we urge future studies to continue qualitatively investigating the role of quality of government in governments' efforts to pursue environmental sustainability goals, including how different forms of corruption, as well as politicized bureaucracy and judicial systems, hamper implementation of environmental laws. While the mechanisms of how corruption hampers environmental sustainability are uncovered in the previous literature, the connection between other aspects of governmental quality and environmental sustainability remain underexplored. The field would benefit from more thorough enquiries and elaborate unpacking of the mechanisms on both macro and micro levels. This is because QoG, treated as a contextual variable, can condition the effects of previously established factors driving policymaking, policy implementation, and policy behavior in relation to environmental sustainability.

Previous research also has a number of important limitations. From the previous studies, we cannot draw definite conclusions about how big of an impact QoG has on environmental sustainability. First, there are numerous other factors that affect the observable environmental outcomes, such as geography, economy, demographics, as well as other political and institutional factors than QoG. Second, the relationship between high QoG and strong economy means, somewhat paradoxically, that countries with high QoG used to be the world's largest polluters and are still major contributors to the depletion of natural resources, but at the same time are at the forefront of addressing the issues of environmental sustainability today. We therefore encourage the future large-N quantitative studies to focus more on subnational variation in the quality of government and its implications for the uneven distribution of environmental quality and environmental justice within countries (see chapter by Drápalová in Part II of this volume). This will help isolate the effect of QoG from that of economic development and bring us closer to estimating the relative effect size of QoG on environmental sustainability outcomes.

Another limitation of the previous large-N research is a lack of good quality data on environmental sustainability outcomes, not only on the state of the natural resources and levels of pollution, but also on the presence and the quality of environmental laws and policies. Although these are difficult to assess and measure for numerous reasons, there is an enormous potential for future work. There is also an apparent lack of data on the quality of environmental government agencies across the globe, the level of political influence over them, trust in the environmental bureaucracy, and therefore there is still a lot to learn about the bureaucratic impediments to successful environmental management. Future work can address this gap in the current research and collect such data for further rigorous and more thorough analyses than have been conducted previously.

Environmental sustainability is also a major, and growing, empirical focus within policy studies. Although several of the major theoretical frameworks applied to understand the workings of the policy process, including the behavior of actors within it and its resulting outcomes, e.g. the Advocacy Coalition Framework, the Multiple Streams Framework, the Institutional Analysis and Development framework, or the Ecology of Games framework, implicitly acknowledge the importance of a well-functioning administrative apparatus, they do not explicitly incorporate QoG in their models, and there is thus a potential for future studies to address this gap.

Future work should also take into account the new channels of the QoG's influence on environmental sustainability. With the rise of globalization and international trade, this work should explore the role of national enforcement and QoG in particular in tracking the origin of raw materials in international trade, including forest and fisheries certification, as well as detecting the trade of rare animals. Future studies can also investigate whether and how the behavior of international corporations differs depending on QoG in host countries and home countries of the corporations' headquarters.

For this, however, it would be beneficial to further acknowledge the multifaceted character of the quality of government concept, for instance by explicitly addressing other aspects of governmental impartiality besides acts of corruption, and placing a further spotlight on the uneven distribution of access to policymakers at the decision-making stage of the policy process. To this extent, future research should also pay more attention to an unexplored role of the quality of government in influencing time horizons of political leaders and investigate whether and how different aspects of QoG contribute to the adoption of policies oriented towards future generations and sustainability, including environmental sustainability. Conclusions from such studies can improve our understanding of how to make country leaders prioritize environmental sustainability goals among other pressing issues societies face.

REFERENCES

Acemoglu, Daron, and Thierry Verdier. 2000. "The Choice between Market Failures and Corruption." *American Economic Review* 90 (1): 194–211. https://doi.org/10.1257/aer.90.1.194

Adger, W. Neil, Shardul Agrawala, M. Monirul Qader Mirza, Cecilia Conde, Karen O'Brien, Juan Pulhin, Roger Pulwarty, Barry Smit, and Kiyoshi Takahashi. 2007. "Assessment of Adaptation Practices, Options, Constraints and Capacity." In *Climate Change 2007: Impacts, Adaptation and Vulnerability. Contribution of Working Group II to the Fourth Assessment Report of the Intergovernmental Panel on Climate Change*, edited by Martin Parry, Martin L. Parry, Osvaldo Canziani, Jean Palutikof, Paul van der Linden, and Clair Hanson, 717–43. Cambridge: Cambridge University Press.

Aghion, Philippe, Yann Algan, Pierre Cahuc, and Andrei Shleifer. 2010. "Regulation and Distrust." *Quarterly Journal of Economics* 125 (3): 1015–49. https://doi.org/10.1162/qjec.2010.125.3.1015

Betsill, Michele, and Harriet Bulkeley. 2007. "Looking Back and Thinking Ahead: A Decade of Cities and Climate Change Research." *Local Environment* 12 (5): 447–56. https://doi.org/10.1080/13549830701659683

Bettinger, Keith Andrew. 2015. "Political Contestation, Resource Control and Conservation in an Era of Decentralisation at Indonesia's Kerinci Seblat National Park." *Asia Pacific Viewpoint* 56 (2): 252–66. https://doi.org/10.1111/apv.12069

Biel, Anders, and John Thøgersen. 2007. "Activation of Social Norms in Social Dilemmas: A Review of the Evidence and Reflections on the Implications for Environmental Behaviour." *Journal of Economic Psychology* 28 (1): 93–112. https://doi.org/10.1016/j.joep.2006.03.003

Bonniface, Leesa, and Nadine Henley. 2008. "'A Drop in the Bucket": Collective Efficacy Perceptions and Environmental Behaviour." *Australian Journal of Social Issues* 43 (3): 345–58. https://doi.org/10.1002/j.1839-4655.2008.tb00107.x

Braithwaite, Valerie, and Margaret Levi. 1998. *Trust and Governance.* New York: Russell Sage Foundation.

Breitmeier, Helmut, Arild Underdal, and Oran R. Young. 2011. "The Effectiveness of International Environmental Regimes: Comparing and Contrasting Findings from Quantitative Research." *International Studies Review* 13 (4): 579–605. https://doi.org/10.1111/j.1468-2486.2011.01045.x

Bulkeley, Harriet. 2013. *Cities and Climate Change.* New York: Routledge.

Bulkeley, Harriet, and Kristine Kern. 2006. "Local Government and the Governing of Climate Change in Germany and the UK." *Urban Studies* 43 (12): 2237–59. https://doi.org/10.1080/00420980600936491

Burstein, Paul. 2003. "The Impact of Public Opinion on Public Policy: A Review and an Agenda." *Political Research Quarterly* 56 (1): 29–40. https://doi.org/10.1177/106591290305600103

Campos, Nauro F., and Francesco Giovannoni. 2007. "Lobbying, Corruption and Political Influence." *Public Choice* 131 (1–2): 1–21. https://doi.org/10.1007/s11127-006-9102-4

Carattini, Stefano, Steffen Kallbekken, and Anton Orlov. 2019. "How to Win Public Support for a Global Carbon Tax." *Nature* 565 (7739): 289–91. https://doi.org/10.1038/d41586-019-00124-x

Cherry, Todd L., Jorge H. García, Steffen Kallbekken, and Asbjørn Torvanger. 2014. "The Development and Deployment of Low-Carbon Energy Technologies: The Role of Economic Interests and Cultural Worldviews on Public Support." *Energy Policy* 68: 562–66. https://doi.org/10.1016/j.enpol.2014.01.018

Citrin, Jack, and Christopher Muste. 1999. "Trust in Government." In *Measures of Social Psychological Attitudes. Vol 2. Measures of Political Attitudes,* edited by John P Robinson, Phillip R Shaver, and Lawrence S Wrightsman, 465–532. San Diego, CA, US: Academic Press. https://doi.org/10.1057/9781137273925_13

Cole, Matthew A. 2007. "Corruption, Income and the Environment: An Empirical Analysis." *Ecological Economics* 62 (3–4): 637–47. https://doi.org/10.1016/j.ecolecon.2006.08.003

Connelly, James, Graham Smith, David Benson, and Clare Saunders. 2012. *Politics and the Environment from Theory to Practice.* 3rd ed. London: Routledge.

Cornell, Agnes. 2014. "Why Bureaucratic Stability Matters for the Implementation of Democratic Governance Programs." *Governance* 27 (2): 191–214. https://doi.org/10.1111/gove.12037

Cornell, Agnes, and Victor Lapuente. 2014. "Meritocratic Administration and Democratic Stability." *Democratization* 21 (7): 1286–304. https://doi.org/https://doi.org/10.1080/13510347.2014.960205

Crowley, Kate. 2017. "Up and down with Climate Politics 2013–2016: The Repeal of Carbon Pricing in Australia." *Wiley Interdisciplinary Reviews: Climate Change* 8 (3): e458. https://doi.org/10.1002/wcc.458

D'Arcy, Michelle, and Marina Nistotskaya. 2017. "State First, Then Democracy: Using Cadastral Records to Explain Governmental Performance in Public Goods Provision." *Governance* 30 (2): 193–209. https://doi.org/10.1111/gove.12206

Dahlström, Carl, and Victor Lapuente. 2017. *Organizing Leviathan: Politicians, Bureaucrats, and the Making of Good Government.* Cambridge: Cambridge University Press.

Dahlström, Carl, Johannes Lindvall, and Bo Rothstein. 2013. "Corruption, Bureaucratic Failure and Social Policy Priorities." *Political Studies* 61 (3): 523–42. https://doi.org/10.1111/j.1467-9248.2012.00998.x

Damania, Richard. 2002. "Environmental Controls with Corrupt Bureaucrats." *Environment and Development Economics* 7 (3): 407–27. https://doi.org/10.1017/S1355770X02000256

Damania, Richard, Per G. Fredriksson, and John A. List. 2003. "Trade Liberalization, Corruption, and Environmental Policy Formation: Theory and Evidence." *Journal of Environmental Economics and Management* 46 (3): 490–512. https://doi.org/10.1016/S0095-0696(03)00025-1

Damania, Richard, Per G. Fredriksson, and Muthukumara Mani. 2004. "The Persistence of Corruption and Regulatory Compliance Failures: Theory and Evidence." *Public Choice* 121 (3–4): 363–90. https://doi.org/10.1007/s11127-004-1684-0

Delhey, Jan, and Kenneth Newton. 2005. "Predicting Cross-National Levels of Social Trust: Global Pattern or Nordic Exceptionalism?" *European Sociological Review* 21 (4): 311–27. https://doi.org/10.1093/esr/jci022

Desai, Uday. 1998. "Environment, Economic Growth, and Government." In *Ecological Policy and Politics in Developing Countries*, edited by Uday Desai, 1–45. Albany, NY: State University of New York Press.

Devos, Thierry, Dario Spini, and Shalom H. Schwartz. 2002. "Conflicts among Human Values and Trust in Institutions." *British Journal of Social Psychology* 41 (4): 481–94. https://doi.org/10.1348/014466602321149849

Dietz, Thomas, Amy Dan, and Rachael Shwom. 2007. "Support for Climate Change Policy: Social Psychological and Social Structural Influences." *Rural Sociology* 72 (2): 185–214. https://doi.org/10.1526/003601107781170026

Dinesen, Peter Thisted. 2012. "Does Generalized (Dis)Trust Travel? Examining the Impact of Cultural Heritage and Destination-Country Environment on Trust of Immigrants." *Political Psychology* 33 (4): 495–511. https://doi.org/10.1111/j.1467-9221.2012.00886.x

Dinesen, Peter Thisted. 2013. "Where You Come from or Where You Live? Examining the Cultural and Institutional Explanation of Generalized Trust Using Migration as a Natural Experiment." *European Sociological Review* 29 (1): 114–28. https://doi.org/10.1093/esr/jcr044

Dresner, Simon, Louise Dunne, Peter Clinch, and Christiane Beuermann. 2006. "Social and Political Responses to Ecological Tax Reform in Europe: An Introduction to the Special Issue." *Energy Policy* 34 (8): 895–904. https://doi.org/10.1016/j.enpol.2004.08.043

Drews, Stefan, and Jeroen C.J.M. van den Bergh. 2016. "What Explains Public Support for Climate Policies? A Review of Empirical and Experimental Studies." *Climate Policy* 16 (7): 855–76. https://doi.org/10.1080/14693062.2015.1058240

Duit, Andreas. 2011. "Patterns of Environmental Collective Action: Some Cross-National Findings." *Political Studies* 59 (4): 900–20. https://doi.org/10.1111/j.1467-9248.2010.00858.x

Eckersley, Robyn. 2004. *The Green State: Rethinking Democracy and Sovereignty.* Cambridge, Mass.; London: MIT Press.

Evans, Peter, and James E. Rauch. 1999. "Bureaucracy and Growth: A Cross-National Analysis of the Effects of 'Weberian' State Structures on Economic Growth." *American Sociological Review* 64 (5): 748–65. https://doi.org/10.2307/2657374

Fairbrother, Malcolm. 2016. "Trust and Public Support for Environmental Protection in Diverse National Contexts." *Sociological Science* 3 (June): 359–82. https://doi.org/10.15195/v3.a17

Feiock, Richard C., and Johathan P. West. 1993. "Testing Competing Explanations for Policy Adoption: Municipal Solid Waste Recycling Programs." *Political Research Quarterly* 46 (2): 399–419. https://doi.org/10.1177/106591299304600211

Feldman, Lauren, and P. Sol Hart. 2018. "Is There Any Hope? How Climate Change News Imagery and Text Influence Audience Emotions and Support for Climate Mitigation Policies." *Risk Analysis* 38 (3): 585–602. https://doi.org/10.1111/risa.12868

Finkel, Steven E., and Edward N. Muller. 1998. "Rational Choice and the Dynamics of Collective Political Action: Evaluating Alternative Models with Panel Data." *American Political Science Review* 92 (1): 37–49. https://doi.org/10.2307/2585927

Finkel, Steven E., Edward N. Muller, and Karl-Dieter Opp. 1989. "Personal Influence, Collective Rationality, and Mass Political Action." *American Political Science Review* 83 (3): 885–903. https://doi.org/10.2307/1962065

Foyle, D. C. 2004. "Leading the Public to War? The Influence of American Public Opinion on the Bush Administration's Decision to Go to War in Iraq." *International Journal of Public Opinion Research* 16 (3): 269–94. https://doi.org/10.1093/ijpor/edh025

Fredriksson, Per G., and Jakob Svensson. 2003. "Political Instability, Corruption and Policy Formation: The Case of Environmental Policy." *Journal of Public Economics* 87 (7–8): 1383–405. https://doi.org/10.1016/S0047-2727(02)00036-1

Fukuyama, Francis. 2014. "States and Democracy." *Democratization* 21 (7): 1326–40. https://doi.org/10.4324/9781315623917

Geddes, Barbara. 1994. *Politician's Dilemma: Building State Capacity in Latin America.* Berkeley: University of California Press.

Gleditsch, Kristian Skrede. 2011. "Expanded Trade and GDP Data." 2011. http://privatewww.essex.ac.uk/~ksg/exptradegdp.html

Gore, Meredith L., Jonah Ratsimbazafy, and Michelle L. Lute. 2013. "Rethinking Corruption in Conservation Crime: Insights from Madagascar." *Conservation Letters* 6 (6): 430–38. https://doi.org/10.1111/conl.12032

Grossman, Gene M., and Alan B. Krueger. 1995. "Economic Growth and the Environment." *The Quarterly Journal of Economics* 110 (2): 353–77. https://doi.org/https://doi.org/10.2307/2118443

Hammar, Henrik, Sverker C. Jagers, and Katarina Nordblom. 2009. "Perceived Tax Evasion and the Importance of Trust." *Journal of Socio-Economics* 38 (2): 238–45. https://doi.org/10.1016/j.socec.2008.07.003

Hardin, Garrett. 1982. *Collective Action.* Baltimore, Md.: Johns Hopkins University Press. https://doi.org/10.4337/9781786430144.00008

Harding, R., & Stasavage, D. (2014). What democracy does (and doesn't do) for basic services: School fees, school inputs, and African elections. *The Journal of Politics*, 76 (1): 229–45. https://doi.org/10.1017/S0022381613001254

Harring, Niklas. 2014. "Corruption, Inequalities and the Perceived Effectiveness of Economic pro-Environmental Policy Instruments: A European Cross-National Study." *Environmental Science and Policy* 39: 119–28. https://doi.org/10.1016/j.envsci.2013.08.011

Harring, Niklas. 2016. "Reward or Punish? Understanding Preferences toward Economic or Regulatory Instruments in a Cross-National Perspective." *Political Studies* 64 (3): 573–92. https://doi.org/10.1111/1467-9248.12209

Harring, Niklas, and Sverker C. Jagers. 2013. "Should We Trust in Values? Explaining Public Support for pro-Environmental Taxes." *Sustainability* 5 (1): 210–27. https://doi.org/10.3390/su5010210

Harrison, Kathryn. 2010. "The Comparative Politics of Carbon Taxation." *Annual Review of Law and Social Science* 6 (1): 507–29. https://doi.org/10.1146/annurev.lawsocsci.093008.131545

Harrison, Kathryn. 2012. "A Tale of Two Taxes: The Fate of Environmental Tax Reform in Canada." *Review of Policy Research* 29 (3): 383–407. https://doi.org/10.1111/j.1541-1338.2012.00565.x

Harstad, Bård, and Jakob Svensson. 2011. "Bribes, Lobbying, and Development." *American Political Science Review* 105 (1): 46–63. https://doi.org/https://doi.org/10.1017/S0003055410000523

Hart, Oliver, and Bengt Holmström. 1987. "The Theory of Contracts." In *Advances in Economic Theory: Fifth World Congress*, edited by Truman Fassett Bewley. Cambridge, UK: Cambridge University Press.

Hetherington, Marc J. 1998. "The Political Relevance of Political Trust." *American Political Science Review* 92 (4): 791–808. https://doi.org/10.2307/2586304

Hoch, Stephen J., and George F. Loewenstein. 1991. "Time-Inconsistent Preferences and Consumer Self-Control." *Journal of Consumer Research* 17 (4): 492. https://doi.org/10.1086/208573

Holmberg, Sören, Bo Rothstein, and Naghmeh Nasiritousi. 2009. "Quality of Government: What You Get." *Annual Review of Political Science* 12 (1): 135–61. https://doi.org/10.1146/annurev-polisci-100608-104510

Horn, Murray J. 1995. *The Political Economy of Public Administration: Institutional Choice in the Public Sector*. New York: Cambridge University Press.

Howlett, Michael. 2019. *Designing Public Policies: Principles and Instruments*. London: Routledge.

Huber, John D., and Nolan McCarty. 2004. "Bureaucratic Capacity, Delegation, and Political Reform." *American Political Science Review* 98 (03): 481–94. https://doi.org/https://doi.org/10.1017/S0003055404001297

Jaensirisak, S., Mark Wardman, and A. D. May. 2005. "Explaining Variations in Public Acceptability of Road Pricing Schemes." *Journal of Transport Economics and Policy* 39 (2): 127–53.

Jagers, Sverker C., and Henrik Hammar. 2009. "Environmental Taxation for Good and for Bad: On Individuals' Reluctance to Mitigate Climate Change via CO2-Tax Vis-à-Vis Alternative Policy Instruments." *Environmental Politics* 18 (2): 218–37. https://doi.org/https://doi.org/10.1080/09644010802682601

Jagers, Sverker C., Niklas Harring, Åsa Löfgren, Martin Sjöstedt, Francisco Alpizar, Bengt Brülde, David Langlet, et al. 2020. "On the Preconditions for Large-Scale Collective Action." *Ambio* 49(7):1282-1296. https://doi.org/10.1007/s13280-019-01284-w

Jagers, Sverker C., Åsa Löfgren, and Johannes Stripple. 2010. "Attitudes to Personal Carbon Allowances: Political Trust, Fairness and Ideology." *Climate Policy* 10 (4): 410–31. https://doi.org/10.3763/cpol.2009.0673

Jagers, Sverker C., and Simon Matti. 2018. "Climate Policy Support in a Comparative Perspective: Exploring the Meaning and Significance of Political-Economic Contexts in Sweden and Norway." *Environmental Politics*.

Johansson Sevä, Ingemar, and Joakim Kulin. 2018. "A Little More Action, Please: Increasing the Understanding about Citizens' Lack of Commitment to Protecting the Environment in Different National Contexts." *International Journal of Sociology* 48 (4): 314–39. https://doi.org/10.1080/00207659.2018.1515703

Kallbekken, Steffen, Jorge H. Garcia, and Kristine Korneliussen. 2013. "Determinants of Public Support for Transport Taxes." *Transportation Research Part A: Policy and Practice* 58: 67–78. https://doi.org/10.1016/j.tra.2013.10.004

Kallbekken, Steffen, and Håkon Sælen. 2011. "Public Acceptance for Environmental Taxes: Self-Interest, Environmental and Distributional Concerns." *Energy Policy* 39 (5): 2966–73. https://doi.org/10.1016/j.enpol.2011.03.006

Kamieniecki, Sheldon. 1995. *Political Parties and Environmental Policy. Environmental Politics and Policy: Theories and Evidence.* Durham, NC: Duke University Press.

Kaufman, Herbert. 1960. *The Forest Ranger: A Study in Administrative Behavior.* Washington, DC: Resources for the Future.

Kellstedt, Paul M., Sammy Zahran, and Arnold Vedlitz. 2008. "Personal Efficacy, the Information Environment, and Attitudes toward Global Warming and Climate Change in the United States." *Risk Analysis* 28 (1): 113–26. https://doi.org/10.1111/j.1539-6924.2008.01010.x

Kenny, John. 2018. "The Role of Economic Perceptions in Influencing Views on Climate Change: An Experimental Analysis with British Respondents." *Climate Policy* 18 (5): 581–92. https://doi.org/10.1080/14693062.2017.1414026

Koletsou, Alexia, and Rebecca Mancy. 2011. "Which Efficacy Constructs for Large-Scale Social Dilemma Problems Individual and Collective Forms of Efficacy and Outcome Expectancies in the Context of Climate Change Mitigation." *Risk Management* 13 (4): 184–208. https://doi.org/10.1057/rm.2011.12

Krasner, Stephen D. 1983. *International Regimes.* Ithaca, N.Y: Cornell University Press.

Lægreid, Ole Martin, and Marina Povitkina. 2018. "Do Political Institutions Moderate the GDP-CO 2 Relationship?" *Ecological Economics* 145: 441–50. https://doi.org/10.1016/j.ecolecon.2017.11.014

Laffont, Jean-Jacques. 2008. "Externalities." In *The New Palgrave Dictionary of Economics: Volume 1–8*, edited by Steven N. Durlauf and Lawrence E. Blume, 1998–2000. London: Palgrave Macmillan.

Leal, Donald R. 1994. "Freedom and the Environment: Reply to Critics." *Critical Review* 8 (3): 461–65. https://doi.org/10.1080/08913819408443352

Letki, Natalia. 2006. "Investigating the Roots of Civic Morality: Trust, Social Capital, and Institutional Performance." *Political Behavior* 28 (4): 305–25. https://doi.org/10.1007/s11109-006-9013-6

Levi, Margaret. 1997. *Consent, Dissent, and Patriotism.* Cambridge: Cambridge University Press.

Levi, Margaret, and Laura Stoker. 2000. "Political Trust and Trustworthiness." *Annual Review of Political Science* 3 (1): 475–507. https://doi.org/10.1146/annurev.polisci.3.1.475

Lewis, David E. 2007. "Testing Pendleton's Premise: Do Political Appointees Make Worse Bureaucrats?" *Journal of Politics* 69 (4): 1073–88. https://doi.org/10.1111/j.1468-2508.2007.00608.x

Linde, S. 2018. "Communication and Cooperation: A Study of the Relationship Between Political Communication and Large-Scale Collective Action." Luleå University of Technology. http://www.diva-portal.org/smash/record.jsf?pid=diva2:1183224

Löfgren, Åsa, and Katarina Nordblom. 2009. "Puzzling Tax Attitudes and Labels." *Applied Economics Letters* 16 (18): 1809–12. https://doi.org/10.1080/13504850701719660

López, Ramón, and Siddhartha Mitra. 2000. "Corruption, Pollution, and the Kuznets Environment Curve." *Journal of Environmental Economics and Management* 40 (2): 137–50. https://doi.org/10.1006/jeem.1999.1107

Lövbrand, Eva. 2014. "Knowledge and the Environment." *Advances in International Environmental Politics* 108 (50): 161–84. https://doi.org/10.1057/9781137338976

Lubell, Mark, Sammy Zahran, and Arnold Vedlitz. 2007. "Collective Action and Citizen Responses to Global Warming." *Political Behavior* 29 (3): 391–413. https://doi.org/10.1007/s11109-006-9025-2

Mansbridge, Jane. 2014. "The Role of the State in Governing the Commons." *Environmental Science and Policy* 36: 8–10. https://doi.org/10.1016/j.envsci.2013.07.006

March, James G., and Johan P. Olsen. 2004. "The Logic of Appropriateness." In *The Oxford Handbook of Political Science*, edited by Robert E. Goodin. Oxford: Oxford University Press.

Matti, Simon. 2010. "Sticks, Carrots and Legitimate Policies: Effectiveness and Acceptance in Swedish Environmental Public Policy." In *Environmental Policy and Household Behaviour: Sustainability and Everyday Life*, edited by Patrik Söderholm, 69–98. London, UK: Earthscan.

Mauro, P. 1995. "Corruption and Growth." *The Quarterly Journal of Economics* 110 (3): 681–712. https://doi.org/10.2307/2946696

Milledge, Simon A H, Ised K Gelvas, and Antje Ahrends. 2007. *Forestry, Governance and National Development: Lessons Learned from a Logging Boom in Southern Tanzania*. Dar es Salaam: TRAFFIC East/Southern Africa; Tanzania Development Partners Group; Tanzania Ministry of Natural Resources and Tourism. http://www.unece.lsu.edu/marketing/documents/2007July/3aA_01.pdf

Miller, G. 2000. "Above Politics: Credible Commitment and Efficiency in the Design of Public Agencies." *Journal of Public Administration Research and Theory* 10 (2): 289–328. https://doi.org/10.1093/oxfordjournals.jpart.a024271

Miller, Michael J. 2011. "Persistent Illegal Logging in Costa Rica: The Role of Corruption among Forestry Regulators." *Journal of Environment and Development* 20 (1): 50–68. https://doi.org/10.1177/1070496510394319

Min, Brian. 2015. *Power and the Vote: Elections and Electricity in the Developing World*. Cambridge, UK: Cambridge University Press.

Mitchell, Ronald B. 2017. "International Environmental Agreements (IEA) Database Project (Version 2017.1)." University of Oregon. http://iea.uoregon.edu

Møller, Jørgen, and Svend Erik Skaaning. 2012. "Systematizing Thin and Thick Conceptions of the Rule of Law." *Justice System Journal* 33 (2): 136–53. https://doi.org/10.1080/0098261X.2012.10768008

Nistotskaya, Marina, and Luciana Cingolani. 2016. "Bureaucratic Structure, Regulatory Quality, and Entrepreneurship in a Comparative Perspective: Cross-Sectional and Panel Data Evidence." *Journal of Public Administration Research and Theory* 26 (3): 519–34. https://doi.org/10.1093/jopart/muv026

North, Douglass C. 1990. *Institutions, Institutional Change, and Economic Performance. The Political Economy of Institutions and Decisions*. Cambridge; New York: Cambridge University Press.

O'Connor, David. 1994. *Managing the Environment with Rapid Industrialization: Lessons from the East Asian Experience. Development Center Studies*. Paris: Development Centre, OECD.

Olson, Mancur. 1965. *The Logic of Collective Action: Public Goods and the Theory of Groups*. Cambridge, Mass: Harvard University Press.

Ostrom, Elinor. 1998. "A Behavioral Approach to the Rational Choice Theory of Collective Action: Presidential Address, American Political Science Association, 1997." *American Political Science Review* 92 (1): 1–22. https://doi.org/10.2307/2585925

Ostrom, Elinor. 2005. *Understanding Institutional Diversity*. Prinston, New Jersey: Prinston University Press.

Ostrom, Elinor, Roy Gardner, and James Walker. 1994. *Rules, Games, and Common-Pool Resources*. Ann Arbor, MI: University of Michigan Press.

Ostrom, Elinor, and James Walker. 2003. *Trust and Reciprocity: Interdisciplinary Lessons from Experimental Research*. New York: Russell Sage Foundation.

Page, Benjamin I., and Robert Y. Shapiro. 1983. "Effects of Public Opinion on Policy." *American Political Science Review* 77 (1): 175–90. https://doi.org/10.2307/1956018

Pellegrini, Lorenzo. 2011. *Corruption, Development and the Environment*. Dordrecht: Springer.

Persson, Tove Ahlbom, and Marina Povitkina. 2017. "'Gimme Shelter': The Role of Democracy and Institutional Quality in Disaster Preparedness." *Political Research Quarterly* 70 (4): 833–47. https://doi.org/10.1177/1065912917716335

Povitkina, Marina. 2018. "The Limits of Democracy in Tackling Climate Change." *Environmental Politics* 27 (3): 411–32. https://doi.org/10.1080/09644016.2018.1444723

Povitkina, Marina, and Ketevan Bolkvadze. 2019. "Fresh Pipes with Dirty Water: How Quality of Government Shapes the Provision of Public Goods in Democracies." *European Journal of Political Research* 58 (4): 1191–212. https://doi.org/10.1111/1475-6765.12330

Pressman, Jeffrey L., and Aaron B. Wildavsky. 1973. *Implementation. How Great Expectations in Washington Are Dashed in Oakland; Or, Why It's Amazing That Federal Programs Work At All, This Being a Saga of the Economic Development Administration as Told by Two Sympathetic Observers Who Seek to Build Morals*. Berkeley: University of California Press.

Rauch, James E, and Peter B Evans. 2000. "Bureaucratic Structure and Bureaucratic Performance in Less Developed Countries." *Journal of Public Economics* 75 (1): 49–71.

Raz, Joseph. 1979. *The Authority of Law: Essays on Law and Morality*. Oxford: Oxford University Press.

Ringquist, Evan J. 1993. *Environmental Protection at the State Level: Politics and Progress in Controlling Pollution. Bureaucracies, Public Administration, and Public Policy*. Armonk, N.Y.: Sharpe.

Robbins, Paul. 2000. "The Rotten Institution: Corruption in Natural Resource." *Political Geography* 19 (4): 423–43. https://doi.org/https://doi.org/10.1016/S0962-6298(99)00087-6

Rothstein, Bo. 2011. *The Quality of Government: Corruption, Social Trust, and Inequality in International Perspective*. Chicago: University of Chicago Press.

Rothstein, Bo, Marcus Samanni, and Jan Teorell. 2012. "Explaining the Welfare State: Power Resources vs. the Quality of Government." *European Political Science Review* 4 (1): 1–28. https://doi.org/10.1017/S1755773911000051

Rothstein, Bo, and Dietlind Stolle. 2008. "The State and Social Capital: An Institutional Theory of Generalized Trust." *Comparative Politics* 40 (4): 441–59. https://doi.org/doi: 10.2307/20434095

Rothstein, Bo, and Jan Teorell. 2008. "What Is Quality of Government? A Theory of Impartial Government Institutions." *Governance* 21 (2): 165–90. https://doi.org/10.1111/j.1468-0491.2008.00391.x

Rudolph, Thomas J., and Jillian Evans. 2005. "Political Trust, Ideology, and Public Support for Government Spending." *American Journal of Political Science* 49 (3): 660–71. https://doi.org/10.1111/j.1540-5907.2005.00148.x

Sandmo, Agnar. 2005. "The Theory of Tax Evasion: A Retrospective View." *National Tax Journal* 58 (4): 643–63. https://doi.org/10.17310/ntj.2005.4.02

Ščasný, Milan, Iva Zvěřinová, Mikolaj Czajkowski, Eva Kyselá, and Katarzyna Zagórska. 2017. "Public Acceptability of Climate Change Mitigation Policies: A Discrete Choice Experiment." *Climate Policy* 17 (sup1): S111–30. https://doi.org/10.1080/14693062.2016.1248888

Schuitema, Geertje, Linda Steg, and Sonja Forward. 2010. "Explaining Differences in Acceptability before and Acceptance after the Implementation of a Congestion Charge in Stockholm." *Transportation Research Part A: Policy and Practice* 44 (2): 99–109. https://doi.org/10.1016/j.tra.2009.11.005

Scruggs, Lyle A. 1999. "Institutions and Environmental Performance in Seventeen Western Democracies." *British Journal of Political Science* 29 (1): 1–31. https://doi.org/10.1017/S0007123499000010

Shleifer, Andrei, and Robert W Vishny. 1993. "Corruption." *The Quarterly Journal of Economics* 108 (3): 599–617. https://doi.org/https://doi.org/10.2307/2118402

Shwom, Rachael, David Bidwell, Amy Dan, and Thomas Dietz. 2010. "Understanding U.S. Public Support for Domestic Climate Change Policies." *Global Environmental Change* 20 (3): 472–82. https://doi.org/10.1016/j.gloenvcha.2010.02.003

Skaaning, Svend Erik. 2010. "Measuring the Rule of Law." *Political Research Quarterly* 63 (2): 449–60. https://doi.org/10.1177/1065912909346745

Smith, Kevin B., and Christopher W. Larimer. 2018. *The Public Policy Theory Primer.* New York: Routledge. https://doi.org/10.4324/9780429494352

Smith, Steve J, John van Aardenne, Zbigniew Klimont, R J Andres, April Volke, and Sabrina Delgado Arias. 2011. "Anthropogenic Sulfur Dioxide Emissions, 1850–2005: National and Regional Data Set by Source Category, Version 2.86." Palisades, NY: NASA Socioeconomic Data and Applications Center (SEDAC). http://dx.doi.org/10.7927/H49884X9

Sobel, Richard. 2001. *The Impact of Public Opinion on U.S. Foreign Policy since Vietnam: Constraining the Colossus.* New York: Oxford University Press.

Söderberg, Charlotta. 2016. "Complex Governance Structures and Incoherent Policies: Implementing the EU Water Framework Directive in Sweden." *Journal of Environmental Management* 183: 90–7. https://doi.org/10.1016/j.jenvman.2016.08.040

Söderberg, Charlotta, and Katarina Eckerberg. 2013. "Rising Policy Conflicts in Europe over Bioenergy and Forestry." *Forest Policy and Economics* 33: 112–19. https://doi.org/10.1016/j.forpol.2012.09.015

Sønderskov, Kim Mannemar. 2009. "Different Goods, Different Effects: Exploring the Effects of Generalized Social Trust in Large-N Collective Action." *Public Choice* 140 (1–2): 145–60. https://doi.org/10.1007/s11127-009-9416-0

Sønderskov, Kim Mannemar. 2011. "Explaining Large-N Cooperation: Generalized Social Trust and the Social Exchange Heuristic." *Rationality and Society* 23 (1): 51–74. https://doi.org/10.1177/1043463110396058

Soroka, Stuart N., and Christopher Wlezien. 2009. *Degrees of Democracy: Politics, Public Opinion, and Policy.* Cambridge: Cambridge University Press.

Stern, David I. 2002. "Explaining Changes in Global Sulfur Emissions: An Econometric Decomposition Approach." *Ecological Economics* 42 (1–2): 201–20. https://doi.org/10.1016/S0921-8009(02)00050-2

Stiglitz, Joseph. 1998. "Distinguished Lecture on Economics in Government: The Private Uses of Public Interests: Incentives and Institutions." *Journal of Economic Perspectives* 12 (2): 3–22. https://doi.org/10.1257/jep.12.2.3

Stimson, James A. 2007. "Perspectives on Representation: Asking the Right Questions and Getting the Right Answers." In *The Oxford Handbook of Political Behavior*, edited by Russell J. Dalton and Hans-Dieter Klingemann, 850–61. Oxford, UK: Oxford University Press.

Stimson, James A., Michael B. Mackuen, and Robert S. Erikson. 1995. "Dynamic Representation." *American Political Science Review* 89 (3): 543–65. https://doi.org/10.2307/2082973

Strömberg, Håkan, and Bengt Lundell. 2000. *Allmän Förvaltningsrätt*. Malmö: Liber.

Sundström, Aksel. 2015. "Covenants with Broken Swords: Corruption and Law Enforcement in Governance of the Commons." *Global Environmental Change* 31: 253–62. https://doi.org/10.1016/j.gloenvcha.2015.02.002

Sundström, Aksel. 2016. "Understanding Illegality and Corruption in Forest Governance." *Journal of Environmental Management* 181: 779–90. https://doi.org/10.1016/j.jenvman.2016.07.020

Sundström, Aksel, and Tanya Wyatt. 2017. "Corruption and Organized Crime in Conservation." In *Conservation Criminology*, edited by Meredith L. Gore. Wiley Online Books.

Svallfors, Stefan. 2013. "Government Quality, Egalitarianism, and Attitudes to Taxes and Social Spending: A European Comparison." *European Political Science Review* 5 (3): 363–80. https://doi.org/10.1017/S175577391200015X

Switzer, David. 2019. "Citizen Partisanship, Local Government, and Environmental Policy Implementation." *Urban Affairs Review* 55 (3): 675–702. https://doi.org/10.1177/1078087417722863

Taniguchi, Hiromi, and Gul Aldikacti Marshall. 2018. "Trust, Political Orientation, and Environmental Behavior." *Environmental Politics* 27 (3): 385–410. https://doi.org/10.1080/09644016.2018.1425275

Tella, Rafael Di, and Robert MacCulloch. 2007. "Why Doesn't Capitalism Flow to Poor Countries?" *Brookings Papers on Economic Activity*. National Bureau of Economic Research Cambridge, Mass., USA. https://doi.org/10.2139/ssrn.361560

Teodoro, Manuel P. 2010a. "The Institutional Politics of Water Conservation." *Journal / American Water Works Association* 102 (2): 98–111. https://doi.org/10.1002/j.1551-8833.2010.tb10055.x

Teodoro, Manuel P. 2010b. "Contingent Professionalism: Bureaucratic Mobility and the Adoption of Water Conservation Rates." *Journal of Public Administration Research and Theory* 20 (2): 437–59. https://doi.org/10.1093/jopart/mup012

Teorell, Jan, Nicholas Charron, Stefan Dahlberg, Sören Holmberg, Bo Rothstein, Natalia Alvarado Pachon, and Richard Svensson. 2019. The Quality of Government Standard Dataset, Version Jan19. Quality of Government Institute: University of Gothenburg. https://doi.org/10.18157/qogstdjan19

The PRS Group. 2018. *International Country Risk Guide*. New York: Political Risk Services.

Tirole, Jean. 1988. *The Theory of Industrial Organization*. Cambridge, Mass.; London: MIT press.

Torgler, Benno. 2003. "Tax Morale, Rule-Governed Behaviour and Trust." *Constitutional Political Economy* 14 (2): 119–40. https://doi.org/10.1023/A:1023643622283

Tyler, Tom R. 1990. *Why People Obey the Law*. Princeton, NJ: Princeton University Press.

Ujhelyi, Gergely. 2014. "Civil Service Reform." *Journal of Public Economics* 118 (October): 15–25. https://doi.org/https://doi.org/10.1016/j.jpubeco.2014.06.009

Versteeg, Mila, and Tom Ginsburg. 2017. "Measuring the Rule of Law: A Comparison of Indicators." *Law and Social Inquiry* 42 (1): 100–37. https://doi.org/10.1111/lsi.12175

Wallner, Jennifer. 2008. "Legitimacy and Public Policy: Seeing beyond Effectiveness, Efficiency, and Performance." *Policy Studies Journal* 36 (3): 421–43. https://doi.org/10.1111/j.1541-0072.2008.00275.x

Weber, Max. 1978. *Economy and Society: An Outline of Interpretive Sociology*. Berkeley: University of California Press.

Weir, Margaret, and Theda Skocpol. 1985. "State Structures and the Possibilities for 'Keynesian' Responses to the Great Depression in Sweden, Britain, and the United States." In *Bringing the State Back In*, edited by Peter B. Evans, Dietrich Rueschemeyer, and Theda Skocpol, 107–64. Cambridge: Cambridge University Press. https://doi.org/doi:10.1017/CBO9780511628283.006

Welsch, Heinz. 2004. "Corruption, Growth, and the Environment: A Cross-Country Analysis." *Environment and Development Economics* 9 (05): 663–93. https://doi.org/https://doi.org/10.1017/S1355770X04001500

Wendling, Zachary A., John W. Emerson, Daniel C. Esty, Marc A. Levy, and Alex de Sherbinin. 2018. "Environmental Performance Index." Yale Center for Environmental Law & Policy: New Haven, CT, USA. https://epi.envirocenter.yale.edu/

Wilson, John K., and Richard Damania. 2005. "Corruption, Political Competition and Environmental Policy." *Journal of Environmental Economics and Management* 49 (3): 516–35. https://doi.org/10.1016/j.jeem.2004.06.004

World Commission on Environment and Development. 1987. "Our Common Future." Oxford: Oxford University Press. http://www.un-documents.net/wced-ocf.htm

Yamagishi, Toshio. 2003. "Cross-Societal Experimentation on Trust: A Comparison of the United States and Japan." In *Trust and Reciprocity: Interdisciplinary Lessons from Experimental Research*, edited by Elinor Ostrom and James Walker, 352–70. Russell Sage Foundation.

Young, Oran R. 2004. *Regime Consequences: Methodological Challenges and Research Strategies*. Dordrecht: Springer.

CHAPTER 20

INEQUALITY, EDUCATION, AND CORRUPTION

ERIC M. USLANER

CORRUPTION persists over long periods of time. Almost all of the solutions reformers propose are institutional. The "cures" include replacing authoritarian regimes with democracy; the establishment of anticorruption commissions, greater penalties for corrupt officials, and changing the electoral regime to make it easier for voters to punish corrupt leaders.

Each reform has its supporters. New democracies such as Estonia appear to have "conquered" corruption: In 2005, it had a Corruption Perceptions Index (from Transparency International) closer to that of Western countries than to other postcommunist nations (Uslaner 2008, 154). Yet corruption barely budged in most other former countries and remained a dominant way of life in Russia (Karklins 2005; Ledeneva 1998). The history of "machine bosses" in the United States provides evidence that democracy is compatible with corruption. The "boss" of New York (George Washington), "Plunkitt of Tammany Hall" (Riordan 1948, 4–5) "seen my opportunity and I took it" and excelled in collecting "honest graft" (providing jobs and other benefits to political supporters). The journalist Lincoln Steffens (1931, 618) wrote about the political boss of Boston, Martin Lomasny, who promised that "there's got to be in every ward somebody that any bloke can come to—no matter what he's done—and get help . . . none of your law and your justice but help."

None of these institutional reforms will lead to the elimination of corruption. Bad governance stems from social conditions such as inequality and can only be overcome by policies that lead to less inequality. The policy most likely to lead to less inequality is universal public education, which provides upward mobility for ordinary citizens and provides a basis for self-governance. It is not simple to reduce inequality and to provide universal education, which persist over long periods of time, as long as a century and a half. Good governance depends upon a social policy that promotes greater equality, but the impact will not be immediate.

WHY CORRUPTION PERSISTS

Inequality breeds corruption by: (1) leading ordinary citizens to see the system as stacked against them (Uslaner 2002, 181–3); (2) creating a sense of dependency of ordinary citizens and a sense of pessimism for the future, which in turn undermines the moral dictates of treating your neighbors honestly; and (3) distorting the key institutions of fairness in society, the courts, which ordinary citizens see as their protectors against evildoers, especially those with more influence than they have (see also Glaeser, Scheinkman, and Schleifer 2003; and You and Khagram 2005).

Widespread corruption becomes entrenched in a society (Mauro 2002, 16). In an unequal world, people of the dominant group may not see cheating those with fewer resources as immoral (Gambetta 1993). People at the bottom of the economic ladder must play the same game even as they may resent the advantages of the well-off (Gambetta 2002, 55).

As with corruption, inequality is "sticky": Countries that were more (or less) equal in the nineteenth century remain so in the twenty-first century. I use Vanhanen's (1997) measure of the percentage of farms in a country that were owned by families (as opposed to large landholders) in 1878 as the indicator of equality in the nineteenth century and Solt's (2009) measure of net inequality for 2004 (this is the year with the largest number of cases). The simple correlation between the two measures across 35 countries is −0.82.

Income distributions across countries are not widely available in the nineteenth century. The Vanhanen measure is a good approximation. Boix (2008, 207) argues: "The percentage of family farms captures the degree of concentration and therefore inequality in the ownership of land." Easterly and Levine (2012, 15) holds that "the family farm measure from earlier dates since 1858 is a good predictor of inequality today" (cf. Rueschemeyer, Stephens, and Stephens 1992, 139–40; Frankema 2010, 118). Galor, Maov, and Vollrath (2009) show that inequality in the ownership of land led to lower levels of education—and income.

The stickiness of both corruption and inequality are the foundations of what I have previously called the "inequality trap" (and also the "corruption trap," Uslaner 2017, 6–8). The poor become trapped as clients to their patrons in corrupt societies. The well off "redistribute" society's resources to themselves and entrench themselves in power by controlling all of society's institutions (Glaeser, Scheinkman, and Shleifer 2003, 200–1). The poor, who depend upon powerful leaders for their livelihood and for justice, have almost no opportunity to challenge the balance of power (Scott 1972, 149). Corruption stems from inequality and reinforces it.

Glaeser, Scheinkman, and Schleifer (2003, 200) argue:

> inequality ... enables the rich to subvert the political, regulatory, and legal institutions of society for their own benefit.... [I]f political and regulatory institutions can be moved by wealth or influence, they will favor the established.

In addition to the "inequality trap," there may also exist a parallel problem, the "corruption trap." Countries that start out with a high level of corruption will not be able to raise taxes for launching social and educations programs for alleviating poverty because corruption results in a high level of distrust in the ability of the state to collect taxes in a fair and efficient manner and to implement the programs in competent and fair manner. Even people with a preference for more economic equality will refrain from supporting higher levels of public spending (and higher taxes) if they perceive that corruption is high and the competence of administrators is low (Svallfors 2013; Rothstein, Samanni, and Teorell 2012). The countries that have the lowest levels of corruption—and the most extensive school systems—are the most equal, not simply the most democratic.

Corruption is shaped far more by inequality than it is by institutional design. Much of the literature on corruption stresses the need to reform political institutions. Governments also look to structural changes and new institutions to end bad governance. Prominent are anticorruption commissions. Hong Kong residents are called upon to report corruption to the Independent Commission Against Corruption (ICAC). The strong enforcement of this commission is generally credited with the sharp reduction in corruption in Hong Kong (Quah 2013). Yet, anticorruption commissions are often the source of malfeasance (see Uslaner 2008, 212 on Africa and Afghanistan).

A wide variety of institutional reforms are posited to be antidotes to corruption, and I shall discuss them below. Yet the evidence that any of them succeed is limited.

The problem is that corruption levels do not change much over time. Levels of corruption in 2010 (from Transparency International) and 1900 (as estimated from the Varieties of Democracy database. Coppedge et al. 2015) are strongly related: For the 24 countries for which there are corruption estimates in 1900, the R^2 with 2010 correlation is .704 (see Figure 20.1). (I exclude countries that were colonies in 1900 since they did not control their own affairs.)

The persistence of corruption may stem from either factors that do not change (especially factor endowments) or the "stickiness" of social and economic institutions. Structural change is not easy, but institutions are far more malleable than the distribution of resources in a society.

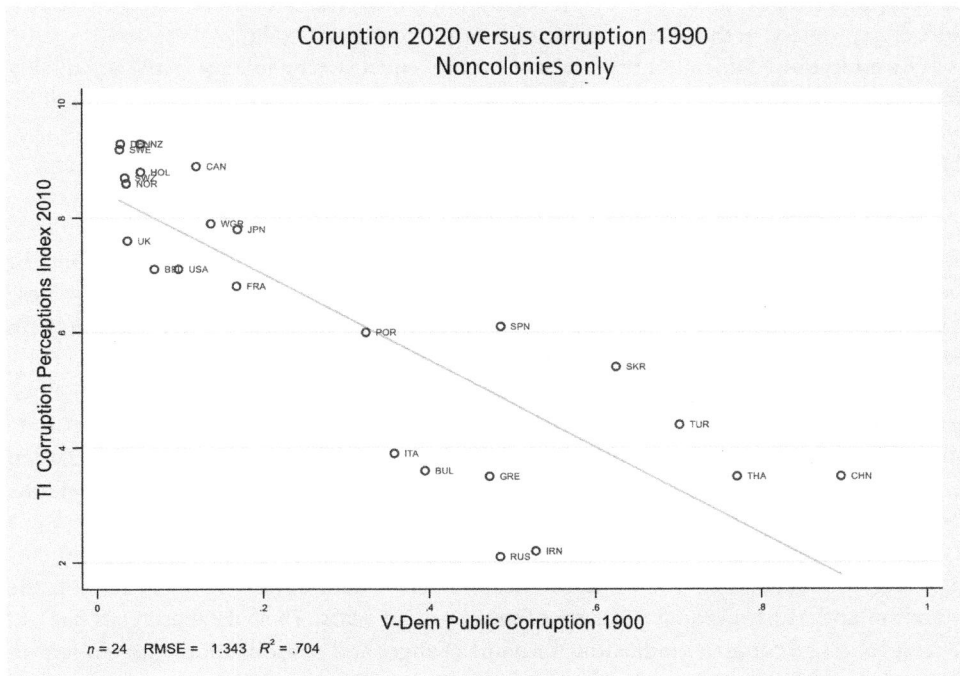

FIGURE 20.1 Corruption 2010 vs corruption 1900

Factor endowments are a society's natural environment: its climate, resources, land, and animals. Areas with temperate climates developed more equal and productive economies, based upon wheat and corn (maize) could be grown by family farmers and wealth would be widely distributed. In "sugar colonies" such as Barbados, Cuba, and Brazil—countries with more tropical climates—economies came to be dominated by large slave plantations and their populations by slaves of African descent. "Where the wealthy enjoyed disproportionate political power, they were able to procure schooling services for their own children and to resist being taxed to underwrite or subsidize services to others" (Engerman and Sokoloff n.d., 6, 13). Natural resources, such as oil or minerals, are easy to steal (Leite and Weidmann 1999). So there may be a "resource curse" of higher corruption.

Yet factor endowments hardly change. Singapore had a hot climate 100 years ago and still does. But it is unquestionably less corrupt. Corruption can be "defeated," but when this occurs, it is part of a broader movement toward more equality (and higher levels of education in a society). This is the role of social policy, notably the introduction of universal public education.

EDUCATION, EQUALITY, AND CORRUPTION

The two "traps" are clearly linked. These parallel trends leave unexplained which policies might lead some countries to become more equal and less corrupt. The universal social welfare program with the greatest effect on corruption is universal education. Universal education, even provided in the "distant" past, leads to less corruption today.

Why education? Education promotes economic equality. The linkage between equality and lower levels of corruption is well established (cf. Uslaner 2008; You 2005). Education promotes the civic values that underlie "good government"—or honesty in government. Education provides the foundation for ordinary people to take part in their governments—and to take power away from corrupt leaders.

Education empowers people to make their own way in the world without having to rely upon clientelistic leaders for their livelihood. When people depend upon "patrons" for their well-being, their welfare is tied to their loyalty. They may "tolerate" corruption by these leaders, either because these "big men" defend them against others who might exploit them even more, or because ordinary people do not have alternative sources of income.

Education also promotes loyalty to the state rather than to local (or tribal) leaders. When governments provide services such as education, people will associate benefits with the state and will be more likely to have a broad sense of solidarity with their fellow citizens (Darden 2013; Peterson 2016; Uslaner 2002, 208), and they will be less likely to cheat (or to condone cheating) their fellow citizens, since they see others as sharing their interests.

There is a strong relationship between early education and contemporary levels of corruption (see Figure 20.2). The earliest indicator of the extent of universal education is the Morrison and Murtin (2009) measure of mean school years. Their database goes back to 1870; it covers 78 countries (adjusting for name changes and consolidations/dissolutions of nations). The R^2 between historical levels of education and corruption in 2010, as measured by the Transparency International Corruption Perceptions Index, is 0.699 across 78 countries. Moving from the fewest years levels of education (01 for four African nations) to the

Corruption 2010 by mean school years 1870

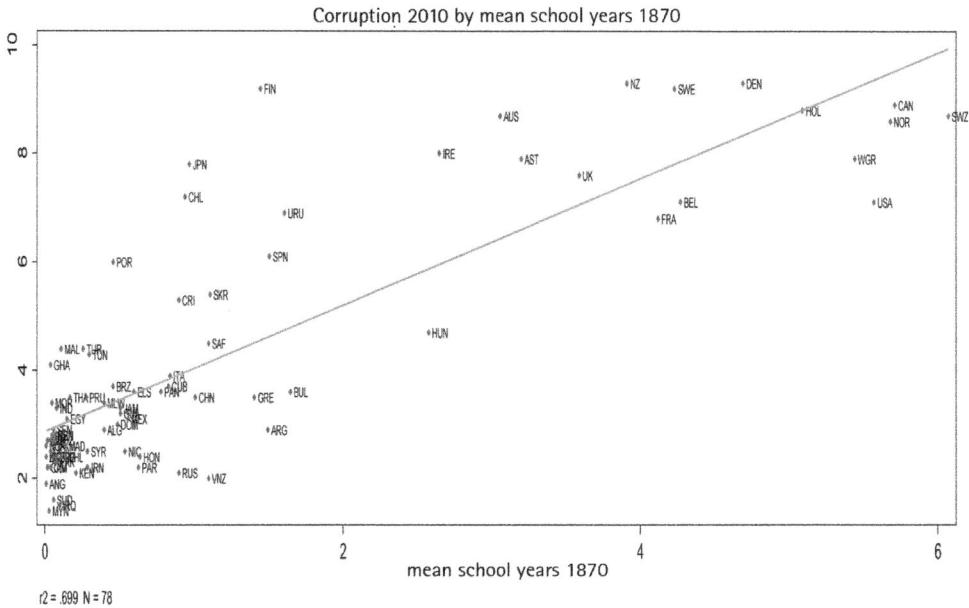

FIGURE 20.2 Corruption 2010 by mean school years 1870

most (67 in Switzerland) leads to an increase in the CPI of 7.0, which is the difference between Angola, the fourth most corrupt country, and Canada, the fifth least corrupt nation.

Universal education implies that every child should attend school. However, there are no comparative data on attendance, so I employ the best proxy, the mean number of years students attend school (which is what others have also used, especially Lindert 2004). Morrison and Murtin (2009, 20) compare estimates of mean school years with the scarce data on attendance and find little to worry about: "Regarding the historical data set, [our] robustness analysis . . . mentions several sources of bias: missing enrolment data, unobserved dropouts, and unknown age pyramids. They turned out to be of modest magnitude." There are data on attendance for the United States from Goldin (2006, 438–46) through 1950 from the United States Census and I interpolate them through 1970. There are only eight cases (1900 through 1970) when there are data from both sources, but the two series—attendance and mean school years—are almost perfectly correlated (R^2=.92; see Uslaner 2017, 111–12).

Other factors that might lead to lower levels of corruption and higher levels of education include democratic institutions. Acemoglu and Robinson (2012, 18–19, 27) argue that political equality, which they see as more important than economic equality, historically triggered a number of important stages of development. Political equality led to political and social stability, which in turn enabled colonies to have stronger economic growth and stability—which led to more widespread public education and especially to "better governance"—including less corruption. Such institutional factors include parliamentary systems which disperse power more widely than presidential systems (Treisman 2007, 22); plurality electoral systems establish a more direct linkage between officeholders and voters than proportional representation (Persson, Tabellini, and Trebbi 2003); closed-list electoral systems which put more emphasis on policy than on providing benefits to voters, such as party loyalty, or effort within the party, as do open-list systems. There are more checks on corrupt leaders in federal systems, where voters may be closer to officials—and where larger shares of a country's budget are spent at subnational levels—than in unitary systems (Fisman and Gatti 2002). There are more checks on corrupt leaders in federal systems, where voters may be closer to officials—and where larger shares of a country's budget are spent at subnational levels (Fisman and Gatti 2002).

Media usage (newspaper readership, newspapers per capita, television sets per capita) should also lead to less corruption by publicizing dishonesty. Countries with greater reliance on trade will be less corrupt, since their economies will be more intertwined with those of other countries. The earlier a country opened its markets, the lower its level of corruption should be.

Mean school years is the strongest predictor of current corruption and is more powerful than a country's wealth, its political institutions (Uslaner 2017, 34–6, 42–8) including the Polity IV measure of democracy in 1870, the years of consecutive democracy, whether a country has always been a democracy, whether a country has a parliamentary or presidential system, district magnitude, whether a country has a federal or unitary system of government, the subnational share of a country's revenue, whether a country has a plurality electoral system (or proportional representation), and the nature of a country's electoral system. It is more important than wealth in 1870, as measured by GNP per capita; imports as a share of the economy, or fuel exports, media usage, factor endowments; or even changes in mean school years from 1870 to 2010 (so that historical levels of education matter more than improvement).

In a regression predicting 2010 levels of corruption, the impact of historical levels of education is 2.5 times that of change in education ($R^2 = 750$). There is evidence of a catch-up effect. Countries with the fewest years of schooling in 1870 (less than two years) had stronger growth in education levels.

But history matters: The correlation between contemporary corruption and levels of education in 1870 is higher ($R^2 = .700$) than between corruption and contemporary mean school years. Countries with high levels of education in 2010 also had more educated publics 140 years ago. Sixteen of the countries with the greatest increase in mean school years were in the 20 most educated countries in 1870; 17 of the 20 countries with the smallest growth in education were among the least educated third in 1870. Aside from changes in education levels, no other factor is significant. These other factors include other measures of factor endowments such as arable land and climate as well as political institutions including press freedom, level of democracy), economic factors (economic inequality, wealth), and demographics (share of population of European origin, share of Protestants), as I show (Uslaner 2017, 42–4).

WHICH SCHOOLING MATTERS

What type of schooling matters? More inclusive education in the latter part of the nineteenth century was more likely to be found where governments, rather than private groups (most notably missionaries), took responsibility for funding and organizing schools—and in countries where there was a greater degree of economic equality. Outside the West, most countries in the late nineteenth century were either colonies or former colonies. The colonies had no control over their own budgets and the colonial powers paid scant attention to educating the public in their colonies. The Protestant churches in Western countries supported public education and worked with the state, financing literary campaigns and promoting public education, even in the less wealthy Scandinavia, lowland Scotland, and Iceland. Before the twentieth century, regions with more Protestant individuals within the same European countries did have higher literacy rates, especially among the lower classes and women (Woodberry 2012).

The Catholic Church invested in education only where it faced competition (such as in Ireland, North America and in the British colonies) or where facing a secularizing state such as France. However, where competition for souls was lacking, education was not a prioritized area for the Catholic Church, as the cases of Italy, Spain, and Portugal clearly show. The Catholic Church feared literacy as this was seen as a means to a Protestant reformation (Gill 1998). Instead, it was the existence of competition for souls and the idea in Protestantism of each individual's access to the word that made education more widespread and equal in Protestant countries. The Catholic Church had a different approach. As the Bible text was read in Latin and hence seldom translated, mass education was not a priority for the Catholic Church, unless it was competing with Protestants or with a secular state.

Historical Education in Western Europe

Universal education began in Europe—first in Prussia. Schooling was more widespread in Protestant Northern Europe than in Catholic Southern Europe. The European advantage over the rest of the world was substantial. The colonial powers mostly invested little in the indigenous peoples they ruled. They provided education mostly to their own citizens—at home. Education was more widespread in Northern and Western Europe, which were also far more equal than Southern Europe. The countries with the highest early levels of education have the lowest corruption scores today. The exception is Finland, which after the Second World War reformed its education system to become a world leader—and has risen to become one of the least corrupt countries in the world.

Education levels were higher in Northern Europe compared to Southern Europe. First, there was more pressure from below in Northern Europe—since land ownership was more egalitarian. Second, Northern European states were generally stronger than those in the South. In the North, the secular state worked with the Protestant Church to provide education to the citizenry. In the South, the Catholic Church was an alternative source of power. The Catholic Church controlled the schools in most Southern European countries.

For the nine countries in the dataset in Northern Europe, the average level of education was 4.5 years (5.1 without the outliers, Finland and the United Kingdom). For Southern Europe (six countries), the mean is 2.1, compared to .47 for the 59 other countries in the dataset excluding the United States, Canada, Australia, and New Zealand.

Northern Europe had higher levels of education because the share of farms held by families was much greater than in Southern Europe—and this equality led to a more widespread provision of public education. Even without a democratic regime, as in Prussia, the peasantry could appeal to the royal courts to reduce their obligations and force large land-holders to provide public education (Lindert 2004, v. 1, 115–23).

The willingness of the Protestant Church to work with the state to promote education was another factor leading to higher levels of universal education in Northern (as opposed to Southern) Europe. Luther's plan to have ordinary people read the Bible (and other books) was essentially egalitarian. Being able to read the Bible in one's own language helped people establish a personal relationship with God (Woodberry 2012). The hierarchical founda-tions of worship and education in Catholic countries reflects the economic inequality in these countries: The correlation between the share of family farms in 1868 with the share of Catholics in a country is .65.

The confluence of forces gave a distinct advantage to Northern Europe. The V-DEM cor-ruption estimate for Northern Europe in 1900 was .55, compared to .33 for Southern Europe, and .51 for other countries (outside the United States, Canada, Australia, and New Zealand).

The new systems of mass education that arose in Denmark, France, Prussia, and Sweden were built on principles that citizenship should be based on universality and egalitar-ianism: One of the most striking aspect of the universalism of the law that established free mass education in Sweden in 1842 was that boys and girls would be treated equally in the new system and that they were to be taught together (Boli 1989, 34, 232).

In Denmark, the church and the state worked together to provide education to all chil-dren: "every child, however destitute, has an inherent and indisputable right to be educated" (Hald 1857, 45). Denmark enacted a law in 1814 requiring that every 14 year-old had to pass an examination to prove that (s)he has "received at least the minimum of education de-manded by law; so that all children are obliged regularly to attend the public school" (Hald 1857, 46) Schools had been run by the Catholic Church until the Reformation in the early six-teenth century, when they were taken over by the state. The Lutheran Church worked with the state to promote universal education.

An exception to the general pattern of more widespread education in Protestant Northern Europe is England. England was the leader in the industrial revolution (Gillard 2011) and it reputedly bequeathed good institutions to its colonies (Acemoglu and Robinson 2012, 18–19, 27). Yet it lagged behind most other European Protestant countries as well as its former col-onies in North America, Australia, and New Zealand in mean school years.

England was an early leader in education but fell behind in the late eighteenth century. Lindert (2004, 113) called the education system a "haphazard system of parish and private ad-venture schools." The upper classes "objected to all forms of education for the poor" Gillard (2011). Schools run by the Church of England refused to allow the children of nonbelievers to enroll.

Even in the first half of the nineteenth century, "the school life of most children was short." As late as 1864, two-thirds of English towns did not have a secondary school. Gillard wrote: "by the start of the nineteenth century, education was organised, like English society as a whole, on a more rigid class basis." In 1911, only 8% of children aged 14–15 were being educated at state schools. By 1938, more than twice as many students went on to higher edu-cation in Germany, France, and Switzerland and over ten times as many in the United States.

Lindert (2004, 113–15) attributed England's poor performance to the centralization of edu-cation funding by Parliament—so that local government had no authority to set their own spending levels. A more compelling explanation is that England was a highly unequal so-ciety in the nineteenth century. Only 5% of its farms were family owned. England stood out as highly unequal in Northern Europe, even more so than its former colonies (the United States, Canada, Australia, and New Zealand).

EDUCATION IN SOUTHERN EUROPE

Education was far less common for children in Southern Europe. The educational system was largely run by the Catholic Church and each society was as hierarchical as the church leadership. The legacy of this inequality is corruption, which persists today from the previous two centuries.

Italy is a prime example of how the Catholic Church failed to promote universal education. Italy introduced a law to promote universal education in 1859, but since Italy was not a unified nation-state, the implementation of the school reform was much more efficient in the northern regions, whereas little was done in the southern regions before 1900. Even as the country adopted universal education by statute in 1859, there was no attempt to enforce the law. In 1870, Italy ranked behind Chile, China, and Russia in mean school years. It also had a highly unequal distribution of land: Only 18% of its farms were family owned in the late nineteenth century. Truancy was rampant and illiteracy was widespread (Clark 1984, 36; di Scala 2004, 161).

There is a similar pattern in both Spain and Portugal, each overwhelmingly Catholic. Spain's education level ranked 19th of the 78 countries, below its former colony Uruguay. Portugal was tied with its former colony Brazil for 42nd. In 2010, Spain and Portugal had CPI scores of 6.1 and 6, respectively, ranking 30th and 32nd. In 1868, 15% of farms in Spain and 20% in Portugal were owned by families. And education was controlled by the Catholic Church.

In Spain, all 6–12 year-old children were required to attend school by a 1901 law. However, poor areas were unable to comply with this requirement, and there was little funding from the central government. In 1940 a quarter of the population was illiterate. There were educational reforms under left-wing governments in 1931–33 (Garrouste 2010, 32), but they were largely reversed when the right took power in 1933.

Portugal had a similar history. It was ruled by António de Oliveira Salazar, a right-wing authoritarian who became prime minister in 1932 and quickly moved to consolidate his power much as Franco did in Spain. Both before and during the Salazar regime, education was controlled by the Catholic Church. A 1844 law establishing mandatory education was never enforced, and a 1911 law mandated only three years of schooling.

Two Catholic countries stand out as exceptions to the argument that the Church stood in the way of widespread education: France and Belgium. Mean school years in the two countries were 4.12 and 4.27. Theytes were among the most equal countries in Catholic Europe with 29 and 22% of farms owned by families, respectively (ranking tenth and 13th). France and Belgium stood out in two other ways: Even though their populations were overwhelmingly Catholic, the state took responsibility for educating children—and the Church had no say in the curriculum. France and Belgium were also relatively free of corruption: Belgium's CPI score was 7.1 (ranking 22nd) and France's was 6.8 (ranking 25th). By 2010, the education reforms in Spain and Portugal in 1910–11 and in the 1930s placed them right below France on corruption, while Italy was ranked lower.

Belgium is (and was) an overwhelmingly Catholic country, but it is divided between Flemish and French speakers. Its levels of equality in the nineteenth century was about the same as the Netherlands (22% of farms were family owned), although it lagged behind the Dutch in mean school years in 1870: 4.27 compared to 5.09. Yet, Belgium's level of education ranked eighth of the 78 countries, behind Denmark and just above Sweden (and also France).

In 1831 Belgium established the "freedom of education," so that anyone—the Church, parents, or other private bodies—could establish a school that would be funded by the state. The state had established religiously neutral schools that were open to everyone and thus competed with Catholic schools (Witte, Craeybeckx, and Meynen 2009, 250). The guarantee of education to every child and the competition between Belgium's linguistic communities promoted widespread education in Belgium. So did the country's history. Belgium had been ruled by the Netherlands prior to 1831, so the newly independent country "inherited" the colonial power's commitment to education.

EDUCATION BEYOND DEVELOPED EUROPE

The pattern of education—and corruption—outside of Europe (and North America, see below)—is varied, but there are commonalities. Some countries were always (or mostly) independent but less well-off, as well as many "countries" in Asia, Africa, and Latin America that were colonies in 1870 or had been ruled earlier in the nineteenth century by European powers. For almost all of these countries, colonies or independent, the story of their nineteenth-century education levels is similar: Relatively small shares of the population were educated and the schools were more likely to be run by religious authorities than by the state. Education by religious authorities was aimed more at indoctrination than at original thinking—or teaching the skills needed for gainful employment. Religious education was usually aimed at establishing the church as an alternative source of power to the secular state—and as an institution that reinforced existing inequalities. Where educational opportunities were restricted, there were also high levels of corruption. In Japan, as in Finland, reform of the education system led to lower levels of corruption (see also the cases of Botswana, Hong Kong, Singapore, and Taiwan in Uslaner 2017, 147–8). For most of the cases below, education levels remain low and inequality and corruption are high—in Turkey, India, Latin America, and especially Africa. In Africa, the legacies of colonialism, inequality, and corruption are especially strong. The exceptions in Latin America are Argentina and Uruguay, where education levels are higher than elsewhere and inequality is lower. In both of these countries, the legacy of colonialism is lower because a large share of the population is of European heritage. Uruguay is the least corrupt of the Latin American countries—because it is the most equal, has a well-developed welfare state, and has placed strong emphasis on universal education.

JAPAN

Japan had a central authority (the shogun), but his authority was limited. From 1603 to 1868, a feudal system run by local lords ran schools that we primarily aimed at the children of the samurai, members of high military castes. Other schools aimed at commoners required parents to pay fees to have their children educated. The local feudal governments did little to promote public education until 1870 (Dore 1964).

A national primary school system was only established in 1872. As late as 1947, only nine years of schooling were required. Education was largely restricted to boys from wealthy families until the end of the Second World War, when the entire system was redesigned under management by the United States. The reform of the education system went hand in hand with broader land reform in Japan, as with South Korea and Taiwan (You 2005). Each of these countries had lower levels of corruption after the reforms were implemented.

TURKEY

Under the Ottoman Empire, which lasted from 1299 to 1922, Turkish society was a highly inegalitarian society, divided between a "ruling elite" and the peasantry. Most schools were religious, run by the Muslim authority, the waqf, and the curriculum was largely religious. The smaller number of secular schools were run by the military. These parallel school systems competed with each other for the few boys (and only boys) who received an education. Only the children of the wealthy were educated. As late as 1928, only 3.7% of the population was in school, with a literacy rate of less than 11% (Frey 1964, 218).

The waqfs were the agencies of religious charity in Islamic societies. The waqf was "an unincorporated trust established under Islamic law by a living man or woman for the provision of a designated social service in perpetuity. Its activities are financed by revenue-bearing assets that have been rendered forever inalienable" (Kuran 2001, 842). These Islamic institutions were essentially private funds, run by wealthy landowners, which provided public services that ordinarily night be run by state institutions (Kuran 2014, 18). At the founding of the Republic of Turkey in 1923, three-quarters of the arable land belonged to waqfs (Kuran 2001, 842). In the Ottoman Empire (Turkey), only 7% of their contributions were devoted to education (Cizakca ND, 34).

The waqfs were unregulated. Assets were extensive—up to half of all real estate in some regions in the Middle East—and sheltered from public authorities, which turned a blind eye in return for bribes (Kuran 2013, 400, 402). Even in contemporary Turkey, the educational system is marked by corruption: In 2010/11 people saw education as the most corrupt government institution. Over a quarter of Turks said that they paid bribes to educational institutions in 2013, compared to 4% in the European Union (Hyll-Larsen 2013, 55).

Corruption persists in Turkey. The V-DEM estimate for corruption in 2012 is .424, not much different from .451 in 1920.

INDIA

India is renowned for its intellectual contributions in literature, science, economics, and many other fields. Yet, it is also a laggard in how widespread educational opportunities are. In 1870, the mean school years for India was lower than Madagascar, Malaysia, or Sierra

Leone. By 2010, average education had risen to levels of Malawi and Nigeria and below Ghana and Myanmar.

The historically low levels of education in India reflect the legacy of colonial rule by Great Britain. Even at Indian independence in 1947, 88% of the population was illiterate. Britain abolished traditional Indian schools (madrasahs or pathashalas) in the nineteenth century and replaced them with curricula imported from England and taught in English and targeted toward the upper castes (Altbach and Umakoshi 2004, 15; Chaudhary 2007, 2). Only one in ten children were enrolled in primary schools in the late nineteenth century, but even by 1941 only a third of eligible children were in school. Male literacy was less than 20% by 1931 and female literacy was below 5% (Chaudhary 2012, 6, 8).

The major factor underlying the low levels of education in India was neglect by the colonial power. Britain simply didn't invest much in public services such as education. When Indians had control over their own services, they were more attentive to people's needs. Iyer (2010, 697) argues that "colonial rulers … set up poor institutions in places where they do not intend to settle over the long term." Britain did not impose direct rule over all parts of its colony, so some areas controlled their own budgets. Iyer (2010, 703) shows that "districts that were part of the British Empire have 37% fewer villages with middle schools, 70% fewer villages equipped with primary health subcenters, and 46% fewer villages with access to good roads."

Colonial government in India, as elsewhere, was more designed to exploit resources for the colonial power than to provide public services or good government for the local population. The legacies of low levels of education were poverty, inequality, and corruption. The level of corruption, from V-DEM estimates, is higher in 2012 (0.568) than at independence (0.269)

AFRICA

Colonial exploitation was most dramatic in Africa, where poverty, inequality, and corruption are pervasive. Africans had an average of .16 years of schooling in 1870 compared to 1.68 for all other countries and 2.88 for noncolonies. The mean corruption score in 2010 is 2.82 compared to 43.91. The 2004 Solt net Gini index is 43.4 compared to 37.3 for all other countries.

Indigenous governments had few resources to spend on public goods—and colonial powers had little interest in providing services such as education. The only source of schooling for most Africans was the support of missionaries. While missionaries were the dominant providers of education, their limited resources and resistance by the local populations meant that only a small share of Africans benefitted from their largesse.

While the British welcomed and facilitated Protestant missionaries, the French were hostile to Catholic missionaries in their colonies and tried to restrict their activities. The French provided few resources for African schools because they wanted to train a small elite to serve as administrators (Frankema 2011, 337). The French saw black Africans as having only "an elementary civilisation," in the words of an Inspector-General in French West Africa (Charton 1970, 97). "The French wanted to develop their Algerian subjects, to assimilate them; the Algerians generally wanted to remain what they were, Algerian Muslims—they did not want to become Frenchmen" (Heggoy 1973, 196). While British officials may have been less openly biased, they were not much more tolerant in their racial views (Bledsoe 1992, 188).

France contributed just 2% of annual revenue for the colonies in French West Africa and just 0.29% was devoted to education (Huillery 2014, 32). The share of government expenditures devoted to education was the same in British Africa (Frankema 2011, 142).

The minuscule support for education by all colonial powers was part of a broader pattern of exploitation. Colonialism led to a "severe deterioration in living standards," a reduction of up to 50%, and a sharp increase in inequality as the colonial powers extracted land, resources, and especially people—sent to the "New World" as slaves (Heldring and Robinson 2012, 3, 19, 21).

Slave exports (Nunn and Wantchekon 2011) are a proxy for the level of inequality in a country. The greater the share of slaves exported, the smaller the change in mean school years over time (as these former colonies became independent). Demography has lasting effects: Countries with large shares of Europeans in 1900 had greater increases (from 1870) in education (in 2010). And mean school year change (as instrumented by slaves exported to the West) shaped contemporary levels of corruption.

Even as some African countries increased their mean levels of education from 1870 to 2010, they did not "catch up" to the more well-off nation. The country with the second greatest gain, South Africa is plagued by the poor quality of its schools. Education spending has increased sharply, but an increasing share of students are repeating grades.

LATIN AMERICA

Latin America is marked by relatively high levels of education and low levels of inequality. Independence for most Latin American countries came earlier than for other colonies, and the major colonial power promoted rather than restricted education. While the English and especially the French invested little in education for their colonists in Asia and Africa, Spain was proactive in promoting education in its colonies. The two countries with the highest levels of European population, Argentina and Uruguay, have relatively high levels of education that track each other closely over time. However, Uruguay has a much lower level of corruption than does Argentina.

Most Latin American countries nevertheless lagged behind the developed countries. Yet, the mean levels of schooling in Argentina and Uruguay in 1870 were almost identical to that of the former colonial power, Spain. Argentina and Uruguay each had 60% Europeans in their populations. Chile followed at 50%—and a mean level of education almost equal to Japan. Costa Rica was not far behind, despite having only 20% of its population of European origin.

Argentina and Uruguay stand out. In both Argentina and Uruguay, universal education was established to integrate immigrants from Europe and to instill a sense of identification with the nation and to create a sense of social solidarity (Ignacio and Hamilton 2005; Arocena and Sutz 2008, 13). Uruguay's 2010 TI Corruption Perceptions Index was 6.9, between that of Belgium and France. Argentina's TI corruption score is 2.9, which puts it barely above the median for former colonies, but below the median for Latin American nations.

Why is Uruguay less corrupt? Neither factor endowments nor institutional design offer satisfactory answers. The two countries are similar in terms of climate and resources. Throughout the twentieth century, they each had periods of military rule and democracy. Buquet and Piñeiro (2014) argue that low levels of corruption in Uruguay reflect the transition from clientelistic to programmatic parties in the 1960s. Yet, Uruguay was less corrupt than Argentina well before the changes in the party systems in the 1960s. The V-DEM corruption score for Argentina in 1900 is .224, compared to .112 for Uruguay. Argentina's score was equal to many African countries, while Uruguay tracked Canada, the United States, and Finland.

A better answer focuses on inequality, which has been consistently higher in Argentina than in Uruguay. In 1870 the Gini index was 52.2 in Argentina and 48.1 in Uruguay. A "pseudo-Gini" index, reflecting income from diverse sources including investments and property, showed greater disparities: 39.1 for Argentina and 29.6 for Uruguay (Williamson 2010 236, 247). Public policy in Uruguay has been more focused on inequality. Uruguay had Latin America's first welfare state, with government control of the railroads, gas stations, water and mail services, and even the production of rum (Krauss 1998). In 1991–2001, the poverty rate in Uruguay was 5.6%, compared to 18.7% in Argentina. Uruguay spent 18% of its GDP in the 1990s on social security and welfare compared to 7.6% for Argentina (Huber and Stevens 2005, 4, 5). It is not surprising, then, that there is less corruption in Uruguay than in Argentina.

SUMMARY

In independent countries, in former colonies—in India, Africa, and Latin America—the levels of education over time stem from historical levels of inequality. Colonialism exacted a particularly strong price. The colonial powers had little interest in providing education or any other social service to the colonists—unless the colonists looked like them (being of European background).

Historical inequality and the failure of the colonial powers to deliver basic services (such as education) have long-lasting effects. Inattention to the needs of the population—through poor governance—sustains itself.

THE UNITED STATES AND OTHER "NEW" ANGLO-AMERICAN COUNTRIES

The United States and other English-speaking former British colonies—Canada, Australia, and New Zealand—offer a key test of the argument that good institutions lead to strong economic growth and to better governance. These four countries—and notably the United States and Canada—had among the highest levels of education by the measure of mean school years.

Acemoglu, Johnson, and Robinson (2001, 1266, 1395) point to democracy and property rights in the United States, Australia, and New Zealand as the keys to success for these countries. They argue that democratic and legal institutions (elections and courts) were the key to understanding why these former British colonies developed good government. We should not be so quick to accept the argument that institutions inherited from Britain were the key to understanding the performance of these countries. First, the institutions of these nations were not uniform. The United States declared independence in 1776. Canada did not become independent until 1865. Australia separated from Britain in 1901. New Zealand statehood emerged in a sequence of events, from a Maori (native) declaration of independence in 1835, the establishment of the country as a British Crown Colony five years later. The institutional foundations of each country's government were different from each other. And each country had greater levels of education than the "mother country" (England)—even before most of these countries "inherited" their institutions from England.

An alternative account is that public education was built upon egalitarian social structures, notably in the United States, without a history of feudalism (Sombart 1976). In 1868, Canada and the United States ranked second and third in the percentage of farms owned by families, behind only Norway. (There are no data for Australia or New Zealand.) The skills learned in public schools furthered economic equality. And they also fostered good governance.

The American public, especially in the Northern states, was willing to tax itself to provide for schools. American education was distinguished by (Goldin and Katz 2008, 133, 166): (1) widespread availability regardless of income; (2) greater gender equality: An almost equal share of girls and boys attended public schools; and (3) the separation of church and state, with a secular rather than religious curriculum.

In the middle of the nineteenth century, states enacted legislation requiring that local districts provide funding for public schools (Goldin and Katz 2008, 161). Between 1830 and 1870, school enrollment rates for 5–19 year-old whites rose from 35 to 61% (Cremin 1980, 178). In the United States, education was perceived as a means for young people to advance into professional jobs that required literacy and rewarded them with middle-class incomes. Education was also seen as the path to good governance.

American inequality was much lower than most other countries, traceable to the lack of a feudal past (Sombart 1976). And there was greater economic mobility: By the early twentieth century, a quarter of young men and women held jobs that required a high-school education or more. Each additional year of secondary school led to gains of 10% or more in salaries. Education was open to both boys and girls. Schools also groomed boys and girls with the "education needed to allow Americans to perform civic duties such as voting and to prepare them to run for office and to lead the nation" (Goldin and Katz 2008, 135–6).

The United States was hardly free from corruption: Most large cities (and many states) were run by political machines (such as those led by Plunkitt and Lomasny). But some places were less corrupt than others. Wisconsin was the home of the major reform movement of the early twentieth century, the Progressives. And reformers saw the solution to the problem of malfeasance to be education: A legislative committee on industrial and agricultural training reported in 1911 (quoted in McCarthy 1912, 148): "We may pass all the resolutions we want to, but the only way to cure political corruption in our cities is to cure it in the way we are stamping out tuberculosis—by education." As education levels rose, political machines became less influential—and the level of corruption in the country declined. The corruption measure is an annual number of mentions of "fraud" and "corruption" in large newspapers across the country from 1816 to 1974 divided by mentions of politics (Glaeser and Goldin

2006). I show (Uslaner 2019, 111–17) that corruption levels decline as school attendance (Goldin 2006) rose and the share of income of the top 1% of the American population from 1913 to 2012 (Saez and Zuckman, 2014) falls.

Corruption and education levels are strongly related in the United States—and what distinguishes the United States, together with Canada, Australia, and New Zealand, are high levels of equality and education—levels greater than the "mother country," England.

IS PATH DEPENDENCE FOREVER?

The strong relationship between historical levels of education and contemporary corruption is evidence of "path dependence," in which the past shapes the present. Is "path dependence" forever? How strongly does history shape the contemporary levels of corruption?

Cross-national educational inequality fell sharply from 1890 to 2010. Most of the countries with low levels of education in 1870 did not catch up to the leaders. There are upward trends in mean school years for every group of countries, but the initial "leaders"—the Anglo-American countries excluding Britain and Northern Europe–showed the greatest increases in education, while African nations lagged behind every other group. And I have shown that the countries that were corrupt in 1900 largely remain the most corrupt in 2010.

Some countries do "beat the system"—they reduce corruption by increasing (or adopting) universal education. The common denominator of most of the success stories is external threat. The first country to adopt widespread education was Prussia. External conflict may (as many of the cases show) destroy the political institutions of countries. So new structures will be established. The redesigned institutions may be better able to provide public services—since political leaders want to establish greater loyalty among the citizenry. In some cases, the institutions may be rebuilt by external forces (such as the American role in restructuring Japanese education after the Second World War). External threats, especially if they have led to war, destroy institutions and test public loyalty. Some countries react to external threat after a major crisis. Others may develop social welfare policies, most notably education, as a political "safety device," to ensure the loyalty of their citizens. Hong Kong and Singapore are the most prominent examples; other such countries include Botswana, Georgia, Hong Kong, Singapore, Taiwan, Barbados, Bhutan, Israel (6.1), Qatar (7.7), Slovenia, and the United Arab Emirates (Uslaner 2017, ch. 6).

Remaining unexplained—and worthy of more detailed study—are countries that have increased education and decreased corruption without external threat. These countries include Barbados, Mauritius, and Slovenia. There is no clear common thread among these countries.

Path dependence is not forever, but it is not common for countries to change course and adopt large-scale social welfare programs such as universal education. The failure to do so explains why bad governance—notably corruption—persists.

REFERENCES

Acemoglu, Daron, and James A. Robinson. 2012. *Why Nations Fail: The Origins of Power, Prosperity and Poverty.* New York: Crown Business.

Acemoglu, Daron, Simon Johnson, and James A. Robinson. 2001. "The Colonial Origins of Comparative Development: An Empirical Investigation." *American Economic Review* 91: 1369–401.

Altbach, Philip G., and Toru Umakoshi. 2004. Asian Universities: *Historical Perspectives and Contemporary Challenges*. Baltimore: Johns Hopkins University Press.

Arocena, Rodgrigo, and Judith Sutz. 2008. "Uruguay: Higher Education, National System of Innovation and Economic Development in a Small Peripheral Country." Lund University Research Policy Institute. www.fpi.lu.se/_mdia/en/research/UniDev_DP_Uruguay.pdf

Bledsoe, Caroline. 1992. "The Cultural Transformation of Western Education in Sierra Leone." *Africa: Journal of the International African Institute* 62: 182–202.

Boix, Carles. 2008. "Civil Wars and Guerrilla Warfare in the Contemporary World: Toward a Joint Theory of Motivations and Opportunities." In *Order, Conflict and Violence*, edited by Stathis Kalyvas, Ian Shapiro, and Tarek Masoud, 197–218. New York: Cambridge University Press.

Boli, John. 1989. *New Citizens for a New Society: The Institutional Origins of Mass Schooling in Sweden*. Oxford: Pergamon.

Buquet, Daniel, and Rafael Piñeiro. 2014. "Corruption and Government Improvement in Uruguay." Presented at the Annual Meeting of the American Political Science Association. Washington, DC. http://papers.ssrn.com/sol3/papers.cfm?abstract_id=2479528

Charton, Albert. 1970. "The Social Function of Education in French West Africa." In *Africans Learn to Be French*, edited by W. Bryant Mumford in consultation with Major G. St. J. Orde-Brown, 97–112. New York: Negro Universities Press.

Chaudhary, Latika. 2007. "An Economic History of Education in Colonial India." http://economics.ucr.edu/seminars_colloquia/2007/political_economy_development/LatikaChaudhary5-6-07.pdf

Chaudhary, Latika. 2012. "Chapter 10: Caste, Colonialism and Schooling: Education in British India." http://papers.ssrn.com/sol3/papers.cfm?abstract_id=2087140

Cizakca, Murat. ND. "Economic Dimensions of Foundations in the Ottoman Era." In *Philanthropy in Turkey: Citizens, Foundations, and the Pursuit of Social Justice*, edited by Davut Aydin, Ali Carkoglu, Murat Cizakca, and Afatos Goksen, 27–42. Istanbul: TUSEV (Third Sector Foundation of Turkey). http://www.tusev.org.tr/usrfiles/files/economic_dimensions_of_foundations_in_the_ottoman_era.pdf

Clark, Martin. 1984. *Modern Italy 1971–1982*. London: Longman.

Coppedge, Michael, John Gerring, Staffan I. Lindberg, Svend-Erik Skaaning, Jan Teorell, David Altman, Michael Bernhard, M. Steven Fish, Adam Glynn, and Allen Hicken. 2015. "V-Dem [Country-Year/Country-Date] Dataset v5." Varieties of Democracy (V-Dem) Project. https://www.v-dem.net/en/data/

Cremin, Lawrence A. 1980. *American Education: The National Experience 1783–1876*. New York: Harper and Row.

Darden, Keith. 2013. *Resisting Occupation: Mass Literacy and the Creation of Durable National Loyalties*. New York: Cambridge University Press.

Di Scala, Spencer M. 2004. *Italy: From Revolution to Republic 1700 to the Present*. Boulder: Westview Press.

Dore, R.P. 1964. "Education: Japan." In *Political Modernization in Japan and Turkey*, edited by Robert E. Ward and Dankwart A. Rustow, 176–204. Princeton: Princeton University Press.

Easterly, William and Ross Levine. 2012. "The European Origins of Economic Development," http://www.nyudri.org/wp-content/uploads/2013/10/European-Origins-Development-Nov2013.pdf

Engerman, Stanley L., and Kenneth L. Sokoloff. n.d. "The Long-Term Persistence of Inequality in the Americas Since European Colonization." Unpublished paper.

Fisman, Raymond, and Roberta Gatti. 2002. "Decentralization and Corruption: Evidence Across Countries." *Journal of Public Economics* 83 (3): 325–45.

Frankema, Ewout. 2010. "The Colonial Roots of Land Inequality: Geography, Factor Endowments, or Institutions?" *Economic History Review* 63 (2): 418–51.

Frankema, Ewout. 2011. "Colonial Taxation and Government Spending in British Africa, 1880–1940: Maximizing Revenue or Minimizing Effort?" *Explorations in Economic History* 48: 136–49. http://dx.doi.org/10.1016/j.eeh.2010.10.002

Frey, Frederick W. 1964. "Education: Turkey." In Political Modernization in Japan and Turkey, edited by Robert E. Ward and Dankwart A. Rustow, 205–35. Princeton: Princeton University Press.

Galor, Oded, Omer Moav, and Dietrich Vollrath. 2009. "Inequality in Landownership, the Emergence of Human-Capital Promoting Institutions, and the Great Divergence." *Review of Economic Studies* 76 (1): 143–79.

Gambetta, Diego. 1993. *The Italian Mafia: The Business of Private Protection.* Cambridge, MA: Harvard University Press.

Gambetta, Diego. 2002. "Corruption: An Analytical Map." In *Political Corruption in Transition: A Skeptic's Handbook*, edited by Stephen Kotkin and Andras Sajo, 69–73. Budapest: CEU Press.

Garrouste, Christelle. 2010. "100 Years of Educational Reforms in Europe: A Contextual Database." European Commission Joint Research Centre. http://publications.jrc.ec.europa.eu/repository/bitstream/JRC57357/reqno_jrc57357.pdf

Gill, Anthony. 1998. *Rendering Unto Caesar: The Catholic Church and the State in Latin America.* Chicago: University of Chicago Press.

Gillard, Derek. 2011. "Education in England: A Brief History." www.educationengland.org.uk/history

Glaeser, Edward L., and Claudia Goldin. 2006. "Corruption and Reform: Introduction." In *Corruption and Reform: Lessons from America's Economic History*, edited by Edward L. Glaeser and Claudia Goldin, 3–22. Chicago: University of Chicago Press.

Glaeser, Edward L., Jose Scheinkman, and Andrei Shleifer. 2003. "The Injustice of Inequality." *Journal of Monetary Economics* 50: 199–222. doi:10.1016/S0304-3932(02)00204-0.

Goldin, Claudia. 2006. "School Enrollment Rates, by Sex and Race: 1850–1994." In *Historical Statistics of the United States, Millennial Edition*, edited by Susan B. Carter, Scott Sigmund Gartner, Michael R. Haines, Alan L. Olmstead, Richard Sutch, and Gavin Wright, 438–46. Online. New York: Cambridge University Press, at http://hsus.cambridge.org/HSUSWeb/toc/showChapter.do?id=Bc

Goldin, Claudia, and Lawrence F. Katz. 2008. The *Race between Education and Technology.* Cambridge, MA: Belknap Press.

Hald, Ernhard. 1857. "On National Education in Denmark." Presented to the National Statistical Society. http://books.google.com/books/about/On_National_Education_in_Denmark.html?id=WUnocQAACAAJ

Heggoy, Alf Andrew. 1973. "Education in French Algeria: An Essay on Cultural Conflict." *Comparative Education Review* 17 (2): 180–97.

Heldring, Leander, and James A. Robinson. 2012. "Colonialism and Economic Development in Africa." National Bureau of Economic Research Working Paper 18566, http://www.nber.org/papers/w18566

Huber, Evelyne, and John D. Stephens. 2005. "Successful Social Policy Regimes? Political Economy, Politics, and the Structure of Social Policy in Argentina, Chile, Uruguay, and Costa Rica." *Conference on Democratic Governability*. Kellogg Institute, University of Notre Dame, October 7–8, 2005. https://kellogg.nd.edu/faculty/research/pdfs/huber.pdf

Huillery, Elise. 2014. "The Black Man's Burden: The Cost of Colonization of French West Africa." *Journal of Economic History* 74 (1): 1–38.

Hyll-Larsen, Peter. 2013. "Free or Fee: Corruption in Primary School Admisisons." In *Transparency International, Global Corruption Report: Education*. Oxon, UK: Routledge.

Ignacio, Jose, and Garcia Hamilton. 2005. "Historical Reflections on the Splendor and Decline of Argentina." *Cato Journal* 25 (3): 521–40.

Iyer, Lakshmi. 2010. "Direct Versus Indirect Colonial Rule in India." *Review of Economics and Statistics* 92 (4): 693–713.

Karklins, Rasma. 2005. *The System Made Me Do It: Corruption in Post-Communist Societies*. Armonk. New York: M.E. Sharpe.

Krauss, Clifford. 1998. "The Welfare State Is Alive, if Besieged, in Uruguay." *New York Times*, May 3, 1998. http://www.nytimes.com/1998/05/03/world/the-welfare-state-is-alive-if-besieged-in-uruguay.html

Kuran, Timur. 2001. "The Provision of Public Goods under Islamic Law: Origins, Impact, and Limitations of the Waqf System." *Law and Society Review* 35 (4): 841–98.

Kuran, Timur. 2013. "The Political Consequences of Islam's Economic Legacy." *Philosophy and Social Criticism* 39 (4) (May): 395–405.

Kuran, Timur. 2014. "Institutional Roots of Authoritarian Rule in the Middle East: Civic Legacies of the Islamic Waqf." Economic Research Initiatives at Duke Working Paper 171. http://ssrn.com/abstract=2449569

Ledeneva, Alena. 1998. *Russia's Economy of Favours*. Cambridge: Cambridge University Press.

Leite, Carlos, and Jens Weidmann. 1999. "Does Mother Nature Corrupt? Natural Resources, Corruption, and Economic Growth?" Washington: International Monetary Fund Working Paper WP. https://www.imf.org/external/pubs/ft/wp/1999/wp9985.pdf

Lindert, Peter. 2004. *Growing Public: Social Spending and Economic Growth since the Eighteenth Century*. 2 vols. New York: Cambridge University Press.

Mauro, Paolo. 2002. "The Effects of Corruption on Growth and Public Expenditure." In. *Political Corruption*, 3rd ed., edited by Arnold Heidenheimer and Michael Johnston, 339–52. New Brunswick, NJ: Transaction.

McCarthy, Charles. 1912. *The Wisconsin Idea*. New York: Macmillan.

Morrison, Christian, and Fabrice Murtin. 2009. "The Century of Education." *Journal of Human Capital* 3 (1): 1–42.

Nunn, Nathan, and Leonard Wantcheckon. 2011. "The Slave Trade and the Origins of Mistrust in Africa." *American Economic Review* 101 (7): 3221–52.

Persson, Torsten, Guido Tabellini, and Francesco Trebbi. 2003. "Electoral Rules and Corruption," *Journal of the European Economic Association* 1 (4): 958–89.

Peterson, Brenton D. 2016. "Kikuyu or Kenyan? Government Service Provision and the Salience of Ethnic Identities." http://papers.ssrn.com/sol3/papers.cfm?abstract_id=2773896

Quah, Jon S.T. 2013. "Curbing Corruption and Enhancing Trust in Government." In *Handbook of Asian Criminology*, edited by Jianhong Liu, Bill Hebenton, and Susyan Jou, 25–48. New York: Springer.

Riordan, William. 1948. *Plunkitt of Tammany Hall*. New York: Alfred A. Knopf.

Rothstein, B., Samanni, M., and Teorell, J. 2012. "Explaining the welfare state: Power resources vs. the Quality of Government." *European Political Science Review* 4 (1): 1–28.

Rueschemeyer, Dietrich, Evelyne Huber Stephens, and John D. Stephens. 1992. *Capitalist Development and Democracy*. Chicago: University of Chicago Press.

Saez, Emmanuel and Gabriel Zucman. 2014. "Wealth Inequality in the United States Since 1913: Evidence from Capitalized Income Tax Data." National Bureau of Economic Research Working Paper. http://www.nber.org/papers/w20625.

Scott, James C. 1972. *Comparative Political Corruption*. Englewood Cliffs, NJ: Prentice-Hall.

Solt, Frederick. 2009. "Standardizing the World Income Inequality Database." *Social Science Quarterly* 90 (2): 231–42.

Sombart, Werner. 1976. *Why Is There No Socialism in the United States?* White Plains: M.E. Sharpe.

Steffens, Lincoln. 1931. *The Autobiography of Lincoln Steffens*. New York: Literary Guild.

Svallfors, Stefan. 2013. "Government Quality, Egalitarianism, and Attitudes to Taxes and Social Spending: A European Comparison." *European Political Science Review* 5 (3): 363–80.

Treisman, Daniel. 2007. "What Have We Learned About the Causes of Corruption from Ten Years of Cross-National Empirical Research?" *Annual Review of Political Science* 10: 211–44. doi: 10.1146/annurev.polisci.10.081205.095418.

Uslaner, Eric M. 2002. *The Moral Foundations of Trust*. New York: Cambridge University Press.

Uslaner, Eric M. 2008. *Corruption, Inequality, and the Rule of Law*. New York: Cambridge University Press.

Uslaner, Eric M. 2017. *The Historical Roots of Corruption*. New York: Cambridge University Press.

Vanhanen, Tatu. 1997. *Prospects of Democracy: A Study of 172 Countries*. London: Routledge.

Williamson, Jeffrey G. 2010. "Five Centuries of Latin American Income Inequality." *Revista de Historia Económica /Journal of Iberian and Latin American Economic History* 28 (2): 227–52.

Witte, Els, Jan Craeybeckx, and Alain Meynen. 2009. *Political History of Belgium: From 1830 Onwards*. Brussels, Belgium: ASP-Academic and Scientific Publishers.

Woodberry, Robert D. 2012. "The Missionary Roots of Liberal Democracy." *American Political Science Review* 106 (2): 244–74.

You, Jong-sung. 2005. "A Comparative Study of Income Inequality, Corruption, and Social Trust: How Inequality and Corruption Reinforce Each Other and Erode Social Trust." Unpublished Ph.D. dissertation (draft). Department of Government, Harvard University.

You, Jong-sung, and Sanjeev Khagram. 2005. "A Comparative Study of Inequality and Corruption." *American Sociological Review* 70 (1): 136–57.

PART V

INTERNATIONAL POLICIES AND GLOBAL STRATEGIES

....

CHAPTER 21

FOREIGN AID AND QUALITY OF GOVERNMENT

....

SIMONE DIETRICH AND MATTHEW S. WINTERS

INTRODUCTION

....

UNDER what conditions does foreign aid improve quality of government (QoG) in recipient countries? Does QoG enhance the effectiveness of foreign aid, and if so, should donors target their aid based on QoG? During the Cold War, aid agencies largely ignored questions of governance, anticorruption, and transparency in their decision-making. Since the mid-1990s, however, these concepts have become central to policymaking in the development sphere, yielding a multitude of aid projects and programs aimed at strengthening QoG in poor countries and an impulse toward selectivity on QoG characteristics in aid allocation. Empirical research both has laid the foundation for some of this real-world decision-making and also has examined the extent to which donor actions match with their announced intentions.

This chapter begins with a historical account of how scholars and practitioners have interacted over time: donor efforts in promoting aid effectiveness or QoG in recipient countries have responded to the creation of systematic evidence, while scholars have identified research questions by looking at practical challenges faced by the development community.

Then we review empirical scholarship interested in uncovering the conditions under which aid improves growth and development. One prominent claim in the aid effectiveness literature is that aid leads to growth in countries with high QoG. More recent literature, however, has called into question the robustness of evidence for this claim. The initial finding nonetheless has motivated donor agencies to condition aid policy and delivery on QoG, spurring further research that aims to understand how QoG levels shape decision-making about foreign aid. This research agenda has been productive for better understanding the behavior of aid agencies, and there are areas for further development. One concern raised by development practitioners and academics alike is that foreign aid flows might undermine QoG. We review this literature, noting the mixed evidence and the analytical challenges to reaching firm conclusions. We argue that this literature needs to move forward with collecting new measures of and data on the alleged mechanisms by which aid supports or hinders growth in QoG.

QUALITY OF GOVERNMENT, FOREIGN
AID EFFECTIVENESS, AND FOREIGN AID
DECISION-MAKING

Historically, foreign aid has served a dual purpose of trying to achieve strategic goals desired by the wealthy countries of the world while also looking to support economic development in aid-receiving countries (Morgenthau 1962). The earliest theories of how foreign aid would spur economic development were largely mechanical, assuming that there was a financing gap created by low savings rates that foreign aid could fill, quickly propelling poor countries into a self-sustaining circle of economic growth (Easterly 2006). Given strategic motivations and a simple theory of foreign aid effectiveness, aid agencies during the Cold War largely ignored questions of governance, anticorruption, and transparency in their decision-making.

In the 1980s, the structural adjustment era was characterized by the idea that foreign aid could be used to incentivize good economic policies, defined as policies that limited the role of the state in economic management (Williamson 1990; Mosley, Harrigan, and Toye 1991). Structural adjustment lending allowed borrowing countries to reduce fiscal imbalances, while conditions attached to the loans required the governments to dismantle state structures and implement market-oriented policies such as deregulation and privatization. The underlying logic was that market-friendly policies, macroeconomic stability, and openness to trade would enable a transition to development (World Bank 2005).

Yet by the early 1990s, this new theory of how foreign aid could be used to promote growth had been thoroughly challenged by the setbacks experienced by developing countries over the previous decade (Boone 1996; Easterly 2005). One dominant reaction was to insist that the failure had been one of implementation, not of policy design (World Bank 1989; Mosley, Harrigan, and Toye 1991; Killick, Gunatilaka, and Marr 1998; Dollar and Svensson 2000; Svensson 2003). These discussions raised the issue of the extent to which political elites in aid-receiving countries were interested in promoting economic growth or rather were simply seeking rents. Other scholars pointed to donor failures to contextualize the reforms (Rodrik 2006) or the difficulties of donors actually enforcing the conditions contained in structural adjustment programs (Easterly 2005).

The shortcomings of structural adjustment and the end of the Cold War opened the door to increased attention to the on-the-ground politics in developing countries. As early as 1989, the World Bank described the underlying development problem in Africa as a "crisis of governance" (World Bank 1989). It began to dawn on practitioners that structural adjustment programs could not produce lasting effects when recipient QoG was poor. In 1990, the World Banks general counsel issued a legal memorandum to its Board of Directors that set out a framework for dealing with the issue of governance "as prelude to any future analysis of the manner in which the WB may take it on operationally" (Lateef 2016). This was a clear signal from the world's leading development actor that QoG should be a part of the language of development (Weaver 2008; Winters and Kulkarni 2014). By 1997, the World Bank`s flagship publication, the *World Development Report*, reflected this major shift in thinking: that year, the report focused on the central role of the state in development and noted the need to reinvigorate public institutions that had been dismantled by structural reforms; the report also highlighted the importance of effective rules and restraints, competitive pressures from within the civil service and outside, and increased citizen's voice and participation (World Bank 1997).

The end of the Cold War also meant that, with less strategic motivation for aid, aid budgets started to decline. This incentivized aid agencies to think more deeply about how to demonstrate that foreign aid could be effective. As a result of the studies that we describe in the next section, from the mid-1990s, the governance agenda grew significantly. No longer focused only on strengthening the state, development actors interested in QoG looked also at democratization, security, justice, strengthening civil society, and much more. Still riding the wave of euphoria that followed the fall of communism and recent democratization trends in sub-Saharan Africa and Latin America, international development actors contributed financing for elections, independent courts, and representative parliaments, among other institutions, recognizing the centrality of politics in development.[1]

Evidence on the link between QoG and foreign aid

One component of the intellectual trends undergirding policy changes in the development community during the 1990s was the increased interest in institutions in economics and political science. Advances by North (1990), Ostrom (1990), Tilly (1990), and Evans (1995) on the importance of institutions for growth and development influenced the debate on foreign aid effectiveness. In a seminal study originally circulated as a World Bank working paper in 1997 as background to the *Assessing Aid* report (World Bank 1998), Burnside and Dollar (2000) represents the seminal quantitative attempt at evaluating the role of sound macroeconomic policies for aid effectiveness. They measure sound macroeconomic policies based on the level of inflation, the size of the budget deficit, and the degree of trade openness. Looking at the period from 1973 to 1993, they find that foreign aid is effective at promoting growth *but only when policies are good* (i.e., when inflation and budget deficits are relatively low and when the country is relatively open to trade).[2] This finding seemed to confirm an emerging consensus about the centrality of good policy in the aid effectiveness debate. It also motivated central players in the aid area, like the World Bank, to recommend that donor governments and their aid agencies condition aid policy on the soundness of recipients' macroeconomic foundations (Pronk 2001). In the 1998 *Assessing Aid* report, the World Bank went as far as suggesting that "an increase of USD 10 billion in aid, favoring countries with sound management, would lift 25 million people per year out of poverty. By contrast, an across the board increase would lift only 7 million out of poverty" (World Bank 1998, 16).

---

[1] Although we do not review it here, there is a substantial body of work that examines the link between foreign aid and democratic change in recipient countries; see, for example, Finkel, Pérez-Liñán, and Seligson (2007), Wright (2009), Bermeo (2011), Kersting and Kilby (2014), and DiLorenzo (2018) and the review in Dijkstra (2018).

[2] In a subsequent working paper, Burnside and Dollar (2004) more directly focused on "institutional quality" as the key moderating variable, finding strong empirical support in their data for the idea that aid leads to economic growth in the presence of QoG (defined as the average of the six indicators that today are known as the Worldwide Governance Indicators).

The initial Burnside and Dollar (2000) finding of a conditional effect of aid on growth was widely cited in the practitioner community and used to justify the emerging focus on governance in the realm of aid-giving.[3] To identify the causal effect of aid on growth, Burnside and Dollar (2000)—building on Boone (1996)—included a set of instrumental variables in a first-stage equation: population, arms imports, and indicators for Egypt, membership in the Franc zone, and Central American countries. They argue that these variables will predict variation in aid flows that is exogenous to economic growth, allowing them to capture the causal effects of aid.

Work that replicates Burnside and Dollar (2000) (e.g., Easterly, Levine, and Roodman 2004) has tended to use these same instruments. It is easy, however, to imagine violations of the exclusion restriction. Arms imports and the Central America indicator are meant to proxy for an aid-receiving country's strategic importance, something that should increase aid flows. Insofar as these measures proxy for armed conflict, however, it is easy to imagine that conflict affecting growth through a channel that does not involve foreign aid—a violation of the exclusion restriction (Wright and Winters 2010). These concerns have led some authors to eschew instrumental variables completely and argue that the best that we can do is attempt to model plausible time frames in which aid might have had an effect (Clemens et al. 2012).

From the perspective of causal identification, the literature needs more attempts to find exogenous variation in aid. Galiani et al. (2017) treat countries losing access to funding from the International Development Association (IDA), the World Bank's concessional lending wing, as exogenous to growth in a small window around an eligibility threshold. They estimate a significant relationship between aid and growth by studying differences in countries that have remained eligible for IDA financing and those that have lost eligibility. These authors do not, however, look at whether or not this affect is moderated by QoG. Carnegie and Marinov (2017) study the effects of aid flows associated with rotation in the European Union Council presidency on human rights and democracy (but not on economic growth). Like Galiani et al. (2017), they identify a specific process that predicts aid increases and decreases and study the effects of those changes in aid. The literature on how QoG moderates aid effectiveness needs to engage with these creative attempts to identify exogenous variation in aid.

The original Burnside and Dollar (2000) spurred numerous studies that investigate the robustness of the finding. The subsequent evidence suggests that the conditional effect where foreign aid promotes growth only under good policies is not, in fact, robust to different data or model specifications (Hansen and Tarp 2000; Lensink and White 2000; Easterly, Levine, and Roodman 2004; Roodman 2007; Rajan and Subramanian 2008; Clemens et al. 2012).

Ultimately, however, the donor community took the original Burnside and Dollar (2000) finding to heart insofar as it supported the practice of conditionality in foreign aid-giving, where tranched foreign aid is disbursed only as aid-receiving countries meet a set of prespecified conditions. This form of aid rewards countries for taking strong measures to

---

[3] It also inspired scholarship to theorize beyond the conditioning effect of good policies. Kosack and Tobin (2006), for example, find that aid is effective at promoting human development in recipient countries that exhibit higher levels of human capital; the authors understand higher human capital as representing government preferences for spending on human development.

promote sound macroeconomic policies as identified by the donor (Gwin and Nelson 1997; Girod 2018).

Despite the failures of structural adjustment conditionality in the 1980s, there is some evidence that donors who seek to promote development have become more vigilant about implementing conditionality since the 1990s (Dunning 2004; Bearce and Tirone 2010; Dietrich and Wright 2015, Dietrich 2017). Ultimately, however, the efficacy of aid as a tool for promoting good policy and QoG depends not only on donors and their development orientation but also on the interests of recipient governments (Mosley, Harrigan, and Toye 1991; Collier et al. 1997; Killick, Gunatilaka, and Marr 1998). Policy conditionality only works if foreign aid succeeds in realigning domestic incentives in favor of reform. Empirical evidence suggests that donor`s ability to realign government incentives depends on conditions in the recipient country. For example, in a study about recipient compliance with World Bank conditionality, Girod and Tobin (2016) find that governments that are more dependent on donor assistance to stay in power are more likely to comply with the World Bank`s conditions than those who are less dependent and have more non-aid revenue at their disposal.

Aid selectivity

Many scholars and aid industry practitioners alike remain skeptical of the possibilities of policy conditionality (Collier et al. 1997). An alternative to using policy conditionality is allocating aid to countries that *already* have a good QoG record, having demonstrated effort in the context of institutional reform and development. Collier and Dollar (2002), for example, posit that outcome-oriented donors should condition their aid flows on the policies of aid recipients. This type of conditioning of aid flows on existing characteristics of aid-receiving countries is known as selectivity.

Beyond good policy, scholars and practitioners have expanded the criteria for selectivity to include broader measures of QoG that proxy government effort and capacity to reform, including corruption, rule of law, regulatory quality, and government effectiveness, as well as political rights, liberties, and institutions. For example, the World Bank`s "Country Policy and Institutional Assessment" index rates developing countries on indicators along four dimensions including macroeconomic and structural policies, as well as social policies, and public sector management and institutions.

What does the evidence say about the extent to which donors implement selectivity? Consistent with Collier and Dollar (2002), early works that examine foreign aid allocation patterns during the Cold War do not find evidence for donor selectivity with regard to policy or institutions. Neither bilateral nor multilateral donors, on average, systematically reduce aid flows when corruption in aid recipient countries is high (Svensson 2000; Alesina and Weder 2002; Neumayer 2003).

On the other hand, when scholars expand the temporal domain or focus only on the post–Cold War period, the empirical evidence shows increasing evidence of selectivity. A series of papers show that, starting in the 1990s, donors begin, on average, to systematically reward sound macroeconomic policy or a good governance environment with more aid (Berthélemy and Tichit 2004; Dollar and Levin 2006; Bandyopadhyay and Wall 2007; Claessens, Cassimon, and Van Campenhout 2009; Knack, Rogers, and Heckelman 2012; Annen and Knack 2018).

The literature reveals, however, important cross-donor differences in selectivity with some donors being more responsive to policy or QoG when making aid allocation decisions (Schudel 2008; Isopi and Mattesini 2008; Easterly and Pfutze 2008; Clist 2011). Recently, Annen and Knack (2019) find that the proportion of policy-selective aid in the global aid budget varies over time, with substantial increases between 1990 and 2001 from zero to 60%, followed by a steep decline to only 20% in 2014.

In one prominent example, this performance-based view of foreign aid allocation is embodied in the United States' Millennium Challenge Account (MCA) program. Created in 2004, the MCA closely aligns foreign aid funding decisions with a country`s performance on governance dimensions: only countries that meet specific policy and QoG criteria receive the generous aid packages that the institution can offer (Mawdsley 2007; Girod, Krasner, and Stoner-Weiss 2009; Goldsmith 2011). These criteria included quantitative, publicly accessible indicators from a variety of different sources that include corruption control, government effectiveness, rule of law, and/or macroeconomic indicators such as inflation or fiscal policy. According to the MCA, high scores on these indicators signal that a country has assumed responsibility for promoting change and development. While the MCA principle of picking winners may reduce the risk that foreign aid goes to waste, it also excludes many of the world's poorest countries—which do not have a record of good policy or high QoG—from funding.

While the notion of selectivity has traditionally revolved around overall aid allocation to countries with better policies and governance, recent scholarly advances have investigated selectivity for other aspects of donor decision-making. Explicitly recognizing the heterogeneity of aid delivery tools, Radelet (2004) advocates that "aid should be delivered to countries with better governance very differently than to countries with poor governance" (12). In line with this thinking, recent evidence suggests that donors look to recipient QoG when making decisions about the sectors to which they will allocate foreign aid sectors and the modalities through which they will do so.

As argued by Svensson (2000), recipient QoG is linked to the risk of aid capture through agency problems and bureaucratic inefficiencies. Some evidence shows that donors reduce the risk of aid capture in low QoG environments by decreasing the amount of aid over which the government has control, such as programmable or budget aid (Winters 2010; Clist, Isopi, and Morrissey 2012; Winters and Martinez 2015). Others find that concerns about aid capture lead donor governments to alter their aid delivery tactics: when the risk of aid capture is high, as is the case in low QoG environments, donor governments, on average, decrease the share of government-to-government aid, while increasing the share of aid channeled through bypass actors (Dietrich 2013; Bermeo 2018). These bypass actors include international organizations, nongovernmental organizations, and private sector contractors. A recent study by Eichenauer and Reinsberg (2017) finds evidence that the selectivity logic explains why bilateral aid donors sometimes channel resources through multilateral organizations for implementation (what the authors call "multi-bi aid"): when the quality of recipient governance is low, donors increase the amount of multi-bi aid, while decreasing the share of government-to-government aid.

What remains less well understood is how donor governments differentiate among the different possible bypass channels. Are there specific QoG concerns that lead donors to prefer NGOs instead of multilateral organizations? When do donors prefer to use private sector contractors over NGOs? Future research should continue to disaggregate bypass channels to better understand the effect of QoG on the choice among the various nonstate delivery channels.

Recent studies also have revealed that aid donors differ in the extent to which they engage in aid channel selectivity. Comparing the predictive power of recipient QoG (measured as an average of five of the six Worldwide Governance Indicators) across individual donor regressions, Bermeo (2018) finds that, on average, donors condition foreign aid delivery on the quality of governance in the recipient country. Dietrich (2016, 2021) shows that not all donors do so to the same degree. She explains that differences in the use of bypass aid across donor governments result, in part, from differences in governance orientations across donors, as donors hold contrasting conceptions about the role of the state in public sector governance. These contrasting views, in turn, influence their propensity to work with or around the recipient public sector. These findings receive robust empirical support at the level of cross-country spending as well as in data from individual aid agency decision-makers. In the context of multilateral aid, Dietrich, Reinsberg, and Steinwand (2021) find that differences in views about the appropriate role of the state in public sector governance systematically influence funding decisions across different types of World Bank trust funds. The existence of donor heterogeneity in aid delivery may help explain conflicting results in the literature that studies aid flows more broadly and cautions us from generalizing findings found in studies of a single donor.

Finally, the literature on public opinion and foreign aid also indicates that donor publics are selective and condition their support for foreign aid on the quality of governance in the recipient country. Both Bauhr, Charron, and Nasiritousi (2013) and Bauhr and Charron (2018) find that perceived corruption in recipient countries reduces support for foreign aid. Examining selectivity at the level of foreign aid channels, Dietrich (2021) finds that information about low levels of QoG in recipient countries increase support for aid through bypass channels.

THE EFFECTS OF FOREIGN AID ON QUALITY OF GOVERNMENT

As donors became increasingly interested in the possibility that foreign aid effectiveness depends on QoG in aid-receiving countries and the possibility that they might therefore make better use of scarce aid dollars by conditioning their allocation of aid on QoG, the academic community and some practitioners simultaneously began to raise concerns that one of the very reasons for poor QoG in aid-receiving countries might be the presence of aid itself. Some authors went so far as to claim the existence of an "aid curse" akin to the "natural resource curse" (Djankov, Montalvo, and Reynal-Querol 2008), while more recent entries argue that the concern that aid hinders the development of QoG have been overblown (Jones and Tarp 2016; Dijkstra 2018). In this section of the chapter, we describe the theoretical reasons why aid might either help or hurt QoG and the indeterminate state of the existing literature, and then we suggest some ways that the literature might move forward.

Table 21.1 Theorized Links Between Aid and QoG

Mechanisms Connecting Aid to Improved QoG
- (1) Ex ante conditionality (i.e., selectivity)
- (2) Traditional conditionality
- (3) Investment in processes and human capital (i.e., technical assistance)
- (4) Best practice examples in investment projects
- (5) Financing higher salaries for bureaucrats
- (6) Increasing human capital in society
- (7) Survival of reform-oriented government

Mechanisms Connecting Aid to Worsened QoG
- (1) Reduced development of infrastructure for taxation
- (2) Less monitoring and fewer demands for accountability
- (3) Less civil society development
- (4) Debilitating transaction costs
- (5) Decreased human capital in government
- (6) Increased use of patronage in public employment
- (7) Increased rent-seeking behavior among elites
- (8) Increased conflict among elites
- (9) Survival of poor-governance governments

Should aid improve or worsen QoG?

Although the literature on aid and QoG—particularly in the earliest entries (e.g., Knack 2001; Bräutigam and Knack 2004)—has focused on the apparent negative consequences of aid on QoG, there are a number of theoretical reasons to believe that aid should improve QoG. We have outlined seven in the top half of Table 21.1.

First, as described in the previous section, donors might condition their aid-giving on governance quality. While aid selectivity is motivated, on the one hand, by a desire to send aid to environments where it is likely to be used well, it also, on the other hand, serves as a form of conditionality. Insofar as recipient governments know that that donors provide more aid to countries with higher levels of QoG, governments now have an incentive to improve QoG in order to attract foreign development assistance (Mosley, Hudson, and Verschoor 2004). Such a mechanism is contingent on recipient governments believing that their allotments of aid will increase if they undertake governance reforms.

Second, donors have frequently included QoG-related conditionality in their aid programs, requiring the meeting of QoG-related policy and institutional targets in order to release tranches of aid. The threat of losing out on promised resources should incentivize aid-receiving countries to improve their QoG. As mentioned above, however, the evidence suggests that poverty-averse donors frequently have been unwilling to enforce conditionality (Svensson 2003) and that the reforms linked to conditionality are typically achieved only in countries where they would have been achieved even in the absence of foreign aid (Killick, Gunatilaka, and Marr 1998). Recent work has suggested that donors have incentives to tailor conditions in such a way that they appear to imply meaningful institutional change and yet stop short of actually reforming functions and capacities (Buntaine, Parks, and Buch 2017; see also Bräutigam and Knack 2004; Pritchett, Woolcock, and Andrews 2013).

Third, donors have provided significant amounts of technical assistance to poor countries over time, aiming to finance trainings and consultancies that lead to improved governance processes and the presence of more human capital in government. Technical assistance aims to directly improve state capacity by funding the provision of knowledge, tools, and education. On the one hand, stories of technical assistance programs failing to effect meaningful change are widespread (Bräutigam 2000), and as just described, states are known for engaging in "isomorphic mimicry" where—in response to donor demands—they create institutions that look like they will perform a function that they actually do not or cannot perform (Pritchett, Woolcock, and Andrews 2013). On the other hand, several studies of technical assistance have found positive impacts of technical assistance on democratization and QoG (Ear 2007; Gibson, Hoffman, and Jablonski 2015; Jones and Tarp 2016; Ariotti, Dietrich, and Wright Forthcoming).

Fourth, even if not specifically aiming at transferring processes or human capital, the presence of foreign aid investment projects may provide best practice examples of good governance, and this information may diffuse back to the aid-receiving government. If, however, incentives for meaningful institutional change are not in place, then knowledge is unlikely to transfer in this way, as the critics of technical assistance would imply more generally. For example, government officials who are content with the existing state of QoG because they benefit from the rents that are a part of it will not seek out reform-related knowledge (Persson, Rothstein, and Teorell 2013).

Fifth, foreign aid may increase salaries among government officials and thereby reduce QoG problems related to corruption or shirking (Bräutigam and Knack 2004). Higher wages have been shown to reduce corruption in some contexts (Di Tella and Schargrodsky 2003), and insofar as foreign aid funds public sector wages paid to capable workers, aid might catalyze improved QoG.

Sixth, if foreign aid achieves its long-term objectives related to improving education and bringing about economic growth (which also improves education), then levels of human capital in society will increase, giving the government a more capable workforce (Askarov and Doucouliagos 2013; Dijkstra 2018). Assuming that incentives are in place for the government to hire capable workers and for those workers to then provide expected services, foreign aid might thereby indirectly finance improved QoG.

Finally, literature has shown that foreign aid promotes government stability and survival (Morrison 2009; Licht 2010; Ahmed 2012). If a government is reform-oriented, foreign aid inflows may give that government the breathing room that it needs to undertake reforms and improve QoG.

While many in the aid industry spend their time designing reform-oriented aid projects and seeking strategic openings for reform in aid-receiving countries, the literature also has provided a number of reasons as to why aid actually might undermine QoG. These alleged negative impacts of aid have been viewed as "unintended effects" (Dijkstra 2018). We describe nine logics for how aid might lead to diminished QoG—or at least diminished growth in QoG—in the bottom half of Table 21.1.

First, foreign aid flows undercut the need for governments to tax their citizens. In early modern Europe, monarchs in need of revenue created bureaucracies to monitor economic activity and collect taxes from citizens; the need to staff such bureaucracies also encouraged state investment in human capital development (Tilly 1985; Bräutigam 2008). In contemporary low-income countries, foreign aid has supplanted tax revenues and so has hindered state development and possibly human capital development and therefore the development of QoG.

Second, insofar as taxation stimulates monitoring of the government and demands for appropriate government behavior by tax-paying citizens, the absence of taxation makes it less likely that citizens will demand accountability from an aid-receiving government (Bräutigam and Knack 2004; Dijkstra 2018). Without societal demands for accountability, levels of QoG are likely to be lower. Eubank (2012) provides a particularly compelling depiction of such dynamics in a comparison of aid-receiving Somalia to the quasi-state of Somaliland, which has not received aid from the international community and therefore has had to engage in revenue bargaining with local citizens.

Third and relatedly, a lack of mobilization among citizens to hold government accountable implies that civil society more generally is less developed (i.e., that the organizations that try to account for taxpayer dollars in wealthy countries do not exist in poor countries). If this is true, then even a citizenry that wants to monitor or threaten sanctions against a government may lack the capacity for collective mobilization that would allow it to do so.

Fourth, the presence of development industry actors—and particular multiple foreign aid actors—in a poor country may impose debilitating transaction costs on a government that lacks QoG. As donors demand meetings and reports from government officials, those officials may develop skills that are useful for that delimited sphere of action and not useful for provision of overall QoG to the populace (Bräutigam and Knack 2004; Acharya, Lima, and Moore 2006; Knack and Rahman 2007). On the other hand, as described above, interacting with donors in these terms may lead to knowledge and skills transfer that is useful in the long term for governance.

Fifth, if donors hire highly capable individuals to work for their country offices or in nongovernmental or quasi-governmental parallel implementing units that they establish for specific projects, these individuals will not be available to take positions in government or will be distracted from fulfilling their duties (Knack and Rahman 2007). This is particularly problematic because donors typically are able to pay larger salaries than aid-receiving governments. While bureaucrats or would-be bureaucrats may acquire skills through working with donors, the continued career opportunities working with foreign donors makes it unlikely that these skilled individuals will return to work in government, thereby limiting the extent to which they can contribute to improving QoG.

Sixth, while the presence of foreign aid may increase government salaries, as described above, governments can also use foreign aid flows to grow the ranks of government, creating meaningless positions that serve only to provide patronage to favored constituencies (Ahmed 2012). To the extent that foreign aid leads to government bloat, we expect QoG to suffer, as well-meaning and capable staff become less incentivized to do their jobs and citizens have increased difficulty in discovering the right pathways for addressing their concerns through government.

Seventh and relatedly, foreign aid flows can incentivize rent-seeking behaviors among elites (Svensson 2000). Rather than investing in productive activities, elites may seek to gain access to the rents generated by foreign aid. By maneuvering to put themselves in charge of government programs, these rent-seeking elites can undermine QoG by making government more responsive to their individual interests than to societal interests.

Eighth, at an extreme, this rent-seeking behavior might devolve into conflict. If foreign aid flows increase the value of being in control of the state, elite political actors within or outside of the regime will be incentivized to take control of the regime, perhaps through violent means (Grossman 1992; Nielsen et al. 2011). Intrastate conflict makes it more difficult to build QoG.

Finally, in contrast to the idea that aid might foment conflict and as described above, existing evidence suggests that aid may prolong government stability (Morrison 2009; Licht 2010; Ahmed 2012). Above we suggested that this could mean that aid facilitates institution building by keeping a reform-oriented government in power; however, it is equally plausible that aid—to the extent it prolongs government survival—may keep an anti-reform government in power, thereby preventing the development of QoG in a low-QoG country.

What does the evidence about aid's effects on QoG say?

As described above, some of the most prominent entries in the literature addressing aid's effects on QoG paint a rather negative portrait. In his seminal article, Knack (2001) finds "evidence that higher aid levels erode the quality of governance" (defined as the sum of three measures from the International Country Risk Guide dataset) while Djankov, Montalvo, and Reynal-Querol (2008) conclude that "aid has a negative impact on institutions" (defined as the measure of checks and balances included in the Database of Political Institutions) and indeed "is a bigger curse than oil." More recent literature, however, has been more positive. Jones and Tarp (2016) find a "small positive net effect of total aid on political institutions ... driven primarily by ... stable inflows of 'governance aid.'" The authors use a composite measure of QoG, drawing on data about democracy, veto players, executive constraints, political terror, and judicial independence. Charron (2011) finds that multilateral aid is associated with *lower* corruption levels (as measured by the International Country Risk Guide) since 1997, while bilateral aid and corruption bear no relationship. Brazys (2016) finds that aid generally has a positive relationship with governance, entering negative territory only at very high levels of aid; the results vary somewhat depending on whether the outcome is from the International Country Risk Guide or the Worldwide Governance Indicators.

Looking at 22 studies published between 1999 (the working paper version of Knack (2001)) and 2012 in a meta-analysis, Askarov and Doucouliagos (2013) find that the overall results in the literature are almost evenly split. Across 620 statistical estimates of the relationship between aid and QoG in their study, slightly more than half are positive and slightly less than half are negative, and in each case, about half of those are statistically significant. That is, 25% of the 620 estimates suggest a positive and significant effect of aid on QoG, and 25% of them suggest a negative and significant effect. When reducing the sample to 385 estimates from 13 studies that attempt to address endogeneity in some way, these proportions remain essentially unchanged: 26.5% of the estimates in that subsample are positive and significant, and 23.4% of them are negative and significant.

Regressing these different statistical estimates on the characteristics of the models that produced them, Askarov and Doucouliagos (2013) find that models that account for endogeneity produce more positive coefficient estimates and that models that study technical assistance produce more positive coefficient estimates (in line with the findings of Jones and Tarp (2016). They also find that larger standard errors predict more negative estimates, which they interpret as providing evidence that the "literature is affected by publication selection bias, with a preference for reporting adverse aid-on-governance effects" (Askarov and Doucouliagos 2013, 622). In other words, studies finding null or positive effects of aid on QoG may not have seen the light of day relative to those that estimate negative impacts. Producing an average estimated effect from the underlying analyses in the meta-analysis, they find a positive relationship between aid and governance that is statistically distinguishable from zero for analyses that rely on data from the pre-1991 period. This analysis, however, uses only 5% of the statistical estimates included in the meta-data. For the average estimated effect based on the 95% of analyses in the meta-data that include post-1991 data, the average estimated effect is small, negative, and not distinguishable from zero. That is, ultimately, the evidence seems to say that the average result in the literature is null, suggesting that aid neither improves nor undermines QoG.

In a nonquantitative systematic review, Dijkstra (2018) reaches a somewhat different conclusion about the earlier time period. She argues that studies employing data that goes up until 1995 or 2000 "show that aid, in particular aid proliferation and fragmentation, leads to a *lowering* of the quality of bureaucratic governance" (Dijkstra 2018, 230; emphasis added). On the other hand, her conclusions are in line with Askarov and Doucouliagos (2013) for the more recent period, as she says that those "studies ... conclude that there are no significant effects" (Dijkstra 2018, 230). Looking separately at studies where corruption is the outcome variable, she similarly concludes that "there is little proof that aid flows systematically lead to an increase in corruption" (Dijkstra 2018, 231).

Assessing the state of the evidence

Like identifying a causal relationship between aid and growth, identifying a causal relationship between aid and QoG is a challenging enterprise. As described above in the discussion of aid selectivity, we have good reasons to expect a reverse causal relationship in which QoG predicts aid flows. Given the slow-moving nature of QoG, the strategy of lagging aid flows to predict QoG is unlikely to address this source of endogeneity. In addition, it is easy to come up with plausible stories about potential background covariates that might affect both aid flows and QoG. For instance, involvement in interstate conflict might both bring about changing aid flows and changing levels of QoG.

Of the 22 studies included in Askarov and Doucouliagos's (2013) meta-analysis, 13 attempt to address endogeneity through either an instrumental variables strategy or generalized method of moments (GMM) estimation. Knack (2001) uses "[e]xogenous instruments for aid [that] are nearly identical to those used by Burnside and Dollar (2000)" (319). Specifically, Knack instruments for average aid/GNP or average aid/government expenditures over the period 1982–95 using infant mortality in 1980, population in 1980, GDP per capita in 1980, and indicators for whether the country was in the Franc Zone or located in Central America, and then estimates the effect of instrumented aid on the change in QoG over 1982–95. The two-stage least squares (2SLS) estimates are twice the magnitude of the negative coefficients estimated in an OLS model. These same instruments are used in Djankov, Montalvo, and Reynal-Querol (2008), whereas Bräutigam and Knack (2004) use infant mortality, population, GDP per capita, and a set of colonial power indicators. Both of those studies estimate a negative relationship between aid and QoG. Ear (2007), on the other hand, relies only on infant mortality as an instrument for aid flows and finds that aid is either not related to QoG or else may have positive effects in some cases.

Despite the efforts to obtain causal estimates with an instrumentation strategy, the particular instruments employed in the literature—like those found in the literatures on aid effectiveness and selectivity reviewed above—raise concerns about whether the exclusion restriction is satisfied or not. Development variables like infant mortality and initial level of development might plausibly affect changing QoG by affecting human capital or by affecting patterns of foreign investment in the country (and not just by affecting the magnitude of aid flows). The indicators for a country's strategic importance might predict both levels of foreign aid and other forms of strategic support provided by wealthy countries to keep a ruling government in power.

Similar concerns can be raised about alternative instruments that have been employed in the literature. Svensson (2000) instruments for aid with past levels of corruption and population. Tavares (2003) instruments for aid with bilateral distance and indicators for a shared land border, shared majority religion, and shared official language. Charron (2011) instruments for aid with indicators for the colonial origins of the aid-receiving country, the region in which the country is located, and past corruption. Asongu and Nwachukwu (2016) instrument for aid with a set of indicator variables categorizing countries by their income level, legal origin, and majority religion. Jones and Tarp (2016) use two sets of instruments that include colonial history variables either separately or alongside life expectancy and population. In all cases, it is possible to think of violations of the exclusion restriction and question the extent to which the authors are successfully manipulating the data into an "as-if random" situation.

A number of studies also include GMM estimates that aim to address simultaneity bias by using past-period changes in aid as instruments for present-period changes in aid. In Djankov, Montalvo, and Reynal-Querol (2008), the GMM models estimate a negative relationship between the change in aid dependence and the change in QoG (operationalized as a measure of checks and balances from the Database of Political Institutions) that is very similar to the relationship estimated using instrumental variables methods (and larger than that estimated using OLS). Brazys (2016) and Jones and Tarp (2016) provide GMM estimates of a positive relationship between aid and institutions that are very similar to the OLS estimates that they produce.

It is surprising that similar strategies for dealing with endogeneity nonetheless lead to different conclusions across different studies. One explanation for this—favored by Dijkstra (2018)—is that donors have become more conscientious over time and have improved the ways in which their aid flows are organized and have taken steps to mitigate potential negative consequences of aid. This then would lead to different conclusions for studies that look at one time period or another. Charron (2011) looks for variation in the relationship between aid and corruption before and after the development community embraced the anticorruption agenda in the mid-1990s; as one would anticipate if donors have changed their behavior, he finds that aid is associated with reduced corruption in the more recent

period. Jones and Tarp (2016) summarize their evidence as indicating that "a positive relation between Aid/GDP and political institutions appears more robust since the mid-1990s"
(274). These findings are in line with those of Dunning (2004) and Dietrich and Wright
(2015), who show that aid flows are more likely to predict democratization in the post–Cold
War era. Asongu and Nwachukwu (2016), on the other hand, study the post–Cold War
period in Africa and continue to find negative effects of aid on QoG.

Discriminating across types of aid

Foreign aid is not monolithic, but rather comes in different forms and is given for different
reasons. As described above, some donors appear to prefer different forms of aid in different
QoG contexts. In the literature looking at the effects of aid, a number of authors have broken
down foreign aid by type as well. In doing so, they generally have been more likely to identify
a *positive* association between (some types of) aid and QoG.

Charron (2011) not only looks for variation in the time period when aid might reduce corruption but also for variation in the type of aid that would reduce corruption. In line with
expectations that multilateral donors more fully (or at least more quickly) embraced the
anticorruption agenda, he finds that multilateral aid is associated with reduced corruption
beginning in the mid-1990s. Okada and Samreth (2012) similarly find evidence that foreign
aid from multilateral donors—although also from France and Japan—predicts less corruption (as measured in the Worldwide Governance Indicators). Dadasov (2017) compared aid
from European countries to aid from the European Union, and once again finds that aid
from the multilateral donor has a positive association with QoG (as measured by an average
of four of the Worldwide Governance Indicators).

Looking at the terms on which aid is given, Selaya and Thiele (2012) find that grants harm
QoG (measured as bureaucratic quality according to the International Country Risk Guide),
while loans have no effect, and they find that budget support in the form of grants is particularly deleterious. In their study finding that aid helps build QoG, Jones and Tarp (2016) find
the largest associations for aid aimed explicitly at improving QoG (i.e., governance aid or
technical assistance). In their data, economic aid and other forms of aid produce positive associations with QoG, but they are not statistically significant.

Future research

For the literature going forward, we recommend that more attempts be made to study specific mechanisms through which aid might either improve or worsen QoG. For example,
the comparison between the Selaya and Thiele (2012) finding that budget support correlates
with reduced QoG and the Jones and Tarp (2016) finding that governance aid correlates with
improved QoG may point toward the usefulness of thinking through which of the mechanisms described in Table 21.1 can be supported by patterns in the data in order to reconcile
contrasting findings in the literature. The Jones and Tarp (2016) study should support beliefs
that technical assistance can work, transferring better governance processes to aid-receiving
countries and improving the skill levels of government bureaucrats. The Selaya and Thiele
(2012) finding, on the other hand, may be indicative of how aid can drive rent-seeking or

conflict among elites or else help low-QoG governments to stay in power. It would be harder to think of their finding as supporting a transactions costs mechanism (since budget support is designed to reduce transaction costs). And while budget support may inhibit the development of accountability because of reduced taxation, it is not necessarily clear why it would do so to a greater extent than other forms of aid.

Drawing on interview evidence from Bolivia and Peru, Cornell (2014) describes pathways by which technical assistance might fail to lead to government reforms: if government bureaucrats lack experience, have short time horizons, or do not want to be associated with programs begun under a different political administration. The description of "isomorphic mimicry" found in Pritchett, Woolcock, and Andrews (2013) might also point toward how we can understand cases where aid-motivated reforms appear to happen but do not actually make a difference. In addition to disaggregating aid, we anticipate that this may also necessitate moving away from studying preexisting indices of QoG and thinking about new ways to measure the size of government, the quality of bureaucrats within the government, the extent to which government positions are awarded as patronage, rent-seeking behavior among elites, and so on. The most theoretically advanced articles in the literature (e.g., Svensson 2000; Knack and Rahman 2007) have tended to continue to rely on the general International Country Risk Guide (ICRG) measure of QoG or its bureaucratic quality component, rather than presenting data that truly hones in on the mechanism.

With regard to the "fiscal contract" mechanisms presented in Table 21.1, a recent set of country-specific studies that look to see how the presence of foreign aid impacts government legitimacy provides insight into the extent to which aid substituting for taxation might reduce citizen interest in interacting with or holding the government accountable. These studies have generally found little evidence that foreign aid undermines government legitimacy or reduces citizen interaction with their governments (Sacks 2012; Dietrich and Winters 2015; Blair and Roessler 2018; Dietrich, Mahmud, and Winters 2018; Baldwin and Winters 2020). This work on how aid may make citizens think differently about their government as compared to how citizens in Organization for Economic Co-operation and Development (OECD) countries think about theirs continues and may hold important clues for the ways in which aid can most effectively promote QoG.

Beyond the fiscal contract channels, researchers should think about other ways to collect micro-level data for the other mechanisms linking aid to QoG. Do parts of a government with greater foreign aid flows accomplish fewer things than other parts of the same government because of transaction costs? Do increases in aid lead to a thinning out of the government bureaucracy? Alternatively, do increases in aid lead to higher government salaries and the retention of higher quality workers? Is there evidence of governments incorporating best practices observed in investment projects? Answering questions like these with more precise data is another way of helping the literature to move beyond contrasting macro-level associations.

Finally, we believe it worthwhile to evaluate the extent to which foreign aid that is conditioned on the QoG in recipient countries really makes for better development outcomes. The question of what has resulted from more aid selectivity in allocation and delivery is an important one. Yet it is not at all simple. As Annen and Knack (2019) remind us, such a test requires us to disentangle donor selection effects from recipient incentive effects. In their paper, the authors find that a 10% increase in the global share of policy-selective aid yields small but statistically significant improvements in policy or QoG, as measured by the World

Bank's Country Policy and Institutional Assessment (CPIA) index. We recommend further work in this direction, based on careful QoG measurement choices.

CONCLUSIONS

Up until the late 1990s, the international development industry did not advance an agenda that could be considered a QoG agenda. During the 1980s, the accepted international development paradigm was decidedly neoliberal: Its central aim was to dismantle the state through structural adjustment reforms that would promote the free reign of market forces. The failure of structural adjustment to spur global economic growth, alongside global shifts in response to the end of the Cold War, however, had ramifications for how the international community saw the development process. The recognition that international actors needed to acknowledge the possibility of a central role in the development process for states—and for how those states were governed—yielded shifts in development thinking: The concept of QoG entered development programming across the donor community.

In this chapter, we have reviewed empirical research that laid the foundation for this shift in thinking. Empirical scholarship interested in uncovering the conditions under which aid effectively improves growth and development investigates the moderating role of QoG. Perhaps the most prominent finding in this body of work, Burnside and Dollar (2000), which argues that foreign aid causes growth only in countries with high QoG, was a catalyst not only for further research on the role of QoG on aid effectiveness but also for encouraging international development actors to promote the nascent governance agendas. Subsequent studies, however, have called into question the robustness of the Burnside and Dollar (2000) result. The strand of the aid effectiveness literature that focuses on QoG—like the aid effectiveness literature more generally—needs to concentrate on finding instances where exogenous variation in aid flows can be identified and more rigorous causal claims about the impact of aid can be made. Going forward, we recommend that scholars interested in the relationship between aid and governance consider joining forces and coordinate experimental research in ways that help overcome external validity concerns associated with isolated, individual impact studies; with a view towards producing more reliable answers across different institutional contexts.

Given the growth in a doctrine that QoG moderates aid effectiveness, we assessed the evidence of whether the donor community's increasing commitment to QoG was reflected in their actions. The literature suggests that, in the post–Cold War context, there is relatively robust empirical evidence that donors condition aid policy and the forms of aid delivery on QoG. We believe that there is much still to be learned from this literature about how aid agencies make decisions and how they negotiate with aid-receiving governments. Variation in donor relations across low- and high-QoG countries should teach us both about how the development industry works and about the possibilities for successful promotion of development objectives through foreign aid.

Our review then examined the literature on the effects of foreign aid on QoG in aid-receiving countries. One concern raised by development practitioners and academics alike is that foreign aid flows might undermine QoG. The evidence base is mixed, although, as with the selectivity literature, there is some suggestion that problematic patterns found in

Cold War data do not persist in the post–Cold War era. To move forward in this literature, we suggest that scholars devote more attention to testing the multiple mechanisms by which foreign aid is alleged to affect QoG and collecting the micro-level data necessary for testing those mechanisms.[4]

References

Acharya, Arnab, Ana de Lima, and Mick Moore. 2006. "Proliferation and Fragmentation: Transactions Costs and the Value of Aid." *Journal of Development Studies* 42 (1): 1–21. https://doi.org/10.1080/00220380500356225

Ahmed, Faisal Z. 2012. "The Perils of Unearned Foreign Income: Aid, Remittances, and Government Survival." *American Political Science Review* 106 (1): 146–65.

Alesina, Alberto, and Beatrice Weder. 2002. "Do Corrupt Governments Receive Less Foreign Aid?" *American Economic Review* 92 (4): 1126–37.

Annen, Kurt, and Stephen Knack. 2018. "On the Delegation of Aid Implementation to Multilateral Agencies." *Journal of Development Economics* 133 (July): 295–305. https://doi.org/10.1016/j.jdeveco.2018.02.007

Annen, Kurt, and Stephen Knack. 2019. *Better Policies from Policy-Selective Aid?* Policy Research Working Papers. The World Bank. https://doi.org/10.1596/1813-9450-8889

Ariotti, Margaret, Simone Dietrich, and Joseph Wright. Forthcoming. "Foreign Aid and Judicial Autonomy." *Review of International Organizations.*

Askarov, Zohid, and Hristos Doucouliagos. 2013. "Does Aid Improve Democracy and Governance? A Meta-Regression Analysis." *Public Choice* 157 (3–4): 601–28. https://doi.org/10.1007/s11127-013-0081-y

Asongu, Simplice A., and Jacinta C. Nwachukwu. 2016. "Foreign Aid and Governance in Africa." *International Review of Applied Economics* 30 (1): 69–88. https://doi.org/10.1080/02692171.2015.1074164

Baldwin, Kate, and Matthew S. Winters. 2020. "How Do Different Forms of Foreign Aid Affect Government Legitimacy? Evidence from an Informational Experiment in Uganda." *Studies in Comparative International Development* 55 (2): 160-83. https://doi.org/10.1007/s12116-020-09303-8

Bandyopadhyay, Subhayu, and Howard J. Wall. 2007. "The Determinants of Aid in the Post-Cold War Era." *Federal Reserve Bank of St. Louis Review* 89 (6): 533–48.

Bauhr, Monika, and Nicholas Charron. 2018. "Why Support International Redistribution? Corruption and Public Support for Aid in the Eurozone." *European Union Politics* 19 (2): 233–54. https://doi.org/10.1177/1465116518757702

Bauhr, Monika, Nicholas Charron, and Naghmeh Nasiritousi. 2013. "Does Corruption Cause Aid Fatigue? Public Opinion and the Aid-Corruption Paradox." *International Studies Quarterly* 57 (3): 568–79.

Bearce, David H., and Daniel C. Tirone. 2010. "Foreign Aid Effectiveness and the Strategic Goals of Donor Governments." *The Journal of Politics* 72 (03): 837–51. https://doi.org/10.1017/S0022381610000204

Bermeo, Sarah Blodgett. 2011. "Foreign Aid and Regime Change: A Role for Donor Intent." *World Development* 39 (11): 2021–31. https://doi.org/10.1016/j.worlddev.2011.07.019

[4] Thanks to Miles Williams and Katharina Fleiner for valuable research assistance.

Bermeo, Sarah Blodgett. 2018. *Targeted Development: Industrialized Country Strategy in a Globalizing World.* New York: Oxford University Press.

Berthélemy, Jean-Claude, and Ariane Tichit. 2004. "Bilateral Donors' Aid Allocation Decisions—a Three-Dimensional Panel Analysis." *International Review of Economics & Finance* 13 (3): 253–74. https://doi.org/10.1016/j.iref.2003.11.004

Blair, Robert A., and Philip Roessler. 2018. "The Effects of Chinese Aid on State Legitimacy in Africa: Cross-National and Sub-National Evidence from Surveys, Survey Experiments, and Behavioral Games." AidData Working Paper 59 (July). http://docs.aiddata.org/ad4/pdfs/WPS59_The_Effects_of_Chinese_Aid_on_State_Legitmacy_in_Africa.pdf

Boone, Peter. 1996. "Politics and the Effectiveness of Foreign Aid." *European Economic Review* 40 (2): 289–329.

Bräutigam, Deborah A. 2000. "Aid Dependence and Governance." 2000:1. Expert Group on Development Issues. Washington, D.C.: American University. http://www1.american.edu/faculty/brautigam/Aid%20Dependence%20and%20Governance.pdf

Bräutigam, Deborah A. 2008. "Introduction: Taxation and State-Buildiing in Developing Countries." In *Taxation and State-Building in Developing Countries: Capacity and Consent*, edited by Deborah A. Bräutigam, Odd-Helge Fjeldstad, and Mick Moore. New York: Cambridge University Press.

Bräutigam, Deborah A., and Stephen Knack. 2004. "Foreign Aid, Institutions, and Governance in Sub-Saharan Africa." *Economic Development and Cultural Change* 52 (2): 255–85. https://doi.org/10.1086/380592

Brazys, Samuel. 2016. "Aid and Governance: Negative Returns?" *The European Journal of Development Research* 28 (2): 294–313. https://doi.org/10.1057/ejdr.2014.77

Buntaine, Mark T., Bradley C. Parks, and Benjamin P. Buch. 2017. "Aiming at the Wrong Targets: The Domestic Consequences of International Efforts to Build Institutions." *International Studies Quarterly* 61 (2): 471–88. https://doi.org/10.1093/isq/sqx013

Burnside, Craig, and David Dollar. 2000. "Aid, Policies and Growth." *American Economic Review* 90 (4): 847–68.

Burnside, Craig, and David Dollar. 2004. "Aid, Policies and Growth: Revisiting the Evidence." World Bank Policy Research Working Paper 3251. Washington, D.C. http://www-wds.worldbank.org/servlet/WDSContentServer/WDSP/IB/2004/04/21/000009486_20040421103444/Rendered/PDF/wps3251Aid.pdf

Carnegie, Allison, and Nikolay Marinov. 2017. "Foreign Aid, Human Rights, and Democracy Promotion: Evidence from a Natural Experiment." *American Journal of Political Science* 61 (3): 671–83.

Charron, Nicholas. 2011. "Exploring the Impact of Foreign Aid on Corrption: Has the 'Anti-Corruption Movement' Been Effective?" *The Developing Economies* 49 (1): 66–88. https://doi.org/10.1111/j.1746-1049.2010.00122.x

Claessens, Stijn, Danny Cassimon, and Bjorn Van Campenhout. 2009. "Evidence on Changes in Aid Allocation Criteria." *The World Bank Economic Review* 23 (2): 185–208.

Clemens, Michael A., Steven Radelet, Rikhil R. Bhavnani, and Samuel Bazzi. 2012. "Counting Chickens When They Hatch: Timing and the Effects of Aid on Growth*." *The Economic Journal* 122 (561): 590–617. https://doi.org/10.1111/j.1468-0297.2011.02482.x

Clist, Paul. 2011. "25 Years of Aid Allocation Practice: Whither Selectivity?" *World Development* 39 (10): 1724–34. https://doi.org/10.1016/j.worlddev.2011.04.031

Clist, Paul, Alessia Isopi, and Oliver Morrissey. 2012. "Selectivity on Aid Modality: Determinants of Budget Support from Multilateral Donors." *The Review of International Organizations* 7 (3): 267–84. https://doi.org/10.1007/s11558-011-9137-2

Collier, Paul, and David Dollar. 2002. "Aid Allocation and Poverty Reduction." *European Economic Review* 46 (8): 1475–500.

Collier, Paul, Patrick Guillaumont, Sylviane Guillaumont, and Jan Willem Gunning. 1997. "Redesigning Conditionality." *World Development* 25 (9): 1399–407. https://doi.org/10.1016/S0305-750X(97)00053-3

Cornell, Agnes. 2014. "Why Bureaucratic Stability Matters for the Implementation of Democratic Governance Programs." *Governance* 27 (2): 191–214. https://doi.org/10.1111/gove.12037

Dadasov, Ramin. 2017. "European Aid and Governance: Does the Source Matter?" *The European Journal of Development Research* 29 (2): 269–88. https://doi.org/10.1057/ejdr.2016.16

Di Tella, Rafael, and Ernesto Schargrodsky. 2003. "The Role of Wages and Auditing during a Crackdown on Corruption in the City of Buenos Aires." *The Journal of Law and Economics* 46 (1): 269–92. https://doi.org/10.1086/345578

Dietrich, Simone. 2013. "Bypass or Engage? Explaining Donor Delivery Tactics in Foreign Aid Allocation." *International Studies Quarterly* 57 (4): 698–712. https://doi.org/10.1111/isqu.12041

Dietrich, Simone. 2016. "Donor Political Economies and the Pursuit of Aid Effectiveness." *International Organization* 70 (1): 65–102.

Dietrich, Simone. 2017. "EU Democracy Promotion, Conditionality, and Judicial Autonomy." In *Beyond the Panama Papers. The Performance of EU Good Governance Promotion. The Anticorruption Report 4*, edited by Mungiu, Alina and Jana Warkotsch. Budrich Publishers.

Dietrich, Simone. 2021. *States, Markets, and Foreign Aid*. Cambridge University Press.

Dietrich, Simone, Minhaj Mahmud, and Matthew S. Winters. 2018. "Foreign Aid, Foreign Policy, and Domestic Government Legitimacy: Experimental Evidence from Bangladesh." *Journal of Politics* 80 (1): 133–48.

Dietrich, Simone, Bernhard Reinsberg, and Martin C. Steinwand. 2021. "Donor Political Economies and the Rise of Performance-Based Aid through Trustfunds." Unpublished manuscript. University of Geneva.

Dietrich, Simone, and Matthew S. Winters. 2015. "Foreign Aid and Government Legitimacy." *Journal of Experimental Political Science* 2: 164–71. https://doi.org/10.1017/XPS.2014.31

Dietrich, Simone, and Joseph Wright. 2015. "Foreign Aid Allocation Tactics and Democratic Change in Africa." *The Journal of Politics* 77 (1): 216–34. https://doi.org/10.1086/678976

Dijkstra, Geske. 2018. "Aid and Good Governance: Examining Aggregate Unintended Effects of Aid." *Evaluation and Program Planning* 68 (June): 225–32. https://doi.org/10.1016/j.evalprogplan.2017.09.004

DiLorenzo, Matthew. 2018. "Bypass Aid and Unrest in Autocracies." *International Studies Quarterly* 62 (1): 208–19. https://doi.org/10.1093/isq/sqx084

Djankov, Simeon, Jose G. Montalvo, and Marta Reynal-Querol. 2008. "The Curse of Aid." *Journal of Economic Growth* 13 (3): 169–94. https://doi.org/10.1007/s10887-008-9032-8

Dollar, David, and Victoria Levin. 2006. "The Increasing Selectivity of Foreign Aid, 1984–2003." *World Development* 34 (12): 2034–46. https://doi.org/10.1016/j.worlddev.2006.06.002

Dollar, David, and Jakob Svensson. 2000. "What Explains the Success or Failure of Structural Adjustment Programmes?" *The Economic Journal* 110 (466): 894–917.

Dunning, Thad. 2004. "Conditioning the Effects of Aid: Cold War Politics, Donor Credibility, and Democracy in Africa." *International Organization* 58 (02). https://doi.org/10.1017/S0020818304582073

Ear, Sophal. 2007. "Does Aid Dependence Worsen Governance?" *International Public Management Journal* 10 (3): 259–86.

Easterly, William. 2005. "What Did Structural Adjustment Adjust? The Association of Policies and Growth with Repeated IMF and World Bank Adjustment Loans." *Journal of Development Economics* 76 (1): 1–22.

Easterly, William. 2006. *The White Man's Burden: Why the West's Efforts to Aid the Rest Have Done So Much Ill and So Little Good.* New York: Penguin Press.

Easterly, William, Ross Levine, and David Roodman. 2004. "Aid, Policies and Growth: Comment." *American Economic Review* 94 (3): 774–80.

Easterly, William, and Tobias Pfutze. 2008. "Where Does the Money Go? Best and Worst Practices in Foreign Aid." *The Journal of Economic Perspectives* 22 (2): 29–52.

Eichenauer, Vera Z., and Bernhard Reinsberg. 2017. "What Determines Earmarked Funding to International Development Organizations? Evidence from the New Multi-Bi Aid Data." *The Review of International Organizations* 12 (2): 171–97. https://doi.org/10.1007/s11558-017-9267-2

Eubank, Nicholas. 2012. "Taxation, Political Accountability and Foreign Aid: Lessons from Somaliland." *Journal of Development Studies* 48 (4): 465–80. https://doi.org/10.1080/00220388.2011.598510

Evans, Peter. 1995. *Embedded Autonomy: States and Industrial Transformation.* Princeton, NJ: Princeton University Press.

Finkel, Steven E., Aníbal Pérez-Liñán, and Mitchell A. Seligson. 2007. "The Effects of US Foreign Assistance on Democracy Building, 1990–2003." *World Politics* 59 (3): 404–40.

Galiani, Sebastian, Stephen Knack, Lixin Colin Xu, and Ben Zou. 2017. "The Effect of Aid on Growth: Evidence from a Quasi-Experiment." *Journal of Economic Growth* 22 (1): 1–33. https://doi.org/10.1007/s10887-016-9137-4

Gibson, Clark C., Barak D. Hoffman, and Ryan S. Jablonski. 2015. "Did Aid Promote Democracy in Africa? The Role of Technical Assistance in Africa's Transitions." *World Development* 68 (April): 323–35. https://doi.org/10.1016/j.worlddev.2014.11.009

Girod, Desha M. 2018. "The Political Economy of Aid Conditionality." In *Oxford Research Encyclopedia of Politics*, edited by James A. Caporaso. 10.1093/acrefore/9780190228637.013.597

Girod, Desha M., Stephen D. Krasner, and Kathryn Stoner-Weiss. 2009. "Governance and Foreign Assistance: The Imperfect Translation of Ideas into Outcomes." In *Promoting Democracy and the Rule of Law: American and European Strategies*, edited by Amichai Magen, Thomas Risse, and Michael A. McFaul. New York: Palgrave Macmillan.

Girod, Desha M., and Jennifer L. Tobin. 2016. "Take the Money and Run: The Determinants of Compliance with Aid Agreements." *International Organization* 70 (01): 209–39. https://doi.org/10.1017/S0020818315000326

Goldsmith, Arthur A. 2011. "No Country Left Behind? Performance Standards and Accountability in US Foreign Assistance." *Development Policy Review* 29 (s1): s157–76. https://doi.org/10.1111/j.1467-7679.2011.00524.x

Grossman, Herschel I. 1992. "Foreign Aid and Insurrection." *Defence Economics* 3 (4): 275–88. https://doi.org/10.1080/10430719208404737

Gwin, Catherine, and Joan M. Nelson, eds. 1997. *Perspectives on Aid and Development.* Washington, D.C.: Overseas Development Council.

Hansen, Henrik, and Finn Tarp. 2000. "Aid Effectiveness Disputed." *Journal of International Development* 12 (3): 375–98. https://doi.org/10.1002/(SICI)1099-1328(200004)12:3<375::AID-JID657>3.0.CO;2-M

Isopi, Alessia, and Fabrizio Mattesini. 2008. "Aid and Corruption: Do Donors Use Development Assistance to Provide the 'Right' Incentives." *CEIS Tor Vergata Research Paper Series* 6 (6). ftp://160.80.46.20/RePEc/rpaper/RP121.pdf

Jones, Sam, and Finn Tarp. 2016. "Does Foreign Aid Harm Political Institutions?" *Journal of Development Economics* 118 (January): 266–81. https://doi.org/10.1016/j.jdeveco.2015.09.004

Kersting, Erasmus, and Christopher Kilby. 2014. "Aid and Democracy Redux." *European Economic Review* 67 (April): 125–43. https://doi.org/10.1016/j.euroecorev.2014.01.016

Killick, Tony, Ramani Gunatilaka, and Ana Marr. 1998. *Aid and the Political Economy of Policy Change*. New York: Routledge.

Knack, Stephen. 2001. "Aid Dependence and the Quality of Governance: Cross-Country Empirical Tests." *Southern Economic Journal* 68 (2): 310–29.

Knack, Stephen, and Aminur Rahman. 2007. "Donor Fragmentation and Bureaucratic Quality in Aid Recipients." *Journal of Development Economics* 83 (1): 176–97.

Knack, Stephen, F. Halsey Rogers, and Jac C. Heckelman. 2012. "Crossing the Threshold: A Positive Analysis of IBRD Graduation Policy." *The Review of International Organizations* 7 (2): 145–76. https://doi.org/10.1007/s11558-011-9136-3

Kosack, Stephen, and Jennifer Tobin. 2006. "Funding Self-Sustaining Development: The Role of Aid, FDI and Government in Economic Success." *International Organization* 60 (1). https://doi.org/10.1017/S0020818306060097

Lateef, K. Sarwar. 2016. "Evolution of the World Bank's Thinking on Governance." *World Development Report 2017: Background Paper* (January).

Lensink, Robert, and Howard White. 2000. "Aid Allocation, Poverty Reduction and the Assessing Aid Report." *Journal of International Development* 12 (3): 399–412. https://doi.org/10.1002/(SICI)1099-1328(200004)12:3<399::AID-JID658>3.0.CO;2-5

Licht, Amanda A. 2010. "Coming into Money: The Impact of Foreign Aid on Leader Survival." *Journal of Conflict Resolution* 54 (1): 58–87. https://doi.org/10.1177/0022002709351104

Mawdsley, Emma. 2007. "The Millennium Challenge Account: Neo-Liberalism, Poverty and Security." *Review of International Political Economy* 14 (3): 487–509.

Morgenthau, Hans J. 1962. "A Political Theory of Foreign Aid." *American Political Science Review* 56 (2): 301–9.

Morrison, Kevin M. 2009. "Oil, Nontax Revenue, and the Redistributional Foundations of Regime Stability." *International Organization* 63 (1): 107–38.

Mosley, Paul, Jane Harrigan, and John Toye. 1991. *Aid and Power: The World Bank and Policy-Based Lending*. Vol. 1. New York: Routledge.

Mosley, Paul, John Hudson, and Arjan Verschoor. 2004. "Aid, Poverty Reduction and the 'New Conditionality'." *The Economic Journal* 114 (496): F217–43. https://doi.org/10.1111/j.1468-0297.2004.00220.x

Neumayer, Eric. 2003. *The Pattern of Aid Giving: The Impact of Good Governance on Development Assistance*. New York: Routledge.

Nielsen, Richard A., Michael G. Findley, Zachary S. Davis, Tara Candland, and Daniel L. Nielson. 2011. "Foreign Aid Shocks as a Cause of Violent Armed Conflict." *American Journal of Political Science* 55 (2): 219–32. https://doi.org/10.1111/j.1540-5907.2010.00492.x

North, Douglass C. 1990. *Institutions, Institutional Change and Economic Performance*. New York: Cambridge University Press.

Okada, Keisuke, and Sovannroeun Samreth. 2012. "The Effect of Foreign Aid on Corruption: A Quantile Regression Approach." *Economics Letters* 115 (2): 240–43. https://doi.org/10.1016/j.econlet.2011.12.051

Ostrom, Elinor. 1990. *Governing the Commons: The Evolution of Institutions for Collective Action*. New York: Cambridge University Press.

Persson, Anna, Bo Rothstein, and Jan Teorell. 2013. "Why Anticorruption Reforms Fail— Systemic Corruption as a Collective Action Problem." *Governance* 26 (3): 449–71. https://doi.org/10.1111/j.1468-0491.2012.01604.x

Pritchett, Lant, Michael Woolcock, and Matt Andrews. 2013. "Looking Like a State: Techniques of Persistent Failure in State Capability for Implementation." *Journal of Development Studies* 49 (1): 1–18. https://doi.org/10.1080/00220388.2012.709614

Pronk, Jan P. 2001. "Aid as a Catalyst." *Development and Change* 32: 611–29.

Radelet, Steven. 2004. "Aid Effectiveness and the Millennium Development Goals." Center for Global Development Working Paper 39. Washington, D.C.: Google Scholar.

Rajan, Raghuram G., and Arvind Subramanian. 2008. "Aid and Growth: What Does the Cross-Country Evidence Really Show?" *Review of Economics and Statistics* 90 (4): 643–65.

Rodrik, Dani. 2006. "Goodbye Washington Consensus, Hello Washington Confusion? A Review of the World Bank's Economic Growth in the 1990s: Learning from a Decade of Reform." *Journal of Economic Literature* 44 (4): 973–87.

Roodman, David. 2007. "The Anarchy of Numbers: Aid, Development, and Cross-Country Empirics." *The World Bank Economic Review* 21 (2): 255–77. https://doi.org/10.1093/wber/lhm004

Sacks, Audrey. 2012. "Can Donors and Non-State Actors Undermine Citizens' Legitimating Beliefs?" Policy Research Working Paper 6158. Washington, D.C.: World Bank.

Schudel, Carl Jan Willem. 2008. "Corruption and Bilateral Aid: A Dyadic Approach." *Journal of Conflict Resolution* 52 (4): 507–26. https://doi.org/10.1177/0022002708316646

Selaya, Pablo, and Rainer Thiele. 2012. "The Impact of Aid on Bureaucratic Quality: Does the Mode of Delivery Matter?" *Journal of International Development* 24 (3): 379–86. https://doi.org/10.1002/jid.1759

Svensson, Jakob. 2000. "Foreign Aid and Rent-Seeking." *Journal of International Economics* 51 (2): 437–61.

Svensson, Jakob. 2003. "Why Conditional Aid Does Not Work And What Can Be Done About It?" *Journal of Development Economics* 70 (2): 381–402.

Tavares, José. 2003. "Does Foreign Aid Corrupt?" *Economics Letters* 79 (1): 99–106. https://doi.org/10.1016/S0165-1765(02)00293-8

Tilly, Charles. 1985. "Warmaking and State Making as Organized Crime." In *Bringing the State Back In*, edited by Peter B. Evans, Dietrich Rueschmeyer, and Theda Skocpol. New York: Cambridge University Press.

Tilly, Charles. 1990. *Coercion, Capital and European States: AD 990–1990*. Cambridge, MA: Blackwell.

Weaver, Catherine. 2008. *Hypocrisy Trap: The World Bank and the Poverty of Reform*. Princeton, NJ: Princeton University Press.

Williamson, John. 1990. "What Washington Means by Policy Reform." In *Latin American Adjustment: How Much Has Happened?* http://www.iie.com/publications/papers/paper.cfm?researchid=486

Winters, Matthew S. 2010. "Choosing to Target: What Types of Countries Get Different Types of World Bank Projects." *World Politics* 62 (3): 422–58. https://doi.org/10.1017/S0043887110000092

Winters, Matthew S., and Shyam Kulkarni. 2014. "The World Bank in the Post-Structural Adjustment Era." In *Handbook of Global Economic Governance: Players, Power and Paradigms*, edited by Manuela Moschella and Catherine Weaver, 249–64. New York: Routledge.

Winters, Matthew S., and Gina Martinez. 2015. "The Role of Governance in Determining Foreign Aid Flow Composition." *World Development* 66 (February): 516–31. https://doi.org/10.1016/j.worlddev.2014.09.020

World Bank. 1989. *Sub-Saharan Africa: From Crisis to Sustainable Growth—A Long-Term Perspective Study.* Washington, D.C.: The World Bank. http://www.springerlink.com/index/F820T52U5M3J4762.pdf

World Bank. 1997. *World Development Report 1997: The State in a Changing World.* New York: Oxford University Press.

World Bank. 1998. *Assessing Aid: What Works, What Doesn't, and Why.* New York: Oxford University Press.

World Bank. 2005. *Economic Growth in the 1990s: Learning from a Decade of Reform.* Washington, D.C.: The World Bank Group. http://documents.worldbank.org/curated/en/664481468315296721/pdf/32692.pdf

Wright, Joseph. 2009. "How Foreign Aid Can Foster Democratization in Authoritarian Regimes." *American Journal of Political Science* 53 (3): 552–71.

Wright, Joseph, and Matthew Winters. 2010. "The Politics of Effective Foreign Aid." *Annual Review of Political Science* 13 (1): 61–80. https://doi.org/10.1146/annurev.polisci.032708.143524

CHAPTER 22

··

CORRUPTION, ELITES, AND POWER: AN OVERVIEW OF INTERNATIONAL POLICY EFFORTS TO IMPROVE THE QUALITY OF GOVERNMENT

··

FRANCIS FUKUYAMA AND
FRANCESCA RECANATINI

INTRODUCTION

··

IN the 1980s and early 1990s, corruption was considered a taboo issue for policymakers and outside the scope of the policy debate. In 1993, Peter Eigen created Transparency International (TI), building on his firsthand experience of promoting development while dealing with corruption and in an attempt to bring this issue to the center of the development agenda (https://transparencyschool.org/lecturer/prof-dr-peter-eigen-2/). In 1995, TI released its first Corruption Perceptions Index, which was followed in 1999 by the release of the Worldwide Governance Indicators by Daniel Kaufmann, Aart Kraay and Pablo Zoido-Lobaton (1999).

The creation and publication of these datasets have allowed a more open discussion of these issues and have led to the first real wave of empirical analysis and reforms to address this problem. More than 20 years later, however, the glass remains half empty, and progress appears to be elusive: corruption remains a challenge in many countries around the world despite their level of development and income and despite the greater amount of information available to practitioners and policymakers. The progress that has been made appears sometimes to be easy to reverse (International Monetary Fund 2016; International Monetary Fund 2019; World Bank 2017). Why is this the case? Are the policy tools available not adequate to address this challenge? Is the information available not appropriate for the design and implementation of effective anticorruption policies? Or has the practitioner community been thinking about anticorruption without taking into consideration some critical aspects of this problem, such as its political nature?

This paper explores the policy tools and approaches used in the past two decades to address corruption in an attempt to answer these questions. Our exploration builds on the renewed efforts in the anticorruption community (Mungiu-Pippidi and Johnston 2017; World Bank 2017; International Monetary Fund 2016, 2018) and suggests that while some progress has been made on this agenda, there is now a need for a change in focus. Practitioners have concentrated on measuring and understanding corruption, as the wealth of existing empirical analysis and studies suggest. Despite the challenges that the phenomenon of corruption poses and the multiple forms it can take, this empirical focus has been useful to move corruption to the center of the policy debate.

But evaluating and understanding the extent of the problem is only the starting point for anticorruption reforms. The real challenge has been designing and implementing reforms on the ground. The evidence collected over the past two decades highlights that significant improvements at the country level have been elusive, with a few exceptions like Georgia, Botswana, and, in the late nineteenth century, the United States (Mungiu-Pippidi 2015; Mungiu-Pippidi and Johnston 2017; World Bank 2012; International Monetary Fund 2019), and that they often have been driven by profound political changes long-term vision and political commitment. This has also pointed to the need for a significant reallocation of power and incentives within the country in question to systematically address corruption (and improving the quality of government). This reallocation cannot be achieved without the emergence of a coalition of actors within the political system in support of a modern public sector (based on transparency, accountability, and inclusiveness principles), that are sufficiently powerful to overcome resistance from those stakeholders who will lose power and wealth. Furthermore, because corruption reforms are about power reallocation and changing the existing incentive system, the sequencing of the different measures proposed and/or implemented is critical for the success and sustainability of a reform.

Corruption can manifest itself in different forms, from administrative/petty corruption to corruption in procurement and state capture, and that to address different types of corruption requires different policy tools able to reallocate powers among actors. Such reallocation of powers can only be successful if policymakers are pragmatic in the reform design, able to understand reform space in which they are working at each point in time and operate through a long-term vision that includes mechanisms to sustain the reform effort in the long run. This review thus provides evidence of the importance of implementing reforms that support changes in behavior (of civil servants, citizens, and businesspeople in the country of focus)[1] in addition to changes in its laws and regulations. Such changes, while necessary, are harder to foster and to sustain over the long periods of time needed to ensure a change in behavior. Doing so requires a more profound understanding of the system of incentives of the actors involved and affected by corrupt activities within the country and globally, not just the costs and the extent of corruption.

Finally, it has become evident that policymakers need to have a medium- to long-term approach to reform that allows for adaptation and learning. If, to reduce the risk and extent of corruption, policymakers need to change behaviors and reallocate power, then it follows that addressing corruption requires time and flexibility, not just data and tools. The

---

[1] We do not discuss in this chapter reforms that support changes in behavior of donor partners and international organizations.

implementation of anticorruption reforms will thus need to be sustained over time to ensure the possibility for adaptation and changes as reforms are implemented. To implement structural reforms and sustain change in behavior is one of the most challenging tasks for policymakers, the most important of whom inevitably need to be indigenous to the society in question and not driven by external donors or advisors.

The fact that both corruption and its cure are a matter of power and thus essentially political also points to the limitations of the conceptual models currently used to understand and address corruption. For the past couple of decades, the primary model used to understand corruption has been principal–agent theory (see Jain 2001 for a comprehensive survey), in which corruption is seen as a consequence of agents following their own self-interest rather than the mandates of the principal. Fixing corruption then entails aligning the agents' interest with that of the principal, primarily through the use of material incentives.

Principal–agent works reasonably well if we assume that there is a single principal and that that principal is actually pursuing something like the common good (e.g. provision of public goods for all citizens). However, the fact of the matter is that in many circumstances the principal is the problem: the principal is using political power to benefit themselves, their family and connections rather than the public. Alternatively, there could be multiple principals, who either collectively act in a predatory fashion or else seek their own separate self-interested goals while imposing contradictory mandates on the agents. In situations like this, principal–agent theory provides no guidance as to how to improve the quality of government (Denisova-Schmidt 2018; Persson, Rothstein, and Teorell 2018).

SETTING THE STAGE

Since the early 1990s, researchers and practitioners have more systematically analyzed the role of corruption and poor quality of government on growth and development, defined, for the purpose of this chapter, as "the traditions and institutions by which authority in a country is exercised" (Kraay, Zoido-Lobatón, and Kaufmann 1999, 1). This move toward deeper analytical work started with the research of Rose-Ackerman (1978), Murphy, Shleifer, and Vishny (1991), and Mauro (1995), among others. In parallel, a similar shift toward greater awareness took place within the civil society community, and TI began pushing the issue of corruption within the policy arena by releasing annual indicators of corruption. This interest led to an unprecedented degree of awareness among the public and to the first wave of corruption indicators. These indicators, based on experts' opinion and citizens' perceptions, provided broad cross-country coverage and long-time series (Kaufmann, Kraay, and Zoido-Lobatón 1999), but, while helping to raise awareness about the issue, did not help policymakers to identify the potential causes or the consequences of corruption. This triggered a second wave of more disaggregated corruption indicators, focused more on experiences and less on perceptions of corruption (see Mungiu-Pippidi and Kukutschka 2018; Fazekas, Cingolani and Toth 2018; Recanatini 2011; and Trapnell 2015).

This evidence has allowed policymakers to treat corruption as a development issue and to more systematically explore its causes and consequences. The emerging body of work has shown that corruption is harmful for standards of living and the distribution of income among citizens—reducing literacy and per capita income while increasing infant mortality (for a comprehensive review of the costs and impact of corruption, please see International Monetary Fund 2016). Despite progress in the analysis of the phenomenon and its impact, corruption remains a significant challenge for both developed and developing countries. Some progress has been made especially in a few selected countries (Mungiu-Pippidi 2016), but much remains to be done.

Practitioners have thus started to question their approaches, increasingly focusing on the nature of corruption and its different forms and manifestations (Heidenheimer and Johnston, 2002). There is now a growing recognition that corruption is a multidimensional, complex phenomenon that manifests itself differently in different countries and affects sectors and citizens in different ways. Empirical work focused on different forms of corruption at the country level shows that progress has been made with some types of corruption, especially when it comes to administrative corruption, while less progress has been achieved with other types of corruption like corruption in public procurement (see Anderson and Gray, 2006). Additional empirical analysis has focused instead on the differences in the extent and type of corruption across different regions within the same country (Kisunko and Knack 2013; Charron et al. 2016).

The new available information stresses the importance of targeted, specific policy solutions that can consider and address such heterogeneity. Existing indicators have also come under more severe scrutiny, and practitioners are now pushing for a new wave of experiential and actionable indicators for corruption as a means to develop more effective policies (Mungiu-Pippidi 2016).

But the most commonly used definition of corruption—the abuse of public office for private gain—has evolved over time not only in terms of the forms of corruption or the unit of observation (for a comprehensive discussion of alternative definitions, see Fisman and Golden 2017). Practitioners have come to accept that corruption is about incentives and power, and that in order to address corruption governments, businesspeople, and citizens need to be willing to significantly reallocate power within their countries and among different economic actors (World Bank 2017). This can make reforms less appealing to ruling governments (and to business elites de facto benefitting from the existing power arrangements). It can also make reforms more challenging to implement unless there is a strong support and long-term collaboration with citizens and businesspeople, partially explaining the uneven progress we observe having been made in tackling corruption at the country level around the world.

The next sections highlight the different approaches and tools used to address corruption, from structural reforms to reforms aimed at increasing transparency and accountability and the use of specialized agencies, emphasizing the advantages and limits of each policy measure through the lens of incentives and power. This overview should be considered a starting point for a new approach to think about policy solutions that reduce the risk and extent of corruption at the country level.

Structural State Reform

After the mid-1990s and World Bank President James Wolfensohn's "cancer of corruption" speech, donor emphasis switched from structural adjustment to much more explicit targeting of government quality and anticorruption. There was a steady rise in the amount of World Bank lending tied to public sector reform and parallel efforts at places like the U.K. Department for International Development and the U.S. Agency for International Development.

There were three structural reforms of state sectors attempted during this period. A more comprehensive approach to civil service reform, focused on improving the performance of governments, sought to reshape core national bureaucracies through job reclassifications and wage decompression (that is, by specifying and rewarding higher-skilled jobs) along the lines of the practices of civil services in existing developed countries (World Bank 1999, 91–6). A second approach was decentralization of government functions from national governments to states, province, municipalities, and even neighborhoods. The theory was that decentralization would move service provision closer to citizens, who would then be able to hold governments more accountable for poor performance. In the parlance of the 2004 World Development Report, this would shorten the so-called "route of accountability" (World Bank 2004). The third approach was to promote outsourcing of actual service provision to third party providers along the lines of New Public Management in developed countries. By "separating the service provider from the policymaker" (World Bank 2004: 98), there could be greater specialization among service providers, competition on the basis of cost and effectiveness, and more accountability.

The actual impact of these broad initiatives on the quality of government institutions and corruption was both hard to measure and often very mixed. Perhaps the least effective initiatives—and those that remain the least measured—were those aimed at comprehensive reform of core bureaucracies. In a study by Engberg-Pedersen and Levy (2004) of 15 World Bank initiatives to improve public sector performance, those that focused on broad public administration reform were less effective than those that more narrowly targeted, improving public financial management. The authors hypothesized that broad procedural reform threatened a wide range of vested interests and did not promise clear near-term benefits when compared to more technocratic efforts to fix specific problems. This was also the conclusion of a broader study by the World Bank's Independent Evaluation Group (Independent Evaluation Group 2008). The report noted that, by the mid-2000s, some 15–20% of all World Bank lending had a major public-sector reform component. While there was some improvement brought about by projects targeting public expenditure and financial management, civil service and administrative reform results led to frequent disappointments over the lifetime of these projects (Independent Evaluation Group 2008). Similarly, anticorruption and transparency strategies, while bringing about some increase in transparency and accountability in specific transactions (World Bank 2017), have not led to measurable improvement in overall rates of corruption at the country level (Independent Evaluation Group 2008). A follow-up work by Johnston (2014) reinforces these findings, adding that anticorruption authorities, traditional civil service reforms, and the use of corruption conditionality in aid allocation decisions in general have not been as effective as practitioners had hoped in curbing the risk of corruption.

The results of administrative decentralization initiatives, which were supported by many multilateral and bilateral organizations in a wide variety of countries including Indonesia, Bolivia, Peru, Kenya, and Ukraine were more mixed. The impact of such measures on the quality of government is highly dependent both on context (Diamond 1999) and on the specific design of the decentralization (World Bank 2004). For example, federalism often works better—indeed, may be politically necessary—in large, diverse countries like India, Brazil, or the U.S., but it is much less necessary in small, relatively homogeneous ones like Israel or the Netherlands. One common mistake in the design of decentralized systems is to promote political decentralization without a corresponding administrative decentralization. That is, voters are given the opportunity to elect local representatives, but the latter are not given adequate resources or power to fulfill citizen demands. Such was the case in the Peruvian decentralization plan begun in the early 2000s by President Alejandro Toledo (McNulty 2011; Toledo Manrique 2015). Conversely, both Brazil and Argentina have suffered in the past from the fact that subnational units could run up budget deficits that then needed to be covered by their national government. This mismatch in powers then led to accountability failures in which governments failed to deliver on promised services (Grindle 2007). On the other hand, there were cases in which decentralization provided greater local control and led to higher rates of citizen participation, just as the theory advertised (Grindle 2000).

With respect to corruption, it is not clear that decentralization decreased aggregate levels as opposed to changing its locus, despite general support for decentralization reforms among international donors. Critical is the realization that decentralization reforms (in the form of power transfer from the center to the local level) have often been implemented separately from the necessary reforms aimed at increasing institutions of accountability at the local level. This has led to a simple move of power and of corruption from one level of the government to another one. It was frequently said that after Indonesia democratized and devolved powers to its provinces after 1999, corruption shifted from wholesale to retail; that is, rather than being a monopoly of the Suharto family, it is now more widely practiced by the newly empowered provincial and municipal governors. Corruption on a local level was also a large problem in Peru, where local governments lacked the basic institutional and organizational capacity to perform many of the tasks now assigned to them (McNulty 2011). This weak capacity translated into significant inefficiency in subnational governments' functions, leading to lower accountability (of civil servants) and transparency and in turn to more opportunities for engaging in corrupt activities.

The governance impact of widespread outsourcing—separating the service provider from the policymaker—is a subject that is only beginning to be studied systematically (see for example Charron, Dahlstrom, Fazekas, and Lapuente 2017), particularly with regard to contractor performance in comparison to the same services provided inhouse. One would imagine that the record here is very mixed, as in the case of decentralization. Many forms of outsourcing are perfectly innocuous and should lead to better service delivery than that provided by governments with weak capacity. Indeed, in many fragile or conflict-afflicted states, basic government functions up through to the provision of basic citizen security could not be performed on any level without help from for- and nonprofit contractors, often from within the donor community.

Corruption has always existed in government procurement (Fazekas and Kocsis 2017). There is, however, a growing body of literature coming out of the experiences of developed countries that suggests that the widespread use of contractors to substitute for core government services could have negative effects, particularly for government accountability even when procurements were done cleanly (DiIulio 2014; Freeman and Minow 2009; Verkuil 2007; Kettl 2016). Contracting complicates principal–agent relationships, since most contractors have two principals: the government agency that is procuring its services for an immediate task and the owners of the organization itself, which may either be operating on behalf of profit-maximizing shareholders or of nonprofit stakeholders who may have social objectives different from those of the government in question. Delegation of government functions to a contractor is often done as a workaround to complex and cumbersome civil service rules but at the same time potentially decreases transparency and accountability. The lack of transparency in outsourcing arrangements provides new opportunities for corruption, particularly when multiple levels of subcontractors are involved. Finally, the ability of developing countries' governments to delegate governmental functions to outside (and often foreign) partners may impede the building of capacity within the state to perform core functions. This was a worry in sub-Saharan Africa and in many fragile states, where foreign aid could constitute a majority of the national budget. Overall, this is an area where much more empirical research and analysis needs to be done.

SIMPLIFICATION AND REDUCTION OF ADMINISTRATIVE DISCRETION

Corruption materializes when there is a transaction or an exchange between economic actors that involves some degree of discretion. The structural reforms described in the previous section are one option to improve governance systems and reduce the risk of corruption at the country level. An alternative approach is to improve regulatory quality and reduce administrative discretion by simplifying the process through which a transaction among economic agents can be completed. The simplification of existing regulations and administrative procedures reduces opportunities for discretion and abuse by civil servants and in turn can promote private sector development.

Researchers have empirically analyzed the links among market restrictions, excessive regulations, and rent-seeking activities. Several studies (Ades and Di Tella 1999; Krueger 1974; Zoido-Lobatón, Johnson, and Kaufmann 1999) show that market restrictions create incentives for rent-seeking behavior, especially when they require the approval of a public official exercising discretion. Broadman and Recanatini (2000) show using a sample of transition economies that higher barriers to market entry can lead to a higher level of corruption in a country. Other studies (Svensson 2005; Djankov et al. 2002; Madani and Licetti 2010) find that corruption at the country level is positively correlated with the number of administrative procedures and the time necessary to start a new business. The quality of the regulatory system and the ability of a firm to comply with regulations are also linked to a lower probability that a firm will be asked for a bribe (Alaimo et al. 2009). Freund, Nucifera, and Rijkers (2014) provide novel evidence of the (mis)use of administrative regulations to create and extract rents in selected sectors in Tunisia between 1994 and 2010. The evidence shows that Tunisia's industrial policy was used as a vehicle for rent creation for the president and his family. World Bank (2006) examines the patterns and trends of corruption in business–government interactions in Europe and Central Asia using data from large-scale surveys of firms on many aspects of the business environment. The report suggests that firms experienced a reduction in bribe payment over a period of three years as result of a simplification in administrative procedures. At the same time, state capture as well as corruption in the judiciary and government procurement may be exacerbated by faster growth, particularly if driven largely by natural resources as in some countries in Central Asia.

This body of empirical research suggesting that the simplification and reduction of administrative procedures can help reduce the risk of corruption has influenced donors' approaches to anticorruption and has led to a series of country-level initiatives (International Monetary Fund 2016). These initiatives have focused on streamlining and simplifying existing administrative procedures and regulations in order to improve efficiency and reduce corruption. Some of these initiatives have taken the form of e-governance innovations and have led to significant simplification of administrative procedures and to a decline in incentives for corrupt activities (Bhatnagar and Deane 2004).

Administrative simplification has been increasingly used to address corruption at the sector level. Successful reforms of customs systems, tax administration systems, and procurement have included a mix of policy tools, from simplification and reduction of processes to increased transparency and reduction in discretionary decisions (Hors 2001; Zuleta, Leyton, and Fanta Ivanovic 2012; OECD and World Bank 2018). The simplification of administrative procedures not only reduces opportunities for abuse by public officials but can also create a better environment for institutional reforms. Highly corrupt environments are associated with strong incentives to delay reforms (Shah 2006; Svensson 2005).

It is important to emphasize that while excessive regulation can breed corruption, its simplification and elimination can also create some challenges, especially when operating in countries where the broad institutional environment is weak and/or undergoing significant transformations. This is especially relevant for understanding some of the current institutional challenges faced by the countries of the former Soviet Union and Eastern Europe. The slow introduction of new regulations and checks-and-balances institutions led to an opaque process of privatization of existing state-owned assets and a subsequent creation of industrial groups and monopolies that fostered new forms of corruption and misgovernance (Kaufmann and Siegelbaum 1996; Tanzi 1999). This also led to the emergence in some of these countries of the phenomenon of state capture, in which these newly created economic actors can affect and effectively capture state institutions, preventing reforms in order to maintain their own interests (see Hellman and Kaufmann 2001 for their seminal piece on state capture; see also Johnston 2005; Kenny and Soreide 2009; World Bank 2006; White 2009; Diwan, Keefer, and Schiffbauer, 2015; and Bussolo, Commander, and Poupakis 2018 for illustrations of the impact of state capture).

TRANSPARENCY AND ACCOUNTABILITY

Since the early to mid-2000s, many anticorruption measures have focused on donor community efforts to increase government transparency and accountability. Examples include large multistakeholder initiatives (MSIs) like the Open Government Partnership and the Extractive Industries Transparency Initiative, both of which were designed to encourage governments of developing countries to voluntarily publish data on budgets, revenues, contracts, and the like. Other initiatives included conflict of interest legislation and income and asset disclosure, which aim at strengthening the accountability of civil servants and elected officials (Della Porta and Vannucci 2012; World Bank and UNODC 2012). In addition, a host of nongovernmental organizations have sprung up trying to encourage transparency, such as the International Budget Partnership, the Natural Resource Governance Institute, Publish What You Pay, and I Paid a Bribe, among others.

The underlying idea behind transparency and accountability initiatives is derived from principal–agent theory, namely that agents like legislators or bureaucrats would not be accountable to their principals—the voters—unless the latter had good information about their behavior. The theory assumes that ordinary voters and in particular the poor do not like corruption, want impersonal service delivery, and will act on information about malfeasance to correct abuses through the ballot box.

A host of empirical studies has examined the relationship between the availability of information and a variety of behavioral outcomes including corruption, service delivery, and electoral accountability (Druckman and Lupia 2016). A number of studies has found the anticipated positive correlations between information and reduced corruption (Blumkin and Gradstein 2002; Etter 2014; Reinikka and Svensson 2004), better service delivery (Islam 2006; Peisakhin and Pinto 2010), and factors affecting economic growth (Glennerster and Shin 2003). A recent analysis (de Renzio and Wehner 2017) provides new evidence on the link between fiscal transparency, reduced corruption and improved allocation of resources.

A World Bank program in Uganda aimed at tracing the flow of funds for education through a public expenditure tracking survey (PETS) is one of the most well-known examples of transparency efforts. The program has led to a substantial improvement in the flow of funds reaching the schools from the treasury: leakage reduced from 87% in 1991–95 to about 18% in 1999 and 2000. These results show the value of transparency and the efficiency of mobilizing civil society against corruption (Reinikka and Svensson 2004; Sundet 2007). Similar initiatives have been introduced in other countries. More recently, a PETS in Tanzania in 2009 found that about 37% of money intended for education had been lost (Bold et al. 2011).

Despite these examples, it soon became apparent that transparency by itself was often insufficient to affect behavioral outcomes (Fox 2007; Posner, Tsai, and Lieberman 2014) and that many of the assumptions of the underlying principal–agent theory may be incorrect. Voters may not care about corruption, may want targeted services rather than impersonal service delivery, may have priorities other than holding their elected representatives accountable for misbehavior (e.g. receiving patronage), may not have mechanisms for actually imposing accountability on officials, and may face collective action problems in acting on information about corruption.

The focus of many efforts in the 2000s therefore shifted to efforts to strengthen civil society and its accountability mechanisms, as noted in the World Bank's 2004 World Development Report, *Making Services Work for the Poor* (World Bank 2004). This stream of work included initiatives like participatory budgeting, litigation-based advocacy, and what the World Bank called "shortening the route of accountability," that is, moving the locus of decision-making closer to the citizens being affected (see previous section). A robust civil society or other forms of outside pressure must be in place for positive effects to occur (Kaufmann and Bellver 2005; Kolstad and Wiig 2009; Mauro 2004; Mungiu-Pippidi 2016; Rose-Ackerman and Truex 2013). Even when such accountability mechanisms exist through regular democratic elections, voters may still choose corrupt officials of their own ethnic group over more honest ones from different groups, on the grounds that "it's our turn to eat" (Wrong 2010). The World Bank study on Uganda cited above (Reinikka and Svensson 2004) has been criticized on the grounds that the country's educational system underwent a large expansion in the year that the expenditure tracking survey was completed, which better explained the apparent drop in resource diversion (Sundet 2007). A replication study by Kuecken and Valfort (2019) showed an increase in enrollments but not in schooling.

Within the focus on transparency, a special mention should be given to e-governance tools and their potential applicability as anticorruption measures as part of government's efforts to improve the quality of institutions. In particular, Adam and Fazekas (2019) stresses that more research is needed, as there is little scientific evidence on the impact of e-governance tools on extent and frequency of corruption. Information and Communication Technology (ICT) can remove opportunities for public officials to misuse discretionary powers and increases oversight and downward transparency, can create greater transparency for citizens to report corruption, exchange information, organize collective action, and can promote accountability, advocacy, and citizen participation. At the same time, ICT can shift corruption opportunities to other areas and create new vulnerabilities for hacking and manipulation, can support the diffusion of false information, or facilitate criminal activity with new opportunities related to the dark web, cryptocurrencies, or misuse of well-intentioned digital services like centralized databases (Kopp, Kaffenberger, and Wilson 2017).

In general, transparency by itself is not sufficient to change outcomes unless they are linked to robust accountability mechanisms. A review of the effectiveness of accountability mechanisms has pointed to several context-specific conditions in which they have been effective in reducing corruption (Joshi 2010; Gaventa and Barrett 2010; Gaventa and McGee 2013). On the supply side, accountability mechanisms work best in democratic countries in which governments, or specific actors within governments, are sympathetic to demands for reform, and in which institutional frameworks exist for translating citizen demand into implementable reform. On the demand or citizen side, they work best when citizens have the capacity to process information, when they are connected to broader mobilizations, and when citizens are involved not just in implementing but in formulating reforms. Accountability channels do not necessarily have to be traditional mechanisms like elections, lobbying, and interest group pressure, but can come through newer participatory methods through which citizen pressure can be mounted. However, the empirical literature points to the central conclusion of this article: control of corruption is fundamentally political phenomena that has to be addressed through political rather than technocratic mechanisms (Newell and Wheeler 2006). Where political pressure does not exist, accountability will not occur. This perhaps explains the outcome of a review of five large MSIs including the Extractive Industries Transparency Initiative and the Open Government Partnership:

> Looking across all five public governance multi-stakeholder initiatives, the evidence collected to date suggests that these initiatives are still operating within the early stages of their proposed results frameworks. While public sector MSIs have made some notable progress promoting information disclosure and participation, there is little evidence thus far that these reforms have been effective at improving government accountability or achieving broader social, economic, and/or environmental impacts (Brockmyer and Fox 2015).

INTERNATIONAL AGREEMENTS
AND CONVENTIONS

The increased focus from international organizations on corruption has led to a wave of international agreements and initiatives as an attempt to resolve corruption by standardizing approaches. Since the early 1990s several international conventions and initiatives building on the experience of the Foreign Corrupt Practice Act (FCPA), passed in 1977 in the US, were launched (for a detailed discussion, see Rose-Ackerman and Palifka 2016), including:

- the Financial Action Task Force, addressing money laundering and introduced in 1989;
- the Inter-American Convention Against Corruption (IACAC), adopted in 1996 by the member countries of the Organization of American States;
- the OECD Convention on Combating Bribery of Foreign Public Officials in International Business Transactions, introduced in 1997;
- the Protocol Against Corruption, adopted in 2001 by the Southern African Development Community;
- the Extractive Industries Transparency Initiative (EITI), launched in 2002, and its sister initiatives, the Construction Sector Transparency (CoST) Initiative, launched in 2012, and the Medicine Transparency Alliance, launched in 2009 and now in its second phase;
- the United Nations Convention Against Corruption (UNCAC), introduced in 2003; and
- the Stolen Asset Recovery Initiative, established by the World Bank and the United Nations Office on Drugs and Crime in 2007.

These conventions and initiatives aim at establishing a common set of rules and incentives for countries committed to fighting corruption. They often require the introduction of laws and specialized bodies to address corruption. These initiatives suffer, however, from the same implementation challenges faced by national anticorruption laws (Heimann, Földes, and Báthory 2014; Mungiu-Pippidi 2016). In addition, governments' participation in these initiatives may be driven by considerations other than sincere commitment to anticorruption, such as access to donor and foreign aid, foreign investment, membership in economic and trade agreements, and internal unrest. For this reason, their impact and effectiveness as a policy tool are under discussion.

Mungiu-Pippidi et al. (2011) focus on the role of UNCAC and highlight the limited impact of this convention. Wei (2000) and Cuervo-Cazurra (2008) provide evidence of the limited impact of the FCPA on U.S. firms, showing that their investment in corrupt countries has not fallen more than that of other countries' firms. Furthermore, Cuervo-Cazurra (2008) and David-Barrett and Okamura (2013) explore the country-level impacts of joining the OECD Anti-Bribery Convention and the EITI respectively, showing how participating in the OECD convention may discourage businesses from investing in corrupt countries rather than encourage those countries to improve the quality of government institutions, while participation in initiatives like the EITI instead appears to attract additional aid, at least at the early stages, as countries can signal through these actions their commitment to greater transparency.

CORRUPTION, ELITES, AND POWER   483

A few lessons emerge from this body of work. The signing of such treaties is just the first step. The political economy issue surrounding participation in such agreements and the challenges to implementing and enforcing them are the factors undermining the effectiveness of such international tools. Governments often have an incentive only to sign these agreements and not to ratify them and adopt them within their countries.

SPECIALIZED ANTICORRUPTION BODIES

Policy efforts to address corruption have focused not only on changing incentive systems existing within public administration but also on establishing and strengthening specialized institutions (Independent Evaluation Group 2008). The presence of these specialized anticorruption agencies (ACAs) has grown significantly in the last two decades, in part following the introduction of several international conventions aimed at addressing corruption (Recanatini 2011). These conventions endorse the view that specialized ACAs can be the optimal policy tool to address rampant corruption in a country (Doig 1995; 2009; Pope and Vogl 2000; Quah 2010).

These agencies are still viewed, however, with scepticism by practitioners, as they have been unable to show a clear and significant impact on corruption (Doig 2009; Hussmann 2007; Huther and Shah 2000; Meagher 2005; Mungiu-Pippidi et al. 2011). As a result, some experts question the ability of ACAs to address corruption (Kuris 2014; UNDP 2006).

Practitioners have increasingly focused on factors that can help to identify the possible reasons for the limited impact of ACAs. Some practitioners have analyzed a few well-known cases (De Speville 2000, 2008). Although rich in details and history, these country-specific studies often have limited utility for policymaking. A few others have focused on countries within the same region (Doig, Watt, and Williams 2005; Meagher 2005; Quah 2010). The lessons for policy purposes are similarly difficult to generalize. Finally, others have taken a broader approach (De Sousa 2010; Kuris 2014; Recanatini 2011; Doig and Recanatini 2020) to identify a common set of policy recommendations.

The main message that emerges from this wealth of studies is that these specialized agencies can have some impact but alone these bodies are not the solution to corruption within a country. The effectiveness of these agencies is affected by institutional and political factors introducing additional complexity to an already complex challenge (Recanatini 2011; Doig and Recanatini 2020). For example, strong political support from country leadership emerges as the cornerstone of ACA effectiveness and their ability to have some impact (Doig, Watt, and Williams 2007; Meagher 2005; Quah 2010). Without clear commitment and support from top leadership, these specialized agencies are short-lived and often marginalized (Doig, Watt, and Williams 2007). Support from the top is a necessary but not a sufficient condition. In order to promote change, support from middle management is crucial as well. This calls for a revised approach to anticorruption reforms, one that seeks to change the incentives of middle management so that they act to improve transparency and promote accountability as part of the reform process (Doig and Recanatini 2020).

The introduction of a comprehensive and clear legal framework for anticorruption work is an additional factor that can contribute to the ability of ACAs to have impact (Meagher 2005). Merely introducing such a legal framework, although necessary, is not sufficient: laws and regulations need to be applied in order to bring change. Furthermore, interagency co-ordination and cooperation among different jurisdictions are required to enhance the investigative capacity (and effectiveness) of ACAs. Clarity of legal mandate and interagency coordination are especially important for investigative and prosecutorial work, as these functions are often split across different government agencies.

Adequate resources and a clear role and position within the country's institutional system are two additional dimensions that can determine whether an ACA will be able to make significant progress in the fight against corruption (De Sousa 2010; Meagher 2005). Without a well-defined legislative mandate specifying the agency's powers and its relations with other entities responsible for anticorruption policy, the agency's effectiveness can be greatly undermined (Recanatini 2011).

Independence and accountability are also crucial factors for effective ACAs. De Sousa (2010) suggests that ACAs need operational autonomy—the capacity to carry out the agency's mission and objectives—to be effective. These agencies should, however, not be immune to scrutiny or regulation; they must have oversight and be responsive to the constituents they are charged with serving (Meagher 2005). In some cases, procedures to appoint and remove the heads of these agencies have been exploited by governments not committed to the anticorruption agenda (Schütte 2015).

Other, less often emphasized factors can affect the effectiveness of ACAs. The existence of an adequate budget, independently managed, can help sustain ACA efforts. Measures promoting ACA accountability and relationship with citizens and the media (including social media) can be powerful tools to create an enabling environment when facing faltering political support. ACAs should set an example and make themselves accountable for their work by regularly sharing the outcomes of their efforts and initiatives. Finally, ACA leadership should not underestimate the role of civil society for their survival. Civil society, through monitoring exercises and demand for better governance, can help counterbalance resistance from politicians and civil servants to transparency and accountability reforms that ACAs often try to implement (Recanatini 2011).

In the end, these specialized agencies are a tool that can be shaped and adapted depending on a country's circumstances and the real commitment of its government to address corruption. In some cases, ACAs have brought some changes (for example, in Hong Kong, Indonesia, Slovenia, and Latvia), while in others these agencies have been created without sufficient consideration of the institutional issues and commitment of resources, as a quick and cheap solution in response to internal and external pressures to act against corruption proving to be an ineffective tool against corruption (De Sousa, Hindess, and Larmour 2009; Meagher 2005; Recanatini 2011; Doig and Recanatini, 2020).

THE HALF-FULL GLASS AND THE POLITICAL NATURE OF CORRUPTION

In the more than two decades that the academic and international donor communities have been focused on the problem of anticorruption, the aggregate picture has been very mixed. There is no question that global consciousness of the problem of corruption has shifted and that a great deal of world politics now focuses on this issue rather than the ideo-logical questions that underlay the Cold War. Accountability for corruption has reached the highest levels of politics in recent years, with former presidents and prime ministers being prosecuted, jailed, or driven from office in a wide variety of countries including Argentina, Brazil, Italy, Iceland, South Korea, Romania, Peru, Ukraine, Thailand, and the Philippines. One of the sparks for the Arab Spring in 2011 was broad indignation throughout the Arab world at corrupt and unaccountable regimes. The People's Republic of China has been en-gaged in a huge anticorruption drive since 2013, though it is unclear whether this represents a sustainable application of law or a purge of one part of the ruling Communist Party of China by another part.

Global attention to the problem of corruption has also led to the creation of a broad net-work of institutions devoted to promoting this agenda. This includes donor-sponsored organizations like the EITI as well as a wide variety of civil society groups demanding trans-parency and accountability of developing country governments. Since the 1990s there has also been a far higher level of attention paid to the problems of corruption by researchers inside and outside of academia. This has led to the development of an array of new indicators that did not exist 20 years ago, like the Worldwide Governance Indicators, the Corruption Perceptions Index, the Bertelsmann Transformation Index, and the Varieties of Democracy indicators (Fukuyama 2013).

There have been some clear gains in government performance across the developing world and lower levels of corruption in certain specific sectors. The bulk of these gains have occurred in narrowly targeted areas like public financial management, tax administration, public health, and customs collection. What is less apparent is improvement in broader areas of public administration, particularly in areas involving large numbers of frontline service providers, such as public education, criminal justice, and the like.

There is also a question of displacement. Decentralization programs have given local officials in Indonesia, Peru, and Kenya new opportunities to participate in corruption. Alternative anticorruption initiatives have driven the locus of corruption out of the hands of low-level bureaucrats and into other, more lucrative areas higher up the food chain. We have relatively little data on grand corruption by high officials like presidents, prime ministers, Cabinet ministers, and so forth, except when one of them gets caught in a major scandal; in aggregate, one suspects that overall levels have not changed substantially in recent years. An interesting study supporting this point with data from businesses in former Soviet Union countries shows a fairly clear trend of decline in administrative and petty corruption while other types of corruption remain at the same level or increase (World Bank 2006).

Why, despite all the global attention paid to this issue, has it been so hard to root out sys-temic corruption and improve government performance? And why have existing gains tended to cluster in certain specific government sectors like public financial management?

The answer to the first of these questions lies in understanding what causes corruption in the first place. Corruption does not exist because leaders or politicians are ignorant and do not know how an accountable government is supposed to be run. Nor is it the case that corruption is a strange pathology that happens to affect a small minority of contem-porary developing countries. Corruption has rather been a historical norm (Denisova-Schmidt 2018). In most human societies for most of human history, governments existed not to provide citizens with public goods on an impersonal basis but because political power was a route to personal enrichment. Indeed, in premodern times, kings and queens ran patrimonial states in which dynasties literally owned the territories over which they ruled and could bequeath their lands to friends and relatives as a form of private property. As North, Wallis, and Weingast (2009) have argued, elite pacts to share rents were important mechanisms for controlling violence, a pattern that in part continues to the present day in countries like Nigeria, Russia, Bosnia, Angola, Iraq, and Somalia.

When corruption is systemic, no individual has an incentive to behave in a noncorrupt fashion; shifting out of this equilibrium into one in which corruption is routinely punished therefore poses a major collective action problem (Mungiu-Pippidi 2015). Impersonal governments providing public goods are a modern phenomenon and one that has emerged only in a small handful of developed countries in the past couple of centuries; what needs to be explained is, therefore, not why corruption continues to exist but rather how certain select countries have managed to shift to a different equilibrium.

The answer to this question is, broadly, that governments shift out of a corrupt equilibrium only when they are forced to do so because of very strong internal political pressure or because of sudden changes in regimes. Corruption exists because it is in the self-interest of entrenched, dominating elites to behave in a corrupt fashion. The system can change only if these elites are forced out of power or if their source of rents is at risk; lectures or incentives offered by donor agencies will typically not do the job (Mungiu-Pippidi et al. 2011). In addition, elites not only do not have an incentive to improve governance; they also have an incentive to improve it only on paper (by signing conventions, for example) to keep geo-economic interests, the donor community and potential foreign investors satisfied. It should be emphasized however that the removal of the past elites is only a necessary but not sufficient condition for change and more inclusive reallocation of powers since past elites may be replaced by new elites operating with similar corrupt incentives. Thus, more inclusive and accountable institutions need to be established following the removal of less inclusive or predatory elites. Without such institutional change, the removal of existing elites will not lead to less corrupt regimes.[2]

The shift to a new equilibrium has happened in the past because other groups with a self-interest in promoting impersonal and more inclusive government gained political power and pushed the old elites out of the way.[3] Such groups come into existence oftentimes because of ecnomic modernization and social change as well as in reaction to profound inequality; They have to be organized by strong, visionary leaders into a coalition and mobilized to take on the old elites.

The political nature of anticorruption efforts can be illustrated by reference to the experience of the U.S. in the nineteenth century (see Fukuyama 2014). American politics during that period were not too different from politics in contemporary developing democratic countries like India, Brazil, Argentina, or Indonesia. Beginning in the 1820s, U.S. states began expanding the franchise to include all white males, vastly enlarging the voter base and presenting politicians with the challenge of mobilizing relatively poor and poorly educated voters. The solution, which appeared particularly after the 1828 presidential election that brought Andrew Jackson to power, was the creation of a vast clientelistic system by which elected politicians appointed their supporters to positions in the bureaucracy or rewarded them with individual payoffs like Christmas turkeys or bottles of bourbon. This system, known as the spoils or patronage system, characterized American government for the next century, from the highest federal offices down to local postmasters in every American town

---

[2] As some of the countries involved in the Arab Spring and countries like Peru and Ukraine illustrate.
[3] An example is Georgia in 2003 (World Bank 2012).

or city. As with other clientelistic systems, patronage led to astonishing levels of corruption and abuse, particularly in eastern cities like New York, Boston, or Chicago where machine politicians had ruled for generations.

This system began to change only in the 1880s as a consequence of economic development and pressures for social change. The country at that point was being transformed by new technologies like railroads and the telegraph from a primarily agrarian society into an urban industrial one. There were increasing demands both on the part of business leaders and from a newly emerging civil society for a different, more modern form of government that would prioritize merit and knowledge over political connections (Kuo 2018). Following the assassination of newly elected President James A. Garfield in 1881 by a would-be office seeker, Congress was embarrassed into voting for the Pendleton Civil Service Reform Act, which for the first time established a U.S. Civil Service Commission and the principle that public officials should be chosen on the basis of merit. Even so, expanding the number of classified (i.e. merit-based) officials met strong resistance and did not become widespread until after the First World War. Individual municipal political machines like Tammany Hall in New York were not dismantled completely until the middle of the twentieth century.

The U.S. experience illustrates a number of features of both corruption and reform of corrupt systems. First, the incentives that had led to the creation of the clientelistic system in the first place were deeply political and based on rent extraction: politicians, who got into office via their ability to distribute patronage, had no incentive to vote in favor of something like the Pendleton Act that would take away those privileges. The only reason it passed was a tragic exogenous event, the Garfield assassination, which mobilized public opinion in favor of a more modern and accountable governmental system. Second, the reform of the system was similarly political. The Progressive Era saw the emergence of a vast reform coalition made up of progressive business leaders, urban activists, farmers, and ordinary citizens who were fed up with the existing exclusionary patronage system and the associated lack of accountability. It required good leadership and vision from politicians like Theodore Roosevelt, himself head of the U.S. Civil Service Commission, and Gifford Pinchot, head of the U.S. Forest Service to foster change. And it required a clear reform agenda pointing toward modern government, one that was formulated by intellectuals like Frank Goodnow, Dorman Eaton, and Woodrow Wilson and that was built on transparency and accountability principles. Finally, reform was helped along by economic development. Industrialization in the U.S. created greater wealth and produced new social groups, like business leaders who needed efficient and reliable government services, a broad and better educated middle class who could mobilize for reform, and grassroots organization of civil society groups. It was only the creation of a progressive reform coalition under strong leadership that succeeded in bringing about the political changes necessary to overcome resistance from the older generation of patronage politicians and to introduce a new system of government institutions based on greater accountability and broader inclusion that has lasted until today.

Conclusions

This article has explored alternative policies and tools used to address corruption. The overview provided highlights the progress achieved and the need for further work and a new approach. The past few decades have witnessed significant efforts aimed at understanding and measuring corruption. This focus on indicators has been useful to move corruption to the center stage of the policy debate. However, measuring the problem is only the starting point for anticorruption reforms. The real challenge remains at the design and implementation stages: How to support the transition from a corrupt government system to a more accountable and inclusive one.

The American case illustrates how corruption—and the poor quality of government institutions that results from it—is deeply political insofar as it confers power and wealth on those who practice it. Reducing the risk of corruption therefore requires generating countervailing political power to change the existing incentive system, create new and more inclusive institutional rules, and force the old entrenched actors out of power. Such efforts are sometimes described as political will, a poor metaphor to the extent that it analogizes politics to individual will and fails to understand that institutions need to change and not only political actors. Developing political will is nothing more or less than building and sustaining a coalition of political actors who aim at a common objective, something that the progressive coalition succeeded in doing at the turn of the twentieth century in the U.S.

In light of the disappointing results of earlier efforts at combatting corruption, development policy has not shifted in a single coherent direction. There continues to be an emphasis on transparency and accountability, with an increasing emphasis on mechanisms for improving the latter. There has been a shift away from broad anticorruption efforts to ones targeted at specific sectors, as well as a recognition that the first generation measures of government quality needed to be replaced by disaggregated ones focusing on specific sectors, levels of government, and regions. While development agencies have paid lip service to understanding the political economy of corruption in their field operations, it is not clear the degree to which they have been able to move beyond the dominant economic paradigm in practice.

From a pragmatic point of view, policymakers may internalize these challenges by thinking about addressing corruption through a series of gradual reforms aimed at changing the existing system of incentives, beginning by addressing less significant types of corruption (i.e. petty corruption) that can provide concrete and visible results. This gradual approach can help to weaken the existing power structure without threatening it upfront and creating significant resistance to reforms, and to create a broader coalition for change. Following these initial reforms and their visible results, policymakers can mobilize more resources and support for more systematic reforms aimed at addressing more entrenched types of corruption, like corruption in public procurement and state capture. Only a few countries have been able to implement such an incremental approach over the past 20 years (Mungiu-Pippidi 2016; Mungiu-Pippidi and Johnston, 2017). The question, however, remains as to why a policymaker would have an incentive to begin such a process of reform and reallocation of powers within a country.

References

Adam, Isabelle, and Mihaly Fazekas. 2019. "Are Emerging Technologies Helping Win the Fight against Corruption in Developing Countries?" Pathways for Prosperity Commission Background Paper Series no. 21. Oxford, United Kingdom.

Ades, Alberto, and Rafael Di Tella. 1999. "Rents, Competition, and Corruption." *American Economic Review* 89 (4): 982–93.

Alaimo, Veronica, Pablo Fajnzylber, Jose Luis Guasch, Jose Humberto Lopez, and Ana Oviedo. 2009. "Behind the Investment Climate: Back to Basic—Determinants of Corruption." In *Does the Investment Climate Matter? Microeconomic Foundations of Growth in Latin America*, edited by Pablo Fajnzylber, Jose Luis. Guasch, and Jose Humberto Lopez, 139–78. Washington, DC, Houndmills, Basingstoke, Hampshire, New York: Palgrave Macmillan.

Anderson, James, and Cheryl Gray. 2006. *Anticorruption in Transition 3: Who is Succeeding... and Why?* Washington, DC: The World Bank.

Bhatnagar, Subhash, and Arsala Deane. 2004. "Building Blocks of E-government. Lessons From Developing Countries." PREM Notes 91. Washington, DC: The World Bank.

Blumkin, Tomer, and Mark Gradstein. 2002. "Transparency Gloves for Grabbing Hands? Politics and (Mis)Governance." CEPR Discussion Papers No 3668. London: CEPR.

Bold, Tessa, Jakob Svensson, Bernard Gauthier, Ottar Mæstad, and Waly Wane. 2011. *Service Delivery Indicators. Pilot in Education and Health Care in Africa.* CMI Report 2011:8. Bergen: Chr. Michelsen Institute.

Broadman, Harry, and Francesca Recanatini. 2000. "Seeds of Corruption. Do Market Institutions Matter?" Policy Research Working Paper 2368. Washington, DC: The World Bank.

Brockmyer, Brandon, and Jonathan Fox. 2015. *The Effectiveness and Impact of Public Governance-Oriented Multi-Stakeholder Initiatives.* London: Transparency and Accountability Initiative.

Bussolo, Maurizio, Simon Commander, and Poupakis Stavros. 2018. "Political Connections and Firms: Network Dimensions." Policy Research Working Papers, WSP 8428. Washington DC: The World Bank.

Charron, Nicholas, Stefan Dahlberg, Soren Holmberg, Bo Rothstein, Anna Khomenko, and Richard Svensson. 2016. *The Quality of Government EU Regional Dataset.* Gothenburg: The University of Gothenburg.

Charron, Nicholas, Carl Dalhstrom, Mihaly Fazekas, and Victor Lapuente. 2017. "Careers, Connections, and Corruption Risks: Investigating the Impact of Bureaucratic Meritocracy on Public Procurement Processes." *The Journal of Politics* 79: 89–104.

Cuervo-Cazurra, Alvaro. 2008. "The Multinationalization of Developing Country MNEs: The Case of Multilatinas." *Journal of International Management* 14 (2): 138–54.

David-Barrett, Liz, and Ken Okamura. 2013. "The Transparency Paradox: Why do Corrupt Countries Join EITI?" Paper presented at the *Annual American Political Science Association Meeting.* Chicago, August 29–September 1, 2013.

De Sousa, Luis. 2010. "Anti-corruption Agencies: Between Empowerment and Irrelevance." *Crime, Law and Social Change* 53 (1): 5–22.

De Sousa, Luis, Barry Hindess, and Peter Larmour, eds. 2009. *Governments, NGOs and Anti-corruption: The New Integrity Warriors.* London: Routledge.

De Speville, Bertrand. 2008. "Failing Anticorruption Agencies? Causes and Cures." Paper presented at the *ISCTE Conference.* Lisbon, May 14–16.

De Speville, Bertrand. 2000. "Why do Anti-corruption Agencies Fail?" In *UNCICP, Implementation Tools, the Development on an Anti-corruption Tool Kit: Inputs for a United Nations Expert Group Meeting.* Vienna: UNODC.

Della Porta, Donatella, and Andrea Vannucci. 2012. *The Hidden Order of Corruption: An Institutional Approach.* Farnham: Ashgate.

Denisova-Schmidt, Elena. 2018. "Corruption, the Lack of Academic Integrity and Other Ethical Issues in Higher Education: What Can Be Done with the Bologna Process?"

In *European Higher Education Area: The Impact of Past and Future Policies*, edited by Curaj, A., L. Deca and R. Pricopie, 43–59. Springer International Publishing.

Diamond, Larry. 1999. *Developing Democracy: Toward Consolidation.* Baltimore, London: Johns Hopkins University Press.

DiIulio, John. 2014. *Bring Back the Bureaucrats: Why More Federal Workers Will Lead to Better (and Smaller!) Government.* West Conshohocken: Templeton Press.

Diwan, Ishac, Philip Keefer, and Marc Schiffbauer. 2015. "Pyramid Capitalism: Political Connections, Regulations and Firm Productivity in Egypt." Policy Research Working Paper WSP 7354. Washington DC: The World Bank.

Djankov, Simeon, Rafael La Porta, Florencio Lopes-de-Silanes, and Andrei Shleifer. 2002. "The Regulation of Entry." *Quarterly Journal of Economics* 117 (1): 1–37.

Doig, Alan. 2009. "Matching Workload, Management and Resources: Setting the Context for "Effective" Anti-corruption Commissions." In *Governments, NGOs and Anti-corruption: The New Integrity Warriors*, edited by L. De Sousa, B. Hindess, and P. Larmour, 65–84. London: Routledge.

Doig, Alan. 1995. "Good Government and Sustainable Anti-corruption Strategies: A Role for Independent Anti-corruption Agencies?" *Public Administration and Development* 15 (2): 151–65.

Doig, Alan and Francesca Recanatini. 2020. "Anticorruption Agencies" in Bajpai, Rajni; Myers, Bernard, 2020, *Enhancing Government Effectiveness and Transparency: The Fight Against Corruption.* Washington, D.C.: World Bank Group.

Doig, Alan, David Watt, and Robert Williams. 2007. "Why do Developing Country Anti-corruption Commissions Fail to Deal With Corruption? Understanding the Three Dilemmas of Organisational Development, Performance Expectation, and Donor and Government Cycles." *Public Administration and Development* 27 (3): 251–9.

Doig, Alan, David Watt, and Robert Williams. 2005. *Measuring "Success" in Five African Anti-corruption Commissions. The Cases of Ghana, Malawi, Tanzania, Uganda and Zambia.* U4 Reports 2005: 1. Bergen: Chr. Michelsen Institute.

Druckman, James, and Arthur Lupia. 2016. "Preference Change in Competitive Political Environments." *Annual Review of Political Science* 19 (1): 13–31.

Engberg-Pedersen, Poul, and Brian Levy. 2004. "Building State Capacity in Africa: Learning From Performance and Results." In *Building State Capacity in Africa*, edited by S. Kpundeh, and B. Levy, 87–108. Washington, DC: The World Bank.

Etter, Luca. 2014. "Can Transparency Reduce Corruption?" Paper presented at *the Doing Business Conference 2014.* Washington, DC, February 20-21. https://eiti.org/document/can-transparency-reduce-corruption

Fazekas, Mihaly, and Gabor Kocsis. 2017. "Uncovering High-level Corruption: Cross-national Objective Corruption Risk Indicators Using Public Procurement Data." *British Journal of Political Science* 1–10.

Fazekas, Mihaly, Gabor Kocsis, Luciana Cingolani, and Bence Toth. 2018. "Innovations in Objectively Measuring Corruption in Public Procurement." In *Governance Indicators: Approaches, Progress, Promise*, edited by Anheier, Haber, and Kayser, 154–85. Oxford: Oxford University Press.

Fisman, Ray, and Miriam Golden. 2017. *Corruption: What Everyone Needs to Know.* Oxford: Oxford University Press.

Fox, Jonathan. 2007. "The Uncertain Relationship between Transparency and Accountability." *Development in Practice* 17: 663–71.

Freeman, Jody, and Martha Minow, eds. 2009. *Government by Contract*. Cambridge: Harvard University Press.

Freund, Caroline, Antonio Nucifora, and Bob Rijkers. 2014. "All in the Family. State Capture in Tunisia." Policy Research Working Paper No. 6810. Washington, DC: The World Bank.

Fukuyama, Frank. 2014. *Political Order and Political Decay: From the Industrial Revolution to the Globalization of Democracy*. New York: Macmillan.

Fukuyama, Frank. 2013. "What Is Governance?" *Governance* 26 (3): 347–68.

Gaventa, John, and Gregory Barrett. 2010. "So What Difference Does It Make? Mapping The Outcomes Of Citizen Engagement." IDS Working Papers. London: Institute for Development Studies.

Gaventa, John, and Rosemary McGee. 2013. "The Impact of Transparency and Accountability Initiatives." *Development Policy Review* 31: 3–28.

Glennerster, Rachel, and Yongseok Shin. 2003. "Is Transparency Good for You, and Can the IMF Help?" IMF Working Paper No 03/132. Washington, DC: International Monetary Fund.

Grindle, Merilee. 2007. *Going Local: Decentralization, Democratization, and the Promise of Good Governance*. Princeton: Princeton University Press.

Grindle, Merilee. 2000. *Audacious Reforms: Institutional Invention and Democracy in Latin America*. Baltimore: Johns Hopkins University Press.

Heidenheimer, Arnold, and Michael Johnston. 2002. *Corruption: Concepts and Contexts*, Routledge Press.

Heimann, Fritz, Adam Földes, and Gabor Báthory. 2014. *Exporting Corruption*. Progress Report 2014: Enforcement of the OECD Convention of Combating Foreign Bribery. Berlin: Transparency International.

Hellman, Joel, and Kaufmann, Daniel. 2001. "Confronting the Challenge of State Capture in Transition Economies." *Finance & Development* 38 (3). Washington DC: IMF.

Hors, Irene. 2001. *Fighting Corruption in Customs Administration: What Can we Learn From Recent Experiences?* Paris: OECD.

Hussmann, Karen. 2007. *Anti-corruption Policy Making in Practice. What Can be Learned for Implementing Article 5 of UNCAC?* U4 Reports 2007:1. Bergen: Chr. Michelsen Institute.

Huther, Jeff, and Shah, Anwar. 2000. "Anti-corruption Policies and Programs: A Framework for Evaluation." Policy Research Working Paper No 2501. Washington, DC: The World Bank.

International Monetary Fund. 2019. *Fiscal Monitor: Curbing Corruption*, April 2019. Washington DC: IMF.

International Monetary Fund. 2018. "Review of 1997 Guidance Note on Governance – A proposed Framework for Enhanced Fund Engagement." IMF Policy Paper. Washington, DC: IMF. http://www.imf.org/external/pp/ppindex.aspx

International Monetary Fund. 2016. "Corruption. Costs and Mitigation Strategies." IMF Staff Discussion Note SDN/16/05. Washington, DC: IMF.

Independent Evaluation Group. 2008. *Public Sector Reform: What Works and Why? An IEG Evaluation of World Bank Support*. Washington, DC: The World Bank.

Islam, Roumeen. 2006. "Does More Transparency go Along With Better Governance?" *Economics and Politics* 18 (2): 121–67.

Jain, Arvind. 2001. "Corruption: A Review." *Journal of Economic Surveys* 15 (1): 71–121.

Johnston, Michael. 2014. *Corruption, Contention, and Reform: The Power of Deep Democratization*. Cambridge: Cambridge University Press.

Johnston, Michael. 2005. *Syndromes of Corruption: Wealth, Power, and Democracy*. Cambridge, New York, Melbourne: Cambridge University Press.

Joshi, Anuradha. 2010. *Service Delivery: Review of Impact and Effectiveness of Transparency and Accountability Initiatives.* London: Transparency and Accountability Initiative.

Kaufmann, Daniel, and Ana Bellver. 2005. "Transparenting Transparency. Initial Empirics and Policy Applications." Available at SSRN: https://ssrn.com/abstract=808664 or http://dx.doi.org/10.2139/ssrn.808664

Kaufmann, Daniel, Aart Kraay, and Pablo Zoido-Lobatón. 1999. "Aggregating Governance Indicators." Policy Research Working Paper No 2195. Washington, DC: The World Bank.

Kaufmann, Daniel, and Paul Siegelbaum. 1996. "Privatization and Corruption in Transition Economies." *Journal of International Affairs* 50 (2): 419–58.

Kenny, Charles, and Tina Soreide. 2009. "Grand Corruption in Utilities." Policy Research Working Paper No 4805. Washington, DC: The World Bank.

Kettl, Donald. 2016. *Politics of Administrative Process.* Los Angeles: CQ Press.

Kisunko, Gregory, and Stephen Knack. 2013. "Russian Federation: National and Regional Trends in Regulatory Burden and Corruption." Policy Note, April 2013, World Bank.

Kolstad, Ivar, and Arne Wiig. 2009. "Is Transparency the Key to Reducing Corruption in Resource-rich Countries?" *World Development* 37 (3): 521–32.

Emanuel Kopp, Lincoln Kaffernberger, and Christopher Wilson. 2017. "Cyber Risks, Market Failures and Financial Stability." IMF Working Papers, No. 17/185. Washington DC: The International Monetary Fund.

Kraay, Aart, Pablo Zoido-Lobatón, and Daniel Kaufmann. 1999. "Governance Matters." Policy Research Working Paper No 2196. Washington, DC: The World Bank.

Krueger, Anne. 1974. "The Political Economy of the Rent-Seeking Society." *American Economic Review* 64 (3): 291–303.

Kuecken, Maria, and Marie-Anne Valfort. 2019. "Information Reduces Corruption And Improves Enrolment (but Not Schooling): A Replication Study Of A Newspaper Campaign In Uganda." *The Journal of Development Studies* 55: 1007–1029.

Kuo, Didi. 2018. *Clientelism, Capitalism, and Democracy: The Rise of Programmatic Politics in the United States and Britain.* Cambridge: Cambridge University Press.

Kuris, Gabe. 2014. *From Underdogs to Watchdogs. How Anti-corruption Agencies Can Hold Off Potent Adversaries.* Princeton: Innovations for Successful Societies.

Madani, Dorsati, and Martha Licetti. 2010. "Business Regulation, Reform and Corruption." *PREM Notes 155.* Washington DC: The World Bank.

Mauro, Paolo. 2004. "The Persistence of Corruption and Slow Economic Growth." *IMF Staff Papers* 51 (1). Washington DC: IMF.

Mauro, Paolo. 1995. "Corruption and Growth." *Quarterly Journal of Economics* 110 (3): 681–712.

McNulty, Stephanie. 2011. *Voice and Vote: Decentralization and Participation in Post-Fujimori Peru.* Stanford: Stanford University Press.

Meagher, Patrick. 2005. "Anti-corruption Agencies: Rhetoric Versus Reality." *The Journal of Policy Reform* 8 (1): 69–103.

Mungiu-Pippidi, Alina. 2016. "For a New Generation of Objective Indicators in Governance and Corruption Studies." *European Journal on Criminal Policy and Research* 22 (3): 363–7.

Mungiu-Pippidi, Alina. 2015. *The Quest for Good Governance: How Societies Develop Control of Corruption.* Cambridge: Cambridge University Press.

Mungiu-Pippidi, Alina and Roberto Kukutschka. 2018. "Can a Civilization Know its own Institutional Decline? A Tale of Indicators." In *Governance Indicators: Approaches, Progress, Promise,* edited by Anheier, Haber, and Kayser, 71–102. Oxford: Oxford University Press.

Mungiu-Pippidi, Alina and Johnston Michael, eds. 2017. *Transitions to Good Governance: Creating Virtuous Circles of Anticorruption.* Cheltenham: Edward Elgar.

Mungiu-Pippidi, Alina, Mette Jensen, Marsa Loncaric, et al. 2011. *Contextual Choices in Fighting Corruption. Lessons Learned.* Oslo: Norwegian Agency for Development Cooperation.

Murphy, Kevin, Andrei Shleifer, and Robert Vishny. 1991. "The Allocation of Talent: Implications for Growth." *The Quarterly Journal of Economics* 106 (2): 503.

Newell, Peter, and Joanna Wheeler. 2006. *Making Accountability Count.* IDS Policy Briefing, No. 33. London: Institute for Development Studies.

North, Douglas, John Wallis, and Barry Weingast. 2009. *Violence and Social Orders: A Conceptual Framework for Interpreting Recorded Human History.* Cambridge: Cambridge University Press.

OECD and World Bank. 2018. *Improving Co-operation between Tax Authorities and Anti-corruption Authorities in Combating Tax Crime and Corruption.* OECD: Paris.

Peisakhin, Leonid, and Paul Pinto. 2010. "Is Transparency an Effective Anti-corruption Strategy? Evidence From a Field Experiment in India." *Regulation & Governance* 4 (3): 261–80.

Persson, Anna, Bo Rothstein, and Jan Teorell. 2018. "What Anticorruption Reforms Fail--Systemic Corruption as a Collective Action Problem." *Governance* 26: 449–71.

Pope, Jeremy, and Frank Vogl. 2000. "Making Anticorruption Agencies More Effective." *Finance and Development* 37 (2). Washington DC: IMF.

Posner, Daniel, Lily Tsai, and Evan Lieberman. 2014. "Does Information Lead to More Active Citizenship? Evidence from an Education Intervention in Rural Kenya." *World Development* 60: 69–83.

Quah, Jon. 2010. "Defying Institutional Failure: Learning From the Experiences of Anti-corruption Agencies in Four Asian Countries." *Crime, Law and Social Change* 53 (1): 23–54.

Recanatini, Francesca. 2011. "Anti-corruption Authorities: An Effective Tool to Curb Corruption?" In *International Handbook on the Economics of Corruption: Volume 2*, edited by Susan Rose-Ackerman and Tina Søreide, 528–70. Cheltenham: Edward Elgar.

Reinikka, Ritva, and Svensson, Jakob. 2004. "Local Capture: Evidence from a Central Government Transfer Program in Uganda." *The Quarterly Journal of Economic* 119 (2): 679–705.

de Renzio, Paolo, and Joachim Wehner. 2017. "The Impact of Fiscal Openness." SSRN Working Paper. https://papers.ssrn.com/sol3/papers.cfm?abstract_id=2602439

Rose-Ackerman, Susan. 1978. *Corruption: A Study in Political Economy.* New York: Academic Press.

Rose-Ackerman, Susan, and Bonnie Palifka. 2016. *Corruption and Government: Causes, Consequences, and Reform.* 2nd ed. New York, Cambridge: Cambridge University Press.

Rose-Ackerman, Susan, and Rory Truex. 2013. "Corruption and Policy Reform." In *Global Problems, Smart Solutions: Costs and Benefits*, edited by B. Lomborg, 632–672. Cambridge: Cambridge University Press.

Schütte, Sofie Arjon. 2015. "The Fish's Head. Appointment and Removal Procedures for Anti-corruption Agency Leadership." *U4 Issue no 12.* Bergen: Chr. Michelsen Institute.

Shah, Anwar. 2006. "Corruption and Decentralized Public Governance." Policy Research Working Paper No 3824. Washington, DC: The World Bank.

Sundet, Geir. 2007. "Public Expenditure Tracking Surveys. Lessons From Tanzania." *U4 Brief No 14.* Bergen: Chr. Michelsen Institute.

Svensson, Jakob. 2005. "Eight Questions About Corruption." *Journal of Economic Perspectives* 19 (3): 19–42.

Tanzi, Vito. 1999. "The Quality of the Public Sector." Paper presented at the *IMF Conference on Second Generation Reforms.* Washington, DC, November 8–9, 1999. Washington, DC: International Monetary Fund.

Trapnell, Stephanie. 2015. *User's Guide to Measuring Corruption and Anti-Corruption*. New York: UNDP Global Anti-corruption Initiative.

United Nations Development Programme. 2006. *Institutional Arrangements to Combat Corruption: A Comparative Study*. Bangkok: United Nations Development Programme.

Verkuil, Paul. 2007. *Outsourcing Sovereignty: Why Privatization of Government Functions Threatens Democracy and What We Can do About it*. New York: Cambridge University Press.

Wei, Shang-Jin. 2000. "How Taxing Is Corruption on International Investors?" *Review of Economics and Statistics* 82 (1): 1–11.

White, Colin. 2009. *Understanding Economic Development: A Global Transition From Poverty to Prosperity*. Cheltenham, Northampton: Edward Elgar.

World Bank. 2017. *Governance and the Law*. Washington, DC: The World Bank.

World Bank. 2012. *Fighting Corruption in Public Services: Chronicling Georgia's Reforms*. Washington, DC: The World Bank.

World Bank. 2006. *The Many Faces of Corruption: Tracking Vulnerabilities at the Sector Level*. Washington, DC: The World Bank.

World Bank. 2004. *Making Services Work for Poor People: World Development Report 2004*. Washington, DC: The World Bank.

World Bank. 1999. *Civil Society Reform. A Review of World Bank Assistance*. Report No. 19211. Washington, DC: (The World Bank).

World Bank and United Nations Office on Drugs and Crime. 2012. *Public Office, Private Interests: Accountability Through Income and Asset Disclosure*. Washington, DC: The World Bank.

Wrong, Monica. 2010. *It's our Turn to Eat: The Story of a Kenyan Whistle-blower*. New York: Harper Perennial.

Zoido-Lobatón, Pablo, Simon Johnson, and Daniel Kaufmann. 1999. *Corruption, Public Finances, and the Unofficial Economy*. Washington, DC: The World Bank.

Zuleta, Juan Carlos, Alberto Leyton, and Enrique Fanta Ivanovic. 2012. "Combating Corruption in Revenue Administration: The Case of VAT Refunds in Bolivia." In *The Many Faces of Corruption: Tracking Vulnerabilities at the Sector Level*, edited by J. E. Campos and S. Pradhan, 339–66. Washington, DC: The World Bank.

....

CHAPTER 23

INTERNATIONAL EFFORTS TO COMBAT CORRUPTION

....

MATHIS LOHAUS AND ELLEN GUTTERMAN

INTRODUCTION

ATTEMPTS to improve the domestic quality of government often involve international actors. The fight against corruption is no exception. Such efforts are often labeled as matters of good governance. In other instances, corruption has been linked to standards of democracy, to more procedural concerns about the rule of law, and (by some) as a matter of human rights. Irrespective of the framing in individual cases, fighting corruption can be seen as a necessary condition for quality of government: Impartial governance, the gold standard of QoG, is impossible under conditions of systematic corruption, which is always about providing benefits to some at the expense of others (Rothstein and Teorell 2008; Kurer 2005).

After early efforts to address the global challenge of corruption during the 1970s had failed, the issue rapidly gathered momentum during the 1990s. Today, the United Nations Convention against Corruption (UNCAC) has been ratified by 187 states and laws to curb corruption are commonplace around the world. At the same time, however, there is no evidence that quality of government has improved across the board. Corruption remains a crucial challenge for domestic governance as well as international cooperation. This chapter provides an overview of international efforts to combat corruption. It is guided by two broad questions: First, what is known about the emergence and characteristics of the various types of anticorruption efforts? Second, how do they affect the quality of government?

The remainder of this chapter is divided into two parts. First, the following section surveys global and regional anticorruption initiatives. This includes nonbinding initiatives, such as high-level declarations resulting from regional or global summits. Moreover, anticorruption is codified in various international treaties as well as in the rules of multilateral institutions. These commitments are briefly described to provide a bird's-eye view. Second, several issues are discussed in more detail: The linkage between international law and domestic implementation; the roles played by international mechanisms to prod governments towards compliance; and matters relating to the quality of government in the member states of the Organisation for Economic Co-operation and Development (OECD), which are crucial for effectively curtailing bribe payments and money laundering. The chapter concludes with a summary and future directions for international anticorruption research and policy.

WHAT IS INTERNATIONAL ABOUT THE FIGHT AGAINST CORRUPTION?

As a prerequisite, one needs to clarify why corruption necessitates an international response in the first place. Most corrupt practices, after all, likely occur within national boundaries. So, what is international about the fight against corruption? This agenda gained momentum in the 1990s in response to a number of global developments (George, Lacey, and Birmele 1999; McCoy and Heckel 2001). Two main factors are often named: The end of the Cold War and the global trend towards democratization. As competition between the blocs ceased to be the primary concern of foreign policy, it was no longer necessary for the major powers to protect allied but deeply corrupt regimes at all costs. The spread of democratic forms of government, at the same time, put pressure on political elites. Freedom of speech and other political rights translated into demands for more accountability, which prompted newly democratic governments to express their commitment to anticorruption measures. These two trends thus allowed anticorruption to take hold on the global stage.

In addition to the structural changes, the literature points to several political dynamics. In Europe, the end of the Cold War translated into efforts to admit new members into regional institutions. Seeing a need for harmonization before and during accession, the Council of Europe and the European Union (EC at the time) promoted reforms in the neighborhood. Some authors also point to the role of corruption scandals in Europe and other developed countries, triggering public outrage and demands for reform. In the meantime, the United States emerged as a powerful government advocate for anticorruption in the field of transnational business. U.S. exporters were bound by the 1977 Foreign Corrupt Practices Act (FCPA), which made it illegal to bribe foreign officials. For competitors from the rest of the OECD world, such practices were legal and often tax-deductible. As globalization led to more competition for global market shares, U.S. negotiators sought to level the playing field through an international agreement (Abbott and Snidal 2002). Finally, expert opinions on corruption shifted during the early 1990s. While previous works had speculated that corrupt practices might be useful to grease the wheels of commerce and bypass inefficient bureaucrats, new methods and evidence pointed to the detrimental effects of corruption on social and economic development. The famous "cancer of corruption" speech by World Bank president Wolfensohn illustrates this change of heart among academics and policy experts (Wolfensohn 1996). Since then, anticorruption has become a key objective for multilateral institutions and bilateral donors.

Trying to assess the relative importance of different explanatory factors seems moot at this point. One way or the other, anticorruption rapidly gained prominence, causing some to speak of a "corruption eruption" (Glynn, Kobrin, and Naím 1997). Critics refer to an "industry" or "gospel" of anticorruption (Sampson 2010; Wedel 2015). In any case, the mushrooming of initiatives (see below) stands in dramatic contrast to the situation up until 1995, when no international organization had yet adopted binding anticorruption commitments.

Now almost every sovereign state in the international system has ratified at least one international treaty designed to combat corruption; some have joined five global and regional conventions (Lohaus 2019b, 3).

Overview of International Law and Other Initiatives

Following the eruption during the 1990s and early 2000s, anticorruption is now well established on the global political agenda. This section surveys the literature regarding the emergence and characteristics of four types of initiatives: Political declarations adopted at high-level international summits; international treaties and protocols with some degree of legal obligation; anticorruption provisions in multilateral frameworks for development cooperation; and transnational initiatives involving nonstate actors. Research on their effects on the quality of government will be considered in the subsequent sections.

High-level political declarations

For decades, government representatives have used international gatherings to declare their intention to combat corruption. One of the earliest cases is the 1975 UN General Assembly Resolution 3514 on corrupt practices of transnational corporations. In this brief declaration, the General Assembly urged corporations to respect local laws while calling on governments to adopt anti-bribery legislation and gather data on corrupt practices. Several months earlier, a similar statement had been issued by the Organization of American States (OAS), in which the 35 members declared that transnational enterprises ought to act in accordance with the economic and social development goals of host countries. However, these early proposals regarding anticorruption were split between different interpretations of the problem. Among G-77 members, for instance, the view was that anticorruption policies were needed to constrain corporate conduct generally and to prevent the political interference of multinational corporations in democratic processes. In contrast, the United States emphasized a focus on illicit payments and corporate bribery as isolated transactions to be controlled (Katzarova 2019). As no coalition was able to sustain diplomatic efforts, the early initiatives fizzled out.

At the 1994 Summit of the Americas, corruption again appeared as a concern for heads of state. Seeking to energize the OAS and pave the way for closer cooperation across the Americas, the U.S. government provided organizational leadership for a new "hemispheric approach" to anticorruption. The summit's declaration recognized corruption as a challenge to democracy and multiple Latin American states backed the new agenda. Leaders in other regions issued similar declarations, for instance the 1999 "Principles for Combating Corruption in Africa" (Marong 2002).

Further high-level declarations have been made in the context of the G7/G8 and G20 meetings of powerful states. Participants of the G20 created an "anti-corruption working group" at the Toronto summit in 2010, followed by an "action plan" at the Seoul summit later that year. Since then, the G20 declarations have regularly mentioned corruption, and the action plan was recently updated for the 2019–21 period. Individual members have complemented this agenda. The British government, for instance, invited heads of state and other representatives from more than 40 countries to a 2016 anticorruption summit in London. While Transparency International (TI) deemed the meeting a success, other observers were less positive and demanded more concrete steps (Transparency International 2016).

With the establishment of the 2015 Sustainable Development Goals (SDGs), anticorruption took center stage in international development cooperation, too. With SDG 16.5, UN members vouch to "substantially reduce corruption and bribery in all their forms." Importantly from a QoG perspective, this commitment is linked to a benchmark. Success regarding SDG 16.5 is measured by how often public officials are bribed or ask for a bribe. This data is to be collected for two groups: The general public on the one hand, business actors on the other. Corruption has thus been established as a priority for development cooperation under the UN umbrella—albeit as one item among many.

International treaties and protocols

The most widely ratified international treaty to curb corruption is the 2003 United Nations Convention against Corruption, which has 187 state parties at the time of writing. In addition to its unparalleled reach, UNCAC stands out because it is very broad. The treaty encompasses 71 articles with provisions on preventive measures, rules regarding criminalization and jurisdiction, domestic standards of enforcement, and international cooperation (UNODC 2012). In 2009, a few years after UNCAC had been ratified, member states agreed to create a peer review system. The Implementation Review Mechanism (IRM) is meant to assess how member states implement different parts of UNCAC, with the current (second) cycle focused on prevention and asset recovery. The IRM employs a combination of self-assessment and (optional) country visits. Each country under review works to produce a consensus report with delegates from two peer states at similar levels of government performance. The consensus requirement means that countries under review can modify or even block publication of their IRM report. Other aspects of the IRM process also permit states to exploit lenient procedures and potentially manipulate the review process, which has lessened the perceived authority of the IRM among some parties (Jongen 2018). Regardless of these limitations, the IRM remains an active and vital component of the UNCAC and a significant accomplishment among international anticorruption efforts; its very creation surprised experts at the time, who had not expected the diverse UN membership to agree on such a mechanism (Chaikin and Sharman 2009, 41–2; Joutsen and Graycar 2012).

In contrast to the broad UNCAC, the OECD Convention on Combating Bribery of Foreign Public Officials in International Business Transactions is focused on transnational bribery. It was adopted in 1997 and has since been ratified by all OECD states as well as several nonmembers. As already mentioned, the origins of this agreement can be traced to lobbying by the United States, which sought to internationalize domestic legislation against the payment of bribes to secure business deals. In the absence of a global standard, governments would always be tempted to allow their businesses to pay bribes to gain a competitive advantage. That is why the OECD, whose members compete for the exports of goods and services, was seen as the optimal venue to solve this cooperation problem (Pieth 1997; Abbott and Snidal 2002; Gutterman 2015).

While UNCAC and the OECD convention receive the most academic and political attention, anticorruption was addressed in regional forums first. The OAS was the pioneer among regional organizations, adopting its anticorruption convention in 1996. The Council of Europe and European Union both adopted regional conventions, which focused mostly on harmonizing criminal law.[1] On the African continent, the Economic Commission for West Africa (ECOWAS) and the Southern African Development Community (SADC) adopted anticorruption protocols in 2001, shortly before the African Union (AU) finalized its anticorruption convention in 2003. Asia appears to be an outlier, although some regional groups cooperate with the OECD in nonbinding forums. Including the 2010 Arab anticorruption convention, largely ignored in the literature, at least nine international and regional organizations have thus adopted treaties to combat corruption.

While these documents share many elements, they are not identical in how they cover prevention, criminalization, enforcement, and international cooperation (Arnone and Borlini 2014; Lohaus 2019b; Snider and Kidane 2007; Wouters, Ryngaert, and Cloots 2013). Some organizations focus on a narrow range of corruption offenses. The OECD is primarily concerned with transnational bribery of foreign public officials related to business transactions, while the European Union initially created a treaty to ban bribery of its own officials. Enforcement cooperation in these cases relies on monitoring and peer pressure mechanisms to supervise member state compliance. Other cases combine binding language on a few core commitments with many optional clauses. The OAS convention, for instance, obliges members to ban a narrow range of corrupt behavior. It also allows states to establish illicit enrichment as a corruption offense—but leaves this as purely optional, because the concept was contested among member states. In contrast, the African anticorruption agreements stand out because they include many provisions with seemingly obligatory language. Not just far-reaching criminalization but also preventive measures, such as standards of procurement and public sector hiring, are mandatory in these cases. However, the high proportion of mandatory clauses is undermined by a lack of monitoring and enforcement, which arguably turns the African regional agreements into "illusionary giants" (Lohaus 2019b, chapter 2).

What explains this multitude of agreements? U.S. diplomats played a decisive role as advocates for the OAS, OECD, and UN conventions. As a result, Katzarova argues, the dominant American conception of corruption as transactional rather than systemic—that is, limited to bribery—has prevailed at the expense of alternative conceptions which may have otherwise challenged the rules of the international economic system, demanded curbs to the power of multinational corporations, and tackled networked aspects of corruption across the licit and illicit economic spheres (Katzarova 2019). In her book on the emergence of anticorruption efforts, Rose also emphasizes the influence of U.S. negotiators on the UNCAC and other initiatives (Rose 2015). Gutterman argues that international anticorruption efforts unfold within an American-dominated regime of extraterritoriality, fundamentally grounded in U.S.-based social, legal, and political concepts and diffused through distinctly American

---

[1] The European Union stands out among regional organizations. Its dedicated anticorruption agreements are relatively narrow; at the same time, many rules concerning procurement and other standards of public administration and good governance are regulated in other parts of EU legislation.

legal norms and practices (Gutterman 2019b). In his account of the fight against kleptocratic "grand corruption," Sharman identifies a more decentralized, undirected, and coincidental process of change and responses to development policy failures (Sharman 2017). Jakobi places the fight against corruption in the context of a broader trend towards global governance to curb criminal behavior. In line with similar measures against money laundering and other "evils," corruption thus became institutionalized in world society (Jakobi 2013). Lohaus argues that diffusion processes, such as learning and emulation, influenced the drafting of anticorruption treaties. The documents vary in content because they are designed to send signals to different audiences: domestic constituents, states in the same organization, or external development partners (Lohaus 2019b).

Multilateral institutions

The World Bank has incorporated anticorruption into its lending practices since the late 1990s when corruption was named as an obstacle to development. As with its policy on other issues of public administration and the rule of law, the Bank seeks to avoid inefficiencies or the misappropriation of funds. This was controversial at first, seeing how corruption was understood as a "political" concern. However, since the landmark "cancer of corruption" speech, the fight against corruption is established in the Bank's policy portfolio. The strongest enforcement mechanism, however, does not address the governments of recipient countries, but the behavior of companies competing for public tenders. When a company is found guilty of using bribery to win a procurement contract, it can be barred from future World Bank tenders. This debarment procedure was reformed multiple times during the 2000s and 2010s and is now managed by the Integrity Vice Presidency. Information on offenders is shared with regional development banks in Europe, Asia, Africa, and Latin America. This virtually always leads to cross-debarment since 2010 (Leroy and Fariello 2012; Søreide, Gröning, and Wandall 2016).

The effectiveness of the World Bank's measures is debated in the literature (e.g., Bauhr and Nasiritousi 2012; Marquette 2003; Weaver 2008). The same is true for measures adopted by the International Monetary Fund as well as the development agencies in the United Nations system. Because development cooperation is covered elsewhere in this volume (see Dietrich and Winters, this volume), we will not discuss these institutions further.

NGOs, professional associations, and business

Transparency International is arguably the leading transnational NGO in the field of anticorruption (Wang and Rosenau 2001; Gutterman 2014). It was founded in 1993 by a group of experienced development professionals. According to one of the founding members, the group was motivated by frustration with how development efforts were undermined by corruption (Vogl 2012, 61–3). While Transparency International's global headquarters—the TI Secretariat—are in Berlin, it has independent chapters at the national level. The chapters have country-specific priorities, but all parts of TI broadly follow three goals: raise public awareness about corruption, lobby governments and businesses, and keep track of developments around the globe. In 2006, TI started the UNCAC coalition together with other civil society actors. This loose network of NGOs now encompasses more than 300 partners. The coalition reflects TI's goal of organizing and exchanging ideas among anticorruption activists, also driven by the desire to present a unified position vis-a-vis government and business actors.

TI's best-known initiative is the Corruption Perceptions Index (CPI). Since 1995, the organization publishes an annual ranking of countries meant to reflect the levels of corrupt behavior perceived by citizens and business actors. The CPI has been praised for its enormous awareness-raising effect and criticized for methodological shortcomings (Heywood and Rose 2014). In addition to the CPI, the organization has published multiple iterations of the Bribe Payers Index (BPI), asking corporate actors to report illicit payments. TI also publishes reports on country compliance with the OECD convention. Yet overall, Transparency International's approach has been characterized as "non-confrontational" (Gutterman 2014). Particularly in the early years of (successful) agenda-setting, the organization often relied on high-level contacts and the persuasion of key government officials rather than mass mobilization or "naming and shaming" corrupt actors. Funding for TI mainly comes from government and multilateral development agencies.

Business actors have become active in international anticorruption, too. Business associations in multiple industries with high corruption risk have committed to codes of conduct and other nonbinding principles. The International Chamber of Commerce (ICC) published its first anticorruption rules in 1977; the document has been updated several times since, with the latest edition published in 2011 (ICC 2011). Additionally, business actors cooperate with governments and civil society. The Publish What You Pay (PWYP) initiative asks its member firms to publicize the conditions of deals related to natural resources. If fees and profits were public, so it was thought, citizens would be better able to hold their officials accountable (Getz 2006). A similar logic is enshrined in the multi-stakeholder Extractive Industries Transparency Initiative (EITI), founded in 2003 (Eigen 2009). This group includes multinational corporations (MNCs) in the extractive industries, host governments in mineral-rich countries, and MNC home governments. Initially designed as a voluntary process of revenue disclosure for payments from companies to governments, EITI has evolved into a global standard for the management and accountability of extractive industries and their value chains in resource rich countries. EITI rules now encompass a wide range of practices relating to contract transparency, beneficial ownership, and commodity trading (Lujala, Rustad, and Le Billon 2017). However, critics argue that certain exclusions from the reporting requirements—for instance, states do not have to disclose line-by-line sums regarding licensing fees—limit the EITI's potential to create full transparency (Rose 2015, 133–75).

In recent years, other NGOs, government-sponsored groups, and business-led initiatives have begun to champion anticorruption policies and practices of various kinds. Some take a more confrontational stance towards North American and European governments and private actors. Global Witness, a founding member of both PWYP and EITI, has exposed U.S. law firms that seemed all too willing to provide services to corrupt foreign officials seeking to hide the proceeds of corruption in American investments (Global Witness 2016). Investigative-reporting collectives and organizations working with whistleblowers have highlighted the flows of corruption-related funds in reports such as the "Panama Papers" and "Paradise Papers" (AIPC 2017). The Tax Justice Network, a small transnational NGO, advocates for reforms to curtail "financial secrecy" (Tax Justice Network 2018). These efforts put the spotlight on OECD member states, urging them to exclude ill-gotten gains from their financial systems. Integrity Initiatives International advocates the establishment of a permanent International Anticorruption Court to prosecute corrupt government leaders, on a jurisdictional basis akin to that of the International Criminal Court (Wolf 2018).

Increasingly, various organizations address corruption as part of their broader advocacy efforts.[2] The Open Government Partnership (OGP) has made anticorruption a key policy area in its work to enhance governance and "democracy beyond the ballot box" among national and local level participants. OGP has teamed with the organization OpenOwnership to establish a peer learning network for the promotion of beneficial ownership transparency in line with open data principles. By making company records publicly accessible, activists hope to improve governments' and other actors' ability to track corruption and related illicit financial flows. On the business side, the B Team is a not-for-profit initiative founded by prominent global business leaders. In addition to anticorruption initiatives and beneficial ownership transparency, the B Team encourages global business attention to broad social purposes including climate change and human rights. Under the umbrella of the World Economic Forum, corporate leaders have created the Partnering Against Corruption Initiative (PACI). By addressing corporate transparency and emerging market-risk, they seek to promote anticorruption practices that improve the ease of doing business. In sum, a new generation of NGOs, public–private partnerships, and business groups is adding to the range of anticorruption demands and policy proposals on the international scene.

THE IMPACT(S) OF ANTICORRUPTION EFFORTS

Since the 1990s, anticorruption pledges, international treaties, and other commitments have proliferated. Assessing the impact of such efforts is no easy task given the breadth of the literature and the difficulty of obtaining empirical evidence; corrupt practices are hard to study. It seems more appropriate to speak of multiple impacts on a wide range of actors and outcomes including discourse, laws, and behavior. This section first discusses how international law shapes the conditions for domestic governance. Focusing on literature from International Relations, the next part addresses how governments can be influenced through peer pressure and reputational costs. This is followed by a section on an underappreciated aspect of global anticorruption: The quality of government in OECD countries. In contrast to the usual targets of anticorruption reforms, the governments of highly developed states are crucial when it comes to controlling business-related bribery, money laundering, and illicit financial flows.

---

[2] See: www.opengovpartnership.org/policy-areas/, www.openownership.org/, www.bteam.org, and www.weforum.org/communities/partnering-against-corruption-initiative

International treaties and domestic implementation

International agreements prescribing standards are one part of the equation; yet their implementation depends on laws and practices at the national level. Both legal scholars and political scientists have analyzed the contents of anticorruption agreements, usually by comparing the range of issues addressed in the documents, their level of detail, and the degree of legal obligation for different provisions (Snider and Kidane 2007; Webb 2005; Wouters, Ryngaert, and Cloots 2013). Due to its importance as the only agreement with a global reach, UNCAC has received the lion's share of attention. The range of issues covered by the treaty is ambitiously broad. UNCAC features "no fewer than a dozen different levels of implementation obligations [...] from hard (mandatory requirements) to very soft" (Arnone and Borlini 2014, 258). In the words of one critic, the many escape clauses and concessions to domestic concerns work like "termites," undermining the potential of UNCAC as a serious commitment (Schroth 2005). Looking beyond UNCAC, some of the regional treaties and protocols have narrowly focused and obligatory clauses, while others resemble "illusionary giants" whose commitments seem less impressive upon closer inspection (Lohaus 2019b).

More fundamentally, some legal scholars debate whether international law can be expected to be an effective remedy against corruption (Davis 2012). Optimists would stress that international agreements indeed have made a mark. While certain aspects of corruption were illegal in many countries long before the 2000s, the adoption of UNCAC and regional treaties sparked further change. Many African states, for instance, introduced new anticorruption laws and institutions to comply with treaty commitments (Hatchard 2014, 33). This effect becomes obvious when looking at national anticorruption laws and authorities from Afghanistan to Zimbabwe, which often bear recent dates of adoption or amendment (UNODC 2019). One of the most widespread institutional reforms has been the creation of national anticorruption agencies, although enthusiasm about such institutions has since dampened among academics and policy experts (de Sousa 2010).

This brings us to the skeptical perspective, according to which anticorruption efforts are unlikely to systematically change incentives or serve as sources of moral persuasion. Critics contend that anticorruption institutions might be captured by elites and that legal rules have little traction in the context of limited statehood or developing economies. In addition to such general concerns, skeptics argue that international (and thus: external) actors are often unable to effectively tackle corruption because of their limited willingness, power, knowledge, and/or legitimacy (Davis 2012, 333–5).

To be sure, no robust link between the ratification of anticorruption treaties and subsequent improvements in the quality of government has been found (Mungiu-Pippidi et al. 2011). The consensus in the literature holds that three decades of international anticorruption efforts have yielded few, if any, positive results (Heywood 2018; Johnston 2018). Clearly, the implementation of treaties in national law is no panacea: Implementation guarantees neither enforcement nor effectiveness, especially in states with a strong executive and weak judiciary. While countries often implemented new policies shortly after they ratified UNCAC, for example, these were not necessarily effective (Buscaglia 2011). One study based on data from over one hundred countries between 1984 and 2012 has even argued that the flurry of initiatives led to an *increase* in perceived corruption, simply because citizens and business actors became more sensitive to corrupt practices (Cole 2015). Another recent quantitative study suggests that international organizations with relatively corrupt member states are unlikely to enforce anticorruption agreements. In other words, initiatives to address domestic corruption likely remain ineffective "cheap talk" in exactly those cases where they would be most useful (Hafner-Burton and Schneider 2019).

With respect to implementation of the OECD Convention to curb transnational bribery, the empirical evidence of impact is decidedly mixed. One study of foreign firms operating in Vietnam found that those from countries party to the Convention reduced their payments of certain kinds of illicit fees when the chances of discovery increased due to the Convention's monitoring and enforcement processes. However, the same study also observed an *increase* in corruption among firms from nonsignatory states during the same period (Jensen and Malesky 2018). Even among the Convention's signatory states, only a few countries are active enforcers. Countervailing pressures and electoral incentives in wealthy democracies sometimes promote *non*compliance with international anti-bribery rules (Gilbert and Sharman 2016; Gutterman 2017).

These empirical findings are difficult to generalize and compare because of diverging theoretical assumptions, statistical techniques, and operationalizations of the notoriously slippery concept of corruption. All quantitative studies relying on country-level corruption data should be taken with a grain of salt given the questionable quality of comparative data (Heywood and Rose 2014; Knack 2007). Yet overall, the skeptical perspective seems to prevail. In many countries, corruption does not appear to be a principal–agent problem amenable to legal-technical intervention. When the highest political elites are entrenched in corrupt networks, international commitments cannot change the fundamental incentives—even when they do lead to new implementing laws. The best bet for anticorruption activists might then be to think of corruption as a collective action problem. Seen through this lens, international instruments should not be expected to change the balance of power directly—but they might be useful to rally and empower domestic actors (Persson, Rothstein, and Teorell 2012; Mungiu-Pippidi 2015, 221–6).

In an alternative approach, "anticorruption" and the pursuit of "good governance" from above might be reconsidered completely, in favor of an explicitly political and normative approach premised on the cultivation of "deep democratization" from below (Johnston 2005, ch. 8; Johnston 2014; see also Sparling 2018). Pushing past a focus on impartiality as a procedural norm, this approach entails the promotion of domestic processes to increase pluralism, to open political and economic space for people to pursue their own interests in "safe" activism, and to maintain accountability among those in power. The goal is to enable citizens to defend themselves and their interests by political means, with an emphasis on the aspirations and grievances *they* care about. Rather than an implementation of international rules or an outcome of political activity, therefore, anticorruption is thus reconceived as a "continuing process of setting limits to power, building accountability, and establishing social and political foundations of support for reforms by bringing more voices and interests into the governing process" (Johnston 2013, 1238) This approach to "deep democratization" requires gradual reform over the long term, and it is difficult: It requires social and political actors to confront head-on what are real political disagreements about the nature of politics (Sparling 2018)—at base, questions about the appropriate relationships among states, markets, and bureaucracies—that international anticorruption treaties elide.

The political dynamics of peer pressure, persuasion, and reputation

International efforts may have a limited potential to affect the domestic quality of government. But that does not mean they have no impact whatsoever. Membership conditionality might be the strongest mechanism available to international organizations. The most likely case for this mechanism to be effective is the European Union, where membership rights are tied to enormous economic benefits. The EU's policy towards candidates and neighboring countries is the most widely cited success story when it comes to the promotion of QoG norms by international organizations (Sandholtz and Gray 2003; Szarek-Mason 2010; Börzel, Stahn, and Pamuk 2010). However, the EU's policy toolkit loses its bite as soon as the target state has acquired membership rights, which can lead to a "backsliding" dynamic that undoes previous reforms (Kartal 2014; van Hüllen and Börzel 2015).

A softer form of international pressure is exerted by peer review mechanisms, which are used in the anticorruption regimes of the Council of Europe, OECD, Organization of American States, and United Nations. In all four, member states periodically report on their efforts to implement the rules of the respective agreement, and other members of the organization provide their own assessments. While such reviews do not include sanctions, their effects as exchanges of information and venues for peer pressure are said to improve compliance with international standards. However, the existing anticorruption peer reviews differ regarding transparency towards the public, the formal rules of procedure, and the informal rules of criticism among members. The widely lauded OECD model of peer review might be difficult to replicate in other contexts (Jongen 2018; Carraro, Conzelmann, and Jongen 2019).

In addition to monitoring among peers, international anticorruption efforts routinely target the reputation of states that are found to violate global norms. In the field of anticorruption, such measures can be grouped in two camps. On the one hand, there are some state-led initiatives to single out offending businesses or governments. This includes the World Bank debarment measures and its rankings of good governance and the rule of law. The Financial Action Task Force (FATF)[3] and the European Union also publish "blacklists" to pressure governments into complying with standards against money laundering and tax evasion (Sharman 2010; Nance 2015). On the other hand, naming and shaming is often used by nongovernmental actors, which have no other leverage over governments. In addition to raising public awareness, assessment tools such as the Corruption Perceptions Index or the Financial Secrecy Index are designed to push governments towards behavioral change (Urueña 2018; Seabrooke and Wigan 2015). Corruption is also seen as a risk to transnational business and thus assessed by commercial services like the Economist Intelligence Unit and the PRS Group.

The International Relations literature discusses such mechanisms under the terms "naming and shaming," "ranking," "benchmarking," and the "politics of numbers" (Busby and Greenhill 2015; Broome and Quirk 2015; Kelley and Simmons 2015; Merry 2018; Cooley and Snyder 2015; Merry, Davis, and Kingsbury 2015). Several effects of such rankings and benchmarks can be distinguished. Some researchers stress that governments accused of

---

[3] The FATF was created in 1989 following a G-7 initiative to address money laundering. Its mandate has since been expanded to include measures against terrorist financing and corruption (Kahler 2018).

corruption might enact new policies because they genuinely seek the approval of their peers and the public; they are persuaded and socialized into tackling corruption. Other authors argue that rankings and blacklists constitute pressure rather than persuasion. When a government is labeled as corrupt, it will scramble to pay lip service to global norms, with the goal of appeasing constituents, donors, and/or investors. Critics of the various rankings thus emphasize the power relations hidden behind seemingly technical indicators. Examinees are taken to be *responsible* for a negative classification in the rankings, and for future improvement under the guidance of those who wield the power to set the standards in the first place (Löwenheim 2008).

At the same time, rankings obscure the responsibility of the multiplicity of actors and systems implicated in *transnational* (as opposed to purely domestic) corrupt practices and illicit financial flows. Rankings may thus depoliticize the problems they purport to measure (Merry, Davis, and Kingsbury 2015). The premise of country-level corruption rankings, furthermore, entails a methodological nationalism that is incompatible with transnational notions of corruption. They hardly account for the globalized networks of professionals and elites which facilitate corruption via cross-border illicit finance and offshore transactions (Cooley and Sharman 2017; Cooley 2018). In sum, the emphasis on country-level measures and rankings in analyses of corruption is not in line with how many forms of corruption operate in practice (Heywood 2017).

Transnational corruption and quality of government within the OECD

The most widely discussed element of transnational corruption is bribery in the context of cross-border trade and investment. All parties to the 1997 OECD Convention declared their willingness to stop corporations based in their territory from offering and paying bribes abroad. By curtailing the supply of bribery payments, quality of government can be improved to the extent that politicians in the receiving countries have fewer incentives to deviate from the public good. However, it is worth noting that the OECD agreement is not designed to address regulation in countries with low QoG scores (as much of development policy does). Instead, rules against foreign bribery concern law enforcement *in the exporting countries*—which are not normally worried about their own quality of government.

Based on the long history of the U.S. Foreign Corruption Practices Act, U.S. government agencies have become the most stringent enforcers of such laws, with the frequency of enforcement increasing over time (Gutterman 2019a). Due to the importance of U.S. markets, they also have the furthest reach, paired with enormous sanctioning power. No matter where multinational businesses are domiciled, they can be subject to U.S. enforcement actions. If a firm has ties to American markets, for instance via stock listings or dollar-denominated assets, or even simply makes use of financial instruments and communications that pass through the U.S., it can be prosecuted. By contrast, many other OECD member states seem to enforce their rules only infrequently. Half of them, in fact, had not ordered criminal sanctions once during the first twenty years of the Convention (OECD 2017). According to Transparency International, just a handful of OECD states can be considered "active enforcers" (Heimann, Földes, and Coles 2015).

How can this variation be explained? For the German case, local state attorneys appear to be crucial—which stands in contrast to the U.S., which has centralized enforcement at the federal level (Hoven 2018). Moreover, there seems to be a domino effect. Quantitative evidence suggests that countries are more likely to start enforcing their laws against foreign bribery once a company from their own jurisdiction has been targeted by enforcement from elsewhere (Kaczmarek and Newman 2011). While extraterritoriality is highly contested, it thus seems to have had a positive effect in the eyes of some anticorruption activists. However, relying on unilateral, extraterritorial action might become more difficult to stomach once other actors begin to play a more active role. Chinese foreign policy and legal doctrine, for instance, is increasingly assertive about pursuing disgraced officials and businesspeople abroad (Lang 2018; Quah 2018). The line between so-called "political" prosecutions and straightforward application of (international) law will remain contentious.

Money laundering, illicit financial flows, and international asset recovery all resemble transnational bribery: Effective regulation can only occur when OECD countries implement the respective standards, because that is where banks and financial intermediaries are concentrated. Another similarity is that unilateral actions by the U.S. government have been instrumental in triggering global change (e.g., Bean 2018). Driven by antidrug and anti-terrorism demands, the U.S. has strongly promoted the FATF, which has become the de facto standard setter on anti-money laundering (Kahler 2018). Together with the UN Office on Drugs and Crime, the World Bank has launched the Stolen Assets Recovery Initiative, which aims to help governments recover funds that (former) corrupt officials have stashed in financial centers abroad. Yet success has been limited due to the difficulties of acquiring evidence and building solid transnational cases (Pieth 2008; Fenner Zinkernagel, Monteith, and Gomes Pereira 2013; Gray, et al. 2014; Sharman 2017; Lohaus 2019a).

These aspects of illicit transnational finance are connected by two common threads. First, they are intimately connected to domestic corruption, which is often the predicate offense and the source of the funds channeled abroad (Chaikin and Sharman 2009) as well as a key driver of illicit trade in drugs, people, natural resources, and counterfeit goods (Shelley 2018). Second, the success of international efforts to curb these practices depends on governance and political will in highly developed states home to sophisticated financial institutions. It may not be feasible to completely alter incentives so that large-scale corruption simply becomes unattractive; but improved money laundering prevention and asset recovery mechanisms could contribute to justice and improved funding for development initiatives (Lohaus 2019a). Several scholars are advocating for this *transnational* view on anticorruption—either in addition to or instead of the predominant focus on improving QoG in developing countries (Cooley and Sharman 2017; Forstater 2018; Sharman 2017; Reuter 2012). Put differently, opposing corruption might require a look beyond the "usual suspects."

CONCLUSION

International efforts against corruption come in many shapes and forms not limited to intergovernmental treaties. They include soft law, self-regulation, naming and shaming, and hard law under various headings, like in parts of broader EU regulations. Thus, many international standards and tools are available to those willing to use them. However, enforcement remains selective. This is true even for the OECD anti-bribery rules, which can be considered the "gold standard" in terms of rule precision and the efficacy of peer review.

Some authors emphasize how anticorruption constitutes a success of nonstate activism, norm entrepreneurs, and moral arguments (Wang and Rosenau 2001; McCoy and Heckel 2001). Others focus on the success of foreign policy interests, most notably U.S. efforts to internationalize domestic norms against foreign bribery and, more recently, money laundering (Abbott and Snidal 2002; Kahler 2018; Katzarova 2019). Another perspective is centered on diffusion processes, with some authors emphasizing agents and mechanisms (Lohaus 2019b) and others choosing a structural lens, arguing that anticorruption conforms to broader (neoliberal) ideas (Bukovansky 2006; Jakobi 2013).

How do these international efforts affect the quality of government? So far, the debate between optimists and skeptics has yielded some empirical evidence in both directions: It seems that international measures led to legal and policy changes around the world but failed to trigger fundamental improvements in practice. At the same time, there is a lack of reliable and comparable data on corruption, money laundering, and other illicit financial flows. A first promising research agenda thus concerns measures of corruption. New and carefully calibrated expert assessments allow for methodologically sound comparisons over time (McMann et al. 2016). However, measures based on expert perceptions are no panacea. Empirical research can also benefit from creative ways to leverage objective and direct measures of corrupt behavior (for a special issue on this topic, see Mungiu-Pippidi 2016). Measurement is crucial not least because the Sustainable Development Goals include illicit financial flows as a phenomenon to be addressed.

Second, researchers trying to assess the impact of international efforts on the domestic quality of government should consider replicating and refining previous quantitative studies. This literature would benefit tremendously from a careful meta-analysis of how effects are conditioned by the choice of dependent variable, statistical techniques, range of covariates, timeframe under analysis, and regional variations. This call for careful stocktaking is closely linked to a third research objective: Qualitative case study evidence is necessary to probe the causal mechanisms driving statistical correlations. The effects of international anticorruption agreements most likely vary depending on the context, as illustrated by statistical analyses suggesting that preexisting corruption levels shape how governments respond to international commitments (Hafner-Burton and Schneider 2019). To explore the scope conditions for different causal arguments, case studies should be designed to complement previous research.

Fourth, corruption is closely connected to other dimensions of the quality of government. It thus seems logical to draw parallels when it comes to the politics of implementation. Conceptually, anticorruption measures resemble international democracy promotion and human rights treaties, which also seek to shape domestic governance and legal structures in pursuit of universalist standards. Political scientists and legal scholars have studied the effects of these international regimes—including unintended consequences and shortcomings—for decades. Given that democracy and human rights precede anticorruption on the global agenda, they may provide inspiration for successful strategies (e.g., Sikkink 2017). At the same time, corruption is linked to international political economy. Curbing money laundering, for instance, is not that different from other types of financial standard-setting, while transnational bribery poses challenges of monitoring and enforcement similar to other unwanted business practices. Anticorruption research could benefit from exploring these conceptual and methodological parallels more systematically by drawing on multiple streams of literature.

Finally, future research could broaden the scope of inquiry by investigating how global and regional debates on anticorruption evolve. Overall, the quantity of commitments and institutional support for initiatives like UNCAC suggests that anticorruption has become a robust international norm, although some aspects remain contested (Gutterman and Lohaus 2018). International efforts were propelled by the concerns of domestic actors—specifically American ones—and domestic enforcement, often including an element of extraterritoriality (Gutterman 2019b). Impending shifts in global leadership, most notably the rise of China and other emerging powers paired with the decline of U.S. hegemony, might thus alter the international anticorruption agenda. Assertive rising powers could seek to use anticorruption measures to crack down on political opponents. At the same time, critics of the status quo may hope that future initiatives change the long-standing notions of what is inside and outside of definitional boundaries. A shift in the discourse might, for example, put more emphasis on political corruption within the OECD world. Analyzing interference in elections, the influence of lobby groups, executive overreach, or the involvement of financial institutions in illicit transnational flows would open new avenues for considering the quality of government in the twenty-first century.

REFERENCES

Abbott, Kenneth W., and Duncan Snidal. 2002. "Values and Interests: International Legalization in the Fight Against Corruption." *Journal of Legal Studies* 31 (S1): 141–77. https://doi.org/10.1086/342006

AIPC. 2017. "The Plunder Route to Panama: How African Oligarchs Steal from Their Countries." https://www.zammagazine.com/images/pdf/documents/African_Oligarchs.pdf

Arnone, Marco, and Leonardo S. Borlini. 2014. *Corruption: Economic Analysis and International Law.* Cheltenham: Edward Elgar Publishing.

Bauhr, Monika, and Naghmeh Nasiritousi. 2012. "How Do International Organizations Promote Quality of Government? Contestation, Integration, and the Limits of IO Power." *International Studies Review* 14 (4): 541–66. https://doi.org/10.1111/misr.12009

Bean, Elise J. 2018. *Financial Exposure: Carl Levin's Senate Investigations into Finance and Tax Abuse.* Cham: Springer International Publishing.

Börzel, Tanja A., Andreas Stahn, and Yasemin Pamuk. 2010. "The European Union and the Fight Against Corruption in Its Near Abroad: Can It Make a Difference?" *Global Crime* 11 (2): 122–44. https://doi.org/10.1080/17440571003669142

Broome, André, and Joel Quirk. 2015. "Governing the World at a Distance: The Practice of Global Benchmarking." Special Issue: The Politics of Numbers. *Review of International Studies* 41 (05): 819–41. https://doi.org/10.1017/S0260210515000340

Bukovansky, Mlada. 2006. "The Hollowness of Anti-Corruption Discourse." *Review of International Political Economy* 13 (2): 181–209. https://doi.org/10.1080/09692290600625413

Busby, Joshua W., and Kelly M. Greenhill. 2015. "Ain't That a Shame? Hypocrisy, Punishment, and Weak Actor Influence in International Politics." In *The Politics of Leverage in International Relations: Name, Shame, and Sanction*, edited by Richard H. Friman, 105–22. United Kingdom: Palgrave Macmillan UK.

Buscaglia, Edgardo. 2011. "On Best and Not so Good Practices for Addressing High-Level Corruption Worldwide: An Empirical Assessment." In *International Handbook on the Economics of Corruption, Volume 2*, edited by Susan Rose-Ackerman and Tina Søreide, 453–77. Cheltenham: Edward Elgar Publishing.

Carraro, Valentina, Thomas Conzelmann, and Hortense Jongen. 2019. "Fears of Peers? Explaining Peer and Public Shaming in Global Governance." *Cooperation and Conflict* 24 (4): 001083671881672. https://doi.org/10.1177/0010836718816729

Chaikin, David, and J. C. Sharman. 2009. *Corruption and Money Laundering: A Symbiotic Relationship*. Basingstoke: Palgrave Macmillan.

Cole, W. M. 2015. "Institutionalizing a Global Anti-Corruption Regime: Perverse Effects on Country Outcomes, 1984–2012." *International Journal of Comparative Sociology* 56 (1): 53–80. https://doi.org/10.1177/0020715215578885

Cooley, Alexander. 2018. "How International Rankings Constitute and Limit Our Understanding of Global Governance Challenges: The Case of Corruption." In *The Palgrave Handbook of Indicators in Global Governance*, edited by Debora Valentina Malito, Gaby Umbach, and Nehal Bhuta, 49–67. Cham: Palgrave Macmillan.

Cooley, Alexander, and J. C. Sharman. 2017. "Transnational Corruption and the Globalized Individual." *Perspectives on Politics* 15 (03): 732–53. https://doi.org/10.1017/S1537592717000937

Cooley, Alexander, and Jack Snyder, eds. 2015. *Ranking the World: Grading States as a Tool of Global Governance*. Cambridge: Cambridge University Press.

Davis, Kevin E. 2012. "The Prospects for Anti-Corruption Law: Optimists Versus Skeptics." *Hague Journal on the Rule of Law* 4 (02): 319–36. https://doi.org/10.1017/S1876404512000188

de Sousa, Luís. 2010. "Anti-Corruption Agencies Between Empowerment and Irrelevance." *Crime, Law and Social Change* 53 (1): 5–22.

Eigen, Peter. 2009. "A Coalition to Combat Corruption: TI, EITI, and Civil Society." In *Corruption, Global Security, and World Order*, edited by Robert I. Rotberg, 416–29. Washington, D.C. Brookings Institution Press.

Fenner Zinkernagel, Gretta, Charles Monteith, and Pedro Gomes Pereira, eds. 2013. *Emerging Trends in Asset Recovery*. Bern: Peter Lang.

Forstater, Maya. 2018. "Defining and Measuring Illicit Financial Flows." In *Global Governance to Combat Illicit Financial Flows: Measurement, Evaluation, Innovation*, edited by Miles Kahler, Maya Forstater, Michael G. Findley, Jodi Vittori, Erica Westenberg, and Yaya J. Fanusie, 12–29. New York: Council on Foreign Relations International Institutions and Global Governance Program. https://www.cfr.org/report/global-governance-combat-illicit-financial-flows

Friman, H. Richard, ed. 2015. *The Politics of Leverage in International Relations: Name, Shame, and Sanction*. Houndmills: Palgrave Macmillan.

George, Barbara C., Kathleen A. Lacey, and Jutta Birmele. 1999. "On the Threshold of the Adoption of Global Antibribery Legislation: A Critical Analysis of Current Domestic and International Efforts Toward the Reduction of Business Corruption." *Vanderbilt Journal of Transnational Law* 32 (1): 1–37.

Getz, Kathleen A. 2006. "The Effectiveness of Global Prohibition Regimes: Corruption and the Antibribery Convention." *Business & Society* 45 (3): 254–81. https://doi.org/10.1177/0007650306286738

Gilbert, Jo-Anne, and Jason C. Sharman. 2016. "Turning a Blind Eye to Bribery: Explaining Failures to Comply with the International Anti-Corruption Regime." *Political Studies* 64 (1): 74–89. https://doi.org/10.1111/1467-9248.12153

Global Witness. 2016. "Lowering the Bar: How American Lawyers Told Us How to Funnel Suspect Funds into the United States." https://www.globalwitness.org/documents/18208/Lowering_the_Bar.pdf

Glynn, Patrick, Stephen J. Kobrin, and Moisés Naím. 1997. "The Globalization of Corruption." In *Corruption and the Global Economy*, edited by Kimberly Ann Elliott, 7–27. Washington, D.C.: Institute for International Economics.

Gray, Larissa, Kjetil Hansen, Pranvera Recica-Kirkbride, and Linnea Mills. 2014. *Few and Far: The Hard Facts on Stolen Asset Recovery*. Washington, D.C.: World Bank.

Gutterman, Ellen. 2014. "The Legitimacy of Transnational NGOs. Lessons from the Experience of Transparency International in Germany and France." *Review of International Studies* 40 (2): 391–418. https://doi.org/10.1017/S0260210513000363

Gutterman, Ellen. 2015. "Easier Done Than Said: Transnational Bribery, Norm Resonance, and the Origins of the US Foreign Corrupt Practices Act." *Foreign Policy Analysis* 11 (1): 109–28. https://doi.org/10.1111/fpa.12027

Gutterman, Ellen. 2017. "Poverty, Corruption, Trade, or Terrorism? Strategic Framing in the Politics of UK Anti-Bribery Compliance." *The British Journal of Politics and International Relations* 19 (1): 152–71. https://doi.org/10.1177/1369148116681731

Gutterman, Ellen. 2019a. "Banning Bribes Abroad: US Enforcement of the Foreign Corrupt Practices Act and Its Impact on the Global Governance of Corruption." *European Political Science* 18 (2): 205–16. https://doi.org/10.1057/s41304-018-0153-z

Gutterman, Ellen. 2019b. "Extraterritoriality as an Analytic Lens: Examining the Global Governance of Transnational Bribery and Corruption." In *the Extraterritoriality of Law: History, Theory, Politics*, edited by Daniel S. Margolies, Umut Özsu, Maïa Pal, and Ntina Tzouvala. Abingdon, Oxon: Routledge.

Gutterman, Ellen, and Mathis Lohaus. 2018. "What Is the 'Anti-Corruption' Norm in Global Politics?" In *Corruption and Norms: Why Informal Rules Matter*, edited by Ina Kubbe and Annika Engelbert, 241–68. London: Palgrave Macmillan.

Hafner-Burton, Emilie M., and Christina J. Schneider. 2019. "The Dark Side of Cooperation: International Organizations and Member Corruption." *International Studies Quarterly*. https://doi.org/10.1093/isq/sqz064

Hatchard, John. 2014. *Combating Corruption: Legal Approaches to Supporting Good Governance and Integrity in Africa*. Cheltenham: Edward Elgar Publishing.

Heimann, Fritz, Ádám Földes, and Sophia Coles. 2015. "Exporting Corruption. Progress Report 2015: Assessing Enforcement of the OECD Convention on Combating Foreign Bribery". *Transparency International* https://www.transparency.org/en/publications/exporting-corruption-progress-report-2015-assessing-enforcement-of-the-oecd

Heywood, Paul M. 2017. "Rethinking Corruption: Hocus-Pocus, Locus and Focus." *The Slavonic and East European Review* 95 (1): 21. https://doi.org/10.5699/slaveasteurorev2.95.1.0021

Heywood, Paul M. 2018. "Combating Corruption in the Twenty-First Century: New Approaches." *Daedalus* 147 (3): 83–97. https://doi.org/10.1162/daed_a_00504

Heywood, Paul M., and Jonathan Rose. 2014. ""Close but No Cigar": The Measurement of Corruption." *Journal of Public Policy* 34 (3): 507–29. https://doi.org/10.1017/S0143814X14000099

Hoven, Elisa. 2018. *Auslandsbestechung: Eine Rechtsdogmatische und Rechtstatsächliche Untersuchung*. Neue Schriften zum Strafrecht 15. Baden-Baden: Nomos Verlagsgesellschaft.

ICC. 2011. "ICC Rules on Combating Corruption: 2011 Edition." https://iccwbo.org/publication/icc-rules-on-combating-corruption/

Jakobi, Anja P. 2013. *Common Goods and Evils? The Formation of Global Crime Governance.* Oxford: Oxford University Press.

Jensen, Nathan M., and Edmund J. Malesky. 2018. "Nonstate Actors and Compliance with International Agreements: An Empirical Analysis of the OECD Anti-Bribery Convention." *International Organization* 72 (1): 33–69. https://doi.org/10.1017/S0020818317000443

Johnston, Michael. 2005. *Syndromes of Corruption: Wealth, Power and Democracy.* Cambridge: Cambridge University Press.

Johnston, Michael. 2013. "More than Necessary, Less than Sufficient: Democratization and the Control of Corruption." *Social Research* 80 (4): 1237–58.

Johnston, Michael. 2014. *Corruption, Contention, and Reform: The Power of Deep Democratization.* Cambridge: Cambridge University Press.

Johnston, Michael. 2018. "Reforming Reform: Revising the Anticorruption Playbook." *Daedalus* 147 (3): 50–62. https://doi.org/10.1162/daed_a_00502

Jongen, Hortense. 2018. "The Authority of Peer Reviews Among States in the Global Governance of Corruption." *Review of International Political Economy* 25 (6): 909–35. https://doi.org/10.1080/09692290.2018.1512891

Joutsen, Matti, and Adam Graycar. 2012. "When Experts and Diplomats Agree: Negotiating Peer Review of the UN Convention Against Corruption." *Global Governance* 18: 425–39. https://doi.org/10.5555/1075-2846-17.4.425

Kaczmarek, Sarah C., and Abraham L. Newman. 2011. "The Long Arm of the Law: Extraterritoriality and the National Implementation of Foreign Bribery Legislation." *International Organization* 65 (04): 745–70. https://doi.org/10.1017/S0020818311000270

Kahler, Miles. 2018. "Countering Illicit Financial Flows: Expanding Agenda, Fragmented Governance." In *Global Governance to Combat Illicit Financial Flows: Measurement, Evaluation, Innovation*, edited by Miles Kahler, Maya Forstater, Michael G. Findley, Jodi Vittori, Erica Westenberg, and Yaya J. Fanusie, 1–11. New York: Council on Foreign Relations International Institutions and Global Governance Program. https://www.cfr.org/report/global-governance-combat-illicit-financial-flows

Kartal, Mert. 2014. "Accounting for the Bad Apples: The EU's Impact on National Corruption Before and After Accession." *Journal of European Public Policy* 21 (6): 941–59. https://doi.org/10.1080/13501763.2014.910820

Katzarova, Elitza. 2019. *The Social Construction of Global Corruption: From Utopia to Neoliberalism.* Basingstoke: Palgrave Macmillan.

Kelley, Judith G., and Beth A. Simmons. 2015. "Politics by Number: Indicators as Social Pressure in International Relations." *American Journal of Political Science* 59 (1): 55–70. https://doi.org/10.1111/ajps.12119

Knack, Stephen. 2007. "Measuring Corruption: A Critique of Indicators in Eastern Europe and Central Asia." *Journal of Public Policy* 27 (03). https://doi.org/10.1017/S0143814X07000748

Kurer, Oskar. 2005. "Corruption: An Alternative Approach to Its Definition and Measurement." *Political Studies* 53 (1): 222–39. https://doi.org/10.1111/j.1467-9248.2005.00525.x

Lang, Bertram. 2018. "China's Anti-Graft Campaign and International Anti-Corruption Norms: Towards a "New International Anti-Corruption Order"?" *Crime, Law and Social Change* 70 (3): 331–47. https://doi.org/10.1007/s10611-017-9742-y

Leroy, Anne-Marie, and Frank Fariello. 2012. "The World Bank Group Sanctions Process and Its Recent Reforms." Washington, D.C.: The World Bank. http://pubdocs.worldbank.org/en/447971449169634017/Sanctions-Process.pdf

Lohaus, Mathis. 2019a. "Asset Recovery and Illicit Financial Flows from a Developmental Perspective: Concepts, Scope, and Potential." *U4 Issue* 2019:12. http://dx.doi.org/10.17169/refubium-25404.2

Lohaus, Mathis. 2019b. *Towards a Global Consensus Against Corruption: International Agreements as Products of Diffusion and Signals of Commitment.* Abingdon, Oxon: Routledge.

Löwenheim, Oded. 2008. "Examining the State: A Foucauldian Perspective on International 'Governance Indicators." *Third World Quarterly* 29 (2): 255–74. https://doi.org/10.1080/01436590701806814

Lujala, Päivi, Siri Aas Rustad, and Philippe Le Billon. 2017. "Has the EITI Been Successful? Reviewing Evaluations of the Extractive Industries Transparency Initiative." *U4 Brief* August 2017:5.

Marong, Alhaji B.M. 2002. "Toward a Normative Consensus Against Corruption: Legal Effects of the Principles to Combat Corruption in Africa." *Denver Journal of International Law and Policy* 30 (2): 99–129.

Marquette, Heather. 2003. *Corruption, Politics and Development: The Role of the World Bank.* http://dx.doi.org/10.1057/9781403943736

McCoy, Jennifer L., and Heather Heckel. 2001. "The Emergence of a Global Anti-Corruption Norm." *International Politics* 38 (1): 65–90.

McMann, Kelly, Daniel Pemstein, Brigitte Seim, Jan Teorell, and Staffan I. Lindberg. 2016. "Strategies of Validation: Assessing the Varieties of Democracy Corruption Data." V-DEM Institute Working Paper Series 2016:23.

Merry, Sally Engle. 2018. "Measuring the World: Indicators, Human Rights, and Global Governance." In *The Palgrave Handbook of Indicators in Global Governance*, edited by Debora Valentina Malito, Gaby Umbach and Nehal Bhuta, 477–501. Cham: Palgrave Macmillan.

Merry, Sally Engle, Kevin E. Davis, and Benedict Kingsbury, eds. 2015. *The Quiet Power of Indicators.* Cambridge: Cambridge University Press.

Mungiu-Pippidi, Alina. 2015. *The Quest for Good Governance: How Societies Develop Control of Corruption.* Cambridge: Cambridge University Press.

Mungiu-Pippidi, Alina. 2016. "For a New Generation of Objective Indicators in Governance and Corruption Studies." Special Issue: Measuring Corruption In Europe And Beyond. *European Journal on Criminal Policy and Research* 22 (3): 363–67. https://doi.org/10.1007/s10610-016-9322-1

Mungiu-Pippidi, Alina, Masa Loncaric, Bianca Vaz Mundo, Sponza Braga, Ana Carolina, Michael Weinhardt, Angelica Pulido Solares, Aiste Skardziute et al. 2011. "Contextual Choices in Fighting Corruption: Lessons Learned." Draft report commissioned by Norad, c/o ANKOR (the Anti-corruption Project) in cooperation with the Evaluation Department ("Contextual Choices for Results in Fighting Corruption", Reference number: 1001232). Accessed on January 6, 2021. https://papers.ssrn.com/sol3/papers.cfm?abstract_id=2042021

Nance, Mark T. 2015. "Naming and Shaming in Financial Regulation: Explaining Variation in the Financial Action Task Force on Money Laundering." In Friman 2015, 123–42.

OECD. 2017. "2016 Data on Enforcement of the Anti-Bribery Convention: Special Focus on International Co-Operation." http://www.oecd.org/daf/anti-bribery/Anti-Bribery-Convention-Enforcement-Data-2016.pdf

Persson, Anna, Bo Rothstein, and Jan Teorell. 2012. "Why Anticorruption Reforms Fail. Systemic Corruption as a Collective Action Problem." *Governance.* https://doi.org/10.1111/j.1468-0491.2012.01604.x

Pieth, Mark. 1997. "International Cooperation to Combat Corruption." In *Corruption and the Global Economy*, edited by Kimberly Ann Elliott, 119–31. Washington, D.C.: Institute for International Economics.

Pieth, Mark, ed. 2008. *Recovering Stolen Assets*. Bern: Peter Lang.

Quah, Jon S.T. 2018. "Combating Corruption in Asian Countries: Learning from Success & Failure." *Daedalus* 147 (3): 202–15. https://doi.org/10.1162/daed_a_00511

Reuter, Peter, ed. 2012. *Draining Development? Controlling Flows of Illicit Funds from Developing Countries*. Washington, D.C.: The World Bank.

Rose, Cecily. 2015. *International Anti-Corruption Norms: Their Creation and Influence on Domestic Legal Systems*. Oxford: Oxford University Press.

Rothstein, Bo, and Jan Teorell. 2008. "What Is Quality of Government? A Theory of Impartial Government Institutions." *Governance* 21 (2): 165–90.

Sampson, Steven. 2010. "The Anti-Corruption Industry: From Movement to Institution." *Global Crime* 11 (2): 261–78. https://doi.org/10.1080/17440571003669258

Sandholtz, Wayne, and Mark M. Gray. 2003. "International Integration and National Corruption." *International Organization* 57 (4): 761–800. https://doi.org/10.1017/S0020818303574045

Schroth, Peter W. 2005. "The United Nations Convention Against Doing Anything Serious About Corruption." *Journal of Legal Studies in Business* 12 (2): 1–22.

Seabrooke, Leonard, and Duncan Wigan. 2015. "How Activists Use Benchmarks: Reformist and Revolutionary Benchmarks for Global Economic Justice." Special Issue: The Politics of Numbers. *Review of International Studies* 41 (05): 887–904. https://doi.org/10.1017/S0260210515000376

Sharman, J. C. 2010. "Dysfunctional Policy Transfer in National Tax Blacklists." *Governance* 23 (4): 623–39. https://doi.org/10.1111/j.1468-0491.2010.01501.x

Sharman, J. C. 2017. *The Despot's Guide to Wealth Management: On the International Campaign Against Grand Corruption*. Ithaca: Cornell University Press.

Shelley, Louise I. 2018. "Corruption & Illicit Trade." *Daedalus* 147 (3): 127–43. https://doi.org/10.1162/daed_a_00506

Sikkink, Kathryn. 2017. *Evidence for Hope: Making Human Rights Work in the 21st Century*. Princeton: Princeton University Press.

Snider, Thomas R., and Won Kidane. 2007. "Combating Corruption Through International Law in Africa: A Comparative Analysis." *Cornell International Law Journal* 40 (3): 691–748.

Søreide, Tina, Linda Gröning, and Rasmus Wandall. 2016. "An Efficient Anticorruption Sanctions Regime? The Case of the World Bank." *Chicago Journal of International Law* 16 (2): 523–52.

Sparling, Robert Alan. 2018. "Impartiality and the Definition of Corruption." *Political Studies* 66 (2): 376–91. https://doi.org/10.1177/0032321717722360

Szarek-Mason, Patrycja. 2010. *The European Union's Fight Against Corruption: The Evolving Policy Towards Member States and Candidate Countries*. Cambridge Studies in European Law and Policy. Cambridge: Cambridge University Press.

Tax Justice Network. 2018. "Financial Secrecy Index - 2018 Results." Accessed January 30, 2018. https://www.financialsecrecyindex.com/introduction/fsi-2018-results

Transparency International. 2016. "Was It Worth It? Assessing Government Promises at the 2016 Anti-Corruption Summit." Accessed on January 6, 2021. https://www.transparency.org/en/publications/assessing-government-promises-at-the-2016-anti-corruption-summit

UNODC. 2012. "TRAVAUX PRÉPARATOIRES of the Negotiations for the Elaboration of the United Nations Convention Against Corruption: Electronic Version Incl. The Corrigenda

Issued in March and July 2012." Accessed on January 6, 2021. http://www.unodc.org/documents/treaties/UNCAC/Publications/Travaux/Travaux_Preparatoires_-_UNCAC_E.pdf

UNODC. 2019. "TRACK Legal Library." Accessed March 8, 2019. http://www.track.unodc.org/LegalLibrary/Pages/default.aspx

Urueña, René. 2018. "Activism Through Numbers? The Corruption Perception Index and the Use of Indicators by Civil Society Organisations." In *The Palgrave Handbook of Indicators in Global Governance*, edited by Debora Valentina Malito, Gaby Umbach, and Nehal Bhuta, 371–87. Cham: Palgrave Macmillan.

van Hüllen, Vera, and Tanja A. Börzel. 2015. "Why Being Democratic Is Just Not Enough: The EU's Governance Transfer." In *Governance Transfer by Regional Organizations: Patching Together a Global Script*, edited by Tanja A. Börzel and Vera van Hüllen, 227–41. Houndmills: Palgrave Macmillan.

Vogl, Frank. 2012. *Waging War on Corruption: Inside the Movement Fighting the Abuse of Power.* Lanham: Rowman & Littlefield.

Wang, Hongying, and James N. Rosenau. 2001. "Transparency International and Corruption as an Issue of Global Governance." *Global Governance* 7 (1): 25–49.

Weaver, Catherine. 2008. *Hypocrisy Trap: The World Bank and the Poverty of Reform.* Princeton: Princeton University Press.

Webb, Philippa. 2005. "The United Nations Convention Against Corruption: Global Achievement or Missed Opportunity?" *Journal of International Economic Law* 8 (1): 191–229. https://doi.org/10.1093/jielaw/jgi009

Wedel, Janine R. 2015. "High Priests and the Gospel of Anti-Corruption." *Challenge* 58 (1): 4–22. https://doi.org/10.1080/01603477.2015.990831

Wolf, Mark L. 2018. "The World Needs an International Anti-Corruption Court." *Daedalus* 147 (3): 144–56. https://doi.org/10.1162/daed_a_00507

Wolfensohn, James D. (1996): "People and Development". Annual Meetings Address by James D. Wolfensohn, President. World Bank. Washington, D.C. Accessed January 6, 2021. http://documents.worldbank.org/curated/en/135801467993234363

Wouters, Jan, Cedric Ryngaert, and Ann Sofie Cloots. 2013. "The International Legal Framework Against Corruption: Achievements and Challenges." *Melbourne Journal of International Law* 14 (1): 1–76.

....

CHAPTER 24

CONTROLLING CORRUPTION
Institutional Strategies

....

MICHAEL JOHNSTON

ANTICORRUPTION INSTITUTIONS AND WHAT THEY DO

....

MANY institutions contribute to the success or failure of anticorruption efforts. While a full listing of types and examples lies well beyond the scope of this discussion, we can note major categories and activities of institutions directly aimed at corruption control (see also Heywood 2018), and of others that make essential contributions in the course of doing other things (Rothstein 2011).

Corruption itself is a diverse, contextually rooted and rapidly evolving bundle of problems with no fixed analytical definition, and no universally accepted standards of measurement. As a consequence, institutional controls come in many forms and do not fall into neat categories. Still, we might consider them in terms of whether they are aimed primarily at bureaucratic or political corruption—or at both—acknowledging that such distinctions are far from precise. Then comes a discussion of the effectiveness of these controls, and a concluding survey of the "research frontier": Kinds of questions that must be raised, and the evidence and methodology that will be needed to sort them out.

Initial truths

Anyone hoping to understand corruption—much less, to control or reduce it—will have to start with some basic facts. One is that corruption itself can be an institution (Teorell 2007). Opportunistic smash-and-grab cases are common, and it is therefore tempting to think of corruption as one-off bad deeds done by bad people—and thus, as a straightforward crime-and-punishment issue. But dominant political machine parties and patronage networks, corruption linked to drug and arms cartels, bureaucracies captured by business interests, and rings of colluding officials in the customs sector (just as examples) can be long-lived and deeply entrenched, developing their own networks and incentive systems. They can entrench themselves by political and sometimes legal means—or through violence. Formal organizations can become largely or completely corrupt, with their budgets and leadership structures helping to perpetuate corruption rather than inhibit it; examples might include a systemically corrupted police force. Some clearly legal activities—or at least, ones that are not clearly illegal—can nonetheless be seriously corrupt. Lessig (2013) and Thompson (2018) have shown how "institutional corruption"—corporations that pay for favorable legal testimony and "scientific" findings regarding their products and activities, or distorted policy and decision-making flowing from legal political contributions, for example—can embed itself in the workings of legitimate organizations, simultaneously helping and undermining those institutions and their activities.

Variations on such themes are numerous, but all hold a critical lesson for reformers: Corruption is not necessarily a marginal form of deviance that will go away once we bring it to light. It can become stronger and better organized than the institutions intended to bring it under control. Not only powerful corrupt elites, but sometimes powerless and vulnerable citizens, can have a stake in the corrupt status quo, or believe they stand to benefit from it in the future. Reform groups often find it difficult to earn public credibility, while bad experiences may have persuaded many citizens that change is more likely to be for the worse than for the better. Often, serious corruption is described in language usually reserved for dread diseases: Corruption as "the cancer of democracy" is a favorite theme. Few would dispute that significant corruption does great social, political and economic damage, but it does not necessarily follow that unchecked corruption will lead directly to systemic collapse. Indeed, the case of the old Soviet Union and its client states suggests that pervasive, entrenched corruption can help prop up a dysfunctional regime.

Sorting out Institutions and their Roles

Table 24.1 offers an inventory of institutional approaches to corruption control. It divides institutions into those dealing directly with corruption problems, and those making more general contributions. Corruption itself is divided into bureaucratic and political varieties—the former referring to administrative and implementation functions, and the latter involving parties, elections and campaigns, and efforts by private parties to influence the substance of policy. The boundary between bureaucratic and political corruption is depicted as a broad gray line to acknowledge that the two categories are not always sharply demarcated. In the bottom section of the table the bureaucratic/political distinction disappears because institutions in that area can restrain corruption indirectly and in both domains.

Bureaucratic and Political Corruption Control: General Purpose Institutions

Anticorruption Agencies

Over one hundred dedicated anticorruption agencies (ACAs) have been established around the world (Quah 2017). They vary in many ways: Some have constitutional status while

Table 24.1 Illustrative institutional checks on corruption

	Bureaucratic corruption	Political corruption
Dedicated institutions	Anticorruption agencies (ACAs)	
	Investigation (and prosecution in some cases) Public liaison and education Corruption prevention (functions vary among ACAs)	
	General judicial systems Special corruption courts Prosecutors	
	Transparency procedures Conflict of interest rules/financial Disclosures	
	Police	Protections for electoral processes
	Audit agencies Legislative oversight Internal affairs processes	Party and Campaign funding rules – limits on contributors – limits on spending – subsidies, matching funds
	Whistleblower protection	– "blinding"
		Civil Service/merit system protections/ controls on "spoils systems" – limits on political activity of public employees
Supporting institutions	Political/structural (electoral/party systems, representation)	
	International agreements and cooperation ISO standards	
	Civil society organizations, pressure Civil liberties Free press, news media Political norms	

Note: The gray boundary between the bureaucratic and political cells indicates that the distinction between bureaucratic and political corruption is not always clear-cut.

others have been established by ordinary legislation or by executive order. As will be noted below, ACAs vary in terms of their powers, main strategies, and relationships with other state institutions. Some are generally successful; others are generally regarded as failures, or as helping a regime to use corruption control as a pretext for moving against its critics. DeSousa defines ACAs as "public bodies of a durable nature, with a specific mission to fight corruption and reducing the opportunity structures propitious for its occurrence in society through preventive and/or repressive measures" (de Sousa 2009, 5).

An ACA can focus on corruption problems in some depth and may be given special powers to investigate and prosecute cases, and even to reverse burdens of proof. In some cases it can also have broad responsibilities in the private sector, and for corruption prevention within organizations both public and private. ACAs generally come in three varieties: *Multipurpose agencies* possessing all of the powers noted here; Hong Kong's Independent Commission Against Corruption (ICAC) with its "three-pronged strategy" (investigation and prosecution, prevention, and public education), is a primary example. Similar agencies are found in New South Wales and other states of Australia; Lithuania; and Botswana, with several Asian countries such as the Republic of Korea emulating the ICAC model in some respects. *Law enforcement agencies*, of which Singapore's Corrupt Practices Investigation Bureau (CPIB), dating from 1952, is the oldest and best-known, emphasize detection, investigation, and punishment; similar agencies have been established in Belgium, Norway, Malta, and Romania. Finally there are *prevention-focused agencies*—some of which work by coordinating the efforts of other institutions (e.g. Georgia, Albania, Azerbaijan) and some of which (Slovenia, Montenegro, Serbia, France) assume direct responsibility for prevention. The categories and examples here are drawn from International Association of Prosecutors (2019).

Courts and judiciaries

Courts and judiciaries are a critical part of any anticorruption regime, but they can be problematical as well. Their capacity and quality can vary tremendously. Corruption cases in Japan, the Philippines, and elsewhere may take seven or eight years before a verdict is reached. In Nigeria, for example, if a judge retires, is moved to another court, dies, or for other reasons leaves a case in progress, the trial must be started over with a new judge from day one. Long backlogs of cases mean that witnesses may leave the jurisdiction or lose their nerve; memories fade, records and other evidence can be destroyed, and key participants—including defendants—may die. In Japan, among other examples, lawyers for elderly persons accused of corruption have been known to file one motion after another, and to seek repeated postponements and continuance rulings, in effect to "run out the clock" so that their clients will never be convicted (on the case of Tanaka Kakuei see Mitchell 1996). The Republic of the Philippines has addressed those issues by setting up a special corruption court, the *Sandiganbayan*, but it has never been fully staffed. Some cases arising in the "pork barrel" scandals during the Noy Aquino presidency involved over 30 defendants and may well have stretched the court beyond its limits. A related issue is the scale of penalties that may be imposed; some in the Philippines were defined long ago and are not commensurate with the gains corrupt figures can realize.

Transparency: Let the Sun Shine in?

Transparency principles and practices have major implications for both the political arena and administration. Transparency "refers to the principle that information about, and used by, major institutions and actors in both the public and (in somewhat different ways) private sectors, should be widely available, in the belief that the public both has a right to know about activities affecting their lives and can use information to hold the powerful accountable" (Johnston 2019, 2).

Transparency is a widely supported value in most democracies, and has been a key part of corruption control since the days of Jeremy Bentham, who emphasized "publicity," and

Justice Brandeis, who may or may not have told us that "sunlight is the best disinfectant" (Johnston 2019). At times, "transparency" is used as a general synonym for good government and corruption control, yet few reform ideas have experienced as little critical evaluation. From the balance sheets of publicly held corporations to the budgets of government entities at all levels—and, within many systems, the financing of parties and election campaigns too—transparency is held to be a fundamental value. The core notion is that an informed public, aided by free and independent news media, will have a vested interest in scrutinizing what government, interest groups, parties and their candidates, and political contributors, do, and in checking revealed abuses either at the polls or by other sorts of political pressure.

Stated thus, the argument seems plausible, but in practice there are difficulties. Publishing government budgets and reports on policy implementation may well inhibit egregious abuses—to what extent, we may never know, as corruption that does not occur is even more difficult to measure than that which does—and few would recommend that public funds be raised and spent, and policy be made in total secrecy. "Sunshine laws" allowing public attendance at government meetings may have similar democratic appeal. But ordinary citizens generally spend little time reading official budgets and attending public meetings,[1] and if they do they will usually find that organized interests got there first and have a superior grasp of details. Similarly, open-meeting "sunshine" laws can be quite useful to other officials: In a large U.S. state years ago, I heard a heated conversation between two officials which ended with "Fine, if you won't tell me what you're doing about (Issue X), I'll sunshine your meeting...."

Conflict-of-Interest laws and disclosures

Institutions of several sorts can focus on officials' personal financial interests and ties. Conflict-of-Interest (COI) rules and financial disclosure procedures are of particular importance in both the bureaucratic and political arenas: An official who, say, owns property that might be earmarked for a public use—the classic case is George Washington Plunkitt's soliloquy on "honest graft" (Riordon 1995)—or whose relatives own a firm that is a government vendor is in a COI situation. Those financial interests may encourage decisions or actions contrary to the best interests of the public, even if the assets in question are fully legal; and at other times, the issue might be aiding criminal activities or enterprises. The basic idea of COI is often misunderstood, not only by the public but by the political official who says, "yes, my family does have large investments in government vendor X, but I don't do anything to help them." COI is a *situation*, not an action, which is the rationale for requirements that officials and/or family members declare their financial interests, and divest themselves of assets creating possible conflicts, before the official takes office.

COI controls have widespread support as a corruption-controlling institution, but they are not without their drawbacks, particularly on the implementation side. Overly intrusive financial disclosure requirements and investigations may well deter able and creative

---

[1] A video clip from an open meeting in one American town features two officials who stand at the front table, pledge their allegiance to the flag, and then sit down and look out at an empty room. They are the only two in attendance. See https://www.youtube.com/watch?v=RTXUIVmJQmQ. Accessed November 22, 2019. Thanks to Jennifer Kartner for spotting it.

individuals from entering, or staying in, government service. A culture of caution and intimidation can take hold in which officials become reluctant to innovate, or even to excel, lest they draw unwelcome attention. Values of integrity and public service may give way to rule-following and box-checking for their own sakes. Those rules, moreover, may impose inefficiency or reduce the quality of performance, perhaps inhibiting some forms of corruption but in the process impairing the overall quality of government (Anechiarico and Jacobs 1996).

Institutions Focused Primarily upon Bureaucratic Corruption

Police

In societies influenced by British control such as Hong Kong, for many years the police had primary responsibility for detecting and punishing corrupt activities. That was often a lamentable choice, one akin to having a fox guard the chicken coop, as police have many opportunities to engage in misconduct of their own. In part for those reasons, police authorities as frontline anticorruption institutions have become less prominent, often giving way to ACAs as corruption has become a more prominent concern. At the same time, ACA investigation and enforcement activities often have much in common with policing, and cooperation with police forces (particularly when it comes to alleged corruption within police agencies which, after all, are bureaucracies in their own right) can be essential.

Audit agencies

For transparency and scrutiny by the courts, legislators, and the public to be effective, high-integrity audit agencies are essential. While they do not focus solely on corruption, they can investigate, make rules, enforce transparency, and mete out penalties. Given sufficient resources, independence, and leadership, they can reveal suspect activities and provide critical evidence to prosecutors and other investigators. Their effectiveness—particularly with respect to transparency—requires political actors, interest groups, journalists and citizens with lasting reasons to look at what transparency reveals and act upon it.

Legislative oversight may be most effective in separation-of-powers systems with competing political parties; there, it can involve investigation, law- and rulemaking, budgetary and regulatory sanctions or incentives, and the like. McCubbins and Schwartz (1984) have distinguished between "police patrol" and "fire alarm" styles of oversight; routine monitoring of procedures is the main emphasis of the former style, while the latter involves direct responses to problems as they come to light. Both styles have their uses: Institutionalized "police patrols" can enforce long-standing norms to be internalized by staffers but can also become a *pro forma* exercise in which larger questions of integrity are forgotten and venal staffers learn how to avoid detection. High-profile "fire alarm" responses can attract public and political support, but because of their intermittent and likely inconsistent nature, may have little effect once a scandal fades from view. In some parliamentary systems parliamentary committees ordinarily have little or no independence from the government of the day, and legislative oversight may be weak; professional civil servants might be more effective at imposing informal constraints on political figures (for humorous but realistic examples see Lynn and Jay 1987).

Internal affairs processes

Many bureaucratic agencies—notably, police authorities—treat corruption as an internal matter. It may well be that relatively minor corrupt dealings can best be handled that way, rather than immediately escalating them to matters of criminal justice: That would quickly overburden judicial systems that are often struggling with the caseloads they have at present. Moreover, internal adjudication enables punishments that are proportional to minor offenses, and that can be levied quickly and with less stringent burdens of proof. But too often the internal affairs approach can be a way to keep significant corruption problems out of the public eye, and to avoid scrutiny by other governmental and political bodies. Particularly in police departments, where an "us-*versus*-them" culture may already be strongly institutionalized, internal adjudication can amount to more of a cover-up than a control.

Whistleblower protection

The term "whistleblower" likely dates from the nineteenth century or before, when police were often summoned with whistles, and police themselves found them useful for getting citizens' attention. In 1778 the U.S. Continental Congress intervened in the prosecution of two Rhode Island citizens who had reported misconduct by a high naval official, providing funds for their legal defense. Later that year, it unanimously approved legislation, providing "That it is the duty of all persons in the service of the United States, as well as all other inhabitants thereof, to give the earliest information to Congress or any other proper authority of any misconduct, frauds or misdemeanors committed by any persons in the service of these states, which may come to their knowledge" (National Whistleblower Center 2019). "Whistleblower" continues to refer to a person who reveals, or makes key allegations of, corrupt behavior, often within the organization where they are employed.

Such reports can be important in checking corruption, but not surprisingly they—and the people who make them—are often unpopular with top leadership. Examples abound of whistleblowers who are fired, suspended, ostracized, or kept on the payroll but stripped of their responsibilities. Whistleblowing is more common in the bureaucratic realm; it can occur in politics too, but corruption allegations there tend to become parts of routine political contention. Clearly, however, whistleblower reports within an agency can have more general political consequences.

Whistleblower protections are written into law, or specified by regulation, in many contemporary societies (European Commission 2018; U.S. Department of Labor 2019). Actual protection, however, is uneven at best, particularly within the private sector, and there are numerous ways managers or coworkers can make a whistleblower's situation extremely difficult without actually resorting to dismissal or punishment. At the same time, protection can be abused: Some incompetent employees on the verge of being fired have produced last-minute evidence or allegation of corruption by others and fallen back upon whistleblower protection to avoid dismissal (Anechiarico and Jacobs 1996).

Institutions Focusing Primarily upon Political Corruption

Corruption issues in politics are more diverse and contested than in the bureaucratic and administrative worlds: Elections, campaigns, the flow of funding, and voting can all become corrupted, and other issues, such as agency capture, may involve elected officials too. "Political" corruption can thus be a very broad category, yet institutional oversight is often limited. That is in some respects a good thing, as—particularly in emerging democracies—administrative interventions into political processes can become abusive in their own right. In authoritarian systems, by contrast, elections may happen as a public exercise but power is claimed and used in ways that have little to do with day-to-day politics.

Political corruption can be a matter of perceptions. If citizens believe they are excluded from decision making by conniving elites, a democratic system (or an aspiring democracy) has a corruption problem, at least at the level of public credibility. Those issues are often overlaid with concerns like inequality; regional, ethnic, religious, and cultural divisions; and historical events of many sorts. Legality may be beside the point: In the United States, for example, the vast majority of political contributions are given, received, and disclosed within the law—or at least, not clearly in violation of it—yet large majorities have long seen the system as corrupted (Johnston 2005, ch. 4; Johnston 2014, ch. 7). Warren's (2004) argument, that the essence of corruption in a democracy is the "duplicitous exclusion" of people from processes and decisions affecting their lives, is instructive. Most will agree that elections should be *fair*, with all eligible voters able to participate, and parties and candidates able to compete on a fundamentally equal footing. At the same time, we want them to be *free*, in the sense that preferences and (within limits) their intensity may be expressed without restriction. In competitive systems, that often involves spending private funds, sometimes supplemented by public money.

But there can be trade-offs between "free" and "fair." Regulating processes in the name of fairness will be seen by some as compromising freedom, while where the financing and conduct of campaigns is left up to competitors themselves, fairness may suffer. Further complicating the situation is that in democracies, election rules are generally written by incumbent officials with a stake in the status quo, and are closely watched by parties, interest groups, and private contributors who have helped put those legislators in office. In authoritarian systems electoral oversight, if any, is likely to reflect the interests of those at the top.

Electoral procedures and administration

Ensuring that parties and candidates are placed on the ballot within consistent eligibility rules, that all persons eligible to vote may do so (and those who are not, cannot), and that eligible voters know where, when, and how to vote, are critical to checking electoral corruption. Votes must be cast, collected, and counted honestly, and results must be promptly and accurately reported to the public. Those processes are governed by election legislation, and often by constitutional provisions, in nearly every country. The Electoral Integrity Project (EIP) has identified 11 dimensions on which electoral procedures may be evaluated: Electoral laws; electoral procedures; district boundaries; voter registration; party registration; media coverage; campaign finance; voting process; vote count; results; and electoral authorities (Norris and Grömping 2019). That list shows how complex and challenging it can be to maintain high-quality electoral procedures. EIP's annual reports include a Perceptions of Electoral Integrity Index, an expert survey giving numerical scores for 166 countries tabulated by region, regime type, electoral process, and the like. Not surprisingly, scores cover a wide range: Denmark leads the list with an aggregate score of 86 on a 100-point scale, while three countries (Burundi, Equatorial Guinea, and Ethiopia) score only 24.[2] The International Foundation for Electoral Systems (IFES)[3] emphasizes similar concerns, with a focus on new and emerging democracies. It conducts frequent Electoral Integrity Assessments and issues White Papers, on a rapid response basis when necessary, and publishes a range of other materials on an election-by-election basis.

Party and campaign funding

The tension between "free" and "fair" is more acute when it comes to party, candidate and campaign funding. Here again, most countries have political party legislation, in some cases grounded in constitutional provisions, and many have laws on party financing (a comparative framework and cases appear in Norris and van Es 2016). An election administration body may be a referee, ensuring that procedures are followed and rules fairly enforced; in other systems that body, or the national treasury, may distribute subsidies or matching funds linked to small private contributions, numbers of members or registered voters, or vote shares in past elections.

Major policy types include:

- Limits on contributors: Who may contribute funds or in-kind support, to whom, by what routes, within what limits and during what time periods, are important issues. Some countries allow only their own nationals to contribute; others place limits on various categories of contributors and support, distinguishing between monetary and in-kind support; contributions directly to candidate or party organizations versus expenditures made independently, and so forth (a comparison of Mexican, Canadian, and American policies appears in Tokaji 2018).
- Limits on spending: Other interventions may limit spending by parties and candidates. That can raise complex questions in countries where speech, or political speech, receives constitutional or legal protection—not least about the inherent relationship (if any) between political money and speech. Free elections would seem to encourage as

[2] As with other such rankings, we should not necessarily see those three countries as "worst in the world," as there are others that could not be included in the ranking at all.
[3] https://www.ifes.org/

much speech as possible, in all forms and by all contenders, but fairness may be endangered if one party or candidate can finance so much advertising as to drown out other voices. There is no way to strike a definitive balance. Spending may be limited overall, or in categories such as advertising, by parties or by individual candidates, and at various levels of jurisdiction within federal systems. Other restrictions may apply to spending on voter registration and get-out-the-vote activities, party conferences, and compliance with regulations. Outright vote-buying is generally banned yet remains commonplace in a number of societies (Nichter 2014; Schaffer 2007).

- Transparency and financial disclosures are among the most basic controls on electoral corruption. Making problems visible, the argument runs, will elicit legal and political punishment of wrongdoers, but most data emerge well after elections and in such a flood that all but the worst transgressions can be difficult to spot. It was also hoped that publishing financial data would build trust in the political process, but they have likely done more to persuade citizens that politics is awash in money. Since the Federal Election Campaign Act of 1973[4] and court cases beginning with *Buckley v. Valeo* (1976)[5], American political finance regulation has heavily relied upon transparency— all the more so in recent years as courts have tended to equate political money with speech. Citizen perceptions of corruption in American politics have worsened in recent years, and while some voters consider financial reports as they vote, contributors and fundraisers arguably use them as "target lists" (Levine and Johnston 2016; Johnston 2019; on other unintended consequences of transparency see Sebold and Dowdle 2018). Such data also help contributors insist that elected recipients give them value for money (D'Angelo, Ranalli, and King 2017).

"Blinding" in place of transparency

An alternative to publishing contributions is to make them confidential, or at least unverifiable (Ackerman and Ayres 2002; Levine and Johnston 2016). Contributions might be made to a central agency, credited to candidate accounts, and periodically distributed *en bloc* with donors names removed, on a smoothed-out basis so that a large contribution would not easily show up as a bulge in receipts. All contributions in money or in kind would be subject to a ten-day take-back option. Even if a donor told a candidate a contribution had been made, or if a candidate demanded to be told, such claims would thus be unverifiable. Ironically, this system would work better if some were to lie about whether or not they had contributed. Donor records would be retained by the agency for enforcement purposes but not otherwise disclosed. Such a scheme has yet to be fully implemented anywhere; an experiment by the UK Labour Party in 1997 turned out badly when data on tobacco industry contributions were leaked to journalists. But with a reliable central agency, the "blinding" scheme might have considerable merit; it has attracted interest in Korea and Chile in years past.

---

[4] 2 U.S.C. Ch. 14 § 431 *et seq.*
[5] 424 U.S. 1.

Subsidies and matching funds

In the name of fairness public funding, raised either by contributions or out of general budgets, could be used to put "floors" under spending by qualified candidates, or to amplify the influence of small contributions by matching them at various levels. Alternatively, Germany provides subsidies to parties in order to facilitate equal public participation. Subsidies and matching funds can be deployed in creative ways (Malbin and Parrott 2017) to counteract influence by large contributors. Some American states and cities require candidates to qualify by raising some quota of small contributions, at which point they are given the option of accepting only public funds for the rest of the campaign or going it alone with private contributions. Public funding schemes have encountered opposition from critics seeing them as threatening the freedom side of the electoral trade-off.

Limits on the "spoils system"

A final set of interventions are aimed at the "spoils system"—political favoritism in hiring, firing, and disciplining the government work force, in awarding contracts, and policy decisions. Civil Service procedures require that workers pass examinations, and provide some protection against political pressures. While patronage practices were once defended as a way to build parties and bring people into politics (Riordon 1995 ed.), more recent jurisprudence (cf. *Rutan v. Republican Party of Illinois*[6]) has taken a much dimmer view. Arguments that political activity on the part of public employees threatens a fair electoral system underlie laws such as the Hatch Act,[7] enacted in 1939 and subsequently amended, prohibiting all but a few top officials in the federal executive branch from participating in electoral campaigns and fundraising.

SUPPORTING INSTITUTIONS

Institutions dedicated to corruption control usually depend upon support from others carrying out more general functions. Sound administration of their routine functions, supported by appropriate resources, personnel, and legal tools, is important; so too are legitimacy and public support, which can be deepened by consistent processes and outcomes. Key institutions serving such supporting functions include those conferring authority (e.g. constitutions and electoral systems); those charged with using and restraining authority (legislative, executive, and judicial institutions within parliamentary and, in differing ways, within separation-of-powers frameworks); those facilitating implementation of policy and enforcement of laws (law enforcement, courts, bureaucracies and, at times, federalism); and those facilitating participation and social feedback (civil liberties, free press, self-organizing

---

[6]   497 U.S. 62 (1990).
[7]   Public Law 76-252, 53 *Stat.* 1147; officially, An Act to Prevent Pernicious Political Activities.

civil society, and channels of dissent). That list also highlights the breadth of support and co-ordination that successful control can require.

Categorizing an institution as "supporting" does not imply secondary importance. A number of ACAs lack the power to lodge legal charges and prosecute cases, for example, and must depend upon prosecutors and courts. A free press can bring cases to light, and a strong civil society can put pressure upon government to enforce laws. Electoral systems may create—or weaken—incentives for parties to watch each other closely, and for voters to respond to corrupt activities. Political norms are intangible and diffuse but can be of critical importance: In the United Kingdom, for example, a number of important ethical standards (e.g. the notion of an MP's overriding loyalty to the House of Commons) amount to un-written law. The drawback, of course, is that norms may be disregarded with impunity—witness the former U.S. President's refusal to disclose his tax returns despite a fifty-year tradition that candidates and winners will do so.

Constitutional architecture and electoral arrangements

Gerring and Thacker (2004, 2008) have developed a "centripetal" theory of government, supported by empirical data, suggesting that unitary and parliamentary systems, rather than federal and separation-of-powers/presidential models, are better at corruption con-trol. Closed-list Proportional Representation, in which party leaders decide who will appear on its candidate list and in what order candidates will be allocated seats, confers analogous centripetal advantages. Decentralizing institutions, a characteristic common to many well-governed societies, are often proposed (see Karlström 2015) as opening up government to greater scrutiny and bringing it "closer to the people." That same openness, on the other hand, may create points of access for potential corrupt actors. Parliamentary and unitary states—as the term "centripetal" suggests—facilitate politics and institutions that are inclu-sive yet authoritative, "focusing political energies toward the center" (Gerring and Thacker 2008). Tighter controls over agendas, decisions, and implementation, and greater ability to broker among the diverse interests that back a party, should help make "centripetal" systems better at corruption control. Karlström (2015) argues that the implications of decentraliza-tion for corruption control depend upon the presence or absence of other institutions that provide citizens with information and enable them to act on it. Decentralization may well help check corruption in democratic societies, but under authoritarian regimes it will likely make matters worse.

International agreements and cooperation

Corruption respects no national boundaries and, increasingly, seems to capitalize on off-shore dealings, weak institutions wherever they may be, and business activities that seem to take place everywhere yet be taxed and regulated nowhere. International agreements and cooperation are increasingly critical for corruption control; they began in 1977 with the United States Foreign Corrupt Practices Act (FCPA) and include, more recently, the OECD Anti-Bribery Convention, the United Nations Convention Against Corruption (UNCAC), regional agreements in Latin America and Africa, and new national regulations on international bribery in the United Kingdom and France. In some respects these international initiatives are a category of controls all their own: They are agreements among sovereign states, but often they require signatories to change their legal frameworks and enforcement priorities. In that sense, such agreements are more than just supporting institutions, but since they are implemented largely through domestic institutions they are categorized here.

International initiatives are significant not only for their scope but also for their potential to inhibit the sort of corruption that originates, and serves interests in, the affluent North and West, but is carried out in developing countries. Some such corruption facilitates international trafficking in drugs, arms, and human beings. In some respects, international anticorruption initiatives emulate law enforcement and ACA activities, but they also emphasize sharing of information and expertise and coordination of activities. Larger countries that are party to such agreements can use the clout of their banks, markets, and regulatory agencies to put pressure upon international bad actors and the movements of funds and people they exploit. A chronic difficulty, however, is that some governments' commitment to treaties and compacts may be more symbolic than real. Domestic politics and poor institutional capacity are just two reasons why actual compliance may be elusive.

ISO standards

A final, and recent, international initiative comes from the International Organization for Standardization (ISO). Its relatively new (2016) ISO 37001 series of Anti-Bribery Management Standards—part of a larger 37000 series on Guidance for the Governance of Organizations—lays down detailed practices for detecting and responding to bribery by and within businesses and other organizations. Along with FCPA and similar legislation, it has spawned an active global "compliance" industry. A firm that does not follow ISO standards covering a wide range of activities in many series other than 37000 cannot be certified as being in compliance. The hope is that corrupt operators will find it difficult to do business with those in compliance, and that compliant practices will become general practice. The scope and detail of the ISO standards are remarkable, and their potential impact will be worth careful study as time passes. One concern is that by treating those organizations as isolated yet isomorphic, ignoring the broader systemic causes of corruption and impediments to reform, and restricting the view of corruption primarily to bribery, they will reduce concerns of integrity and justice to codified rule-following.

Civil society

For many reasons a strong and diverse civil society—self-organizing citizen activity in the realm between the household and the state—can help control corruption. A robust civil society can build mutual trust and legitimate leadership, diffuse organizational skills, communicate and reinforce shared values, encourage awareness and participation in public affairs, and build shared organizational and social resources useful for dealing with a variety of problems. Nearly every comprehensive anticorruption strategy will incorporate civil society into its repertoire.

But civil-society action against corruption is plagued by constraints, misunderstandings, and chronic problems. In undemocratic societies civil society may not exist, may be manipulated from above, or may be intimidated, deeply divided, and plagued by violence or poverty. Even in established democracies, civil society may be far weaker than we expect (Putnam 2000). Too many reformers understand "civil society" to mean only formal organizations dedicated to corruption control; groups seeking such public goods, however, are frequently vulnerable to collective action problems, and to being compromised or destroyed by the regime. Where civil society has helped check abuses of power, it has often been via informal, multipurpose, and socially rooted shared activities, demanding better government by pushing for changes or services in which its members have a lasting stake. The formal-organizations approach, by contrast, often devolves into a handful of donor-supported organizations in and around the national capital—organizations with few deep social roots and little connection to the problems of most citizens. Not surprisingly, some of those organizations evolve into grant-seeking vehicles for their leaders rather than means of popular mobilization. Those reform efforts might do better to support socially rooted groups and movements with a variety of agendas—social activity and mutual aid, local economic development, education—to build grassroots leadership and social networks sufficient to help citizens resist exploitation and demand fair treatment.

A few more general institutions are worth mention here. *Civil liberties*—even de facto liberties that fall short of functioning democracy but still allow some criticism of a regime—can become a useful force for better government (Isham, Kaufmann, and Pritchett 1997). *Political norms* and commitment to the *rule of law* may likewise seem only theoretical constraints on those in power, but the current travails of established democracies in the face of so-called "populist" movements and rulers convinced of their own impunity shows their importance. As with many other things, we may not fully appreciate them until they are gone, or in crisis. Finally, *free, independent, and credible news media* help keep the public informed, contribute to vital social conversations and values, and can be watchdogs in their own right. The steep decline in print journalism seen in recent years has made it more difficult to check corruption with the force of an informed public. American communities that lose a local newspaper tend to see local government borrowing costs increase significantly (Gao, Lee, and Murphy 2018). Whether that signals increases in actual corruption is impossible to say, but it seems likely that public scrutiny of local governments and politics have been weakened.

Do They Work?

The effectiveness of corruption controls is a critical question with few clear answers because we lack a consensus definition of corruption itself. Moreover, we lack valid, reliable measures of corruption—particularly, of those applying to a level of detail comparable to specific controls—as it is frequently a clandestine activity. ACAs and other reform groups often publish data on their activities—cases handled, conferences held, testimony offered—but have little hard evidence on trends in corruption itself. A further question is, progress toward *what*? What is the opposite of corruption, and what do we seek in the long term? "Less corruption" is a natural response, but without good metrics, how can we know? "Less corruption" also overlooks the possibility that corruption comes in different varieties reflecting distinctive origins, having contrasting effects, and requiring differing responses—all of which complicates the question of causality for any trends.

We might, for example, seek greater trust in government, or a general sense that justice, fairness, and the rule of law prevail. Polling data on political trust are available in most democracies, but even where positive trends are indicated—not a common result, as of late—it is hard to know just what creates or sustains them. Indeed, some transparency measures seem to have backfired: For example, revelations of campaign contribution levels that may have been common may appear to signal a flood of private money and influence.

Indeed, beyond a few specific cases there seems to be little clear-cut success to account for. Indeed, Transparency International (TI) notes that its 2018 Corruption Perception Index

> reveals that the continued failure of most countries to significantly control corruption is contributing to a **crisis in democracy** around the world. While there are exceptions, the data shows that despite some progress, most countries are failing to make serious inroads against corruption (Transparency International, 2019 emphasis in original; see also Drapalova 2019).

Process-tracing evidence from the European Union's ANTICORRP project (Mungiu-Pippidi and Johnston 2017) highlights Chile, Costa Rica, Estonia, Georgia, South Korea, Taiwan, and Uruguay as having reduced corruption to varying extents; Rwanda and Botswana might be added to that list. Those cases offer valuable lessons, but most are comparatively small societies and (with the major exception of Rwanda) socially relatively homogeneous. Several (e.g. Chile, Estonia, Georgia, Rwanda) likely owe recent progress more to the effects of system-shaking crises than to any impact of the international reform movement.

Lasting successes in larger, diverse societies are few and hard to document. Affluent democracies generally receive high ratings on perception-based indices, and most well-rated countries—with notable exceptions—are democracies. But those assessments are open to question: Such countries are likely to be home to "institutional corruption" (Lessig 2013; Thompson 2018) or "influence markets" (Johnston 2005; Johnston 2014) in which activities many see as corrupt, or corrupting, carry on within the law and are protected by legal and political institutions. Furthermore, some unknown share of corrupt activity occurring in developing societies originates in, and benefits, more fortunate developed countries. Even if we trust the indices, causality is complex: Does Sweden (say) check corruption because it is affluent and democratic; is it affluent and democratic because it limits corruption; or does it enjoy all of those advantages because of other developments dating back many generations? Uslaner (2017), for example, makes a strong case that contemporary levels of corruption in many countries can be traced to the availability of public education *in 1870*.

Alternatively, consider ACAs: While the category reflects wide variations in structure, powers, control tactics, and backing, in most countries an ACA is still the best-resourced anticorruption institution—at least, at the outset. If a *bona fide* ACA must struggle to make progress in a society, more modest approaches are less than promising as well. Here again, the evidence is not particularly encouraging. The Hong Kong and Singapore stories are familiar history, well-documented in Quah's (2017) comparative assessment of several Asian ACAs. Both are atypical, however, because of the small scale of the two societies. Neither is a democracy, meaning that anticorruption action organized from above could proceed with relatively few constraints. Other ACAs in the region—notably Korea, the Philippines,

Taiwan, and Japan—have produced only limited benefits at best. Some ACAs are far from fully staffed, and some face political headwinds if they become overly ambitious in their efforts. Quah rightly notes that the "policy context"—political alignments, history, economics and demographics—can limit ACA efforts and results.

Meagher (2005) tells a similar story based on rigorous evidence that cuts through the rhetorical claims made on ACAs' behalf. Where the legal, institutional, political, and social environment is supportive (and where, we might speculate, corruption control might have taken root without an ACA), success can be demonstrated. But in countries that are poorly governed overall and suffer serious economic problems, ACAs are unlikely to succeed— and might even do harm. Meagher's lesson is important for mainstream reformers, from whom "establish an ICAC" is a frequent recommendation. Far better, it would seem, to build stronger social and political foundations for governing institutions, and for citizens demanding better government, than to expect an ACA to produce quick benefits. De Sousa (2009), while correctly seeing ACAs as among the more innovative reform ideas in current discussions, similarly sees their results as "meagre" in many cases.

Heilbrunn sums up the situation best:

> [A]nti-corruption commissions fail to reduce public sector venality in all but a few special circumstances.... [G]overnments that have established successful anticorruption commissions have done so in response to demands for reform from a broad base of domestic constituents. Demands for reform generally occur after a precipitating crisis has caused deep economic hardship and a national consensus exists that reforms must be implemented. Anticorruption commissions are effective when they respond to that national consensus and a broad domestic coalition supports reform. Without the precipitating crisis, building such domestic coalitions is a challenge for even the most popular leaders. When support is more tenuous, policymakers have an incentive to weaken reforms and avoid any threat to powerful constituents who profit from official inattention to expenditures, access to governments contracts, and other manifestations of public sector inefficiency (Heilbrunn 2004, 2).

These shortcomings have recently led to a welcome reconsideration of the ACA model. The Jakarta Statement on Principles for Anti-Corruption Agencies (UNODC 2012) was developed in conjunction with the UNCAC process, and in 2015 TI launched its Anti-Corruption Agencies Strengthening Initiative, beginning with the Asia-Pacific region. The former advances key principles regarding resources, leadership and independence, adherence to the rule of law, and agencies' own integrity and internal accountability, among others, while the latter seeks to mobilize support from TI country chapters and other partners. Both initiatives reflect a much-needed rethinking of the ACA concept; a problematical aspect of the Jakarta Statement, however, is that it proposes a lack of "political will" as a core problem. Political will is a tempting idea but is fundamentally a slogan whose validity cannot be demonstrated until after the fact (Johnston 2018).

The safest verdict with respect to the effects of institutional corruption controls is usually "not proven." There may be benefits at the level of public perceptions from being *seen* *to* make a significant reform effort. Against that, however, is the possibility "reforms" might do actual harm (e.g., setting political spending limits so low that campaigns cannot be waged without illicit funds, as has been the case at times in the past in both Italy and Brazil); might be a pretext for locking up opposition leaders and chilling dissent; might place citizen supporters at risk; or might merely waste reform opportunities and squander public support.

THE RESEARCH FRONTIER

What sort of research agenda, then, do we need? There are many goals we could choose. A top priority would be to develop more valid and reliable proxy indicators for trends in corruption. The "proxy" notion is important because we are unlikely ever to get around the fundamental problems of measuring activities that are usually kept secret. Instead of attempting to measure the problem directly, or settling for compilations of various observers' perceptions, proxies can draw upon some of the consequences or enabling conditions of corruption to identify "hot spots" of vulnerability. Measurements of government performance—the speed and accuracy of processes, the variability and negotiability of taxation and regulatory processes, the quality of outcomes—and benchmarking them over time and across jurisdictions (Johnston 2010) is one option. A bureaucratic function that is unusually fast or slow, and that involves unusually numerous or few steps by comparison to similar processes elsewhere, might signal the frequent use of "speed" money or a past history of bribes that encourages functionaries to drag their feet until a payment is made. The assumption here is not that the fastest process is the best one—few would want to see power plants licensed in 48 hours—but rather that such indicators and benchmarks can indicate vulnerabilities and steps to be taken in response. Because this approach can be focused upon specific locations, agencies, and functions, it can provide reformers with detailed knowledge of whether anticorruption measures are having any effect. Proxy indicators can come in many forms: Consider the U4 (2016) "proxy challenge" competition, or Integrity Action's (2016) "fix rate." If they are inexpensive, replicable, policy-neutral, and non-intrusive, they can be of immense value in corruption control (Stephenson 2019).

Another important challenge is to differentiate among kinds of corruption, their origins, dynamics, and consequences. One-dimensional corruption rankings obscure more than they reveal: In effect they tell us that corruption is the same thing everywhere, varying only in terms of more versus less. Incorporated into statistical models, those index scores suggest that the causes and effects of corruption are also the same wherever it occurs. Stated thus, the idea has obvious flaws; we should not keep falling back on perception scores simply because they are convenient (for alternatives see Rothstein, Charron, and Lapuente 2013; Mungiu-Pippidi and Dadašov 2016).

More emphasis on "legal corruption," as discussed earlier, would also help us understand the political (as well as administrative) dynamics of corruption, its link to developments such as so-called "populism," and the wide gaps between what citizens think is corrupt—or corrupting—and what most contemporary reforms actually address (Thompson 2018; Lessig 2013; Dinçer and Johnston 2015; 2017). It would be facilitated by the improved proxy measures suggested above and would direct useful attention to parts of the private sector that deserve much closer scrutiny. Such analysis would closely link corruption studies to emerging concerns about inequalities—not only of wealth and income, but also of power—and to more complete understandings of fairness and justice. They, after all, are why corruption is worth studying in the first place.

A final research focus may be most important of all. We need a far better understanding of how corruption and reforms fit into the societies and institutions surrounding them. That would entail, first, working definitions of corruption that forego the search for sharp distinctions between corrupt and acceptable actions, and for subtle elaborations on cultural and linguistic concepts that bear little resemblance to corruption issues as real people understand them, and that instead begin with the conflicts, grievances, aspirations, and expectations that lead various situations and actions to be characterized as corrupt. The resulting definitions would not point toward consensus, nor should they be intended to. Indeed, they may well highlight contention and disagreement over the nature of power, who should hold it, and how it should and should not be used (a modest attempt at such a definition appears in Johnston 2014, ch. 1). But if the effectiveness of ACAs, for example, depends upon political support, then which (and whose) grievances they take on, how they communicate and justify their agendas, and the specific sorts of outcomes they aim to produce will be matters of critical importance. Arid, process-oriented notions of "good governance" may be appealing when viewed from 30,000 feet, but dealing with the day-to-day problems of citizens on the ground may be the real challenge an ACA confronts. Much the same goes for understanding the opposition reformers will always encounter. Like "legal corruption," these ideas can change our thinking about corruption in fundamental ways—away from seeing it as a clearly defined sort of deviance and toward a much broader and more political view. Research that emphasizes sophisticated process-tracing methods and longer-term historical linkages—that relies upon what Geertz (1973) called "thick description"—might, much more than work employing statistical methods alone, *tell us a story* that guides reform and our expectations of it, and that shows clearly why corruption control will never be finished.

None of that is to suggest that quantitative work and the study of administrative processes should cease. Far from it: Good data and case studies in particular will always be needed. But we who worry about corruption must be equally concerned about fairness and justice in people's lives, both in the public and private sectors and those murky regions that are part of both. That sort of research agenda will be long term in nature—as will the reforms it suggests. But corruption has been with us throughout history, and shows no signs of fading away, so we continue to have time—and good reason—to get the research right.

REFERENCES

Ackerman, Bruce, and Ian Ayres. 2002. *Voting with Dollars: A New Paradigm for Campaign Finance.* New Haven: Yale University Press.

Anechiarico, Frank, and James B. Jacobs. 1996. *The Pursuit of Absolute Integrity: How Corruption Control Makes Government Ineffective.* Chicago: University of Chicago Press.

D'Angelo, James, David C. King and Brent Ranalli. 2017. "The Evolution of Transparent Corruption." Unpublished manuscript. Accessed November 22, 2019. http://congressionalresearch.org/extrafiles/images/DAngelo2017EvolutionOfTransparentCorruption.pdf

de Sousa, Luis. 2009. "Anti-corruption Agencies: Between Empowerment and Irrelevance." *Crime, Law and Social Change* 53 (1) (February): 5–22. https://doi.org/10.1007/s10611-009-9211-3

Dinçer, Oguzhan C., and Michael Johnston. 2015. "Measuring Illegal and Legal Corruption in American States: Some Results from the Edmond J. Safra Center for Ethics Corruption in America Survey." Working paper number 58, Edmond J. Safra Center for Ethics, Harvard University (March 16). https://dx.doi.org/10.2139/ssrn.2579300

Dinçer, Oguzhan C., and Michael Johnston. 2017. "Political Culture and Corruption Issues in State Politics: A New Measure of Corruption Issues and a Test of Relationships to Political Culture." *Publius* 47 (1): 131–48. https://doi.org/10.1093/publius/pjw026

Drapalova, Eliska. 2019. "Corruption and the Crisis of Democracy." Transparency International Anti-Corruption Helpdesk Answer. (6 March). Accessed November 22, 2019. https://docs.google.com/viewer?url=https%3A%2F%2Fknowledgehub.transparency.org%2Fassets%2Fuploads%2Fhelpdesk%2FCorruption-and-Crisis-of-Democracy_2019.pdf

European Commission. 2018. "Whistleblowers Protection." Accessed November 22, 2019. https://ec.europa.eu/info/aid-development-cooperation-fundamental-rights/your-rights-eu/whistleblowers-protection_en

Gao, Pengjie, Chang Lee, and Dermot Murphy. 2018. "Financing Dies in Darkness? The Impact of Newspaper Closures on Public Finance." *Journal of Financial Economics* (forthcoming). https://dx.doi.org/10.2139/ssrn.3175555

Geertz, Clifford. 1973. "Thick Description: Toward an Interpretive Theory of Culture." In *The Interpretation of Cultures*, edited by Clifford Geertz, 310–73. New York: Basic Books.

Gerring, John, and Strom C. Thacker. 2004. "Political Institutions and Corruption: The Role of Unitarism and Parliamentarism." *British Journal of Political Science* 34 (2): 295–330. https://doi.org/10.1017/S0007123404000067

Gerring, John and Strom C. Thacker. 2008. *A Centripetal Theory of Democratic Governance.* Cambridge: Cambridge University Press.

Heilbrunn, John R. 2004. "Anti-Corruption Agencies: Panacea or Real Medicine to Fight Corruption?" Washington, DC: World Bank Working Paper 37234. 21pp. Accessed November 22, 2019. https://docs.google.com/viewer?url=http%3A%2F%2Fsiteresources.worldbank.org%2FWBI%2FResources%2Fwbi37234Heilbrunn.pdf

Heywood, Paul M. 2018. "Combating Corruption in the Twenty-First Century: New Approaches." *Daedalus* 147: 83–97. https://doi:10.1162/DAED_a_00504

Integrity Action. 2016. "The Fix Rate: A Key Metric for Transparency and Accountability." London: Integrity Action (March 29). 28 pp. Accessed November 22, 2019. https://docs.google.com/viewer?url=https%3A%2F%2Fintegrityaction.org%2Fsites%2Fdefault%2Ffiles%2Ftraining_materials%2FThe%2520Fix%2520Rate%252C%2520English.pdf

International Association of Prosecutors. 2019. "Anti-Corruption Models." Accessed November 22, 2019. https://www.iap-association.org/NACP/Anti-Corruption-Models

International Organization for Standardization. 2016. "ISO 37001 Anti-Bribery Management Systems." Accessed November 22, 2019. https://www.iso.org/iso-37001-anti-bribery-management.html#page-top

Isham, Jonathan, Daniel Kaufmann, and Lant Pritchett. 1997. "Civil Liberties, Democracy, and the Performance of Government Projects." *World Bank Economic Review* 11 (2): 219–242. https://doi.org/10.1093/wber/11.2.219

Johnston, Michael. 2005. *Syndromes of Corruption: Wealth, Power, and Democracy.* Cambridge and New York: Cambridge University Press.

Johnston, Michael. 2010. "Assessing Vulnerabilities to Corruption: Indicators and Benchmarks of Government Performance." *Public Integrity* 12 (2): 125–42. https://doi.org/10.2753/PIN1099-9922120202

Johnston, Michael. 2014. *Corruption, Contention, and Reform: The Power of Deep Democratization.* Cambridge and New York: Cambridge University Press.

Johnston, Michael. 2018. "Reforming Reform: Revising the Anticorruption Playbook" *Daedalus* 147 (3): 50–62. https://doi:10.1162/DAED_a_00502

Johnston, Michael. 2019. "Limits and Ironies of Transparency: Controlling Corruption in American Elections." *Election Law Journal: Rules, Politics, and Policy* 18 (3): 282–96. doi: 10.1089/elj.2018.0530

Karlström, Kajsa. 2015. "Decentralization, Corruption and the Role of Democracy." Working Paper Series 2015: 14 (August), Quality of Government Institute, University of Gothenburg, Sweden. 54 pp. Accessed November 22, 2019. https://docs.google.com/viewer?url=https%3A%2F%2Fqog. pol.gu.se%2FdigitalAssets%2F1538%2F1538165_2015_14_karlstr--m.pdf

Lessig, Lawrence. 2013. "'Institutional Corruption' Defined." *Journal of Law, Medicine, and Ethics* 41 (3): 2–4. https://doi.org/10.1111%2Fjlme.12063

Levine, Bertram J., and Michael Johnston. 2016. "The Compliance Equation: Creating a More Ethical and Equitable Campaign Financing System by Blinding Contributions to Federal Candidates." In *Blinding as a Solution to Bias: Strengthening Biomedical Science, Forensic Science, and Law*, edited by Christopher T. Robertson and Aaron S. Kesselheim, 277–96. Cambridge, MA: Academic Press.

Lynn, Jonathan, and Antony Jay. 1987. *The Complete Yes Minister*. Topsfield, MA: Salem House.

McCubbins, Mathew D., and Thomas Schwartz. 1984. "Congressional Oversight Overlooked: Police Patrols versus Fire Alarms." *American Journal of Political Science* 28 (1): 165–79. doi: 10.2307/2110792.

Malbin, Michael J., and Michael Parrott. 2017. "Small Donor Empowerment Depends on the Details: Comparing Matching Fund Programs in New York and Los Angeles." *The Forum* 15 (2): 219–50. https://doi.org/10.1515/for-2017-0015

Meagher, Patrick. 2005. "Anti-Corruption Agencies: Rhetoric Versus Reality." *Journal of Policy Reform* 8 (1): 69–103. https://doi.org/10.1080/1384128042000328950

Mitchell, Richard H. 1996. *Political Bribery in Japan*. Honolulu: University of Hawaii Press.

Mungiu-Pippidi, Alina, and Ramin Dadašov. 2016. "Measuring Control of Corruption by a New Index of Public Integrity." *European Journal of Criminal Policy and Research* 22 (3): 415–38. https://doi.org/10.1007/s10610-016-9324-z

Mungiu-Pippidi, Alina, and Michael Johnston. 2017. *Transitions to Good Governance*. Cheltenham: Edward Elgar.

National Whistleblower Center. 2019. "Celebrate National Whistleblower Appreciation Day!" Accessed November 22, 2019. https://www.whistleblowers.org/news/ celebrate-national-whistleblower-appreciation-day/

Nichter, Simeon. 2014. "Conceptualizing Vote Buying." *Electoral Studies* 35 (September): 315–27. https://doi.org/10.1016/j.electstud.2014.02.008

Norris, Pippa, and Andrea Abel van Es. 2016. *Checkbook Elections? Political Finance in Comparative Perspective*. Oxford and New York: Oxford University Press.

Norris, Pippa, and Max Grömping. 2019. *Electoral Integrity Worldwide*. Sydney: The Electoral Integrity Project. https://www.electoralintegrityproject.com/the-year-in-elections-2017

Putnam, Robert D. 2000. *Bowling Alone: The Collapse and Revival of American Community*. New York: Simon and Schuster.

Quah, Jon S. T. 2017. "Anti-Corruption Agencies in Asia Pacific Countries: An Evaluation of their Performance and Challenges." Berlin: Transparency International. 32 pp. Accessed November 22, 2019. https://docs.google.com/viewer?url=http%3A%2F%2Fwww.transpar-ency.org%2Ffiles%2Fcontent%2Ffeature%2F2017_ACA_Background_Paper.pdf

Riordon, William L., ed. 1995. *Plunkitt of Tammany Hall*. New York: Signet.

Rothstein, Bo. 2011. *The Quality of Government: Corruption, Social Trust, and Inequality in International Perspective*. Chicago: University of Chicago Press.

Rothstein, Bo, Nicholas Charron, and Victor Lapuente. 2013. *Quality of Government and Corruption from a European Perspective: A Comparative Study of Good Government in EU Regions.* Cheltenham: Edward Elgar.

Schaffer, Frederic C., ed. 2007. *Elections for Sale: The Causes and Consequences of Vote Buying.* Boulder, CA: Lynne Rienner.

Sebold, Karen, and Andrew J. Dowdle. 2018. "Can Letting in Sunlight; Lead to Accidental Sunburn? The Unintended Consequences of Campaign Finance Reform on the Financing of U.S. Presidential Candidates." *Election Law Journal: Rules, Politics, and Policy* 17 (3): 209–20. https://doi.org/10.1089/elj.2018.0517

Stephenson, Matthew. 2019. "Some Good News and Bad News about Transparency International's Interpretation of its Latest Corruption Perceptions Index." *GAB: The Global Anticorruption Blog* (February 7). Accessed November 22, 2019. https://globalanticorruptionblog.com/2019/02/07/some-good-news-and-bad-news-about-transparency-internationals-interpretation-of-its-latest-corruption-perceptions-index/#more-13249

Teorell, Jan. 2007. "Corruption as an Institution: Rethinking the Nature and Origins of the Grabbing Hand." Working Paper 2007: 5. 26 pp. Gothenburg, Sweden: The Quality of Government Institute, University of Gothenburg. Accessed November 22, 2019. http://www.qog.pol.gu.se/digitalAssets/1350/1350653_2007_5_teorell.pdf

Thompson, Dennis F. 2018. "Theories of Institutional Corruption." *Annual Review of Political Science* 21: 495–513. https://www.annualreviews.org/doi/pdf/10.1146/annurev-polisci-120117-110316

Tokaji, Daniel P. 2018. "Campaign Finance Regulation in North America: An Institutional Perspective." *Election Law Journal: Rules, Politics, and Policy* 17 (3): 188–208. https://doi.org/10.1089/elj.2018.0512

Transparency International. 2019. "How Corruption Weakens Democracy." (January 29). Accessed November 22, 2019. https://www.transparency.org/news/feature/cpi_2018_global_analysis

U4 Anti-Corruption Resource Center. 2016. "The Proxy Challenge Award 2016." December 9. Accessed November 22, 2019. https://www.cmi.no/news/1751-the-proxy-challenge-award

United Nations. Office on Drugs and Crime. 2012. "Jakarta Statement on Principles for Anti-Corruption Agencies." November 26–27. Accessed November 22, 2019. http://www.unodc.org/documents/corruption/WG-Prevention/Art_6_Preventive_anti-corruption_bodies/JAKARTA_STATEMENT_en.pdf

United States. Department of Labor. 2019. Accessed November 22, 2019. "The Whistleblower Protection Program." https://www.whistleblowers.gov/

Uslaner, Eric M. 2017. *The Historical Roots of Corruption: Mass Education, Economic Inequality, and State Capacity.* Cambridge and New York: Cambridge University Press.

Warren, Mark. 2004. "What Does Corruption Mean in a Democracy?" *American Journal of Political Science* 48 (2): 328–43. doi: 10.2307/1519886.

PART VI

DIVERSITY, SOCIAL COHESION, AND WELL-BEING

CHAPTER 25

QUALITY OF GOVERNMENT AND SOCIAL TRUST

PETER THISTED DINESEN AND
KIM MANNEMAR SØNDERSKOV

INTRODUCTION

DOES a trusting citizenry beget well-functioning government institutions? Or do high-quality government institutions lay the foundation for trust between citizens? The question of the relationship between quality of government and generalized social trust is an important derivative of the wider academic debate about the interconnections between political institutions and political culture (Almond and Verba 1963; Inglehart 1997). From a policy perspective, the relationship between trust and quality of government is ultimately the question of the recipe for successful societies. Are these achieved through policies strengthening bonds between citizens, or rather via policies promoting good governance? Or, to cast this in more substantive terms: Did the Nordic societies become the most trustful in the world because of low corruption or other features of good government? Or did trust between citizens enable the establishment of well-functioning institutions?

This chapter reviews existing work—both theoretical and empirical—on the connection between quality of government and generalized social trust.[1] We start out by delineating the core concepts—social trust and quality of government—to clarify their meaning and distinguish them from related concepts. Then we review the theoretical mechanisms—in both directions—proposed to link social trust and quality of government. We next move to the empirical evidence. Here we distinguish between macro-level (aggregate) and micro-level (individual) work. Given the disputed "chicken-and-egg" nature of the relationship, we pay special attention to the strength of the empirical evidence vis-à-vis causal claims. Lastly, based on the review of the literature, we propose a number of avenues for future research, specifically emphasizing firmer theorization and corresponding empirical testing of observable implications.

---

[1] For a review of the related question of the relationship between corruption and trust, see Serritzlew, Sønderskov, and Svendsen (2014) and You (2018).

Conceptual Clarification

Both quality of government and social trust are broad concepts with a range of connotations. Following from this there is also a potential confusion with their putative downstream consequences alluded to in the introduction. It is therefore useful to clarify how we understand both concepts before we scrutinize their linkages.

The first core concept, *quality of government*, can be conceived both broadly and more narrowly based on the literature (Rothstein and Teorell 2008). The broader conception stresses a wide range of institutions/institutional features often associated with good government, including democracy and rule of law. In contrast, the narrow conception highlights "impartiality of institutions that exercise government authority" (Rothstein and Teorell 2008) as the specific institutional feature characterizing of high-quality government. Here, we position ourselves closer to the narrow conception and understand "government" to include state institutions in general. The narrow conceptualization implies a focus on the output side of government (i.e. the branches of government that implement and enforce rather than formulate policies), which has generally been considered more consequential for social trust than the input side (i.e. political actors), as we will explain below (Rothstein and Stolle 2008). Consequently, we do not focus on the input side of government including the democratic institutions that channel citizens' demand into the political system (for a relevant discussion of this, see Warren 1999).

It is particularly important to distinguish quality of government from *government performance* (however defined)—an outcome it is often purported to explain. The two are arguably conceptually distinct; quality of government refers to the functioning of government institutions, while government performance denotes the societal outcomes that these institutions produce. Yet, in practice, quality of government is often inferred from indicators of government performance; if, for example, governments spend more on public goods or are perceived as more responsive, this is taken as an indication of high-quality government (Putnam 1993, see especially ch. 3). Or put differently: measures of government performance can be viewed as both an outcome (*i*) and an indicator (*ii*) of quality of government. This highlights the problem of empirically distinguishing between the two. While this is clearly an important issue within the literature on quality of government, we approach this pragmatically and therefore consider theoretical arguments and empirical analyses relying on both approaches.

The second core concept, *social trust*, refers to trust in other people with a range of potential targets (family, neighbors, strangers etc.). Following the literature, our specific focus is on trust in unknown others (strangers)—what is known as *generalized social trust*. It is this form of generalized trust in other people—rather than more particularized forms of trust (e.g. trust in one's own family or ethnic group)—that is expected to be beneficial in modern societies characterized by a multitude of interactions between strangers on an everyday basis (Sønderskov and Dinesen 2014). Generalized social trust relates to a number of other concepts. Most pertinently, it is often considered a core element of the wider concept of social capital (Putnam 1993), around which much theorizing vis-à-vis the connection with quality of government has evolved.

Lastly, in considering the relationship between quality of government and social trust, the level of analysis is important; specifically, the distinction between the macro (societal) and the micro (individual) level is central. While institutions are inherently macro-level phenomena, they have a meaningful micro-level manifestation in terms of individuals' perceptions of and trust in state institutions. Similarly, social trust is inherently a micro-level concept, but can also meaningfully be aggregated to the macro level to capture societies with a higher or lower density of trustful individuals. It therefore makes sense to analyze the relationship at both the micro and the macro level, and we will review studies conducted at both level of analysis.

THEORETICAL LINKAGES

In the following, we review the mechanisms purported to lead from social trust to quality of government and vice versa.

Social trust as the cause of quality of government

A distinguished line of research going back at least to Tocqueville [1840] (1969) posits that a vibrant civil society furthers better government. In their classic five-country study, Almond and Verba (1963) argued that a civic culture—of which social trust is a central component—undergirds effective democratic governance. Putnam (1993) reiterated this idea—now incarnated in the concept of social capital—in his path-breaking study explaining the dramatic differences in government performance between the northern and the southern regions of Italy. Putnam's account strongly emphasized the path-dependency in regional political culture founded by different forms of rule dating back centuries.

The common idea underlying this line of work is that high levels of trust enable co-operation to overcome collective action problems and ultimately achieve better societal outcomes. Yet, as highlighted by Boix and Posner (1998), the specific mechanisms by which collective action dilemmas are overcome were often left vaguely specified in earlier work. They articulate a range of mechanisms, often implicitly alluded to in the previous literature, through which the wider concept of social capital could influence government performance. Relating to the discussion in the previous section, this perspective typically implicitly interprets government performance as an indication of quality of government.

Four mechanisms relevant for social trust can be distilled based on Boix and Posner's work. One mechanism posits that trusting others implies a feeling of solidarity toward others, and therefore a greater tendency to take their interest into account (i.e. displaying altruism) when expressing political preferences. Collectively more optimal solutions can therefore be obtained when people tend to think more in terms of "we" than "I," and are willing to forego short-term self-interest (Boix and Posner 1998, 691; Putnam 1995). A second mechanism, with weaker assumptions about altruistic motives, concerns citizens' ability and willingness to engage in politics. When citizens trust each other, they can more easily overcome problems of collective action enabling them to congregate in common interest groups, and they also have a higher willingness to accept the opportunity costs of participating in politics because they trust others to do the same. This makes for a more competitive democracy through higher participation and by securing a wider representation of interests. This in turn animates politicians to be politically responsive and to enact policies that benefit a broader cross-section of citizens. A third mechanism relates to rule compliance. When people trust their fellow citizens—specifically in terms of observing formal rules (e.g. taxpaying) as well as informal norms (e.g. engaging in pro-environmental behaviors)—they are also more likely to follow these regulations themselves. As a consequence, fewer resources have to be spent on enforcing rules and implementing policies, which can then in turn be channeled toward public goods. Finally, a fourth mechanism implies that the pro-social motivations associated with trust are also manifested among civil servants—drawn from a pool of high-trusting citizens—who therefore feel obligated to work for the common interest.

The above mechanisms all explain how living in a society of trustful individuals can have aggregate consequences on the quality of government. Yet, the individual-level relationship between social trust and institutional trust has also been scrutinized, although generally with limited theoretical underpinning. The primary argument appears to be that a trusting view of other people is extrapolated to include institutions and the individuals that represent these institutions (Brehm and Rahn 1997; Rosenberg 1956). However, an argument for the reverse extrapolation could of course also be made (we return to this below).

Quality of government as the cause of social trust

In response to the approach assuming a causal role of social trust for quality of government—and prompted by the reinvigoration of this line of research with *Making Democracy Work*—a literature arguing for the reverse relationship has developed. Levi's (1996, 1998) review essay of *Making Democracy Work* and subsequent theorization was among the first to highlight the role of state institutions—as an alternative to civil society—in creating social trust (see also Tarrow 1996 and Fukuyama 1995). In subsequent work, Rothstein and Stolle (2008) and others have built on and extended Levi's argument regarding the role of institutions, particularly articulating the micro foundations of this relationship.

The literature highlights a range of intertwined mechanisms by which quality of government may engender social trust. In our view, they can be condensed to two general (and interrelated) mechanisms: one mechanism relating to the state's role in deterring untrustworthy behavior and another relating to the role of state institutions in signaling fairness.

A quintessential role of a state is to secure productive interactions—in which mutual trust is crucial—between its citizens. By *deterrence of untrustworthy behavior*, the state is able to foster trust between citizens. Levi (1998) writes about the states' trust-generating role: "The most important attributes would seem to be the capacity to monitor laws, bring sanctions against lawbreakers, and provide information and guarantees about those seeking to be trusted" (Levi 1998, 85). In other words, by monitoring, exposing, and sanctioning untrustworthy behavior, state institutions enable trust between individuals. This would manifest itself in the form of efficient and fair law-and-order institutions (e.g. the police and the judiciary), which directly sanction untrustworthy behavior. However, equally importantly, fair and efficient state institutions more broadly (especially on the output side of government, see below), serves an important role in signaling that such behavior does not pay off in the first place (Rothstein and Stolle 2008).

It is worth stressing that this is not simply a matter of eliminating risks, and thus potentially crowding out the actual need to trust as some have argued (Bohnet and Baytelman 2007). Firstly, such effective policing of untrustworthy behavior is not realistic (at least not at present), and judging others' intentions will therefore still be a matter of placing trust in them (but with a low likelihood of having trust betrayed). Secondly, by regulating some domains of life and therefore enabling trustful interaction with others, the state lays the foundation for learning about the benefits of trust and trustworthiness, which in turn leads such "nice" strategies to spread to other domains that are not guided by the same regulations (Levi 1998; Farell and Knight 2001). For example, if one learns that people generally fulfill their contractual agreements and are therefore generally trustworthy (because state institutions strongly incentivize them to do so), this might engender trust that can be applied in one's private life.

Institutional fairness in terms of impartiality in the application of institutional procedures signifies that other individuals or groups cannot abuse the system to their own advantage, which deters untrustworthy behavior as just noted. However, institutions also "set the tone" for what is acceptable behavior, and thus influence the norms of individuals by *signaling fairness* (or the opposite). As Rothstein and Stolle (2008, 446) write "Police officers, social service bureaucrats, and judges are both representatives of the people and exhibitors of institutionalized values. In short, their behaviors function as important signals to citizens about the moral standard of the society in which they live." In other words, even if someone could get away with untrustworthy behavior, she would be inclined to see it as an unacceptable option given that she lives under institutions that do not espouse such values. That is, the moral costs of engaging in untrustworthy behavior become higher, and therefore people are more likely to act in a trustworthy manner.

The two noted mechanisms both relate to the output side of government, which—as noted earlier—is considered to be more consequential for social trust than the input side. The input side—politicians, parties, and other political actors—are designed to represent the interest of groups of voters, and thus to be *partial* (Rothstein and Teorell 2008). For that reason, institutions on the input side of government are unlikely to signify impartiality and concomitant trustworthiness, and therefore in turn hold less potential for creating social trust. Conversely, the output side of government—that is, the bureaucracy and street-level bureaucrats (i.e. the aforementioned law-and-order institutions, but also doctors, for example)—must be *impartial* in the implementation of a given policy. Everyone in the same position (e.g. in a lawsuit) should be treated according to the same procedures by the output side of government. These institutions therefore hold greater potential for engendering trust in others by both deterring untrustworthy behavior and signaling fairness.

As already mentioned, trust in institutions can be viewed as a micro-level manifestation of high-quality state institutions, and there is research suggesting that better "objective" state institutions lead to higher "subjective" trust in institutions. As such, trust in institutions can be viewed as a *mediator* vis-à-vis social trust (see below). However, complicating things further, the literature also highlights trust in institutions as a *moderator* of the influence of quality of government, in particular in relation to the mechanism relating to deterrence of untrustworthy behavior. As Levi (1998, 85) notes:

> Infrastructure and resources are necessary but not sufficient conditions. If citizens doubt the state's commitments to enforce the laws and if its information and guarantees are not credible, then the state's capacity to generate interpersonal trust will diminish. If the state is one of the institutions—and, in many cases, the most important institution—for promoting generalized trust, it can play this role only if the recipients of these services consider the state itself to be trustworthy. Subjects and citizens must trust the competence of the state to perform its trust-producing roles.

In other words, the state's capacity for producing social trust critically hinges on whether it is perceived as trustworthy itself. This points to a self-reinforcing influence of quality of government on social trust: high-quality government produces trust in state institutions, which may have a positive influence on social trust in itself, but it may also accentuate the positive effects of quality of government on social trust.

Linking macro-level quality of government with micro-level social trust

The theoretical mechanisms reviewed above all focus on the macro level as a consequence of quality of government being a societal-level phenomenon. Yet, in order to establish a relationship between macro-level institutions and individual-level trust, one must specify an individual level mechanism. In a series of studies with various co-authors, Rothstein (Kumlin and Rothstein 2005; Rothstein and Stolle 2008; Rothstein and Eek 2009) has suggested that citizens' everyday interactions with government representatives provide an experiential foundation for their perceptions of various states institutions (see also Dinesen 2012a). When these institutions fulfill the functions stipulated in the mechanisms highlighted above, this results in increased trust in institutions, and ultimately higher trust in other people. For example, experiencing a corrupt doctor or police officer, signifies that institutions are not fair, and also unlikely to be efficient in sanctioning untrustworthy behavior (as bribing is possible). Consequently, individuals develop lower levels of trust in institutions, including in their ability to perform the key functions that enable trust in other individuals.

Rothstein's experiential theory also helps explain the importance of the output side of government further. It is representatives on this side of government—doctors, teachers, bureaucrats, police officers, and others working in the public sector—that citizens interact with most frequently, and these interactions therefore provide an experience-based foundation for trust in such institutions and, ultimately, trust in other people. Conversely, people rarely have direct experiences with the input side of government—politicians and the legislative institutions therefore instead operate—and trust in these institutions therefore instead tend to vary by whether the party one supports is in power or not.

In this account, trust in (certain) government institutions is the mediator linking individual experiences with government representatives to social trust (Sønderskov and Dinesen 2014, 2016). While the causal influence of institutional trust on social trust is arguably more richly theorized, the reverse relationship is of course also possible, as noted above. Ultimately, the relationship between the two forms of trust remains an empirical question. Below, we discuss the evidence accumulated in this regard.

A dissenting perspective: quality of government depresses social trust

While the abovementioned mechanisms share an expectation about a positive effect of high-quality government institutions on social trust, other theories propose a negative relationship. From this perspective, well-functioning institutions may depress social trust (and related outcomes) by the process of *motivational crowding*. Effective state institutions centralize social control, which can crowd out intrinsic motivations to trust and behave in a trustworthy way (Bohnet and Baytelman 2007; Robbins 2011). A related argument rests on *institutional attribution*—i.e. that citizens attribute others' trustworthy behavior to the existence of effective institutions and consequently underestimate the trustworthiness of their fellow citizens (Irwin, Mulder, and Simpson 2014; Malhotra and Murnighan 2002). Thus, effective institutions may result in some of the same beneficial outcomes as trust would (e.g. cooperation), but trust itself may be lost in the process, which may have further downstream consequences (Cook 2001, xxvii).

REVIEW OF EMPIRICAL EVIDENCE

In the following, we review the empirical evidence for the relationship between quality of government and social trust. To structure the overview, we distinguish between macro-level (societal aggregates as analytical units) and micro-level studies (individuals as analytical units), although some studies combine both (e.g. multilevel studies focusing on how macro-level institutions shape individual social trust). The latter are reviewed under micro-level studies. The reviewed studies vary in methodological sophistication, including the attention paid to problems of causal inference (i.e. can quality of government be claimed to *causally* influence social trust and vice versa). We therefore highlight studies' relative strength vis-à-vis credibly identifying causal effects.

Lastly, it is important to note that while the studies reviewed use largely the same indicator(s) of social trust, they differ markedly in their operationalization of quality of government. This in turn raises the question of what should (and should not) be considered relevant indicators of quality of government. An exhaustive discussion of this point is outside the scope of this chapter, but we will focus on operationalizations that we find roughly in line with our definition of quality of government laid out above.

Macro-level studies

Early studies focused on social trust as the causal operator influencing quality of government. Interestingly, despite being a central influence in the literature about the relationship between social trust and quality of government, Putnam's (1993) famous study of Italian regions did in fact not analyze this relationship directly. Instead, it only addressed this indirectly via the association between aggregate social trust and a "civic community index," which was in turn strongly related to institutional performance at the regional level (Putnam 1993,

111–12). Further, civicness is stable over long periods, thereby suggesting it is a stable cultural trait, which influences contemporary institutional performance.

Following Putnam, several studies examined the conditional relationship between social trust (considered the independent variable) and various indicators of quality of government. In a sample of countries (27–33), La Porta et al. (1997) find that after controlling for GNP per capita, trust is strongly and statistically significantly associated with four indicators of quality of government taken from international databases: Efficiency of the judiciary, absence of corruption, bureaucratic quality, and tax compliance. For example, a standard deviation change in trust is associated with 0.7 standard deviation change in judicial efficiency and a 0.3 standard deviation reduction in corruption. Knack and Keefer (1997) report largely similar results, including for security of property rights and aggregate confidence in government, while additionally controlling for schooling in 1960. Cusack (1999), in a creative study, finds a positive effect (borderline statistically significant) of trust among local elites on government performance in German municipalities.

A number of studies also find evidence for the "reverse" relationship—i.e. that a range of indicators of quality of government predicts social trust. Zak and Knack (2001), for example, show that contract enforceability and freedom from corruption are strongly positively associated with trust in others in cross-country models based on 33–7 countries controlling for, among other things, GDP and schooling. Delhey and Newton (2005) confirm this finding for a quality of government factor (of which rule of law is an integral part) in a larger sample of countries (55–60) and while controlling for religious heritage (Protestantism) and ethnic heterogeneity—variables plausibly preceding quality of government. Similarly, Rothstein and Stolle (2008) find a strong relationship between variables tapping institutional effectiveness and institutional impartiality, as well as an interaction between them, in a slightly larger country-sample and controlling for a few extra potential confounders. Finally, Tsai, Laczko, and Bjørnskov (2011) expand Delhey and Newton's analysis by adding additional countries (98), and employ ridge regression to deal with multicollinearity, which is an obvious concern in this line of macro-level work given the small number of cases. Similar to Rothstein and Stolle, Tsai, Laczko, and Bjørnskov find evidence of conditional effects in that the relationship between quality of government and social trust is stronger in countries with higher levels of democracy and workers' rights. Interestingly, Tsai, Laczko, and Bjørnskov also find evidence of a nonlinear relationship between quality of government and social trust, where the relationship is negative—or close to zero—in countries with poor institutional quality.

The studies reviewed in the previous paragraphs report conditional statistical relationships between social trust and quality of government, but say little about the causal direction. Further, the relationships reported are likely confounded by unobserved confounders—something that is further accentuated by the small sample size and the concomitant limited number of control variables. A number of macro-level studies have tried to address the issue of causality using various strategies.

A large number of studies attempt to establish causality by applying instrumental variable techniques. Therefore, it is worth clarifying the rationale behind this approach and the assumptions it hinges on. The intuition behind instrumental variables techniques is that the effect of one variable X on another variable Y can be identified by using only variation in X that is exogenous to Y and all confounders. Such exogenous variation in X must be induced by a third variable, IV (the instrumental variable), which is exogeneous and only influences Y through its effect on X. A classic example uses the draft lottery (IV), which induces exogeneous variation in individuals' propensity to serve in the military (X). The causal effect of military service on various outcomes (Y) can then be identified by instrumenting military service with the lottery number. Angrist (1990), for example, studies the effect of military service on lifetime earnings by instrumenting military service with the lottery number. In this example, it is intuitive that the IV is exogenous to all potential confounders and to life-time earnings given that the IV is randomly assigned. It is also plausible that the IV will not affect lifetime earnings through other channels than through military service (but see the discussion in Angrist, Imbens, and Rubin (1996)). Under these conditions, the IV-technique allows for identifying causal effects (Angrist, Imbens, and Rubin 1996). However, the applic-ability of IV approaches to study the relationship between social trust and the quality of gov-ernment is severely challenged by the absence of true exogenous variation that affects social trust or the quality of government.

Knack (2002) uses an IV approach and instruments social trust (and other indicators of social capital) with state-level religious composition in a sample of American states, and reports a significant positive effect of trust on various indicators of quality of govern-ment. The problem is obviously that religious composition—unlike lottery numbers—is not randomly assigned to states and therefore likely to be correlated with a host of factors that may also affect quality of government (e.g. a combination of geography and immigra-tion patterns.). It is also likely that religiosity affects quality of government through other channels than social trust (e.g. other features of state culture). These challenges imply that the estimated relationship may not be closer to the true causal effect of trust on government than the estimate obtained using multivariate cross-sectional analyses.

A number of other studies employ similar instrumental variables strategies based on cross-sectional country-level analyses, and most find the expected relationship (e.g., Berggren and Jordahl 2006; Bjørnskov 2010; Robbins 2012a). Examples include lin-guistic characteristics (pronoun drop and second person differentiation), monarchy, and temperature as instruments for social trust (Bjørnskov 2010; Bjørnskov and Méon 2013; Robbins 2012a; Tabellini 2008), and information technologies, press freedom, and legal tradition as instruments for institutional quality (Berggren and Jordahl 2006; Bjørnskov 2007; Robbins 2012a). Although most of these instruments are temporally distant and generally stable, and, consequently, exogeneous to present-day levels of institutional quality or social trust, it is hard to rule out that they do not correlate with other factors that affect the outcome or that they do not affect the outcome through other channels than the endogenous variable. Related to the latter problem, other studies have used some of the noted instruments when exploring other determinants of trust or institutional quality. Licht, Goldschmidt, and Schwartz (2007), for example, use linguistic characteristics to in-strument the effect of autonomy on institutional quality, which thus suggests that these characteristics also affect institutional quality through other channels than social trust. It is perhaps also indicative of this problem that many of those instruments that have applied in the literature for either institutional quality or social trust just as well could have been an instrument for the other variable. Therefore, in conclusion, while an IV approach is in principle an attractive strategy to tease out causal relationships between variables that may have common causes and/or may cause each other, the lack of truly exogeneous vari-ation at the country-level makes this a less viable strategy for exploring the nexus between institutions and trust.

A few macro-level studies have used other—generally better suited—techniques to examine the causal relationship. Keele (2007) relies on a long time series of U.S. data (1972–2000) on aggregate social trust, trust in government, and perceptions of governmental performance measured on a quarterly basis. Using a granger causality test (i.e. regressing the dependent variable on lagged values of the dependent variable and the explanatory variable), Keele first rejects that trust in government causes social trust. Second, using an Error Correction Model, he shows that perceptions of governmental performance and especially social trust are strong predictors of trust in government in that short-term fluctuations in perceptions and social trust are followed by fluctuations in Americans' trust in government.

Robbins (2012b) uses aggregate panel data on social trust based on a sample of 74 countries. Using random and fixed effects models, he analyzes the impact of various institutional features (e.g. the extension of property rights and workers' rights[2]) on social trust. Interestingly, he finds notable differences between the random effects models resembling those employed in the previous literature, and the fixed effects models. The latter, which are arguably better suited to handle confounding by unobserved covariates (see below), indicate that, e.g., extensive workers' rights do not promote social trust. On the other hand, the fixed effects results do support the role of property rights in relation to social trust. Furthermore, and in line with the findings by Tsai Laczko and Bjørnskov (2011) mentioned above, the results from this study support the notion of a nonlinear relationship between institutions and social trust. In all specifications, Robbins finds evidence of a curvilinear relationship with negative effects of improved property rights in countries with only limited protection of property.

Micro-level studies

The micro-level relationship between social trust and individual-level manifestations of quality of government has been examined through a range of approaches. We review them in turn.

A large set of studies has explored the relationship between social trust and trust in various institutions (with the latter being a purported outcome and mediator of macro-level institutional quality). Although most of these studies theorize a causal relationship, they employ—with a few exceptions— research design that are not well suited to test causal claims. Interestingly, some early studies found only little to no connection between social trust and various forms of institutional trust in pooled and country-specific bi- and multivariate analyses (Kaase 1999; Newton 2001; Newton and Norris 2000). However, subsequent studies found strong associations between the two types of trust in multivariate models (Freitag 2003; Schyns and Koop 2010; Newton and Zmerli 2011; Rothstein and Stolle 2008), which is partly attributed to more precise and reliable measurement of the two types of trust (Zmerli and Newton 2008). Generally, studies examine trust in institutions *in toto* (averaging across institutions) without paying attention to the potential heterogeneouos

---

[2] Admittedly, both measures—especially the latter—are arguably stretching our conceptions of quality of government.

association with social trust across different institutions, but the analysis by Rothstein and Stolle (2008) constitutes a notable exception. Consistent with their theorization of the importance of the output side of government for social trust, they find a stronger association between "order institutions" (e.g. the police and the civil service) and social trust than similarly for political (partisan) institutions in country-level and Swedish individual-level data. However, in the pooled World Value Survey individual-level data, they find the opposite. Regardless, their efforts to differentiate between institutions is theoretically fruitful and something that should be explored further.

On balance, there is thus substantial evidence that social trust and institutional trust are closely connected. This in turn raises the question of causality—both in terms of direction (what causes what?) and potential confounding, e.g. from an inherent disposition to trust in general (e.g. personality traits influencing both institutional and social trust) (Sønderskov and Dinesen 2016). As in the macro-level work reviewed above, a number of studies have employed instrumental variable methods. Results range from absence of an effect (in postcommunist countries) (Mishler and Rose 2001) to strong effects of trust in government on social trust (in the U.S. and Russia) (Brehm and Rahn 1997; Mishler and Rose 2005), and some reciprocal effects of social trust (in the U.S.) (Brehm and Rahn 1997). This line of instrumental variable studies suffers from the same methodological problems highlighted above; the instruments cannot credibly be claimed to be exogeneous to potential confounders, nor can it be ruled out that the instruments do not influence the outcome through other channels. These analyses are therefore inconclusive vis-à-vis the causal effects of one form of trust on the other.

A recent line of studies has addressed the question of causality between institutional trust and social trust using individual-level panel data. The longitudinal aspect can be used to illuminate causal relationship in different ways. Most importantly, studying the relationship between the two types of trust *within* rather than *between* individuals (typically by means of individual fixed effects), allow for bypassing confounding by all time-*invariant* confounding variables including stable predispositions or personality traits. This can effectively rule out that an association between the two types of trust is driven by a common underlying disposition to trust as raised above. Further, under certain assumptions, panel data can be used for assessing the direction of causality by means of so-called Granger causality tests in which contemporary values of one form of trust is regressed on lagged (previous) values of that variable plus the independent variable in question (*in casu*, the other form of trust). While this test has been criticized, it arguably provides a tentative indication of the direction of causality between the two forms of trust. Based on two different panel data sets from Denmark, and employing both cross-lagged and fixed effects models, Sønderskov and Dinesen (2014, 2016) show that institutional trust consistently has a strong positive effect on social trust, whereas there is only a weak feedback effect from social trust. Seifert (2018) confirms the effect of institutional trust on social trust in fixed effects analyses of panel data from both the Netherlands and Switzerland. Taken together, the best available evidence thus suggests that institutional trust and social trust are closely connected. Further, while not definitive, there are relatively strong indications that institutional trust causally influences social trust, with none or only limited reciprocal effects.

Moving beyond the relationship between institutional and social trust, another line of work scrutinizes how experiencing different institutions shapes social trust. One strand of this research program scrutinizes how living under certain institutions—measured at the macro level—correlate with social trust at the micro level. This approach is closely related to the analyses conducted exclusively at the macro level reviewed above, but with trust measured at its locus (the individual). In line with the macro-level evidence reviewed above, both Freitag and Buhlmann (2009) and You (2012) find, in multilevel models, that country-level corruption is strongly negatively correlated with individual-level social trust. In the former study, corruption matters above other indicators of quality of government including rule of law and independence of the judiciary, which are not significantly related to trust. In a similar setup, Robbins (2011) does not confirm the negative influence of corruption, but report that enhanced property rights are related to higher social trust. Wang and Gordon (2011) confirm the latter results.

The noted multilevel studies are based on cross-sectional data and it is therefore difficult to rule out confounding factors. Two studies go some way in addressing this issue. Dinesen (2013) focuses specifically of immigrants to separate corruption from other noninstitutional enculturation processes (e.g., socialization by parents or in the educational system).[3] In multivariate models, he finds that corruption strongly (negatively) predicts trust of immigrants, thus demonstrating that corruption is not merely a placeholder for informal socialization. Charron and Rothstein (2014) employ a strategy of focusing on within-country (regional) variation in quality of government (aggregated survey responses based on experiences and perceptions). This is a marked improvement over traditional country-level studies as it allows for excluding any confounding of the relationship between quality of government and social trust stemming from country-level explanations (e.g. culture, inequality etc.) by means of country fixed effects analyses. Using this more rigorous analytical strategy, they replicate the strong relationship between quality of government and trust (measured both at the regional and the individual level). While the two latter studies do not provide definitive evidence of a causal effect of quality of institutions on individual-level social trust, they at least bolster our confidence that a number of plausible confounders do not confound this relationship.

A related line of work examined how individual-level experiences of quality of government, or perceptions of institutional quality shape social trust. For example, Kumlin and Rothstein (2010) find a strong positive relationship between experiences of equal treatment in personal contacts with public authorities and social trust in Sweden. Interestingly, the relationship is even stronger for individuals with a non-Nordic background. The trust gap for this group vis-à-vis individuals with a Nordic background is more than halved for those with the most positive experiences of equal treatment compared to those with the least. This indicates that institutional quality is particularly important for ethnic minorities, who may be targets of (perceived) discrimination from representatives of the state. Dinesen's (2012a) results based on first- and second-generation immigrants and native-born adolescents in 7–9th grade (age 13–16) in public schools in Denmark support this notion further. He finds that perceptions of institutional fairness are positively associated with social trust, but more

---

[3] See Dinesen (2012b) and Nannestad et al. (2014) for related approaches comparing immigrants in specific destination countries to comparable residents in their ancestral country. Both also find indications of effects of quality of institutions in the destination country on social trust (although they do not control for other explanations at the destination country level).

strongly so for first and second-generation immigrants.[4] Further, perceptions of institutional fairness are shaped by experiences of equal treatment by teachers in school, and again significantly stronger for first- and second-generation immigrants. This suggests that early-life experiences with representatives of (fair) government institutions may be important in shaping social trust, especially for groups with less prior experience with such institutions. In a related vein, Nannestad et al. (2014) show that perceptions of institutional fairness correlate with institutional trust, which in turn strongly predicts social trust among four immigrant groups in Denmark.

Another set of studies indirectly explores the importance of personal experiences of quality of government by examining how contact with different welfare state institutions shapes social trust (Rothstein and Uslaner 2005; Kumlin and Rothstein 2005). Selective welfare institutions are hypothesized to erode trust based on the following rationale: "because selective welfare institutions must test each case individually, they are to a greater extent subject to suspicions of cheating, arbitrariness, and discrimination compared with universal public agencies" (Kumlin and Rothstein 2005, 349). In contrast, universal programs "may give rise to a sense of equal treatment and that the 'rules of the game' in society are based on principles of fairness" (Kumlin and Rothstein 2005, 349). These predictions are borne out in Swedish and American data (only for selective welfare institutions in the latter) using multivariate models (Kumlin and Rothstein 2005; Rothstein & Uslaner 2005).

While there is strong evidence for a positive relationship between experiences of institutional quality and social trust, causality remains a weak point in the empirical analyses as they are based on observational cross-sectional data (see the criticisms raised above). However, using a vignette experiment, Rothstein and Eek (2009) experimentally manipulate (imagined) experiences of corruption, and find that this negatively influences trust in the authorities in general as well as social trust. While imagined scenarios are obviously not equivalent to actually experiencing corruption, the experiment still provides an indication that experiences of corrupt institutions may have a negative causal effect on social trust.

Finally, a few results from a different strand of literature are worth mentioning. Irwin, Mulder, and Simpson (2014), Malhotra and Murnighan (2002), and Mulder et al. (2006) use economic experimental games to study the effect of introducing various institutions (e.g. sanction systems and binding contracts) on trusting behavior. These studies focus on trust between economic agents who interacted personally and as such, they conceptualize trust as trust in specific targets rather than generalized social trust. Nevertheless, the results are interesting given the few experiments in the remaining literature. In contrast to the extensive support for the positive consequences of high-quality government found in the studies reviewed above, these three laboratory experiments find evidence of a negative impact of institutions on trust. The differences in conceptualization of trust aside, these results link to the macro-level findings of the potential curvilinear relationship between institutions and trust discussed above, where the impact of institutions could be negative in countries with poor institutions (Robbins 2012b; Tsai, Laczko, and Bjørnskov 2011). The economic experiments are typically comparing a situation without any institutions to a situation with some institutions, which in some sense could be seen as simulating the improvement of

---

[4] It bears mentioning that Dinesen (2010), in another (earlier) sample of young immigrants in Denmark, finds a positive (although statistically insignificant) relationship between feelings of discrimination by teachers and social trust.

institutions in a context with poor institutions to begin with (cf. Robbins 2012b). Either way, the laboratory experiments suggest that institutions may not always enhance (certain forms of) trust. Given the lack of experiments in the literature on quality of government and social trust, more studies scrutinizing this relationship using economic games would make an interesting contribution going forward.

Summary of empirical evidence

Having reviewed a wealth of empirical studies of the connection between quality of government and social trust, we briefly summarize the main conclusions. Firstly, there is ample evidence of a positive relationship between various manifestations of quality of government and social trust, both at the macro and the micro level. Secondly, while several macro-level analyses have attempted to sort out the causal relationship between institutional quality and social trust, they generally apply research designs that do not credibly identify causal effects of one variable on the other. A few notable exceptions stand out, of which one credibly indicates that macro-level social trust predicts trust in government in time-series data from the United States (Keele 2007). Thirdly, micro-level work is richer, both theoretically and methodologically, as it allows for testing more empirical implications of existing theories, as well as more credibly identifying causal effects of social trust on institutional trust (and vice versa) in large-n individual-level panel data. There are generally strong indications of a positive effect of trust in state institutions on social trust based on causally oriented analyses of panel data from Denmark, the Netherlands, and Switzerland (Sønderskov and Dinesen 2014, 2016; Seifert 2018). Further, several individual-level analyses indicate—some with increased causal leverage—that experiencing quality of government through experiences with representatives of the output side of government positively influences social trust. This suggests a causal chain running from high-quality institutions at the societal level (i) via individual-level experiences (ii) and subsequent perceptions of institutional fairness (iii), to, ultimately, trust in other people (iv).

Paths for Future Research

Having reviewed the rich theoretical and empirical literature concerning the relationship between quality of government and social trust, we conclude our review by highlighting what we perceive to be three prominent avenues for future research on the relationship.

Testing theories of social trust's influence on quality of government more rigorously

While the rich theorization of quality of government's influence on social trust has been met with corresponding thorough empirical testing of observable implications, the same cannot be said for the reverse relationship. The theoretical arguments regarding the effect of trust on quality of government are relatively elaborate, but they have rarely been rigorously tested. Conversely, this relationship has been modeled crudely at the macro level in models that provide little causal leverage. While the choice of the macro level is probably a function of quality of government (the dependent variable) inherently being a macro-level factor, several observable implications derived from existing theorizations (or new ones) could be examined at the individual level. For example, in line with one of Boix & Posner's (1998) conjectures noted above, it could be examined whether trusting individuals are more likely to select into the public sector in countries with high quality of government (and vice versa for countries with poor institutions). This would probe a mechanism regarding selection of bureaucrats underlying a positive effect of trust on quality of government. Related research on honesty suggests that this is indeed the case (Barfort et al. 2019).

Macro-level research is certainly also still valid, but moving away from (or at least supplementing) traditional cross-country models would be fruitful. Following the general "subnational turn" in comparative politics and thus, ironically, returning to Putnam's within-country focus seems like a logical path in this regard. Cusack's study of (1999) German municipalities is one of the few existing examples that use local variation in trust (specifically among local elites) to explain government performance (measured as citizens' satisfaction). While the subnational focus cannot resolve problems of reverse causality, it can help test more implications of existing theories of social trust's influence on (local) quality of government by studying this relationship between many more administrative units within a controlled setting in terms of one or more countries.

Further fleshing out which aspects of quality of government that matter for social trust

As noted from the outset, quality of government is a broad concept, which is also reflected in the fact that it has been operationalized in a number of different ways. While the theorizations by Rothstein and others have made important inroads in articulating exactly how and which aspects of (quality of) government that matter for social trust, this could be further elaborated theoretically, and, not least, tested empirically. Differentiating between different branches of government (Rothstein and Stolle 2008), and how perceptions of these institutions are shaped, are especially important to develop the micro-level linkage between macro-level institutions and social trust further. The existing focus on personal experiences with government representatives is indeed meaningful, but it could be expanded in several ways. One may, for example, question whether people have enough experiences with representatives of (ostensibly) key government institutions on which to base their institutional perceptions and, ultimately, trust in others. In this regard, and still viewed through an experiential lens, vicarious experiences—i.e. experiences via others—with government officials seem like a plausible supplementary source of perceptions of quality of government. It may not only be our own experiences with government officials, but also experiences of others, socially transmitted to us, which shape our perceptions of the way government institutions work. Further, beyond personal and vicarious experiences, alternative sources may also plausibly influence institutional perceptions. Along the lines of Dinesen (2012a), it is relevant to understand to which extent institutional perceptions are founded in primary socialization in the family. It seems plausible that one learns about institutional quality from one's parents (partly based on their personal experiences), and then subsequently adjust these perceptions based on one's own experiences (personal and vicarious). Finally, in line with perceptions of other properties of society—e.g. the state of the economy (Soroka 2006)—it is relevant to ask which role the mass media plays in shaping institutional perceptions.

Improved research designs

While some strands of the literature on the relationship between quality of government and social trust have begun employing more rigorous research designs better suited for addressing causality, this has been a soft spot in the bulk of existing work; most studies are essentially looking at conditional associations. It therefore seems appropriate for this literature to follow the lead of related literatures and move towards increased methodological sophistication. Using panel data, as some of the studies of the relationship between institutional trust and social trust have done, is a logical next step for improving causal inference. This need not be limited to individual-level studies, as panel data at the country-level have become available (Robbins 2012b). The European Social Survey (ESS) is a very good data source in this regard with biannual data collections. Further, the ESS also enables the use of panel data at subnational levels, as it holds regional identifiers. As argued above, this is an underutilized approach, which combines the qualities of control for a host of plausibly country-level confounders by design (Charron and Rothstein 2014), and more observations, and hence more statistical power for detecting relationships and differentiating between alternative explanations. Natural experiments—prominent in related literatures—is another promising approach. Yet, as this approach would often be applied in an instrumental variables framework, researchers would have to justify how a given instrument only affects the dependent variable through the independent variable of interest, as discussed above.

Finally, by calling for increased methodological sophistication, we are obviously not suggesting that there is no room for further theorization, even if this cannot be substantiated in more sophisticated empirical analyses. Quite the opposite—both theoretical and methodological sophistication are warranted, and ideally, of course, in combination.

REPRISE

In this chapter we have reviewed the literature on the relationship between quality of government—conceptualized as quality of institutions at the output side of government—and generalized social trust (trust in strangers). We reviewed the relatively rich theorizations—in both directions—of the link between social trust and quality of government, as well as the concomitant empirical evidence. More observable implications have been deducted for the literature emphasizing the effect of quality of government on social trust, and this has therefore been scrutinized more rigorously empirically. There is very considerable evidence for a positive relationship between social trust and various manifestations of quality of government at both the societal level (macro) and the individual level (micro). Most studies are strictly correlational, but a few studies—primarily at the individual level—employ designs allowing for stronger (if not definitive) causal statements. These studies suggest a positive effect of institutional quality on social trust. We concluded the review by discussing paths for further research, emphasizing theoretical development and, especially, more rigorous empirical testing.

References

Almond Gabriel, A., and Sidney Verba. 1963. *The Civic Culture: Political Attitudes and Democracy in Five Nations.* Princeton: Princeton University.

Angrist, Joshua D. 1990. "Lifetime Earnings and the Vietnam Era Draft Lottery: Evidence from Social Security." *The American Economic Review* 80 (3): 313–36.

Angrist, Joshua D., Guido W. Imbens, and Donald B. Rubin. 1996. "Identification of Causal Effects Using Instrumental Variables." *Journal of the American Statistical Association* 91 (434): 444–55.

Barfort, Sebastian, Nikolaj A. Harmon, Frederik Hjorth, and Asmus L. Olsen. 2019. "Sustaining Honesty in Public Service: The Role of Selection." *American Economic Journal: Economic Policy* 11 (4): 96–123.

Berggren, Niclas, and Henrik Jordahl. 2006. "Free to Trust: Economic Freedom and Social Capital." *Kyklos* 59 (2): 141–69.

Bjørnskov, Christian. 2007. "Determinants of Generalized Trust: A Cross-Country Comparison." *Public Choice* 130 (1–2): 1–21.

Bjørnskov, Christian. 2010. "How Does Social Trust Lead to Better Governance? an Attempt to Separate Electoral and Bureaucratic Mechanisms." *Public Choice* 144(1–2): 323–46.

Bjørnskov, Christian, and Pierre-Guillaume Méon. 2013. "Is Trust the Missing Root of Institutions, Education, and Development?" *Public Choice* 157 (3–4): 641–69.

Bohnet, Iris, and Yael Baytelman. 2007. "Institutions and Trust: Implications for Preferences, Beliefs and Behavior." *Rationality and Society* 19 (1): 99–135.

Boix, Carles, and Daniel N. Posner. 1998. "Social Capital: Explaining Its Origins and Effects on Government Performance." *British Journal of Political Science* 28 (4): 686–93.

Brehm, John, and Wendy Rahn. 1997. "Individual-Level Evidence for the Causes and Consequences of Social Capital." *American Journal of Political Science* 41 (3): 999–1023.

Charron, Nicholas, and Bo Rothstein. 2014. "Social Trust, Quality of Government and Ethnic Diversity." QoG Working Paper Series 2014 (20).

Cook, Karen. 2001. "Trust in Society." In *Trust in Society*, edited by Karen Cook, xi–xxviii. New York: Russell Sage Foundation.

Cusack, Thomas R. 1999. "Social Capital, Institutional Structures, and Democratic Performance: A Comparative Study of German Local Governments." *European Journal of Political Research* 35 (1): 1–34.

Delhey, Jan, and Kenneth Newton. 2005. "Predicting Cross-National Levels of Social Trust: Global Pattern or Nordic Exceptionalism?" *European Sociological Review* 21 (4): 311–27.

Dinesen, Peter T. 2010. "Upbringing, Early Experiences of Discrimination and Social Identity: Explaining Generalised Trust among Immigrants in Denmark." *Scandinavian Political Studies* 33 (1): 93–111.

Dinesen, Peter T. 2012a. "Parental Transmission of Trust or Perceptions of Institutional Fairness: Generalized Trust of Non-western Immigrants in a High-Trust Society." *Comparative Politics* 44 (3): 273–89.

Dinesen, Peter T. 2012b. "Does Generalized (Dist)Trust Travel? Examining the Impact of Cultural Heritage and Destination-Country Environment on Trust of Immigrants." *Political Psychology* 33 (4): 495–511.

Dinesen, Peter T. 2013. "Where You Come from or Where You Live?: Examining the Cultural and Institutional Explanation of Generalized Trust Using Migration as a Natural Experiment." *European Sociological Review* 29 (1): 114–28.

Farrell, Henry, and Jack Knight. 2001. "Trust, Institutions, and Institutional Change: Industrial Districts and the Social Capital Hypothesis." *Politics and Society* 31 (4): 537–66.

Freitag, Markus, and Marc Bühlmann. 2009. "Crafting Trust: The Role of Political Institutions in a Comparative Perspective." *Comparative Political Studies* 42 (12): 1537–66.

Freitag, Markus. 2003. "Social Capital in (Dis) Similar Democracies: The Development of Generalized Trust in Japan and Switzerland." *Comparative Political Studies* 36 (8): 936–66.

Fukuyama, Francis. 1995. *Trust: The Social Virtues and the Creation of Prosperity*. New York: Free Press.

Inglehart, Ronald. 1997. *Modernization and Postmodernization: Cultural, Economic, and Political Change in 43 Societies*. Princeton: Princeton University Press.

Irwin, Kyle, Laetitia Mulder, and Brent Simpson. 2014. "The Detrimental Effects of Sanctions on Intragroup Trust: Comparing Punishments and Rewards." *Social Psychology Quarterly* 77 (3): 253–72.

Kaase, Max. 1999. "Interpersonal Trust, Political Trust and Non-Institutionalised Political Participation in Western Europe." *West European Politics* 22 (3): 1–21.

Keele, Luke. 2007. "Social Capital and the Dynamics of Trust in Government." *American Journal of Political Science* 51 (2): 241–54.

Knack, Stephen. 2002. "Social Capital and the Quality of Government: Evidence from the Us States." *American Journal of Political Science* 46 (4): 772–85.

Knack, Stephen, and Philip Keefer. 1997. "Does Social Capital Have an Economic Payoff? a Cross-Country Investigation." *The Quarterly Journal of Economics* 112 (4): 1251–88.

Kumlin, Staffan, and Bo Rothstein. 2005. "Making and Breaking Social Capital: The Impact of Welfare-State Institutions." *Comparative political studies* 38 (4): 339–65.

Kumlin, Staffan, and Bo Rothstein. 2010. "Questioning the New Liberal Dilemma: Immigrants, Social Networks, and Institutional Fairness!" *Comparative Politics* 43 (1): 63–80.

La Porta, Rafael, Florancio Lopez-De-Silane, Andrei Shleifer, and Robert W. Vishny. 1997. "Trust in Large Organizations." *The American Economic Review* 87 (2): 333–8.

Levi, Margaret. 1996. "Social and Unsocial Capital: A Review Essay of Robert Putnam's Making Democracy Work." *Politics and Society* 24 (1): 45–55.

Levi, Margaret. 1998. "A State of Trust." In *Trust and governance,* edited by Valerie Braithwaite, and Margaret Levi, 77–101. New York: Russell Sage Foundation.

Licht, Amir N., Chanan Goldschmidt, and Shalom H. Schwartz. 2007. "Culture Rules: The Foundations of the Rule of Law and Other Norms of Governance." *Journal of Comparative Economics* 35 (4): 659–88.

Malhotra, Deepak, and J. Keith Murnighan. 2002. "The Effects of Contracts on Interpersonal Trust." *Administrative Science Quarterly* 47 (3): 534–59.

Mishler, William, and Richard Rose. 2001. "What Are the Origins of Political Trust? Testing Institutional and Cultural Theories in Post-communist Societies." *Comparative Political Studies* 34 (1): 30–62.

Mishler, William, and Richard Rose. 2005. "What Are the Political Consequences of Trust? a Test of Cultural and Institutional Theories in Russia." *Comparative Political Studies* 38 (9): 1050–78.

Mulder, Laetitia B., Eric van Dijk, Davis De Cremer, and Henk A.M. Wilke. 2006. "Undermining Trust and Cooperation: The Paradox of Sanctioning Systems in Social Dilemmas." *Journal of Experimental Social Psychology* 42 (2): 147–62.

Nannestad, Peter, Gert T. Svendsen, Peter T. Dinesen, and Kim M. Sønderskov. 2014. "Do Institutions or Culture Determine the Level of Social Trust? the Natural Experiment of Migration from Non-western to Western Countries." *Journal of Ethnic and Migration Studies* 40 (4): 544–65.

Newton, Kenneth, and Pippa Norris. 2000. "Confidence in Public Institutions." In *Disaffected Democracies. What's Troubling the Trilateral Countries?*, edited by Susan J. Pharr and Robert D. Putnam, 52–73. Princeton: Princeton University Press.

Newton, Kenneth, and Sonja Zmerli. 2011. "Three Forms of Trust and Their Association." *European Political Science Review* 3 (2): 169–200.

Newton, Kenneth. 2001. "Trust, Social Capital, Civil Society, and Democracy." *International Political Science Review* 22 (2): 201–14.

Putnam, Robert D. 1993. *Making Democracy Work: Civic Traditions in Modern Italy*. Princeton: Princeton University Press.

Putnam, Robert D. 1995. "Tuning in, Tuning Out: The Strange Disappearance of Social Capital in America." *PS: Political Science and Politics* 28 (4): 664–83.

Robbins, Blaine G. 2011. "Neither Government nor Community Alone: A Test of State-Centered Models of Generalized Trust." *Rationality and Society* 23 (3): 304–46.

Robbins, Blaine G. 2012a. "Institutional Quality and Generalized Trust: A Nonrecursive Causal Model." *Social Indicators Research* 107 (2): 235–58.

Robbins, Blaine G. 2012b. "A Blessing and a Curse? Political Institutions in the Growth and Decay of Generalized Trust: A Cross-National Panel Analysis, 1980–2009." *PloS one* 7 (4): e35120.

Rosenberg, Morris. 1956. "Misanthropy and Political Ideology." *American Sociological Review* 21 (6): 690–95.

Rothstein, Bo, and Daniel Eek. 2009. "Political Corruption and Social Trust: An Experimental Approach." *Rationality and Society* 21 (1): 81–112.

Rothstein, Bo, and Dietlind Stolle. 2008. "The State and Social Capital: An Institutional Theory of Generalized Trust." *Comparative Politics* 40 (4): 441–59.

Rothstein, Bo, and Jan Teorell. 2008. "What Is Quality of Government? a Theory of Impartial Government Institutions." *Governance* 21 (2): 165–90.

Rothstein, Bo, and Eric M. Uslaner. 2005. "All for All: Equality, Corruption, and Social Trust." *World Politics* 58 (1): 41–72.

Schyns, Peggy, and Christel Koop. 2010. "Political Distrust and Social Capital in Europe and the USA." *Social Indicators Research* 96 (1): 145–67.

Seifert, Nico. 2018. "Yet Another Case of Nordic Exceptionalism? Extending Existing Evidence for a Causal Relationship between Institutional and Social Trust to the Netherlands and Switzerland." *Social Indicators Research* 136 (2): 539–55.

Serritzlew, Søren, Kim M. Sønderskov, and Gert T. Svendsen. 2014. "Do Corruption and Social Trust Affect Economic Growth? a Review." *Journal of Comparative Policy Analysis: Research and Practice* 16 (2): 121–39.

Soroka, Stuart. 2006. "Good News and Bad News: Asymmetric Responses to Economic Information." *The Journal of Politics* 68 (2): 372–85.

Sønderskov, Kim M., and Peter T. Dinesen. 2014. "Danish Exceptionalism: Explaining the Unique Increase in Social Trust over the past 30 Years." *European Sociological Review* 30 (6): 782–95.

Sønderskov, Kim M., and Peter T. Dinesen. 2016. "Trusting the State, Trusting Each Other? the Effect of Institutional Trust on Social Trust." *Political Behavior* 38 (1): 179–202.

Tabellini, Guido. 2008. "Institutions and Culture." *Journal of the European Economic Association* 6 (2–3): 255–94.

Tarrow, Sidney. 1996. "Making Social Science Work across Space and Time: A Critical Reflection on Robert Putnam's Making Democracy Work." *American Political Science Review* 90 (2): 389–97.

Tocqueville, Alexis. [1840] 1969. *Democracy in America*. New York: Anchor Books.

Tsai, Ming-Chang, Leslie Laczko, and Christian Bjørnskov. 2011. "Social Diversity, Institutions and Trust: A Cross-National Analysis." *Social Indicators Research* 101 (3): 305–22.

Wang, Lanlan, and Peter Gordon. 2011. "Trust and Institutions: A Multilevel Analysis." *The Journal of Socio-Economics* 40 (5): 583–93.

Warren, Mark E. 1999. *Democracy and Trust*. Cambridge: Cambridge University Press.

You, Jong-sung. 2012. "Social Trust: Fairness Matters More Than Homogeneity." *Political Psychology* 33 (5): 701–21.

You, Jong-sung. 2018. "Trust and Corruption" in *The Oxford Handbook of Social and Political Trust*, edited by Eric Uslaner. New York: Oxford University Press.

Zak, Paul J., and Stephen Knack. 2001. "Trust and Growth." *The Economic Journal* 111 (470): 295–321.

Zmerli, Sonja, and Ken Newton. 2008. "Social Trust and Attitudes Toward Democracy." *Public Opinion Quarterly* 72 (4): 706–24.

CHAPTER 26

....

GENDER, GENDER EQUALITY, AND CORRUPTION
A Review of Theory and Evidence

....

AMY C. ALEXANDER

INTRODUCTION

....

IN the early 2000s, two studies, one by Dollar, Fisman, and Gatti (2001) and the other by Swamy et al. (2001), sparked a wealth of research on gender, gender equality and corruption. One line continues to explore the relationship between gender and corruption among individuals and another continues to explore the relationship between levels of gender equality and corruption across various social units (e.g., countries or municipalities). A rather substantial body of evidence supports robust relationships at both the individual and societal levels: women tend to be less tolerant of corruption and higher levels of gender equality correlate with lower levels of corruption. Given the substantial evidence base, these relationships have attracted serious attention from the world's most important intergovernmental organizations, such as the United Nations and the World Bank. This has led to their widespread investment in the gender/gender equality perspective as a strategy to better understand corruption and how to combat it (see, for instance, United Nations Development Programme 2012; World Bank 2001). Nevertheless, after nearly two decades of research, the theories behind the relationship at both the individual and societal levels remain contested: Whether the relationships are conditional on particular contexts and why needs further inquiry and, at the societal level, the direction of the relationship is not entirely clear.

This chapter thus covers the state of the art in theory and evidence on the relationship between gender and corruption among individuals and gender equality and corruption across governing units. Section 1 of the chapter reviews the contested theory behind the relationships. Starting with the theoretical assumptions that link individuals' gender to the likelihood to engage in corruption, I cover the four mechanisms proposed throughout the literature for expecting women to engage less: gender role socialization, power marginalization, the greater importance of an effective state for women's self-determination, and the tendency to hold women to higher standards. From here, I review additional societal level theories on gender equality and corruption: 1) theory assuming that gender equality lowers corruption by empowering women, promoting women's interests, and generating norms of impartiality; and, 2) theory assuming that lower corruption increases gender equality.

Section 2 of this chapter turns to the evidence in support of the various theories. This section reviews individual-level evidence from observational studies and experiments and societal-level evidence from observational studies.

Section 3 concludes with a critical assessment of the literature given the state of theory and evidence. The section identifies gaps and suggests future research.

Section 1: Theoretical Underpinnings

Micro-Theoretical Assumptions Linking Individuals' Gender to Likelihood to Engage in Corruption

Individuals have the potential to engage in corruption as ordinary people attempting to secure goods and services in their everyday lives or as public authorities using the power of their position for private gains. Thus, the corrupt transactions that individuals engage in can be observed among both masses and elites. Theories on gender and corruption expect greater intolerance and engagement by women compared to men among both masses and elites. I review each of these theories below and discuss their applicability to the mass and elite levels.

Women are socialized to react more ethically. In one of the seminal pieces that ignited gender and corruption research, the social role theory of gender (Eagly and Crowley 1986) and evidence of its impact on behavior is used to motivate assumptions about women, men, and corruption. Indeed, the first two lines of Dollar et al.'s (2001, 423) abstract notes the following: "Numerous behavioral studies have found women to be more trustworthy and public-spirited than men. These results suggest that women should be particularly effective in promoting honest government." Eagly's work is among the studies highlighted. According to Eagly, Wood, and Diekman (2000, 175), social role theory:

> argues that the beliefs that people hold about the sexes are derived from observations of the role performances of men and women and thus reflect the sexual division of labor and gender hierarchy of society. In their abstract and general form, these beliefs constitute gender roles, which, through a variety of mediating processes, foster real differences in behavior.

In particular, Eagly et al. (2000) note the emphasis that has traditionally been placed on communalism and nurturing to socialize girls into roles that accord with the sexual division of labor and gender hierarchies observed across the globe. The emphasis on communalism and nurturing generates a greater tendency among girls/women towards helping behavior, selflessness, and concern for the welfare of others compared to boys/men.

Dollar et al. (2001), among others, have drawn on this perspective and evidence from social role theory to propose one of the mechanisms behind greater female intolerance of and engagement in corruption. Cumming, Leung, and Rui (2015, 1572–1573) label this the "ethicality" mechanism, noting that "if it is assumed that women are socialized to embody communal values more than are men, women would be more likely to react ethically in dilemma situations." The decision to engage in corruption creates a classic dilemma between one's private gain and the public good which provokes the decision to behave ethically or not. Thus, as one competing theoretical mechanism in the literature, it may be women's socialized predisposition to react more ethically that drives greater female intolerance of corruption.[1]

This mechanism applies equally to women's tendency compared to men to be more intolerant of corruption or not engage in it at both the mass and elite levels. For instance, both offering a bribe to an official for a public service and embezzling money through one's position of authority create an ethical dilemma between one's private gain and the public good. Thus, if women are socialized to react more ethically, this will lower their tendency to tolerate or engage in corruption as both ordinary people and elites.

Women are risk averse. The difference in male and female socialization to take risks is also adopted in theorizing the link between gender and corruption (Gustafsod 1998). For instance, some suggest that this is a deeply grounded gender difference using the perspective of evolutionary psychology and emphasize the role of the hunter-gather sexual division of labor that characterized a large span of humanity's early existence (Tooby and Cosmides 1990, 1992). Scholars presume that as hunters, male psychology evolved to be more risk acceptant, and this evolutionary footprint continues to differentiate women and men on risk-taking today. Other researchers are less concerned with the sources of gender differences in risk and risk aversion and simply take note of the rather large experimental literature supporting the female tendency to be more risk averse (Charness and Gneezy 2012). Largely drawing on this evidence, gender and corruption scholars have argued that women may be less likely to engage in corruption because, under many circumstances, doing so requires one to take risks.

Similar to the ethicality mechanism, this mechanism is applicable to gender differences in tolerance of and engagement in corruption at both the mass and elite levels. If we take the example of bribery, in contexts where corruption is risky, both giving and receiving bribes are punishable by law. In this case, risk is involved for both an ordinary person and a public authority. Thus, it is plausible to expect a risk aversion effect among women across levels. However, we might expect the gender gap to be larger when it comes to tolerance and engagement in forms of corruption that are large in scale and fall outside the realm of petty corruption. These forms of corruption are most severely punishable by law and therefore carry the highest risks. Carrying out such large-scale corruption requires that one occupy an influential position of power. In this case, if risk aversion underlies gender differences, the gap between women and men may be wider at the elite level and particularly among those with the power to consider such large-scale corruption.

Finally, it should be noted that this theory is contingent on the assumption that corruption is risky, which is not the case in contexts where corruption is systemic. To the contrary, in contexts where corruption is the norm, failing to tolerate this or refusing to engage in it can be extremely risky. Thus, from the perspective of the risk aversion mechanism, there is no

---

[1] A related literature on the pronounced tendency for women/girls to engage less in delinquent and criminal behavior also supports the ethicality mechanism (see for instance, Bennett, Farrington, and Huesmann 2005; Mears, Ploeger, and Warr 1998; Walters 2017).

expectation for the effect of gender on corruption in contexts where corruption is systemic and the norm.

Women are marginalized from power. The idea that women are somehow the "fairer," more "risk adverse" sex due to their socialized nature has been criticized from the perspective of gendered opportunities (Goetz 2007). Women share the experience of being members of a marginalized group which restricts their opportunities for engaging in corrupt activities. Given their history of marginalization, women are less likely to hold positions of public authority leaving them with fewer opportunities to abuse power for private gain. As a result, patronage networks tend to be highly male dominant. This, in turn, sends the signal that a man is more likely to agree to engage in corruption, which further reduces opportunities for women to become involved, since this lowers the likelihood that they are asked to take part in corrupt activities.

Given that the power marginalization mechanism focuses entirely on women's access to power, this is only applicable to expecting gender differences among elites. In this case, the mechanism fails to offer a good theoretical reason for gender differences in tolerance of and engagement in corruption at the mass level.

Women depend on an effective state for their autonomy. Women make up some of the most vulnerable populations in the world (United Nations Development Programme 2012). They are also disproportionately responsible for unpaid domestic and care-taking labor in every country in the world, which adds to their vulnerability under conditions of poverty (United Nations Development Programme 2012). As a result, a strong state that effectively provides social services is especially important for women's level of self-determination. Thus, this dependency on an extensive and effective state for their autonomy potentially incentivizes women to shun and refuse to engage in corruption relative to men (Alexander, Bågenholm and Charron 2019; Stensöta, Wängnerud, and Agerberg 2015a; United Nations Development Programme 2012).

An effective and extensive state is important for service provision on a mass level that improves female autonomy, which, in turn, generates resources and opportunities for increasing women's presence as elites. In this case, the dependency on an effective state is relevant to both the mass and elite levels. Women tend to gain from such a state in their ability to lead self-determined, empowered lives at both levels. Thus, this mechanism can be used to expect gender differences in tolerance of and engagement in corruption across both levels.

Women are held to higher standards. Referring to this as the "differential treatment theory of gender and corruption," Schwindt-Bayer, Esarey, and Schumacher (2018, 60) note that women are stereotypically perceived as more honest than men, which could lead to stronger punishment of women compared to men by the public or authorities if they engage in corruption. If women are held to higher standards, women will eventually become aware of this likelihood for differential treatment, which will reduce women's willingness to engage in such behavior. All in all, the mechanism operating here would be the deterring effect on women of their awareness of the societal tendency to hold them to higher standards and punish them more harshly compared to men if they are caught engaging in corruption.

An assumption behind the higher standards mechanism is that women become aware of a societal tendency to treat them more harshly than men for corrupt behavior. Such a tendency is more likely to become visible through societal reactions to elite women and men

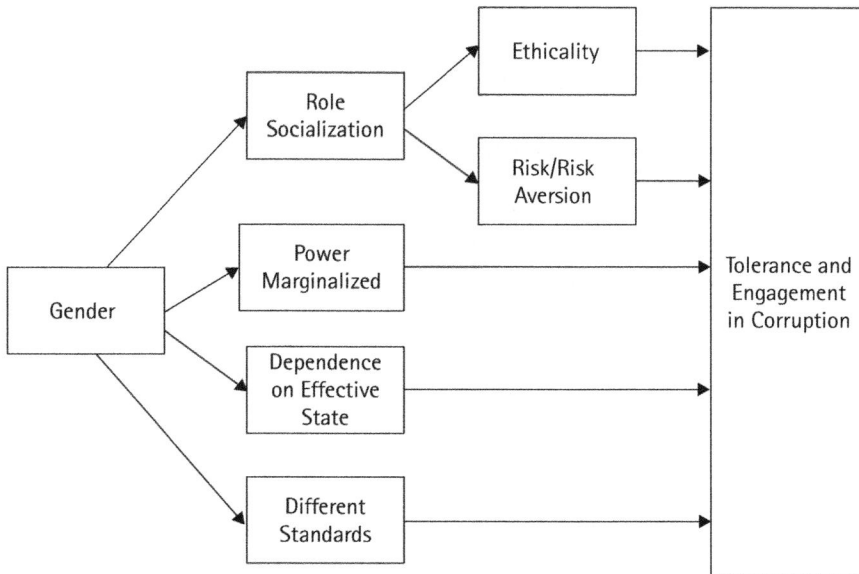

FIGURE 26.1 Summary of micro theoretical assumptions

and is therefore also likely to be most deterring for elite women. It is these instances that receive widespread media attention, for instance. Thus, this mechanism is most plausible for understanding gender differences in tolerance of and engagement in corruption among elites.

Figure 26.1 summarizes the micro-theoretical assumptions linking gender and corruption. While I have described how the theories link gender to tolerance and engagement in corruption independent of one another, in reality, many of the sources of gender differences on which the theories are based could operate simultaneously in decreasing women's tolerance and behavior compared to men's. This is where empirical work has begun to make headway, but it is by no means definitive on which is the most plausible mechanism. Before turning to that evidence, the following section continues with the theoretical work in the field by reviewing macro-theoretical assumptions.

Macro-Theoretical Assumptions: Gender Equality Lowers Corruption across Social Units

Empowers women. Five strands of theory reviewed above *expect women to be less tolerant of corruption* compared to their male counterparts either by a socialization (ethicality and risk aversion), opportunity, state dependency, or higher standards mechanism. If we follow the implications of this expectation to the level of societal units, then expectations that gains in gender equality across various social units will decrease corruption follows rather obviously. Given that women continue to be the "disempowered sex" in every country in the world, gains in gender equality will necessarily empower women in some capacity and, with this, generate a greater tendency for the public and decision-makers to be less susceptible to corrupt behavior.

There is an assumption behind this mechanism that challenging actions taken by women are behind the relationship between gender equality and lower corruption when observed across social units. However, gender equality may also negatively impact corruption in other ways that do not operate directly through the actions taken by women. The next two mechanisms suggest additional, more indirect ways that gains in gender equality potentially lower corruption by seeing this as a process connected to policies that strengthen accountability and diversity and as a socialization agent with the potential to impact societal norms.

Improves the adoption and enforcement of women's interests' policies. In addition to generating greater empowerment of women, in contexts of higher gender equality there is a higher adoption and enforcement of what we might call "women's interests policies." This covers a broad spectrum of policies aimed at combating discrimination and poor, limited service provision that hinder women's self-determination, resources, and achievements. Higher adoption and enforcement of such policies require strategies of increased monitoring, transparency, auditing, and diversity in recruitment of public and elected officials. All of these strategies have the potential to indirectly combat corruption by shedding light on shady practices and/or opening up closed, collusive networks. Scholars refer to this as the women's interests mechanism in the literature (Alexander and Ravlik 2015; Agerberg et al. 2018; Bauhr, Charron, and Wängnerud 2019).

Develops and strengthens impartiality norms. As an alternative perspective, in addition to leading to higher adoption and enforcement of women's interests policies, higher gender equality may socialize a higher respect for impartiality norms among elites and masses, which lowers tolerance of corruption throughout populations as a whole (Alexander 2018; Rothstein 2018, 49). Greater gender equality leads to both private and public experiences of universal treatment that increase the understanding and value of treating people impartially. This generates and reinforces new norms that prioritize universal value, dignity, and capability irrespective of sex differences, transforms the informal practice of power in everyday interactions and, thereby, develops and strengthens anticorruption norms (Alexander 2018; Rothstein 2018).

Macro-Theoretical Assumptions: Lower Corruption Increases Gender Equality across Social Units

One of the better known, colloquial ways to describe corrupt networks is to make reference to "good ole boy" networks. Such reference casts a particular light onto the world of corruption and its players: these are generally closed, collusive, shadowy networks generated and passed on by men. Due to the male-dominated nature of such networks, corrupt systems tend to benefit men and thereby create and/or fuel gender inequality (Bjarnegård 2018; 2013; Stockemer and Sundström 2019; Sundström and Wängnerud 2016). In this case, the relationship between gender equality and corruption is largely driven by corruption suppressing gender equality and not the other way around.[2]

---

[2] There has been an additional theory proposed in the field that the relationship between gender equality and lower corruption is spurious, with both being driven by a fairer system, such as democracy

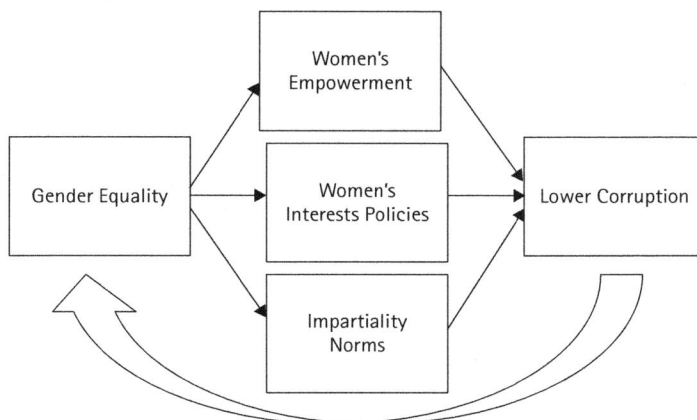

FIGURE 26.2 Macro theoretical assumptions

Figure 26.2 summarizes the macro-theoretical assumptions linking gender equality and corruption. In the interests of offering a clear and parsimonious summary of this strand of theory in the field, I have depicted the mechanisms that link gender equality and corruption as operating independently of one another. However, the picture is plausibly more complex.

For instance, a large body of literature suggests that when women are empowered they are more likely to advocate for women's interests (Wängnerud 2009) and women's interest policies should increase the empowerment of women. Moreover, in contexts where impartiality is strongly valued, gender discrimination is less likely to be tolerated. Finally, a bidirectional relationship between gender equality and lower corruption where both directions operate over time is plausibly the more accurate depiction of reality. Thus, there are virtuous interconnections between these mechanisms. All and all, gender equality most likely has the greatest impact on corruption through their mutually reinforcing interplay.

SECTION 2: EVIDENCE

Micro Evidence: Perception Based and Behavior Based

Perception-Based Evidence. When it comes to gender differences in individuals' perceptions of corrupt behavior, evidence is predominantly drawn from large-scale, global surveys of mass populations. These survey projects ask respondents, for instance, how justifiable they find bribery with response options ranging from (1) always justifiable to (10) never justifiable. Or, respondents are asked whether they have engaged in bribery. In addition, respondents may be asked how severe the problem of corruption is in their country.

(Sung 2003). As empirical work grew, this theory became implausible given findings that there are gender differences at the individual level and that the relationship between gender equality and lower corruption is likely to only be observed among democracies and to be strongest in more accountable democracies. These findings are covered in the sections on evidence below.

This is one of the evidence bases drawn on in the seminal study of Swamy et al. (2001). Swamy et al. (2000, 28) analyze data from over 40 countries across the globe and two time points spanning ten years and find "that about one-fifth more men than women believe that bribery can sometimes or always be justified." Following this tradition, one of the more recent studies of gender differences in perceptions of corrupt behavior finds a similar result: Women are less tolerant of such behavior when compared to men, and this is an enduring difference (Torgler and Valev 2010). In this study, Torgler and Valev (2010) work with data from eight Western European countries over 20 years and find that these gender gaps are surprisingly persistent. They persist to a similar degree over time and even among women and men surveyed from countries high in gender equality, where we would expect women's power marginalization to be weakest.

Based on this evidence, the authors conclude that the status and opportunity gap explanation most indicative of the power marginalization mechanism is less convincing as the factor behind the gender/corruption link. Given the persistence of the differences over time and observations of a larger gap where women are more empowered, deeply rooted, socialized differences between women and men, such as differences in ethicality and risk aversion, are more plausible mechanisms.

In addition to these role socialization mechanisms, although not mentioned by the authors, the study generates evidence in support of the dependence on an effective state mechanism as well. Along these lines, Torlger and Valev's (2010) findings show that social democratic states such as Denmark and the Netherlands have some of the highest marginal effects of being female on aversion to bribery. This finding suggests that attributing greater importance to an effective state among women compared to men may also be behind these gender effects. Women are likely most attuned to the importance of an effective state for their self-determination in social democratic states with extensive welfare provision, since this is where they will have the strongest experience with the state in offsetting barriers to their self-determination in their everyday lives.

In addition to the more comprehensive research conducted by Torlger and Valev (2010), Hernandez and McGee (2013, 2014a, 2014b, 2014c; 2014d) conduct a series of cross-sectional comparative studies across countries from various global regions including Latin America, Africa, and the Middle East. For the most part, their research finds a similar gender gap in opposition to bribery. It is only in the Middle East where they find no significant differences (Hernandez and McGee 2014d). Finally, Bowman and Gilligan (2008) find that women are more likely to consider corruption a problem based on survey data from Australia. Thus, data from public opinion of mass populations is rather consistent in revealing greater female aversion to corruption.

Similar data on the elite level from surveys of politicians or public servants is severely limited. One study is conducted in Ghana. Contrary to the mass evidence, this study does not find gender differences in the level of disapproval of acts of corruption among public servants in the police and education service (Alhassan-Alolo 2007). Thus, more research on elite-level perceptions is needed to determine whether the perception based gender gaps largely observed among masses hold among elites.

Other perception based research evaluates gender differences in *voter reactions* to corruption (Alexander, Bågenholm and Charron 2019; Stensöta et al. 2015a). For instance, some studies examine whether women differ from men in the tendency to vote for another party or candidate when their preferred party or candidate has been involved in corruption

(Alexander, Bågenholm and Charron 2019; Stensöta et al. 2015a). These studies find that women are *less likely* to remain loyal when compared to men: Women are more likely to not vote or to vote for an alternative candidate or party.

This evidence of gender differences in perceptions of voting behavior in reaction to corruption lends the least support to the risk aversion mechanism. Remaining *loyal* to a corrupt candidate or party is, in many instances, the risk-averse option if risk is involved at all. Hence, role socialization in the form of ethicality seems to be the more plausible mechanism for understanding these results. In addition, interestingly, similar to Torlger and Valev (2010), both Alexander et al. (2019) and Stensöta et al. (2015a) find that the effect of gender is even stronger in countries with stronger welfare states and in regions with a more extensive provision of public services. Thus, here again, the dependence on an effective state mechanism finds some support.

Studies also examine how voters treat women relative to men when they are involved in a corruption scandal, which is directly relevant to the higher standards mechanism (Barnes and Beaulieu 2019; Eggers, Vivyan and Wagner 2018; Schwindt-Bayer, Esarey, and Schumacher 2018; Żemojtel-Piotrowska et al. 2017). These studies have produced mixed results. Żemojtel-Piotrowska et al. (2016) find some evidence that female politicians are more harshly evaluated when they are associated with a corruption scandal, and Barnes and Beaulieu (2014) find that the presence of women in government reduces suspicions of fraud based on a national survey experiment in the U.S. Yet, survey experiments conducted on populations from the U.S. and Brazil found no evidence that voters disproportionately punish women at the ballot box for engaging in corruption (Schwindt-Bayer, Esarey and Schumacher 2018). In addition, a survey experiment conducted on populations in the U.K. found that female politicians do not face significantly greater punishment for misconduct among male voters, but they do among female voters (Eggers et al. 2018).

Overall, then, survey data from mass populations on perceptions of the justifiability of corrupt behavior like bribery, whether corruption is a problem, and how one would vote in reaction to corruption offer evidence supporting a tendency for women to show more aversion to corruption compared to men. The persistence of gender differences in some of this research and findings across studies that gender differences appear to be larger in countries and regions with more extensive welfare provision lend greater support to the role socialization mechanism, particularly in the form of ethicality, and the dependence on an effective state mechanism.

On another note, one should weight the value of this evidence with some caution. Social desirability response bias creates a major limitation for perception-based research on ethics, such as perceptions of the justifiability of corruption. Under this limitation, it is difficult to rule out the possibility of a greater tendency among women to answer survey questions in a socially desirable manner but in actual situations to behave similarly to men. And, indeed, broader research on gender differences in ethics finds that "the effect of gender on ethical decision-making is largely attenuated once social desirability is included in [their] analysis" (Dalton and Ortegren 2011, 73). This is a limitation that warrants more attention in future perception-based research on gender and corruption.

Behavior-Based Evidence. An additional take on evaluating gender differences among individuals comes with experimental evidence, which moves us out of the realm of simply evaluating people's attitudes toward corrupt behavior and into the realm of evaluating how people actually behave when confronted with the opportunity to hypothetically engage in a corrupt transaction.

On this front, scholars have designed experiments, typically games where individuals play the roles of firms and public officials, to gauge gender differences in engagement and reciprocity in corruption and corrupt transactions both with and without threat of punishment (Chaudhari 2012). When experimenting with engaging and reciprocating in corruption with no threat of punishment, studies find that women are less likely to offer a bribe, deceive another for personal benefit, and reciprocate a bribe by extending an undue favor to the briber (Chaudhari 2012, 39; Dreber and Johannesson 2008; Lambsdorf and Frank 2011; Rivas 2013). When threat of punishment comes into play, the evidence is more mixed. While Schulze and Frank (2003) find that women are less inclined to participate in corruption under threat of punishment, other experiment-based studies lean more towards a general tendency that is not contingent on the threat of punishment (Chaudari 2012; Rivas 2013; Waithima 2011).

In addition to threat of punishment, Rivas (2013) tests whether women and men behave differently according to their partner's gender in a bribery game. This offers a way to gauge whether stereotypical expectations of women versus men affect inclinations to bribe. Rivas (2013) finds that women are offered lower bribes than men, and, when both partners are women, bribe offering and taking is lower. Moreover, when experimental subjects are asked their beliefs of the probability of women to offer and take bribes compared to men, they expect this to be lower.

Fišar et al. (2016) conduct an experimental study that allows them to elicit both actions and beliefs and thereby analyze not only gender differences in corrupt behavior but also how differences in corrupt behavior relate to gender differences in beliefs about the behavior of others. Under this approach, they find that women are less likely to engage in punishment of corruption and believe corruption to be more prevalent than men. Additionally, whether men act corruptly is more robustly related to their belief that a bribe will be accepted and the probability that they will be reported. Thus, they conclude that men are more likely than women to offer a bribe in the game particularly given the belief that the bribe is likely to be accepted or unlikely to be reported. They interpret this evidence to indicate that there is greater sensitivity among men to social concerns in the context of corruption compared to women and, therefore, men are more likely to conform to a culture of bribe-giving compared to women.

It is also important to note that some of the experimental work that has been cross-nationally comparative finds gender differences only in more highly developed countries (Alatas et al. 2009; Chaudari 2012; Waithima 2010).

Finally, there is a legacy of related experimental work that attempts to assess individuals' tendency to behave in the interest of the public good that has also evaluated gender differences. This research presents rather strong evidence that women are more likely to behave in the interest of the public good through tax compliance (D'Attoma, Volintiru, and Steinmo 2017) and honesty (Rosenbaum, Billinger, and Stieglitz 2014).

All and all, the experimental research supports a tendency among women to engage less in corruption compared to men. Does the evidence also tell us something about mechanisms? There are some insights to be gained here. Adding threat of punishment to corruption experiments seems to return underwhelming results in terms of moderating the effect of gender; in some studies, gender differences are similar regardless of the addition of threat of punishment. This goes against the risk/risk aversion mechanism, since adding a threat of punishment increases the risk of behaving corruptly in a hypothetical experimental game.

Moreover, the finding that men are more likely to behave corruptly particularly if they believe that this is likely to be accepted or unlikely to be reported, while women demonstrate less norm conformity also runs contrary to expectations of the risk/risk aversion mechanism. A tendency to conform to a culture of bribe-giving is arguably risk averse compared to nonconformity, and the evidence points to women as the more likely nonconformists in Fišar et al.'s (2016) study.

Furthermore, many of these studies do not generate much support for the power marginalization mechanism. In these experimental games, both men and women have an equal chance of being assigned a status position, thus holding status marginalization constant. And, yet, gender differences continue to be observed. In addition, interesting contextual patterns that we saw in the research working with perceptions repeat across these studies. To this effect, the likelihood to find gender differences seems to be conditional on whether the experiments were conducted in highly developed societies, which also speaks against the power marginalization mechanism. Gains in gender equality are substantially higher in highly developed societies and, therefore, status gaps between women and men lower. Thus, it is unlikely that status gap biases how women play the experimental corruption games.

Thus, the more plausible mechanisms that remain are the role socialization mechanism in the form of ethicality and the dependence on an effective state mechanism. Indeed, Rivas (2013) found that women were expected to behave more ethically and were involved in less bribery when they played the game. Moreover, women showed a tendency towards nonconformity in the ethical direction in the Fišar et al. (2016) study. And, comparative work suggests that gender differences may be more likely to arise in experiments conducted in highly developed countries, countries that likely are most effective in public service provision that improves women's self-determination.

That said, future experimental work can do a better job of attempting to directly tackle the competing micro mechanisms in the literature. Along these lines, it appears it is particularly informative to elicit beliefs in addition to actions to gauge why players played the game in the way that they did (Fišar et al. 2016). This generates more direct evidence for evaluating mechanisms than simply relying on behavior based measures.

Macro Evidence of Gender Equality Lowering Corruption: Variation across Governing Units

Elected Office. The largest evidence base linking gender equality to lower corruption comes out of studies focused on women's inclusion in elected office (Alexander and Bågenholm 2018; Bauhr, Charron, and Wängnerud 2018; Esarey and Chirillo 2013; Esarey and Schwindt-Bayer 2018; Grimes and Wängnerud 2018; Jha and Sarangi 2018; Watson and Moreland 2014). Scholars have evaluated the impact of women's inclusion across levels and types of office, covering municipal and national legislatures as well as executive offices, such as the office of mayor. The evidence from research focused on legislatures strongly suggests that a higher inclusion of women in elected bodies decreases societal corruption across democracies (Bauhr, Charron and Wängnerud 2018; Esarey and Chirillo 2013; Esarey and Schwindt-Bayer 2018;

Jha and Sarangi 2018). In young democracies that have weak institutions for ensuring demo-cratic accountability and in outright autocracies, this relationship is weak or nonexistent (Alexander 2019; Bjarnegård, Yoon, and Zetterberg 2018; Esarey and Chirillo 2013). Higher levels of women's inclusion in elected office also lowers public perceptions of corruption (Watson and Moreland 2014; Bauhr, Charron and Wängnerud 2018). Finally, while Grimes and Wängnerud (2018, 205) ultimately theorize and evidence a bidirectional relationship between women's presence in elected office and lower corruption, their study across 31 states in Mexico finds "robust support for the contention that women in political office may affect the prevalence of corruption."

The work on executive positions, such as the position of mayor or chief councilor, is also supportive (Beaman et al. 2009; Brollo and Troiano 2016). Brollo and Troiano (2016) look at the effect of the gender of the mayor on corruption episodes with random auditing data across municipalities in Brazil. According to their results, "the probability of observing a corruption episode is 33 to 28 percent lower in municipalities with female mayors than in those with male mayors" (Brollo and Troiano 2016, 3). In addition, Beaman et al. (2009) find that when exposed to a chief female councilor, households report less bribe paying across villages in India.

When it comes to understanding how women lower corruption through their inclusion in elected office, more research is badly needed. Alexander and Bågenholm (2018) identify this as a black box in the literature. To my knowledge, this study is the only study to work with data that captures differences in behavior related to corruption across female and male politicians. In this case, they evaluate differences in the politicization of corruption during election campaigns among presidential candidates in Latin America (from 2000 to 2014) and party leaders in Europe (from 1990 to 2015). They find evidence that women are more likely to politicize corruption, but women's inclusion among both samples of politicians is so small that it is unlikely that this actually curbs corruption.

Other research attempts to shed light on how women's inclusion in elected office lowers corruption by looking at whether the relationship is conditional on some set of factors, mediated by some set of factors, differs depending on the type of corruption or, in the case of survey-based corruption indicators, differs by different public service experiences or the gender of the respondent. I highlight three studies at the forefront of such strategies.

Esarey and Schwindt-Bayer (2018) attempt to better understand what drives the women's representation–corruption link by focusing on whether the relationship is conditional on the strength of electoral accountability across countries. Their assumption is that a female tendency towards risk aversion compared to men is behind the relationship. Thus, they ex-pect the women's representation–corruption link to be strongest when the risk of corruption being detected and punished by voters is high. This is expected to be the case in countries where corruption is not the norm, press freedom is respected, there is a parliamentary system, and electoral rules are personalistic. Drawing on a time-series, cross-sectional dataset of 76 democratic-leaning countries, their results show that all measures of electoral accountability moderate the link between women's representation and corruption in the expected direction. In this case, the risk aversion mechanism finds support, but this amounts to lower levels of corruption with women's inclusion in elected office *only* in contexts where accountability is high and corruption is therefore risky.

Agerberg et al. (2018) attempt to better understand the women's representation–corruption link by determining whether the effect of the level of women's inclusion on corruption is mediated by a set of relevant factors. Under this design, the authors are particularly interested in testing the women's interests' mechanism. Following this theoretical angle, the authors presume that women's inclusion in elected office is likely to indirectly lower corruption through increasing an overall emphasis on monitoring and transparency and through greater efforts to adopt and enforce policies particularly important for women's self-determination. To test this, the authors conduct a cross-national, mediation analysis on over 100 countries and indeed find that the influence of higher levels of women in national parliaments channels indirectly via higher levels of auditing and stronger adoption and enforcement of women-friendly policies in negatively effecting levels of corruption. Based on this mediation evidence, their study lends support to the women's interests' mechanism.

Finally, Bauhr, Charron, and Wängnerud (2018) look at whether the effect of the percentage of women on local councils throughout Europe on the level of corruption differs depending on whether one is measuring petty or grand corruption. They measure petty corruption with survey data that captures corruption experiences among citizens and grand corruption with a novel measure of risk of corruption in high-level procurement. With survey-based measures that capture petty corruption, they additionally look at whether the effect of women's representation varies across types of service delivery experienced by individuals and the gender of the individuals. They find that women's inclusion on local councils reduces levels of both petty and grand corruption. Based on the grand corruption finding, they argue that female politicians likely reduce corruption by supporting monitoring and policy strategies that combat exclusionary power networks. In understanding the effect on petty corruption, they dig deeper with a set of survey-based measures and look at whether the effect varies across types of service delivery experienced by individuals and by the gender of individuals. Ultimately, they find that while reported bribe paying decreases generally with higher levels of women on local councils, the effect is stronger in the area of education and health services compared to law enforcement and particularly among women.

Based on these findings, they conclude that women in elected office lower grand corruption because of their marginalized status and consequent desire to break up exclusionary power networks, while they lower petty corruption because they more strongly support women's interests policies that strengthen clean public service provision in areas that are particularly important for women, such as in the education and health sectors.

To sum up this section on the relationship between women's presence in elected office and lower corruption, I turn to whether there is evidence that adopting quotas to increase women's presence in elected office leads to lower corruption, as this is a key policy implication that emerges from this research. I alert readers to two studies on this research frontier. Bjarnegård, Yoon, and Zetterberg (2018) and Esarey and Valdes (2019) find no or weak evidence that the adoption of gender quotas lower corruption. For Bjarnegård, Yoon, and Zetterberg (2018), this is dependent on whether quota policies result in the election of women that are recruited from new networks and have the potential to operate independently on a range of issues. For Esarey and Valdes (2019), taking into consideration a range of variation in how and where quotas are adopted and implemented, including how this varies the level of improvement in women's seat shares, the level of women's accountability to voters and the level of women's agency to participate in policymaking, their study finds little evidence that gender quotas substantially lower corruption.

Bureaucracy. Unlike the evidence from research on elected offices, evidence from research on bureaucracies is much weaker (Stensöta, Wängnerud, and Svensson 2015b; Stensöta 2018). In a recent publication, Stensöta (2018) theoretically and empirically interrogates this relationship. She theorizes that gender effects are suppressed among bureaucrats due to the emphasis on expertise and meritocracy that sets the standards for effective bureaucratic practice. Compared to politicians who are more likely to be evaluated according to personal characteristics in assessments of their performance, bureaucrats tend to be constrained by standards of formal and informal institutions that emphasize proper procedure and impartial treatment. This suppresses the saliency of personal characteristics, like gender, and thereby reduces differences in behavior between men and women. Thus, the rule-bound nature of these bureaucratic contexts suppresses differences that might otherwise surface in more personalistic contexts, such as legislatures. The evidence from Stensöta's (2018) study supports the theory insofar as the relationship between the percentage of women in the bureaucracy and corruption is much weaker when compared to the relationship between the percentage of women in the legislature and corruption analyzing the same country-level dataset.

The finding suggesting that bureaucratic contexts suppress gender differences in engagement in corruption could be interpreted to support several micro-level mechanisms in the literature. Given the rule-bound nature of bureaucratic environments, perhaps those who select into these positions are more homogeneously high in respect for ethical standards which minimizes any gender differences that might otherwise surface due to role socialization. From another perspective, the rule-bound nature of bureaucratic environments might also raise the level of risk in engaging in corruption to so high a level that this source of gender difference becomes minimized. Similarly, the rule-bound nature of these environments might also generate higher expectations of ethical behavior under which men are held to as high of standards as women. Finally, it is likely that bureaucrats attribute greater importance to widespread, effective public services since their livelihood in many ways depend on this. This may minimize differences by making men as concerned as women in this direction. Thus, more research should be done to tease out more precisely how bureaucratic environments suppress gender differences compared to more personalistic environments such as those characteristic of elected offices.

Legacies of Gender Equality and Impartiality Norms. Alexander (2018) posits that variation in countries' gender norms and practices begin early in their historical trajectories and it is through these norms and practices that individuals internalize some of the most pervasive grassroots' experiences with power, which, in turn, generate and reinforce norms important for the quality of government. Thus, legacies of gender equality are vital as a key socialization agent of norms behind countries' historical trajectories in quality of government. Alexander (2018) works with large-scale cross-national and longitudinal data and finds robust relationships between countries' pre-industrial gender equality patterns within households and their levels of quality of government and trust across the globe, from 1800 to 2012 (Alexander 2018).

In a similar vein but with a very different research design, a study conducted in India finds that whether individuals reside in villages that vary in historic systems of gendered power, matrilineal versus patrilineal, affects whether they tend towards public goods provision or free riding when participating in an experiment (Andersen, Bulte, Gneezy, and List 2008). In particular, the authors find that 1) fewer individuals that played an experimental game were strong free riders in villages with a matrilineal system compared to the villages with nonmatrilineal systems; 2) public goods provision was highest among players in the villages with a matrilineal system; and, 3) the higher level of provision was primarily due to male, rather than female, differences among players in contributing to the public good in the game. Taken together, these findings suggest that more gender egalitarian systems, in this case matrilineal systems, socialize *both men and women* to support public goods. The results support the idea that legacies of gender equality may generate widespread impartiality norms that decrease their vulnerability to corruption.

Finally, Merkle and Wong's (2019) study of Ghana, Nigeria, Rwanda, South Africa, and Zimbabwe relies on World Value Survey data and finds that people who agree *that men are better political leaders than women*, regardless of their gender, are more likely to state that corruption is justifiable. They interpret their findings as corroborating "the argument that corruption is deeply rooted in patriarchal structures, which need to be addressed to achieve both higher political participation of women and lower levels of corruption" (Merkle and Wong 2019: 353).

Macro Evidence of Corruption Lowering Gender Equality

As this chapter noted in the review of theory, it is as plausible to assume that there is a relationship between gender equality and corruption because women are more likely to be excluded from power and depleted of resources under environments with widespread corruption. In this case, the causal direction of the relationship may run from higher (lower) levels of corruption to lower (higher) gender equality. Some key studies provide evidence to support this direction of the relationship. For instance, Bjarnegård (2013) conducts statistical analyses of parliamentary compositions worldwide and extensive fieldwork in Thailand and concludes that electoral corruption is particularly likely to benefit men and thereby negatively influence gender equality in politics. Men are considered assets in the clientelistic networks that underlie electoral corruption, because they have access to those networks and the resources to finance those networks. Thus, corruption functions to the exclusion of women and to the benefit of men in clientelistic systems. Sundström and Wängnerud (2016) find support with data covering 167 regions in 18 European countries. Through their analyses, they find that where levels of corruption are high, the proportion of women elected to local councils is low and vice versa: Where levels of corruption are low, the proportion of women elected to local councils is higher. In addition, in a study of the African region, Stockemer (2011) finds evidence that corruption prevents gender equal representation. Finally, Esarey and Schwindt-Bayer (2017) and Grimes and Wängnerud (2018) are two of the few studies to build the notion of bidirectionality into their theory and analysis of the women's representation–lower corruption link. Esarey and Schwindt-Bayer use and instrumental variable approach and find evidence of a bidirectional relationship: Women's representation decreases corruption and corruption decreases women's participation in government. Grimes and Wängnerud (2018) argue that a new impetus for anticorruption reforms opens opportunities for women's inclusion in elected office, which then, in turn, may further strengthen anticorruption norm compliance and lower corruption. Thus, in this case, efforts to lower corruption are a key initiating force behind increases in women's inclusion and an eventual decline in actual levels of corruption. Findings from their study of

31 states across Mexico support this direction of influence from anticorruption reforms to greater female inclusion.

SECTION 3: CONCLUSION

The field of gender, gender equality, and corruption research is developing rapidly and, perhaps, even more importantly, it is capturing the attention of the larger anticorruption international policy and activist communities. While the field has seen tremendous development, there is room for improvement.

First and foremost, the field is largely silent on how socializing masculinity and perpetuating patriarchal structures generates vulnerability to corrupt behavior and institutions. The theoretical and empirical frontlines are overwhelmingly focused on the positive impact of more feminine socialization, female investment in the state, societal expectations of female incorruptibility, greater empowerment of women, adoption and enforcement of women-friendly policies, and norms supporting women's equality. Future research should work to balance this bias with more theory on and observation of the link between masculinity, patriarchy, and corruption. Thus it is important that future research build on recent calls in the literature to move in this direction (Bjarnegård 2018).

The field is also relatively silent on how corruption harms women and men differently and how corrupt transactions may play out differently for women compared to men. Expanding the gender perspective in this direction will improve our ability to identify corruption and understand the true scope of the problem. Recent interesting work on this front, for instance, has called for rethinking corruption from the perspective of sexual exploitation (Lindberg and Stensöta 2018).

There is also room for improvement within the current framework for approaching gender, gender equality, and corruption. Starting with gender differences at the individual level and the role socialization mechanisms, ethicality, and risk aversion, the near total lack of data on female and male elites for gauging gender differences at this level and linking this to anticorruption support and behavior is a serious gap. As the field currently stands, whenever this mechanism is invoked to anticipate elite-level differences, it is not directly tested with perception-based or behavior-based data from elite surveys or experiments. Instead, studies extrapolate to the elite-level based on mass-level data. This is problematic as it ignores selection biases that may be operating behind who eventually holds elite positions, which, for instance, might attenuate gender differences in socialization among elites. For instance, more risk-acceptant women may be more likely to achieve elite positions.

In terms of the power marginalization mechanism for understanding individual-level differences, theory and observation is unclear on whether marginalized status deters female engagement in corruption due to a lack of network resources or whether it deters female engagement because of lower recruitment into such opportunities based on assumptions of incapability and unwillingness to engage in corruption. Thus, how marginalized status is operating needs to be interrogated more thoroughly given these divergent possibilities.

Turning to the individual-level dependence on an effective state mechanism, more work is needed to differentiate which areas of state dependency are most mobilizing of female intolerance of corruption and how. The theory emphasizes both employment opportunities and the provision of an array of public services that open up to women under a more expansive and effective state and, in turn, mobilize their investment in combatting state waste. Future research needs to look deeper into how these mobilizing processes are occurring.

Finally, in terms of the different standards mechanism, existing studies run into a similar data gap faced by the theory on socialization. We need more data on whether elite women perceive themselves as held to higher standards compared to their male counterparts and whether this correlates with their perceptions and/or behavior related to corruption. Moreover, we need more research on whether differential treatment varies depending on the type of corruption scandal elites engage in or the position of power they hold.

I now move on to the most important gaps remaining in research linking gender equality and corruption. This research focuses relationships among societal units. I begin with the most simple, direct mechanism: Gender equality lowers corruption by empowering women. On this front, the existing literature largely fails to adopt empirical strategies for observing differences in the anticorruption behavior of empowered women (e.g., female politicians) compared to their male counterparts. Instead, the bulk of this literature assumes these individual-level effects based on correlations between the percentage of women in a given organizational unit and the unit's corresponding level of corruption. Future research should begin to fill this gap.

Turning to the second macro-level mechanism, the women's interests mechanism, I see the following need for more work. There are two primary ways that the adoption and enforcement of women's interests policies indirectly lower corruption: Through diversifying recruitment and breaking up corrupt networks or through the increased monitoring and transparency necessary for realizing the enforcement of women's interests' policies. Future research needs to do a better job interrogating the indirect effects of gains in women's interests' policies given these divergent possibilities.

On the third mechanism, operating through norm generation, future research could unpack the notion of impartiality norms into more specific forms of impartiality values, such as anti-discrimination, anti-authoritarianism, generalized trust or universalism, and attempt to evaluate which aspects of impartiality are most strongly impacted through experiences of higher gender equality.

Finally, we come to the reverse causality mechanism: lower corruption leads to gender equality. In moving the field forward, a "directionality war" is not useful. Indeed, the evidence is rather convincing in both directions of influence (Esarey and Schwindt-Bayer 2017; Grimes and Wängnerud 2018). Thus, what should be focused on is the mutually reinforcing and virtuously cyclical capacity between gender equality and lower corruption in increasing countries' quality of government. If gender equality and lower corruption are so profoundly interconnected such that a boost in one kicks off a boost in the other and vice versa, then for anticorruption researchers, policymakers, and activists, the gender perspective offers us multiple avenues for theorizing and testing ways to punctuate corruption equilibria.

References

Andersen, Steffen, Erwin Bulte, Uri Gneezy, and John A. List. 2008. "Do Women Supply More Public Goods Than Men? Preliminary Experimental Evidence from Matrilineal and Patriarchal Societies." *American Economic Review* 98 (2): 376–81.

Agerberg, Mattias, Maria Gustavson, Aksel Sundström, and Lena Wängnerud. 2018. "Gender aspects of government auditing." In *Gender and Corruption*, edited by Helena Stensöta, Lena Wängnerud, 213–33. London: Palgrave Macmillan.

Alatas, Vivi, Lisa Cameron, Ananish Chaudhuri, Nisvan Erkal, and Lata Gangadharan. 2009. "Gender, Culture, and Corruption: Insights from an Experimental Analysis." *Southern Economic Journal*: 663–80.

Alexander, Amy. 2019. "Is Poor Performance in Gender Equality Linked to Higher Corruption in the Middle East?" In *Corruption and Informal Practices in the Middle East and North Africa*, edited by Ina Kubbe and Aiysha Varraich, 154. New York: Routledge.

Alexander, Amy C. 2018. "The Historic Roots of Quality of Government: The Role of Gender Equality." In *Gender and Corruption*, edited by Helena Stensöta and Lena Wängnerud, 21–36. London: Palgrave Macmillan.

Alexander, Amy C., and Andreas Bågenholm. 2018. "Does Gender Matter? Female Politicians' Engagement in Anti-corruption Efforts." In *Gender and Corruption*, 171–89. London: Palgrave Macmillan.

Alexander, Amy. C., Andreas Bågenholm, and Nicholas Charron. (2019). "Are women more likely to throw the rascals out? The mobilizing effect of social service spending on female voters." *Public Choice*, 1–27.

Alexander, Amy C., and Maria Ravlik. 2015. "Responsiveness to Women's Interests as a Quality of Government Mechanism: A Global Analysis of Women's Presence in National Legislatures and Anti-trafficking Enforcement." In American Political Science Association's Annual Meeting, San Francisco.

Alhassan-Alolo, Namawu. 2007. "Gender and Corruption: Testing the New Consensus." *Public Administration and Development: The International Journal of Management Research and Practice* 27 (3): 227–37.

Bennett, Sarah, David P. Farrington, and L. Rowell Huesmann. 2005. "Explaining Gender Differences in Crime and Violence: The Importance of Social Cognitive Skills." *Aggression and violent behavior* 10 (3): 263–88.

Bjarnegård, Elin. 2013. *Gender, Informal Institutions and Political Recruitment: Explaining Male Dominance in Parliamentary Representation*. London: Springer.

Bjarnegård, Elin. 2018. "Focusing on Masculinity and Male-Dominated Networks in Corruption." In *Gender and Corruption*, 257–73. London: Palgrave Macmillan.

Bjarnegård, Elin, Mi Yung Yoon, and Pär Zetterberg. 2018. "Gender Quotas and the Re (pro) duction of Corruption." In *Gender and Corruption*, 105–24. London: Palgrave Macmillan.

Barnes, Tiffany D., and Emily Beaulieu. 2019. "Women Politicians, Institutions, and Perceptions of Corruption." *Comparative Political Studies* 52 (1): 134–67.

Bauhr, Monika, Nicholas Charron, and Lena Wängnerud. 2019. "Exclusion or Interests? Why Females in Elected Office Reduce Petty and Grand Corruption." *European Journal of Political Research* 58 (4): 1043–1065.

Beaman, Lori, Raghabendra Chattopadhyay, Esther Duflo, Rohini Pande, and Petia Topalova. 2009. "Powerful Women: Does Exposure Reduce Bias?" *The Quarterly journal of economics* 124 (4): 1497–540.

Bowman, Diana M., and Georg Gilligan. 2008. "Australian Women and Corruption: The Gender Dimension in Perceptions of Corruption." *JOAAG* 3 (1): 1–9.

Brollo, Fernanda, and Ugo Troiano. 2016. "What Happens When a Woman Wins an Election? Evidence from Close Races in Brazil." *Journal of Development Economics* 122: 28–45.

Charness, Gary, and Uri Gneezy. 2012. "Strong Evidence for Gender Differences in Risk Taking." *Journal of Economic Behavior & Organization* 83 (1): 50–8.

Chaudhuri, Ananish. 2012. "Chapter 2 Gender and Corruption: A Survey of the Experimental Evidence." In *New Advances in Experimental Research on Corruption*, 13–49. Bingley: Emerald Group Publishing Limited.

Cumming, Douglas, Tak Yan Leung, and Oliver Rui. 2015. "Gender Diversity and Securities Fraud." *Academy of management Journal* 58 (5): 1572–93.

Dalton, Derek, and Marc Ortegren. 2011. "Gender Differences in Ethics Research: The Importance of Controlling for the Social Desirability Response Bias." *Journal of Business Ethics* 103 (1): 73–93.

D'Attoma, John, Clara Volintiru, and Sven Steinmo. 2017. "Willing to Share? Tax Compliance and Gender in Europe and America." *Research & Politics* 4 (2): 2053168017707151.

Dollar, David, Raymond Fisman, and Roberta Gatti. 2001. "Are Women Really the "Fairer" Sex? Corruption and Women in Government." *Journal of Economic Behavior & Organization* 46 (4): 423–29.

Dreber, Anna, and Magnus Johannesson. 2008. "Gender Differences in Deception." *Economics Letters* 99 (1): 197–9.

Eagly, Alice H., and Maureen Crowley. 1986. "Gender and Helping Behavior: A Meta-Analytic Review of the Social Psychological Literature." *Psychological Bulletin* 100 (3): 283.

Eagly, Alice H., Wendy Wood, and Amanda B. Diekman. 2000. "Social Role Theory of Sex Differences and Similarities: A Current Appraisal." *The Developmental Social Psychology of Gender* 12: 174.

Eggers, Andrew C., Nick Vivyan, and Markus Wagner. 2018. "Corruption, Accountability, and Gender: Do Female Politicians Face Higher Standards in Public Life?" *The Journal of Politics* 80 (1): 321–26.

Esarey, Justin, and Gina Chirillo. 2013. "'Fairer Sex' or Purity Myth? Corruption, Gender, and Institutional Context." *Politics & Gender* 9 (4): 361–89.

Esarey, Justin, and Leslie Schwindt-Bayer. 2017. "Estimating Causal Relationships between Women's Representation in Government and Corruption." *Comparative Political Studies.* 0010414019830744.

Esarey, Justin, and Leslie A. Schwindt-Bayer. 2018. "Women's Representation, Accountability and Corruption in Democracies." *British Journal of Political Science* 48 (3): 659–90.

Esarey, Justin, and Natalie Valdes. 2019. "Do Legislative Gender Quotas Lower Corruption?" Working paper retrievable from http://www.justinesarey.com/research

Fišar, Miloš, Matúš Kubák, Jiři Špalek, and James Tremewan. 2016. "Gender Differences in Beliefs and Actions in a Framed Corruption Experiment." *Journal of Behavioral and Experimental Economics* 63: 69–82.

Goetz, Anne Marie. 2007. "Political Cleaners: Women as the New Anti-Corruption Force?" *Development and Change* 38 (1): 87–105.

Jha, Chandan Kumar, and Sudipta Sarangi. 2018. "Women and Corruption: What Positions Must They Hold to Make a Difference?" *Journal of Economic Behavior & Organization* 151: 219–33.

Grimes, Marcia, and Lena Wängnerud. 2018. "Gender and Corruption in Mexico: Building a Theory of Conditioned Causality." In *Gender and Corruption*, 191–211. London: Palgrave Macmillan.

Gustafsod, Per E. 1998. "Gender Differences in Risk Perception: Theoretical and Methodological Perspectives." *Risk analysis* 18 (6): 805–11.

Hernandez, Teresa, and Robert W. McGee. 2013. "The Ethics of Accepting a Bribe: A Comparative Study of Opinion in the USA, Canada and Mexico." *Journal of Accounting, Ethics and Public Policy* 14 (4).

Hernandez, Teresa, and Robert W. McGee. 2014a. "Ethical Attitudes toward Taking a Bribe: A Study of Three Latin American Countries." Available at SSRN 2426955.

Hernandez, Teresa, and Robert W. McGee. 2014b. "The Ethics of Accepting a Bribe: An Empirical Study of Opinion in the USA, Brazil, Germany and ChinPa." Brazil, Germany and China (April 20, 2014). Available at SSRN: https://ssrn.com/abstract=2426956 or http://dx.doi.org/10.2139/ssrn.2426956

Hernandez, Teresa, and Robert W. McGee. 2014c. "A Demographic Study of African Attitudes on Bribery." *Journal of Accounting, Ethics and Public Policy* 15 (2).

Hernandez, Teresa, and Robert W. McGee. 2014d. "The Ethical Perceptions of Bribe Taking in Four Muslim Countries." *Journal of Accounting, Ethics and Public Policy* 15 (1).

Lambsdorff, Johann Graf, and Björn Frank. 2011. "Corrupt Reciprocity: Experimental Evidence on a Men's Game." *International review of Law and economics* 31 (2): 116–25.

Lindberg, Helen, and Helena Stensöta. 2018. "Corruption as Exploitation: Feminist Exchange Theories and the Link between Gender and Corruption." In *Gender and Corruption*, edited by Helena Stensöta and Lena Wängnerud, 237–56. London: Palgrave Macmillan.

Mears, Daniel P., Matthew Ploeger, and Mark Warr. 1998. "Explaining the Gender Gap in Delinquency: Peer Influence and Moral Evaluations of Behavior." *Journal of research in crime and delinquency* 35 (3): 251–66.

Merkle, Ortrun, and Pui-Hang Wong. 2019. "It Is All about Power: Corruption, Patriarchy and the Political Participation of Women." In *Women and Sustainable Human Development*, 353–68. London: Palgrave Macmillan.

Rivas, M. Fernanda. 2013. "An Experiment on Corruption and Gender." *Bulletin of Economic Research* 65 (1): 10–42.

Rothstein, Bo. 2018. "Corruption, Gender Equality and Meritocracy." In *Gender and Corruption*, edited by Helena Stensöta and Lena Wängnerud, 37–56. London: Palgrave Macmillan.

Rosenbaum, Stephen Mark, Stephan Billinger, and Nils Stieglitz. 2014. "Let's Be Honest: A Review of Experimental Evidence of Honesty and Truth-Telling." *Journal of Economic Psychology* 45: 181–96.

Schulze, Günther G., and Björn Frank. 2003. "Deterrence versus Intrinsic Motivation: Experimental Evidence on the Determinants of Corruptibility." *Economics of governance* 4 (2): 143–60.

Schwindt-Bayer, Leslie A., Justin Esarey, and Erika Schumacher. 2018. "Gender and Citizen Responses to Corruption among Politicians: The Us and Brazil." In *Gender and Corruption*, edited by Helena Stensöta and Lena Wängnerud, 59–82. London: Palgrave Macmillan, 2018.

Swamy, Anand, Stephen Knack, Young Lee, and Omar Azfar. 2001. "Gender and Corruption." *Journal of development economics* 64 (1): 25–55.

Stensöta, Helena. 2018. "Corruption and Female Representation in the Bureaucracy." In *Gender and Corruption*, 127–44. London: Palgrave Macmillan.

Stensöta, Helena Olofsdotter, Lena Wängnerud, and Mattias Agerberg. 2015a. "Why Women in Encompassing Welfare States Punish Corrupt Political Parties." In *Elites, Institutions and the Quality of Government*, 245–62. London: Palgrave Macmillan.

Stensöta, Helena, Lena Wängnerud, and Richard Svensson. 2015b. "Gender and Corruption: The Mediating Power of Institutional Logics." *Governance* 28 (4): 475–96.

Stockemer, Daniel. 2011. "Women's Parliamentary Representation in Africa: The Impact of Democracy and Corruption on the Number of Female Deputies in National Parliaments." *Political Studies* 59 (3): 693–712.

Stockemer, Daniel, and Aksel Sundström. 2019. "Corruption and Women in Cabinets: Informal Barriers to Recruitment in the Executive." *Governance* 32 (1): 83–102.

Sundström, Aksel, and Lena Wängnerud. 2016. "Corruption as an Obstacle to Women's Political Representation: Evidence from Local Councils in 18 European Countries." *Party Politics* 22 (3): 354–69.

Sung, Hung-En. 2003. "Fairer Sex or Fairer System? Gender and Corruption Revisited." *Social Forces* 82 (2): 703–23.

Tooby, John, and Leda Cosmides. 1992. "The Psychological Foundations of Culture." *The adapted mind: Evolutionary psychology and the generation of culture* , ed. JH Barkow, L Cosmides, J Tooby, pp. 19–136. New York: Oxford University Press.

Tooby, John, and Leda Cosmides. 1990. "The Past Explains the Present: Emotional Adaptations and the Structure of Ancestral Environments." *Ethology and Sociobiology* 11 (4–5): 375–424.

Torgler, Benno, and Neven T. Valev. 2010. "Gender and Public Attitudes toward Corruption and Tax Evasion." *Contemporary Economic Policy* 28 (4): 554–68.

United Nations Development Programme. 2012. "Seeing Beyond the State: Grassroots Women's Perspectives on Corruption and Anti-Corruption." New York: Bureau for Development Policy.

Walters, Glenn D. 2017. "Viewing the Cycle of Violence through a Gendered Pathways Lens: Perceived Parental Tolerance of Violence, Peer Influence, and Child Aggressive Behavior." *Journal of Interpersonal Violence*. 35: 2189–209.

Waithima, Abraham K. 2011. "The Role of Gender, Ethnicity and Harambee in Corruption: Experimental Evidence from Kenya." Ph.D. diss. University of Cape Town.

Wängnerud, Lena. 2009. "Women in Parliaments: Descriptive and Substantive Representation." *Annual Review of Political Science* 12: 51–69.

Watson, David, and Amy Moreland. 2014. "Perceptions of Corruption and the Dynamics of Women's Representation." *Politics & Gender* 10 (3): 392–412.

World Bank. 2001. *Engendering Development through Gender Equality in Rights, Resources and Voice*. Oxford: Oxford University Press.

Żemojtel-Piotrowska, Magdalena Anna, Alison Marganski, Tomasz Baran, and Jarosław Piotrowski. 2017. "Corruption and Sexual Scandal: The Importance of Politician Gender." *Anales de Psicología/Annals of Psychology* 33 (1): 133–41.

CHAPTER 27

....

BRINGING POLITICS
BACK IN

*Ethnic Fractionalization, Quality of
Government, and Public Goods
Provision Revisited*

....

ANNA PERSSON

INTRODUCTION

....

WHY are some states able to provide public goods and promote broad-based development whereas other states do not have the capacity to do any of these things, and might even have to rely on international aid in order to realize even the most minimal tasks of the modern state? The recent literature examining this question has typically emphasized one of two factors in an attempt to explain this. On the one hand, an increasingly vocational literature points to the vital role played by the factor in focus of this volume: The *Quality of Government*, henceforth *QoG* (Acemoglu and Robinson 2012; Fukuyama 2011; Holmberg, Rothstein, and Nasiritousi 2009; Rodrik, Subramanian, and Trebbi 2004; Svallfors 2013). On the other hand, parallel to the development of this prominent field of research, the past few decades have witnessed a radical increase also in studies putting forward a presumed negative impact of *ethnic fractionalization* on a variety of outcomes. Ethnic fractionalization has thus been linked to suboptimal public goods provision and subpar development outcomes within a wide range of areas, including infrastructure, education, health, economic growth, and taxation (Easterly and Levine 1997; Alesina and La Ferrara 2000; Alesina, Baqir, and Easterly 1999; Miguel and Gugerty 2005; Baldwin and Huber 2010; Habyarimana et al. 2007; Lieberman 2003; Khwaja 2009; Banarjee, Iyer, and Somanathan 2005; Lassen 2007; Montalvo and Reynal-Querol 2005). In fact, having been referred to as "one of the most powerful hypotheses in political economy" (Banerjee, Iyer, and Somanathan 2005, 639), the negative association between ethnic fractionalization and public goods provision is now so widely accepted that it has become a "standard" control in regressions explaining cross-national differences in various aspects of political, social, and economic development. Following from this, rather than being concerned with further establishing the relationship between ethnic fractionalization and public goods provision empirically, scholars are now primarily concentrating on exploring the various possible mechanisms that can account for the association (cf. Habyarimana et al. 2007). As such, with a few exceptions, the emphasis in contemporary research is typically "not on *whether* ethnic diversity undermines public goods provision, but on *why*" (2007, 709; for a critique of the focus on mechanisms in the current literature, see Gisselquist 2014, 1623).

The aim of this chapter is to introduce, revisit, and challenge the suggested negative causal relationship between ethnic fractionalization and public goods provision, with a particular focus on the role of QoG. In the endeavor to do so, the chapter is organized as follows. In the next section, the argument that ethnic fractionalization undermines public goods provision is explored in greater detail. What notion of ethnic fractionalization does the argument rely on, and through what micro and macro mechanisms is the relationship presumed to work? As this section reveals, QoG has typically played quite an important role in the relationship, if yet not always being explicitly acknowledged. The next section turns to the empirical study of the relationship; what does the empirical evidence demonstrating a negative effect of ethnic fractionalization on public goods provision consist of? The subsequent section then proceeds to revisit the suggested relationship between ethnic fractionalization and public goods provision, theoretically as well as empirically. What are the main theoretical and empirical criticisms that have been directed towards the argument? As will be demonstrated, with the quite extensive empirical variation as regards the effects of ethnic fractionalization, across contexts and over time, as a backdrop, the criticism against the so-called "diversity debit hypothesis" (Gerring et al. 2015) has typically taken its point of departure in social constructivist theories of ethnicity and ethnic relations and can be divided into four broad categories; one critique which is mainly concerned with measurement problems, one approach which argues that the relationship is subject to conditioned causality, one which holds that the relationship is spurious, and one which holds that the relationship is reverse and that ethnic fractionalization is thus in fact endogenous to the very outcomes it seeks to explain. The final section offers some concluding remarks, as well as a number of ideas about potential future avenues to pursue within the field. Most prominently, the final section emphasizes the need to endogenize the relationship between ethnic fractionalization and public goods provision by bringing the state up front of the analysis as a social force in its own right (cf. Grafstein 1992, 1), with the power to shape notions of "us" and "them" and, thus, development outcomes.

Ethnic Fractionalization and Public Goods Provision: The Argument

While the argument that ethnic fractionalization undermines public goods provision has gained substantial attention in more recent work, particularly in the political economy literature within the fields of political science and economics (Alesina, Baqir, and Easterly 1999; Miguel and Gugerty 2005; Banerjee and Somanathan 2007; Easterly and Levine 1997;

Alesina and La Ferrara 2000; Habyarimana et al. 2007; Kimenyi 2006), it corresponds well also to the insights offered by more classical work on governance and public goods provision. Already John Stuart Mill (1991 [1861]), for instance, declared "free institutions" to be "next to impossible in a country made up of different nationalities." Moreover, the argument parallels a large literature within the fields of anthropology and sociology, and to some extent even political science, which focuses on the ways in which states in much of the contemporary developing world, and particularly in sub-Saharan Africa—due to them being exogenously imposed, "artificial" state constructions, and thus also comparatively more ethnically heterogeneous—are typically driven by an ethnic-based, neo-patrimonial type of logic and thus, as the argument goes, extraordinarily ill-equipped to provide public goods and promote broad-based development (Sandbrook 1972; Lemarchand 1972; Ekeh 1975; Migdal 1988; Englebert 2000; Médard 1986).[1]

Whereas a clear conceptualization of the term *ethnic fractionalization* is certainly necessary to interpret the relationship between ethnic fractionalization and public goods provision, as argued by Chandra and Wilkinson (2008, 516), recent political economy-oriented research in the field has typically proceeded without such a conceptual foundation. As a result, what is meant by the term ethnic fractionalization in each particular study is often left to the reader to interpret. Having said this, acknowledging the fact that the lion's share of political economy-oriented studies rely on the so-called Ethno-Linguistic Fractionalization (ELF) index, or some measure closely related to this index (cf. Posner 2004a)—most notably the measure of ethnic fractionalization provided by Alesina et al. (2003)—the majority of studies in the field promote an, if yet implicit, "umbrella" definition of the first component of the term, i.e. *ethnic*, as signifying a person's demographically defined cultural, religious, linguistic, tribal, racial, or regional identity, or some combination of the foregoing. For example, the original version of the ELF index, which is available for 129 countries, indicates the likelihood that two randomly drawn individuals from a particular population belong to different ethnic groups, the term ethnic being understood in cultural-linguistic terms.[2] In Alesina et al.'s (2003) measurement for 190 countries, religion is added to

---

[1] However, probably due to differences in methodological approach, the different literatures only seldom interact.

[2] The ELF index is calculated using a Herfindahl concentration index from data compiled by a team of Soviet ethnographers in the early 1960s and published in the Atlas Narodov Mira in 1964. It is calculated as follows. Let us consider a country with a total population N that is in turn divided into J groups, each group's population denoted by n. ELF is then given by

$$\text{ELF} = 1 - \sum_{j=1}^{J} \left(\frac{n_j}{N} \right)^2$$

ELF increases with the number of groups *n*. The index also increases the more equal the sizes of each of these groups. The consequence of the latter characteristic added to the first is that very different societies can despite of this fact have a quite similar ELF.

the picture. The influential measurements developed by Roeder (2001) similarly provide multiple measures of ethnic diversity, each using slightly different rules for what constitutes an ethnic group.

Regarding the second component of the term, i.e. *fractionalization*, whereas the majority of authors in the field, as aforementioned, rely on *demographic* measures of ethnic *diversity*— and in fact also often talk about diversity or heterogeneity rather than fractionalization—as noted by Posner (2004a) and Singh (2010), a close reading of the literature shows that the underlying theoretical construct in most studies is in fact not ethnic diversity—i.e. a concept with strong demographic connotations—but ethnic *divisions* (or, in other words, *fractionalization, polarization,* or *mobilization)*—i.e. a political concept, signifying a notion of "us" versus "them." As emphasized by Singh (2010), this widespread conceptual confusion is brought out strikingly in, for example, Alesina et al.'s (1999, 1243) introduction to their seminal work, where they claim: "This paper argues that certain public goods supplied by US cities ... are inversely related to ethnic fragmentation in those cities. In cities where ethnic groups are polarized ... the share of spending that goes to public goods is low." Similarly, in their influential piece on Africa's growth tragedy, Easterly and Levine (1997) use the concepts of heterogeneity and polarization interchangeably. That is, notwithstanding the tendency to use the concepts of diversity and heterogeneity, and despite the heavy reliance on demographic measures of ethnic *diversity*, the majority of political economy-oriented studies in fact argue that ethnic *polarization*—i.e. the existence of a dividing line between "us" and "them"—and not ethnic diversity, is what negatively affects public goods provision (cf. Cheeseman 2018; Posner 2004a).

In terms of the mechanisms connecting ethnic fractionalization to subpar development outcomes, the explicit focus of the recent literature has almost exclusively been with the micro-level mechanisms. The literature to date provides three broad sets of micro-level mechanisms that could help explain the assumed negative impact of ethnic fractionalization on public goods provision. *First,* in line with the insights offered by Social Identity Theory (Tajfel and Turner, 1986), it has been argued that group identification serves to reduce the perceived distance between the members of that group so that they are less likely to make a distinction between their own and others' welfare and more likely to view each other as having common goals (Rabushka and Shepsle 1972; Alesina and La Ferrara, 2000; Luttmer 2001; Miguel 2004; Singh 2010). In the context of such an "other-regarding preferences mechanism," "taste for discrimination," or "ethnic bias," community members are likely to be willing to bear the cost of public goods only if they believe that most of the beneficiaries belong to their own group (Habyarimana et al. 2007). As a result, insofar as various ethnic identities become politically mobilized *within* the territorial boundaries of the nation-state, this is likely to generate an important and non-universalistic set of views regarding who should be eligible to public goods, undermining the prospects for public goods provision. An early spokesperson for this view was T. H. Marshall (1950), who found citizens' entitlement to an expanded range of public goods in Great Britain to be the result of the emergence of a national consciousness that transcended sectoral group identification. In a famous passage, Marshall (1950, 8) stated: "Citizenship requires a bond of a different kind, a direct sense of community membership based on loyalty to a civilisation that is a common possession."

A *second* mechanism conjectures that different ethnic groups have different preferences, making the provision of public goods less likely in ethnically divided settings (Alesina,

Baqir, and Easterly 1999; Alesina and LaFerrara 2000; Vigdor 2004; Lieberman and McClendon 2013; Horowitz 1985). As pointed out by Chandra (2001), as well as Lieberman and McClendon (2012, 577), the preference divergence mechanism can concern slightly different things. It can be about the *salience* of an issue, i.e. the issues that the members of different ethnic groups think that the government should devote resources to. For example, studying U.S. municipalities, Alesina et al. (1999) have argued that individuals from different ethnic groups prefer distinct types of public goods—roads versus libraries, for instance— and that this disagreement on public goods is what leads to lower funding in diverse areas. Ethnic groups might also have conflicting preferences regarding *how* the government should go about addressing an issue, once it has been labeled a priority. For example, as argued by Bates (1973), to the extent that ethnic groups are geographically concentrated, they may have divergent interests over outcomes that have a geographic component, notably the location of public investments.

The most serious form of conflicting preferences—in terms of the risk of them undermining public goods provision—are presumably diverging preferences based on *symbolic values*. As argued by Horowitz (1985, 223), this is because "[s]ymbolic claims are not readily amenable to compromise. In this, they differ from claims deriving wholly from material interests. Whereas material advancement can be measured both relatively and absolutely, the status advancement of one ethnic group is entirely relative to the status of others." For example, the different languages and cultures that ethnic groups possess may make collectively-agreed-upon decisions regarding what the language of instruction in schools should be, or what religious holidays that should be nationally observed, difficult to reach (Miguel 2004; Persson 2008). As forcefully summarized by Rustow (1970, 359–60): "On matters of economic policy and social expenditure you can always split the difference. [...] But there is no middle position between Flemish and French as official languages or between Calvinism, Catholicism and Secularism as principles of education."

In short, as concluded by Habyarimana et al. (2007, 710), insofar as preferences are correlated with ethnic group identities in one of the described ways, ethnic fractionalization is likely to lead to the underprovision of public goods (cf. Alesina et al. 1999). Ultimately, this is because, if faced with so-called "multiple principals" in the form of an uncoordinated public with conflicting preferences, the political elites will have no real impetus to prioritize public goods since the demand for such goods, as well as the level of monitoring and control in the system, are likely to be low. In fact, the incentives for elites to provide public goods in ethnically divided settings might even be *negative* in the sense that elites might be punished for serving the public good (Persson and Sjöstedt 2012). Conflicting preferences across ethnic groups can as such be interpreted as struggles for the collective goods of the nation-state (Wimmer 1997) or, in the words of Horowitz (1985, 189); as battles over "who are the 'real owners of the country' and of who [should] rule over whom."

Thirdly, it has been argued that the level of public goods will be lower in ethnically fractionalized societies since such societies lack a shared set of norms which serve to facilitate sanctioning, reciprocity and, subsequently, collective action in favor of public goods (Miguel and Gugerty, 2005; Miguel 2004; Banerjee and Somanathan 2007). An early exponent of this view is the political theorist David Miller (1995; 1998). According to Miller, national identity is key to generating a sense of trust and, thus, collective action in favor of public goods. "In states lacking a common national identity," Miller argues, "[...] trust may exist within the groups, but not across them" (1995, 92). A similar case has been made by Brian Barry (1991,

174–7), who argued that nationhood facilitates a sense of "trust in the willingness of others to reciprocate benefits when the need arises." In a study of the impact of ethnic diversity on local school funding and the quality of school facilities in Kenya, Miguel and Gugerty (2005) similarly propose that the comparatively lower public good contributions found in more heterogeneous areas can be linked to free riding in the absence of effective community sanctions. In a study that links ethnic fractionalization to subpar levels of tax collection, Lassen (2007) similarly points to less effective social sanctions in ethnically heterogeneous societies as the key mechanism driving the relationship.

Whereas the more recent literature linking ethnic fractionalization to subpar development outcomes has quite a lot to say about the micro mechanisms involved, the literature has been much more quiet in terms of potential macro mechanisms. To the extent that such mechanisms are implicitly or explicitly discussed or mentioned, however, they often relate to low QoG—in the literature typically conceptualized in terms of nonprogrammatic, patronage, or clientelistic politics. The, at least implicit, focus on the supposedly important role played by QoG in the relationship is decisively backed up by a significant number of studies in the field, which, on the one hand, demonstrate a direct and negative effect of ethnic fractionalization on QoG, and, on the other hand, a strong association between low QoG and subpar public goods provision (Kimenyi 2006; Easterly and Levine 1997; Alesina et al. 1999; La Porta et al. 1999; Khemani 2015).

The argument linking ethnic fractionalization to negative development outcomes via QoG comes in two main versions. In the first version, QoG is typically understood as an *independent, intervening mechanism.* That is, ethnic fractionalization is assumed to negatively affect public goods provision *via* low QoG. In a nutshell, in this interpretation, on the other side of the coin of the claimed negative effects of ethnic fractionalization on public goods provision, there seems to be a positive association between ethnic fractionalization and low QoG (cf. Kimenyi 2006; Easterly and Levine 1997; Alesina et al. 1999; Keefer and Khemani 2005; Khemani 2015; Kimenyi 2006; Vicente and Wantchekon 2009; Bratton and van de Walle 1994). An example of this interpretation of the relationship would be Kimenyi's (2006) and Alesina et al.'s (1999) studies, which both reveal how ethnic polarization increases the share of patronage goods in a polity, at the expense of the provision of public goods.

In the second, related but yet distinct, version, ethnic fractionalization and low QoG are rather treated as a largely *inseparable, joint force.* In line with this thinking, in ethnically fractionalized societies the whole idea of the state is presumably different in the sense that it is not even likely to be thought of as a public good but instead as a potential resource to be appropriated, or even an instrument to be used in the domination of other groups—as effectively captured in terms such as the "neo-patrimonial" or "clientelistic" state. This line of reasoning is probably most prominent in the discussion about sub-Saharan Africa; the source of the region's suffering is routinely understood through the lenses of the African state being ruled by a completely different, ethnic-based, and thus also—as the argument unfolds—inevitably non-universal and patronage-based rationale. Within the framework of this "neo-patrimonial" type of state, the *"modus operandi"* guiding the political elite is either to disproportionately favor the own ethnic group or to use public goods and services to "buy" support from non-coethnics (cf. Franck and Rainer 2012; Kimenyi 2006; Vicente and Wantchekon 2009; Bratton and van de Walle 1994; Kasara 2007; Azam 2001). In fact, a whole branch of political economy studies are now concerned with exploring the more exact ways in which the distribution of ethnic patronage varies across African states, without acknowledging that even these states in fact vary quite a lot in terms of the extent to which a neo-patrimonial logic of rule *at all* guides state action in the region (cf. Kramon and Posner 2013).

By way of conclusion, the argument about the negative impact of ethnic fractionalization on public goods provision holds that, depending on the degree to which ethnic cleavages are politically mobilized, this will trigger a set of micro- and macro-level mechanisms that together serve to undermine the prospects for public goods provision, through channels of both *demand* and *supply*. The next section explores the empirical evidence in support of this claim.

ETHNIC FRACTIONALIZATION AND PUBLIC GOODS PROVISION: THE EMPIRICS

In reviewing the empirical evidence in support of the diversity debit hypothesis, as aforementioned, it soon becomes evident that almost all recent analyses in the field are large-N statistical studies that take their point of departure in the ELF index, or some related measurement of ethnic heterogeneity. In the lion's share of models, ethnic fractionalization is thus operationalized in demographic terms and measured by the use of data compiled either in the early 1960s by a team of Soviet ethnographers and as summarized in the Atlas Naradov Mira (1964) or in the 1990s by Alesina et al. (2003) or Roeder (2001). Ethnic fractionalization is thus typically employed as an *exogenous, independent* variable, similar to variables such as climate or topography, in the search for explanations to variation in different economic, social, and political outcomes (cf. Singh and vom Hau 2016).

For example, in their seminal work on "Africa's Growth Tragedy," Easterly and Levine (1997) show ethnic fractionalization—as measured by the ELF index—to be a significant factor in explaining Africa's slow economic growth relative to East Asia, through its negative effects on schooling, infrastructure, political stability, financial systems, foreign exchange markets, and government budget. Similarly, in a highly influential study which draws on census data and budget information from cities, metropolitan areas, and urban counties in the United States, Alesina et al. (1999) show that ethnic heterogeneity—in this case measured in racial terms—is negatively and statistically significantly associated with the share of public spending on roads, education, welfare, sewage, and trash collection. In line with the findings presented by Alesina et al. (1999), but at the local level of analysis in Kenya and Tanzania, Miguel (2004), as well as Miguel and Gugerty (2005), find evidence of a negative effect of ethnic heterogeneity on public goods provision, including education and the maintenance of water wells. The same kind of analysis has typically been employed also in studies arguing that ethnic fractionalization undermines the prospects for public goods provision indirectly by undermining QoG through the fueling of patronage goods (Kimenyi 2006; Easterly and Levine 1997; Alesina et al. 1999; La Porta et al. 1999).

To sum up, as summarized by Singh and Vom Hau (2016), on the basis of the conceptualizations and measurements described above, ethnic fractionalization has been empirically linked to subpar development outcomes across countries (Gerring et al. 2015; Alesina et al. 2003; Baldwin and Huber 2010; La Porta et al. 1999); in different regions, including sub-Saharan Africa (Easterly and Levine 1997) and South Asia (Banerjee, Iyer, and Somanathan 2005); in different countries, including Kenya (Miguel and Gugerty 2005), the United States (Alesina et al. 1999), and Indonesia (Alesina, Gennaioli, and Lovo 2019); and, across cities, local districts, and municipalities (Alesina et al. 1999; Habyarimana et al. 2007). The negative effects of ethnic fractionalization have moreover been demonstrated for various types of public goods, as well as outcomes closely related to effective public goods provision, including social capital and trust (Knack and Keefer 1997; Alesina and La Ferrara 2000); quality of government (La Porta et al. 1999); taxation (Lassen 2007); economic development and growth (Easterly and Levine 1997; Montalvo and Reynal-Querol 2005); the provision of basic infrastructure such as water and electricity (Alesina et al. 1999; Khwaja 2009); the provision of healthcare (Banerjee, Iyer, and Somanathan 2005); and the provision of high-quality education (Miguel and Gugerty 2005).

However, important to note is that, although there is a large empirical literature that points to a negative impact of ethnic fractionalization on public goods provision, there is also empirical evidence in favor of a more nuanced approach, and even evidence that calls for the need to reconsider the relationship between ethnic fractionalization and public goods provision altogether. For example, using a global sample of countries in the developing world, Gerring at al. (2015) find no evidence whatsoever at the subnational level that ethnic diversity negatively affects the provision of public goods, including children's health status, education, and welfare. In fact, the authors even find evidence of a *positive* effect of ethnic fractionalization on these outcomes. On a similar note, Gisselquist's (2014) re-analysis of the data used in the agenda-setting study by Alesina et al. (1999) shows no negative effects of ethnic fractionalization on public goods provision at the local level. In fact, in line with Gerring et al.'s (2015) study, quite on the contrary, Gisselquist and her collaborators even find strong evidence of a *positive* relationship between ethnic diversity and public goods provision at the subnational level (Gisselquist, Leiderer, and Niño-Zarazúa 2016). Moreover, in Gisselquist's single-authored study, the relationship between ethnic diversity and public goods provision comes out as mixed for different goods at the national level, i.e. the relationship is sometimes positive, sometimes negative, and sometimes insignificant.

These latter findings raise the question of whether it might be the case that some public goods are more sensitive to ethnic claims than others and, if so; why? Related to this, on the basis of the aforementioned insight provided by the literature of the sometimes symbolic, and thus indivisible, character of ethnic preferences (Horowitz 1985), there is an ongoing discussion in the empirical literature regarding the question of whether all *types* of ethnic cleavages are equally harmful to public goods provision. For instance, whereas Gerring et al. (2015) find evidence of that ethno-linguistic and religious fractionalization are both negatively associated with public goods provision, Gurr (2000) argues that religious cleavages are in fact considerably more likely to lead to the underprovision of public goods and other undesired outcomes, including violent conflict, since such cleavages are comparatively more symbolically laden and, thus, not easily resolved through compromise. However, in some respects, Fearon (2008) undermines this proposition by pointing to the fact that membership in religious groups is often (if yet not always) reckoned by faith rather than descent, and is as such potentially more fluid in character. Young (1976), on the other hand, argues that racial fractionalization is probably most problematic in terms of public goods provision, whereas Safran (2004) recognizes the mobilizing potential especially of linguistic cleavages.

Yet another set of researchers point to the need not only to nuance the relationship depending on the type of public good or ethnic cleavage but also depending on the *number* of such cleavages in a particular society. Perhaps most prominently, Montalvo and Reynal-Querol (2005) have argued that the relationship between ethnic fractionalization and suboptimal development outcomes are not monotonic, but the "highest risk" type of society is likely to be a society with a middle-range level of ethnic fractionalization (cf. Horowitz 1985; Collier 2001). In particular, the countries at the highest risk of negative effects of ethnic fractionalization are likely to be the ones in which a large ethnic minority faces an ethnic majority (Montalvo and Reynal-Querol 2005). On a similar but yet slightly different note, building on the work by, among others, Chandra (2005), Laitin (1986), and Posner (2005), Dunning and Harrison (2010) advance the argument—as well as provide a measurement in support of it—that the societies at the highest risk of negative effects of ethnic fractionalization will be societies in which different types of ethnic cleavages—for example linguistic, racial, religious, caste or clan—are *overlapping* (cf. Dahl 1956; Lipset and Rokkan 1967). On the same note, by limiting the potential for political mobilization along any one dimension of identity, cross-cutting cleavages are on the other hand likely to dampen the risk of violent conflict and instead promote development, democratic stability and public goods provision (cf. Chandra 2005; Persson 2008).

In the end, independently of the more specific nuances of the argument and the more exact conceptualizations and measurements used, the core assumption underlying the argument that ethnic fractionalization undermines public goods provision—as well as the empirical evidence both in support of and against this hypothesis—is that ethnic fractionalization constitutes a potentially important *exogenous* force in the development process. In the next section, the most common critique directed against the underlying assumptions of this argument—and the implications following from it—are explored in greater detail.

Ethnic Fractionalization and Public Goods Provision: The Critique

The critique against the diversity debit hypothesis has been substantial and has typically taken its point of departure in, on the one hand, social constructivist theories of ethnicity and ethnic relations, and, on the other hand, factual empirical variation in the extent to which ethnic fractionalization is indeed associated with public goods provision.

The social constructivist perspective stands in direct contrast to the so-called primordial view of ethnic identities and relations, which understands ethnic identities as inherently political "givens" of social life, as it separates the notion of ethnic diversity from the notion of ethnic polarization. Ethnic diversity can, according to the social constructivist perspective, in other words exist in anthropological categorization without necessarily being politically relevant. This is because, in line with the social constructivist perspective, it is not ethnic diversity *per se* that forms the basis for social and political mobilization but an "imagined community" (Anderson 1983), which separates "us" from "them" (Barth 1969). Important to note is that, in this context, the word "imagined" does not simply mean "invented" in the sense of the creation or invention of a myth of a common historical past. Instead, it signifies a contemporary belief in shared cultural and historical ties and a shared destiny created by myth (Smith 1997, 609). As such, an imagined community—in the form of a nation or an ethnic group—has the potential to tie millions of people together and create a bond between past and future generations. That is, more than merely serving as a form of political organization, the nation or ethnic group as an imagined community appeals to fundamental needs of belonging and as such becomes central to the formulation of collective identities and political mobilization.

As an imagined community, the nation or ethnic group is in addition *limited* in the sense that it has finite if yet elastic boundaries, beyond which lie other nations or ethnic groups (Anderson 1983). As such, national and ethnic identities are relational and shaped by the nature of the relevant "others" in the social and political arena. In other words, while a sense of membership in a given community involves recognition of certain features of the group which make it distinctive, implicitly, these attributes are contrastive in the sense that the production, reproduction, as well as transformation of the boundaries of national and ethnic identities are two-way processes that take place across the boundary of "us" and "them" (Barth 1969). As such, what matters for political outcomes is not the sum of objective differences between different groups but only those which the actors themselves regard as significant. As a result, national and ethnic identities cannot be treated as an immutable bundle of reciprocity and equal preferences, which are sufficient to refer to in order to identify a person as an "X" or "Y" or locate the boundary between different groups. Instead, national and ethnic identities are situationally defined concepts. That is, as emphasized by Posner (2005, 11), from this perspective, individuals are not being hardwired with a single ethnic identity but instead they possess repertoires of identities whose relevance "wax and wane" over time and with change in context (cf. Barth 1969; Hobsbawm 1990).

The implications of the social constructivist perspective for studying the relationship between ethnic fractionalization and public goods provision are multifold. To the extent that the relevance of ethnic identities is identified by boundary markers rather than by cultural traits, it becomes problematic to use demographic measures of ethnic diversity—such as the ELF index and other related measures—as indicators of the political relevance of ethnic groups. In other words, from the social constructivist perspective, one form of critique that can be directed against the diversity debit thesis is that it is plagued by problems related to content validity in the form of a mismatch between the theoretical foundations of the argument that ethnic polarization undermines public goods provision and the indicators used to measure this polarization. In fact, as Figure 27.1 effectively demonstrates, notions of "us" and "them"—as measured by actual political mobilization of ethnic cleavages—only occasionally overlap with demographic categorizations of ethnic groups, making any argument about the relationship between ethnic fractionalization and public goods provision that relies on demographic data analytically problematic.[3]

---

[3] N = 142, Adjusted R^2 = 21.74. Ethnic diversity is measured by the ELF index, which indicates the chance between 0 and 1 that two randomly drawn individuals from a population in a country belong to different ethnic groups. The higher is the score, the greater is this probability. An indicator developed by Vanhanen (1999) is used to measure the level of ethnic polarization. This indicator runs from 0 to 200 and captures both non-violent and violent forms of ethnic mobilization. The maximum value 200 means that the share of ethnic parties exceeds 90 percent; that all significant interest organizations are ethnic-based; that practically all interest conflict takes place along ethnic lines; that ethnic war dominates politics; and that there have been occasions of genocidal ethnic violence.

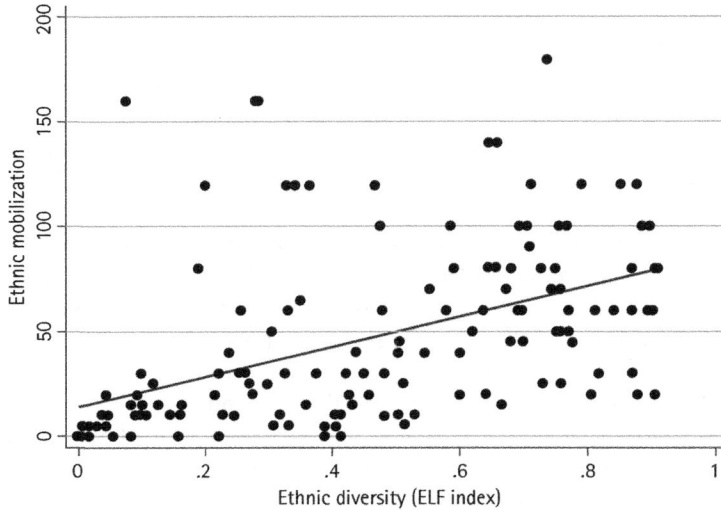

FIGURE 27.1 Ethnic diversity versus ethnic polarization

Note: N = 142, Adjusted R² = 21.74. Ethnic diversity is measured by the ELF index, which indicates the chance between 0 and 1 that two randomly drawn individuals from a population in a country belong to different ethnic groups. The higher the score, the greater is this probability. An indicator developed by Vanhanen (1999) is used to measure the level of ethnic polarization. This indicator runs from 0 to 200 and captures both nonviolent and violent forms of ethnic mobilization. The maximum value 200 means that the share of ethnic parties exceeds 90%; that all significant interest organizations are ethnic based; that practically all interest conflict takes place along ethnic lines; that ethnic war dominates politics; and that there have been occasions of genocidal ethnic violence.

The reasons for the mismatch between demographic measures and actual political polarization are potentially multiple. One reason is the fact that while there are typically many ethnic groups along multiple dimensions of ethnic identity (e.g. tribal, linguistic, territorial etc.) in any society, societies vary substantially in terms of how many of these identities, if any, serve as a platform for political mobilization (Posner 2004a; Chazan 1982). For instance, Fearon and Laitin (1996) estimate that there has only been one instance of ethnic violence in Africa for every 2,000 cases that would have been predicted on the basis of demographic differences alone. Similarly, on the basis of a historical analysis of social development in Kerala, Singh (2010) shows how it is not so much objective diversity that affects public goods provision but the extent to which people share a subjective sense of belonging—a factor that has indeed no necessary relation to objective diversity. Another clarifying case in point is the insight advanced by Posner (2004b) that, while the objective cultural differences between Chewas and Tumbukas are identical in Zambia and Malawi, the two groups are political allies in Zambia but adversaries in Malawi. Along the same line of thought, whereas, for example, language group distinctions might be central to the political process by which various social, economic, and political outcomes are determined in some countries—such as, for example, Belgium—linguistic diversity might exist but yet be irrelevant for politics in other countries, for example Madagascar. Such an insight is highly important for analytical purposes, particularly given the risk of the potential errors that the failure to capture the right cleavage dimension in terms of actual political salience may cause.

With the above discussion in mind, as argued by Posner (2004a), if the aim is to assess the general effect of ethnic fractionalization on public goods provision, what is required is a case-by-case identification of the relevant cleavage line in each country. Only then can the right headcount of ethnic groups be undertaken and a meaningful calculation of the country's de facto ethnic polarization be made. In line with this insight, a few attempts to capture ethnic polarization for a larger number of cases already exist, for example the PREG (Politically Relevant Ethnic Groups) index developed by Posner (2004a), which covers politically relevant ethnic groups in sub-Saharan Africa. Another attempt is Fearon's (2003) index, developed for 160 countries, which uses the structural difference between languages as a proxy for the cultural distance between groups in a country.

Yet another insight generated by social constructivism and of greatest analytical relevance has to do with *time*. Whereas the vast majority of studies exploring the effect of ethnic fractionalization on public goods provision treat ethnic fractionalization as a factor that is fixed in time, many real-life events convey how the political salience of different ethnic cleavages is a product of historical and political processes and, as such, varies quite substantially not only across context but also over time. For example, a large scholarship has demonstrated how the salience of different ethnic identities in sub-Saharan Africa has varied quite substantially throughout modern history (Posner 2005; Persson 2008, 2018). From this perspective, as emphasized by Posner (2004a), even if we accepted the relevance of existing quantitative indices for measuring ethnic fractionalization, such as the ELF index, the fact that most indices only capture one, or occasionally two (as is the case for Roeder's measure), point/s in time becomes problematic given constantly shifting patterns of migration and immigration. Throughout history, processes of both democratization (Mann 1999) and state formation (Tilly 1990; Smith 1987) have moreover been intimately associated with both the desire and the power to commit genocide, as well as to rearrange external borders, leaving a direct and substantial imprint on the national composition of ethnic groups.

By way of conclusion, much of the literature on the relationship between ethnic fractionalization and public goods provision can be—and has been—criticized for violating key constructivist findings about the fluid, multidimensional, and sociopolitically manufactured nature of ethnicity (Chandra and Wilkinson 2008; Laitin and Posner 2001; Posner 2004a). From the perspective that ethnic identities are socially constructed and as such politically relevant only in relation to an "other" it simply becomes problematic to assume that ethnic diversity automatically implies ethnic polarization, as well as to treat ethnic fractionalization as an exogenous variable. Instead, once we recognize that ethnic identities are fluid, it becomes critical to consider the potential that the relationship between ethnic fractionalization and public goods provision might be conditioned by other factors, be spurious, endogenous, or even characterized by reverse causality.

ETHNIC FRACTIONALIZATION AND PUBLIC GOODS PROVISION REVISITED

With the point of departure in the empirical variation in the ways in which ethnic fractionalization is indeed associated with subpar development outcomes, as well as in the social constructivist critique, an increasingly influential literature has begun to revisit the argument that ethnic fractionalization serves to undermine public goods provision. So far, the lion's share of studies adhering to a revisionist approach have focused on finding out which are the more specific factors that *condition* the relationship between ethnic diversity and public goods provision by asking: "Under what circumstances does ethnic diversity become a problem for public goods provision?" While there are certainly many factors at play in this process, the vast majority of previous studies have focused on *competition*—for political power or scarce economic resources—as the main conditioning factor (cf. Eifert, Miguel, and Posner, 2010). For example, in a well-cited article focusing on the role of political competition, Posner (2004b) argues that the varying salience of ethnic divisions can be explained by the different sizes of different ethnic groups in a particular country relative to the size of that particular country's political arena. In the end, ethnic group differences will only be mobilized as to matter for social, economic, and political outcomes in countries in which the ethnic groups are large enough to serve as viable bases for political coalition building. Focusing on the role of economic competition, Fearon and Laitin (2003), as well as Collier and Hoeffler (2004), suggest that the importance of ethnic identities as a platform for social, economic and political mobilization diminishes, even washes away, once material factors, such as per capita income, are controlled for. In a similar vein, Cederman, Weidmann, and Gleditsch (2011) argue that development outcomes—in this case intrastate warfare—is highly contingent upon horizontal political and economic inequalities between politically relevant ethnic groups and states at large. Similar to Cederman et al.'s argument but focusing explicitly on public goods provision, Alesina, Michalopolous, and Papaioannou (2016), as well as Baldwin and Huber (2010), emphasize how it is the different economic statuses of groups that serve as the main driver of the relationship between ethnic fractionalization and public goods provision; if groups have different economic statuses, it will be difficult for them to reach agreement on which public goods that should be provided, leading to a situation in which political elites' incentives will be skewed in favor of patronage rather than public goods.

Among the explanations focusing on potential mitigating factors, even QoG and other aspects of state capacity have gained some recognition. Most prominently, in a widely cited article, Easterly (2001) reruns the analysis from his own and Levine's influential study on "Africa's Growth Tragedy," and finds that high QoG—conceptualized in terms of an impartial and trustworthy bureaucracy, governed by the rule of law—in fact washes away the negative effects of ethnic fractionalization found in the original analysis. Moving beyond the focus on potential mitigating factors but still focusing on the role played by QoG and related aspects of state capacity, another, if yet so far largely unrecognized, strand of work within the revisionist scholarship has instead argued that the observed causal relationship between ethnic fractionalization and public goods provision is either *spurious* or *reverse*.

The most advanced account forwarding the argument that the relationship is spurious is probably the one promoted by Wimmer (2016) and which holds that both contemporary ethnic heterogeneity and low public goods provision represent legacies of a weakly developed state capacity inherited from the past. More specifically, according to Wimmer's argument, the association between today's levels of ethnic diversity and public goods provision is brought about not by direct causal connection but by historical patterns of state strength in two different ways. On the one hand, strong states offered incentives for minorities to adopt the language and culture of the politically dominant group, thus decreasing ethnic diversity over time. On the other hand, strong states left a legacy of indigenous bureaucratic capacity, which shapes contemporary abilities to provide public goods in path-dependent ways.

Related to Wimmer's (2016) argument in the way that ethnic fractionalization is understood to be *endogenous* to other factors, another set of scholars have argued that the causality of the relationship between ethnic diversity and public goods provision is instead likely to be *reverse* in the sense that the level of public goods provision is what leads to ethnic polarization and not vice versa. One of the most prominent accounts within this line of thought is probably Azam's (2001) study, according to which ethnic capital arises as a direct *response* to a limited capacity of the central state to ensure the provision of public goods and services. In a related but yet distinct fashion, Ahlerup and Olsson (2012) present a model in which new ethnic groups endogenously emerge among peripheral populations in response to an insufficient supply of collective goods.

In the end, whereas all these abovementioned studies certainly contribute important insights, despite adhering to the social constructivist view, they can still be criticized for treating ethnic identities largely as "givens." That is, despite the fact that these accounts rely on a notion of ethnic identities as being socially constructed, the political importance of ethnic group identities is typically still already built into the explanation. For instance, it remains unclear why competition for scarce resources should lead to individual actors turning to their ethnic fellows rather than to people with a similar income level. Similarly, why do people in some countries turn to individuals speaking the same language in times of economic hardship whereas in other countries tribal loyalties seem to prevail? As will be further developed in the concluding section, with the lack of satisfactory answers to these and similar questions as a backdrop, the mainstream revisionist literature needs to be supplemented with approaches that go even further back in the causal chain, particularly approaches that try to explain under what circumstances political coalitions are likely to form along ethnic lines rather than some other line in the *first* place, or why certain aspects of one's identity—for example language—becomes vital for politics whereas others—for example tribe—remain unimportant.

SUMMARY AND CONCLUSIONS: BRINGING POLITICS BACK IN

What distinguishes the modern state from most other large-scale political organizations in history, such as empires, has been its insinuation into the core identities of its subjects (thus the emphasis on the nation-state) (Migdal 1994, 13).

The state constitutes the nation, in the full sense, by giving it body and by ordering the social system around it ... The institutions of the state anchor the nation in historical continuity (Schnapper 1998, 97).

Despite the fact that anthropologists began to move away from a "primordial" understanding of ethnicity towards a more "constructivist" point of view already in the late 1960s (Barth 1969), the lion's share of studies in the field continue to treat ethnic identities as "givens" of social and political life. This counts for both the political economy literature, which customarily incorporates ethnic fractionalization as an exogenous factor in the analysis, and more critical studies, which typically acknowledge the socially constructed nature of ethnic identities but despite this tend to treat such identities as stable categories. As a consequence, even though the revisionist strand of literature has made a considerable effort in demonstrating the ways in which the relationship between ethnic fractionalization and public goods provision might be conditioned by other factors, be spurious, or even be subject to reverse causality what has typically been left out from the discussion is the important question of under what circumstances political coalitions are likely to form along ethnic lines rather than some other line in the *first* place. For example, why do Kenyan voters tend to think of themselves—and others—in terms of belonging to one ethnic group or another, even to the extent that it at times spurs interethnic violence, whereas Swedish voters instead think of the electoral arena as an arena for competition primarily between different ideological standpoints, running from left to right? On a similar if yet different note; how can we understand the fact that the Ugandan state is rife with ethnic-based patronage while the Botswanan state seems to have been able to escape such an outcome and has even been able to establish a relatively impartial bureaucracy despite being ethnically diverse and with a history of ethnic competition even on the basis of membership in different Tswana tribes (cf. Persson 2008)?

In an attempt to answer these and similar questions, an increasingly vocational literature emphasizes the need to endogenize the relationship between ethnic diversity and public goods provision in a way that moves beyond the idea of the state as a neutral arena. In short, according to this scholarship, we need to bring politics back in. In particular, what this literature calls for is the need to bring the state up front of the analysis, by focusing on the state's role in the creation of notions of "us" and "them" (cf. Persson 2008; Persson 2018; Singh and vom Hau 2016). At the heart of this call is, as such, a view of the state that goes beyond an understanding of the state as merely an *arena* for political competition among ethnic groups, or as a simple neutral broker of competing ethnic interests. Instead, quite in line with the historical institutional perspective, the state and its institutions are understood as "social forces in their own right" (Grafstein 1992, 1). As such, by recognizing or targeting a given ethnic region or a population, state policies may draw new boundaries around ethnic subunits, as well as excite old ones, giving them legitimacy and a political forum at the national level (Nagel & Olzak 1982). Moreover, as an *autonomous* and *political* actor, the state has the potential to influence how various individual and collective actors come to define their political interests and worldviews, as well as their very identities.

In line with this view, an increasingly rich case study literature has provided important insights regarding the colonial state's role in the creation of modern ethnic identities (e.g. Laitin 1986; Lieberman 2003; Posner 2005). An influential literature has moreover begun to focus on how the modern state—set against the fact that nationalism is indeed the central organizing principle for political communities in the contemporary world, and particularly the consequences this brings in terms of modern states having to confront the question of how to define membership in the national political community, as well as how to govern the expression of ethnic diversity—serves as an important actor in shaping notions of "us" and "them" and, subsequently, public goods provision. For example, conducting comparative case study research, Miguel (2004) and Persson (2008) both show how government nation-building policies—in the form of either policies of assimilation or ethnic-based group recognition—have led to radically different outcomes in the postcolonial sub-Saharan

African context in terms of patterns of inter-ethnic cooperation and conflict and the de-velopment of a shared sense of belonging, with important consequences for contemporary public goods provision. In a different study, Persson (2018) has moreover demonstrated how the degree and character of what is referred to as *postcolonial indirect rule* have played an important role in shaping notions of "us" and "them," as well as subsequent institutional quality and public goods provision, in the former British colonies, adopting an approach which emphasizes the critical but yet probably unintended role played by policies aimed at securing territorial integrity, adopted by the new national elites at the time of independence. Lieberman and Singh (2012) in turn highlight the substantial effects of the state's institution-alization of ethnic categorizations in the national census on the likelihood of violent conflict between ethnic groups.

By way of conclusion, insofar as one takes the socially constructed nature of ethnic identities seriously, future research should continue focusing on the role played by the state in constructing and reconstructing such identities. In its capacity to provide the "highest-level definition" of the national political community, as institutionalized in the consti-tution, citizenship laws, as well as various state policies, on both the "input" and "output" side of politics, the state has extensive power when it comes to shaping notions of "us" and "them" and, thus, development outcomes. In short, depending on how the national polit-ical community gets defined and depending on how power is exercised towards different ethnic groups, certain identities, including regional, religious, racial, and linguistic ones, are more likely to become not only more politically salient but also more powerful as pol-itical platforms than others (Brubaker 1992; Lieberman 2003; Persson 2008).[4] In line with this argument, low QoG, as far as it is associated with favoritism, discrimination, and the provision of goods and services on the principle of ethnic differentiation—such as is indeed common practice in many parts of particularly the developing world—may certainly play an important role in mobilizing ethnic cleavages, with potentially decisively negative effects in terms of the prospects for broad-based development (see Leeson 2005 for a first account of this). However, the more exact role and impact of such practices remain to be explored by future studies.

References

Acemoglu, Daron, and James Robinson. 2012. *Why Nations Fail: The Origins of Power, Prosperity, and Poverty*. New York: Crown Business.
Ahlerup, Pelle, and Ola Olsson. 2012. "The roots of ethnic diversity." *Journal of Economic Growth* 17: 71–102.

---

[4] As should be evident, inherent in any discussion about the state's role in identity construction and reconstruction is the inevitable importance of taking into serious consideration the balancing of minority versus majority rights, as well as carefully considering how procedural versus outcome-oriented standards of fairness do and should play into the picture. In the end, as a social force in its own right (cf. Grafstein 1992), the state has an enormous power to do not only good but also bad, with fundamental consequences not only for policy but for the vast majority of the world's population, who do in fact not reside in de facto "nation states" but rather in what can be described in terms of "state nations" (cf. Stepan, Linz, and Yadav 2010).

Alesina, Alberto, Reza Baqir, and William Easterly. 1999. "Public Goods and Ethnic Divisions." *The Quarterly Journal of Economics* 114 (4): 1243–84.

Alesina, Alberto, Arnaud Devleeschauwer, William Easterly, Sergio Kurlat, and Romain Wacziarg. 2003. "Fractionalization." *Journal of Economic Growth* 8: 155–94.

Alesina, Alberto, Caterina Gennaioli, and Stefania Lovo 2019. "Public Goods and Ethnic Diversity: Evidence from Deforestation in Indonesia." *Economica* 86 (341): 32–66.

Alesina, Alberto, and Eliana La Ferrara. 2000. "Participation in Heterogeneous Communities." *The Quarterly Journal of Economics* 115 (3): 847–904.

Alesina, Alberto, Stelios Michalopolous, and Elias Papaioannou. 2016. "Ethnic Inequality." *Journal of Political Economy* 124 (2): 428–88.

Anderson, Benedict. 1983. *Imagined Communities*. London & New York: Verso.

Azam, Jean Paul. 2001. "The Redistributive State and Conflicts in Africa." *Journal of Peace Research* 38 (4): 429–44.

Atlas Naradov Mira. 1964. Moscow: Miklukho Maklai Ethnological Institute at the Department of Geodesy and Cartography of the State Geological Committee of the Soviet Union.

Baldwin, Kate, and John D. Huber. 2010. "Economic versus Cultural Differences: Forms of Ethnic Diversity and Public Goods Provision." *American Political Science Review* 104 (4): 644–62.

Banerjee, Abhijit, Lakshmi Iyer, and Rohini Somanathan. 2005. "History, Social Divisions, and Public Goods in Rural India." *Journal of the European Economic Association* 3 (2–3): 639–47.

Banerjee, Abhijit, and Rohini Somanathan. 2007. "The Political Economy of Public Goods: Some Evidence from India." *Journal of Development Economics* 82 (2): 287–314.

Barth, Fredrik. 1969. *Ethnic Groups and Boundaries: The Social Organization of Culture Difference*. London: Allen & Unwin.

Barry, Brian. 1991. *Democracy and Power: Essays in Political Theory*. Oxford: Oxford University Press.

Bates, Robert. 1973. *Ethnicity in Contemporary Africa*. Syracuse: Program in East African Studies.

Bratton, Michael, and Nicholas Van de Walle. 1994. "Neopatrimonial Regimes and Political Transitions in Africa." *World Politics* 46 (4): 453–89.

Brubaker, Rogers. 1992. *Citizenship and Nationhood in France and Germany*. Cambridge: Harvard University Press.

Cederman, Lars-Erik, Nils B. Weidmann, and Kristian Skrede Gleditsch. 2011. "Horizontal Inequalities and Ethnonationalist Civil War: A Global Comparison." *American Political Science Review* 105: 478–95.

Chandra, Kanchan. 2001. "Ethnic Bargains, Group Instability, and Social Choice Theory." *Politics and Society* 29 (3): 337–62.

Chandra, Kanchan. 2005. "Ethnic Parties and Democratic Stability." *Perspectives on Politics* 3 (2): 235–52.

Chandra, Kanchan, and Steven Wilkinson. 2008. "Measuring the Effect of 'Ethnicity'." *Comparative Political Studies* 41 (4–5): 515–63.

Chazan, Naomi. 1982. "Ethnicity and Politics in Ghana." *Political Science Quarterly* 97 (3): 461–85.

Cheeseman, Nic. 2018. "Ethnicity and Development." In *The Oxford Handbook of the Politics of Development*, edited by Carol Lancaster and Nicolas van de Walle, 162–76. Oxford: Oxford University Press.

Collier, David, and Anke Hoeffler. 2004. "Greed and Grievance in Civil War." *Oxford Economic Papers* 56: 563–95.

Collier, Paul. 2001. "Implications of Ethnic Diversity." *Economic Policy* 16 (32): 127–66.

Dahl, Robert A. 1956. *A Preface to Democratic Theory*. Chicago: The University of Chicago Press.

Dunning, Thad, and Lauren Harrison. 2010. "Cross-Cutting Cleavages and Ethnic Voting: An Experimental Study of Cousinage in Mali." *American Political Science Review* 104 (1): 21–39.

Easterly, William. 2001. "Can Institutions Resolve Ethnic Conflict?" *Economic Development and Cultural Change* 49 (4): 687–706.

Easterly, William, and Ross Levine. 1997. "Africa's Growth Tragedy: Policies and Ethnic Divisions." *The Quarterly Journal of Economics* 112 (4): 1203–50.

Eifert, Benn, Edward Miguel, and Daniel N. Posner. 2010. "Political Competition and Ethnic Identification in Africa." *American Journal of Political Science* 54 (2): 494–510.

Ekeh, Peter. 1975. "Colonialism and the Two Publics in Africa: A Theoretical Statement." *Comparative Studies in Society and History* 17 (1): 91–112.

Englebert, Pierre. 2000. "Solving the Mystery of the AFRICA Dummy." *World Development* 28 (10): 1821–35.

Fearon, James D. 2003. "Ethnic and Cultural Diversity by Country." *Journal of Economic Growth* 8: 195–222.

Fearon, James D. 2008. "Ethnic Mobilization and Ethnic Violence." In *The Oxford Handbook of Political Economy*, edited by Donald A. Wittman and Barry R. Weingast, 852–68. Oxford: Oxford University Press.

Fearon, James D., and David D. Laitin. 1996. "Explaining Interethnic Cooperation." *American Political Science Review* 90 (4): 715–35.

Fearon, James D., and David D. Laitin. 2003. "Ethnicity, Insurgency, and Civil War." *American Political Science Review* 97 (1): 75–90.

Franck, Raphaël, and Ilia Rainer. 2012. "Does the Leader's Ethnicity Matter? Ethnic Favoritism, Education, and Health in Sub-Saharan Africa." *American Political Science Review* 106 (2): 294–325.

Fukuyama, Francis. 2011. *The Origins of Political Order: From Prehuman Times to the French Revolution*. New York: Farrar, Straus, and Giroux.

Gerring, John, Strom C. Thacker, Yuan Lu, and Wei Huang. 2015. "Does Diversity Impair Human Development? A Multiple-Level Analysis." *World Development* 66: 166–88.

Gisselquist, Rachel M. 2014. "Ethnic Divisions and Public Goods Provision, Revisited." *Ethnic and Racial Studies* 37 (9): 1605–627.

Gisselquist, Rachel M., Stefan Leiderer, and Miguel Niño-Zarazúa. 2016. "Ethnic Heterogeneity and Public Goods Provision in Zambia: Evidence of a Subnational 'Diversity Dividend.'" *World Development* 78: 308–23.

Grafstein, Robert. 1992. *Institutional Realism: Social and Practical Constraints on Rational Actors*. New Haven, Connecticut: Yale University Press.

Gurr, Ted R. 2000. *Peoples v. States*. Washington D.C.: U.S. Institute of Peace.

Habyarimana, James, Macartan Humphreys, Daniel N. Posner, and Jeremy M. Weinstein. 2007. "Why Does Ethnic Diversity Undermine Public Goods Provision?" *American Political Science Review* 101 (4): 709–25.

Hobsbawm, Eric J. 1990. *Nations and Nationalism Since 1780: Programme, Myth, Reality*. New York, NY: Cambridge University Press.

Holmberg, Sören, Bo Rothstein, and Nagmeh Nasiritousi. 2009. "Quality of Government: What You Get." *Annual Review of Political Science* 12: 135–61.

Horowitz, Donald L. 1985. *Ethnic Groups in Conflict*. Berkeley: University of California Press.

Kasara, Kimuli. 2007. "Tax Me If You Can: Ethnic Geography, Democracy, and the Taxation of Agriculture in Africa." *The American Political Science Review* 101 (1): 159–72.

Keefer, Philip, and Stuti Khemani. 2005. "Democracy, Public Spending, and the Poor: Understanding Political Incentives for Providing Public Services." *The World Bank Research Observer* 20 (1): 1–27.

Khemani, Stuti. 2015. "Buying Votes versus Supplying Public Services: Political Incentives to Under-invest in Pro-poor Policies." *Journal of Development Economics* 117: 84–93.

Khwaja, Asim. 2009. "Can Good Projects Succeed in Bad Communities?" *Journal of Public Economics* 93 (7–8): 899–916.

Kimenyi, Mwangi S. 2006. "Ethnicity, Governance and the Provision of Public Goods." *Journal of African Economies* 15: 62–99.

Knack, Stephen, and Philip Keefer. 1997. "Does Social Capital have an Economic Payoff? A Cross-Country Investigation." *The Quarterly Journal of Economics* 112 (4): 1251–88.

Kramon, Eric, and Daniel N. Posner. 2013. "Who Benefits From Distributive Politics? How the Outcome One Studies Affects the Answer One Gets." *Perspectives on Politics* 11 (2): 461–74.

LaPorta, Rafael, Florencio Lopez-de-Silanes, Andrei Shleifer, and Robert Vishny. 1999. "The Quality of Government." *Journal of Law and Economic Organization* 15 (1): 222–79.

Laitin, David. 1986. *Hegemony and Culture: Politics and Religious Change Among the Yoruba.* Chicago: The University of Chicago Press.

Laitin, David D., and Daniel N. Posner. 2001. "The Implications of Constructivism for Constructing Ethnic Fractionalization Indices." *APSA-CP* 12 (3): 3–17.

Lassen, David D. 2007. "Ethnic Divisions, Trust, and the Size of the Informal Sector." *Journal of Economic Behavior and Organization* 63 (3): 423–38.

Leeson, Peter. 2005. "Endogenizing fractionalization." *Journal of Institutional Economics* 1 (1): 75–98.

Lemarchand, René. 1972. "Political Clientelism and Ethnicity in Tropical Africa: Competing Solidarities in Nation-Building." *American Political Science Review* 66 (1): 68–90.

Lieberman, Evan S. 2003. *Race and Regionalism in the Politics of Taxation.* Cambridge, New York: Cambridge University Press.

Lieberman, Evan S. and Gwyneth H. McClendon. 2013. "The Ethnicity-Policy Preference Link in Sub-Saharan Africa." *Comparative Political Studies* 46 (5): 574–602.

Lieberman, Evan S., and Prerna Singh. 2012. "The Institutional Origins of Ethnic Violence." *Comparative Politics* 45 (1): 1–24.

Lipset, Seymour Martin, and Stein Rokkan. 1967. "Cleavage Structures, Party Systems, and Voter Alignments." In *Party Systems and Voter Alignments: Cross-National Perspectives*, edited by Seymour Martin Lipset and Stein Rokkan, 1–64. New York: The Free Press.

Luttmer, Erzo. 2001. "Group Loyalty and the Taste for Redistribution." *Journal of Political Economy* 10: 500–28.

Mann, Michael. 1999. "The Dark Side of Democracy." *New Left Review* 235: 18–45.

Marshall, T. H. 1950. *Citizenship and Social Class.* Cambridge: Cambridge University Press.

Médard, Jean-Francois. 1986. "Public Corruption in Africa—A Comparative Perspective." *Corruption and Reform* 1 (2): 115–31.

Migdal, Joel. 1988. *Strong Societies and Weak States.* Princeton, NJ: Princeton University Press.

Migdal, Joel. 1994. "The State in Society: An Approach to Struggles for Domination." In *State Power and Social Forces*, eds. Migdal, Joel S. Atul Kohli and Vivienne Shue, 7–34. Cambridge: Cambridge University Press.

Miguel, Edward. 2004. "Tribe or Nation? Nation Building and Public Goods in Kenya Versus Tanzania." *World Politics* 56 (3): 327–62.

Miguel, Edward and Mary Kay Gugerty. 2005. "Ethnic Diversity, Social Sanctions, and Public Goods in Kenya." *Journal of Public Economics* 89 (11–12): 2325–68.

Mill, John Stuart. 1991 [1861]. "Considerations on Representative Government." In *On Liberty and Other Essays*, edited by John M. Gray. Oxford: Oxford University Press.

Miller, David. 1995. *On Nationality*. Oxford: Oxford University Press.

Miller, David. 1998. "The Left, The Nation-State and European Citizenship." *Dissent* (Summer): 47–51.

Montalvo, Jose G., and Marta Reynal-Querol. 2005. "Ethnic Diversity and Economic Development." *Journal of Development Economics* 76: 293–323.

Nagel, Joane, and Susan Olzak. 1982. "Ethnic Mobilization in New and Old States: An Extension of the Competition Model." *Social Problems* 30 (2): 127–43.

Persson, Anna. 2008. *The Institutional Sources of Statehood: Assimilation, Multiculturalism, and Taxation in Sub-Saharan Africa*. Ph.D. diss. Included as number 111 in Goteborg Studies in Political Science. Gothenburg, Sweden: University of Gothenburg.

Persson, Anna. 2018. "The Historical-Institutional Sources of Statehood: Postcolonial Direct versus Indirect Direct Rule and State Development in British Ex-Colonies." Paper presented at APSA. Boston, August 30–September 2.

Persson, Anna, and Martin Sjöstedt. 2012. Responsive and Responsible Leaders: A Matter of Political Will? *Perspectives on Politics* 10 (3): 617–32.

Posner, Daniel N. 2004a. "Measuring Ethnic Fractionalization in Africa." *American Journal of Political Science* 48 (4): 849–63.

Posner, Daniel N. 2004b. "The Political Salience of Cultural Difference: Why Chewas and Tumbukas are Allies in Zambia and Adversaries in Malawi." *American Political Science Review* 98 (4): 529–45.

Posner, Daniel N. 2005. *Institutions and Ethnic Politics in Africa*. Cambridge: Cambridge University Press.

Rabushka, Alvin, and Kenneth A. Shepsle. 1972. *Politics in Plural Societies: A Theory of Democratic Instability*. Columbus: Charles E. Merrill Publishing Company.

Rodrik, Dani, Arvind Subramanian, and Francesco Trebbi. 2004. "Institutions Rule: The Primacy of Institutions Over Geography and Integration in Economic Development." *Journal of Economic Growth* 9 (2): 131–65.

Roeder, Philip G. 2001. *Ethnolinguistic Fractionalization (ELF) Indices, 1961 and 1985*. http//: weber.ucsd.edu/proeder/elf.htm

Rustow, Dankwart. 1970. "Transitions to Democracy." *Comparative Politics* 12 (3): 337–64.

Safran, William. 2004. "Introduction: The Political Aspects of Language." *Nationalism and Ethnic Politics* 10: 1–14.

Sandbrook, Richard. 1972. "Patrons, Clients and Factions: New Dimensions of Conflict Analysis in Africa." *Canadian Journal of Political Science* 5 (1): 104–19.

Schnapper, Dominique. 1998. *Community of Citizens: On the Modern Idea of Nationality*. New Brunswick, N.J.: Transaction Publishers.

Singh, Prerna. 2010. "We-ness and Welfare: A Longitudinal Analysis of Social Development in Kerala, India." *World Development* 39 (2): 282–93.

Singh, Prerna, and Matthias vom Hau. 2016. "Ethnicity in Time: Politics, History, and the Relationship between Ethnic Diversity and Public Goods Provision." *Comparative Political Studies* 49 (10): 1303–40.

Smith, Roger. 1987. "Human Destructiveness and Politics: The Twentieth Century as an Age of Genocide." In *Genocide and the Modern Age*, edited by Isidor Walliman and Michael N. Dobkowski, 21–39. New York: Greenwood Press.

Smith, Charles D. 1997. "Imagined Identities, Imagined Nationalisms: Print Culture and Egyptian Nationalism in Light of Recent Scholarship." *International Journal of Middle East Studies* 29: 607–22.

Stepan, Alfred, Juan Linz, and Yogendra Yadav. 2010. "The Rise of State-Nations." *Journal of Democracy* 21 (3): 50–68.

Svallfors, Stefan. 2013. "Government Quality, Egalitarianism, and Attitudes to Taxes and Social Spending: A European Comparison." *European Political Science Review* 5 (3): 363–80.

Tajfel, Henri, and John C. Turner. 1986. "The Social Identity Theory of Intergroup Behavior." In *Psychology of Intergroup Relations*, edited by Stephen Worchel and William G. Austin, 7–24. Chicago: Nelson-Hall.

Tilly, Charles. 1990. *Coercion, Capital, and European States*. Cambridge, MA: Blackwell.

Vanhanen, Tatu. 1999. "Domestic Ethnic conflict and Ethnic Nepotism." *Journal of Peace Research*, 36 (1): 55–73.

Vicente, Pedro. C., and Leonard Wantchekon. 2009. "Clientelism and Vote Buying: Lessons from Field Experiments in African Elections." *Oxford Review of Economic Policy* 25 (2): 292–305.

Vigdor, Jacob L. 2004. "Interpreting Ethnic Fragmentation Effects." *Economic Letters* 75: 271–76.

Wimmer, Andreas. 1997. "Who Owns the State? Understanding Ethnic Conflict in Post-Colonial Societies." *Nations and Nationalism* 3 (4): 631–65.

Wimmer, Andreas. 2016. "Is Diversity Detrimental? Ethnic Fractionalization, Public Goods Provision, and the Historical Legacies of Stateness." *Comparative Political Studies* 49 (11): 1407–45.

Young, Crawford. 1976. *The Politics of Cultural Pluralism*. Madison: University of Wisconsin Press.

CHAPTER 28

HAPPINESS AND THE QUALITY OF GOVERNMENT

JOHN F. HELLIWELL, HAIFANG HUANG, AND
SHUN WANG

INTRODUCTION

THIS chapter has three main purposes. The first is to explain how and why there is increasing interest in using happiness data and research to measure the quality of life, to help governments make policy choices, and to evaluate the effects of government policies. A review of important milestones marking the changes in policy perspective is presented.

The second purpose is to bring together the largest available sets of existing national-level measures of the quality of governance, and to assess the extent to which they contribute to explaining the levels and changes in life evaluations in more than 150 countries over the years 2005–17, using data from the Gallup World Poll. In our view, happiness data provide the most appropriate means for learning what types and styles of government are most helpful, as experienced by each country's residents.

The third purpose is to dig slightly deeper into some of the channels whereby happiness and government quality are linked. We emphasize three channels: conflict, trust, and inequality. Conflict and inequality are *partly created by governments*, and make other policy objectives harder to reach. Trust is an asset *partly due to government actions*, and is good for happiness in its own right as well as aiding the achievement of other policy objectives.

A short concluding section summarizes what has thus far been learned about how governments could be changed so as to improve well-being in all countries, as measured by people's own evaluations of their lives.

SETTING THE STAGE

There is now widespread interest in refocusing government policies with the explicit aim of increasing equitable and sustainable human well-being. This change in policy perspective has been decades in the making, built on a growing dissatisfaction with using GDP per capita as a sufficient measure of human progress (Stiglitz, Sen, and Fitoussi 2009), inspired by the Bhutanese choice more than 40 years ago to make happiness a national objective, and fueled by decades of research aimed at creating a transdisciplinary science of happiness (Ura et al. 2015). These converging threads came together on July 19, 2011, when the United Nations General Assembly adopted a Bhutan-sponsored resolution that "called on United Nations Member States to undertake steps that give more importance to happiness and well-being in determining how to achieve and measure social and economic development."[1]

That resolution then led to a High Level Meeting on Well-Being and Happiness: Defining a New Economic Paradigm,[2] convened by Jigme Y. Thinley, Prime Minister of Bhutan, at the United Nations on April 2, 2012. That meeting marked the release of the first *World Happiness Report* (Helliwell, Layard, and Sachs 2012), bringing together the available global data on national happiness and reviewing related evidence from the emerging science of happiness. That report, which in turn built on many other reviews of the science of well-being, provided strong support for the view that the quality of people's lives can be coherently and reliably assessed by a variety of subjective well-being measures, collectively referred to in this chapter as "happiness." It also built upon, as did the UN meeting itself, the UK launch of a well-being initiative in November 2010, still unique in combining engagement at the highest level from the political, administrative, and data-gathering pillars of government. The initial constellation of these three supporting pillars was probably crucial in establishing widespread data-gathering and discussions. Once started, these data and discussions have fueled a broad swath of innovations in firms and communities, and a variety of within-government and cross-pillar organizations that have continued to deliver research and applications despite not being a central feature of the political environment.

Life evaluations were granted a central role in the *World Happiness Reports* because they provide an umbrella that can enable comparisons of the relative importance of the supporting pillars for good lives. The *OECD Guidelines on Measuring Subjective Well-Being* (OECD 2013) also emphasize the need to measure life evaluations as a primary indicator, ideally in concert with monitoring affect (i.e., both positive and negative aspects of people's more daily emotions and experiences); "Eudaimonia" (i.e. measures of life purpose); and other factors that have been found to support better lives (e.g. income, health, good jobs, family and friends, welcoming communities, good government, trust, and generosity). Having an umbrella measure of subjective well-being permits the relative importance of these factors supporting well-being to be assessed, making it possible to move beyond a general wish to improve well-being towards some specific policies with established credentials for supporting better lives.

Both before and after the April 2012 UN meeting, attempts were made to sketch the possible implications of happiness research for public policies. A number of national and

[1] Resolution 65/309. See http://www.un.org/apps/news/story.asp?NewsID=39084#.WhdoDLYZP3h
[2] For the report of the meeting, see: https://sustainabledevelopment.un.org/index.php?page=view&type=400&nr=617&menu=35

international efforts also aim to develop a well-being policy framework, as summarized in Durand and Exton (2019). Using happiness data and research to assess the value of political institutions and policies seems especially appropriate, since many national constitutions and most policy platforms relate to the quality of life, and the existence and reelection of democratic governments depend on maintaining a sufficient level of citizen satisfaction with the quality of life. Nonetheless, until recently, most studies of the sources of electoral support have focused on economic conditions rather than more general measures of the quality of life. More recently, when comparisons have been made between economic performance and life satisfaction as determinants of electoral outcomes, the latter has been found to be more important (Esaiasson, Dahlberg, and Kokkonen 2019; Ward 2019a, 2019b). If these results are confirmed more broadly, they will tend to give happiness a more central role in political science, political platforms and public policies.

There are three key components required to support systematic attempts to design and evaluate government institutions and policies in terms of their likely effects on people's own evaluations of the quality of their lives. The first is the collection of happiness data in sufficient detail to support research into the reasons why some neighborhoods and nations are happier than others. Relatively few countries are yet assessing subjective well-being in enough detail and frequency to support research sufficient to formulate policies focused on well-being.

Second, governments are unlikely to change their policy objectives unless supported by public opinion. There is already apparent support, in most countries, for a policy framework designed to deliver sustainability, as witnessed by the breadth of national commitments to the Paris Accord establishing the Sustainable Development Goals. Subjective well-being is included among the many goals, but more importantly has the potential for being used as an umbrella welfare measure to help to establish the relative importance of what otherwise risk being too many unrelated goals. In this important area, as in others, the availability of an empirically useful measure of individual and societal well-being can help to galvanize as well as direct public and political thought and actions.

Third, to convert broad objectives to specific policies, and to effectively rank alternative ways to design and deliver public services, requires a much broader and more comprehensive form of cost–benefit analysis. The basic idea is simple. Many policies have expected consequences for a variety of economic and social outcomes, for a range of beneficiaries, and with various ways of distributing the costs and efforts of policy design and delivery. Traditional cost–benefit analysis includes costs and consequences that are directly measured at market prices, with nonmarket outcomes, such as the level of social trust in a community, being mentioned in discussions as being relevant, but being left out of any explicit calculations used to support the ranking of alternative policies. To go further requires extending the evaluation of alternative policies to include their expected contributions to subjective well-being, using empirical research to establish the weights assigned to the various outcomes when measuring the overall costs and benefits. These practices are increasingly established within the policy green books and evaluation practices used in departments and Cabinet offices in several countries, and probably represent the most important shift required to implement a well-being approach to the evaluation and design of government institutions and policies.

HAPPINESS AND THE QUALITY OF
NATIONAL GOVERNMENTS

We use "happiness" as a shorthand way of describing a three-member family of measures of subjective well-being comprising life evaluations, positive affect, and negative affect (Durand and Smith 2013; OECD 2013).[3] Happiness as an emotion is part of positive affect, while happiness about one's overall life is an evaluative judgment. Judgments about life satisfaction or happiness with life deliver quite different answers than do questions about happiness as an emotion, with life evaluations being more reflective of a wide range of life circumstances. Most of the research linking happiness and the quality of government has made use of some form of life evaluations, whether happiness with life, satisfaction with life, or the Cantril ladder question asking people to think of their lives as a ladder, with the best possible life for them as a 10 and the worst possible life as a zero, and to rate their current lives on that scale. There is good reason for this preference for life evaluations. They vary more across countries than do emotional measures, and these differences are much more explicable in terms of national variations in the social, political, and economic circumstances of life than is the case for either positive or negative emotions. Life evaluations are themselves supported also by positive emotions, without being strongly affected by negative ones, as shown in Table 2.1 of Helliwell, Layard, and Sachs (2019, 20). Life evaluations thus provide a more powerful tool for assessing the importance of various aspects of the quality of government. Good government may or may not make you feel happy, but does, as we shall show, make you happier with your life as a whole.

Most of the existing literature on the empirical linkages between happiness and government quality have been cross-sectional in nature, mainly because of the relatively short time span of suitable survey evidence, coupled with the frequently slow pace of change in the quality of the political institutions being studied. One frequent finding of this research has been that if the six World Bank measures of government quality (Kaufmann, Kraay, and Zoido-Lobaton 1999) are divided into two groups, one related to the honesty and effectiveness of policy design and delivery, and the other related to the quality of the electoral process, that quality of delivery is more important than democracy as a support for higher life evaluations (e.g. Helliwell and Huang 2008; Ott 2010), especially for countries with lower levels of delivery quality (Helliwell et al. 2018).

Only recently has the run of available data come to be long enough to permit the analysis to focus on the consequences of within-country changes rather than long-standing differences between countries (e.g. Diaz-Serrano and Rodríguez-Pose 2012; Helliwell et al. 2018; Nikolova 2016; Ovaska and Takashima 2010; Whiteley et al. 2010; Yamamura 2011). The ability to study changes within a given set of national institutions enables attribution of changes in life satisfaction to changes in the quality of government within a policy-relevant time horizon, even if it limits the scope for the study of the effects of broader systemic

---

[3] The OECD also proposed having a measure of life purpose, and such a question is one of the four key well-being questions used by the UK Office for National Statistics. In our Aristotelian view, a sense of purpose should be a strong support for life evaluations, but there is unfortunately not yet such a question in the Gallup World Poll.

changes in the nature of public institutions. These broad systemic changes are perhaps best assessed by cross-sectional analysis combined with a closer examination of the time series evidence in those cases where an important institutional change takes place.

Since our interest in this chapter includes the analysis of different types of institutions that change very slowly, and of changes of government quality that occur reasonably often within the period covered by the available data, our analysis makes use of pooled samples of data covering more than a dozen years for more than 150 countries, doing our analysis with and without country fixed effects, with the latter delivering results that depend on what is happening within individual countries.

Our main analysis makes use of data from the Gallup World Poll, starting in 2005 and extending to 2017 or 2018, producing a panel of generally more than 1500 observations. Our analysis ends in 2017 in those cases where the quality of government variables are not available for 2018. Table A1 describes the main variables used in analysis and their sources, while Statistical Appendix 2 of *World Happiness Report 2019* (WHR 2019 SA2) has more details and also shows the correlations among the variables (Helliwell, Huang, and Wang 2019).

Delivery quality and democratic quality

Table 28.1 shows our latest results comparing the life evaluation effects of the World Bank government quality variables divided into two groups, as we and others have done in previous work. This new estimation involves more data than we and others have used previously, and is mainly based on analysis employing country fixed effects. The new results replicate the basic earlier finding that within-country differences in the quality of delivery (the average for effectiveness, rule of law,[4] regulatory quality, and absence of corruption) have significant linkages to life evaluations. As before, there is no such linkage for differences in democratic quality, as represented by two measures, one capturing voice and accountability, and the other stability and freedom from violence. We shall return later to consider the democratic and violence aspects.

There are three equations in Table 28.1. The first just includes the delivery and democratic variables, and shows a substantial link between a country's delivery quality and average life evaluations, with an increase in governmental quality equal to one standard deviation associated with a 0.7 point increase in average life evaluations. The second equation adds GDP per capita, which attracts a significant positive coefficient, and lowers the coefficient on delivery quality by about one-third. Such a reduction is to be expected, as better government should improve the ability to produce GDP. The third equation adds the three social variables included in the *World Happiness Report* framework for explaining this same sample of life evaluations. Healthy life expectancy is not included, since the country fixed effects estimation excludes the effects of inter-country differences, and the healthy life expectancy data follow simple time trends and hence do not add to the explanation of within-country changes. The corruption variable is excluded because it is a key part of the delivery variable. Adding the social variables reduces the remaining impact from delivery quality,

---

[4] Nikolova (2016) finds the rule of law to help explain changes in the happiness gap between the transition and nontransition countries of Europe.

Table 28.1 Subjective well-being and quality of government measured by WGI indicators of governance, country fixed effects regressions, sample period 2005–17

	Dependent variable		
Independent variable	SWB	SWB	SWB
Democratic quality	0.19	0.12	0.09
	(0.13)	(0.12)	(0.11)
Delivery quality	0.69	0.45	0.28
	(0.2)***	(0.19)**	(0.17)*
Log GDP per capita		0.84	0.77
		(0.23)***	(0.2)***
Freedom to make life choices			0.92
			(0.21)***
Generosity			0.29
			(0.18)
Social support			1.61
			(0.29)***
Year fixed effects	Included	Included	Included
Country fixed effects	Included	Included	Included
Number of countries	162	162	160
Number of obs.	1,548	1,548	1,469
Within-country R-squared	0.08	0.11	0.19

Notes: Standard errors in parentheses are cluster adjusted at the country level. *, **, and *** indicate statistical significance at 10%, 5%, and 1% levels respectively.

and for mostly the same reasons as for income. For example, countries where delivery quality is high are also likely to provide the breadth and quality of public services that permit higher fractions of the population to feel that they are free to make key life decisions. Indeed, in these data the simple correlation between delivery and freedom (+0.48) is even higher than that between democratic quality and freedom (+0.45). In none of the equations does democratic quality show a significant additional linkage to life evaluations once the other variables in the equation are taken into account, despite the high simple correlation (which includes differences among countries as well as over time) between democratic quality and life evaluations (+0.62), which is nonetheless less than between delivery quality and life evaluations (+0.71).[5]

---

[5] We also ran regressions that replace the democratic and delivery indicator with a single measure of governance, the absence of corruption from the World Bank government quality indicators. Corruption control has a positive and statistically significant effect in the simplest specification. But when GDP per

When we previously divided our sample of countries into those with high and low delivery quality, we found that the democratic quality variable did have positive linkages to life evaluations in countries with higher than average delivery quality. However, that result is not replicated in our new longer data sample, where we find that changes in democratic quality have no impact in either group of countries. This result is not driven by the infrequency of within-country changes in democratic quality, since it is also found in a pure cross-sectional analysis.[6]

Assessing other measures of government quality

Besides the World Bank government quality variables that we use to construct the delivery and democratic quality measures, the literature has other frequently used measures of government quality. In chapter 2 of the *World Happiness Report 2019* we consider five of them— corruption perceptions, political rights, civil liberties, economic freedom, and political freedom[7]—in a regression model identical to those reported in Table 28.1, except that the variables for delivery and democratic quality are replaced by the five alternative measures. We find that only the corruption index has a significant positive effect in the first equation, where no other variables are included. The same result is found even if the variables are tested one by one within the fixed effects framework. This lack of correlation is of course strongly influenced by the use of country fixed effects, which transfer the cross-country linkages into the country-specific fixed effects. If instead, we look at the simple correlations for the whole data sample, with most of their variation coming from differences across countries, then there are significant linkages for each of these variables, although only for the corruption perceptions index is the correlation with life evaluations (+0.68) close to that of the delivery variable (+0.70). This similarity is to be expected, as corruption perceptions are a key variable in explaining life evaluations, and are also a key element in the delivery quality variable. If we add GDP per capita to the right-hand side of the regression, even the within-country changes in corruption are no longer significant incremental contributors to life evaluations, suggesting that much of their influence is mediated by changes in GDP per capita. When the social variables are added in the third column, they keep their importance, while the government quality indicators remain insignificant.[8]

To confirm the robustness of this empirical preference for delivery quality over the other measures of the quality of governance, Table 28.2 shows pure cross-section results for changes from 2005–8 to 2016–18. The first column shows life evaluations to have increased more in countries where delivery quality has increased, even excluding effects flowing

person is added to the right-hand side as a control variable, the estimated effect of corruption control drops by half and the statistical significance disappears. When other control variables in Table 28.1 are included, the estimated effect of the corruption variable is close to zero.

[6] See columns 1 and 2 of Table 14 of Statistical Appendix 2 of *World Happiness Report 2019*.

[7] Political Rights (PR) and Civil Liberties (CL) indices are from the Freedom House. Corruption Perception Index (CPI) is from the Transparency International. World Press Freedom Index (WPFI) is from the Reporters without Borders. Index of Economic Freedom (WEFI) is from the Heritage Foundation.

[8] See Table 12 of Statistical Appendix 2 of *World Happiness Report 2019*.

Table 28.2 Cross-sectional regressions of changes from 2005–8 to 2016–18

Independent variable	Dependent variable		
	SWB	SWB	SWB
Democratic quality	−0.04		
	(0.18)		
Delivery quality	0.53		0.68
	(0.26)**		(0.39)*
Log GDP per capita	0.65	1.04	0.9
	(0.28)**	(0.33)***	(0.34)***
Corruption Perception Index on standardized scale		−0.18	−0.43
		(0.21)	(0.25)*
Political rights on standardized scale		−0.19	−0.14
		(0.31)	(0.31)
Civil liberties on standardized scale		0.2	0.14
		(0.34)	(0.34)
World Press Freedom Index on standardized scale		−0.06	−0.02
		(0.15)	(0.15)
Index of Economic Freedom on standardized scale		0.26	0.16
		(0.14)*	(0.15)
Number of countries	128	112	112
Number of obs.	128	112	112
R-squared	0.14	0.15	0.17

Note: Standard errors are in parentheses. *, **, and *** indicate statistical significance at 10%, 5%, and 1% levels respectively.

through increases in GDP. Column 2 takes out the delivery quality index, and includes the five alternative quality measures, for the smaller number of countries for which these variables are available. In this cross-section, the economic freedom index acquires significance at the 10% level, but this is lost in column 3 when the delivery quality variable is reintroduced. We therefore conclude that changes in delivery quality, whether on a year-to-year basis, or over a decade, contribute to national average life evaluations, and that nothing further is added from any of the other quality measures tested in Table 28.2.

Confidence in government

The Gallup World Poll asks respondents, yes or no, whether they have confidence in their national governments. The fraction of respondents answering "yes" can be used as a supplementary subjective measure of the quality of governance, as seen by those living within that system. Table 28.3 presents some results from country fixed effects regressions showing that changes within the sample period contribute to average life evaluations above and beyond what is explained by delivery quality, GDP per capita, and the three social variables. The same pattern of results holds both with and without adding the social variables, so Table 28.3 adopts the simpler structure. Column 1 includes confidence in government on its own, while column 2 adds GDP per capita, and column 3 adds democratic and delivery quality. Confidence in government retains explanatory power when delivery quality is introduced. Delivery quality itself has a lower effect when confidence in government is included. Although the two variables have essentially no correlation in the full sample, within-country changes are significantly positively related, thereby increasing confidence in both variables as indicators of changes within a country, and reducing their coefficients in fixed effects specifications where both are included.

Experiments using the data from one half of each year's sample to measure the average confidence in government to explain the life evaluations of the other half of the sample would slightly reduce these effects (as shown in WHR 2018 for other variables), but leave their structure intact. Here we can report a similar experiment, replacing the confidence measure from the same survey with the confidence measure from the survey done in the year before. This way the key explanatory variable (the confidence measure) and the variable to be explained (the happiness measure) come from different respondents and also different,

Table 28.3 Gallup World Poll's measure of confidence in national government; country fixed effects regressions; sample period 2005–17/18

Independent variable	Dependent variable		
	SWB	SWB	SWB
Confidence in national government	0.83	0.68	0.6
	(0.18)***	(0.15)***	(0.16)***
Log GDP per capita		1.08	0.93
		(0.28)***	(0.27)***
Democratic quality			−0.003
			(0.11)
Delivery quality			0.39
			(0.21)*
Year fixed effects	Included	Included	Included
Country fixed effects	Included	Included	Included
Number of countries	152	152	152
Number of obs.	1,504	1,504	1,388
Within-country R-squared	0.09	0.13	0.14

Notes: Standard errors in parentheses are cluster adjusted at the country level. *, **, and *** indicate statistical significance at 10%, 5%, and 1% levels respectively.

though adjacent, years. The estimated effects of the confidence measure drop slightly (by about 20%) but retain all their statistical significance.

Forms of governments and how governments are elected

Here we return to the question of the structure and operation of the electoral system. The results reported above attach only modest importance, in life satisfaction terms, to whether a system is or is not a functioning democracy. Of the total observations in our dataset, slightly more than half (54%) are recorded as democracies,[9] and those recorded as democracies on average have higher life evaluations than those which are not, 5.9 vs 4.9 on the 0 to 10 scale, using all data from 2005 to 2018. And within democracies, parliamentary democracies with proportional representation have the highest average life evaluations, averaging 6.4. Digging deeper into these simple averages, Table 28.4 contains six equations including the three variables reflecting political structure: democracy, democracy with proportional representation, and parliamentary democracy, with year fixed effects (but not with country fixed effects) and a variety of other control variables. Altman, Flavin, and Radcliff (2017) reported, among the OECD countries, higher life satisfaction in those with a parliamentary or proportional representation systems. Columns 1 to 3 are without regional control variables, while columns 3 to 6 include them. The first column includes just the three political structure variables, while column 2 adds GDP per capita and column 3 also adds delivery quality, perceptions of corruption, and the three social variables. In all three cases, being democratic is estimated to have a significant positive impact, ranging from +0.67 in the simplest case to +0.42 in the case with the most controls, but still without regional fixed effects. Proportional representation and a parliamentary form both add some positive contribution in the simplest case, with coefficients for the three variables summing to over +1.5 points.[10] But by the time the column 3 controls have been added, the net effect for the proportional parliamentary democracies is down to +0.3 points. Columns 3 to 6 repeat the same equations with the addition of control variables for each of the ten global regions. In these equations, the effects of different political systems are estimated relative to other countries in the same continental region, as well as the relatively rare within-country changes. In none of the cases with regional controls are there any significant effects from the political system variables. Thus, we conclude that the effects found in columns 1 to 3 risk being based on differences in life circumstances across global regions that are possibly attributable to factors beyond the ways in which governments are elected. We do not present results with country fixed effects, since they are even less able than columns 3 to 6 to show any impact from systemic variables.

How governments spend

In chapter 2 of the *World Happiness Report 2019* we also tested some particular government expenditure patterns that might have possible implications for average life evaluations. In

---

[9] We follow the regime classification in Authoritarian Regimes Dataset (Wahman, Teorell, and Hadenius, 2013; Hadenius and Teorell, 2007).

[10] This is consistent with the results of Altman, Flavin, and Radcliff (2017) for the OECD countries.

Table 28.4 Happiness, forms of government, and electoral systems; pooled regressions without and with regional fixed effects; sample period 2005–18

Independent variable	Dependent variable					
	SWB	SWB	SWB	SWB	SWB	SWB
Democracy, QGI	0.67	0.51	0.42	0.28	0.14	0.1
	(0.2)***	(0.12)***	(0.12)***	(0.18)	(0.09)	(0.09)
Proportional representation	0.47	0.16	0.07	0.09	0.07	0.01
	(0.2)**	(0.14)	(0.11)	(0.14)	(0.11)	(0.1)
Parliamentary democracy	0.35	−0.33	−0.28	0.1	0.04	0.04
	(0.2)*	(0.15)**	(0.13)**	(0.22)	(0.17)	(0.14)
Log GDP per capita		0.68	0.45		0.62	0.35
		(0.04)***	(0.06)***		(0.06)***	(0.07)***
Year fixed effects	Included	Included	Included	Included	Included	Included
Regional fixed effects				Included	Included	Included
Social variable controls			Included			Included
Number of countries	144	144	136	144	144	136
Number of obs.	1,453	1,453	1,212	1,453	1,453	1,212
R-squared	0.28	0.65	0.76	0.6	0.73	0.8

Notes: The social variable controls in columns 4 and 6 are the same ones that are used in Table 28.1, namely the perception of corruption, freedom to make life choices, generosity, and social support, all from the Gallup World Poll. Standard errors in parentheses are cluster adjusted at the level of countries. *, **, and *** indicate statistical significance at 10%, 5%, and 1% levels respectively.

a full equilibrium, if every country had the structure of government that was best for the subjective well-being of its citizens, then spending patterns in each country would simply reflect the preferences of that country's voters, and international variations would reflect differences in tastes and circumstances across countries. This may also explain the mixed findings linking government size to happiness (Bjørnskov, Dreher, and Fischer 2007; Flavin, Pacek, and Radcliff 2014; Ott 2010, 2011, 2015; Persson and Rothstein 2015; Ram 2009; Yamamura 2011). The four variables we consider are government education spending, government healthcare spending, and military spending (all as percentage of GDP) and a cross-sectional measure of the breadth of coverage of a country's social safety net system, on a scale of 1 to 10. Here we briefly summarize the key findings.[11] We find that social safety net coverage takes a significant positive coefficient, with or without regional fixed effects, but only in the simplest form excluding income and other control variables. Government spending on education has no impact in any of the equations, with or without regional fixed

[11] Detailed estimates are reported in Tables 16–18 of Statistical Appendix 2 of *World Happiness Report 2019.*

effects, while healthcare spending has a positive coefficient, and military spending a negative one in the equations with the largest set of control variables, both with and without the additional of regional fixed effects. But these effects disappear when country fixed effects are used. This indicates that statistical significance for healthcare and military spending mostly arises from differences across countries.

MEDIATING FACTORS: CONFLICT, TRUST, AND INEQUALITY

Here we consider some factors that are important for subjective well-being and are also affected by the quality of government. We look especially at conflicts, trust and inequality of well-being.

War and peace

In this section, we show that conflicts[12] and the global peace index[13] both provide important channels by which good government helps to support high life evaluations.

One of the benefits of good government should be to reduce the incidence of violence, and more generally to enable citizens to live in peace. Indeed, the absence of conflict is one of the components of the World Bank's measure of political stability. Since that measure was not found earlier to significantly affect life evaluations, we return to the issue here more directly. We look first at the incidence of violence, and then consider the global peace index. To assess whether the prevalence of violence is associated with lower life evaluations, we make use of data published by the Uppsala Conflict Data Program. Table 28.5 shows two sets of three columns each. In every column there are two conflict variables, each on a zero to 1 basis. The first conflict variable indicates a country and year in which there were any conflict deaths recorded, and the second takes the value of 1.0 for any country-year where the conflict death rate was in the 90th percentile of all cases where conflict deaths were recorded. In our sample of 2,100 country-years, about 600 had some conflict deaths recorded, while in 60 country-years (the top decile) the conflict death rates ranged from 7.5 to 70 deaths per 100 thousand population. There were 14 different countries that had one or more years of conflict deaths in the 90th percentile.[14]

The results reported in columns 1–3 of Table 28.5 are all from regressions that include country fixed effects. The first column contains only the conflict variables, the second adds the log of GDP per capita, and the third adds corruption, freedom to make life choices, generosity, and social support. The estimates suggest negative impacts from any conflict deaths,

[12] For single country evidence for Ukraine, see Coupe and Obrizan (2016). For estimates of the well-being consequences of terrorism in France and the United Kingdom, see Frey, Luechinger, and Stutzer (2009).

[13] See http://visionofhumanity.org/indexes/global-peace-index/.

[14] These countries are listed in Table 20 of Statistical Appendix 2. Note that Syria is not one of these countries, since their data are not included the version 18.1 of the Uppsala data.

Table 28.5 Happiness, conflicts, and peace; country fixed effects regressions; sample period 2005–17

Independent variable	Dependent variable					
	SWB	SWB	SWB	SWB	SWB	SWB
Having conflict deaths reported in Uppsala GED (0 or 1)	−0.08	−0.04	−0.01			
	(0.04)*	(0.04)	(0.04)			
Conflict death rate ranked above 90th percentile (0 or 1)	−0.18	−0.02	−0.06			
	(0.09)**	(0.08)	(0.08)			
Global Peace Index				−0.60	−0.37	−0.32
				(0.18)***	(0.17)**	(0.18)*
Log GDP per capita		1.07	0.95		1.02	0.95
		(0.24)***	(0.26)***		(0.29)***	(0.33)***
Year fixed effects	Included	Included	Included	Included	Included	Included
Country fixed effects	Included	Included	Included	Included	Included	Included
Social variable controls			Included			Included
Number of countries	161	161	157	154	154	151
Number of obs.	1,542	1,542	1,402	1,416	1,416	1,318
Within-country R-squared	0.04	0.09	0.18	0.05	0.08	0.18

Notes: The social variable controls in columns 4 and 6 are the same ones that are used in Table 28.1, namely the perception of corruption, freedom to make life choices, generosity, and social support, all from the Gallup World Poll. Standard errors in parentheses are cluster adjusted at the level of countries. *, **, and *** indicate statistical significance at 10%, 5%, and 1% levels respectively.

and a much greater impact for those countries in the 90th percentile. They also suggest that when GDP and other social variables are added, there is a substantial reduction in the negative impacts of conflicts, indicating that some of the adverse effect of conflicts on population happiness is likely due to weakening economic activity and damage to the social fabric.

Columns 4–6 of Table 28.5 present the results when the conflict-death variables are replaced by the Global Peace Index in regressions with country and year fixed effects. The Global Peace Index takes a negative sign in almost all specifications because the index is defined so that higher values indicate a less peaceful country. The variable rates each of more than 160 countries in each year from 2008 to 2018 in three domains: societal safety and security, the extent of continuing domestic and international conflict, and the degree of militarization. The estimated happiness effects for the peace index are significant in all three cases, even though with a smaller estimated effect in the final column with the fullest set of economic and social control variables. Thus, part of the negative effect from conflict and violence flows through the economic and social channels.

Trust and inequality

We consider trust and inequality together, since some recent evidence shows them to have interrelated impacts on life evaluations. For example, there is substantial evidence that high-trust societies are more resilient in the face of external shocks including earthquakes, floods, and economic crises (Helliwell, Huang, and Wang 2014). In a parallel way, individuals who feel that others can be trusted, and have a sense of belonging to their communities, are more resilient in the face of hardships ranging from unemployment and ill-health to discrimination. Although any of those adverse situations significantly reduces an individual's life evaluations, the loss is less for those who live in a high-trust environment (Helliwell, Huang, and Wang 2018). Similarly, the well-being costs to children facing discrimination because of their disabilities are much less for those who feel a sense of belonging in their local communities (Daley, Phipps, and Branscombe 2018). Trust and belonging thereby not only raise subjective well-being for all, they reduce inequality of well-being. They do so by providing larger gains for those who are subject to conditions—such as illness, unemployment, and discrimination—that would otherwise be likely to place them at the bottom of the happiness distribution.[15]

Many countries have had sharply growing inequality of income and wealth in the last decades of the twentieth century and the first two decades of this century. These increases have had political salience in many countries, and have been linked to changes in a variety of measures of well-being (e.g. Pickett and Wilkinson 2015). However, if income is too narrow a measure for human progress, then inequality of the distributions of income and wealth is also too narrow an indicator of inequality. Goff, Helliwell, and Mayraz (2018), making use of individual-level data from three large international surveys, found that inequality of the distribution of happiness, as measured by the standard deviation of the within-country distribution of individual life evaluations, is more closely linked to average life evaluations than are the usual measures of inequality in the distribution of income. This continues to be the case even when efforts are made to reduce the risk posed by possible mechanical linkages between the mean and the standard deviation of life evaluations. Another link between inequality and trust enters here, as the same study finds that well-being inequality is stronger than income inequality as a predictor of international differences in average rates of social trust, even when average well-being levels are among the predictors. This is so despite the fact that income inequality has been found to be a strong predictor of international trust differences (Rothstein and Uslaner 2005). A final empirical support for the greater generality of well-being inequality is that it has a greater well-being effect than does income inequality to an extent that is greater for those who report themselves in surveys to favor more equality.[16]

Another way of measuring well-being inequality is to look at the quantile averages or percentile boundaries, thereby reducing the possibilities for end-point effects to influence the measure. Recent research has shown a growing spread of the global distribution of well-being scores, especially since 2010 (Nichols and Reinhart 2019). And this growing

---

[15] See Ovaska and Takashima (2010) for discussion of other likely factors influencing well-being inequality.
[16] All three of these results are from Goff et al. (2018).

dispersion, which has happened much more in some countries than others, has been found to significantly reduce average life evaluations, even more than found for income inequality or the standard deviation of life evaluations.

Choosing Government Policies
to Improve Lives

One advantage of focusing policy attention on well-being inequality rather than income inequality is that there are many more win–win policy options for reducing well-being inequality. When it comes to the distribution of income and wealth, most policy options involve targeted transfer of financial resources from the top to the bottom, sometimes angering those being taxed and stigmatizing the recipients. By contrast, creating happiness for those who have little does not require any transfers from those who are already happier. In fact, recent research has shown that a wide range of prosocial actions are likely to improve the subjective well-being of both the givers and receivers of such kindness (for a recent survey, see Aknin et al. 2019), especially when under the volition of the donor.

More generally, changes in the structure of government to increase the options for individuals and communities to share in the design and implementation of their own institutions is likely to improve outcomes in several ways, because such collaborations encourage engagement, increase the scope for innovation, and build social connections that raise subjective well-being above and beyond what they contribute to solving the specific problems at hand. This may be part of the reason why studies find that people are happier in more decentralized systems (Flavin, Pacek, and Radcliff 2014; Rodríguez-Pose and Maslauskaite 2012), especially for the raising of revenues (Diaz-Serrano and Rodríguez-Pose 2012), and are happier when they share the political views of the party in power (Di Tella and MacCullough 2005; Tavits 2008) and are more directly involved in policy choices (Stutzer and Frey 2006). The large negative effects of corruption on happiness (Helliwell, Layard, and Sachs 2019, 20) may reflect in part that corruption must lessen the extent to which citizens see themselves as parts of trustworthy collaborations to improve lives. Emphasis on the "how" of policy design and delivery is still much less central to policy thinking than it should be.[17]

There is a growing range of evaluations of government policies intended to improve happiness in many policy areas. At the broadest level, the OECD has recommended that countries adopt a whole-of-government approach to improving well-being, supported by broader and more systematic collection of well-being data, and the development and application of policy evaluation tools that use subjective well-being as the objective and as the means for comparing monetary and nonmonetary costs and outcomes (Durand and Exton 2019). Within healthcare, using the happiness lens to evaluate different treatment alternatives has been advocated as a means of producing much better health and more happiness with less drain on scarce resources (Peasgood, Foster, and Dolan 2019). Within schools, positive

---

[17] For an example of evidence showing that procedural utility has empirical relevance, see Stutzer and Frey (2006), and Helliwell et al. (2014).

education policies designed to produce better lives for students have been tested and affirmed in large-scale trials in countries around the world (Seligman and Adler 2019). Finally, a large variety of urban policies, frequently involving a mix of bottom-up and top-down collaboration to build successful communities, has exposed the importance and value of enabling people to work together in creating happier communities, especially in urban areas, where such connections require more innovation to create (Bin Bishr et al. 2019).

There is a growing body of evidence illustrating feasible changes in the structure of government that are likely to improve population well-being, as measured by people's own life evaluations (Diener and Biswas-Diener 2019). What is required to move beyond the possible to the actual? The case studies reviewed above are replete with reasons why existing policies and approaches tend to stick to time-tested procedures. Risk minimization is the norm, and innovation remains exceptional, especially that required to build cross-silo cooperation of the sort required. It is simply very hard to change the course of the ship of state, especially when it requires top-to-bottom and ministry-to-ministry collaboration. Add in the growing climate of risk aversion, and innovation looks to be ever more difficult. One way of establishing entry points, and building up experience and experimental evidence about what works to deliver more happiness, might be to establish "partnerships for happiness" (Helliwell 2019). These could take different forms in different circumstances, but essentially they would typically start small and explicitly experimental, providing freedom of action and innovation for those willing to collaborate. Such partnerships would ideally involve cooperation across policy silos and from up and down the administrative structure. It would probably be important to keep the initial efforts explicitly experimental, accepting that failures are to be expected in any well-designed learning strategy, and to give higher levels of government the distance and deniability they may at first require.

From either a scientific or a political perspective, the small scale and flexible nature of partnerships for happiness make them perhaps the most efficient way of acquiring enough information to inform future choices. Although the logic of redesigning government to build happiness may be very strong, there is still much to be learned about the best ways of doing so. Opening the doors to innovation may be difficult, but it remains the essential next step. The related research agenda is both pressing and increasingly feasible as the range of available happiness data continues to grow alongside a parallel growth in policy interest.[18]

References

Aknin, Lara B., Ashley V. Whillans, Michael I. Norton, and Elizabeth W. Dunn. 2019. "Happiness and Prosocial Behavior: An Evaluation of the Evidence." In *World Happiness Report 2019*, edited by John F. Helliwell, Richard Layard, and Jeffrey D. Sachs, 67–86. New York: UN Sustainable Development Solutions Network.

Altman, David, Patrick Flavin, and Benjamin Radcliff. 2017. "Democratic Institutions and Subjective Well-being." *Political Studies* 65 (3): 685–704.

[18] Helliwell's research has been supported by the Canadian Institute for Advanced Research (CIFAR). Wang gratefully acknowledges financial support from the KDI School of Public Policy and Management. We thank the Gallup Organization for access to data from the Gallup World Poll.

Bin Bishr, Aisha, Ali al-Azzawi, Ger Baron, Charles Montgomery, Mauricio Rodas, and Nicola Yates. 2019. "Happy Cities Agenda." In *Global Happiness and Wellbeing Policy Report 2019*, Global Happiness Council, 112–39.

Bjørnskov, Christian, Axel Dreher, and Justina A. V. Fischer. 2007. "The Bigger the Better? Evidence of the Effect of Government Size on Life Satisfaction around the World." *Public Choice* 130 (3–4): 267–92.

Coupe, Tom, and Maksym Obrizan. 2016. "The Impact of War on Happiness: The Case of Ukraine." *Journal of Economic Behavior & Organization* 132: 228–42.

Daley, Angela, Shelley Phipps, and Nyla R. Branscombe. 2018. "The Social Complexities of Disability: Discrimination, Belonging and Life Satisfaction among Canadian Youth." *SSM - Population Health* 5: 55–63.

Diaz-Serrano, Luis, and Andrés Rodríguez-Pose. 2012. "Decentralization, Subjective Well-being, and the Perception of Institutions." *Kyklos* 65 (2): 179–93.

Diener, Ed, and Robert Biswas-Diener. 2019. "Well-being Interventions to Improve Societies." In *Global Happiness and Wellbeing Policy Report 2019*, Global Happiness Council, 95–110.

Di Tella, Rafael, and Robert MacCullough. 2005. "Partisan Social Happiness." *Review of Economic Studies* 72 (2): 367–93.

Durand, Martine, and Carrie Exton. 2019. "Adopting a Well-being Approach in Central Government: Policy Mechanisms and Practical Tools." In *Global Happiness and Wellbeing Policy Report* 2019, Global Happiness Council, 140–62.

Durand, Martine, and Conal Smith. 2013. "The OECD Approach to Measuring Subjective Well-being." In *World Happiness Report 2013*, edited by John F. Helliwell, Richard Layard, and Jeffrey D. Sachs, 112–37. New York: UN Sustainable Development Solutions Network.

Esaiasson, Peter, Stefan Dahlberg, and Andrej Kokkonen. 2019. "In Pursuit of Happiness: Life Satisfaction Drives Political Support." *European Journal of Political Research*. https://doi.org/10.1111/1475-6765.12335

Flavin, Patrick, Alexander C. Pacek, and Benjamin Radcliff. 2014. "Assessing the Impact of the Size and Scope of Government on Human Well-being." *Social Forces* 92 (4): 1241–58.

Frey, Bruno S., Simon Luechinger, and Alois Stutzer. 2009. "The Life Satisfaction Approach to Valuing Public Goods: The Case of Terrorism." *Public Choice* 138 (3/4): 317–45.

Goff, Leonard, John F. Helliwell, and Guy Mayraz. 2018. "Inequality of Subjective Well-being as a Comprehensive Measure of Inequality." *Economic Inquiry* 56 (4): 2177–94.

Hadenius, Axel, and Jan Teorell. 2007. Pathways from Authoritarianism. *Journal of Democracy* 18 (1): 143–56.

Helliwell, John F. 2019. "How to Open Doors to Happiness." In *Global Happiness and Wellbeing Policy Report* 2019, Global Happiness Council, 9–26.

Helliwell, John F., and Haifang Huang. 2008. "How's Your Government? International Evidence Linking Good Government and Well-being." *British Journal of Political Science* 38 (4): 595–619.

Helliwell, John F., Haifang Huang, Shawn Grover, and Shun Wang. 2014. "Good Governance and National Well-being: What are the Linkages?" OECD Working Papers on Public Governance No 25. doi: 10.1787/5jxv9f651hvj-en

Helliwell, John F., Haifang Huang, Shawn Grover, and Shun Wang. 2018. "Empirical Linkages between Good Governance and National Well-being." *Journal of Comparative Economics* 46 (4): 1332–46.

Helliwell, John F., Haifang Huang, and Shun Wang. 2014. "Social Capital and Well-being in Times of Crisis." *Journal of Happiness Studies* 15 (1): 145–62.

Helliwell, John F., Haifang Huang, and Shun Wang. 2018. "New Evidence on Trust and Well-being." In *The Oxford Handbook of Social and Political Trust*, edited by Eric M. Uslaner, 409–46. New York: Oxford University Press.

Helliwell, John F., Haifang Huang, and Shun Wang. 2019. "Changing World Happiness." In *World Happiness Report 2013*, edited by John F. Helliwell, Richard Layard, and Jeffrey D. Sachs, 11–46. New York: UN Sustainable Development Solutions Network.

Helliwell, John F., Richard Layard, and Jeffrey D. Sachs, eds. 2012. *World Happiness Report*. New York: UN Sustainable Development Solutions Network.

Helliwell, John F., Richard Layard, and Jeffrey D. Sachs, eds. 2019. *World Happiness Report 2019*. New York: UN Sustainable Development Solutions Network.

Kaufmann, Daniel, Aart Kraay, and Pablo Zoido-Lobaton. 1999. "Governance Matters." *Policy Research Working Paper no. 2196*. Washington, D.C.: The World Bank.

Nichols, Stafford, and R. J. Reinhart. 2019. "Well-Being Inequality May Tell Us More about Life Than Income." Gallup Blog, March 14, 2019. https://news.gallup.com/opinion/gallup/247754/wellbeing-inequality-may-tell-life-income.aspx

Nikolova, Milena. 2016. "Minding the Happiness Gap: Political Institutions and Perceived Quality of Life in Transition." *European Journal of Political Economy* 45: 129–48.

OECD. 2013. *OECD Guidelines on Measuring Subjective Well-being*. Paris: OECD Publishing. http://www.oecd.org/statistics/Guidelines%20on%20Measuring%20Subjective%20Well-being.pdf

Ott, Jan C. 2010. "Good Governance and Happiness in Nations: Technical Quality Precedes Democracy and Quality Beats Size." *Journal of Happiness Studies* 11 (3): 353–68.

Ott, Jan C. 2011. "Government and Happiness in 130 Nations: Good Governance Fosters Higher Level and More Equality of Happiness." *Social Indicators Research* 102 (1): 3–22.

Ott, Jan C. 2015. "Impact of Size and Quality of Governments on Happiness: Financial Insecurity as a Key-Problem in Market-Democracies." *Journal of Happiness Studies* 16 (6): 1639–47.

Ovaska, Tomi, and Ryo Takashima. 2010. "Does a Rising Tide Lift All the Boats? Explaining the National Inequality of Happiness." *Journal of Economic Issues* 44 (1): 205–24.

Peasgood, Tessa, Derek Foster, and Paul Dolan. 2019. "Priority Setting in Healthcare through the Lens of Happiness." In *Global Happiness and Wellbeing Policy Report* 2019, Global Happiness Council, 27–52.

Persson, Anna, and Bo Rothstein. 2015. "It's My Money: Why Big Government May Be Good Government." *Comparative Politics* 47 (2): 231–49.

Pickett, Kate E., and Richard G. Wilkinson. 2015. "Income Inequality and Health: A Causal Review." *Social Science & Medicine* 128: 316–26.

Ram, Rati. 2009. "Government Spending and Happiness of the Population: Additional Evidence from Large Cross-Country Samples." *Public Choice* 138 (3/4): 483–90.

Rodríguez-Pose, Andrés, and Kristina Maslauskaite. 2012. "Can Policy Make Us Happier? Individual Characteristics, Socio-Economic Factors and Life Satisfaction in Central and Eastern Europe." *Cambridge Journal of Regions, Economy and Society* 5 (1): 77–96.

Rothstein, Bo, and Eric M. Uslaner. 2005. "All for All: Equality, Corruption, and Social trust." *World Politics* 58 (1): 41–72.

Seligman, Martin, and Alejandro Adler. 2019. "Positive Education." In *Global Happiness and Wellbeing Policy Report* 2019, Global Happiness Council, 53–72.

Stiglitz, Joseph, Amartya K. Sen, and Jean-Paul Fitoussi. 2009. *The Measurement of Economic Performance and Social Progress Revisited: Reflections and Overview*. Paris: Commission on the Measurement of Economic Performance and Social Progress.

Stutzer, Alois, and Bruno S. Frey. 2006. "Political Participation and Procedural Utility: An Empirical Study." *European Journal of Political Research* 45 (3): 391–418.

Tavits, Margit. 2008. "Representation, Corruption, and Subjective Well-being." *Comparative Political Studies* 41 (12): 1607–30.

Ura, Karma, Sabina Alkire, Tshoki Zangmo, and Karma Wangdi. 2015. *Provisional Findings of 2015 GNH Survey.* Thimphu, Bhutan: Centre for Bhutan Studies & GNH Research.

Wahman, Michael, Jan Teorell, and Axel Hadenius. 2013. Authoritarian Regime Types Revisited: Updated Data in Comparative Perspective. *Contemporary Politics* 19 (1): 19–34.

Ward, George. 2019a. "Happiness and Voting Behaviour." In *World Happiness Report 2013*, edited by John F. Helliwell, Richard Layard, and Jeffrey D. Sachs, 47–66. New York: UN Sustainable Development Solutions Network.

Ward, George. 2019b. "Happiness and Voting: Evidence from Four Decades of Elections in Europe." *American Journal of Political Science.* https://doi.org/10.1111/ajps.12492

Whiteley, Paul, Harold D. Clarke, David Sanders, and Marianne C. Stewart. 2010. "Government Performance and Life Satisfaction in Contemporary Britain." *The Journal of Politics* 72 (3): 733–46.

Yamamura, Eiji. 2011. "The Influence of Government Size on Economic Growth and Life Satisfaction: A Case Study from Japan." *Japanese Economy* 38 (4): 28–64.

CHAPTER 29

....

GOVERNANCE BEYOND THE STATE

Social Institutions and Service Delivery

....

RUTH CARLITZ AND ELLEN LUST

INTRODUCTION

....

THE past two decades have seen a "good governance" agenda rise to prominence among both scholars and practitioners. This trend—visualized in Figure 29.1, which depicts the frequency of the term in all books in Google's English text corpora[1]—reflects two phenomena that serve to reinforce each other. First, since the 1990s international development practitioners have increasingly realized that initiatives that looked good on paper frequently failed due to gaps in policy implementation (Rakner 2017). This shift in thinking led international financial institutions such as the World Bank and the International Monetary Fund

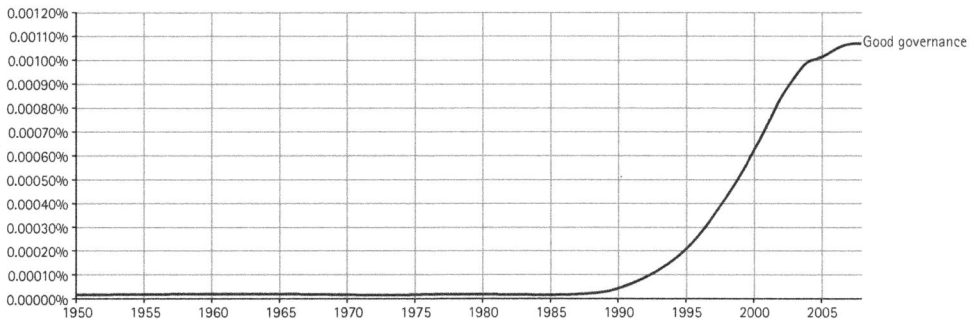

FIGURE 29.1 Frequency of term "good governance" in all books in Google's English text corpora, 1950–2008

---

[1] https://books.google.com/ngrams

to focus on governance reforms as a linchpin of their development assistance programs. At the same time, social scientists were becoming increasingly dissatisfied with their inability to describe and explain the "real world" (Jessop 1998). This motivated a number of disciplinary reorientations, including the rise of new institutional economics. In shifting their focus to institutions—i.e. "the humanly devised constraints that shape human interaction" (North 1990, 3)—economists paved the way for political scientists to develop new research agendas examining the form and functioning of state institutions, and the implications of institutional variation for a range of outcomes.

A fundamental premise of this line of thinking is that when the state performs well, a number of positive consequences will follow as a result. Scholars understand sound state policies, efficient administration, and control of state corruption as the engines of economic development (Knack and Keefer 1995; La Porta et al. 1999). Contexts characterized by high quality of government (QoG) are also thought to perform better when it comes to providing public services. Recent empirical work suggests QoG may be even more important than democracy and GDP per capita when it comes to explaining cross-national variation in access to safe water, child nutrition, quality healthcare, and access to information (Halleröd et al. 2013).

However, state institutions are not the sole determinants of development outcomes, particularly the quality of service provision. Scholars have increasingly recognized this, highlighting the role of nonstate actors such as NGOs (Brass et al. 2018; Bueno 2018; MacLean and Brass 2015), sectarian organizations (Cammett 2014), and unofficial arms of political parties (Thachil 2014) in complementing state governance and providing services. The most comprehensive effort in this regard is likely Post, Bronsoler, and Salman (2017), who develop a descriptive typology of "hybrid" local public goods regimes, or systems in which both state and nonstate actors contribute to provision. Their framework emphasizes two dimensions: the type of state involvement (direct versus indirect provision), and the degree of formal state penetration. The politics of producing local public goods, they argue, takes on distinct forms depending on the configuration of actors and roles. For instance, in "state dominant" systems, where the state is the main service provider and provides services effectively, the politics of service production and allocation is likely to be affected by factors such as the number of political parties and levels of political competition or decentralization. On the other hand, studies of "independent" provision, where the state is relatively absent, require theorization and measurement tailored to contexts where nonstate actors provide most services, often while being informally regulated by state agents.

Understanding the role that nonstate actors play in delivering public services is an important contribution. To date, however, there has been relatively little attention paid to nonstate (social) *institutions,* or, "the rules—written or unwritten—that govern social relations within a community, the rewards of compliance, and the costs of transgression" (Lust and Rakner 2018, 278).[2] Importantly, social institutions can influence the nature of service provision and contribute to variation in outcomes, even when state actors are the predominant providers of services.

[2] Notable exceptions include MacLean (2010), Tsai (2007), Singh (2015), and Lust and Rakner (2018).

Thus, in this chapter, we highlight the role of social institutions, exploring how they affect governance and service delivery in four key service sectors: education, electricity, health, and water. These services have been singled out to receive global funding and policy priority through the Sustainable Development Goals (SDGs)[3] and their predecessors, the Millennium Development Goals. We focus on low- and middle-income countries, given how important public services are for the lives of people in these settings and the consensus on their priority by the international development community.[4]

In many ways, our focus is in line with the work of Elinor Ostrom (1990), who paid particular attention to how communities designed and enforced rules in their attempts to solve common pool resource problems. Like Ostrom, we note that the rules governing social interactions can be exercised through formal procedures (e.g., written, or "parchment," rules) or informal (e.g., unwritten) ones, as is often the case with expectations regarding obligations to kin, elders, or other actors, norms of reciprocity, etc. (Ostrom 1990, 67; Lust 2018). However, while Ostrom focuses on community governance as a *substitute* for state institutions, we see social institutions at times as interacting with state institutions to shape behavior. Social institutions may influence governance and service provision directly, as when rules over managing irrigation systems regulate water use, or tithing and religious duties to provide for the poor facilitate basic service provision. But social institutions can also interact with, or affect, the ways in which state institutions influence service provision. Indeed, what is frequently labeled "corruption" and "clientelism" may be better understood as the interaction between the social institutions requiring individuals to favor kin or coethnics and the state institution of elections as a means of selecting representatives and holding them accountable.[5] In many contexts, it is the two sets of institutions together that drive voting patterns and subsequent distribution of resources.

---

[3] In particular, Goals 3, 4, 6, and 7 define targets related to the improvement of these services to be achieved by 2030. The cross-cutting nature of the SDG framework also recognizes their importance to the achievement of other goals (United Nations 2015)

[4] We used the Scopus API to identify relevant literature on governance of each of these sectors in low- and middle-income countries. Specifically, we identified articles where the words "water," "health," "education," or "electricity" appear in combination with the words "governance," "institutions," "accountability," "representation," or "community monitoring" in the title, abstract, or keywords of articles published in 14 top Political Science, Economics, and Development Studies journals. The journals are: *Quarterly Journal of Economics, Journal of Political Economy, American Economic Review, American Political Science Review, American Journal of Political Science, Perspectives on Politics, World Development, Journal of Development Economics, Journal of Development Studies, Economic Development and Cultural Change, Journal of African Economics, World Bank Research Observer, Development Policy Review,* and *Public Administration and Development*. We then manually excluded articles that focused exclusively on the governance of service delivery in high-income countries as well as those that did not deal directly with household-level service delivery (e.g. articles on health insurance or renewable energy). We supplemented this with select additional articles and books that concerned the governance of service delivery by nonstate institutions. This yielded 20 works pertaining to education, 10 on electricity, 12 pertaining to health, and 17 on water provision. Note that in a number of cases, an article that came up as a result of a search in one sector ended up being relevant for multiple sectors. In such cases we only count the article for the sector for which it first appeared—that is, we do not double-count articles. The full list of works reviewed is available upon request.

[5] This line of reasoning is in keeping with Peter Ekeh (1975)'s notion of "two publics" in postcolonial Africa. He argues that while the "civic public" structures formal state interactions, people's loyalties tend to lie with the "primordial public." Such divided loyalties in turn can engender tribalism and corruption.

Thus, this chapter focuses on how social institutions influence service provision, both directly and indirectly. We show how they can affect the targeting of goods and services; the information that citizens have regarding service delivery; and the willingness or ability of citizens to make demands for improved services. We conclude by proposing a research agenda that more fully incorporates social institutions. This is key to identify the drivers of improved service delivery and to more accurately understand the relationship between social institutions, state capacity, and quality of government.

SOCIAL INSTITUTIONS AND SERVICE DELIVERY

An increasingly robust literature on the comparative politics of service delivery in developing countries provides important insights into the substantial differences we frequently observe across and within countries. Lieberman's (2018) recent review summarizes some of the main findings emerging from this literature. First, democracies tend to spend more and generally provide more public services than do autocratic regimes, *ceteris paribus*. Second, ethnic heterogeneity has been shown to undermine public goods provision, especially when ethnic identity is socially or politically salient. One reason for this may be the tendency of ruling political regimes in many African countries to allocate public goods in favor of their coethnics, rather than targeting services based on need (Burgess et al. 2015; Franck and Rainer 2012). Furthermore, ethnic diversity can hinder effective provision of goods that are highly dependent upon collective action within communities. Lieberman (2018) also highlights how the structure of governance conditions public service delivery, particularly regarding whether services are delivered through decentralized means. While decentralization reforms were enacted in large part with the goal of improving service delivery, there is mixed evidence of their ability to do so. Finally, international influences—particularly foreign aid and donor-driven reforms—are shown to have a positive impact on service delivery in terms of mobilizing resources and encouraging policy responses. However, the impact of specific global initiatives has been harder to identify and remains an area to be studied in further detail.

While extant research on the comparative politics of service delivery is enlightening, the drivers of access to and quality of service provision are frequently not uniform across services. For instance, while there is substantial evidence for a link between democracy and education provision across countries (Brown 1999; Kaufman and Segura-Ubiergo 2001; Brown and Hunter 2004; Stasavage 2005), the relationship between democracy and public health is much less apparent. There is some evidence that democracy is associated with better access to clean water (Lake and Baum 2001) but not necessarily with access to sanitation services (McGuire 2010). Furthermore, regime type appears to have little bearing on governments' responses to HIV/AIDS (Lieberman 2007, 2009).

We also frequently observe considerable variation in access to and quality of public services *within* countries. For instance, Graetz et al. (2018) show that despite marked progress in educational attainment from 2000 to 2015 across Africa, substantial differences persist within countries across locations and by gender. Moreover, these differences have widened in many countries, particularly across the Sahel. Similarly, a recent study from Tanzania finds significant subnational variation for rural care in birth outcomes, health systems inputs, and contextual indicators (Armstrong et al. 2016). Focusing on the Middle East, Brixi, Lust, and Woolcock (2015) find notable differences in access, quality, and satisfaction with services, including education, electricity, health, sanitation, security, and roads. Service delivery not only varies by gender, locality, and class, but as the case of Tunisia shows, individuals evaluate the quality of services differently across different sectors (Brixi, Lust, and Woolcock 2015, 58–9).

What explains why we see such variation? A small but growing literature considers how subnational differences in the abovementioned factors and other aspects of state institutions affect the quality of service provision within countries. For instance, studying Tanzanian districts, Rosenzweig (2015) finds that greater local electoral competition leads to substantially greater access to local public goods. Looking within Russia, Rosenberg, Kozlov, and Libman (2018) find that in poor regions, political pluralism and competition have an adverse impact on health, whereas in rich regions, political pluralism and competition produce better results. However, such explanations still leave a considerable amount of variation unexplained. Our review therefore focuses on the role of social institutions, highlighting factors that have largely been overlooked in the literature that focuses primarily on the state's role in service provision. We do not expect that social institutions explain all of the variance we see across service sectors, communities, or countries; however, as we demonstrate, there is reason to believe that social institutions are an important source of variation and deserving of further attention.

Examining governance and outcomes in the education, electricity, health, and water sectors, we consider three sets of explanations. First, we examine how social institutions can affect the targeting of goods and services. Next, we describe how these institutions condition the information that citizens have about the quality and nature of service delivery. Finally, we explain how social institutions affect the willingness and ability of citizens to make demands for improved services. For each, we consider how these institutions might explain sub- and cross-national variation, as well as variation across service sectors.

Targeting

Scholars have only somewhat recently begun to investigate distributive politics in low-income countries (Golden and Min 2013), with studies centered primarily on the role of state institutions and actors in targeting service provision. Political incentives help to explain which services governments prioritize, and which constituents receive services. While scholars have paid some attention to how social identities and expectations shape service provision, more research needs to be done to examine explicitly the role of social institutions and how this role may vary across time and space.

A growing body of work provides evidence of resources being distributed in a manner consistent with political incentives shaped by state institutions. For instance, in many low- and middle-income countries, ruling parties reward supporters, while punishing those that defect to the opposition (Carlitz 2017; Weinstein 2011; Magaloni 2006; Blaydes 2011).

State institutions also influence which service sectors receive attention. From a politician's point of view, more visible aspects of service delivery should receive priority, particularly before elections. As such, processes of state governance are more likely to influence *access* to a given service rather than determine their *quality*. For example, politicians frequently promote investing in building schools and clinics, but do not necessarily train teachers or health workers to staff these facilities and ultimately provide quality services. Combes (2016) provides compelling evidence of this phenomenon in Kenya, where local politicians allocate resources to constructing new dispensaries but construction is rarely completed. His interview data shows that local politicians acknowledge their electoral motivation to provide visible health services. Harding and Stasavage (2014) show that increased electoral competition has prompted African governments to abolish school fees (a more visible policy outcome), but has had less of an impact on the provision of school supplies and school quality. This appears to be precisely because executive actions related to these latter policies are more difficult to monitor and thus less likely to foster electoral support.

Conversely, when crises are highly visible and costly, policymakers have an incentive to change policies and are frequently better able to rally the public behind their proposed policy solutions, thereby concentrating power to overcome traditional veto points. For example, Murillo and Le Foulon (2006) document how Chile's 1998–99 electricity crisis was visible and costly enough to generate public pressure on policymakers to change the status quo and generate opportunities for a technical reform of the sector.

The factors influencing the targeting of service provision go beyond state institutions, however. In many low- and middle-income countries, the relevant constituencies targeted for favoritism in distributive allocations are groups formed around socially constructed identities, such as ethnic or religious groups, rather than organized political parties (Golden and Min 2013). For example, Franck and Rainer (2012) find that ethnic favoritism is an important determinant of education and health outcomes—specifically infant mortality—in sub-Saharan Africa. Their results suggest that people who share the ethnicity of the leaders of the 18 African countries in their sample enjoy significantly higher rates of primary school attendance, completion, and literacy, and lower rates of infant mortality. Relatedly, Kramon and Posner (2013) study ethnic favoritism in six African countries and find that coethnics of the President are more likely to finish primary school in Kenya and Malawi, more likely to survive their first year in Benin and Malawi, and more likely to have access to improved water sources and household electricity in Zambia. Identities other than ethnicity can also structure clientelist exchanges and the distribution of state resources. For instance, in Jordan, and elsewhere in the Middle East and North Africa, tribal and family ties structure expectations over exchange, ultimately influencing electoral politics and the distribution of services (Kao 2015; Lust 2009; Lust-Okar 2006). Meanwhile, connections, networks, and relations in Lebanon, often shaped around sectarian identities, influence service provision (Stel and Naudé 2016; Cammett 2014: Cammett and Issar 2010).

The motivations for distributing resources to groups formed around socially constructed identities are deeply rooted in social institutions. The predominant explanations for ethnic favoritism in the distribution of state resources derive from instrumentalist theories of ethnic voting (Ferree 2006; Ichino and Nathan 2013; Posner 2005; Wantchekon 2003). As Carlson (2015) explains, such models reflect political contexts in which voters and politicians participate in clientelist exchanges structured along ethnic lines. She points out that ethnicity has several advantages as a social cleavage along which to make clientelist bargains, which require that clients actually vote for their designated patrons—something difficult to enforce in the presence of a secret ballot—and that patrons follow through and deliver the goods to their designated clients. The ascriptive nature of ethnic identity and the ability of tight social networks to police their own members helps to promote credibility and enforcement of the clientelist exchange on both sides.

Habyarimana et al. (2007) identify two families of mechanisms that suggest social institutions around ethnicity may promote targeting. The first of these is other-regarding preferences, or the idea that individuals attach positive utility to the welfare of their fellow coethnics but no utility (or negative utility) to the welfare of non-coethnics. We contend that these preferences are borne out of and reinforced, at least in part, by social rules that oblige individuals to benefit coethnics above others. The second family of mechanisms more explicitly focuses on social institutions, positing that people will behave differently with coethnics vs. non-coethnics; specifically, coethnics share norms of reciprocity and the ability to sanction the failure to cooperate. This can make it easier for voters to hold coethnic politicians accountable through informal channels.

Moreover, social institutions shape targeting of service provision in ways that go beyond clientelism. Branisa, Klasen, and Ziegler (2013) find that social institutions around gender inequality, including rules that shape women's decision-making power,[6] help to explain cross-national variation in female secondary education, fertility rates, and child mortality. Social institutions appear to shape the extent to which education and health resources are targeted at women and men, thereby helping to explain subnational and cross-national variation in service provision.

Finally, there is reason to believe that social institutions also contribute to cross-sectoral variation in service delivery. In their study of ethnic favoritism, Kramon and Posner (2013) point out that inferences about ethnic favoritism may depend on the country and the outcome one chooses to analyze—that is, coethnics do not always favor their own, or may only do so with respect to certain services in certain contexts. We anticipate that social institutions may be driving such variation. Rules regarding in-group favoritism or clientelistic exchanges vary across countries, and within them. More work needs to be done to thoroughly examine these institutions, and to understand how and when they impact service delivery.

Information

Beyond conditioning the provision and targeting practices of state and other authorities, social institutions also affect the information that citizens have about the nature and quality of service provision. This is important given the considerable research on accountability highlighting the role that information can play in allowing citizens to demand and receive public goods. The underlying notion is that citizens can monitor and hold accountable public service providers and state officials when they possess information on the quantity and

---

[6] The authors measure gendered social institutions with the Social Institution and Gender Index (SIGI), which includes the following sub-indices (and measures): Family Code (including parental authority, inheritance, early marriage, and polygamy), Civil Liberties (including freedom of movement and freedom of dress), Physical Integrity (including violence against women and female genital mutilation), son preference (including gender bias in mortality), Ownership Rights (including women's access to land, women's access to bank loans, and women's access to property other than land). For more information, see OECD Development Centre (2019).

quality of service provision, their rights as citizens, and the processes of provision (Keefer and Khemani 2005; Mani and Mukand 2007; Besley 2007).

These ideas about the nature of accountability for service provision received a boost with the publication of the World Bank's influential 2004 *World Development Report (WDR)*. The *WDR* distinguished two forms of accountability: a traditional "long route," through which citizens delegate authority to political representatives, who in turn influence service provision through management of the bureaucracy and a "short route," linking citizens directly to service providers through various oversight, voice, and exit mechanisms (World Bank 2003). Development specialists and scholars have promoted the "short route" in contexts where the "long route" is seen as dysfunctional due to the absence of programmatic parties competing for people's votes, a lack of open and informed public debate, and constraints on the functioning of democracy (Joshi and Houtzager 2012). The articulation of the "short route" has motivated a raft of "social accountability" (SA) initiatives designed to promote citizen-led efforts to monitor and demand (Joshi 2017). Most initiatives have aimed at enhancing information and monitoring, and studies examining their impact have focused on administrative and political factors that shape information access. Yet, the literature suggests that social institutions play an important role as well.

Perhaps the most influential SA initiative in health is the Ugandan community-based monitoring experiment analyzed by Björkman and Svensson (2009). A year after the intervention, their study found that treatment communities were more involved in monitoring and health workers appeared to exert a greater effort. This generated substantial increases in utilization and improved health outcomes including reduced child mortality and increased child weight. Subsequent randomized control trials (RCTs) of SA initiatives, many of which focused specifically on the provision of information, have had mixed results. Some have demonstrated that SA initiatives have reduced provider absenteeism and improved service provision outcomes (Sebert Kuhlmann et al. 2017), while other studies have found null results (Arkedis et al. 2019; Joshi 2014; Grossman Platas and Rodden 2018; and Lieberman, Posner, and Tsai 2014). Notably, a recent near replication of Björkman and Svensson (2009) finds that the intervention had only a modest positive impact on treatment quality and patient satisfaction, and the community monitoring intervention had *no effect* on utilization rates or health outcomes (including child mortality). These authors also find no evidence that the channel through which the intervention affected treatment quality was citizen monitoring (Raffler, Posner, and Parkerson 2020).

To some extent, such inconsistent findings may be explained by differences across service sectors. The degree of *information asymmetry*, which can limit the ability of citizens to make choices based on an evaluation of the quality and efficiency of the services offered (Batley and Mcloughlin 2015), may be most pronounced in highly professionalized domains where technical expertise is required to deliver high-quality services, and to know when quality services are being provided. For example, Das and Hammer (2014) characterize healthcare as a "credence good," reflecting substantial information asymmetries between patients and providers. Electricity provision arguably requires a similarly high degree of technical expertise. The relative *visibility* of different public goods also influences the extent to which citizens can assess provider effort based on observed outcomes (Mani and Mukand 2007). Finally, services may vary in their *complexity*—the extent to which multiple factors that affect the outcome may obscure individuals' information on provider effort. Extant evidence, focused on voters' responses to provision of different goods, suggests that such differences affect monitoring and accountability. Analyzing survey data from Kenya, Harding and Stasavage (2014) show that citizens condition their voting intentions on improved service delivery outcomes for which executive action is verifiable, but not for outcomes where the influence of politicians is more indirect. Harding (2015) further shows how vote shares for the President in Ghana respond positively to changes in the condition of local roads—an outcome that is clearly attributable to central government effort in the Ghanaian context. On the other hand, numbers of classrooms, textbooks, seats, school services, and facilities—outcomes over which the central government has less clear influence—did not appear to influence vote shares.

However, sectoral differences do not fully explain the inconsistent findings regarding information and service provision. The null findings of Raffler, Posner, and Parkerson's (2020) near replication of the Björkman and Svensson (2009) health intervention cannot be explained by sectoral differences. Similarly, Joshi (2014) notes that very similar initiatives intended to promote demands for accountability and improve educational outcomes have had different impacts despite being implemented in similar (macro) country contexts. She suggests that such mixed findings reflect issues of context at the local level.

Social institutions provide a useful lens on how the "local context" affects the implementation of social accountability initiatives. To understand how they may do so, we consider a model of information and service provision set forth by Lieberman, Posner, and Tsai (2014). Reflecting on the null findings from a study of transparency and accountability in the education sector in Kenya, they argue that scholars and policymakers need to adopt a more nuanced, and somewhat more sober, understanding of how information can affect service provision:

> Specifically, we suggest that for information to generate citizen action it must be understood; it must cause people to update their prior beliefs in some manner; and it must speak to an issue that people prioritize and also believe is their responsibility to address. In addition, the people at whom the information is directed must know what actions to take and possess the skills for taking these actions; they must believe that authorities will respond to their actions; and, to the extent that the outcome in question requires collective action, they must believe that others in the community will act as well. And, of course, they cannot already be doing everything that is possible for them to do (Lieberman et al. 2014, 70).

There is reason to believe that social institutions influence a number of these linkages. First, they may affect the extent to which individuals update their beliefs in the face of new information. In their influential discussion of the mechanisms underlying ethnicity and service provision, Habyarimana et al. (2007) argue that coethnics may perceive each other to share tastes, and conversely, different ethnic groups may perceive each other to care about different types of public goods. For example, one who cares about education may anticipate that coethnic teachers are similarly interested in their children's education, and non-coethnic teachers less so. Information can cause people to update such beliefs—demonstrating, for instance, that coethnic teachers are less committed to children's education than previously believed, or that non-coethnic teachers are more committed to their education. Studies in psychology (following Festinger 1962) suggest two potential responses when individuals face new, conflicting (dissonant) information: they may dismiss the information, thereby maintaining their beliefs, or they may update their expectations. In either case, the expectations—which are based on social institutions and may vary in ways not yet incorporated into analyses—affect the impact of information on accountability and service provision.

Social institutions may also affect citizens' perceived efficacy and thus the likelihood that "they believe the authorities will respond to their actions; and to the extent that the outcome in question requires collective action . . . that others in the community will act as well" (Lieberman, Posner, and Tsai 2014, 70). Again, Habyarimana et al's. (2007) discussion is helpful. They point to the technology mechanism, which suggests that ethnically homogenous communities are better at promoting collective action given higher levels of efficacy and findability of coethnics in social networks. Information should be expected to be more effective where such institutions are present.

The social institutions that aid collective action may be based on tribe or locality, as well as ethnic identity. For example, a case study of health centers in Jordan found strong observational evidence that tribal leaders worked with health centers, youth leaders, and others to improve healthcare (Brixi, Lust, and Woolcock 2015). Similarly, Tsai (2007) shows how social institutions allow villagers in China to enforce local government obligations in some settings. She finds that public goods and services such as running water and upgraded classrooms were more likely to be found in villages where "solidary groups" such as churches and fraternal organizations exist. Such groups are both *encompassing* (open to everyone) and *embedded* (incorporating local officials), and thus function as informal accountability institutions. This helps to explain the significant observed variation in the quality of local public goods provision in China.

Conversely, information may have little effect when social institutions repress community action. Our review of the literature on the governance of service provision revealed a number of ways in which social institutions can determine whose voice gets heard, and who is silenced. We discuss this further in the following section, showing how social institutions can condition the expectations that citizens have of service providers, and the likelihood that citizens make demands for improved service delivery.

CITIZEN DEMAND AND EXPECTATIONS

If citizens have low expectations or undervalue services, then they are less likely to use information to hold service providers accountable. Additionally, such circumstances make it difficult for public officials and service providers to target services to them. We therefore need to consider how social institutions can affect the expression of demand for improved service delivery.

To some extent, demand is driven by the type of service. Services differ in the *frequency* and *predictability* with which individuals encounter them. For instance, drinking water is a basic, daily need for all people; in contrast, many people only encounter education if they have children, or health services when they need treatment, particularly in less developed settings, where access to and take-up of preventative healthcare is much lower than in richer countries (Dupas 2011). Services which are encountered frequently and with predictability should have higher unity of demand, serving to increase users' power over providers (Batley and Mcloughlin 2015). Services also differ in the availability of *exit options*. In the case of the water sector, for instance, exit options might include the existence of renewable surface water resources. Surface water can subject water users to health risks they could avoid by using "improved" sources provided by the state, but the residents of many poorer countries tend to lack awareness of such risks.

Beyond service characteristics, social institutions have an impact on the expression of demands. Bicchieri and Noah (2003) highlight the importance of socially conditional preferences, which characterize situations in which people prefer to engage in a given behavior because others are engaging in the behavior, or because others think that they should engage in the behavior. These preferences are based on empirical and/or normative expectations about people in their "reference network," composed of those individuals whose behaviors and beliefs matter to their choices. The composition of different reference networks is often a function of social institutions. For instance, as discussed above, "solidary groups" in China affect who is perceived to be accountable to whom (Tsai 2007). Similarly, Diaz-Cayeros, Magaloni, and Ruiz-Euler (2014) show that indigenous communities in Mexico that have chosen to govern themselves through *usos y costumbres*[7] experienced improvements in the quality of electricity, education, and sewerage. The authors attribute this in part to the collective decision-making processes in these communities.

The norms transmitted through different reference networks can also be a function of social institutions. A poignant example of this is found in India. Examining education in Northern India, Johnson and Bowles (2010) argue that families are reluctant to invest in girls' education because "excessive education" may increase their daughters' bride prices to a point that makes them unmarriageable. The social institution of the dowry, and specifically the positive association of education and bride price, reduces investment in education and demand for improved services in this sector.

Gender can also condition the expression of demand in terms of the investments that different citizens make to access and make use of different public services. For example, Chicoine and Guzman (2017) examine a citizen-monitoring initiative at a public health clinic in rural Uganda. The program sent text messages regarding confirmed attendance of clinic staff and activities to randomly selected cell phone–owning households in the local community. Such monitoring led to an increase in clinic attendance and the receipt of medicine, and reduced the duration of illness for young children aged six and under. However, benefits were only realized for children who were the same gender as the cell phone owner, suggesting favoritism of sons by fathers, and of daughters by mothers.

Furthermore, making demands on a service provider (e.g., via what the *WDR 2004* termed the "short route of accountability") may go against socially conditioned preferences, particularly in communities where social hierarchies are strongly enforced and where service providers such as teachers or doctors are considered to be authority figures. For instance, women and girls tend to have primary responsibility for the daily collection of water in many contexts (Graham, Hirai, and Kim 2016). As such, they are more likely to be aware of the particular service delivery challenges affecting their communities. However, engrained social norms frequently prevent women from advocating individually or collectively for improved services, while other (adult male) end-users may be insufficiently aware of problems related to water provision (Mason, Batley, and Harris, 2014). For example, Nagrah, Chaudhry, and Giordano (2016) note that despite their central role in agricultural labor, women in Pakistan are not as engaged in the irrigation-related community meetings or activities.

---

[7] A traditional form of participatory democracy given full legal standing in 1995.

As another example of how social institutions condition the expression of demand, Schnegg's (2016) study of pastoralists in rural Namibia finds that equal contributions to communal water supplies (a "flat rate rule") is the dominant institutional arrangement in many communities. This is in spite of the fact that the majority of households would benefit from a "per-head-of-cattle rule," where contributions are proportional to the number of livestock a household owns. However, wealthier households prefer the flat rate rule since they would pay proportionally more under the "per-head-of-cattle rule." Since community elders typically come from wealthier households, they use their social status to push for institutional arrangements that favor them. Respect for elders can make it difficult even for elected officials to go against the will of the older, wealthier minority. Dense kinship networks and normative expectations also contribute to maintaining the inequitable status quo. Furthermore, per-household contributions are the norm in other arenas of social life, so it is natural to many communities to apply them to water.

Social institutions can also constrain the expression of demand for improved service delivery in terms by generating well-founded fear of consequences for raising one's voice (Fox 2015). For example, Pande (2015) documents violent reprisals against information-requestors acting in accordance with India's landmark Right to Information (RTI) Act. These include 50 reported cases of RTI-related deaths (including three suicides), 84 reported cases of assault, and 101 reported cases of harassment. Moreover, the likelihood that victims will follow up on a police inquiry and pursue judicial action or litigation largely depends on their social and economic background (i.e., caste and class). This is a chilling example of how one of India's most influential social institutions (caste) conditions the expression of demand.

The expectations that citizens have of service providers, and the consequent demands they make, are not static. As Joshi observes, "If one views social accountability as part of a longer political process of citizen engagement with the state, then histories of prior engagement will shape expectations of stakeholders, expectations that will change over time" (2014, 32). The same can be said of changing expectations and social institutions, as individuals in communities engage with each other over time. This suggests the importance of considering when and how social institutions evolve in ways that may influence the likelihood or ability of citizens to make demands for improved service delivery.

Conclusions

This chapter turns our attention to the ways in which social institutions shape service provision and development outcomes. We explore how social institutions influence targeting—that is, which communities enjoy higher quality service provision and which service sectors receive the most attention; how these institutions affect the information that individuals have about service provision, thus influencing their ability to hold providers accountable; and how they shape citizens' demands and expectations. Our argument is not that social institutions are the *sole* factor affecting service provision; to the contrary, we note how state institutions and the distinct nature of different services help explain outcomes. We argue that social institutions are an important, yet undertheorized, factor affecting service provision outcomes, and that they are distinct from both nonstate actors and state institutions.

By highlighting the importance of social institutions, we hope to encourage an exciting research agenda. There are important questions to be asked regarding how social institutions interact with state institutions. Scholars have begun to examine the extent to which, and under what circumstances, state and nonstate actors function as complements or substitutes. More often than not, they have viewed state and nonstate realms as substitutes. For instance, Bodea and LeBas (2016) argue that people are less tax compliant when they can access nonstate goods and services that would otherwise be funded through public revenue. Brixi, Lust, and Woolcock (2015) make this implicit assumption as well, arguing that citizens fail to make demands on the state to improve public services when their needs are met by nonstate actors: thus, nonstate provision promotes weak state institutions. Similarly, Batley and Mcloughlin (2015) argue that the existence of exit options can make the exercise of voice less pressing. However, an emerging literature on hybrid political orders and "twilight institutions" suggests that state and nonstate actors may serve to complement each other (Boege, Brown, and Clements 2009; Lund 2006).

The questions of what influences service provision by state and nonstate actors, and how this varies across different service sectors, only tangentially considers the intersection of state and social *institutions*. How, and when, are the rules governing social interactions and administrative or political rules mutually compatible, and when do they conflict? How do individuals navigate tensions when they exist?

Examining the potential conflict or complementarity of state and nonstate institutions suggests the need for more nuanced thinking about state capacity and the nature of governance in different contexts. Focusing on the strength of the state, without considering governance by nonstate actors and institutions, tells us little about the overall quality of governance and outcomes. Rather, we need to study the full set of institutions shaping governance and development outcomes. Moreover, we need to recognize that the extent to which state or social institutions guide citizens' demands and expectations, the information they have, and their ability to hold state and nonstate providers accountable, may vary subnationally, and across domains. This is important both in terms of the "outputs" of governance, i.e. services that the state is often expected to provide (such as education, electricity, health, and water) as well as overarching governance qualities such as participation, transparency, and accountability.

Taking social institutions into account more explicitly in analyses of the quality of government also requires greater attention to how these institutions are constructed and evolve over time. One of the major challenges in the study of institutions is the selection problem: Are governance outcomes the result of the relationships between social and state institutions or, rather, are they driven by the conditions that give rise to these institutions? Some scholars are beginning to grapple directly with such questions. For instance, Robinson and Gottlieb (2019) argue that the matrilineal institutions, which they find are related to smaller gender gaps in participation, arose historically and relatively independently of other conditions that may influence gender differences in participation. Other scholars have paid attention to the factors that lead, for instance, to the evolution of social institutions promoting cooperation (e.g., Axelrod 1984; Bowles and Gintis 2013; Ostrom 1990). Such efforts are important, yet more research remains to be done for us to fully understand the origins and evolution of social institutions.

Engaging meaningfully with social institutions not only advances our scholarly work on governance and service provision, it also paves the way for better development programming. Much of the "good governance" literature focuses solely on the need to improve state institutions in order to improve service delivery. The dominant approaches to defining and measuring governance, and policy prescriptions emanating therefrom, tend to reflect a one-size-fits-all model of government that encourages "isomorphic mimicry," where "governments change what they look like, not what they do" (Andrews, Pritchett, and Woolcock 2013, 234). Expecting low-income countries to "catch up" with better governed Western nations that have experienced very different histories may be unrealistic (Grindle 2004). Furthermore, using development assistance to promote "good governance" of the sort that exists in present-day Western countries may fail to provide poorer countries with effective strategies for addressing the specific challenges they face (Centre for the Future State 2010).

As a corrective to this, an emerging literature on policy implementation in the developing world highlights the importance of "going with the grain" (Booth 2011; Kelsall 2008). In this spirit, Andrews, Pritchett, and Woolcock (2013) develop a new approach to "doing development" that they term Problem-Driven Iterative Adaptation (PDIA). PDIA focuses on solving locally nominated and prioritized performance problems, instead of transplanting "best practice" solutions. This approach encourages positive deviance and experimentation, instead of requiring that agents implement policies as designed. By working with, rather than against, the local context, going with the grain and PDIA inherently acknowledge the role of social institutions. However, there is still more work to be done to develop a systematic framework that elucidates specific dimensions of nonstate institutions and where they matter more or less, sheds light on what "the grain" is in different contexts, and relates this to programmatic guidance and better service provision outcomes. That is, in order to "go with the grain," we need a better understanding of what "the grain" is.

We need to consider social institutions more carefully if we are to understand the drivers of good governance and improved service delivery. Social institutions can be critical to understanding variation we observe across communities and within countries, and they can help explain differences in state capacity and the interaction between state and nonstate actors. A better understanding of social institutions can also help development specialists and policymakers craft programs that engage meaningfully with the local contexts in which policies are being implemented. In short, bringing social institutions into the study of governance represents both an important theoretical advance and a key step in developing more effective development policies.

References

Andrews, Matt, Lant Pritchett, and Michael Woolcock. 2013. "Escaping Capability Traps through Problem Driven Iterative Adaptation (PDIA)." *World Development* 51 (November): 234–44.

Arkedis, Jean, Jessica Creighton, Akshay Dixit, Archon Fung, Stephen Kosack, Dan Levy, and Courtney Tolmie. 2019. "Can Transparency and Accountability Programs Improve Health? Experimental Evidence from Indonesia and Tanzania." *HKS Faculty Research Working Paper Series* (May): RWP 19-020.

Armstrong, Corinne E., Melisa Martínez-Álvarez, Neha S. Singh, Theopista John, Hoviyeh Afnan-Holmes, Chris Grundy, Corrine W. Ruktanochai, Josephine Borghi, Moke Magoma, Georgina Msemo et al. 2016. "Subnational Variation for Care at Birth in Tanzania: Is This Explained by Place, People, Money or Drugs?" *BMC Public Health* 16 (795): 83–101.

Axelrod, Robert. 1984. *The Evolution of Cooperation*. New York: Basic Books.

Batley, Richard, and Claire Mcloughlin. 2015. "The Politics of Public Services: A Service Characteristics Approach." *World Development* 74 (October): 275–85.

Besley, Timothy. 2007. *Principled Agents?: The Political Economy of Good Government.* Oxford: Oxford University Press.

Bicchieri, Cristina, and Thomas Noah. 2003. "Applying Social Norms Theory in CATS Programming." UNICEF.

Björkman, Martina, and Jakob Svensson. 2009. "Power to the People: Evidence from a Randomized Field Experiment on Community-Based Monitoring in Uganda." *The Quarterly Journal of Economics* 124 (2): 735–69.

Blaydes, Lisa. 2011. *Elections and Distributive Politics in Mubarak's Egypt.* Cambridge: Cambridge University Press.

Bodea, Cristina, and Adrienne LeBas. 2016. "The Origins of Voluntary Compliance: Attitudes Toward Taxation in Urban Nigeria." *British Journal of Political Science* 46 (1): 215–38.

Boege, Volker, M., Anne Brown, and Kevin P Clements. 2009. "Hybrid Political Orders, Not Fragile States." *Peace Review* 21 (1): 13–21.

Booth, David. 2011. "Introduction: Working with the Grain? The Africa Power and Politics Programme." *IDS Bulletin* 42 (2): 1–10.

Bowles, Samuel, and Herbert Gintis. 2013. *A Cooperative Species: Human Reciprocity and Its Evolution*. Princeton: Princeton University Press.

Brass, Jennifer N., Wesley Longhofer, Rachel S. Robinson, and Allison Schnable. 2018. "NGOs and International Development: A Review of Thirty-Five Years of Scholarship." *World Development* 112 (December): 136–49.

Branisa, Boris, Stephan Klasen, and Maria Ziegler. 2013. "Gender Inequality in Social Institutions and Gendered Development Outcomes." *World Development* 45 (May): 252–68.

Brixi, Hana, Ellen Lust, and Michael Woolcock. 2015. *Making Trust, Voice, and Incentives.* Washington, D.C.: World Bank Group.

Brown, David S. 1999. "Reading, Writing, and Regime Type: Democracy's Impact on Primary School Enrollment." *Political Research Quarterly* 52 (4): 681–707.

Brown, David S., and Wendy Hunter. 2004. "Democracy and Human Capital Formation: Education Spending in Latin America, 1980 to 1997." *Comparative Political Studies* 37 (7): 842–64.

Bueno, Natália S. 2018. "Bypassing the Enemy: Distributive Politics, Credit Claiming, and Nonstate Organizations in Brazil." *Comparative Political Studies* 51 (3): 304–40.

Burgess, Robin, Remi Jedwab, Edward Miguel, Ameet Morjaria et al. 2015. "The Value of Democracy: Evidence from Road Building in Kenya." *The American Economic Review* 105 (6): 1817–51.

Cammett, Melani. 2014. *Compassionate Communalism: Welfare and Sectarianism in Lebanon.* Ithaca: Cornell University Press.

Cammett, Melani, and Sukriti Issar. 2010. "Bricks and Mortar Clientelism: The Political Geography of Welfare in Lebanon." *World Politics* 62 (3): 381–421.

Carlitz, Ruth D. 2017. "Money Flows, Water Trickles: Understanding Patterns of Decentralized Water Provision in Tanzania." *World Development* 93 (May): 16–30.

Carlson, Elizabeth. 2015. "Ethnic Voting and Accountability in Africa: A Choice Experiment In Uganda." *World Politics* 67 (April): 353–85.

Centre for the Future State. 2010. *An Upside Down View of Governance.* Brighton, UK: Institute of Development Studies.

Chicoine, Luke, and Juan Guzman. 2017. "Increasing Rural Health Clinic Utilization with SMS Updates: Evidence from a Randomized Evaluation in Uganda." *SSRN Electronic Journal.*

Combes, Nathan John. 2016. "Preventable Deaths: Children, Diarrhea, and the Politics of Oral Rehydration Solution in Kenya." Ph.D. diss. UC San Diego.

Das, Jishnu, and Jeffrey Hammer. 2014. "Quality of primary care in low-income countries: facts and economics." Annual Review of Economics 6 (1): 525–553.

Díaz-Cayeros, Alberto, Beatriz Magaloni, and Alexander Ruiz-Euler. 2014. "Traditional Governance, Citizen Engagement, and Local Public Goods: Evidence from Mexico." *World Development* 53 (January): 80–93.

Dupas, Pascaline. 2011. "Health Behavior in Developing Countries." *Annual Review of Economics* 3 (1): 425–49.

Ekeh, Peter P. 1975. "Colonialism and the two publics in Africa: A theoretical statement." *Comparative Studies in Society and History* 17 (1): 91–112.

Ferree, Karen E. 2006. "Explaining South Africa's Racial Census." *Journal of Politics* 68 (4): 803–15.

Festinger, Leon. 1962. "Cognitive Dissonance." *Scientific American* 207 (4): 93–106.

Fox, Jonathan A. 2015. "Social Accountability: What Does the Evidence Really Say?" *World Development* 72 (August): 346–61.

Franck, Raphael, and Ilia Rainer. 2012. "Does the Leader's Ethnicity Matter? Ethnic Favoritism, Education, and Health in Sub-Saharan Africa." *American Political Science Review* 106 (2): 294–325.

Golden, Miriam, and Brian Min. 2013. "Distributive Politics Around the World." *Annual Review of Political Science* 16 (1): 73–99.

Graetz, Nicholas, Joseph Friedman, Aaron Osgood-Zimmerman, Roy Burstein, Molly H. Biehl, Chloe Shields, and Jonathan F. Mosser et al. 2018. "Mapping Local Variation in Educational Attainment Across Africa". *Nature* 555 (7694): 48–53.

Graham, Jay P., Mitsuaki Hirai, and Seung-Sup Kim. 2016. "An Analysis of Water Collection Labor among Women and Children in 24 Sub-Saharan African Countries." *PLoS ONE* 11 (6): e0155981.

Grindle, Merilee S. 2004. "Good Enough Governance: Poverty Reduction and Reform in Developing Countries." *Governance* 17 (4): 525–48.

Grossman, Guy, Melina R. Platas, and Jonathan Rodden. 2018. "Crowdsourcing Accountability: ICT for Service Delivery." *World Development* 112 (December): 74–87.

Habyarimana, James, Macartan Humphreys, Daniel N. Posner and Jeremy M. Weinstein. 2007. "Why Does Ethnic Diversity Undermine Public Goods Provision?" *American Political Science Review* 101 (4): 709–25.

Halleröd, Björn, Bo Rothstein, Adel Daoud, and Shailen Nandy. 2013. "Bad Governance and Poor Children: A Comparative Analysis of Government Efficiency and Severe Child Deprivation in 68 Low-and Middle-Income Countries." *World Development* 48 (August): 19–31.

Harding, Robin. 2015. "Attribution and Accountability: Voting for Roads in Ghana." *World Politics* 67 (04): 656–89.

Harding, Robin, and David Stasavage. 2014. "What Democracy Does (and Doesn't Do) for Basic Services: School Fees, School Inputs, and African Elections." *Journal of Politics* 76 (1): 229–45.

Ichino, Nahomi, and Noah L. Nathan. 2013. "Crossing the Line: Local Ethnic Geography and Voting in Ghana." *American Political Science Review* 107 (2): 344–61.

Johnson, Craig, and Michael T. Bowles (2010). "Making the Grade? Private Education in Northern India." *The Journal of Development Studies* 46 (3): 485–505.

Jessop, Bob. 1998. "The Rise of Governance and the Risks of Failure: The Case of Economic Development." *International Social Science Journal* 50 (155): 29–45.

Joshi, Anuradha. 2014. "Reading the Local Context: A Causal Chain Approach to Social Accountability." *IDS Bulletin* 45 (5): 23–35.

Joshi, Anuradha. 2017. "Legal Empowerment and Social Accountability: Complementary Strategies Toward Rights-Based Development in Health?" *World Development* 99 (November): 160–72.

Joshi, Anuradha, and Peter P. Houtzager. 2012. "Widgets or Watchdogs? Conceptual Explorations in Social Accountability." *Public Management Review* 14 (2): 145–62.

Kao, Kristen E. 2015. "Ethnicity, Electoral Institutions, and Clientelism: Authoritarianism in Jordan." Ph.D. diss. UCLA.

Kaufman, Robert R., and Alex Segura-Ubiergo. 2001. "Globalization, Domestic Politics, and Social Spending in Latin America." *World Politics* 53 (4): 553–87.

Keefer, Philip, and Stuti Khemani. 2005. "Democracy, Public Expenditures, and the Poor: Understanding Political Incentives for Providing Public Services." *The World Bank Research Observer* 20 (1): 1–27.

Kelsall, Tim. 2008. "Going with the Grain in African Development?" *Development Policy Review* 26 (6): 627–55.

Knack, Stephen, and Philip Keefer. 1995. "Institutions and Economic Performance: Cross-Country Tests Using Alternative Institutional Measures." *Economics & Politics* 7 (3): 207–27.

Kramon, Eric, and Daniel N. Posner. 2013. "Who Benefits from Distributive Politics? How the Outcome One Studies Affects the Answer One Gets." *Perspectives on Politics* 11 (2): 461–74.

La Porta, Rafael, Florencio Lopez-de Silanes, Andrei Shleifer, and Robert Vishny. 1999. "The Quality of Government." *Journal of Law, Economics, and Organization* 15 (1): 222–79.

Lake, David A., and Matthew A. Baum. 2001. "The Invisible Hand of Democracy Political Control and the Provision of Public Services." *Comparative Political Studies* 34 (6): 587–621.

Lieberman, Evan S. 2007. "Ethnic Politics, Risk, and Policy-Making A Cross-National Statistical Analysis of Government Responses to HIV/AIDS." *Comparative Political Studies* 40 (12): 1407–32.

Lieberman, Evan S. 2009. *Boundaries of Contagion: How Ethnic Politics Have Shaped Government Responses to AIDS*. Princeton (N.J.): Princeton University Press.

Lieberman, Evan S. 2018. "The Comparative Politics of Service Delivery in Developing Countries." In *The Oxford Handbook of Politics of Development*, edited by Carol Lancaster and Nicholas van de Walle. Oxford: Oxford University Press.

Lieberman, Evan S., Daniel N. Posner, and Lily L. Tsai. 2014. "Does Information Lead to More Active Citizenship? Evidence from an Education Intervention in Rural Kenya." *World Development* 60 (August): 69–83.

Lund, Christian. 2006. "Twilight Institutions: An Introduction." *Development and Change* 37 (4): 673–84.

Lust, Ellen. 2009. "Legislative Elections in Authoritarian Regimes: Competitive Clientelism and Regime Stability." *Journal of Democracy* 20 (3): 122–35.

Lust, Ellen. 2018. "Layered Authority and Social Institutions: Reconsidering State-Centric Theory and Development Policy." *International Journal of Middle East Studies* 50 (2): 333–6.

Lust, Ellen, and Lise Rakner. 2018. "The Other Side of Taxation: Extraction and Social Institutions in the Developing World." *Annual Review of Political Science* 21 (1): 277–94.

Lust-Okar, Ellen. 2006. "Elections Under Authoritarianism: Preliminary Lessons from Jordan." *Democratization* 13 (3): 456–71.

MacLean, Lauren M. 2010. *Informal Institutions and Citizenship in Rural Africa: Risk and Reciprocity in Ghana and Cote d'Ivoire.* Cambridge: Cambridge University Press.

MacLean, Lauren M., and Jennifer N. Brass. 2015. "Foreign Aid, NGOs and the Private Sector: New Forms of Hybridity in Renewable Energy Provision in Kenya and Uganda." *Africa Today* 62 (1): 57–82.

Magaloni, Beatriz. 2006. *Voting for Autocracy: Hegemonic Party Survival and its Demise in Mexico.* Cambridge: Cambridge University Press.

Mani, Anandi, and Sharun Mukand. 2007. "Democracy, Visibility and Public Good Provision." Journal of Development Economics 83 (2): 506–29.

Mason, Nathaniel, Richard Batley, and Daniel Harris. 2014. *The Technical is Political: Understanding the Political Implications of Sector Characteristics for the Delivery of Drinking Water Services.* Birmingham: ODI. https://www.odi.org/publications/8254-technical-political-understanding-political-implications-sector-characteristics-delivery-sanitation

McGuire, James W. 2010. *Wealth, Health, and Democracy in East Asia and Latin America.* Cambridge: Cambridge University Press.

Murillo, Maria Victoria, and Carmen Le Foulon. 2006. "Crisis and Policymaking in Latin America: The Case of Chile's 1998–99 Electricity Crisis." *World Development* 34 (9): 1580–96.

Nagrah, Aatika, Anita M. Chaudhry, and Mark Giordano. 2016. "Collective Action in Decentralized Irrigation Systems: Evidence from Pakistan." *World Development* 84 (August): 282–98.

North, Douglass C. 1990. *Institutions, Institutional Change and Economic Performance.* Cambridge: Cambridge University Press.

OECD Development Centre. 2019. "Social Institutions and Gender Index (SIGI)." Accessed November 5, 2019. http://genderindex.org/

Ostrom, Elinor. 1990. *Governing the Commons: The Evolution of Institutions for Collective Action.* Cambridge: Cambridge University Press.

Pande, Suchi. 2015. "Dying for Information: Right to Information and Whistleblower Protection in India." *U4 Brief* 2015 (3). http://www.u4.no/publications/dying-for-information-right-to-information-and-whistleblower-protection-in-india/

Posner, Daniel N. 2005. *Institutions and Ethnic Politics in Africa.* Cambridge: Cambridge University Press.

Post, Alison E., Vivian Bronsoler, and Lana Salman. 2017. "Hybrid Regimes for Local Public Goods Provision: A Framework for Analysis." *Perspectives on Politics* 15 (4): 952–66.

Raffler, Pia, Daniel N. Posner, and Doug Parkerson. 2020. "Can Citizen Pressure be Induced to Improve Public Service Provision?" October 28. http://piaraffler.com/wp-content/uploads/2020/10/Citizen-Pressure_Oct2020.pdf

Rakner, Lise. 2017. "Governance." In *Politics in the Developing World*, ed. Peter Burnell, Vicky Randall, and Lise Rakner, 5th ed. Oxford: Oxford University Press.

Robinson, Amanda Lea, and Jessica Gottlieb. 2019. "How to Close the Gender Gap in Political Participation: Lessons from Matrilineal Societies in Africa." *British Journal of Political Science*, 1–25. doi:10.1017/S0007123418000650

Rosenberg, Dina, Vladimir Kozlov, and Alexander Libman. 2018. "Political Regimes, Income and Health: Evidence from Sub-National Comparative Method." *Social Science Research* 72: 20–37.

Rosenzweig, Steven C. 2015. "Does Electoral Competition Affect Public Goods Provision in Dominant-Party Regimes? Evidence from Tanzania." *Electoral Studies* 39 (September): 72–84.

Schnegg, Michael. 2016. "Lost in Translation: State Policies and Micro-politics of Water Governance in Namibia." *Human Ecology* 44 (2): 245–55.

Sebert Kuhlmann, Anne K., Sara Gullo, Christine Galavotti, Carolyn Grant, Maria Cavatore, and Samuel Posnock. 2017. "Women's and Health Workers' Voices in Open, Inclusive Communities and Effective Spaces (VOICES): Measuring Governance Outcomes in Reproductive and Maternal Health Programmes." *Development Policy Review* 35 (2): 289–311.

Singh, Prerna. 2015. *How Solidarity Works for Welfare: Subnationalism and Social Development in India*. Cambridge: Cambridge University Press.

Stasavage, David. 2005. "Democracy and Education Spending in Africa." *American Journal of Political Science* 49 (2): 343–58.

Stel, Nora, and Wim Naudé. 2016. "'Public–Private Entanglement': Entrepreneurship in Lebanon's Hybrid Political Order." *The Journal of Development Studies* 52 (2): 254–68.

Thachil, Tariq. 2014. "Elite Parties and Poor Voters: Theory and Evidence from India." American Political Science Review 108 (2): 454–77.

Tsai, Lily L. 2007. *Accountability Without Democracy: Solidary Groups and Public Goods Provision in Rural China*. New York, N.Y.: Cambridge University Press.

United Nations. 2015. "Transforming Our World: The 2030 Agenda for Sustainable Development." Resolution adopted by the General Assembly on 25 September 2015. http://www.un.org/ga/search/view_doc.asp?symbol=A/RES/70/1&Lang=E

Wantchekon, Leonard. 2003. "Clientelism and Voting Behavior: Evidence from a Field Experiment in Benin." *World Politics* 55 (3): 399–422.

Weinstein, Laura. 2011. "The Politics of Government Expenditures in Tanzania, 1999–2007." *African Studies Review* 54 (1): 33–57.

World Bank. 2003. *Making Services Work for Poor People*. Washington D.C.: World Bank.

PART VII

STATE STRUCTURE AND POLICY

CHAPTER 30

BUREAUCRACY AND GOVERNMENT QUALITY

CARL DAHLSTRÖM AND VICTOR LAPUENTE

INTRODUCTION

THE organization of bureaucracy is of fundamental importance to the study of government but is not always treated as such (Lægreid 2018). Most comparative studies are instead focused on the institutions shaping incentives and ultimately the behavior of politicians, such as, for example, electoral systems and political regimes. Yet, for most citizens across the globe, the public face of politics is not that of a politician but of a bureaucrat (Pepinsky, Pierskalla, and Sacks 2017).

The internal workings of the state and the incentives of public employees administrating state business and providing public services are often, despite their capital importance, overlooked by scholars of government (Finan, Olken, and Pande 2017). This is unfortunate for at least three reasons. First, the capacity of the state is limited by the reach and competence of the administration (D'Arcy and Nistotskaya 2017; Dahlström and Lapuente 2017). Second, the organization of the administration, and not least its personnel politics, can both invite and hamper opportunistic behavior from politicians as well as from bureaucrats (Miller and Whitford 2016; Grindle 2012; Lewis 2008). Third, citizens' perceptions of the quality of government is, to a large extent, a result of their interactions with public employees (Rothstein 2005). Consequently, comparativists and other students of government should try to better understand the workings, attitudes, and incentives of bureaucrats—and not only of their political masters.

This chapter offers an overview of the existing research linking bureaucrats with the quality of government. We use the term bureaucrat for the nonelected personnel working in administrative or managerial positions within the state. This includes the civil service but is not limited to it. We thus take into account all public employees, irrespective of their position within the public sector hierarchy.

We focus primarily on the role that human resources plays in bureaucracies in achieving good government (Lewis 2011). We are well aware that personnel politics is not the only significant part of a bureaucracy. Indeed, Max Weber's (1978 [1921]) definition of a bureaucracy involves other relevant aspects, such as a hierarchical organization and the routinization of tasks. These elements undoubtedly have consequences for government quality, both positive and negative. Influential economists have, for example, been mostly interested in the potentially negative aspects of a bureaucratic organization, such as red tape, as explored in James Q. Wilson's (1991) classical analysis of the American bureaucracy. Likewise, James Buchanan (1968) and William Niskanen (1971) identified the potential problem with "slack" in bureaucracies as they are monopolist markets. The theoretical and empirical research this chapter is interested in is, however, concentrated on personnel politics: how bureaucrats are recruited, promoted, dismissed, payed, and how they are in other ways incentivized. The chapter will thus be mostly concerned with the characteristics of what public administration scholars refer to as "civil service system" (Bekke and van der Meer 2000) and economists as the "personnel economics" of government (Finan, Olken, and Pande 2017).

The rest of the chapter is organized as follows: the next section describes two opposing views of what constitutes a bureaucracy's prime quality. Should it merely be an instrument for political leaders, or should it be to some extent autonomous? The answer is not self-evident and the debate is longstanding. We use the more than 75-year-old discussion between Carl Friedrich (1940) and Herman Finer (1941) to structure the pros and cons of the different viewpoints. The section is then followed by two sections in which we review recent empirical scholarly work that tries to address the consequences for the quality of government of different levels of bureaucratic autonomy. In the chapter's final section, we summarize the findings from the field, and suggest what we think could be promising avenues for future research.

THE IDEAL BUREAUCRACY: ACCOUNTABLE OR AUTONOMOUS?

Most constitutions do not discuss how to organize the bureaucracy, and barely mention its personnel (see Schuster 2017 for an overview of countries that mention recruitment practices in the constitution). In spite of the importance of the administration for policymaking and implementation, neither the founding fathers of the United States constitution nor the European constitutions that followed the United States example a few decades later give much guidance. To some extent this might be explained by the fact that the potential problems presented by bureaucratic organization seemed small at the time. In the newly formed United States of America, the bureaucracy consisted of a few hundred civil servants, with, for instance, the whole state department fitting in two rooms. This changed quickly however, and not only in the United States. With millions of state employees, the problem of governing them soon became obvious, and the consequences of such governing decisions for the quality of government far-reaching.

Looking back at the scholarly discussion during the last century, we can distinguish two distinct answers to the fundamental problem of how to organize the administration. The first one emphasizes political accountability. It is originally inspired by the experience of the (American) private sector. It is based on the power of incentives, explained by extrinsic motivations, and is theoretically rooted in the work of Frederick W. Taylor (1911). The idea is that in order to have an effective bureaucracy, bureaucrats should be as accountable as possible to their (political) masters. Public employees are thus, like their private sector counterparts in a standard corporation, accountable to the chief executive officer, in this case to their political superior (Frant 1993). Bureaucrats have no legitimate agency of their own; they should simply be instruments for fulfilling political decisions taken elsewhere (Finer 1941).

In a diametrically opposite point of view, the second answer to the organizational problem of bureaucracies emphasizes autonomy, and it is originally inspired by the experience of the (Prussian) public sector. It is based on the importance of intrinsic motivations, created by norms and a strong *esprit de corps*, and is theoretically rooted in the work of Max Weber (1978 [1921]). According to this view, the idea is to rely on the professional norms of bureaucrats and grant them autonomy, which makes them a lever for rationality and gives them authority to act against opportunistic (partisan) behavior. From this perspective bureaucrats thus have autonomy, and should sometimes use it to stand up to elected political leaders in order to serve the public good (Miller 2000).

There are different risks that come with each perspective. In a bureaucracy highly accountable to politics, the danger is that the public employee follows politicians' opportunistic orders by, for example, taking partisan considerations into account instead of implementing policies impartially. In a highly autonomous bureaucracy, the risk is that the bureaucrat uses this autonomy to fulfill her own goals at the expense of the public good. Both perils are real, but proponents of these stylized views of bureaucracy make very different assessments about the main threats to high-quality government. While the first view emphasizes jeopardies related to runaway bureaucrats, and wants to incentivize them to function as the extended arm of politicians, the second is concerned with the moral hazards related to politics and wants to introduce a counterbalance against self-serving politicians.

These two polar views of what constitutes a good bureaucracy are clearly portrayed in the influential debate between Carl Friedrich (1940) and Herman Finer (1941) in the 1930s and 1940s. In the aftermath of the Great Depression and on the eve of the Second World War, there was a huge expansion of government activities throughout the Western world. Therefore, the question of why bureaucrats would be willing to sacrifice their own interests for those of the organization was a poignant one for influential thinkers (Barnard 1938).

Finer argued for "a relationship of obedience" (1936, 580) between politicians and bureaucrats. Civil servants are instruments, not agents, he argued. Following Hobbes' Leviathan, he suggested that civil servants are no more than the "nerves and tendons" of the sovereign (Jackson 2009, 74). In opposition, Friedrich argued for the civil servants' own agency, as a *corps*; for their inner motivation, their "sense of duty." While Finer claimed civil servants should be directly accountable to their political masters, Friedrich considered that civil servants should respond to their collegial associations.

At the root of the Finer–Friedrich debate lies a radically divergent view of government. Finer believed that politics and administration belong to entirely different spheres. But for those, like Friedrich, advocating the inner responsibility of civil servants, the assumption is that politics and administration cannot be separated. In the day-to-day operations of government, the design and implementation of policies are blended. Even the execution of most technical matters, such as how to build a public road or bridge, requires bureaucrats to take decisions that have policy consequences, such as the social disruption generated by the building of the infrastructure, and they become de facto policymakers (Lipsky 1980). Since bureaucrats get involved in policy design and, equally, politicians also take part in policy implementation, in the Friedrich view of bureaucracy politicians and bureaucrats are partners. On the contrary, for those, like Finer, defending a command and control bureaucracy, politics and administration can be neatly distinguished: Politics directs, and administration obeys (Jackson 2009).

The discussion between Friedrich and Finer is also interesting because it reveals a deeply divergent assumption on the nature of public employees, which is fundamental for today's discussion about management reforms in the public sector. Are public employees intrinsically motivated workers, and drawn to the public sector for a genuine will to serve the public interest? Or are they self-interested individuals with a poor work ethic? Recent empirical evidence sheds some light on this debate. On the one hand, surveys indicate that public employees are more intrinsically motivated than private sector workers, even after controlling for socioeconomic characteristics (Cowley and Smith 2014). And experiments show that public employees are also more prosocial (Banuri and Keefer 2013). But this public sector motivation depends, crucially, on the corruption level of the country. In highly corrupt settings, public employees are not more intrinsically motivated than their private sector counterparts, but rather, quite the opposite. For instance, experiments in India—a highly corrupt country according to most comparative indicators—suggest that individuals who cheat in games express a higher interest in joining the public sector (Hanna and Wang 2017).

Friedrich's emphasis on professional public service prevailed in the postwar years over Finer's more instrumental view of bureaucracy. While the size of government was growing, and was seen as an embodiment of public interest, Friedrich's view was preferred to Finer's (Jackson 2009). Yet, when the size of government stopped being seen as an avatar of the public interest, and the suspicion about government activities (and employees) rose in the 1970s and 1980s, Finer's perspective that bureaucrats must follow politicians' instructions seemed to gain priority for policymakers and scholars alike (Buchanan 1968; Niskanen 1971).

All in all, the opposite implications emerging from Finer's (accountability) and Friedrich's (autonomy) approaches have determined the design and reform of public administrations worldwide for over a century. Finer's view permeates the prescriptions of the principal–agent theory (Dixit 2002) for public bureaucracies, embodied in the New Public Management movement (NPM) (Hood 1991). The NPM movement aims to transform public administrations within organizations to become as similar as possible to those within private firms (Lægreid 2018). This means, among other reforms, the introduction of rewards for bureaucrats who follow politicians' explicit instructions, and punishments for those who do not. Conversely, Friedrich's view is reflected in the (Neo) Weberian approach: the motivation of civil servants is not through extrinsic motivations, but through the internal motivation inherent in the *esprit de corps* of civil servants. Through strict selection procedures, training, and socialization in public service values, civil servants will pursue the public interest, and not their own.

In the next two sections we discuss the potential effects of bureaucratic autonomy and accountability, and the empirical support for these contrasting views on how bureaucracies should be organized: with autonomous and responsible civil servants, or with accountable and responsive civil servants? We will review recent empirical work that evaluates aspects of bureaucracy that can be broadly sorted under Finer's and Friedrich's different views and the consequences of this for the quality of government. We start by discussing the effects of an autonomous bureaucracy.

Autonomous Bureaucracies and The Quality of Government

Cross-country analysis indicates that the highest levels of quality of government are achieved in countries where politicians are accountable to their citizens—i.e. there are free and fair elections—and, at the same time, bureaucrats are not accountable to their political masters—i.e. there is an autonomous bureaucracy (Dahlström and Lapuente 2017). Yet, in the public debate, an autonomous bureaucracy is often seen as an "organizational dinosaur" (Olsen 2006, 1), at best, and as a wasteful and perverse machinery, at worst; a fear expressed by President Trump's recent offensive against the "deep state," and underlying the unwritten rule in American politics that says that no candidate can lose an election by criticizing the bureaucracy.

Although classics in public administration, such as Weber (1978 [1921]), Wilson (1887), and Goodnow (1900), note the importance of a bureaucracy that is autonomous from its political masters for good government, such a notion was, for a long time, absent from scholarly studies of comparative politics. Both mainstream economics and political science literature largely overlooked the potential effect of bureaucratic structures on government performance until fairly recently.

The significance of autonomous bureaucracies for quality of government regained more scholarly attention after the economic miracles of the so-called Asian tigers (see Johnson 1982 on Japan; Amsten 1989 on Korea; Wade 1990 on Taiwan). Evans (1995, 9) coined the term "embedded autonomy" to remark on the subtle equilibrium that these countries achieved between two, at first sight, contradictory goals of a bureaucracy. On the one hand, an autonomous public workforce—where civil servants were recruited and promoted depending on their abilities and competences, not their political loyalty. On the other hand, a bureaucracy embedded in the society, serving the public interest and not their own.

An illustrative and more recent study of the different fortunes of Jamaica and Singapore, two islands that became independent from Britain in the early 1960s, describes how this was partly the result of two opposing ways of building a state bureaucracy (Rothstein 2011). Jamaica, despite having a democratic system, built an administration populated by at-will appointments who, in turn, implemented policies that exclusively benefitted core constituencies of the ruling party. Singapore, despite its authoritarian turn, created a merit-based administration that was able to provide public services in an impartial way, which is the essence of quality of government (Rothstein and Teorell 2008).

This first wave of studies that was interested in how bureaucratic structure, and more specifically the personnel politics of the administration, affected the quality of government often utilized case studies or few case comparisons. The first broader comparisons saw the light of day at the end of the 1990s, and cross-country studies have indicated since then that countries with more meritocratic (versus politicized) recruitment and promotion systems in the administration also have higher levels of economic development (Evans and Rauch 1999;

Cingolani, Thomsson, and de Crombrugghe 2015), lower poverty (Henderson et al. 2007), lower corruption levels (Rauch and Evans 2000; Dahlström, Lapuente, and Teorell 2012), and more effective and flexible governments (Dahlström and Lapuente 2017). Moreover, administrative reforms are significantly more likely in those administrations, such as the Nordic countries, where bureaucrats enjoy autonomy and are not politicized (Dahlström and Lapuente 2010; Greve, Lægreid, and Rykkja 2016). Subnational studies point out that this relationship, between a merit-based autonomous bureaucracy and government performance, also holds among regions within EU countries (Charron et al. 2017).

Similarly, historical studies on the success of democracy and the industrial revolution in Britain, and subsequently in the United States, have long emphasized the "political foundations" of the rule of law (Weingast 1997, 245). Democratic arrangements, and respect for the rule of law, have been suggested to be a self-enforcing equilibrium among political elites or parties. Political checks and balances—for instance, a bicameral legislature, and separate elections for the executive and the legislature—are examples of how to limit the concentration of powers in the same political hands, and thus the likelihood of abuse. However, more recently, economic historians have challenged this view, noting that the checks and balances that prevented monarchs in Early Modern Britain from undertaking opportunistic actions against the public interest were not of a political as much as of bureaucratic nature (Greif 2008; González de Lara, Greif, and Jha 2008). Unlike most of their counterparts in the European continent, English, and later British, monarchs could not command and control their administrative apparatus. This bureaucratic autonomy was de facto a key constraint on the executive. Centuries later, in the process of state-building, European powers correspondingly created autonomous administrative bodies in order to signal their commitment to the rule of law (Lapuente 2007). One conclusion that comes out of this line of historical research is that it makes as much sense to talk about the "administrative" as the "political" "foundations" of the rule of law.

So, there seems to be a correlation between autonomous bureaucracies and the quality of government. And even if it is uncertain if the relationship is causal—there are few, if any, studies with designs that allow for definite causal inference in the field—there are suggestions of at least four mechanisms through which an autonomous bureaucracy trumps a politically dependent bureaucracy when it comes to providing high-quality government.

In the first place, an autonomous bureaucracy may help the state to *select better types* thorough a meritocratic recruitment system. Nevertheless, this does not mean recruitment of bureaucrats must be done through (nationwide) competitive exams, like the *concours* and *oposiciones* prevailing in, respectively, the French and Spanish public administrations as well as in most of their former colonies. While such a strict system of recruitment is indeed associated with a better administration in emerging economies with high levels of corruption, it does not have a significant effect in advanced democracies (Sundell 2014). For instance, countries like New Zealand, Denmark, or Sweden have high-performing governments and, nevertheless, possess recruitment systems for the public service similar to those prevailing in the private sector, such as CV screening and job interviews (Peters and Painter 2010). Contrariwise, traces of nepotism have been found in the theoretically meritocratic nationwide competitive exams of countries like Spain (Bagüés 2005).

A second mechanism linking an autonomous bureaucracy to good government is civil servants' relatively high *salaries*. Scholars have long argued that if bureaucrats get high salaries they will not have as strong incentives to demand side payments or accept bribes if they are offered them, which in turn increases the quality of government (Becker and Stigler 1974). However, most comparative studies do not find a statistically significant association between high salaries in the public sector and lower levels of corruption, once confounding factors are included (Rauch and Evans 2000; Treisman 2000; Dahlström, Lapuente, and Teorell 2012). Additionally, it has been suggested that high salaries may attract the wrong type of civil servants, quite contrary to what is intended. Offering higher wages may be especially tempting for corruption-prone candidates (Prendergast 2007). It has even been argued that, in order to convince publicly minded and intrinsically motivated "zealots," public sector wages should thus be lower than market wages (Gailmard and Patty 2007). Interestingly, an empirical regularity reported in the literature is that public employees enjoy a significant wage premium over their private sector counterparts worldwide (Finan, Olken, and Pande 2017). One reason for this large wage premium in the public sector might be that in developing countries state capture by rent-seeking elites is more common.

A third mechanism potentially explaining the association between an autonomous bureaucracy and quality of government is the *internalization of norms of conduct*. By joining an administrative body at a very early stage in their careers and moving up slowly in the hierarchical ladder with internal promotions, young public servants are socialized over many years in a set of public values—such as equity and impartiality. In turn, these values induce civil servants to act in pursuit of the broad and long-term public interest instead of their own, or their political superior's narrow and short-term interest. This *"esprit de corps,"* created thanks to life tenure, would account for the higher performance of autonomous bureaucracies (Evans and Rauch 1999; Rauch and Evans 2000). The intrinsic motivation that the *esprit de corps* gives to civil servants may be a crucial factor in explaining the overall productivity of a bureaucracy (Perry and Hondegheim 2008). Nevertheless, cross-country studies do not find a robust effect of the bureaucratic characteristics associated with the *esprit de corps*, such as life tenure or internal promotions, over different indicators of quality of government (Dahlström, Lapuente, and Teorell 2012; Dahlström and Lapuente 2017).

A fourth mechanism connecting autonomous bureaucracies with good government comes from the incentives shaped by the *separation of careers* between bureaucrats and political officials that a merit-based administration creates (Dahlström and Lapuente 2017). If politicians appoint public servants at-will, the latter have no interest in reporting their superiors' malfeasances to the opposition parties, the media, or the corresponding judicial authority, as the subsequent political scandal would not only damage the politician's career but also the whistleblower's. Consequently, bureaucrats in politically dependent administrations have an incentive to either turn a blind eye or take part in any abuse of public office for private gain that they witness. Conversely, if the professional fates of politicians and bureaucrats are separated—with politicians being accountable to their voters and bureaucrats to their peers—both groups are free to report each other's misbehaviors. And, as empirical analyses indicate, merit recruitment encourages civil servants to be frank and fearless when speaking to power (Cooper 2018).

One interesting implication from this fourth mechanism is that the key feature of an autonomous bureaucracy is a merit-based civil service system, not an isolated civil service, or a "closed Weberian administration" (Dahlström and Lapuente 2017). What is required in order to have an effective administration is that bureaucrats be recruited and promoted according to merit, not recruitment of civil servants to an administrative body through competitive examinations, with guarantees of life tenure. A bureaucracy can be politically autonomous and, at the same time, free from special privileges for civil servants, such as life tenure, internal promotions (i.e. preventing lateral entries), and special employment laws in comparison to those prevailing in the private sector. This "managerial administration" (Dahlström and Lapuente 2017) operates in the countries with the highest quality of government in the world, such as the Nordic countries, Australia, and New Zealand.

These studies, mostly cross-sectional comparisons, raise the issue of endogeneity. Bureaucratic structures, such as a merit-based recruitment system or life tenure, could be both endogenous to unobserved efforts to improve quality of government, and correlated to other sources of good performance (Pepinsky, Pierskalla, and Sacks 2017). The observational studies come with a number of well-known caveats, as credible causal identification designs are lacking. Researchers have, however, tried to address these limitations using a number of strategies, such as employing instrumental variables (for example, historic bureaucratic features), and including previous levels of the dependent variable on the independent side (which, in effect, makes us focus more on changes in the dependent variable, instead of levels). This is, for example, how Dahlström, Lapuente, and Teorell (2012) approach questions of reversed causality and potential omitted variable bias when they study the effect of meritocracy over corruption in their worldwide comparison of contemporary administrations. Another method to check for endogeneity is through a qualitative study of some cases in which the proper sequence—that is, in this case, from a meritocratic administration to lower levels of corruption—is identified. In particular, the historical account of how the U.S., the U.K., and the Nordic countries effectively curbed their relatively high levels of corruption in the late nineteenth century indicates that the reform of the civil service— replacing political loyalty with merit—came first (see, for instance, Rubinstein 1983 for the U.K., or Teaford 1983 for the U.S.).

The most promising way of addressing the endogeneity problem is, however, with experiments. Conjoint experiments, like those conducted in the Dominican Republic by Oliveros and Schuster (2018) indicate that an autonomous bureaucracy does contribute to good government. The existence of meritocratic recruitment curbs corruption among Dominican Republic civil servants and, at the same time, enhances their work motivation. In contrast, the existence of job stability does not have such a significant effect on quality of government—for it only decreases the participation of bureaucrats in electoral mobilization. In other words, this experimental evidence provides further support for the normative argument of the fourth mechanism discussed above: What matters is whether merit (versus political loyalty) is rewarded within the public sector, and not so much whether public employees spend their whole careers in the public sector—via formal entry examinations, internal promotions, and life tenure—or not.

POLITICALLY ACCOUNTABLE BUREAUCRACIES AND THE QUALITY OF GOVERNMENT

After exploring Friedrich's suggestion that an autonomous bureaucracy, in which civil servants follow their peers and internal norms, and not only their political superiors, leads to better outcomes, let us now analyze Finer's idea that bureaucrats' good performance originates from orders by their political superiors, elicited with a system of extrinsic rewards and punishments. Before going into the details of suggestions as to how to control the bureaucracy, and the effects thereof, let us remind ourselves of the strong foundations the argument rests upon. For a person with strong democratic convictions, what could really be said against the idea that the bureaucracy should follow democratically elected leaders to the letter? To understand how this could be even questioned we have to consider, first, that democratically elected leaders can be shortsighted and self-interested and therefore may need to be counterbalanced; second, that what may motivate bureaucrats to do a good job is the desire to not simply be an instrument in the hands of others; and, third, the empirical effects of more or less accountable bureaucracies, which do not always speak in favor of direct accountability for bureaucrats.

Finer's hypothesis sits very well with the standard take on principal–agent theory, according to which there is an inherent divergence between the goals of the principal (i.e. the political masters) and the actions of the agent (i.e. the civil servants). The informational asymmetry between the elected politician—a dilettante in Max Weber's (1978 [1921]) words—and the clever, experienced public servant, a la *Sir Humphrey*, who appeared in the British sitcom *Yes Minister*, gives the latter opportunities to take advantage of the former, at a cost to social welfare at large. Principal–agent theory has, during the last decades, become the primary framework to analyze bureaucracies in both political science and economics, which has brought Finer's hypothesis to the center of the discussion. Scholars have explored several incentive-compatible solutions aimed at minimizing the twin problems of principal–agent models: adverse selection and moral hazard. Both are fundamental problems for politicians delegating power to bureaucrats (for overviews, see Bendor, Glazer and Hammond 2001; Gailmard and Patty 2012; Pepinsky, Pierskalla, and Sacks 2017).

The idea behind all standard principal–agent solutions is to align the principal's (politicians) and the agent's (bureaucrats) incentives. One way of doing it is through monetary compensation. We should remind ourselves that from the principal–agent perspective, it is worrying that the principal would like the agent to work hard while the agent might want to use her time for other things (sometimes this is referred to as "slack"). Introducing *performance-based payments* into the bureaucracy is a way of handling this problem, as bureaucrats would then have increased incentives for intensifying their efforts. And indeed, randomized controlled field trials indicate that monetary rewards work under several circumstances. For instance, Pakistani tax inspectors with high-powered economic incentives achieved a 46% higher growth rate in tax revenue (Khan, Khwaja and Olken 2015). And monetary incentives may help in reducing the widespread absenteeism of education and healthcare personnel so prevalent in emerging economies (Duflo, Hanna, and Ryan 2012; Hasnain, Manning, and Pierskalla 2014). This is extremely relevant for many countries in the world, if we take into account that between one-fifth and one-third of primary school teachers and public healthcare workers are absent from work on a daily basis in many developing countries (Chaudhury et al. 2006). Additionally, a randomized school-level study in India documented an improvement on math and language tests in those schools where teachers were paid modest incentives (of around 3% of their annual salary) (Muralidharan and Sundararaman 2011). Likewise, the measurement of performance has produced some beneficial effects in advanced democracies. In the U.K., the government's control of performance in healthcare has managed to reduce waiting times in hospitals (Kelman and Friedman 2009).

Nevertheless, performance-based incentives face some well-known problems, because while the system might improve in some respects (those measured), it might be at the expense of other very relevant aspects (those not measured). This is illustrated by what could be called the "quarterback" problem, as defined by Prendergast (1999). In the 1980s, a promising young quarterback in American football was offered a contract that penalized him every time he lost the ball to the opposing team. As a result, he avoided throwing the ball in dangerous situations as well as in less dangerous (and potentially excellent) situations. Overall, his performance diminished. Likewise, the multitasking inherent to public activities makes it very difficult to design incentives that do not hamper overall performance. Bureaucrats may concentrate their efforts on the incentivized dimension of their work, while ignoring other important tasks (Holmstrom and Milgrom 1987). If teachers are rewarded according to the test results of their students, they may simply teach to the test, disregarding a more encompassing education (Pepinsky, Pierskalla, and Sacks 2017). Another example of where the same type of negative externalities was observable was when police agencies were allowed to keep the revenue from assets seized in drug arrests, and therefore targeted drug dealers at the expense of fighting other crimes (Baiker and Jacobsson 2007). Generally speaking, the problem of multitasking is probably more severe in public than in private organizations. The latter aims at maximizing profit, a measurable dimension, while the former aspires to public service, a concept more difficult to operationalize (Finan, Olken, and Pande 2017), and thus easier to game. Furthermore, the level of compensations offered to civil servants cannot, because of ethical restrictions, equate the bonuses private sector CEOs get from their shareholders.

Additionally, thinking about performance-related payments is relevant also because it concerns another aspect of the Friedrich–Finer discussion, namely the balance between intrinsic and extrinsic motivation. Performance-related pay for bureaucrats may generate an undesirable trade-off between external rewards and inner motivation. Paying bureaucrats for undertaking what they see as their duties could lead to demoralization (Banuri and Keefer 2013). Financial incentives may actually reduce effort in those individuals who are prosocially motivated (Bénabou and Tirole 2006). Having said this, the empirical support for this trade-off is not conclusive (Pepinsky, Pierskalla, and Sacks 2017). On the one hand, it has been found that higher wages may actually attract high-quality candidates to the public sector. In an experiment for recruiting employees in a Mexican regional development program, in which the program offered a monthly salary of 5,000 pesos, the average applicant was smarter and had better personality traits than where the program only offered a salary of 3,750 pesos (Dal Bó, Finan and Rossi 2013). On the other hand, an experiment in Uganda indicated that the high-pay treatment attracted more applicants, but these were less motivated for public service and more motivated for "earning money" (Deserrano 2019). Curiously, those workers recruited under the low-pay treatment performed better and were more prosocial. In addition, the experimental study on tax collection in Pakistan, mentioned earlier, found that despite economic incentives significantly raised tax revenue, the downside was that, in the incentivized areas, bribe rates also increased (Khan, Khwaja, and Olken 2015). Other nonexperimental studies of incentives in tax collection, such as the analysis of a tax collection reform in Brazil, also cited above, did not find this negative increased bribery effect (Khan, Silva, and Ziliak 2001).

Another type of answer to the problem of how to align the incentives of bureaucrats with the incentives of politicians, and ultimately the electorate, is to increase competition. A flagship of the NPM movement has thus been *contracting out* activities to competing nonprofit organizations or private firms. Increasing competition should stimulate both production and creativity, so that efficiency also increases (Le Grand 2007; Shleifer 1998). The asymmetries of information between politicians and bureaucrats would simply be by-passed by setting contracts with providers based on obtaining the desired results. Nevertheless, the empirical evidence on contracting out is mixed (Broms, Dahlström, and Nistotskaya 2020) and has shown both positive (Bergman et al. 2016; Castle, Engberg, and Liu 2007), negative, and no effects on performance (Dahlström, Nistotskaya, and Tyrberg 2018; Dunleavy and Carrera 2013; Forder and Allan 2014). Contracting out may increase efficiency in the delivery of public policies, significantly reducing costs in some studies, but it might be at the expense of equal treatment of all citizens (Hodge 2000; Andrews 2011), or the quality of services (Hart, Shleifer, and Vishny 1997). For instance, the Swedish government, in order to increase the performance of healthcare and education, has created a system of vouchers that allows citizens to freely choose their schools and hospitals, and there are indications that this system has led to social segregation, negatively affecting equity (Blomqvist and Rothstein 2000). A similar result has been found in Denmark (Andersen and Serritzlew 2007), and, in general, contracting out has not delivered the expected results according to the theory (Hood and Dixon 2015). Principal–agent theory predicts that a contract based on results might be an ideal incentive-compatible mechanism to improve service delivery, but this proposition only seems to work in some particular administrative contexts. And, even in the most amicable contexts for reform, such as the Nordic countries (Greve, Lægreid, and Rykkja 2016), contracting out implies equity losses (Blomqvist and Rothstein 2000).

Another principal–agent solution to motivate bureaucrats is *rotation*. This was traditionally used in pre- and Modern Europe to increase the efficiency of tax collection (Kiser and Kane 2001). Rulers shifted skillful tax collectors to regions where tax revenue was low. Rotation also minimizes the development of strong, and potentially dangerous, links between public officials and entrenched local interests (Pepinsky, Pierskalla, and Sacks 2017). Additionally, rotations are easier to implement in civil service systems than firing or pay incentives—which tend to be more constrained by regulations—and the preliminary results from field experiments are supportive (Finan, Olken, and Pande 2017). A randomized study in India indicated that those police officials who, as an incentive, had the possibility of a transfer to another station performed significantly better than those officials who had no transfer incentives (Banerjee et al. 2012). It should, however, also be kept in mind that rotation strategies can be used by politicians to control bureaucrats. Another study of Indian political-bureaucracy relations shows exactly that, and, in addition, that it is low-, rather than high-skilled bureaucrats that are transferred (Iyer and Mani 2012).

A final remark should be made about the principal–agent relationship and the problems that might emerge from it. The standard assumption in principal–agent theory is that the source of problems is the agent, who, through adverse selection and moral hazard, may take advantage of her informational advantage over the principal. But what about the problems created by an opportunistic principal? For instance, what incentives do politicians have to control the bureaucrat? The literature on Western bureaucracies, and in particular on the American administration, has long noted that the existence of multiple principals (i.e.

House, Senate, and Presidency) in relation to a single bureaucratic agency (e.g. Food and Drug Agency) leads to poor monitoring and agency slack (Kiewiet and McCubbins 1991; Hammond and Knott 1996), although an important caveat is in order here. For some scholars, the existence of several political principals may prevent them from taking advantage of the bureaucrats working for the agency, because it is more difficult for two or three political institutions (or parties)—than for a single principal—to suddenly shift the goal of a bureaucratic agency or cut its budget by half. Consequently, multiple principals have been shown to have positive effects under certain circumstances in democracies such as the United States (Miller 1992; Miller and Falaschetti 2001) or Spain (Lapuente 2007). Regarding emerging economies, multiple principals have, on the contrary, been found to lead to worse bureaucratic outcomes. For instance, a study in India shows that bureaucrats perform better when they are accountable to a single politician rather than to several (Gulzar and Pasquale 2017).

Moreover, electoral competition may alter politicians' incentives to control bureaucrats, but it is difficult to assert in which direction this is (Pepinsky, Pierskalla, and Sacks 2017). On the one hand, evidence from Nigeria (Rasul and Rogger 2017), Pakistan (Callen et al. 2013), Italy (Coviello and Gagliarducci 2017), Romania (Klašnja 2015), and Sweden (Broms, Dahlström, and Fazekas 2019) indicates that the more electoral competition a politician faces, the better the bureaucratic output. On the other hand, there is evidence from India (Nath 2015) indicating that the longer the tenure of a politician, the more she will invest in properly incentivizing bureaucrats, designing contracts that are more appropriate. Evidence is thus mixed, but it leans towards a positive influence of political competition.

Main Findings and New Challenges

The Friedrich–Finer discussion is interesting partly because it is unresolvable. Ideally, we would like to have both bureaucratic autonomy and a bureaucracy directly accountable to the elected politicians, but there is an inherent tension between these two values (Lægreid 2018). In the best of worlds we should not have to choose between them, but when autonomy and accountability are tested, one against the other, the increase in bureaucratic autonomy is associated with higher productivity of bureaucrats while the increase in monitoring is associated with lower bureaucratic output (Rasul and Rogger 2017). Moreover, monitoring may lead to excessive prudence in the public sector. For instance, Brazilian municipalities expecting to be audited tend to reduce public spending, with a notable worsening of health indicators, such as hospital beds and immunization coverage (Lichand, Lopes and Medeiros 2017). Being afraid of punishment for procurement mistakes when monitoring is extremely detailed, public officials may simply prefer to cut purchases, at the expense of overall social welfare.

More generally, the picture is one of a robust correlation between the prevalence of autonomous bureaucracies and largely uncorrupt, highly effective governments, with sound theoretical reasons for assuming that the relationship could be causal (Dahlström and Lapuente 2017; Miller 2000; Miller and Whitford 2016; Nistotskaya and Cingolani 2016; Rauch and Evans 2000).

This does not mean that total bureaucratic autonomy is desirable. In order to perform well, bureaucracies need to be embedded in their societies, both at the central level (Evans 1995) as well as on the frontlines (Pepinsky, Pierskalla, and Sacks 2017). Contact by bureaucrats with the beneficiaries of policies is essential for good performance (Ricks 2016), maybe even more so than the formal education skills of the bureaucrats (Bhavnani and Lee 2018). Absence of that link may be devastating. As Fukuyama (2013) notes, the extremely autonomous military Japanese and German bureaucracies in the first decades of the twentieth century fostered a dangerous arms race that was at odds with the wishes of most citizens, and which ended up being disastrous for their countries and the whole world.

In order to secure high quality of government, bureaucrats should probably be autonomous in the sense that they are nonpartisan, so that their professional life is not tied to one or a set of politicians, but they should not be unaccountable. Bureaucrats should be accountable to their peers. This means that the future career prospects of bureaucrats—either within the public or private sector—should be determined by their professional colleagues. In a setting where the use of economic incentives is constrained, as in the public sector, career prospects seem to be the key feature in molding public officials' behavior. Both quantitative and qualitative evidence indicates that the concern of civil servants for their career trajectories determines policy decisions as diverse as the monetary policies chosen by central bankers (Adolph 2013) or the building of a public library or a highway (Dahlström and Lapuente 2017). The prospect of attractive career opportunities is one of, or *the* key factor in recruiting high-quality applicants to the public sector (Ashraf, Bandiera, and Jack 2014; Finan, Olken, and Pande 2017).

Ideally, such a system selects and promotes intrinsically motivated individuals, and public service motivation is empirically linked to better performance (Perry and Hondeghem 2008) and lower shirking (Callen et al. 2015). For instance, a fascinating field experiment in Zambia with public health workers showed that intrinsic motivation may trump extrinsic incentives: The employees who got nonfinancial "stars" on a "thermometer" display performed significantly better than the employees who got (large) financial incentives (Ashraf, Bandiera, and Jack 2014). Intrinsic motivation is, in addition, crucial for public organizations in which, unlike private firms, most goods and services cannot be priced in the market, making the design of incentives more difficult (Besley and Ghatak 2005). Yet we do not know which specific recruitment system selects more intrinsically motivated employees, and the fact that there is an association between public service motivation and job performance does not mean that there is a causal relationship, nor, in such an eventuality, does it indicate in which direction the causality moves (Finan, Olken, and Pande 2017).

What is less clear from research today, especially in cross-country comparisons, is where to draw the line for bureaucratic autonomy. As indicated by Fukuyama (2013) above, it is easy to imagine that bureaucratic autonomy can go too far. If left to their own devices, bureaucrats might prioritize their self-interest, the interest of their corps, or the interests of some other external group, for example business, at the expense of the public interest (Dal Bó 2006). Acknowledging that there is an upper limit to bureaucratic autonomy indicates that the relationship between autonomy and the quality of government should not be expected to be linear, but rather curvilinear. And there is some evidence pointing in this direction, for example on the performance of agencies in the United States (Krause and Meier 2005). Moreover, using data from public sector workers in Brazil, Bersch and Fukuyama (2019) find an inverted U-shaped relationship between one type of bureaucratic discretion and government quality. Such a U-shaped relationship is also implied by the mutual-monitoring mechanism of bureaucrats and politicians, as suggested in Dahlström and Lapuente (2017); if left alone, politicians might indeed act in a short-sighted and self-interested manner, but the same may be said to be true for bureaucrats. These observations and theoretical suggestions, taken at the national level, point towards exciting new studies, exploring more intricate aspects of the Friedrich–Finer discussion.

Over the last two decades, we have substantially advanced our knowledge of central bureaucracies in cross-country (Evans and Rauch 1999; Dahlström and Lapuente 2017; Nistotskaya and Cingolani 2016) and national (Lewis 2008; Miller and Whitford 2016) analyses. There are, however, few studies that go beyond the national level. The studies that do so are rarely designed in ways that allow for certain causal inference, and measures rely too much on citizen and expert perceptions. These shortcomings open up exciting new opportunities for research in the field.

For instance, we know quite a lot about the selection and incentives of civil servants working at central departments, but relatively little about those working at regional and local entities (for an exception, see Charron et al. 2017), and, in general, on those working in frontline service delivery (Pepinsky, Pierskalla, and Sacks 2017). Future research should thus focus more on within-country variations, both geographically (with more subnational studies), and organizationally (with more studies comparing institutions). These meso-level differences offer one promising avenue for future research. One of the reasons for this is that the effects of bureaucratic features, and reforms, seem to be more context-dependent than general. If that is indeed the case, then we might disregard the elaboration of "global recipes," and opt instead for more limited and conditional recommendations (Lægreid 2018). It has been found that the particular organizational context determines the success of major bureaucratic reforms. For example, in developing countries, formal reform of the civil service by instituting meritocratic hiring may not work (Grindle 2012; Pritchett, Woolcock, and Andrews 2013). And we have not been able to assess the success of large, all-encompassing reforms, such as NPM, in general (Hammerschmid et al. 2016) but only in certain contexts (Lapuente and Van de Walle 2020).

Moreover, different types of quasi-experiments offer the possibility of isolating the effects of bureaucratic features (e.g. type of recruitment, level of wages, tenure, economic incentives) on performance, but this experimental research is still in its infancy (Finan, Olken, and Pande 2017). This is probably the methodological research niche that should be expanded the most in future public administration scholarship. For instance, what happens when we introduce secure tenure or economic incentives to police forces in a country? Do incentives in the public sector increase performance, as is usually the case in the private sector, or do they reduce effort among public employees, similar to what usually happens in the nonprofit sector, such as the famously documented reduction in blood donation when financial incentives are introduced (Mellstrom and Johanesson 2008)?

Another promising avenue for future research is in improving data collection, which should probably be done both by the collection of objective data on units such as agencies, municipalities, and countries, and individual micro-level data. Big Data techniques offer opportunities to tap into previously unanalyzable sources, with forerunners in, for example, public procurement. The relevance of the individual level is illustrated by the fact that there are indications that personality traits, such as the Big Five, do seem to affect bureaucratic performance in experiments (e.g. Callen et al. 2015). Collecting a large dataset with individual personality traits may help us in understanding the comparative performance of sectoral, regional, or national bureaucracies.

Nevertheless, these empirical efforts should not come at the expense of theoretical cohesion. The fact that there are no easy panaceas on how to improve bureaucratic performance, and that we need to be more humble than idealistic (Lægreid 2018), should not preclude us from developing theories that establish, at the very least, conditional generalizations that can be transferred across countries, sectors, and administrative levels (Pollitt and Bouckaert 2017). In particular, future research should provide a more coherent theory on how bureaucratic autonomy—and which particular features of it—systematically affect government performance. We know that bureaucracies matter. The question is, how?

References

Adolph, Christopher. 2013. *Bankers, Bureaucrats, and Central Bank Politics: The Myth of Neutrality*. New York: Cambridge University Press.

Amsten, Alice. 1989. *Asia's Next Giant: South Korea and Late Industrialization*. New York: Oxford University Press.

Andersen, Simon, and Sören Serritzlew. 2007. "The Unintended Effects of Private School Competition." *Journal of Public Administration Research and Theory* 17 (2): 335–56.

Andrews, Rhys. 2011. "NPM and the Search for Efficiency." In *The Ashgate Research Companion to New Public Management*, edited by Tom Christensen and Per Lægreid. Burlington: Ashgate.

Ashraf, Nava, Oriana Bandiera, and B. Kelsey Jack. 2014. "No Margin, No Mission? A Field Experiment on Incentives for Public Service Delivery." *Journal of Public Economics* 120 (December): 1–17.

Bagüés, Manuel F. 2005. "¿Qué determina el éxito en unas oposiciones?" In XII Encuentro de Economía Pública: Evaluación de las Políticas Públicas: Palma de Mallorca los días 3 y 4 de febrero de 2005: 13.

Baicker, Katherine, and Mireille Jacobson. 2007. "Finders Keepers: Forfeiture Laws, Policing Incentives, and Local Budgets." *Journal of Public Economics* 91 (11–12): 2113–36.

Banerjee, Abhijit V., Raghabendra Chattopadhyay, Esther Duflo, Daniel Keniston, and Nina Singh. 2012. "Can Institutions be Reformed from Within? Evidence from a Randomized Experiment with the Rajasthan Police." MIT Department of Economics Working Paper No. 12-04: https://papers.ssrn.com/sol3/papers.cfm?abstract_id=2010854

Banuri, Sheheryar, and Philip Keefer. 2013. "Intrinsic Motivation, Effort and the Call to Public Service." World Bank Policy Research Working Paper 6729. https://elibrary.worldbank.org/doi/abs/10.1596/1813-9450-6729

Barnard, Chester. 1938. *The Functions of the Executive*. Cambridge, MA: Harvard University Press.

Becker, Gary S., and George J. Stigler. 1974. "Law Enforcement, Malfeasance, and Compensation of Enforcers." *The Journal of Legal Studies* 3 (1) (January): 1–18.

Bekke, Hans, and Frits van der Meer. 2000. "Civil Service Systems in Western Europe: An Introduction." In *Civil Service systems in Western Europe*, edited by Hans Bekke and Frits van der Meer, 1–11. Cheltenham: Edward Elgar.

Bénabou, Roland, and Jean Tirole. 2006. "Incentives and Prosocial Behavior." *American Economic Review* 96 (5): 1652–78.

Bendor, Jonathan, Amihai Glazer, and Thomas Hammond. 2001. "Theories of Delegation." *Annual Review of Political Science* 4: 235–69.

Bersch, Katherine, and Francis Fukuyama. 2019. "Bureaucratic Autonomy, State Capacity, and Government Quality: Evidence from Brazil." Paper presented at the Workshop on State Capacity Research: Conceptual and Methodological Frontiers. University of Gothenburg, June 10–11, 2019.

Bergman, Mats, Per Johansson, Sofia Lundberg, and Giancarlo Spagnolo. 2016. "Privatization and Quality: Evidence from Elderly Care in Sweden." *Journal of Health Economics* 49: 109–19.

Besley, Timothy, and Maitreesh Ghatak. 2005. "Competition and Incentives with Motivated Agents." *American Economic Review* 95 (3): 616–36.

Bhavnani, Rikhel, and Alexander Lee A. 2018. "Local Embeddedness and Bureaucratic Performance: Evidence from India." *Journal of Politics* 80 (1) (January): 71–87.

Blomqvist, Paula, and Bo Rothstein. 2000. *Välfärdsstatens nya ansikte*. Stockholm: Agora.

Broms, Rasmus, Carl Dahlström, and Mihály Fazekas. 2019. "Political Competition and Public Procurement Outcomes." *Comparative Political Studies* 52 (9): 1259–92.

Broms, Rasmus, Carl Dahlström, and Marina Nistotskaya. 2020. "Competition and Service Quality: Evidence from Swedish Residential Care Homes." *Governance* 33 (3): 525–43.

Buchanan, James. 1968. *The Demand and Supply of Public Goods*. Chicago: Rand McNally and Company.

Callen, Michael, Saad Gulzar, Ali Hasanain, and Yasir Khan. 2013. "The Political Economy of Public Employee Absence: Experimental Evidence from Pakistan." Working paper, Rady School Manage., University California, San Diego. https://papers.ssrn.com/sol3/papers.cfm?abstract_id=2316245

Callen, Michael, Saad Gulzar, Ali Hasanain, Yasir Khan, and Arman Rezaee. 2015. "Personalities and Public Sector Performance: Evidence from a Health Experiment in Pakistan." NBER Working Paper 21180. https://www.nber.org/papers/w21180

Castle, Nicholas, John Engberg, and Darren Liu. 2007. "Have Nursing Home Compare quality measure scores changed over time in response to competition?" *BMJ Quality & Safety* 16 (3): 185–91.

Charron, Nicholas, Carl Dahlström, Mihaly Fazekas, and Victor Lapuente. 2017. "Careers, Connections, and Corruption Risks: Investigating the impact of bureaucratic meritocracy on public procurement processes." *The Journal of Politics* 79 (1): 89–104.

Chaudhury, Nazmul, Jeffrey Hammer, Michael Kremer, Karthik Muralidharan, and F. Halsey Rogers. 2006. "Missing in Action: Teacher and Health Worker Absence in Developing Countries." *Journal of Economic Perspectives* 20 (1): 91–116.

Cingolani, Luciana, Kaj Thomsson, and Dennis de Crombrugghe. 2015. "Minding Weber More Than Ever? the Impacts of State Capacity and Bureaucratic Autonomy on Development Goals." *World Development* 72 (August): 191–207.

Cooper, Christopher A. 2018. "Encouraging Civil Servants to Be Frank and Fearless: Merit Recruitment and Employee Voice." *Public Administration* 96 (4): 721–35.

Coviello, Decio, and Stefano Gagliarducci. 2017. "Tenure in Office and Public Procurement." *American Economic Journal: Economic Policy* 9 (3: 59–105.

Cowley, Edd and Sarah Smith. 2014. "Motivation and Mission in the Public Sector: Evidence from the World Values Survey." *Theory and Decision* 76 (2) (February): 241–63.

Dal Bó, Ernesto. 2006. "Regulatory Capture: A Review." *Oxford Review of Economic Policy* 22 (2): 203–25.

Dal Bó, Ernesto, Frederico Finan, and Martín A. Rossi. 2013. "Strengthening State Capabilities: The Role of Financial Incentives in the Call to Public Service." *Quarterly Journal of Economics* 128 (3): 1169–218.

D'Arcy, Michelle, and Marina Nistotskaya. 2017. "State First, Then Democracy: Using Cadastral Records to Explain Governmental Performance in Public Goods Provision." *Governance* 30 (2): 193–209.

Dahlström, Carl, and Victor Lapuente. 2010. "Explaining Cross-Country Differences in Performance-Related Pay in the Public Sector." *Journal of Public Administration Research and Theory* 20 (3): 577–600.

Dahlström, Carl, and Victor Lapuente. 2017. *Organizing Leviathan. Politicians, Bureaucrats, and the Making of Good Government.* Cambridge: Cambridge University Press.

Dahlström, Carl, Victor Lapuente, and Jan Teorell. 2012. "The Merit of Meritocratization: Politics, Bureaucracy, and the Institutional Deterrents of Corruption." *Political Research Quarterly* 65 (3): 656–68.

Dahlström, Carl, Marina Nistotskaya, and Maria Tyrberg. 2018. "Outsourcing, Bureaucratic Personnel Quality and Citizen Satisfaction with Public Services." *Public Administration* 96 (1): 218–233.

Deserranno, Erika. 2019. "Financial Incentives as Signals: Experimental Evidence from the Recruitment of Health Workers." *American Economic Journal: Applied Economics* 11 (1) (January): 277–317.

Dixit, Avinash. 2002. "Incentives and Organizations in the Public Sector: An Interpretative Review." *Journal of Human Recourses* 37 (4): 696–727.

Duflo, Esther, Rema Hanna, and Stephen P. Ryan. 2012. "Incentives Work: Getting Teachers to Come to School." *American Economic Review* 102 (4): 1241–78.

Dunleavy, Patrick, and Leandro Carrera. 2013. *Growing the Productivity of Government Services.* Cheltenham: Edward Elgar.

Evans, Peter. 1995. *Embedded Autonomy: States and Industrial Transformation.* Princeton: Princeton University Press.

Evans, Peter, and James E. Rauch. 1999. "Bureaucracy and Growth: A Cross-National Analysis of the Effects of 'Weberian' State Structures on Economic Growth." *American Sociological Review* 64 (5): 748–65.

Finan, Frederico, Benjamin Olken, and Rohini Pande. 2017. "The Personnel Economics of the Developing State." In *Handbook of Economic Field Experiments,* edited by Abhijit Vinayak Banerjee and Esther Duflo, 467–514. Amsterdam: North-Holland.

Finer, Herman. 1936. "Better Government Personnel." *Political Science Quarterly* 51 (4): 569–99.

Finer, Herman. 1941. "Administrative Responsibility in Democratic Government." *Public Administration Review* 1 (4) (Summer): 335–50.

Forder, Julien, and Stephen Allan. 2014. "The Impact of Competition on Quality and Prices in the English Care Homes Market." *Journal of Health Economics* 34 (March): 73–83.

Frant, Howard. 1993. "Rules and Governance in the Public Sector: The Case of Civil Service." *American Journal of Political Science* 37 (4): 990–1007.

Friedrich, Carl J. 1940. "Public Policy and the Nature of Administrative Responsibility." In *Public Policy: A Yearbook of the Graduate School of Public Administration,* vol. 1, edited by Carl J. Friedrich and E. Mason, 3–24. Cambridge: Harvard University Press.

Fukuyama, Francis. 2013. "What is Governance?" *Governance* 26 (3): 347–68.

Gailmard, Sean, and John Patty. 2007. "Slackers and Zealots: Civil Service, Policy Discretion, and Bureaucratic Expertise." *American Journal of Political Science* 51 (4): 873–89.

Gailmard, Sean, and John Patty. 2012. "Formal Models of Bureaucracy." *Annual Review of Political Science* 15: 353–77.

González De Lara, Yadia, Avner Greif, and Saumitra Jha. 2008. "The Administrative Foundations of Self-enforcing Constitutions." *American Economic Review* 98 (2): 105–109.

Goodnow, Frank. J. 1900. *Politics and Administration*. New York: Macmillan.

Greve, Carsten, Per Lægreid, and Lise Rykkja, eds. 2016. *Nordic Administrative Reforms: Lessons for Public Management*. London: Palgrave Macmillan.

Greif, Avner. 2008. "The Impact of Administrative Power on Political and Economic Development: Toward a Political Economy of Implementation." In *Institutions and Economic Performance*, edited by Elhanan Helpman, 17–63. Cambridge: Harvard University Press.

Grindle, Merilee. 2012. *Jobs for the Boys: Patronage and the State in Comparative Perspective*. Cambridge: Harvard University Press.

Gulzar, Saad, and Benjamin J. Pasquale. 2017. "Politicians, Bureaucrats, and Development: Evidence from India." *American Political Science Review* 111 (1): 162–83.

Hammerschmid, Gerhard, Steven Van de Walle, Rhys Andrews, and Philippe Bezes, eds. 2016. *Public Administration Reforms in Europe: The View from the Top*. Cheltenham: Edward Elgar.

Hammond, Thomas, and Jack Knott. 1996. "Who Controls the Bureaucracy? Presidential Power, Congressional Dominance, Legal Constraints, and Bureaucratic Autonomy in a Model of Multi-Institutional Policy-Making." *Journal of Law, Economics, and Organization* 12 (1): 119–66.

Hanna, Rema, and Shing-Yi Wang. 2017. "Dishonesty and Selection into Public Service: Evidence from India." *American Economic Journal: Economic Policy* 9 (3) (August): 262–90.

Hart, Oliver, Andrei Shleifer, and Robert Vishny. 1997. "The Proper Scope of Government: Theory and an Application to Prisons." *The Quarterly Journal of Economics* 112 (4): 1127–61.

Hasnain, Zahid, Nick Manning, and Jan Henryk Pierskalla. 2014. "The Promise of Performance Pay? Reasons for Caution in Policy Prescriptions in the Core Civil Service." *World Bank Research Observer* 29 (2): 235–64.

Henderson, Jeffrey, David Hulme, Hossein Jalilian, and Richard Phillips. 2007. "Bureaucratic Effects: Weberian State Agencies and Poverty Reduction." *Sociology* 41 (3): 515–32.

Hodge, Graeme. 2000. *Privatization: An International Review of Performance*. Boulder, CO: Westview.

Hood, Christopher. 1991. "A Public Management for All Seasons?" *Public Administration* 69 (1): 3–19.

Hood, Christopher, and Ruth Dixon. 2015. *A Government That Worked Better and Cost Less? Evaluating Three Decades of Reform and Change in UK Central Government*. Oxford: Oxford University Press.

Holmstrom, Bengt, and Paul Milgrom. 1987. "Aggregation and Linearity in the Provision of Intertemporal Incentives." *Econometrica* 55 (2): 303–28.

Iyer, Lakshmi, and Anandi Mani. 2012. "Traveling Agents: Political Change and Bureaucratic Turnover in India." *The Review of Economics and Statistics* 94 (3): 723–39.

Jackson, Michael. 2009. "Responsibility versus Accountability in the Friedrich-Finer Debate." *Journal of Management History* 15 (1): 66–77.

Johnson, Chalmers. 1982. *MITI and the Japanese Miracle. The Growth of Industrial Policy, 1925–1975*. Stanford: Stanford University Press.

Kelman, Steven, and John Friedman. 2009. "Performance Improvements and Performance Dysfunctions." *Journal of Public Administration Research and Theory* 19 (4): 917–46.

Khan, Adnan Q., Asim I. Khwaja, and Benjamin A. Olken. 2015. "Tax Farming Redux: Experimental Evidence on Performance Pay for Tax Collectors." *The Quarterly Journal of Economics* 131 (1): 219–71.

Khan, Charles M., Emilson C. D. Silva, and James P. Ziliak. 2001. "Performance-Based Wages in Tax Collection: The Brazilian Tax Collection Reform and its Effects." *Economic Journal* 111 (468): 188–205.

Kiewiet, Roderick, and Mathew McCubbins. 1991. *The Logic of Delegation*. Chicago: University of Chicago Press.

Kiser, Edgar, and Joshua Kane J. 2001. "Revolution and State Structure: The Bureaucratization of Tax Administration in Early Modern England and France." *American Journal of Sociology* 107 (1): 183–223.

Klašnja, Marko. 2015. "Corruption and the Incumbency Disadvantage: Theory and Evidence." *Journal of Politics* 77 (4) (October): 928–42.

Krause, George A., and Kenneth J. Meier, eds. 2005. *Politics, Policy, and Organizations: Frontiers in the Scientific Study of Bureaucracy*. University of Michigan Press.

Lapuente, Victor. 2007. *A Political Economy Approach to Bureaucracies*. Ph.D. diss. University of Oxford.

Lapuente Victor and Steven Van de Walle. 2020. "The effects of new public management on the quality of public services." *Governance* 33 (3): 461–75.

Le Grand, Julian. 2007. *The Other Invisible Hand: Delivering Public Services through Choice and Competition*. Princeton: Princeton University Press.

Lewis, David. 2008. *The Politics of Presidential Appointments*. Princeton: Princeton University Press.

Lewis, David. 2011. "Presidential Appointments and Personnel." *Annual Review of Political Science* 14 (June): 47–66.

Lipsky, Michael. 1980. *Street-level Bureaucracy. Dilemmas of the Individual in Public Service*. New York: Russell Sage Foundation.

Lægreid, Per. 2018. "Designing Organizational Tools: Tool Choices as Administrative Reforms." In *Routledge Handbook of Policy Design*, edited by Michael Howlett and Ishani Mukherjee, 274–87. London: Routledge.

Lichand, Guilherme, Marcos FM Lopes, and Marcelo C Medeiros. 2017. "Is Corruption Good for Your Health?" Working Paper. https://pdfs.semanticscholar.org/d7f4/b3b83e1b0d2c6226 00758bd8031fb7a3f74d.pdf

Mellstrom, Carl, and Magnus Johannesson. 2008. "Crowding Out in Blood Donation: Was Titmuss Right?" *Journal of the European Economic Association* 6 (4): 845–63.

Miller, Gary. 1992. *Managerial Dilemmas: The Political Economy of Hierarchy*. Cambridge: Cambridge University Press.

Miller, Gary. 2000. "Above Politics." *Journal of Public Administration Research and Theory* 10 (2) (April): 289–328.

Miller, Gary J., and Dino Falaschetti. 2001. "Constraining Leviathan: Moral Hazard and Credible Commitment in Institutional Design." *Journal of Theoretical Politics* 13 (4): 389–411.

Miller, Gary, and Andrew Whitford. 2016. *Above Politics*. New York: Cambridge University Press.

Muralidharan, Karthik, and Venkatesh Sundararaman. 2011. "Teacher Performance Pay: Experimental Evidence from India." *Journal of Political Economy* 119 (1): 39–77.

Nistotskaya, Marina, and Luciana Cingolani. 2016. "Bureaucratic Structure, Regulatory Quality, and Entrepreneurship in a Comparative Perspective: Cross-Sectional and Panel Data Evidence." *Journal of Public Administration Research and Theory* 26 (3): 519–34.

Nath, Anusha. 2015. "Bureaucrats and Politicians: How Does Electoral Competition Affect Bureaucratic Performance?" Institute for Economic Development (IED) Working Paper 269. https://pdfs.semanticscholar.org/fda3/8621315199d05d28149373263b41c751bc07.pdf

Niskanen, William. 1971. *Bureaucracy and Representative Government*. Chicago: Aldine Atherton.

Oliveros, Virginia, and Christian Schuster. 2018. "Merit, Tenure, and Bureaucratic Behavior: Evidence from a Conjoint Experiment in the Dominican Republic." *Comparative Political Studies* 51 (6): 759–92.

Olsen, Johan P. 2006. "Maybe it is Time to Rediscover Bureaucracy." *Journal of Public Administration Research and Theory* 16 (1) (January): 1–24.

Painter, Martin, and B. Guy Peters. 2010. *Tradition and Public Administration*. Basingstoke: Palgrave Macmillan.

Pepinsky, Thomas, Jan Pierskalla, and Audrey Sacks. 2017. "Bureaucracy and Service." *Annual Review of Political Science* 20 (May): 249–68.

Perry, James L., and Annie Hondeghem. 2008. "Building Theory and Empirical Evidence about Public Service Motivation." *International Public Management Journal* 11 (1): 3–12.

Pollitt, Christopher, and Geert Bouckaert. 2017. *Public Management Reform*. 4th ed. Oxford: Oxford University Press.

Prendergast, Canice. 1999. "The Provision of Incentives in Firms." *Journal of Economic Literature* 37 (1): 7–63.

Prendergast, Canice. 2007. "The Motivation and Bias of Bureaucrats." *American Economic Review* 97 (1): 180–96.

Pritchett, Lant, Michael Woolcock, and Matt Andrews. 2013. "Looking like a State: Techniques of Persistent Failure in State Capability for Implementation." *The Journal of Development Studies* 49 (1): 1–18.

Rauch, James, and Peter Evans. 2000. "Bureaucratic Structure and Bureaucratic Performance in Less Developed Countries." *Journal of Public Economics* 75 (1): 49–71.

Rasul, Imran, and Daniel Rogger. 2017. "Management of Bureaucrats and Public Service Delivery: Evidence from the Nigerian Civil Service." *The Economic Journal* 128 (608): 413–46.

Ricks, Jacob. 2016. "Building Participatory Organizations for Common Pool Resource Management: Water User Group Promotion in Indonesia." *World Development* 77 (January): 34–47.

Rothstein, Bo. 2005. *Social traps and the problem of trust*. Cambridge: Cambridge University Press.

Rothstein, Bo. 2011. *The Quality of Government: Corruption, Social Trust and Inequality in International Perspective*. Chicago: University of Chicago Press.

Rothstein, Bo, and Jan Teorell. 2008. "What Is Quality of Government? a Theory of Impartial Government Institutions." *Governance* 21 (2): 165–90.

Rubinstein, W. D. 1983. "The End of Old Corruption in Britain, 1780–1860." *Past & Present* 101 (1): 55–86.

Schuster, Christian. 2017. "Legal Reform Need Not Come First: Merit-Based Civil Service Management in Law and Practice." *Public Administration* 95 (3): 571–88.

Shleifer, Andrei. 1998. "State versus Private Ownership." *Journal of Economic Perspectives* 12 (4): 133–50.

Sundell, Anders. 2014. "Are Formal Examinations the most Meritocratic Way to recruit Civil Servants? Not in all Countries." *Public Administration* 92 (2): 440–57.

Taylor, Frederick. 1911. *The Principles of Scientific Management*. New York and London: Harper & brothers.

Teaford, Jon. 1983. *The Unheralded Triumph: City Government in America, 1870–1900*. Baltimore: Johns Hopkins University Press.

Treisman, Daniel. 2000. "The Causes of Corruption: A Cross-National Study." *Journal of Public Economics* 76 (3): 399–457.

Wade, Robert. 1990. *Governing the Market: Economic Theory and the Role of Government in East Asian Industrialization*. Princeton: Princeton University Press.

Weber, Max. 1978. *Economy and Society*, edited by G. Roth and C. Wittich. Berkeley: University of California Press.

Weingast, Barry. 1997. "The Political Foundations of Democracy and the Rule of the Law." *American Political Science Review* 91 (2): 245–63.

Wilson, James Q. 1991. *Bureaucracy: What Government Agencies Do and Why They Do It*. New York: Basic Books.

Wilson, Woodrow. 1887. "Study of Administration." *Political Science Quarterly* 2 (2): 197–222.

CHAPTER 31

....

POCKETS OF EFFECTIVENESS AND ISLANDS OF INTEGRITY

Variation in Quality of Government within Central State Administrations

....

ERIN METZ MCDONNELL AND LUIZ VILAÇA

INTRODUCTION

....

WHY do some state organizations perform effectively and honestly, despite working in incredibly inhospitable environments where many peer organizations struggle? This is a particularly pressing question in low-income states, where the stereotypical belief is that the public sector works poorly, if at all. This belief is reinforced by global efforts to compare the quality of government between states, such as the World Bank's widely used Worldwide Governance Indicators (WGI). Such efforts offer a single measure of the administrative quality of "the state," which is thereby tacitly presumed to be evenly distributed throughout the many organizations comprising the administrative central state (Dahlström et al. 2015; Howell 2011; Kaufmann, Kraay, and Mastruzzi 2010; Knack and Keefer 1995). Scholars' focus on variation in quality of government between states has overlooked extensive variation *within* states. The difference in administrative quality between the best- and worst-rated state agencies in Ghana or Indonesia approximates the distance between "the state" of Japan (WGI of 1.48) and Sierra Leone (WGI of −0.411), spanning the chasm of so-called developed and developing worlds.[1] A rising body of scholarship finds that even within states conventionally regarded as weak, there are some state organizations that perform unusually well, acting honestly and effectively in pursuit

---

[1] Within-country range calculated using the World Bank Governance and Anti-Corruption Diagnostic Survey series (World Bank 1999), rescaled to the more familiar Worldwide Governance Indicators control of corruption measure (2019).

of the public interest despite substantial obstacles (Leonard 2010; McDonnell 2017; Roll 2014).[2]

Understanding high-performing state agencies in challenging contexts has interested scholars and practitioners for more than fifty years. However, consolidation of scholarly dialogue was hampered by terminological diversity and tendencies to cite within geographic silos. High-performing public sector organizations in otherwise weak contexts have been described variously as "islands," "pockets," or "niches" of "excellence," "effectiveness," "efficiency," or "integrity." However varied, these terms all have a similar metaphorical imagery at their core: A demarcated group that is positively distinguished yet inextricably embedded within a larger environment that is inimical or unfavorable. Work in this spirit is increasingly converging on the term "pockets of effectiveness" (POEs), which we use here to describe all work analyzing organizations performing at the high-end of within-state variation on administrative quality. This chapter first examines the historical origins of the POE perspective, identifying a first wave of scholarship emerging out of work on Brazil, the expansion of the perspective to different fields and geographies, and the contemporary consolidation of a subfield that takes as its explicit theoretical focus understanding positive outliers in the variation in quality of government within central state administrations. We then analyze four major theoretical areas that have received greatest attention as explanations for why some state organizations are particularly honest and effective while others are not: external networks, autonomy, technical competence and incentives, and organizational culture. Collectively, these works call for a concerted theoretical agenda, and we conclude by pointing toward some productive directions for future scholarship in this tradition.

KEY CONCEPTS AND METHODOLOGICAL CHALLENGES OF WITHIN-STATE VARIATION

Some POE scholarship focuses explicitly on integrity, others on organizational effectiveness, and still others analyze both dimensions. Integrity involves acting in accordance with explicit organizational rules, typically entailing impersonal administration in pursuit of the public interest. Integrity thus defined entails eschewing different forms of corruption, whereby officials leverage their public office for private gain. Organizational effectiveness is defined as accomplishing explicit organizational goals. Theoretically, integrity and effectiveness are conceptually distinct. However, thus defined, both integrity and effectiveness converge empirically on the impartial pursuit of stated organizational goals, so we treat both outcomes together within this review. We focus on effectiveness (attaining goals) rather than efficiency (conserving resources expended) because 1) relative success attaining explicit goals aligns with most analyses in this body of work, and 2) efficiency

---

[2] We do not engage the conceptually analogous question of variation within a single program across space—for example, differences in the performance of police or municipal water across different municipalities—because such subnational variation is conceptually and methodologically distinct, and is addressed elsewhere in this volume.

may not correlate with effectiveness because these high-performing organizations may enable effectiveness by incorporating excess organizational slack (like high-reliability engineering, some POEs leverage redundancies to mitigate uncertainty and risk from the surrounding environment; see McDonnell 2020). POE scholarship examines public sector organizations, therefore stated organizational goals overwhelmingly incorporate some overt appeal to the public interest framed in ways that are resonant within local standards—hitting at the heart of impartiality in quality of government theory (Rothstein and Teorell 2008). Thus understood, a police organization that effectively generated personal payments through bribes and rackets might be very good at extortion, but would not qualify as an "effective" POE by our definition unless that was a publicly stated goal of the organization.

POE scholars confront distinctive methodological challenges when seeking to identify relative integrity or effectiveness, because comparisons to the performance of other organizations within the central administrative state must grapple with incomparability of outputs. The organizational model of states that has proliferated globally is grounded in discrete jurisdictions, creating an apples-to-oranges problem that makes it difficult to compare objective outcome measures across organizations governing different sectors.[3] How can researchers measure whether the Ministry of Education's increases in literacy are evidence of superior organizational performance relative to Agriculture's promotion of high-yielding seeds or Transport's construction of new roads? The ministries pursue incommensurate goals, and moreover each may confront differently challenging structural constraints beyond their immediate control, such as a drought.

To address this challenge, some scholars have intentionally selected POE cases of state organizations with a very limited range of outputs believed to be relatively comparable across countries (Grindle 1997a).[4] However, a similar challenge can arise even when comparing the performance of ministries in the same sector in different countries. Unlike the crisp and universal metric of profit in corporations, ministries in the same sector may pursue different organizational goals even when acting competently in the public interest. One ministry of agriculture might pursue high-yielding seeds and increased fertilizer usage among small peasant farmers, while in the adjacent country the "same" ministry may focus on controlling pests blighting a critical crop and fostering farmer cooperatives for global export. In light of these measurement challenges, much POE scholarship has relied on *reputational measures* to identify cases of high-performing agencies, whether through media reports (Tendler 1997), key informants (Therkildsen and Tidemand 2007), or surveying major organizations with high-frequency government contact (McDonnell 2017).

Comparing the *integrity* of state organizations poses some parallel challenges, though research in this vein has tended to use both reputational measures as well as specific behavioral outcomes. Integrity and corruption encompass a wide range of behaviors, which may be differently visible to everyday citizens and may vary by sector. Large global measurement efforts, such as Transparency International, navigate these difficulties by focusing

---

[3] This is the most significant methodological difference between POE research and the analogous field of subnational variation, which analyzes the performance of functionally similar organization in different regions.

[4] Grindle (1997a) conducts a six-country comparison but purposively focuses on a few state organizations performing functions that are narrowly similar across context, such as controlling the macro-economy.

on street-level bribery. Transparency International's Global Corruption Barometer asks a sample of citizens if they have interacted with a public service organization and, if so, whether they have offered or solicited a bribe. This provides a more comparable metric, but also excludes other corrupt practices, such as kickbacks for contracts. Scholars have credible reasons to believe that parts of the state may be systematically more vulnerable to different types of corruption, so measuring only a narrow practice may produce a skewed picture of integrity broadly across state organizations. Attention to street-level bribery also tends to force measurement to focus on a few parts of the administrative state with which citizens have relatively routine direct contact, such as utilities, police, health, and education. Few citizens have regular direct contact with ministries of finance, which makes it illegible through the lens of citizen reports of bribery, though its integrity is still crucial to the functioning of the state.

BRIEF HISTORY OF THE SUBFIELD

Focused attention on within-state variation in the performance of government administration first emerged in Brazil. There is general consensus that enhanced administrative capacities in Brazil initially emerged within isolated pockets of the state or "*bolsões de eficiência*" (Evans 1992; Geddes 1996; Lafer 1970; Nunes 1984). The mid-twentieth-century Brazilian state seems to have been the first state to have reflexively and explicitly understood itself as *intentionally* creating clusters of technocratic strength while foregoing reforms elsewhere, which enabled political elites to achieve important development goals while leaving vast swaths of the state available for patronage hiring to shore up support in a fragile party system. President Vargas experimented with creating *autarquias*, semi-autonomous administrative agencies, as early as 1938, when he created the Administrative Department of Public Service (DASP), an agency dedicated to rationalizing public administration in Brazil and providing technical assistance to the president (Nunes 1997; Wahrlich 1983).[5]

After President Kubitschek was elected in 1956, Helio Jaguaribe published an influential editorial, writing on behalf of a salon of Brazilian intellectuals,[6] arguing that sweeping reforms to the whole Brazilian administrative system were infeasible. They suggested instead that the state create a few strong organizations capable of implementing President Kubitschek's ambitious development plan (Jaguaribe 1956). This was precisely what Kubitschek eventually did. Following DASP, a handful of other POEs emerged in Brazil, including the National Development Bank (BNDES, founded in 1952), the Superintendency of Currency and Credit (SUMOC, founded in 1945) and, later, several of Kubitschek's Executive Groups (*Grupos Executivos*, founded 1956–60), all depicted in excellent case studies (Graham 2014; Lafer 1970; Wahrlich 1983; Willis 1986). Seemingly unaware of the great Brazilian experiment already under way, almost a decade later a research report by the Economic Development Institute, the World Bank's predecessor, would muse about the

---

[5] DASP was conceived by Luis Simões Lopes, a close friend of Vargas who "sought to create a technical service with admission on a purely universalistic basis" (Daland 1981, 355).

[6] For more information on Jaguaribe and the group, known as IBESP, see Fundação Getúlio Vargas (2001).

theoretical possibility of a "nuclei" approach to administrative reform when comprehensive reforms proved infeasible. Echoing observations no less true today, the report's author Waterston suggested, "Instead of insisting on an 'all or nothing' basis, on drastic, across-the-board changes in personnel practices, administrative procedures and organization, it might be better to select a few large or otherwise important projects or programs and concentrate on improving administration and organization" (1965, 285).

Concentrated and explicit academic attention on effective "pockets" or "islands" emerged first from Brazilians studying abroad (Lafer 1970; Nunes 1984; Pinto 1969), and later among American scholars studying Brazil (Daland 1981; Evans 1992; Geddes 1990; Schneider 1992; Tendler 1997; Willis 1986). But scholars beyond Brazil also noticed uneven administrative capacity as a structural feature of states, from the U.S. to many so-called "developing" or "third-world" states in Latin America, Africa, and Asia. Historian Leonard White (1954) noted the unevenness of administrative quality in the early U.S. state, with a few agencies acting effectively in the public interest during the Jacksonian era famed for its patronage politics. Similarly, in their comparative analysis of New Deal agencies, Skocpol and Finegold (1982, 271) observed that "the U.S. Department of Agriculture was, so to speak, an island of state strength in an ocean of weakness" demonstrating strong administrative capacities at a time when, in general, "the civil administrative capacities of the U.S. national state in the 1930s were weak and poorly coordinated." Other scholars have observed, often just briefly in passing, that even in the contemporary U.S., "pockets of effectiveness" exist within U.S. public schools (Crew 1998; Wikeley 1998) and labor unions (Boxall and Haynes 1997). Some work was explicitly interventionist and prescriptive, wrapped up in the rise of the Western-based global aid industry in the 1990s. For example, the founding of Transparency International catalyzed a stream of writing on "islands of integrity," a plan for intentionally improving good governance through localized "integrity pacts" (Eigen 1996; Ocampo 2000).

Much of the expansion of the POE perspective that flourished in the 1990s sought to understand high-performing agencies in otherwise weak contexts as not merely a passing descriptive observation, but increasingly as a core research focus in its own right (Grindle 1997a, 1997b; Israel 1987; Leonard 1991; Matsuda 1997; Strauss 1998; Uphoff 1994). There was a cluster of researchers embracing that project with ties to Berkeley: Judith Tendler and David Leonard worked closely together on a USAID project at Berkeley around 1979–81; Leonard and Peter Evans served together on several dissertations; several authors whose work includes POE-style thinking were graduate students at Berkeley during the 1980s, including Edson de Oliveira Nunes ('84), Barbara Grosh ('88), Rwekaza Mukandala ('88), Julia Strauss ('91), Barbara Geddes ('86), and Ben Ross Schneider ('87). Apart from the cluster of scholars with ties to Berkeley, however, much of the first-wave POE scholarship took place largely in isolation without concerted dialogue among scholars.

Scholars in a variety of disciplines and working in different geographic areas converged on studying public sector *success cases* as an antidote to the dominant intellectual trends of the time: A post–Washington Consensus that was highly critical of states, denigrated the public sector of low-income countries in particular, and which sought to impose Western-generated solutions universally (see for example Tendler 1997). Some POE scholars were inspired by lived experiences that contradicted the assumption that public sectors in developing countries were universally doomed. David Leonard had previously worked on agricultural extension management for the Institute for Development Studies in Nairobi

(Leonard, personal communication, April 3, 2019). Similarly, Merilee Grindle, another early leader in the subfield, had experiences that contrasted sharply with the prevailing stereotypes of public sector work in low-income countries. Grindle observed,

> when I did the research for my dissertation, I worked with people who worked in government and found many of them to be deeply committed and intelligent—and then at the Kennedy School I regularly taught mid-career people from governments in developing countries who were courageous, idealistic, and strategic in their efforts to make change happen (Grindle, personal communication, April 14, 2019).

Post-2000 scholarship in the subfield constitutes a second wave of POE studies, characterized by a proliferation of scholars working in the area, a greater move towards within- and between-country comparison studies, and importantly increasing dialogue between studies, consolidating into a discernible interdisciplinary scholarly subfield (Andrews 2015; Barma, Huybens, and Viñuela 2014; Bersch, Praça, and Taylor 2017; Booth and Cammack 2013; Crook 2010; Hertog 2010; Johnson 2015; McDonnell 2017; Owusu 2006). This consolidation was facilitated by several key contributions, particularly David Leonard's (2010) meta-analysis and Michael Roll's (2014) edited volume.

Across a wide range of countries and government functions, these varied POE studies collectively demonstrate the need for a consolidated theory of organizational-level resiliency. For too long there was a tacit assumption that conditions promoting high-quality administration were merely the absence of conditions enabling corruption, such as the lightly monitored access to valued resources (Campos and Pradhan 2007; Flatters and Macleod 1995). Across a range of studies, POE scholarship consistently demonstrates that explaining honest and effective state administration in challenging contexts depends on more than merely the absence of the conditions enabling corruption. This subfield has now matured into a scholarly agenda ripe for theoretically informed case selection and theory refinement, therefore it is important to take stock of some of the major areas of consensus within the literature as well as key differences. Below we identify four major theoretical themes in analyses of POEs: technical competence and incentives, external networks, autonomy, and organizational culture.

Prevailing Explanations for POEs

To analyze systematically the trends in POE scholarship, we developed a qualitative content analysis of the academic POE subfield. We identified 86 distinct POEs, located in 55 different studies, using major academic search engines and the reference lists of identified POE works, including key review pieces (Leonard 2010; Roll 2014). We had two primary criteria for inclusion: 1) the study presented empirical evidence on at least one successful POE, defined as a relatively high-performing public sector organization embedded in a generally challenging organizational environment where many peer organizations fail; and 2) the study demonstrated sufficient depth of discussion, including information about data collection and analysis.

Because some publications analyzed multiple different POEs and sometimes advanced different explanations for them, we use the POE, rather than the publication, as our unit of analysis. We coded studies using deductive codes drawn from previous works (Leonard 2010; McDonnell 2017; Roll 2014), coupled with emergent codes. Our final coding scheme contained four aggregate categories, each of which included subcategorical codes (see Appendix A). Categories are not mutually exclusive; for example, a case could emphasize both elite alliances and organizational culture in the explanation for why the POE succeeded.

At times we report how common a particular theoretical condition is across the body of studies reviewed here, giving a sense of the relatively scholarly attention different conditions have received. However, these numbers must be interpreted with caution. These should not be interpreted as evidence of which aspects empirically matter more for POEs because the data used in this analysis is not representative of the general population of pockets (indeed, no exhaustive list of all pockets exists), and does not include nonpockets, that is, organizations in the same environment that failed to become successful.

Merit-Oriented Recruitment, Training, and Material Incentives

Our analysis of major themes in POE research raises thorny questions about how to operationally distinguish "causal factors" that explain POE emergence and "defining features" that characterize effective POEs. This is perhaps most clear with respect to meritocracy. Nearly two-thirds of POE cases (62%) cite the relatively high technical competence of organizations as a key explanation for their effectiveness.[7] Sometimes meritocracy is seen as a causal factor contributing to productivity, and elsewhere it is interpreted as so axiomatically synonymous with organizational productivity that it might be conceptualized more as a dependent variable that signals the presence of a POE. We include it as an explanatory theme because we argue it should not go without saying that a concentration of technical competence is a potentially critical foundation for POEs, and that changes to organizational routines for recruitment, training, and incentives may be temporally prior to the emergence of distinctive organizational effectiveness. The underlying theory of emergence here is that governments struggle administratively because they lack personnel with the requisite skills, so organizational practices that address human resources gaps will foster the emergence of POEs. Because skilled, performance-oriented personnel are scarce in the local environments, a concentration of personnel sufficient to catalyze organizational change may only be possible when distinctive human resources are clustered (McDonnell 2020), which helps explain why there is uneven organizational performance among state organizations.

Technical competence enables POE functioning by optimizing resource management (Larizza and Glynn 2014), enhancing the ability to respond to exogenous shocks (Viñuela and Ousman 2014), understanding the agency's organizational field (Whitfield et al. 2015), finding creative new solutions that enhance performance (Leonard 1991; McDonnell 2020; Strauss 1998), and interpreting relevant laws and regulations (Strauss 2014). For example, technocratically skilled staff were crucial for the success of the Brazilian National

---

[7] It is possible the seemingly taken-for-granted relationship between technical competence and organizational performance suppressed the number of cases explicitly mentioning this condition.

Development Bank (BNDE). Willis argues "the early managers of the BNDES were dedicated to enhancing the skills and knowledge of the technical staff," which they hoped would contribute to building technocratic competence in the economy broadly (1995, 219).

Authors seeking to understand how unusual levels of technical competence came to be vested in some pockets of the state have typically emphasized three mechanisms: 1) merit-based recruitment (cited by 51% studies); 2) training (57%), and 3) incentives (65%). Enacting *merit-based recruitment* typically faces challenges and pushback in contexts where patronage is the norm (Grindle 2012). Pursuing merit is not merely a choice, but also a genuine practical question of *how* to enact that change. For example, successful reform programs in a Brazilian province were able to enact merit-based local recruitment because the reformist governor provided political cover (Tendler 1997). Other POEs explicitly outsourced aspects of recruitment to international consultants or implemented merit-based exams, both of which buffered the organization from patronage influence by deferring to outsiders or mechanical objectivity in the selection process (Geddes 1990; Willis 1986; Strauss 1998). For example, Nigeria's successful Food and Drug Agency (NAFDAC) outsourced significant aspects of recruitment to external consultants, who halved the initial applicant pool and then administered an aptitude test; only the most successful candidates on the test were then interviewed by the organization (Roll 2011).

In addition to selecting competent personnel, often successful pockets have also invested in developing technical skills by *training* existing personnel, both locally (Kuwajima 2016; Larizza and Glynn 2014; Roll 2011; Samford 2017; Tendler 1997) and internationally (Abah 2012; Viñuela 2014; Willis 1995; Roll 2014; McDonnell 2020). According to some studies, training was particularly important because in addition to developing technical skills within staff members, it "contributed to the diffusion of professional norms and beliefs about what the proper structures for a [specific] agency are" (Viñuela and Ousman 2014, 204). Training periods could thereby provide both explicit knowledge in technical skills but also lived exposure to technocratic organizational environments that helped shape new understandings of desirable organizational practice (McDonnell 2020).

A focus on *incentives* as a pathway to technical competence echoes the global dominance of economics in policy thinking, which casts incentives as a key means of recruiting and retaining highly skilled staff. Perhaps surprisingly, *financial* incentives were only mentioned in 24% of cases, which may reflect the unfortunate reality that POEs are located within resource-scarce states and donors generally refuse to give aid to enhance public-sector salaries. Nevertheless, some scholars argue that relatively higher salaries and welfare benefits can help attract high-skilled and effective candidates from the labor pool (Roll 2011; Barma and Osken 2014a). Other authors emphasize financial incentives not only for recruitment (selection effects) but also to motivate existing personnel (influence effects). In Booth's analysis of public health agencies in Rwanda, financial awards were used to "encourage staff to find innovative ways of implementing health policies" (Booth and Cammack 2013, 64; see also Whitfield and Buur 2014). Similarly, agricultural and health organizations in Burundi improved performance after financial rewards were put in place that provided staff incentives to perform better (Chemouni 2016). Nigeria's Food and Drug agency offered financial incentives to whistleblowers who identified corruption within the organization (Akunyili 2013). Though financial incentives may play a role in some POEs, financial incentives are not a necessary condition for the emergence of pockets: Most POEs improved organizational performance *despite* little financial reward.

Relatively high incentives may also discipline public servants by increasing the opportunity costs of losing employment for poor performance or corruption, a kind of negative incentive. Negative incentives usually appeared in two forms: sanctions (Booth and
Cammack 2013; Peiffer and Armytage 2018; Roll 2011) and dismissals (Roll 2014; Kuwajima
2016; McDonnell 2017; Leonard 1991; Strauss 1998). The rationale here is that alongside
rewarding good performers, pockets also punish those who underperform or fail to abide
by organizational rules and expectations. Anderson, for example, notes that removing
corrupt agents was quite important to ensure the continuity of high-performing social
welfare agencies in Timor-Leste, in which "one director and two senior staff were recently
removed, and some 21 staff under temporary contracts with the HHF did not have their
contracts renewed due to questionable administrative practices" (Anderson 2014b, 286).
Negative incentives may both directly affect productivity by removing or reforming poor
performers, and may also have indirect effects on other workers by serving as cautionary
tales (McDonnell 2017).

EXTERNAL NETWORKS

Alliances outside the organization are another core explanation for successful POEs.
Engagement with actors outside the organization was an explanatory factor in the vast
majority of POE studies (88%). Explanations focused on network connections to different
types of actors: 1) political elites (70% of all cases); 2) private sectors (43%); 3) international
organizations (51%); 4) civil society (52%); and 5) other state agencies (47%). Case by case,
scholars typically emphasize the importance of a particular type of network alliance.
However, looking comparatively, we argue external networks are more parsimoniously
understood as roughly equifinal pathways.[8] We therefore group them together because
they share a similar underlying theory of POE emergence: Organizations struggle because
they lack various critical resources, and network connections can provide sufficient access
to resources thereby enabling organizational performance. Because these are typically
resource-constrained environments, a sufficient endowment of resources is only possible
when investments are concentrated, therefore we would again expect to observe uneven organizational performance among state organizations. Secondarily, external networks may
support POE emergence because they may also provide pressure to perform and protection
from influences suborning organizational performance.

Different cases emphasize different types of networks, however meta-analytically external networks appear to provide a similar set of resources, suggesting that alliances to
different external actors may be theoretically equivalent. Access to *financial resources*,
which can be converted into other needs, can be enhanced by connections to political elites
(Huntington and Wibbels 2014; Samatar and Oldfield 1995; Whitfield et al. 2015), private
sector actors (Whitfield and Buur 2014), or international organizations (Anderson 2014b;
Chemouni 2016; Fairfield 2006; Johnson 2015; Larizza and Glynn 2014; Noy 2017; Roll
2011; Whitfield et al. 2015; Willis 1995). *Personnel training* may be supplemented by other

---

[8] For equifinality, see SUIN causes (Mahoney, Kimball, and Koivu 2009).

public sector organizations (Daland 1981; McDonnell 2020), private sectors (Barma and Osken 2014a; Herrera 2017; Samford 2017), international organizations or civil society (Roll 2011). *Technical assistance* may be provided by other state agencies (Korten 1980; Strauss 2014; Viñuela and Alvesson 2014; Willis 1995), private companies (Hout 2014; Whitfield et al. 2015), or international organizations (Anderson 2014b; Chemouni 2016; Fairfield 2006; Johnson 2015; Larizza and Glynn 2014; Noy 2017; Roll 2011; Whitfield et al. 2015; Willis 1995). Operational support *implementing programs* may be aided by networks with other public-sector organizations (McDonnell 2020), the private sector (Barma and Osken 2014b; Evans 1995; Muilerman and Vellema 2017; Tendler 1997) or civil society (Fairfield 2006; Herrera 2017; Korten 1980; Kuwajima 2016; Tendler 1997). For example, public prosecutors in Brazil became more effective at fighting corruption when they cultivated networks with federal detectives and tax inspectors (Vilaça 2019). Similarly, connections to other state organizations in the same country can facilitate implementation by improving workflow efficiency (Fairfield 2006) and boosting coordination across different agencies (Geddes 1996; Samford 2017; Whitfield et al. 2015; Willis 1995), which can be a key ingredient for the effective implementation of public policies and management of the external environment (Viñuela and Alvesson 2014).

Most cases emphasize alliances with only a few different types of external actors, which makes intuitive sense if, as we argue, these networks provide similar benefits. Nearly half (48%) of the studies emphasized two or fewer different types of external alliances—for example, connections to elites *and* international organizations—while 10.5% mentioned all five different external networks types. Among organizations with multiple connections, there is some evidence that there may be patterns to the types of connections that co-occur: Meta-analytically, alliances to international organizations are correlated positively with alliances to elites, other agencies, and civil society. Conversely, alliances to the private sector were not significantly correlated to any other forms of network ties.

Beyond the primary emphasis on resource attainment, external networks may also facilitate the emergence of POEs by *shifting the balance of pressures* on an agency towards an organizational performance orientation, by increasing pressure on the POE to perform or protecting a POE from other pressures that might suborn a performance orientation. The tacit theory of change here is that organizations fail to perform because the local environment does not reward organizational output or because their efforts are divided among sometimes irreconcilable goals. Pressure to perform well can emerge from political elites (Geddes 1996; Hertog 2010; Ricks 2017), international organizations (Muilerman and Vellema 2017; Shrank 2016; Whitfield et al. 2015), or civil society (Crook 2010; Tendler 1997). For example, among effective water management organizations in Mexico, Herrera (2017, 19–20) observed that "business, even when acting in its own material interests, can be an effective ally for infrastructure-based public service reforms, and its support of these reform initiatives can translate into considerable material improvements that serve the public good." Conversely, the balance of pressures on organizations may be improved when networks reduce external pressures that otherwise interfere with pursuing the organization's stated public goals, including patronage hiring or politicizing the production or distribution of outputs. Organizations may obtain protection from other political pressures through relationships with supportive high-level political elites (Leonard 1991), private sector groups (Whitfield and Buur 2014), international organizations (Leonard 1991), or local civil society (Rich 2013).

We have argued many external network ties provide functionally equivalent benefits to POEs, however there are some areas where particular types of actors enjoy distinct advantages. Unlike other actors, political elites can grant organizations new legal powers. For example, a Nigerian anti-human-trafficking agency was granted power to prosecute as a result of an alliance with political elites (Roll 2011). Conversely, civil society organizations such as NGOs (Rich 2013; Viñuela and Alvesson 2014), media outlets (Anderson 2014b), academics (Korten 1980), and community leaders (Samford 2017) are particularly well positioned to affect public attitudes and engage citizens (Anderson 2014b; Booth and Cammack 2013; Brinkerhoff and Wetterberg 2013; Rich 2013; Vanderhurst 2017), and thereby build public support to protect the organization against threats (Carpenter 2001; Hout 2014; Vilaça 2019).

Autonomy

Autonomy features prominently in both scholarly accounts of POE success (Bersch et al. 2017; Herrera 2017; Matsuda 1997) and in the toolkit of development practitioners seeking to enhance state capacity (Barma et al. 2014). Three-quarters of the cases emphasized some form of autonomy, whether political autonomy (57% of all cases), personnel autonomy (51%), or financial autonomy (16%). The underlying theory of emergence here is that organizations struggle to perform because they are subject to political pressures that direct effort away from explicit organizational goals, so providing autonomy buffers an organization from contrary pressures, allowing it to become more technocratic. Competing political pressures that divide organizational effort include providing patronage employment to technically un-qualified political supporters, or distributing outputs at heavily subsidized rates that garner political goodwill but decimate financial sustainability (Hertog 2010). Hertog captures this view: "the immediate cause [of relative organizational success] is a profit- and market-oriented management that is autonomous in its daily operations, hence insulated against political and bureaucratic predation, and receives clear incentives from a strictly limited, coherent group of high-level principals in the political regime" (2010, 263). However, pa-tronage employment and political distribution of state goods are prominent means of or-dering political power and ensuring stability in many polities (Mungiu-Pippidi 2015; Prasad, Martins da Silva, and Nickow 2018), which is why protection from those pressures are fi-nite, helping explain the observed uneven distribution of government quality within state administrations.

In some scholarly literatures, meritocracy is presented as almost synonymous with pol-itical autonomy. We treat them as separate themes because first, autonomy may not always lead to meritocracy and vice versa. Second, meritocracy may be independently caused by other factors, apart from autonomy. Finally, even if meritocracy and autonomy have elective affinities resulting in a virtuous mutually reinforcing cycle, whether the cycle starts with merit, autonomy, or either remains an open question of considerable theoretical and prac-tical importance.

Some autonomy or informal discretion over personnel (cited in 51% of cases) enables POEs to exert local influence over the factors prioritized in hiring, which matters because it enables POEs to assert technical or meritocratic selection criteria in contexts where patronage is common. Localized hiring may also enhance identification with the specific POE organization in contrast to the "spoiled" identity of public service generally (McDonnell 2020). Though control over personnel does not require full formal legal autonomy, organizations that had full formal legal autonomy typically also had autonomy over personnel decisions, recruiting and dismissing staff outside of conventional civil service regulations and procedures (Strauss 1998; Willis 1995). Autonomy over personnel enables discretion not only to select new recruits, but also to discipline poor-performing or corrupt officials (Leonard, 1991; Strauss 1998). However, even where organizations were formally subject to general civil service hiring procedures, POEs could still gain a measure of discretion over personnel through informal means, such as hiring candidates after provisional observation during national service or refusing new recruits who do not meet POE standards (McDonnell 2017).

Scholarly emphasis on autonomy highlights an interesting tension with the prior section: Emphasizing the critical importance of close *alliances with* political elites seems to be at odds with *autonomy from* political elites. Interestingly, 24% of studies emphasize neither condition, 26% emphasize one but not the other, and half emphasize *both* alliances with elites and autonomy from political elites. Reading comparatively across cases suggests that alliances with elites or autonomy from political elites can be functionally equivalent, different means of protecting the organization from outside influences that subvert resources from its primary organizational goal. Formal autonomy may reduce political elite interference. On the other hand, a sufficiently motivated political elite who sees it in his interest for the organization to perform, such as when facing existential threat, can use his political power to protect an organization from his own and others' efforts to exert patronage or political calculus over the organization (Ricks 2017).

Alternatively, Leonard's account of successful agricultural POEs in Kenya argues elite alliances and autonomy may work together, emphasizing interpersonal connections with elites as the essential foundation for securing organizational autonomy in fact as well as law. He observes,

> the autonomy of an organization from undue politicization is not something that can simply be granted to it in a single constitutional act. It has to be earned and then maintained through political connections … Power in African political systems is aggregated out of patronage networks, is highly personalized and generally is concentrated in the hands of the head of state (Leonard 1991, 258).

For example, by leveraging his interpersonal relationship with Kenya's President, the head of the Kenyan Tea Development Agency was able to gain greater discretion over hiring, firing, and operations, including expanding into new domains that benefited the organization but were opposed by existing vested interests (Leonard 1991).

Organizational Culture

Finally, there is a longstanding strand of scholarship in the subfield that sees organizational culture as central to POE emergence (Grindle 1997a; McDonnell 2020; Tendler 1997), drawing on an august tradition within organizational scholarship that highlights the "spirit" or "character" of an organization as an essential component of its success (Barnard 1938; Roethlisberger and

Dickson 1939; Selznick 1957). We include within this category aspects of organizational culture, leadership, and staff who identify strongly with the organization. Three-quarters of the cases mentioned at least one of these conditions, with half (52%) focusing on organizational culture. The tacit theory of emergence here is that improving worker morale and intrinsic or social motivation can jumpstart organizational performance even without other material changes. Grindle's (1997a) pathbreaking comparative study of 29 organizations in six countries found that leadership and "organizational mystique" were two of the strongest factors differentiating strong organizations from poor performers. She describes organizational mystique as "well-defined missions that were widely ascribed to by employees ... [which] amounted to a mystique about the organization and the importance of the task it was performing. Employees internalized the organization's goals and saw themselves as vital contributors to its accomplishment" (Grindle 1997a, 486). Tendler observes a similar phenomenon among highly effective state programs in a poor region of Brazil, where workers "demonstrated unusual dedication to their jobs" that was enabled by government "creat[ing] a strong sense of 'calling' and mission around these particular programs and their workers" (1997a, 14). McDonnell (2017) refers to this as the bureaucratic ethos, the convergence on a shared set of practices and comportment oriented to achieving the organization's goals.

These studies view organizational culture as a foundation that can directly affect organizational performance. Due to longstanding traditions within macro-institutional and political economy research, there can be a tendency to endow factors like "elite interests" with causal weight and to discount organizational culture as merely a defining feature of successful organizations rather than a contributing factor. However, generations of organizational scholars have argued that the features characterizing an organization are key explanations for why some organizations are more effective than others, which dovetails with calls from comparative institutionalists to take seriously endogenous institutional change (Mahoney and Thelen 2010). Development practice has also begun to seriously investigate the idea that enhancing organizational performance may begin with efforts to improve organizational culture, even with no change to personnel, compensation, or the material conditions of work. This approach features prominently in the "Field Level Leadership" initiative designed and developed by public servants in southern India, and supported by the World Bank (Pahuja and Johnson forthcoming).

POE scholars who analyze organizational culture argue that strongly identifying with organizational mission enhances worker effort, as "[c]ivil servants internalise a belief that employment in the [POE] unit is a privilege ... They bragged of their long hours and intense work expectations" (Johnson 2015, 787).[9] A shared sense of identification with organizational mission can promote a tangible sense of *esprit de corps* among staff, facilitating better coordination to improve performance (Anderson 2014a; Leonard 1991; Viñuela and Alvesson 2014; Willis 1995). A strong organizational culture also acts as an "implicit contract" between leaders and workers, which enhances trust, reduces principal–agent problems, and fosters performance (Grindle 1997a, 488).

Strong organizational culture can also indirectly enable POEs by bringing into being other advantages mentioned in prior sections. An agency with a strong organizational culture

---

[9] Meta-analytically, a strong organizational culture is significantly correlated with committed staff ($r=0.52$, $p<0.001$), with 36% of studies mentioning both features.

around mission and staff who deeply identify with that mission is better able to cultivate beneficial external networks (Vilaça 2020). Organizational leaders can create greater autonomy, either formally or informally (Hout 2014; Johnson 2015; Leonard, 1991; McDonnell 2017). A positive organizational culture is also a kind of nonfinancial incentive that aids in recruiting talented staff who are professionally drawn to working in an enabling environment with committed colleagues (McDonnell 2020).

There is, however, disagreement about the relative importance of leadership even among proponents of the organizational culture perspective. Tendler explicitly eschewed analyzing leadership because she believed leadership was analytically intractable and impractical for policy recommendations, though she does state "I do not question the importance of leadership" (1997, 18). By contrast, Grindle (1997a, 487) views leadership and management style as essential for cultivating a performance-oriented organizational culture, observing that high-performers had a management style that "encourage[d] participation, flexibility, teamwork, problem solving, and equity" compared to "top-down decision making, favoritism, lack of consultation, and poor capacity to organize work" among the weak agencies. Organizational leaders may also be essential enforcers of positive incentives for performance and negative sanctions for failures. Strauss (1998, 68) and Leonard (1991, 141) both agree that maintaining a results-oriented organizational culture depended on the "eternal vigilance" of management. In several notable cases, POEs emerged from the reform of existing but ineffective organizations, and those rapid reforms coincide closely with the appointment of a new leader (Roll 2014).

Leadership may foster the cultivation of a mission-focused organizational culture and employee identification. In Lao's electricity utility, "its management systems and organizational culture are such that those workers feel themselves valued members of the institution" (Barma and Osken 2014, 121) resulting in workers who have "a strong professional identity as power sector engineers, which contributes to an organizational mystique and sense of belonging" (136). Similarly, analysis of Timor-Leste's central bank demonstrates how leadership, organizational culture, and staff dedication can be intertwined:

> There is a strong emphasis on professionalism and work ethic, as well as a merit culture that is promoted at all levels of leadership. Employees refer to these values as the features that distinguish the Central Bank from the rest of public administration ... To them, their professional standing results from their belonging to the organization (Viñuela 2014, 367).

McDonnell (2020) observes that leaders may be particularly influential in countries where patronage is common because staff are already accustomed to acting to please a leader's wishes, a habit that can diffuse performance orientation when the "big man" atop an organization makes clear a desire for merit, integrity, and performance.

Towards Theoretical Synthesis: A Virtuous Cycle?

A key question that emerges from our analysis is how these four categories—merit, networks, autonomy, and organizational culture—relate to each other. Figure 31.1 depicts a hypothetical virtuous cycle, intentionally agnostic to the unresolved question of a starting point such that

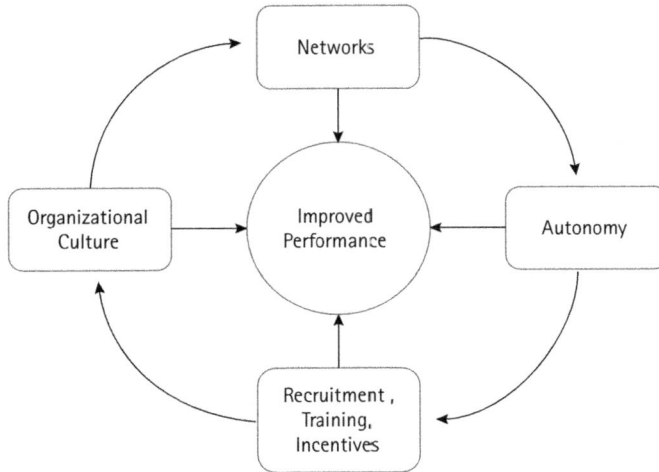

FIGURE 31.1 Virtuous cycle hypothesis

any of the aforementioned themes may act as an "on-ramp" to a process of POEs emergence and consolidation (Figure 31.1). For example, support from networks may be instrumental for POEs to secure political and administrative autonomy (Abah 2012; Anderson 2014a; Leonard, 1991; Muilerman and Vellema 2017; Viñuela 2014). In turn, obtaining legal autonomy or practical discretion may enable merit-oriented changes in how agencies recruit, train, manage, and reward staff. Merit-oriented procedures to select, promote, and dismiss officials can help organizations build a cohesive shared understanding, resulting in an organizational culture that reinforces impersonal and effective performance (McDonnell 2017). However, it is important to emphasize that as currently hypothesized, the virtuous cycle is agnostic as to a starting point. For example, the virtuous cycle could begin with organizational culture. Several studies see the rapid onset of organizational reform from a poor-performer into a POE coinciding with a new leader who occasioned a new organizational culture that signaled performance would be taken seriously. Those changes then set off observable improvements in organizational effectiveness, which cultivated public reputations that in turn were leveraged into external networks of support, which made possible putting into place more merit-based recruitment in the future (Akunyili 2013; Strauss 1998).

Alternatively, instead of a single virtuous cycle, the discrepant emphases found in the literature could suggest a second approach to theoretical synthesis: multiple distinctive equifinal pathways. That is, as the subfield advances towards more theory testing and refinement, we may be able to identify whether there are multiple different *configurations of conditions* that are collectively sufficient to generate a POE. For example, we might hypothesize a distinctive "regard" pathway for street-level bureaucracies that provide desired public goods directly to citizens, such as Tendler's public health workers (1997), in which external public network connections enhance social incentives to perform by providing social regard or risking social sanction from the community, resulting in a POE when coupled with sufficient merit in recruitment and resources to perform tasks. Conversely, Hertog (2010) and Israel (1987) may represent a "rational" pathway that emphasizes not social or intrinsic incentives to perform, but rather focused and agreed-upon metrics for performance coupled with leadership that monitors and rewards organizational outcomes. Differentiating whether there is a single virtuous cycle or multiple configurational pathways remains important work for future theoretical refinement in the subfield.

SUGGESTIONS FOR FUTURE RESEARCH

This growing literature has multiple promising avenues for future research. Consolidation of prior findings in the field can influence future research by informing case selection as the field matures towards a third wave of POE scholarship focused on theory refinement. First, the field should engage in methodological refinement around how to identify POE cases systematically and with high inter-coder reliability, grappling with issues of cross-cultural variation in reputational assessment and perceptual biases that make some POEs less externally legible to the public. Second, theoretical refinement to eliminate idiosyncratic features depends on selecting cases of multiple POEs within or across countries (Barma et al. 2014; Grindle 1997a; Johnson 2015; Leonard 1991). Third, research should increasingly incorporate negative or control cases to help identify spurious characteristics present both in successful POEs and poor-performing counterparts (McDonnell 2017). Fourth, future case selection could systematically address potential differences in the conditions under which POEs emerge as a result of the founding of a new organization versus reforming an existing but ineffectual organization. Cases of both types are clearly present in the literature but rarely explicitly contrasted. Fifth, future work could apply comparative logic to systematically look for theoretically significant cases—for example, selecting a distinctively high-performing case that does not have organizational mystique. Similarly, selecting cases of *failed* POEs, organizations that initially improved performance but then failed, can also contribute to our understanding of the processes by which pockets emerge *and stabilize*. Finally, future case analysis could seek more intensively triangulated data to simultaneously evaluate internal and external forces, gathering information directly from public servants in POEs, political elites, and civil society. This would be particularly advantageous data to collect in the early emergence of a POE.

Future POE work should also pay greater attention to specifying the temporal sequencing of different features associated with POE success. It may be that the elements identified in this review have strong elective affinities (Weber 1978), mutually reinforcing one another such that pulling on any one thread draws tighter the weave of organizational capacity—if so, gains in any condition could initiate a virtuous cycle. Alternatively, the temporal sequencing of conditions could affect POE outcomes. For example, does worker attachment to organizational mission emerge first and then lead the organization to acquire valuable external networks and resources to further enhance capacity? Or do external networks and resources come first and then lead to the emergence of a changed organizational culture around mission? Does organizational autonomy precede and enable organizational performance, or are high-achieving organizations the only ones able to assert and maintain autonomy in predominantly neopatrimonial contexts? Many such questions could be established through fine-grained case analysis, process tracing, experiments, or randomized controlled trials. However measured, careful attention to establishing the temporal ordering and relationships among dominant theoretical elements explaining POEs, and the outcomes themselves, would both result in greater theoretical parsimony and also be an invaluable contribution to development practitioners interested in practical applications.

This chapter addressed theories across the subfield, however our analysis also uncovered interesting regional differences in explanations for the success of POEs, which are not addressed above. For example, compared to other regions, analyses of Latin American POEs more frequently emphasized political autonomy and networks to private companies. Connections to private companies appear in nearly two-thirds of the Latin American cases, compared to one-third of cases in Africa or Asia. By contrast, 70% of authors examining Asian POEs cite organizational culture, compared to 52% of cases in Latin America and 44% in Africa. As scholarly dialogue across area studies boundaries expands, future work should systematically examine whether these regional trends are merely differences in scholarly attention or reflect underlying empirical differences in the conditions that promote POEs in different regions, and if so, why.

The maturing subfield also raises questions about the implications of POE findings for other fields beyond conventional cases of high-performing public sector organizations in low-income countries with typically weak state institutions. Do similar factors explain unusually strong organizational performance in the private sectors of the same countries or is there something distinctive about the public sector organizational field? We have some sense that, historically, some Western states shared the basic structure of a few distinctively high-performing organizations. Do similar mechanics explain where and how POEs emerged in historic early modern European state-building, or were there particularities of the world-historic timeline that made the process fundamentally different than today? POE literature also offers an incisive lens into understanding fundamental cultural change within organizations that may yield relevant insights for organizational scholars more generally, for example, illuminating questions about how to change intransigent corporate cultures so they are more gender or racially inclusive. It may be that the structure of pockets embedded within a dissimilar surrounding context is a much more general feature of organizational fields than we have previously realized.

REFERENCES

Abah, Joe. 2012. "Strong Organisations in Weak States. Atypical Public Sector Performance in Dysfunctional Environments." Ph.D. diss. Maastricht University.
Akunyili, Dora N. 2013. *The War Against Counterfeit Medicine: My Story*. Ibadan, Nigeria: Safari Books Ltd.
Alvesson, Helle, and Lorena Viñuela. 2014. "The Gambia Case Study: Ministry of Basic and Secondary Education." In *Institutions Taking Root: Building State Capacity in Challenging Contexts*, edited by Naazneen Barma, Elisabeth Huybens, and Lorena Viñuela, 71–108. Washington, D.C.: World Bank.
Anderson, Catherine. 2014a. "Timor-Leste Case Study: Ministry of Health." In *Institutions Taking Root: Building State Capacity in Challenging Contexts*, edited by N. Barma, E. Huybens, and L. Viñuela, 303–46. Washington, D.C.: World Bank Group.
Anderson, Catherine. 2014b. "Timor-Leste Case Study: Ministry of Social Solidarity." In *Institutions Taking Root: Building State Capacity in Challenging Contexts*, edited by Naazneen Barma, Elisabeth Huybens, and Lorena Viñuela, 261–302. Washington, D.C.: World Bank.
Andrews, Matt. 2015. "Explaining Positive Deviance in Public Sector Reforms in Development." *World Development* 74: 197–208.
Barma, Naazneen, Elisabeth Huybens, and Lorena Viñuela, eds. 2014. *Institutions Taking Root: Building State Capacity in Challenging Contexts*. Washington, D.C.: World Bank.

Barma, Naazneen, and Stephanie Osken. 2014. "Lao PDR Case Study: Électricité Du Laos." In *Institutions Taking Root: Building State Capacity in Challenging Contexts*, edited by Naazneen Barma, Elisabeth Huybens, and Lorena Viñuela, 119–50. Washington, D.C.: World Bank.

Barnard, Chester. 1938. *The Functions of the Executive*. Cambridge, MA: Harvard University Press.

Bersch, Katherine, Sérgio Praça, and Matthew M. Taylor. 2017. "Bureaucratic Capacity and Political Autonomy within National States: Mapping the Archipelago of Excellence in Brazil." In *States in the Developing World*, edited by Miguel Centeno, Atul Kohli, and Deborah Yashar, 157–83. Cambridge, UK: Cambridge University Press.

Booth, David, and Diana Rose Cammack. 2013. *Governance for Development in Africa: Solving Collective Action Problems*. New York: Zed Books.

Boxall, Peter, and Peter Haynes. 1997. "Strategy and Trade Union Effectiveness in a Neo-Liberal Environment." *British Journal of Industrial Relations* 35 (4): 567–91.

Brinkerhoff, Derick W., and Anna Wetterberg. 2013. "Performance-Based Public Management Reforms: Experience and Emerging Lessons from Service Delivery Improvement in Indonesia." *International Review of Administrative Sciences* 79 (3): 433–57.

Campos, J. Edgardo and Sanjay Pradhan. 2007. *The Many Faces of Corruption: Tracking Vulnerabilities at the Sector Level*. Washington, D.C.: The World Bank.

Carpenter, Daniel P. 2001. *The Forging of Bureaucratic Autonomy: Reputations, Networks, and Policy Innovation in Executive Agencies, 1862–1928*. Princeton: Princeton University Press.

Chemouni, Benjamin. 2016. "The Politics of State Effectiveness in Burundi and Rwanda. Ruling Elite Legitimacy and the Imperative of State Performance." Ph.D. diss. London School of Economics.

Crew, Rudolph. 1998. "Creating a Performance-Driven System." *Economic Policy Review* 4 (1): 7–9.

Crook, Richard C. 2010. "Rethinking Civil Service Reform in Africa: 'Islands of Effectiveness' and Organisational Commitment." *Commonwealth & Comparative Politics* 48 (4): 479–504.

Dahlström, Carl, Jan Teorell, Stefan Dahlberg, Felix Hartmann, Annika Lindberg, and Marina Nistotskaya. 2015. *The QoG Expert Survey Dataset II*. Gothenburg: The Quality of Government Institute.

Daland, Robert T. 1981. *Exploring Brazilian Bureaucracy: Performance and Pathology*. Washington, D.C.: University Press of America.

Eigen, Peter. 1996. "Combatting Corruption around the World." *Journal of Democracy* 7 (1): 158–68.

Evans, Peter. 1992. "The State as Problem and Solution: Predation, Embedded Autonomy, and Structural Change." In *The Politics of Economic Adjustment: International Constraints, Distributive Conflicts and the State*, edited by Stephan Haggard and Robert Kaufman, 139–81. Princeton: Princeton University Press.

Evans, Peter. 1995. *Embedded Autonomy: States and Industrial Transformation*. Princeton: Princeton University Press.

Fairfield, Tasha. 2006. "The Politics of Livestock Sector Policy and the Rural Poor in Peru." Working Paper. Berkeley: Pro-Poor Livestock Policy Initiative.

Flatters, Frank, and W. Bentley Macleod. 1995. "Administrative Corruption and Taxation." *International Tax and Public Finance* 2 (3): 397–417.

Fundação Getúlio Vargas. 2001. "Helio Jaguaribe (Biography)." In *Brazilian Biographical Historical Dictionary Post-1930*. Rio de Janeiro: Fundação Getúlio Vargas.

Geddes, Barbara. 1990. "Building 'State' Autonomy in Brazil, 1930–1964." *Comparative Politics* 22 (2): 217–35.

Geddes, Barbara. 1996. *Politician's Dilemma: Building State Capacity in Latin America*. Berkeley: University of California Press.

Graham, Lawrence S. 2014. *Civil Service Reform in Brazil: Principles Versus Practice*. Austin: University of Texas Press.

Grindle, Merilee S. 1997a. "Divergent Cultures? When Public Organizations Perform Well in Developing Countries." *World Development* 25 (4): 481–95.

Grindle, Merilee S., ed. 1997b. *Getting Good Government: Capacity Building in the Public Sectors of Developing Countries*. Cambridge, MA: Harvard University Press.

Grindle, Merilee S. 2012. *Jobs for the Boys: Patronage and the State in Comparative Perspective*. Cambridge, MA: Harvard University Press.

Herrera, Veronica M. 2017. *Water and Politics: Clientelism and Reform in Urban Mexico*. Ann Arbor, MI: University of Michigan Press.

Hertog, Steffen. 2010. "Defying the Resource Curse: Explaining Successful State-Owned Enterprises in Rentier States." *World Politics* 62 (2): 261–301.

Hout, Wil. 2014. "'Confidence in Our Own Abilities': Suriname's State Oil Company as a Pocket of Effectiveness." In *The Politics of Public Sector Performance. Pockets of Effectiveness in Developing Countries*, edited by Michael Roll, 147–72. London; New York: Routledge.

Howell, Llewellyn D. 2011. *International Country Risk Guide Methodology*. East Syracuse, NY: PRS Group.

Huntington, Heather, and Erik Wibbels. 2014. "The Geography of Governance in Africa: New Tools from Satellites, Surveys and Mapping Initiatives." *Regional & Federal Studies* 24 (5): 625–45.

Israel, Arturo. 1987. *Institutional Development: Incentives to Performance*. Baltimore: Johns Hopkins University Press.

Jaguaribe, Helio. 1956. "Sentido e Perspectivas Do Governo Kubitschek." *Cadernos Do Nosso Tempo* 1 (5): 11–12.

Johnson, Martha C. 2015. "Donor Requirements and Pockets of Effectiveness in Senegal's Bureaucracy." *Development Policy Review* 33 (6): 783–804.

Kaufmann, Daniel, Aart Kraay, and Massimo Mastruzzi. 2010. "Worldwide Governance Indicators." Working paper. The World Bank.

Knack, Stephen, and Philip Keefer. 1995. "Institutions and Economic Performance: Cross-Country Tests Using Alternative Institutional Measures." *Economics & Politics* 7 (3): 207–27.

Korten, David. 1980. "Community Organization and Rural Development: A Learning Process Approach." *Public Administration Review* 40 (5): 480.

Kuwajima, Kyoko. 2016. "Deciphering Capacity Development through the Lenses of 'Pockets of Effectiveness' —A Case of Innovative Turnaround of the Phnom Penh Water Supply Authority, Cambodia." Working Paper. Tokyo: JICA Research Institute.

Lafer, Celso. 1970. "The Planning Process and the Political System in Brazil—A Study of Kubitschek's Target Plan—1956–1961." Ph.D. diss. Cornell University.

Larizza, Marco, and Brendan Glynn. 2014. "Sierra Leone Case Study: Local Councils." In *Institutions Taking Root: Building State Capacity in Challenging Contexts*, edited by Naazneen Barma, Elisabeth Huybens, and Lorena Viñuela, 219–51. Washington, D.C.: World Bank.

Leonard, David K. 1991. *African Successes: Four Public Managers of Kenyan Rural Development*. Berkeley: University of California Press.

Leonard, David K. 2010. "'Pockets' of Effective Agencies in Weak Governance States: Where Are They Likely and Why Does It Matter?" *Public Administration and Development* 30 (2): 91–101.

Mahoney, James, Erin Kimball, and Kendra L. Koivu. 2009. "The Logic of Historical Explanation in the Social Sciences." *Comparative Political Studies* 42 (1): 114–46.

Mahoney, James, and Kathleen Thelen. 2010. "A Theory of Gradual Institutional Change." In *Explaining Institutional Change: Ambiguity, Agency, and Power*, edited by James Mahoney and Kathleen Thelen, 1–37. Cambridge: Cambridge University Press.

Matsuda, Yasuhiko. 1997. "An Island of Excellence: Petroleos de Venezuela and the Political Economy of Technocratic Agency Autonomy." Ph.D. diss. University of Pittsburgh.

McDonnell, Erin Metz. 2017. "Patchwork Leviathan: How Pockets of Bureaucratic Governance Flourish within Institutionally Diverse Developing States." *American Sociological Review* 82 (3): 476–510.

McDonnell, Erin Metz. 2020. *Patchwork Leviathan: Pockets of Bureaucratic Effectiveness in Developing States*. Princeton, NJ: Princeton University Press.

Muilerman, Sander, and Sietze Vellema. 2017. "Scaling Service Delivery in a Failed State: Cocoa Smallholders, Farmer Field Schools, Persistent Bureaucrats and Institutional Work in Côte d'Ivoire." *International Journal of Agricultural Sustainability* 15 (1): 83–98.

Mungiu-Pippidi, Alina. 2015. *The Quest for Good Governance: How Societies Develop Control of Corruption*. Cambridge, UK: Cambridge University Press.

Noy, Shiri. 2017. *Banking on Health: The World Bank and Health Sector Reform in Latin America*. New York: Springer Berlin Heidelberg.

Nunes, Edson de Oliveira. 1984. "Bureaucratic Insulation and Clientelism in Contemporary Brazil: Uneven State-Building and the Taming of Modernity." Ph.D. diss. University of California Berkeley.

Nunes, Edson de Oliveira. 1997. *A gramática política do Brasil: clientelismo e insulamento burocrático*. Rio de Janeiro: Escola Nacional de Administração Pública.

Ocampo, Luis Moreno. 2000. "Structural Corruption and Normative Systems: The Role of Integrity Pacts." *Combating Corruption in Latin America* 2: 53–70.

Owusu, Francis. 2006. "On Public Organizations in Ghana: What Differentiates Good Performers from Poor Performers?" *African Development Review* 18 (3): 471–85.

Pahuja, Sanjay and Hirut Johnson. Forthcoming. "Field Level Leadership: Interim Information Paper". Washington, D.C.: World Bank.

Peiffer, Caryn, and R. Armytage. 2018. "Searching for Success: A Mixed Methods Approach to Identifying and Examining Positive Outliers in Development Outcomes." *World Development* 121: 97–107.

Pinto, Rogerio. 1969. *The Political Ecology of the Brazilian National Bank for Development (BNDE)*. Washington, D.C.: Organization of American States.

Prasad, Monica, Mariana Borges Martins da Silva, and Andre Nickow. 2018. "Approaches to Corruption: A Synthesis of the Scholarship." *Studies in Comparative International Development* 54 (1): 96–132.

Rich, Jessica. 2013. "Grassroots Bureaucracy: Intergovernmental Relations and Popular Mobilization in Brazil's AIDS Policy Sector." *Latin American Politics and Society* 55 (2): 1–25.

Ricks, Jacob I. 2017. "Sector-Specific Development and Policy Vulnerability in the Philippines." *Development and Change* 48 (3): 567–89.

Roethlisberger, Fritz Jules, and William J. Dickson. 1939. *Management and the Worker*. Cambridge, MA: Harvard University Press.

Roll, Michael. 2011. "The State That Works: "Pockets of Effectiveness" as a Perspective on Stateness in Developing Countries." Working Paper. Johannes Gutenberg University Mainz: Department of Anthropology and African Studies.

Roll, Michael, ed. 2014. *The Politics of Public Sector Performance: Pockets of Effectiveness in Developing Countries*. London; New York: Routledge.

Rothstein, Bo, and Jan Teorell. 2008. "What Is Quality of Government? A Theory of Impartial Government Institutions." *Governance* 21 (2): 165–90.

Samatar, Abdi Ismail, and Sophie Oldfield. 1995. "Class and Effective State Institutions: The Botswana Meat Commission." *The Journal of Modern African Studies* 33 (4): 651–68.

Samford, Steven. 2017. "Networks, Brokerage, and State-Led Technology Diffusion in Small Industry." *American Journal of Sociology* 122 (5): 1339–70.

Schneider, Ben Ross. 1992. *Politics within the State: Elite Bureaucrats and Industrial Policy in Authoritarian Brazil.* Pittsburgh, PA: University of Pittsburgh Press.

Selznick, Philip. 1957. *Leadership in Administration: A Sociological Interpretation.* Berkeley, CA: University of California Press.

Shrank, Andrew. 2016. "Imported Institutions: Boon or Bane in the Developing World?" *Conference on Weak Institutions in Latin America: New Theoretical and Empirical Approaches.* Harvard University, Cambridge, MA.

Skocpol, Theda, and Kenneth Finegold. 1982. "State Capacity and Economic Intervention in the Early New Deal." *Political Science Quarterly* 97 (2): 255–78.

Strauss, Julia C. 1998. *Strong Institutions in Weak Polities: State Building in Republican China, 1927–1940.* Oxford, UK: Clarendon Press.

Strauss, Julia C. 2014. "Pockets of Effectiveness: Lessons from the Long Twentieth Century in China and Taiwan." In *The Politics of Public Sector Performance. Pockets of Effectiveness in Developing Countries,* edited by Michael Roll, 43–73. London; New York: Routledge.

Tendler, Judith. 1997. *Good Government in the Tropics.* Baltimore: Johns Hopkins University Press.

Therkildsen, Ole, and Per Tidemand. 2007. *Staff Management and Organisational Performance in Tanzania and Uganda: Public Servant Perspectives.* København, Denmark: Danish Institute for International Studies.

Uphoff, Norman. 1994. *Puzzles of Productivity in Public Organizations.* San Francisco, CA: ICS Press.

Vanderhurst, Stacey. 2017. "Governing with God: Religion, Resistance, and the State in Nigeria's Counter-Trafficking Programs." *PoLAR: Political and Legal Anthropology Review* 40 (2): 194–209.

Vilaça, Luiz. 2020. "When Bureaucrats Become Activists." *Mobilization: An International Journal* 25 (3): 405–24.

Vilaça, Luiz. 2019. "Subterranean and Public Activism: Anti-Corruption Reform in Brazil." Paper presented at the American Sociological Association Annual Meeting. New York City, NY, August 10–13, 2019.

Viñuela, Lorena. 2014. "Timor-Leste Case Study: The Central Bank of Timor-Leste." In *Institutions Taking Root: Building State Capacity in Challenging Contexts,* edited by Naazneen Barma, Elisabeth Huybens, and Lorena Viñuela, 347–80. Washington, D.C.: World Bank.

Viñuela, Lorena, and Barrie Ousman. 2014. "Sierra Leone Case Study: Ministry of Finance and Economic Development." In *Institutions Taking Root: Building State Capacity in Challenging Contexts,* edited by Naazneen Barma, Elisabeth Huybens, and Lorena Viñuela, 189–218. Washington, D.C.: World Bank.

Viñuela, Lorena, and Helle Alvesson. 2014. "The Gambia Case Study: Ministry of Finance and Economic Affairs." In *Institutions Taking Root: Building State Capacity in Challenging Contexts,* edited by Naazneen Barma, Elisabeth Huybens, and Lorena Viñuela, 41–70. Washington, D.C.: World Bank.

Wahrlich, Beatriz. 1983. *Reforma Administrativa Na Era de Vargas.* Rio de Janeiro, RJ: FGV.

Waterston, Albert. 1965. *Development Planning: Lessons of Experience.* Baltimore: Johns Hopkins University Press.

Weber, Max. 1978. *Economy and Society: An Outline of Interpretive Sociology.* Berkeley, CA: University of California Press.

White, Leonard. 1954. *The Jacksonians: A Study of Administrative History: 1829–1861.* New York: Macmillan.

Whitfield, Lindsay, and Lars Buur. 2014. "The Politics of Industrial Policy: Ruling Elites and Their Alliances." *Third World Quarterly* 35 (1): 126–44.

Whitfield, Lindsay, Ole Therkildsen, Lars Buur, and Anne Mette Kjær. 2015. *The Politics of African Industrial Policy: A Comparative Perspective.* New York: Cambridge University Press.

Wikeley, Felicity. 1998. "Dissemination of Research as a Tool for School Improvement?" *School Leadership & Management* 18 (1): 59–73.

Willis, Eliza J. 1986. "The State as Banker: The Expansion of the Public Sector in Brazil." Ph.D. diss. University of Texas at Austin.

Willis, Eliza J. 1995. "Explaining Bureaucratic Independence in Brazil: The Experience of the National Economic Development Bank." *Journal of Latin American Studies* 27 (3): 625–61.

World Bank. 1999. *Governance & Anti-Corruption Country Diagnostic Survey Series.* Washington, D.C.: World Bank.

APPENDIX A

CODING SCHEME FOR CONTENT ANALYSIS

Category	Subcategories
Networks	Private sector
	Political elites
	International organizations
	State agencies
	Civil society
Merit, technical competence, and incentives	Merit-based recruitment
	Technical competence
	Training
	Financial incentives
	Nonfinancial incentives
Autonomy	Political
	Financial
	Personnel
Culture	Organizational culture
	Leadership
	Committed officials

......

CHAPTER 32

IMPROVING GOVERNANCE IN TIGHTLY CONTROLLED SOCIETIES

The Importance of Transformational Leadership

......

ROBERT I. ROTBERG

QUALITY of government (QoG) in all societies depends upon structural and contingent forces, the availability of favorable human and natural resources, fortunate geophysical locations, and political cultures that enshrine democratic values, social tolerance, and individuality. This chapter argues, additionally, that QoG depends on transformational political leadership. The leadership factor, often overlooked, is formidable, especially in the fragile states of the developing world where political institutions are largely embryonic, democratic political cultures are still being consolidated, and partiality prevails.

Given the dependence of QoG on democratic inspiration and its usual association as both a normative and an empirical outcome with competitive, open, fully tolerant, politically participatory undertakings, how and why is it that some peoples can enjoy very high qualities of government within nations that are ruled undemocratically? A few nations provide high government quality to their citizens, but restrict some fundamental freedoms (and thus are less than democratic). How can that be? Is there a contradiction in terms, or should we reconceptualize QoG to take account of these "imperfect" governmental providers? This chapter confronts such fundamental puzzles.

The introduction in this *handbook* poses the same question, informing us that China exceeds India in terms of delivering quality and that Singapore outperforms Jamaica.

> Human well-being in democratic Jamaica is much worse than in autocratic Singapore. However, both these former British colonies were equally poor in the early 1960s and if things like ethnic diversity, level of education, natural resources, and access to markets are considered, Jamaica had the better situation. Thus, democratic but highly corrupt Jamaica has been clearly outperformed by autocratic but less corrupt Singapore.

Rothstein's chapter in this book reminds us that strong leaders often abridge rule of law principles, violate human rights, manipulate elections, and engage in clientelism—all to the detriment of their constituents. They thus offend QoG by behaving partially. Yet, Singapore globally, and Rwanda, in today's Africa, see no contradiction in combining authoritarianism with the delivery of among the highest qualities of government among their peers. Indeed, their past and present leaders would doubtless argue that only tough-minded, determined, leaders can uplift their peoples—to give them QoG that is "directed," but still uplifting in terms of quality of life betterments.

This chapter consequently examines the Singaporean and Rwandan cases in some detail. It also studies Botswana, to provide a thoroughgoing democratic contrast to both Singapore and Rwanda. Further, it emphasizes the impact of leadership in molding the kinds of QoG that these countries developed. Finally, but only in an understated manner, it offers measurable "good governance" as an equivalent optic for quality of government. But this "good governance" goes well beyond that discussed at the end of Rothstein's chapter in this handbook.

Quality of Governance is broader than QoG, as used in this handbook. In brief, governance is the effective performance of government. Thus, quality of governance includes deliverables that enhance the lives and livelihoods of citizens in a manner that extends beyond the administrative and procedural confines of government. It includes at least 57 measures of governance, and encompasses such major variable categories as Safety and Security; Rule of Law and Transparency; Political Participation and Human Rights; Sustainable Economic Development; and Human Development, the last which includes educational opportunity and accessible health outcomes. (For detailed definitions and the extended argument, see the references immediately below. This discussion has been carried on elsewhere, and needs only to be referred to here, not repeated. (Rotberg 2004, Rotberg 2014; Rotberg 2015). Quantifying the attainment of governance strikes me as much more objective and empirical than trying to judge the normative (subjectively determined) differences of quality. In that last sentence I also respond to Rothstein.

In the developing world, at least, creating higher rather than lower qualities of government or, as I propose, good governance outcomes, largely depends on committed, responsible political leadership. Today's more highly rated developing countries—on good governance rating scales—all have benefitted and been shaped by determined, far-seeing, and courageous political leaders. These leaders have emphasized performance—the delivery of desired and desirable political goods to constituents, foremost of which was and is economic betterment, even prosperity. These leaders also delivered security and safety, developmental advantages such as expanded educational opportunities and advances in public health attention and treatment, and other life improvements. Across several dimensions, these political leaders were and are transformational, behaving in ways that far exceed the usual, every day, transactional behavior of most of the world's elected political leaders (Rotberg 2012).

Transformational Leadership

When political leaders translate their visions into comprehensive programs of action, and arouse and motivate followers to respond (a critical criterion), they are behaving transformationally, not transactionally. These leaders challenge settled expectations and elucidate new, even unexpected, paradigms of performance from citizens. They elevate their followers' "level of consciousness" and encourage citizens to embrace forward-looking, pathbreaking, objectives that surmount their own, more limited, personal goals. A transforming political leader uplifts the "level of human conduct and ethical aspirations of both leader and led" (Burns 1978, 20). In other words, transformational leaders enable citizens to "self-actualize" at an elevated level—to achieve a form of transcendence (Rotberg 2012, 22). Transformational leaders challenge existing processes, take risks, are open to new ideas, inspire shared visions, promote collaboration, establish trust, empower, and encourage high expectations (Kouzes and Posner 1987).

Avery (2004, 96–8); Avolio (2010, 742–4); Burns (1978); Nye (2008, 61–9); and Podsakoff, Mackenzie, Moorman, et al. (1987, 177–92) write tellingly about the rare quality and necessity of transformational political leadership. Zaleznick (1977, 67–80) places the same phenomenon in the corporate context. Willner (1984, 46–7) and Conger and Kanungo (1998), show that transformational leaders need not be charismatic leaders. Each of these writers builds upon and echoes the pioneering work on political leadership of Weber (1958, 77–8), Shannon (1949), Seligman (1950, 904–15), Pye (1967, 43–6), Easton (1965, 212–16, 302–7), and Rustow (1970 687–90). Each, and there were others, argued that political leadership was central and integral to political transformation, writ large.

Transformational leaders exercise political will to improve the QoG of their constituents (followers). "Political will ... [is] ... the demonstrated credible intent of ... [leaders] ... to attack perceived causes or effects of corruption at a systemic level" (Kpundeh 1998, 68). Consummate transformational political leaders like President Nelson Mandela exercise political will when they insist on bettering outcomes for their followers: "Listen to me ... I am your leader [and] I am going to give you leadership" (Quoted in Greenberg 2009, 145). Persson and Sjöstedt rightly caution against equating "voluntarism" as explanatory, preferring to place more emphasis on context and circumstance (Persson and Sjöstedt 2012). Their analysis suggests (as do other writers) that expressions of political will—of transformative leadership—depend on political leaders creating positive political cultures. Such an exercise of political will and transformational leadership, especially in pre-institutional states (where corruption is commonly prevalent) is essential to enhance sustainable qualities of government. Exercising political will means leadership from in front, Mandela-like, not from behind. It means sharing diagnoses of societal ills and articulated remedies with followers, and selling positive answers to skeptics. Political will and transformational leadership are both active, never passive. The objectives of new expressions of political will are only achieved as a result of deep teaching, committed persuasion, and the effective mobilization of large arrays of people to solve a (national) problem.

A foremost exponent of this kind of transformational leadership and political will in enhancing QoG was U.S. President Theodore K. Roosevelt. Consciously working to alter the prevailing national political culture that he had inherited, Roosevelt focused on corrupt dealings first at the municipal and then at the national level, decisively shifting his nation's perspective. Railing at personal indulgences and political felonies, he declared that corruption struck at the "foundation of all law" (Teachout 2014, 107). US Senators were jailed for taking bribes. At his urging, Congress passed the Tillman Act of 1907, which banned corporate contributions to political campaigns, and the Federal Corrupt Practices Act of 1910, which limited party and candidate spending in Senate races. Roosevelt's efforts, and his gift for transformational leadership, greatly improved QoG in the United States for about a century.

Good Governance

Citizens in every jurisdiction want to be secure within their national borders and safe on their urban streets or in their rural villages. They seek stability and order. They want as much schooling as possible for their children. They want access to the best possible health facilities and to clinics with modern treatment and medicines available. They want clean water and, if possible, waterborne sanitation. They want the ability to prosper to the fullness of their natural abilities. They therefore prefer money and banking systems that work and do not cheat, and a national currency that keeps its value. They want roads and railways—the arteries of commerce. Nowadays, too, citizens look to their governments for connectivity— to mobile telephones and to the Internet. When they become even somewhat engaged in the political process, citizens also demand predictable, fair ways of adjudicating disputes without violence, and contracts that can similarly be enforced under an impartial rule of law. Accountability and transparency for their political leaders goes hand in hand with access to fair justice. Even where corrupt practices are common and a way of life, citizens are still intolerant of those who steal and cheat.

The above are all essential political goods, the provision of which can be measured and quantified as well as their qualities roughly assessed. Good governance (or quality of government) exists when most of these political goods are delivered by political leaders and their governing elites to citizens in sufficient quantity and adequate quality (see Rotberg and Gisselquist 2009).

Another critical political good that is delivered by well-governed states is political participation—the ability of citizens to voice their policy preferences freely and to play a full role in the national political process. That could mean campaigning for political office, voicing dissent with accepted leadership preferences, freedom of assembly, freedom of speech, and the rest. Harmfully run countries—dictatorships, despotisms, autocracies, and nonconstitutional monarchies—where governance is delivered by fiat and citizens are fortunate if they can obtain any of the desired political goods, and where they are at risk of detention for requesting basic services, provide none of these qualities of government. However, there is a rare category of nation-state that for the most part gives its citizens many political goods of high quality and reasonable quantity without extending to them the freedom to participate openly in a society's political decision-making process. Singapore and Rwanda are examples.

Most highly rated countries, according to governance measurement metrics, are democratic. But there are a small handful of states that are undeniably well governed except for this last political good. Because they are quasi- or nondemocratic they extend the forms of democratic practice, including elections and the like, without permitting much dissent, much real opposition, and very little freedom of speech or assembly. Those who dare to oppose the political leadership cadres of these only quasi-democratic but otherwise well-managed states are harassed, prosecuted, detained, and sometimes even eliminated. This chapter is about the seeming contradiction—QoG without full democracy. It focuses on

Singapore and Rwanda, the two best examples of good governance and QoG in polities with incomplete democracy. In order to understand how Singapore and Rwanda deviate from their peers in good governance, this chapter also contrasts the highly ranked good governance states of Africa with Rwanda and Singapore.

It is important when comparing the democratic and the quasi-democratic examples of nation-states to do so objectively. It is of little epistemological use to employ subjectively derived appellations such as Freedom House's "free," "partly free," and "not free," to designate the differences between and among polities. Nor is it very helpful to employ the UNDP's Human Development Index (HDI), again somewhat subjectively derived, or a variety of similarly directed but insufficient indexing methods to capture differences and congruencies between the good governance performers that are democratic and those that are not. (Freedom House and the HDI use largely nonobjective methods—mostly the opinions of supposed "experts"—to rate countries in terms of criteria that are often fuzzy or at least ambiguous. Their results are prey to selection bias, and useful only as approximations. For the many indexes and their methodologies, see Rotberg and Bhushan (2015a)).

That is why Harvard Kennedy School graduate students and I originally created an elaborate method of scoring countries across the globe according to their delivery of the essential political goods sketched above. Building on this globally tested methodological foundation, and thanks to a thoughtful financial supporter, Rachel Gisselquist and I produced the first three published Indexes of African Governance. After scouring existing databases and ones that we created ourselves, with help from in-country associates, we compared first the 49 and then the 54 nation states of Africa to each other in terms of how secure they were (their civil conflict fatalities each year), how safe they were (homicide numbers), what percentages of their pupils completed primary and secondary school, how available potable water was, how long were their total paved roads, their per capita wealth, their life expectancies, and so on. We ended up with 57 governing qualities—political goods—the provision of which could be quantified. To us, and to those who now continue the pioneering indexing work that we inaugurated, the delivery of adequate quantities and high qualities of political goods equals good governance, and -- from at least one point of view -- with what is popularly thought of as quality of government. Several mostly democratic African nations now rate highly on the latest iterations of the index because they do provide high qualities of government. How did one of those early achievers deliver what so many of their peers did not, would not, and still do not?

BOTSWANA: FROM NOTHING TO SOMETHING

Botswana, along with Mauritius, the Seychelles, and Cape Verde, has always scored at the top of the Index of African Governance, trailed by South Africa, Namibia, Senegal, and Ghana in recent scorings. But Botswana, like Singapore and Rwanda (as we shall see), had no natural advantages that would automatically give it prominence in the good governance sweepstakes. Like Singapore and Rwanda, it also came to independence in 1966 with many potentially serious handicaps: it was landlocked (as is Rwanda, but not Singapore or the other top governing African island states); it was two-thirds desert; its only paved roads were

12 kms long and in two mining towns; it had beef cattle but no abattoir (until 1967); there were as yet no diamonds and no tourism; its population was small; and, although it appeared homogeneous and many of its eight ethnic groups discoursed in the same language, rival chiefs and rival peoples squabbled. Botswana could easily have become an autocratically ruled, poorly governed, parlous economic dependency of apartheid-ruled South Africa.

What Botswana had, however, was Seretse Khama. He came to power at the head of the Botswana Democratic Party (BDP). Better yet, he acceded in 1966 to the presidency of Botswana with both traditional legitimacy (he was heir to the throne of the largest ethnic entity in Botswana) and rational legitimacy (after the country's first, very open, and thoroughly transparent) election. All around him, in newly independent Africa, regimes were rapidly shedding their colonial legacies. Nearby Zambia was shifting from multiparty to single-party rule. Under gentle and humane President Kenneth Kaunda, the ruling political party was soon to bar dissent and nationalize its productive copper mines. Malawi was growing accustomed to the despotism of President Hasting Banda. Farther afield, but beloved by Scandinavians, was President Julius Nyerere's Tanzania. Preaching Afro-Socialism, he was shortly to trash trade unions, try to collectivize African agriculturalists, compel pastoralists to remain in one locale and become villagers, and imprison opponents. On the West Coast, Nigeria and Dahomey (now Benin) were experiencing their first military coups, with authoritarian rule to follow. Ghana was about to have its first of several coups, too, but in that country President Kwame Nkrumah had already displayed a profound intolerance for dissent and democratic political participation. The new paradigm said that state-controlled development trumped democratic norms; open discussion should not stand in the way of dominant political party and executive decision-making. Furthermore, in all of these domains, corruption flourished.

When Botswana gained independence it was dirt poor, with an average annual per capita GDP of $50. Khama, arguing that he needed to uplift his people, could have taken critical decisions on his own. Given the political and security overhang of South Africa, Khama could have argued that only a strong (read authoritarian) president could provide for the country. He could have abridged democracy in the nascent country. But Khama was never comfortable with easy answers and the postures of his contemporaries. He was too intellectually honest to pursue such tendentious shortcuts or to trot out specious arguments that neutered basic freedoms and, deep down, were meant to entrench the first liberationists and to enrich them and their followers.

Khama easily could have joined the crowd. Given his overwhelming legitimacy and standing within the protean ex-protectorate, Khama could have become an autocrat with almost no one gainsaying his decision. Indeed, Nkrumah had backed a left-leaning political alternative to Khama. Following Nyerere and Kaunda, Khama could have taken the customary African route of the day and bashed his opponents. Instead, to the eventual benefit of the peoples of Botswana, Khama decided to rule as a tolerant, transparent, impartial, open democrat. As president, he instructed, explained, guided, cajoled, and ultimately led his constituents forward by example. Lee Kuan Yew in Singapore did much the same, minus the adverb cajole, and substituting "coercing when necessary" in its place. Paul Kagame follows Lee (and Khama) in this respect, but for his reign we should also add "waving and using a heavy stick whenever necessary." In contrast to virtually all of their peers, moreover, each (has) eschewed corruption—Kagame somewhat later in his rule than the other two.

Khama did not necessarily conceptualize either good governance or QoG to describe what he was hoping to achieve for the people of Botswana. But he was a fully transformative leader. Poor, disadvantaged Africans slowly understood that he was attempting to make a salutary difference to their lives and that, unlike the subjects of neighboring autocrats, Khama and his government were in fact dedicated to making Botswana a better place than it had been under British colonial rule and better than it might have developed under the independent African rule of someone like Nkrumah or Nyerere.

From the start, Khama insisted that his followers and constituents should retain their own voice, and not let the political regime speak for them. That was in keeping with Tswana tradition, of course, and also consonant with the teaching of the British Congregationalist missionaries who had tutored the early Tswana and nurtured men and women of character. But Khama's leadership formula was the sum of far more than the wise stew of his forefathers.

For him, leadership was a calling that could, if he were deft and decisive, deliver the essence of good governance to his people, and to deliver it sustainably. As early as 1956, long before he could have anticipated being president, he told reporters that he sought to help his people "to develop a democratic system, raise the standard of living, and establish a happy healthy nationhood" (Tlou et al. 1995, 148). As a Legislative Council speaker, he (like the later Nelson Mandela) preached nonracial inclusionism, not wanting to marginalize the whites or tribesmen from ethnicities other than his own who were contributing in their diverse ways to the growth of a land that was short of educated and skilled indigenous contributors. Adjacent to South Africa, he had reason to establish a regime where no one was discriminated against on racial grounds and in which living standards were being raised for all, not just for a favored class. On the eve of independence, Khama hence insisted that the national bureaucracy should not be Africanized prematurely.

During the run-up to independence, Khama demonstrated a quiet vision, gained support for that vision among his party and his peers and followers, and made loyal followers of sometime opponents. He also forged a critical bond with Quett (later Sir Ketumile). Masire, a journalist and agro-businessman who was his loyal associate and successor. They worked hand in glove from the beginning, trusting each other and, in both cases, reconsidering their views if the other held contrary opinions.

Both were determined, consciously, to act on behalf of the nation, not themselves or their families. Khama claimed that to do good, following Thomas Paine, was his real religion (Tlou et al. 1995, 61). Without using or knowing the jargon of American political scientists of his era, Khama was determined as president to instill an ethos—an embryonic political culture—on the basis of which his country could grow enduring and democratic political institutions. Creating that system of values for political discourse, and growing the strong political institutions that were its product, were among Khama (and Masire's) signal contributions to government quality. Those institutions were "structures by which national objectives could be achieved" (Tlou et al. 1995, 271). There was never any question in Khama's British-trained mind that the nation's courts should be genuinely independent and that the national parliament should have a real voice. But these were leadership decisions; others elsewhere—Rwanda's Kagame, for example—charted a contrary course.

Fundamental to Khama's ability to muster followers beyond his vision for a united, economically growing, inclusive nation was his demonstrated integrity. Lee knew, and Kagame seems to appreciate, that a lack of honesty in personal dealings—ostentation, motorcades, accumulations of wealth, favoritism, and nepotism—all erode legitimacy and ultimately undermine the national enterprise. Khama even insisted that Cabinet ministers should pay their personal debts promptly and cover all bank overdrafts, something that Lee also emphasized. Khama—in a very un-African manner—refused to permit his vice-president or his Cabinet ministers to travel anywhere by air other than in coach class. He also purposely refused to allow any of his subordinates to accumulate too much power. Major moves, especially in mining or construction, had to be made by the entire Cabinet, with open consultation. Responsibility was thus collectivized and potential temptations limited. He believed both in transparency and accountability in a manner that many of his fellow African presidents could not. As a testament to Khama's determination and to his implantation of a political culture of integrity, and to Masire's continuation of this initiative, the Corruption Perceptions Index has consistently rated Botswana the least corrupt country in Africa since 1996, and (in 2020) the 35th least corrupt country in the world along with the Seychelles.

Khama ran a thoroughly open society. He was consultative to a fault and as impartial as possible, but, like Lee and Kagame, he was intolerant of backstabbing, corruption, and anything that detracted from responsible nation-building. Kagame, of course, tolerates less, especially the dissenting voices that Khama always welcomed.

As Khama enunciated before parliament: "Democracy, like a little plant, does not grow or develop on its own. It must be nursed and nurtured if it is to grow and flourish. It must be believed in and practiced if it is to survive" (Tlou et al. 1995, 364). Within his own ministerial Cabinet, unlike Kagame, Khama encouraged free-ranging discussions and decisions were made consensually, sometimes guided in the direction of his own not immediately declared preferences.

QoG for Khama meant taking his poor nation's destiny out of the hands of its former colonial rulers. Unlike so many of his aid-dependent (and rent-seeking) peers, Khama therefore insisted that Botswana should balance its budget, and from its own means. That fiscal objective he accomplished in year six (1972), together with a favorable customs agreement forged with South Africa, the collection of tax payments from an emerging local middle class, and a wise break from the South African rand and the printing of his own currency, the pula.

When the possibility of gem diamonds underneath Botswana became real in the mid-1970s, Khama opted not to nationalize the endeavor but to create a joint company with Cecil Rhodes' old De Beers Co. Ltd. to exploit and manage the bonanza. That decision delivered Botswana's current prosperity and its 7% per year per capita GDP growth for much of the past 30 years. It is now the fifth richest per capita entity in Africa, after the Seychelles, Mauritius, the oil kleptocracy of Equatorial Guinea, and mineral-rich and autocratic Gabon. Khama's Botswana has delivered the economic wherewithal by which quality of life and QoG can be sustained.

In other African locales, such as Equatorial Guinea and Gabon, massive corruption and intensive rent-seeking accompanied the exploitation of petroleum or precious metal resources. So did Dutch disease, as in Nigeria. But not in Botswana, where the per capita yearly GDP in 2019 was more than $17,000. Zambia's comparable figure is $4,056, and Tanzania's $2,946.

QoG or good governance depends on the delivery of the kinds of political goods mentioned earlier. Khama created a primary and secondary school system from nothing. At independence there were only 22 university graduates. Now the University of Botswana is an effective teaching institution, focusing on undergraduate subjects. Its graduates have assumed major governmental and corporate roles locally, but also have held major leadership positions in a host of international bodies, such as the WHO.

Khama's great gift to his country and to the issues discussed from various perspectives in this *handbook* is the democratic political culture that he and Masire gestated and sustained. Rare south of the Sahara, where most states are still pre-institutional, Botswana enjoys positive political institutions that now are more important politically than executive leaders or political party chiefs. Its good governance and high QoG stems from the implanting of such institutions, and the socialization of all of the human components of the polity to the value systems embedded in the new institutions. Khama created a nation in the way that few of his peers ever did or have yet done. (Kagame is one of the few others who have built a nation.) Together, Botswana lives within a democratic political culture that is largely responsible for its empirically tested, elevated QoG.

Khama (later Sir Seretse) set the tone for, and charted the path that Botswana has followed to reach its esteemed level of good governance. Like Lee in Singapore, Khama delivered on an improbable vision and established one of the most prosperous, stable, contented, self-satisfied, and unregimented nations on mainland Africa. Human agency—consummate leadership in the political sphere—was critical, and determinative.

SINGAPORE, THE "FIRST WORLD OASIS"

Lee was always more heavy-handed than Khama. But he operated within a much more hardscrabble, bitterly contested, arena. He had to fend off Sukarno's Indonesian ambitions and, after Singapore was tossed out of Malaysia, he worried about how their jealous rulers would attack his much smaller city-state. Most of all, however, Lee's ambitions for himself and Singapore had to overcome the Chinese triad gangs that had, with British connivance and complicity, long run amok in the corrupt pirate swamp that was colonial Singapore. The gangs specialized in extortion, kidnapping for ransom, and other forms of criminality. They had a huge stake in everything shady, everything that had made Singapore one of the wildest places in the East. Additionally, Singapore had its communists, mostly of Malay descent and linked closely to the Peninsula's Malaysian Communist Party. Finally, in this great mix, Singapore was a mélange of several nonMandarin-speaking south Chinese ethnic groups. There were Malays, too, Tamils from South India, Hindi-speakers from northern India, Buddhists, Taoists, and a Straits Settlement English-speaking elite of which Lee was himself one.

The city-state was an entrepôt. Its main resource was its British naval base, together with its commanding (and yet vulnerable) position at the entrance to the Malacca Straits (a choke point for shipping from Asia to Europe). There were no deposits of oil, no minerals, no palm oil, and no timber. Lee's vision, to transform his decrepit third world collection of problems into a first world oasis, was believed by many to be but a fantasy.

Lee, a lawyer, was determined to remake Singapore along modern lines. He did so with a vengeance, but largely (not exclusively) by persuading his voters (and although no elections were blatantly rigged, opposition freedoms to campaign and to articulate full-throated arguments were curtailed) that he alone knew what was good for them. If the Singapore electorate let him and his People's Action Party win, he promised his constituents that he would transform Singapore into a well-behaved model society where everyone would prosper (equally as it transpired), be educated, receive excellent health services, and be protected against depredations from Indonesia and Malaysia. Everyone would be able to do what they wished—provided of course that kept themselves within the societal outcomes that Lee believed were fitting and attainable. The most talented young people would be rewarded with bursaries and further training well beyond secondary school. There would be no limits on what they could achieve and what they could do—providing, of course, that their ambitions fit within Lee's overall plan.

Conformity was not the goal, but Singapore became a collection of peoples who were accustomed to living within specified parameters. Singapore, after all, is but 580 sq km—not a large city-state geographically—and its population, today, is just under 6 million. Drugs and drug-taking and such antisocial behaviors as spitting on pavements and urinating in high-rise lifts were among the deviant pursuits that Lee outlawed. Lee instituted severe punishment for minor offenses. He believed that dangerous crimes were deterred by severe physical retributions, like caning. Narcotics pushers and those unfortunate foreigners who dabbled in opium or heroin were flogged and sometimes sentenced to death. Giving his people physical safety was one of Lee's chief goals.

Most of all, Lee was zealous in eradicating corruption in public *and* private life—a feat that is almost unparalleled (except for Hong Kong, under determined British rule) in Asia and in settings that had been steeped in corrupt practices for more than a century, and without serious challenge. Lee, almost singlehandedly, took a deviant, amoral society accustomed to living uproariously and dangerously and rapidly transformed it into the punctiliously law-abiding, obedient society that it is today. His partiality, Lee would doubtless argue, made Singapore effectively impartial (despite devolving the premiership on his son).

Lee accomplished this remarkable transformation by tweaking common law principles to give the state serious legal advantages in its pursuit of corruption: defendants had to explain how they managed to live beyond their means; evidence of excess spending or assets that could not be accounted for were virtual admissions of guilt. But beyond using retributive justice to bring corrupt politicians and offenders to book, Lee also fired from high or low office those who appeared to be living too lavishly—persons whom Lee suspected (often with very good reason) to have been bribed by a housing developer, an aircraft supplier, or someone seeking permits or concessions. Famously, when Lee saw an associate's wife wearing expensive gold jewelry at a cocktail party, he knew that her husband had transgressed. The miscreant was soon dismissed.

All of these early actions on behalf of what Lee liked to believe were sanctity and purity accomplished their cleansing purpose. Setting these examples, plus the investigatory activities of an anticorruption commission, and draconian prosecutions, soon produced a society in which corruption was rare. Additionally, and more important, citizens came to understand that Lee meant what he said; they themselves came to see corruption as an unacceptable pursuit. They adopted the ethical universalism that Lee's efforts had made an expectation, and a norm. Yet, Lee also acknowledged that he had bent the law to his own purpose: "You know," he candidly admitted to the Singapore Advocates and Solicitors Society in 1967, "we have paid a very heavy price. We have departed in quite a number of material aspects ... from the principles of justice and the liberty of the individual ... in order to maintain ... [First World] standards" (Han 1998, 205).

None of this quick popular shift from accepting corruption as a way of life to deriding it as shameful and antisocial could have happened if Lee and his family were seen to be living unusually well. Lee's personal financial integrity preserved the legitimacy of his anticorruption crusade. So did his delivery of full employment and steady increases in annual GDP per capita—from about US$250 per head in 1965 to $80,000 per head in 2019 (unadjusted).

Singapore's growth record is remarkable. That individuals could feel secure and safe, that they were gainfully employed and well remunerated, that they received the best schooling and medical care in Asia, and—for the most part—that they were socially rewarded, meant that they willingly reelected Lee and his party on a regular basis—without overt coercion. Lee was never a charismatic personality. But always he was straight and frank and told Singaporeans that his instructions, if followed, would be to their benefit. They bought that (Faustian) message.

They also agreed to forsake random, low-rise living arrangements for blocks of high-rise boring flats, color-coded so no one would get lost. They even agreed to become English speakers; Lee knew that they and the city-state would grow more rapidly if everyone spoke the tongue of traders. (Lee, himself, learned Mandarin so that he could speak to all of the different Chinese linguistic groups.) For the sake of increased productivity, he also air-conditioned the entire city-state in 1982. The torrid tropics were antithetical to productivity, so he improved their health and working conditions.

Naturally, amid all of this possibly overdetermined but well-thought-out approach to societal gain, Lee kept a tight hold on his party, grooming his eldest son, Harvard-educated, eventually to succeed him as prime minister. He kept an equally tight hold on political discourse, curtailed freedom of speech, and successfully limited press and media freedom inside and outside Singapore by the (excessive) use of prosecutions for libel, followed regularly by financial punishments that were confiscatory. Just as Lee managed in this manner to silence criticisms that he believed were inappropriate, so he created an atmosphere of conformity and obedience.

As Lee articulated in a speech at the Singapore Press Club: "When any newspaper pours a daily dose of language, cultural or religious poison, I put my knuckle-dusters on. Do not believe that you can beat the state." Moreover, he determined, "Freedom of the Press, freedom of the news media, must be subordinated to the overriding needs of Singapore, and to the primacy of purpose of an elected government" (Han 212).

In all but this last area, the court system was free to rule according to common law practices. It enforced contracts fairly and without requiring the kinds of under-the-table payments that were common elsewhere in Asia (and in Africa). Citizens found its judgments largely straightforward in matters that were criminal and civil, but not political. In the last dimension, the judges knew to whom they reported.

Lee bankrupted many who opposed him, or critiqued his policies, and did so "legally." He managed to jail persons who behaved corruptly. In a relatively short time after 1965, Lee had created a comparatively chaste, disciplined, hardworking, and relatively boring (a Western notion) society in which virtually everyone had station and standing, provided that they let Lee and his successors rule the political realm.

Coercion was rarely physical. The police presence was light. The military stayed in its barracks. Lee's administration was effectively coercive only to the extent that it rounded up those who disposed of chewing gum improperly or caused public commotions. Assembly during political campaigns was monitored and the campaigns themselves were constrained by rules that all parties had to obey. "We will allow feedback," a follower said, "but we don't accept all their concerns." (Richmond 2008, 359).

Lee argued, as his son and other successors have done, that his sometimes heavy-handed methods were all employed with but one goal in mind: to make Singapore a better place. He wanted to make Singapore a great, if small, nation.

Could Lee have created such high qualities of government and such a high-scoring model of good governance without employing questionable antidemocratic methods? He argued that within the Asian context, especially within a city-state housing so many potential disharmonies, that he simply could not. Anyway, Lee was never patient enough to find out whether Khama-like methods would have worked just as well. He was in a hurry to make Singapore the kind of platform on which a man as talented as he believed himself to be could stand tall, and be acclaimed a genuine world leader. What he may have done for himself, he also did for Singapore, where authoritarianism created a nation with unquestioned quality of government, as commonly understood.

Leadership skills again made the difference. Singapore's good governance is where it is today because of one man's consummate ability to articulate a persuasive and politically sale-able vision to a mixed mass of unruly and undisciplined immigrants. "To build a country," Lee famously wrote, "you need passion. If you just do your sums—pluses, minuses, credit, debit—you are a washout" (Han 1998, 101). It was also critical for a leader who wanted to accomplish major transformative moves to be transparent, accountable, and consistent. "I don't say one thing today and another tomorrow" (Lee 2000a). The task of a leader in a new nation, he articulated fairly early in his prime ministerial career, was to create "a strong framework within which [the people] can learn, work hard, be productive and be rewarded accordingly" (Lee 2000b, I, 132). According to one acute observer, Lee and Singapore always placed "national interests, albeit narrowly defined by a narrow elite ... ahead of any par-ticular benefits for the rulers" (Bellows 1985, 1096).

Lee was the ultimate Faustian. If Singaporeans would accept limitations to their freedoms and natural liberties, he would provide order under law, rock-ribbed safety and security, and steady improvements in real standards of living. He would also give all Singaporeans a sense of larger purpose—a profound meaning to their lives as citizens. He provided grandeur and glory (and real advances) to all of those who accepted his hardworking leadership as they sought "virtue together" (Minchin 1990, 317). That virtue together notion corresponds to Rawls' "consensus" and includes qualities of government.

Kagame and the Wages of War

Unlike Khama and Mandela, the president of Rwanda can hardly claim to be a thorough-going democrat, or even a consensus-building quasi-democrat. He is a naked authoritarian, with substantial legitimacy as a genuine modernizer. But what truly distinguishes him and his long reign as the *chef* of Rwanda is his close attention to improving the public good and the daily lives and outcomes of his 13 million densely packed constituents.

As a Ugandan-based military commander who had undergone training in the United States and had been the sometime intelligence chief of Uganda's army, Kagame responded to the horrific 1994 genocide in Rwanda by entering Rwanda at the head of a Tutsi army to save as many remaining Tutsi lives as possible and to restore order in his country. Initially that meant imprisoning Hutu perpetrators of genocide and pursuing them and their ethnic compatriots into the nearby forests of the Congo. Subsequently, after Kagame had become prime minister (under a titular but powerless president), he focused on rebuilding, stabilizing, and pacifying the desperate land that had lost at least 800,000 Tutsi and had seen another 200,000 Hutu flee into the Congo, Burundi, Tanzania, Uganda, and overseas.

Kagame was no mere military leader with rudimentary ideas about organizing a re-born state and a responsible government. By 2000, when Kagame acceded to the nation's presidency, he had articulated a vision for the emergence of war-damaged Rwanda as the Singapore of Africa. Lacking most of Singapore's advantages: Its perfectly positioned harbor, its geographical location at the crossroads of a good third of the globe's commerce, its well-educated and advanced-skilled population, and its greatly appreciated wealth per capita, Kagame nevertheless became determined—at least by 2005, if not before, to transform a very poor state with natural resources no more promising than shade-grown coffee (subject as it is to fluctuating world prices) into a well-functioning, potentially middle-income juris-diction in the heart of equatorial Africa.

What Kagame presumably admired most about Singapore, the city-state that Lee had willed into modern existence, was the careful and conciliatory manner in which Lee had transformed an unruly port city into a thriving metropolis obedient to and willing to be confirmed by the vision of Lee and the centralized manner in which he and his government made decisions. They took those policy initiatives in the public interest, as defined by Lee, but were punctilious about not stealing from the people. Most of all, in Singapore, innovations such as shifting the Chinese-speaking populace to English as a common tongue, the compulsory mixing of ethnic groups in high-rise housing estates (to prohibit ghettos and ensure comity), had a modernizing purpose. Lee's government delivered progress (as enunciated from above) but also gave the city-state the stability, the rule of law, an emphasis on education, attention to medical services, and the prosperity that attracted international investment and soon increased the per capita GDP of its citizens many times over. In 1994, Rwanda's GDP per capita was $205. It rose to $698 in 2014 and to $765 in 2017. In 2019, Rwanda's GDP per capita was $2,325.

Kagame's goal has been to bring first world educational opportunities to Rwanda, along with major improvements in life expectancies and other medical outcomes. NonRwandans have been assisted in their efforts to upgrade healthcare in rural areas. Such technological initiatives as drone deliveries of blood plasma to rural clinics have been pioneered. From 2005 to 2018, Rwanda experienced falling rates of maternal and infant mortality, and mildly rising life expectancy rates. Educationally, primary school persistence rates have climbed from low levels to 57% in 2017. Life expectancy rose from 48 years in 2000 to 69 years in 2020.

Kagame has thus performed as a leader on those dimensions. But he has also echoed Lee (and Khama) by greatly lowering crime rates in Kigali, Rwanda's capital city of 921,000. Newly professionalized police (after 2004) even pursue litterers, making Kigali a compul-sorily pristine locale (certainly by the standards of African cities). Kagame simply refused as a leader to countenance crime, thus delivering levels of safety and security that are unknown in most other capitals in contemporary Africa outside of Botswana.

The president tellingly also virtually eliminated what had been a casual epidemic of corruption throughout the country. His method copied Lee: to preach against the evils of corruption (there were billboards throughout Kigali warning of its evils and forbidding such behavior: "He Who Practices Corruption Destroys His Country"); mercilessly to prosecute alleged offenders; to remove from office any elected or appointed public officials, even associates of the president; and—most of all—to remain untainted himself by accusations of improper enrichment. Rwanda is still perceived as more corrupt in Africa than Botswana, the Seychelles, and Cape Verde (and less corrupt than Namibia, Mauritius, South Africa, and all other sub-Saharan African states), but its rating by the Corruption Perceptions Index has increased from 83rd place in 2005 to 49th place in 2020—a remarkable jump in perceived probity and one mostly unprecedented in Africa.

When Kagame's great reform program had begun to accelerate after 2005, he copied President Mikheil Saakashvili's Georgia and significantly downsized the civil service, finding ghost workers, and removed existing bureaucrats who were inefficient or deemed superfluous. Competitive tests were introduced for the first time to improve competency and make merit appointments. Rwanda has also raised civil service salaries consistently.

In order to improve Rwanda's ratings by the World Bank's Doing Business reports, Kagame reduced bureaucratic controls and the number of permits required to open commercial concerns. His government removed regulatory burdens and red tape of most kinds. His aim was to produce a more investor-friendly (and Singapore-like) corporate environment, but also to make it at least conceivable that isolated and remote Rwanda could boast some of the advantages that accrued to Singapore.

As a result of all of these and many other innovations and initiatives, not least the careful subordination of Rwanda's peoples to the clear-minded edicts of its president, the country's governance ratings have risen, its civil service is better motivated than others in its African neighborhood, its peoples are relatively prosperous compared to past decades, and Kagame can assert that he has brought stability and improved living standards to his disciplined polity. Rwanda's quality of government, as commonly construed, is robust.

Free speech, media, assembly, and association are not permitted, however, and Kagame has imprisoned or assassinated a number of his vocal opponents. Rwanda is tightly regimented, but Kagame would argue that his leadership abilities have produced more and better personal and national outcomes for his peoples than those supposed deficiencies would imply. Kagame also says that his decision to rewrite constitutional prohibitions against becoming a virtual president for life were essential if Rwanda were to keep moving ahead on its developmental trajectory, and continue to provide good returns to its citizens. These are high-flown rationalizations, of course, but Kagame has nevertheless remained popular among his people. Like Lee, he has produced the returns that he said he would produce. In good governance scoring, Kagame's Rwanda gets high marks for education and medical advances, for reducing civil conflict, crime, and random killings, and for rising levels of incomes and productivity. Kagame has brought honor and a sense of impending greatness to Rwandans.

As an uncompromising leader, Kagame's tenure demonstrates the importance of an ambitious vision, the virtue of mobilizing behind such a vision, the impact of intellectual honesty and self-mastery in pursuing visionary objectives, the relevance of legitimacy and the personal integrity that supports legitimacy, and the attributes that flow from the construction of a national edifice (and a nation) of which its citizens can be proud.

But Kagame's version of QoG comes with high doses of coercion. The instincts of his people are held very much in check by fear of the state, fear of informers, and fear of breaking rules. Rwandans, enjoying their positive quality of government, nevertheless do so knowing that they have paid a price. Instead of freedom of expression, one kind of positive political good, they benefit from physical deliveries of medicine and blood plasma to remote regions of the country by drone aircraft. They have better schools, even if schoolchildren know that complaining about governmental edicts would be unwise. Nor would competing for political office without permission, or arguing policy too loudly with the president or his colleagues. Rwanda runs well, as its index rankings demonstrate, and Kagame's constituents welcome the political goods that his leadership has delivered.

QoG and Coercion

If strong-minded, intellectually capable, self-possessed, and impatient leaders genuinely seek to make the lives of their constituents significantly better—*if* they actually have a plan to establish a well-functioning society for their people rather than for themselves—then it is understandable (but not excusable) that they should brook as little opposition as possible and employ coercion more than persuasion to accomplish their objectives. We can applaud the result and condemn the method. Certainly, as the discussion of Khama's Botswana has shown, Lee and Kagame's techniques are not the only or the best ways of eradicating corruption, introducing robust rules of law, and bringing material betterments to fragile states and to masses of disadvantaged citizens. But their method also works. In all three cases, consummate leadership skills made a difference and delivered large quantities of QoG and, empirically, good governance.

Benevolent autocrats occasionally have their uses. But the cases of Botswana, Cape Verde, Mauritius, today's Ghana, and the new dispensation in South Africa and Malawi, demonstrate that excellent qualities of government can be achieved in developing countries by fully democratic means, employing the usual political stratagems of consensus-building, compromise, accommodation, and—where necessary—healthy competition. But gifted, preferably transformational, leadership is required. (Transactional leaders have other, personal or small-group interests in mind.) Without that critical ingredient, little can be achieved, and governance scores correspondingly remain low.

Can Kagame argue that because his country is more than twice the size of Singapore and four times the populations of Botswana and Mauritius, that the gentle techniques that work to uplift those small polities would not work in Rwanda? It is the same rationale that Prime Minister Sheikh Hasina might advance to justify her nondemocratic methods in Bangladesh, a much improved, very large, society. Or perhaps, as Rothstein suggests, President Xi Jinping could claim the same for the new, tightly orchestrated, China.

Perhaps scale does have saliency. But, in Africa, Ghana is larger than Rwanda, and has progressed substantially using very democratic techniques. So has Senegal. Likewise, Prime Minister and Nobel Laureate Abiy Ahmed in Ethiopia, Africa's second most populous state, started to establish better governance and more QoG by relaxing the authoritarian approaches of his two predecessors, the first of whom could have claimed the benevolent autocrat title. More recently, Abiy's methods have been genocidal, especially in Tigray province.

There are no examples anywhere of benevolent political leaders who meant well but simply failed to achieve improved qualities of government because of circumstances beyond their control. Across a vast range of African, Asian, and Latin American cases, the occasional well-intended but not already deeply corrupted head of state or head of government never pursues the kinds of courageous political initiatives that are required to pry the tentacles of corruption off a national body politic.

If, as Rothstein (this volume) draws on Rawls, "political legitimacy requires an 'overlapping consensus' about the basic institutions for justice in a society, so that citizens will continue to support them even when they have incommensurable conceptions of 'the meaning, value and purpose of human life' ... even if their group would lose political power," then Lee and Kagame, as well as Khama and others, have done well to create an overlapping consensus that now deeply infuses their states. QoG can thus be created exceptionally in both democratic and nondemocratic (but well-led) nations.

FURTHER RESEARCH

Lee believed that transformational leaders were born, not made. In order to suggest, even prescribe, routes that will take citizens to improved QoG regimes, much more deep psychological study of motive is essential. Why did Khama, Lee, and Kagame break with the received paradigms of their peers, eschew corruption, and focus on uplifting their peoples more than themselves and their coteries? Is it something inborn or learned that drives them? And why did President John Magufuli of Tanzania, who started out well, regress to the mean of his many predecessors and contemporaries? What makes exceptions to the (corrupt) leadership norm? Did contextual constraints inhibit humane and well-meaning former political leaders such as Presidents Kenneth David Kaunda of Zambia or Julius K. Nyerere of Tanzania? Do they curtail current leaders such as President Joko Widodo of Indonesia and President Cyril Ramaphosa of South Africa from wholesale assaults on bad governance and improvements of quality of government, or are their hesitancies failures of political will and influenced by the terribly disruptive coronavirus pandemic?

Achieving positive qualities of government (and good governance) depends on capable transformational leadership and the exercise of consummate political will. Since both of those assertions are often contested, more research to confirm or refute such propositions would be welcome. So would further work on the nature of political will itself.

REFERENCES

Avery, Gayle C. 2004. *Understanding Leadership: Paradigms and Cases.* London: Sage.
Avolio, Bruce J. 2010. "Pursuing Authentic Leadership Development." In *Handbook of Leadership Theory and Practice,* edited by Nitin Nohria and Rakesh Khurana, 739–68. Boston: Harvard Business Press.
Bellows, Thomas. 1985. Book review, in *Third World Quarterly,* VII.
Burns, James Macgregor. 1978. *Leadership.* New York: Harper & Row.
Conger, Jay A., and Rabinda N. Kanungo. 1998. *Charismatic Leadership in Organizations.* Thousand Oaks: Sage.
Easton, David A. 1965. *A Systems Analysis of Political Life.* Chicago: University of Chicago Press.
Greenberg, Stanley B. 2009. *Dispatches from the War Room: In the Trenches with Five Extraordinary Leaders.* New York: Macmillan.

Han Fook Kwang, Warren Fernandez, and Sumiko Tan. 1998. *Lee Kuan Yew: The Man and His Ideas*. Singapore: Marshall Cavendish.

Kouzes, James M., and Barry Z. Posner. 1987. *The Leadership Challenge: How to Get Extraordinary Things Done in Organizations*. San Francisco: Wiley.

Kpundeh, Sahr J. 1998. "Political Will in Fighting Corruption." In *Corruption and Integrity Improvement Initiatives in Developing Countries*, edited by Kpundeh and Irene Kors. New York: UNDP.

Lee Kuan Yew. 2000a. Interview at Harvard Kennedy School, Oct. 17, 2000, unpublished.

Lee Kuan Yew. 2000b. *From Third World to First: The Singapore Story*. Singapore: Times Media.

Manchin, James. 1990. *No Man Is an Island: A Portrait of Singapore's Lee Kuan Yew*. 2nd ed. London: Allen & Unwin.

Nye, Joseph S. Jr. 2008. *The Power to Lead*. New York: Oxford University Press.

Persson, Anna, and Martin Sjöstedt. 2012. "Responsive and Responsible Leaders: A Matter of Political Will?" *Perspectives on Politics* VII: 364–66.

Podsakoff, Philip M., S. B. Mackenzie, and R. H. Moorman, et al. 1990. "Transformational Leadership Behaviors." *Leadership Quarterly* I: 107–42.

Pye, Lucian W. 1967. *Politics, Personality, and Nation Building*. New Haven: Yale University Press.

Richmond, Jonathan E. D. 2008. "Transporting Singapore: the Air-Conditioned Nation." *Transport Reviews* XXVIII: 357–90.

Rotberg, Robert I. 2004. Strengthening Governance: Ranking Countries Would Help." *Washington Quarterly* XXVIII: 71–81.

Rotberg, Robert I. 2012. *Transformative Political Leadership*. Chicago: University of Chicago Press.

Rotberg, Robert I. 2014. "Good Governance Means Performance and Results." *Governance* XXVII: 511–18.

Rotberg, Robert I. 2015. "The Governance of Nations: Definitions and Measures" In *On Governance: What it Is, What it Measures, and its Policy Uses*, edited by Robert I. Rotberg, 7–21. Waterloo: ON, CIGI.

Rotberg, Robert I., and Aniket Bhushan. 2015a. "The Indexes of Governance." In *On Governance: What it Is, What it Measures, and its Policy Uses*, edited by Robert I. Rotberg, 55–90. Waterloo: ON, CIGI.

Rotberg, Robert I., and Rachel Gisselquist. 2009. *Strengthening African Governance: The 2009 Index of African Governance*. Cambridge, MA: World peace Foundation.

Rustow, Dankwart A., ed. 1970. *Philosophers and Kings: Studies in Leadership*. New York: Braziller.

Seligman, Lester G. 1950. "The Study of Political Leadership." *American Political Science Review* XLIV: 904–15.

Shannon, Jasper B. 1949. "The Study of Political Leadership." In Shannon. *The Study of Comparative Government*. New York: Appleton Century.

Teachout, Zephyr. 2016. *Corruption in America: From Benjamin Franklin's Snuff Box to Citizens United*. Cambridge, MA: Harvard University Press.

Tlou, Thomas, Neil Parsons, and Willie Henderson. 1995. *Seretse Khama, 1921–80*. Gaborone: Botswana Society.

Weber, Max. 1958. "Politics as a Vocation." In *From Max Weber: Essays in Sociology*, edited by H. H. Gerth and C. Wright Mills, 77–128. New York: Oxford University Press.

Willner, Ann Ruth. 1984. *The Spellbinders: Charismatic Political Leadership*. New Haven: Yale University Press.

Zaleznick, Abraham. 1977. "Managers and Leaders: Are They Different?" *Harvard Business Review* LV. 74–81.

CHAPTER 33

....

TAXATION AND THE QUALITY OF GOVERNMENT*

....

STEVEN M. KARCESKI AND EDGAR KISER

THIS chapter explores the relationship between taxation and quality of government by summarizing the many ways in which different features of tax systems relate various ways of thinking about of the quality of government. Taxation structures key interactions between citizens and the state and it is essential to understand how it fits within notions of quality of government. We begin with a broad conception of quality of government and then identify three unique and competing theoretical perspectives. The first focuses on administrative impartiality, the second on state size and economic growth, and the third on democracy. The position of the editors of this volume is that quality of government is best represented by administrative impartiality. While we largely agree with them, we also believe there is utility in exploring other perspectives as to which characteristics determine quality of government.

Each of the three perspective has several distinct prescriptive implications for taxation. In order to explore these implications systematically, it is necessary to distinguish between three different dimensions of tax systems. We focus on the following dimensions: (1) total tax revenue (what percentage of GDP the state takes); (2) tax structure (what and who is taxed); and (3) tax implementation (including both tax administration and taxpayer compliance). The general structure of the chapter follows from these distinctions—we will look at how each of these three dimensions of taxation will affect each of the three definitions of quality of government.

Each perspective has clear implications for taxation. The perspective of administrative impartiality prescribes a simple tax structure with horizontal equity and an impartial tax administration. The perspective concerned with a small state and economic growth emphasizes minimal revenues and the structure that offers the minimal market distortions. The democracy perspective suggests tax revenues should meet the public goods demanded by the population according to a structure deemed fair, which is of course dependent upon

* We would like to thank Michelle O'Brien and Steven Pfaff for taking the time to carefully read and provide thoughtful comments on earlier drafts of this chapter.

context. The relationship between taxation and quality of government varies in different historical contexts, so our analysis necessarily has a historical dimension. In the historical section of the chapter, we trace the best examples in the relationship between taxation and quality of government for each perspective in four different historical periods: ancient states, medieval states, early modern states, and contemporary states.

We want to note, however, that it is not possible to completely understand the effects of taxation on quality of government without simultaneously considering how tax revenue is spent. For example, a regressive sales tax would have more positive effects on quality of government if it funded a universal healthcare system than an unpopular war. Although we do not systematically assess the effects of state spending on quality of government in this chapter, we do argue that the general relationship between taxation and spending—a function of the structure of political institutions—affects quality of government. When taxing a spending are unrelated (e.g. tribute systems) quality of government will be low, when they are tightly related (e.g. earmarking) it will be higher but lack flexibility, and when they are loosely related (e.g. general fund taxation) quality of government will depend on the specific features of political institutions.

THREE VIEWS ON TAXATION AND THE QUALITY OF GOVERNMENT

There are three main perspectives on quality of government. The most developed and empirically tested perspective, coming from the work of Rothstein and his many collaborators (Rothstein 2009, 2013; Rothstein and Eek 2009), focuses on the impartiality of administration. A second view, derived from Smith (1776), but common in contemporary economics (Barzel 2002; La Porta et al. 1999; North 1981; North and Thomas 1973), defines good government as a small state that intervenes in markets as little as possible. A third theory, most common in political science (Dahl 1971, 1989; Wolfe 1977), views quality of government in terms of formal democratic institutions and responsiveness to the will of the majority.

There are also several composite definitions of quality of government that combine aspects of these three general definitions in various ways. Agnafors (2013) presents a comprehensive critique of each of the definitions above and offers a more complex definition containing seven important aspects of government: public ethos, good decision-making, reason giving/transparency, principle of beneficence, rule of law, efficiency, and intrinsic stability. The World Bank defines good governance as a combination of a number of indicators deemed to be inputs to, aspects of, and results of good government, including measures for (1) voice and accountability, (2) political stability and absence of violence, (3) government effectiveness, (4) regulatory quality, (5) rule of law, and (6) control of corruption (Kaufman and Kraay 2019). Kaufmann, Kraay, and Mastruzzi (2010, 2–6) organize the six areas of good governance around (a) constitutive institutions; (b) government capacity; and (c) legitimacy of economic and social institutions. While composite measures are certainly useful in many cases, we focus on three separate views, as the distinct nature of each allows us to deduce specific implications for taxation.

QUALITY OF GOVERNMENT AS ADMINISTRATIVE
IMPARTIALITY: IMPLICATIONS FOR TAXATION

Rothstein's (2011, 2013) definition of quality of government is based on the procedural impartiality of the "output" side of the citizen–government relationship. Good government can be measured by how effectively and fairly public officials enact policy in a noncorrupt manner. This entails that officials enact policy in the absence of preferential treatment based on social group membership. Fukuyama agrees that quality of government is about outputs, not inputs, arguing that "governance is about the performance of agents in carrying out the wishes of principals, and not about the goals that principals set ... governance is thus about execution, or what has traditionally fallen within the domain of public administration, as opposed to politics or public policy" (2013, 350–1). Both Fukuyama and Rothstein argue that both large and small states and democratic and autocratic regimes can be considered quality governments if their administrations are impartial.[1]

The administrative impartiality view of quality of government has two important implications for tax structure. First, tax structure must be impartial, so the incidence of taxation cannot vary by social group membership (aristocratic status, race, etc.). All people in similar economic positions (income, etc.) must be treated the same. Second, simple tax structures are preferred to more complex tax structures. Tax structures allowing for more exemptions and rebates according to differential income classifications make it easier for some taxpayers to avoid or evade some of all of their tax obligations, and thus make administrative impartiality more difficult to achieve. Moreover, simple tax structures are more transparent to the public, making it easier to see whether tax administration is impartial or biased.

Regarding tax administration, administrative impartiality arguments focus mainly on bureaucratization. The classical source for definitions of quality of government in terms of administrative effectiveness and impartiality is Max Weber (1978). Weber argued bureaucratic administration, and the rational-legal authority on which it is based, facilitated fair and equitable treatment of subjects or citizens, as opposed to the pervasive personal and group biases that characterized patrimonial administration.[2] The history of administrative impartiality is thus in part the history of bureaucratization. However, the Weberian

---

[1] Fukuyama (2013) identifies bureaucratic autonomy as a key feature of good governance. This means that bureaucrats need to have the autonomy that allows them to act impartially, and bureaucratic autonomy is "inversely related to the number and nature of the mandates issued by the principal" (2013, 357). This means that agents should be given broad goals to achieve, without specific, partial instructions to act specifically with other actors. According to Lipsky (2010), the autonomy of bureaucrats is inevitable. "Street-level bureaucrats," the people on the ground who put policy into practice, typically operate with discretion because the real-life situations they deal with are complex and difficult to monitor. Their autonomy means there is slippage between formal rules and action. Discretion and slippage are often much more efficient than following every rule.

[2] Empirical research has generally shown that bureaucracy decreases corruption (Evans and Rauch 1999; Rauch and Evans 2000). Dahlström, Lapuente, and Teorell (2012) show bureaucratic professionalization is linked to lower corruption. Bureaucratic professionalization is characterized by a separation of interests between politicians and bureaucrats, achieved through meritocratic recruitment, the nonpoliticization of bureaucratic positions and agencies, and the use of internal promotions.

approach is limited by its overemphasis on the formal institutions of bureaucracy. The fact that bureaucratic organization is not a sufficient condition for the effectiveness or impartiality of administration has been widely demonstrated (Blau 1956; Kiser 1999; Rothstein 2011).

Impartial tax administration has important feedback effects on levels of tax compliance. It creates a high level of social trust that improves many aspects of state functioning, including tax collection (Rothstein 2013; Rothstein and Eek 2009; Steinmo 2018). Levi (1988) argues that people will be more likely to pay their taxes if they think other taxpayers are also paying theirs—in other words, if they think the system is fair. Williamson (2017) finds that American taxpayers view their taxpaying status as a mark of citizenship—people who pay taxes are the ones who contribute to society, who deserve the benefits of various public goods and social programs. However, this status hinges on whether individuals pay income taxes. This leads to distaste for the tax system because taxes paid by everyone, like sales and excise taxes, are underestimated leading to the belief that poor people generally pay nothing whatsoever in taxes. Consistent with the findings of Lieberman (2003), Williamson links much of the anti-tax sentiment in the U.S. to the fact that people underestimate the taxes paid by the poor, especially marginalized racial groups (not part of the mainstream, white political community), meaning benefits are perceived to be going to some "other," undeserving group. Williamson (2017) also finds that willingness to pay taxes is conditional on citizen's perceptions of how revenues are spent. In her study, government waste not only included inefficiencies and funds allocated to connected constituents, but also funds that go to other groups and the perception of lavish spending by politicians (dinners, travel, housing, etc.). When these categories of "government waste" are salient, citizens don't feel as proud to pay their taxes.

An interesting anomaly from this perspective is the extreme unpopularity of the Internal Revenue Service in the United States. The arguments made by Rothstein and Levi, and the findings of several ultimatum game experiments all imply that citizens should like administrative organizations that enforce tax payments and catch tax evaders. However, in the United States the IRS is one of the least liked government agencies (Desilver 2013) and as a result is seriously underfunded by the government, resulting in higher rates of unpunished tax evasion. This is very different than in Sweden, where the tax administration ("Skatteverket") was recently found to be the most favored among a list of 25 major government institutions (Holmberg 2015).

QUALITY OF GOVERNMENT AS SMITHIAN EFFICIENCY: IMPLICATIONS FOR TAXATION

Going back as far as Adam Smith (1776), economic theories of quality of government have stressed the importance of small, noninterventionist government, on the grounds that it maximizes economic growth.[3] Contemporary neoliberal economic theories follow in this

---

[3] Not all economists are advocates of small states that intervene as little as possible in markets. Keynesians, for example, also define quality of government by its ability to generate economic growth, but argue that this is often (especially during periods of economic contraction) facilitated by more state spending and economic intervention. The World Bank used to consider small government the

Smithian tradition.[4] Adam Smith (1776) outlined several roles for governments necessary to facilitate a well-functioning free market society. This list includes a judicial system to enforce contracts, the granting and enforcing of intellectual property rights/patents, the building and maintenance of public goods such as infrastructure, providing national defense, supporting education, and regulating banks. Beyond this set of activities, Smith advocated limited state intervention in the economy (laissez-faire). Building upon this idea, public choice scholarship has equated *good* government with *small* government. If the government is small, it will intervene in the economy to a lesser degree, thus allowing markets to function optimally and efficiently.

One of the main implications of the Smithian perspective for taxation concerns total revenue—high quality of government is associated with low taxation. From the neoliberal and public choice perspectives (each in the Smithian camp), high taxation is viewed as undesirable because it represents excessive government intervention that disrupts market equilibria and distorts individuals' incentives (La Porta et al. 1999). In this perspective, it follows that minimal government intervention through taxation leads to greater economic growth. Yet, despite holding the belief that small governments are better, one of the major pieces of scholarship in this area concludes, "we have consistently found that the better performing governments are larger and collect higher taxes. Poorly performing governments, in contrast, are smaller and collect fewer taxes" (La Porta et al. 1999, 266; also see Persson and Rothstein 2015).

Regarding tax structure, Smithians favor taxes that distort markets and economic choices least. For example, Smith (1776) argued against customs because they decreased the amount of trade between nations, thus lessening the gains from comparative advantage. Consumption taxes are preferred over income taxes because the latter decrease participation in labor markets. Indeed, scholarship has linked a greater reliance on indirect taxation to higher rates of economic growth (Lindert 2004). A second argument from the Smithian camp is that the amount of tax individuals pay should equal the value of the benefits they get from public goods provided by the state (Buchanan and Tullock 1962; Wicksell 1958). According to this perspective, when individuals pay more in taxes than they get back in spending benefits, they are being coerced (Martinez-Vazquez and Winer 2014). This rules out the use of taxation for redistribution, and suggests that high-quality governments cannot use highly progressive taxes, unless the rich are getting a very large share of the benefits.

The Smithian perspective focuses on the efficiency of tax administration, not its administrative impartiality. As a result, they advocate for different types of administrative systems than scholars who stress administrative impartiality. For example, some arguments using agency theory to evaluate alternative systems of tax administration have advocated tax-farming (Kiser 1994) or contemporary variants of shifting residual claimancy to tax collectors (Kiser and Sacks 2011), even though it often results in unfair surcharges on the weakest taxpayers.

---

benchmark of "good" government, more recently the language has changed to focus on "effective" government, although some have challenged that the changes in policy reflect this change in language when pointing out that policy recommendations continue along a neoliberal/limited government path (Crawford 2007).

   [4] A number of scholars correctly point out that the mainstream representation of Adam Smith's views is misleading (see Rothschild 2002). We use "Smithian" to represent the dominant understanding of his work but do not claim it to be the view he would hold if he were alive today.

QUALITY OF GOVERNMENT
AS DEMOCRACY: IMPLICATIONS FOR TAXATION

Many scholars have defined quality of government in terms of the input side of political systems (Dahl 1971; Wolfe 1977). Good government is democratic government—the electoral process must be impartial so that all citizens share an equal chance at affecting political decisions. A number of scholars point out that impartial electoral institutions (political inputs) do not necessarily lead to policies that align with popular opinion (Achen and Bartels 2016; Bartels 2016; Gilens and Page 2014), policy implementations (political outputs) aside. However, many maintain preferences for majority rule through pluralistic electoral systems, particularly due to the absence of viable alternatives (Page and Gilens 2017).

Many scholars criticize the use of democracy in defining quality of government. Rothstein (2011, ch. 4) argues that, while democracy is a noble and desirable end in itself, democracy does not necessarily lead to political legitimacy or high quality of government unless other political institutions on the output end of politics are impartial. Fukuyama agrees, arguing the distinction between the two is important because "we will later want to theorize the relationship between governance and democracy" (2013, 350). We cannot assume that democracy is related to good governance, therefore they should be defined separately to test their relationship. Several countries have managed to achieve a high quality of government in the absence of democracy, most notably Singapore, and many countries with formal democratic electoral institutions still end up with low quality of government (Rothstein 2011; also see Charron and Lapuente 2010, 2011). High quality of government likely requires input from citizens through the political process (the "input" side of the citizen–government relationship), but democracy on its own will not be a sufficient indicator of good government.

For democracy to be associated with a high quality of government a relatively high national income may be a necessary condition. Charron and Lapuente (2010) find that in poorer democracies, long-term demand for expanding the administrative capacity is low, resulting in quality of government levels lower than some authoritarian states. In wealthier democracies, there is demand for mid- and long-term investment in administrative capacity. In other words, a democracy tends to need a wealthy population in order to result in high quality of government.

In terms of total tax revenue, a high quality of government from the democracy perspective is one that taxes as much as necessary to meet the public demand for state spending, and not more. In nondemocratic states, where there is often a loose relationship between taxing and spending, rulers tax as much as their power and administrative capacity will allow, and spend the money based on their preferences—in pre-modern states, mostly on war and personal consumption (Acemoglu and Robinson 2012; Kiser and Karceski 2017). In democratic states, taxation and spending can be related in two ways. The first is often referred to as earmarking—a particular tax is devoted to fund a particular type of spending. This was common in most states up until the nineteenth century (Barzel and Kiser 2002; Webber and Wildavsky 1986) and many states today use benefit-linked taxes to fund social insurance programs (Kesselman 1996). In democratic contexts, the transparency of this approach makes it easier for the public to link taxation to demands for spending.

The second way the two can be related—and by far the most common in complex, modern states—is through general fund taxation. Here tax payments enter into a general fund and dispersed to a variety programs, agencies, and spending projects. The complexity of this system, and the lack of a transparent connection between taxes and spending, makes it difficult for citizens to adequately control tax policy even in democratic states. In these cases, high trust in government is especially important (Rothstein 2013; Steinmo 2018). Democracy facilitates the development of trust, state legitimacy, and quasi-voluntary compliance, decreasing the costs of tax collection and the amount of tax evasion (Levi 1988).

Progressivity is the most studied issue related to tax structure and democratic theory. Many have argued (and some have feared) the working classes and poor would use their numerical advantage in democratic elections to "soak the rich" with highly progressive taxes. This has happened to some extent in certain democratic states, but not in others. The largest difference in tax structure in modern Western states is between Northern European social democratic states' high reliance on regressive indirect consumption taxes and the reliance on more progressive direct income taxes in the United States (Prasad and Deng 2009). One of the main determinants of this difference are differences in political institutions—in the form or type of democracy. Steinmo (1993) and Beramendi and Rueda (2007) argue that the combination of social democracy (stable left party power) and corporatism (facilitating bargaining and credible commitments between capital and labor) leads to more regressive taxation, high tax revenue, and large welfare states. Workers are willing to pay high indirect taxes because they trust the state to use revenues to provide public goods, and this trust is provided by corporatist and social democratic institutions. Another analysis by Hays (2003) shows that majoritarian political institutions, compared to institutions of proportional representation, result in the reliance on progressive income taxes, as working-class voters try to extract resources from the rich.

With respect to tax administration, one of the most important findings concerns the effects of the temporal ordering of the origins of democracy and bureaucracy. When democracy developed before bureaucratic tax administration, tax (and other) administrative institutions were often used for patronage by elected officials (see Orloff and Skocpol 1984 on the United States). But when bureaucracy developed prior to democracy, bureaucratic rules prevented this form of corruption and tax administration was both more impartial and more effective.

We conclude by summarizing the key points from this section in a table. Table 33.1 displays the implications from each of the three perspectives on quality of government

Table 33.1 Implications for three dimensions of taxation from three perspectives

	Admin. impartiality	Smithian	Democracy
Tax revenue	NA	Low tax revenue	A function of the demand for spending
Tax structure	Simple, clear, horizontal equity	Benefit-linked and minimally distortive for markets	Determined democratically
Tax administration & compliance	Impartial	Efficient	NA

(impartiality, Smithian, and democracy) with respect to the three areas of taxation (total revenue, tax structure, and tax administration/compliance). Each perspective offers distinct prescriptions for how good government might organize tax policy.

HISTORY OF TAXATION AND THE QUALITY OF GOVERNMENT FROM THREE PERSPECTIVES

Due to the vast differences in environmental and institutional conditions, quality of government means different things in different historical eras. This section provides a broad survey of political and fiscal history over the past two millennia from the perspective of each of the three definitions of quality of government. Our goal is to identify the best examples of high quality of government from three different perspectives over four main historical eras: ancient states (roughly 500 BC–400 AD), medieval states (1100–1500), early modern states (1500–1800), and contemporary states (1800–present). In all cases, we compare states in the same general time period, since high quality of government means something very different in 500 BCE or 1500 than it does now. Needless to say, our arguments will be suggestive rather than definitive, as we cannot in this short chapter provide adequate empirical support for our claims. Our hope is that by addressing such a wide array of cases, even in a fairly cursory manner, we can expand and sharpen the three perspectives on quality of government. Table 33.2 provides our summary of the evolution of quality of government over time.

Table 33.2 Taxation and the quality of government through history from three different theoretical perspectives

	Administrative impartiality	Smithian perspective	Democratic perspective
Ancient states	Qin/Han China Athens	Athens	Athens
Medieval States	Italian city-states	Italian city-states	England Italian city-states
Early modern states	Britain	Britain	Britain
Contemporary states	Denmark Sweden Singapore	United States Singapore	Sweden Denmark

The History of Taxation and the Quality of Government from the Administrative Impartiality Perspective

Almost all pre-modern states used various forms of patrimonial administration marked by very low levels of administrative impartiality. Patrimonialism is a broad concept referring to several different types of administrative forms usually associated with traditional authority, including the use of kin, slaves, patronage, feudalism, prebendalism, local notables, sale of offices, and tax-farming (Weber 1978, 228–34, 1028–64). Its core features are administration based on personal ties to or dependence on rulers (kin, slaves, patronage), privatization of offices (sale of offices and tax-farming), and extreme forms of decentralization (local notables, feudalism, and prebendalism).[5]

How can states move from inefficient and inequitable tax administration to efficient and equitable tax administration? To begin to answer these questions, we explore the causes of the replacement of patrimonial by bureaucratic tax administration. Both Weber (1978) and contemporary agency theories (Adams 1996; Kiser 1999; Kiser and Schneider 1994) suggest that adequate monitoring capacity (the ability of rulers to gather information on the actions of officials) is a necessary condition for bureaucratization. Since the main agency problem rulers face is information asymmetry (officials know more about what they are doing than rulers do), monitoring problems are central in agency relations. When monitoring is poor, rulers must compensate either by recruiting agents who are dependent on them (Kiser and Schneider 1994; Weber 1978), or by increasing the strength of sanctions (for example by using tax farmers [Kiser 1994]). Bureaucracy does not permit these compensatory strategies (hiring must be merit-based and salaries must be fixed), so it will not be an effective organizational form when monitoring is poor.

The level of technological development is one of the main determinants of monitoring capacity. Economic development brings improvements in technologies of communications, transportation, and record-keeping, and thus contributes significantly to centralization and bureaucratization (Ardant 1975; Kiser 1994; Weber 1978). Prior to the development of efficient communications, transportation, and record-keeping technologies, size was one of the most important barriers to centralization and bureaucratization (Ardant 1975; Weber 1978, 1051). Holding technology constant, small countries bureaucratize earlier than larger ones.

However, on their own, these technological developments are often not sufficient to bring about bureaucratization. Officials within the state often have entrenched power to block reforms, so bureaucratization may not occur even if monitoring capacity improves. Revolutions and major wars facilitate bureaucratization in this instance by breaking the power of entrenched officials opposed to reform (Goldstone 1991; Kiser and Kane 2001; Kiser and Schneider 1994; Skocpol 1979). Revolution and major war are neither sufficient nor necessary conditions for bureaucratization, but both are contributory.

---

[5] All forms of decentralization are not patrimonial, of course. Decentralized administration can be run as a small-scale bureaucracy, or can include patrimonial elements like rule by local notables, elected officials, or privatized collection.

The history of bureaucratization of tax administration is far from linear. It begins in Qin and Han China but doesn't develop in Europe until approximately 2000 years later. The origins of bureaucratic administration occurred in two distinct phases: Qin China (221–206 BCE) was the best example of administrative bureaucratization (Fukuyama 2011, 110–24; Kiser and Cai 2003), but it didn't diffuse to Europe until the eighteenth century.[6] Why did a partially bureaucratized administrative system develop in Qin China about two millennia before it did in European states? The Warring States era (481–221 BCE) that preceded the Qin unification of China created the necessary conditions for bureaucratization by creating a bureaucratic model (based on Legalist philosophy), facilitating the development of roads, and providing trained and disciplined personnel. The Chinese case illustrates that bureaucratization of tax administration is not just a function of efficiency considerations, but of power, as well. The weakening of the power of aristocrats is a necessary condition for bureaucratization, because aristocrats were embedded in lucrative positions in patrimonial administrations, and didn't want to give them up. The main factor differentiating Qin China from other ancient states and empires was the extreme weakness of the aristocracy produced by an unusually long period of severe warfare. Extensive aristocratic warfare killed much of the dominant class, allowing rulers to hire agents on the basis of merit rather than aristocratic status (Fukuyama 2011, 110–24; Kiser and Cai 2003).[7]

The government of ancient Athens (from roughly 500 to 300 BC) was much less bureaucratic than Qin and Han China, but it had even higher administrative impartiality. Athenian tax administration was derived from its participatory democratic ideology and institutions. It was run by citizen amateurs, chosen by lottery or elected, working in collegial boards on short (usually one year) terms (Ober 2015, 496–7). Even the council in charge of monitoring tax collectors and other officials was composed of citizens chosen by lottery. The corruption of officials was unusually low, and as a result the Athenian state was able to extract 10–15% of GDP in taxes, more than almost all states prior to the nineteenth century (Ober 2015, 496, 504).

The next important exemplary case in high-quality tax administration comes with the Italian city-states (Venice, Florence, Genoa, and Milan were the most prominent) that broke away from the Holy Roman Empire in the eleventh and twelfth centuries and flourished until the fourteenth to fifteenth centuries. European states in this period were ruled by patrimonial monarchs and collected their taxes using various forms of patrimonial administration dominated by aristocratic elites. The Italian city-states had much higher administrative impartiality (and effectiveness) for two main reasons. First, many of them replaced hereditary autocratic rulers with Podesta—foreign rulers without local ties serving very short terms (often only one year). This significantly reduced corruption at the top of the system (Mungiu-Pippidi 2013, 1266–7). The second thing they did was pass laws limiting the ability

---

[6] Of course, other pre-modern states also had some bureaucratic elements. Pharaonic Egypt was partially bureaucratic, but there are too few documents related directly to their tax administration to say much with certainty (Jursa and Garcia 2015, 139).

[7] Although Qin China was more bureaucratic than any other state or empire prior to the seventeenth century, bureaucratization was limited to top officials in central administration located in the capital. The reason is that top officials are much easier to monitor—they are less numerous and less distant than lower level officials. The lower levels of Chinese administration were patrimonial, relying on local notables, and ad hoc clerks and "runners" to collect taxes (Huang 1974).

of aristocratic elites to control politics and administration (the 1293 Ordinances of Justice in Florence is a prominent example). As a result, their tax administrations were more effective than those of competing states, and tax collectors were better controlled (Jones 1997; Mungiu-Pippidi 2013, 1265–7).

In the early modern era, it is Britain that stands out for its administrative quality of government. After the revolution of 1640–88, Britain developed aspects of bureaucratic tax administration (especially in excise taxation) prior to other European states (Brewer 1990; Ertman 1997), due mainly to its relatively small size and more rapid development of effective communications and transportation systems (Geiger 1994, 19; Szostak 1991, 55–7), but also due to its early revolution. The revolution was important because it dramatically decreased dominant class control of tax administration, and facilitated partial bureaucratization (Kiser and Kane 2001). Reforms at the end of the early modern era (1780–1840) further decreased administrative corruption (Mungiu-Pippidi 2013, 1274).

One of the best indications of the advances in British administration is that they were able to implement the first income tax. The most important turning point in the history of premodern tax structure, marking the transition to modern taxation, is the development of the income tax. Britain is the exemplary case of this transition, experimenting with the income tax in 1798–1802 (to pay for the Napoleonic wars) and instituting it permanently in 1842. The income tax diffused throughout Europe fairly quickly, and by 1920 it was being used in almost all developed European economies (Scheve and Stasavage 2016). The main virtue of the income tax was that it linked taxation to economic production more tightly than any prior tax, so states could better ensure that economic growth produced more tax revenue.

In the beginning of the modern era, Denmark and Sweden developed the highest quality of government from the administrative impartiality perspective.[8] Mungiu-Pippidi (2013, 1273) notes that Danish absolute monarchs provided much of the foundation of high administrative impartiality in Denmark. The reforms in the second half of the nineteenth century built on this early advantage, giving Denmark the first "modern control of corruption." The trust in government created by these impartial administrations was one of the main determinants of the development of large welfare states in both Denmark and Sweden (Rothstein 2013; Steinmo 2010, 2018). One of the most important determinants of administrative impartiality in both Sweden and Denmark is that the development of bureaucracy preceded the development of democracy (Mungiu-Pippidi 2013; Rothstein 2013; Uslaner and Rothstein 2016). The early development of democracy can produce low administrative impartiality, as democratic leaders can use nonbureaucratic administration for patronage and other forms of corruption. Many scholars agree that the high levels of administrative impartiality in contemporary Denmark and Sweden are the product of long-term historical causes, not just contemporary institutional arrangements. Uslander and Rothstein

---

[8] We will discuss these two cases together (both here and in the section on democracy), because they share many important features. The similarities between these two countries in levels of administrative impartiality raises an interesting question about the importance of diffusion, often referred to as "Galton's problem"—is the similarity a function of similar internal causal processes or diffusion from a common source? We can only raise this issue here, but it is an important topic for future research. The fact that former British colonies tend to rank higher on administrative impartiality than other states at similar levels of economic development also suggests that diffusion may be an important determinant of quality of government.

(2016) demonstrate that levels of education and wealth equality one century ago are strong predictors of corruption in contemporary states. Steinmo (2018) argues that long-term causes creating virtuous cycles are the main determinants of low corruption and high trust in government in contemporary Sweden.

Among contemporary states, Singapore also measures quite high in terms of administrative impartiality (Hong Kong could be included here as well). Bureaucrats in Singapore are honest and effective, in part because they are paid unusually high salaries, and this is reflected in the fact that Singapore always ranks close to the top (higher rankings indicate lower corruption) of the Corruption Perception Index (Transparency International 2019). The high quality of tax administration and administrative impartiality in Singapore is one of the main determinants of their economic prosperity (Quah 1982, 1984). The case of Singapore is especially interesting because it demonstrates how democracy is not a necessary condition for high administrative impartiality (Rothstein 2011).

A SMITHIAN HISTORY OF TAXATION AND THE QUALITY OF GOVERNMENT

It is hard to judge pre-modern states from a Smithian perspective, since markets were absent or minimally developed in most of them. For most of pre-modern history, states were small in size by default because very few states were able to extract much revenue from their populations. Pre-modern states and empires were "low taxation societies" (Bang 2015, 552; see also Monson 2015; O'Brien 2012; Scheidel 2015) that rarely extracted more than 5% of GDP (Bean 1973, 212; Mann 1993, 369), meaning there was relatively little government intervention through taxation.

There are several reasons these states couldn't get much tax revenue. First, there wasn't much to tax. Economic growth is the main long-term motor of increasing tax revenue/GDP (Wagner 1958). Because there was little or no growth in per capita income prior to the industrial revolution (Clark 2007; North, Wallis, and Weingast 2009, 3), we should not expect much growth in tax revenue.[9] Second, class power limited state revenue. Pre-modern autocrats needed the support of aristocratic landowners (and often the leaders of religious organizations) to maintain their power, and they purchased that support almost everywhere by giving them an exemption from (at least direct) taxation. Third, the demand for state spending was limited. War was the main source of the demand for tax revenue in all pre-modern states (Ertman 1997; Kiser and Linton 2002; Tilly 1990), and the tax revenue of states did begin to increase in early modern Europe due to a dramatic increase in the frequency and scale of warfare (O'Brien 2012). However, the part of this argument that is rarely noted is that war was practically the *only* source of demand for taxation prior to the nineteenth century (only a few pre-modern states provided infrastructure like irrigation systems or welfare such as grain redistribution). Fourth, the capacity of the state to collect taxes was very limited. Rulers of states could neither afford nor control a sufficient number of officials to adequately

---

[9] Of course, there were significant variations in levels of economic development in pre-modern states, and where capitalism developed earlier, tax revenue was higher (Tilly 1990).

assess and collect taxes. Over time these stable, low tax levels came to be viewed as "customary" or based on tradition, making them even more resistant to change (Weber 1978).

Among ancient political systems, the Athenian city-state (especially from 500 to 300 BCE) had by far the best quality of government from the Smithian perspective, in spite of these structural limitations.[10] The Athenian city-state was a central node in Mediterranean trade, and merchants' interests were paramount in the political and tax system. The result was unprecedented economic growth compared to other ancient states. Athens was among the most urbanized regions in the world, had an unusually large middle class, and per capita GDP higher not only the ancient states but most pre-modern states (Ober 2015, 493). Their fiscal institutions were one of the main determinants of their economic success (Ober 2015, 494).

In the later medieval era (eleventh to fifteenth centuries), the Italian city-states best approximated the Smithian ideal of good government.[11] This is not surprising, since they were run by and for capitalists—guilds and merchants. Capitalism indeed flourished in this period, as these small city-states had the highest per capita incomes in the world (Stark 2005). There were also substantial advances in credit and insurance markets, and double-entry bookkeeping was developed (Carruthers and Espeland 1991; Ferguson 2008). Several scholars have noted that the tax policies of these city-states were important determinants of their economic growth (Grief 1998; Mungiu-Pippidi 2013, 1269).

Early modern Britain is the exemplary Smithian case in the early modern era. The early democratic revolution in Britain (1640–88) paved the way for merchants and producers in towns to gain more control over state policy (Moore 1966). The power of parliament facilitated the formation of credible commitments in the political and fiscal systems, increasing the rule of law and the predictability of state policy (North and Weingast 1989; Weber 1978). These political and fiscal developments laid the foundation for the industrial revolution and Britain's rise to global hegemon; it's no wonder Smith (1776) often used Britain as a positive example of his model, in contrast to continental states.

Among contemporary states, Singapore is one of the most Smithian. The government of Singapore is based on free trade—they are one of the most open economies in the world. They have very low taxes for a country at their level of economic development, only about 14% of GDP, and have no capital gains tax. Yet, it scores remarkably high on measures of government effectiveness (Fukuyama 2015). In the most recent release of the Index of Economic Freedom—a composite score based on rule of law, government size, regulatory efficiency, and market openness—Singapore is number two on the list, behind only Hong Kong (Miller, Kim, and Roberts 2019). Other countries ranking high on the list include New Zealand, Switzerland, Australia, and Ireland.

The contemporary United States is also a leader in quality of government from the Smithian perspective. Smithian ideologies have been dominant for most of U.S. history, with the exceptions of the Populist/Progressive and New Deal eras. This has become even

---

[10] Other Greek city-states could be included here, and Temin (2006) makes a good argument that the Roman Empire had many Smithian elements.

[11] A partial breakthrough from the Smithian perspective comes with the tax system of medieval England, where there was a link between those who paid the tax and who got the benefits. The tax structure created and enforced by the parliament was fundamentally Smithian, using earmarking to tie tax payments closely to public and collective goods provision (Barzel and Kiser 1997).

more pronounced in the post-Reagan era, as advocates of smaller government have successfully implemented a low-tax and low-regulation regime. The contemporary United States gets much less revenue than most other states at a similar level of development (Kenworthy 2014; Prasad 2018) and recent changes to tax policy under Trump have followed this trend.

A History of Taxation and the Quality of Government from the Democratic Perspective

The model case of quality of government defined as democratic control of taxation in the ancient world was Athens (roughly 500–300 BCE).[12] Although voting rights were extremely restricted by modern standards (slaves and women were excluded), Athens was far more democratic than other states at the time. Ober (2015, 493) describes Athens as a "strikingly egalitarian" citizen republic based on "participatory democracy." Tax laws were passed by a majority vote of the citizen assembly, and citizens were even paid to participate (Ober 2015, 496–9). Revenues were earmarked for particular spending projects, making it easier for citizens to monitor the link between taxation and spending (Ober 2015, 496–7).

The next exemplary case in the development of democratic control of taxation comes with the origins of the English Parliament, although scholars disagree about what caused voting institutions to emerge at that time. Weber (1978, 1057, 1352) argues that medieval rulers bargained with subjects in voting institutions only when they lacked the power to coerce tax payments from them beyond their customary feudal obligations. There are serious empirical problems with this power/conflict argument. The historical record shows that voting institutions initially developed in both England and France under relatively strong rulers (Barzel and Kiser 1997; Major 1960; Strayer 1955, 18). Moreover, English rulers were far more powerful than their French counterparts prior to the development of voting institutions (Lewis 1962; McIlwain 1932), but voting developed first and was strongest in England.

An alternative argument suggests that voting institutions such as the English Parliament emerged as an unintended outcome of wealth-seeking by rulers and subjects (Bates and Lien 1985; Kiser and Barzel 1991). In the context of the Middle Ages, national voting institutions were mechanisms that allowed rulers and subjects to cooperate with each other on mutually profitable projects by enabling rulers to make credible commitments to subjects.[13] Rulers

---

[12] Other Greek city-states and the Roman Republic (which copied many Greek political institutions) could also be considered here. Republican Rome even taxed the rich in order to redistribute to the poor (Ober 2015, 494), but aristocratic power over state policy was much greater than in Athens (Tan 2015, 208).

[13] The stress on the need for credible commitments in the relationship between rulers and subjects has created a new view of the state that models conditions in which rulers will willingly cede power to some of their subjects (Barzel and Kiser 1997; Bates and Lien 1985; Kiser and Barzel 1991; North and Weingast 1989; Root 1994).

will choose to share residual claimancy (a claim on profit or loss from generated by a joint venture) with participating subjects in projects like war to provide their partners with adequate incentives to ensure sufficient effort. Voting institutions are created to help resolve three sets of problems that arise in joint ventures between rulers and subjects: decision-making by multiple individuals, rulers' confiscation of subjects' gains, and subjects' confiscation from each other.

Another model case of democratization of taxation in the medieval era was in the Italian city-states. Although they are perhaps best characterized as republican rather than democratic, because they were controlled mainly by corporate groups like the guilds, policymaking was much more inclusive and participatory than in other states at this time (Mungiu-Pippidi 2013, 1268). For most of the period, they were often dominated not by aristocrats, but by the "*popolo grasso*" (lawyers, merchants, guilds), although the Ciompi rebellion in Florence in 1378 ushered in a brief period on broader participation by the "*popolo minuto*." This proto-democracy was supported by a large literature on the virtues of republican government.

In the early modern period, Britain was the leader in democratic quality of government.[14] Although the franchise was still very limited, its early revolution (1640–88) dramatically decreased the power of both the monarchy and the aristocracy. The increasing power of parliament significantly increased the number of social groups with influence over state tax policy. The development of democratic institutions dramatically lowered the transaction costs of creating and enforcing fiscal contracts between taxpayers and rulers. North and Weingast (1989) show how the Glorious Revolution of 1688 increased tax revenue by increasing the ability of monarchs to bargain with and to make credible commitments to taxpayers.

Denmark and Sweden are the best examples of democratic control of taxation in the modern era, and also illustrate the ways in which the type of democracy matters for quality of government. Sweden was already more democratic than other monarchies in the early modern period, since its aristocracy was relatively weak and peasants had seats in the legislative assembly (Steinmo 2010), illustrating the importance of long-term path-dependent processes for contemporary quality of government. The tax systems of both Sweden and Denmark are characterized by very high revenues and a heavy reliance on regressive indirect taxes. This has only been possible because of the very high rates of trust in government (OECD 2015) created in part by strong democratic institutions (Steinmo 1993).

In addition to the effects of the amount of democracy on quality of government, it is also important to look at differences in the type of democracy. The parliamentary and corporatist nature of political institutions in both Sweden and Denmark are important determinants of the democratic nature of their tax policy. As we noted above, when spending comes from a general fund (as opposed to having revenues earmarked for particular spending), it is very difficult for taxpayers to understand and thus democratically control the relationship between what they pay and what they get. Corporatist political institutions help reduce the information asymmetry between the state and the citizens by providing collective bargaining units that are better informed and can better advocate for their constituencies (Streeck and Kenworthy 2005). Parliamentary systems force parties to

---

[14] Both the Netherlands and the United States after its war of independence should also be considered here.

take more precise positions on taxation (compared to the broad and heterogeneous political parties in presidential systems), and thus serve a similar function. As a result of the particular form of their democratic institutions, Sweden and Denmark are able to extract more revenue than most contemporary states. However, Rothstein (2011) argues that administrative impartiality, not democratic institutions, is the main determinant of high taxes in Sweden and Denmark.

CONCLUSION

The brief survey of the exemplary cases in quality of government through history summarized in Table 33.2 shows that there is substantial agreement across the three different perspectives on quality of government. In the ancient world, all three perspectives rate Athens at the top. In the medieval world, all three perspectives argue that tax systems in the Italian city-states had the highest quality of government. In the early modern era, all agree on ranking Britain at the top. Among contemporary states there is some divergence, but both administrative impartiality and democracy see Sweden and Denmark as having the highest quality of government. Given the extent of theoretical disagreement across these perspectives, that seems like a lot of consensus.

Surveying the history of quality of government reveals another important fact: High quality of government is very rare. This is true regardless of which of the three perspectives we use. We argue that this is true for two main reasons: (1) Path dependence makes it difficult to move out of low quality of government; and (2) strategic innovation makes it difficult to maintain high quality of government.

The vast majority of states throughout history (and still today) have low quality of government, and path-dependent constraints make it difficult for them to improve. Rothstein (2011) uses the example of "social traps" common in poorer countries (which would include all pre-modern states), and shows their effect on taxation. In this context, citizens do not see the government as trustworthy and therefore are unlikely to believe the government would put tax revenues to good use. This absence of sufficient revenues limits the state's ability to provide adequate public goods. Causation is often endogenous to the institutional context as the result of multiple feedback loops, consistent with theories of path dependence (Rothstein and Eek 2009, 85; Pierson 2000; Mahoney 2000). This creates a viscous cycle: Low trust leads to low tax morale, which leads to lower revenues, which does not allow a state to provide the public goods that would build trust in the state (Steinmo 2018).

There are reasons to believe that the virtuous cycles supporting high quality of government may not last. Impartial, noncorrupt tax institutions may have a long-term limit, due to learning effects. Will actors in the long run learn how to game the system and capture it to their benefit? We can see this in the persistent long term, and often successful effort of elites to reduce taxes via the political system (Martin 2013; Prasad 2006; Scheve and Stasavage 2016; Page, Seawright, and Lacombe 2019). None of the cases in Table 33.2 that were benchmarks of good government retained that position forever. The best examples of high quality of government today (Denmark, Sweden, even Singapore) have not been around very long relative to the rise and fall of these other historical examples of good government. Time will tell if they prove to be exceptions to the rule.

References

Acemoglu, Daron, and James A. Robinson. 2012. *Why Nations Fail: The Origins of Power, Prosperity and Poverty*. 1st ed. New York: Crown Publishers.

Achen, Christopher H., and Larry M. Bartels. 2016. *Democracy for Realists: Why Elections Do Not Produce Responsive Government*. Princeton Studies in Political Behavior. Princeton: Princeton University Press.

Adams, Julia. 1996. "Principals and Agents, Colonialists and Company Men: The Decay of Colonial Control in the Dutch East Indies." *American Sociological Review* 61 (1): 12–28. https://doi.org/10.2307/2096404

Agnafors, Marcus. 2013. "Quality of Government: Toward a More Complex Definition." *American Political Science Review* 107 (3): 433–45. https://doi.org/10.1017/S0003055413000191

Ardant, Gabriel. 1975. "Financial Policy and Economic Infrastructure of Modern States and Nations." In *The Formation of National States in Western Europe*, edited by Charles Tilly, 164–242. Studies in Political Development. Princeton, N.J.: Princeton University Press.

Bang, Peter Fibiger. 2015. "Tributary Empires and the New Fiscal Sociology: Some Comparative Reflections." *Fiscal Regimes and the Political Economy of Premodern States*: 537–56.

Bartels, Larry M. 2016. *Unequal Democracy: the Political Economy of the New Gilded Age*. Princeton: Princeton University Press. http://public.eblib.com/choice/publicfullrecord.aspx?p=4694159

Barzel, Yoram. 2002. *A Theory of the State: Economic Rights, Legal Rights, and the Scope of the State*. Political Economy of Institutions and Decisions. Cambridge; New York: Cambridge University Press.

Barzel, Yoram, and Edgar Kiser. 1997. "The Development and Decline of Medieval Voting Institutions: A Comparison of England and France." *Economic Inquiry* 35 (2): 244–60. https://doi.org/10.1111/j.1465-7295.1997.tb01907.x

Barzel, Yoram, and Edgar Kiser. 2002. "Taxation and Voting Rights in Medieval England and France." *Rationality and Society* 14 (4): 473–507. https://doi.org/10.1177/1043463102014004003

Bates, Robert H., and Da-Hsiang Donald Lien. 1985. "A Note on Taxation, Development, and Representative Government." *Politics & Society* 14 (1): 53–70. https://doi.org/10.1177/003232928501400102

Bean, Richard. 1973. "War and the Birth of the Nation State." *The Journal of Economic History* 33 (01): 203–21. https://doi.org/10.1017/S0022050700076531

Beramendi, Pablo, and David Rueda. 2007. "Social Democracy Constrained: Indirect Taxation in Industrialized Democracies." *British Journal of Political Science* 37 (04): 619–41. https://doi.org/10.1017/S0007123407000348

Blau, Peter. 1956. *Bureaucracy in Modern Society*. New York, N.Y.: Random House.

Brewer, John. 1990. *The Sinews of Power: War, Money, and the English State, 1688–1783*. 1st Harvard University pbk. ed. Cambridge, MA: Harvard University Press.

Buchanan, James M., and Gordon Tullock. 1962. *The Calculus of Consent: Logical Foundations of Constitutional Democracy*. Ann Arbor, MI: University of Michigan Press.

Carruthers, Bruce G., and Wendy Nelson Espeland. 1991. "Accounting for Rationality: Double-Entry Bookkeeping and the Rhetoric of Economic Rationality." *American Journal of Sociology* 97 (1): 31–69. https://doi.org/10.1086/229739

Charron, Nicholas, and Victor Lapuente. 2010. "Does Democracy Produce Quality of Government?" *European Journal of Political Research* 49 (4): 443–70. https://doi.org/10.1111/j.1475-6765.2009.01906.x

Charron, Nicholas, and Victor Lapuente. 2011. "Which Dictators Produce Quality of Government?" *Studies in Comparative International Development* 46 (4): 397–423. https://doi.org/10.1007/s12116-011-9093-0

Clark, Gregory. 2007. *A Farewell to Alms: A Brief Economic History of the World*. The Princeton Economic History of the Western World. Princeton, NJ: Princeton University Press.

Crawford, Gordon. 2007. "The World Bank and Good Governance." In *IMF, World Bank and Policy Reform*, edited by Alberto Paloni and Maurizio Zanardi, 109–34. Place of publication not identified: Routledge.

Dahl, Robert Alan. 1971. *Polyarchy: Participation and Opposition*. New Haven: Yale University Press.

Dahl, Robert Alan. 1989. *Who Governs?: Democracy and Power in an American City*. New Haven, CT; London: Yale University Press.

Dahlström, Carl, Victor Lapuente, and Jan Teorell. 2012. "The Merit of Meritocratization: Politics, Bureaucracy, and the Institutional Deterrents of Corruption." *Political Research Quarterly* 65 (3): 656–68. https://doi.org/10.1177/1065912911408109

Desilver, Drew. 2013. "IRS Among Least-Popular Federal Agencies." *Fact Tank at the Pew Research Center* (blog). May 16, 2013. https://www.pewresearch.org/fact-tank/2013/05/16/irs-among-least-popular-federal-agencies/

Ertman, Thomas. 1997. *Birth of the Leviathan: Building States and Regimes in Medieval and Early Modern Europe*. Cambridge, UK; New York: Cambridge University Press.

Evans, Peter, and James E. Rauch. 1999. "Bureaucracy and Growth: A Cross-National Analysis of the Effects of 'Weberian' State Structures on Economic Growth." *American Sociological Review* 64 (5): 748–65. https://doi.org/10.2307/2657374

Ferguson, Niall. 2008. *The Ascent of Money: A Financial History of the World*. New York Times Best Sellers. New York: Penguin Press.

Fukuyama, Francis. 2011. *The Origins of Political Order: From Prehuman Times to the French Revolution*. 1st ed. New York: Farrar, Straus and Giroux.

Fukuyama, Francis. 2013. "What Is Governance?" *Governance* 26 (3): 347–68. https://doi.org/10.1111/gove.12035

Fukuyama, Francis. 2015. *Political Order and Political Decay: From the Industrial Revolution to the Globalization of Democracy*. New York, N.Y.: Farrar, Straus and Giroux.

Geiger, Reed G. 1994. *Planning the French Canals: Bureaucracy, Politics, and Enterprise under the Restoration*. Newark; London; Cranbury, NJ: University of Delaware Press; Associated University Presses.

Gilens, Martin, and Benjamin I. Page. 2014. "Testing Theories of American Politics: Elites, Interest Groups, and Average Citizens." *Perspectives on Politics* 12 (3): 564–81. https://doi.org/10.1017/S1537592714001595

Goldstone, Jack A. 1991. *Revolution and Rebellion in the Early Modern World*. Berkeley, CA: University of California Press.

Grief, Avner. 1998. "Self-Enforcing Political Systems and Economic Growth: Late Medieval Genoa." In *Analytic Narratives*, edited by Robert H. Bates, Avner Grief, Margaret Levi, Jean-Laurent Rosenthal, and Barry R. Weingast, 23–63. Princeton, N.J.: Princeton University Press.

Hays, Jude C. 2003. "Globalization and Capital Taxation in Consensus and Majoritarian Democracies." *World Politics* 56 (01): 79–113. https://doi.org/10.1353/wp.2004.0004

Holmberg, Sören. 2015. "Mycket höga krav på offentlig verksamhet." Gothenburg, Sweden: Society Opinion and Media Institute.

Huang, Ray. 1974. *Taxation and Governmental Finance in Sixteenth-Century Ming China*. Cambridge Studies in Chinese History, Literature and Institutions. New York, N.Y.: Cambridge University Press.

Jones, P. J. Philip James. 1997. *The Italian City-State: From Commune to Signoria*. Oxford; New York: Clarendon Press.

Jursa, Michael, and John Carlos Moreno Garcia. 2015. "The Ancient Near East and Egypt." In *Fiscal Regimes and the Political Economy of Premodern States*, edited by Andrew Monson and Walter Scheidel, 115–65. Cambridge, United Kingdom; New York, NY: Cambridge University Press.

Kaufman, Daniel, and Aart Kraay. 2019. "The Worldwide Governance Indicators Project." The World Bank. 2019. http://info.worldbank.org/governance/wgi/index.aspx

Kaufmann, Daniel, Aart Kraay, and Massimo Mastruzzi. 2010. "The Worldwide Governance Indicators: Methodology and Analytical Issues." SSRN Scholarly Paper ID 1682130. Rochester, NY: Social Science Research Network. https://papers.ssrn.com/abstract=1682130

Kenworthy, Lane. 2014. *Social Democratic America*. Oxford; New York: Oxford University Press.

Kesselman, Jonathan R. 1996. "Payroll Taxes Around the World: Concepts and Practice." *Canadian Tax Journal* 44 (1): 59–84.

Kiser, Edgar. 1994. "Markets and Hierarchies in Early Modern Tax Systems: A Principal-Agent Analysis." *Politics & Society* 22 (3): 284–315. https://doi.org/10.1177/0032329294022003003

Kiser, Edgar. 1999. "Comparing Varieties of Agency Theory in Economics, Political Science, and Sociology: An Illustration from State Policy Implementation." *Sociological Theory* 17 (2): 146–70. https://doi.org/10.1111/0735-2751.00073

Kiser, Edgar, and Yoram Barzel. 1991. "The Origins of Democracy in England." *Rationality and Society* 3 (4): 396–422. https://doi.org/10.1177/1043463191003004002

Kiser, Edgar, and Yong Cai. 2003. "War and Bureaucratization in Qin China: Exploring an Anomalous Case." *American Sociological Review* 68 (4): 511–39. https://doi.org/10.2307/1519737

Kiser, Edgar, and Joshua Kane. 2001. "Revolution and State Structure: The Bureaucratization of Tax Administration in Early Modern England and France." *American Journal of Sociology* 107 (1): 183–223. https://doi.org/10.1086/323656

Kiser, Edgar, and Steven M. Karceski. 2017. "Political Economy of Taxation." *Annual Review of Political Science* 20 (1): 75–92. https://doi.org/10.1146/annurev-polisci-052615-025442

Kiser, Edgar, and April Linton. 2002. "The Hinges of History: State-Making and Revolt in Early Modern France." *American Sociological Review* 67 (6): 889–910. https://doi.org/10.2307/3088975

Kiser, Edgar, and Audrey Sacks. 2011. "African Patrimonialism in Historical Perspective Assessing Decentralized and Privatized Tax Administration." *The ANNALS of the American Academy of Political and Social Science* 636 (1): 129–49. https://doi.org/10.1177/0002716211399067

Kiser, Edgar, and Joachim Schneider. 1994. "Bureaucracy and Efficiency: An Analysis of Taxation in Early Modern Prussia." *American Sociological Review* 59 (2): 187–204. https://doi.org/10.2307/2096226

La Porta, R., F. Lopez-de-Silanes, A. Shleifer, and R. Vishny. 1999. "The Quality of Government." *The Journal of Law, Economics, and Organization* 15 (1): 222–79. https://doi.org/10.1093/jleo/15.1.222

Levi, Margaret. 1988. *Of Rule and Revenue*. California Series on Social Choice and Political Economy 13. Berkeley, C.A.: University of California Press.

Lewis, P. S. 1962. "The Failure of the French Medieval Estates." *Past & Present* 23: 3–24.

Lieberman, Evan S. 2003. *Race and Regionalism in the Politics of Taxation in Brazil and South Africa*. Cambridge Studies in Comparative Politics. Cambridge; New York: Cambridge University Press.

Lindert, Peter H. 2004. *Growing Public: Social Spending and Economic Growth since the Eighteenth Century*. Cambridge, UK; New York: Cambridge.

Lipsky, Michael. 2010. *Street-Level Bureaucracy: Dilemmas of the Individual in Public Services*. 30th anniversary expanded ed. New York: Russell Sage Foundation.

Mahoney, James. 2000. "Path Dependence in Historical Sociology." *Theory and Society* 29 (4): 507–48. https://doi.org/10.1023/A:1007113830879

Major, James Russell. 1960. *Representative Institutions in Renaissance France, 1421–1559*. Etudes Présentées à La Commission Internationale Pour l'histoire Des Assemblées d'Etats 22. Madison: University of Wisconsin Press.

Mann, Michael. 1993. *The Sources of Social Power: Volume 2, The Rise of Classes and Nation States 1760–1914*. Cambridge, U.K.; New York: Cambridge University Press.

Martin, Isaac William. 2013. *Rich People's Movements: Grassroots Campaigns to Untax the One Percent*. Studies in Postwar American Political Development. Oxford; New York: Oxford University Press.

Martinez-Vazquez, Jorge, and Stanley L. Winer. 2014. *Coercion and Social Welfare in Public Finance: Economic and Political Perspectives*. New York: Cambridge University Press.

McIlwain, Charles Howard. 1932. "Medieval Estates." In *Cambridge Medieval History*, edited by Joseph Robson Tanner, Charles William Previte-Orton, and Zachary Nugent Brooke, 665–715. New York: Macmillan.

Miller, Terry, Anthony B. Kim, and James M. Roberts. 2019. *2019 Index of Economic Freedom: 25th Anniversary Edition*. Washington, D.C.: The Heritage Foundation.

Monson, Andrew. 2015. "Hellenistic Empires." In *Fiscal Regimes and the Political Economy of Premodern States*, edited by Andrew Monson and Walter Scheidel, 169–207. Cambridge; New York: Cambridge University Press.

Moore, Barrington. 1966. *Social Origins of Dictatorship and Democracy: Lord and Peasant in the Making of the Modern World*. Boston: Beacon Press.

Mungiu-Pippidi, Alina. 2013. "Becoming Denmark: Historical Designs of Corruption Control." *Social Research: An International Quarterly* 80 (4): 1259–86.

North, Douglass C., John Joseph Wallis, and Barry R. Weingast. 2009. *Violence and Social Orders: A Conceptual Framework for Interpreting Recorded Human History*. Cambridge; New York: Cambridge University Press.

North, Douglass C., and Barry R. Weingast. 1989. "Constitutions and Commitment: The Evolution of Institutions Governing Public Choice in Seventeenth-Century England." *The Journal of Economic History* 49 (04): 803–32. https://doi.org/10.1017/S0022050700009451

North, Douglass Cecil. 1981. *Structure and Change in Economic History*. New York London: W. W. Norton Company.

North, Douglass Cecil, and Robert Paul Thomas. 1973. *The Rise of the Western World: A New Economic History*. Cambridge: Cambridge University Press.

Ober, Josiah. 2015. "Classical Athens." In *Fiscal Regimes and the Political Economy of Premodern States*, edited by Andrew Monson and Walter Scheidel, 492–522. Cambridge; New York: Cambridge University Press.

O'Brien, Patrick Karl. 2012. "Fiscal and Financial Preconditions for the Formation of Developmental States in the West and the East from the Conquest of Ceuta (1415) to the

Opium War (1839)." *Journal of World History* 23 (3): 513–53. https://doi.org/10.1353/jwh.2012.0090

OECD. 2015. *How's Life? 2015: Measuring Well-Being*. Paris: OECD Publishing.

Orloff, Ann Shola, and Theda Skocpol. 1984. "Why Not Equal Protection? Explaining the Politics of Public Social Spending in Britain, 1900–1911, and the United States, 1880s–1920." *American Sociological Review* 49 (6): 726–50.

Page, Benjamin I., and Martin Gilens. 2017. *Democracy in America? What Has Gone Wrong and What We Can Do about It*. Chicago; London: The University of Chicago Press.

Page, Benjamin I., Jason Seawright, and Matthew J. Lacombe. 2019. *Billionaires and Stealth Politics*. Chicago; London: The University of Chicago Press.

Persson, Anna, and Bo Rothstein. 2015. "It's My Money: Why Big Government May Be Good Government." *Comparative Politics* 47 (2): 231–49.

Pierson, Paul. 2000. "Increasing Returns, Path Dependence, and the Study of Politics." *American Political Science Review* 94 (2): 251–67. https://doi.org/10.2307/2586011

Prasad, Monica. 2006. *The Politics of Free Markets: The Rise of Neoliberal Economic Policies in Britain, France, Germany, and the United States*. Chicago: University of Chicago Press.

Prasad, Monica. 2018. *Starving the Beast: Ronald Reagan and the Tax Cut Revolution*. New York: Russell Sage Foundation.

Prasad, Monica, and Yingying Deng. 2009. "Taxation and the Worlds of Welfare." *Socio-Economic Review* 7 (3): 431–57. https://doi.org/10.1093/ser/mwp005

Quah, Jon S. T. 1982. "Bureaucratic Corruption in the ASEAN Countries: A Comparative Analysis of Their Anti-Corruption Strategies." *Journal of Southeast Asian Studies* 13 (1): 153–77. https://doi.org/10.1017/S0022463400014041

Quah, Jon S. T. 1984. "The Public Policy-Making Process in Singapore." *Asian Journal of Public Administration* 6 (2): 108–26. https://doi.org/10.1080/02598272.1984.10800148

Rauch, James E., and Peter B. Evans. 2000. "Bureaucratic Structure and Bureaucratic Performance in Less Developed Countries." *Journal of Public Economics* 75 (1): 49–71. https://doi.org/10.1016/S0047-2727(99)00044-4

Root, Hilton L. 1994. *The Fountain of Privilege: Political Foundations of Markets in Old Regime France and England*. California Series on Social Choice and Political Economy 26. Berkeley, C.A.: University of California Press.

Rothschild, Emma. 2002. *Economic Sentiments: Adam Smith, Condorcet, and the Enlightenment*. Cambridge, MA; London: Harvard University Press.

Rothstein, Bo. 2009. "Creating Political Legitimacy: Electoral Democracy Versus Quality of Government." *American Behavioral Scientist* 53 (3): 311–30. https://doi.org/10.1177/0002764209338795

Rothstein, Bo. 2011. *The Quality of Government: Corruption, Social Trust, and Inequality in International Perspective*. Chicago; London: University of Chicago Press.

Rothstein, Bo. 2013. "Corruption and Social Trust: Why the Fish Rots from the Head Down." *Social Research* 80 (4): 1009–32.

Rothstein, Bo, and Daniel Eek. 2009. "Political Corruption and Social Trust: An Experimental Approach." *Rationality and Society* 21 (1): 81–112. https://doi.org/10.1177/1043463108099349

Scheidel, Walter. 2015. "The Early Roman Empire." In *Fiscal Regimes and the Political Economy of Premodern States*, edited by Andrew Monson and Walter Scheidel, 229–57. Cambridge; New York: Cambridge University Press.

Scheve, Kenneth, and David Stasavage. 2016. *Taxing the Rich: A History of Fiscal Fairness in the United States and Europe*. Princeton, N.J.: Princeton University Press.

Skocpol, Theda. 1979. *States and Social Revolutions: A Comparative Analysis of France, Russia, and China*. Cambridge; New York: Cambridge University Press.

Smith, Adam. 1776. *The Wealth of Nations*. Bantam classic ed. New York, N.Y.: Bantam Classic.

Stark, Rodney. 2005. *The Victory of Reason: How Christianity Led to Freedom, Capitalism, and Western Success*. 1st ed. New York: Random House.

Steinmo, Sven. 1993. *Taxation and Democracy: Swedish, British, and American Approaches to Financing the Modern State*. New Haven: Yale University Press.

Steinmo, Sven. 2010. *The Evolution of Modern States: Sweden, Japan, and the United States*. Cambridge Studies in Comparative Politics. Cambridge; New York: Cambridge University Press.

Steinmo, Sven, ed. 2018. *The Leap of Faith: The Fiscal Foundations of Successful Government in Europe and America*. 1st ed. Oxford: Oxford University Press.

Strayer, Joseph Reese. 1955. *Western Europe in the Middle Ages, a Short History*. Appleton-Century-Crofts. http://hdl.handle.net/2027/mdp.39015063777968

Streeck, Wolfgang, and Lane Kenworthy. 2005. "Theories and Practices of Neocorporatism." In *The Handbook of Political Sociology: States, Civil Societies, and Globalization*, edited by Thomas Janoski, Robert Alford, Alexander Hicks, and Mildred A. Schwartz. New York: Cambridge University Press.

Szostak, Rick. 1991. *The Role of Transportation in the Industrial Revolution: A Comparison of England and France*. Montreal; Buffalo: McGill-Queen's University Press.

Tan, James. 2015. "The Roman Republic." In *Fiscal Regimes and the Political Economy of Premodern States*, edited by Andrew Monson and Walter Scheidel, 208–28. Cambridge; New York: Cambridge University Press.

Temin, Peter. 2006. "The Economy of the Early Roman Empire." *Journal of Economic Perspectives* 20 (1): 133–51. https://doi.org/10.1257/089533006776526148

Tilly, Charles. 1990. *Coercion, Capital, and European States, AD 990–1990*. Studies in Social Discontinuity. Cambridge, MA: Basil Blackwell.

Transparency International. 2019. "Corruption Perception Index 2018." Berlin: Transparency International.

Uslaner, Eric M., and Bo Rothstein. 2016. "The Historical Roots of Corruption: State Building, Economic Inequality, and Mass Education." *Comparative Politics* 48 (2): 227–48. https://doi.org/info:doi/10.5129/001041516817037736

Wagner, Adolph. 1958. "Three Extracts on Public Finance." In *Classics in the Theory of Public Finance*, edited by Richard A. Musgrave and Alan T. Peacock, translated by Nancy Cooke. New York: The MacMillan Company.

Webber, Carolyn, and Aaron B. Wildavsky. 1986. *A History of Taxation and Expenditure in the Western World*. New York: Simon and Schuster.

Weber, Max. 1978. *Economy and Society: An Outline of Interpretive Sociology*, edited by Guenther Roth and Wittich Claus. Nachdr. Berkeley, C.A.: University of California Press.

Wicksell, Knut. 1958. "A New Principle of Just Taxation (1896)." In *Classics in the Theory of Public Finance*, edited by Richard A. Musgrave and Alan T. Peacock, translated by Gustav Fischer. New York: The MacMillan Company.

Williamson, Vanessa S. 2017. *Read My Lips: Why Americans Are Proud to Pay Taxes*. Princeton, N.J.: Princeton University Press.

Wolfe, Alan. 1977. *The Limits of Legitimacy: Political Contradictions of Contemporary Capitalism*. New York: Free Press.

CHAPTER 34

··

QUALITY OF GOVERNMENT AND WELFARE STATE SUPPORT

··

STAFFAN KUMLIN

MANY readers probably picked up this book as they already suspected that "quality of government" influences politics and society. They now wanted to learn about the details of theories, concepts, and evidence. For these readers it may come as a surprise that research on citizens' support for government redistribution, social protection, and services (shorthand: welfare state support) has been late to examine quality of government explanations. As described in general overviews of this large field (Kumlin 2007b; Svallfors 2010) scholars long emphasized individual-level explanations such as class, self-interest, and values. Alternatively, they considered macro explanations related to the institutional logic of the welfare state itself (i.e. "welfare regimes") or various "functional pressures" (i.e. economic development and crisis, population aging, and globalization). By contrast, factors related to the quality and performance of policies were until recently not part of the standard set of explanatory variables. An influential article written less than a decade ago even went so far as to describe work on quality of government and welfare attitudes as "separate corpora of research." Indeed, the attitudinal effects of perceptions of government quality in terms of effectiveness and fairness had "hardly been studied at all" (Svallfors 2013, 365–6).

This verdict now seems on the harsh side. Slowly but surely in roughly the 2000s, scholars have compensated a previous neglect. Interestingly, and thankfully, this literature is also one where research on welfare state attitudes has been able to expand beyond the much-studied rich Western welfare states and more often include, for example, Eurasian countries, Latin America, and China. In terms of substantive questions, scholars in this field ask questions such as: Are citizens' assessments of various "quality of government" aspects positive or negative across space and time? Are such assessments multi- or unidimensional? What aspects of quality of government do citizens assess? Are evaluations rooted in relevant information and objective facts? And finally, do quality of government factors affect normative support for the welfare state and its constituent policies and aspects?

Improved data availability in comparative surveys has helped this budding research program on its way. As noted elsewhere (Kumlin and Stadelmann-Steffen 2016), older comparative surveys paid little attention to views on how the welfare state actually functions in practice. They typically offered a reasonable selection of *normative* welfare support measures; examples include if people generally want more or less redistribution and social spending in society as well as whether they support "government responsibility" in specific areas such as pensions, healthcare, unemployment benefits, social assistance, and so on. By contrast, more *evaluative* measures of "performance" were unusual. However, this has changed in the 2000s, as evidenced especially by the 2008 and 2016 "welfare modules" in the European Social Survey, but also by other data sources such as the International Social Survey Program.

The growing empirical evidence is discussed below. A first section highlights research on *general* evaluations of public services and transfer schemes. These studies use broad evaluative survey questions that do not tell us exactly what it is people are (dis)satisfied with. For example, they cannot tell us if people evaluate only the outcomes of welfare state schemes or (also) specific aspects that are key in the "quality of government" debate, such as procedural fairness and bureaucratic impartiality. Still, general evaluative measures allow us to gauge how believable it is that normative welfare support can be *at all* rooted in *some kind* of output performance evaluation. A subsequent section discusses the sources behind these general evaluations. Do they meaningfully reflect actual experiences and information about quality of government or are they rather rooted in culture and ideology? The two final chapter sections concentrate on evaluative measures that are closer to the core of the quality of government debate as discussed in Chapter 1. This includes studies of "institutional trust," as well as even more specific evaluations of procedural and distributive fairness aspects in the delivery of public services and social protection.

General Performance Evaluations

The much-improved data situation has allowed more comparative work on the levels, dimensionality, causes, and consequences of welfare state related performance evaluations. For example, Roosma, van Oorschot and Gelissen (2014) demonstrated the usefulness of separating between normative and evaluative dimensions of welfare state attitudes. Their analysis of the 2008 ESS module and over 20 European countries showed that there are meaningful "clusters" in all four corners of a two-dimensional normative-evaluative space. Said differently, all over Europe we find all the possible combinations of strong/weak normative welfare state support and good/poor perceived welfare state performance, respectively.

In another article, the same authors went on to separate between no less than seven manifestations of welfare state related attitudes (Roosma, Gelissen, and van Oorschot 2013). The evaluative performance dimension was represented by multiple survey questions. Some asked if healthcare and the tax system are "efficient" in handling queries on time, avoiding mistakes, and preventing fraud. Other items tapped people's perception of benefit abuse as well as underuse (i.e. people not using benefits/services they are entitled to). Finally, evaluations of "outcomes" involved perceptions of whether benefits and services generate more equality, less poverty, and facilitate work–family balance. Outcome evaluations were also tapped by items on "the state" of education, healthcare, the standard of living of the old, the unemployed, affordable child care services, and job opportunities for the young.

Other outcomes were more economic in nature and tapped welfare state consequences for the country's economy and for immoral behavior (laziness, unwillingness to look after themselves and their family, etc.). Based on all this information, Roosma, Gelissen, and van Oorschot (2013, 250) came to a simple but startling conclusion:

> people in European countries are very positive about the welfare state's goals and range, while simultaneously feeling critical about its efficiency, effectiveness and policy outcomes. Perceived ineffectiveness of the welfare state and the perception of abuse and underuse of welfare state benefits and services are clearly the weakest link in welfare state support.

What is striking here is that even in Europe, with arguably the most developed welfare states, we typically find a gap between positive normative support and more critical evaluations of actual performance. A question for future research is if this gap can be found also in other global regions. It may well be. Mares and Carnes' (2009, 94) overview of social policy in developing countries emphasized how in Latin America and Africa "governments have reneged [...] on many of the social policy promises enshrined in their legislation. In both regions, highly uneven social protection resulted because governments either lacked the administrative capacity to enforce contributions to social insurance or deliberately chose to manipulate social insurance to benefit particular sectors."

Some studies have analyzed how general performance evaluations *affect* normative support (and sometimes vice versa). Kumlin (2007a) studied how performance evaluations in the education and healthcare areas affect a host of political orientations and behavior. A key conclusion was that the dissatisfied only to a modest extent draw substantive political conclusions. Thus, effects on normative general support for redistribution were weak and variable across countries. And only in some contexts did those dissatisfied seem to exercise "electoral accountability," i.e. withdrawing support for incumbent government parties (see also Giger 2011). Instead, dissatisfaction seemed to damage trust in the actors and institutions of representative democracy more generally.

Importantly, this weak substantive impact of quality of government evaluations concerns very generalized attitudes such as "the government should reduce differences between the rich and the poor." More significant and reoccurring dissatisfaction effects are found in studies of concrete spending preferences on particular policy areas. Importantly, these effects are often in accordance with Wlezien's (1995) "thermostat model" (see also Soroka and Wlezien 2010). That is, dissatisfaction with performance makes people *more* inclined "to throw money on the problem," i.e. spend more on the specific policy area where performance is poorly evaluated. Such effects have been uncovered in Europe-wide comparisons (van Oorschot and Meuleman 2012) as well as country studies of, for example, Spain (Calzada and del Pino 2008), Sweden (Edlund 2006), and Denmark (Hedegaard and Larsen 2014). The latter study is especially interesting as it tests a larger causal model. First, and unsurprisingly, public service users are prone to support spending on policy areas they themselves use. Second however, users are also more generally satisfied with the performance of the areas they use, which—perhaps more surprisingly, but consistent with the thermostat model—tempers spending demands.

Not all studies reveal such "thermostatic" impact. Habibov et al. (2018) studied "willingness to pay for health care" in 29 postcommunist countries over time across Eurasia and Europe (i.e. comparing countries as diverse as Albania, Estonia, Kyrgyzstan, and Mongolia).

Output satisfaction was one of only three explanations that consistently had an impact across these diverse countries, with satisfaction consistently associated with *more* willingness to pay. What could explain these differences across studies? A partial explanation may be country coverage: Perhaps dissatisfaction triggers calls for more spending mainly in mature and less corrupt welfare states? A second possibility is that that Habibov et al.'s willingness to pay measure makes additional clarifications over and above standard "more-or-less" spending questions. For example, the measure emphasizes personal taxation contributions to improving healthcare. Perhaps throwing one's *own* money on a perceived problem is less attractive and more dependent on prior satisfaction? Be that as it may, understanding why output dissatisfaction usually, but not always, boosts concrete welfare demand, will be an important avenue for further research.

Note that all the studies discussed in this section are cross-sectional. That is, they generally assume a causal direction and test whether there is static association between evaluations and normative welfare preferences. A smaller number of studies have used two wave panel data and estimated cross-lagged models, so far suggestive of more complex reciprocal relationship where evaluations and preferences adjust to each other over time (Kumlin and Goerres forthcoming). More work along these lines, preferably extending the number of panel waves and countries, as well as estimating also other types of dynamic models (i.e. fixed effects and hybrid models) seems like a fruitful direction for this research field.

Sources of "Quality of Government" Performance Evaluations

Assuming quality of government evaluations have some sort of causal impact we want to know what explains them. As discussed by de Blok, Haugsgjerd, and Kumlin (2020), two perspectives can be extracted from the literature. One sees performance evaluations as stable attitudes rooted in culture and psychological predispositions like ideology or partisanship. Here, there is little reason to think that welfare support attitudes are causally affected by output evaluations of quality of government. Another perspective, however, holds that performance evaluations are "cognitive" and experiential. They depend on objective performance conditions and relevant information about such conditions. Output performance views are thus open to new influences and can shift over time.

Several studies pursuing different research designs and country coverage suggest that quality of government evaluations are at least in part cognitive in nature. Schneider and Popic (2018), for example, found that the large European East–West differences in healthcare evaluations can be explained by specific perceptions of efficiency in services, perceived equality in treatment, and perceived health status of the population. Of these three, perceived efficiency was clearly the most important factor. The "equal treatment" item (asking if doctors and nurses give special advantages to some or deal with everyone equally) came out as the second most important cognitive factor. A study of China comes to similar conclusions (Munro and Duckett 2016). This study reported weak associations between performance satisfaction and sociodemographic variables, self-reported health, and income.

Satisfaction was more strongly linked to coverage and utilization, as well as perceptions of access as unequal, or of service providers as "unethical." Overall results such as these indicate that general performance assessments do have a cognitive basis in more specified evaluations.

But do general performance evaluations also reflect objectively measured performance? The answer seems to be a cautious and provisionary "yes." Having said this, there is little established consensus as to which objective factors matter. Some studies find the strongest effects of broad contextual variables such as inequality levels and corruption. Of course, the corruption–inequality nexus is central to the debate over quality of government and may affect quality of service delivery through multiple mechanisms (see Uslaner this volume; You this volume). It is therefore interesting that associations between these macro variables and individual-level heath care assessments are found in several studies and regions.

For example, a study of post-socialist Eurasian countries used an instrument variable approach and found that experiencing corruption significantly reduces healthcare satisfaction (Habibov 2016). Similar conclusions have been drawn in comparative studies in Europe (Nikoloski and Mossialos 2013). Another European study concluded that there was a "strong congruence between experts and the general population in their perceptions of the quality of government" in terms of effectiveness and impartiality (Svallfors 2013, 376–7). Finally, a study of Latin America finds that factors related to basic healthcare access are more important for healthcare satisfaction than corruption and other governance indicators (Kim, Blendon, and Benson 2013).

Other studies have analyzed how evaluations are affected by properties of the policy regimes in which they are made. Still focusing on healthcare, Wendt et al. (2010) noted that while normative support for healthcare is high everywhere in Western Europe, the same is not true for performance satisfaction. The latter is relatively strongly related to "specific institutional arrangements" such as the number of practitioners, the prices of co-payments, and the like. The countries with the lowest satisfaction levels, notably Southern Europe, are also marked by clear social group differences in evaluations. Similar findings apply to more high-spending "social insurance" systems that build on free choice of providers, whereas the universal Scandinavian systems and the U.K.'s National Health Service produce more homogenous satisfaction patterns at high levels.

Further studies assess individual-level information within countries. Kumlin (2004) studied effects of personal welfare state experiences in Sweden, and found that the nature of experience effects vary with the design of policies. Experiences of "customer institutions"— where bureaucratic discretion and means-testing are relatively absent, but exit-options frequent—are associated with positive perceptions of distributive and procedural fairness aspects of these institutions. The opposite was true for "client institutions," where discretion and means-testing are rather frequent but exit-options unusual. In a similar vein, Laenen (2018) uses Dutch data showing how within-country variations in institutional design meaningfully structures output performance evaluations and in turn the normative legitimacy of the schemes in question.

Again, the studies just cited draw on static cross-sectional data. This raises the issue of whether relationships hold up also using dynamic data such that correlations more credibly reflect causality. An example in this regard is Rönnerstrand and Oskarson (2018, early view) who found that a waiting-time guarantee reform (that drastically reduced waiting times) also resulted in substantially increased healthcare satisfaction. And a study by Kumlin (2014) used survey experiments combined with panel data on which specific TV programs respondents had watched during an election campaign. Results showed that "expert facts" about welfare state performance, as well as extensive exposure to political debate over these facts, usually generated meaningful adjustments in general evaluations of welfare state performance over time.

Finally, a growing literature examines perceptions of welfare state performance quality in terms of how fiscally sustainable the welfare state is. These studies capture an evaluative aspect that should become more relevant as welfare states progress into what Pierson (1996) called the era of "permanent austerity." Results so far point to a political importance of sustainability perceptions and their underlying objective conditions. For example, experiments suggest that citizens develop sustainability perceptions using incoming information about "fiscal pressure," in particular costs associated with groups seen as "undeserving" (Naumann 2017; Goerres, Karlsen, and Kumlin 2018, first view). Moreover, real-world reform pressures and perceptions thereof may depress welfare state support. Here, Naumann (2014) studied the relationships between ageing populations and acceptance of pension reforms. Using aggregate data from a large number of time points, he concluded that Europeans have adjusted their pension preferences to new fiscal realities produced by demographic change. Relatedly, Jensen and Naumann (2016) used the outbreaks of influenza epidemics as a natural experiment on how increasing fiscal pressure on public healthcare affects its support negatively.

These studies provide some sound causal evidence that objective conditions and relevant information about quality of government can have meaningful effects on evaluations of welfare performance. What is more, such evaluations may apparently impact on key aspects of normative welfare state support, although the direction and strength of impact is a complex matter. Such effects will be probed more in-depth in the remainder of the chapter, now focusing on studies that measure quality of government in more specified ways.

INSTITUTIONAL TRUST AND WELFARE STATE SUPPORT

We first come to an accumulation of studies on how "institutional trust" in welfare state institutions and services impacts on welfare state support. These studies are worth treating separately as the concept of trust takes us closer to the core of the "quality of government" debate (see Chapter 1). The concept of "trust," after all, has connotations to actors (also) being fair and impartial rather than (only) "performing" well in some unspecified or outcome-related sense. Additionally, empirical evidence suggests that institutional trust reflects objective "quality of government" measures such as corruption (Dinesen and Sønderskov, this volume).

Again however, there is little consensus about the finer nuances of definition and measurement. Thus, in a study of postcommunist countries Habibov, Cheung, and Auchynnikava (2018:54), define institutional trust "as trust in national, regional, and local governments, parliament, political parties, the court, the police, the army, trade unions, non-governmental organizations, financial institutions, foreign investors, and religious organizations." Using instrumental variables techniques to address reciprocal causality, their results revealed that higher values along this broad trust continuum enhance willingness to pay taxes to help the needy, and support healthcare and education.

A much more specific approach to institutional trust was taken by Edlund and Lindh (2013). Their measures pinpoint people's specific faith in concrete public service institutions related to healthcare, childcare, education, and so on. Using a multidimensional framework for welfare state support variables, also their results suggest that most indicators of such support are boosted by trust. The specificity in their conceptualization is further underscored by multivariate controls for trust in market institutions. Controlling for trust in market institutions is pivotal, Edlund and Lindh argue, as the different trust types are positively correlated but have offsetting effects on welfare state support. Said differently, trust in market institutions has a suppressing function on the estimates of institutional trust. We may not notice this impact unless we control for trust in market institutions.

SPECIFIC EVALUATIONS OF QUALITY OF GOVERNMENT IN RESEARCH ON WELFARE STATE SUPPORT

We now turn to studies that take us to the core of the quality of government debate as discussed in Chapter 1. These studies use independent variables that tap more directly into issues of government effectiveness and fairness. A previous review (Kumlin 2007b) discussed "social justice" in personal welfare state experiences and how this impacts on welfare state support. The idea underlying the social justice perspective is that people do not just evaluate personal and economic interests. They also assess whether practices are "fair," based on some normative expectation about quality of government beyond one's own economic interests. Such assumptions are rooted in theoretical debates over how citizens may have "dual utility functions" (Rothstein 1998) and are concerned with achieving a "moral economy" (Mau 2003).

Building on these debates, Kumlin (2004) operationalized two types of perceived fairness in personal welfare state experiences: "distributive justice," where welfare support is contingent on whether such institutions are perceived to distribute outcomes fairly, and "procedural justice," where support depends on service delivery processes matching normative expectations. The latter concept is complex, with several potential subdimensions, including whether people are treated with equal respect (Rothstein 1998), and whether authorities are impartial. The most common procedural aspect in empirical research, however, is probably "voice opportunities," i.e., if citizens feel they can influence and express views to public employees (Thibaut and Walker 1975).

Kumlin (2004) is still one of few studies that incorporates multiple measures of distributive and procedural fairness, while still controlling for economic self-interest. Importantly, fairness evaluations were relatively uncorrelated with subjective self-interest evaluations. This is crucial, as fairness variables lose appeal if they are "self-interest in disguise," i.e. merely reflections of personal material gain (cf. Lind and Tyler 1988). That said, perceptions of distributive and procedural fairness were strongly correlated with each other, suggesting that people do not differentiate much between complex types of fairness. Still, both perceptions of distributive justice and procedural justice in experiences with welfare state institutions had some impact on political orientations, controlling for one another. Again however, such effects were stronger for political trust than for welfare state support. Conversely, economic self-interest appeared to be more important for these latter variables. These lukewarm results for quality of government effects on welfare support echo those discussed earlier for general evaluations, and resonate with another review article on how political trust seems clearly affected by welfare state polices and evaluations (Kumlin and Haugsgjerd 2017). What could possibly explain these patterns? We do not know, but Kumlin (2004) suggests that welfare state policy choices are more naturally linked to economic wins and losses than the question of whether political institutions can be trusted. This may partly crowd out fairness evaluations as explanations of welfare state support.

A more recent study by Svallfors (2013) examines perceptions of government quality in terms of "efficiency" and the specific procedural value of "impartiality." As Rothstein (this volume) discussed, the latter procedural aspect is key in the broader debate about quality of government. European Social Survey questions about efficiency and impartiality (whether healthcare/tax authorities "give special advantages to certain people") were posed next to each other, enabling respondents to distinguish between them. Nonetheless, they formed one overall dimension of quality of government evaluation. Moreover, and as mentioned earlier, Svallfors finds that such evaluations correlate strongly with expert judgments across countries. Finally, quality of government perceptions are found to affect a single-item in-dicator of generalized attitudes towards taxation and social spending. Those who see institutions as efficient and fair are more supportive of increasing taxes and spending on so-cial benefits and services. More than this, however, Svallfors introduces an original hypoth-esis by arguing (and finding) that government quality enables preexisting egalitarian values to translate into political welfare state support. From this standpoint, it is the *combination* of preexisting egalitarianism, and presumably malleable perceptions of effective and impar-tial bureaucracy, that breeds generalized support for spending and taxation. Overall, this study is probably the one that finds the most unequivocal support for the view that quality of government boosts welfare state support. These findings can be contrasted against the pre-viously discussed results suggesting that effects may be stronger for political trust as well as be "thermostatic" in nature for more concrete attitudes, where poor outputs breed increased support for specific spending.

A couple of studies have added insights by reanalyzing the same ESS 2008 "welfare module" as that used by Svallfors. Baslevent and Kirmanoglu (2015) studied a wider range of dependent variables, examining not just generalized support for spending/taxation but also well-known measures of support for "government responsibility" for helping specific groups (the old, the sick, the unemployed, working parents, etc.). They also directly gauge the attitu-dinal impact of "objective" country-level data on impartiality and efficiency from the World Bank, Transparency International, and similar. The findings show that while quality of gov-ernment boosts generalized welfare state support more concrete preferences for government responsibility to specific groups react mostly in the negative thermostatic direction.

Finally, in a further study building on the same data, Mizrahi (2016) focused en-tirely on specific government responsibility preferences as the dependent variable. This study disregards objective measures of quality of government but introduces subjective perceptions of living conditions of vulnerable groups. Negative perceptions about living conditions correlate with negative perceptions about quality of government. This helps explain why, perhaps paradoxically, support for very specific government action sometimes increases in low-quality government contexts. The thermostatic interpretation discussed earlier is again useful here. It would appear that a syndrome of poor government quality and bad conditions for vulnerable groups triggers a thermostatic response that boosts demands for the government to address problems. At the same time, however, this negative syndrome may have undermining effects on support conceptualized at a more general level. Continued debate around these issues using the valuable ESS data should prove fruitful.

Note that the research discussed so far exclusively concerns attitudes towards domestic redistribution and welfare policy. However, some studies indicate that support for international redistribution beyond national borders may be affected by quality of government. Thus, Bauhr and Charron (2019, 2018) find that support for E.U.-wide redistribution depends on domestic quality of government factors such as corruption. In a similar vein, Kumlin (2009) found that national public service dissatisfaction hampers generalized E.U. trust, controlling for a host of domestic political orientations such as national political trust.

All the studies discussed so far in this section concentrate on procedural aspects such as impartiality or absence of corruption, or more general perceived "efficiency" in process of social services. They do not necessarily include "distributive justice," i.e. the idea that support may also depend on whether services and benefits go to those who deserve it. In recent years, however, a distinct research program has grown around "deservingness theory" (see van Oorschot 2006; Petersen et al. 2010; Goerres, Karlsen, and Kumlin 2018, first view; Mau 2003; van Oorschot 2000; Aalberg 2003; Hochschild 1981; Petersen et al. 2012). This literature increasingly applies a five-dimensional framework, now called the "CARIN" criteria (van Oorschot et al. 2017). First, people are thought to assess "control" (C) where those who cannot help their predicament are more deserving. Second, the A criterion taps desirable and likable attitudes among beneficiaries. Third, R stands for reciprocity, where solidarity hinges on recipients adhering to key behavioral norms. Fourth, I stands for identity, with those who somehow "belong to us" being seen as more deserving. Fifth, N denotes the perceived needs among recipients. Although the evidence is complex and incomplete, research does suggest that these deservingness dimensions are partly cognitive in nature (i.e. depend on information at hand) and that they in turn structure support for redistribution.

This literature, then, provides additional evidence that fairness aspects of distributive processes are important for welfare state support. Of course, positively evaluated deservingness is not exactly the same thing as perceived quality of government, as defined in Chapter 1. After all, deservingness theory is about the *recipients* of policy processes, and quality of government explanations are more concerned with *institutions and employees*. In principle, one could imagine that well-functioning impartial institutions nonetheless distribute to undeserving individuals, and conversely that low-quality institutions still manage to find deserving recipients. Nonetheless, the findings on deservingness should probably be seen as a "smoking gun" also for the validity of quality of government explanations. After all, if citizens are preoccupied with deservingness of recipients, it would be curious if they were not interested in how public institutions and employees function. Said differently, there is a cognitive/conceptual closeness between deservingness and quality of government. This likely also accounts for the empirical closeness noted above between measures of perceived distributive and procedural justice measures.

CONCLUSIONS AND DIRECTIONS
FOR FUTURE RESEARCH

This chapter has documented growing scholarly interest in how quality of government, and perceptions thereof, influence attitudes towards redistribution and welfare state policies. If nothing else, the study of government quality and welfare state support can no longer be described as "separate corpora of research," although there is still a bias towards the oldest European and Anglo-Saxon welfares states. At the same time, we have seen growing evidence from post-soviet Eurasian countries, Latin America, and China. Although we clearly need more work from across the globe, there are few indications that basic correlations and patterns are wildly different across regions.

What stylized facts can we currently extract from this evolving research program? To begin with, even in the comparatively rich European welfare states perceived ineffectiveness and abuse/underuse of benefits and services may be "the weakest link" of welfare state support. Moreover, such perceptions do seem to partly reflect objective systemic features and meaningful information. Having said this, there is little consensus about which underlying objective/informational factors that are important for which quality of government evaluations, and why. Advancing and testing a theoretical framework that addresses this big question should be a high priority in future work. One insight to take on board in such a framework is that citizens may not make finer distinctions in evaluating the "fairness" of welfare state delivery processes. While fairness perceptions may reflect some underlying reality, and while such perceptions do not seem to be merely "self-interest in disguise," we have also seen indications that procedural and distributive fairness aspects are not very distinct from each other.

Do quality of government variables affect normative welfare state support? Here, there is more uncertainty and complexity. While most studies find some significant impact, several studies report that effects are quite weak. The political ramifications of poor quality of government may strike harder against trust in political institutions and actors, than against normative support for the welfare state itself. Plausible reasons for such differences in impact have been suggested (see Kumlin and Haugsgjerd 2017), but we need more solid evidence for why citizens are prone to certain types of political inferences and reactions. Meanwhile, multiple studies show that effects on very concrete preferences for more or less spending in particular areas display "thermostatic" patterns. That is, poor quality of government actually drives up immediate demands for government action as much as it hollows out more general support. Future work should try to advance systematic theories for why quality of government dissatisfaction may boost concrete welfare demand—and simultaneously have no or even negative effects on generalized aspects of welfare state support.

A final unresolved issue concerns the relative weight of perceived "quality" and fiscal "sustainability" of the welfare state. The current evidence certainly demonstrates the potential usefulness of going beyond fairness and efficiency measures and explicitly model beliefs about whether we can afford the welfare state given growing fiscal challenges. Of course, a near-consensual view is that especially the oldest and most expensive European welfare states are facing growing "reform pressures." Complex reform patterns underscore how welfare states must handle growing needs with constant or smaller resources (Beramendi et al. 2015; van Kersbergen, Vis, and Hemerijck 2014). Recent research also shows that political leaders in Europe provide citizens with much information about these challenges (Goerres, Kumlin, and Karlsen 2019, first view). We have discussed evidence that this information may affect sustainability perceptions, which may in turn undermine aspects of welfare state support (Jensen and Naumann 2016). More evidence on these processes is sorely needed, however, not least as the political implications are severe. If the legitimacy-building effects of perceived fiscal sustainability match those of output quality evaluations, and procedural/distributive fairness, then welfare reforms that reduce quality and fairness—but improve fiscal sustainability—may have no negative, or even positive net effects on welfare state support.[1]

REFERENCES

Aalberg, Toril. 2003. *Achieving Justice: Comparative Public Opinion on Income Distribution*. Leiden: Brill.

Baslevent, Cem, and Hasan Kirmanoglu. 2015. "Quality of Government, Egalitarianism, and Welfare State Attitudes." *Economics Bulletin* 35 (4): 2877–87.

Bauhr, Monika, and Nicholas Charron. 2018. "Why Support International Redistribution? Corruption and Public Support for Aid in the Eurozone." *European Union Politics* 19 (2): 233–54.

Bauhr, Monika, and Nicholas Charron. 2019. "The EU as a Savior and a Saint? Corruption and Public Support for Redistribution." *Journal of European Public Policy*. doi: 10.1080/13501763.2019.1578816.

Beramendi, Pablo, Silja Häusermann, Herbert Kitschelt, and Hanspeter Kriesi, eds. 2015. *The Politics of Advanced Capitalism*. Cambridge: Cambridge University Press.

Calzada, Inés, and Eloísa del Pino. 2008. "Perceived Efficacy and Citizens' Attitudes toward Welfare State Reform." *International Review of Administrative Sciences* 74 (4): 555–74. doi: https://doi.org/10.1177/0020852308098468.

de Blok, Lisanne, Atle Haugsgjerd, and Staffan Kumlin. 2020. "Increasingly Connected? Political Distrust and Dissatisfaction with Public Services in Europe, 2008–2016." In *Welfare State Legitimacy in Times of Crisis and Austerity*, edited by Bart Meuleman, Wim van Oorschot and Tijs Laenen. Cheltenham, UK: Edward Elgar Publishing.

Edlund, Jonas. 2006. "Trust in the Capability of the Welfare State and General Welfare State Support: Sweden 1997–2002." *Acta Sociologica* 49 (4): 395–417.

Edlund, Jonas, and Arvid Lindh. 2013. "Institutional Trust and Welfare State Support: On the role of Trust in Market Institutions." *Journal of Public Policy* 33 (3): 295–317. doi: doi:10.1017/S0143814X13000160.

Giger, Nathalie. 2011. *The Risk of Social Policy: The Electoral Consequences of Welfare State Retrenchment and Social Policy Performance in OECD Countries*. London: Routledge.

---

[1] I draw in some parts on my contributions to *The Oxford Handbook of Political Behavior* (see Kumlin 2007b) and *The Oxford Handbook of the Welfare State* (2nd edition, Kumlin, Goerres, and Spies, forthcoming 2021).

Goerres, Achim, Rune Karlsen, and Staffan Kumlin. 2020. "What Makes People Worry about the Welfare State? A Three-Country Experiment." *British Journal of Political Science* 50 (4): 1519–37. doi: https://doi.org/10.1017/S0007123418000224.

Goerres, Achim, Staffan Kumlin, and Rune Karlsen. 2019, first view. "Pressure without Pain: What Politicians (Don't) Tell You about Welfare State Change." *Journal of Social Policy*.

Habibov, Nazim. 2016. "Effect of Corruption on Healthcare Satisfaction in Post-Soviet Nations: A Cross-Country Instrumental Variable Analysis of Twelve Countries." *Social Science & Medicine* 152: 119–24.

Habibov, Nazim, Alena Auchynnikava, Rong Luo, and Lida Fan. 2018. "Who Wants to Pay More Taxes to Improve Public Health Care?" *International journal of health planning and management* 33: 944–59. doi: https://doi.org/10.1002/hpm.2572.

Habibov, Nazim, Alex Cheung, and Alena Auchynnikava. 2018. "Does Institutional Trust Increase Willingness to Pay More Taxes to Support the Welfare State?" *Sociological Spectrum* 8 (1): 51–68.

Hedegaard, Troels Fage, and Christian Albrekt Larsen. 2014. "How Proximate and Visable Polices Shape Self-Interest, Satisfaction, and Spending Support: The Case of Public Service Production." In *How Welfare States Shape the Democratic Public: Policy Feedback, Participation, Voting, and Attitudes*, edited by Staffan Kumlin and Isabelle Stadelmann-Steffen, 269–88. Cheltenham, UK: Edward Elgar Publishing.

Hochschild, Jennifer L. 1981. *What's Fair: American Beliefs about Distributive Justice.* Cambridge: Harvard University Press.

Jensen, Carsten, and Elias Naumann. 2016. "Increasing Pressures and Support for Public Healthcare in Europe." *Health Policy* 120 (120): 698–705.

Kim, Minah K., Robert J. Blendon, and John M. Benson. 2013. "What is Driving People's Dissatisfaction with their own Health Care in 17 Latin American Countries?" *Health Expectatoins* 16 (2): 155–63 doi: https://doi.org/10.1111/j.1369-7625.2012.00777.x.

Kumlin, Staffan. 2004. *The Personal and the Political: How Personal Welfare State Experiences Affect Political Trust and Ideology.* New York: Palgrave-Macmillan.

Kumlin, Staffan. 2007a. "Overloaded or Undermined? European Welfare States in the Face of Performance Dissatisfaction." In *The Political Sociology of the Welfare State: Institutions, Social Cleavages, and Orientations*, edited by Stefan Svallfors, 80–116. Stanford: Stanford University Press.

Kumlin, Staffan. 2007b. "The Welfare State: Values, Policy Preferences, and Performance Evaluations." In *The Oxford Handbook of Political Behavior*, edited by Russel J. Dalton and Hans-Dieter Klingemann, 362–82. New York: Oxford University Press.

Kumlin, Staffan. 2009. "Blaming Europe: Exploring the Variable Impact of National Public Service Dissatisfaction on EU Trust." *Journal of European Social Policy* 19 (5): 408–20.

Kumlin, Staffan. 2014. "Informed Performance Evaluation of the Welfare State? Experimental and Real-World Findings." In *How Welfare States Shape the Democratic Public: Policy Feedback, Participation, and Attitudes*, edited by Staffan Kumlin and Isabelle Stadelmann-Steffen, 289–310. Cheltenham, UK: Edward Elgar Publishing.

Kumlin, Staffan, and Achim Goerres. forthcoming. *Election Campaigns and Welfare State Change: Democratic Linkage and Leadership under Pressure.*

Kumlin, Staffan, and Atle Haugsgjerd. 2017. "The Welfare State and Political Trust: Bringing Performance Back In." In *Handbook on Political Trust*, edited by Sonja Zmerli and Tom van der Meer, 285–301. Cheltenham, UK.

Kumlin, Staffan, and Isabelle Stadelmann-Steffen. 2016. "Studying How Policies Affect the People: Grappling with Measurement, Causality, and the Macro-Micro Divide." In *Handbook of Research Methods and Applications in Political Science*, edited by Hans Keman and Jaap J. Woldendorp, 343–58. Cheltenham, UK: Edward Elgar Publishing.

Laenen, Tijs 2018. "Do Institutions Matter? The Interplay between Income Benefit Design, Popular Perceptions, and the Social Legitimacy of Targeted Welfare." *Journal of European Social Policy* 28 (1): 4–17. doi: 10.1177/0958928718755777.

Lind, Allan E., and Tom R. Tyler. 1988. *The Social Psychology of Procedural Justice*. New York: Plenum Press.

Mares, Isabela, and Matthew E. Carnes. 2009. "Social Policy in Developing Countries." *Annual Review of Political Science* 12: 93–113.

Mau, Steffen. 2003. *The Moral Economy of Welfare States: Britain and Germany Compared*. London: Routledge.

Mizrahi, Shlomo. 2016. "Economic Conditions, Government Effectiveness and Public Attitudes towards the Welfare State." *Journal of Poverty and Social Justice* Volume 24 (2): 157–70.

Munro, Neil, and Jane Duckett. 2016. "Explaining Public Satisfaction with Health-care Systems: Findings from a Nationwide Survey in China." *Health Expectations* 19 (3): 654–66. doi: https://doi.org/10.1111/hex.12429.

Naumann, Elias. 2014. "Raising the Retirement Age: Retrenchment, Feedback, and Attitudes." In *How Welfare States Shape the Democratic Public: Policy Feedback, Participation, and Attitudes*, edited by Staffan Kumlin and Isabelle Stadelmann-Steffen, 223–43. Cheltenham, UK: Edward Elgar Publishing.

Naumann, Elias. 2017. "Do Increasing Reform Pressures Change Welfare State Attitudes? An experimental study on population ageing, pension reform preferences, political knowledge, and ideology." *Ageing and Society* 37 (2): 266–94

Nikoloski, Zlatko, and Elias Mossialos. 2013. "Corruption, Inequality and Population Perception of Healthcare Quality in Europe." *BMC Health Services Research* 13: 472. doi: https://doi.org/10.1186/1472-6963-13-472.

Petersen, Michael Bang, Rune Slothuus, Rune Stubager, and Lise Togeby. 2010. "Deservingness versus Values in Public Opinion on Welfare: The Automaticity of the Deservingness Heuristic." *European Journal of Political Research* 50: 24–52.

Petersen, Michael, Daniel Sznycer, Leda Cosmides, and John Tooby. 2012. "Who Deserves Help? Evolutionary Psychology, Social Emotions, and Public Opinion about Welfare." *Political Psychology* 33 (3): 395–418.

Pierson, Paul. 1996. "The New Politics of the Welfare State." *World Politics* 48 (2): 143–79.

Roosma, Femke, John Gelissen, and Wim van Oorschot. 2013. "The Multidimensionality of Welfare State Attitudes: A European Cross-National Study." *Social Indicators Research* 113: 235–55.

Roosma, Femke, Wim van Oorschot, and John Gelissen. 2014. "The Preferred Role and Perceived Performance of the Welfare State: European Welfare Attitudes from a Multidimensional Perspective." *Social Science Research* 44: 200–10. doi: http://dx.doi.org/10.1016/j.ssresearch.2013.12.005.

Rothstein, Bo. 1998. *Just Institutions Matter. The Moral and Political Logic of the Universal Welfare State*. Cambridge: Cambridge University Press.

Rönnerstrand, Björn, and Maria Oskarson. 2018, early view. "Standing in Line When Queues Are on the Decline: Services Satisfaction Following the Swedish Health Care Waiting Time Guarantee." *Policy Studies Journal* 48 (2): 469–93. doi: https://doi.org/10.1111/psj.12277.

Schneider, Simone M., and Tamara Popic. 2018. "Cognitive Determinants of Healthcare Evaluations—a Comparison of Eastern and Western European Countries." *Health Policy* 122 (3): 269–78. doi: https://doi.org/10.1016/j.healthpol.2017.12.012.

Soroka, Stuart N., and Christopher Wlezien. 2010. *Degrees of Democracy: Politics, Public Opinion, and Policy*. Cambridge: Cambridge University Press.

Svallfors, Stefan. 2010. "Public Opinion." In *The Oxford Handbook of the Welfare State*, edited by Francis G. Castles, Stephan Leibfried, Jane Lewis, Herbert Obinger, and Christopher Pierson. Oxford: Oxford University Press.

Svallfors, Stefan. 2013. "Government Quality, Egalitarianism, and Attitudes to Taxes and Social spending: A European Comparison." *European Political Science Review* 5 (3): 363–80.

Thibaut, John, and Laurens Walker. 1975. *Procedural Justice: A Psychological Analysis*. Hillsdale, N.J.: L. Erlbaum Associates.

van Kersbergen, Kees, Barbara Vis, and Anton Hemerijck. 2014. "The Great Recession and Welfare State Reform: Is Retrenchment Really the Only Game Left in Town?" *Social Policy & Administration* 48 (7): 883–904.

van Oorschot, Wim. 2000. "Who Should Get What, and Why? on Deservingness Criteria and the Conditionality of Solidarity among the Public." *Policy & Politics* 28 (1): 33–48.

van Oorschot, Wim. 2006. "Making the Difference in Social Europe: Deservingness Perceptions among Citizens of European Welfare States." *Journal of European Social Policy* 16: 23–42.

van Oorschot, Wim, and Bart Meuleman. 2012. "Welfare Performance and Welfare Support." In *Contested Welfare States: Welfare Attitudes in Europe and Beyond*, edited by Stefan Svallfors, 25–57. Stanford: Stanford University Press.

van Oorschot, Wim, Femke Roosma, Bart Meuleman, and Tim Reeskens, eds. 2017. *The Social Legitimacy of Targeted Welfare: Attitudes to Welfare Deservingness*. Cheltenham, UK: Edward Elgar Publishing.

Wendt, Claus, Jürgen Kohl, Monika Mischke, and Michaela Pfeifer. 2010. "How Do Europeans Perceive Their Healthcare System? Patterns of Satisfaction and Preference for State Involvement in the Field of Healthcare." *European Sociological Review* 26 (2): 177–92.

Wlezien, Christopher. 1995. "The Public as a Thermostat: Dynamics of Preferences for Spending." *American Journal of Political Science* 39 (4): 981–1000.

PART VIII

STATE-BUILDING AND BREAKDOWN

CHAPTER 35

....

THE CHALLENGE OF STATE-BUILDING IN HISTORICAL PERSPECTIVE
How States are Built Critically Affects Political Development and Quality of Government

....

SHERI BERMAN

OVER the past decades, scholars have increasingly recognized that strong, effective states are an essential prerequisite for a wide variety of political and economic goods. In particular, high-quality government entails a state able to implement policies, maintain the rule of law, collect resources from and deliver resources to citizens and so on (Rothstein 2011; Mungiu-Pippidi 2015). Yet while many recent studies remind us that strong, effective states are important and explain how they differ from weak, predatory ones (North, Wallis and Weingast 2009; Acemoglu and Robinson 2017) few focus on *how* such states actually develop (Fukuyama 2012, 2015).

This is partially because the existing state-building literature has focused primarily on understanding *why* states develop and looks to structural variables such as the development of trade or capitalism (Strayer 2016; Gellner 1997; Poggi 1990; Anderson 1974; Wallerstein 2011), geography (Stasavage 2015), resource endowment (Herbst 2000; Dunning 2008; Bates 2008), particular ideas (Dyson 1980; Bendix 1978; Nexon 2009; Gorski 2003) or, of course, war-making, to explain outcomes (Tilly 1975b, 1990). But even if we accept that broad structural forces help explain *why* state-building occurs, such explanations tell us little about *how* it actually does, and such questions are of critical theoretical and practical import (Ghani and Lockhart 2008). How does political authority get centralized? How are the institutions that implement policy, collect resources from and deliver resources to citizens constructed? How do state-builders overcome their adversaries to achieve their goals? Answering these questions requires analyzing how state-building occurs and in particular investigating the mechanisms involved in state-building (Berman 2019).

Examining the historical record provides a good starting point for such an analysis. Much historical research on early modern Europe zeroes in on the essential prerequisite or first stage of state-building: centralizing authority in contexts where there are powerful opponents of it (Reinhard 1966; Fulbrook 1993; Bickle 1997; Boone 2003; Rosenthal 1998). Just as in many parts of the world today, authority in Europe up through the early modern period was segmented or fragmented, held largely by local and/or or religious elites. Today we refer to the former as chiefs, tribal leaders or most often, warlords (Marten 2011; Reno 1998), in the past they were referred to as nobles, dukes, princes, or lords, and any successful attempt at state-building had to include strategies for outmaneuvering, undermining or destroying them as well as religious authorities. As one observer notes,

> it was only in the destruction of the "segmentary" character of medieval society that the formation of a territorial sovereign authority became possible. Clearly, state sovereignty cannot exist where real authority rests with subordinate social units. This is why many 'third world' states are states in name only ... they are states attempting to rule essentially segmental societies based on tribal or other local units that are the locus of political loyalty that strive to function independently of the states. These states are still in the state building process and face, in essentials, the same dilemmas that the modern Western state faced in overcoming the centripetal forces of their own segmental societies (Nelson 2006, 9).

While state-building today will not follow the same patterns it did in the past, any understanding of how state-building occurs that builds on cases across time and space will be richer than one that does not (Tilly 1975a, 3, 14; Callaghy 1994; Barkey and Prikh 1991). What an examination of the European experience reveals is that in the past as today, centralizing authority was an extremely difficult process, marred by conflicts and setbacks, and requiring compromises and concessions along the way. When centralizing rulers embarked on the task of state-building they faced adversaries who had much to lose from centralization and resisted it accordingly (Christia and Semple 2009). Unable initially to defeat their opponents solely through coercion, many European state-builders tried to co-opt them, and employed material incentives or "carrots" to bribe or entice adversaries into gradually abandoning their opposition to centralization. The particular strategies state-builders used to defeat or at least gain the acquiescence of their adversaries profoundly impacted subsequent political development in general and the challenges associated with establishing high-quality government in particular since these strategies critically influenced whether or how easily a state capable of implementing policies, maintaining the rule of law, and collecting and delivering resources from and to citizens could develop.

The European Background

Up through the early modern period, Europe was divided into many small political units with porous, undefined borders. A map of Europe in 1500 would show hundreds of entities claiming some authority over people or territory; for every one of these that survived (say, France or Prussia) several did not (say, Burgundy or Lucca) (Davies 2011). During this time, the borders between political entities "were ... poorly defined, zones of contact between neighboring powers rather than lines clearly demarcated" (Anderson 1998, 15). The hold of central leaders over border areas was incomplete and they were accordingly areas of violence and disorder (Greengrass 1991; Sassen 2006). Although border regions were particularly un-stable, a king's hold over the rest of his ostensible territories was often not much stronger; indeed, most of the "countries" of the day were really loose collections of provinces, regions, and people, effectively governed by local rulers, legal systems, and traditions rather than central governments (Nexon 2009, 7; Elliot 1992). In short, where kings existed, they were more titular than actual rulers: They had little power outside of a "capital" city; most people had little contact with or even knowledge of the king and the king's authority was "constantly challenged." To maintain power a king needed "the loyalty and goodwill of his magnates" (Elliot 1968, 73).

Indeed, the dominant authority in most peoples' lives during this time was local or re-ligious. Direct responsibility for the provision of defense and welfare up through the early modern period lay primarily with nobles rather than kings. In general, kings could not en-gage in warfare on their own; they needed the support of nobles who provided the necessary resources and men. Far from central leaders having a "monopoly over the use of violence," (to use Weber's classic definition of "stateness"), control over the use of violence in pre-modern Europe "was dispersed, overlapping and democratized" (Thomson 1994, 3). Nobles retained their own arsenals, armed forces, and fortresses and used them to defend their land. In addition, the Church and ecclesiastical figures exerted immense social, cultural, and pol-itical influence and carried out many of the functions we would today associate with "states" (e.g. education, care for the poor, running hospitals, etc.). In short, before the early modern period, authority in Europe was segmented and fragmented and most Europeans' identities were accordingly regional, local, or religious rather than national. The geographical, ethnic, or linguistic unity that we associate with modern states, in other words, did not exist in Europe at this time.

The lack of a single central authority with a monopoly over the means of violence or overarching authority made the period lawless and violent: Banditry and piracy were rife, as were international and domestic conflicts. The most important of the former was the Thirty Years' War (1618–48). Although it had its origins in religious conflict between Catholics and Protestants, it developed into a more generalized conflagration that destroyed entire regions of Europe (Wilson 2009). As for domestic conflicts, when monarchs attempted to centralize authority, local, regional, and religious elites as well as many ordinary people rebelled against their efforts (Anderson 1998; Tilly, Tilly, and Tilly 1975; Mann 1993; Best 1982). Indeed, so frequent and severe were such confrontations, and so acute and disorienting was the larger debate about the nature and locus of authority occurring during this time that many historians view them as the cause of a "general crisis" that Europe experienced during this era (Parker and Smith 1997; Zagorian 1982; Rabb 1975; Aston 1965; Goldstone 1991; Treasure 1985). Indeed, the "blowback" many European monarchs faced in response to attempts to centralize authority was so great that many wondered if Europe would survive; as one con-temporary observer wrote "if one ever had to believe in the Last Judgment . . . I believe it is happening right now" (Parker 2008, 1057).

These conflicts left many Europeans longing for an authority to end the disorder. This was the era when theorists like Bodin and Hobbes argued that only strong, unitary sovereigns who had "high, absolute and perpetual power over . . . citizens and subjects" could "prevent society from lapsing into the 'state of nature,' a constant war of everyman against every man that made life solitary, poor, nasty, brutish, and short" (Keohane 1980, 70; Hobbes 1982). By the seventeenth century, in other words, many had accepted the need to move beyond the decentralized political arrangements that existed in much of Europe and build new political forms that were capable of controlling violence and lawlessness, building and maintaining armies capable of deterring and if necessary fighting wars and raising the necessary funds for such tasks.

Even where successful, state-building was extremely difficult, marred by constant conflicts and setbacks, and, as we will see, requiring significant trade-offs and bargaining. This is because even when faced with a need to raise revenue to fight wars, most European rulers were unable to eliminate those opposed to the centralization of authority or rapidly reshape existing loyalties. They therefore had to make a variety of compromises to get the job done. Although these compromises varied from case to case, with critical implications for subsequent political development, one common feature was that rulers left in place many of their opponents' social and economic privileges while undermining or at least weakening their political power.

Privilege was a central feature of this time. Today, this word has pejorative connotations and is viewed as antithetical to good government, the rule of law, meritocracy and so on, but in pre-modern Europe it simply described rights people enjoyed by virtue of belonging to a particular social group (or estate). Privilege was sanctified by law; one contemporary definition described it as "distinctions, whether useful or honorific, which are enjoyed by certain members of society and denied to others" (Jones 1995, 58). These distinctions extended into almost all spheres of life, governing everything from access to economic resources and property, to the payment (or nonpayment) of taxes, to the type of justice one was subjected to. In contrast to the contemporary advanced industrial world, in other words, where rights are generally viewed either as national—deriving from membership in a particular state—or universal—inhering in all human beings—in pre-modern Europe rights were often inherited (or, as we will see, sometimes purchased) and depended on membership in a particular group. The "privileged" groups during this era—the nobility and the clergy—originally derived their privileges from functions they carried out, such as the provision of justice or defense. The result was a world where identities were communal or status based rather than national and, since access to political, social, and economic resources and rights was largely determined by group membership, social inequality and divisions were the norm. Modern notions of rights, corruption, rule of law, etc. made no sense in this context.

Beginning in the early modern period, however, kings in France and some other parts of Europe began to change this system—or rather, parts of it. Eager to centralize political power, monarchs in France and elsewhere made trade-offs, exchanging support for or at least acquiescence in centralization of political power for a reconfirmation and in some cases even augmentation of the nobility and the Church's social and economic privileges. The early modern period was thus a transitional era, a time when key features of the modern political world like states were emerging, while at the same time critical traditional or pre-modern socioeconomic features of European societies like the system of privilege and the inequality, corruption, nepotism and inherent in it, remained.

To illustrate how early modern state-building occurred, this essay examines the French case in some depth and other cases briefly in comparison. France is often held up as the first modern state, and it is the one that contemporaries looked upon with awe. It is also, of course, the case that gave rise to the French revolution, and how state-building occurred is a critical part of the revolution's "backstory." Furthermore, although much about the French case was distinctive, the basic challenge confronting French kings during the early modern period—centralizing authority in the face of widespread opposition—was confronted by all European rulers, as it is by many rulers today.

France

When Hugh Capet, the first king of the Capetian dynasty, came to power in 987 he ruled over an assortment of lands collectively much smaller than the territory we now recognize as France (Parker 1983; Clark 1995). In addition, of the territory ostensibly within France's borders, much of it was out of the king's direct control: "large parts of what subsequently would become the territorial state of the French monarchy were in practice independent and often belligerent states, imperial cities and principalities, dependent on the counts of Flanders, the dukes of Burgundy, the kings of England and of Aragon, to name but a few of the long series" (Isaac and Prak 1978, 214; Clark 2006, 38ff). Hugh Capet's kingdom also lacked well-defined frontiers, a common language, or a unified legal system (Knecht 1996, 1; Briggs 1998).

Given the obstacles to the centralization of power in France—strong traditions of local sovereignty, powerful nobles,[1] institutional, linguistic, and legal diversity—kings only fitfully expanded their territorial reach over the following centuries. And when new territories were incorporated into France, they often kept their old customs, currencies, and languages and kings often confirmed and even their enhanced traditional privileges, most notably control over how they were governed and taxed (Hoffman and Noberg 1994, 227; Zagorin 1982; Lublinskaya 1968; Goubert 1996). The Church also retained control over education and poor relief. In short, up through the sixteenth century France did not resemble a modern state, much less a nation-state, at all. Instead it was "a collection of 'nations,' pays, seignories, fiefs and parishes," each of which kept its own customs, privileges, and even languages (Bendix 1978, 339; Zagorin 1982; Collins 1995). Given traditions of independence, attempts by kings to centralize power often provoked bloody reactions (Bohanan 2001, 32). Indeed, during the sixteenth and early seventeenth centuries, conflicts over centralization became so frequent and serious that the "French monarchy seemed to be disintegrating in civil and religious war" (Whiting 1991, 6; Johnson 1993, 43; Church 1969).

Yet this eventually changed. Louis XIII (1619–43) and especially Louis XIV (1643/54–1715) made great strides in subduing the opponents of centralization and expanding their military forces, lawmaking authority, and bureaucratic apparatus (Woloch 1982, 8–10). When Cardinal Richelieu looked back on his service to Louis XIII he wrote that when he became chief minister in 1624, "the Huguenots shared the state with [Your Majesty] ... the *grands* (essentially the nobility) behaved as if they were not your subjects, and the governors of the provinces as if they were sovereign powers" (Elliot 1984, 64–5). However, by the end of Louis

---

[1] And lest we romanticize early modern nobles, especially in comparison to their contemporary counterparts, here is one scholar's description of them: "Many noblemen ... were nothing short of petty tyrants or gangsters who embraced violence as a way of life. Not only did they take up arms against royal magistrates and tax officials ... they also waged war against the peasantry, and frequently fought to the death among themselves as a matter of course .... Moliere, of course, has given us an enduring image of this petty tyrant in the character of Don Juan, a blasphemer, womanizer, duelist, thief and murderer who recognizes no law, either earthly or divine, except that of his own sadistic will." (Schneider 1984, 273–4).

XIV's reign, these forces had been weakened and the French monarchy and state were the envy of Europe. How did this transformation occur?

Perhaps the most obvious characteristics of this period were violence and conflict. As Charles Tilly noted, "during the seventeenth century France passed through a significant revolutionary situation almost one year in two" (Tilly 2004, 99). Peasant revolts, uprisings by the Protestant minority, and resistance by provincial authorities and local nobles marked the period.[2] However, the most consequential conflicts for French state-building were the civil wars known as the *Fronde* (1648–53).

The *Fronde* was a result of the monarchy's centralizing aspirations. In the years preceding its outbreak, the French monarchy had to deal with domestic unrest as well as the Thirty Years' War, straining its finances. The king thus needed to raise revenue, which would require expanding his control over individuals, areas, and corporate bodies hitherto largely free from central interference. The response was predictable: violent rebellions led by those committed to protecting privileges from royal authority. The first of these, referred to as the first *Fronde* or the *La Fronde parlementaire*, was led by the Paris *Parlement*, which refused to pay proposed taxes and, in order to avoid future incursions, called for explicit limits on the king's powers. This revolt was put down when the king's army returned home after the peace of Westphalia, but in 1650 a second *Fronde des princes* broke out spurred by the nobility's determination to protect its power and privileges from the monarchy. These *frondeurs* were gradually beaten back and by 1653 the *Fronde* was over, but the cost was very high: provinces were devastated and trade and economic life disrupted (Doyle 2001, 3; Bickle 1997, 68ff). Nonetheless, the *Fronde* opened a new political era. It did not eliminate opposition to centralization nor clear a direct path to more extensive taxation or the construction of other institutions associated with modern states, but it changed the dynamic between the king and nobility. Many nobles, after losing a military confrontation with the king, recognized the advantages of compromise. And the king, although victorious in the *Fronde*, recognized that defeating the nobles through coercion alone was very costly. The *Fronde* ultimately therefore "led both king and nobles to realize that cooperation could be mutually advantageous. After decades of revolts and conflict, this realization came nearly as an epiphany to both sides" (Bohanan 2001, 61; Kiser and Linton 2002).[3]

Instead of relying purely on coercion, Louis XIII and Louis XIV and their ministers began enticing opponents into a new relationship with the crown using venality, bribery, patronage and the dispersal of privileges—what we would today consider corruption (Root 1994). Such tools were not new in France, but Louis XIII and Louis XIV made more extensive and innovative use of them than their predecessors.

For example, even after his military victory in the *Fronde*, Louis recognized that he could not pay off the debts associated with war through taxation alone. In the past, attempts to expand taxation had caused rebellions and so the king understood the need to move slowly and indirectly. Louis XIII, Louis XIV, and their successors therefore turned to a less politically problematic way of raising funds—the sale of offices. Venality has obvious advantages to leaders desperate for money. First, it is quick and easy, requiring limited personnel to

---

[2] Again, to quote Bacon on this period: "The Kingdom of France ... is now fallen into those calamities, that, as the prophet saith, 'From the crown of the head to the sole of the foot, there is no whole place'" (Zagorin 1982, 58).

[3] Bohanan (2001, 61); Root (1994, 14, 15, 18); Kiser and Linton (2002).

administer and little in the way of institution-building. Second, it does not require directly confronting the nobility or other taxation-resistant actors. Accordingly, the sale of offices went into "overdrive" after the *Fronde*; by the eighteenth century, everything from the right to be an auctioneer, a bailiff, or an oyster seller to the ability to collect taxes and or be a judge was auctioned off (Doyle 1996a; Doyle 1995; Jones 2002, 57; Swart, 1949).

Many offices were lucrative, bringing annual income as well as revenue produced by the office itself; some also conferred privileges on the holder, including ennoblement, and eventually the ability to pass the office to descendants. The holders of such offices thus developed a stake in this system. And because offices were for sale to those who could afford them, they were often purchased by what we might now consider to be the well-off middle class. In addition, therefore, to providing access to funds, venality enabled the king to create a new nobility as a counterweight to the old (Gagliardo 1970, 62) by turning rich and ambitious local merchants, businessmen, etc. into his own clients (Doyle 1996, 9–10). The sale of offices thereby became a "key prop of royal absolutism" (Moore 1966, 59).

Alongside selling offices, the king also doled out or confirmed a variety of other privileges to increase loyalty to the crown and expand his authority. One of the most important was exemption from certain taxes (Doyle 1996, 12). The Church, meanwhile, was allowed to keep the revenue generated from its land (between 6% and 10% of the country's total), making modest "gifts" to the king in lieu of many taxes. The Church also collected the *tithe*, which theoretically entitled it to a tenth of every person's livelihood. Such measures helped the king buy off his opponents, but the price was high, not merely in lost revenue (Cobban 1961, 13; Root 1994, 18) but because these measures created deep divisions and inequalities in society (Beik 1985; Doyle 1996b).

Other trade-offs were required to expand the king's administrative capacity. Precisely because they had traditionally lacked the authority or institutions to control their territories directly, French kings relied on brokers. These brokers, often the great nobles, were not however fully loyal or subservient to them. As one observer noted, "Of all the dangers that menace France there is none greater … than the tyrannical enterprises of the governor … who by means of their governments of provinces and towns have made themselves lords, practically sovereign lords of their regions" (Harding 1978, 7). Richelieu in particular recognized that successful centralization required replacing this system and created his own network of brokers, purposefully bypassing the *grands* and instead searching out men who were not members of the old nobility. Lacking the independent power of the *grands*, these men became Richelieu's *creatures* alone (Bohanan 2001, 57). Richelieu then funneled resources to his brokers, who then bought the support of other key local figures. These brokers also acted as Richelieu's "eyes and ears," facilitating information flows, acting as mediators between different interests, and lobbying for the king's policies (Kettering 1986, 99ff). Richelieu's successors, Mazarin and Colbert, continued along these lines, bypassing and undermining the *grands'* networks, and creating a new web of relationships reaching into provincial France. French kings thus initially relied on traditional means (distributing resources) and networks (local notables) to expand control and only gradually constructed something resembling a modern administration with the *intendants*, a sort of royal bureaucracy that operated parallel to the system of venal offices.[4]

---

[4] These *intendants'* positions were salaried rather than venal and appointed rather than purchased. Since they were "removable at the King's pleasure, they were in every respect the King's men and could at

Alongside venality, patronage and clientelism, the King also used the palace of Versailles to co-opt and control the nobles. After the *Fronde*, Louis XIV made presence at Versailles a prerequisite for currying favor. Once at Versailles, the king created an elaborate court and set of rituals emphasizing the king's differentiation from the nobles. The king devoted immense time and energy to cultivating social distinctions that played to the aristocracy's belief in a natural and clearly differentiated social hierarchy—but one with the king firmly at its apex (Dunn 1970, 138ff; Maczak 1966, 245; Beik 1985, 318; Goubert 1996, 89). In addition, by assembling the nobility at Versailles, Louis XIV was better able to "control them. Those who came were richly rewarded" as well as "domesticated and made dependent" (Doyle 2002, 41–2). In addition, bringing the nobles to Versailles had the advantage of physically removing them from their local power bases (Collins 1995, 136ff). With more time spent at Versailles, noble households, entourages, gendarmes, and so on shrank. Versailles, in other words, helped direct nobles' wealth and energy away from the administration of their land and people and toward trying to impress the king and the other aristocrats. Conspicuous consumption, rather than politics, became the French aristocracy's focus (Doyle 2001, 59).[5]

These trade-offs were in many ways successful. During Louis XIV's reign in particular the monarch's power increased. Although Louis XIV confirmed the Church's enormous financial resources, he also declared his right to make ecclesiastical laws; to approve all declarations by the Pope before they took force in France; to regulate bishops' travel outside of France; and to protect royal officials from excommunication. Similarly, while the king confirmed the nobility's social and economic privileges, their political power was undermined. As nobles lost authority at the local level, they were increasingly viewed as parasites by the wider population. Tocqueville's remains the classic analysis of this transformation:

> when nobles had real power as well as privileges, when they governed and administered, their rights could be at once greater and less open to attack. In fact, [in a previous age] the nobility was regarded ... much as the government is regarded today; its exactions were tolerated in view of the protection and security it provided. [By the eighteenth century, however they had ceased] to act as leaders of the people [but had] not only retained but greatly increased their fiscal immunities and the advantages accruing to them individually (de Tocqueville, 1955, 30, 204).

Having co-opted or weakened his opposition, Louis XIV made great strides in centralization and state-building: He increased France's territory by nearly 10% and added one and half million new subjects to his realm (Jones 2002, 53). He gave his territories something resembling a single system of civil law for the first time and eliminated some local, provincial, and municipal institutions (Parker 1983, 122). He made his population more religiously homogenous by revoking the Edict of Nantes[6] and forcing two or three hundred thousand Huguenots who had

---

least rival if not altogether displace the local elites" (Woloch 1982, 8–10; Gruder 1968). Although they had existed in the past, by the 1630s *intendants* had become more numerous and more powerful and began developing "many of the features of a permanent organization" (Briggs 1998, 119–20; Bonney 1978, 30; Harding 1978, 216–17; Godard 1969).

[5] As one observer put it, "A nobleman, if he lives at home in his province, lives free but without substance; if he lives at court, he is taken care of, but enslaved" (Ford 1953, vii).

[6] Which had granted toleration to Protestants. With this move, Louis XIV forced Protestants to choose between conversion and exile: After 1685, French Protestants no longer had civil rights; their clergy were exiled or jailed, their possessions could be confiscated, and their children were encouraged to

previously resisted centralization to flee the country.[7] (It is worth remembering that during this time it was widely accepted that religious diversity made a country unviable—as the old proverb had it: "one faith, one law, one king." (Koeningsberger and Mosse 1968, 252)). And Louis XIV expanded the monarchy's administrative and military power by making increasing use of *intendants* and expanding and professionalizing the army.[8]

In short, during the seventeenth century, French kings centralized authority and laid the foundations of a modern state. By so doing, they transformed France from a kingdom that had seemed on the verge of disintegration at the beginning of the seventeenth century to one that possessed a monarchy and state that were the envy of Europe by the century's end.[9] However, although the monarchy's political power increased, a nobility and Church with immense social and economic privileges was embedded within the *ancien régime*, creating critical perhaps even fatal flaws in it. These flaws would come back to haunt French kings and the French people during the late eighteenth century and beyond.

Other Cases

Although there is much distinctive about France, the basic challenge confronting French kings during the early modern period—centralizing authority—was confronted by all European rulers. Not all succeeded, however, in outmaneuvering or undermining the opponents of centralization. Indeed, the majority did not, which is why most of the political entities existing in Europe in 1500 disappeared.

Once particularly consequential, if unusual (since it was later reversed), example of state-building failure was Poland. Indeed, during the early modern period Poland went in the opposite direction from many of its neighbors, with its nobility consolidating its dominance over the king. The nobility preserved and even strengthened its traditional social, economic, and political power at the local and national level. It retained authority over own its lands and peoples as well as its own independent military capabilities; it also controlled a national political assembly, the *Sejm*, which elected the king, thereby limiting his independence and power.[10] Poland was accordingly known as "The Paradise of the Nobility" (Davies 1982, 160, 386; Stokes 1997, 12). Although many favorably contrasted Poland's "Golden Liberty" to the absolutism developing in France and other parts of Europe, the nobility's ability to block the

---

convert to Catholicism. Of course, the departure of many Huguenots had many negative consequences as well, especially in the economic realm.

[7] As noted earlier, religious conflict had torn France apart during the previous century and the Huguenots had resisted encroachments upon their privileges. As Richelieu put it, "As long as the Huguenots have a foothold in France, the king will never be master in his own house" (Tapié, 1975, 148).

[8] At the time of Louis XIV accession the French army had about 20,000 men; by 1688 it had between 150,000–400,000 men depending on whether it was peace or wartime (Woloch 1982, 51; Koenigsberger 1987a, 185; Briggs 1998, 141–2; Parker 2008, 149; Rowlands 2002).

[9] This transformation is the reason why so many praised Louis XIV as the savior of France. As Voltaire put it, "the spirit of faction, strife and rebellion which had possessed the people since the time of Francis II, was transformed into a rivalry to serve their king" (Church 1969, 137–8; Church 1959; Goubert 1966).

[10] The *liberium veto* allowed any member of the Sejm to veto legislation or end a session of the parliament.

centralization of authority was calamitous. Lacking a strong central authority, Poland failed to develop the national-level administrative, fiscal, or military resources or the consistent, forceful foreign policy that would allow it to successfully confront those neighbors that did develop these capacities. As any victim of European imperialism could predict, it was thus gobbled up by them during the eighteenth century, only reappearing when Europe's continental empires collapsed at the end of the First World War.

Poland and France were on opposite ends of the state-building spectrum, but there were variations in-between. In Spain, for example, the centralization of authority went in reverse: At the beginning of the early modern period the country had a strong military and a fairly strong monarchy, but by the period's end both were in decline (Glete 2002). The Spanish nobility and Church held on to political as well as social and economic power and the Spanish crown was unable to develop its own administrative institutions or complete authority over the provinces (Rude 2002; Thompson 1993; Williams 1970). During the seventeenth century, centrifugal tendencies increased and the crown faced revolts in Portugal (linked to Spain at the time), Catalonia, and elsewhere. By the end of the century "the focus of loyalties for ... Spaniards was becoming increasingly diffused" with identities becoming narrower and more localized (Thompson 1993, 84). As one of Charles III's (1759–88) ministers put it, Spain remained "a body composed of other smaller bodies, separated and in opposition to one another, which oppress and despise each other and are in a continuous state of war" (Williams 1970, 121–2; Treasure 1985, 340; Thompson 1994; Scott 1990).

The Spanish state that emerged from the early modern period was thus weak—kings were not as powerless as their Polish counterparts, but neither did they undermine or co-opt the opponents of centralization as thoroughly as had their French counterparts. Without a strong central authority or national-level institutions, Spain began a period of international decline and domestic disorder. "By the mid-seventeenth century, banditry was widespread ... and there were enormous crime waves in both the countryside and the cities. In the 'dark corners of the land' ... gang warfare and clan faction were the rule. Even in the capital Madrid, it was impossible to go out at night except in large numbers and armed to the teeth." Many began to fear that "royal jurisdiction" was on the verge of "extinction" (Thompson 1993, 89–90). Spain thus entered the modern era with an unintegrated territory, recalcitrant and fractious nobility, and an unreformed and reactionary Church—all of which critically affected political development up through the twentieth century.

Another interesting case is Prussia. Up through the early modern period, Prussia was composed of discontinuous territories lacking natural boundaries or strong economic or cultural ties. Indeed, so disjointed were these territories that they were not yet generally even known as "Prussia" (Rosenberg 1958, 27–8). The titular rulers of Prussia, moreover, had historically been weak and faced extremely powerful nobles. Little suggested, in short, that Prussia was an auspicious setting for state-building (Clark 2006, xvi; Williams 1970, 292). Yet during the late seventeenth and early eighteenth centuries a series of remarkable Hohenzollern rulers—the Great Elector, Frederick William (1640–1688), Frederick I (1688–1713), and Frederick William I (1713–40)—managed to achieve what the Prussian historian Otto Hintze referred to as "the perfection of absolutism," creating a strong state ruling over consolidated territories (Clark 2006, 111). Prussian absolutism differed, however, from its French counterpart. Rather than the monarch undermining the nobility as in France, or the nobility undermining the monarchy as in Poland, in Prussia a symbiosis emerged between the crown and the nobility.

The Hohenzollerns eliminated the nobles' assemblies and created a national bureaucracy and army. Indeed, so formidable did both become that Prussia became known as a "bureaucratic-absolutist" state; a famous quip had it that "Prussia was not a country with an army, but an army with a country."[11] But rather than severing the central state from the nobility, Prussian kings integrated them into it, allowing them to dominate high-status posts in the bureaucracy and army, and turning them into a "class of hereditary state servants" (Rude 2002, 75; Clark, 2006 99; Woloch 1982, 89ff; Fulbrook 1983). (Like many contemporary rulers, in other words, they rewarded their supporters by granting them access to state offices and resources, but rather than support coming from a particular communal group as it often does today, in Prussia it came from a socioeconomic one.) Also, while the Hohenzollerns strengthened their power at the national level, they left much of rural Prussia under the nobility's control (Clark 2006, 155; Williams 1970, 326; Rosenberg 1958; Berdhal 1988). Thus, despite losing power to central rulers, the Junkers remained "miniature kings" on their own lands and traditional social and economic hierarchies remained relatively untouched (Greenfeld 1992, 289, 292). Prussia thus entered the modern age in paradoxical way—with a strong monarchy *and* a strong nobility, and with a comparatively modern state but one dominated by a pre-modern elite. This crucially shaped subsequent Prussian and later German political development.

Lest we assume that the only successful states during the early modern period were absolutist, Britain followed another political trajectory. In comparison to France or Prussia, the obstacles to territorial centralization were relatively low in England, since it had a fairly small territory that was easily navigable and somewhat removed from the main power struggles of the continent. Indeed, the country we now think of as England was unified earlier than France or Prussia (Koeningsberger 1987a; Boucoyannis n.d.). Nonetheless during the early modern period, the British Isles were disordered, with kings constantly driven from the throne, rulers often meeting violent ends, and endemic rebellions. One sociologist calculated that "between 1450 and 1640 there were more internal disturbances in England than in any other European country" (Hill 1969, 119; Plumb 1967, 1; Mervyn 1986). This instability peaked with the War of the Roses (approximately 1455–85), a decades-long series of conflicts between powerful magnates for control of the crown. When the war finally ended with the victory of a somewhat obscure Henry Tudor, Earl of Richmond, a crucial task facing the new king was to assert himself vis-a-vis his "over mighty subjects." As one analyst of the period put it, "a poor and weak crown was confronted by wealthy and arrogant magnates: there lay the crux of the problem" (Elton 1955, 10). Henry VII (1485–1509) and his successors did increase the power of the crown and began what some scholars refer to as a "Tudor revolution" in government (Coleman and Starkey 1986; Bradshaw 1979; Stone 1965, 119, 218).

Henry VIII (1509–47) continued along the path laid out by his predecessor, and took a major step forward by "nationalizing" the English Church, thereby removing an opponent to his authority and using expropriated Church land to fund expenditures and buy the loyalty of elites. Meanwhile, Cromwell, Henry VIII's key minister (1532–40), reorganized the government, making it less an extension of the king and his household and creating new institutions

---

[11] Probably originally said by Friedrich von Schrötter (1743–1815) Prussian Junker and government minister (Blackbourn 2003, 17).

to handle various administrative functions. The process picked up under Elizabeth (1558–1603) who further strengthened loyalty to the crown (MacCaffrey 1961; MacColluh, 1986). Under the Tudors, in short, government became less personalistic and more bureaucratic; whereas Henry VII had himself managed most governing functions from his private chambers, Elizabeth left much day-to-day governing in the hands of advisors and administrators. In short, after the War of the Roses, the crown reasserted its authority in England. However, when seventeenth-century monarchs tried to further centralize their authority by moving towards the type of absolutist dictatorships that their counterparts in France and elsewhere were developing, they failed. Indeed, by the end of the seventeenth century the absolutist "option" had been rejected in England. England's ability to avoid the absolutist "wave" that swept other parts of Europe during the early modern period and continue its state-building process under a constitutional regime after 1688, had immense consequences for its subsequent political development.

Conclusions and Future Research

Partially because the state-building literature emphasizes structural variables that help explain *why* state-building happens, we don't know enough about *how* it does—how centralization occurs, how state institutions are constructed, how state-builders overcome their adversaries to achieve their goals, and more. But, as we have seen, even when state-building occurs, how it does varies, and these variations critically influence subsequent political development in general and the likelihood of high-quality government emerging in particular.

Regardless of how state-building occurred, all successful cases of state-building began with bargains between rulers and the opponents of centralization.[12] State-building only got underway once the interests of elites and religious authorities had been transformed: they needed to acquiesce in, or at least cease actively opposing, the centralization of authority. To achieve this, state-builders relied on a variety of "carrots" or practices that would be considered corrupt today.

French kings used things like venality, clientelism, and patronage to defang their opponents. The genius of Louis XIV, as one observer put it, lay in his "ability to translate royal aspiration towards greater and more centralized power into terms which appealed to the provincial ruling class and which enhanced their class position even while strengthening the state and the monarchy" (Beik 1985, 280; Bonney 1978, 447). But the state created by these means had critical, perhaps fatal, flaws. The French state rested on a narrow social base, with the king and the nobility locked into an unhealthy embrace. By confirming and expanding an elaborate system of privileges, and by exempting many of the wealthiest groups in society from taxation, the system ensured that taxation ended up falling on those least able to pay (especially peasants), thus exacerbating conflict between the poor and the privileged. The nature of the French state thereby helped create a "society divided into closed, self-regarding groups" (Root 1994, 236) "whose members" as one of Louis XVI's own ministers once put it,

---

[12] Through this prism, it is possible that empires are best viewed as "stalled" cases of state-building where centralizing rulers are unable to complete this process.

"have so few links between themselves that everyone thinks solely of his own interests, no trace of any feeling for the public weal is anywhere to be found" (Tocqueville 1955, 107).

Furthermore, the French state's dependence on a narrow social base and a system of privilege to keep its supporters happy also limited its ability to reform. By the second half of the eighteenth century, largely as a result of several expensive and disastrous wars, the French state's fiscal position had become precarious. Unable to significantly raise taxes, it increasingly borrowed, but by the 1780s its debt burden had become unsustainable.[13] However, despite the regime's existence being at stake, attempts at reform were rejected because they threatened the social base and system of privileges upon which the state was built. Indeed, so entrenched was this system, so central was it to the state's nature, that it took the French revolution to finally get rid of it.

But it's not just France, of course: Examining how state-building occurs enables us to better understand political development in all European countries (Berman 2019). The nature of Prussian state-building, for example, critically shaped how the German Empire was founded, the nature of its political system as well as the political divisions and conflicts plaguing it, the challenges Germany's first democracy—the Weimar Republic—inherited, and finally, the rise and nature of the Nazi regime. The English civil war(s) and the Glorious Revolution are hard to understand without a consideration of the state-building process up through the seventeenth century—and these conflicts are the essential backstory to Britain's modern political development. The conflicts within and the breakup of the Habsburg Empire flowed from its stalled centralization and state-building process, as did the economic underdevelopment and political conflicts plaguing Spain up through the twentieth century.

Conclusions

In short, even a brief examination of European history makes clear that is impossible to understand political development without understanding *how* state-building occurs. Social scientists should, accordingly, spend more time examining not just why, but also how states develop and how variations in state development influence political development overall (Berman 2019).

In addition to illuminating political development, studying state-building in Europe also provides the backstory of the development of high-quality government. High-quality government requires a state capable of implementing policies, maintaining the rule of law, collecting resources from and delivering resources to citizens, and so on. How state-building occurs critically influences whether or to what degree states develop such capacities.

One illustration of this is the connection between corruption and state-building. In Europe, state-building involved practices that would be considered corrupt today (Rothstein and Varraich 2017; Rose-Ackerman 2016). This may indicate that many practices we frown upon may be "natural" or necessary parts of the early state-building process. In particular,

---

[13] By 1788, the payment of interest on France's debt was by some estimates eating up almost 50% of state expenditures and the interest the *ancien régime* had to pay on it was itself partially a consequence of the particular nature of the French state, i.e. its narrow social base and inability to raise taxes (Berman 2019).

when national rulers lack the strength to eliminate the opponents of centralization through coercion alone, they must co-opt them, and material incentives are a common way of doing so. Similarly, when national rulers can't build their own institutions capable of collecting resources from and delivering resources to their citizens, they often rely on "intermediaries" whose interests don't full coincide with theirs. Such "principal–agent" problems, in political science parlance, help explain why clientelism, patronage, venality, and nepotism exist in all but the most developed states today.

But while various forms of corruption were common in Europe and may be "natural" parts of the early state-building process, eliminating or at least weakening them is necessary to transition to astate capable of high-quality government. There is some evidence, however, that some forms of corruption are more pernicious and difficult to uproot than others (Root 1994). Over the past years, excellent work has begun analyzing conditions conducive to overcoming corruption (Mungiu-Pippidi 2015; Dahlström and Wängerud 2015; Rose-Ackerman 2015; Dahlström and Lapuente 2017; Rothstein 2015). More research into how corrupt practices are intertwined with state-building, and the differing political, economic, and social consequences of various corrupt practices, would provide further insight to the precise nature of the challenges that need to be overcome in order to transition from weak to strong states.

In conclusion, a reconsideration of the French and other European cases has a lot to offer students of state-building today. First, and most obviously, it reminds us of how difficult centralizing authority is—which makes perfect sense once one recognizes that it involves displacing longstanding authority patterns, relationships, and elites. Second, historical cases reveal how misleading it is to view state-building as a straightforward process of transforming pre-modern political institutions into modern ones. As the French and other European cases highlight, the evolution from pre-modern to modern political arrangements was far from linear or clear-cut. Instead, rather than directly building modern state institutions, French and other European monarchs made use of traditional means and relationships when pursuing centralization: Clientelism replaced feudal relations, patrimonial ties replaced local ones; only relatively late in the game did modern state institutions like rational bureaucracies and independent extractive capacities or truly national sentiment emerge. State-building in France and Europe, in other words, entailed an intermediary phase of institution-building that exhibited at least as much continuity with the past as it did with the future.

And third, the French and other European cases make clear the necessity of further research into the mechanisms of state-building. Such research would help us better understand the development of democracies and dictatorships, the conditions under which effective, high-quality political institutions develop, the reason why some societies are riven by various forms of social and economic cleavages, and much more (Berman 2019).

References

Acemoglu, Daron, and James Robinson. 2017. *Why Nations Fail.* N.Y.: Crown.

Anderson, M.S. 1998. *War and Society in Europe of the Old Regime 1618–1789.* Montreal: McGill-Queen's University Press.

Anderson, Perry. 1974. *Lineages of the Absolutist State.* London: Verso.

Aston, Trevor, ed. 1965. *Crisis in Europe 1560-1660*. N.Y.: Routledge.

Barkey, Karen, and Sunita Parikh. 1991. "Comparative Perspectives on the State." *American Review of Sociology* 17 (1): 523-49.

Bates, Robert. 2008. *When Things Fell Apart*. N.Y.: Cambridge University Press.

Beik, William. 1985. *Absolutism and Society in Seventeenth Century France*. N.Y.: Cambridge University Press.

Bendix, Reinhard. 1978. *Kings or People. Power and the Mandate to Rule*. Los Angeles: University of California Press.

Berman, Sheri. 2019. *Democracy and Dictatorship in Europe. From the Ancient Régime to the Present Day*. N.Y.: Oxford University Press.

Berdhal, Robert. 1988. *The Politics of the Prussia Nobility*. Princeton: Princeton University Press.

Best, Geoffrey. 1982. *War and Society in Revolutionary Europe*. N.Y.: St Martin's Press.

Bickle, Peter. 1997. *Resistance, Repression and Community*. London: Clarendon Press.

Blackbourn, David. 2003. A History of Germany. N.Y.: Blackwell.

Bohanan, Donna. 2001. *Crown and Nobility in Early Modern France*. N.Y.: Palgrave.

Bonney, Richard. 1978, *Political Change in France Under Richelieu and Mazarin 1624-1661*. N.Y.: Oxford University Press.

Boone, Catherine. 2003. *Political Topographies of the African State*. N.Y.: Cambridge University Press.

Boucoyannis, Deborah. n.d. *Laws, Courts and Parliaments: The Hidden Sinews of Power in the Emergence of Constitutionalism*. Unpublished manuscript.

Bradshaw, Breden. 1979. "The Tudor Commonwealth: Reform and Revision." *The Historical Journal* 22 (2): 455-76.

Briggs, Robin. 1998. *Early Modern France 1560-1715*. N.Y.: Oxford University Press.

Callaghy, Thomas M. 1994. *The State-Society Struggle. Zaire in Comparative Perspective*. N.Y.: Columbia University Press.

Christia, Fontini, and Michael Semple. 2009. "Flipping the Taliban," *Foreign Affairs* 88 (4) (July/August).

Church, William, ed. 1959. *The Greatness of Louis XIV*. Boston: Heath and Co.

Church, William, ed. 1969. *The Impact of Absolutism in France*. N.Y.: John Wiley & Sons.

Clark, Christopher. 2006. *Iron Kingdom. The Rise and Downfall of Prussia, 1600-1947*. Cambridge, MA: Harvard University Press.

Clark, Samuel. 1995. *State and Status*. Montreal: McGill-Queen's University Press.

Cobban, Alfred. 1961. *A History of Modern France. Volume I 1715-1799*. Baltimore: Penguin.

Coleman, Christopher and David Starkey 1986. *Revolution Reassessed*. Oxford: Clarendon Press.

Collins, James. 1995. *The State in Early Modern France*. N.Y.: Cambridge University Press.

Dahlström, Carl, and Lena Wängnerud. 2015. "How Institutions Constrain Elites from Destructive Behavior." In *Elites, Institutions, and the Quality of Government. How Institutions Constrain Elites from Destructive Behavior*, edited by Dahlström Carl and Lena Wängnerud, 3-12. N.Y.: Palgrave Macmillan.

Dahlström, Carl, and Victor Lapuente. 2017. *Organizing Leviathan: Politicians, Bureaucrats, and the Making of Good Government*. N.Y.: Cambridge University Press.

Davis, Norman. 1982. *God's Playground: A History of Poland*. N.Y.: Columbia University Press.

Davies, Norman. 2011. *Vanished Kingdoms: The Rise and Fall of States and Nations*. N.Y.: Viking.

de Tocqueville, Alexis. 1955. *The Old Regime and the French Revolution*. N.Y.: Anchor Books.

Doyle, William. 1995. *Officers, Nobles, and Revolutionaries*. London: Hambledon Press.

Doyle, William. 1996a. *Venality. The Sale of Offices in Eighteenth Century France*. N.Y.: Oxford University Press.

Doyle, William. 1996ba. "The Sale of Offices in French History." *History Today* 46: 39-449.

Doyle, William. 2001. *Old Regime France, 1648–1788*. N.Y.: Oxford University Press.

Doyle, William. 2002. *The Oxford History of the French Revolution*. N.Y.: Oxford University Press.

Dunn, Richard. 1970. *The Age of Religious Wars, 1559–1689*. N.Y.: W.W. Norton & Co.

Dunning, Thad. 2008. *Crude Democracy*. N.Y.: Cambridge University Press.

Dyson, Kenneth. 1980. *The State Tradition in Western Europe*. Oxford: Martin Robertson.

Elliot, J.H. 1968. *Europe Divided 1559–1598*. N.Y.: Harper and Row.

Elliott, J. H. 1984. *Richelieu and Olivares*. N.Y.: Cambridge University Press.

Elliot, J.H. 1992. "A Europe of Composite Monarchies." *Past and Present* 137 (November): 48–71.

Elton, G.R. 1955. *England Under the Tudors*. London: Methuen & Co.

Ford, Franklin. 1953. *Robe and Sword. The Regrouping of the French Aristocracy after Louis XIV*. Cambridge: Harvard University Press.

Fulbrook, Mary, ed. 1993. *National Histories and European History*. London: Routledge.

Fukuyama, Francis. 2012. *The Origins of Political Order*. N.Y. Farrar, Strauss and Giroux.

Fukuyama, Francis. 2015. *Political Order and Political Decay*. N.Y. Farrar, Strauss and Giroux.

Gagliardo, John. 1970. *Enlightened Despotism*. N.Y.: Thomas Cromwell Co.

Gellner, Ernst. 1997. *Nationalism*. N.Y.: NYU Press.

Ghani, Ashraf and Clare Lockhart. 2008. *Fixing Failed States*. N.Y.: Oxford University Press.

Glete, Jan. 2002. *War and the State in Early Modern Europe*. N.Y.: Routledge.

Godard, Charles. 1969, ed. "The Historical Role of the Intendants." In *The Impact of Absolutism*, 159–65. Church, William.

Goldstone, Jack. 1991. *Revolution and Rebellion in the Early Modern World*. Berkeley: University of California Press.

Gorski, Philip. 2003. *The Disciplinary Revolution*. Chicago: University of Chicago Press.

Goubert, Pierre. 1996. *Louis XIV and Twenty Million Frenchmen*. N.Y.: Pantheon Books.

Greenfeld, Liah. 1992. *Nationalism. Five Roads to Modernity*. Cambridge: Harvard University Press.

Greengrass, Mark. 1991. *Conquest and Coalescence*. N.Y.: Edward Arnold.

Gruder, Vivian. 1968. *The Royal Provincial Intendants*. Ithaca: Cornell University Press.

Harding, Robert. 1978. *Anatomy of a Power Elite*. New Haven: Yale University Press.

Herbst, Jeffrey. 2000. *States and Power in Africa*. Princeton: Princeton University Press.

Hill, Christopher. 1969. *Reformation to Industrial Revolution*. Baltimore, MD: Penguin Books.

Hobbes, Thomas. 1982. *Leviathan*. N.Y.: Penguin.

Hoffman, Philip. 1994. "Early Modern France, 1450–1700." In *Fiscal Crises, Liberty, and Representative Government, 1450–1789*, edited by Philip Hoffman and Katherine Noberg, 226–52. Palo Alto: Stanford University Press.

Hoffman, Philip, and Katherine Noberg, eds. 1994. *Fiscal Crises, Liberty, and Representative Government, 1450–1789*. Palo Alto: Stanford University Press.

Isaac, Ann Katherine, and Maarten Prak, eds. 1996. "Cities, Bourgeoisies and States." In *Power Elites and State Building*. London: Clarendon Press.

Johnson, Douglas. 1993. "The Making of the French Nation." In *The National Question in Europe in Historical Context*, edited by Mikulas Teich and Roy Porter, 35–62. N.Y.: Cambridge University Press.

Jones, Colin. 2002. *The Great Nation*. N.Y.: Columbia University Press.

Jones, Peter M. 1995. *Reform and Revolution in France: The Politics of Transition, 1774–1791* N.Y.: Cambridge University Press, 1995.

Kettering, Sharon. 1986. *Patrons, Brokers and Clients in Seventeenth Century France*. N.Y.: Oxford University Press.

Keohane, Nannerl. 1980. *Philosophy and the State in France: The Renaissance to the Enlightenment*. Princeton, NJ: Princeton University Press.

Kiser, Edgar, and April Linton. 2002. "The Hinges of History: State-Making and Revolt in Early Modern France," *American Sociological Review* 67 (6): 889–910.

Knecht, R. J. 1996. *French Renaissance Monarchy*. London: Longman Group.

Koenigsberger, H.G. 1987a. *Early Modern Europe*. London: Longman Group.

Koenigsberger, H.G. 1987b. *Medieval Europe, 400–1500*. London: Longman.

Koenigsberger, H.G., and George Mosse. 1968. *Europe in the Sixteenth Century*. N.Y.: Holt, Rinehart and Winston, Inc.

Lublinskaya, A.D. 1968. *French Absolutism*. N.Y.: Cambridge University Press.

MacColluh, Diarmaid. 1986. *Suffolk and the Tudors*. Oxford: Clarendon Press.

Mann, Michael. 1993. *The Sources of Social Power*. N.Y.: Cambridge University Press.

Marten, Kimberly. 2011. "Warlords." In *The Changing Character of War*, edited by Hew Strachan and Sibylle Scheiper, 302–14. N.Y.: Oxford University Press.

Maczak, Antoni. 1966. "The Nobility-State Relationship." In *Power Elites and State Building*, edited by Wolfgang Reinhard, 189–206, London: Clarendon.

Mervyn, James. 1986. *Society, Politics, and Culture: Studies in Early Modern England*. N.Y.: Cambridge University Press.

Moore, Barrington. 1966. *Social Origins of Dictatorship and Democracy*. Boston: Beacon Press.

Mungiu-Pippidi, Alina. 2015. *The Quest for Good Governance. How Societies Develop Control of Corruption*. N.Y.: Cambridge University Press.

Nelson, Brian. 2006. *The Making of the Modern State*. N.Y.: Palgrave MacMillan.

Nexon, Daniel. 2009. *The Struggle for Power in Early Modern Europe*. Princeton: Princeton University Press.

North, Douglass, John Joseph Wallis, and Barry Weingast. 2009. *Violence and Social Orders*. N.Y.: Cambridge University Press.

Parker, David. 1983. *The Making of French Absolutism*. N.Y.: St. Martin's Press.

Parker, Geoffrey. 2008. "Crisis and Catastrophe: The Global Crisis of the Seventeenth Century." *American Historical Review* 113 (4) (October): 1053–1079.

Parker Geoffrey, and Lesley Smith. 1997. *The General Crisis of the Seventeenth Century* N.Y.: Routledge.

Plumb, J.H. 1967. *The Growth of Political Stability in England 1675–1725*. London: MacMillan.

Poggi, Gianfranco. 1990. *The State*. Palo Alto: Stanford: Stanford University Press.

Rabb, Theodore K. 1975. *The Struggle for Stability in Early Modern Europe*. N.Y.: Oxford University Press.

Reinhard, Wolfgang ed. 1966. *Power Elites and State Building*. London: Clarendon Press.

Reno, Willia. 1998. *Warlord Politics and African States*. Boulder, CO: Lynne Rienner.

Root, Hilton. 1994. *The Fountain of Privileges*. Berkeley: University of California Press.

Rose-Ackerman, Susan. 2015. "Are Corrupt Elites Necessary for Corrupt Countries?" In *Elites, Institutions, and the Quality of Government*, edited by Dahlström Carl & Lena Wängnerud, 33–47. London: Palgrave Macmillan.

Rose-Ackerman, Susan. 2016. *Corruption and Government: Causes, Consequences, and Reform*. N.Y.: Cambridge University Press.

Rosenberg, Hans. 1958. *Bureaucracy, Aristocracy and Autocracy*. Boston: Beacon.

Rosenthal, Jean-Laurent. 1998. "The Political Economy of Absolutism Reconsidered." In *Analytic Narratives*, edited by Robert Bates, Avner Grief, Margaret Levi, Jean-Laurent Rosenthal, and Barry Weingast, 64–108. Princeton: Princeton University Press.

Rothstein, Bo. 2011. *The Quality of Government*. Chicago: University of Chicago Press.

Rothstein, Bo. 2015. *Political Corruption—A Research Collection*. Cheltenham: Edward Elgar.

Rothstein, Bo and Aiysha Varraich. 2017. *Making Sense of Corruption*. N.Y.: Cambridge University Press.

Rowlands, Guy. 2002. *The Dynastic State and the Army Under Louis XIV*. N.Y.: Cambridge University Press.

Rude, George. 2002. *Europe in the Eighteenth Century. Aristocracy and the Bourgeois Challenge*. London: Phoenix Press.

Sassen, Saskia. 2006. *Territory, Authority, and Rights. From Medieval to Global Assemblages* Princeton: Princeton University Press.

Scott, H.M. 1990. *Enlightened Absolutism. Reform and Reformers in Later Eighteenth Century Europe*. Ann Arbor: University of Michigan Press.

Schneider, Robert. 1984. "Swordplay and Statemaking." In *Statemaking and Social Movements*, edited by Charles Bright and Susan Harding, 265–96. Ann Arbor: University of Michigan Press.

Stasavage, David. 2015. *States of Credit. Size, Power and the Development of European Polities*. Princeton: Princeton University Press.

Stokes, Gale. 1997. *Three Eras of Political Change in Eastern Europe*. New York. Oxford University Press.

Stone, Lawrence. 1965. *Crisis of the Aristocracy, 1558–1641*. N.Y.: Oxford University Press.

Strayer, Joseph. 2016. *On the Medieval Origins of the Modern State*. Princeton: Princeton Classics.

Swart, K.W. 1949. *Sale of Offices in the Seventeenth Century*. The Hague: M. Nijhoff.

Tapié, Victor-L. 1975. *France in the Age of Louis XIII and Richelieu*. N.Y.: Prager.

Thomson, Janice. 1994. *Mercenaries, Pirates and Sovereigns*. Princeton: Princeton University.

Thompson, I.A.A. 1993. *Crown and Cortes*. Ann Arbor: University of Michigan.

Thompson, I. A.A. 1994. "Castile: Polity, Fiscality and Fiscal Crisis." In *Fiscal Crises, Liberty, and Representative Government, 1450–1789*, edited by Hoffman and Norberg. Stanford: Stanford University Press.

Tilly, Charles. 1975a. "Reflections on the History of European State-Making." In *The Formation of National States in Western Europe*, edited by Charles Tilly, 3–83. Princeton: Princeton University Press.

Tilly, Charles, ed. 1975b. *The Formation of National States in Western Europe*. Princeton: Princeton University Press.

Tilly, Charles. 1990. *Coercion, Capital, and European States, AD 990–1990*. Cambridge, Mass: Blackwell Publishers.

Tilly, Charles. 2004. *Contention and Democracy in Europe, 1650-2000*. N.Y.: Cambridge University Press.

Tilly, Charles, Louise Tilly, and Richard Tilly. 1975. *The Rebellious Century, 1830–1930*. Cambridge, MA: Harvard University Press.

Treasure, Geoffrey. 1985. *The Making of Modern Europe*. N.Y.: Methuen & Co.

Wallerstein, Immanuel. 2011. *The Modern World System*. Berkeley: University of California Press.

Whiting, Edward Fox. 1991. *The Emergence of the Modern European World*. Cambridge: Blackwell.

Williams. E. N. 1970. *The Ancien Régime in Europe*. N.Y.: Harper and Row.

Wilson, Peter H. 2009. *The Thirty Years War. Europe's Tragedy*. Cambridge, MA: Harvard University Press.

Woloch, Isser. 1982. *Eighteenth Century Europe*. N.Y.: W.W. Norton & Co.

Zagorin, Perez. 1982. *Rebels and Rulers, 1500–1660*. N.Y.: Cambridge University Press.

....

CHAPTER 36

STATE CAPACITY, QUALITY OF GOVERNMENT, SEQUENCING, AND DEVELOPMENT OUTCOMES

....

MICHELLE D'ARCY AND MARINA NISTOTSKAYA

INTRODUCTION

....

THE idea that state capacity plays an important role in achieving human development is now widely accepted by academics and practitioners. Strong states lead to development through property rights and contract enforcement (North 1981) and also through their role in the provision of common-interest goods, such as security, a sustainable environment, public health or education (Acemoglu, Garia-Jimeno, and Robinson 2015; Cole 2015; D'Arcy and Nistotskaya 2017; Fearon and Laitin 2003; Hanson 2015; Povitkina 2018). However, it has also been recognized that the powers of the state can be used to not only promote the welfare of society as a whole (thereafter social welfare), but to serve the private interests of those who control the state. As Barry Weingast (1995, 1) famously said: "A government strong enough to protect property rights and enforce contracts is also strong enough to confiscate the wealth of its citizens." In other words, the state is like double-faced Janus: One face is benign and the other malevolent.[1] Consequently, one strand of the state-centered literature has been concerned with the state's predatory powers and ways to constrain them, and the other with how the state's powers are beneficial for human development (Figure 36.1).

Much of the "state as malevolent Janus" literature has concentrated on the need to constrain powerholders through, for example, constitutional separation of political power and regular elections. The system of institutional checks and balances ensures that no political actor is able to use the power of the state for the benefit of narrow or selfish interests (North and Weingast 1989), while regular competitive elections is another measure ensuring rulers' credible commitment to social welfare (Fearon 1999). Furthermore, in their influential

---

[1] We borrow this metaphor from Miller (2000).

Views of the state

| State as a malevolent Janus | | State as a benign Janus |

The Basic solution

| Constrain power holders | | Build capacities of the state |

Specific solutions

Input side of politics   Output side of politics

Bureaucratic competence
Bureaucratic reach
Information resources
Infrastructure (roads, etc.)

1. Constitutional   Impartiality (QoG): Meritocratic
   separation of   recrutiment
   powers
2. Elections

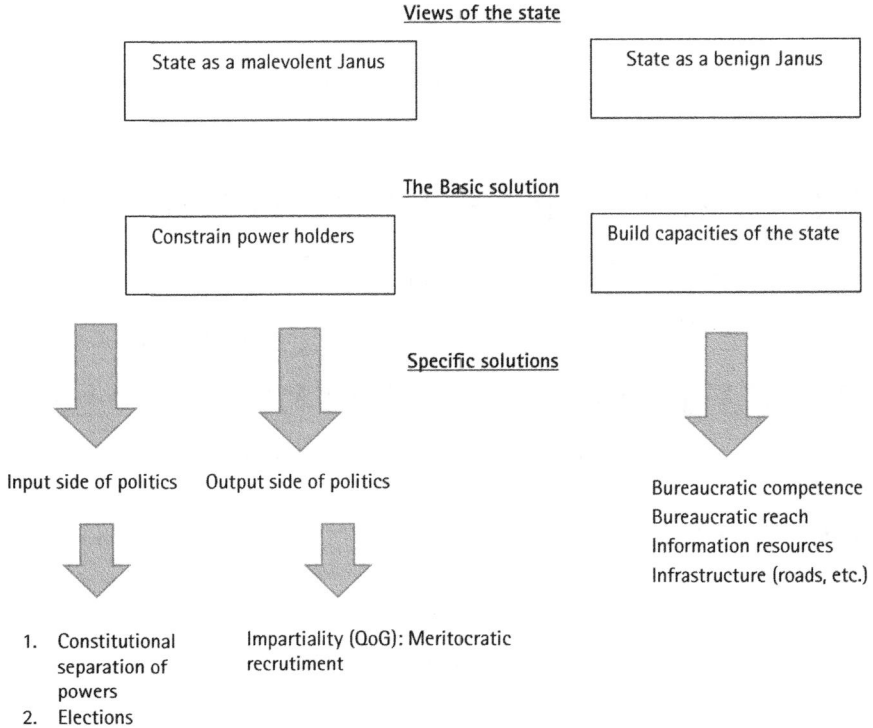

FIGURE 36.1 Views on the nature of the state and basic solutions

article Rothstein and Teorell (2008) called for more attention not only to the constitutional arrangements and the input side of politics (such as elections), but also to the output side of politics, specifically to impartiality in the implementation of laws and policies by executives, bureaucrats, and judges. "When implementing laws and policies, government officials shall not take into consideration anything... that is not beforehand stipulated in the policy or the law" (Rothstein and Teorell (2008, 170). In other words, impartiality in the exercise of public authority is conducive to human development as it ensures that the malevolent preferences of individual officeholders do not jeopardize the welfare-enhancing intent of public policies during implementation. In the light of this definition, the literature on the quality of government as impartiality (QoG) could be seen as part of the "state as malevolent Janus" literature, since its major concern is the risk of the use of state power for particularistic ends.[2] On the other hand, the "state as benign Janus" literature is concerned not with constraints on powerholders, but with how the powers of the state affect important societal outcomes

[2] It is important to note that the literature that we labeled the "state as malevolent Janus," including the QoG literature, is not equivalent of the neoclassical economics view of the state as an inherently "predatory" organization (Becker, Lazear, and Murphy 2003; Friedman 2003). On the contrary, this literature recognizes the state as a necessary determinant of human well-being, but also warns against welfare-undermining preferences of individual power holders (Fukuyama 2014; Miller 2000; North 1981; Rothstein and Teorell 2008).

such as economic growth, civil conflict, public goods provision, sustainable environment, and consolidation of democracy. Understanding of the Janus-faced nature of the state has produced a third distinct literature on institutional sequencing—the ordering of the institutionalization of state powers and constraints to generate the best development outcomes.

This chapter provides a review of the state capacity and sequencing literatures. It discusses how scholars conceptualize and measure state capacity, the debate on sequencing, as well as the existing evidence of its effects on development outcomes. The final section summarizes the state of the art, reflecting on challenges and outlining possible avenues for future research.

Conceptualizing State Capacity

The state capacity literature builds on the idea that the ability of the state to enforce political decisions is a property that greatly varies across polities, and is also independent from political regime type (democracy/autocracy). As Samuel Huntington (1968, 1) argued: "The most important political distinction among countries concerns not their form of government but their degree of government." Although the background concept of state capacity as the ability of the state to effectively implement official goals is intuitively straightforward, it has been conceptualized and measured in many different ways (Figure 36.2). There are two broad approaches to conceptualization of state capacity: One is the functional approach,

Generalist

Implementation of *any* political decision

Bureaucratic quality

- Competence
- Cohesion
- Adherence to professional standards

Territorial reach

- Presence of functionaries & agencies
- Rail/automobile roads

Information resources

- Census (quality, scope, regularity)
- Civil registration and vital statistics
- Digital identification documents (Sweden's *personnummer*, India's *Aadhaar*, Kenya's *Huduma Numba*)
- Cadastral records

Functionalist

Specific functions of the state/specific policy aim

- Coercive/military
- Extractive/fiscal
- Administrative
- Provision of public goods

FIGURE 36.2 Conceptualizations of state capacity

which focuses on specific capacities, such as fiscal or coercive, and another-generalist-that sees state capacity as the ability to implement any political decision.

Functional Approach

The functional approach to conceptualization of state capacity is based on considering "the form and function of existing capabilities," however, the specific choice often depends on what part of state capacity researchers come up against (Berwick and Christia 2018, 71). For example, for many economists, the capacity to collect revenue (extractive/fiscal capacity) and to enforce contractual agreements (legal capacity) constitute state capacity (Besley and Persson 2011; Dincecco and Katz 2016). On the other hand, scholars of international relations and peace and conflict tend to see monopoly of violence as a key attribute of the concept (DeRouen and Sobek 2004; Risse 2011). This situation, in which the concept changes meaning depending on the context, is a clear example of "conceptual stretching," which has haunted state capacity research for some time, undermining the accumulation of knowledge (Soifer and vom Hau 2008).

In the quest for greater generalizability across contexts, there are attempts to identify several key state functions that together constitute the notion of state capacity. For example, Hanson and Sigman (2013) argue that any modern state has three key functions: extractive, coercive, and administrative, and measure these through about 30 indicators. Similarly, Luna and Soifer (2017) build a three-pillar concept of state capacity that includes territorial control, ability to tax, and protection of property rights. Many other scholars have offered their own version of the most important set of government functions (Andersen et al. 2014; Besley and Persson 2011; Hendrix 2010). The problem with this approach is that while state capacity manifests itself in numerous forms and functions, the prospect of a broad consensus of what constitutes key state functions is elusive, as it inevitably involves a normative stand on the scope of the state (Soifer 2012).

Another functional approach to the conceptualization (and measurement) of state capacity is through policy outputs and outcomes, such as investor protection laws, tax, or vaccination rates (Besley and Persson 2010; Soifer 2012). A serious problem of the outcome-based approach is that arguments about the effects of state capacity on policies and outcomes risk becoming circular. As Kocher (2010, 139) notes, "the claim that an insurgency broke out because the state lacked the capacity to prevent an insurgency" is tautological and therefore trivially true (see also Brambor et al. 2019; Centeno, Kohli, and Yashar 2017; Soifer 2008).[3] Furthermore, defining state capacity through policy outputs and outcomes makes it difficult to separate the *ability to implement* policies from 1) *impartiality* of policy implementation and 2) policy *content*. In sum, the problems of conceptual stretching, tautology, and ambiguity with regard to the underlying mechanisms makes the functionalist approach to the conceptualization of state capacity a suboptimal choice for comparative research.

---

[3] If Kocher's (2010) example of tautology is hypothetical, consider Besley and Persson's (2010, 1) statement that "The absence of state capacities to raise revenue and to support markets is a key factor in explaining the persistence of weak states."

Generalist Approach

The generalist approach sees state capacity as the ability to implement *any* political decision and focuses on the endowments needed for the successful implementation of a broad range of political decisions. One of the most established generalist conceptualizations of state capacity relates to *bureaucratic quality*, where "quality" is understood differently by scholars. The oldest—Weberian—tradition understands quality as *competence* or *epistemic quality*, which is a function of professionalization (Weber 1978). The abridged form of the argument holds that professional bureaucracy—permanent organization, staffed with educated experts, whose actions are guided not only by legal, but also by professional norms—is a bureaucracy of high epistemic quality and is, therefore, a more able implementation tool than the alternatives (Bersch, Praca, and Taylor 2017; Evans and Rauch 1999; Nistotskaya and Cingolani 2016). Another conceptualization holds that effective policy implementation requires bureaucratic *autonomy*, which allows bureaucrats a degree of freedom from external pressures (societal, interest-based, and political) in the choice of methods through which to achieve politically mandated policies (Bersch, Praca, and Taylor 2017; Brieba 2018; Fukuyama 2013; Mann 1984; Skocpol 1985). Finally, some scholars claim that *absence of corruption* is a key feature of bureaucracies in high capacity states (Charron and Lapuente 2010; Povitkina 2018). Competence, autonomy, and noncorruptibility have been identified by the literature as attributes of public bureaucracy associated with high state capacity.

There are several problems with the conceptualization of bureaucratic capacity as (the absence of) corruption and autonomy. First, these two properties do not exclusively tap into state capacity, but also into impartiality (Boräng et al 2018; Dahlström and Lapuente 2017; Miller 2000; Nistotskaya and Cingolani 2016)—the core concept of a related, yet distinct quality of government literature (Rothstein and Teorell 2008), which is concerned with "constraints" and not "capacity." This is problematic because, as Fukuyama noted, it is "entirely possible that a state could be highly impartial and still lack the capacity . . . to effectively deliver services" (2013, 349).

Second, the concept of bureaucratic autonomy does not only imply the choice of means of implementation, but also suggests autonomy with regard to policy content. For example, discussing the autonomy of the National Health Service of Chile, Brieba (2018, 45) explicitly refers to its ability to set public health policy priorities independently from the preferences of both politicians and the public at large. Of course, one can argue that the ability to *make* rules is as important a property of state capacity as the ability to *enforce* rules, and such conceptualizations are not unusual in the literature (Mann 1984; Skocpol 1985; Ziblatt 2008). For example, Michael Mann (1984) distinguishes between the "despotic" and "infrastructural" powers of the state, where despotic power refers to decisions that the state can take without consultation with society and infrastructural power refers to implementational capacity. In Mann's analogy, based on *Alice in Wonderland*, the despotic power of the Red Queen is her prerogative to *order* Alice's head to be cut off, while infrastructural power is the Red Queen's ability to hunt Alice down and *enforce* her decapitation.[4]

---

[4] Mann's conceptualization is often plainly misunderstood (for example, despotic power is often confused with coercive capacity (White 2018)), which hinders knowledge accumulation.

Most of the recent literature finds it necessary to analytically separate the implementational capacities of the state from the content of public policies and the extent to which different actors influence it (Besley and Persson 2011; Brambor et al. 2019; D'Arcy and Nistotskaya 2017; Fukuyama 2013; Hanson and Sigman 2013; Soifer and vom Hau 2008). The inclusion of the latter (for example, the extent of citizens' influence over public policies) conflates the notion of state capacity with concepts related to regime type, such as democracy and accountability (Fukuyama 2013, 350–1), which it is better to avoid if the aim is to understand the independent effects of regime type and state capacity. Similarly, the inclusion of the former (the content of public policies, reflecting, for example, preferences for the degree of state interventionism and the scope of redistribution) may obscure the true effects of state capacity. Is low tax revenue in polity A caused by low collection effort (state capacity effect) or low tax rate (policy content effect)? For instance, it is well established that tax rates in late imperial China were low in comparative perspective and impacted the tax revenue (Deng 2015). Therefore, direct comparison between the tax revenue of late Qing China and other countries would not reveal a true picture of China's state capacity. In order to be able to isolate state capacity and policy effects, conceptualizations and measures of state capacity that relate to policy content and organization of decision-making processes should be avoided.

The second generalist conceptualization of state capacity relates to the *territorial reach* of the state, spurred by Michael Mann's notion of infrastructural power: The "institutional capacity of a central state … to penetrate its territories and logistically implement [political] decisions" (Mann 1984: 113; 1986, 170; 1993, 59; 2008, 355). Infrastructural power is concerned with the "logistics" of implementation—that is "technologies" or "know hows" integral to the enforcement process—and with the territorial reach of the state. Mann did not develop his "logistics" of policy implementation in great detail, instead cursorily pointing to bureaucracy, information (for example data on earned income, allowing the state to tax effectively), as well as transportation networks as possible institutional forms of infrastructural capacity (Mann 1984, 2008). However, his insight about territorial reach as a crucial dimension of state capacity is an important conceptual advancement. Territorial reach is independent from the quality of bureaucracy, which can be high, but geographically circumscribed, meaning that in some areas rules are not enforced and services underprovided. For example, if the ability of the state to enforce the laws governing property rights is a key ingredient for economic development (North 1981; Besley and Persson 2011), consider the implications of Herbst's (2000) observation that in many African countries state authority is high in areas around the capital, but diminishes as distance from the capital increases. One of the consequences of Mann's focus on territorial reach has been an increased attention to subnational variation in territorial penetration by the state, generating a separate body of literature (Acemoglu, Garcia-Jimeno, and Robinson 2015; Acemoglu, Moscona, and Robinson 2016; Ch et al. 2018; Harbers 2015; Just Quiles 2019; Luna and Soifer 2017; Soifer 2015; Ziblatt 2008).

The most recent addition to the conceptual literature on state capacity focuses on information as its most distinctive attribute. The methodological stance at the heart of this approach is the idea that while state capacity cannot be measured directly (Hanson and Sigman 2013), the resources a state deploys can (Brambor et al. 2019). Building on James Scott's (1998) observation that the modern state relies on information to govern territory and people, several scholars put forward a conceptualization of state capacity as information resources that states deploy to achieve policy goals (Brambor et al. 2019; Lee and Zhang 2017; D'Arcy and Nistotskaya 2017; Soifer 2013). Information that provides an overview of the physical landscape of the state and of individuals and groups is crucial for policy implementation. For example, there is a cross-disciplinary consensus that systematic land surveying by the state led to efficient tax extraction (D'Arcy and Nistotskaya 2017; Kain and Baigent 1992; Nistotskaya and D'Arcy 2018; Scott 1998). Similarly, public health research acknowledges that statistics produced by civil registration and vital statistics systems provide information essential for the implementation of health promotion and disease prevention policies (Phillips et al. 2015).

In summary, there is a wide variety of definitions of state capacity, which frequently overlap with concepts such as impartiality or regime type, leading to a fragmented conceptual space and impeding the accumulation of knowledge. Bureaucratic competence, territorial reach, and informational inputs emerged as the types of capacity that states need for the successful implementation of a broad range of political decisions. They represent distinctive dimensions of state capacity without bleeding over into distinct concepts such as impartiality or democracy.

MEASURING STATE CAPACITY

Within the generalist conceptualization of state capacity, measures capturing bureaucratic quality have been most frequently used in the literature. Regarding the epistemic qualities of bureaucracy, they have been empirically captured through direct indicators such as meritocratic recruitment (Dahlström et al 2015; Evans and Rauch 1999; Geddes 1994), share of expert civil servants in the total number of bureaucrats (Bersch, Praca, and Taylor 2017), security of tenure (Cornell 2014; Nistotskaya and Cingolani 2016), or indirectly through such measures as *ICRG Bureaucratic Quality* from the International Country Risk Guide (PRS 2010) or *Government Effectiveness* from the World Bank's Worldwide Governance Indicators (WGI). Research that utilizes meritocratic recruitment as a measure of epistemic quality relies heavily on the Quality of Government Institute-generated expert-based data, the major drawbacks of which are the possible contamination of expert assessments of meritocracy in bureaucratic recruitment by other environmental factors and the lack of data over time (Dahlström et al. 2015). The availability of time-series observations makes ICRG data a preferred option for many researchers, but the multidimensional character of the measures (for example, Bureaucratic Quality pertains to professionalism, autonomy, and efficacy in delivering public goods) makes it impossible to discern the probable cause driving outcomes. The methodology of ICRG data is highly opaque, generating concerns about its validity (Bersch, Praca, and Taylor 2017; Knutsen 2013). Both ICRG and WGI have an indicator for corruption that has been widely used in the research on state capacity (Bäck and Hadenius 2008; Charron and Lapuente 2010). Recent studies that view state capacity as corruption have made use of new data-collection efforts, such as the Varieties of Democracy project (Povitkina 2018).

The lack of reliable comparative data on the organizational design and behavior of public bureaucracies has long been recognized as a "sore point" for several social science disciplines and fields within them (Lapuente and Nistotskaya 2009; Fukuyama 2013), and a concerted effort to collect such data would move the research frontier forwards. Important steps forward are being made by scholars associated with the Governance Project at Stanford University (e.g. Bersch, Praca and Taylor 2017) and a U.K. based project that surveyed civil service management practices in ten developing countries (Meyer-Sahling, Schuster, and Mikkelsen 2018). Another important effort is being made by the World Bank's Bureaucracy Lab, which harnessed large administrative data on public sector employment and wages for 115 countries for 2000–16 (World Bank 2018b).

In large-N empirical studies bureaucratic autonomy has mostly been studied in terms of the insulation of bureaucratic agents from the pressures of their political principals (Bersch, Praca, and Taylor 2017; Boräng et al. 2018; Cingolani, Thomsson, and De Crombrugghe 2015; Dahlström and Lapuente 2017; Nistotskaya and Cingolani 2016), which, as discussed above, does not solely capture the notion of state capacity, but spills over into the concept of QoG as impartiality. Bersch, Praca, and Taylor (2017) and Cingolani, Thomsson, and De Crombrugghe (2015) examined the correlation between measures of bureaucratic autonomy and state capacity, finding it to be of weak to medium strength. Furthermore, both studies found the indicators for state capacity and autonomy to have independent effects on their outcome variables—a result that calls for further scrutiny, both theoretical and empirical, of the relationships between state capacity, bureaucratic autonomy, and development.

When it comes to territorial reach, measurement has been through road density indicators (Herbst 2000), censuses (Centeno 2002; Soifer 2013), and quality of cadastral records, which involves the evaluation of the extent of spatial implementation of cadastral surveying (D'Arcy, Nistotskaya, and Ellis 2019). These measures focus on the overall presence of the state over space, rather than "the depth of the state's reach into any given location" (Soifer 2012, 588)—something that has been scrutinized in a growing literature on subnational variations in state capacity, in which scholars have experimented with such diverse indicators of territorial reach as density of salaried government officials (Bensel 1990) and post offices (Acemoglu, Moscona, and Robinson 2016) or survey-based time estimates of police reaching respondents' homes for emergency purposes (Luna and Soifer 2017).

A relatively new enterprise of measuring the information resources required for successful policy implementation has produced several indicators related to censuses. These measures capture methodology, sources and periodicity (World Bank 2018a), organizations that collect and analyze information on people (Brambor et al. 2019) and the accuracy of census data (Lee and Zhang 2017), cadasters (D'Arcy and Nistotskaya 2017) or biometrical IDs (Muralidharan, Niehaus, and Sukhtankar 2016) and other digital technology enabling implementation of policies (Cingolani 2019). Due to their high congruence with the conceptualization of state capacity as information, fungibility, (transferability from one policy area to another) and good temporal and spatial coverage, these indicators will potentially be of wide use in empirical research. Time-trends in these datasets, however, point to convergence in state capacity between countries across the most recent observations, which may make them a less sensitive indicator of state capacity for the time period since the Second World War.

A popular approach to measuring state capacity is through policy outputs and outcomes. One of the most popular indicators here is tax revenue[5] (Besley and Persson 2010, 2011;

---

[5] Most often operationalized as per capita or in relation to GDP, but also as tax effort, which is tax collected over the expected tax revenue, given the underlying productivity of the economy.

Dincecco and Katz 2016; Ziblatt 2008), which some argue is "the most valid general measure of state capacity" (Andersen et al. 2014: 1310) or even *sine qua non* (Hendrix 2010, 283). State capacity has also been measured as life expectancy (DeRouen and Bercovitch 2008), school enrollment (Migdal 1988), or crime rates (Soifer 2012). As argued above, such indicators conflate extant political preferences for the size of the state/scope of redistribution (policy effect) with implementation (capacity effect), thereby impeding a meaningful evaluation of their independent effects. While scholars are paying more attention to the issue of concept-measure congruence, many measures employed in empirical research still exhibit a large gap between the theoretical construct and the indicator used to operationalize it. Perhaps an even greater threat to inference comes from the fact that measures do not discern be-tween competing mechanisms. For example, meritocracy in bureaucratic recruitment has been linked to economic development through increased bureaucratic competence and also bureaucratic cohesion (Evans and Rauch 1999), however it is also plausibly connected to economic development through a competing causal channel—impartiality (Miller 2000; Nistotskaya and Cingolani 2016).

Sequencing Debate

This section reviews the so-called sequencing debate, which addresses the question: Can the state expand its power under the constraint of democratic institutions? And thus, is a strong state necessary prior to democratization? The roots of this debate lie in Huntington's (1968) observation that countries going through the Third Wave of democratization were following a reverse sequence to that which unfolded in the West historically: While Western states were strong before democratization, most contemporary developing countries democra-tize at low levels of state capacity. This insight spurred rich theoretical and normative debate focused on the relationship between state capacity and democratization a) in the West and b) in the contemporary developing world. While there is agreement that a strong state is neces-sary for democracy itself to consolidate, there is much less consensus about whether democ-racy is essential to or a barrier for state-building. Overall, this literature has been dominated by polarization and has not yet fully harnessed the advancements in the state capacity litera-ture discussed above.

Within the literature on Western institutional development, some have seen the emer-gence of proto-democratic institutions as a consequence of state-building processes in the early modern period. During this period states acquired capacity, particular in terms of co-ercion and extraction (Dincecco 2011; Tilly 1990). The expansion of state power under the pressures of warfare incentivized some powerful societal actors to bargain with rulers over revenue, leading to the establishment of representative institutions (Levi 1989; Tilly 1990). Neo-institutionalists extended this perspective by arguing that concessions made by rulers strengthened fiscal capacity through increased consent to pay taxes and rulers' access to credit, which had implications for long-term economic development (North and Weingast 1989). Although this theoretical perspective, with its emphasis on credible commitment and executive constraints, is often employed to argue for the necessity of democratic institutions for development (Knutsen 2011), its origins lie in a historical sequence in which these constraints emerge *in response* to state strength (Boucoyannis 2015). It is important to note that during the early modern period representative institutions represented a narrow section of the population whose motivations were focused on the defense of their own economic interests.

After the establishment of centralized political power, the monopoly on coercion, and a degree of state capacity, the institutional development of Western countries in the nineteenth century focused on quality of government matters—such as improvements in bureaucratic quality—and the institutions of mass democracy. There are sequencing arguments relating to this specific phase of institutional development. Some argue that where the establishment of a Weberian bureaucracy preceded mass democratization, programmatic rather than clientelist parties emerged and, consequently, the scope of welfare was broader (Skocpol 1992; Kamens 1986; Shefter 1994). This scenario is observed in many European states (Flora and Alber 1981), but not in the United States, where democratization preceded the emergence of QoG, especially in terms of Weberian bureaucracy. Consequently, welfare provision became part of the system of political clientelism, making its benefits partisan and generating resistance to its expansion (Hacker 1998). Others argue that some democratic institutions that emerged in this period also bolstered state capacity: For example, the extension of suffrage stimulated the state to gather more information on the population (Brambor et al. 2019). In sum, where democratic institutions emerged in a context of high state capacity and quality of government this paved the way for broader public goods provision.

Although this evolution is neither uniform nor linear, it has provided the empirical grounding for the central theoretical assertions of the "state-first" literature: a) state capacity and democracy are conceptually distinct and b) as they are interrelated but not mutually dependent historical processes, there is an inherent tension between state-building and democracy. Exemplifying the first point, Rose and Shin (2001, 333) argued that "democracy is not a necessary attribute of the modern state, as is shown by the absolutist character of the initial modern states, monarchical France and Prussia." State capacity developed in many countries in the absence of democracy, and the emergence of democratic institutions was not an inevitable outcome of state-building, as the case of Germany exemplifies. This point is taken a step further by Fukuyama (2007, 2014) who argues that state capacity and democracy are not only distinct but in tension. He sees state-building as being fundamentally about "the concentration of the means of coercion," while "both liberal rule of law and democracy, by contrast, involve limiting the central state's authority to coerce," which causes problems for state-building because "stable states must often be constructed through violent means" (2007, 11). The focus on these inherent tensions highlights the importance of sequencing: "state, law and accountability can impede one another's development … this is why the sequence in which institutions were introduced becomes important" (Fukuyama 2014: 534).

As democratic institutions spread in the twentieth and twenty-first centuries to parts of the world with different formal and informal institutions and levels of economic development than the West, the issue of institutional sequencing—state first, then democracy or vice versa—has been the subject of intense debate. On the one hand, there are those who identify in the contemporary developing world the axiom of the historical literature: Consolidation of democracy requires a functioning state. This perspective explains many of the political pathologies of developing countries—especially corruption, poor public goods provision, and the risk of conflict—in terms of the interactive effects of democratizing at low levels of state capacity. However, there are also those who reject the "state first" argument and see democracy as a complementary or even necessary condition for state-building.

Most of the literature considers democracy as the outcome variable and examines the effects of state capacity on the quality of democracy, with many arguing that "no modern polity can become democratically consolidated unless it is first a state" (Linz and Stepan (1996, 7). At the most basic level, a certain degree of state capacity is required to run free and fair elections (Slater 2008; Piccolino 2016). With capacity, the state can provide rule of law and the public goods needed to cement its authority and consolidate democratic institutions (Fortin 2012; Møller and Skaaning 2011). Without capacity, politicians and voters often choose clientelist strategies as a substitute for the public goods that the state cannot adequately provide (Kitschelt and Wilkenson 2007). This then further erodes state capacity and also QoG, making consolidation of democracy more difficult. In the worst cases, it leads politicians to resort to nationalist mobilization and even war (Mansfield and Snyder 2007a). Overall, this literature argues that a certain degree of stateness is a prerequisite for successful democratic consolidation and that, much as it did in the nineteenth-century West, state capacity mediates the quality of democracy.

In contrast to this literature, there are those who argue that higher state capacity actually inhibits democratization. A history of early statehood influenced patterns of colonial settlement, with strong states better able to resist and therefore less likely to experience institutional transfer through settlers (Hariri 2012). The ability to use coercive force to repress is seen as a key factor in stabilizing authoritarian regimes in the Arab world (Bellin 2012). In Southeast Asia, united elites with shared incentives to strengthen the state are better able to resist popular pressures for reform (Slater 2010).

The literature that has taken democratization as an independent variable and considered its effect on state capacity and quality of government has been the subject of heated debate. While many scholars emphasize the need for state-building first, especially for post-conflict and otherwise "weak" states (Fearon and Laitin 2004; Fukuyama 2004a, 2004b, 2004c, 2007; Mansfield and Snyder 1995, 2007a, 2007b; Krasner 2004), this position was subjected to intense critique—see the exchange in the Journal of Democracy (Carothers 2007a, 2007b; Fukuyama 2007; Mansfield and Snyder 2007b).

The arguments in support of the "state first" position have pointed to the adverse effects of democracy on the quality of government in particular. For example, evidence from panel cross-country data suggests that bureaucratic quality suffers in young democracies (Bäck and Hadenius 2008). Explanations of this so-called J-shaped relationship have focused on "democratization" of the patronage networks that often follow the introduction of competitive elections (Cheeseman 2015; D'Arcy and Cornell 2016); the escalating effects this has on campaign spending and thus the incentives this creates for graft between election cycles (Cheeseman 2015; Lindberg 2003); and the new elite-ruler dynamics that pave the way for corruption as a means of cementing intra-elite alliances (D'Arcy 2015).

The second line of research considers the inherent tensions between democratization and state capacity. Here, the portrayal of governance as a series of collective action problems (Mansbridge 2014) revealed the magnitude of challenges faced by democratic governments in low capacity states. In order to effectively solve large-scale collective action problems, governments have to be "credible enforcers" of collective agreements (D'Arcy and Nistotskaya 2017). For example, in order to fund public goods and services, governments have to compel citizens to pay their tax obligations—something that high capacity states do through enumeration of taxpayers (Lee and Zhang 2017; Scott 1989) and their economic assets (Nistotskaya and D'Arcy 2018). When state capacity is low and government is not a "credible enforcer," individual rational strategy is to free ride. This means that in order to govern for the benefit of people, governments have to override such preferences. However, as democratic government is, per definition, reflective of citizens' preferences, democracy impedes its ability to override the welfare-undermining preferences of citizens. In other words, democracy before state capacity traps polities in a suboptimal equilibrium where citizens have weak incentives to comply and government cannot legitimately force citizens to comply.

However, some scholars argue that democracy bears no negative consequences for state capacity and see the two processes as mutually reinforcing. Many authors see democratic institutions and processes as essential for fighting corruption (Hollyer, Rosendorff, and Vreeland 2011; Kolstad and Wiig 2016); for increasing the legitimacy of the state and thus levels of voluntary compliance (Bratton and Chang 2006; Mazzuca and Munck 2014; Carbone and Memoli 2015); and as impetus for the expansion of state capacity through requirements for voter registration (Brambor et al. 2019) and the need to build mass parties (Slater 2010). To put it shortly, democracy is seen as "a meta-institution for building good institutions" (Rodrik 2000, 3).

While there is broad agreement on the historical evolution of the West, the debate on the implications of different sequences for development in the contemporary period is at an impasse. Critics of the "state first" perspective are correct to resist a teleological reasoning derived from the particular history of the West. However, they are too quick to dismiss the highly suggestive evidence of this historical record and the valid questions raised about the compatibility of democracy and state-building given the inherent tension of the "Janus-faced" state. Given its polarization, the literature could be more fruitfully progressed 1) by accepting that this tension exists and that there may be a number of sequences leading to development, and 2) by investigating these sequences using the refined concepts and measures of state capacity discussed in the previous section.

State Capacity and Development Outcomes: Empirical Evidence

Recent decades have seen the proliferation of empirical research on the effects of state capacity. This section discusses the empirical literature that has examined its role in achieving important development outcomes, including economic development and the provision of public goods and services (see the chapter by Deglow and Fjelde in this volume reviewing state capacity's impact on internal conflict). Table 36.1 provides a review of the most important studies.

Table 36.1 State capacity and developmental outcomes: Main studies

Author	Data and scope	Conceptualization of state capacity	Measurement of state capacity	Outcome Variable	Main Findings
Economic Development					
Evans and Rauch 1999	Cross-sectional 1970–90 averages 35 less developed countries	Bureaucratic quality	Meritocratic recruitment	GDPpc growth	Positive relationships
Besley and Persson 2010, 2011	Cross-sectional Global	Fiscal and legal capacities	Fiscal: trade or trade & indirect taxes/ total tax, income taxes/GDP; total taxes/GDP Legal: private credit/GDP; ease of acess to credit (collateral & bankruptcy laws, credit information index, public credit registry coverage, private credit bureau coverage); investor protection (transparency of transactions, liability for self-dealing, shareholders can sue for misconduct).	Economic growth, efficient production	Formal model of the link between state capacity and the outcomes, correlation between state capacity and GDPpc
Knutsen 2013	Panel 1984–2004 sub-Saharan Africa and globally	Bureaucratic quality (autonomy)	ICRG Bureaucratic Quality and State Antiquity Index	GDPpc growth	When state capacity is low, democracy matters
Dincecco and Katz 2016	Panel 1650–1913 11 European countries	Fiscal centralization	Government revenue pc and nonmilitary expenditure pc	GDPpc growth	Positive direct relationships
Acemoglu et al. 2016	Panel 1804–99 U.S. counties	Territorial reach (implicitly)	Density of post offices	GDPpc growth	Positive relationships

(continued)

Table 36.1 Continued

Author	Data and scope	Conceptualization of state capacity	Measurement of state capacity	Outcome Variable	Main Findings
Nistotskaya and Cingolani 2016	Cross-country and panel time: various countries (global)	Bureaucratic competence	Mritocratic recruitement, security of tenure	Enterpreneurship rates	Positive relationships
Public Goods Provision					
Acemoglu et al 2015	Cross-section c.1000 municipalities of Colombia	Territorial reach	Number of government agencies, number of national-level and municipal-level employees	Life quality, public unitilities coverage, poverty, primary, and secondary enrollment rate, vaccination coverage	State capacity is a first-order determinant of current prosperity
Cingolani et al. 2015	Panel 1990–2010 158 countries	Bureaucratic autonomy	Bureaucratic Autonomy Index (BAI), capturing early termination of the contracts of central bankers in countries where such officials enjoy formal fixed-term tenure	Child mortality and tuberculosis prevalence	Stronger impact of BAI than other measures of state capacity
Hanson 2015	Panel 1965–2010 162 countries	Territorial reach	State Antiquity Index and census frequency	Secondary school enrollment and infant mortality	Once accounting for state capacity, democracy leads to better development outcomes
D'Arcy and Nistotskaya 2017	Cross-section democracies	Territorial reach, information	Cadastral records	Index of quality of 11 public services, quality of primary education, PISA scores, infant mortality	States that democritized at higher levels of state capacity produce better public goods
Brieba 2018	1960–present case study (Chile and Argentina)	Bureaucratic quality and territorial reach	Territorial reach, homogenity, and quality of health bureaucracies	Infant and maternal mortality	Chile achieved a "reversal of fortune" compared to Argentina, and also markedly brought down territorial inequalities

Economic Development

The main portrayal of the state in the economic growth literature is of a "malevolent Janus." Since North (1981) the dominant narratives have been concerned with the extent to which powerholders are constrained in their own predatory tendencies to confiscate private property or to renege on sovereign debt, and scholars have examined the role of constraints on powerholders (credible commitment effect) on both the "input" (Acemoglu, Johnson, and Robinsson 2001; North and Weingast 1989) and "output" side of politics (Miller 2000; Nistotskaya and Cingolani 2016). Meanwhile, the New Institutional Economic account of development also emphasizes clear property rights and contract enforcement as important predictors, which intrinsically embraces the notion of state capacity (Besley and Persson 2011; North 1981; Weingast 1995). Johnson and Koyama (2017) and Dincecco (2018) provide a good review of the "capacity" and "constraints" mechanisms through which sustained economic growth is achieved.

The empirical literature, however, has not reached the same clarity, often not being able to separate between "capacity" and "constraints" mechanisms. For example, PRS's *Risk of Expropriation and Repudiation of Government Contracts* has been employed both as a measure of constraints on powerholders (Acemoglu et al. 2001) and as a measure of state capacity (Fearon 2005). Similarly, some measures of fiscal and legal capacities in Besley and Persson (2010, 2011) do not uniquely measure state capacity (for example, investor protection), thereby precluding the interpretation of the findings exclusively in terms of state capacity effects.

Consequently, there are only a few empirical studies that have examined the role of state capacity without conflating it, either theoretically or empirically, with the "constraints" argument. One of those is by Dincecco and Katz (2016), in which they explore the impact of both state capacity, proxied through tax revenue per capita, and constraints, measured as the existence of parliament, on economic growth in 11 European countries over 250 years. Similarly, Acemoglu, Moscona, and Robinson (2016) measure state capacity through the presence of post offices across U.S. counties (thereby alluding to Mann's (1984) idea of territorial reach, although providing no explanation of the concept behind their key explanatory variable), finding positive relationships between the density of post offices and subsequent economic development.

There is also a literature that explores the association between bureaucratic quality and economic outcomes. In their seminal article, Evans and Rauch (1999) make a commendable effort to separate capacity from outcomes by assessing (with the help of expert knowledge) a number of organizational features of bureaucratic units responsible for economic policy in 35 less developed countries. They found robust associations between the extent of meritocratic recruitment and economic growth, pointing to a number of capacity-related causal paths: competence, organizational cohesion (*esprit de corps*) and institutionalization of the professional criteria for success. Knutsen (2013) makes a point to distinguish between regime type and state capacity, and finds in the context of sub-Saharan countries that in low-capacity states democracy has a substantial positive effect on growth, while in high-capacity states, the type of regime does not matter. However, the adopted conceptualization (bureaucratic quality) and its operationalization (ICRG Bureaucratic Quality) do not convincingly attribute the discovered empirical link to the "capacity" argument. Conceptually, Knutsen's (2013, 2) bureaucratic quality, which is "independent, rule-following bureaucratic apparatus," is much closer to Rothstein and Teorell's (2008) concept of QoG as impartiality than to any conceptualizations of state capacity. Therefore, a better interpretation of Knutsen's results is not that of state capacity matters, but that "constraints" on the "output" side of politics matter more than those on the "input" side. Finally, Nistotskaya, and Cingolani (2016) argue that merit-based bureaucracies promote economic development both through the "capacity" effect (improved epistemic qualities) and "constraints" effect. They report supporting empirical evidence from cross-sectional and panel data, but to further substantiate this claim indicators that would capture competence and impartiality in meritocratic bureaucracies separately are needed.

Public goods provision

The literature that examines the link between state capacity and public goods provision has recently advanced through engaging with the conceptual literature on state capacity using formal modeling, novel measures, and sophisticated empirical analysis, both quantitative and qualitative, to examine the relationship (Acemoglu, Garcia-Jimeno, and Robinson 2015; Brieba 2018; Cingolani, Thomsson, and Denis De Crombrugghe 2015; D'Arcy and Nistotskaya 2017; Hanson 2015). Acemoglu, Garcia-Jimeno, and Robinson (2015, 2364) study the impact of state capacity, explicitly conceptualized as "the presence of state functionaries and agencies," on public goods provision in Colombian municipalities. Theoretically, the focus of their inquiry is the spillovers that municipalities create on their neighbors, which is formally modeled. Empirically, the authors leverage cross-sectional data on the number of national- and municipal-level employees and government agencies against six measures of public goods provision and employ a wide range of estimation techniques to conclude that "local state presence is indeed a first-order determinant of current prosperity" (Acemoglu, Garcia-Jimeno, and Robinson 2015, 2405). Similarly to Knutsen (2013), Hanson's (2015) main aim is to evaluate regime type and state capacity effects independently and in interaction. Hanson adopts the territorial reach conceptualization of state capacity and shows that once state capacity is accounted for, democracy leads to higher secondary school enrollment and low child mortality. Cingolani, Thomsson, and Denis De Crombrugghe (2015) examine the independent effects of state capacity and bureaucratic autonomy—which is defined as nonalignment of bureaucratic and political cycles, and therefore is close to the idea of constraints on powerholders through some organizational forms of bureaucracy (Miller 2000). Using a novel measure of bureaucratic autonomy, they find that it has a larger impact on several important public goods than several measures of capacity. In other words, the study shows that "constraints" outperform "capacity." D'Arcy and Nistotskaya (2017) argue that state capacity, conceptualized in terms of territorial reach and information resources, facilitates legibility of people and their economic resources, which is key for solving the collective action problems at the heart of public goods production. They use a novel measure on the quality of cadastral records to show that countries that had higher levels of accumulated state capacity at the moment of democratization perform better in terms of public goods provision today.

The work of Brieba (2018) is an example of careful empirical work on the link between state capacity and infant and maternal mortality, using cross-case comparison of Chile and Argentina and within-case process tracing over a period of 50 years. Brieba shows that both countries had fairly similar policy priorities, but different economic and regime type conditions, which should have favored Argentina. He also shows that the two countries are markedly different in terms of investment into public health bureaucracies and that the better educated, more adherent to standard protocols of services and territorially omnipresent health bureaucracy of Chile eventually manages to reverse the country's fortune in terms of mother and child mortality. Brieba's (2018) paper is important in unpacking the specific mechanism with high-resolution evidence and showing that investment in state capacity can be made in relatively poor countries and that the return on investment can be expected within a relatively short period of time.

Conclusion

Despite a growing consensus that state capacity refers to the logistics of implementation of political decisions, the conceptual space remains fragmented and conceptual stretching persists. Concept-measure congruence is often compromised and the same measure is used in references to different conceptualizations of state capacity or no conceptualization at all, generating no payoff for knowledge accumulation. The literature, however, has moved away from excessively generic measures of state capacity (such as GDPpc) and is increasingly critical about the usefulness of output-based measures. Measuring state capacity accurately remains a formidable challenge, both in terms of getting better data (for example, on bureaucratic structures), but also in terms of coming up with innovative measurements. However, the emergence of detailed time-series data on censuses, cadastral records, biometric smart cards, and other technologies suggests that this is not impossible. There has also been considerable progress in terms of subnational data and research, but there is plenty of room for improvement in this subfield, which is a clear avenue for future research.

There have also been important developments on the theoretical front. The days of research that only examines a broad link between state capacity and outcome without postulating the specific mechanisms through which the causal influence operates are coming to a close. The literature has advanced a number of theoretical accounts, explicating the association between state capacity and economic development, civil war, public goods provision, and consolidation of democracy. However, there are only a few empirical studies that have examined the "capacity" effect without conflating it, either theoretically or empirically, with the "constraints" effect, be it on the "input" (democracy) or "output" (impartiality) sides of the political process. This is a major challenge and also an apparent avenue for future research. Without clarity in these matters it will remain hard for practitioners to draw policy lessons from this literature. There is also a need for qualitative research that brings high-resolution evidence, from which the policy community can extract specific "know hows" pertaining to the "logistics" of implementation.

The concept of state capacity came into being as an analytical tool to help us understand the mechanisms of development. While there is general agreement that this is a highly potent tool, evidenced by the fact that state capacity is routinely considered, at the least, as a control variable in comparative research on development outcomes, it is still not at its optimum, particularly with regard to conceptualization, measurement, and causal mechanisms. The conceptual literature on state capacity has yet to explicitly engage with the scholarship on symbolic power (Bourdier 1991; Loveman 2005), something that presents itself as an obvious avenue for future research. The lack of reliable comparative data on the organizational design and behavior of public bureaucracies has long been recognized as a "sore point" for several social science disciplines and fields within them (Lapuente and Nistotskaya 2009; Fukuyama 2013), and a concerted effort to collect such data would move the research frontier forwards. More fine-grained measures would then enable better investigation of mechanisms. For example, since it is conceivable that noncorrupt and autonomous bureaucracies are attributes of both high capacity and high QoG states, more work is needed to illuminate the specific causal paths through which these properties improve the implementational capacities of states and those through which they increase impartiality. The literature on the sequencing debate could further benefit from cross-pollination from the increasingly sophisticated conceptualizations and measures of state capacity. With engagement from scholars from different disciplines, the research frontier on state capacity has advanced, and demonstrated the field's own capacity to address its challenges.

REFERENCES

Acemoglu, Daron, Simon Johnson, and James Robinson. 2001. "The Colonial Origins of Comparative Development: An Empirical Investigation." *American Economic Review* 91 (5): 1369–401.

Acemoglu, Daron, Jacob Moscona, and James Robinson. 2016. "State Capacity and American Technology: Evidence from the Nineteenth Century." *The American Economic Review* 196 (5): 61–7.

Acemoglu, Daron, Camilo Garcia-Jimeno, and James Robinson. 2015. "State Capacity and Economic Development: A Network Approach." *American Economic Review* 105 (8): 2364–409.

Andersen, David, Jørgen Møller, Lasse Rørbæk, and Svend-Erik Skaaning. 2014. "State Capacity and Political Regime Stability." *Democratization* 21 (7): 1305–25.

Becker, Gary, Edward Lazear, and Kevin Murphy. 2003. "The Double Benefit of Tax Cuts." *The Wall Street Journal*, October 7, 2003. https://www.wsj.com/articles/SB106548881712135300

Bellin, Eva. 2012. "Reconsidering the Robustness of Authoritarianism in the Middle East: Lessons from the Arab Spring." *Comparative Politics* 44 (2): 127–49.

Bensel, Richard. 1990. *Yankee Leviathan: The Origins of Central State Authority in America, 1859–1877.* Cambridge: Cambridge University Press.

Bersch, Katherine, Sergio Praca, and Mattew Taylor. 2017. "Bureaucratic Capacity and Political Autonomy within National States: Mapping the Archipelago of Excellence in Brazil." In *States in the Developing World*, edited by Miguel Centeno, Atul Kohli, and Deborah Yashar, 157–83. Cambridge: Cambridge University Press.

Berwick, Elissa, and Fotini Christia. 2018. "State Capacity Redux: Integrating Classical and Experimental Contributions to an Enduring Debate." *Annual Review of Political Science* 21: 71–91.

Besley, Timothy, and Torsten Persson. 2011. *Pillars of Prosperity: The Political Economics of Development Clusters.* Princeton: Princeton University Press.

Besley, Timothy, and Torsten Persson. 2010. "State Capacity, Conflict, and Development." *Econometrica* 78 (1): 1–34.

Boräng, Frida, Agnes Cornell, Marcia Grimes, and Christian Schuster. 2018. "Cooking the Books: Bureaucratic Politicization and Policy Knowledge." *Governance* 31 (1): 7–26

Boucoyannis, Deborah. 2015. "No Taxation of Elites, No Representation: State Capacity and the Origins of Representation." *Politics & Society* 43 (3): 303–32.

Bourdieu, Pierre. 1991. *Language and Symbolic Power*. Cambridge: Cambridge University Press.

Brambor, Thomas, Agustín Goenaga, Johannes Lindvall, and Jan Teorell. 2019. "The Lay of the Land: Information Capacity and the Modern State." *Comparative Political Studies* advance online publication. https://doi.org/10.1177/0010414019843432

Bratton, Michael, and Eric Chang. 2006. "State Building and Democratization in Sub-Saharan Africa: Forwards, Backwards, or Together?" *Comparative Political Studies* 39 (9): 1059–83.

Brieba, Daniel. 2018. "State Capacity and Health Outcomes: Comparing Argentina's and Chile's Reduction of Infant and Maternal Mortality, 1960–2013." *World Development* 101: 37–53.

Bäck, Hanna and Alexis Hadenius. 2008. "Democracy and State Capacity: Exploring a J-Shaped Relationship." *Governance* 21 (1): 1–24.

Carbone, Giovanni, and Vincenzo Memoli. 2015. "Does Democratization Foster State Consolidation? Democratic Rule, Political Order, and Administrative Capacity." *Governance* 28 (1): 5–24.

Carothers, Thomas. 2007a. "How Democracies Emerge: The 'Sequencing' Fallacy." *Journal of Democracy* 18 (1): 12–27.

Carothers, Thomas. 2007b. "Misunderstanding Gradualism." *Journal of Democracy* 18 (3): 18–22.

Centeno, Miguel. 2002. *Blood and Debt: War and the Nation-State in Latin America*. University Park, PA: Penn State Press.

Centeno, Miguel, Atul Kohli, and Deborah Yashar. 2017. "Unpacking States in the Developing World: Capacity. Performance, and Politics." In *States in the Developing World*, edited by Miguel Centeno, Atul Kohli, and Deborah Yashar,1–32. Cambridge: Cambridge University Press.

Ch, Rafael, Jacob Shapiro, Abbey Steele, and Juan Vargas. 2018. "Endogenous Taxation in Ongoing Internal Conflict: The Case of Colombia." *American Political Science Review* 112 (4): 996–1015.

Charron, Nicholas, and Victor Lapuente. 2010. "Does Democracy Produce Quality of Government?" *European Journal of Political Research* 49 (4): 443–70.

Cheeseman, Nic. 2015. *Democracy in Africa: Successes, Failures, and the Struggle for Political Reform*. Cambridge: Cambridge University Press.

Cingolani, Luciana. 2019. "Digital State Capacities: The Impact of Fiscal Digital Technology on Tax Performance in Europe." Paper presented at the workshop *State Capacity Research: Advancing Conceptual and Methodological Frontier*. Gothenburg, June 10–11.

Cingolani, Luciana, Kaj Thomsson, and Denis De Crombrugghe. 2015. "Minding Weber more than Ever: The Impacts of State Capacity and Bureaucratic Autonomy on Development Goals." *World Development* 72: 191–207.

Cole, Wade. 2015. "Mind the Gap: State Capacity and the Implementation of Human Rights Treaties." *International Organization* 69: 405–41.

Cornell, Agnes. 2014. "Why Bureaucratic Stability Matters for the Implementation of Democratic Governance Programs." *Governance* 27 (2): 191–214.

Dahlström, Carl, and Victor Lapuente. 2017. *Organizing Leviathan: Politicians, Bureaucrats, and the Making of Good Government*. Cambridge: Cambridge University Press.

Dahlström, Carl, Jan Teorell, Stefan Dahlberg, Felix Hartmann, Annika Lindberg, and Marina Nistotskaya. 2015. *The QoG Expert Survey Dataset II*. University of Gothenburg: The Quality of Government Institute.

D'Arcy, Michelle. 2015. "Rulers and Their Elite Rivals: How Democratization Has Increased Incentives for Corruption in Sub-Saharan Africa." In *Elites, Institutions and the Quality of Government*, edited by Carl Dahlström and Lena Wängnerud, 111–27. London: Palgrave Macmillan.

D'Arcy, Michelle, and Agnes Cornell. 2016. "Devolution and Corruption in Kenya: Everyone's Turn to Eat?" *African Affairs* 115 (459): 246–73.

D'Arcy, Michelle, and Marina Nistotskaya. 2017. "State First, Then Democracy: Using Cadastral Records to Explain Governmental Performance in Public Goods Provision." *Governance* 30 (2): 193–209.

D'Arcy, Michelle, Marina Nistotskaya, and Robert Ellis. 2019. "Mapping the State: Measuring Infrastructural Power through Cadastral Records." *Proceedings of the International Federation of Surveyors' Working Week*. Hanoi, April. https://www.fig.net/resources/proceedings/fig_proceedings/fig2019/papers/ts04j/TS04J_nistotskaya_darcy_et_al_9784.pdf

Deng, Kent. 2015. "Imperial China Under the Song and Late Imperial Qing." In *Fiscal Regimes and the Political Economy of Premodern States*, edited by Andrew Monson and Walter Scheidel, 308–42. Cambridge: Cambridge University Press.

DeRouen, Karl, and Jacob Bercovitch. 2008. "Enduring Internal Rivalries: A New Framework for the Study of Civil War." *Journal of Peace Research* 45 (1): 55–74.

DeRouen, Karl, and David Sobek. 2004. "The Dynamics of Civil War Duration and Outcome." *Journal of Peace Research* 41 (3): 303–20.

Dincecco, Mark. 2018. *State Capacity and Economic Development: Present and Past*. Cambridge: Cambridge University Press.

Dincecco, Mark. 2011. *Political transformations and public finances: Europe, 1650–1913*. Cambridge: Cambridge University Press.

Dincecco, Mark, and Gabriel Katz. 2016. "State Capacity and Long-run Economic Performance." *The Economic Journal* 126 (590): 189–218.

Evans, Peter, and James Rauch. 1999. "Bureaucracy and Growth: A Cross-National Analysis of the Effects of 'Weberian' State Structures on Economic Growth." *American Sociological Review* 64 (5): 748–65.

Fearon, James. 2005. "Primary Commodity Exports and Civil War." *Journal of Conflict Resolution* 49 (4): 483–507.

Fearon, James. 1999. "Electoral Accountability and the Control of Politicians: Selecting Good Types versus Sanctioning Poor Performance." In *Democracy, Accountability, and Representation*, edited by Adam Przeworski, Susan Stokes, and Bernard Manin. 55–97. New York: Cambridge University Press.

Fearon, James, and David Laitin. 2004. "Neotrusteeship and the Problem of Weak States." *International security* 28 (4): 5–43.

Fearon, James, and David Laitin. 2003. "Ethnicity, Insurgency, and Civil War." *American Political Science Review* 97 (1): 75–90.

Flora, Peter, and Jens Alber. 1981. "Modernization, Democratization, and the Development of Welfare States in Western Europe." In *The Development of Welfare State in Europe and America*, edited by Peter Flora and Albert Heidenheimer, 37–80. New Brunswick: Transaction Books.

Fortin, Jessica. 2012. "Is There a Necessary Condition for Democracy? The Role of State Capacity in Postcommunist Countries." *Comparative Political Studies* 45 (7): 903–30.

Friedman, Milton. 2003. "What Every American Wants." *The Wall Street Journal*, January 15, 2003. https://www.wsj.com/articles/SB10425937967041880064

Fukuyama, Francis. 2014. *Political Order and Political Decay: From the Industrial Revolution to the Globalization of Democracy*. New York: Macmillan.

Fukuyama, Francis. 2013. "What is Governance?" *Governance* 26 (3): 347–68.

Fukuyama, Francis. 2007. "Exchange: Liberalism versus State-Building." *Journal of Democracy* 18 (3): 10–13.

Fukuyama, Francis. 2004a. *State-Building: Governance and World Order in the 21st Century*. Ithaca, NY: Cornell University Press.

Fukuyama, Francis. 2004b. "The Imperative of State-Building." *Journal of Democracy* 15 (2): 17–31.

Fukuyama, Francis. 2004c. "Stateness First." *Journal of Democracy* 16 (1): 84–8.

Geddes, Barbara. 1994. *Politician's Dilemma: Building State Capacity in Latin America*. Oakland: University of California Press.

Hacker, Jacob. 1998. "The Historical Logic of National Health Insurance: Structure and Sequence in the Development of British, Canadian, and US Medical Policy." *Studies in American Political Development* 12 (1): 57–130.

Hanson, Jonathan. 2015. "Democracy and State Capacity: Complements or Substitutes." *Studies in Comparative International Development* 50 (3): 304–30.

Hanson, Jonathan, and Rachel Sigman. 2013. "Leviathan's Latent Dimensions: Measuring State Capacity for Comparative Political Research." Unpublished manuscript. https://papers.ssrn.com/sol3/papers.cfm?abstract_id=1899933

Harbers, Imke. 2015. "Taxation and Unequal Reach of the State: Mapping State Capacity in Ecuador." *Governance* 28 (3): 373–91.

Hariri, Jacob Gerner. 2012. "The Autocratic Legacy of Early Statehood." *American Political Science Review* 106 (3): 471–94.

Hendrix, Cullen. 2010. "Measuring State Capacity: Theoretical and Empirical Implications for the Study of Civil Conflict." *Journal of Peace Research* 47 (3): 273–85.

Herbst, Jeffrey. 2000. *States and Power in Africa: Comparative Lessons in Authority and Control*. Princeton: Princeton University Press.

Hollyer, James, Peter Rosendorff, and James Vreeland. 2011. "Democracy and Transparency." *The Journal of Politics* 73 (4): 1191–205.

Huntington, Samuel. 1968. *Political Order in Changing Societies*. New Haven: Yale University Press.

Just Quiles, Marco. 2019. *Fragmented State Capacity External Dependencies, Subnational Actors, and Local Public Services in Bolivia*. Wiesbaden: Springer.

Johnson, Noel, and Mark Koyama. 2017. "States and Economic Growth: Capacity and Constraints." *Explorations in Economic History* 64: 1–20.

Kain, Roger, and Elizabeth Baigent. 1992. *The Cadastral Map in the Service of the State—A History of Property Mapping*. Chicago: University of Chicago Press.

Kamens, David. 1986. "The Importance of Historical Sequencing: Party Legitimacy in the United States and Europe." *Comparative Social Research* 9: 331–45.

Kitschelt, Herbert, and Steven Wilkinson. 2007. *Patrons, Clients and Policies: Patterns of Democratic Accountability and Political Competition*. Cambridge: Cambridge University Press.

Kolstad, Ivar, and Arne Wiig. 2016. "Does Democracy Reduce Corruption?" *Democratization* 23 (7): 1198–215.

Knutsen, Carl-Henrik. 2013. "Democracy, State Capacity, and Economic growth." *World Development* 43: 1–18.

Knutsen, Carl-Henrik. 2011. "Democracy, Dictatorship and Protection of Property Rights." *The Journal of Development Studies* 47 (1): 164–82.

Kocher, Matthew. 2010. "State Capacity as a Conceptual Variable." *Yale Journal of International Affairs* 5 (2): 137–45.

Krasner, Stephen. 2004. "Sharing Sovereignty: New Institutions for Collapsed and Failing States." *International security* 29 (2): 85–120.

Lapuente, Victor, and Marina Nistotskaya. 2009. "To the Short-Sighted Victor Belong the Spoils: Politics and Merit Adoption in Comparative Perspective." *Governance* 22 (3): 431–58.

Lee, Melissa, and Nan Zhang. 2017. "Legibility and the Informational Foundations of State Capacity." *Journal of Politics* 79 (1): 118–32.

Levi, Margaret. 1989. *Of Rule and Revenue.* Oakland, CA: University of California Press.

Lindberg, Staffan. 2003. "'It's Our Time to 'Chop': Do Elections in Africa Feed Neo-Patrimonialism rather than Counter-Act It?" *Democratization* 10 (2): 121–40.

Linz, Juan, and Alfred Stepan. 1996. *Problems of Democratic Transition and Consolidation: Southern Europe, South America, and Post-Communist Europe.* Washington DC: Johns Hopkins University Press.

Loveman, Mara. 2005. "The Modern State and the Primitive Accumulation of Power." *American Journal of Sociology* 110 (6): 1651–83.

Luna, Juan Publo, and Hillel Soifer. 2017. "Capturing Sub-National Variation in State Capacity: A Survey-based Approach." *American Behavioral Scientist* 61 (8): 887–907.

Mann, Michael. 2008. "Infrastructural Power Revisited." *Studies in Comparative International Development* 43 (3): 355–65.

Mann, Michael. 1993. *The Sources of Social Power: The Rise of Classes and Nation-States, 1760–1914.* Cambridge: Cambridge University Press.

Mann, Michael. 1986. *The Sources of Social Power: A History of Power from the Beginning to AD 1760.* Cambridge: Cambridge University Press.

Mann, Michael. 1984. "The Autonomous Power of the State: Its Origins, Mechanisms and Results." *European Journal of Sociology* 25 (2): 185–213.

Mansbridge, Jane. 2014 "What Is Political Science for?" *Perspectives on Politics* 12 (1): 8–17.

Mansfield, Edward, and Jack Snyder. 2007a. *Electing to Fight: Why Emerging Democracies Go to War.* Cambridge, MA: MIT Press.

Mansfield, Edward, and Jack Snyder. 2007b. "The Sequencing 'Fallacy'." *Journal of Democracy* 18 (3): 5–9.

Mansfield, Edward, and Jack Snyder. 1995. "Democratization and the Danger of War." *International Security* 20 (1): 5–38.

Mazzuca, Sebastián, and Gerardo Munck. 2014. "State or Democracy First? Alternative Perspectives on the State-Democracy Nexus." *Democratization* 21 (7): 1221–43.

Meyer-Sahling, Jan-Hinrik, Christian Schuster, and Kim Mikkelsen. 2018. "Civil Service Management in Developing Countries: What Works?" Report for the UK Department for International Development. https://forskning.ruc.dk/en/publications/civil-forvaltning-i-udviklingslandene-hvad-virker-fund-fra-en-und

Migdal, Joel. 1988. *Strong Societies and Weak States: State-Society Relations and State Capabilities in the Third World.* Princeton: Princeton University Press.

Miller, Gary. 2000. "Above Politics: Credible Commitment and Efficiency in the Design of Public Agencies." *Journal of Public Administration Research and Theory* 10 (2): 289–327.

Møller, Jørgen, and Svend-Erik Skaaning. 2011. "Stateness First?" *Democratization* 18 (1): 1–24.

Muralidharan, Karthik, Paul Niehaus, and Sandip Sukhtankar. 2016. "Building State Capacity: Evidence from Biometric Startcards in India." *American Economic Review* 106 (10): 2895–929.

Nistotskaya, Marina, and Luciana Cingolani. 2016. "Bureaucratic Structure, Regulatory Quality, and Entrepreneurship in a Comparative Perspective: Cross-Sectional and Panel Data Evidence." *Journal of Public Administration Research and Theory* 26 (3): 519–34.

Nistotskaya, Marina, and Michelle D'Arcy. 2018. "Getting to Sweden: The Origins of High Tax Compliance in the Swedish Tax State." In *The Leap of Faith: The Fiscal Foundations of Successful Government in Europe and America*, edited by Sven Steinmo, 33–55. Oxford: Oxford University Press.

North, Douglass. 1981. *Structure and Change in Economic History*. New York: Norton.

North, Douglass and Barry Weingast. 1989. "Constitutions and Commitment: The Evolution of Institutions Governing Public Choice in Seventeenth-Century England." *The Journal of Economic History* 49 (4): 803–32.

Phillips, David, Carla AbouZahr, Alan Lopez, Lene Mikkelsen, Don de Savigny, Rafael Lozano, John Wilmoth, and Philip Setel. 2015. "Are Well Functioning Civil Registration and Vital Statistics Systems Associated with Better Health Outcomes?" *The Lancet* 386 (10001): 1386–94.

Piccolino, Giulia. 2016. "Infrastructural State Capacity for Democratization? Voter Registration and Identification in Côte d'Ivoire and Ghana compared." *Democratization* 23 (3): 498–519.

PRS, Political Risk Services Group. 2010. International Country Risk Guide Methodology. http://www.prsgroup.com/wp-content/uploads/2012/11/icrgmethodology.pdf

Povitkina, Marina. 2018. "The Limits of Democracy in Tackling Climate Change." *Environmental Politics* 27 (3): 411–32.

Risse, Thomas. 2011. "Governance in Areas of Limited Statehood." In *Governance without a State? Policies and Politics in Areas of Limited Statehood*, edited by Thomas Risse, 1–36. New York: Columbia University Press.

Rodrik, Dani. 2000. "Institutions for High-Quality Growth: What they are and How to Acquire Them." *Studies in Comparative International Development* 35 (3): 3–32.

Rose, Richard, and Doh Chull Shin. 2001. "Democratization Backwards: The Problem of Third-Wave Democracies." *British Journal of Political Science* 31 (2): 331–54.

Rothstein, Bo, and Jan Teorell. 2008. "What is Quality of Government? A Theory of Impartial Government Institutions." *Governance* 21 (2): 165–90.

Scott, James. 1998. *Seeing Like a State: How Certain Schemes to Improve the Human Condition Have Failed*. New Haven, CT: Yale University Press.

Shefter, Martin. 1994. *Political Parties and the State: The American Historical Experience*. Princeton: Princeton University Press.

Skocpol, Theda. 1992. "State Formation and Social Policy in the United States." *American Behavioral Scientist* 35 (4–5): 559–84.

Skocpol, Theda. 1985. "Bringing the State Back in: Strategies of Analysis in Current Research." In *Bringing the State Back In*, edited by Peter Evans, Dietrich Rueschemeyer, and Theda Skocpol, 3–37. Cambridge: Cambridge University Press.

Slater, Dan. 2010. *Ordering Power: Contentious Politics and Authoritarian Leviathans in Southeast Asia*. Cambridge: Cambridge University Press.

Slater, Dan. 2008. "Can Leviathan be Democratic? Competitive Elections, Robust Mass Politics, and State Infrastructural Power." *Studies in Comparative International Development* 43 (3–4): 252–72.

Soifer, Hillel. 2015. *State Building in Latin America*. Cambridge: Cambridge University Press.

Soifer, Hillel. 2013. "State Power and the Economic Origins of Democracy." *Studies in Comparative International Development* 48 (1): 1–22.

Soifer, Hillel. 2012. "Measuring State Capacity in Contemporary Latin America." *Revista De Ciencia Politica* 32 (3): 585–98.

Soifer, Hillel. 2008. "State Infrastructural Power: Approaches to Conceptualization and Measurement." *Studies in Comparative International Development* 43 (3–4): 231–51.

Soifer, Hillel, and Matthias Vom Hau. 2008. "Unpacking the Strength of the State: The Utility of State Infrastructural Power." *Studies in Comparative International Development* 43 (3): 219–30.

Tilly, Charles. 1990. *Coercion, Capital, and European States, AD 990–1990.* London: Blackwell.

Weber, Max. 1978 [1922]. *Economy and Society: An Outline of Interpretative Sociology.* Oakland, CA: University of California Press.

Weingast, Barry. 1995. "The Economic Role of Political Institutions: Market-Preserving Federalism and Economic Development." *Journal of Law, Economics and Organization* 11 (1): 1–31.

White, David. 2018. "State Capacity and Regime Resilience in Putin's Russia." *International Political Science Review* 39 (1): 130–43.

World Bank. 2018a. Data on Statistical Capacity. http://datatopics.worldbank.org/statisticalcapacity/

World Bank. 2018b. Worldwide Bureaucracy Indicators. https://datacatalog.worldbank.org/dataset/worldwide-bureaucracy-indicators

Ziblatt, Daniel. 2008. "Why Some Cities Provide More Public Goods than Others: A Subnational Comparison of the Provision of Public Goods in German Cities in 1912." *Studies in Comparative International Development* 43 (3–4): 273–89.

CHAPTER 37

THE QUALITY OF GOVERNMENT AND CIVIL CONFLICT

ANNEKATRIN DEGLOW AND HANNE FJELDE

INTRODUCTION

How does the quality of government influence the risk of armed conflict within countries and the prospect for a stable and durable peace in postconflict societies? And how does civil conflict, in turn, affect the way in which government power is exercised? In this chapter we discuss the research on the relationship between quality of government and civil conflict. Whereas much existing literature directly or indirectly places variations in how governments exercise power at the core of their arguments for where and why armed conflict breaks out, there is no clearly delineated literature that scholars interested in the relationship between the quality of government and civil conflict ascribe to. Except from a handful of studies that explicitly frame their work in terms of the quality of political institutions (see, for instance, Fearon 2010; Fjelde and De Soysa 2009; Lapuente and Rothstein 2014; Rothstein 2009; Taydas, Peksen, and James 2010; Teorell 2015; Walter 2015; Wig and Tollefsen 2015), relevant work is scattered across different strands of literature that deal with concepts more or less directly associated with the quality of government. These include for example regime type, (in)equality, state capacity, state repression, institutional trust, political participation, democratic attitudes, and informal governance.

In our mapping of the literature relevant for understanding the relationship between quality of government and civil conflict, we make several observations. First, it is clear that scholars of conflict have been more preoccupied with examining variations in the outlook of the formal institutions of the state, rather than how governance has been exercised within these structures. This applies in particular to scholars interested in macro-level political determinants of conflict onset and recurrence. Second, much of the relevant macro-level research regarding the relationship between the quality of government and civil conflict is conducted under the conceptual umbrella of state capacity. Yet, a clearer distinction between the two is important since many states possess strong capacity for enforcement but exercise this capacity in ways that do not benefit the population at large. Third, we also note a burgeoning literature that moves away from the macro level to the micro level, studying people's perceptions of governance within their countries. So far, however, this literature has primarily dealt with the legacies of armed conflict. In other words, it examines how the population in conflict-affected states perceive the state and their agents many but focuses less on how these individual perceptions may also feed into violent mobilization and conflict outbreak. Fourth, we identify a growing research field relating to the role of informal governance structures. Whereas the quality of government is commonly thought of in relation to formal institutions of the state, the particular context of armed conflict and state breakdown makes it important to consider also the role of governance provided by actors other than the state.

Through this discussion, we want to point to important findings of relevance to the relationship between quality of government and civil conflict, but also highlight some of the conceptual and empirical challenges that this research agenda is facing. We conclude by suggesting several ways forward that we believe could help to expand our knowledge on the relationship between civil conflict and the quality of government.

What We Mean by "Quality of Government" and "Civil Conflict"?

Before outlining our main observations in more detail, we briefly discuss what we mean by the "quality of government" and "civil conflict." According to Rothstein and Teorell (2008, 166) a core feature of the quality of government is "impartiality in the exercise of public authority." In this conceptualization, quality of government is related to impartiality in the output, rather than the input side of the political system. It is consequently distinct from democracy, which relates to equal access to political power and institutions, but not (necessarily) to how power is exercised within such institutions. For instance, a country may have formal institutions that ensure inclusion and contestation, e.g. universal suffrage and the right of opposition candidates to compete in election and assume office if they win. Yet, politicians and civil servants working within such formal institutions can still exercise their power and implement laws and policies in ways that are highly partial (e.g. Rothstein 2009; Taydas, Peksen, and James 2010). Corruption, property rights violations, unequal provision of services and public goods across strata of society, weak rule of law, as well as biased law enforcement agencies and judiciaries are indicators of a low quality of government.

The research that speaks to the relationship between the quality of government and civil conflict is not itself united around a shared set of concepts and definitions. Considering the centrality of the state and its agents in many theoretical accounts of armed conflict, it is surprising, perhaps, that a clearer research agenda related to the quality of government is yet to coalesce. For our review, we use the conceptualization by Rothstein and Teorell (2008) as our theoretical reference point. Yet, to be able to properly convey relevant research within this quite disparate research field, we adopt a broader approach including theoretical concepts more indirectly related to the quality of government, such as regime type, democratic institutions, state capacity, as well as institutional trust and democratic attitudes.

By civil conflict we mean large-scale dissent, involving an organized, armed nonstate group, which challenges either the government or the territorial integrity of the state through violent means (Gleditsch et al. 2002). We will use this term interchangeably with "civil war" and "internal armed conflict." While we focus our discussion on civil conflict in particular, the research on the quality of government also focuses on other forms of organized political violence that take place within a country. This includes, amongst others, terrorism, protests, riots, and election-related violence. We include studies that focus more broadly on political violence whenever we deem them to be of relevance. For coherence, we have chosen not to focus on the relationship between interstate armed conflicts and the quality of government throughout this chapter, but we return briefly to this relationship towards the end.

INSTITUTIONS THAT REGULATE ACCESS TO POLITICAL POWER

Much of the quantitative literature on the political determinants of armed conflict has focused on the role of formal political institutions that regulate the access to political power. Central to this literature is the claim that regimes that combine democratic and autocratic features are more likely to experience armed challenges to their rule, compared to fully democratic or nondemocratic regimes (Hegre et al. 2001; Regan and Bell 2010; Jones and Lupu 2018). Interestingly, the theoretical accounts for this relationship tend to focus on how formal institutions shape the exercise of authority. Whereas the most harshly authoritarian regimes display coercive powers that effectively deter or suppress would-be insurgents, regimes "in the middle" are held to be particularly prone to civil conflict. These regimes are institutionally constrained in their reliance on repression to quell dissent. Meanwhile, the institutional avenues for accommodating political discontent are not sufficiently strong to facilitate a substitution to nonviolent means to redress grievances (Hegre et al. 2001; Muller and Weede 1990; Reynal-Querol 2002).

Different theoretical accounts point to the importance of different aspects of democratic institutions. Some highlight the role of institutional avenues that accommodate broad societal demands for participation and influence that install popular legitimacy on the regime, such as elections (Gurr 1971; Carey 2007; Bartusevicius and Skaaning 2018). Others emphasize the importance of institutions that ensure government accountability through horizontal checks on executive power, such as a powerful legislature and independent courts (Walter 2015; Hafner-Burton, Hyde, and Jablonski 2014). These constraining institutions may be associated with a lower risk of conflict through different mechanisms. In autocratic settings, legislatures and regime parties, for example, have been argued to reduce the risk of rebellion because they present credible avenues for elite co-optation and control (Gandhi and Przeworski 2006; Svolik 2012). In less autocratic regimes, these institutions of oversight and control gain more independent power, and could more clearly serve to constrain the regime in its discretionary use of power for the narrow interest of those holding power (Fjelde et al. in press). Accountability mechanisms, in the form of both electoral and executive constraints, may indirectly reduce popular incentives for rebellion, for example by curtailing elite-predation (Bates 2008). They may also more directly curb political violence, through constraining human rights violations and regime-perpetrated violence (Davenport 2007). Hafner-Burton, Hyde, and Jablonski (2014) note, for example, that limits on executives' decision-making powers make them less able to resort to violence during electoral periods to manipulate electoral outcomes.

As noted above, the peace-inducing impact of democratic institutions is partly explained by these regimes' inclusive and participatory practices. At the same time, studies also suggest an association between democratization and conflict, noting that the political competition induced by popular elections might also aggravate societal tension (Mansfield and Snyder 1995; Snyder 2000; Cederman, Hug, and Krebs 2010). If elections are held in a context where civil society is weak, media is controlled, and the protection of political and civil liberties are weak, elites may resort to noninclusionary and violence-prone rhetoric to mobilize voters and demobilize others, thus increasing the risk of civil war (e.g. Snyder 2000). Studies of postconflict democratization also warn that within the framework of nominally democratic institutions, such as elections, elites may practice democracy in ways that precipitate a return to civil war (e.g. Brancati and Snyder 2013). This suggests that it may be useful to separate between the formal institutions that regulate access to power, and how power is exercised within these institutions, even in states with nominally democratic institutions.

Another challenge for the literature on regime type and armed conflict relates to the empirical evidence, which to a large extent relies on regressing conflict on aggregate democracy indices, such as the Polity scale. This could be problematic since the theoretical expectation of a nonmonotonic relationship between democracy and armed conflict is underpinned by different mechanisms that relate to distinct components of governance. As one moves from the authoritarian towards the democratic end point of a polity scale, repression is assumed to decrease, while accommodation is assumed to increase. Using a unidimensional measures of democracy to proxy for two countervailing practices makes it difficult to validate specific arguments (Gleditsch and Ruggeri 2010). Indeed, a general problem with Polity, which aggregate various features of democratic institutions into one linear scale, is that many different institutional configurations may underlie the same score, leading users to conflate a very heterogenous set of regime characteristics under the same classification.[1] Although some research has focused on more specific regime characteristics, such as type of electoral system, mode of executive recruitment, or form of authoritarian government (e.g. Reynal-Querol 2002; Carey 2007; Fjelde 2010; Bartusevicius and Skaaning 2018), more work could be done in this direction.

THE QUALITY OF GOVERNMENT AND THE ONSET AND RECURRENCE OF CIVIL CONFLICT

The literature more specifically dealing with the quality of government and conflict onset can be divided into two broad strands. First, there is a handful of studies that look at specific dimensions of governance, such as the role of corruption, influence of weak bureaucratic

---

[1] The Polity scale has also been shown to contain subcomponents that are endogenous to civil war, making the original index unsuitable for civil war scholars (Vreeland 2008).

quality, and the weak rule of law. Second, a large literature examines the link between inequality and conflict. This latter body of work does not specifically study the conduct of civil servants, judiciary, politicians, or other agents of the state—as the quality of government perspective would entail. Yet, it does highlight systematic inequalities in the access to state power, in the distribution of economic resources, and in the protection of political and civil rights, which is so profound and politically salient that they are hard to imagine short of a context in which state power is also being exercised in the interest of more narrow segments of society.

Cutting across both of these strands of literature are theoretical accounts that invoke at least three different mechanisms, depending on how scholars perceive the key drivers of armed conflict. These quality of government variables are held to shape (1) incentives (grievances) underlying violent mobilization, (2) opportunities for doing so, as well as (3) credibility, accountability, and transparency of political rule—all of which influence the risk of armed conflict.

One central account focuses on the role of popular grievances as drivers of conflict. It argues that where the formulation and implementation of policies reflect the narrow interests of a particular segment of society, rather than that of the population at large, aggrieved population groups are more likely to rebel to change the distribution of political and economic power in society. Much of the early literature focused on vertical inequalities between aggrieved versus privileged segments of the population, facilitating the mobilization of rebellion (Gurr 1971). Some of the research on how bad governance leads to armed conflict also draws on these arguments, highlighting how corruption and elite predation divert funds from the public good towards private interest and breed popular grievances (Le Billon 2003; Fjelde 2009; Bates 2008). The most systematic evidence relating grievances to conflict pertain to the role of horizontal inequalities, i.e. large disparities in the distribution of political power and economic resources along ethnic or other group lines. Exclusion and outright discrimination of ethnic groups increase the risk of armed conflict outbreak (Stewart 2008; Østby 2008; Cederman, Weidmann, and Gleditsch 2011; Cederman, Gleditsch, and Buhaug 2013), and makes conflicts, once they have broken out, more intractable (Wucherpfennig et al. 2011).[2]

Another strand of the literature focuses on how the quality of government influences the opportunity structures for nonstate actors to mobilize, take up arms against the regime, and sustain a rebellion, inspired by the work of e.g. Tilly (1978). Governments that lack an efficient and capable state bureaucracy, that have their power narrowly concentrated in the state capital (not present in state peripheries), and maintain understaffed, corrupt, and undisciplined police and military forces also lack the ability to detect a mounting rebellion or engage in effective counterinsurgency campaigns (Fearon and Laitin 2003). Weak military capacities and absence of state authority in state hinterlands can facilitate the outbreak of armed conflict, by making it more feasible for armed groups to set up their bases and mobilize to become a significant challenge to state authority.

At the same time, the literature on state repression documents how strong coercive powers can also be used to repress the citizenry and significantly constrain their civil and

---

[2] There is also a substantial body of literature that links gender inequality (and in particular lack of female political representation) to a higher risk of armed conflict (e.g. Melander 2005).

political freedoms. A strong and permanent influence of military in politics and potent repressive apparatus may denote governments with high military capacity, but "the dark side of the force"—to use Hirshleifer (1994) conceptualization—is an unstable peace based on coercion (Davenport and Inman 2012). If states violate the physical, economic, or political integrity of their citizens, they are likely to engender grievances that facilitate mobilization, increasing the likelihood of violence (e.g. Cingranelli et al. 2019; Gurr and Moore 1997; Regan and Norton 2005; Davenport and Inman 2012; Skarstad and Strand 2016; Young 2013; Hatz 2019). In other words, problems with poor governance may stem from both the lack of *capacity* to formulate and implement policies that benefit the population at large, and from the lack of *incentives* to use the power of the state to formulate and implement decisions in the interest of the public good. As such, a clearer conceptual distinction between state capacity and quality of government would be helpful in the conflict literature (see D'Arcy and Nistotskaya, this volume).

Interestingly, the literature on state repression might be the one that comes closest to studying variations in the quality of government understood as (im)partiality of the exercise of public authority. It is the strand of literature that most thoroughly goes beyond the input side, and focuses on the output side of government. There are, however, theoretical and methodological challenges distinguishing cause and effect in the relationship between state repression and armed challenges to state authority (Ritter and Conrad, 2016). Many scholars have thus moved away from theorizing about whether state repression triggers civil conflict and towards theorizing the dissent–repression nexus as an escalatory process (Davenport and Inman 2012).

Importantly, then, the importance of state capacity on civil peace must be traced along additional dimensions besides capacity for coercion and military deterrence. Scholars interested in the output side of government should also focus on states' ability to formulate and enact policies that benefit the society at large, for example, generating and redistributing resources, and investing in public goods (Fjelde and De Soysa 2009; Hendrix 2010). In terms of attracting support and legitimacy from the citizenry, governments that work to enhance the welfare of their societies may "outperform" groups that challenge their rule. Effective governments, according to Margaret Levi "offer powerful constituents enough in the way of benefits to retain their loyalty and to desist from violent predation" (2006, 9). This suggests an alternative pathway through which strong states reduce the risk of conflict: by building what Levi (2006, 7) refers to as "quasi-voluntary compliance," that is, compliance backed by a credible threat of coercion, but motivated by a perception that the social contract is fair. Citizens consent to being governed, conditional on the government's provision of political goods in return.

Consistent with such arguments, there is cross-country evidence showing that countries with high-quality bureaucracy see a lower risk of conflict incidence (Hegre and Nygård 2015) and a lower risk of rebel groups successfully defeating the regime in conflict (DeRouen and Sobek 2004). Also, low corruption, rule of law, and strong property rights have been found to correlate positively with civil peace (Fjelde 2009; Fjelde and De Soysa 2009; Taydas, Peksen, and James 2010). Governments that rule by these principles may also be in a better position to manage periods of crisis, because impartial and capable bureaucracies with low corruption may convey transparency and legitimacy in public spending, even when the size of the pie is shrinking (Andersen and Krishnarajan 2018).

Governments that politicize their bureaucracies and rely on state resources for patronage are more likely to see elite fragmentation and violence in situations of economic downturn (Bates 2008; Reno 2005).[3]

Finally, some studies have highlighted the centrality of quality of government variables, not primarily for influencing grievances or the opportunities for sustaining a rebellion, but for enhancing credibility, accountability, and transparency in the exercise of public authority. At the core of these explanations is the observation that armed conflicts often occur in situations where both adversaries would be better off with a bargained outcome that saved them the cost of war. It is information asymmetries, combined with difficulties of credibly committing not to renege on negotiated agreements, which precipitate armed conflict (Fearon 1995). According to this account, quality of government has a central role to play: Impartial and capable state bureaucracies insulated from politics, civil servants that function autonomously of political pressures, and an impartial enforcement of the law all strengthen the transmission of information and the credibility of government decision-making (e.g. Walter 2015; Andersen and Krishnarajan 2018; Lapuente and Rothstein 2014).[4] High-quality governance, in turn, allows regimes to credibly commit to peaceful compromises that reduce the risk of violent escalation, facilitate efforts to reach durable settlements that end conflict, and can reduce the risk of conflict recurrence by offering more credibility in that negotiated settlements will be upheld (Fearon 2005; Hegre and Nygård 2015; Shair-Rosenfield and Wood 2017; Walter 2015; Andersen and Krishnarajan 2018). For instance, Lapuente and Rothstein (2014) argue that one reason why Sweden's late nineteenth-century class conflict was peacefully resolved through collaboration, while Spain's class conflict led to the outbreak of the Spanish Civil War, was that the former had a meritocratic autonomous—and therefore more impartial—bureaucracy, while the latter had a patronage-based—and therefore more partial—bureaucracy. The separation of elected politicians and civil servants helped preserve the rule of law in Sweden, allowing the government to make credible commitments to their political opponents not to abuse their power, thereby preventing the outbreak of armed conflict. In Spain, the patronage-based administrative system did not allow the government to signal such constraints, thereby precipitating violent conflict.

THE QUALITY OF GOVERNMENT AND
THE LEGACY OF CIVIL CONFLICT

So far, our discussion has focused on the role that various aspects related to the quality of government play for the onset, dynamics, and recurrence of armed conflicts within states. However, civil conflict is also likely to have profound *consequences* on political institutions and how authority within such institutions is exercised. As many countries in the developing world are postconflict, the impact of conflict on institutions generally and governance

---

[3] See also Rothstein (2009), who argues that the outbreak of violence in the former Yugoslavia was the result of a systematic lack of government impartiality in the implementation of public policies.

[4] See also Teorell (2015) for a parallel argument related to interstate peace.

specifically is a salient concern (e.g. Fearon 2010). It is therefore not surprising that the last decade has witnessed a burgeoning literature studying the legacies of civil conflict for a range of political outcomes. While the vast majority of scholarly work in this literature is not framed as being directly concerned with how government power is exercised, it touches upon concepts that are more or less directly linked to the quality of governance and political institutions. Interestingly, in contrast to research on the political determinants of civil conflict, the literature on the political outcomes of civil conflict is characterized by a focus on micro-level perceptions of governance. Relatively fewer studies assess the impact of conflict on macro-level institutions, as we discuss in detail below.

Whereas research on the political determinants of civil conflict is dominated by cross-national comparisons that focus on macro-level variations in institutions, such studies are comparatively fewer in the literature on the consequences of civil conflict. This is somewhat surprising, given that the earliest work on state- and nation-building processes has stressed the role of external warfare as a driving force of institutional development (e.g. Tilly 1975, 1990). Scholars focusing more specifically on conflict within states disagree on what to expect with regard to the political legacies of civil conflict: Some have argued civil wars to be "development in reverse" (Collier et al. 2003, 13), as they weaken state capacity and therefore lead to institutional decay (see also Le Billon 2008). Cervellati, Fortunato, and Sunde (2014), for instance, find that violent conflict during democratic transitions leaves persistent negative effects on the institutional quality of emerging democracies. Others, however have noted that civil war termination may also under some conditions be associated with the emergence of more liberal political systems (Wantchekon and Neeman 2002; Wantchekon 2004; Wood 2001). Scholars have therefore started to investigate the effects of particular civil war dynamics on the prospects of postwar democratization. Empirical evidence remains ambiguous, in part due to different measurements and definitions of what constitutes a postwar period (e.g. Fortna and Huang 2012). While some find that variations in civil war characteristics translate into variations in postwar democratization (Gurses and Mason 2008; Hartzell and Hoddie 2015; Huang 2016) others do not find such an effect (Fortna and Huang 2012), or provide evidence for path dependency (Haggard and Tiede 2014). Focusing on a different outcome, Keels and Nichols (2018) find a relationship between the type of conflict termination and postwar state repression, with negotiated settlements producing more repressive postwar states than military victories. Note that existing country-level studies on how civil conflict shape political institutions tend to explore the question within a sample of conflict-affected countries only. Hence, we generally lack more systematic comparisons between countries that did and that did not experience civil conflict. In sum, while the link between quality of government–related features (e.g. regime type, democratic institutions, and state capacity) and the onset and recurrence of civil conflict has been scrutinized in a wealth of studies, we know comparatively little about how civil conflict affects the institutional outlook of the political system or governance outputs.

When it comes to consequences, scholars have primarily focused on the political legacies of civil conflict at the subnational and individual level (Davenport et al. 2019). The last decade has seen the emergence of a promising literature studying micro-level perceptions of governance. This literature focuses in particular on levels of trust in various institutions, such as the central and local government, parliament, presidency, judiciary, armed forces, and police. If we believe that nonbiased and impartial institutions are the ones citizens are most likely to trust, this literature might be significant from a quality of government per-spective (e.g. Wig and Tollefsen 2015).

An often-articulated theoretical argument in these studies builds on the notion of a social contract between states and its citizens: Civil conflicts signal low government competence, which is punished by the citizenry through the withdrawal of trust (Bakke et al. 2014; De Juan and Pierskalla 2016; Lake 2010). Empirical evidence for trust-reducing effects of armed conflict, however, remain ambiguous, with some studies finding support for the suggested relationship (Deglow and Sundberg in press; De Juan and Pierskalla 2016; Grosjean 2014; Hutchison and Johnson 2011; Wig and Tollefsen 2015; Voors and Bulte 2014), others finding no support, or even a relationship in the opposite direction (Bakke et al. 2014; Gates and Justesen 2016; Hong and Kang 2017). While some explain divergent findings by pointing to differences in methodological approaches, case selection, and measurement (De Juan and Pierskalla 2016), others have noted that whether armed conflict leads to increases, decreases, or no changes in trust in political institutions depends on more substantial conditionalities. The type of state institution under study, to what extent individuals are exposed to violence, as well as the perpetrator, victim, and type of violence are likely to determine direction and magnitude of effects (Deglow 2018).

While this literature predominantly studies postconflict societies, there is also some work focusing more explicitly on wartime institutional processes. Wood (2008) for in-stance, notes that modes of governance might change in the course of armed conflict as institutions become militarized. A prime example of this is the police, whose involvement in counterinsurgency operations during armed conflict might lead to more militarized and harsh policing conduct that is likely to reduce perceptions of state legitimacy and in-stitutional trust among targeted populations (Bayley and Perito 2010; Brewer and Magee 1991; Deglow 2016; Deglow and Sundberg in press; Weitzer 1995). This line of research is promising, as it explicitly studies conflict-induced changes in the exercise of public authority and their potentially destructive consequences for the impartiality of state governance.

There are two adjacent strands of literature that also provide interesting insights into the effects of civil conflict on the micro-determinants of the quality of democratic govern-ance. First, several scholars have assessed the consequences of different forms of political violence—including civil war, terrorism, and electoral violence—for individual-level pol-itical participation, such as voting behavior, vote choice, and civic engagement (e.g. Balcells 2012; Bellows and Miguel 2006, 2009; Blattman 2009; Bratton 2008; Costalli and Ruggeri 2014; Grossman, Manekin, and Miodownik 2015; Gutierrez-Romero 2014; Lupu and Peisakhin 2017; Rozenas, Schutte, and Zhukov 2017). Empirical evidence to date remains inconclusive. Whether violence increases or decreases political participation, and how it affects vote choice, seem highly dependent on both the form of participation, as well as the type of violence. While not being a direct measure of the quality of government in terms of the public exercise of authority, these studies provide insights into the effects of civil conflict on the health of (post)conflict societies with regard to important bottom-up processes of democratic governance. The second, and related strand of literature, focuses on the effects of violence on political attitudes in the form of support for democratic or authoritarian rule (e.g. Dyrstad 2013; Burchard 2015). This literature is informative as it shows that exposure to political violence has the potential to stifle democratization by weakening democratic norms among the citizenry.

THE ROLE OF INFORMAL GOVERNANCE

While the concept of "quality of government"—at least within the conflict literature—is commonly used with reference to state institutions, an emerging literature on what has come to be labeled "rebel governance" suggests that governance provided by nonstate actors is an important feature of many contemporary civil wars (Arjona 2016; Huang 2016; Kasfir 2015; Mampilly 2011; Metelits 2009; Stewart 2018; Weinstein 2007).[5] "Rebel governance" in its broadest definition refers to "the organization of civilians within rebel held territories for a public purpose" (Kasfir 2015, 23). Insurgent groups oftentimes co-opt formal modes of governance by taking over service provision related to, for instance, welfare, education, and security in the areas they control. Scholars interested in this phenomenon have so far been preoccupied with studying the conditions under which rebel governance emerges, as well as what explains variations in the type of governance rebels engage in. Several of these studies hereby touch upon notions of institutional quality.

For instance, Arjona (2016) shows that when prewar local institutions are of high quality—that is legitimate and efficient—rebels settle for a minimal involvement in governance as civilians are likely to resist intrusion by nonstate actors. When institutional quality is low, however, they engage more broadly in civilian affairs by establishing local rule, or what she calls "rebelocracy." Stewart (2018) further finds that secessionist groups are more likely to provide inclusive governance—that is, provide services independent from whether individuals support the group's goal—than rebels aspiring to take over government power. She argues that secessionist rebels cannot afford to rely on exclusive service provision that merely targets their supporter base as they need to establish legitimacy among a broader subset of the population that could form part of a future autonomous territorial entity.

Less well understood, however, are the consequences that rebel governance has for the development trajectory of formal institutions, though some tentative empirical evidence suggests that it may also leave important political legacies. Huang (2016), for example, relies on quantitative data and case study evidence from Nepal, Mozambique, Tajikistan, and Uganda to show that the way rebels govern during civil war can have important implications for postwar democratization. Some rebel groups directly involve ordinary people and encourage their active support during conflict, while others fight with little regard for popular involvement. Huang shows that how rebel groups appeal to the citizenry influences state–society relations and, in turn, postconflict regime trajectories. Focusing on the micro level, Kubota (2017) draws on survey data from Sri Lanka to show that rebel governance at the subnational level might shape individual-level perceptions of legitimacy and therefore civilian political identities far into the postwar period. Costalli and Ruggeri (2018) study the legacy of civil war on electoral behavior in Italy. They show that the rebel groups' organizational advantage during armed conflict can be institutionalized after the conflict and translated into higher vote shares for rebel-affiliated parties. While not providing an

---

[5] There is also an emerging literature that focuses on how the risk of political violence is shaped by the presence of traditional governance structures, for example customary courts or traditional leaders. These often have precolonial roots—established before the development of modern state structures (e.g. Mustasilta 2019; Wig and Kromrey 2018).

exhaustive overview of the literature on wartime informal governance, these findings indicate that a discussion of the relationship between the quality of government and civil conflict is incomplete without referring to the role that informal governance plays—both as a factor shaping the quality of formal institutions, and as an outcome thereof.

THE QUALITY OF GOVERNMENT AND INTERSTATE ARMED CONFLICTS

In this chapter, we have focused on the relationship between the quality of government and civil conflict, that is, violent conflicts within states. Before we conclude, we provide a brief discussion of the quality of government as it has been studied in relation to the risk of interstate war. The overall observation for this entire chapter applies also here: There is no coherent research agenda on the quality of government and the risk of war between states. Relevant studies, when we look at the mechanisms they invoke, can particularly be found in the study of the democratic peace proposition, as well as the broader literature on state-building.

Interstate war has been put forward as a central driving force behind the development of European states. Seminal work on European state-formation processes has argued that external warfare is crucial for institutional development, as it required rulers to raise revenues through taxation and thereby expanded fiscal state capacity (Tilly 1975, 1990). Empirical support for this argument has more recently been provided by Besley and Persson (2009) and Scheve and Stasavage (2010). Summarizing research on state formation processes outside of Europe (for instance, Centeno 2002, 2003; Desch 1996; Herbst 2001; Migdal 1988), Taylor and Botea (2008, 23) note that on the flip side of the coin, the absence of war—or less intense wars—might lead to weaker states.[6] Associated with the argument that war increases state capacity is the notion that conflict between states created incentives to expand suffrage (e.g. Krebs 2009; Ticchi and Vindigni 2008). In other words, warfare might affect institutional development by leading to an expansion of citizens' political rights.

With regard to how the quality of government influences the risk of interstate war, the most relevant efforts have been made by scholars of the democratic peace. However, as Teorell (2015) notes, while quantitative evidence has consistently shown that democracies are unlikely to fight each other (see, for instance, Dafoe, Oneal, and Russett 2013), we know little about the effect that factors at the output side of a political system have on the likelihood that interstate armed conflicts occur. Addressing this gap, Teorell (2015) finds that the quality of government, measured as the absence of corruption, bureaucratic quality, and law and order, are correlated with a lower risk of militarized disputes between states. The suggested mechanism is parallel to some of the arguments made in the literature on the effects of institutional quality on the occurrence of civil conflict, namely that impartial

---

[6] For a detailed review of the literature on the ability of interstate armed conflicts to increase state capacity, the effect of interstate rivalries on state capacity, as well as scholarly criticism of this argument, see Taylor and Botea (2008).

modes of governance reduce information uncertainty and increases governments' ability to credibly commit to political promises.

Concluding Remarks

As is evident from this chapter, the literature on the quality of government and civil conflict does not represent a coherent research agenda. The sum of our knowledge about this relationship is derived from contributions initially made to quite different strands of literature, which has evolved, at least partly, in isolation from each other. At the same time, the centrality of the state in many of our accounts for why civil conflict occurs provides a red thread through which the importance of governance features can be traced. By way of conclusion, we point to three avenues of research where gaps in our knowledge are particularly apparent, and where we hope to see more research in the future.

First, on a general level, we believe that our understanding of the relationship between the quality of government and civil conflict would be improved if more research was to focus specifically on the output side of government. As noted in this chapter, most research—may it be on the quality of government as a predictor or as an outcome of civil conflict—focuses on aspects that are associated with, yet not directly measuring, the extent to which governance is exercised in an impartial manner. We therefore think it is relevant to reiterate the concern raised by others (for instance, Rothstein and Teorell 2008; Taydas, Peksen, and James 2010; Teorell 2015) that principles of equality and inclusiveness when it comes to the input side of political systems (e.g. universal suffrage) can very well be accompanied by partiality at the output side. While research on aspects such as regime type, (in)equality, state capacity, state repression, institutional trust, political participation, democratic attitudes, or informal governance has significantly contributed to our understanding of the relationship between civil conflict and institutional quality, assessing more directly how the exercise of political authority affects armed conflict, and vice versa, would be an important addition to this research agenda.

Second, and moving towards more specific avenues, the literature on the quality of government and the outbreak of armed conflict is predominantly built around country-level analysis of aggregate indicators. We lack both theory and evidence on the micro-level underpinnings of these relationships. This gap is particularly glaring compared to the booming micro-level research on the legacies of armed conflict. We hope that the turn towards increased reliance on survey data, lab-in-the-field, or other experimental designs currently taking place across political science can also move into in this subfield. This could lead researchers to address questions of how individuals' perceptions of corruption or other features of how governments exercise their power, shape for example the support for violence or individual willingness to take to the street to challenge current political orders. Such a turn to the micro level could be particularly useful in this research field, since existing data sources have significant limitations. Predominantly, macro-level studies measure the quality of government through expert assessment, and with relatively short time-series. Experimental approaches and survey data could help to address concerns of endogeneity and reverse causality. Better identification of theoretical mechanisms could also speak to the issue of theoretical equifinality. In the literature on the determinants of armed conflict, a more coherent effort to provide micro-level evidence for theoretical conjectures is still lacking (for an exception see Wig and Tollefsen (2016)). In a situation where many of our macro-level relationships are consistent with different theoretical interpretations, survey data could perhaps be particularly useful to probe the particular mechanism at play.

A third research gap relates to the literature on the legacies of armed conflict for the quality of government. For this relationship the challenge is the opposite: Whereas there has been a surge in the literature on the micro-level impact of exposure to violence across a number of different conflict contexts, the impact of armed conflict on the development trajectory of state institutions is relatively poorly understood. Individual-level data is helpful for understanding the micro-level foundations for how armed conflict shapes political outcomes (e.g. through voter turnout or vote choice). Experimental methods associated with much of this research also enhance our ability to draw causal inference. Yet, these approaches have limitations. Although many scholars treat survey responses as indicators of the actual quality of institutions, they tend to be individual perceptions, which—for a variety of reasons—may not neatly map on to actual variation in the development of formal institutions. In other words, the quality of government might not be easily aggregated from the preferences of ordinary citizens that populate most existing survey samples to macro-level outcomes. Complementing existing approaches with more macro-level, comparative analysis would also allow us to better understand long-term historical political trajectories that follow from armed conflict.[7]

References

Andersen, David Delfs Erbo, and Suthan Krishnarajan. 2019. "Economic Crisis, Bureaucratic Quality and Democratic Breakdown." *Government and Opposition* 54(4): 715–744. doi:10.1017/ gov.2017.37.

Arjona, Ana. 2016. *Rebelocracy. Social Order in the Colombian Civil War*. Cambridge, UK: Cambridge University Press.

Bakke, Kristin M., John O'Loughlin, Gerard Toal, and Michael D. Ward. 2014. "Convincing State-Builders? Disaggregating Internal Legitimacy in Abkhazia." *International Studies Quarterly* 58 (3): 591–607. doi:10.1111/isqu.12110.

Balcells, Laia. 2012. "The Consequences of Victimization on Political Identities: Evidence from Spain." *Politics and Society* 40 (3): 311–47. doi:10.1177/0032329211424721.

Bartusevicius, Henrikas, and Svend Erik Skaaning. 2018. "Revisiting Democratic Civil Peace: Electoral Regimes and Civil Conflict." *Journal of Peace Research* 55 (5): 625–40. doi:10.1177/0022343318765607.

Bates, Robert. 2008. *When Things Fell Apart. State Failure in Late-Century Africa*. New York, NY: Cambridge University Press.

Bayley, David H., and Robert M Perito. 2010. *The Police in War. Fighting Insurgency, Terrorism, and Crime*. Boulder, CO: Lynne Rienner Publishers.

Bellows, John, and Edward Miguel. 2006. "War and Institutions: New Evidence from Sierra Leone." *American Economic Review* 96 (2): 394–99. doi:10.1257/000282806777212323.

---

[7] The authors thank Jenniina Kotajoki for excellent research assistance.

Bellows, John, and Edward Miguel. 2009. "War and Local Collective Action in Sierra Leone." *Journal of Public Economics* 93 (11–12): 1144–57. doi:10.1016/j.jpubeco.2009.07.012.

Besley, Timothy, and Torsten Persson. 2009. "The Origins of State Capacity: Property Rights, Taxation, and Politics Author." *American Economic Review, American Economic Association* 99 (4): 1218–44. doi:10.1257/aer.99.4.1218.

Blattman, Christopher. 2009. "From Violence to Voting: War and Political Participation in Uganda." *American Political Science Review* 103 (2): 231–47. doi:10.2139/ssrn.1100110.

Brancati, Dawn, and Jack L. Snyder. 2013. "Time to Kill: The Impact of Election Timing on Postconflict Stability." *Journal of Conflict Resolution* 57 (5): 822–53. doi: 10.1177/0022002712449328

Bratton, Michael. 2008. "Vote Buying and Violence in Nigerian Election Campaigns." *Electoral Studies* 27 (4): 621–32. doi:10.1016/j.electstud.2008.04.013.

Brewer, John, and Kathleen Magee. 1991. *Inside the RUC: Routine Policing in a Divided Society.* New York: Clarendon Press.

Burchard, Stephanie M. 2015. *Electoral Violence in Sub-Saharan Africa: Causes and Consequences.* Boulder, CO: Lynne Rienner Publishers.

Carey, Sabine C. 2007. "Rebellion in Africa: Disaggregating the effect of political regimes." *Journal of Peace Research* 44 (1): 47–64. doi: 10.1177/0022343307072176.

Cederman, Lars Erik, Simon Hug, and Lutz F. Krebs. 2010. "Democratization and Civil War: Empirical Evidence." *Journal of Peace Research* 47 (4): 377–94. doi:10.1177/0022343310368336.

Cederman, Lars-Erik, Kristian Skrede Gleditsch, and Halvard Buhaug. 2013. *Inequality, Grievances, and Civil War.* New York: Cambridge University Press.

Cederman, Lars-Erik, Nils B. Weidmann, and Kristian Skrede Gleditsch. 2011. "Horizontal Inequalities and Ethnonationalist Civil War: A Global Comparison." *American Political Science Review* 105 (3): 478–95. doi: 10.1017/S0003055411000207

Centeno, Miguel Angel. 2002. *War and the Nation-State in Latin America.* University Park, PA: The Pennsylvania State University Press.

Centeno, Miguel Angel. 2003. "Limited War and Limited States." In *Irregular armed forces and their role in politics and state formation*, edited by Diane E. Davis and Anthony W. Pereira, 82–95. Cambridge, UK: Cambridge University Press.

Cervellati, Matteo, Piergiuseppe Fortunato, and Uwe Sunde. 2014. "Violence during Democratization and the Quality of Democratic Institutions." *European Economic Review* 66: 226–47. doi:10.1016/j.euroecorev.2013.12.001.

Cingranelli, David, Skip Mark, Mark Gibney, Peter Haschke, Reed Wood, and Daniel Arnon. 2019. "Human Rights Violations and Violent Internal Conflict." *Social Sciences* 8 (2): 1–33. doi:10.3390/socsci8020041.

Collier, Paul, Lani Elliott, H˚avard Hegre, Anke Hoeffler, Marta Reynal-Querol, and Nicholas Sambanis. 2003. *Breaking the Conflict Trap: Civil War and Development Policy.* Oxford: Oxford University Press.

Costalli, Stefano, and Andrea Ruggeri. 2014. "Forging Political Entrepreneurs: Civil War Effects on Post-conflict Politics in Italy." *Political Geography* 44: 40–9. doi:10.1016/j.polgeo.2014.08.008.

Costalli, Stefano, and Andrea Ruggeri. 2018. "The Long-Term Electoral Legacies of Civil War in Young Democracies: Italy, 1946–1968." *Comparative Political Studies.* doi:10.1177/0010414018784057.

Dafoe, Allan, John R. Oneal, and Bruce Russett. 2013. "The Democratic Peace: Weighing the Evidence and Cautious Inference." *International Studies Quarterly* 57 (1): 201–14. doi:10.1111/isqu.12055.

Davenport, Christian. 2007. *State Repression and the Domestic Democratic Peace.* Cambridge: Cambridge University Press.

Davenport, Christian, and Molly Inman. 2012. "The State of State Repression Research Since the 1990s." *Terrorism and Political Violence* 24 (4): 619–34. doi: 10.1080/09546553.2012.700619

Davenport, Christian, Håvard Mokleiv Nygård, Hanne Fjelde, and David Armstrong. 2019. "The Consequences of Contention: Understanding the Aftereffects of Political Conflict and Violence." *Annual Review of Political Science* 22 (1): 361–77. doi:10.1146/annurev-polisci-050317-064057.

De Juan, Alexander, and Jan Henryk Pierskalla. 2016. "Civil War Violence and Political Trust: Microlevel Evidence from Nepal." *Conflict Management and Peace Science* 33 (1): 67–88. doi:10.1177/0738894214544612.

Deglow, Annekatrin. 2016. "Localized Legacies of Civil War: Postwar Violent Crime in Northern Ireland." *Journal of Peace Research* 53 (6): 786–99. doi:10.1177/0022343316659692.

Deglow, Annekatrin. 2018 "Forces of Destruction and Construction. Local Conflict Dynamics, Institutional Trust and Postwar Crime." Ph.D. diss. Uppsala University.

Deglow, Annekatrin, and Ralph Sundberg (In press). "Local Conflict Intensity and Public Perceptions of the Police: Evidence from Afghanistan." *The Journal of Politics.* doi: https://doi.org/10.1086/711559.

DeRouen, Karl, and David Sobek. 2004. "The Dynamics of Civil War Duration and Outcome." *Journal of Peace Research* 41 (3): 303–20. doi:10.1177/0022343304043771.

Desch, Michael C. 1996. "War and Strong States, Peace and Weak States?" *International Organization* 50 (2): 237–68. doi:10.1017/s0020818300028551.

Dyrstad, Karin. 2013. "Does civil war breed authoritarian values? An empirical study of Bosnia-Herzegovina, Kosovo and Croatia." *Democratization* 20 (7): 1219–42. doi:10.1080/13510347.2012.688032.

Fearon, James D. 1995. "Rationalist Explanations for War." *International Organization* 49 (3): 379–414. doi:https://www.jstor.org/stable/2706903.

Fearon, James D 2005. "Primary Commodity Exports and Civil War." *Journal of Conflict Resolution* 49 (4): 483–507. doi:10.1177/0022002705277544.

Fearon, James D. 2010. "Governance and Civil War Onset." World Development Report 2011 Background Paper. Washington, DC.

Fearon, James D, and David D. Laitin. 2003. "Ethnicity, Insurgency, and Civil." *American Political Science Review* 97 (1): 75–90. doi:10.1017/s0003055403000534.

Fjelde, H. 2009. "Buying Peace? Oil Wealth, Corruption and Civil War, 1985–99." *Journal of Peace Research* 46 (2): 199–218. doi:10.1177/0022343308100715.

Fjelde, H. 2010. "Generals, Dictators, and Kings: Authoritarian Regimes and Civil Conflict, 1973–2004." *Conflict Management and Peace Science* 27 (3): 195–218. doi:10.1177/0738894210366507.

Fjelde, Hanne, and Indra De Soysa. 2009. "Coercion, Co-optation, or Cooperation?" *Conflict Management and Peace Science* 26 (1): 5–25. doi:10.1177/0738894208097664.

Fjelde, Hanne, Carl Henrik Knutsen and Håvard Mokleiv Nygård. In press. "Which Institutions Matter? Re-considering the Democratic Civil Peace" *International Studies Quarterly.* https://doi.org/10.1093/isq/sqaa076

Fortna, Virginia Page, and Reyko Huang. 2012. "Democratization after Civil War: A Brush-Clearing Exercise." *International Studies Quarterly* 56 (4): 801–808. doi:10.1111/j.1468-2478.2012.00730.x.

Gandhi, Jennifer, and Adam Przeworski. 2006. "Cooperation, Cooptation and Rebellion Under Dictatorships." *Economics and Politics* 18 (1): 1–26. doi:10.1111/j.1468-0343.2006.00160.x.

Gates, Scott, and Mogens K. Justesen. 2020. "Political Trust, Shocks, and Accountability: Quasi-Experimental Evidence from a Rebel Attack." *Journal of Conflict Resolution* 64 (9): 1693–1723. doi: 10.1177/0022002720906446

Gleditsch, Kristian Skrede, and Andrea Ruggeri. 2010. "Political Opportunity Structures, Democracy, and Civil War." *Journal of Peace Research* 47 (3): 299–310. doi:10.1177/0022343310362293

Gleditsch, Nils Petter, Peter Wallensteen, Mikael Eriksson, Margareta Sollenberg, and Håvard Strand. 2002. "Armed Conflict 1946–2001: A New Dataset." *Journal of Peace Research* 39 (5): 615–37. doi:10.1177/0022343302039005007.

Grosjean, Pauline. 2014. "Conflict and Social and Political Preferences: Evidence from World War II and Civil Conflict in 35 European Countries." *Comparative Economic Studies* 56 (3): 424–51. doi:10.1057/ces.2014.2

Grossman, Guy, Devorah Manekin, and Dan Miodownik. 2015. "The Political Legacies of Combat: Attitudes Toward War and Peace Among Israeli Ex-Combatants." *International Organization* 69 (4): 981–1009. doi:10.1017/s002081831500020x

Gurr, Ted Robert. 1971. *Why Men Rebel*. Princeton, NJ: Princeton University Press.

Gurr, Ted Robert, and Will H Moore. 1997. "Ethnopolitical Rebellion: A Cross-Sectional Analysis of the 1980s with Risk Assessments for the 1990s." *American Journal of Political Science* 41 (4): 1079–103. doi:10.2307/2960482

Gurses, Mehmet, and T. David Mason. 2008. "Democracy Out of Anarchy: The Prospects for Post-Civil War Democracy." *Social Science Quarterly* 89 (2): 315–36.

Gutierrez-Romero, Roxana. 2014. "An Inquiry into the Use of Illegal Electoral Practices and Effects of Political Violence and Vote-buying." *Journal of Conflict Resolution* 58 (8): 1500–27. doi:10.1177/0022002714547902

Hafner-Burton, Emilie M., Susan D. Hyde, and Ryan S. Jablonski. 2014. "When Do Governments Resort to Election Violence?" *British Journal of Political Science* 44 (1): 149–79. doi: 10.1017/S0007123412000671

Haggard, Stephan, and Lydia Tiede. 2014. "The Rule of Law in Post-conflict Settings: The Empirical Record." *International Studies Quarterly* 58 (2): 405–17. doi:10.1111/isqu.12103

Hartzell, Caroline A., and Matthew Hoddie. 2015. "The Art of the Possible: Power Sharing and Post—Civil War Democracy." *World Politics* 67 (1): 37–71. doi:10.1017/s0043887114000306.

Hatz, Sophia. 2019. "Israeli Demolition Orders and Palestinian Preferences for Dissent." *Journal of Politics* 81 (3): 1069–1074. doi:10.1086/703211

Hegre, Håvard, Tanja Ellingsen, Scott Gates, and Nils Petter Gleditsch. 2001. "Toward a Democratic Civil Peace? Democracy, Political Chance and Civil War, 1816–1992." *American Political Science Review* 95 (1): 33–48. doi:http://www.jstor.org/stable/3117627

Hegre, Håvard, and Håvard Mokleiv Nygård. 2015. "Governance and Conflict Relapse." *Journal of Conflict Resolution* 59 (6): 984–1016. doi:10.1177/0022002713520591

Hendrix, Cullen S. 2010. "Measuring State Capacity: Theoretical and Empirical Implications for the Study of Civil Conflict." *Journal of Peace Research* 47 (3): 273–85. doi:10.1177/0022343310361838

Herbst, Jeffrey. 2001. *States and Power in Africa*. 280. Princeton, NJ: Princeton University Press.

Hirshleifer, Jack. 1994. "The Dark Side of the Force." *Economic Inquiry* 32 (1): 1–10.

Hong, Ji Yeon, and Woo Chang Kang. 2017. "Trauma and Stigma: The Long-Term Effects of Wartime Violence on Political Attitudes." *Conflict Management and Peace Science* 34 (3): 264–86. doi:10.1177/0738894215593683

Huang, Reyko. 2016. *The Wartime Origins of Democratization. Civil War, Rebel Governance, and Political Regimes*. 229. New York: Cambridge University Press.

Hutchison, Marc L., and Kristin Johnson. 2011. "Capacity to Trust? Institutional Capacity, Conflict, and Political Trust in Africa, 2000–2005." *Journal of Peace Research* 48 (6): 737–52. doi:10.1177/0022343311417981

Jones, Zachary M., and Yonatan Lupu. 2018. "Is There More Violence in the Middle?" *American Journal of Political Science* 62 (3): 652–67. doi:10.1111/ajps.12373

Kasfir, Nelson. 2015. "Rebel Governance—Constructing a Field of Inquiry: Definitions, Scope, Patterns, Order, Causes." In *Rebel Governance in Civil War*, 21–46. Cambridge: Cambridge University Press.

Keels, Eric, and Angela D. Nichols. 2018. "State Repression and Post-conflict Peace Failure." *Conflict, Security and Development* 18 (1): 17–37. doi:10.1080/14678802.2017.1420313.

Krebs, Ronald R. 2009. "In the Shadow of War: The Effects of Conflict on Liberal Democracy." *International Organization* 63 (1): 177–210. doi:10.1017/S0020818309090067.

Kubota, Yuichi. 2017. "Imagined Statehood: Wartime Rebel Governance and Post-war Sub-national Identity in Sri Lanka." *World Development* 90: 199–212. doi:10.1016/j.worlddev.2016.09.007.

Lake, David. 2010. "Building Legitimate States after Civil War." In *Strengthening Peace in Post–Civil War States*, edited by Matthew Hoddie and Caroline A. Hartzell, 29–51. Chicago: University of Chicago Press.

Lapuente, Victor, and Bo Rothstein. 2014. "Civil War Spain Versus Swedish Harmony: The Quality of Government Factor." *Comparative Political Studies* 47 (10): 1416–41. doi:10. 1177/0010414013512598.

Le Billon, Philippe. 2003. "Buying Peace or Fuelling War: The Role of Corruption in Armed Conflicts." *Journal of International Development* 15 (4): 413–26. doi: 10.1002/jid.993.

Le Billon, Philippe. 2008. "Corrupting Peace? Peacebuilding and Post-conflict Corruption." *International Peacekeeping* 15 (3): 344–61. doi:10.1080/13533310802058851.

Levi, Margaret. 2006. "Why We Need a New Theory." *Perspectives on Politics* 4 (1): 5–19. doi:10.1017/S1537592706060038.

Lupu, Noam, and Leonid Peisakhin. 2017. "The Legacy of Political Violence across Generations." *American Journal of Political Science* 61 (4): 836–51. doi:10.1111/ajps.12327.

Mampilly, Zachariah Cherian. 2011. *Rebel Rulers: Insurgent Governance and Civilian Live During War*. Ithaca, NY: Cornell University Press.

Mansfield, Edward D, and Jack Snyder. 1995. "Democratization and the Danger of War." *International security* 20 (1): 5–38.

Melander, Erik. 2005. "Gender Equality and Intrastate Armed Conflict." *International Studies Quarterly* 49 (4): 695–714. doi:10.1111/j.1468-2478.2005.00384.x.

Metelits, Claire. 2009. *Inside Insurgency. Violence, Civilians, and Revolutionary Group Behavior*. New York and London: New York University Press.

Migdal, Joe S. 1988. *Strong Societies and Weak States: State-Society Relations and State Capabilities in the Third World*. Princeton, NJ: Princeton University Press.

Muller, Edward N., and Erich Weede. 1990. "Cross-National Variation in Political Violence: A Rational Action Approach." *Journal of Conflict Resolution* 34 (4): 624–651. doi:http: //www.jstor.org/stable/174182.

Mustasilta, Katariina. 2019. "Including Chiefs, Maintaining Peace? Examining the Effects of State–Traditional Governance Interaction on Civil Peace in sub-Saharan Africa." *Journal of Peace Research* 56 (2): 203–19. doi: 10.1177/0022343318790780.

Østby, Gudrun. 2008. "Polarization, Horizontal Inequalities and Violent Civil Conflict." *Journal of Peace Research* 45 (2): 143–62. doi:10.1177/0022343307087169.

Regan, Patrick M., and Sam R. Bell. 2010. "Changing Lanes or Stuck in the Middle: Why Are Anocracies More Prone to Civil Wars?" *Political Research Quarterly* 63 (4): 747–59. doi: 10.1177/1065912909336274.

Regan, Patrick M., and Daniel Norton. 2005. "Greed, Grievance and Mobilization in Civil Wars." *Journal of Conflict Resolution* 49 (3): 319–36. doi:10.1177/0022002704273441.

Reno, William. 2005. "The Politics of Violent Opposition in Collapsing States." *Government and Opposition* 40 (2): 1–25. doi: 10.1111/j.1477-7053.2005.00147.x

Reynal-Querol, Marta. 2002. "Political Systems, Stability and Civil Wars." *Defence and Peace Economics* 13 (6): 465–83. doi:10.1080=102426902000006150.

Ritter, Emily Hencken and Conrad, Courtenay R. 2016. "Preventing and responding to dissent: The observational challenges of explaining strategic repression" *American Political Science Review* 110 (1):85–99. doi: 10.1017/S0003055415000623

Rothstein, Bo. 2009. "Creating Political Legitimacy. Electoral Democracy Versus Quality of Government." *American Behavioral Scientist* 53 (3): 311–30. doi: 10.1177/0002764209338795.

Rothstein, Bo, and Jan Teorell. 2008. "What Is Quality of Government? a Theory of Impartial Government Institutions." *Governance* 21 (2): 165–90. doi:10.1111/j.14680491.2008.00391.x

Rozenas, Arturas, Sebastian Schutte, and Yuri Zhukov. 2017. "The Political Legacy of Violence: The Long-Term Impact of Stalin's Repression in Ukraine." *The Journal of Politics* 79 (4): 1147–61. doi: 10.1086/692964

Scheve, Kenneth, and David Stasavage. 2010. "The Conscription of Wealth: Mass Warfare and the Demand for Progressive Taxation." *International Organization* 64: 529–61. doi:10. 1017/S0020818310000226

Shair-Rosenfield, Sarah, and Reed M. Wood. 2017. "Governing Well after War: How Improving Female Representation Prolongs Post-Conflict Peace." *The Journal of Politics* 79 (3): 995–1009. doi:10.1086/691056

Skarstad, Kjersti, and H°avard Strand. 2016. "Do Human Rights Violations Increase the Risk of Civil War?" *International Area Studies Review* 19 (2): 107–30. doi:10.1177/2233865916629567

Snyder, Jack. 2000. *From Voting to Violence. Democratization and Nationalist Violence.* New York/ London: Norton.

Stewart, Frances. 2008. *Horizontal Inequalities and Conflict: Understanding Group Violence in Multiethnic Societies.* New York: Palgrave Macmillan.

Stewart, Megan A. 2018. "Civil War as State-Making: Strategic Governance in Civil War." *International Organization* 72 (1): 205–26. doi:10.1017/S0020818317000418

Svolik, Milan W. 2012. *The Politics of Authoritarian Rule.* Cambridge: Cambridge University Press.

Taydas, Zeynep, Dursun Peksen, and Patrick James. 2010. "Why Do Civil Wars Occur? Understanding the Importance of Institutional Quality." *Civil Wars* 12 (3): 195–217. doi:10.1080/13698249.2010.509544

Taylor, Brian D., and Roxana Botea. 2008. "Tilly Tally: War-Making and State-Making in the Contemporary Third World." *International Studies Review* 10 (1): 27–56. doi:10.1111/j.1468-2486.2008.00746.x

Teorell, Jan. 2015. "A Quality of Government Peace? Explaining the Onset of Militarized Interstate Disputes, 1985–2001." *International Interactions* 41 (4): 648–73. doi:10.1080/03050629.2015.1023434

Ticchi, Davide, and Andrea Vindigni. 2008. "War and Endogenous Democracy." IZA Working Paper No. 3397, Available at SSRN: https://ssrn.com/abstract=1136202 or http://dx.doi.org/10.1111/j.0042-7092.2007.00700.x

Tilly, Charles. 1975. *The Formation of National States in Europe*. Princeton: Princeton University Press.

Tilly, Charles. 1978. *From Mobilization to Revolution*. Reading, Massachusetts: Addison-Wesley.

Tilly, Charles. 1990. *Coercion, Capital, and European States: A.D. 990–1990*. Cambridge, Mass: Blackwell.

Voors, Maarten J., and Erwin H. Bulte. 2014. "Conflict and the Evolution of Institutions: Unbundling Institutions at the Local Level in Burundi." *Journal of Peace Research* 51 (4): 455–69. doi:10.1177/0022343314531264

Vreeland, James Raymond. 2008. "The Effect of Political Regime on Civil War: Unpacking Anocracy." *Journal of Conflict Resolution* 52(3): 401–25. doi: doi.org/10.1177/0022002708315594

Walter, Barbara F. 2015. "Why Bad Governance Leads to Repeat Civil War." *Journal of Conflict Resolution* 59 (7): 1242–72. doi:10.1177/0022002714528006.

Wantchekon, Leonard. 2004. "The Paradox of 'Warlord' Democracy: A Theoretical Investigation." *The American Political Science Review* 98 (1): 17–33. doi:10.1017/S0003055404000978

Wantchekon, Leonard, and Zvika Neeman. 2002. "A Theory of Post-Civil War Democratization." *Journal of Theoretical Politics* 14 (4): 439–64. doi:10.1177/095162902774006822

Weinstein, Jeremy M. 2007. *Inside Rebellion. The Politics of Insurgent Violence.* Cambridge: Cambridge University Press.

Weitzer, Ronald. 1995. *Policing Under Fire. Ethnic Conflict and Police Community Relations in Northern Ireland.* Albany: State University of New York Press.

Wig, Tore, and Daniela Kromrey. 2018. "Which Groups Fight? Customary Institutions and Communal Conflicts in Africa." *Journal of Peace Research* 55 (4): 415–29. doi:10.1177/0022343317740416

Wig, Tore, and Andreas Forø Tollefsen. 2015. "The Institutional Legacies of Local Conflict Violence: Perception-Based Evidence from the Afrobarometer Surveys." In *Beyond the Civil Democratic Peace: Subnational Political Institutions and Internal Armed Conflict*, 163–90. Ph.D. diss. University of Oslo.

Wig, Tore, and Andreas Forø Tollefsen. 2016. "Local Institutional Quality and Conflict Violence in Africa." *Political Geography* 53: 30–42. doi:10.1016/j.polgeo.2016.01.003

Wood, Elisabeth Jean. 2001. "An Insurgent Path to Democracy: Popular Mobilization, Economic Interests, and Regime Transition in South Africa and El Salvador." 34 (8): 862–88. doi:10.1177/0010414001034008002

Wood, Elisabeth Jean. 2008. "The Social Processes of Civil War: The Wartime Transformation of Social Networks." *Annual Review of Political Science* 11 (1): 539–61. doi:10.1146/annurev.polisci.8.082103.104832

Wucherpfennig, Julian, Nils W Metternich, Lars-Erik Cederman, and Kristian Skrede Gleditsch. 2012. "Ethnicity, the State, and the Duration of Civil War." *World Politics* 64 (1): 79–115. doi: 10.1017/S004388711100030X

Young, Joseph K. 2013. "Repression, Dissent, and the Onset of Civil War." *Political Research Quarterly* 66 (3): 516–32. doi: 10.1177/1065912912452485

CHAPTER 38

....

ORGANIZED CRIME AND THE QUALITY OF GOVERNMENT

....

LESLIE HOLMES

INTRODUCTION

....

UNTIL the 1990s, organized crime (hereafter OC) was usually treated by both states and analysts as a form of criminality, but not a political phenomenon. The main exception to this general observation is that some criminologists drew a distinction between OC and "mafias" (Finkenauer 2007, 16–19). For some such analysts, the principal difference was that mafias were a particular type of organized criminal group (OCG) that either deliberately interacted with state authorities—usually by corrupting elected and/or appointed officials—or else partly supplanted the state, whereas other OCGs preferred to avoid the authorities.[1] In this chapter, no distinction is drawn between "mafias" and other OCGs, since *both* impact on the quality of government.

The perception of OC has changed significantly since the end of the Cold War (1991), and it is now typically treated as a security threat that can also exert serious disruptive effects on the quality of government. Regarding security—a major reason for the changed perception is the growing awareness of the frequent connections between OCGs and terrorist groups. Since many serious criminal acts are committed by persons under the influence of illicit drugs, the fact that such drugs are primarily supplied by OCGs represents another way in which OC constitutes a major security issue. As for the quality of government, OCGs impact negatively on the rule of law and, at least in democratic and hybrid (e.g. "competitive authoritarian"—Levitsky and Way 2010) states, can also undermine the democratic political process. Two common ways in which this occurs, though these can overlap, are "state capture" (see below) and interference in elections (Gilligan 1999; Alesina, Piccolo, and Pinotti 2019). High levels of OC activity can hinder or prevent states from pursuing goals important

---

[1] A second way of distinguishing "mafias" from other types of OCG is favored by inter alia Diego Gambetta (1993) and Federico Varese (2001), who see the former as specializing in just one commodity, namely protection. For further distinctions see Sergi (2017, 21–59); Testa and Sergi (2018, 18–56).

to them. For example, both Bulgaria and Romania have long had admission to Europe's borderless Schengen Area blocked, primarily because they are perceived to have unacceptably high levels of OC and corruption. OC can even undermine the legitimacy of states, both authoritarian and democratic.

Yet despite the increase in official awareness of the dangers from OC, analyses of the linkages and resonances between OC and the state are still rare: In the words of Susan Karstedt (2014, 303), despite substantial growth in the number of official assessments of the scale and dangers of OC, "The state as actor on its own account or even only as facilitator of organized crime is conspicuously absent from all of these reports." A major objective of this chapter is to address this lacuna.

Following a definitional section and consideration of the changed climate in which OC is operating, this chapter provides an original taxonomy of the numerous ways in which OC and the state interact and may even mimic each other. This is followed by the conclusions and an agenda for future research. The underlying argument is that the clear distinction usually drawn between the state and OC is sometimes inappropriate and that the boundaries between the two are in practice frequently blurred, impacting negatively on the quality of government.

Before proceeding, an important caveat needs to be emphasized. The problems of obtaining reliable data are even more severe in the cases of OC and corruption (the latter will be a major aspect of the interaction between OC and government analyzed here) than for most sociopolitical phenomena. Hence, more extensive use is made here of serious investigative journalism and research conducted by international organizations (IOs) and NGOs than is customary in academic analyses. Furthermore, the murky nature of the topic means that in some cases, only allegations—not proven evidence—can be cited.

DEFINITIONAL ISSUES

It is impossible to provide a universally accepted definition of either OC or corruption. Despite concerted efforts since the 1990s to standardize definitions of both phenomena, cultural and other differences mean that progress has been slow and agreed interpretations remain elusive. Nevertheless, there is much common ground across jurisdictions, and it is possible to reach acceptable working definitions.

Organized crime—OC is "one of the most contested terms in academic criminology" (Sheptycki 2003, 489). As James Finkenauer (2007, 9) has noted, that there is no universal agreement on the meaning of OC is reflected in the fact that the most widely cited definition, that in the UN's *Convention against Transnational Organized Crime* (UNCTOC, adopted 2000, effective 2003—UNODC 2004a), is vague because its framers could not agree on a more precise one.

Klaus von Lampe (2018) has identified more than 200 definitions of OC: Despite considerable overlap between many of these, there are also important differences. The most significant is that several are now dated, having overly narrow interpretations of OC and OCGs. Such definitions typically include references to strict hierarchies, exclusive membership, and the use or threat of violence. While these criteria still apply to some OCGs, the rise of cybercrime and networked groupings means that much contemporary OC does not fit this description (UNODC 2002; Choo and Grabosky 2014; UNODC 2017, 15–18). At the other end of the spectrum is the approach of Felia Allum and Panos Kostakos (2010, 3), who argue for a postmodern approach to OC, maintaining that "we all are 'organized crime'." While punchy, such an approach is too imprecise for empirical research.

Another debate directly relevant to this chapter concerns the political role of OC. The claim (e.g. Abadinsky 2017, 2) that OCGs have no political goals is not only incorrect for many newer OCGs but was never true of several of the best-known traditional ones. The Sicilian Mafia (Lupo 1996, 2009, esp. 142–276), the Japanese Yakuza (Siniawer 2008; Kaplan and Dubro 2012), and the Chinese Triads (Maguire 1997) have all in the past provided support for right-wing governments.

An increasing number of government authorities prefer the term "serious and organized crime" to OC. This too is problematic. For example, most would consider rape, aggravated home burglary, or murder to be serious crimes but not OC unless perpetrated by enduring organized groups. But we here overlook the issues with the term "serious crime" and instead cite from an appropriate definition of contemporary OC, that of the UK's National Crime Agency (NCA 2014, 7):

> ... serious crime planned, co-ordinated and conducted by people working together on a continuing basis. Their motivation is often, but not always, financial gain ... Organised crime ... recognises neither national borders nor national interests ... Generally, serious and organised crime ... operates in loose networks ... to work on particular enterprises across multiple crime types. Some ... organised crime is perpetrated by hierarchically structured groups comprising close associates and/or family members, some of whom are based overseas.

The reference to "often, but not always" allows for the fact that OCGs are sometimes motivated by factors other than material gain (e.g. revenge killings, such as the Sicilian Mafia's attacks on Italian judges in the early 1990s) while also distinguishing them from terrorist groups whose motivation is primarily ideological.

Quality of government—In line with the general approach in this volume, government is here defined broadly to include all agencies of the state—not only the legislature and central executive, but also law enforcement, the military, and local government. As for quality, Bo Rothstein (2013, 16) argues persuasively that quality of government "should be defined as having impartial government institutions for the *exercise* of public power" (emphasis in original). The concept will be analyzed here in terms of four variables: the assessed level of corruption (the worse it is, the lower the quality of government), budget transparency (as a proxy for transparency more generally—the more transparent the budget, the higher the quality of government), the rule of law (the more extensive this is, the higher the quality of government), and functioning of government (the better this is, the higher the quality of government). All of these variables relate in some way to the concept of state impartiality. For instance, a key feature of the concept of rule of law is that no one, not even the highest members of the political elite, is above the law.

Corruption—As with OC, so in the case of corruption, the UN's inability to reach agreement on what the term connotes means that what is widely seen as the most significant global document on it—the *UN Convention against Corruption* (UNCAC—adopted 2003, effective 2005)—does not include a definition of corruption as such (UNODC 2004b, esp. 7–8). Since the focus here is on the impact of OC on the quality of government, the most common definition—"the abuse of public office for private gain"—is adopted.

Before concluding this section, note that the terms "corruption" and "organized crime" have been separated here for the sake of definitional clarity, and because there *are* important conceptual differences between them. But moving from *de jure* to de facto differentiation, the distinctions become hazier. Thus, criminologists such as Donald Cressey (1969), Vincenzo Ruggiero (1996), and Petrus van Duyne (2007) have argued that there is in practice considerable overlap between OC, corporate crime, and corruption. For instance, while violence may initially appear to be a variable that clearly distinguishes OC from corruption, the fact that corrupt police officers sometimes engage in its inappropriate use, while some OC does not involve even the threat of violence, exemplifies this blurring.

THE CHANGED CLIMATE

As suggested by the date of UNCTOC, the global focus on OC—particularly transnational OC (TOC)—is relatively recent, essentially dating from the 1990s. Several related factors help to explain this.

First, there has been increasing transnationalization of OC, so that in many countries in which OC was once a minor problem it has become far more significant. Germany is a good example. OC was not even a criminal policy issue in Germany until the 1960s (Lampe 1995), but has grown in significance since the 1980s because of an influx of foreign OCGs (Kilchling 2004; Kinzig and Luczak 2004; Olterman and Tondo 2017). Another example of TOC's growth is the marked increase since the early 1990s in both people smuggling and human trafficking across borders (Stoecker and Shelley 2005; Shelley 2010; Piotrowicz, Rijken and Heide Uhl 2018). In the 1990s, Claire Sterling (1994) triggered a heated debate on the changing nature (or otherwise) of OC. The dominant traditional view was that OCGs were essentially monopolistic and engaged in turf wars as part of this. Sterling argued that the situation was changing, and that OCGs were increasingly cooperating with groups in other countries, with an international division of labor emerging. She called this change the *pax mafiosa* (i.e. mafia peace). While some (e.g. Freemantle 1995) strongly challenged this claim, there is much empirical evidence to show that the *pax mafiosa* does apply in some cases, particularly at the international or transnational level: At the domestic and local level, as Dick Hobbs (1998) argues, there is still plenty of competition among OCGs.

Second, globalization and its ideology of neoliberalism has blossomed since the 1980s. This has been seen by various commentators to have assisted OC, while at the same time weakening states, both in terms of controlling OC and more generally. Thus, Moisés Naím maintained in a 2003 article (29–30) that:

> ... globalization has not only expanded illegal markets and boosted the size and the resources of criminal networks, it has also imposed more burdens on governments: Tighter public budgets, decentralization, privatization, deregulation, and a more open environment for international trade and investment all make the task of fighting global criminals more difficult.

Implicitly, this explains one of the most significant ways in which OC, particularly TOC, undermines the quality of national governments. Naím's argument resonates with that of Felia Allum and Panos Kostakos (2010), who maintain that the rise of TOC is an indicator of the declining sovereignty of states. While quantity is not to be confused with quality, losing control over a phenomenon that impacts directly on security does indicate a reduction in the quality—here in the sense of effectiveness—of government. Fabio Armao (2015) takes the argument further, maintaining that the globalization ideology of neoliberalism actually encourages collusion between OCGs, corrupt politicians, and business entrepreneurs. He calls the collaboration between these three elements a "mafia" and cites Italy and Mexico as the best examples of this phenomenon. This said, note that neoliberal policies can sometimes contribute to a *reduction* in corruption, and hence to less collusion with OC: examples include Estonia and Poland (Holmes 2006, 208).

Third, the rise of the Internet has dramatically increased the number of individuals and institutions that become victims of OCGs engaged in cybercrime (Martellozzo and Jane 2017; Viano 2017). With the emergence of Tim Berners-Lee's World Wide Web in 1989/90, the Internet began to be a part of everyday life and susceptible to misuse by OCGs (Wall 2001; Gillespie 2016). Of major concern is the fact that hackers can cause significant problems not only for private citizens, but even for state authorities. While most attacks on government websites and computer systems in recent years are believed to have been the work of hostile states for political reasons (e.g. on Estonia in 2007 and Georgia in 2008, both allegedly by Russia—McGuinness 2017), some have been attributed to OC, in some cases purportedly working on behalf of government authorities (Tamkin 2017). However sophisticated authorities have been at protecting the web, the fact that even Interpol and the Pentagon have been hacked is evidence of the limits of both international and domestic official agencies to protect themselves and citizenries from Internet criminality.

Fourth, national boundaries, at least within Europe, have become less rigid. While the concept of a "borderless world" (Ohmae 1990) is often exaggerated or misused—the term applies much more to capital than to people—the establishment of the Schengen Area in 1995 made it easy for OCGs to move across national boundaries once inside that zone.

Fifth, awareness of links between terrorists and OCGs, and of how one can mimic and sometimes mutate into the other, has grown, especially since the 9/11 events. One sign of this is the broader focus of the Financial Action Task Force (FATF) in the twenty-first century. Established in 1989 and originally targeting money-laundering mainly by OC, FATF has in recent years also devoted considerable attention to money-laundering by terrorist groups and corrupt officials.

A sixth factor emerged in the 1960s but has intensified in recent years, namely the demand for illegal or illicit goods and services. The most obvious example is demand for recreational drugs. This trend originated in affluent countries but is increasingly visible also in developing and transition states (Uchtenhagen 2004; Brown 2014; Vandam et al. 2017). OC has benefitted from and encouraged this growth.

Finally, there is the impact of the collapse of most Communist systems between 1989 and 1991 and the concomitant end of the Cold War. This had numerous implications for the rise of OC, but five are particularly relevant to this analysis. First, the new postcommunist states were initially fragile and had limited capacity for combating OC. Second, every postcommunist state experienced serious economic problems in the 1990s (high rates of inflation and unemployment, negative GDP growth, etc.) that were compounded by the fact that none had a well-developed state-run welfare system to cushion citizens from the pain these were causing (Holmes 1997, 218–21 and 240–9). Third, value systems—including moral codes—were destabilized. Fourth, many former officers of the state's security organs were dismissed as postcommunist governments sought to distance themselves from their predecessors: Some then joined OCGs, a point explored below. Finally, the collapse of the U.S.S.R. in 1991 witnessed a marked decline in successor states' control of weapons and materiel. There were numerous warnings (Lee 1997, 1998—but see too Davis, Hirst, and Mariani 2001, 17–18), that poor security meant that even nuclear materials were being smuggled out of Russian military establishments by corrupt officials and sold to OC gangs, who then on-sold these. While this factor appears in hindsight to have been either exaggerated or erroneous, some OCGs have undoubtedly been colluding with terrorist organizations (e.g. both Afghan and foreign OCGs with the Taliban—UN 2015) in recent years, often trading weapons for drugs.

A TAXONOMY OF OC–STATE INTERACTIONS AND MIMICRY

The ways in—and extent to—which OCGs interact with the state, and how states and their officers sometimes act like OCGs, vary considerably across jurisdictions. We produce here an original classification of these many variations.[2] This novel taxonomy—not a typology, since it is inappropriate to rank-order them—identifies the principal forms such interaction and mimicry assumes and provides examples of each. While examples have been cited from many countries, there is a focus on four to include a developing state (Mexico), a Communist state (China), a non-Communist authoritarian state (Russia) and a developed democratic state (the U.S.). Despite significant differences between these countries' systems and cultures, it will be demonstrated that there are similarities and resonances across all four regarding OC and corruption and their impact on the quality of government.

Police collusion with OC

Police corruption matters in numerous ways. For example, unlike most officers of the state, law enforcement agents are often armed, giving them the potential to use inappropriate violence against citizens. Furthermore, high levels of corruption among police officers lead citizens to mistrust them, resulting in the public reporting less crime and a reduced willingness to assist the police in combating crime. Police corruption can thus lead to higher crime rates and lower crime clearance rates, negatively impacting on a government's image and even legitimacy.

Of particular concern is police collusion with OC, which seriously undermines the public's confidence in law enforcement. Such collusion assumes many forms. These range from tip-offs (e.g. of an imminent raid on an illegal gambling establishment or brothel) to

---

[2] For alternative classifications see Koivu 2018, who suggests a four-fold typology of state–OCG relationships (collaborative; supportive; competitive; evasive), and Lampe (2016, 261–92).

active involvement in the trafficking of drugs, weapons, and humans, and occasionally even contract killing (for a Slovak case see Flash News 2006; US Department of State 2009).

Links between OC and law enforcement are not restricted to developing, transition, or hybrid states. In both the 1970s and the 1990s, investigations of corruption in the New York Police Department by the Knapp and Mollen Commissions found abundant evidence of police collusion with OCGs, often in the form of accepting bribes to overlook illegal brothels, drug-dealing, etc. Even more serious is the case of two New York police officers who were sentenced to life imprisonment in 2006 for numerous crimes, including committing several murders on behalf of New York OC (Lawson and Oldham 2006: On police corruption and collusion in the U.S. see Punch 2009, 53–92). Research on collusion between OC and law enforcement in Europe suggests that both foreign and traditional domestic OCGs are much more likely to attempt to influence police officers (and judges) than other state officials (Sberna and Vannucci 2015, 109–10).

While the focus here has been on collusion between domestic police officers and OC, such linkages sometimes involve international law enforcement officials. In 2010, Jackie Selebi was sentenced by a South African court to 15 years' imprisonment for accepting more than US$156,000 in bribes from a drug smuggler during his period as President of Interpol (2004–8).

Other state officials' collusion with OC

As with police collusion, that between other officers of the state and OCGs assumes many forms. A common one is where border guards and customs officials assist OCGs in various ways (e.g. by turning a blind eye) to smuggle goods and people across borders (Gounev and Bezlov 2010, 16–17 and 93–104; Dandurand and Bullock 2013, esp. 11–13). Another is where immigration officials provide genuine documentation to assist people smugglers or human traffickers in irregular migration (Dandurand and Bullock 2013, esp. 15 and 18–19). While concrete evidence of collusion between members of the military and OCGs is relatively scarce, cases have been reported in countries such as Iraq and Russia (Muravska, Hughes, and Pyman 2011).

But in terms of governance, even more serious is collusion between judges, politicians, and OCGs. There is evidence of this from many types of political system. A Mexican case is of the former governor of Veracruz state, Javier Duarte, who in September 2018 was sentenced to nine years' imprisonment for corruption and criminal association (for examples—both proven and alleged—from Nigeria and several other West African states see Alemika 2013: more generally on OC–state collusion see Cockayne 2016; Lampe 2016, 261–92).

In China, the anticorruption campaign that has been a key feature of Chinese politics since Xi Jinping became the Communist Party General Secretary (2012) and the country's President (2013) has sometimes led the authorities to refer to a "red-black" nexus (see Wang 2017, esp. 143–72). This term refers to collusion between Communist officials (reds) and OCGs (blacks—the Chinese term for OCGs is *hei shehui*, or dark/black societies). One of the key cases mounted against a "tiger" (i.e. a high-level official) in recent years related to both corruption and links to OC: This is the Bo Xilai case that resulted in 2013 in a life sentence for the former Communist Party Secretary of Chongqing (Sichuan) and Politburo member.

Before his fall, Bo had mounted a campaign against OC in Chongqing that revealed that large numbers of Communist Party, government, and judicial officials had been colluding with criminal gangs. More recently, Xi Jinping has been targeting OC specifically: He announced a three-year major crackdown in January 2018, claiming that OC now threatened the very existence of the Communist Party system (Shi 2018; Zhang 2019)—just as he had earlier claimed that corruption could bring about the collapse of the CCP and ultimately the country (China Daily 2012).

Collusion between officials and OC was also a feature of the (Communist) Soviet Union. Thus, according to Marie Lavigne (1999, 9–10), party officials collaborated in the late Communist era with OC to run illegal markets. This helped former Communist Party and state officials to benefit from the privatization process in early postcommunism, which undermined attempts to legitimize the new democratic government and system. But collusion between Russian officials and OC is still all too common. Indeed, based on a case study of Tatarstan, Svetlana Stephenson (2017) provides detailed evidence of "fusion" between the two agencies—i.e. interdependence of political authorities and OCGs. Finally, there are numerous allegations (e.g. Dawisha 2014) that President Putin himself has close links of various kinds to OC.

There is considerable evidence of American politicians colluding with OCGs, dating back at least to the nineteenth century, continuing through the early twentieth century in cities such as Chicago (Landesco 1968), and extending up to the present (Cressey 1969; Allen 1993; Woodiwiss 2001, 2017; Allerfeldt 2018). In an empirical study of Seattle—the city is given the pseudonym "Rainfall West,"[3] but it is claimed that what the research uncovered there would be found in any other US city—William Chambliss (1971, 1151) refers to a "cabal" of OC, politicians, city officials, law enforcement, and businesspeople and argues that OC is "a hidden but nonetheless integral part of the governmental structure." There have certainly been numerous allegations that U.S. President Donald Trump has had connections with OC, both in the U.S. (Drehle 2018) and in Russia (Kirilenko 2018; Unger 2018).

A serious problem of collusion between politicians and OC is state capture. This term was coined by the World Bank at the start of the twenty-first century—though the concept itself is much older—and refers to a situation in which private interests exert "illicit, illegitimate and non-transparent influence" on "the formation of laws, rules and decrees" (Pradhan et al. 2000, 3; see too Hellman, Jones, and Kaufman 2000) through corrupting public officials, especially legislators. It makes sense to broaden the concept of state capture to include the *implementation* of laws and other state regulations. The term was originally applied principally to postcommunist transition states but has recently been applied in the academic literature mainly to African states (e.g. Rijkers, Freund, and Nucifora 2017; Bracking 2018), though sometimes also to other parts of the world (Trantidis and Tsagkroni 2017).

However, most analyses focus on capture by the regular business sector, without considering the potential or actual role of OC (though see e.g. Sitorus 2011; Sberna 2015; Di Cattaldo and Mastrorocco 2019). In fact, OC frequently extorts funds from legitimate businesses that are tendering for public contracts, or else bribes such businesses to in turn bribe public officials to secure contracts. OCGs are in this situation vicariously corrupting

---

[3] Chambliss subsequently published a book-length analysis on this topic (1978, 2nd ed. 1988) in which he acknowledges that his empirical study is of Seattle.

state officials in the procurement process. Another vicarious form is where OC becomes a subcontractor to a legitimate business that has secured a public contract. In a third scenario, OCGs themselves own or directly control enterprises that secure contracts. Italian examples of these diverse phenomena have been analyzed by Stefano Caneppele, Francesco Calderoni, and Sara Martocchia, who note (2009, 154) that, as of the early 2000s, Italy was the only E.U. state to have adopted legislation explicitly targeting infiltration of the public procurement process by OC. The seriousness of this issue has long been underestimated by most governments.

In concluding this subsection, note that OC not infrequently colludes with political parties and presidential candidates that seek electoral victory. Guatemala's Commission against Impunity has stated publicly that some parties and candidates in the 2011 and 2015 Guatemalan parliamentary and presidential elections were largely funded by OC, while presidential candidate Marco Estrada was arrested in April 2019 and charged with conspiring with the Sinaloa drug cartel (Lakhani 2019). Similarly, U.S. courts published statements in 2019 in which confessed drug traffickers claimed to have financed the campaigns of presidential candidates in Honduras since 2004 (ASJ 2019: see too Dudley 2016; Chayes 2017). The negative implications of this kind of collusion for the integrity—and hence quality—of a government are obvious.

Former officers of the state joining OCGs

As noted above, a salient feature of OCGs in many postcommunist states (e.g. Albania, Bulgaria, Russia, and Serbia) is that a major source of recruits has been former members of the state security agencies, both the regular police and in particular the secret police. After the collapse of Communism in Europe, many postcommunist governments were anxious to distance themselves from their predecessors' practices and therefore dramatically reduced the scale of the secret police. Such former officers were highly attractive to OCGs, since they had been well trained in the use of weapons, sometimes had access to such weapons, were often desensitized to killing, knew how the state investigated OC and conducted surveillance, and could in many cases inform their new "employers" about the potential corruptibility of individual officers still working for the state. Many of these former officers felt alienated from the new authorities, which they considered had been disloyal to them. This alienation, combined with the attraction of using their skills, being respected, and potentially earning substantial incomes, helps to explain the appeal of OC to such former officers.

In developed Western states, one major source of new members of OMCGs (outlaw motorcycle gangs) in the U.S., Australia, and elsewhere in recent decades has been former soldiers who miss the camaraderie and excitement of their time in the military (Quinn 2001, 388; Piano 2018, 352; generally on OMCGs see Bain and Lauchs 2017).

Groups of state officials acting like OCGs

All too often, officers of the state engage in criminal activity that closely resembles that of OCGs. For example, a salient trend in the Russian police during the 2000s has been for groups of officers to replace OCGs and act like such groups themselves, as in *reiderstvo* and *kryshevanie*. The first of these terms usually translates as "raiding." However, although the word is said to have been borrowed from Wall Street (as in "corporate raiding" in the private sector), the Russian version involves officers of the state. Sometimes on their own initiative, sometimes in return for material benefits from OCGs or miscreant businesspeople, and sometimes on orders from their political masters, Russian police officers will raid a well-functioning company and falsely accuse it of some impropriety. In one common scenario, the case will then come before a corrupt judge, who will be bribed to find the (innocent) company guilty and fine them so heavily that the owners sell up—in practice, to those behind the raid (see Rochlitz 2014; Shelley and Deane 2016). This problem was explicitly recognized by the then (2008–12) Russian President, Dmitry Medvedev, who strongly condemned such practices (Medvedev 2010).

The second phenomenon, *kryshevanie*, translates literally as "roofing" and refers to improper protection rackets run by police officers. While mostly directed towards shops, restaurants and other small and medium enterprises, even old ladies selling produce from their gardens have been targeted (Taktarov 2012). According to analysts such as Brian Taylor (2011, 164), this is an area where officers of the state have largely replaced OCGs since the 1990s, even though the nature of this protection may have changed somewhat following police reforms and the introduction of tougher controls from above under President Medvedev (Kravtsova 2012; more generally on Russian police corruption see Cheloukhine 2017).

Russia is by no means the only state in which groups of corrupt officers of the state act like OCGs. There is a long history in the U.S., dating back to the nineteenth century, of groups of corrupt police officers not only colluding with OCGs but in some cases themselves acting like OCGs. The most significant nineteenth-century investigation into police corruption in New York—the Lexow Committee of the 1890s—uncovered cases of officers engaging in voter intimidation, extortion, counterfeiting, and other types of unambiguously criminal behavior (Berman 1981).

Border guards constitute another group of officers who sometimes act like OCGs. In 2013, for example, two former border patrol agents in the U.S. were sentenced to 35- and 30-years' imprisonment respectively for assisting at least 500 illegal migrants to enter the U.S., netting the two officers more than US$700,00 in the process (Watson 2013). The problem, particularly as it relates to people smuggling, continues to exist in the U.S. Thus, a 2018 report in *Mother Jones* detailed the issue of corrupt American border guards on the U.S. border with Mexico and maintained that the federal authorities' commitment to a dramatic and swift increase in the number of these guards had the unintended consequence of increasing the proportion of questionable recruits. While these benefitted from assumed de facto immunity, several had in fact been charged with embezzlement, people smuggling, money-laundering and other criminal activities (Schatz 2018; see too Steinle 2018). Mexico has also experienced this problem (MND 2019). This highlights once again that the differences between OC and corruption are *in practice* often hazy.

The state inadvertently—or not so unwittingly—assisting OC

Among the many ways in which states often play into the hands of OC is by adopting legislation that prohibits certain goods or services for which there is popular demand. The best-known example of this is alcohol prohibition in the U.S. 1920–33, which is widely perceived to have promoted the expansion of the Italian Mafia's (La Cosa Nostra's) role in the U.S. during that period.

In other cases, it is the absence of legislation that can assist OCGs. For example, it is only in the 2000s that many states have introduced dedicated laws prohibiting human trafficking: As of 2003 (the year in which the UN's anti-trafficking protocol became effective), less than one-third of states had such legislation.

Another area in which many states have been slow to adopt laws that could at least hinder OCGs (as well as corrupt officials) is in anti-money-laundering legislation. In 2009, the UK-based Tax Justice Network (TJN) began publishing a biennial Financial Secrecy Index, which ranks jurisdictions—60 in 2009, 112 in 2018—"according to their secrecy and the scale of their offshore financial activities" (TJN 2018). This index provides quantitative data on the extent to which jurisdictions facilitate money-laundering. In the 2018 Financial Secrecy Index, the ten worst jurisdictions (the lower the number, the more secretive) were:

1. Switzerland
2. United States
3. Cayman Islands
4. Hong Kong
5. Singapore
6. Luxembourg
7. Germany
8. Taiwan
9. United Arab Emirates (Dubai)
10. Guernsey (TJN 2018)

Contrary to the common perception that it is basically small island-states that are the principal culprits in facilitating money-laundering, it emerges from this index that leading developed states such as the U.S. and Germany have much to answer for (see Findley, Nielsen, and Sharman 2015; Foer 2019).

In some cases, developed states do not fulfill promises they have made to introduce measures putatively designed to combat OC and corruption. A prime example is the UK, which promised in late 2018 to suspend the Tier 1 (a.k.a. Golden Visa) system as part of its anticorruption and anti-OC drive—but then delayed its implementation (Pegg and Grierson 2018). While the UK did replace this system with "Innovator" visas in April 2019, some analysts maintain that the new scheme can still be exploited by OC and corrupt officials (Dawkins 2019; more generally on Golden Visas in Europe see Brillaud and Martini 2018; Pearson 2019).

Before concluding this section, it is worth noting a form of interaction between the state and OC that is not often mentioned, namely "noble cause" corruption—a.k.a. "process corruption" or the "Dirty Harry problem"—in police forces. This is where police officers take the law into their own hands—bending or breaking laws not for personal gain, but because they want to ensure the conviction of persons they believe have been committing serious crimes and getting away with these. They might plant evidence or commit perjury in court ("testilying"), for example (on noble cause see Crank, Flaherty, and Giacomazzi 2007;

Caldero, Dailey, and Withrow 2018). But in states that respect the rule of law, a problem can arise that helps OCG members—namely that convictions can be overturned and the state required to pay compensation if such "noble cause" activity is discovered. In 2018, it was revealed that the Victorian (Australia) police had authorized a defense lawyer for a number of OCG members involved in a gangland "war" in Melbourne to act as an informant. Despite awareness that a number of violent gangsters against whom the lawyer had helped to secure convictions would now be in a position to appeal their sentences, Victorian authorities severely criticized the police and established a Royal Commission to examine the whole affair (Le Grand and Schliebs 2019). In July 2019, the first alleged OC killer to have his sentence quashed because of this case revealed he would be seeking compensation for 12 years' false imprisonment.

The state's positive use of OC for political purposes

A common situation in which states opt to use OC for political purposes is when a country is being subjected to sanctions by much of the international community, and the authorities either "turn a blind eye" to OC sanction-breaking or else actively encourage it (Gounev and Bezlov 2010; Blancke 2014). In January 1996, the Yugoslav Prosecutor-General admitted that his government had turned a blind eye to OC engaged in smuggling items into the Federal Republic of Yugoslavia (comprising Serbia and Montenegro) while the country was subject to UN sanctions (1992–95) because of the Bosnian War (OMRI 1996; more generally see Giatzidis 2007). Another state about which official collusion with OCGs in sanctions-busting has been alleged is Iran. In 2017, the U.S. Treasury Department identified 16 "entities and individuals" it claimed were procuring American military hardware and software for sale to the Iranian government (Calamur 2017). But U.S. authorities have themselves sometimes colluded with OC for political and security reasons, as with Italian OC both within the U.S. and in Italy during the Second World War (Campbell 1977; Newark 2007; Cockayne 2016, 147–68).

A particularly disturbing variant of the state's use of OC for political purposes is where it encourages and possibly finances OC to operate beyond the country's borders on behalf of the government (Filatova 2017). Thus Mark Galeotti (2017: 1) writes of Russia: "Russian-based organised crime groups in Europe have been used for a variety of purposes, including . . . cyber attacks . . . and even to carry out targeted assassinations on behalf of the Kremlin." While the evidence on much of this use of OC by the Russian state remains circumstantial, it is considered sufficiently persuasive to be of concern to many Western governments (on Russian, Chinese, and other states' alleged use of cybercriminals see Maurer 2018; Taylor 2019: on the use of OC "as a covert tool for the 'dark aspects' of its [Russia's—LH] foreign policy," including murder, see Galeotti 2019, and for more detail Galeotti 2018).

There have been unsubstantiated allegations that Hong Kong authorities, possibly with Beijing's backing, hired OCG members to attack protesters during anti-government demonstrations in both 2014 and 2019 (Lim 2014; Varese and Wong 2018; Handley and Zhao 2019). If such allegations are true, this would exemplify state authorities surreptitiously using OCGs to counter political opposition. According to Prof. T. Wing Lo, "All the crime committed by Triads is for money ... sometimes when governments cannot use the formal law enforcement for whatever reason, they pay for it" (cited in Regan 2019).

According to Lynette Ong (2018), local governments in Communist China sometimes use hired "thugs" to assist them in implementing unpopular policies—notably the destruction of existing properties to make way for new developments—that local residents are resisting. Other states that have allegedly outsourced violence against protesting citizens include Egypt, Russia, Syria, and Ukraine (Ong 2019).

States will sometimes tolerate OC subject to tacitly agreed conditions. Thus, the Mexican government's approach towards the drug cartels until the 2000s was de facto to permit them to traffic cocaine into the U.S., on condition that they did not do so within Mexico itself and that they abstained from using violence (Rios 2015, 1436). This was seen to have the twin advantages that the state could profit from the business while maintaining low levels of violence and other forms of crime.

The state's negative use of OC for political purposes

Unlike the situation in the previous category, here politicians will blame OC for problems they perceive the public to be seriously concerned about and will promise to combat OCGs. A recent example is U.S. President Donald Trump's citing of the MS-13 (Mara Salvatrucha 13) gang as symptomatic of the criminality that can be expected from Latin American illegal migrants (Rosenberg 2018), while President Rodrigo Duterte's campaign against drug dealers in the Philippines and President Jair Bolsonaro's campaign against OC in Brazil also typify this. While this approach is sometimes adopted by mainstream politicians genuinely committed to reducing OC because of its pernicious effects on society, it is all too often taken by populists and dictators who pursue such a policy not to foster the rule of law but rather to enhance their own popularity; in these circumstances, this approach undermines the quality of government.

A related phenomenon is where governments, opposition parties, or state agencies use or manipulate data on OC for political purposes. For instance, law enforcement agencies may emphasize—even exaggerate—the threat from OC in a bid to increase their funding. In May 2019, the head of the UK's National Crime Agency warned that law enforcement would lose the fight against OC unless the police were better funded (Townsend 2019).

OC negatively interacting with the state

While the preferred method by which OCGs seek to influence politics is through corrupting or blackmailing politicians (for evidence from Turkey see Cengiz 2017), an alternative approach is the threat or actual use of violence. This has not been widely researched, but Gianmarco Daniele and Gemma Dipoppa (2017) have analyzed the use of OC violence against local Italian politicians, finding that attacks are more likely shortly after an election than before it, especially if there has been a change of ruling party. This suggests that an hypothesis about the reasons for the increase in OC violence in Mexico since 2007—the breakdown of longstanding cosy relations between OC and the ruling party or coalition (Shirk and Wallman 2015, 1359–60)—may be supported by Italian data. However, note that another study (Alesina, Piccolo, and Pinotti 2019) finds that, in Italy at least and in contrast to the situation in local politics, OC threats and use of violence against politicians at the national level are more likely to occur *before* elections.

The state acting like an OCG

In a controversial analysis, Charles Tilly (1985) argued that the modern—primarily European—state has much in common with OC, at least in its origins. He maintained that early states extracted funds from the citizens for war-making, which in turn was seen to legitimize the state, since its ultimate purpose was allegedly to protect the citizenry. It is the focus on protection, violence, and the extraction of funds from citizens that is seen as a common feature of the early modern state and some OCGs. After all, scholars such as Diego Gambetta (1993) and Federico Varese (2001) have argued that weak and corrupt states can encourage the rise of OCGs that offer private protection (for analysis of the connections between weak and corrupt states and OC in Latin America see Yashar 2018).

There are numerous examples of contemporary states acting like OCGs. A term widely attributed to either Alexander Litvinenko or a Spanish prosecutor (this is disputed) to describe the current Russian system—"Mafia state"—has become increasingly popular among journalists (e.g. Harding 2011; Rosenberg 2012). This term has also been applied to several other states, including Afghanistan, Bulgaria, Guinea, Hungary, and Venezuela (Naím 2012; Magyar 2016: see too Chayes 2015). One of the most frequently cited examples of the state acting like an OCG is North Korea, which Wang and Blancke (2014) have also labeled a "mafia state." There has been a strong suspicion in U.S. official agencies, for instance, that North Korean government agencies were behind the large-scale hacking of a Bangladeshi bank in February 2016 (Corkery and Goldstein 2017). A common explanation for such behavior is that the sanctions imposed on North Korea because of its nuclear weapons program encourage the state to circumvent these through criminal activity (Nichols 2019).

The hacking of foreign targets by government agencies, assuming the allegations are justified, are mostly considered to be for political purposes. But there are also numerous allegations that states such as China have engaged in hacking overseas corporations' sites to steal intellectual property (Nakashima 2015; Dilanian 2018). If such claims are true, this is clearly for economic benefit, and thus looks very similar to OCGs' activity and motivations (on "shadow states" and "parapolitics" see Wilson 2009; Decoeur 2018).

OC acting like a state

The previous types elaborated in this taxonomy all focus on either the state or its interactions with OC. But some OCGs have on occasions mimicked governments, themselves acting like surrogate—albeit incomplete—states, carrying out important tasks that the authorities were performing either inadequately or not at all. Perhaps the most obvious example is the early Sicilian Mafia, which many analysts maintain arose primarily to protect landowners by enforcing new land ownership rules introduced in the early nineteenth century at a time when the Sicilian authorities were weak and not fulfilling this role (Gambetta 1993; Bandiera

2003).[4] Another example is the Yakuza, which—while losing popularity since the early 1990s—once enjoyed widespread support partly because it often assisted the public more quickly and efficiently than did the Japanese state following major catastrophes such as earthquakes (Robinson 1995). The fact that it continues to do this (e.g. following the March 2011 earthquake and tsunami—Jones 2011) suggests that many Japanese still either appreciate the Yakuza or have mixed feelings about them.

Conclusions

It is clear that OC can significantly impact negatively on both society generally and the quality of government more specifically. In rare situations, there may even be fears that OCGs will replace a very weak government: In the late 1980s, the Colombian President was reported to have made such a claim about his country's powerful drug cartels (Bagley 1996, 202). While this is an extreme and improbable scenario, it should be obvious that the impact of OC is much greater than it would be were it not for so much corruption among public officials. But this chapter has demonstrated that governments themselves can encourage OC and even act like OCGs. In other words, and as frequently emphasized here, there is all too often a blurring between government and OC.

Occasionally, OC can play a positive role in collaboration with the state. Focusing on Central Asia, Alexander Kupatadze (2012, 1) notes how a Kyrgyz politician involved in drug-trafficking used some of the profit from that trafficking to build a vital bridge for local residents. Yet despite rare situations in which OC can play a positive role, collusion between governments, corrupt officials, and OC, as well as the mimicry of each other by OC and governments, is sooner or later to the serious detriment of the quality of government. In the longer term, cultures of OC and corruption develop that become entrenched and difficult to overcome.

However, a comparison of assessments of the OC, corruption, and quality of government levels in our four targeted states—using the four variables identified in the definitional section—suggests that any relationship between the level of OC, corruption, and the quality of government is more complex than might be assumed.

We begin by comparing the perceived impact of OC, using the World Economic Forum's *Global Competitiveness Report* for 2017. This provides data on the perceived impact of OC on firms and reveals that, in terms of costs to business, the situation in Mexico is much worse than in China or Russia (which have similar scores), while the situation is best in the U.S. (Schwab 2017, 91, 203, 249 and 303).

To assess corruption levels, we can consider both perceptions and actual bribery rates. As regards perceived corruption levels, Mexico and Russia both emerge as far worse than China, with the U.S. again being seen to have much less of a problem than the other three states (Transparency International 2018). The rankings are slightly different when it comes to actual experiences of corruption, with Mexico having a much higher rate than Russia, China

---

[4] While Gambetta (1993, 7) prefers to see the Mafia as a particular type of business rather than a surrogate and incomplete state, his analysis suggests that the protection it sold was in various ways analogous to that provided by states and funded by taxation.

having somewhat less of a problem than either of these, and the U.S. again (probably) having much less of a problem than the other three (Pring 2017a, 17; 2017b, 15; 2016, 18).[5]

Turning now to three variables used for determining the quality of government, an interesting and complex picture emerges. Starting with budget transparency, the Open Budget Survey 2017 assesses the level of transparency in Mexico, Russia, and the U.S. as quite similar (with Mexico enjoying the highest level), while China's budgeting process is significantly more opaque (Lakin 2018, 54–5). Regarding the rule of law, China, Russia, and Mexico all have similar—middling—scores according to the World Justice Project's Rule of Law Index for 2017, with the U.S. faring much better (WJP 2018, 20–1). Finally, the Economist Intelligence Unit produces a score for each country called "Functioning of Government" in its annual *Democracy Index*. This is a composite figure based on 14 variables, such as "Is there an effective system of checks and balances on the exercise of government authority?" and "Is the civil service willing to and capable of implementing government policy?" In the 2017 index, Russia performs far worse on this variable than China, which in turn is ranked below Mexico—with the U.S. again rated as having the best functioning government (EIU 2018, 5–8).

Thus, the data used here suggest that Mexico has a reasonably well-functioning government, even though both OC and corruption are clearly serious problems in that country, so that there is a rule of law issue. While Russia's government is assessed as a poorly functioning one and the country clearly has a serious problem with corruption, OC is not—apparently—nearly as much of an issue for Russians as might be assumed. This is possibly because of the decline of civilian OC and the rise of a corrupt police force engaging in OC activities, plus the reduced visibility of OC as it has moved increasingly online in the twenty-first century. These two examples suggest that a case-by-case approach to the role that OC plays in a given country's politics and government will be at least as instructive as a macro-comparison across a large number of states.

Nevertheless, some generalizations are permissible. Notably, the nature of interaction between OCGs and the state does vary somewhat between developed, transition, and developing states. Overall, the developed democratic state (U.S.) emerges as the one best adhering to the rule of law, having the most effective government and the least problem with OC. This finding is in line with that of Edgardo Buscaglia and Jan van Dijk (2003, 31) who, on the basis of a sophisticated statistical analysis, concluded that it is above all the quality of "core public state institutions," especially law enforcement, that determines levels of OC and corruption. They further maintained that this finding applies across states at all levels of development. In short, the more effective and less corrupt a state's institutions, the less impact OC will have on the overall quality of government. Yet while there is typically greater distance in developed states between the state and OC, the latter nevertheless constitutes a growing problem in even the most law-abiding countries and impacts upon the quality of government.

Whereas most analysts see the linkages between OC and the state as undesirable, Kendra Koivu (2018) argues that OC–state collusion is not invariably a negative phenomenon and that if states criminalize certain markets because of external pressure, they are more likely

---

[5] The U.S. was not surveyed in the 2015–17 *Global Corruption Barometer* (GCB) cited here, so that the result for the previous GCB (Transparency International 2013) was used—hence the use of the term "probably."

to collaborate with the OCGs that emerge. This observation is compatible with the point alluded to above that sanctions against a regime can have the unintended consequence of making that regime turn to OC to overcome shortages. While this does not excuse governments that collaborate with or themselves act like OC, it does mean that international organizations and foreign states should be aware of the likely negative ramifications of imposing sanctions on a given regime—just as they need to accept that over-regulation of goods and services the market demands can stimulate both OC and corruption.

Can OC and corruption be overcome, which would have positive effects on the quality of government? Addressing this warrants a separate chapter, but some broad observations are possible. Eric Uslaner (2008) has argued persuasively that higher levels of inequality lead to higher levels of corruption and lower levels of trust. Given that a major driver of OC is poverty and social inequality, less inequality as reflected in lower Gini coefficients would almost certainly have a positive effect on the level of OC, and, as a knock-on effect, corruption and the quality of government. Governments have the capacity to reduce inequality if they are so inclined. They could also experiment with different policies on recreational drugs, which would impact OC.

But OC, like corruption, is ultimately a so-called wicked problem: It is too complex ever to fully comprehend or eradicate. For instance, states cannot effectively prevent domestic violence, postconflict PTSD, and other factors that can be stimuli to membership of OCGs. Ultimately, the most important factors in reducing OC are political will (of leaders, bureaucrats, and the general public) and state capacity. Unfortunately, even these are insufficient to eradicate OC, since they essentially relate to individual states and territories. The transnationalization of OC is a particularly intractable problem, given that combating this requires a level of cooperation and agreement (e.g. on definitions) that will be difficult to achieve in a world where the self-proclaimed leader of the "free world"—the U.S.—has under President Trump often been more critical of traditional allies than of dictators.

Agenda for Future Research

The agenda for future research in this area is a full one. Among the most pressing topics requiring much more empirical investigation or conceptual clarification and agreement are:

- How best to define and measure OC (on the problems see e.g. Barberet 2014; Hobbs and Antonopoulos 2014).
- The linkages and networks between OCGs and corrupt public officials—including more focus on state capture by OC, as distinct from by more legitimate enterprise.
- OC's involvement in public procurement.
- Corrupt officials assisting people smugglers and human traffickers. One recent analysis (Chêne 2018, 2) noted that there appears to be only one detailed study specifically on corruption among border guards, and that was confined to the EU. Even less researched are the links between corrupt immigration officials in embassies and consulates who provide genuine visas to OCGs involved in people smuggling or human trafficking.

- OC's corruption of politicians and other public officials through either blackmail (e.g. based on past activities or the current use of "honey-pots"—attractive people who lure partnered public officials into inappropriate affairs) or the use of threats or actual violence against those officials or members of their families.
- The technical and cultural factors hindering greater collaboration between law enforcement agencies in combating OC.
- States' use of OC for "arm's length" control of citizens and illegal activities in other countries.
- The most effective methods for combating OC: This must avoid the "one-size-fits all" approach and instead devise methods appropriate for particular kinds of OC activity and particular cultures.
- Legitimacy and its relationship to OC and corruption.
- Finally, while a small number of research projects have analyzed the gender aspects of corruption (e.g. Corsianos 2012; Ionescu 2014; Debski et al. 2018) and OC (e.g. Arsovska and Begum 2014; Simoni 2018) separately, it is time for detailed analyses of gender dimensions of the interplay between OC, corruption, and government (for an earlier analysis of the gaps in researching OC and corruption see Levi and Lord 2011).

While these topics should attract more scholarly analysis, researching them can be not merely challenging but dangerous. This compounds the problems of researching what is already a difficult—yet very important—topic.

References

Abadinsky, Howard. 2017. *Organized Crime*. 11th ed. Boston MA: Cengage Learning.

Alemika, Etannibi, ed. 2013. *The Impact of Organised Crime on Governance in West Africa*. Abuja: Friedrich Ebert Stiftung.

Alesina, Alberto, Salvatore Piccolo, and Paolo Pinotti. 2019. "Organized Crime, Violence, and Politics." *Review of Economic Studies* 86 (2): 457–99.

Allen, Oliver. 1993. *The Tiger: The Rise and Fall of Tammany Hall*. Boston MA: Da Capo.

Allerfeldt, Kristofer. 2018. *Organized Crime in the United States, 1865–1941*. Jefferson NC: McFarland.

Allum, Felia, and Panos Kostakos. 2010. "Deconstruction in Progress: Towards a Better Understanding of Organized Crime?" In *Defining and Defying Organized Crime: Discourse, perceptions and reality*, edited by Felia Allum, Francesca Longo, Daniela Irrera, and Panos Kostakos. 1–12. London: Routledge.

Armao, Fabio. 2015. "Mafia-Owned Democracies. Italy and Mexico as Patterns of Criminal Neoliberalism." *Tiempo Devorado* 2 (1): 4–15.

Arsovska, Jana, and Popy Begum. 2014. "From West Africa to the Balkans: exploring women's roles in transnational organized crime." *Trends in Organized Crime* 17 (1–2): 89–109.

ASJ. 2019. "Public Position of ASJ Regarding Illicit Financing of Political Campaigns." Tegucigalpa and Berlin: Asociación para una Sociedad Más Justa and Transparency International. https://www.transparency.org/news/pressrelease/public_position_of_asj_regarding_illicit_financing_of_political_campaigns?utm

Bagley, Bruce. 1996. "The Drug War in Colombia, 1989." In *Drugs in the Western Hemisphere: An Odyssey of Cultures in Conflict*, edited by William Walker III, 201–15. Wilmington DE: Scholarly Resources.

Bain, Andy, and Mark Lauchs, eds. 2017. *Understanding the Outlaw Motorcycle Gangs: International Perspectives*. Durham NC: Carolina Academic Press.

Bandiera, Oriana. 2003. "Land Reform, the Market for Protection, and the Origins of the Sicilian Mafia: Theory and Evidence." *Journal of Law, Economics and Organization* 19 (1): 218–44.

Barberet, Rosemary. 2014. "Measuring and Researching Transnational Crime." In *Handbook of Transnational Crime and Justice*, 2nd ed., edited by Philip Reichel and Jay Albanese, 47–61. Thousand Oaks CA: Sage.

Berman, Jay. 1981. "The Taming of the Tiger: The Lexow Committee Investigation of Tammany Hall and the Police Department of the City of New York." *Police Studies* 3 (4): 55–65.

Blancke, Stephan. 2014. "Criminal Connections: State Links to Organised Crime in North Korea." *Jane's Intelligence Review* (April): 34–37.

Bracking, Sarah. 2018. "Corruption & State Capture: What Can Citizens Do?" *Daedalus* 147 (3): 169–83.

Brillaud, Laure, and Maíra Martini. 2018. *European Getaway: Inside the Murky World of Golden Visas*. Berlin and London: Transparency International and Global Witness.

Brown, Elizabeth. 2014. "Drug Use in Developing Countries." *The Borgen Project*, January 23, 2014. https://borgenproject.org/drug-use-developing-countries/

Buscaglia, Edgardo, and Jan van Dijk. 2003. "Controlling Organized Crime and Corruption in the Public Sector." *Forum on Crime and Society* 3 (1–2): 3–34.

Calamur, Krishnadev. 2017. "The Latest U.S. Sanctions Against Iran." *The Atlantic*, July 18, 2017. https://www.theatlantic.com/news/archive/2017/07/iran-sanctions/534003/

Caldero, Michael, Jeffrey Dailey, and Brian Withrow. 2018. *Police Ethics: The Corruption of Noble Cause*. 4th ed. New York: Routledge.

Campbell, Rodney. 1977. *The Luciano Project: The Secret Wartime Collaboration of the Mafia and the U.S. Navy*. New York: McGraw Hill.

Caneppele, Stefano, Francesco Calderoni, and Sara Martocchia. 2009. "Not Only Banks: Criminological Models on the Infiltration of Public Contracts by Italian Organized Crime." *Journal of Money Laundering Control* 12 (2): 151–72.

Cengiz, Mahmud. 2017. "Entrenched Political Corruption Squelches New Crime-Fighting Model Designed to Combat Human Trafficking Operations in Turkey." *Global Initiative Against Transnational Organized Crime*, September 4, 2017. https://globalinitiative.net/entrenched-political-corruption-squelches-new-crime-fighting-model-designed-to-combat-human-trafficking-operations-in-turkey/

Chambliss, William. 1971. "Vice, Corruption, Bureaucracy, and Power." *Wisconsin Law Review* 1971 (4): 1150–73.

Chambliss, William. 1988. *On the Take: From Petty Crooks to Presidents*. 2nd ed. Bloomington IN: Indiana University Press.

Chayes, Sarah. 2015. *Thieves of State: Why Corruption Threatens Global Security*. New York: Norton.

Chayes, Sarah. 2017. *When Corruption is the Operating System: The Case of Honduras*. Washington DC: Carnegie Endowment for International Peace.

Cheloukhine, Serguei. 2017. *Policing in Russia: Combating Corruption since the 2009 Police Reforms*. Cham: Springer.

Chêne, Marie. 2018. *Corruption at Borders*. Bergen: U4 Anti-Corruption Resource Centre.

China Daily. 2012. "Resolve to Fight Corruption." *China Daily*, November 20, 2012. http://www.chinadaily.com.cn/cndy/2012-11/20/content_15942999.htm

Choo, Kim-Kwang Raymond, and Peter Grabosky. 2014. "Cybercrime." In Paoli 2014: 482–99.

Cockayne, James. 2016. *Hidden Power: The Strategic Logic of Organized Crime.* New York: Oxford University Press.

Corkery, Michael, and Matthew Goldstein. 2017. "North Korea Said to Be Target of Inquiry Over $81 Million Cyberheist." *New York Times*, March 22, 2017.

Corsianos, Marilyn. 2012. *The Complexities of Police Corruption.* Lanham MD: Rowman and Littlefield.

Crank, John, Dan Flaherty, and Andrew Giacomazzi. 2007. "The Noble Cause: An Empirical Assessment." *Journal of Criminal Justice* 35 (1): 103–16.

Cressey, Donald. 1969. *Theft of the Nation: The Structure and Nature of Organized Crime in America.* New York: Harper and Row.

Dandurand, Yvon, and Shannon Bullock. 2013. *Corruption and the Smuggling of Migrants.* Vienna: United Nations Office on Drugs and Crime.

Daniele, Gianmarco, and Gemma Dipoppa. 2017. "Mafia, Elections and Violence against Politicians." *Journal of Public Economics* 154: 10–33.

Davis, Ian, Chrissie Hirst, and Bernardo Mariani. 2001. *Organised Crime, Corruption and Illicit Arms Trafficking in an Enlarged EU: Challenges and Perspectives.* London: Saferworld.

Dawisha, Karen. 2014. *Putin's Kleptocracy: Who Owns Russia?* New York: Simon and Schuster.

Dawkins, David. 2019. "How The World's Wealthiest Obtain 'Golden Passports' To The U.K. And EU." *Forbes*, July 22, 2019. https://www.forbes.com/sites/daviddawkins/2019/07/22/the-worlds-wealthiest-embrace-covert-and-secretive-service-granting-golden-passports-to-uk-and-eu/#426087d8188f

Debski, Julia, Michael Jetter, Saskia Mösle, and David Stadelmann. 2018. "Gender and Corruption: The Neglected Role of Culture." *European Journal of Political Economy* 55 (December): 526–37.

Decoeur, Henri. 2018. *Confronting the Shadow State: An International Law Perspective on State Organized Crime.* New York: Oxford University Press.

Di Cattaldo, Marco, and Nicola Mastrorocco. 2019. "Organised Crime, Captured Politicians and the Allocation of Public Resources." *Trinity Economics Papers*, Working Paper no.1018.

Dilanian, Ken. 2018. "China's Hackers Are Stealing Secrets from U.S. Firms Again, Experts Say." *NBC News*, October 9, 2018. https://www.nbcnews.com/news/china/china-s-hackers-are-stealing-secrets-u-s-firms-again-n917836

Drehle, David, Von 2018. "Trump's Résumé Is Rife with Mob Connections." *Washington Post*, August 10, 2018.

Dudley, Stephen. 2016. *Honduras Elites and Organized Crime.* Washington DC: InSight Crime.

Duyne, Petrus van. 2007. "All in the Dutch Construction Family: Cartel Building and Organised Crime." In *Terrorism, Organised Crime and Corruption*, edited by Leslie Holmes, 109–29. Cheltenham: Elgar.

EIU. 2018. *Democracy Index 2017: Free Speech under Attack.* London: Economist Intelligence Unit.

Fijnaut, Cyrille, and Letizia Paoli, eds. 2004. *Organised Crime in Europe: Concepts, Patterns and Control Policies in the European Union and Beyond.* Dordrecht: Springer.

Filatova, Irina. 2017. "Russian Mafia Groups Reportedly Operate in Europe on Behalf of the Kremlin." *DW* [*Deutsche Welle*], April 27, 2017. https://www.dw.com/en/russian-mafia-groups-reportedly-operate-in-europe-on-behalf-of-the-kremlin/a-38617828

Findley, Michael, Daniel Nielsen, and Jason Sharman. 2015. "Causes of Noncompliance with International Law: A Field Experiment on Anonymous Incorporation." *American Journal of Political Science* 59 (1): 146–61.

Finkenauer, James. 2007. *Mafia and Organized Crime*. Oxford: One World.

Flash News. 2006. "Brutal murder of businessman was 'highly professional' according to police." *Slovak Spectator*, November 16, 2006. http://spectator.sme.sk/articles/view/25161/10/

Foer, Franklin. 2019. "How Kleptocracy Came to America." *The Atlantic*, March 2019. https://www.theatlantic.com/magazine/archive/2019/03/how-kleptocracy-came-to-america/580471/

Freemantle, Brian. 1995. *The Octopus: Europe in the Grip of Organised Crime*. London: Orion.

Galeotti, Mark. 2017. *Crimintern: How the Kremlin Uses Russia's Criminal Networks in Europe*. London: European Council on Foreign Relations.

Galeotti, Mark. 2018. *The Vory: Russia's Super Mafia*. New Haven: Yale University Press.

Galeotti, Mark. 2019. "Gangster Geopolitics: The Kremlin's Use of Criminals as Assets Abroad." *Moscow Times*, January 18, 2019. https://www.themoscowtimes.com/2019/01/18/gangster-geopolitics-the-kremlins-use-of-criminals-as-assets-abroad-a64204

Gambetta, Diego. 1993. *The Sicilian Mafia: The Business of Private Protection*. Cambridge MA: Harvard University Press.

Giatzidis, Emil. 2007. "The Challenge of Organized Crime in the Balkans and the Political and Economic Implications." *Journal of Communist Studies and Transition Politics* 23 (3): 327–51.

Gillespie, Alisdair. 2016. *Cybercrime: Key Issues and Debates*. Abingdon: Routledge.

Gilligan, George. 1999. "Organised Crime and Corrupting the Political System." *Journal of Financial Crime* 7 (2): 147–54.

Gounev, Philip, and Tihomir Bezlov. 2010. *Examining the Links between Organised Crime and Corruption*. Sofia: Center for the Study of Democracy.

Handley, Erin, and Iris Zhao. 2019. "What Are the Triads behind the Violent Attacks in Hong Kong?" *ABC News*, July 25, 2019. https://www.abc.net.au/news/2019-07-25/what-are-triads-and-were-they-involved-in-attacks-in-hong-kong/11341726

Harding, Luke. 2011. *Mafia State: How one reporter became an enemy of the brutal new Russia*. London: Guardian Books.

Hellman, Joel, Geraint Jones, and Daniel Kaufman. 2000. "Seize the State, Seize the Day: State Capture, Corruption, and Influence in Transition." *World Bank Policy Research Working Papers* (2444).

Hobbs, Dick. 1998. "Going down the Glocal: The Local Context of Organised Crime." *Howard Journal of Criminal Justice* 37 (4): 407–22.

Hobbs, Dick, and Georgios Antonopoulos. 2014. "How to Research Organized Crime." In Paoli 2014: 96–117.

Holmes, Leslie. 1997. *Post-Communism*. Durham NC: Duke University Press.

Holmes, Leslie. 2006. *Rotten States? Corruption, Post-Communism and Neoliberalism*. Durham NC: Duke University Press.

Ionescu, Luminița. 2014. "The Impact of Gender on Corruption." *Journal of Research in Gender Studies* 4 (1): 1044–49.

Jones, Terril Yue. 2011. "Yakuza among First with Relief Supplies in Japan." *Reuters*, March 26, 2011. https://www.reuters.com/article/us-yakuza/yakuza-among-first-with-relief-supplies-in-japan-idUSTRE72O6TF20110325

Kaplan, David, and Alec Dubro. 2012. *Yakuza: Japan's Criminal Underworld*. Rev. ed. Berkeley: University of California Press.

Karstedt, Susanne. 2014. "Organizing Crime: The State as Agent." In Paoli 2014: 303–20.

Kilchling, Michael. 2004. "Organised Crime Policies in Germany." In Fijnaut and Paoli 2004: 717–62.

Kinzig, Jörg, and Anna Luczak. 2004. "Organised Crime in Germany: A Passe-Partout Definition Encompassing Different Phenomena." In Fijnaut and Paoli 2004: 333–56.

Kirilenko, Anastasiya. 2018. "Gangster Party candidate: Trump's ties to Russian organized crime." *The Insider*, April 7, 2018. https://theins.ru/uncategorized/98190?lang=en

Koivu, Kendra. 2018. "Illicit Partners and Political Development: How Organized Crime Made the State." *Studies in Comparative International Development* 53 (1): 47–66.

Kravtsova, Mariya. 2012. "Korruptsiya v politsii: transformatsiya otnoshenii s biznesom." *Ekonomicheskaya Sotsiologiya* 13 (2): 82–98.

Kupatadze, Alexander. 2012. *Organized Crime, Political Transitions and State Formation in Post-Soviet Eurasia*. Basingstoke: Palgrave Macmillan.

Lakhani, Nina. 2019. "Guatemala Elections Show Corruption Rampant Four Years after Uprising Toppled President." *Guardian*, June 13, 2019. https://www.theguardian.com/world/2019/jun/13/guatemala-election-corruption-creeps-in-again-four-years-after-uprising

Lakin, Jason. 2018. *Open Budget Survey 2017*. Washington DC: International Budget Partnership.

Lampe, Klaus von. 1995. "Understanding Organized Crime in Germany." *Organized Crime Research*. http://www.organized-crime.de/IALEtnr1.htm

Lampe, Klaus von. 2016. *Organized Crime: Analyzing Illegal Activities, Criminal Structures, and Extra-legal Governance*. Thousand Oaks, CA: Sage.

Lampe, Klaus von. 2018. "Definitions of Organized Crime." http://www.organized-crime.de/organizedcrimedefinitions.htm

Landesco, John. 1968. *Organized Crime in Chicago: Part III of Illinois Crime Survey 1929*. Chicago: University of Chicago Press.

Lavigne, Marie. 1999. *The Economics of Transition: From Socialist Economy to Market Economy*. 2nd ed. Basingstoke: Macmillan.

Lawson, Guy, and William Oldham. 2006. *The Brotherhoods: The True Story of Two Cops Who Murdered for the Mafia*. New York: Scribner.

Lee, Rensselaer. 1997. "Recent Trends in Nuclear Smuggling." In *Russian Organized Crime*, edited by Phil Williams, 109–21. London: Cass.

Lee, Rensselaer. 1998. *Smuggling Armageddon: The Nuclear Black Market in the Former Soviet Union and Europe*. New York: St. Martin's.

Le Grand, Chip, and Mark Schliebs. 2019. "Lawyer X scandal: police in crosshairs over informants." *Australian*, February 16, 2019: 5.

Levi, Michael, and Nicholas Lord. 2011. "Linkages between Organised Crime and Corruption and Research Gaps." In *Non-State Actors in Asset Recovery*, edited by Daniel Thelesklaf and Pedro Gomes Pereira, 39–61. Bern: Peter Lang.

Levitsky, Steven, and Lucan Way. 2010. *Competitive Authoritarianism: Hybrid Regimes After the Cold War*. New York: Cambridge University Press.

Lim, Louisa. 2014. "The Thugs of Mainland China." *New Yorker*, October 8, 2014. https://www.newyorker.com/news/news-desk/thugs-mainland-china-hong-kong-protests

Lupo, Salvatore. 1996. *Andreotti, la mafia, la storia d'Italia*. Rome: Donzelli.

Lupo, Salvatore. 2009. *History of the Mafia*. New York: Columbia University Press.

Maguire, Keith. 1997. "Modernisation and Clean Government: Tackling Crime, Corruption and Organised Crime in Modern Taiwan." *Crime, Law and Social Change* 28 (1): 73–88.

Magyar, Balint. 2016. *Post-Communist Mafia State: The Case of Hungary*. Budapest: Central European University Press.

Martellozzo, Elena, and Emma Jane, eds. 2017. *Cybercrime and Its Victims*. Abingdon: Routledge.

Maurer, Tim. 2018. *Cyber Mercenaries: The State, Hackers and Power*. New York: Cambridge University Press.

McGuiness, Damien. 2017. "How a Cyber Attack Transformed Estonia." *BBC News—Europe*, April 27, 2017. https://www.bbc.com/news/39655415

Medvedev, Dmitry. 2010. "Stenograficheskii otchet o zasedanii Soveta zakonodatelei." *Website of the President of Russia*, July 14, 2010. http://kremlin.ru/events/president/transcripts/8343

MND. 2019. "Immigration Agency Restructures after Dismissing 500 Agents for Corruption." *Mexico News Daily*, June 25, 2019. https://mexiconewsdaily.com/news/immigration-restructures-after-dismissing-500-agents/

Muravska, Julia, William Hughes, and Mark Pyman. 2011. *Organised Crime, Corruption, and the Vulnerability of Defence and Security Forces*. London: Transparency International UK.

Naím, Moisés. 2003. "The Five Wars of Globalization." *Foreign Policy* 134: 28–36.

Naím, Moisés. 2012. "Mafia States: Organized Crime Takes Office." *Foreign Affairs* 91 (3): 100–11.

Nakashima, Ellen. 2015. "China Still Trying to Hack U.S. Firms despite Xi's Vow to Refrain, Analysts Say." *Washington Post*, October 19, 2015. https://web-b-ebscohost-com.ezp.lib.unimelb.edu.au/ehost/detail/detail?vid=8&sid=55e4a362-8690-4ac4-883f-74ccd1722fed%40pdc-v-sessmgr03&bdata=JnNpdGU9ZWhvc3QtbGl2ZQ%3d%3d#AN=wapo.d9a923fe-75a8-11e5-b9c1-f03c48c96ac2&db=bwh

NCA, 2014. *National Strategic Assessment of Serious and Organised Crime 2014*. London: National Crime Agency.

Newark, Tim. 2007. *Mafia Allies: The True Story of America's Secret Alliance with the Mob in World War II*. St Paul MN: Zenith.

Nichols, Michelle. 2019. "North Korea Took $2 Billion in Cyberattacks to Fund Weapons Program: U.N. Report." *Reuters*, August 6, 2019. https://www.reuters.com/article/us-northkorea-cyber-un/north-korea-took-2-billion-in-cyberattacks-to-fund-weapons-program-u-n-report-idUSKCN1UV1ZX

Ohmae, Kenichi. 1990. *The Borderless World: Power and Strategy in the Interlinked Economy*. New York: Harper Business.

Oltermann, Philip, and Lorenzo Tondo. 2017. "Mafia Gangs Move to Germany as Business Hits Hard Times in Sicily." *Guardian*, June 29, 2017.

OMRI. 1996. "Serbia to Crack Down on Economic Crime?" *Open Media Research Institute Daily Digest II* (16), January 23, 1996. http://www.hri.org/news/balkans/omri/1996/96-01-23.omri.html#5

Ong, Lynette. 2018. "Thugs and Outsourcing of State Repression in China." *China Journal* (80): 94–110.

Ong, Lynette. 2019. "In Hong Kong, Are 'Thugs for Hire' behind the Attacks on Protesters?" *Washington Post*, July 24, 2019. https://www.washingtonpost.com/politics/2019/07/24/hired-guns-attacked-protesters-hong-kong-this-is-who-they-are-want-they-want/?noredirect=on&utm_term=.b1fae590f6a4

Paoli, Letizia, ed. 2014. *The Oxford Handbook of Organized Crime*. New York: Oxford University Press.

Pearson, Lucinda. 2019. "When Will Golden Visas Lose Their Glitter?" *Transparency International EU*, March 21, 2019. https://transparency.eu/when-will-golden-visas-lose-their-glitter/

Pegg, David, and Jamie Grierson. 2018. "Home Office Fails to Suspend "Golden Visa" Scheme." *Guardian*, December 12, 2018. https://www.theguardian.com/uk-news/2018/dec/11/home-office-fails-to-suspend-golden-visa-scheme

Piano, Ennio. 2018. "Outlaw and Economics: Biker Gangs and Club Goods." *Rationality and Society* 30 (3): 350–76.

Piotrowicz, Ryszard, Conny Rijken, and Bärbel Heide Uhl, eds. 2018. *Routledge Handbook of Human Trafficking*. Abingdon: Routledge.

Pradhan, Sanjay, James Anderson, Joel Hellman, Geraint Jones, Bill Moore, Helga Muller, Randi Ryterman, and Helen Sutch. 2000. *Anticorruption in Transition: A Contribution to the Policy Debate*. Washington DC: World Bank.

Pring, Coralie. 2016. *People and Corruption: Europe and Central Asia*. Berlin: Transparency International.

Pring, Coralie. 2017a. *People and Corruption: Asia Pacific*. Berlin: Transparency International.

Pring, Coralie. 2017b. *People and Corruption: Latin America and the Caribbean*. Berlin: Transparency International.

Punch, Maurice. 2009. *Police Corruption: Deviance, Accountability and Reform in Policing*. Cullompton: Willan.

Quinn, James. 2001. "Angels, Bandidos, Outlaws, and Pagans: The Evolution of Organized Crime among the Big Four 1% Motorcycle Clubs." *Deviant Behavior* 22 (4): 379–99.

Regan, Helen. 2019. "Fears of Thugs-for-Hire in Hong Kong after Mob Attack." *CNN*, July 24, 2019. https://edition.cnn.com/2019/07/23/asia/hong-kong-triad-arrests-intl-hnk/index.html

Rijkers, Bob, Caroline Freund, and Antonio Nucifora. 2017. "All in the Family: State Capture in Tunisia." *Journal of Development Economics* 124: 41–59.

Rios, Viridiana. 2015. "How Government Coordination Controlled Organized Crime: The Case of Mexico's Cocaine Markets." *Journal of Conflict Resolution* 59 (8): 1433–54.

Robinson, Gwen. 1995. "Mobsters Hand Out Milk and Noodles." *The Times*, January 20, 1995: 14.

Rochlitz, Michael. 2014. "Corporate Raiding and the Role of the State in Russia." *Post-Soviet Affairs* 30 (2–3): 89–114.

Rosenberg, Chuck. 2018. "Trump's Incendiary Attacks on MS-13 and Immigrants Are Making It Harder to Fight Crime." *USA Today*, October 4, 2018. https://www.usatoday.com/story/opinion/2018/10/04/trump-attacks-ms-13-immigrants-stereotypes-fight-crime-facts-column/1509739002/

Rosenberg, Steve. 2012. "Putin's Russia 'Now a Mafia State'." *BBC News (Europe)*, February 29, 2012. https://www.bbc.com/news/av/world-europe-17200833/putin-s-russia-now-a-mafia-state

Rothstein, Bo. 2013. "Conceptualizing QoG." In *Quality of Government and Corruption from a European Perspective*, edited by Nicholas Charron, Victor Lapuente, and Bo Rothstein, 16–34. Cheltenham: Elgar.

Ruggiero, Vincenzo. 1996. *Organised and Corporate Crime in Europe: Offers That Can't Be Refused*. Aldershot: Dartmouth.

Sberna, Salvatore. 2015. "Criminal-Political Capture and Public Procurement. Some Evidence from Italian Municipalities." Paper presented at the SGOC ECPR Annual Conference, 10–12 December 2015. Naples, Italy.

Sberna Salvatore, and Alberto Vannucci. 2015. "The Criminal Organisation of Political Corruption in Europe." In *Government Favouritism in Europe*, edited by Alina Mungiu-Pippidi, 105–26. Leverkusen Opladen: Barbara Budrich.

Schatz, Bryan. 2018. "New Report Details Dozens of Corrupt Border Patrol Agents—Just As Trump Wants to Hire More." *Mother Jones*, April 24, 2018. https://www.motherjones.com/politics/2018/04/new-report-details-dozens-of-corrupt-border-patrol-agents-just-as-trump-wants-to-hire-more/

Schwab, Klaus, ed. 2017. *The Global Competitiveness Report 2017–2018*. Geneva: World Economic Forum.

Sergi, Anna. 2017. *From Mafia to Organised Crime: A Comparative Analysis of Policing Models*. Cham: Palgrave Macmillan.

Shelley, Louise. 2010. *Human Trafficking: A Global Perspective*. New York: Cambridge University Press.

Shelley, Louise, and Judy Deane. 2016. *The Rise of Reiderstvo: Implications for Russia and the West*. Washington DC: TraCCC Consulting LLC.

Sheptycki, James. 2003. "The Governance of Organised Crime in Canada." *Canadian Journal of Sociology* 28 (4): 489–516.

Shi, Jiangtao. 2018. "Xi Jinping Puts China's Mafia in Cross Hairs, but Fears of Judicial Abuse Remain." *South China Morning Post*, January 26, 2018. https://www.scmp.com/news/china/policies-politics/article/2130629/xi-puts-chinas-mafia-cross-hairs-fears-judicial-abuse

Shirk, David, and Joel Wallman. 2015. "Understanding Mexico's Drug Violence." *Journal of Conflict Resolution* 59 (8): 1348–76.

Simoni, Serena. 2018. "Queens of Narco-trafficking: Breaking Gender Hierarchy in Colombia." *International Affairs* 94 (6): 1257–67.

Siniawer, Eiko Maruko. 2008. *Ruffians, Yakuza, Nationalists: The Violent Politics of Modern Japan, 1860–1960*. Ithaca: Cornell University Press.

Sitorus, Lily. 2011. "State Capture: Is It a Crime? How the World Perceived It." *Indonesia Law Review* 1 (2): 45–68.

Steinle, Mia. 2018. "13 CBP Employees Arrested for Corruption this Administration." *Project on Government Oversight*, April 23, 2018. https://www.pogo.org/investigation/2018/04/13-cbp-employees-arrested-for-corruption-this-administration/

Stephenson, Svetlana. 2017. "It Takes Two to Tango: The State and Organized Crime in Russia." *Current Sociology* 65 (3): 411–26.

Sterling, Claire. 1994. *Thieves World: The Threat of the New Global Network of Organized Crime*. New York: Simon and Schuster; also published as *Crime Without Frontiers: The Worldwide Expansion of Organized Crime and the Pax Mafiosa*. New York: Little Brown.

Stoecker, Sally, and Louise Shelley, eds. 2005. *Human Traffic and Transnational Crime: Eurasian and American Perspectives*. Lanham MD: Rowman and Littlefield.

Taktarov, Vadim. 2012. "Nachal'nik politsii sbezhal za granitsu posle obvinenii v korruptsii." *Izvestiya*, July 6, 2012. https://iz.ru/news/529548

Tamkin, Emily. 2017. "10 Years After the Landmark Attack on Estonia, Is the World Better Prepared for Cyber Threats?" *Foreign Policy*, April 27, 2017. https://foreignpolicy.com/2017/04/27/10-years-after-the-landmark-attack-on-estonia-is-the-world-better-prepared-for-cyber-threats/

Taylor, Brian. 2011. *State Building in Putin's Russia: Policing and Coercion after Communism*. New York: Cambridge University Press.

Taylor, Josh. 2019. "Chinese Cyberhackers 'Blurring Line between State Power and Crime.'" *Guardian*, August 8, 2019. https://www.theguardian.com/technology/2019/aug/08/chinese-cyberhackers-blurring-line-between-state-power-and

Testa, Alberto, and Anna Sergi. 2018. *Corruption, Mafia Power and Italian Soccer*. Abingdon: Routledge.

Tilly, Charles. 1985. "War Making and State Making as Organized Crime." In *Bringing the State Back In*, edited by Peter Evans, Dietrich Rueschemeyer, and Theda Skocpol, 169–91. Cambridge: Cambridge University Press.

TJN. 2018. "Financial Secrecy Index." Chesham: Tax Justice Network. https://www.financialsecrecyindex.com/

Townsend, Mark. 2019. "UK's Organised Crime Threat at Record Level, Warns National Crime Agency." *Observer*, May 12, 2019.

Transparency International. 2013. *Global Corruption Barometer 2013* (GCB2013_DataPack). Berlin: Transparency International. https://www.transparency.org/gcb2013/in_detail

Transparency International. 2018. "Corruption Perceptions Index 2017." https://www.transparency.org/news/feature/corruption_perceptions_index_2017#table

Trantidis, Aris, and Vasiliki Tsagkroni. 2017. "Clientelism and Corruption: Institutional Adaptation of State Capture Strategies in View of Resource Scarcity in Greece." *British Journal of Politics and International Relations* 19 (2): 263–81.

Uchtenhagen, Ambros. 2004. "Substance Use Problems in Developing Countries." *Bulletin of the World Health Organization* 82 (9): 641.

UN. 2015. *Report of the Analytical Support and Sanctions Monitoring Team on specific cases of cooperation between organized crime syndicates and individuals, groups, undertakings and entities eligible for listing under paragraph 1 of Security Council resolution 2160 (2014) – S/2015/79*. New York: United Nations.

Unger, Craig. 2018. *House of Trump, House of Putin: The Untold Story of Donald Trump and the Russian Mafia*. New York: Dutton.

UNODC. 2002. *Results of a Pilot Survey of Forty Selected Organized Criminal Groups in Sixteen Countries*. Vienna: United Nations Office on Drugs and Crime.

UNODC. 2004a. *United Nations Convention against Transnational Organized Crime and the Protocols Thereto*. New York: United Nations.

UNODC. 2004b. *United Nations Convention against Corruption*. New York: United Nations.

UNODC. 2017. *The Drug Problem and Organized Crime, Illicit Financial Flows, Corruption and Terrorism*. Vienna: United Nations Office on Drugs and Crime.

US Department of State. 2009. *2008 Human Rights Report: Slovak Republic*. February 25, 2009. http://www.state.gov/g/drl/rls/hrrpt/2008/eur/119104.htm

Uslaner, Eric. 2008. *Corruption, Inequality, and the Rule of Law: The Bulging Pocket Makes the Easy Life*. New York: Cambridge University Press.

Vandam, Liesbeth, João Matias, Rebecca McKetin, Meredith Meacham, and Paul Griffiths. 2017. "Illicit Drug Trends Globally." In *International Encyclopedia of Public Health*, 2nd ed., edited by Stella Quah, 146–56. London: Academic Press.

Varese, Federico. 2001. *The Russian Mafia: Private Protection in a New Market Economy*. Oxford: Oxford University Press.

Varese, F. and Wong, R. W. Y. 2018. "Resurgent Triads? Democratic mobilization and organized crime in Hong Kong." *Australian & New Zealand Journal of Criminology* 51 (1): 23–39.

Viano, Emilio., ed. 2017. *Cybercrime, Organized Crime, and Societal Responses: International Approaches*. Cham: Springer.

Wall, David, ed. 2001. *Crime and the Internet*. London: Routledge.

Wang, Peng. 2017. *The Chinese Mafia: Organized Crime, Corruption, and Extra-Legal Protection.* Oxford: Oxford University Press.

Wang, Peng, and Blanke, Stephan. 2014. "Mafia State: The Evolving Threat of North Korean Narcotics Trafficking." *RUSI Journal* 159 (5): 52–9.

Watson, Julie. 2013. "Former Border Patrol agents sentenced to 30 years in immigrant smuggling case." *NBC News*, June 21, 2013. http://usnews.nbcnews.com/_news/2013/06/21/19081188-former-border-patrol-agents-sentenced-to-30-years-in-immigrant-smuggling-case?lite

Wilson, Eric, ed. 2009. *Government of the Shadows: Parapolitics and Criminal Sovereignty.* London: Pluto.

WJP. 2018. *Rule of Law Index 2017–2018.* Washington DC: World Justice Project.

Woodiwiss, Michael. 2001. *Organized Crime and American Power.* Toronto: University of Toronto Press.

Woodiwiss, Michael. 2017. *Double-Crossed.* London: Pluto.

Yashar, Deborah. 2018. *Homicidal Ecologies: Illicit Economies and Complicit States in Latin America.* New York: Cambridge University Press.

Zhang, Yi. 2019. "Latest anti-graft campaign focuses on organized crime." *China Daily*, February 14, 2019. http://www.chinadaily.com.cn/a/201902/14/WS5c64a8bca3106c65c34e933a.html

INDEX

....

For the benefit of digital users, indexed terms that span two pages (e.g., 52–53) may, on occasion, appear on only one of those pages.

Tables and figures are indicated by *t* and *f* following the page number